Map Locator

P9-DBX-857

Finland

Russia
106

Est.
Latvia
Belarus
104
Ukraine

102

129

Mongolia

EASTERN ASIA
112
Beijing-Tianjin
114

114

Uzbekistan
Kyr.
Turkmen.
Taj.

132
Turkey
Geo.
Syria
Iraq
Iran
Afghanistan
128

Pakistan
126 Nepal

India

124

Myanmar
Thai-land
Laos
Cam.
120
V. Nam

China

Shanghai
114

N. Korea
115
Seoul
S. Korea
115

Japan
116

Tokyo-Yokohama
119

Ōsaka-Nagoya
119

Taiwan
113
Hong Kong

117

ASIA
109

118

CENTRAL PACIFIC OCEAN
158

Philippines
121

Malaysia

Indonesia
123

Papua New Guinea

176

Libya
Egypt
143
130
Saudi Arabia
Oman
Yemen

Sudan
Somalia
Ethiopia

Cent Afr. Rep.

Uganda
Kenya
Dem. Rep. of the Congo
Tanzania

Malawi
Zambia
Zimb.
Botswana
146

Madagascar
149

149
Mauritius and Réunion

148
Witwatersrand
South Africa
148 Cape Region
148

Sri Lanka

122

E. Timor

154

Perth
154

Adelaide
155

AUSTRALIA
151

Melbourne
157

156

Brisbane
156

Sydney
156

157

159

New Zealand

ANTARCTICA
202

These maps of the World, United States and Europe indicate locations of the regional maps found on pages 69-202. The colored outlines show the scale of each map (per the accompanying legend) and the extent of each map's coverage. Page numbers of the same color are found in the center of each outline. Large scale map insets are noted by outline, name and page number. Small scale maps are indicated by name and page number only. A map of the world appears on pages 64-65.

Europe

73

73
73
18
80 Norway
Sweden
Den.
82
Finland
Est.
Latvia
Lith.

Saint Petersburg

Russia
103

Moscow
103

Ire.
76
U.K.
74
London
72

Neth.
92
Germany
Berlin
Poland
82

Belarus

84
Belg.
94
France
98
Switz.
100
96
Czech
Vienna
91
Aus.
Budapest
Hun.

Ukraine

Mol.
Romania
Georgia

90

Turkey

86
Lisbon
87
Port.

Spain

Madrid
87
Barcelona
87

Italy
Cro.
Bos.
Serb.
91

Bul.
FYROM
Alb.

Greece
Athens
89

88
Malta
88

133
Cyprus
Leb.
Israel
133
Jor.

142
Morocco
142
Algeria
142
Tunisia

Libya
Egypt
Syria
Saudi Arabia

HAMMOND

CONCISE

WORLD
ATLAS

HAMMOND
CONCISE
WORLD
ATLAS

HAMMOND World Atlas Corporation

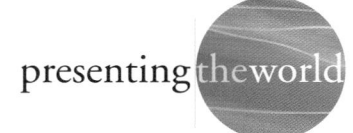

presenting the world

Contents

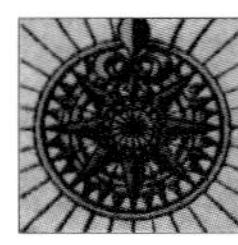

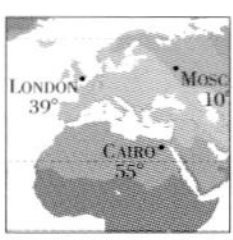

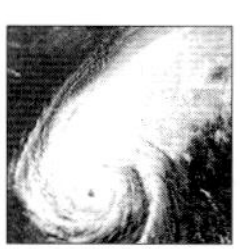

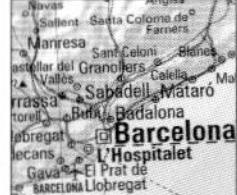

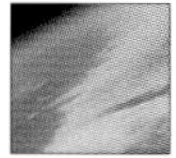

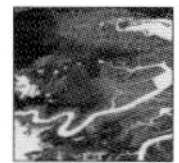

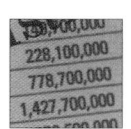

STATISTICS, COUNTRIES OF THE WORLD, TIME ZONES AND INDEX

The section on World Statistics includes the planets of the solar system, dimensions of the earth, oceans and major seas, major mountain peaks, longest rivers, largest lakes and major islands. The Countries of the World section presents the national flag and important geographic data about each independent country, including area, population, capital, largest city, highest point and monetary unit. The computer-generated Time Zones of the World reflects the world's most recent time zone changes. A Master Index lists 70,000 places and other features appearing in this atlas, complete with their page numbers and easy-to-use alpha-numeric references.

Concise World Atlas
SECOND EDITION

ENTIRE CONTENTS
© COPYRIGHT 2008 BY
HAMMOND WORLD ATLAS CORPORATION

PHOTO CREDITS: NASA - National Aeronautics and Space Administration Earth from Space images: Greece-Peloponnesus Peninsula-p.68; Pakistan-Indus River Delta-p.108; Egypt-Sinai Peninsula-p.134; Australia-Lake Eyre-p.150; United States-Grand Canyon-p.160; Argentina/Chile-Andes Mountains-p.188.

LIBRARY OF CONGRESS
CATALOGING-IN-PUBLICATION DATA

Hammond World Atlas Corporation.
        Hammond concise world atlas.
          p. cm.
        Includes index.
        ISBN 9-780843-70965-0
        1. Atlases. I. Title.
        II. Title: Concise world atlas.
        G1021. H2668   2000 <G&M>

        912--DC21   00-038861
                                         CIP
                                        MAPS

Map Projections

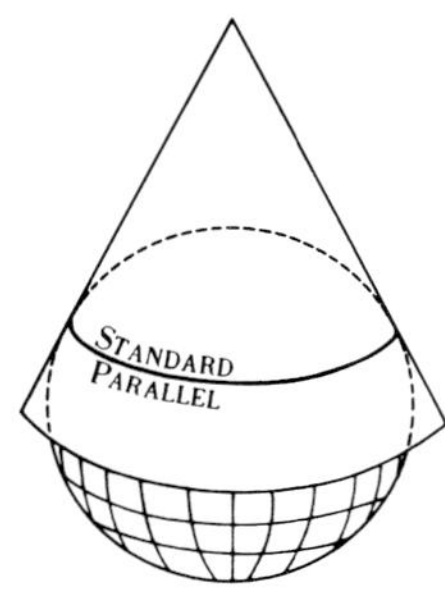

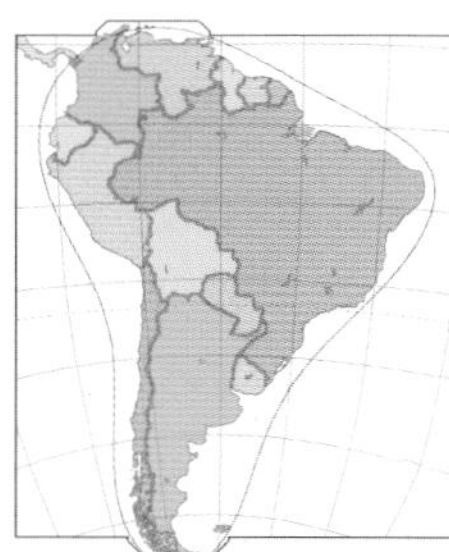

Simply stated, the map-maker's challenge is to project the earth's curved surface onto a flat plane. To achieve this elusive goal, cartographers have developed map projections — equations which govern this conversion of geographic data.

This section explores some of the most widely used projections. It also introduces a new projection, the Hammond Optimal Conformal.

GENERAL PRINCIPLES AND TERMS

The earth rotates around its axis once a day. Its end points are the North and South poles; the line circling the earth midway between the poles is the equator. The arc from the equator to either pole is divided into 90 degrees of latitude. The equator represents 0° latitude. Circles of equal latitude, called parallels, are traditionally shown at every fifth or tenth degree.

The equator is divided into 360 degrees. Lines circling the globe from pole to pole through the degree points on the equator are called meridians, or great circles. All meridians are equal in length, but by international agreement the meridian passing through the Greenwich Observatory near London has been chosen as the prime meridian or 0° longitude. The distance in degrees from the prime meridian to any point east or west is its longitude.

While meridians are all equal in length, parallels become shorter as they approach the poles. Whereas one degree of latitude represents approximately 69 miles (112 km.) anywhere on the globe, a degree of longitude varies from 69 miles (112 km.) at the equator to zero at the poles. Each degree of latitude and longitude is divided into 60 minutes. One minute of latitude equals one nautical mile (1.15 land miles or 1.85 km.).

HOW TO FLATTEN A SPHERE: THE ART OF CONTROLLING DISTORTION

There is only one way to represent a sphere with absolute precision: on a globe. All attempts to project our planet's surface onto a plane unevenly stretch or tear the sphere as it flattens, inevitably distorting shapes, distances, area (sizes appear larger or smaller than actual size), angles or direction.

Since representing a sphere on a flat plane always creates distortion, only the parallels or the meridians (or some other set of lines) can maintain the same length as on a globe of corresponding scale. All other lines must be either too long or too short. Accordingly, the scale on a flat map cannot be true everywhere; there will always be different scales in different parts of a map. On world maps or very large areas, variations in scale may be extreme. Most maps seek to preserve either true area relationships (equal area projections) or true angles and shapes (conformal projections); some attempt to achieve overall balance.

PROJECTIONS: SELECTED EXAMPLES

Mercator (Fig. 1): This projection is especially useful because all compass directions appear as straight lines, making it a valuable navigational tool. Moreover, every small region conforms to its shape on a globe — hence the name conformal. But because its meridians are evenly-spaced vertical lines which never converge (unlike the globe), the horizontal parallels must be drawn farther and farther apart at

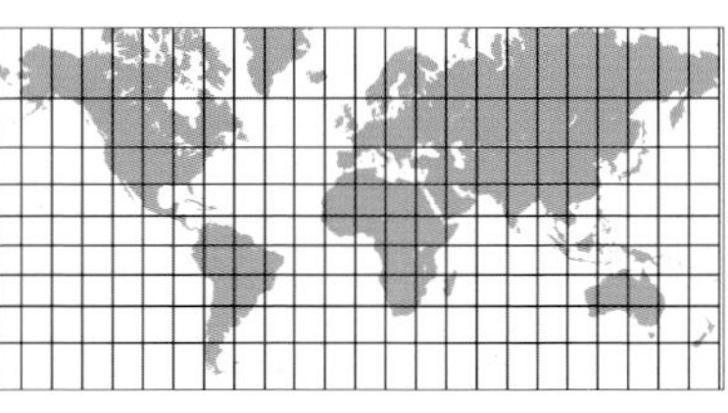

FIGURE 1 **Mercator Projection**

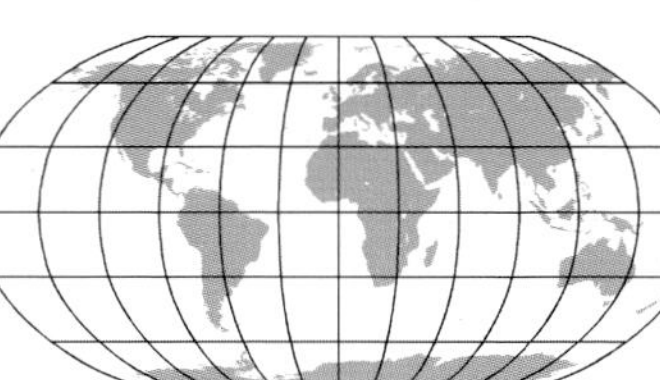

FIGURE 2 **Robinson Projection**

higher latitudes to maintain a correct relationship.

Only the equator is true to scale, and the size of areas in the higher latitudes is dramatically distorted.

Robinson (Fig. 2): To create the World-Political and World-Physical maps on pages 64-67, the Robinson projection was used. It combines elements of both conformal and equal area projections to show the whole earth with relatively true shapes and reasonably equal areas.

Conic (Fig. 3): This projection has been used frequently for air navigation charts and to create most of the national and regional maps in this atlas. (See text in margin at right).

HAMMOND OPTIMAL CONFORMAL

As its name implies, this new conformal projection (Fig. 4) presents the optimal view of an area by reducing shifts in scale over an entire region to the minimum degree possible. While conformal maps generally preserve all small shapes, large shapes can become very distorted because of varying scales, causing considerable inaccuracy in distance measurements. The concept underlying the Optimal Conformal is that for any region on the globe, there is an ideal projection for which scale variation can be made as small as possible. Consequently, unlike other projections, the Optimal Conformal does not use one standard formula to construct a map. Each map is a unique projection — the optimal projection for that particular area.

After a cartographer defines the subject area, a sophisticated computer program evaluates the size and shape of the region, and projects the most distortion-free conformal map possible.

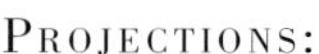

SYMBOLS USED ON MAPS OF THE WORLD

First Order (National) Boundary

Demarcated Land Boundary

Demarcated Water Boundary

Disputed Boundary

Armistice Boundary

De Facto Boundary

Undefined

Second Order (Internal) Boundary

Land/Administrative District Boundary

Water Boundary

Third Order (Internal) Boundary

Land/Administrative District Boundary

Water Boundary

Cities and Towns

Stockholm First Order (National) Capital

Salt Lake City Second Order (Internal) Capital

Manchester Third Order (Internal) Capital

Towns

City District/Neighborhood

City and Urban Area Limits

Transportation

International Airport

Airport

Highways/Roads

Railroads

Ferries

Tunnels (Road, Railroad)

Drainage Features

Shoreline, River

Intermittend River

Canal

Lake, Reservoir

Intermittent Lake

Dry Lake

Salt Pan

Swamp/Marsh

Other Physical Features

▲ Elevation

⤨ Pass

● Falls

✳ Rapids

Desert/Sand Area

Lava Flow

Glacier/Ice Shelf

Cultural Features

⁂ Archeological Sites, Ruins

○ Dam

⚹ Park

✕ Wildlife Area

■ Point of Interest

⌣ Well

⊗ Air Base

⊘ Naval Base

International Date Line

Ancient Walls

Native Reservation/Reserve

Military/Government Reservation

State Park/Recreation Area

National Park/Forest/Recreation/Wildlife Area

Elevation Legend

Height

m. ft.

6000 / 19700

4000 / 13000

2000 / 6500

1500 / 5000

1000 / 3300

500 / 1600

200 / 700

0

200 / 700

500 / 1600

1000 / 3300

2000 / 6500

3000 / 9800

4000 / 13000

5000 / 16400

6000 / 19700

m. ft.

Depth

The color tints in this bar represent both elevation of land areas and depth of the oceans. The changes between colors are labeled in meters and feet. Selective shading for the land areas highlights those regions with significant relief variations. The legend is entered next to each individual map.

ABBREVIATIONS USED IN THE MAPS

Abor. Rsv.	Aboriginal Reserve	Ft.	Fort	NHP	National Historical Park	Pen.	Peninsula
Admin.	Administration	G.	Gulf			Pk.	Peak
AFB	Air Force Base	Govt.	Government	NHS	National Historic Site	Plat.	Plateau
Amm. Dep.	Ammunition Depot	Gd.	Grand			PN	Park National
		Gt.	Great	NL	National Lakeshore	Prom.	Promontory
Arch.	Archipelago	Har.	Harbor			Prsv.	Preserve
Aut.	Autonomous	Hist.	Historic(al)	NM	National Monument	Pt.	Point
B.	Bay	Hts.	Heights			R.	River
Bfld.	Battlefield	I., Is.	Island(s)	NMEM	National Memorial	Rec.	Recreation(al)
Bk.	Brook	Ind. Res.	Indian Reservation			Ref.	Refuge
Br.	Branch	Int'l	International	NMILP	National Military Park	Reg.	Region
C.	Cape	IR	Indian Reservation			Rep.	Republic
Can.	Canal	Isth.	Isthmus	No.	Northern	Res.	Reservoir, Reservation
Cap.	Capital	Jct.	Junction	NP	National Park		
C.G.	Coast Guard	L.	Lake	NPP	National Park and Preserve	Sa.	Sierra
Chan.	Channel	Lag.	Lagoon			Sd.	Sound
Co.	County	Mem.	Memorial			So.	Southern
Consv.	Conservation	Mil.	Military	NPRSV	National Preserve	SP	State Park
Cord.	Cordillera	Mon.	Monument	NRA	National Recreation Area	Spr., Sprgs.	Spring, Springs
Cr.	Creek	Mt.	Mount			St.	State
Ctr.	Center	Mtn.	Mountain	NRIV	National River	Sta.	Station
Dep.	Depot	Mts.	Mountains	NRSV	National Reserve	Stm.	Stream
Depr.	Depression	Nat.	Natural			Str.	Strait
Des.	Desert	Nat'l	National	NS	National Seashore	Terr.	Territory
Dist.	District	Nav.	Naval			Tun.	Tunnel
DMZ	Demilitarized Zone	NB	National Battlefield	NWR	National Wildlife Refuge	Twp.	Township
Est.	Estuary			Obl.	Oblast	UNDOF	United Nations Disengagement Observer Force
Fed.	Federal	NBP	National Battlefield Park	Occ.	Occupied		
Fk.	Fork			Okr.	Okrug	Val.	Valley
For.	Forest	NCA	National Conservation Area	Passg.	Passage	Vill.	Village

<big>T</big>he Concise World Atlas has been designed to be easy and enjoyable to use. Only a short time is neeeded to familiarize yourself with its organization.

MAP SYMBOLS, COLORS AND LABELS

The cartographer selects the natural and cultural features most valuable to the map user. Map legibility requires that small features be represented by symbols that are actually larger than true scale size. Due to the larger symbol sizes and the resulting loss of map space, it is necessary to omit less important features in congested areas.

Most map features are represented by the use of conventional symbols, lines, and patterns printed in appropriate colors. The chart to the left shows the standard symbols used in this atlas. Water features are shown in blue. Lines of various weights, styles, and colors represent the many different linear features in this atlas. Individual point features are represented by a pictorial and/or generic symbol.

Notes may also be added to explain features that cannot be depicted clearly.

MAP SCALES

A map's scale is the relationship of any length on the map to an identical length on the earth's surface. A scale of 1:3M means that one inch on the map represents 3,000,000 inches (47 miles, 76 km.) on the earth's surface. Thus, a 1:1M scale is larger than 1:3M, just as 1/1 is larger than 1/3.

The most densely populated areas are shown at a scale of 1:1M, while selected metropolitan areas are covered at either 1:500,000 or 1:1M. Other populous areas are presented at 1:3M and 1:6M, allowing you to accurately compare areas and distances of similar regions. Remaining regions, including the continent maps, are presented at 1:9M and smaller scales.

BOUNDARY POLICIES

This atlas observes the boundary policies of the U.S. Department of State. Disputed, armistice and de facto boundaries are handled with a special symbol treatment. The portrayal of independent nations follows their recognition by the United Nations and/or United States government.

Map Type Styles

Cartographers use a variety of type styles to differentiate between map features. The following styles are used in this Atlas.

Major Political Areas

LUXEMBOURG

Internal Political Divisions

SAXONY-ANHALT

Regions

Polabská Nížina

Cities and Towns

Norfolk Sumter Smyrna

Neighborhoods

BIGGIN HILL

Points of Interest

MISSION SAN BUENAVENTURA

Water Features

L. Elsinore

Capes, Points, Peaks, Passes

Pt. La Jolla Pacifico Mtn.

Islands, Peninsulas

Cape Breton I.

Mountains, Uplands

Serra do Norte

Deserts, Plains, Valleys

San Fernando Valley

A Word About Names

Our source for all foreign names is the decision lists of the U.S. Board of Geographic Names and/or official foreign government maps and official gazetteers. This atlas also uses accepted conventional names for certain major foreign place names. The U.S. Board of Geographic Names defines a conventional name as "a name approved for use in addition to, or in lieu of, an approved local official name or names."

In order to make the maps more readily understandable to English-speaking readers, many foreign physical features are translated into more recognizable English forms.

The rendering of city, town and village names for the United States follows the forms and spelling of the U.S. Postal Service.

The Solar System

Our Home Star and Its Orbiting Planets

The sun is just one star among billions in our galaxy, the Milky Way. The solar system comprises nine planets (and their named moons): Mercury, Venus, Earth (one moon), Mars (2), Jupiter (48), Saturn (35), Uranus (27), Neptune (9), and the recently "demoted" Pluto (3) (see explanation on bottom of page 9), as well as numerous other smaller objects, such as comets, meteorites, and asteroids. Most asteroids are less than 100 km. in diameter, and nearly all of their paths pass between Mars and Jupiter. Unlike the stars, the planets, their moons, and the small celestial bodies emit no light and are visible to us only because they are illuminated by the sun.

Seen through a telescope, the planets appear as disks of various sizes. Images transmitted from spacecraft provide information about their surface features. The planets move along elliptical orbits on planets which deviate only slightly from that of the earth's orbit. Puzzled by apparent reversals of direction, ancient and medieval observers were unable to explain the motions of the planets as seen from the earth.

Key Data: The Sun	
Diameter:	1,392,000 km
Mass:	333,000 x earth mass
Mean density:	1.409 g/ccm
Distance from earth:	149.6 mill. km
Time of light travel sun—earth:	8 min 20 s

Key Data: The Moon	
Distance earth—moon:	384,403 km
Mass:	0.0123 x earth mass
Mean density:	3.341 g/ccm
Daytime temp.:	214°F
Nighttime temp.:	−240 °F

Planets	Mass (x earth mass)	Density (g/ccm)
Mercury	0.055	5.43
Venus	0.815	5.24
Earth	1.000	5.52
Mars	0.107	3.93
Jupiter	318.0	1.33
Saturn	95.1	0.70
Uranus	14.4	1.30
Neptune	17.2	1.76
Pluto	0.002	1.7

Sizes and Distances

Because the inner, "earthlike" planets Mercury, Venus, Earth, and Mars are composed of metals and rock (rock planets), they are relatively dense. The outer, Jovian planets – Jupiter, Saturn, Uranus, Neptune – and the dwarf planet Pluto consist primarily of gases (including hydrogen, helium, and methane) and frozen water. The asteroid belt lies between the inner and outer planets. The distribution of light and heavy matter took place during the infancy of the solar system, as lighter materials condensed in the colder outer regions of the system. With the exception of Pluto, all of the other planets (known as giant planets) are considerably larger than the earth. The diameter of Jupiter is eleven times greater than that of the earth, that of Saturn almost ten times greater. The sun's diameter is ten times larger than Jupiter's. A comparison of the masses of the objects in the solar system reveals even more marked differences. Added together, the masses of all planets including Pluto amount to only 13% of the sun's mass, and Jupiter alone accounts for 70% of that total. Relative sizes and distances can be illustrated on the basis of the following example: The distance between the sun and Pluto is 5.9 billion kilometers. If the sun had a diameter of one meter, Pluto would measure two millimeters across, and the distance between the two would be four kilometers.

Born of a Cloud of Dust

Some five billion years ago, a cloud of interstellar dust began to condense, a reaction perhaps triggered by a nearby supernova. As gravitational forces increased, the core of the cloud grew increasingly dense, while the concentration of mass in the center accelerated the system's rotation. Gradually, a flat disk formed, from which the planets later emerged. Temperatures at the center of the disk approached eighteen million degrees F, generating nuclear fusion of the hydrogen atoms. The sun began to radiate. At its core, 655 million tons of hydrogen were converted into 650 million tons of helium every second, while nine million tons of matter were transformed into energy. Five billion years from now, when its nuclear energy has been consumed, the sun will enter its final phase, at which point it will turn first into a red giant and later into a white dwarf.

The Earth's Reliable Heater

The sun produces temperatures of up to 27 million degrees F at its core. Pressure at that point is 200 billion times that recorded on the earth's surface. The visible surface of the sun is called the photosphere. It is about 400 km thick and has a mean temperature of 9,900 degrees F. Sunspots form where magnetic-field lines break through the surface. Granules (giant bubbles) measuring about 1,500 km in diameter form on the upper surface of the photosphere and bubble upward. Flames of gas (protuberances) shoot forth from the outer layer (the chromosphere), reaching heights up to tens of thousands of kilometers. The outer atmosphere of the sun (the corona) has a very low density and temperatures around 1.8 million degrees F. It extends beyond the photosphere to heights equivalent to several times the radius of the sun.

The Inner Planets

Mercury, the second-smallest planet after to Pluto, is closest to the sun. Humans could not possibly survive its surface temperatures of 780°F during the day and –325°F during the night. The atmosphere (helium, argon) above the moonlike, cratered landscape is extremely thin.

The surface of Venus is not visible from the earth. Thick clouds of carbon dioxide (96%), nitrogen (3%), and trace amounts of water vapor and other gases reflect 65% of the sun's rays, making Venus the third brightest object in the sky, after the sun and the moon. The greenhouse effect caused by its mantle of gases raises the surface temperatures of the planet's craters and lava fields (80%) to temperatures in the range of 850°F. There is no liquid water, and there are no rivers or oceans, only a few dunes.

The distance between the Earth and the sun is favorable to life as we know it, and temperatures are neither too high nor too low.

People long assumed that there could be some form of life on Mars – intelligent or at least primitive life. The pattern of lines on the planet's surface thought to be a network of irrigation canals proved to be an optical illusion however, although valleys marked by meanders do suggest that rivers must have flowed through them at one time. The cold crater landscapes of the "Red Planet" (with lows at the winter polar caps reading -225°F) are marked by rocky deserts. The largest shield volcano on Mars is 700 km wide, 25 km high and presumably several hundred million years old.

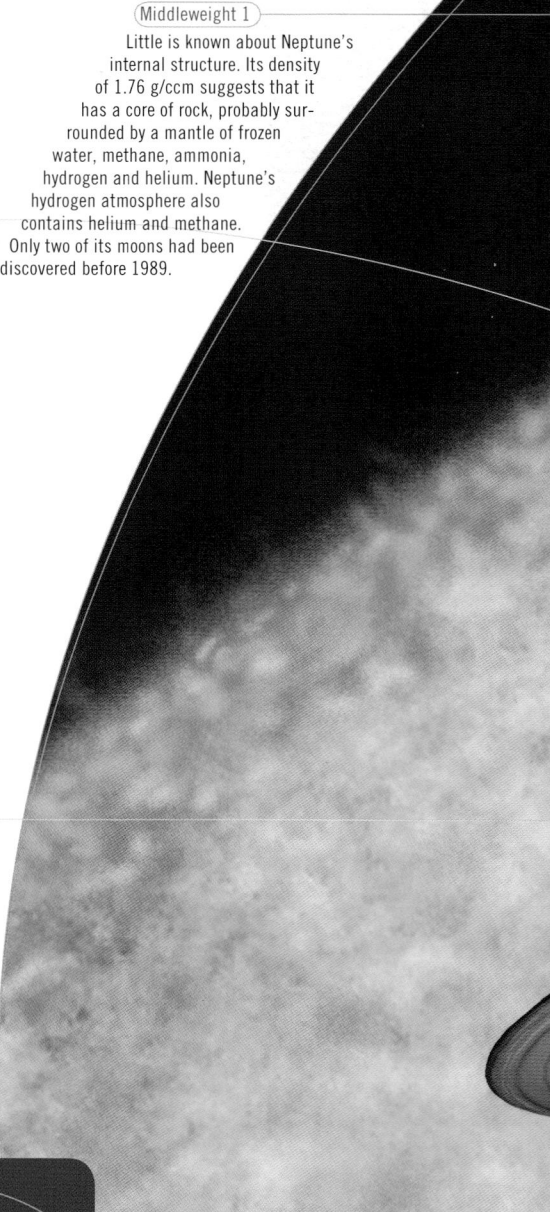

The Smallest of the Group

Pluto, the planet in our solar system, was discovered in 1930. Its low surface temperature (−440 °F) cannot support a gaseous atmosphere, and existing gases were presumably frozen out long ago.

Middleweight 1

Little is known about Neptune's internal structure. Its density of 1.76 g/ccm suggests that it has a core of rock, probably surrounded by a mantle of frozen water, methane, ammonia, hydrogen and helium. Neptune's hydrogen atmosphere also contains helium and methane. Only two of its moons had been discovered before 1989.

Predictable Relationships

The planets travel in elliptical orbits on planes which, unlike those of comet orbits, are "tilted" only slightly off the earth's orbital plane. The inner planets, Mercury, Venus, the earth, and Mars, are closest to the sun and receive more warming solar radiation than the distant outer planets, which are accordingly much colder.

Middleweight 2

Seen through a telescope, Uranus appears as a blue-green disk without visible surface features. It was not until 1986 that Voyager 2 provided a more detailed picture, revealing cloud structures, the presence of a magnetic field, and ten previously undiscovered moons. The planet's greater density indicates a composition containing metals heavier than those on Saturn. Its atmosphere consists primarily of hydrogen and helium.

Neptune · Earth · Venus · Mars · Pluto · Jupiter · Saturn · Sun · Mercury · Uranus

The Solar System

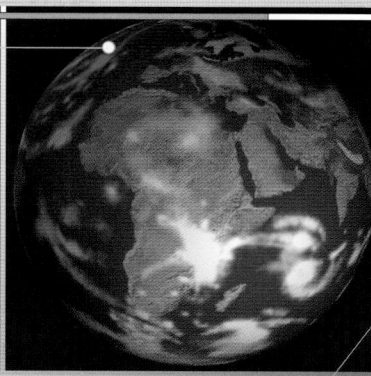

Our Moon

When Astronauts Armstrong and Aldrin took their first steps on the moon on July 21, 1969, they fulfilled an age-old human dream. Since then, plans have been in the making for a manned mission to Mars. Although that goal has yet to be achieved, a number of unmanned spacecraft have explored the depths of space as far away as Neptune.

The Blue Planet

The view from the porthole of a spacecraft shows how lost our planet is in space. Compared with the giant planets or the sun, it seems infinitely small. If mankind is to survive, we must manage our resources wisely. Viewed from outer space, our planet appears predominantly blue.

A Glaring Ball of Fire

Only when the sun is just above the horizon can we gaze at it without protecting our eyes. From this position, sunlight travels farther through the atmosphere, and the energy-laden blue rays are largely filtered out. Looking directly at the sun at midday without protection causes irreparable damage to the retina.

Giant Twins

The rings of Saturn and several of Jupiter's moons are clearly visible through even a small telescope. The giant planets Jupiter and Saturn are so large that the earth is dwarfed in comparison. Like other giant planets, Jupiter also has a system of rings, although it is not as prominent as that of Saturn. Both planets have many moons and are encircled by bands of clouds. Their atmospheres consist of hydrogen, helium and minute admixtures of methane and ammonia. Towards the interior, these gases pass through transitions from gaseous to liquid (on the planet's surface) to solid states (at their cores). The two giants have strong magnetic fields.

Io, the innermost planet of Jupiter, became famous through images sent back to earth by Voyager, which provided the first opportunity to observe extraterrestrial volcanic activity. Fountains of lava expelled at speeds of up to 1,000 m/s traveled as high as 300 m above the surrounding areas covered with multi-colored lava and frozen sulfur-dioxide.

It's not easy being Pluto

Originally considered an official planet, in August of 2006 the International Astronomical Union (IAU) down-graded Pluto to a dwarf planet.

According to new rules established by the IAU an offical planet must meet three criteria: 1) it must orbit the sun, 2) be large enough for gravity to have formed it into a sphere, and 3) it must have cleared other objects out of the way in its orbital neighborhood.

Since Pluto orbits among the many other icy objects of the Kuiper Belt – a distinct region beyond the orbit of Neptune – it does not meet the third criterion.

Mars

Venus

Mercury

Earth

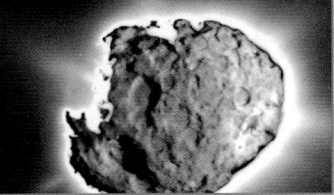

Comets and Asteroids

Space Dust, Science, and Superstition

Comets, and meteors – the streaks of light created by asteroids on a collision course with earth – have inspired awe and fear in cultures around the world since antiquity. To our ancestors, a blazing sword of fire tearing through the heavens was a message from angry, vengeful gods – a symbol of impending death and destruction. Babylonian mythology described fire, brimstone, and flood with the arrival of a comet. Roman prophecies told of a "great conflagration from the sky, falling to earth." Extensive Chinese comet atlases, dating back to at least 240 BC, chronicle the mysterious appearances and trajectories of hundreds of "long-tailed pheasant stars" and associate them with natural disasters. In 1456, Pope Calixtus III went so far as to excommunicate Halley's Comet as an instrument of the devil because it coincided with the Turkish invasion of the Balkans.

Eyes to the Skies

Although most comets are too small or too faint to be seen without the aid of a telescope, the characteristic cosmic glow of Halley's Comet or Comet Hyakutake is clearly visible to the naked eye. In 1997, the most active comet in more than 400 years, Hale-Bopp came to within 197 million kilometers of Earth and wowed scientists and casual observers alike with a spectacular display for some 500 days.

How do these interstellar objects light up the evening sky from hundreds of millions of kilometers away? Comets and asteroids are packed with rocks, ice, dust—and volumes of information about the beginnings of our solar system and the birth of our planet.

Anatomy of a Dirty Snowball

The core, or nucleus, of a comet is a solid ball of ice and gas interspersed with small amounts of dust. A black layer of dust and rock covers most of the ice, which is why comets are sometimes referred to as "dirty snowballs" or "icy mudballs." As the comet's orbit brings it closer to the sun, or inner solar system, ice on the surface of the nucleus is converted to gas and creates the coma – a dense cloud of water, carbon dioxide, and other gases present in the nucleus. The coma grows larger and fluoresces as the comet becomes hotter. The sun's radiation pushes dust particles away from the coma, creating the dust tail, while fast-moving electrically charged particles stream away from the coma to form the ion tail. The dust tail, which is the most visible part of a comet to the naked eye, can reach up to 10 million km; the ion tail can grow to over 100 million km.

Comets lose ice and dust during each journey around the sun and over time can become less active or dormant. If a comet burns off its entire core of ice, it may dissipate into clouds of dust or turn into an inactive rocky formation much like an asteroid.

Origins of Comets – The Oort Cloud and Kuiper Belt

Halley's Comet is not only the most famous "dirty snowball," it is also the first comet to be defined as periodic – it becomes visible to the naked eye once about every 76 years, as its orbit approaches the sun. In his book, A Synopsis of the Astronomy of Comets, Edmund Halley (1656–1742) asserted that the comets of 1531, 1607 and 1682 were in fact a single comet, and predicted that it would return in 1758. Halley was correct, and the comet was named in his honor.

Short-period comets, such as Halley's Comet, take less than 200 years to orbit the sun and move along a path near the orbits of other planets. The gravitational pull of the outer planets can bump objects out of the Kuiper belt – a region beyond Neptune – toward the sun where they become active comets. A dozen or so "new" comets are discovered each year, most of which are short-period comets that orbit the sun in periods ranging between 30 and 200 years.

Comets that take more than 200 years to orbit the sun are known as long-period comets and are far less common than their short-period counterparts. Long-period comets are found in the Oort Cloud around the outer edge of our solar system. Because the sun's physical and gravitational effects are extremely weak in the Oort Cloud – located 1,000 times farther away from the sun than Pluto – the billions of comets and other icy bodies found there are easily nudged out of orbit by the forces exerted by passing stars. Long-period comets bumped out of their orbits in the Oort Cloud may be observed in the inner solar system on occasion, although they will never be seen again – one trip around the sun can take as long as 30 million years.

Close Encounters with Asteroids and Meteorites

Sometimes called minor planets, asteroids are remnant rocks from the formation of the solar system 4.6 billion years ago. They are significantly smaller than comets – the largest asteroid, Ceres, has a diameter of about 1000 km. If the total mass of all asteroids was gathered into a single object, scientists estimate such an object would be less than 1,500 km across (less than half the diameter of our moon).

Asteroids orbit the sun in the Asteroid Belt or Main Belt located between Mars and Jupiter. This area of our solar system probably contains millions of asteroids,

Comet Neat

Comet C/2001 Q4 (NEAT) was discovered on August 24, 2001, by the Near Earth Asteroid Tracking (NEAT) system operated by NASA's Jet Propulsion Laboratory, Pasadena, CA. In the image to the right, a brilliant cloud of dust and gas surround the tail of the comet as it passes through the inner solar system in 2004. The image was taken with the Mosaic I camera, which has a one-square degree field of view, or about five times the size of the Moon. Even with this large field of view, only the comet's coma and the inner portion of its tail are visible. This color image was assembled by combining images taken through blue, green and red filters.

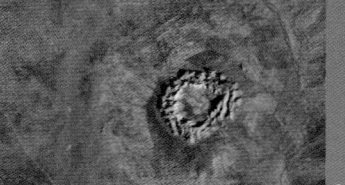

Comets and Asteroids

ranging in size from 1,000 km in diameter to bodies less than 1 km across. As asteroids orbit around the Sun, Jupiter's gravity and close encounters with Mars or nearby asteroids can knock them out of the Main Belt toward the orbits of the planets. For example, some scientists believe Mars' moons, Phobos and Deimos, may be captured asteroids. Near-Earth asteroids (NEAs) have orbits that bring them within 195 million km of the sun. It is believed that most NEAs are fragments jarred from the main belt by a combination of asteroid collisions and the gravitational influence of Jupiter. Some NEAs may be the nuclei of dead, short-period comets.

Scientists classify asteroids according to how well they reflect or absorb light – bright objects reflect light; dark objects absorb light. Using this system, asteroids are sorted into 3 groups: C-type, S-type, M-type. Seventy-five percent of known asteroids are C-type (carbonaceous), a very dark rock with a composition similar to the sun. Seventeen percent are S-type (silicaceous), a relatively bright rock composed of metallic iron mixed with iron and magnesium silicates. The remaining asteroids are relatively bright with a metallic iron composition and are designated M-type (metallic).

Much of our knowledge about asteroids comes from examining space debris that reaches the Earth. An asteroid or asteroid collision fragment with an orbit that will collide with the Earth's is called a meteoroid. The glowing object that zips across the sky is a meteoroid. Often referred to as a falling star, "meteor" is the term for the streak of light that shoots through the sky. When the meteoroid reaches the earth, it is called a "meteorite."

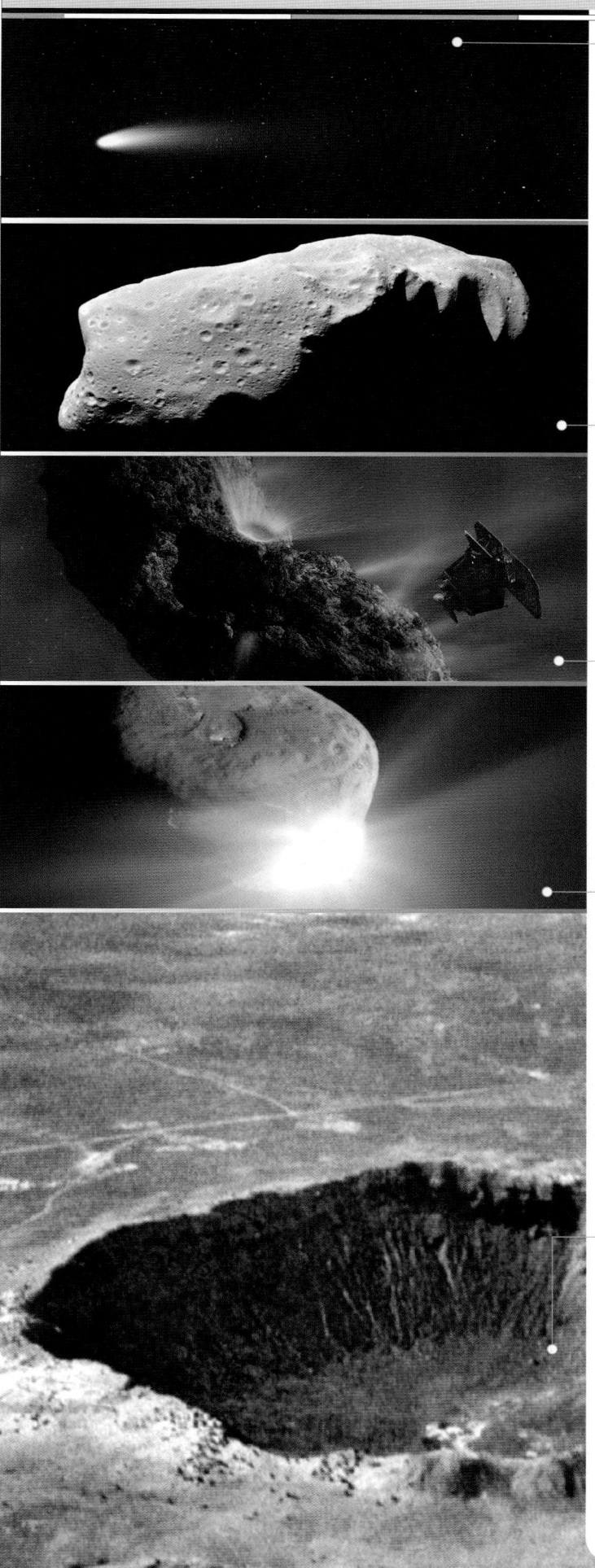

Comet Hale-Bopp is Discovered

On July 23, 1995, an unusually bright comet outside of Jupiter's orbit (7.15 AU!) was discovered independently by Alan Hale, New Mexico and Thomas Bopp, Arizona. The new comet, designated C/1995 01, is the farthest ever discovered by amateurs and appeared 1000 times brighter than Comet Halley did at the same distance. Normally, comets are inert when they are beyond the orbit of Jupiter, so it has been speculated that Comet Hale-Bopp is either rather large, or experienced a bright outburst (or both). The comet is the brightest comet since Comet West in 1976. From Hubble Space Telescope images, the comet's diameter has been determined to be about 40 km.

Asteroid Ida

Ida is the second asteroid ever encountered by a spacecraft. It appears to be about 52 kilometers (32 miles) in length. Ida is an irregularly shaped asteroid placed by scientists in the S class (believed to be like stony or stony iron meteorites). It is a member of the Koronis family, presumed fragments left from the breakup of a precursor asteroid in a catastrophic collision.

Artist's Concept of Deep Impact

Comets are time capsules that hold clues about the formation and evolution of the solar system. They are composed of ice, gas and dust, primitive debris from the solar system's distant and coldest regions that formed 4.5 billion years ago. Deep Impact, a NASA Discovery Mission, is the first space mission to probe beneath the surface of a comet and reveal the secrets of its interior.

Deep Impact Mission Accomplished

On July 4, 2005, the Deep Impact spacecraft arrived at Comet Tempel 1 to impact it with a 370-kg (~820-lbs) mass, creating a crater estimated to be up to 800 feet in diameter. Deep Impact has yielded unexpected results about the structure and composition of comets. Mission scientists found the first definitive evidence of water ice on the surface of a comet. Analysis of the ejection plume indicated that comets contain a substantial amount of organic material and thus could have brought such material to Earth early in the planet's history.

Arizona's Impact Crater

The Meteor Crater in Arizona was the first crater to be identified as an impact crater. It is believed to have been formed 20,000 to 50,000 years ago when a small asteroid about 80 feet in diameter impacted the Earth. The crater is the best preserved crater on Earth and measures 1.2 km in diameter. For many years, scientists had doubted that there were any impact craters on Earth. The origin of this crater has been a source of controversy for many years. The discovery of fragments from the Canyon Diablo Meteorite helped prove that the feature is in fact an impact crater.

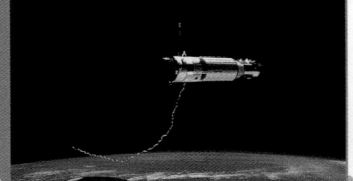

Planet Earth

... and it truly does move!

If we could look from a great distance at the supposedly firm and motionless ground on which we normally stand, we would see that it is anything but motionless. Our Earth is a dynamic celestial body which rotates on its own axis and revolves around the sun. The very point at which we stand moves along a complicated orbit through space.

Dancing on a Volcano

An entirely different kind of motion involving shifts in the positions of points on Earth relative to one another ordinarily takes place unnoticed and so slowly that extraordinarily precise instruments are required to prove that it occurs at all. Yet a time-lapse film in which 10 million years are compressed into a single second would provide striking evidence of how much the Earth's appearance has changed since prehistoric times and become the planet we know today. The key terms used to describe this process are "continental drift" and "plate tectonics." The only effects of these changes we perceive directly are the – often disastrous – earthquakes and seaquakes, frequently followed by massive tidal waves, that frequently accompany movements of the large plates in the uppermost layers of the Earth's crust.

Like our perceptions of the positions and movements of objects in the sky, much of what we experience on Earth – the alternation of day and night, the changing seasons – is caused by the motion of the Earth. The alternation of day and night would seem easy enough to explain: The Earth turns completely around its own axis every 24 hours, and thus every place on Earth experiences a sunrise and a sunset. But wait! There are regions on Earth in which the sun doesn't rise for months and doesn't set

again until more months have passed: the polar zones within the Arctic and Antarctic Circles. These periods of time are referred to as polar nights and polar days.

The cause of both – and for the changing seasons everywhere on Earth – is the fact that the Earth's rotational axis is inclined 23.5 degrees to the plane of the Earth's orbit around the sun. Because the angle of the Earth's axis does not change as it revolves around the sun – its northern extension always points towards the North Star – one hemisphere is always closer to the sun: the northern hemisphere during the northern summer and the southern hemisphere during the northern winter. Only at the spring and fall equinoxes, when days and nights are equally long, are the northern and southern hemispheres exposed to the same intensity of solar radiation.

Moon – Calendar – Clock

The Earth has a constant companion on its journey around the sun – the moon. The movements of the Earth and the moon are the basis for our reckoning of time, the rhythm of our clocks, and our calendar system. The corresponding units of time are days, months, and years – the interval between one arrival of the sun at its zenith and the next; the period between full moons, and the length of time it takes the Earth to complete a full revolution around the sun. Precise astronomical observations are required to measure the lengths of these periods. Ancient astronomers discovered that neither a revolution of the Earth around the sun nor of the moon around the Earth equated to a full number of revolutions of the Earth around its own axis. There are approximately 365 ½ days in a year and about 29 ½ days in a (lunar) month. That is what makes designing a precise, reliable calendar such

a difficult matter. Sophisticated correction systems are required to keep the calendar in step with the movements of the celestial bodies. Depending upon the system in use, these systems involve the addition of additional days or months to the calendar at regular intervals (in leap years, for example).

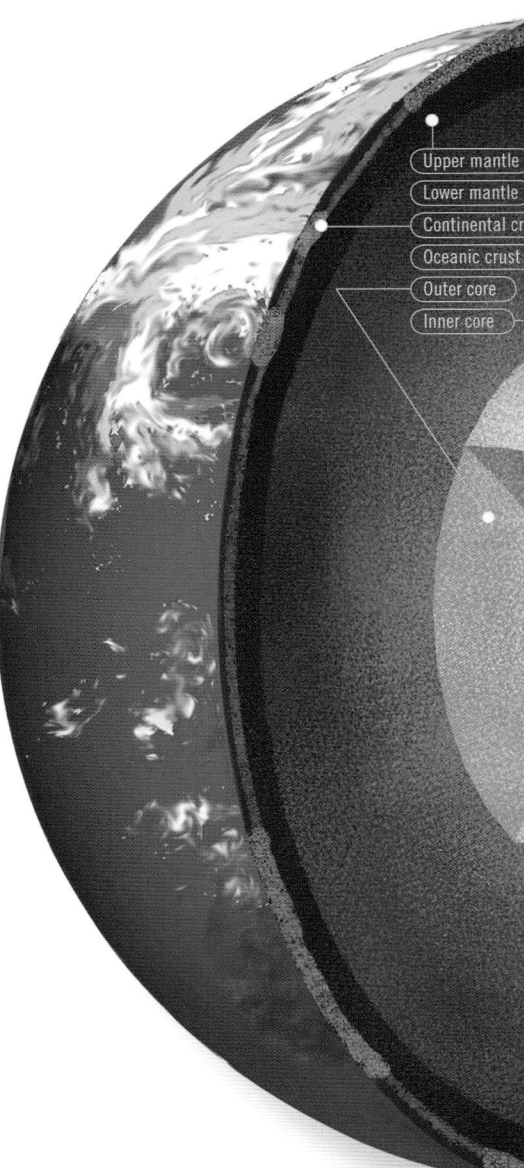

Upper mantle
Lower mantle
Continental crus
Oceanic crust
Outer core
Inner core

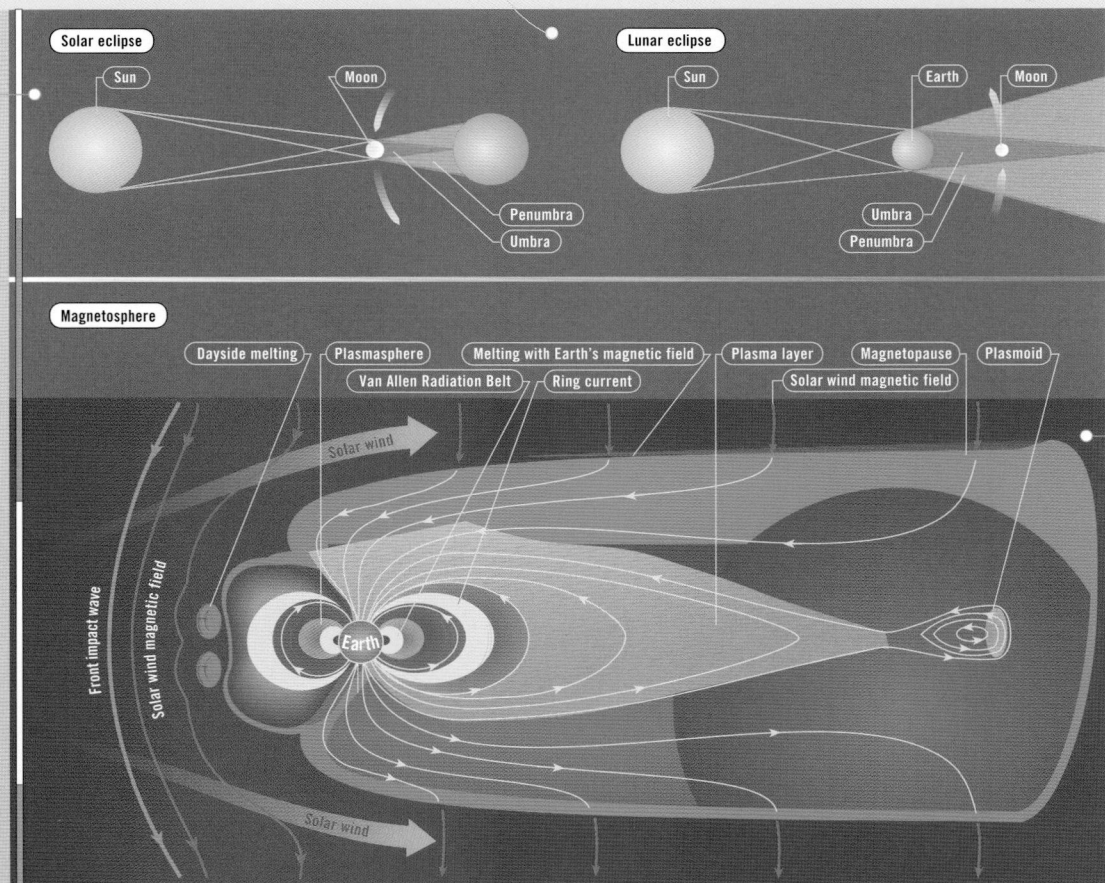

Light and Shadow

During a solar eclipse, the moon passes between the Earth and the sun, whereas a lunar eclipse occurs when the moon moves through the shadow cast by the Earth and thus grows dark. Depending upon their relative positions the sun and the moon may totally or only partially obscured. We can observe a total eclipse of the sun from a place at which the moon's umbra falls. During a total lunar eclipse, the moon is encompassed entirely within the Earth's umbra.

Solar eclipse
Sun
Moon
Penumbra
Umbra

Lunar eclipse
Sun
Earth
Moon
Umbra
Penumbra

Magnetosphere

Dayside melting · Plasmasphere · Melting with Earth's magnetic field · Plasma layer · Magnetopause · Plasmoid
Van Allen Radiation Belt · Ring current · Solar wind magnetic field

Solar wind
Front impact wave
Solar wind magnetic field
Earth
Solar wind

An Invisible Cloak

Generated within the Earth's core, the Earth magnetic field is shaped and limited by solar wind, a stream of electrically charged particles emitted by the sun. The space it encloses is known as the magnetosphere. On the side of the Earth facing the sun, the magnetosphere extends to a distance equivalent to between 10 and 20 Earth radii. On the opposite side of the Earth, it pulls a tail measuring some 1,000 Earth radii in length. In the Van Allen radiation belt, electrically charged particles captured from cosmic radiation by the magnetosphere move back and forth between the Earth's magnetic poles. The term "plasma" denotes a gas consisting of positively and negatively charged particles, whose charges offset one another. Plasmoids are lumps of plasma that are cut off and catapulted from the tail of the magnetosphere.

Occasional corrections to clock time are required, usually in late June and/or late December, for a different reason: the irregular rotation of the Earth. This irregularity was not discovered until the 1930s, following the invention of quarz clocks that were more exact than the Earth's own rotation. These smaller corrections involve the addition of leap seconds.

The Earth Seen from Space

Although mankind has long been aware that the Earth is an object in space, like the sun and the moon, people did not truly appreciate that fact until the age of space exploration began in the early sixties. The image shows an early docking maneuver during the Gemini 8 mission in 1966.

A Glowing Hot Core inside a Cool Shell

In terms of its static structure, the Earth can be divided roughly into a crust, a mantle, and a core. We distinguish between the upper and the lower mantle, while the core consists of an outer and an inner core. The crust and the mantle are composed of rock, while the core consists primarily of iron and nickel. The outer core (iron and iron oxide) is molten liquid. The inner core (iron and nickel) is solid. The continental crust is considerably thicker than the oceanic crust.

Like a Tilted Top

Seasonal temperature differences are attributable to the fact that the Earth's rotational axis is not precisely perpendicular to the plane of its orbit around the sun. As a result, the Earth tips its northern polar region toward the sun during the northern summer, while the southern polar region is inclined toward the sun during the northern winter. In the first case, the northern hemisphere is exposed to stronger solar radiation; in the second, it is the southern hemisphere that is bathed in warmer sunlight. At the spring and autumn equinoxes, when days and nights are of equal length, the northern and southern hemispheres are exposed to the same amount of solar radiation.

The larger figures representing the Earth illustrate the distribution of sunlight at the summer solstice (around June 21st, on the left) and at the winter solstice (around December 21st, on the right).

The amount of warmth received by the various regions of the globe, and thus the temperature characteristics of the four seasons, depend largely upon the angle at which solar radiation reaches the Earth, which is in turn a function of the time of day, geographic latitude, and the time of year.

The elliptical shape of the Earth's orbit also exerts a small influence on temperatures. At the most distant (aphelion) and the nearest points (perihelion) to the sun, the distance between the Earth and the sun is 1.7 per cent greater or smaller than its mean distance. Thus at these points, solar radiation is also nearly 3.5 per cent stronger or weaker, respectively.

The Seasons

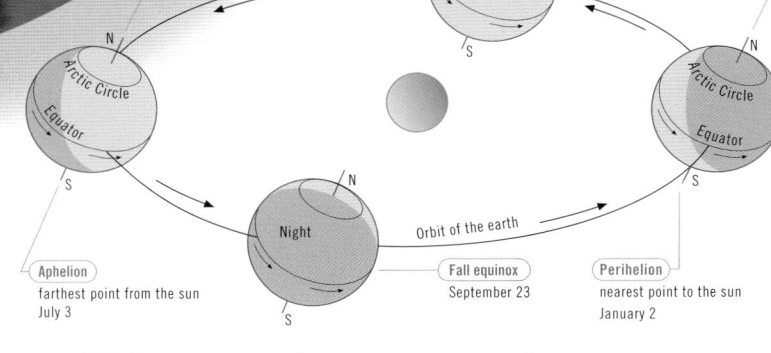

Summer solstice
June 21

Spring equinox
March 21

Day

Winter solstice
December 21

N

Arctic Circle

Equator

S

Arctic Circle

Equator

S

N

Night

Orbit of the earth

Aphelion
farthest point from the sun
July 3

Fall equinox
September 23

Perihelion
nearest point to the sun
January 2

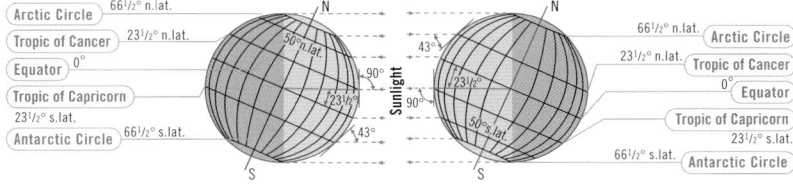

Arctic Circle — 66½° n.lat.
Tropic of Cancer — 23½° n.lat.
Equator — 0°
Tropic of Capricorn — 23½° s.lat.
Antarctic Circle — 66½° s.lat.

66½° n.lat. — Arctic Circle
23½° n.lat. — Tropic of Cancer
0° — Equator
23½° s.lat. — Tropic of Capricorn
66½° s.lat. — Antarctic Circle

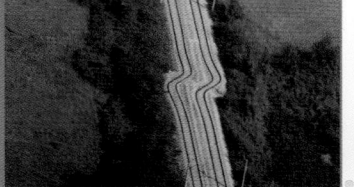

Earthquakes - Danger from the Depths

When the ground begins to shake beneath our feet

Well into the Middle Ages, earthquakes were regarded as the work of mythical, supernatural beings or signs of the wrath of God. The quake that destroyed Lisbon in cataclysmic waves of fire and flooding on November 1, 1775 caused many people to wonder about the validity of prevailing philosophical systems. Could anyone still look upon our world as the "best of all possible worlds," as a planet governed by reliable natural laws?
And why had Lisbon, of all places, a city of churches and monasteries devoted to piety, been singled out by God for such terrible punishment? That earthquake marked the beginning of the science of seismology. The Portuguese minister Pombal had reports compiled by observers all over the country. The British engineer John Michell computed the speed of the shock waves. Questions were raised about the origin and the causes of the quake.

The Restless Earth

Although we rarely notice it, the Earth's crust is constantly moving. The oceans and atmosphere are subject to patterns of natural motion, and so are the seemingly fixed landmasses of the continents, though their movements are so slow that we do not perceive them. Much more obvious – and dangerous – are the brief (lasting less than a minute), abrupt, and rapid shifts of larger segments of crust caused by tensions inside the Earth. The amplitude of these movements of ground may amount to as much as several decimeters. The energy released in the process spreads in the form of elastic waves through the Earth's interior: longitudinal and transverse waves. Longitudinal waves (also known as P or primary waves) move faster and arrive at a given distant point sooner than transverse waves (S or secondary waves). The slowest but most highly energized waves are surface waves (L and Rayleigh waves).

The source of an earthquake, known as the focus or hypocenter, may be near the surface or deep within the Earth's crust. Based upon its distance from the epicenter, the point of greatest surface movement, seismologists distinguish between shallow, intermediate, and deep-focus earthquakes. At depths below 720 km, rock is so soft and malleable that no abrupt shifts occur.

On average, 10,000 earthquakes classified as grade 4 or higher on the Richter Scale are recorded annually. Between 10 and 15 of these cause significant damage. In 1999, more than 22,000 people died as a result of earthquakes, while the average death toll for the preceding years is about 10,000. Some 15 percent of the Earth's land area is subject to severe earthquake activity. Another 40 percent is classified as virtually risk-free.

Measuring Earthquake Energy and Effects

Earthquakes are registered and recorded in seismograms using highly sensitive measuring instruments known as seismographs. The direction, distance, and energy of an earthquake can be derived from the data in the seismogram, i. e. the amplitude of the waves generated by an earthquake. Energy is expressed as magnitude, which is computed on the basis of ground amplitude, wave duration, and a calibration function. Earthquakes are classified on the Richter Scale of Earthquake Magnitude according to the maximum amplitude measured at a distance of 100 km from the epicenter. Magnitude values range from zero to between 7.7 and 8.6, but the scale has no upper limit.

California Awaits "The Big One"

The United States Geological Survey (USGS) estimates the probability of a major earthquake in northern California by the year 2020 at 70 per cent. USGS experts anticipate a seismic event comparable to the San Francisco earthquake of 1906, which measured 8.3 on the Richter Scale and laid much of the city to waste, causing numerous fires and killing some 2,000 people. The quake in Northridge near Los Angeles in 1994 took 60 human lives, and total damage was valued at $ 30–40 billion (a U.S. record). The American West Coast is one of the most severely endangered regions in the world. The Pacific Plate thrusts against the North American Plate along several fault lines, the best known of which is the San Andreas fault. These movements are not gradual and consistent but abrupt and violent, and they are responsible for a seemingly endless series of earthquakes. Some 7,800 earthquakes are registered in California each year, although most of them can only be detected by sensitive seismographic instruments.

Seismic Waves Explore the Earth's Interior

Physical bores are mere pinpricks in the Earth's crust (at about 13 km, the deepest bore ever made reached a depth equivalent to only about 0.2 per cent of the Earth's radius). We learn a great deal more about the structure of the Earth's interior from seismic waves that penetrate to the core and beyond. This method is the basis for the shell model of the Earth, with a crust (50–70 km thick beneath the continents, 5–10 km thick below the oceans), a mantle (2,900 km thick, divided in two by a transition zone), and a core (outer core to a depth of 5,200 km, inner core to a depth of 6,371 km). Correlations between wave speeds and experimental findings generate conclusions about the density, the temperature, and the chemical and mineral composition of the different zones.

Are Earthquakes Predictable?

People in ancient China observed unusual behavior in animals immediately preceding earthquake events, although they realized this only later. Today, even seismologists disagree about whether the location, time, and magnitude of an earthquake can be predicted. Researchers have been trying to identify reliable signs for decades. Using automatic recording devices, they systematically measure changes in specific characteristics – temperature, chemical composition, gas concentration (radon) and electrical groundwater resistance, groundwater levels and spring behavior, movements at fault lines, and deformations of the Earth's surface. All of these phenomena can – but do not necessarily – indicate impending earthquake activity.

Crisis Management – Emergency Disaster Aid

In industrialized countries threatened by earthquakes, such as Japan, the U. S. (especially California), and Italy, plans have been made for responses to natural disasters. Kindergarten and school children in Japan and California learn rules for behavior when danger threatens. Public emergency disaster exercises are conducted on a broad basis in Japan. Plans are modified in response to experience gained in such emergencies. California has established a network of decentralized emergency aid stations staffed and equipped to meet specific local needs. The central Japanese authority failed to respond adequately during the Kobe earthquake.

Earthquake-Proof Construction – Only an Illusion?

The first building designed to resist earthquake shock was erected by American architect Frank Lloyd Wright in Tokyo between 1916 and 1922. It survived the earthquake of 1923 virtually undamaged. In the years since, architects have employed special methods of stable or flexible construction at locations in Japan, California,

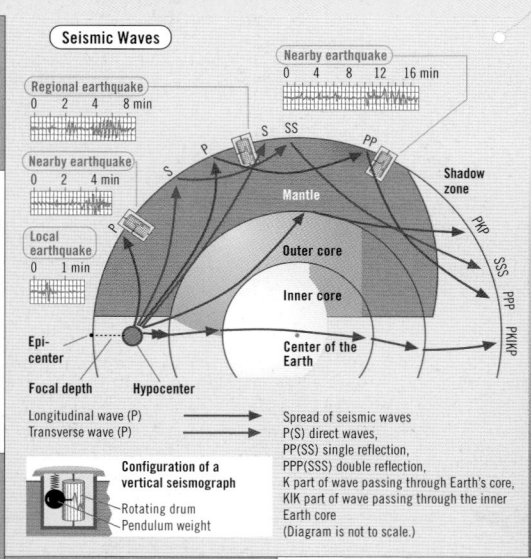

Seismic Waves

Regional earthquake
0   2   4   8 min

Nearby earthquake
0   2   4 min

Local earthquake
0   1 min

Nearby earthquake
0   4   8   12   16 min

Mantle
Outer core
Inner core

Shadow zone

Epi-center
Focal depth   Hypocenter
Center of the Earth

Longitudinal wave (P)
Transverse wave (P)

Spread of seismic waves
P(S) direct waves,
PP(SS) single reflection,
PPP(SSS) double reflection,
K part of wave passing through Earth's core,
KIK part of wave passing through the inner Earth core
(Diagram is not to scale.)

Configuration of a vertical seismograph
Rotating drum
Pendulum weight

Earthquake Epicenters and Plate Boundaries

Zones of Critical Seismic Activity

Ninety per cent of all earthquakes are caused by seismic activity (volcanism and collapsing hollow areas in the Earth account for the remainder). Thus the theory of plate tectonics has given rise to new insights into the causes and distribution of earthquakes. As this map of epicenters shows, seismic activity is most intense along plate margins. The Circum-Pacific Belt coincides primarily with subduction zones (these incline toward the continental interiors, which explains the locations of deep-focus earthquakes), while the Mediterranean-Transasian Belt is aligned with converging continental plates. Weaker earthquakes originate at the edges of plates moving away from another near mid-oceanic ridges.

Eurasian Plate
Philippine Plate
Indo-Australian Plate

Where the Ball Rolls – the First Seismograph

The first device used to register earthquake activity was invented in China in the first century AD. The pot-bellied vessel is adorned with eight dragon figures, each facing a crouching toad positioned on the base below. When a tremor occurs, the pendulum inside begins to swing. The mouth of the dragon on the side opposite the direction of the shock wave opens and drops a ball into the mouth of the toad beneath it. This was believed to indicate the direction of the earthquake.

An Earthquake Exposes Weaknesses in Japanese Society

The quake that shook the Japanese industrial and port city of Kobe in the early morning of January 17, 1995 lasted no more than a few seconds. More than 20,000 buildings were heavily damaged or destroyed; 6,432 people were killed and 350,000 lost their homes. The supports beneath 500 m of the Hanshin Highway collapsed, and the supposedly earthquake-proof elevated road crashed to the ground. The multi-story buildings nearby remained undamaged. The seemingly well-organized disaster aid and rescue system was largely ineffective.

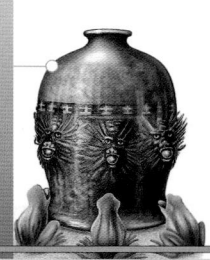

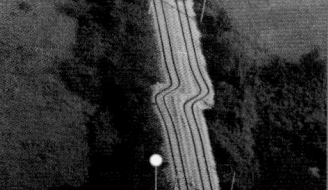

Earthquakes - Danger from the Depths

and other parts of the world. A number of countries have enacted corresponding building regulations in the past few years. Cellular construction techniques and "sandwich structures" comprised of steel and rubber plates built into the foundations of high-rise buildings absorb earthquake shocks. Steel structures are generally safer than stone or brick buildings. Wood-frame buildings may also offer satisfactory earthquake resistance if certain safety requirements are met. Schools, hospitals and other public buildings are subject to particularly stringent regulations. Recent experience has shown that many bridges, highway ramps, and similar structures need upgrading to meet safety requirements. Loose substrata, especially made-made fills or embankments, are very susceptible to earthquake damage. Much depends on the quality of construction – an issue of concern in developing countries. It is important to consider that the greatest damage incurred during major earthquakes (e.g. San Francisco, 1906 and Kobe, 1995) resulted from fire (broken gas lines). Although earthquakes cannot be prevented, precautionary measures reduce damage significantly.

A "Bend" in the Landscape

Only rarely are movements of the Earth's crust as obvious as in this photo: a bend of 3 to 5 meters in the railway line near Izmit, Turkey in August 1999.

Building Structure and Building Damage

With shops and underground parking areas, the basement level is the weakest part of many otherwise robust reinforced concrete structures. When it collapses, the entire building may fall.
(Wufeng, Taiwan, 9/21/1999).

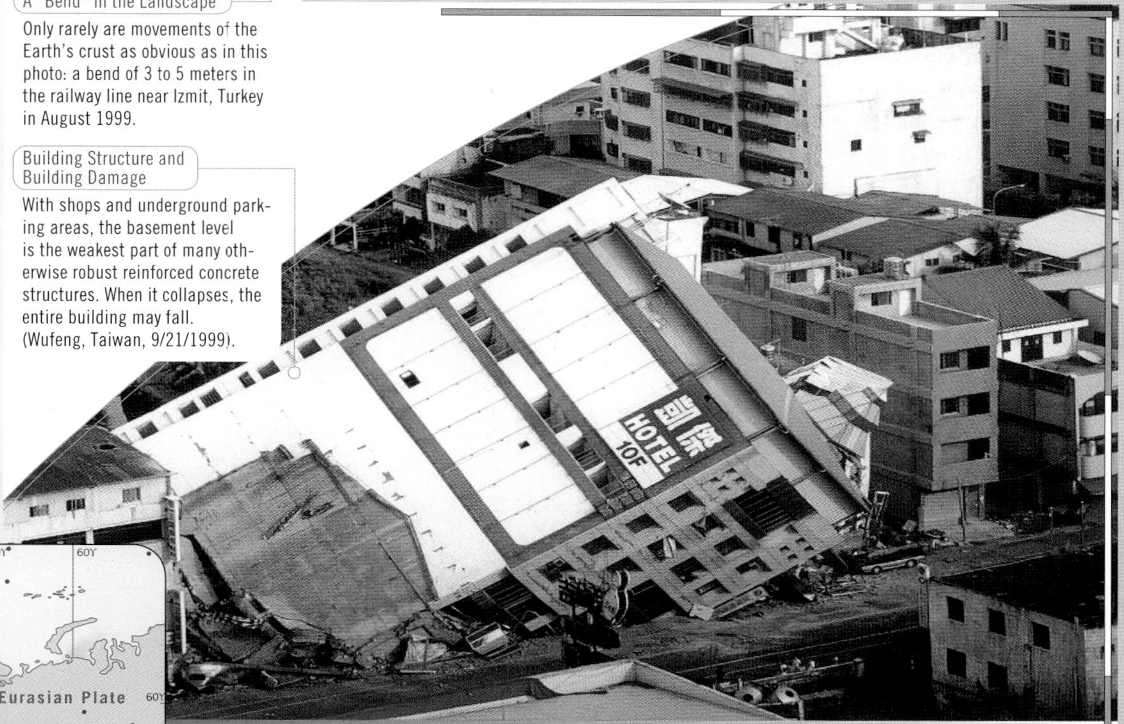

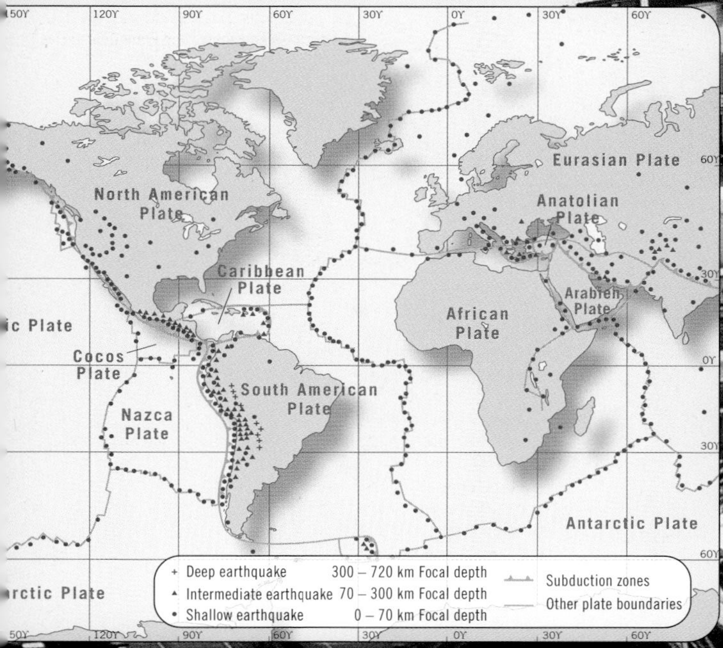

Map legend:
- **+** Deep earthquake — 300 – 720 km Focal depth
- ▲ Intermediate earthquake — 70 – 300 km Focal depth
- ▲ Shallow earthquake — 0 – 70 km Focal depth
- Subduction zones
- Other plate boundaries

Plate labels: North American Plate, Eurasian Plate, Anatolian Plate, Caribbean Plate, Arabien Plate, African Plate, Cocos Plate, Nazca Plate, South American Plate, Antarctic Plate

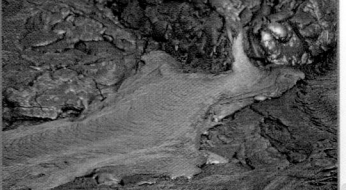

Volcanism - Unbridled Forces from the Earth's Interior

Fertile Soil – Ever-Present Danger

In the early morning hours of August 27, 1883, the small volcanic island of Krakatoa in the Sundra Strait was shaken by violent explosions which virtually blew the island paradise apart. The enormous bang was heard more than 5,000 km away, and atmospheric pressure rose by 1.45 millibars in Tokyo. Massive tremors that triggered tsunamis traveling at the speed of an airliner battered the coastlines of Java and Sumatra. Roughly 36,000 people lost their lives as a direct result of the eruptions. And this was by no means the worst volcanic disaster in history. Eruptions on the Indonesian island of Sumbawa in 1815 ejected more than 180 cubic km of lava and ash (compared to only 20 cubic km on Krakatoa). The volcano, the tidal waves, and the famine that followed were responsible for some 90,000 deaths. Dust in the atmosphere darkened the sky for weeks.

A Bubbling Inferno Beneath Us

The solid crust that floats on the hot molten rock of the upper mantle is actually very thin. Continental crust attains a maximum thickness of 70 km, while oceanic crust is ordinarily between 5 and 10 km thick. (Imagine

An Eruption in Hawaii

An eruption of Kilauea in Hawaii begins with a fountain of lava lasting several hours. Escaping gas catapults the red-hot molten mass hundreds of meters into the air.

"Rushing Stream"

This is the literal translation of the Islandic word for geyser (geysir). Rainwater seeping into the hot volcanic underground is heated and ejected – often at regular intervals – through fissures in the rock. (photo: geysers in the Rotorua region of New Zealand). The process is a part of the waning phase of volcanic activity.

Volcanic Breakthrough in a Glacier

In 1996, the volcano beneath the Vatnajökull Glacier in Iceland melted a hole in the ice cap, sending clouds of ash as high as 4,000 m into the air. The lava eruptions that followed were accompanied by severe earthquakes.

Aa and Pahoehoe Lava

A skin forms on the surface of the thin, red-hot pahoehoe lava as it flows. Once it has cooled and solidified, the lava may look much like lengths of intertwining twisted ropes or strings.

A Volcanic Blessing

Geothermal energy is a readily available alternative energy source in volcanically active regions like Italy, Iceland, and New Zealand.

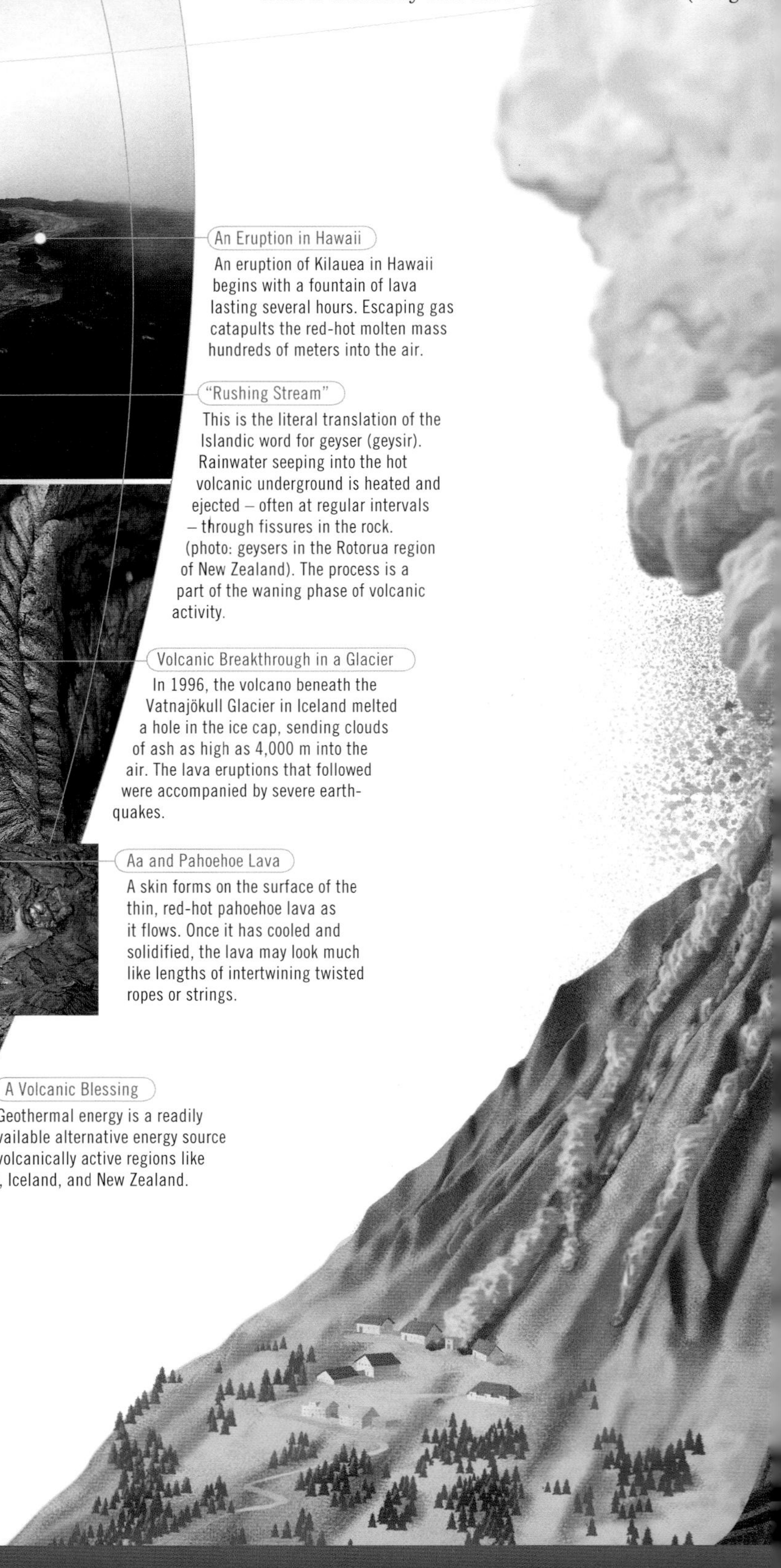

Volcanism - Unbridled Forces from the Earth's Interior

an orange measuring 12 cm in diameter with a peel only 0.3 mm thick!). And thus it is no wonder that the Earth's thin crust is extremely fragile. Molten rock accumulates in large magma chambers beneath the surface and rises where faults or openings develop. Magma that emerges at the surface is called lava.

Harmless and Dangerous Volcanoes

The flow characteristics of lava depend on its chemical composition and gas content. Thin, basaltic lava (50% SiO2) of the kind that erupts from Kilauea (Hawaii) is often ejected in towering fountains which then flow smoothly from the crater. Andesitic magma rich in silicic acid (60 % SiO2) is catapulted from volcanic Mount Saint Helens to heights of several kilometers. Gases escape easily from thin magma, whereas thick, highly gaseous magma builds up high pressures that are released suddenly and explosively near the surface, where outside pressure decreases rapidly. At these points, lava shoots from the volcano like champagne from a shaken bottle. Basaltic lava forms relatively flat (12 degrees) shield volcanoes like those in Hawaii, or basalt floors (Dekkan, India).

Acidic lava tends to erupt violently, although it may also flow quietly down volcanic slopes. Alternating deposits of lava and tuff form cone-shaped stratovolcanoes with slopes as steep as 30 degrees. The most famous volcano of this type is Fujiama in Japan. When underground pressure has no means of escape, domes of lava form, raising the overlying layers and the Earth's surface above. The destructive power of explosive eruptions makes living in these areas extremely dangerous. The worst outbreak of this kind occurred at the Montagne Pelée on the island of Martinique in 1902. Extremely hot air (1,440° F) loaded with ash enveloped the nearby city of Saint-Pierre in a red-hot cloud, killing 29,000 people. The only survivor was found at the island prison.

Volcanoes – Gigantic Dirt Canons

Volcanic eruptions also hurl huge blocks of rock (bombs) far into the surrounding countryside. Fine particles are shot up to 10 km into the atmosphere, where they may circulate around the Earth for years. Bombs, lapilli (fragments measuring from two to 64 mm), and fine ash fall to the ground, forming volcanic tuff. Fragments that have not cooled sufficiently fuse into clinkers. Rock baked from larger masses becomes volcanic breccia. Storms among the high clouds above the volcano bring heavy rains, often causing massive mudflows that obliterate everything in their paths to the valleys below.

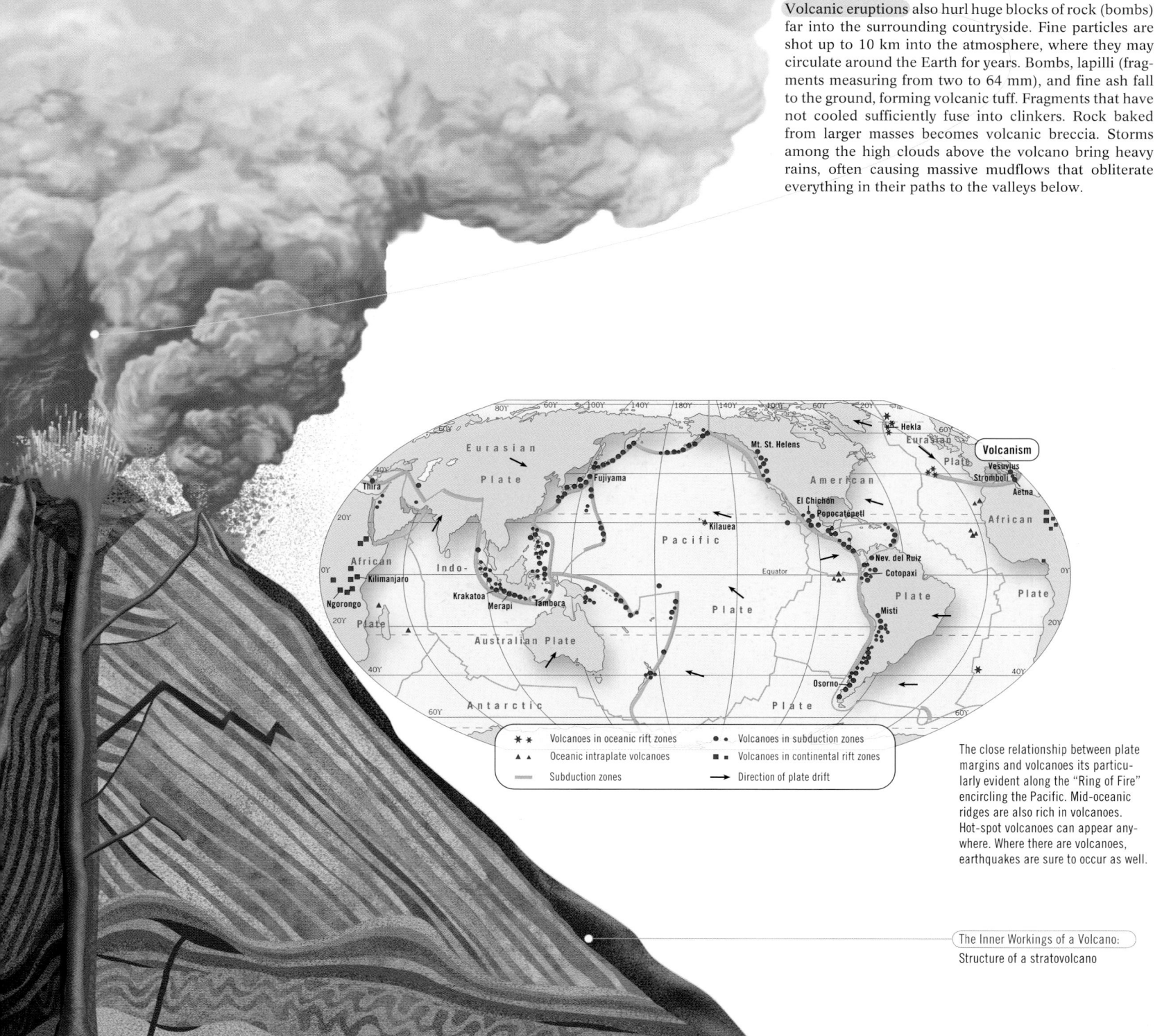

The close relationship between plate margins and volcanoes its particularly evident along the "Ring of Fire" encircling the Pacific. Mid-oceanic ridges are also rich in volcanoes. Hot-spot volcanoes can appear anywhere. Where there are volcanoes, earthquakes are sure to occur as well.

The Inner Workings of a Volcano:
Structure of a stratovolcano

Water Molds the Landscape

Water's Journey from the Sea to the Mountains and Back

Life came to Earth with water, which entered the cloud of gas that surrounds our planet in the form of gas released from molten magma. The cooling process produced the first rains, and the seas began to form. In the protective watery environment and under the influence of rising oxygen concentrations, life burst forth explosively several hundred million years ago. We come from water, and we need water to live. The human body is 70 percent water. Although we can live for weeks without food, we would die within days without water. More than half of the human race suffers from a shortage of clean drinking water. Eighty percent of the diseases responsible for millions of deaths every year are carried by unclean water. Water is an essential, life-giving substance that is unequally distributed. Some people die of thirst, while others drown.

High into the Atmosphere and back to Earth. The Water Cycle

How does water find its way back to the sea? Raindrops falling to earth have several ways of returning to the bodies of water from which they came. They may evaporate, flow over the surface, or seep into the earth, emerging again later through springs. Water that remains on the surface reaches the sea in a matter of weeks. Yet water held captive in a freshwater lake can take years to return to the ocean. Water that falls as snow and turns to ice in cold regions of the Earth like the Antarctic, may not return to the sea for hundreds of thousands of years. Once there, it is ready to embark upon another long journey. Many water molecules take refuge at safe ocean depths, however, thus escaping the routine of constant travel.

The water cycle begins with the evaporation of liquid water, most of which takes place on the ocean surface. At a temperature of 77°F, this process consumes 583 calories per gram of water. Molecules of water vapor transport this kinetic energy over long distances. The water condenses again only after a journey of hours or even days through the air. At this point, raindrops are formed during the transition from the gaseous to the liquid state, and evaporation heat is released again. That is how warmth from the Caribbean, for example, travels via the Gulf Stream to Norway. When raindrops freeze (changing from liquid to solid), 79.4 calories are released per gram of water. Thus, as strange as it may seem, the freezing process generates heat. Molecules move more slowly in ice than in liquid water.

Water Shapes Mountains and Valleys by Day and by Night

With rare exceptions, water flows downhill toward the sea, quickly forming drainage lines on the surface. As the kinetic energy of water rushing downhill tears away material and carries it away, long cuts form in the earth – the valleys of streams and rivers. Naturally, elevated ridges are left standing between these valleys. The product is a relief of mountains and valleys. Depending upon elevation and slope, mountains of different heights are created and cut apart by water and/or ice (glaciers). The higher the mountain range, the steeper the forms carved by the water.

A Steady Drip Hollows the Stone

Water is the most important element in the weathering process that shapes rock – just as it is when automobiles succumb to rust (corrosion). Limestone is one of the most highly soluble types of rock, and large caves and other karsts are often found in limestone formations. Apart from its corrosive effect, moving water also works mechanically to hasten the process of rock destruction.

The effects of wind, water, and salt have combined to undercut a coastal rock formation on the island of Lanzarote.

Crashing waves strike steep coastal formations with incredible force (one cubic meter of water weighs roughly a ton), wielding sand and pebbles as abrasive weapons. Although these forces are weaker in rivers, a substantial amount of material is eroded and carried away from riverbeds and banks over the course of time. Deep, V-shaped valleys and gorges offer striking evidence of the destructive power of water. Bank and bed erosion caused by flowing water forms valleys in a multitude of different shapes.

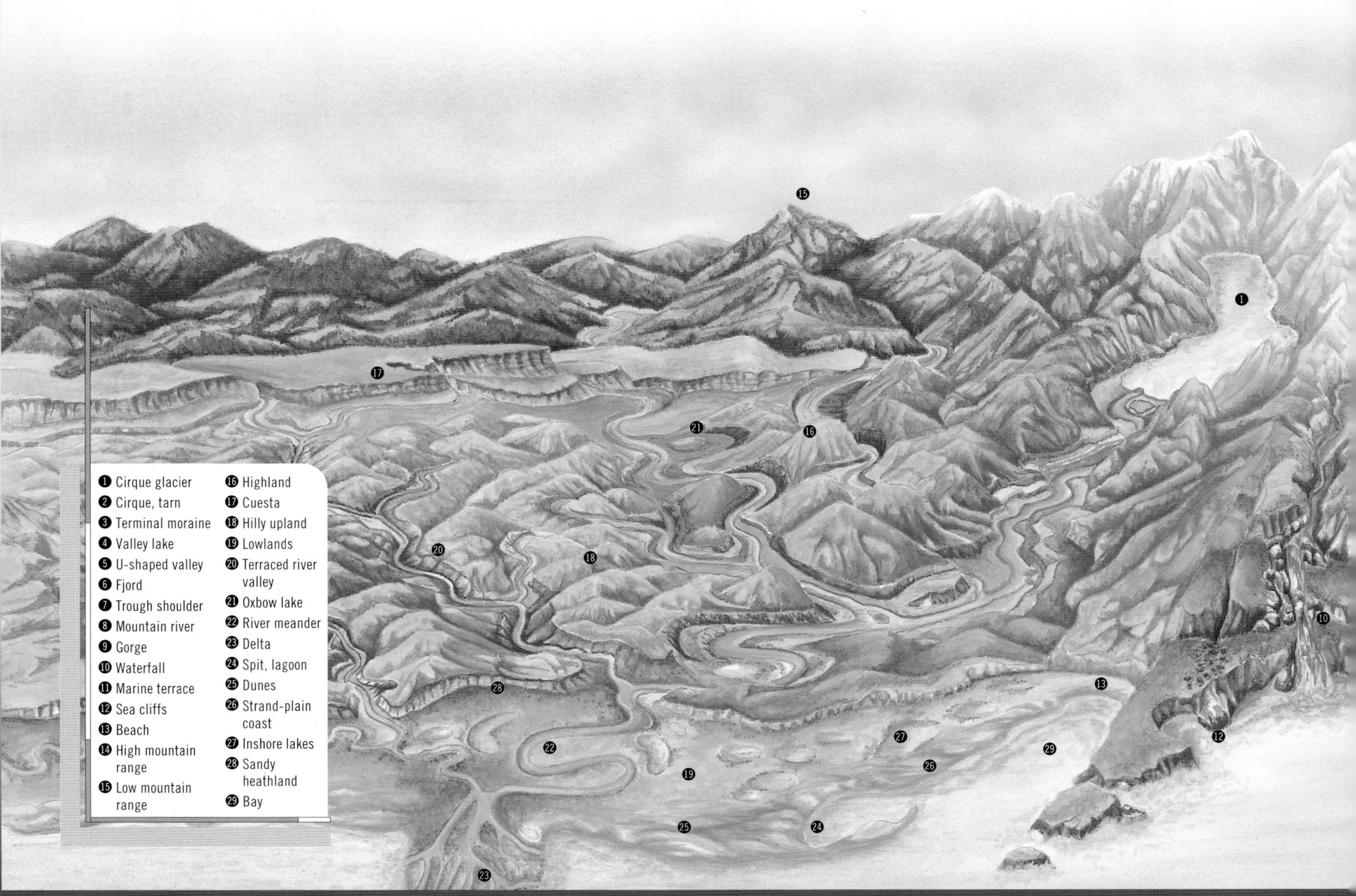

1. Cirque glacier
2. Cirque, tarn
3. Terminal moraine
4. Valley lake
5. U-shaped valley
6. Fjord
7. Trough shoulder
8. Mountain river
9. Gorge
10. Waterfall
11. Marine terrace
12. Sea cliffs
13. Beach
14. High mountain range
15. Low mountain range
16. Highland
17. Cuesta
18. Hilly upland
19. Lowlands
20. Terraced river valley
21. Oxbow lake
22. River meander
23. Delta
24. Spit, lagoon
25. Dunes
26. Strand-plain coast
27. Inshore lakes
28. Sandy heathland
29. Bay

Water Molds the Landscape

Glacial ice has even greater erosive power. The high pressure exerted by the ice causes severe erosion (detersion, exaration) even at low flow speeds. Blocks of stone the size of a house may be torn away and carried downward. This is how deep U-shaped valleys are formed. The eroded material is deposited in glacial moraines. Water and ice cover three-quarters of the Earth's surface. Although the total quantity of water on earth – some 1.4 billion square km – is almost impossible to imagine, this immense treasure is of little use to us, as 96.5 per cent of it is salty. Methods developed for desalinating seawater are too costly for most countries. And it is hardly practical to tow icebergs from the Antarctic to the arid regions of the world. We may expect future water shortages to reach life-threatening proportions in many places on Earth.

No Escape from Water

Although water is in short supply in many parts of the world, thousands die or lose their homes in water-related disasters every year. Floods, typhoons, and tsunamis ravage broad stretches of land. Melting snow and torrential rains cause rivers to swell and overflow their banks in low-lying areas. Dykes often do not hold or are simply not high enough.

When the ground freezes during the winter and is covered by a thick blanket of snow, it takes only a brief interlude of warm temperatures accompanied by heavy rainfall to melt the snow and cause severe flooding in the valleys. The frozen soil prevents water from seeping into the ground and accelerates the speed of surface runoff.

Spectacle of Nature
A thundering waterfall crashes over a steep drop in Iceland. The energy of flowing water, which mankind has not yet begun to exploit significantly, is a powerful force that here continues to erode the step in the terrain.

Planed and Leveled
The surf along the Basque coast near Saint-Jean-de-Luz has worn a flat abrasion plate in the terraced slopes of the Pyrenees.

Source of Life
Water is extremely scarce in deserts. Knowledge of the few, often hidden sources of water is crucial to survival in these extremely arid regions. Surface springs like this one in the Aïr Massif (Niger) are rare, and water must often be drawn from wells or water holes dug in the sands of dry riverbeds.

Unbridled Force
Water from melting snow and ice flows to the sea. In steep terrain, the milky glacial melt rushes unhindered to the valleys below. The fine sand dispersed in the water consists of rock material ground away under massive glacial pressure. In mountainous regions, the force of flowing water is strong enough to move even large blocks of stone.

Floods
When the snows melt in spring or rains are especially heavy in summer, flooding often occurs on the coastal plains and alpine piedmont regions of Europe.

In the Underworld
Underground erosion creates caves (photo: Wyandotte Cave, Indiana). Water acts as a solvent in limestone. This erosive action is enhanced by karst dissolution. In this process, carbon dioxide (CO_2) works as a catalyst in the conversion of calcium carbonate to highly soluble calcium hydrogen-carbonate, which is carried away in the karst water.

Natural Disasters - Human Catastrophes

Does Mankind Pose a Challenge to Nature?

The media provide news about a terrible natural disaster somewhere in the world virtually every day. Our television screens show us images of devastation and often of the dramatic events themselves as they unfold. Sober assessments of underlying causes are often overshadowed in the public mind by such sensational reports.

Yet there are several questions we cannot ignore: "To what extent are we humans at fault?" Is mankind inevitably doomed to destruction, or can we find a way to avert it?

A Devastating Christmas Present

On Christmas Day of 1974, Tropical Storm Tracy battered the city of Darwin in northern Australia. With average wind speeds of 140 kilometers per hour and gusts peaking at 260 kilometers per hour, the storm completely destroyed more than 5,000 of the 8,000 lightweight houses built on stilts. Forty-nine people died, and property damage amounted to 3 billion Australian dollars. Of Darwin's 45,000 inhabitants, 25,000 were evacuated by air, while 10,000 people fled the city by car toward the south. This was the greatest natural disaster in Australia's history.

Flight from the Inferno

In early April 1991, Pinatubo, a volcano on the Philippine island of Luzon, erupted again for the first time in human memory. In June, the mountain collapsed and lost 300 meters of elevation. Red-hot clouds spread like avalanches, covering distances of as much as 20 km. Ten cubic km of ash, gas, and other erupted matter were catapulted into the stratosphere to heights of up to 40 km. Torrential rains generated by a tropical storm turned the accumulated ash into massive streams of mud. More than 200,000 people fled the looming catastrophe; 400 lives were lost. The expulsion of ash and particles containing sulphuric acid caused average temperatures in the atmosphere near ground level to sink by as much as 0.9° F — worldwide.

Tornadoes – Dangerous Twisters

The narrow funnel of a tornado dips threateningly earthward. The air rising inside the funnel rotates at speeds that accelerate to a maximum of 200 kilometers per hour toward the inside. The suction force generated inside the funnel rips buildings apart and bursts lungs and blood vessels in human victims. Objects carried away become dangerous projectiles; dust and water are hurled high into the atmosphere. The path of the funnel, which moves at speeds between 50 and 60 kilometers per hour, is narrow and clearly delineated, and so is its wake of destruction — and destruction is almost always total. The extensive damage is attributable in part to the prevalence of lightweight, wood-frame buildings in the United States.

Disasters Mark the Course of the Earth's History

The history of the Earth teaches us that catastrophic events have always played a role in global and regional developments and have even impacted on the evolution of living organisms. Yet from our somewhat short-sighted present-day perspective, we tend to overlook the length of time involved in these processes. Experts continue to debate the question of whether the mass extinction of life forms some 65 million years ago was caused by a collision with an extraterrestrial body, a severe outbreak of volcanic activity, or other geological, perhaps tectonic events. Most agree, however, that the extinction of the dinosaurs (along with many other forms of animal life) paved the way for the development of mammals and thus ultimately for the origin of Homo sapiens. But when we speak of natural disasters, we are usually thinking of events that affect human beings directly.

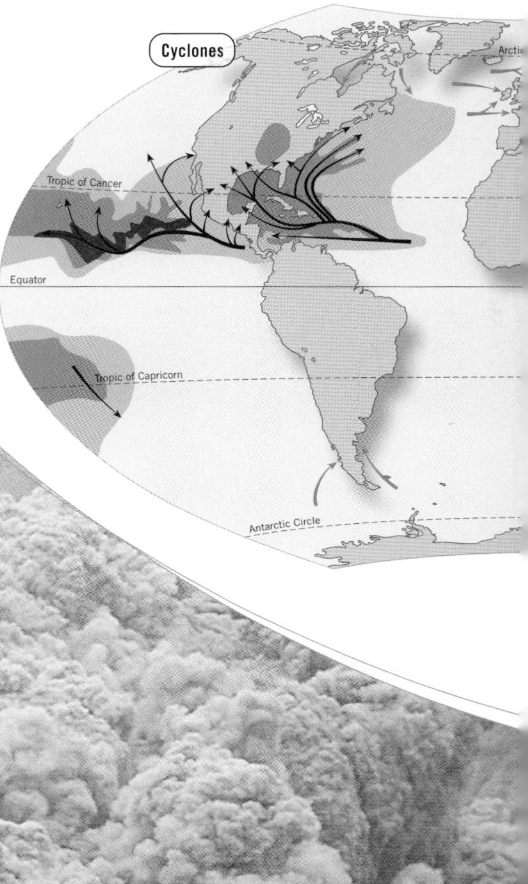

Cyclones

Tropic of Cancer

Equator

Tropic of Capricorn

Antarctic Circle

Arctic

Natural Disasters - Human Catastrophes

The Earth's Vast Destructive Potential

The "restless Earth" poses many dangers. Earthquakes and volcanic eruptions are concentrated in certain regions. While it is impossible to prevent such events from occurring, precautions can be taken against their consequences. The number of severe earthquakes (measuring 7.0 or above on the Richter Scale) did not increase worldwide during the twentieth century. Yet the toll in human lives and property damage has risen steadily, due to increasing population and building density, to the spread of settlements into endangered areas people once avoided, to the increasing value of property and goods (concentrated primarily in metropolitan areas) that has accompanied the rise in living standards, and to the increased susceptibility of modern societies and technologies to damage. Explosive population growth is another significant factor. The Kobe earthquake (1995) clearly showed seismic activity affects not only devel-

oping countries but often industrialized nations as well. And much the same applies to volcanism. We find ourselves in the midst of a heated debate about the dangers posed by the Earth's atmosphere and waters. Is the number of incidents rising? Are they growing in severity? And what or who is to blame – nature or mankind? A closely related issue is the question of mankind's impact on climate. Hurricanes are not the only destructive climatic phenomenon. Extended periods of heavy rain or snow storms; hail, ice, droughts; heat waves and periods of extreme cold; forest, bush, and prairie fires caused by lightning; avalanches, fog and smog all leave destruction in their wake. Excessive precipitation causes floods, landslips, and mudslides.

Stormy Times

The most dangerous storms originate in the Tropics: hurricanes along the coasts of Central and North America, typhoons over the waters off East and Southeast Asia, and cyclones in the Bay of Bengal (Bangladesh). They often wander for days over the sea in a westerly direction, only to turn suddenly north or south just before landfall. Their low pressure areas measure between 300 and 1,000 km in diameter. The center (known as the eye) of such storms is virtually cloudless and calm. It is encircled by a spiral of clouds that rotates at speeds up to 400 kilometers per hour. Torrential rain falls from massive cloud formations towering to heights of more than 15,000 meters. Storms that reach land wreak tremendous destruction, to which tidal waves also contribute, but then quickly lose intensity and dissipate. Hurricane Andrew caused $30 billion in damage. Katrina, ultimately is expected to cost about $200 billion. In Bangladesh, more than 300,000 people lost their lives in flooding caused by cyclones in 1970. The energy bundled in such storms is equivalent to that of several atomic bombs.

The tornadoes that occur frequently in the Midwestern United States are born when warm, moist air from the Gulf of Mexico is overlayered by dry, cool air from the Rocky Mountains or the Arctic. The temperature differential (between 36° and 54°F) generates incredibly high wind speeds. An average of 750 tornadoes are registered in the U.S. every year. They have costs the lives of hundreds of people – despite the well-organized warning system.

Dangerous Tropical Storms

Tropical storms originate over waters with surface temperatures of at least 48°F in northern and southern latitudes between 5° and 30° during the late summer and early fall. A mass of moist, warm air with towering formations of cumulonimbus clouds gathers above the water. Condensation of the water vapor releases huge amounts of heat energy which accelerate the movement of rising air and the speed of the whirling mass of clouds. Tropical storms are generated by wavelike disruptions along the edge of the subtropical high-pressure belt or by the intrusion of low-pressure centers from the west-wind zone into the tropical circulation belt. Due to defrection caused by the Earth's rotation (Coriolis effect), storms spin clockwise in the southern hemisphere and counter-clockwise in the northern hemisphere. Cyclonic storms do not occur near the equator, as the Coriolis effect is too weak to accelerate the rotating masses of air.

When the Earth Slides Away

Saturation of debris or "soft," porous rock on mountain slopes or hillsides by heavy, sustained rainfall or melting snow can cause extensive landslips or mudslides. When these huge masses of mud and debris are carried into the valleys below, the descending wave cuts a broad path of destruction through the landscape. Mudslides of this kind occur often in the Apennines (photo taken near Sarno, east of Mt. Vesuvius), especially in areas where slopes have been stripped of vegetation through deforestation or overgrazing.

Those Who Look for Trouble ...

The map divides the eastern and southeastern coasts of the United States into 58 numbered sections (each 80 km wide). Based on long-term observation, it is possible to estimate the probability of hurricane activity in a given year as a percentage value. The number of "normal" hurricanes (wind speeds higher than 33 meters per second) is entered in the inner row of boxes; "major" hurricanes (56 meters per second and higher) are listed in the outer row, which has several large gaps. Hurricane activity is most frequent in August and September.

Year in, Year out ...

Floods caused by high water on the Rhine (photo: Cologne) and its tributaries are practically a regular occurrence. Data gathered at water-level measuring stations enable authorities to issue advance warnings and initiate evacuation procedures. Dykes and ad hoc precautionary measures (such as mobile protective walls) can help prevent some but by no means all flood damage. Flooding in 1993 and 1995 caused total property damage estimated at five billion dollars.

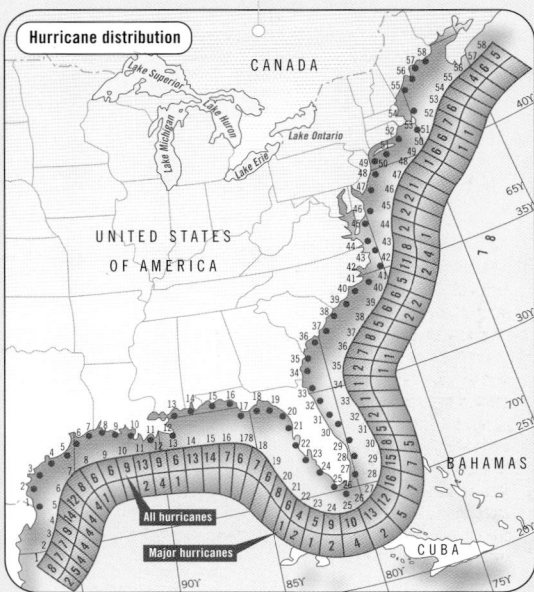

Hurricane distribution

The Great Flood Yet to Come?

High water is ordinarily caused by unusually long periods of heavy precipitation or by rapid melting of winter snows. Repeated reports of catastrophic flooding evoke the impression that these disastrous events are becoming more frequent. Are they a by-product of global climatic changes that are reflected in increasingly heavy precipitation in Central Europe and the American Midwest? Catastrophic floods have occurred often in the past, as high-water marks show, but they had less far-reaching consequences, as agriculture and housing development were much less extensive than they are today. Various human interventions in the balance of nature have accelerated runoff activity and increased the danger of flooding. Prime examples are deforestation, ground-surface sealing (roads, housing developments, etc.), soil compaction (resulting from machine plowing and the conversion of meadowlands to fields), riverbed constriction with dams and dykes, river straightening, and the draining of wetlands (along the Mississippi, Missouri, and Red Rivers, for example), in combination with ground settlement and rising riverbed levels caused by accumulating silt deposits. Awakened from their lethargy by the increasing frequency and impact of floods, experts and regulatory authorities have instituted renaturation programs for river areas. Efforts to restore natural flood plains (retention areas) often encounter stiff opposition from local farmers, however.

Tropical storms (cyclones)

highly destructive severe to very severe weak to moderate

Tornadoes

Major paths of movement

Tropical storms   Non-tropical storms

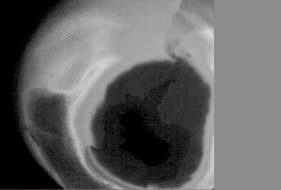

The Changing Global Climate

... and Mankind's Role in the Process

The history of the Earth's climate is one of changes, some gradual, others rapid and dramatic. Periods of relative stability and calm like the Holocene, which began some 10,000 years ago, are the exception rather than the rule. Yet it was precisely this climatic stability that allowed human civilization to develop. Today, the extent of human intervention in climatic processes is increasing. Are we merely a minor disruptive factor in the interplay of these powerful forces of nature, or does mankind pose a serious threat to the global climatic balance?

Variations in the Earth's Orbit

Some 20,000 years ago, at the peak of the last ice age, substantial portions of North America and northern Europe were covered by sheets of ice several thousand meters thick. This ice extended deep into the North American continent to the region now covered by the Great Lakes. The land south of the ice was arctic steppe, much like today's tundra regions. On the basis of bore samples taken from deposits thousands and even millions of years old, from layers of sediment on the ocean floor or from continental ice in Antarctica and Greenland, for example, it has been possible to reconstruct temperature patterns and many other characteristics of past climate. For at least two million years, the Earth's climate has been governed by relatively regular cycles. Ice ages lasting roughly 100,000 years have alternated with warm periods usually about 10,000 years long. These cycles are caused by subtle shifts in the Earth's orbit around the sun and in the inclination of the Earth's axis. These changes, known

as Milankovitch variations, affect the seasonal and geographic distribution of solar radiation – although the total amount of radiation that reaches the Earth remains constant. It is not entirely clear why the Earth's climate reacts so dramatically to these changing radiation patterns. One crucial factor is apparently the intensity of summer sunlight over the continents of the northern hemisphere, for when the snows of the past winter do not melt completely, large sheets of ice begin to form. They reflect solar radiation and thus lead to further cooling. Our understanding of Milankovitch variations suggests that the Holocene is an unusually long warm phase, which would mean that a new ice age is not to be expected for several tens of thousands of years.

Abrupt Climatic Shifts

Scientists have learned only fairly recently that the last ice age was marked by a series of very abrupt and drastic changes in climate. In the course of these so-called

Dansgaard-Oeschger Events (of which more than 20 are known to have occurred during the last ice age), average temperatures in the North Atlantic region rose rapidly – within only a few years – by between 11 and 14°F. These unusually warm periods lasted several hundreds or thousands of years. Their effects were felt around the globe – even in the Antarctic. Evidently, sudden shifts in the course of marine currents played a significant role in these sudden climatic changes.

Even the Holocene, the current, relatively stable warm period, has not been free of climatic changes. Some 5,500 years ago, the Sahara was transformed from a landscape of swamps, lakes and areas of vegetation inhabited by many large animals and human beings into the desert we know today. In all likelihood, this process was set in motion by a shift in the Earth's orbit which triggered a fatal chain of events: a gradual decrease in rainfall resulting in diminished plant growth which led in turn to further reduction in precipitation.

The Radiation Budget

The Earth's temperature is regulated by a simple radiation budget. On average, the energy received from the sun is equal to the energy radiated by the Earth into space. If too much energy is received, temperatures rise and the Earth radiates more heat until balance is

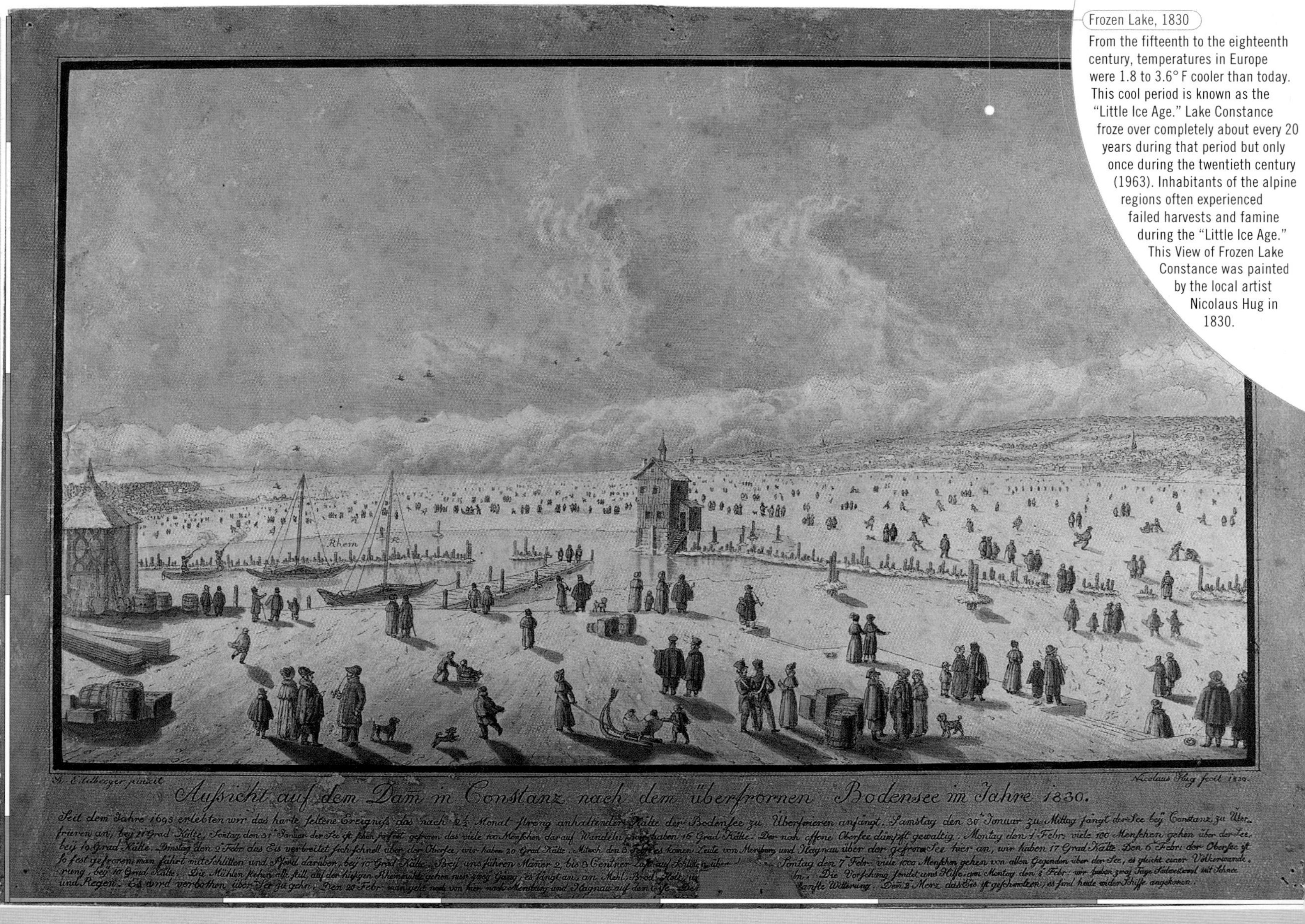

Frozen Lake, 1830
From the fifteenth to the eighteenth century, temperatures in Europe were 1.8 to 3.6° F cooler than today. This cool period is known as the "Little Ice Age." Lake Constance froze over completely about every 20 years during that period but only once during the twentieth century (1963). Inhabitants of the alpine regions often experienced failed harvests and famine during the "Little Ice Age." This View of Frozen Lake Constance was painted by the local artist Nicolaus Hug in 1830.

Aussicht auf dem Dam in Constanz nach dem überfrornen Bodensee im Jahre 1830.

The Changing Global Climate

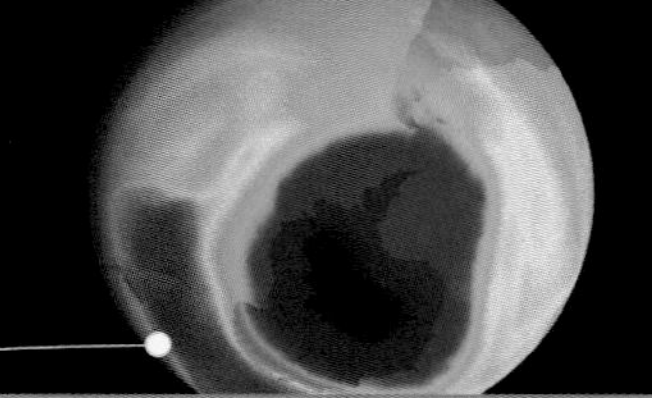

restored. If the Earth had no atmosphere, its average temperature would be somewhere near 0° F. The atmosphere inhibits thermal radiation from the Earth's surface, primarily due to the insulating effect of water vapor and carbon dioxide, the so-called greenhouse gases. Consequently, the Earth's surface warms until the radiation balance is restored at today's average temperature of about 59° F. It is this natural greenhouse effect that makes our planet inhabitable. Changes in the composition of the atmosphere or in the surface area of reflective ice and cloud masses can affect the radiation budget and thus raise or lower temperatures.

The Human Factor

Human impact on the global climate dates back to the Middle Ages, when people began clearing forests to make room for farmland, thereby increasing carbon dioxide levels in the atmosphere and creating lighter areas of surface that reflect more sunlight. But it was not until the Industrial Revolution in the first half of the nineteenth century that mankind developed the means to disrupt the delicate radiation balance significantly. The leading cause of these man-made changes is the use of fossil fuels – coal, petroleum, and natural gas. The fossil fuel we burn in a single year took roughly a million years to accumulate. The carbon contained in these materials oxidizes during combustion and is released into the air as carbon dioxide (CO_2). About half of it remains in the atmosphere, while the remainder is absorbed by the oceans and the biosphere. Since the beginning of the Industrial Age, the carbon-dioxide concentration in the atmosphere has risen from 280 parts per million (ppm) to 360 ppm, and the greenhouse effect has grown stronger accordingly. Other gases released in the course of human activities intensify the greenhouse effect even further. Examples are methane and fluorocarbons, which are also responsible for the ozone hole.

Concentrations of greenhouse gases in the atmosphere have risen in recent years, raising average global temperatures by about 1.25° F – over both land and sea. Mountain glaciers are melting all over the world (total glacier volume in the Alps has already decreased by half). Artic Ice has become almost 40 per cent thinner over the past 30 years.

Using sophisticated pattern-recognition techniques, climatologists have attempted to determine the extent to which these trends are actually attributable to anthropogenic emissions and to identify other possible causes (such as fluctuations in the sun). Their findings indicate that, at the very least, the accelerated warming trend observed since 1970 is largely a man-made phenomenon.

Scientists warned as early as the late nineteenth century on the basis of simple computations that increasing concentrations of carbon dioxide in the atmosphere would lead to global warming. Today, the world's climate can be simulated with the aid of powerful computers, which make it possible both to reconstruct past climate patterns and to project scenarios for the future. If concentrations of greenhouse gases in the atmosphere continue to rise at the current pace, we can expect global temperatures to rise by between 2.7 and 9.9 degrees F over the next hundred years. Should this happen, the earth will be warmer than it has been at any time during the past 100,000 years. One consequence would be a rise in sea level of between 20 and 90 centimeters, which would persist for centuries even if the warming trend were halted. Warming would also lead to changes in precipitation patterns and thus possibly to drought and flooding, endangering many existing ecosystems in the process. Low-lying coastal regions would be threatened by flooding caused by storms, and several island nations in the Pacific would disappear beneath the sea.

In an effort to slow the process of global warming, most of the nations participating in the international conference in Kyōto, Japan in 1997 signed a Climate Treaty that obliges industrial nations to reduce emissions of greenhouse gases to five per cent below 1990 levels by the year 2012. The treaty is not yet in force, as only a few nations have ratified it, and it represents, at best, only a first small step toward effective climate protection.

The Radiation Budget and the Greenhouse Effect

Assuming a value of 100 % for the amount of solar radiation that actually effects the global radiation budget (342.5 Watts per square meter), only 45 % (on long-term, global average) actually reaches the Earth's surface. The remainder is absorbed or scattered. The total reflective capacity of the earth (including the atmosphere and clouds) is referred to as the Earth's albedo, and amounts to 30 % on a yearly average.
The effective heat radiated by the Earth's surface is 18 %. This equates to the difference between 114 % – the value which would be expected if the Earth had no atmosphere – and 96 % – for radiation reflected back by the atmosphere (the greenhouse effect). The difference between incoming solar radiation and outgoing terrestrial radiation (27 %) at the surface is offset by heat currents.

Threatening Hole

In 1985, British researchers discovered a hole in the ozone layer of the upper atmosphere – our shield against dangerous cosmic radiation. One of the causes identified was the release of industrially produced fluorocarbons, such as those used in spray cans, into the atmosphere. The Montreal Protocol of 1987 called for a global ban on these gases, to be achieved in a step-by-step process. They are hardly used at all today, and scientists now predict that the ozone hole will gradually close over the next several decades. It will probably take more than 100 years to restore the ozone layer completely, however.

Global warming trends, 1976 – 1999

Quelle: NCDC

in degrees Fahrenheit per century

| 14°YF | 17.6°YF | 21.2°YF | 24.8°YF | 28.4°YF | 32°YF | 35.6°YF | 39.2°YF | 42.8°YF | 46.4°YF | 50°YF |

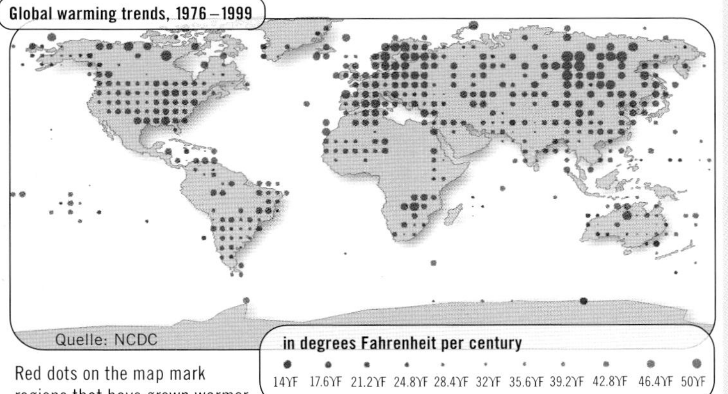

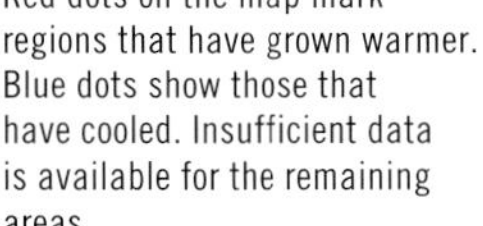

Red dots on the map mark regions that have grown warmer. Blue dots show those that have cooled. Insufficient data is available for the remaining areas.

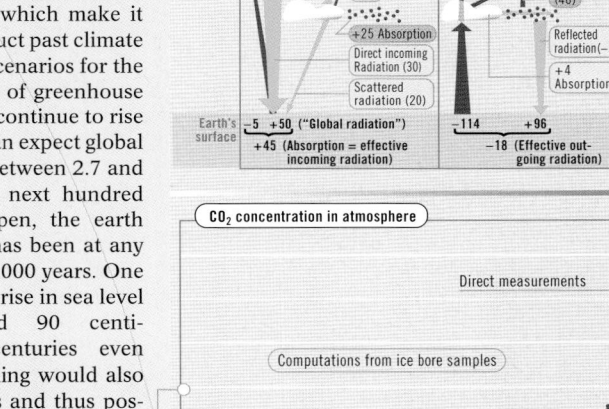

budget and greenhouse effect

Process values	Solar radiation (incoming)			Terrestrial radiation (outgoing)			Radiation budget
Upper boundary of atmosphere	+5 −100	+25	Total −70	+14	+65	Total +70	0
Atmosphere		Reflection (70)		(10)	Outgoing radiation (−56)		
		+25 Absorption			(46)		−27
		Direct incoming Radiation (30)			Reflected radiation(−56)		
		Scattered radiation (20)			+4 Absorption		
Earth's surface	−5 +50 ("Global radiation")			−114	+96		+27
	+45 (Absorption = effective incoming radiation)			−18 (Effective outgoing radiation)			

CO_2 concentration in atmosphere

Direct measurements

Computations from ice bore samples

Compensation curve   Individual readings

Year   800   1000   1000   1400   1600   1800   2000

ppm   360   340   320   300   280

100,000-year temperature curve

Pleistocene   Holocene

ΔT   0   −20

100 000   80 000   60 000   40 000   20 000   Today
Years ago

0 = Average Holocene temperature

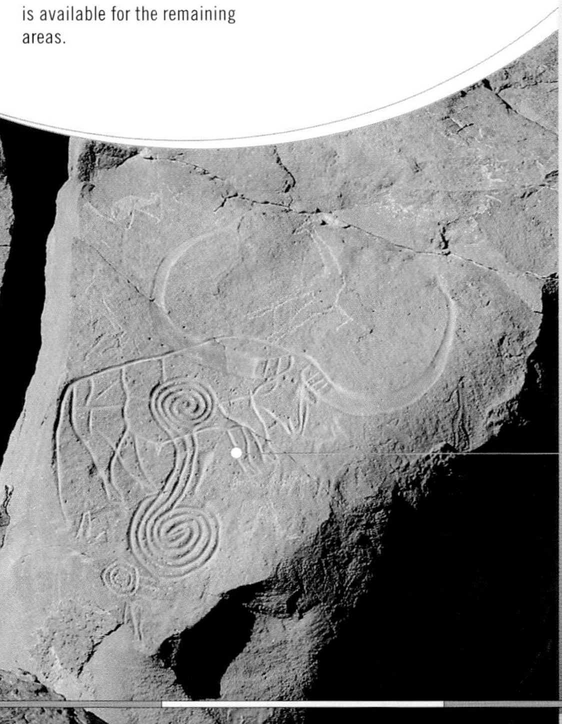

Saharan Rock Painting

Until about 6,000 years ago, the Sahara was much greener than it is today. A large number of rock drawings offer evidence of a much moister climate. The buffalo Homoioceras antiquus (Oued Djerat, Tassili n'Ajjer, Algeria) became extinct during the early Holocene.

Alarming Rise

Analyses of air bubbles in Antarctic ice and measurements taken at Mauna Loa (Hawaii) since 1957 tell us a great deal about carbon-dioxide concentration in the atmosphere: about 280 ppm during warm periods like the Holocene, 200 ppm during the ice ages, and more

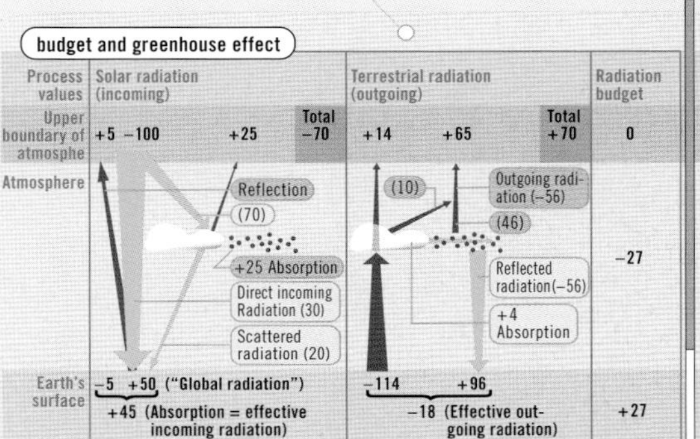

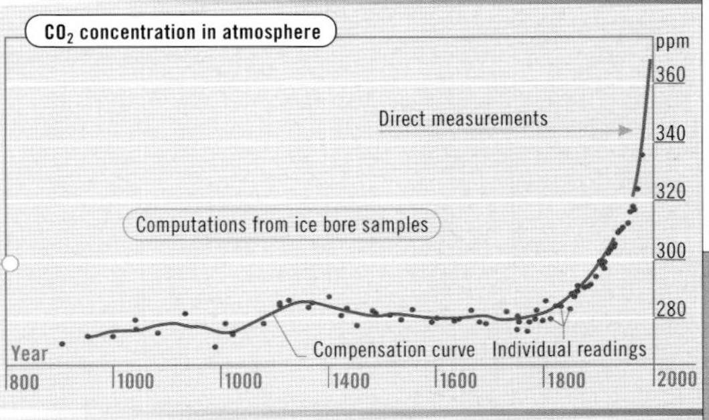

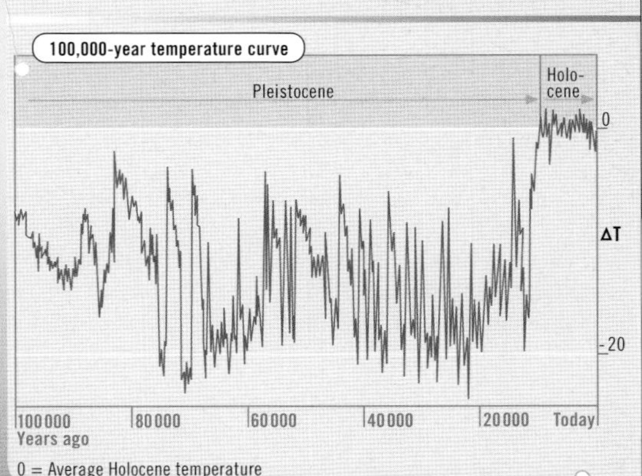

Climate Curves for the Last 100,000 Years from Greenland Ice

This climate curve from Greenland shows the consistently warm climate of the past 10,000 years, the Holocene period. During the preceding 100,000 ice-age years, the climate was not only much colder but also subject to sudden fluctuations.

Vegetation - The Earth's Botanical Cloak

Plant and Human Life – A Reassessment

According to the Book of Genesis, God created plants on the third day, calling upon the Earth to "bring forth grass, the herb yielding seed … and the tree yielding fruit … and God saw that it was good." (Genesis 1:11). Mankind arrived on the scene soon afterward. By current reckoning, human beings have since destroyed about 30% of the original 62 million square kilometers of forest on Earth, transformed much of our planet's vast grasslands into arid wastelands (desertification) through overcultivation, and altered the character of natural vegetation in many regions of the world. We have intervened in natural patterns of growth and distribution, manipulated genetic makeup through breeding experiments, and replaced local flora with secondary growth over wide areas. Yet despite this massive human intervention in the plant kingdom, more than 99% of the Earth's biomass – about 1.8 trillion tons of organic material (300 tons for every living human being) – is vegetable matter.

The Foundation of Human and Animal Life

In his famous "Canticle of the Sun," Saint Francis of Assisi spoke of "… Earth, our Mother, who feeds us in her sovereignty and produces various fruits and colored flowers and herbs." The words of Saint Francis reflect an uncomplicated view of nature and an implicit recognition of the close and vital cosmic relationship between all living organisms (the biosphere) and the Earth's inorganic crust (the lithosphere), a mystery that was not solved by modern biological science until many years later. Biologists, ecologists and biochemists agree that animal, and thus of course human life could not exist in its present form without the Earth's botanical cloak.

Plants as Chemical Factories and Nutrient Pumps

The leaves of plants contain chlorophyll (the pigment that makes them green), which they use to convert water taken up by their roots and carbon dioxide (CO_2) absorbed from the air into glucose (sugar) with the aid of light (solar energy) captured on their surfaces in a complicated process known as photosynthesis. Through their roots, which in some plants (wheat, for example) form networks of microscopically fine fibrous tendrils with combined lengths of up to several hundred kilometers, they absorb a wide variety of elements essential to all life on Earth from the soil. These they process along with the glucose into organic matter, referred to collectively as biomass (the dry weight of organic matter).

Through this process, a number of elements essential to many physiological processes, such as iron, phosphorus, calcium, magnesium, nitrogen, and sulfur, are incorporated into biomass and passed along through the food chain to herbivorous animal organisms and ultimately to carnivores (including humans as well, regardless of whether they actually eat meat or not, since the consumption of animal protein is virtually unavoidable for modern consumers).

In this way, the massive global nutrient pump of natural vegetation extracts more than two cubic kilometers per year – roughly six billion tons – of minerals and substances of all kinds from the Earth's crust and makes them available as sustenance to animals and human beings (approximately one ton for every living human being on Earth).

A root hair launches a biochemical attack on a calcite mineral: the first stage in the transition from mineral to chemical substance.

Soil-Building Vegetation

Vegetable biomass consumed by animal organisms is returned to the eternal mineral cycle as feces or in the bodies of dead organisms themselves. Unconsumed biomass is also remineralized when humus is formed through the decomposition of fallen leaves and dead plants. Mineral replacement resulting from biochemical and physical root activity, on the one hand, and the accumulation of biomass, on the other, are important soil-building processes which work within an ecological network in collaboration with such non-biological factors as the warmth and moisture of vegetation in a specific region.

Trees – Unsung "Environmental Helpers"

Trees are the largest forms of plant life. A deciduous tree between 15 and 20 meters high generates three million liters of oxygen annually (four times as much as a single human being needs in a year) through the process of photosynthesis. In one year, the same tree also filters as much as 7,000 kg of dust from the air with its foliage and extracts up to 7,000 liters of water from the soil through its root system, thus contributing significantly to the prevention of soil erosion – a problem that can assume catastrophic proportions in deforested areas. For every human being on Earth today, there are about 500 trees at work providing these important environmental services.

How Do the Little Flowers Grow, and How Do Plants Give Us Food?

The preceding description shows how very important the plant kingdom is. In light of the crucial role plants play in our lives, it is shocking to realize how little we know about them. Most people in the industrialized countries of the world can name at least 20 different makes of car but not nearly as many kinds of plants! Yet botanists have now identified more than 360,000 varieties, of which about 180,000 are blossoming plants.

It is not the species of so-called "higher plants" classified into families of trees, shrubs, flowers, and grasses that are so difficult to identify with certainty. The real difficulty and suspense begins with the attempt to establish clear scientific distinctions among the varieties of "lower plant organisms" or microflora: fungi, the various species of algae, lichens as symbiotic communities of fungi and algae, and even the types of bacteria that are classified as forms of plant life – the "little beasties" discovered and described by Antonie van Leewenhoek (1632–1723) with the aid of his home-made microscope.

Although between 10,000 and 50,000 edible varieties of plants are available for human consumption, only about 150 to 200 species (between 0.3 and 2%) are actually used for nutritional purposes. Over 75% of all energy consumed by human beings in the form of vegetable matter comes from only about ten crop plants (between 0.002 and 0.1% of all edible species of plants).

The Earth's Coat of Brightly Colored Stripes

Plants have no means of locomotion, and thus the characteristics they exhibit as indicator plants at the present stage of evolutionary development are always evidence of their adaptation to prevailing conditions in their local environments (known as habitat conditions). These include such features as water-retention organs (in cactuses or agaves in arid regions), shallow, broad root systems (like those of the birch tree) in permafrost regions where soil thaws only for a few months during the summer, or a thick coat of hair as protection against evaporation in alpine regions (edelweiss is an example). Thus we understand why belts of vegetation corresponding generally to the Earth's climatic zones, communities of plants known by botanists as vegetation zones, cover the Earth like a brightly-colored striped coat. And the same explanation applies to the typical vegetation patterns in mountainous regions that reflect the increasing lack of heat at progressively higher elevations, a phenomenon described with specific reference to South America by Alexander von Humboldt as early as the late eighteenth century.

(2) Tundra Vegetation

With average annual temperatures normally below 5°F, permafrost soil thaws only briefly to a depth of a few centimeters in the summer. With a growth period of 30–90 days, this type of vegetation, which forms a continuous belt only in the northern hemisphere, is characterized by an extraordinary abundance of lichens (in the Arctic north) and treeless, summer-green, flower-covered meadows (in the subpolar south).

(11) Alpine Vegetation

The most impressive alpine vegetation is found in the Andes (see photographs). Here the hierarchy of vegetation levels, from the tropical rain forest to the Paramo to the high tropical grasslands (moist puna) and the frost-prone, high, cold puna at elevations of about 5,000 m, where grass is sparse but lichens are plentiful, reflect the effects of diminishing warmth at progressively higher elevations.

The upper layer of permafrost soil thaws in the early summer.

Tundra meadows blossom in mid-summer.

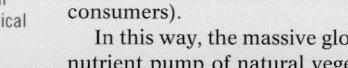
Soil erosion following deforestation in Peru

Vegetation - The Earth's Botanical Cloak

(5) Tropical deciduous forest

Despite annual precipitation often exceeding 1,000 mm, these forests of long-trunked trees that turn fully green only near their tops during the summer rainy season have a relatively short growth period, as water is scarce during the rest of the year (photo: Caprivi, Namibia). The monsoon forests of southern and Southeast Asia represent a special form of this class of vegetation.

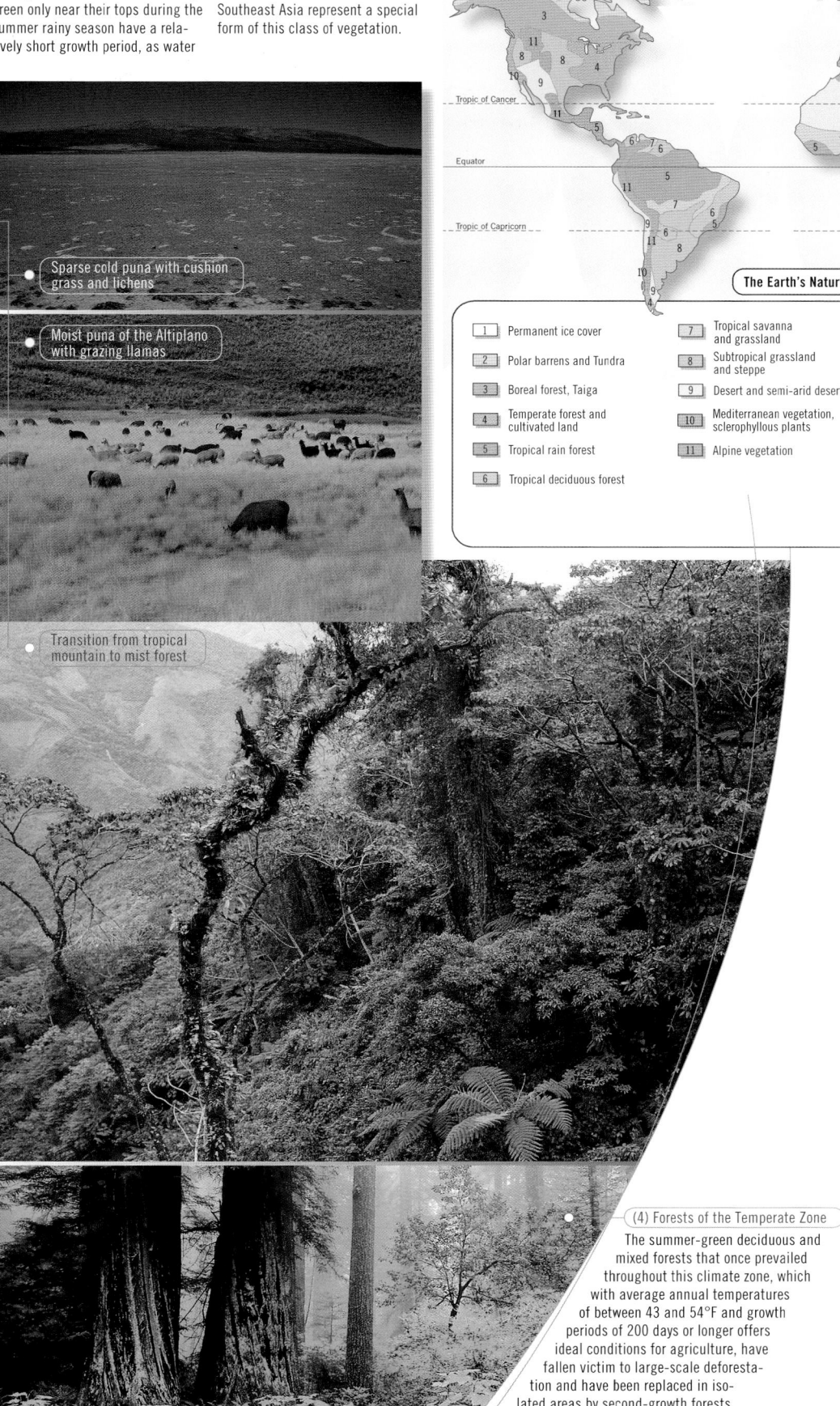

Sparse cold puna with cushion grass and lichens

Moist puna of the Altiplano with grazing llamas

Transition from tropical mountain to mist forest

The Earth's Natural Vegetation Zones

1 Permanent ice cover	7 Tropical savanna and grassland
2 Polar barrens and Tundra	8 Subtropical grassland and steppe
3 Boreal forest, Taiga	9 Desert and semi-arid desert
4 Temperate forest and cultivated land	10 Mediterranean vegetation, sclerophyllous plants
5 Tropical rain forest	11 Alpine vegetation
6 Tropical deciduous forest	

(4) Forests of the Temperate Zone

The summer-green deciduous and mixed forests that once prevailed throughout this climate zone, which with average annual temperatures of between 43 and 54°F and growth periods of 200 days or longer offers ideal conditions for agriculture, have fallen victim to large-scale deforestation and have been replaced in isolated areas by second-growth forests used primarily for wood production.

(3) Taiga – the Northern Continental Vegetation Belt

Average annual temperatures in these regions covered by boreal evergreen and summer-green coniferous forests comprising only a few species, which span the globe only in the permafrost regions of the northern hemisphere, range near 32°F. Covering some 20 million square km (about 13 % of the Earth's dry land), they represent the world's largest forest formation.

(5) Tropical Rain Forest

In the tropics, where rain falls the year round and annual precipitation often exceeds 2,000 mm, temperatures determine the character of forests. Multi-tiered, evergreen equatorial rain forest – a habitat for a wide range of species – is predominant in low-lying areas with mean annual temperatures of 72 – 82°F. Mountain forests with fewer species are prevalent at elevations over 1,000 m and average temperatures of 57 – 72°F. Mist forests characterized by beard lichens, epiphytes, and tree ferns predominate only at elevations of over 2,000 m and at average temperatures of only 40 – 57°F. Together, these three forest types occupy a total area of about 12.5 million square km (approximately 8 % of the dry land on Earth). They are seriously endangered, particularly at lower elevations, by logging operations and large-scale deforestation. The most common natural form of vegetation along the tropical coasts are mangrove forests, although they have now been almost totally destroyed.

(7) Savannas – Maximum Landscape Diversity

Savannas are generally thought of as expansive tropical grasslands (like the Serengeti). Actually, they display a number of different faces. Although grass is the dominant ground cover in all savanna landscapes, the spectrum of plant formations encompasses dry, thorny shrub vegetation, flourishing bush growth, densely wooded areas, and even true forests (such as the gallery forests along riverbanks or the Mopane and Miombo woodlands of southern Africa). Common to all types of savannas are summer rainy seasons and the absence of a thermal winter.

(8) Steppes – Non-Tropical Grasslands Under the Plow

Where grasslands once stretched to the horizon in climates with dry summers and often extremely cold winters (on the North American prairies or the black-earth regions of southern Russia), human beings have replaced the natural vegetation of the dry, short-grass and moister, long-grass steppes with vast grain fields. In many places, such industrial-scale farming operations have contributed to soil deterioration by clearing the way for wind and water erosion.

(9) Desert Vegetation

Vegetation in deserts and semi-arid regions (where climates are only slightly more favorable), is ideally adapted to the extreme conditions of their environments (scarcity of water, heat, nocturnal or winter frost, sand storms, etc.). Higher forms of plant life have developed appropriate survival tools: water-retaining organs, leaf coverings that inhibit evaporation, suspension of metabolic activity during extremely dry periods ("latent life") or disproportionately large (relative to above-ground biomass) underground plant organs (primarily roots). Microflora – ordinarily overlooked by human beings – is represented in abundance on the surface in the form of algae, fungi, and blankets of lichens that can even be seen in satellite images.

(10) Mediterranean Vegetation

The original natural vegetation of the Mediterranean regions, which are classified as subtropical climate zones with wet winters, was evergreen sclerophyllous forest (holm oak forests in the actual Mediterranean region). Extreme overuse by humans has caused much of this original vegetation to be replaced by meager second-growth formations such as broad-leaved shrubs and small trees (matorral, chaparral or maquis) and even poorer scrubland vegetation (garrigue).

Human Migration

A Global View of Shifting Populations

The history of humanity is a history of migration – and has been since the first humans appeared on Earth. Immigrants and emigrants – invading hordes and war refugees – mass migrations: all of these terms describe aspects of a complex problem that is of crucial global importance today.

Causes of Popular Migration

In addition to the natural causes of many major population movements (floods, soil degradation, desertification, etc.), people have tended to migrate primarily for ideological and economic reasons. Aside from the many unfortunate cases of involuntary migration (banishment, deportation, flight from persecution, slavery, etc.), economic push-and-pull factors are among the most common causes of large-scale migration. Overpopulation, a shortage of work, and the corresponding economic and social misery that accompany these phenomena are and always have been important "push" factors contributing to regional migration and emigration. On the other hand, prosperity and an abundance of jobs in other countries attract workers and economic refugees, as "pull" factors, with the promise of better living conditions and opportunities for social advancement. A review of the economic and social history of the modern era clearly shows that political developments in many areas of the world have been shaped by major population movements – from the mass displacement of African slaves to the emigration of Europeans (primarily for economic or political reasons) to the New World, Australia, New Zealand, and South Africa. In the roughly one hundred years between 1830 to 1928, nearly six million Germans emigrated, about 90% of them to the U.S., the remainder to Canada, Brazil, Australia, Argentina, South Africa, and Asia.

Between Hostile Lines
In the fall of 1996, hundreds of thousands of Hutu refugees fled the war zone in eastern Zaire to return to their homelands in war-torn Rwanda.

Skills Wanted Abroad
Young emigrants from Germany in Brazil (1925): automotive knowledge and skills provide the basis for a new start.

Involuntary Exile
African captives were often chained together with their hands bound to a pole during their journey into slavery.

Boat People
Hundreds of thousands of Vietnamese fled their homeland, often in overloaded, unseaworthy boats, seeking refuge in non-communist countries in Southeast Asia even long after the Vietnam War. A favored destination was the former British Crown Colony of Hong Kong.

	16th and 17th c.	Spanish and Portuguese
	17th and 18th c.	Slave trade
	18th and 19th c.	North American continental migration
	18th and 20th c.	Europeans to overseas regions

Human Migration

Streams of Refugees

Probably the most frequent cause of often involuntary mass migrations is war. In addition to the two World Wars, a number of more recent local wars and hostilities have caused huge groups of refugees to leave their homelands in Africa (Congo, Rwanda, the Guineas), Afghanistan, and the Middle East (where unsolved political and military conflicts between Israelis and Palestinians and problems involving Kurdish populations have persisted for decades). Striking evidence that religious and ideological differences as well as ethnic hostilities can lead to major refugee migrations can be found in the Balkan states, Southeast Asia (Christian-Moslem antagonism), and the Indian subcontinent (conflicts between Moslems and Hindus).

Environmental refugees are people who have been compelled to move away from their familiar homelands due to degradation of their natural environments and the resulting deterioration or loss of traditional foundations of life. Water shortages and water pollution, soil erosion, deforestation, desertification, and changes affecting the diversity of animal and plant species are forcing increasing numbers of people, especially in the "Third World," to abandon their native lands.

Economic refugees are prompted to leave their native lands in search of better living conditions – primarily in western industrialized countries – by worsening social and, above all, economic imbalances of regional or global proportions. Noteworthy examples include the immigration of Mexicans into the U.S., the growing stream of eastern European migrants into central and western Europe, and the rising number of Africans and Asians smuggled illegally by organized gangs into the Member States of the European Union.

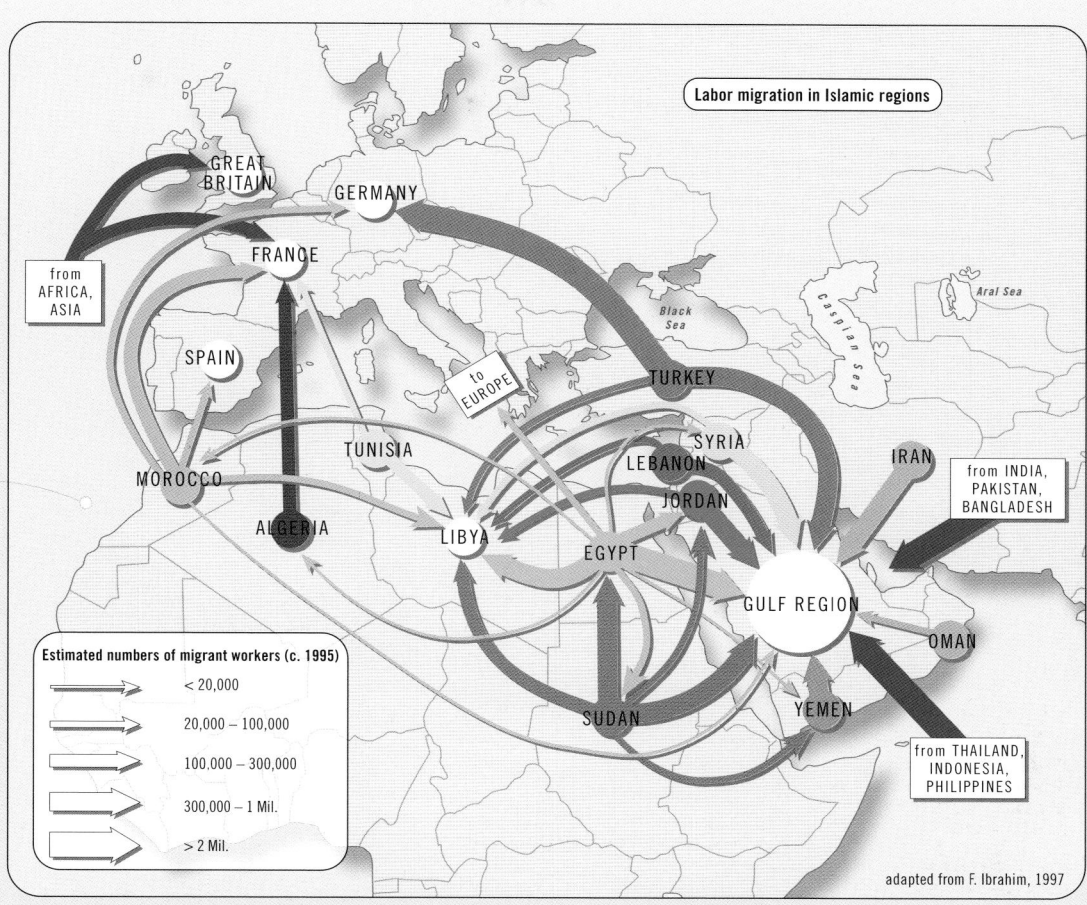

Labor migration in Islamic regions

from AFRICA, ASIA

to EUROPE

from INDIA, PAKISTAN, BANGLADESH

from THAILAND, INDONESIA, PHILIPPINES

Estimated numbers of migrant workers (c. 1995)

	< 20,000
	20,000 – 100,000
	100,000 – 300,000
	300,000 – 1 Mil.
	> 2 Mil.

adapted from F. Ibrahim, 1997

Major migration streams of the past 500 years

	19th c.	Indians
	19th and 20th c.	Russians into Asia
	19th and 20th c.	Chinese (and Japanese) to overseas regions

Effects of disasters on world population, 1969–1993

Type of disaster	affected	No. of persons homeless	Death toll	No. of events
Drought and famine	57,906,000	23,000	74,000	438
Floods	47,850,000	3,178,000	12,000	1,366
Tropical storms	9,417,000	1,066,000	29,000	1,551
Earthquakes	1,765,000	224,000	22,000	640
Landslides	132,000	107,000	1,600	218
Volcanic eruptions	95,000	13,000	1,000	98
Technical accidents	53,000	8,400	600	310
Fire	33,000	88,000	3,300	583

On an Emigrant Ship

During the 19th century, thousands of Irish emigrants embarked on a quest for a better life in the New World, the majority of them fleeing during the Irish potato famine of 1845–50. This 1884 woodcut shows passengers on an emigrant ship being called to breakfast by a bell.

Labor Migration

Unlike the many and diverse groups of more or less involuntary migrants, migrants who leave their homelands in search of work ordinarily do so voluntarily on the basis of personal considerations. Two examples may serve to illustrate this phenomenon.

In North America, migrant workers are needed primarily as unskilled harvest laborers in the agricultural sector. Most of these people come from the south – from Mexico or the Caribbean. According to official estimates, there were approximately 8.5 million Mexicans living and working in the U.S. in 2001, about three million of them illegally. In most cases, these migrant workers have been smuggled into the country by organized gangs. Over the years, specific migration patterns have taken shape in the United States. A significant number of migrant laborers work as fruit pickers in Florida during the winter before moving north to the New England states to help harvest tomatoes, potatoes, and apples in the summer. A second stream of migrant workers moves from Texas into the Midwest or to the West Coast in search of jobs picking fruit, vegetables, sugar beets, or cotton. A third current flows northward along the West Coast from southern California to Washington, working during the fruit and vegetable harvests.

Migrant workers often contribute significantly to the maintenance of living standards and even to increasing prosperity, as the example of the small oil-producing countries along the Persian Gulf clearly shows. Not only do "guest laborers" account for up to 80% of their populations, social institutions and economic sectors – public services, schools, universities, hospitals, private households, national and municipal administrations, the construction business and to a certain extent even the oil industry itself – depend heavily upon foreign workers and could hardly function without them.

Prospects

Environmental catastrophes, rapid population growth, and economic stagnation in some regions; sluggish population growth accompanied by strong economic expansion in others; political disputes and regional conflicts, civil wars, and famines – all of these factors will continue to cause large-scale popular migrations and waves of refugees in the 21st century. In a global economy, hardly a single country will be spared the consequences of these developments.

Religions of the World

One Divine Power? Many Concepts of Divinity

Religion is an expression of human responses to the experience of divinity in ritual and doctrine. It appears in different forms in different cultures and at different times, and though distinct from other manifestations of culture, it both reflects and shapes them at the same time. Religion is always community-oriented and always involves standards of ethics, although these may differ significantly from one set of beliefs and principles to another. Religion takes public form in rituals and pilgrimages, at specific places, and in the teachings of religious leaders. Religious faith informs and molds the lives of those who share it.

A Ubiquitous Phenomenon

All human societies since prehistoric times have embraced religious beliefs of some kind. We distinguish between two basic types of religion. The first is known as "primary religion." The origin and basis for all religions, it is still clearly evident today in "tribal religions" (frequently, though imprecisely and even inaccurately referred to as "natural" or "animistic" religions). These systems of belief have primarily local or regional relevance and generally govern communal life in small societies. They provide guidance and support at critical points in life – birth, puberty, marriage, death and mourning – through "rites of passage." Events marking seasonal transitions, such as planting and harvest or the winter and summer solstices, are also celebrated in rituals and serve as fixed points of reference for communal life, much like Christmas and Easter in western societies.

The second group, "secondary religions," comprises systems of belief and ritual which can be traced to the teachings or activities of founders, reformers, and charismatic leaders. They include the five major religions of the world: Judaism, Christianity, Islam, Buddhism, and Hinduism. They all pose the question of truth, which plays no role at all in primary religions, whose "natural" legitimacy is grounded in the specific societies that embrace them. Many secondary religions have sacred scriptures, which contain the basic tenets of ethics, faith, and behavior to which their adherents subscribe. Because they claim possession of universal truth, they tend to assume a missionary character, and their founders are the central focus of teaching and devotion. Buddhism, Christianity, and Islam are prime examples of this tendency. As they spread throughout the world, these secondary religions have had to come to grips with

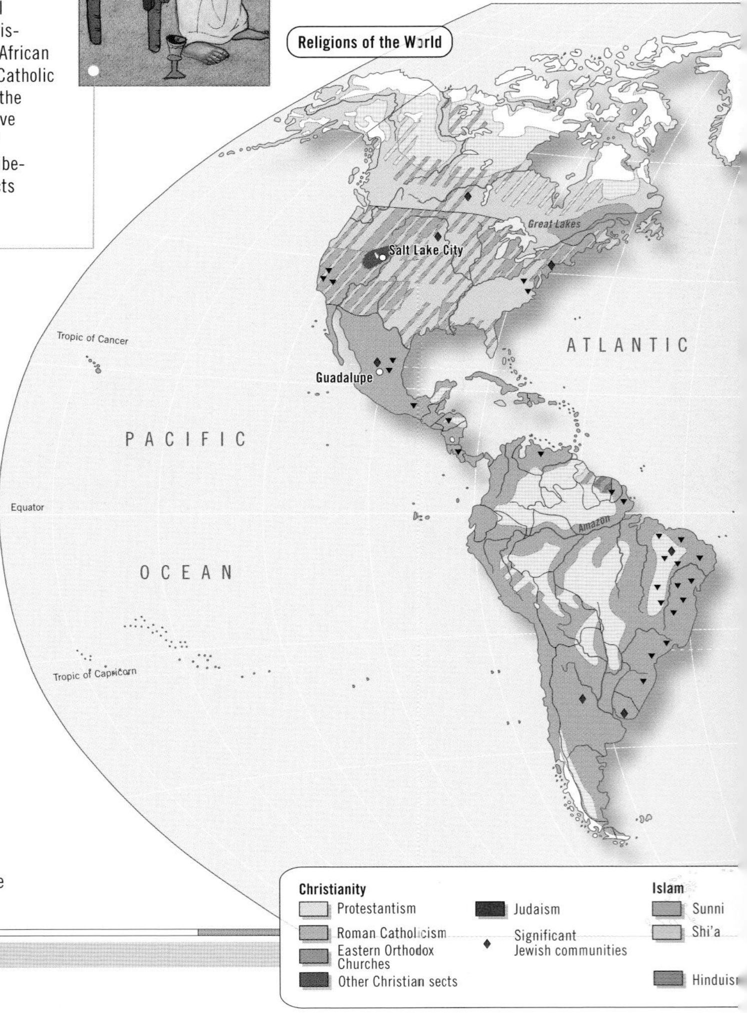

Christian Africa

The majority of people in most of the countries of central and southern Africa are Christians. More than one-third of African Christians are members of the Catholic Church, which actively promotes the education and development of native clerics. The "Independent Churches" embody a form of Christianity that deliberately makes room for traditional aspects of African tribal cultures.

Religion by the Book

An Ethiopian monk demonstrates the art of manuscript illumination while writing a page of the Bible in Amharic, which becomes established as the liturgical language of the Ethiopian Church.

Sacred Waters

A bath in the sacred Ganges River is believed to purify the soul of a Hindu. The ghats (bathing steps) at the pilgrimage center in Varanasi provide easy access to the Ganges.

Traditional Healer

In many African religions, misfortune, disease, and death are attributed to evil spells cast by witches. Only the healer (photo: Susa Madela, Sorcerer of Lightning, 1902–1988) can provide protection.

Islamic Pilgrimage

The Ka'bah, an empty, windowless building inside the Great Mosque in Mecca was a sacred shrine in the city even during pre-Islamic times. All Muslims are obliged to make at least one pilgrimage to Mecca in their lifetime. Pilgrims walk around the shrine seven times.

Religions of the World

Great Lakes
Salt Lake City
Guadalupe
Tropic of Cancer
Equator
Tropic of Capricorn
PACIFIC OCEAN
ATLANTIC

Christianity		Islam
Protestantism	Judaism	Sunni
Roman Catholicism	Significant Jewish communities	Shi'a
Eastern Orthodox Churches		
Other Christian sects		Hinduis

primary religions. In the process, they have adopted and adapted existing sacred rituals, places and times, reinterpreting them and casting out whatever elements could not be reconciled with their teachings. Buddhism developed into Mahayana Buddhism in China, for example, in response to regional influences. Christianity split into an eastern (Orthodox) branch under the influence of the religions of Greece and Asia Minor and a western (Roman) form of Catholicism oriented toward the more dogmatic Roman religions. Islam adopted pre-Islamic and existing Judaic and Christian elements, as the life of Mohammed clearly shows.

When the great religions face a loss of vitality and begin to abandon their original doctrines under the influence of progressive enlightenment, modern patterns of thought, and the pressure of political systems, reformers appear, new sects are founded, and fundamentalist revival movements take shape, as we witness all over the world today. This tendency is reflected in new religious movements and sects in Japan (Tenrykyo and others), the United States (Mormons, Children of God, etc.), Latin America (Umbanda, voodoo cults), India (neo-Hinduism), and Africa (Kimbanguism, Aladura churches, etc.) as well as the emphatically pious New-Age religions.

Religion – a Source of Conflict?

All religions strive to control the lives of their members, and thus they play an important role in public life. Radical, often fundamentalist religious movements also seek to exert political influence, although they often expose themselves to manipulation by political forces as well. In view of the dangers all societies face in today's world, religions would do well to remember their humanitarian function and support the growth of a system of ethics that will enable human beings to live together in peace.

Religions of the World				
Religions	Date of origin	Sacred scriptures	Number of adherents	% of world population
Christianity	30 AD	Bible	2 bn	33 % – increasing in the Third World
Islam	622 AD	Koran	1.3 bn	20 % – increasing
Hinduism and neo-Hinduism	c. 1,500 BC	Vedas, Upanishads	900 mil.	15 % – stagnant
Atheists and agnostics	–	–	900 mil.	15 % – decreasing
Buddhism	c. 530 BC	Tipitaka	360 mil.	6 % – stagnant
Chinese Religious Complex (ancestor and nature worship, Taoism, Confucianism*)	c. 1,500 BC	–	230 mil.	5 %
Tribal religions	prehistoric	Oral tradition	91 mil.	2 %
Yoruba religions: voodoo cults, Umbanda, etc.	?	–	30 mil.	< 1 %
New religious movements (Caodaism, Soka-Gakkai, Ananda Marge, etc.)	19th/20th c.	–	30 mil.	< 1 %
Sikhism	1500 AD	Adi Granth	18 mil.	< 1 %
Judaism	Babylonian exile (587 – 538 BC)	Torah, Talmud	15 mil.	< 1 %
Shamanism	prehistoric	Oral tradition	12 mil.	< 1 %
Spiritism*	after 1800	–	10 mil.	< 1 %
Baha'i	1863 AD	The Most Holy Book	4 mil.	< 1 %
Shintō	6th c. AD	Kojiki, Nihongi, Fudoki	4 mil.	< 1 %
Jainism	6th/5th c. BC	Extensive canon in Prakrit literature	3 mil.	< 1 %
Parsiism	500 – 250 BC	Avesta	150,000	< 1 %

* not a religion in the strict sense

(The Desert – Origin of all Great Religions)

The Israelites were nomads, like these shepherds on the Sinai Peninsula. They are believed to have worshiped protector gods and local divinities originally. Every tribe had its own god, to whom access was gained through the tribal elders ("fathers").

(Harmony and Peace)

Meditation is an important religious exercise for Buddhists, as it relieves the heart of suffering and the mind of ignorance. The simple saffron-colored robe symbolizes simplicity and self-denial; the fig tree recalls the bodhi tree beneath which Buddha achieved enlightenment.

(Jewish Marriage Rites)

Bride and groom cover their heads with a tallit (prayer cloak) during the marriage ceremony.

Northern and southern Buddhism
Lamaistic Buddhism

Chinese Religious Complex (Confucianism, Taoism)
Shinto
Tribal religions, Shamanism

▼ ▼ New religious movements
○ Religious shrines and sites
Unpopulated areas

Global Linguistic Diversity

One World — Thousands of Languages

Europoid			Afri...
French	Indian	Bushman (San)	Massai
Indo-European		Khoisan	Nilo-Sahara...

Depending upon the criteria applied in distinguishing them, between 2,500 and 6,500 languages are spoken on Earth. These widely diverging figures reflect both the difficulty involved in differentiating with certainty between a dialect and a language and our lack of knowledge about many languages spoken by very small groups in regions such as the Amazon Basin, New Guinea, and the African interior.

European languages account for only a small portion of the total. Somewhere between 70 and 165 different tongues are spoken on the continent. More languages (nearly 750!) are spoken in Papua New Guinea than in any other single country in the world. Only very few countries are completely unilingual (Iceland is one). Most countries are home to speakers of several or many different tongues and their variants. A number of languages die out every year, and discoveries of new languages are rare even today.

Dead Languages — Living Legacies

Some languages die out with their last speakers, while others are preserved as funds of knowledge, taught in schools (classical Arabic), used only in religious contexts (Old Hebrew), or studied as fixed points of historical reference in linguistics (Sanskrit). Still others serve as a source of new scientific terminology (Greek, Latin) or retain their vitality as literary languages (classical Chinese).

English — A Dominant World Language

Languages are affected by globalization as well. English has become the dominant language worldwide, although it ranks far behind Chinese in terms of numbers of native speakers. In sports and culture, in the high-tech world of computers and telecommunication, in the realm of travel and leisure activities, in scientific discourse and business correspondence, English has attained a degree of appeal, prestige, and influence that is unrivalled by any other language at the global level. International organizations exert considerable influence on language policy in support of other tongues. At the UN, for example, Arabic, Chinese, French, Russian, and Spanish join English as official languages. The European Union has even awarded official status to the national languages of all its member states.

Ethnic Revival — Grass Roots Resistance

The emancipation movements of the sixties and seventies led to a reassessment of the importance of language within the context of ethnic revival. Emphasis suddenly shifted from "utility" and "suitability" in a global sense to concern for linguistic diversity. "Minority" languages and tongues spoken in now independent former colonies were recognized as worthy of equal status and treatment. Languages which for centuries had been preserved and passed from one generation to the next only in oral form were systematically analyzed and described, transposed into a standardized written form, and documented in learning and reference materials such as textbooks, teachers' guides, dictionaries, and grammars (examples include Faeroese, a Germanic island language, and Swahili, the lingua franca in Africa). Bilingual or trilingual traffic and street signs, multilingual billboards, and enhanced media presence now offer striking visible and audible evidence of the new status of many once-neglected languages.

Writing Systems — Keys to Language

Human beings have employed a wide range of different writing systems to present natural, spoken language in visual form for more than three millennia. People of the ancient Egyptian, Inuit, and Maya cultures developed various forms of hieroglyphics, the Sumerians created a cuneiform system, while people of other civilizations established systems comprised of signs for words or syllables. Most forms of writing employed today make use of letters or symbols representing specific sounds. The writing systems now used in Europe and North America derive from the Phoenician alphabet developed in the 10th century BC, which also provided the basis for both the Arabic and Hebrew writing systems. Linguists have identified four major groups of alphabets: Greek (Latin, Coptic, Cyrillic, Armenian, Georgian), Semitic (Arabic, Hebrew, Ethiopian), Indian (Devanagari, Bengali, Tibetan, Burman, Thai, Khmer), and East Asian (Chinese, Japanese, Korean).

Every human has a language, but not everyone has command of its written form. Illiteracy is actually quite widespread and is particularly prevalant in the Third World. In Haiti, for example, 55% of the population cannot read or write. Illiterates account for 40% of the population of the Central African Republic, and 62% of all Yemeneseare unable to read a newspaper or write even a short note. Even the rich industrialized countries of the world face the problem of illiteracy, with up to 5% of their inhabitants unable to read or express themselves in written form and thus virtually excluded from the mainstream of cultural and economic life.

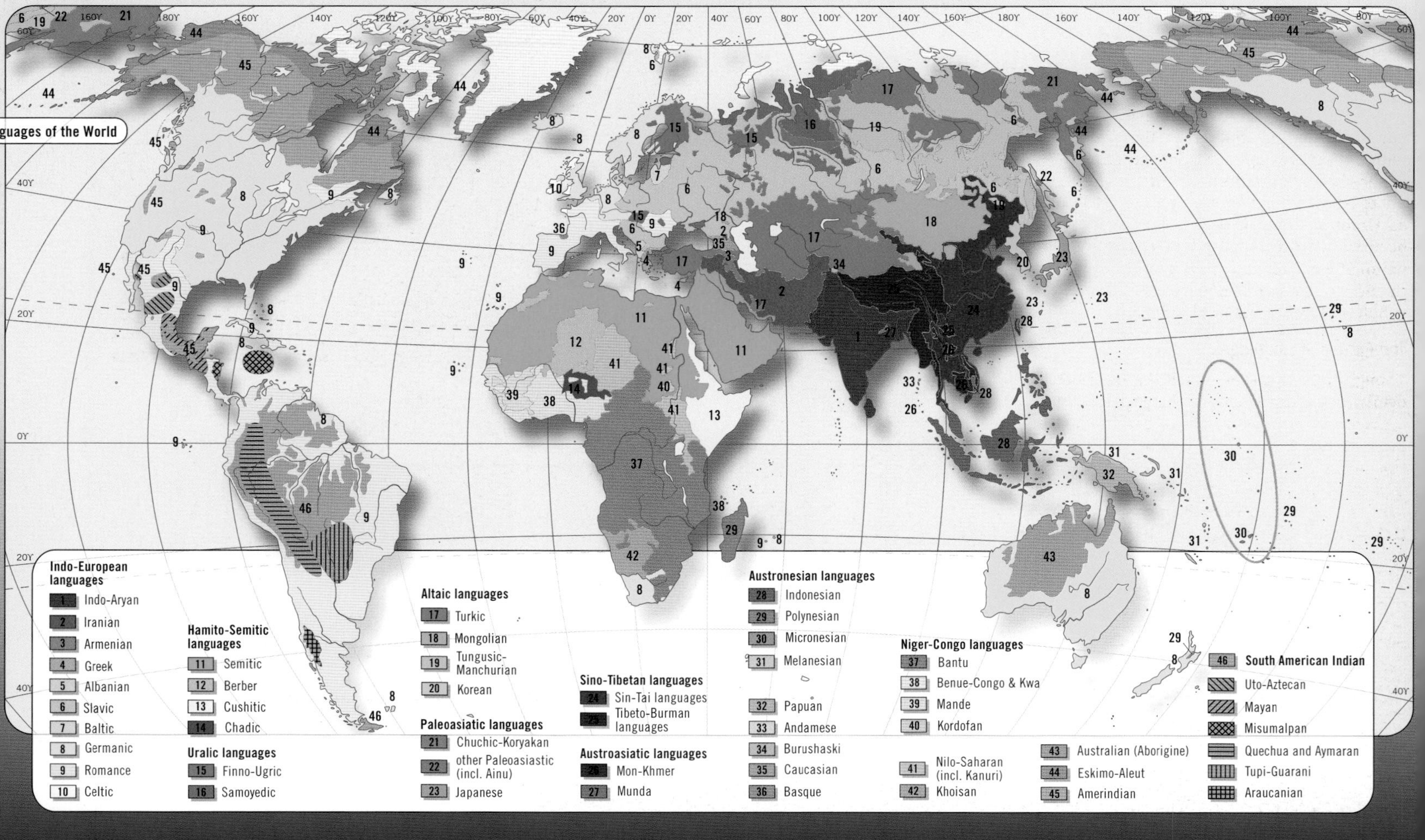

Languages of the World

Indo-European languages
1. Indo-Aryan
2. Iranian
3. Armenian
4. Greek
5. Albanian
6. Slavic
7. Baltic
8. Germanic
9. Romance
10. Celtic

Hamito-Semitic languages
11. Semitic
12. Berber
13. Cushitic
14. Chadic

Uralic languages
15. Finno-Ugric
16. Samoyedic

Altaic languages
17. Turkic
18. Mongolian
19. Tungusic-Manchurian
20. Korean

Paleoasiatic languages
21. Chuchic-Koryakan
22. other Paleoasiastic (incl. Ainu)
23. Japanese

Sino-Tibetan languages
24. Sin-Tai languages
25. Tibeto-Burman languages

Austroasiatic languages
26. Mon-Khmer
27. Munda

Austronesian languages
28. Indonesian
29. Polynesian
30. Micronesian
31. Melanesian
32. Papuan
33. Andamese
34. Burushaski
35. Caucasian
36. Basque

Niger-Congo languages
37. Bantu
38. Benue-Congo & Kwa
39. Mande
40. Kordofan
41. Nilo-Saharan (incl. Kanuri)
42. Khoisan

43. Australian (Aborigine)
44. Eskimo-Aleut
45. Amerindian
46. South American Indian

Uto-Aztecan
Mayan
Misumalpan
Quechua and Aymaran
Tupi-Guarani
Araucanian

Global Linguistic Diversity

East Asian		Arctic	Amerindian		Oceanian		Australian

Pygmy — Chinese — Tibetan — Inuit — Maya — Yanomami — Polynesian — Melanesian — Australian

Niger-Kordofan — Sino-Tibetan — Eskimo-Aleut — Amerindian — Austronesian — Australian

Linguistic Diversity – a Curse?

Did all humans originally speak a single language? The idea (no longer accepted) is expressed in the biblical story of the Tower of Babylon (painting by Pieter Bruegel the Elder, 1563), in which linguistic diversity is described as God's punishment for human pride and greed for power.

Linguistic Exchange – The Foreign Element

All languages have changed over the course of centuries. Apart from natural, organic evolution, languages are influenced significantly by contact among speakers of different linguistic communities – conquerors and conquered peoples, neighboring linguistic groups, etc. In this way, languages enrich one another with "foreign material" (adopted and adapted words and forms). These phenomena are referred to by historical linguistics as strata: Substrates are traces of the language of a conquered or exterminated people left behind in the language of the victors (e.g. remnants of Celtic in the Romance languages). Superstrata are elements introduced by a conquering group into the language of a subjugated people but which do not displace the original language (e.g. Franconian influences on French). Adstrata are linguistic influences which do not reflect hierarchical relationships (e.g. contacts between speakers of Germanic and Romance languages along linguistic boundaries).

The Birth of New Languages: Pidgin and Creole Forms

Pidgin and Creole languages are the products of a special form of linguistic interaction which takes place primarily when speakers of different native tongues communicate with each other. Such languages have developed through trading activity and in economies significantly influenced by slavery in the New World, Africa, Southeast Asia, and Oceania. Pidgin languages are characterized by markedly simplified structures that facilitate communication but are found in neither of the original native languages involved. Pidgin languages that become established and are passed on to succeeding generations are known as Creoles. Many Creole languages have been standardized and adopted as official national languages (in Haiti, Mauritius, and the Seychelles, for example) and thus contribute to local or national identity.

The Future of Languages

Though many have predicted the eventual demise of linguistic diversity, languages have proven astonishingly resilient. Even today, there are those who hope and believe that globalization will result in the establishment of English as the worldwide medium for communication. Yet efforts have also been undertaken to have the right to speak one's native language firmly anchored in international human rights conventions. Slowly but surely, people are beginning to realize that linguistic diversity has the capacity to enrich humanity and is not, as the Bible suggests, God's punishment for human pride, vanity, and greed. In the age of technology, languages that remain open to progress and capable of integrating it into their dynamic systems will survive and ensure the preservation of linguistic diversity in the 21st century.

A Monument to Language

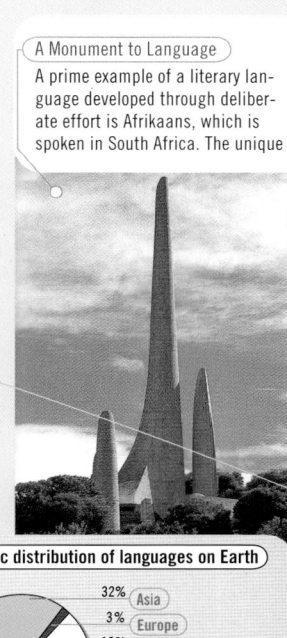

A prime example of a literary language developed through deliberate effort is Afrikaans, which is spoken in South Africa. The unique monument to language erected in Paarl near Cape Town commemorates the linguistic movement founded by the Boers in 1875.

The Physiognomy of Diversity

Portraits of people from selected ethnic groups and their language families (lower print bar).

Geographic distribution of languages on Earth

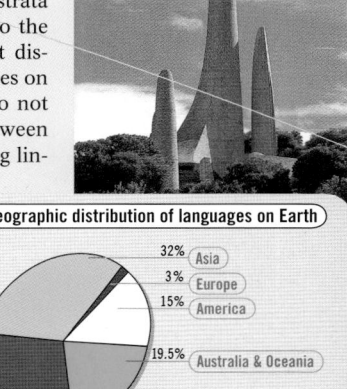

- 32% Asia
- 3% Europe
- 15% America
- 19.5% Australia & Oceania
- 30.5% Africa

Most widely spoken languages by number of speakers
as native and second language

millions	
940	Chinese
475	English
395	Hindi
375	Spanish
300	Russian
215	Arabic
200	Bengali
185	Portuguese
155	Malayan-Indonesian
125	Japanese
122	French
118	German
100	Urdu

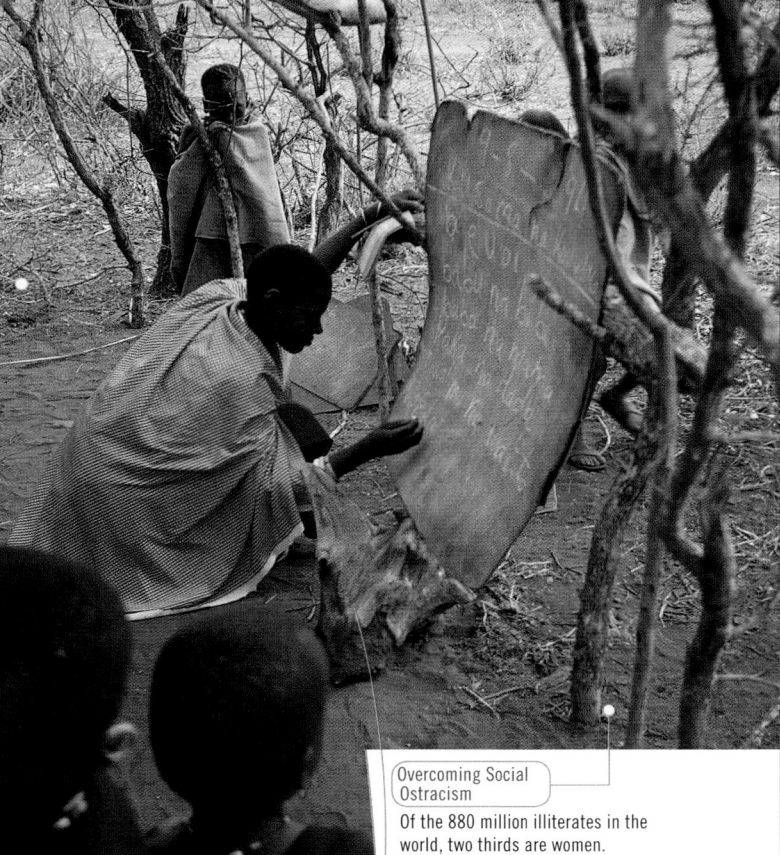

Overcoming Social Ostracism

Of the 880 million illiterates in the world, two thirds are women. 120 million children do not attend proper schools – due primarily to a lack of money. The photo shows a Massai "bush school" in East Africa.

Bilingual Street Sign

Increasing attention is now being given to linguistic minorities in many countries (photo: sign in French and Occitan in Agde). Distinctions are expressed in different print sizes.

Rue
Hôtel du cheval blanc
PORTA DE LA FONT

Water as a Resource & a Source of Conflicts

"Blue Gold" – Our Most Precious Resource

During the International Hydrological Decade (IHD, 1964-1974), a global effort to assess the world's water reserves was launched under the auspices of UNESCO. Based on the results, experts now agree: There is plenty of water in the world – yet not nearly enough to satisfy the needs of the entire human race in the 21st century. According to projections presented at the World Water Conference in The Hague in March 2000, some 3.3 billion people (37% of the world's population) will be directly confronted with a shortage of water by 2025 (the number has already reached two billion), because only about 0.29% of the total water supply on earth is available as fresh water suitable for human use (for drinking, hygiene, and the production of consumer goods), while the population continues to grow at a rapid pace. In the course of the 20th century, the human population grew from 1.6 billion to more than 6 billion people, who now share a maximum total of 4.2 million cubic kilometers of liquid fresh water – a supply that cannot be increased significantly. Thus every new addition to the world's population reduces the amount of water available to each person on earth.

How Much Water Does a Human Being Need?

Inhabitants of temperate climate zones – North Americans, for example – need between two and three liters of water per day to satisfy their basic physical and physiological needs. People who live in hot climes require six or more liters per day. For a worker in the oil fields of Saudi Arabia, a daily ration of twelve liters of liquids is just about sufficient. If he quenches his thirst with beer, the figure of twelve liters must be multiplied by 60 (bringing the total to 720 liters), since up to 60 liters of fresh water are required to produced a single liter of beer. A scholar who stills his thirst for knowledge with three books weighing one kilogram each and places them on his bookshelf must – like the beer-drinking oil field worker – accept responsibility for the consumption of at least 750 liters of water, as it takes roughly 250 liters to produce one kilogram of paper. In light of the worldwide water shortage, the fact that between 20,000 and 30,000 liters of water are required for the production of an average passenger car should give pause for thought, especially when one considers that there are currently 750 million cars on the world's roads and that a country like China (with one-fifth of the world's population) is

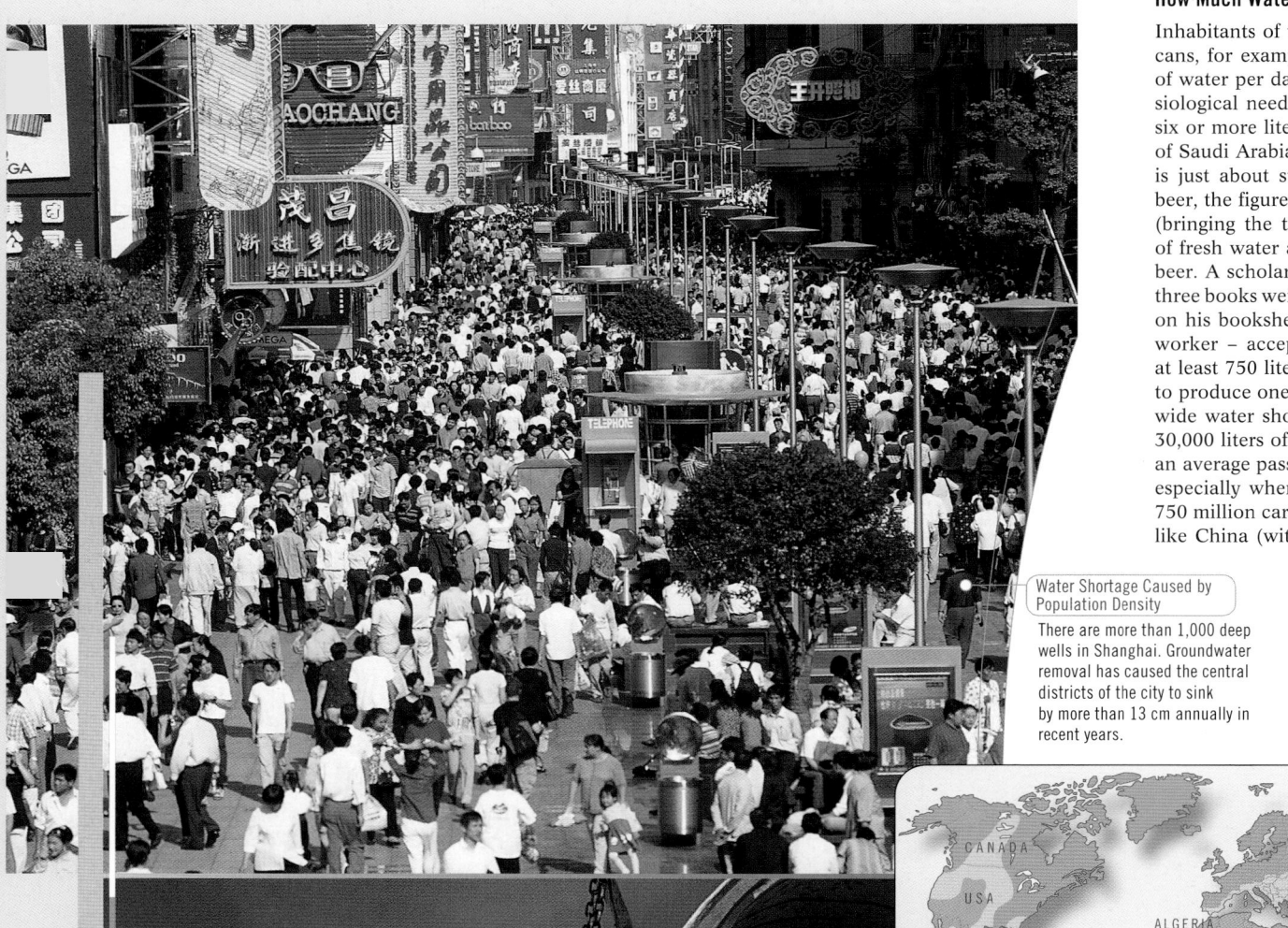

Water Shortage Caused by Population Density

There are more than 1,000 deep wells in Shanghai. Groundwater removal has caused the central districts of the city to sink by more than 13 cm annually in recent years.

Unequal Distribution

Global water resources are unfairly distributed. Only one-fourth of the world's population has access to a sufficient water supply.

World Water Resources

- water surplus
- sufficient supply
- increasing scarcity
- water shortage

Water from the Desert

Muammar Qaddafi's mammoth "Great-Man-Made-River" project has been under construction since 1984. More than 1,000 km of pipelines with a diameter of four meters convey fossil water from depths of 400 to 1,500 m in southeastern Libya to the coastal region.

Water as a Resource & a Source of Conflicts

motorizing in leaps and bounds. Even more alarming is the tremendous amount of fresh water needed to ensure an adequate supply of food for the growing global population. Depending upon climate conditions, the production of one kilogram of grain requires between 1,000 and 2,000 liters of fresh water (or 1,000 to 2,000 tons of water per ton of grain). Thus our daily bread or bowl of rice – like our daily minimum ration of fresh water – is a very important factor in the calculation of per capita consumption of water, although it is seldom given sufficient consideration. The published figures for "average daily water consumption per person per day" (128 liters in Germany and about twice that amount in the U.S.) reflect only measurable household consumption and thus give a false picture of actual water use, which – particularly when viewed from a global perspective – goes far beyond daily household needs.

Who Needs and Uses How Much Water?

According to the most recent precise calculation of the global demand for fresh water (in 1990), private households, which (combined with small businesses and public consumption) account for 7.6% of total consumption, are the smallest but most significant user group, followed in increasing size by industry (24.6%). At 67.8%, agriculture, in its role as the producer of food for the world, is far and away the largest consumer. In contrast to industry, which ordinarily uses water only briefly as utility or process water (which it usually returns to the water cycle as polluted waste water, however), agriculture consumes water in the production of biomass. Despite worldwide efforts to encourage economical use of water resources, the unbridled growth of the world's population is likely to make the water shortage the number-one global problem in the 21st century.

The Statistics of Scarcity

According to guidelines issued by the World Health Organization (WHO), a human being in the 21st century requires a minimum annual per capita ration of 1,000 cubic meters of fresh water (or 2,470 liters per day for food and energy production, industrial products, hygiene, education, traffic, and other purposes) to maintain a living standard appropriate in our time without endangerment to health (current per capita consumption is about 3,000 cubic meters per year in the U.S. and 1,500 cubic meters in other industrialized countries).

The water shortage is not necessarily restricted to specific climate zones. Much more important as a measure of scarcity is the quantity of renewable water resources (precipitation as well as inflowing river and groundwater) available in a given country relative to its population per year. Accordingly, countries with a fresh water supply of less than 1,000 cubic meters per person are classified as water emergency areas. Serious problems arise from water shortage where the natural supply of water falls below 1,700 – 2,000 cubic meters per person (the water stress level). Regions with renewable supplies of between 2,000 and 2,500 cubic meters and above per capita are regarded as non-critical. Africa has the largest number of water-poor countries, in which about 300 million people (one-third of the population) live under conditions of water emergency.

Reasons for Scarcity

Statistically speaking, the fresh water reserves on our "blue planet" are sufficient to serve the needs of humanity as a whole. Yet a number of factors contradict this naive statistical assessment. First of all, fresh water reserves are not equally distributed throughout the world. Nor does the presence of water in a given region necessarily mean that the other living conditions are favorable to human life. Secondly, fresh water that comes from the sky as precipitation rarely stays where it falls. The nature of water – its mobility – causes it to run off, evaporate, or seep to

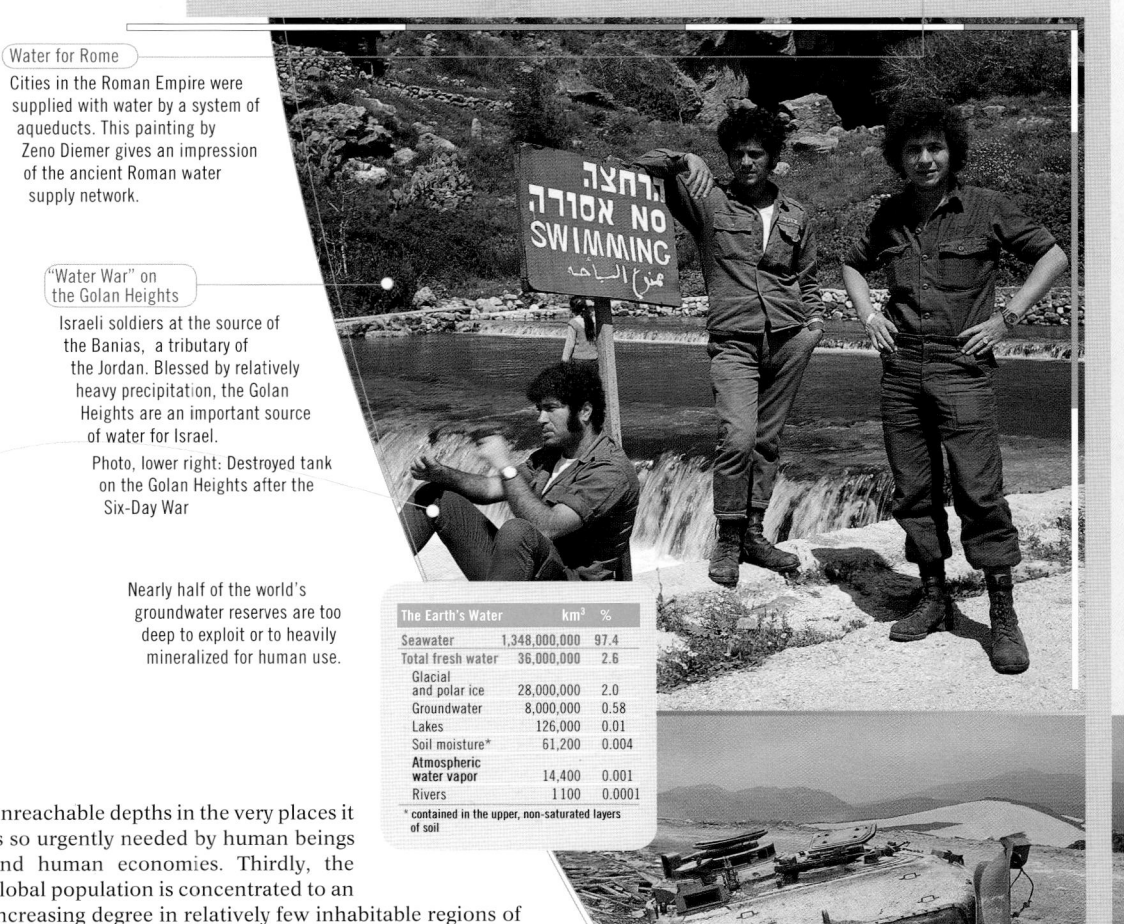

Water for Rome
Cities in the Roman Empire were supplied with water by a system of aqueducts. This painting by Zeno Diemer gives an impression of the ancient Roman water supply network.

"Water War" on the Golan Heights
Israeli soldiers at the source of the Banias, a tributary of the Jordan. Blessed by relatively heavy precipitation, the Golan Heights are an important source of water for Israel.
Photo, lower right: Destroyed tank on the Golan Heights after the Six-Day War

Nearly half of the world's groundwater reserves are too deep to exploit or to heavily mineralized for human use.

The Earth's Water	km³	%
Seawater	1,348,000,000	97.4
Total fresh water	36,000,000	2.6
Glacial and polar ice	28,000,000	2.0
Groundwater	8,000,000	0.58
Lakes	126,000	0.01
Soil moisture*	61,200	0.004
Atmospheric water vapor	14,400	0.001
Rivers	1 100	0.0001

* contained in the upper, non-saturated layers of soil

unreachable depths in the very places it is so urgently needed by human beings and human economies. Thirdly, the global population is concentrated to an increasing degree in relatively few inhabitable regions of the Earth (about 90% of the human race occupies four per cent of the world's dry land) and exceeds the hydrological capacity of these regions by virtue of sheer numbers alone. Finally, humans as economic beings – unlike animals and plants – tend to burden fresh water with many kinds of foreign substances (primarily chemicals) that make it unsuitable for reuse as drinking water and thus exacerbate the water shortage, particularly in densely populated urban agglomerations.

Relief Measures

Advanced cultures with large populations were forced to deal with the problem of water scarcity even in ancient times. Thus hydraulic engineering measures for the procurement and storage of scarce, life-giving water are among the oldest technical structures known to mankind. Remnants of irrigation systems from the 3rd millennium BC have been found in India, China, Yemen, and Egypt. As long ago as 1700 BC, the Babylonian King Hammurabi enacted important laws governing the use of the precious resource of water in the Code of Hammurabi.

Outstanding examples of early urban water supply systems involving technically sophisticated aqueducts are the ancient cities of Pergamum (western Anatolia) and Rome. In the 1st century AD, the Romans moved 600,000 cubic meters of water into their city daily, supplying every inhabitant with 600 liters per day. Modern water procurement systems make use of other means in addition to long-distance water conveyance via pipelines and canals (e.g. the California Aqueduct and the "Great-Man-Made-River" in Libya). Today, some 800,000 small and large dams all over the world prevent rapid water run-off, making more water available for drinking or use in farming or industrial operations than is contained in all of the rivers of the world.

Water Wars?

Experts anticipate population growth of between 30% and 70% in the water-poor regions of the world by the year 2025. It is highly likely that this will lead to increased competition for water, not only among cities and between agriculture and industry but between nations as well.

Forty per cent of the world's population live in regions fed by rivers that flow through more than two countries, and over 200 areas burdened by political conflict largely attributable to disputes over the use of water from such rivers clearly underscore the magnitude of the water shortage as a potential source of political conflict.

The most volatile regions of conflict over water with serious potential for armed hostilities are located along the Ganges (usage disputes between India and Bangladesh), the Tigris and Euphrates (Turkey, Syria, Iraq), the Jordan (Israel, Syria, the West Bank, Jordan), and the Nile (Egypt, Sudan, Ethiopia, Eritrea). "Real" water wars have occurred only rarely in history, but water scarcity has often been the spark that set off the powder keg of existing religious, ethnic, or territorial conflicts.

Fossil Fuels - Production and World Trade

Competition for the Earth's Energy Reserves

The recent rapid rise in prices for fuels and heating oil have reminded us how vulnerable our social and economic systems are and how dependent we are on the oil-producing countries. Our high-tech world consumes vast amounts of energy, and most industrialized countries do not have sufficient resources to cover their own needs. Cartels formed by the oil-producing countries ensure a certain degree of market stability, but they also underscore the dependence of importing countries on the suppliers of raw materials. Transnational and multinational firms operating in the raw materials markets have the power to circumvent cartel agreements more or less at will. Aside from the political and economic problems associated with fossil fuels, environmental issues are now becoming increasingly important.

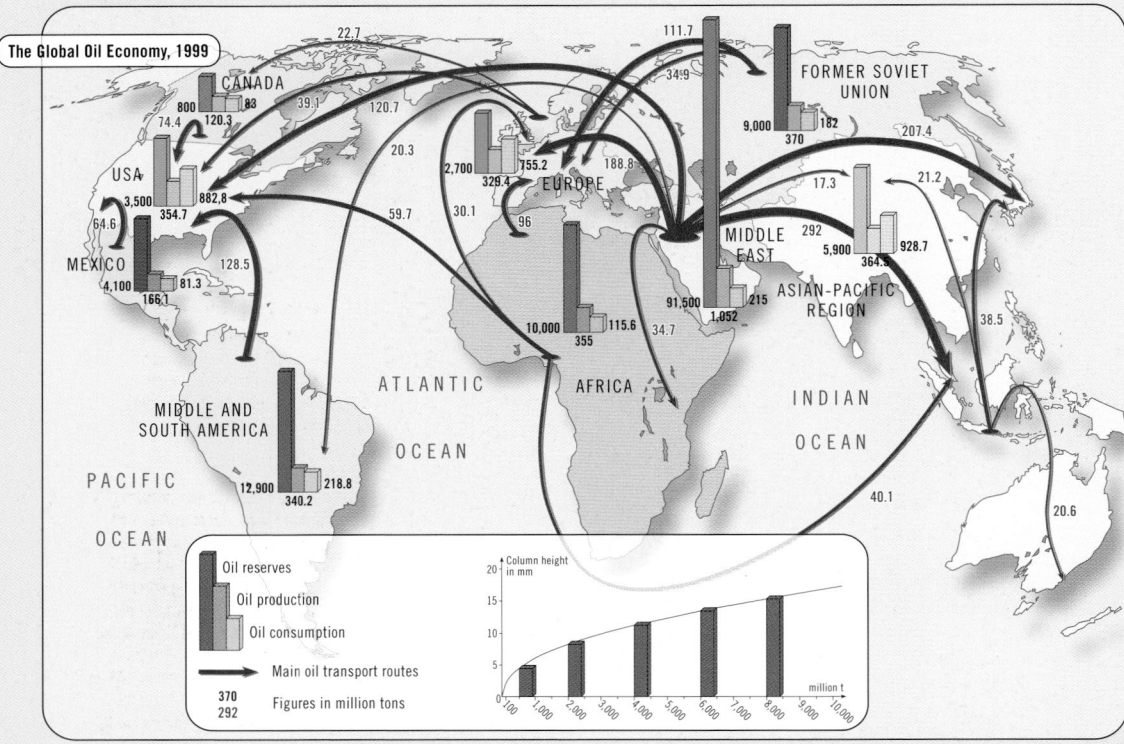

The Global Oil Economy, 1999

Oil reserves
Oil production
Oil consumption

Column height in mm

→ Main oil transport routes

370
292 Figures in million tons

The Growing Hunger for Energy

Hunting and gathering societies met all of their energy needs with wood, a renewable source of energy. This did not change significantly during the transition to farming and animal husbandry, although wood did become scarce in heavily deforested areas. It was not until humans began processing ores to make metal implements using wood or charcoal as fuels that dependence upon renewable energy sources began to pose serious problems. Forests, which had once seemed endless, were destroyed at a pace that far outstripped their capacity to recover. Water and wind mills facilitated the processing of agricultural products and were later employed by the textile industry. The advent of industrialization and mechanized vehicles (steam locomotives) brought the need for higher-energy fossil fuels (coal). In terms of energy output, one ton of coal equated to the annual yield of two acres of forest. Electrification intensified the demand for fossil fuels and also made energy easily transportable. But this applied only to "developed countries." Around 1900, wood, wind, water, and human and animal muscle power still covered two-thirds of the world's energy needs. Only a few decades ago, wood was the only available source of heating and cooking energy for one-third of the world's population. Today, energy consumption and management prognoses must take into account the anticipated rapid rise in energy demand in the Third World.

The Underground Forest

Bituminous coal was used occasionally in ancient civilizations and to an increasing extent during the Middle Ages. Large-scale exploitation, including underground mining, did not begin until the 19th century, when coal became an indispensable source of energy. Worldwide coal production rose rapidly from twelve million tons (1820) to 1.2 billion t (1910), when 85% of all coal produced in the world was mined in Germany, Great Britain, and the U.S.A. Although global production has stagnated in recent years (1998: 3.7 billion t) or grown only marginally, the focal points of mining activity shifted due to cost pressures. Difficult and thus expensive mining operations in the European Union (Great Britain, Germany, France) were cut back drastically in favor of cheaper coal from such countries as the U.S. The German bituminous coal-mining industry, for example, is highly subsidized, as coal costs more than $140 per ton there, while the price of imported coal is below $36. China, Australia, Colombia, South Africa, and other countries increased production, not only to cover domestic demand but for export as well. According to estimates, exploitable coal reserves amount to at least 550 billion tons of bituminous coal units, concentrated mostly in Russia, the U.S., China, Australia, and India. Due to its high water content and low energy output, brown coal is used primarily in the production of electricity and is not transported over long distances.

Petroleum, "Black Gold"

More than 140 years after the discovery of oil in Pennsylvania (1859), global economic and political developments are now more dependent than ever before on the availability of oil. This is primarily the consequence of motorization, and the rise in the use of motor vehicles to transport people and material, although petroleum is also used for heating, in power plants, and as an industrial raw material. After a modest beginning (1900: 20 million t), oil production increased dramatically following the Second World War (1950: 523 million; 1999: 4.1 billion t). Every day, nearly 10 million tons of oil are pumped from several thousand oil wells around the world. The amount of natural gas produced at the same time matches the energy value of six million tons of petroleum.

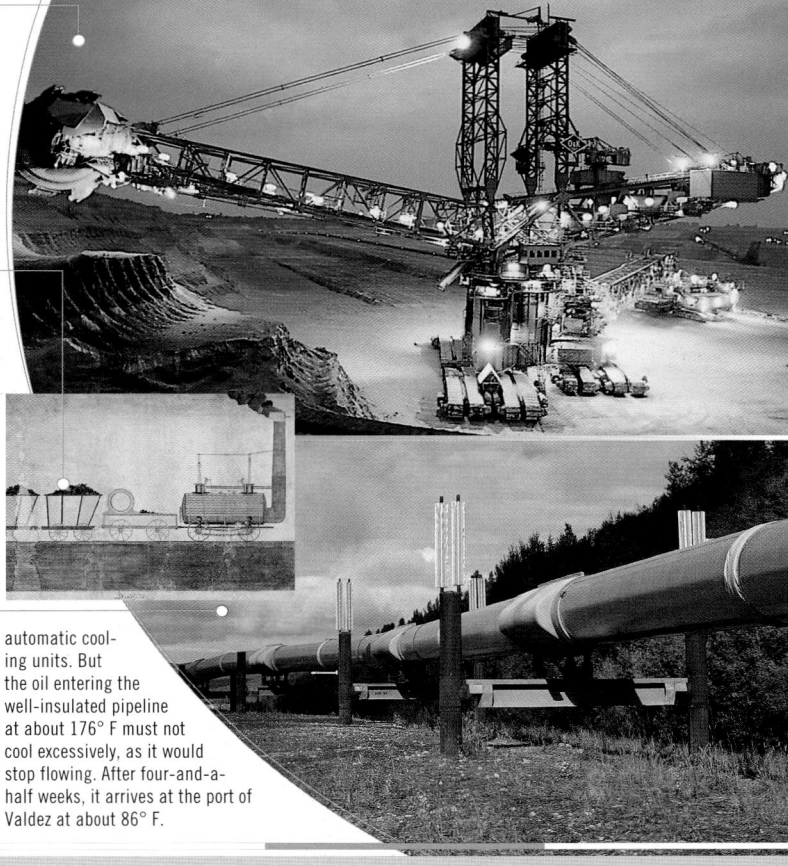

Devouring the Landscape

Brown coal deposits are usually not deep in the earth and are therefore mined almost exclusively in open pits. In the Rhenish brown-coal fields (photo), huge bucket-wheel excavators remove covering layers of sediment and mine the underlying coal. These machines can move more than 200,000 cubic meters of material a day.

Driving Force

The invention of the coal-burning steam engine launched the Industrial Revolution. The development of railroads (photo: steam locomotive built by George Stephenson, c. 1815) made it possible to transport coal, agricultural and industrial goods as well as people quickly, over long distances, and on a large scale. The loud, smoke-spewing engines gave rise to early complaints about environmental pollution.

Protection against Heat and Cold

The designers of the Alaska Pipeline (1,310 km long, 1974-77) had to find ways to protect the delicate permafrost ecosystem, in which soil thaws only near the surface in the summer and would shift if exposed to additional heat. The pipes were laid on supports above ground and equipped with automatic cooling units. But the oil entering the well-insulated pipeline at about 176° F must not cool excessively, as it would stop flowing. After four-and-a-half weeks, it arrives at the port of Valdez at about 86° F.

Fossil Fuels - Production and World Trade

From Crude Oil to the Consumer
Petroleum products such as heating oil, gasoline, diesel fuel, kerosene and bitumen are produced through distillation, refining, and cracking.

Man-Made Islands
Prospecting for oil and natural gas beneath ocean floors and exploiting discovered reserves requires the use of huge platforms, which are towed to the drilling site and anchored with massive steel or concrete constructions. They must be able to withstand heavy tides and severe storms — particularly in the North Sea. The oil or gas is brought to land via pipelines or by shuttle tankers.

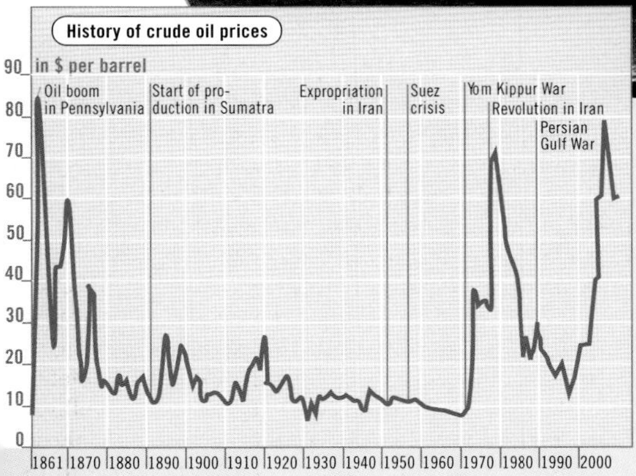

History of crude oil prices

in $ per barrel

90 80 70 60 50 40 30 20 10 0

Oil boom in Pennsylvania | Start of production in Sumatra | Expropriation in Iran | Suez crisis | Yom Kippur War Revolution in Iran | Persian Gulf War

1861 1870 1880 1890 1900 1910 1920 1930 1940 1950 1960 1970 1980 1990 2000

The present tight oil supply situation and accompanying price explosion call to mind the oil crisis of 1973, when the oil price rose 600% as the result of deliberately induced shortages in the aftermath of the Arab-Israeli War. The consequence was a worldwide economic crisis. Years before, in 1960, seven oil-exporting countries formed OPEC (Organization of Petroleum Exporting Countries, which now has eleven members), in the hope of gaining a higher share of oil revenues and exerting greater political influence as a cartel.

The end of the Oil Age predicted by the Club of Rome in 1973 did not come to pass. The sudden rise in prices made it possible to tap petroleum reserves that had previously appeared too expensive to exploit. Thanks to new fields in the North Sea and Alaska, supply rose faster than demand. The power of OPEC waned temporarily.

Natural Gas, an Increasingly Popular Fuel

The demand for natural gas has risen steadily over the past 30 to 40 years. Easily transported via pipelines, it is used to heat buildings and generate electricity. Produc-

tion is concentrated primarily in the CIS countries and the U.S. The United States, which also import natural gas from Canada and Mexico, consume more than one forth of total world production. The largest reserves are in Russia (36%), the other CIS countries, the Middle East, and Southeast Asia. More than 40% are held by the OPEC states. Germany imports nearly 80% of its natural gas (mainly from Russia, Norway, and the Netherlands).

Is an Energy Crisis Looming?

At present, 90% of the world's energy needs are covered by fossil fuels. Industrialized countries account for nearly 60% of total demand. Over the past 30 years, primary energy consumption has risen at a rate of 2% per year, although the collapse of the Eastern Bloc significantly reduced the pace of growth. Increasing motorization in the developing countries could raise the rate of increase to double that figure within the next 20 years.

Half of the energy consumed by the EU countries is imported (Germany: 60%). With only 4.5% of the world's population, the U.S. uses 25% of the annual production of primary energy. Europe (excluding the CIS countries) is not far behind at over 20%.

At present consumption levels, the known reserves of petroleum (approx. 150 billion t) would last for more than 40 years, natural gas reserves (at least 150 trillion cubic meters) for over 60 years. Moreover, new technologies favor more efficient exploitation of deposits and the discovery of new ones. This could result in a doubling of known reserves. And there are also a number of as yet untapped reserves of tar sand, oil shale, and heavy crude oil. These are expensive to exploit, however, and would raise the price of oil accordingly. Since two thirds of the

easily exploitable reserves are located in the Persian Gulf region (chiefly in Saudi Arabia), the power of OPEC is a major factor in the global economy. The OPEC countries currently hold over 75% of known reserves and control 40% of global production. Yet the Middle East, like the oil-rich Caspian Sea region, is politically unstable, which means that disruptions of production are likely.

Protecting the Earth's Atmosphere

Two major themes have dominated discussion with regard to global energy management in recent years: the principle of sustainability and the threat – or reality – of global warming as a consequence of a man-made greenhouse effect. The joint resolution of nearly all industrialized countries (enacted 1992 without the U.S.) calling for reduction of the burning of oil, natural gas, and coal to the 1990 level by the year 2005 has born little fruit thus far. Resistance to nuclear energy (which accounts for 7.4% of primary energy worldwide) and the closing of nuclear power plants could actually result in higher CO_2 emissions due to the increased reliance of oil, gas, and coal. It is likely to take quite some time to achieve large-scale, effective use of renewable energy sources (currently 2.7% of primary energy, primarily from hydroelectric power) – photovoltaic solar cells, solar heating plants, fuel cells, wind and biomass power plants, geothermal energy, heat pumps, ocean energy (wave and tide energy, ocean warmth). It will also be necessary to seek new ways of conserving energy. Regardless of the actual size of current reserves of fossil fuels, they are ultimately limited.

Division of the Globe into Time Zones

The Stock Exchange is Always Open – Somewhere on Earth!

When we want to call someone in Europe, we need to consider the time difference in order to be sure that we don't wake up our party in the middle of the night. Business people and international airlines must be constantly alert to these time differences. Stock-market speculators are happy to know that trading is possible around the clock, as there is always a stock exchange open somewhere in the world, whether in Sydney, New York, or Frankfurt am Main.

Local Time vs. Zone Time

Long ago, local times were different virtually wherever one looked. After all, it is only natural for the noon bell to ring when the sun reaches its highest point in the sky. The time difference between two towns at the same latitude separated by only 50 km is three minutes. Before the railways were built, such discrepancies were of little significance, since travel was always slow at best. Nevertheless, local mean times were introduced toward the end of the 18th century and regarded as binding for a given center and its surrounding region – Geneva time in 1780, Berlin time in 1820, Paris time in 1826, Zurich time in 1832, Pulkow and Greenwich time in 1848, Warsaw and Bern time in 1853. North Americans, in particular, lent strong support to the plan to establish a global system for measuring time. In 1873, 71 different railroad times were still in effect here. That year, Sandford Fleming, Chief Engineer of the Canadian Pacific Railway, proposed setting up a system of 24 meridians spaced at intervals of 15 degrees – a time difference of one hour – and assigning a standard time to each. That would divide the world into 24 time zones. But where was one to start? Which meridian was to get the zero label?

Ignoring the different times in effect in the many different countries of the world, seafarers had generally agreed to go by Greenwich time. But there were also zero meridians in Ferro (now Hierro), in Venice, and in many other places as well. At the Washington conference of 1884, 27 countries agreed to establish the zero meridian at Greenwich and to divide the globe into two geographic hemispheres, the western and the eastern.

Time systems were also standardized in many other European countries in response to the increasing internationalization of travel and transport. In Germany, which was still comprised of many independent states, most of them small, the railroad system could function properly only if agreement was reached on a standard time system. This was achieved with the Reichsgesetz of 1893. France did not join the system until 1911.

Most time zones are 15 degrees wide and cover a section of the globe that lies 7.5 degrees to the east and west of one of the 24 meridians. The standard time is the same everywhere within a given time zone. In some regions, time zone boundaries do not run along lines of longitude but along national borders. This is meant to ensure that the same time applies at every location within a country. Yet , many countries are too large to be accommodated within a single time zone. The U.S. is divided into four time zones, for example.

People living in Los Angeles should call their relatives on the East Coast early in the evening in order to avoid waking them during the night. TV networks must determine the best times to broadcast programs in order to reach the largest possible number of viewers. Under certain circumstances, networks accept the need to broadcast certain programs ("breaking news") at unfavorable times. Countries spanning several time zones require a system that makes it clear which time is meant when times are announced. In the U.S. times are identified by the time zone names: Eastern, Central, Mountain, and Pacific.

Which Island Will Be the First?

As the new year 2000 approached, several island countries in the Pacific set their sights on being the first to ring in the year 2000. The Fiji Islands introduced daylight saving time, turning their clocks ahead in order to be the first to celebrate. Tonga shifted the International Date Line along the eastern edge of its territory, putting itself 13 hours ahead of Greenwich. But the island kingdom had no chance against Kiribati, with its extensive ocean territory measuring 3,870 km from west to east. The eastward protrusion of the Date Line runs along the eastern border of Kiribati. Caroline Island, the easternmost atoll, was given the name Millennium Island (14 hours ahead of Greenwich).

... and the living is easy

Daylight savings time, the practice of turning the clock ahead one hour during the summer months in the northern hemisphere, has existed in Great Britain and Ireland since 1916. In the U.S., it was reintroduced in 1967 after having been used during both World Wars as a means of conserving energy by taking advantage of daylight. The desired energy-saving effect was actually never achieved, but people enjoy having an extra hour of leisure time while the sun shines and see daylight saving time as an improvement in quality of life.

One Day Too Early

People first recognized the need for an international date line when the "Victoria," a ship from Magellan's fleet, returned to Spain after circumnavigating the globe on September 6, 1522. The entries in the ship's log were a day behind the correct date. The expedition had constantly "gained time" on its westward voyage, saving an entire day by the time it had completely circled the globe.

The First Pocket Watch

Peter Henlein is believed to have invented the spring-driven watch. Beginning in 1510, he produced a series of small, portable clocks shaped like a can – the first pocket watches.

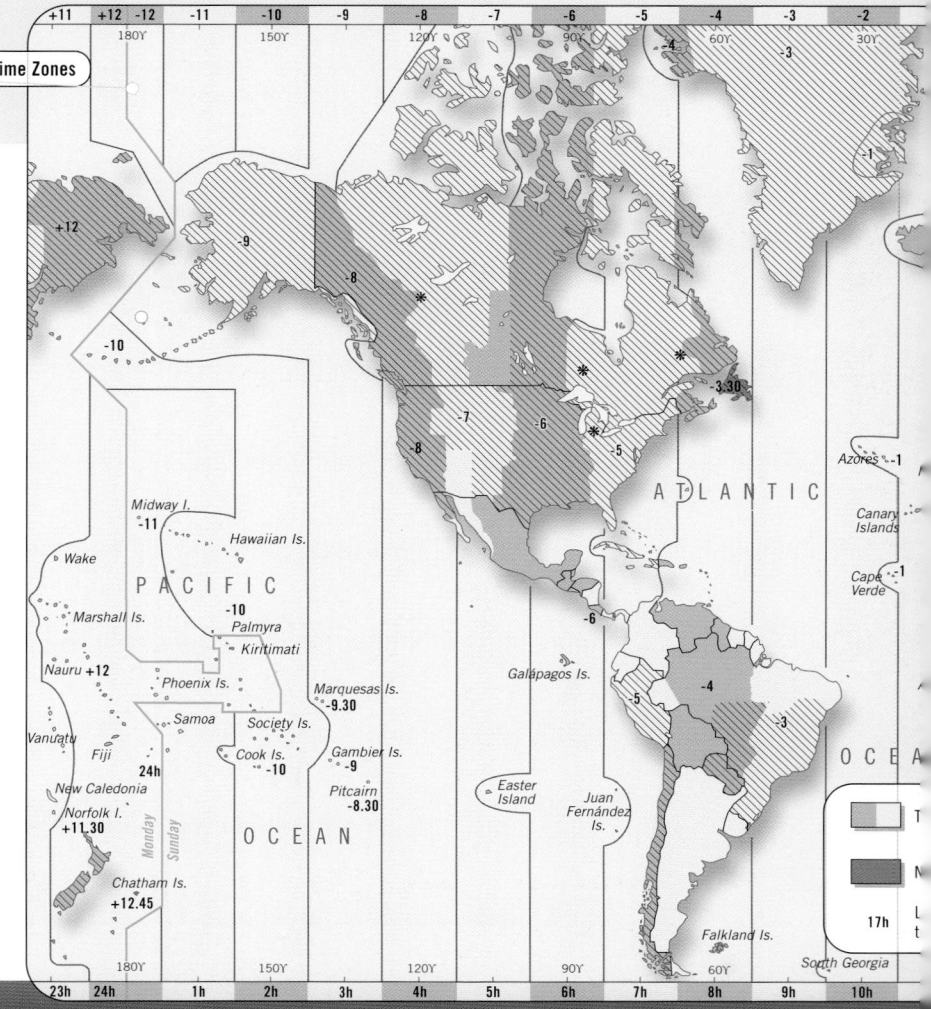

Time Zones

Division of the Globe into Time Zones

I and the Zero Meridian

The seam of our system of measuring time runs through the observatory in Greenwich (now Flamsteed House), which was established in 1675.

People who cross the International Date Line from east to west must move the calendar one day ahead. Those crossing in the reverse direction, from west to east, turn it back one day. A traveler who fails to heed this convention while circling the globe from west to east will find himself a day ahead of the local calendar upon arriving at his starting point. This happened to Phileas Fogg in Jules Verne's famous novel.

Utmost Precision

The CS 2 atomic clock at the Federal Office of Physics and Technology in Braunschweig, Germany is one of the most precise timepieces in the world. It is accurate to within a second even after two million years.

Guardian of Time

The ancient Egyptians amassed a wealth of astronomical knowledge. As early as 2750 BC, they had developed a lunar calendar and a solar calendar that divided the year into 365 days. The sciences and the calculation of time were the domain of the moon god Thot, who was often depicted as a human figure with the head of an ibis (c. 600 BC, Luxor).

International Date Line

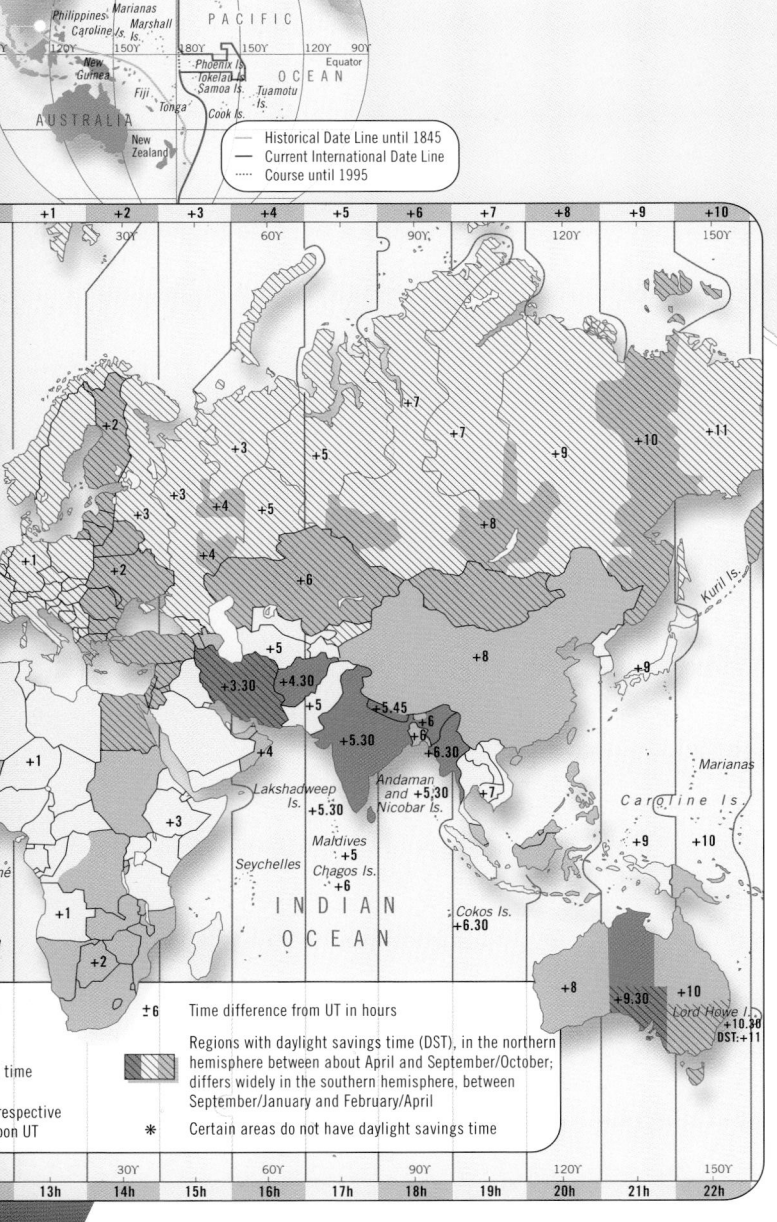

—— Historical Date Line until 1845
—— Current International Date Line
······· Course until 1995

±6   Time difference from UT in hours

Regions with daylight savings time (DST), in the northern hemisphere between about April and September/October; differs widely in the southern hemisphere, between September/January and February/April

time

respective
on UT

＊   Certain areas do not have daylight savings time

An Ingenious Invention

Portable equatorial sundial made by Johann Georg Vogler (1750), with an adjustable hour ring. The clock is positioned facing north with the aid of a compass; the plane of the hour ring is aligned with a point on the curved latitude scale that conforms to the latitude of the measurement site. In this way, the shadow-casting rod of the sundial is positioned parallel to the Earth's axis, so that its tip points to the north celestial pole and the hour ring is parallel to the earth's equator.

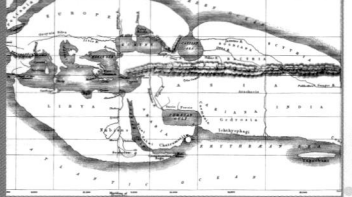

The Evolution of Cartography

Creating a Picture of the World

The first maps provided mankind with a means of creating a highly simplified, abstract image of the Earth. Long before aircraft were invented, the globe had already been depicted – from a bird's-eye view, so to speak – on a smaller, measurable scale in accordance with mathematical principles. Yet maps are never more than a reflection of social reality – of the knowledge, political visions, and religious beliefs of a given age. A map's claim to accuracy and reliability derives from the manner in which it was produced, from the degree of precision achieved by the engraver, lithographer, or draftsman, from the printer's command of his art, and from the ability of map-readers to recognize familiar aspects of their world.

Cartography

Since the mid-19th century, when the term "cartography" was first introduced, the art of map-making developed from a subdiscipline that served the needs of geodesy and geography into a science in its own right. By the early 20th century cartography had developed its own clearly defined concepts and methods.

Because of their military significance, the immense costs of making them, and the detailed nature of their contents, topographic maps remained a monopoly of the state in Europe until the latter half of the 19th century. Around the turn of the 18th to the 19th century, the nations of Europe began to establish statistical services and offices which published some of their data in topical maps intended for broad public use.

From the Disk to the Sphere

Even ancient cultures had maps of known territories showing possessions and boundaries. Excellent examples include the rock drawing of a Neolithic settlement in Çatal Hüyük dated about 6200 BC, the 3,500-year-old city map of Nippur in Babylon, and maps made by the ancient Greeks.

These early map-makers viewed the Earth as a flat disk, inhabited in the center and inaccessible at its outer edges. As knowledge increased, the disk expanded. New insights gained through the conquests of Alexander the Great and the observations of seafarers and scientists gave birth to the idea that the Earth is a sphere, for which Erastosthenes calculated a circumferences of 37,700 km (or 46,250 km, depending upon the conversion method applied) in c. 250 BC. He took his investigations a step further, projecting the three-dimensional segments of the sphere onto a flat surface and overlaying his map with a system of coordinates based upon the length and width of the Mediterranean Sea.

In the 2nd century AD, the astronomer, astrologist, and cartographer Ptolemy of Alexandria developed the first north-oriented map projection with longitudinally true lines of latitude. Ptolemy's instructions for map-making were distributed in copies, commentaries, and translations to geographers and cartographers – and along with them his most glaring error: His globe had a circumference of only 29,000 km.

Immortalized in a Choir Loft: A wood sculpture of Claudius Ptolemaeus (Ptolemy) in the choir loft of the cathedral in Ulm (Michael Erhart, c. 1470). The publication of his Geographia in Ulm in 1482 revived the ancient concept of the shape of the world.

Mappae mundi – The Christian Image of the World

For the next several centuries, theology shaped mankind's view of the world and its representation on maps. Rome's influence waned, and the center of the new Christian world shifted to the east, to Jerusalem. Thus the maps of Christianity were oriented toward the east, and they depicted the earth once again as a flat disk. Like all works of art from this period, they proclaimed the greatness of God and the Church.

The emergence of Islam beginning in the 6th century AD posed a challenge to the dominant Christian view. Arab cartographers incorporated the ancient tradition of Ptolemy (the Earth as a sphere) into their scientific system and expanded their knowledge of the world through extensive travel and the use of astronomical instruments.

Unveiling the Earth

Maps used by seafarers and merchants were not documents of religious philosophy. Their maps were intended for practical use and were therefore as accurate as possible under the given circumstances. Portolan charts of the Mediterranean showed the coasts and major landmarks in detail, and, as studies have proven, contained only minor errors of distance.

However, maps of foreign countries and coastlines were usually kept locked away in the safes of rulers and merchants and were released for public use only after the existence of such regions had become widely known. Even Columbus lacked the most current maps on his journey of "discovery" to America. Although the Vikings had reached North America long before him, Columbus sailed westward into an "unknown" Atlantic (guided by Ptolemy's incorrect estimate of the earth's circumference) hoping to reach India. The newly discovered regions were presented on a world map made by Martin Waldseemüller as early as 1507.

Motivated by the prospect of finding new worlds beyond the horizon and by the lure of endless riches, the nations of Europe launched their campaign of worldwide exploration.

Surveying the Planet

The circumnavigation of the globe by Magellan's expedition had provided practical proof that the Earth is a sphere. Subsequent advances in science and the development of better instruments enabled cartographers to improve the accuracy and detail of their maps of the world over the course of the next several centuries. Unknown regions of the Earth were populated on maps with imaginary beings – an expression of horror vacui, the unwillingness of map-makers to reveal gaps in their knowledge to the general public. Later, they were simply entered as "white spots."

The era of cartographic precision based upon mathematical principles began in the latter half of the 18th century. In the nations of Europe, topographic surveys were carried out for military and administrative purposes, and the data obtained through these efforts serves even today as the basis for planning in modern countries.

Once it became possible to explore the Earth from space in the 20th century, the last remaining white spots disappeared from the maps of the world, and cartographers gained access to all the geographic data they could possibly need. Electronic data processing relieved map-makers of the arduous tasks of drawing and engraving maps, turning them into specialists in graphic communication.

Image of the Medieval World

Produced between 1230 and 1240, the Ebstorf World Map is an example of medieval Christian cartography. Drawn in a TO configuration, it transposes the body of Christ onto the known world. Encircled by the O-shaped ocean, the Earth's landmasses are separated by the T (of the inland seas) – the symbol of Christ's death on the cross. The original map was destroyed by fire in a bombing raid on Hanover in 1943. A copy of the large map (358 x 356 cm) has survived in 30 parts.

The Schematic World

Schematic world map (TO map) by Isidor of Sevilla (1472), illustrating the Christian image of the world.

The Evolution of Cartography

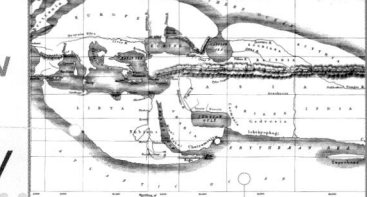

First Coordinate System

This reconstruction of a map by Eratostheus (3rd c. BC) shows the known world in a coordinate system based upon the position of the Mediterranean Sea.

Encircled by the Ocean

Map by Hecataeus of Miletus (c.500 BC) reconstructed from texts, showing the Earth as a disk with the continents of Europe and Asia encircled by an ocean.

Roman Itinerary

The Tabula Peutingeriana illustrates the pragmatic approach of the Roman government. It depicts the network of roads as a schematic itinerary without scale, showing route markers, postal stations, and cities in signature form.

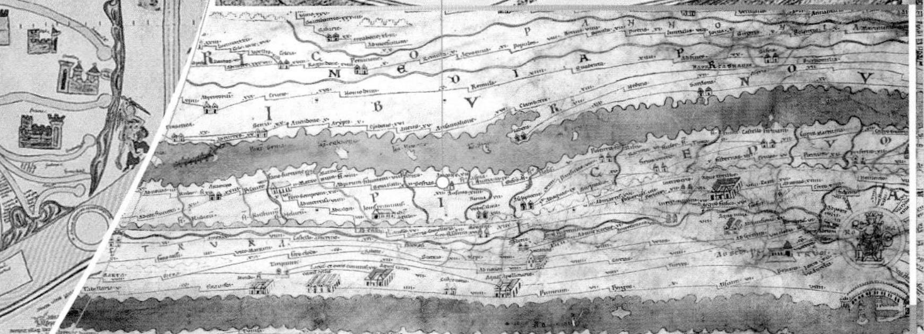

Birth of the Name "America"

Amerigo Vespucci and the regions of South America he discoered. Detail from a map by the Freiburg cartographer Martin Waldseemüller, on which the name "America" (in honor of Vespucci) appeared for the first time. The map was printed in Saint-Dié (Lorraine) in 1507.

The Earth from Space

Topographic Image

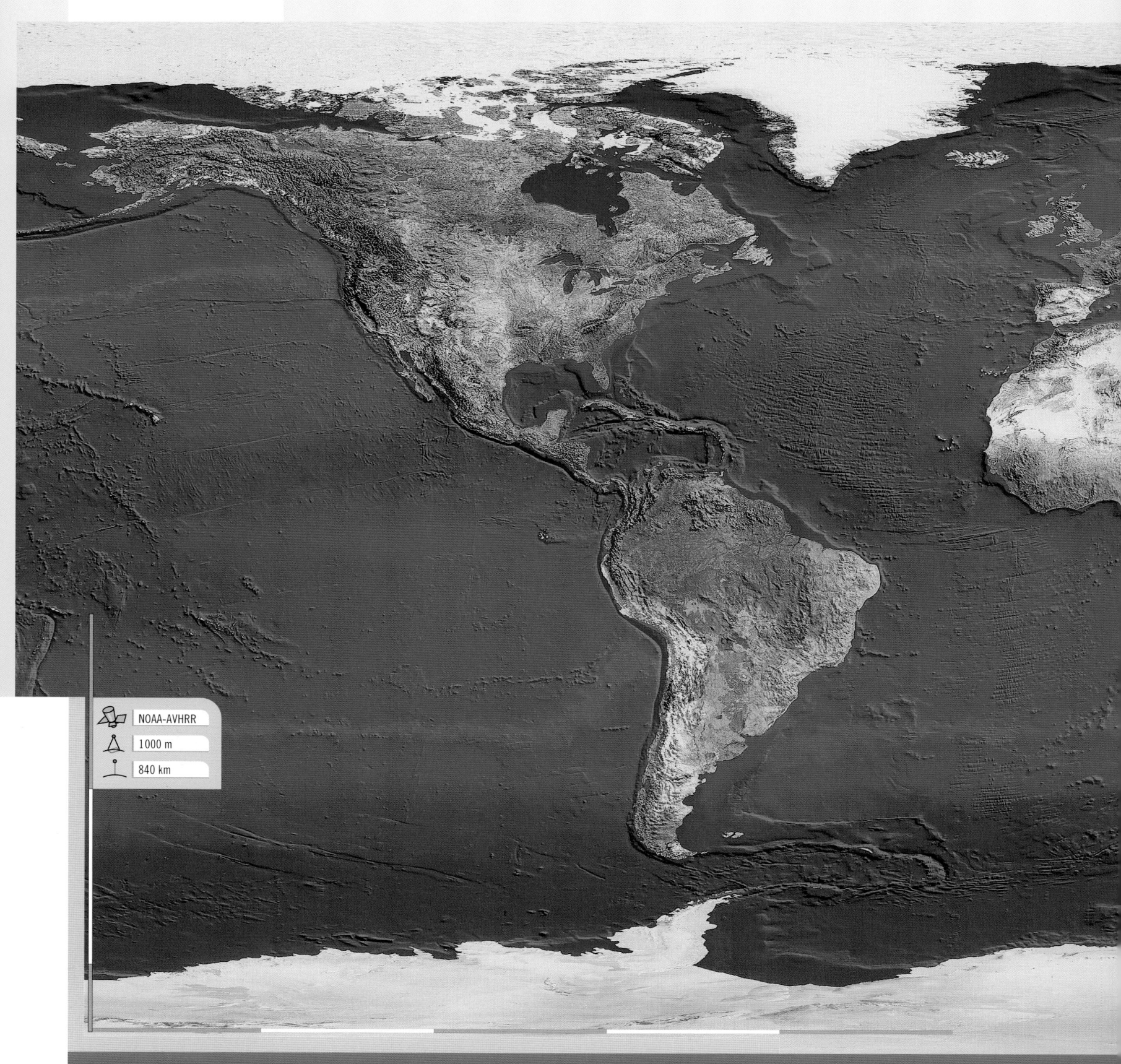

NOAA-AVHRR

1000 m

840 km

View of the Earth from Space

Several thousand images from the U.S. NOAA Satellite Series were required to compile this completely cloudless picture of the Earth.
In the projection selected for this satellite imagery map, the polar regions extend along the full length of the Equator. The continents are true to form to north and south latitudes of about 35 degrees, but distortion grows more extreme toward the poles.
This composite satellite image gives a good overview of major landscapes of the continents and their vegetation patterns. A particularly striking feature is the belt of deserts that encircles the globe.

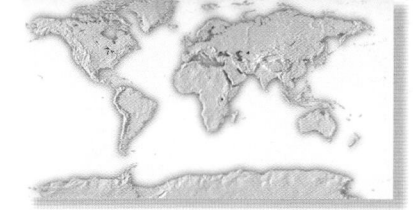

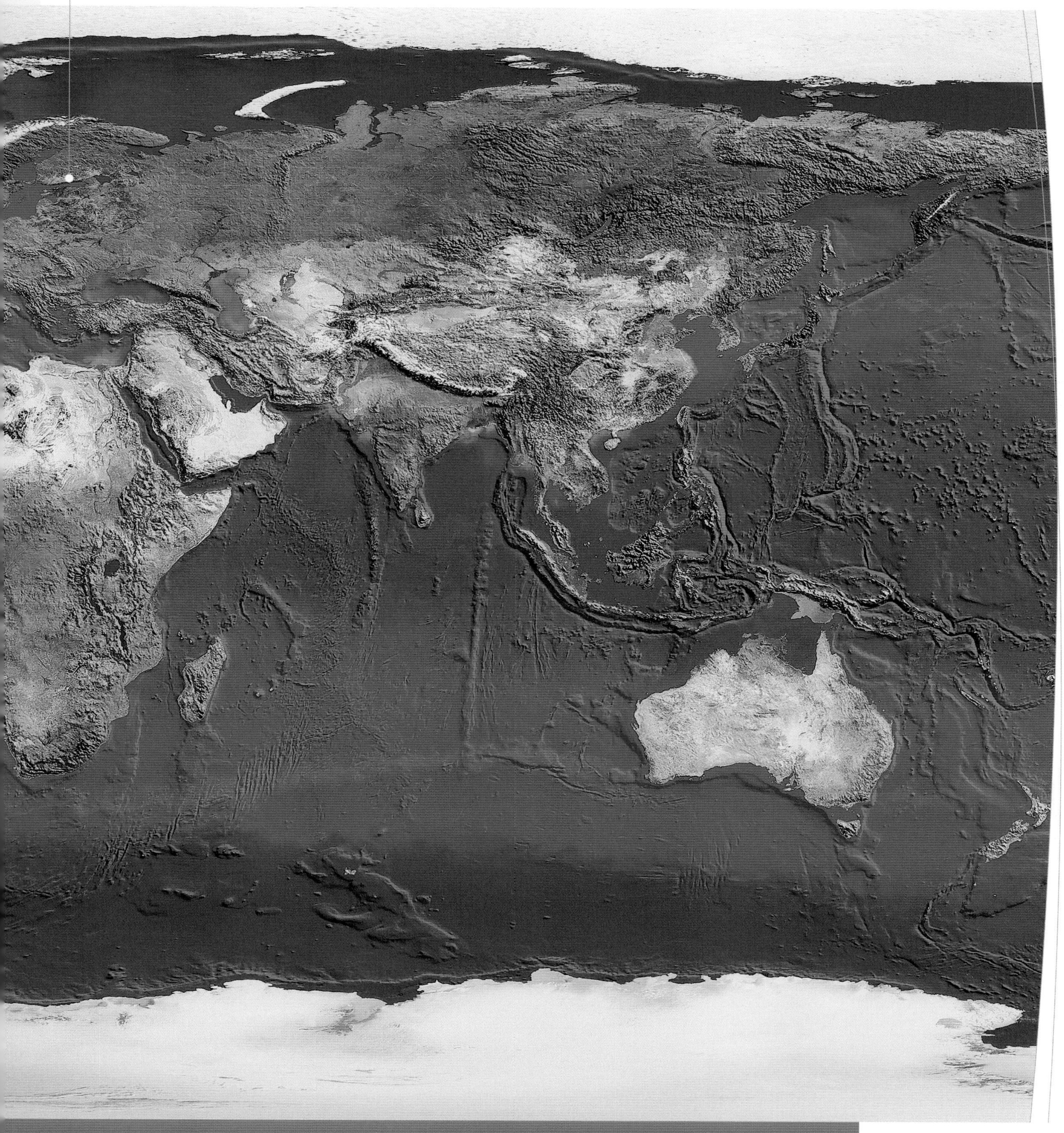

Climate Changes in the Ozone Layer – The Ozone Hole

The large quantities of chlorofluorocarbons (CFC), used in spray dispensers and as coolants in refrigerators for example) released into the atmosphere every year produce chemical changes in the stratosphere which destroy the protective shell of the ozone layer encircling the Earth. The ozone layer absorbs some of the harmful ultra violet B radiation emitted by the Sun and helps regulate the heat budget of the atmosphere. Ozone depletion is most severe above the southern hemisphere during the months of September and October. NASA and the Ozone Research Program of the European Union have been observing changes in the ozone layer for many years. Seasonal fluctuations are illustrated in the series of images below, which show that ozone concentrations can fall to half their normal levels in certain years.

Higher atmospheric temperatures above the Arctic (as compared to the south polar region) reduce the danger of ozone depletion, although the sequence of images shows an increase here as well. The ozone veil above the Arctic is not as thin as that in the Antarctic stratosphere. However, chemical analysis has shown that the composition of the atmosphere above the north polar regions has suffered nearly the same degree of disturbance as that above the Antarctic.

Many of the consequences of atmospheric ozone depletion for mankind are well known. The increased intensity of UV radiation causes a higher incidence of sunburn and skin cancer and a general impairment of the human immune system. High UV radiation levels also have a lasting impact on plant life.

NOAA-AVHRR

1000 m

840 km

Ozone concentration
in the atmosphere

| 100 – 250 |
| 250 – 260 |
| 260 – 270 |
| 270 – 280 |
| 280 – 290 |
| 290 – 300 |
| 300 – 310 |
| 310 – 320 |
| 320 – 330 |
| 330 – 340 |
| 340 – 350 |
| 350 – 360 |
| 360 – 370 |
| 370 – 380 |
| 380 – 390 |
| 390 – 400 |
| 400 – 450 |
| 450 – 500 |
| > 500 |

Ozone concentration per air
column in Dobson Units

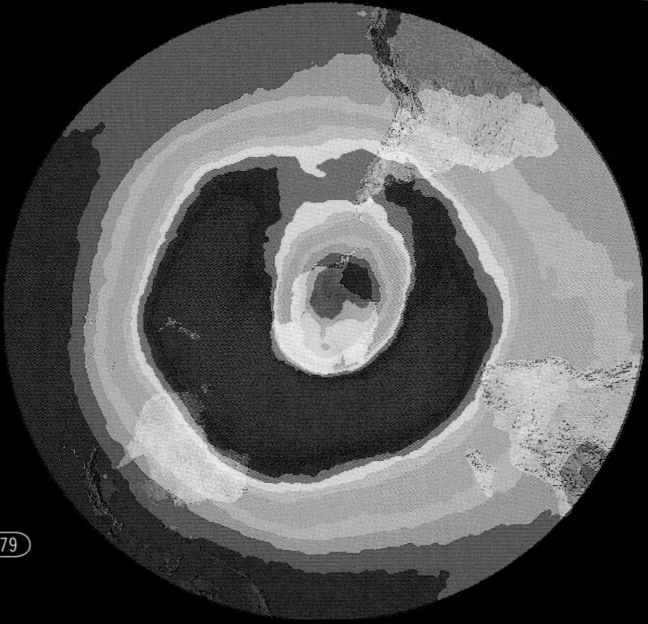

September 1979

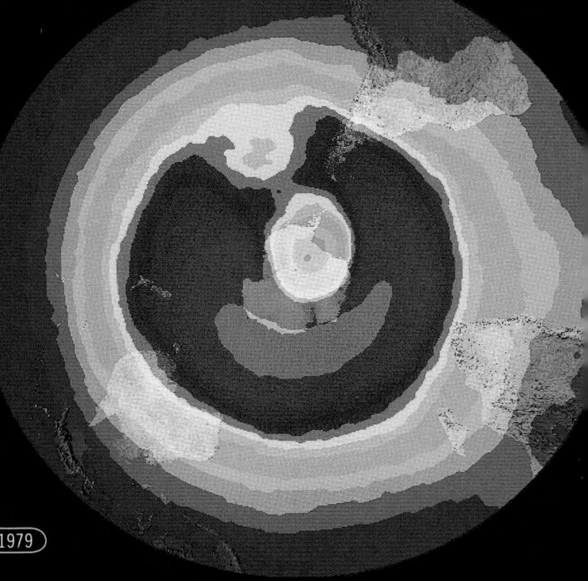

October 1979

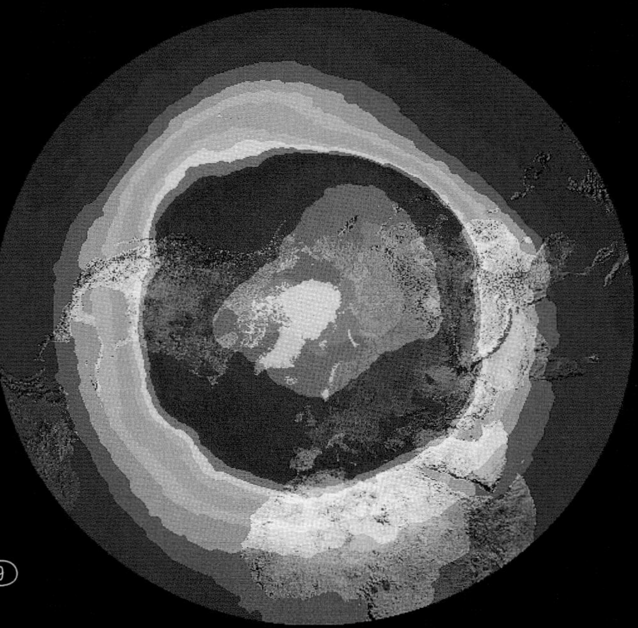

March 1979

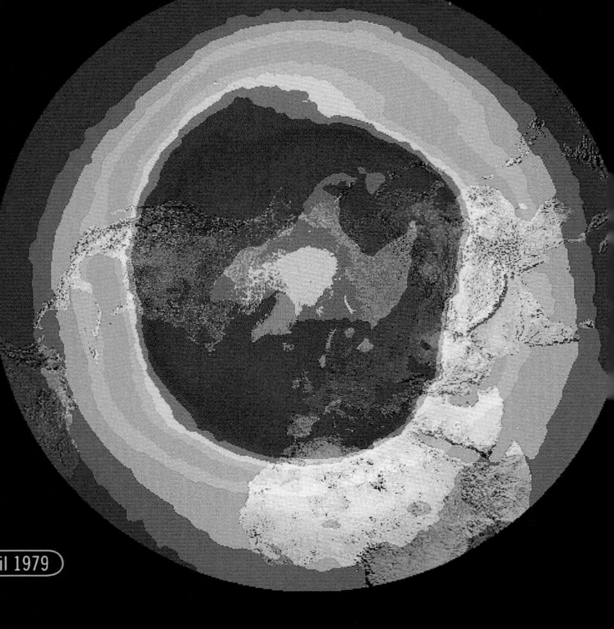

April 1979

Southern hemisphere:
A marked reduction in ozone concentration
is regularly observed in the Antarctic stratosphere
toward the end of the southern winter.

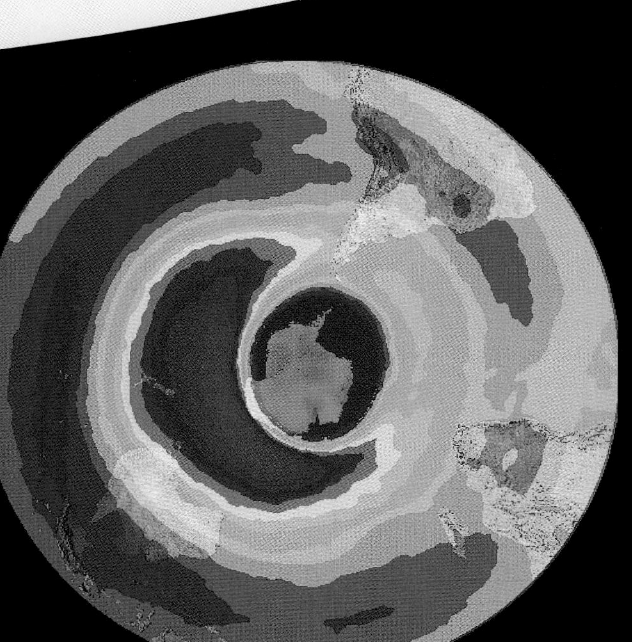

October 1990

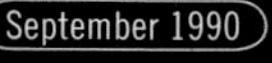

September 1990

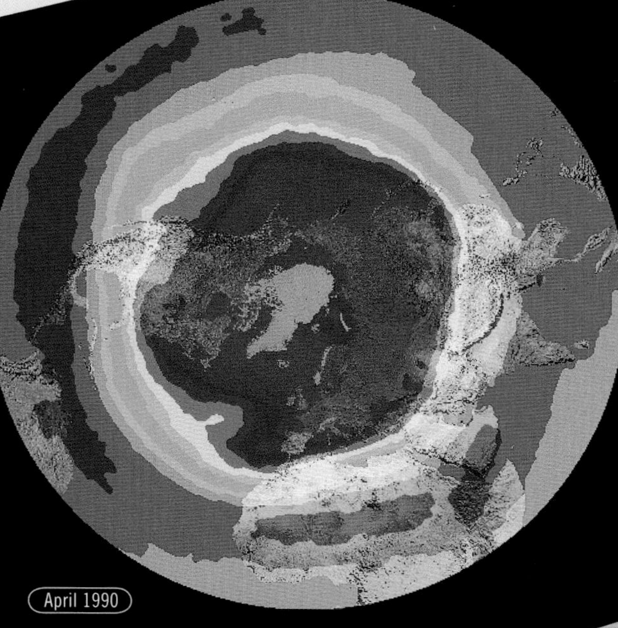

April 1990

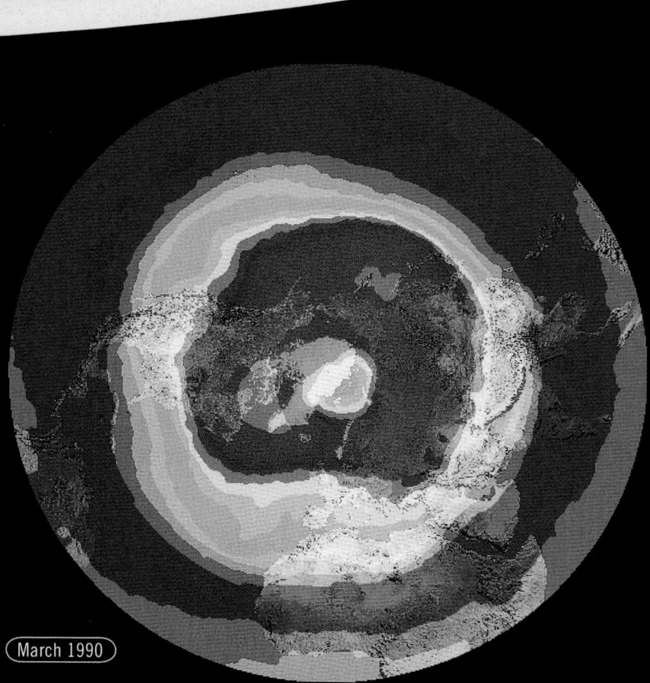

March 1990

Northern hemisphere:
The ozone layer is not as thin above the Arctic as it
is in the Antarctic stratosphere, as average
temperatures in the north polar atmosphere are generally about 18°F higher than above the Antarctic.

Volcanism

Living Links to the Earth's Core

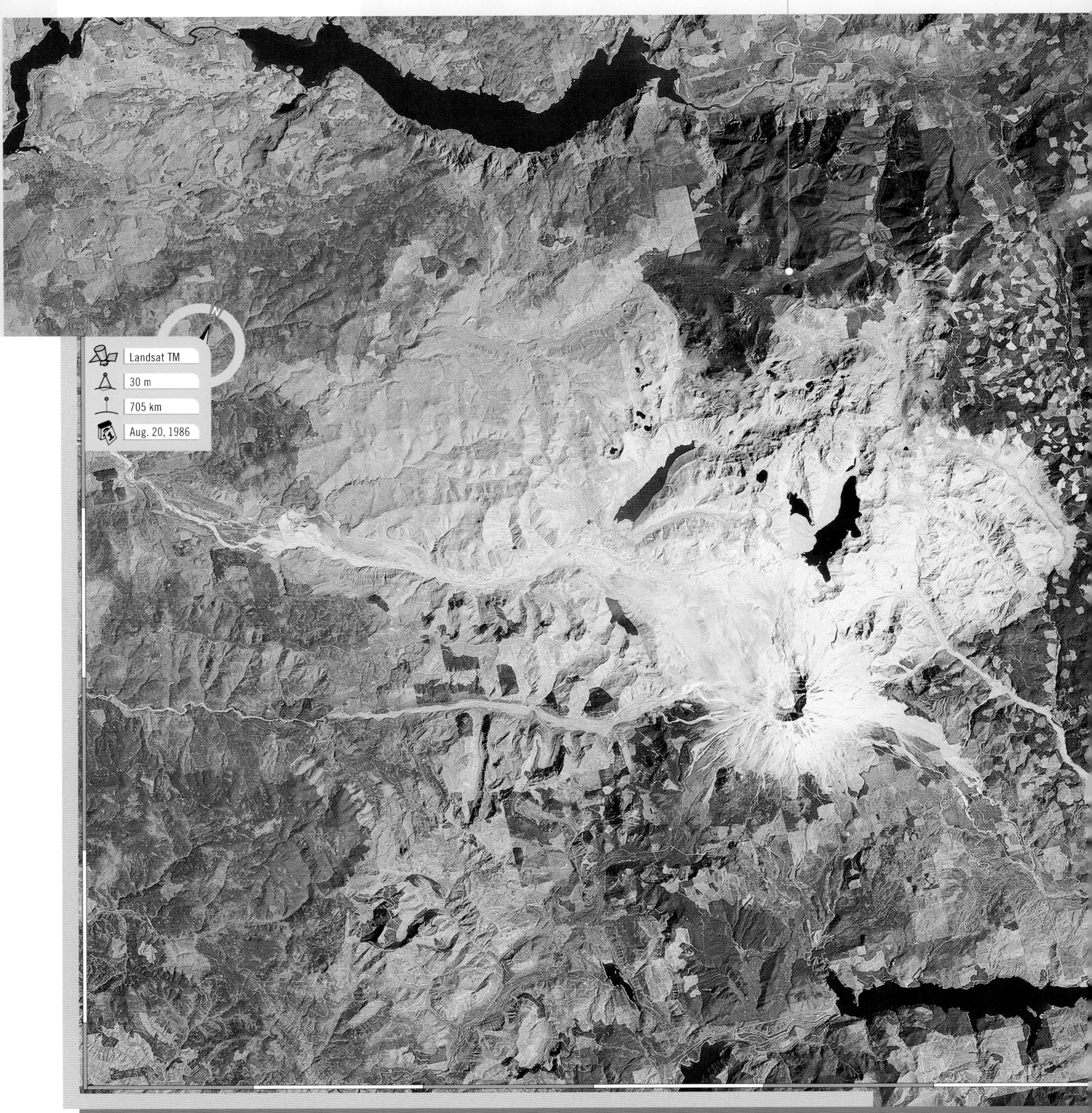

Landsat TM

30 m

705 km

Aug. 20, 1986

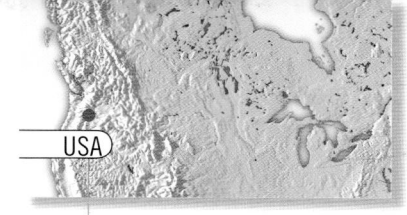

Mt. Saint Helens

One of the most spectacular natural events of the latter half of the 20th century was the eruption of Mount Saint Helens in the Cascade Range in the state of Washington. All of the active volcanoes of North America are located in this chain of mountains that extends from northern California to Canada. The region without vegetation in the center of the image is the area of volcanic devastation surrounding the collapsed oval crater (caldera) and Spirit Lake.

Originally 2,948 m high, the mountain known by the Indians as the "Guardian of Fire" lost about 400 m of elevation during the eruption on May 18, 1980. Avalanches of melted snow, mud, and rock debris rushed down two river valleys, sweeping away bridges and houses and cutting long swaths through the forests. A massive fountain of ash rose up to 23 km into the stratosphere from the mountain's fractured northern flank. The shockwave knocked down all trees within miles of the cone like matches. Sixty people died in the inferno.

Less violent eruptions occurred in 1984, 1986, 1989, and 1991.

Mount Aetna

Mount Aetna, the highest active volcano in Europe, towers above the eastern coast of Sicily between Catania and Taormina on the shores of the Ionian Sea.

The last major eruption of Mount Aetna (present elevation: 3,350 m) occurred in 2001 and threatened the village of Nicolosi. This thermal image shows the pattern of temperature distribution on the surface of the powerful volcano. Red indicates areas of high temperature; blue represents lower surface temperatures. Temperatures are markedly influenced by solar radiation (exposed versus shaded surfaces). Typical of Mount Aetna are its many parasite craters – the largest of which are clearly recognizable on the western and southeastern sides of the volcano. Also evident are the numerous fissures and steam springs through which magma gases are released.

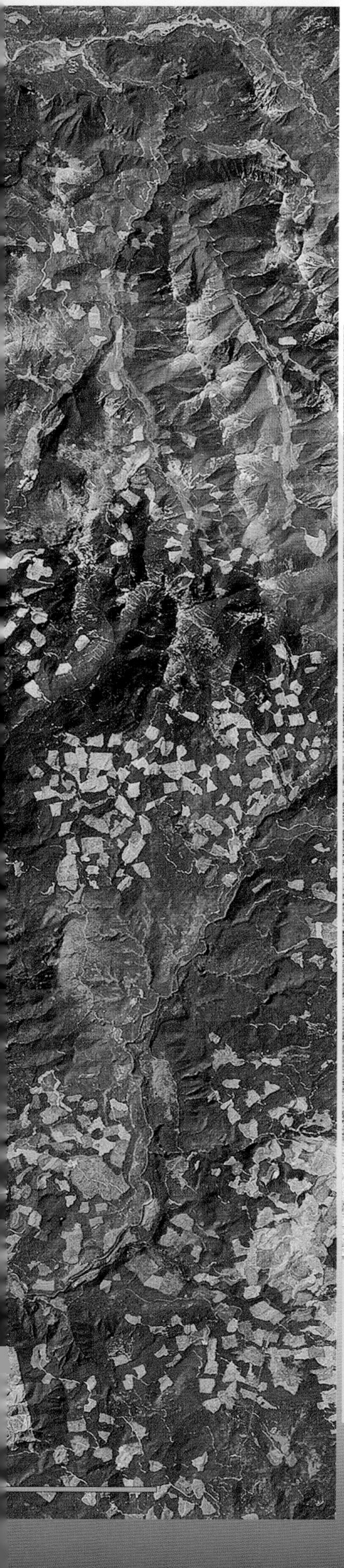

Landsat TM

30 m

705 km

Nov. 27, 1984

Meteorite Crater

Threat from Outer Space

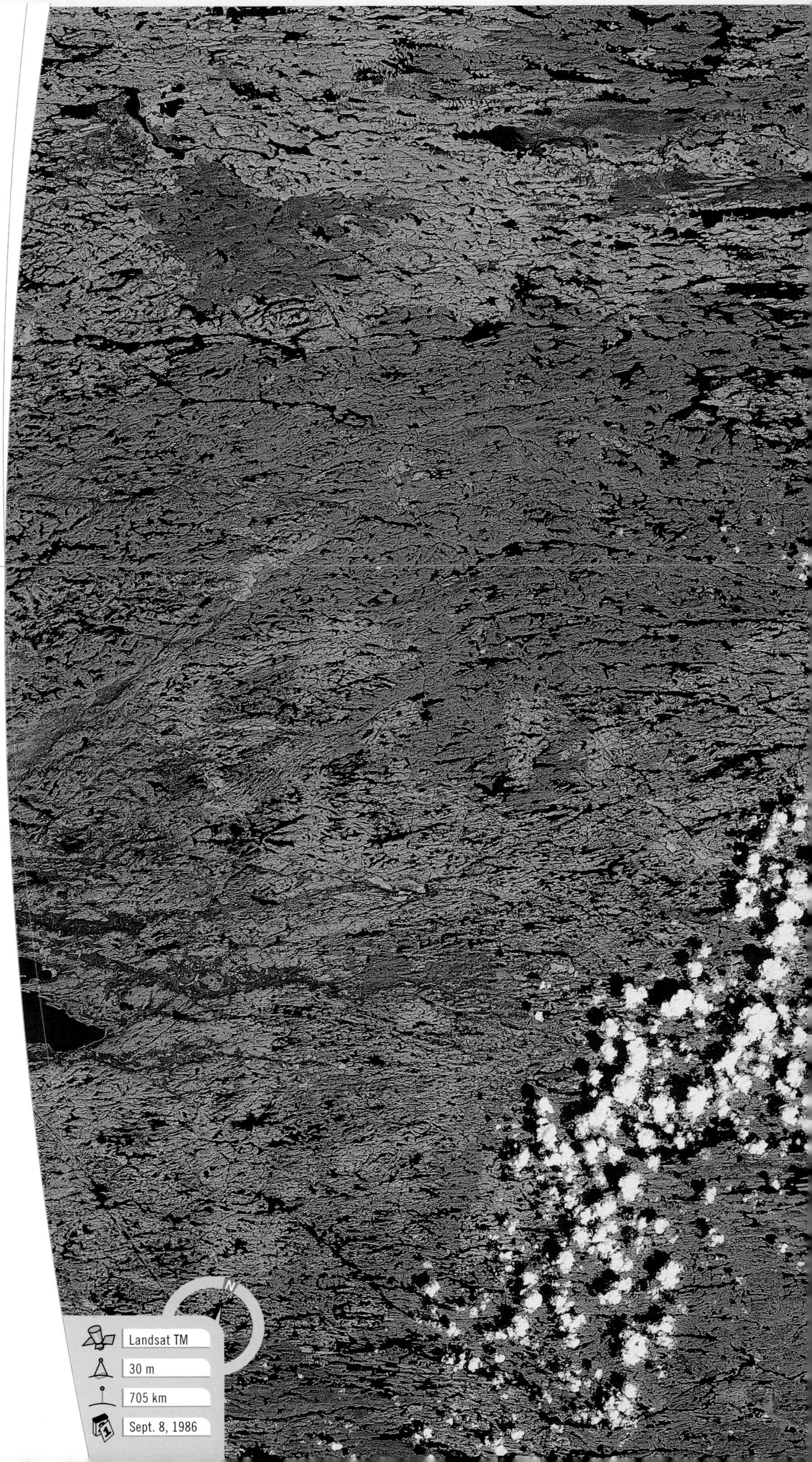

Clearwater Lake

This satellite image shows the two basins
of Clearwater Lake in the Canadian province
of Quebec. The lakebeds are the product of
an extremely rare event — the impact of "twin
meteorites" — that occurs only about once
every one million years, when two presumably
related meteorite fragments strike the earth
in succession. Complex craters formed by
impacts of large meteorites are characterized
by a central mountain formation.
The islands in the larger of the two lakes are
the visible remnants of such a central
mountain formation, left exposed after the
craters filled with water.
The impact that formed the lakes is presumed
to have occurred some 300 million years ago.

Landsat TM	
30 m	
705 km	
Sept. 8, 1986	

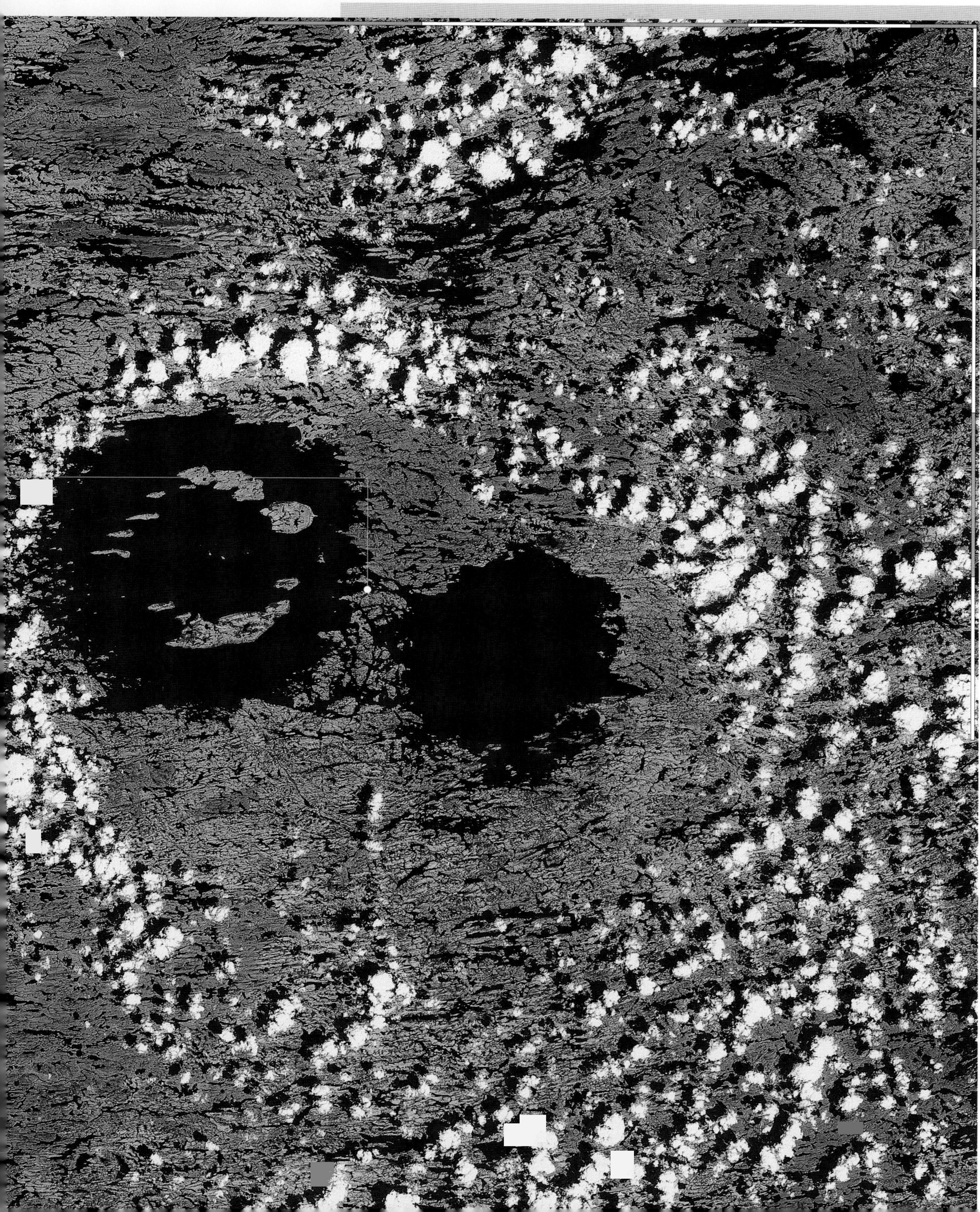

Landsat ETM	
15 m	
705 km	
Nov. 3, 1999	

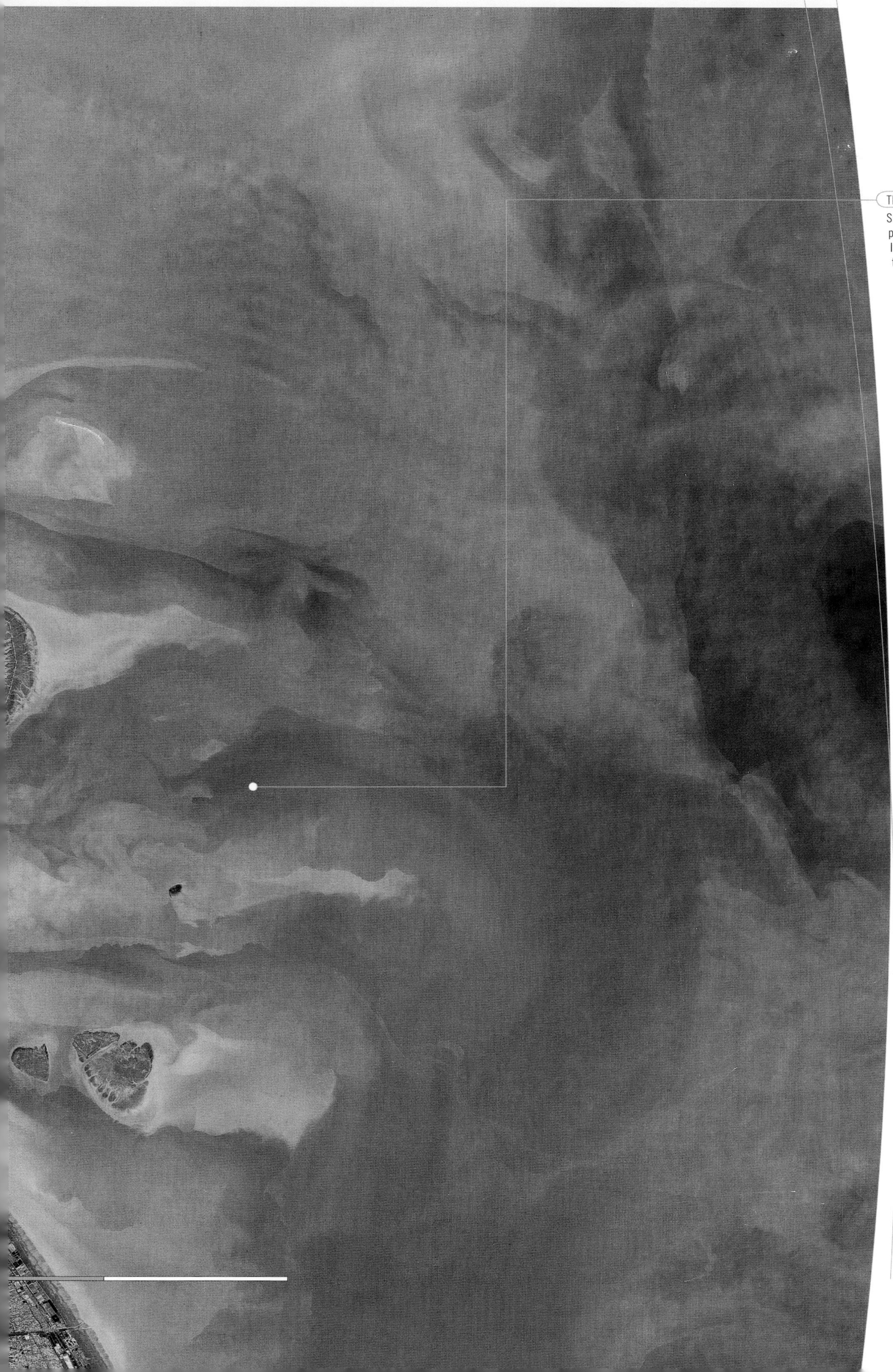

The Mouth of the Yangtze (Chang)

Shanghai is China's most important port and its largest metropolis. It radiates from the confluence of the Huang River and the Yangtze east of Tai Lake. At the turn of the last century, the city was home to some 12 million people, and nearly 20 million people live in greater metropolitan Shanghai. The opening of China to international trade has spurred rapid growth in the city in recent years, to which an expansive system of urban freeways and a number of new high-rise complexes bear witness. The amount of developed land nearly doubled between 1980 and 2000. In the process, the belt of vegetation that once encircled the city (visible in places as spots of light-green coloration in the satellite image) was obliterated. Development has been especially intensive in the Pudong district on the right bank the Huang, where large areas the old city were demolished and replaced by new business and industrial centers.

Deserts

Shifting Seas of Sand

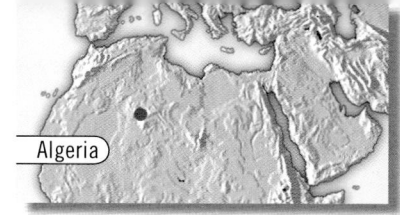

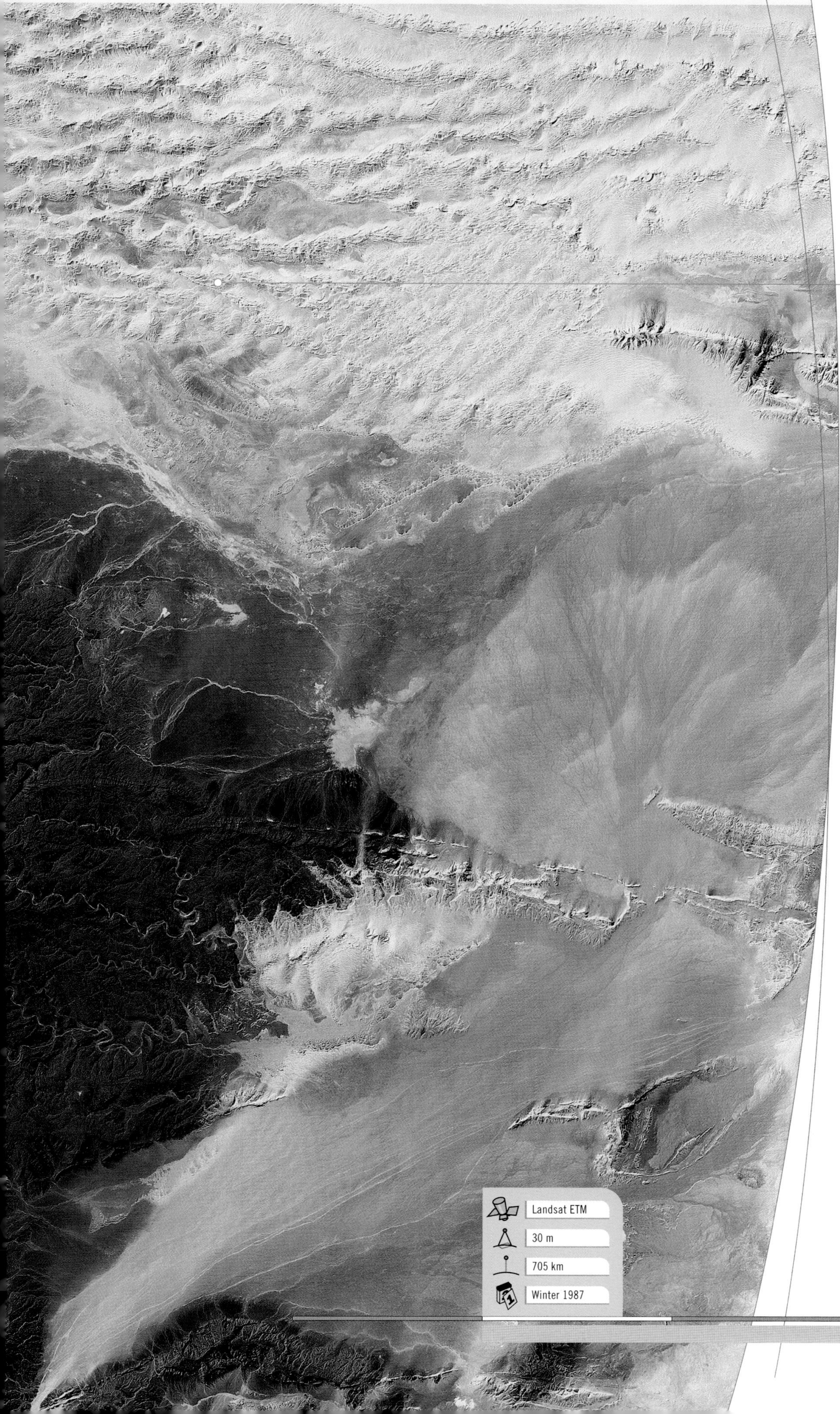

The Sahara near Amguid in Algeria

The Sahara presents a very different
face in many places. Landscapes can
be distinguished on the basis of differences in surface material – exposed
rock, gravel, sand, or salt clay. A large
portion of the image is occupied by the
debris-covered surfaces of the Hamada de Tinrhert (light gray and reddish
brown areas). This bolder-strewn
desert is known as Serir in Algeria. The
second type of desert in the Sahara
is characterized by sand sheets and
dunes. A prominent feature of the
landscape in this satellite image is the
tongue of sand in the upper portion of
the picture, with its regular pattern of
star-shaped figures. Salt clay plains
(bluish-turquoise coloration) are found
in the broad depressions where the
wadis – dry valleys through which
water flows only after heavy rains
– grow wider. The dark brown areas
are the northern fingers of the Tassili-n-Ajjer range, with peaks as high
as 1,800 m.

Landsat ETM	
30 m	
705 km	
Winter 1987	

Coastal Formations

The Largest Reef on Earth

	Landsat TM
	30 m
	705 km
	July 13, 2000

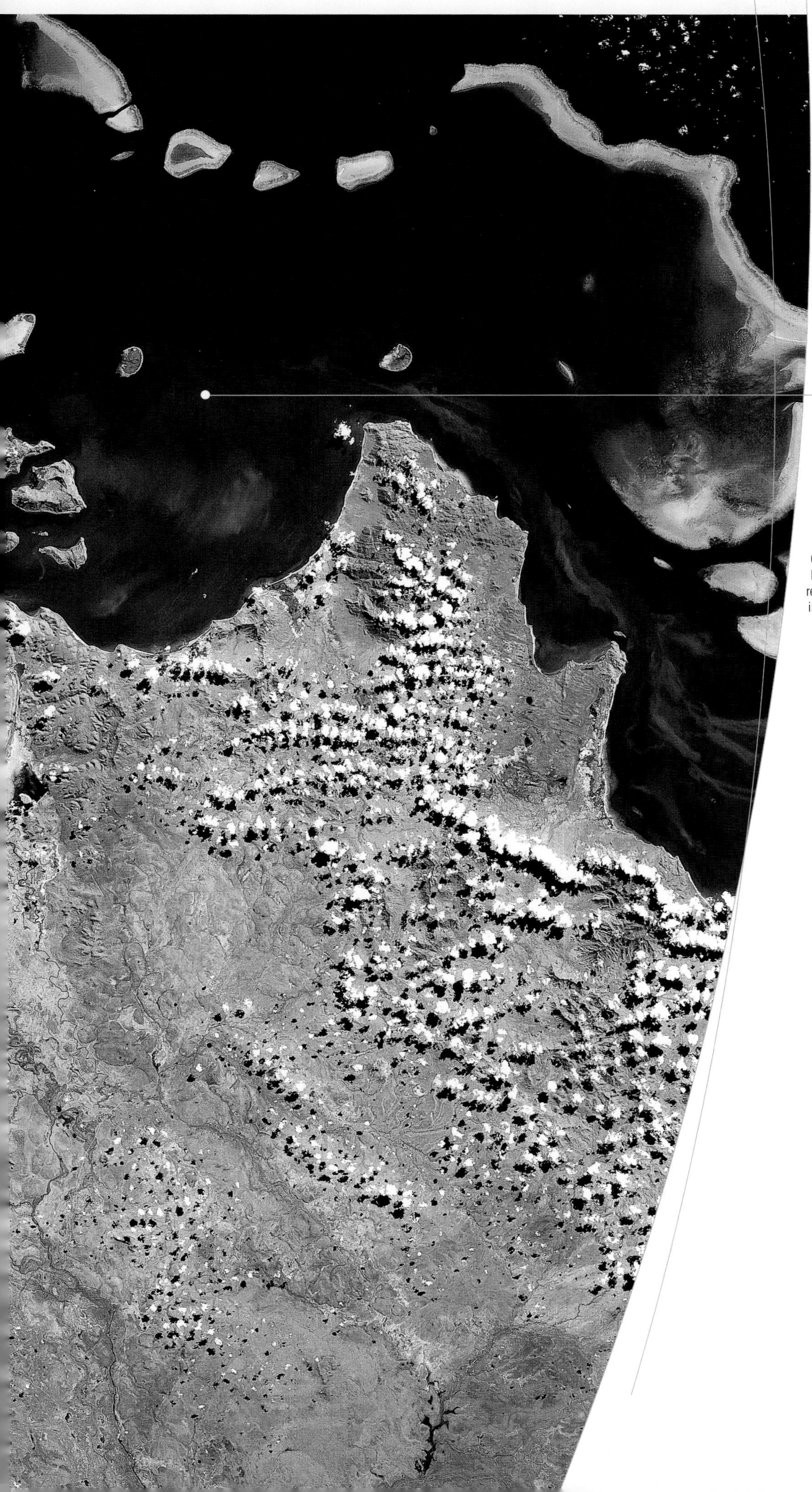

The Great Barrier Reef

The world's largest coral reef runs parallel to the coast
of Australia off the shores of Queensland. This
satellite image shows Princess Charlotte Bay on the
southern coast of the Cape York Peninsula.
The chain of elongated, oval or circular coral reefs
is discernable only from the air. Covered only by shallow waters, they
appear as turquoise and light blue areas that stand out clearly
against the deep blue of the open sea.
The view from the air tells us something else as well. The
Great Barrier Reef is not a continuous, linear reef system
but instead comprises a large number of individual
reefs of different sizes distributed in a picturesque pattern
in the lagoon.

Vegetation and Land Use

Carving New Settlements from the Desert

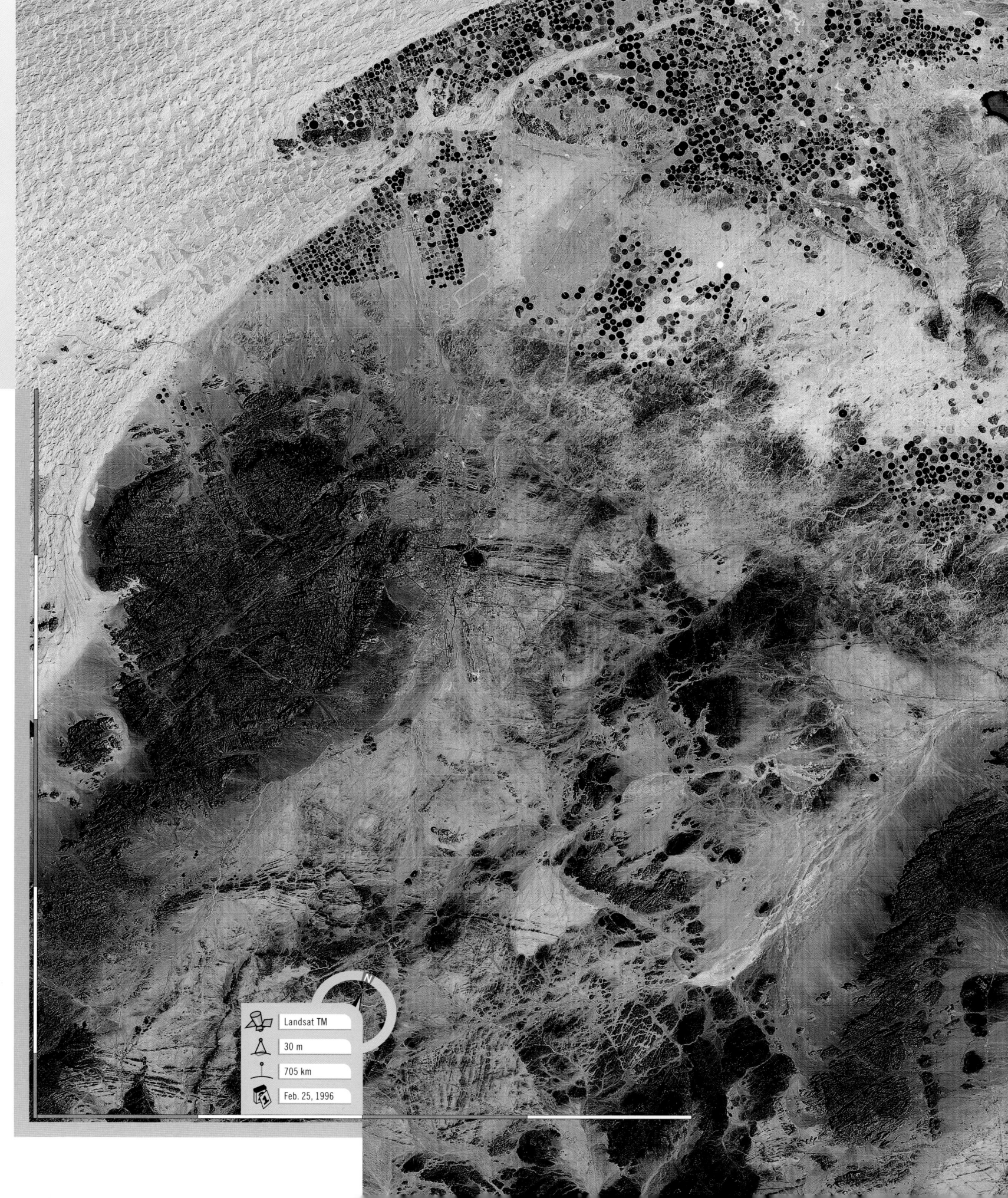

Landsat TM

30 m

705 km

Feb. 25, 1996

Saudi Arabia – Hā'il

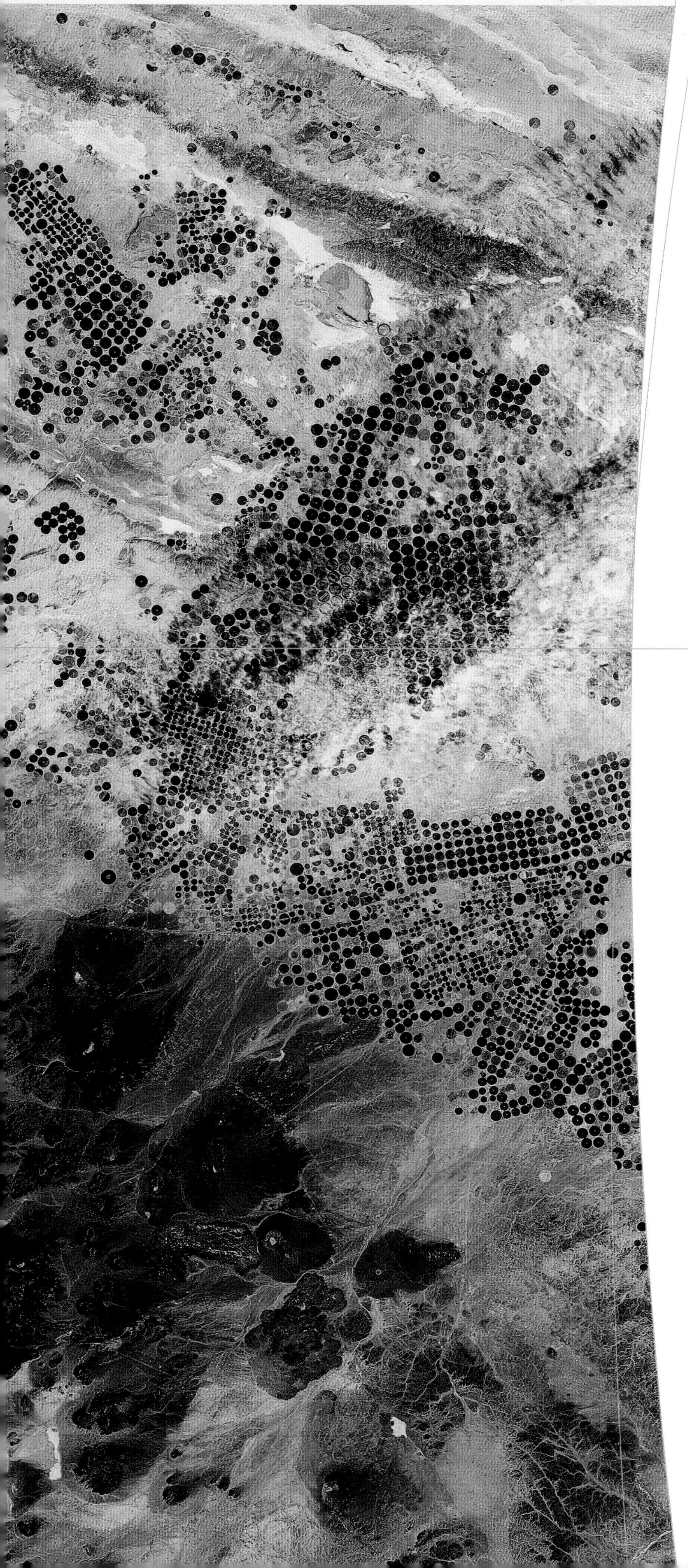

Expansive plateaus irregularly interspersed with ranges of mountains and inselbergs characterize the topography of the Central Arabian Highlands. In the north, the crystalline highlands extend to the edge of the sand desert of An Nafūd. Circular patches are distributed like confetti over the yellow sand of the Wadi Ha'il – small areas of cultivation in the midst of the arid desert, irrigated with rotating sprinkler systems fed to a certain extent with fossil water. Conveyed by pumps and pipelines, the water is distributed for specified periods of time in fine veils of rain. This process enables farmers to fertilize their fields efficiently by adding plant nutrients to the water. Excessive irrigation creates swampy soil conditions, which make the fields difficult to tend. Evaporation rates are extremely high in the hot, arid regions of Saudi Arabia, and changing wind patterns can lead to unequal distribution of water vapor.

Settlement Patterns

City and Country

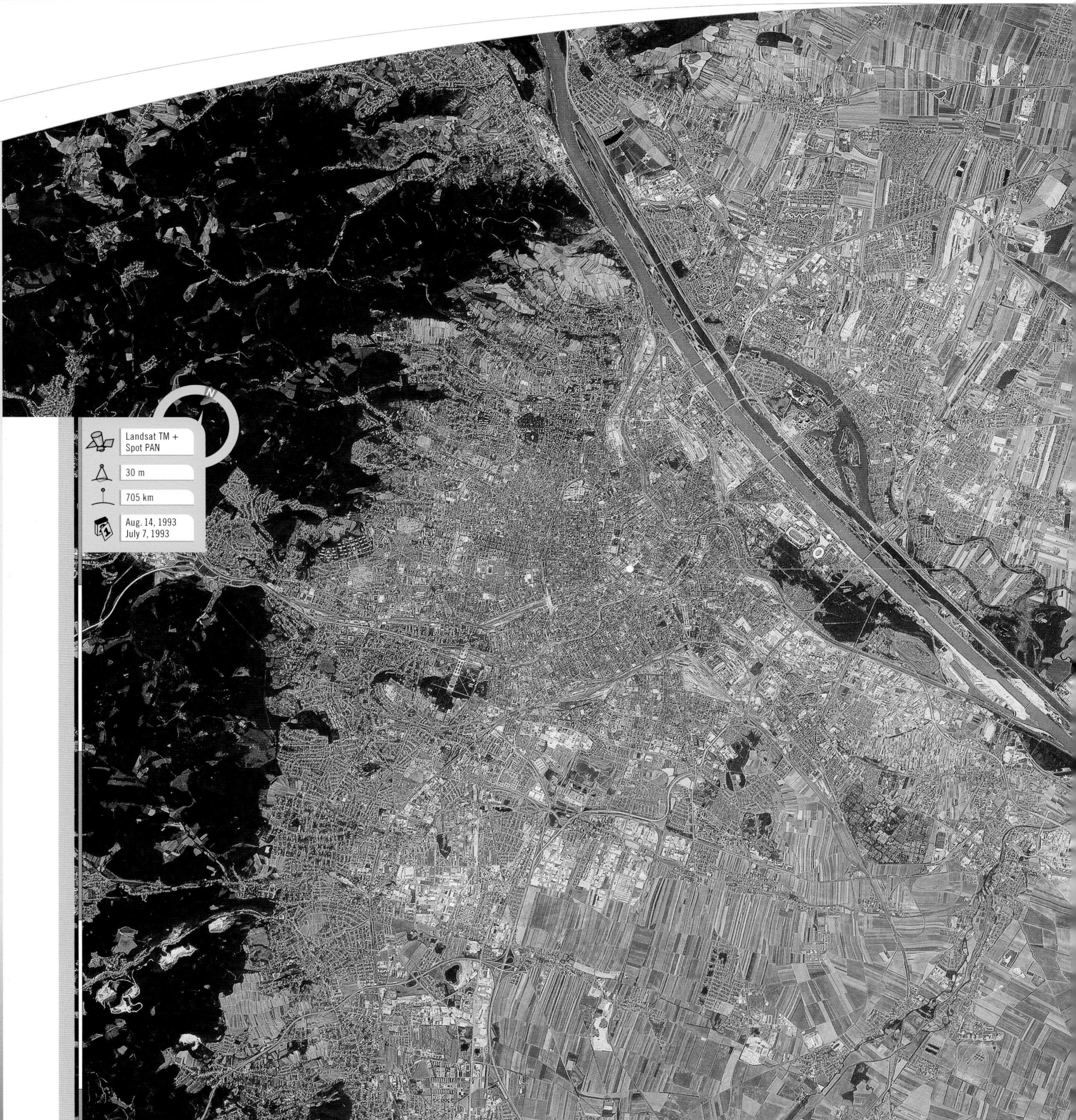

Landsat TM +
Spot PAN

30 m

705 km

Aug. 14, 1993
July 7, 1993

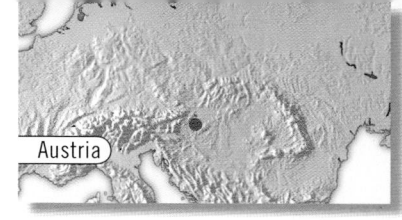

• • • • • •

Vienna

Positioned favorably where the Alps descend to the Great
Hungarian Plain at a major crossroads of traditional
European trading routes from north to south, the Danube
metropolis developed from a village into a world city
within only few centuries.

The Danube, whose course has been artificially altered
twice during the past several centuries, forms the region's
natural axis. The former meanders of the Old Danube
in the northern part of the satellite image serve as important urban recreation areas today.

The New Danube, which runs parallel to the river, was
created in 1970 to prevent flooding. A by-product of this
water-regulation measure is the Danube Island, a
popular park and recreation area for the people of Vienna.

Neusiedler Lake

Despite its size – approximately 296 sq. km, including
120 sq. km of encircling reed growth, Neusiedler
Lake is neither fed nor drained by a river of significant
size. Its cloudy greenish-gray coloration is not
caused by pollution but is a sign of the presence of
billions of suspended particles that never sink
entirely to the bottom of the shallow, windswept lake.
The border between Austria and Hungary is vividly
documented in this satellite image. The landscape
in the Austrian state of Burgenland is covered by an
intricate quilt of small strip parcels indicating intensive cultivation. These stand in stark contrast to
the large block fields on the other side of the border
– remnants of the collective farms of a bygone era.

Landsat TM +
Spot PAN

30 m

705 km

Aug. 14, 1993
Aug. 10, 1992

Environmental Problems

Natural Phenomena and Human Influences

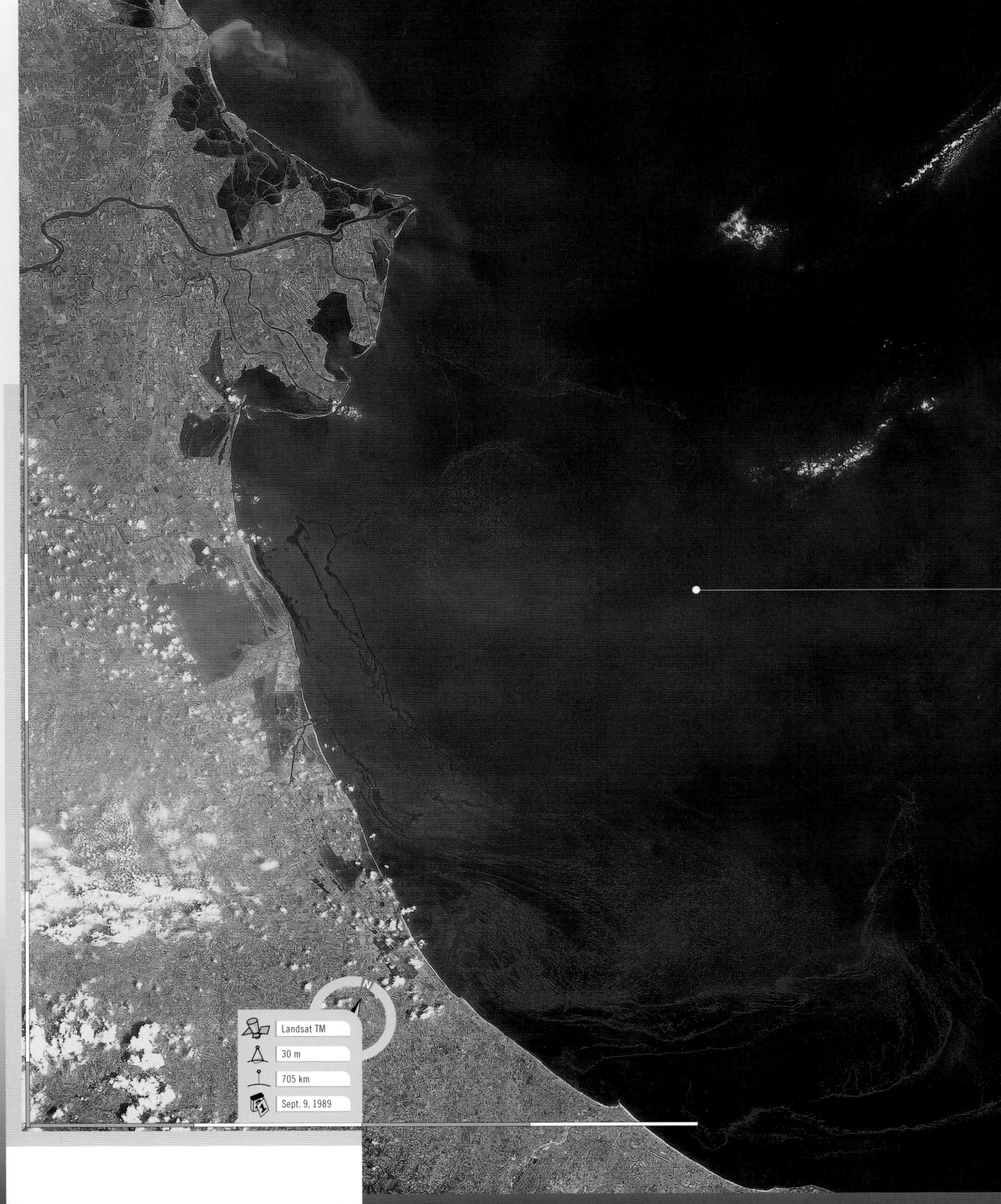

Landsat TM

30 m

705 km

Sept. 9, 1989

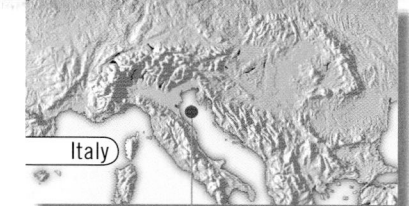 Italy

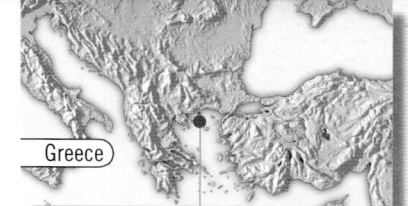 Greece

Carpet of Algae

The satellite image shows a stretch of the Italian Adriatic coastline between Chioggia in the north and Fano in the south. Particularly noticeable are the red streaks in the blue of the Adriatic Sea. Red hues indicate vegetation in the false-color image, and the streaks here represent accumulations of algae floating in the sea.

The formation of algae slime in the Mediterranean is a natural phenomenon that is intensified by long periods of good weather and placid seas. Now a common occurrence in many parts of the Mediterranean, the appearance of huge swarms of jellyfish is attributable to the influx of organic household, industrial, and agricultural waste water, which provides an abundance of nutrients for algae.

This satellite image offers impressive evidence of the expansion of the algae carpet. No other medium is capable of documenting such natural phenomena with this degree of clarity at a comparable cost.

Forest Fires on the Island of Thassos

With an area of 398 sq. km, Thassos is the second-largest island in the northern Aegean Sea and the northernmost Greek isle. The highest mountain on the rugged island is Ipsarion, which rises to an elevation of 1,203 m.

Vast areas of forest in Greece are regularly devastated by fires during the summer months. Such fires are primarily the result of dry periods that often last months at a time, although some are the work of arsonists. Disastrous forest fires on Thassos in 1985 and 1987 destroyed a large portion of the island's trees. Yet, despite the extensive damage caused by these fires, Thassos — once the most heavily forested island in Greece — has remained a green isle. The red areas visible in the southern part of the island show the regions destroyed by the fires of 1985.

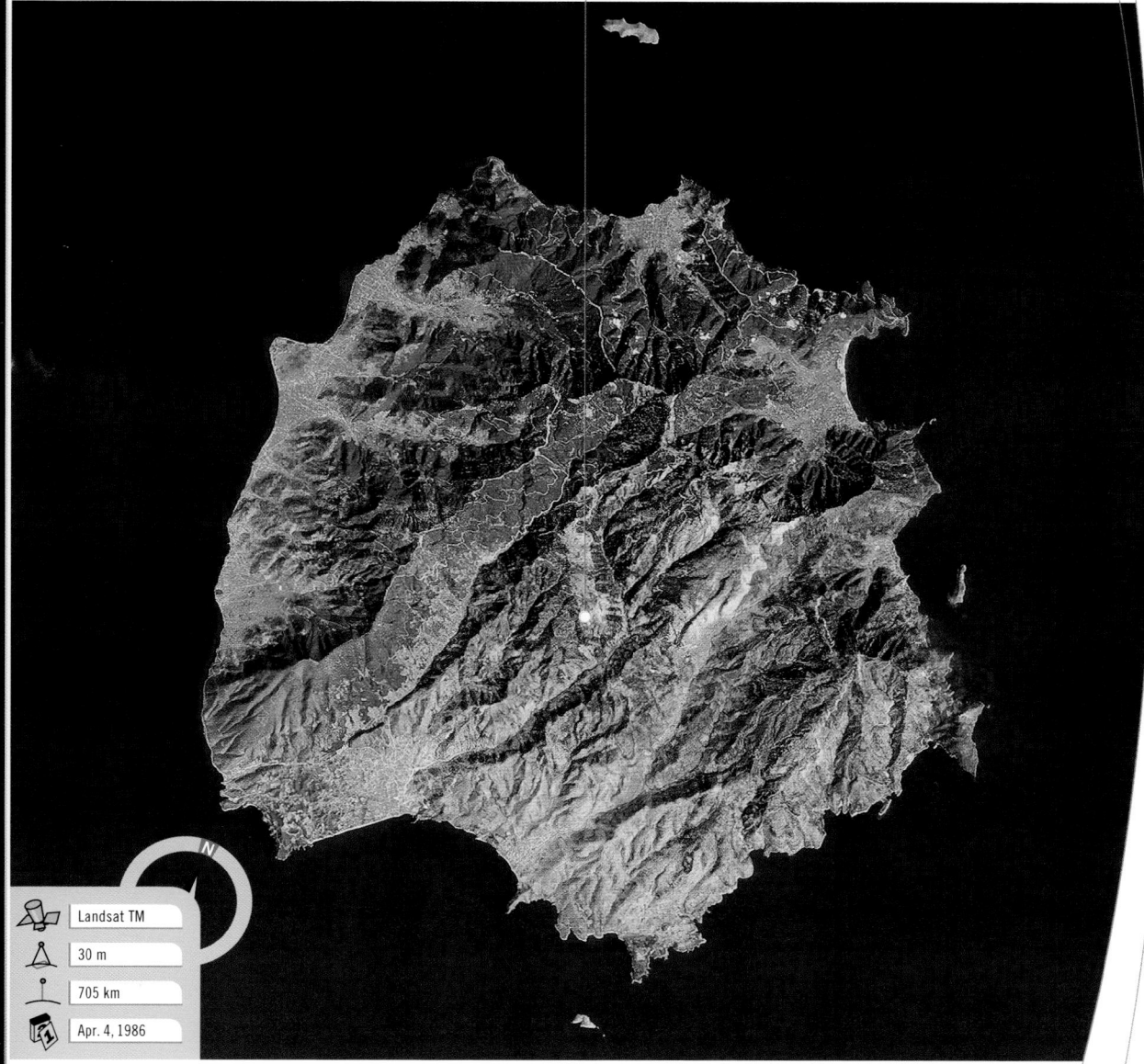

Landsat TM
30 m
705 km
Apr. 4, 1986

Polar Regions   Under the Influence of Cold and Ice

The Arctic

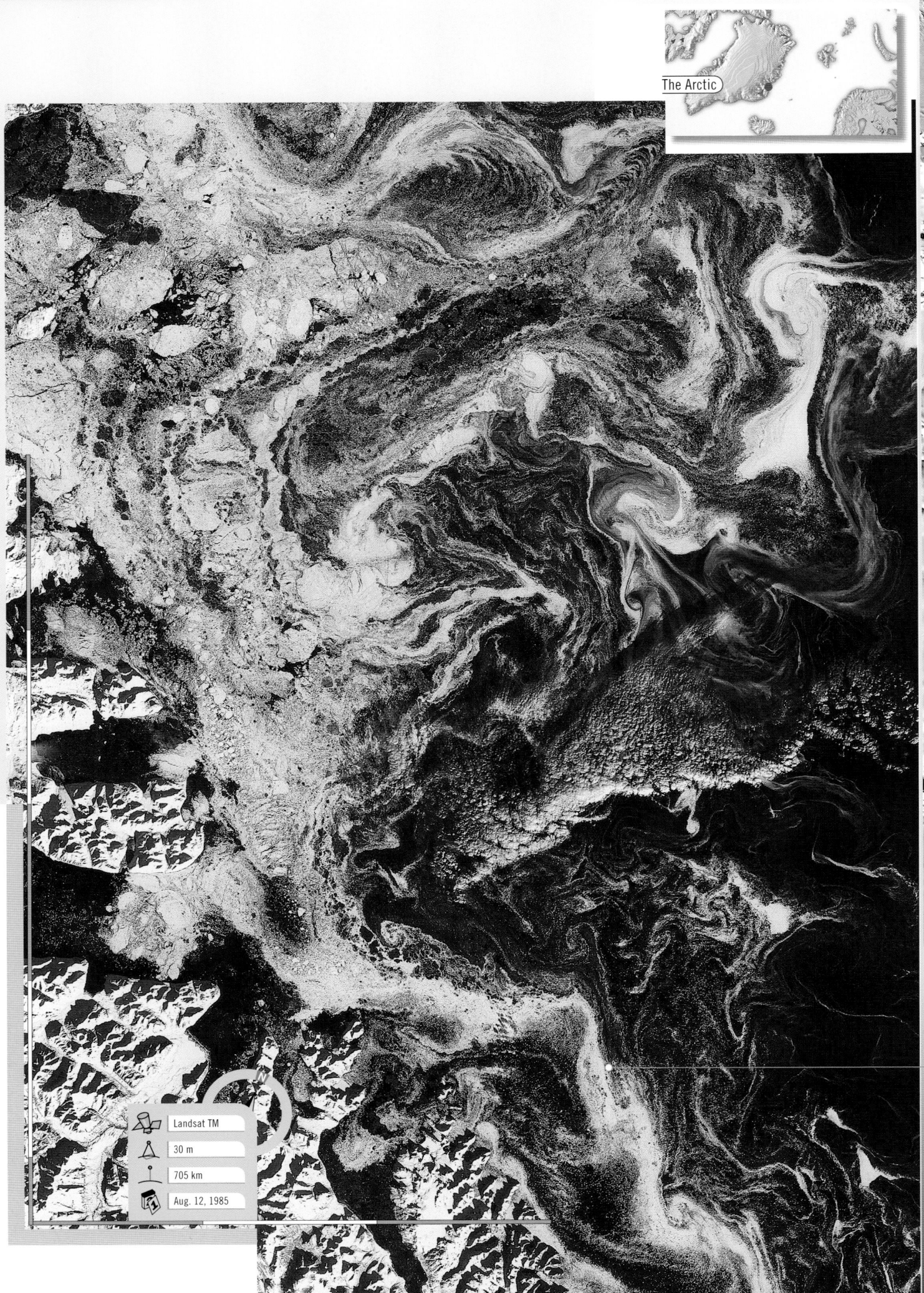

Landsat TM

30 m

705 km

Aug. 12, 1985

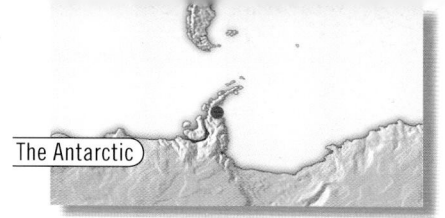

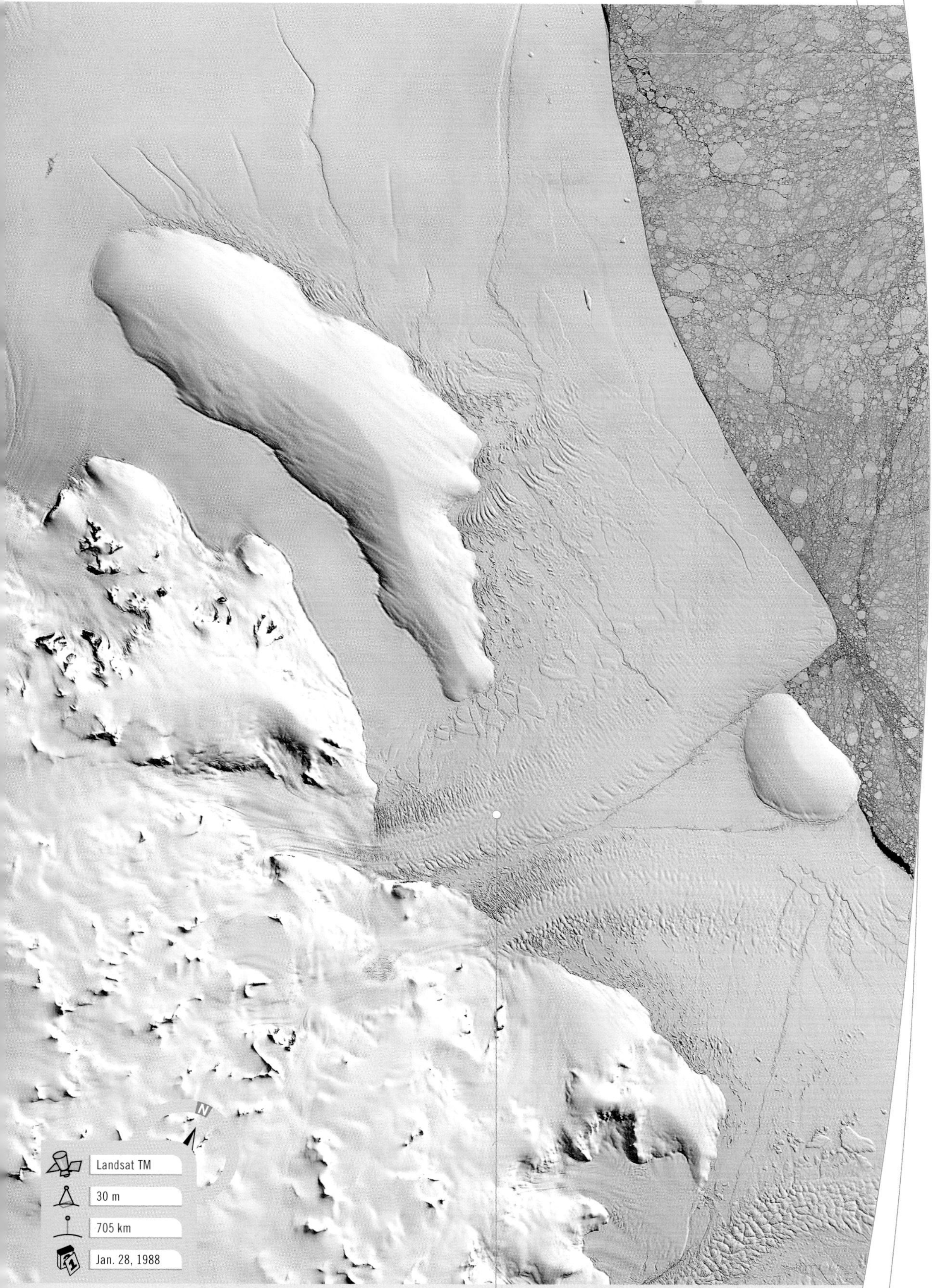

Larsen Ice Shelf in Antarctica

Unlike sea ice, which is created
when seawater freezes, shelf ice consists largely of frozen fresh water,
part of which is the direct, solidified
product of precipitation, although
a much larger share is contributed by
the massive flows of Antarctic inland ice.
Shelf ice reaches a thickness of up to
1,500 m at the line along which
it abuts with the Antarctic ice cap.

Arctic Eddies

Exchange between the warm water advancing from the south
and the colder masses in the polar regions is governed not
only by variations in temperature but also by differences in density
between masses of seawater with varying degrees of salinity.
The convergence of water masses with different properties — in
this case at the eastern coast of Greenland — triggers complex
interactions which in turn create marine gyres or so called eddies.

Mountain Ranges Glacial Heights

Landsat TM

30 m

705 km

Sept. 28, 1985

The Aletsch Glacier

The Aletsch Glacier stands out strikingly against the rugged terrain of the Bernese Alps in this satellite image. With a length of 24.1 km (measured in 1996) and a total area of nearly 87 sq. km (1975), it is both the longest and the most expansive glacier of the Alps. Known as the Great Aletsch, the main glacier flows generally southward from the junction of several other firn fields at Concordia Platz down to the Aletsch Forest.

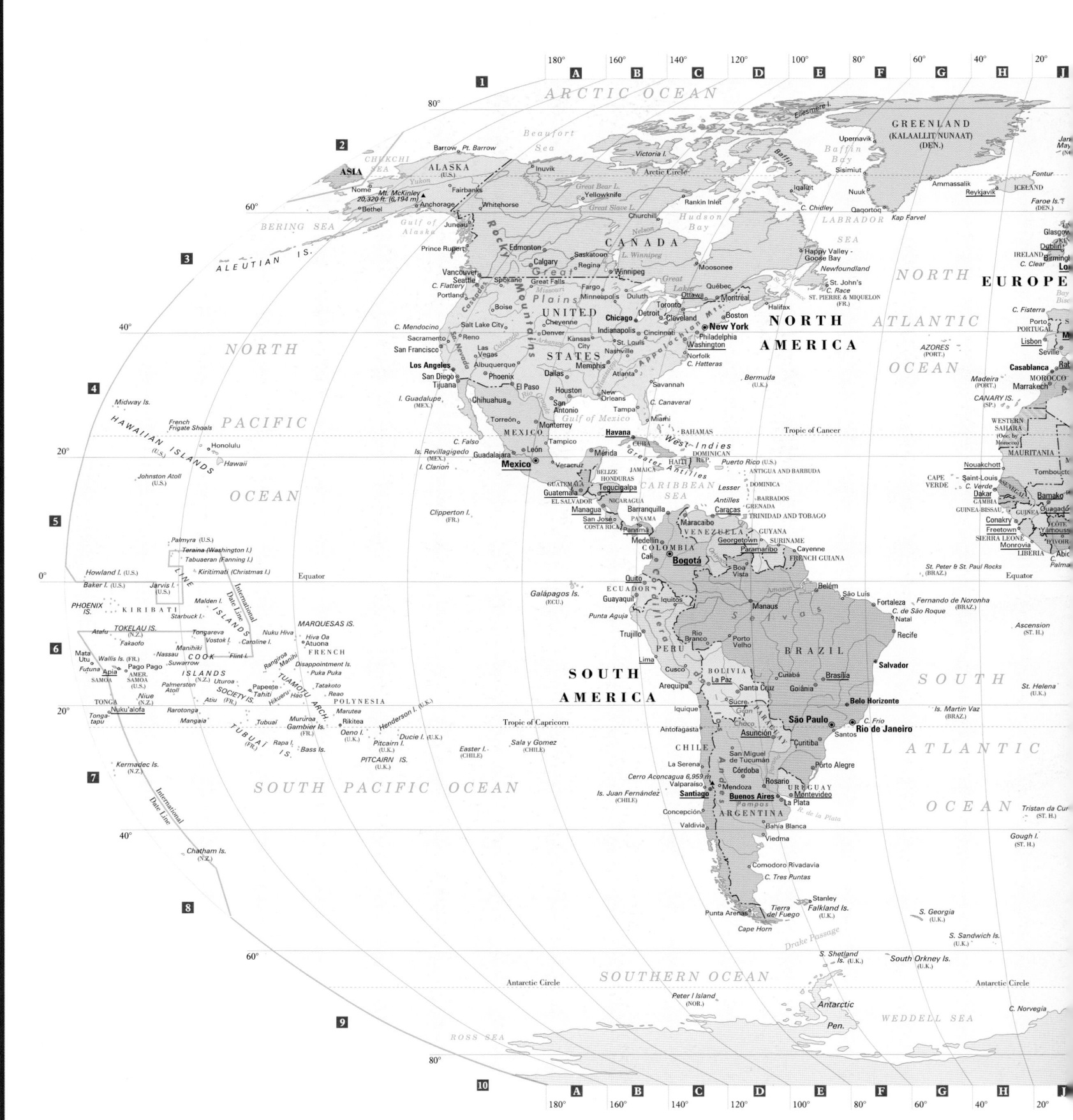

Population
- Over 5,000,000
- 2,000,000 - 4,999,999
- 500,000 - 1,999,999
- Under 500,000

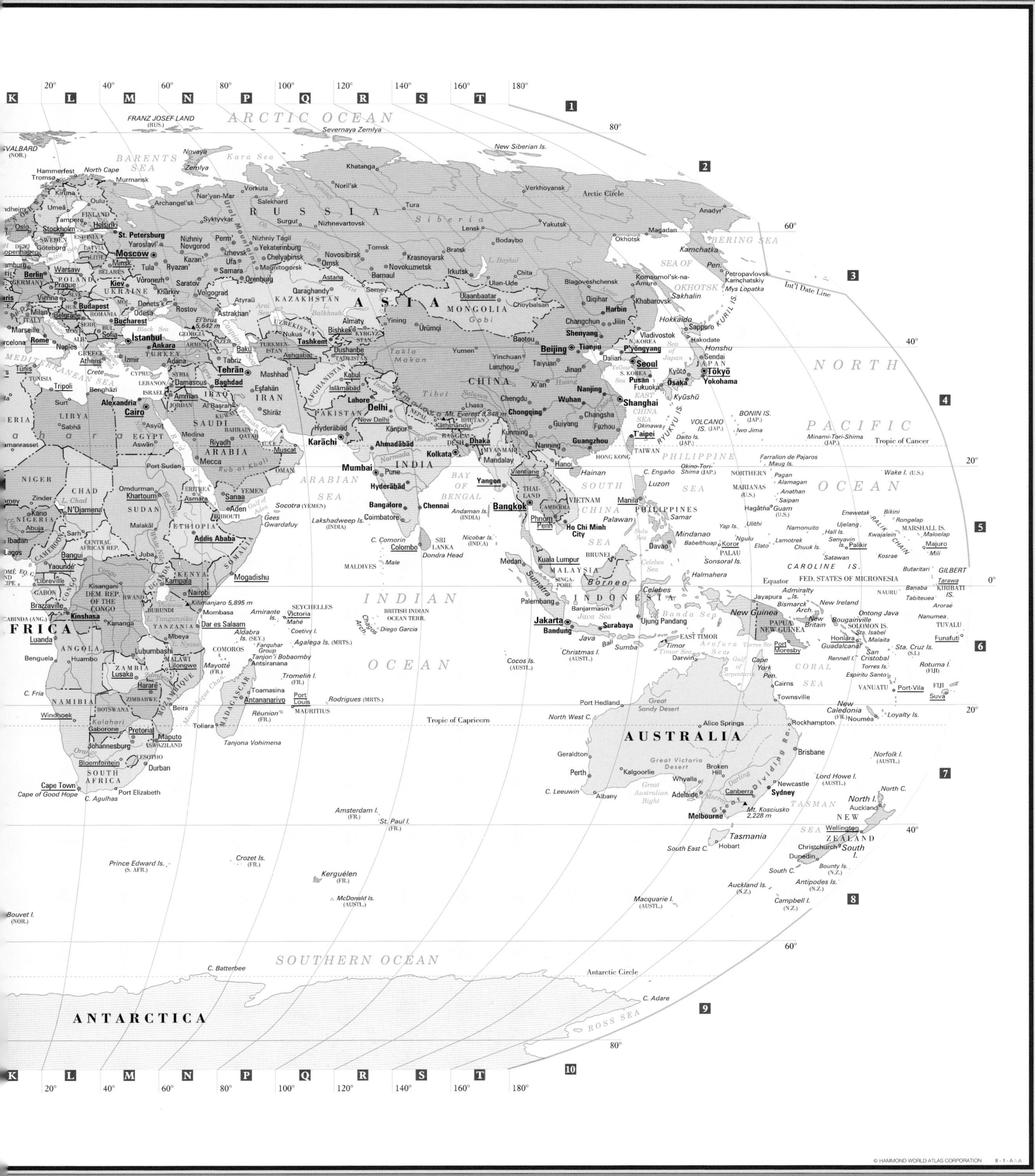

ARCTIC OCEAN

FRANZ JOSEF LAND (RUS.) · Severnaya Zemlya · New Siberian Is. · Novaya Zemlya · Kara Sea · BARENTS SEA · SVALBARD (NOR.) · Hammerfest · North Cape · Tromsø · Murmansk · Kiruna · Khatanga · Noril'sk · Verkhoyansk · Arctic Circle · Anadyr'

RUSSIA · Siberia · Oulu · FINLAND · Archangel'sk · Nar'yan-Mar · Vorkuta · Salekhard · Surgut · Nizhnevartovsk · Tura · Lensk · Bodaybo · Yakutsk · Magadan · BERING SEA · SEA OF OKHOTSK · Kamchatka · Petropavlovsk-Kamchatskiy · Mys Lopatka

Oslo · Stockholm · Tampere · Helsinki · St. Petersburg · Yaroslavl' · Nizhniy Novgorod · Perm' · Nizhniy Tagil · Yekaterinburg · Chelyabinsk · Omsk · Novosibirsk · Tomsk · Krasnoyarsk · Bratsk · Chita · Blagoveshchensk · Komsomol'sk-na-Amure · Okhotsk · Sakhalin · KURIL IS. · Hokkaidō · Sapporo · Hakodate

Copenhagen · GERMANY · Berlin · Warsaw · POLAND · BELARUS · Minsk · Moscow · Tula · Ryazan' · Kazan · Samara · Ufa · Magnitogorsk · Astana · Barnaul · Novokuznetsk · Irkutsk · L. Baykal · Ulan-Ude · Qiqihar · Changchun · Jilin · Vladivostok · Honshu · Sendai

Prague · Vienna · Budapest · Kiev · UKRAINE · Kharkiv · Voronezh · Saratov · Volgograd · Atyraū · KAZAKHSTAN · Qaraghandy · Balkhash · Almaty · Ürümqi · MONGOLIA · Gobi · Ulaanbaatar · Choybalsan · Harbin · Shenyang · N. KOREA · P'yŏngyang · S. KOREA · Seoul · Pusan · JAPAN · Tōkyō · Yokohama · Kyōto · Ōsaka · Fukuoka · Kyūshū

ASIA · Aral Sea · UZBEKISTAN · Nukus · Tashkent · KYRGYZSTAN · Bishkek · Yining · Takla Makan · Yumen · Baotou · Beijing · Tianjin · Dalian · SEA OF JAPAN · EAST CHINA SEA

Rome · Istanbul · Ankara · TURKEY · Baku · GEORGIA · ARMENIA · AZERBAIJAN · TURKMENISTAN · Ashgabat · TAJIKISTAN · Dushanbe · Yinchuan · Lanzhou · Taiyuan · Jinan · Xi'an · Nanjing · Shanghai · Wuhan · VOLCANO IS. (JAP.) · Iwo Jima

Tabrīz · Tehrān · Mashhad · Kabul · AFGHANISTAN · Islāmābād · Lahore · Tibet · Mt. Everest 8,848 m · Chengdu · Chongqing · Changsha · Fuzhou · Taipei · T'aiwan · BONIN IS. (JAP.) · Minami-Tori-Shima (JAP.) · Tropic of Cancer

Damascus · Baghdad · IRAQ · IRAN · Eşfahān · Shīrāz · PAKISTAN · Delhi · New Delhi · NEPAL · Kāthmāndu · BHUTAN · Kunming · Guiyang · Guangzhou · HONG KONG · Okinawa · RYUKYU IS. (JAP.) · Daito Is. (JAP.)

Alexandria · Cairo · JORDAN · Al Başrah · Riyadh · BAHRAIN · QATAR · U.A.E. · Muscat · Karāchi · Hyderābād · Ahmadābād · BANGLADESH · Dhaka · Kānpur · MYANMAR · Mandalay · Nanning · Hainan · C. Engaño · Luzon · NORTHERN MARIANAS (U.S.) · Pagan · Alamagan · Anathan · Saipan

Asyūt · Aswān · Medina · SAUDI ARABIA · Mecca · OMAN · Rub' al Khali · Mumbai · INDIA · Hyderābād · BAY OF BENGAL · Yangon · THAILAND · Vientiane · Hanoi · SOUTH CHINA SEA · Okino-Tori-Shima (JAP.) · Farallon de Pajaros · Maug Is. · Guam (U.S.) · Hagåtña

Port Sudan · NIGER · CHAD · L. Chad · N'Djamena · SUDAN · Khartoum · Omdurman · ERITREA · Asmara · YEMEN · Sanaa · Socotra (YEMEN) · Gulf of Aden · Gees Gwardafuy · ETHIOPIA · Addis Ababa · SOMALIA · Bangalore · Chennai · Coimbatore · ARABIAN SEA · Lakshadweep (INDIA) · Andaman Is. (INDIA) · VIETNAM · Manila · PHILIPPINES · Samar · Davao · Mindanao · MARSHALL IS. · Enewetak · Bikini · Rongelap · Kwajalein · Majuro · Mili

Zinder · NIGERIA · Abuja · Ibadan · Lagos · CAMEROON · Yaoundé · CENTRAL AFRICAN REP. · Bangui · Juba · UGANDA · KENYA · Kampala · Nairobi · C. Comorin · SRI LANKA · Colombo · Dondra Head · MALDIVES · Male · Phnom Penh · Ho Chi Minh City · Palawan · BRUNEI · Sulu Sea · Celebes Sea · Halmahera · Yap Is. · Ulithi · Babelthuap · Koror · PALAU · Ngulu · Namonuito · Hall Is. · Lamotrek · Elato · Satawan · CAROLINE IS. · Senyavin Is. · Ponapé · Kosrae

Libreville · GABON · EQ. GUINEA · SÃO TOMÉ & PRÍNCIPE · CONGO · DEM. REP. OF THE CONGO · Kisangani · RWANDA · BURUNDI · Kilimanjaro 5,895 m · Mombasa · SEYCHELLES · Victoria · Amirante Is. (SEY.) · Mahé · Coëtivy I. · BRITISH INDIAN OCEAN TERR. · Diego Garcia · MALAYSIA · Kuala Lumpur · SINGAPORE · Medan · Sumatra · Borneo · INDONESIA · Palembang · Banjarmasin · Celebes · Jayapura · New Guinea · Admiralty Is. · New Ireland · Bismarck Arch. · FED. STATES OF MICRONESIA · NAURU · Butaritari · Tarawa · KIRIBATI · Tabiteuea · GILBERT IS. · Banaba · Equator · 0°

INDIAN OCEAN · Kananga · TANZANIA · Dar es Salaam · Mbeya · Farquhar Group · Aldabra Is. (SEY.) · Tanjon' i Bobaomby · Antsiranana · COMOROS · Mayotte (FR.) · Agalega Is. (MRTS.) · Jakarta · Bandung · Surabaya · Java · Bali · Ujung Pandang · Banda Sea · New Britain · Bougainville · SOLOMON IS. · Sta. Isabel · Ontong Java · Honiara · Guadalcanal · Malaita · Nanumea · TUVALU · Funafuti · San Cristobal · Rennell I.

Luanda · Benguela · Huambo · ANGOLA · ZAMBIA · Lubumbashi · Lusaka · MALAWI · Lilongwe · L. Tanganyika · MADAGASCAR · Antananarivo · Toamasina · Réunion (FR.) · Port Louis · MAURITIUS · Rodrigues (MRTS.) · Christmas I. (AUSTL.) · Cocos Is. (AUSTL.) · Timor · Sumba · Arafura Sea · EAST TIMOR · Darwin · Gulf of Carpentaria · Cape York Pen. · Torres Str. · PAPUA NEW GUINEA · Port Moresby · CORAL SEA · Sta. Cruz Is. (S.I.) · Rotuma I. (FIJI) · Espiritu Santo · VANUATU · Port-Vila · FIJI · Suva

C. Fria · NAMIBIA · BOTSWANA · ZIMBABWE · Harare · MOZAMBIQUE · Beira · Mozambique Channel · Tromelin I. (FR.) · Tropic of Capricorn · Port Hedland · Great Sandy Desert · North West C. · Alice Springs · Rockhampton · New Caledonia (FR.) · Nouméa · Loyalty Is.

Windhoek · Kalahari · Gaborone · Pretoria · Johannesburg · SWAZILAND · Maputo · Toliara · Tanjona Vohimena · Orange · LESOTHO · Bloemfontein · SOUTH AFRICA · Durban · Geraldton · **AUSTRALIA** · Great Victoria Desert · Perth · Kalgoorlie · Whyalla · Broken Hill · Brisbane · Norfolk I. (AUSTL.) · Lord Howe I. (AUSTL.) · North C.

Cape Town · Cape of Good Hope · C. Agulhas · Port Elizabeth · Amsterdam I. (FR.) · St. Paul I. (FR.) · Great Australian Bight · C. Leeuwin · Albany · Adelaide · Murray · Canberra · Sydney · Mt. Kosciusko 2,228 m · Newcastle · Melbourne · TASMAN SEA · NEW ZEALAND · Auckland · North I. · Wellington · Christchurch · South I.

Prince Edward Is. (S. AFR.) · Crozet Is. (FR.) · Kerguélen (FR.) · McDonald Is. (AUSTL.) · Tasmania · Hobart · South East C. · Dunedin · South C. · Bounty Is. (N.Z.) · Auckland Is. (N.Z.) · Antipodes Is. (N.Z.) · Macquarie I. (AUSTL.) · Campbell I. (N.Z.)

Bouvet I. (NOR.) · **SOUTHERN OCEAN** · C. Batterbee · Antarctic Circle · C. Adare · ROSS SEA · **ANTARCTICA**

NORTH PACIFIC OCEAN · PHILIPPINE SEA · Wake I. (U.S.) · RALIK CHAIN · Ujelang · Maloelap · Arorae

Int'l Date Line

20° 40° 60° 80° 100° 120° 140° 160° 180°

K L M N P Q R S T

1 2 3 4 5 6 7 8 9 10

© HAMMOND WORLD ATLAS CORPORATION

Scale 1:79,500,000 Robinson Projection

MI | 600 | 1200 | 1800 | 2400

KM | 600 | 1200 | 1800 | 2400 | 3000 | 3600

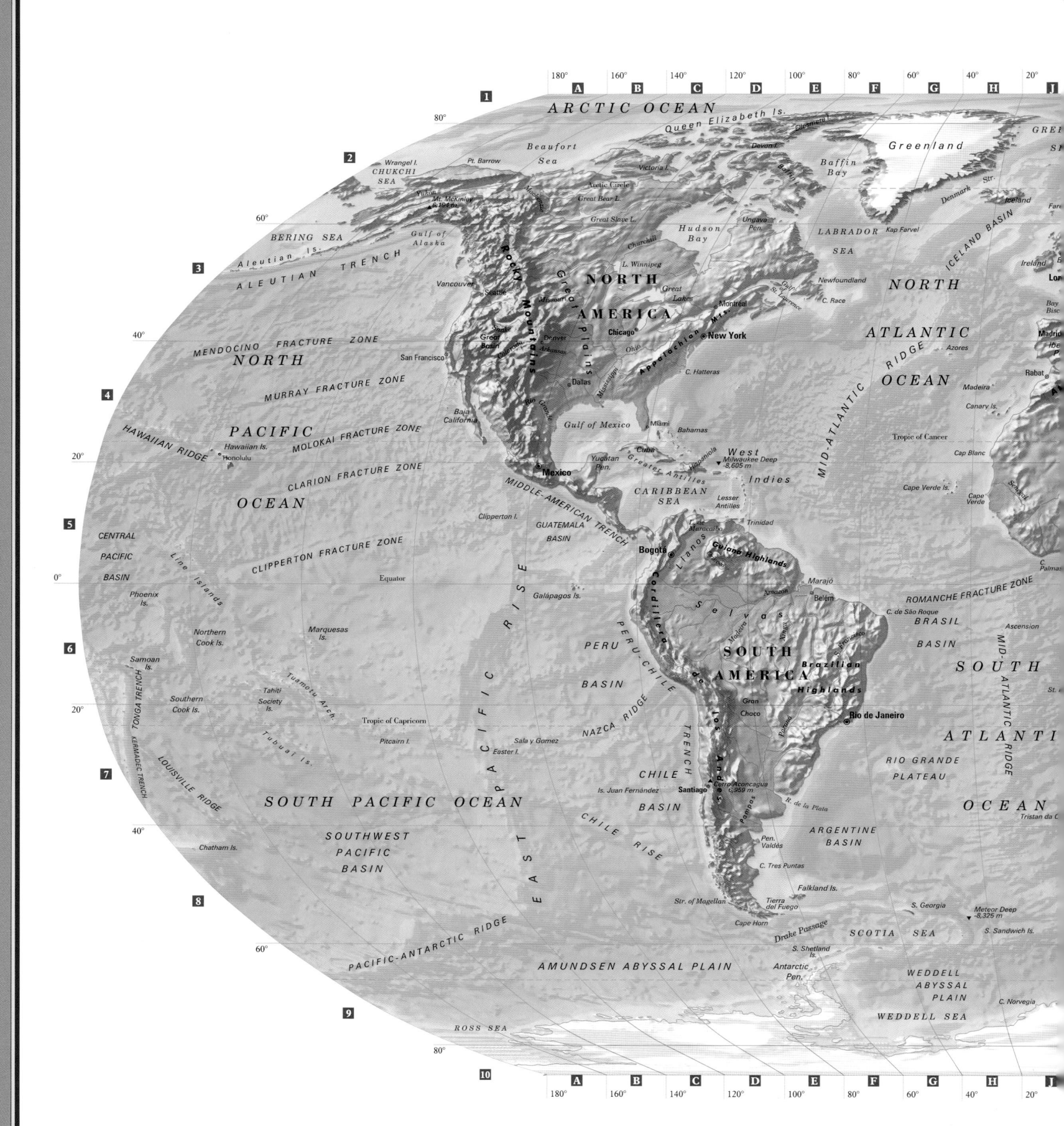

ARCTIC OCEAN

Queen Elizabeth Is.

Ellesmere I.

Greenland

GRE

80°

Beaufort
Sea

Devon I.

SN

2
Wrangel I.
CHUKCHI
SEA

Pt. Barrow

Victoria I.

Baffin
Bay

Denmark
Str.

Iceland

Fare

60°
Yukon
Mt. McKinley
6,194 m

Arctic Circle
Mackenzie

Great Bear L.

ICELAND BASIN

Great Slave L.

LABRADOR

Kap Farvel

Ireland

Lon

3
BERING SEA

Gulf of
Alaska

Churchill

Hudson
Bay

Ungava
Pen.

SEA

Newfoundland

NORTH

Aleutian Is.

ALEUTIAN TRENCH

Vancouver

Rocky Mountains

Great Plains

L. Winnipeg

Great
Lakes

St. Lawrence
Gulf of
St. Lawrence

C. Race

ATLANTIC

Bay
of
Bisc

ALEUTIAN TRENCH

Seattle

NORTH
AMERICA

Montréal

40°
MENDOCINO FRACTURE ZONE

NORTH

San Francisco

Denver
Great
Basin
Colorado

Chicago

Ohio

Appalachian Mts.

New York

OCEAN

MID-ATLANTIC RIDGE

Azores

Madrid

Ibe

4
MURRAY FRACTURE ZONE

PACIFIC

Baja
California

Arkansas

Dallas

Rio Grande

Mississippi

C. Hatteras

Tropic of Cancer

Madeira

Rabat

HAWAIIAN RIDGE

Gulf of Mexico

Miami

Canary Is.

20°
Hawaiian Is.
Honolulu

MOLOKAI FRACTURE ZONE

OCEAN

Yucatan
Pen.

Mexico

Cuba
Greater Antilles

Bahamas

West

Hispaniola

Milwaukee Deep
-8,605 m

Indies

Cap Blanc

Cape Verde Is.

Cape
Verde

CLARION FRACTURE ZONE

CARIBBEAN
SEA

Lesser
Antilles

C.
Palmas

5
CENTRAL
PACIFIC
BASIN

Clipperton I.

GUATEMALA
BASIN

MIDDLE-AMERICAN TRENCH

Trinidad

Maracaibo

Bogotá

Llanos

Guiana Highlands

0°
Line Islands

CLIPPERTON FRACTURE ZONE

Equator

Galápagos Is.

Cordillera

Selvas

Amazon

Marajó

Belém

ROMANCHE FRACTURE ZONE

BRASIL

Phoenix
Is.

PERU

BASIN

PERU-CHILE

Madeira

C. de São Roque

BASIN

Ascension

6
Samoan
Is.

Northern
Cook Is.

Marquesas
Is.

SOUTH
AMERICA

Brazilian

Tocantins

MID-ATLANTIC RIDGE

20°
Southern
Cook Is.

Tahiti
Society
Is.

Tuamotu Arch.

BASIN

Gran
Choco

Highlands

Rio de Janeiro

S
O
U
T
H

Tropic of Capricorn

Pitcairn I.

Sala y Gomez
Easter I.

NAZCA RIDGE

de los Andes

Paraná

ATLANTIC

Tubuai Is.

RIO GRANDE
PLATEAU

7
KERMADEC TRENCH

LOUISVILLE RIDGE

CHILE

Is. Juan Fernández

Santiago

CHILE
BASIN

Pampas

R. de la Plata

OCEAN

Tristan da C

TONGA TRENCH

SOUTH PACIFIC OCEAN

EAST PACIFIC RISE

40°
Chatham Is.

SOUTHWEST
PACIFIC
BASIN

CHILE RISE

ARGENTINE
BASIN

Pen.
Valdés

C. Tres Puntas

Falkland Is.

8
Str. of Magellan

Tierra
del Fuego

S. Georgia

Meteor Deep
-8,325 m

Cape Horn

Drake Passage

SCOTIA
SEA

S. Sandwich Is.

PACIFIC-ANTARCTIC RIDGE

S. Shetland
Is.

60°
AMUNDSEN ABYSSAL PLAIN

Antarctic
Pen.

WEDDELL
ABYSSAL
PLAIN

C. Norvegia

9
ROSS SEA

WEDDELL SEA

80°

K 20° **L** 40° **M** 60° **N** 80° **P** 100° **Q** 120° **R** 140° **S** 160° **T** 180°

1

Svalbard   Franz Josef Land   ARCTIC OCEAN   Severnaya Zemlya

Spitsbergen

BARENTS   Novaya   Kara Sea   New Siberian Is.   **2**
SEA   Zemlya
Nordkapp   Kola   White   Yamal   80°
Kjølen   Pen.   Sea   Pen.   Yenisey   Central   Lower Tunguska   Lena   Arctic Circle
NWEGIAN   Yenisey   Siberian   60°   BERING SEA
SEA   West   Kolyma Ra.   Kamchatka   **3**
Stockholm   Siberian   Plateau   Pen.
L. Ladoga   Ob'   Plain   Lena   SEA OF   EMPEROR SEAMOUNT CHAIN
EUROPE   Moscow   Angara   SAKHALIN   OKHOTSK
Baltic Sea   Kirgiz Steppe   Irtysh   Kamchatka   Hokkaidō   NORTHWEST   NORTH   40°
Alps   Carpathians   Dnepr   A S I A   L. Baykal   Kuril Is.   PACIFIC
ris   Volga   Aral   L. Balkhash   Altai Mts.   Amur   JAPAN TRENCH   BASIN   **4**
Caucasus   Sea   Tian Shan   Gobi Desert   Sea   Hokkaidō
Rome   Black Sea   Elbrus   Takla   Kunlun Mts.   of   Honshū   PACIFIC
Istanbul   5,642 m   Makan   Beijing   Japan   Tōkyō
MEDITERRANEAN SEA   Taurus Mts.   Amu Darya   Hindu Kush   Haung   Yellow   Ryukyu Is.   Tropic of Cancer   20°
Sicily   Caspian Sea   Zagros Mts.   Tehrān   Himalaya   Sea   Taiwan   PHILIPPINE   **5**
Cyprus   Euphrates   Satlej   Mt. Everest   East   RYUKYU TRENCH   OCEAN
Cairo   Tigris   Karāchi   8,848 m   China   PHILIPPINE   Mariana Is.   CENTRAL
ha r a   Red Sea Hills   Arabian   Ganges   Sea   Hainan   SOUTH   SEA   Challenger Deep   PACIFIC
Ahaggar   Pen.   Narmada   BAY   CHINA   Luzon   -11,033 m   Marshall   BASIN
L. Chad   Rub' al Khali   ARABIAN   OF   Manila   PHILIPPINE   Is.
FRICA   Blue Nile   Gulf of Aden   SEA   BENGAL   Andaman   SEA   BASIN   Caroline Is.
Sudan   Ethiopian   Socotra   Is.   Isthmus   Palawan   MELANESIAN
gos   Plateau   CARLSBERG RIDGE   C. Comorin   of Kra   Sula   Mindanao   BASIN   0°
Bioko   White Nile   Maldive   Sri Lanka   Malay   Sea   Celebes
me   Congo   Is.   Equator   Pen.   Borneo   Sea   Halmahera
Kinshasa   CONGO   SOMALI   INDIAN   Sumātra   Celebes   Bismarck Arch.   Solomon   **6**
BASIN   Kilimanjaro   BASIN   Jakarta   Java Sea   New   Is.
ngola   L. Victoria   5,895 m   Seychelles   JAVA TRENCH   Java   -7,450 m   Banda Sea   Guinea   New
BASIN   L. Tanganyika   Chagos   OCEAN   Arafura   Britain   CORAL
Lusaka   Zambezi   Arch.   Cocos Is.   Timor   Sea   Torres Str.   SEA   New Hebrides   20°
VIS RIDGE   L. Nyasa   Comoros   Sea   Gulf of   Great Barrier Reef   Fiji Is.
Namib Desert   Is.   Madagascar   Carpentaria   Cape York Pen.   New
Orange   Mozambique Chan.   Réunion   NINETYEAST RIDGE   BROKEN   C. Leeuwin   Great Victoria   Caledonia
Johannesburg   Mauritius   PLATEAU   A U S T R A L I A   Darling   North C.   **7**
Drakensberg   CENTRAL INDIAN RIDGE   Desert   Great   Sydney
Cape of Good Hope   Great   Australian   Murray   Dividing Ra.   North I.
SOUTHWEST INDIAN RIDGE   Bight   Mt. Kosciusko   TASMAN   40°
Kerguélen   SOUTHEAST   2,228 m   Melbourne   SEA
McDonald Is.   Tasmania   South I.   **8**
KERGUÉLEN   INDIAN
PLATEAU   AUSTRALIAN-ANTARCTIC BASIN   RIDGE   60°
ENDERBY ABYSSAL PLAIN
Antarctic Circle   C. Batterbee   C. Adare   **9**
A N T A R C T I C A   ROSS SEA   80°   **10**

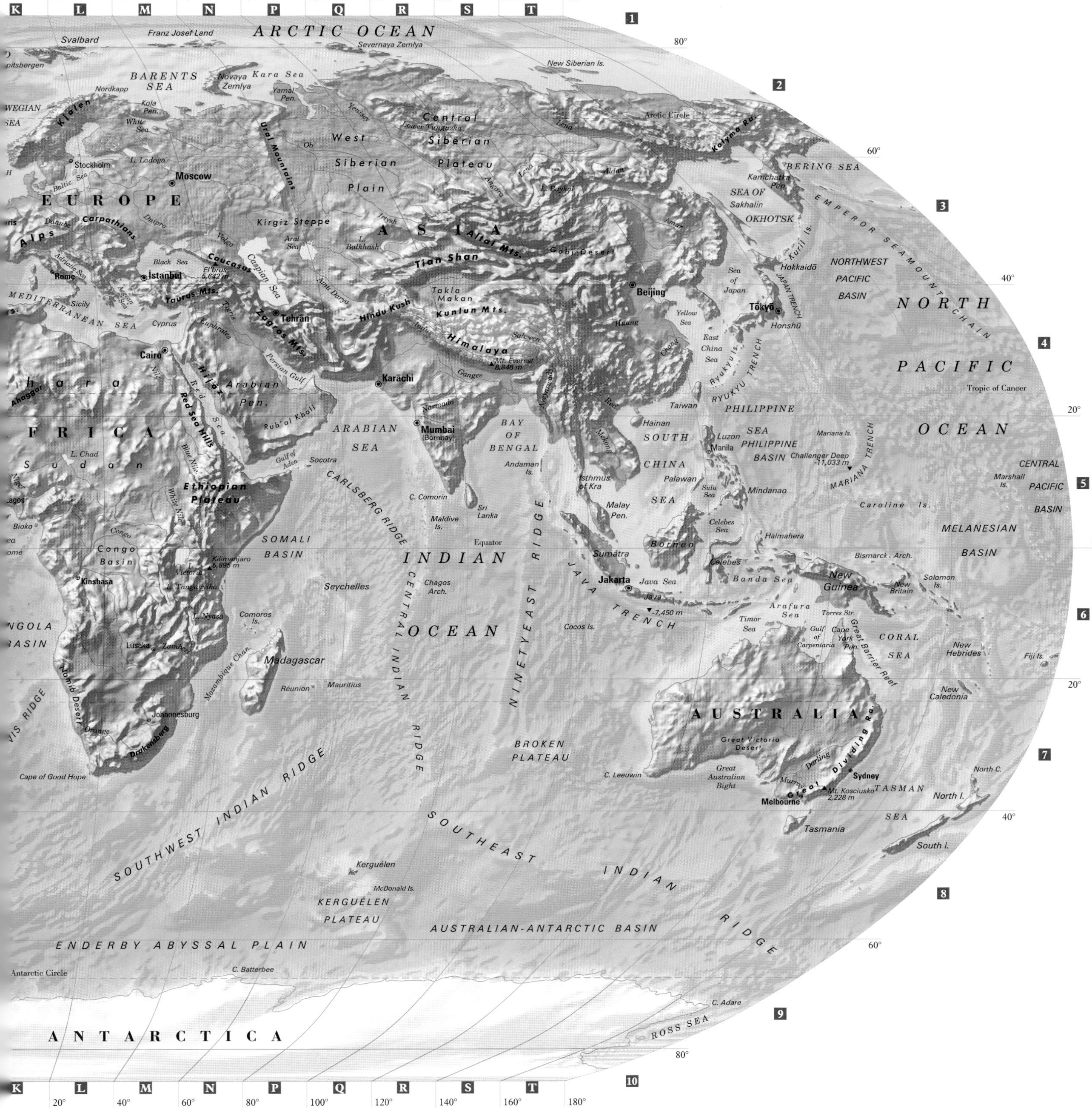

K 20° **L** 40° **M** 60° **N** 80° **P** 100° **Q** 120° **R** 140° **S** 160° **T** 180°

Scale 1:79,500,000   Robinson Projection

MI   600   1200   1800   2400
KM   600   1200   1800   2400   3000   3600

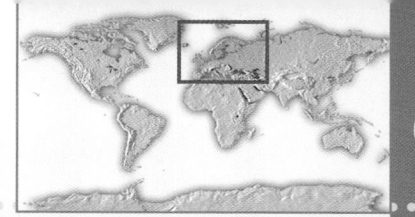

The terrain in this high-oblique, northwest-looking image, is indicative of the rugged, mountainous landscape characterizing most of Greece. Two major landform regions are captured in this image: the northwest to southeast-trending Mountains of Pindus in central Greece (north of the Gulf of Corinth), and the Peloponnisos Peninsula (south of the Gulf of Corinth). The Pindus, a massive continuation of the Dinaric Alps of Albania and the former Yugoslavia, make the land inhospitable and travel difficult. This rugged terrain caused the Greeks to become a seafaring people.

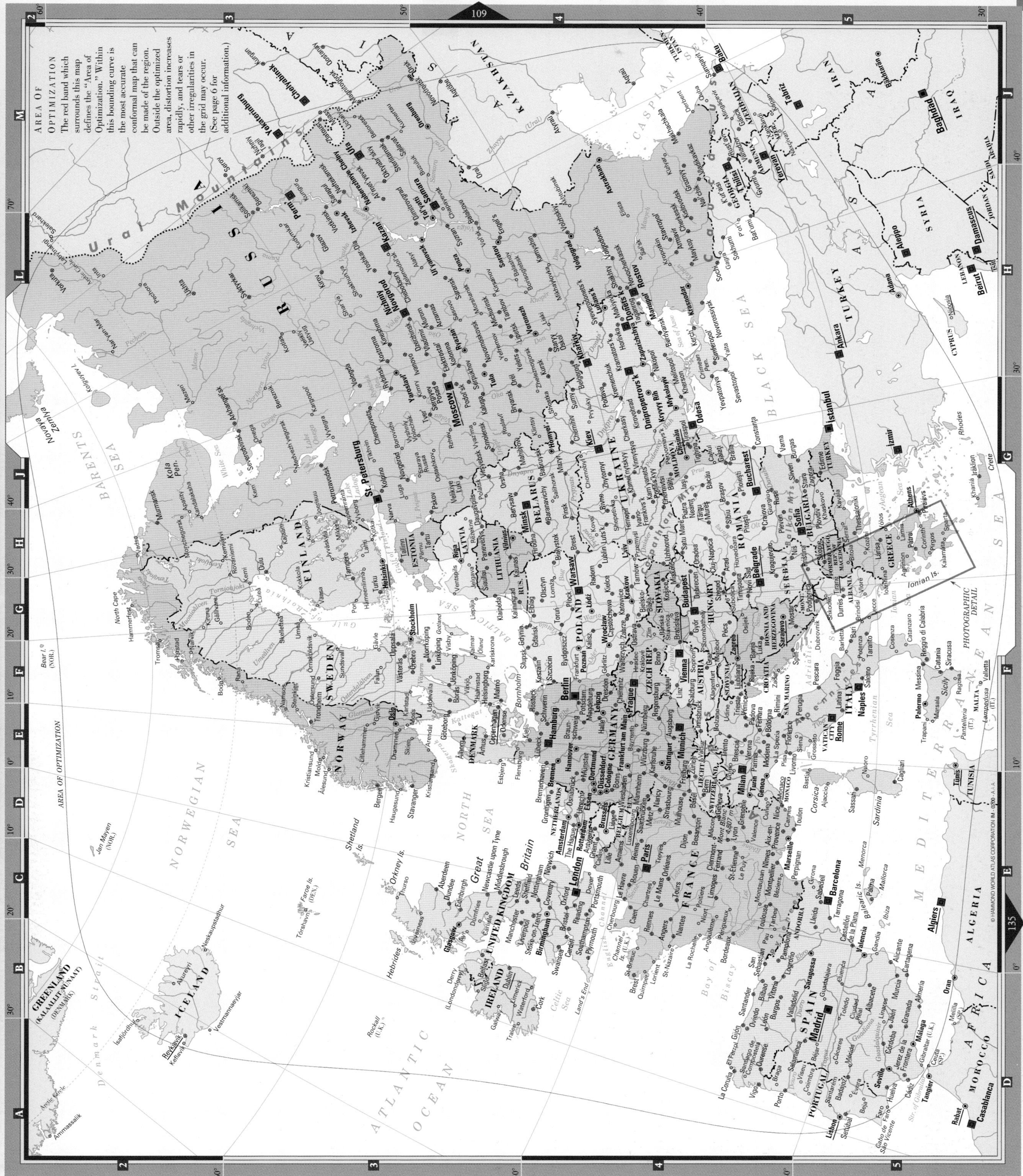

AREA OF OPTIMIZATION
The red band which surrounds this map defines the "Area of Optimization." Within this bounding curve is the most accurate conformal map that can be made of the region. Outside the optimized area, distortion increases rapidly, and tears or other irregularities in the grid may occur. (See page 6 for additional information.)

Population

| ■ Over 3,000,000 | ✳ 500,000 - 999,999 | ○ Under 100,000 |
| ■ 1,000,000 - 2,999,999 | ◉ 100,000 - 499,999 | |

Scale 1:20,500,000   Hammond Optimal Conformal

| MI | 200 | 400 | 600 |
| KM | 200 | 400 | 600 | 800 |

© HAMMOND WORLD ATLAS CORPORATION M-0700-A-A

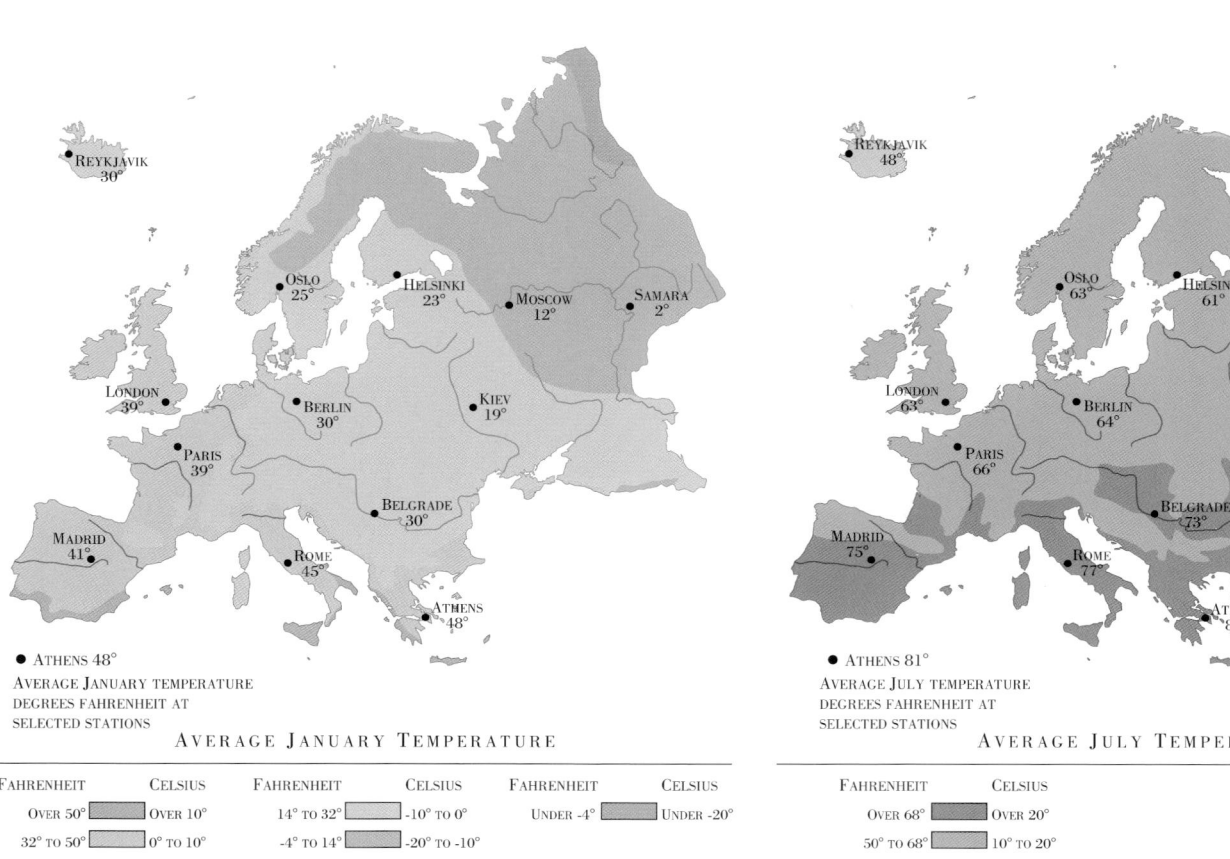

● ATHENS 48°
AVERAGE JANUARY TEMPERATURE
DEGREES FAHRENHEIT AT
SELECTED STATIONS

AVERAGE JANUARY TEMPERATURE

FAHRENHEIT	CELSIUS	FAHRENHEIT	CELSIUS	FAHRENHEIT	CELSIUS
OVER 50°	OVER 10°	14° TO 32°	-10° TO 0°	UNDER -4°	UNDER -20°
32° TO 50°	0° TO 10°	-4° TO 14°	-20° TO -10°		

● ATHENS 81°
AVERAGE JULY TEMPERATURE
DEGREES FAHRENHEIT AT
SELECTED STATIONS

AVERAGE JULY TEMPERATURE

FAHRENHEIT	CELSIUS	FAHRENHEIT	CELSIUS
OVER 68°	OVER 20°	32° TO 50°	0° TO 10°
50° TO 68°	10° TO 20°	UNDER 32°	UNDER 0°

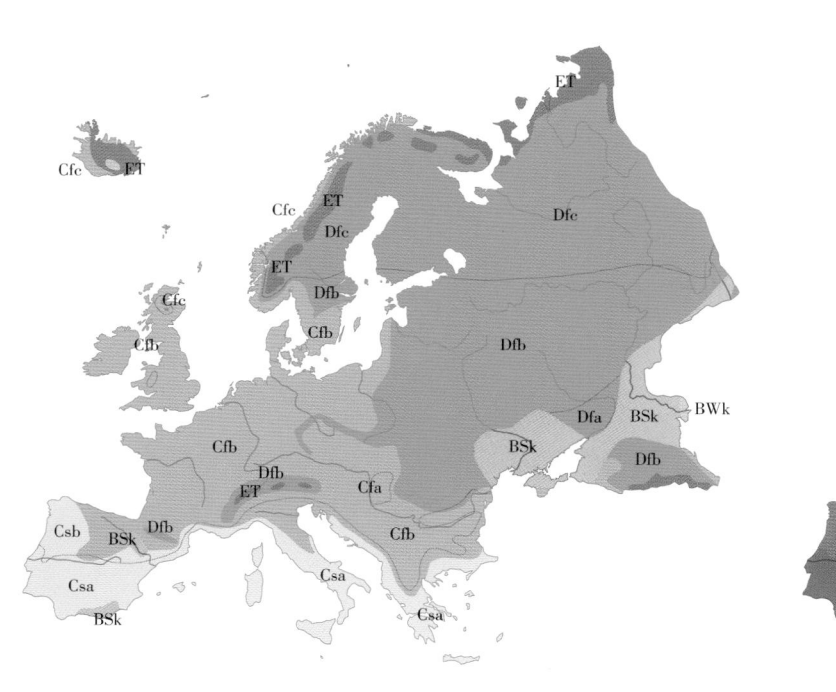

CLIMATE

VEGETATION

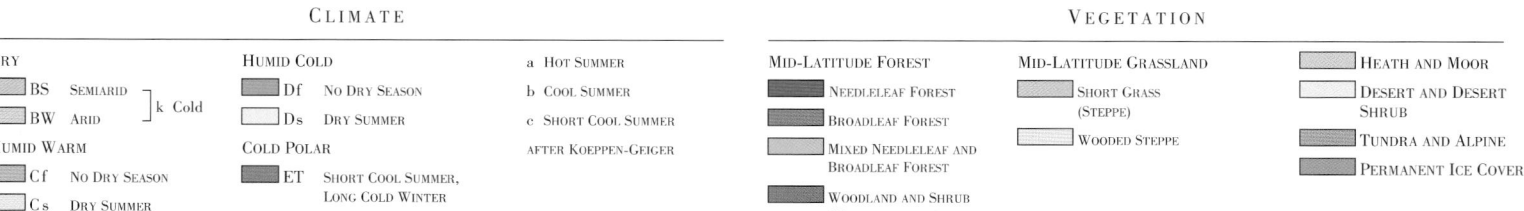

DRY
BS SEMIARID
BW ARID } k Cold

HUMID WARM
Cf NO DRY SEASON
Cs DRY SUMMER

HUMID COLD
Df NO DRY SEASON
Ds DRY SUMMER

COLD POLAR
ET SHORT COOL SUMMER, LONG COLD WINTER
EF PERPETUAL FROST

a HOT SUMMER
b COOL SUMMER
c SHORT COOL SUMMER

AFTER KOEPPEN-GEIGER

MID-LATITUDE FOREST
NEEDLELEAF FOREST
BROADLEAF FOREST
MIXED NEEDLELEAF AND BROADLEAF FOREST
WOODLAND AND SHRUB (MEDITERRANEAN)

MID-LATITUDE GRASSLAND
SHORT GRASS (STEPPE)
WOODED STEPPE

HEATH AND MOOR
DESERT AND DESERT SHRUB
TUNDRA AND ALPINE
PERMANENT ICE COVER

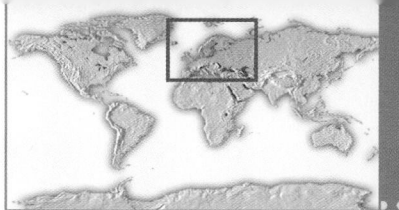

Europe - Geographical Comparisons

REYKJAVIK 31

MURMANSK 15

BERGEN 77

HELSINKI 27

MOSCOW 22

KILLARNEY 67

LONDON 23

BERLIN 23

KIEV 24

ASTRAKHAN 6

PARIS 25

LUGANO 69

ODESSA 15

BELGRADE 27

MADRID 17

ROME 26

TIRANE 46

● BERLIN 23

AVERAGE ANNUAL RAINFALL
IN INCHES AT SELECTED STATIONS

AVERAGE ANNUAL RAINFALL

INCHES	CM	INCHES	CM	INCHES	CM
OVER 80	OVER 200	40 TO 60	100 TO 150	10 TO 20	25 TO 50
60 TO 80	150 TO 200	20 TO 40	50 TO 100	UNDER 10	UNDER 25

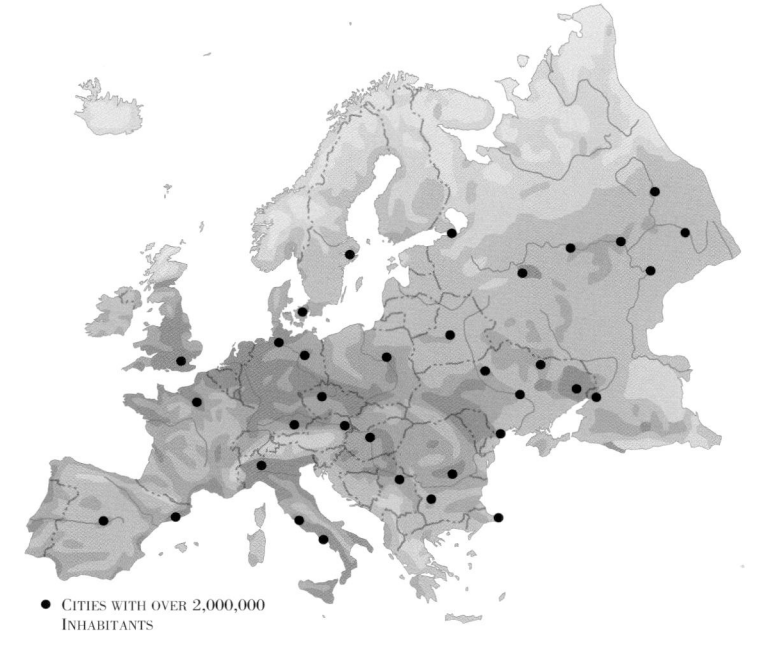

● CITIES WITH OVER 2,000,000 INHABITANTS

POPULATION DISTRIBUTION

DENSITY PER		SQ. MI.	SQ. KM.	SQ. MI.	SQ. KM.
SQ. MI.	SQ. KM.	130 TO 260	50 TO 100	3 TO 25	1 TO 10
OVER 260	OVER 100	25 TO 130	10 TO 50	UNDER 3	UNDER 1

FURS

FURS

FURS

OATS

FLAX

RYE

RYE

WHEAT

DAIRY

RYE

POTATOES

HEMP

RYE

POTATOES

WHEAT

DAIRY

OATS

HOGS

OATS

RYE

SUGAR BEETS

CATTLE

CORN

HOGS

WHEAT

CORN

BARLEY

SHEEP

DAIRY

DAIRY

WINE

CORN

WHEAT

CORN

TOBACCO

TEA

WINE

WINE

WHEAT

WHEAT

WINE

SHEEP

TOBACCO

OLIVES

WINE

FRUIT

SHEEP

WINE

OLIVES

LAND USE

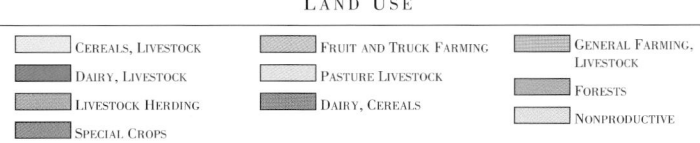

	CEREALS, LIVESTOCK		FRUIT AND TRUCK FARMING		GENERAL FARMING, LIVESTOCK
	DAIRY, LIVESTOCK		PASTURE LIVESTOCK		FORESTS
	LIVESTOCK HERDING		DAIRY, CEREALS		NONPRODUCTIVE
	SPECIAL CROPS				

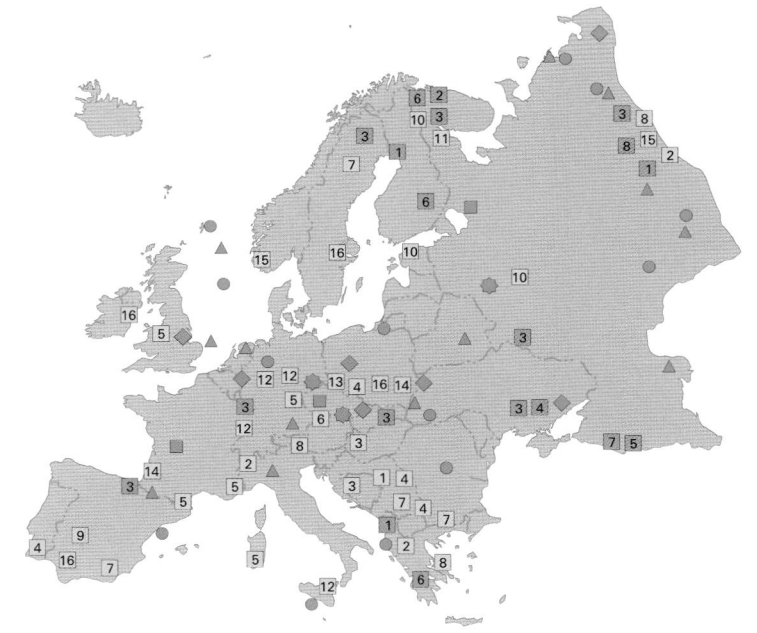

MINERAL RESOURCES

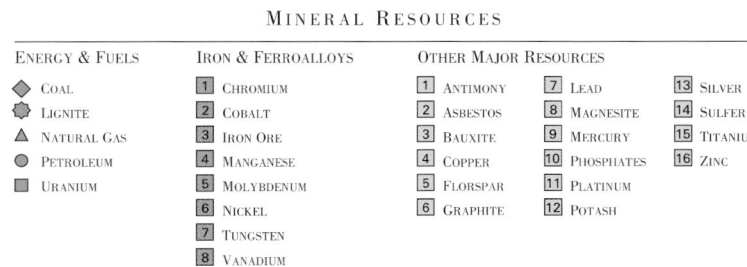

ENERGY & FUELS
◆ COAL
⬠ LIGNITE
▲ NATURAL GAS
● PETROLEUM
■ URANIUM

IRON & FERROALLOYS
1 CHROMIUM
2 COBALT
3 IRON ORE
4 MANGANESE
5 MOLYBDENUM
6 NICKEL
7 TUNGSTEN
8 VANADIUM

OTHER MAJOR RESOURCES
1 ANTIMONY
2 ASBESTOS
3 BAUXITE
4 COPPER
5 FLORSPAR
6 GRAPHITE

7 LEAD
8 MAGNESITE
9 MERCURY
10 PHOSPHATES
11 PLATINUM
12 POTASH

13 SILVER
14 SULFER
15 TITANIUM
16 ZINC

© HAMMOND WORLD ATLAS CORPORATION   CM - A-A

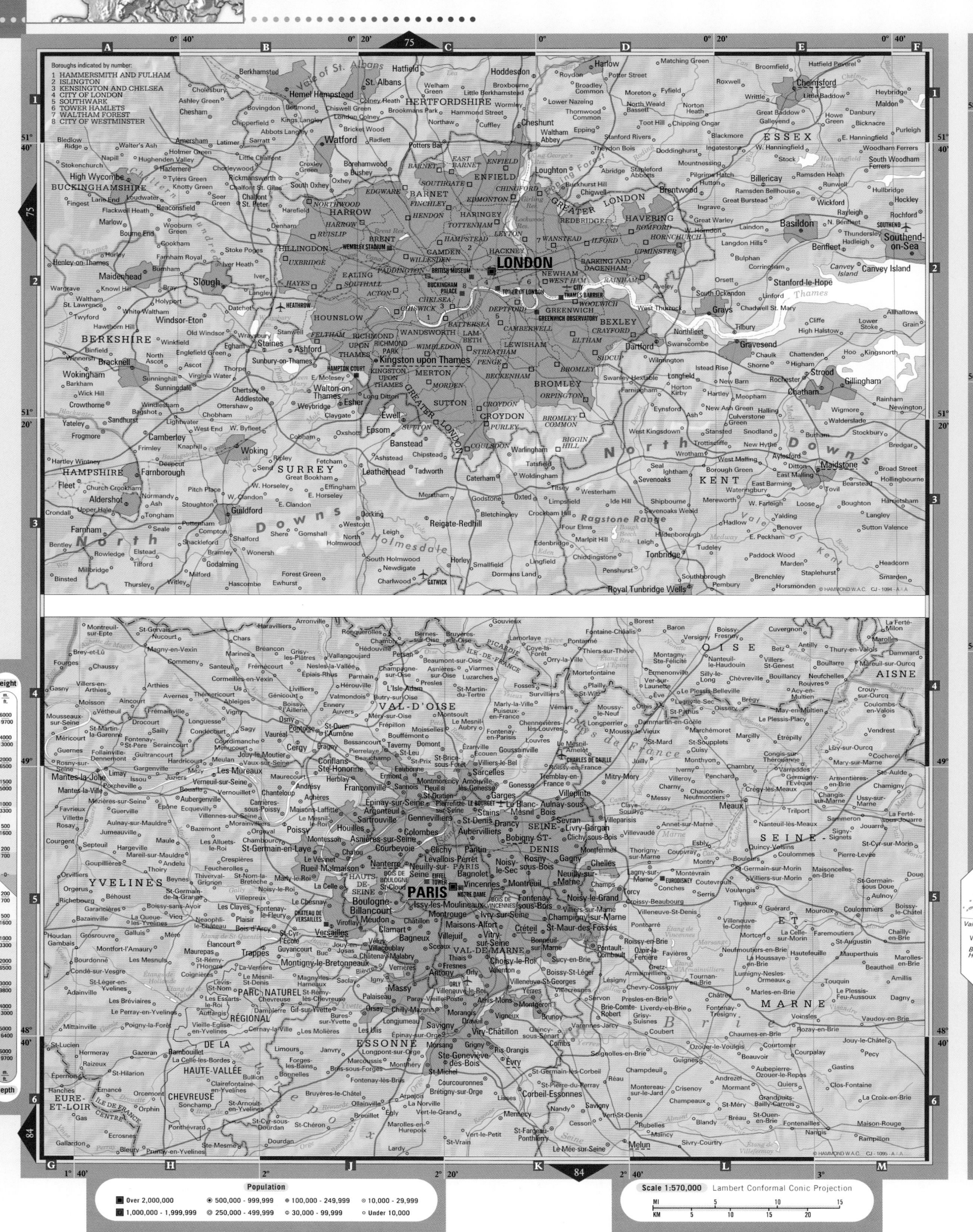

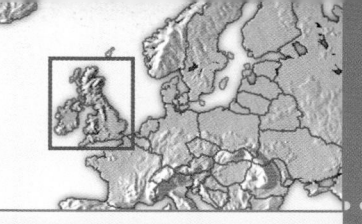

Shetland Is. (U.K.)

Orkney Is. (U.K.)

Same scale as main map

Map continued at left

© HAMMOND W.A.C.
CJ -1096- A - A

ATLANTIC OCEAN

NORTH SEA

SCOTLAND

Great Britain

UNITED KINGDOM

IRELAND

ENGLAND

WALES

NORTHERN IRELAND

Irish Sea

St. George's Channel

CELTIC SEA

ENGLISH CHANNEL

FRANCE

Outer Hebrides

Inner Hebrides

Glasgow · Edinburgh · Aberdeen · Inverness · Dundee · Perth

Belfast · Dublin · Cork · Limerick · Galway · Waterford

Liverpool · Manchester · Sheffield · Leeds · Bradford · Birmingham · Nottingham · Leicester · Coventry

London · Bristol · Cardiff · Swansea · Newport · Plymouth · Exeter · Southampton · Portsmouth · Brighton · Norwich · Cambridge

Isles of Scilly

© Hammond World Atlas Corporation
CM - 1004 - A A A

Scale 1:3,400,000 Lambert Conformal Conic Projection

MI 25 50 75 100

KM 25 50 75 100 125 150

Population

- ▪ Over 2,000,000
- ▪ 1,000,000 – 1,999,999
- ◉ 500,000 – 999,999
- ◉ 250,000 – 499,999
- ◉ 100,000 – 249,999
- ◎ 30,000 – 99,999
- ◯ 10,000 – 29,999
- ∘ Under 10,000

Map of Southeast England

ENGLAND

Counties and Regions
LEICESTERSHIRE · RUTLAND · LINCOLNSHIRE · NORTHAMPTONSHIRE · WARWICKSHIRE · BEDFORDSHIRE · BUCKINGHAMSHIRE · OXFORDSHIRE · CAMBRIDGESHIRE · NORFOLK · SUFFOLK · HERTFORDSHIRE · ESSEX · WEST BERKSHIRE · WINDSOR AND MAIDENHEAD · SLOUGH · WOKINGHAM · BRACKNELL FOREST · SURREY · KENT · WILTSHIRE · HAMPSHIRE · WEST SUSSEX · EAST SUSSEX · ISLE OF WIGHT

East Anglia

Major Cities and Towns
Birmingham · Coventry · Leicester · Peterborough · Northampton · Cambridge · Norwich · Ipswich · Luton · Oxford · GREATER LONDON · LONDON · Reading · Southend-on-Sea · Brighton and Hove · Portsmouth · Southampton · Bournemouth · Canterbury · Dover · Folkestone · Maidstone · Chatham · Gillingham

Water Bodies and Coastal Features
The Wash · The Fens · Bedford Level · NORTH SEA · ENGLISH CHANNEL · Strait of Dover · The Solent · Poole Bay · Rye Bay · Beachy Head · Selsey Bill · Dungeness · North Foreland · South Foreland · Foulness Pt. · Orford Ness · The Naze · Sales Pt.

Highlands
Chiltern Hills · Berkshire Downs · Hampshire Downs · North Downs · South Downs · The Weald · Vale of Sussex · Vale of Kent · The Downs · Milk Hill 294 m · Walbury Hill 297 m · Leith Hill 294 m · Blackdown Hill 280 m · Ditchling Beacon 248 m · Saint Catherine's Hill 236 m · Whitehorse Hill 261 m

FRANCE

PAS-DE-CALAIS · NORD · PICARDIE · SOMME · Calais · Boulogne-sur-Mer · Le Touquet-Paris-Plage · Cap Blanc-Nez · Cap Gris-Nez

ISLE OF WIGHT · THE NEEDLES

© HAMMOND WORLD ATLAS CORPORATION CC - A A A

Scale 1:1,140,000 Lambert Conformal Conic Projection

MI 10 20 30
KM 10 20 30 40

Height

m. / ft.

6000 / 19700
4000 / 13000
2000 / 6500
1500 / 5000
1000 / 3300
500 / 1600
200 / 700
-0-
200 / 700
500 / 1600
1000 / 3300
2000 / 6500
3000 / 9800
4000 / 13000
5000 / 16400
6000 / 19700

Depth

Population

■ Over 2,000,000   ⊙ 500,000 - 999,999   ⊕ 100,000 - 249,999   ⊚ 10,000 - 29,999
■ 1,000,000 - 1,999,999   ⊙ 250,000 - 499,999   ⊙ 30,000 - 99,999   ○ Under 10,000

Northeastern Ireland, Northern England and Wales

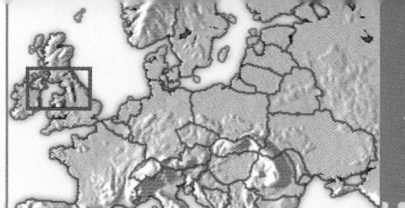

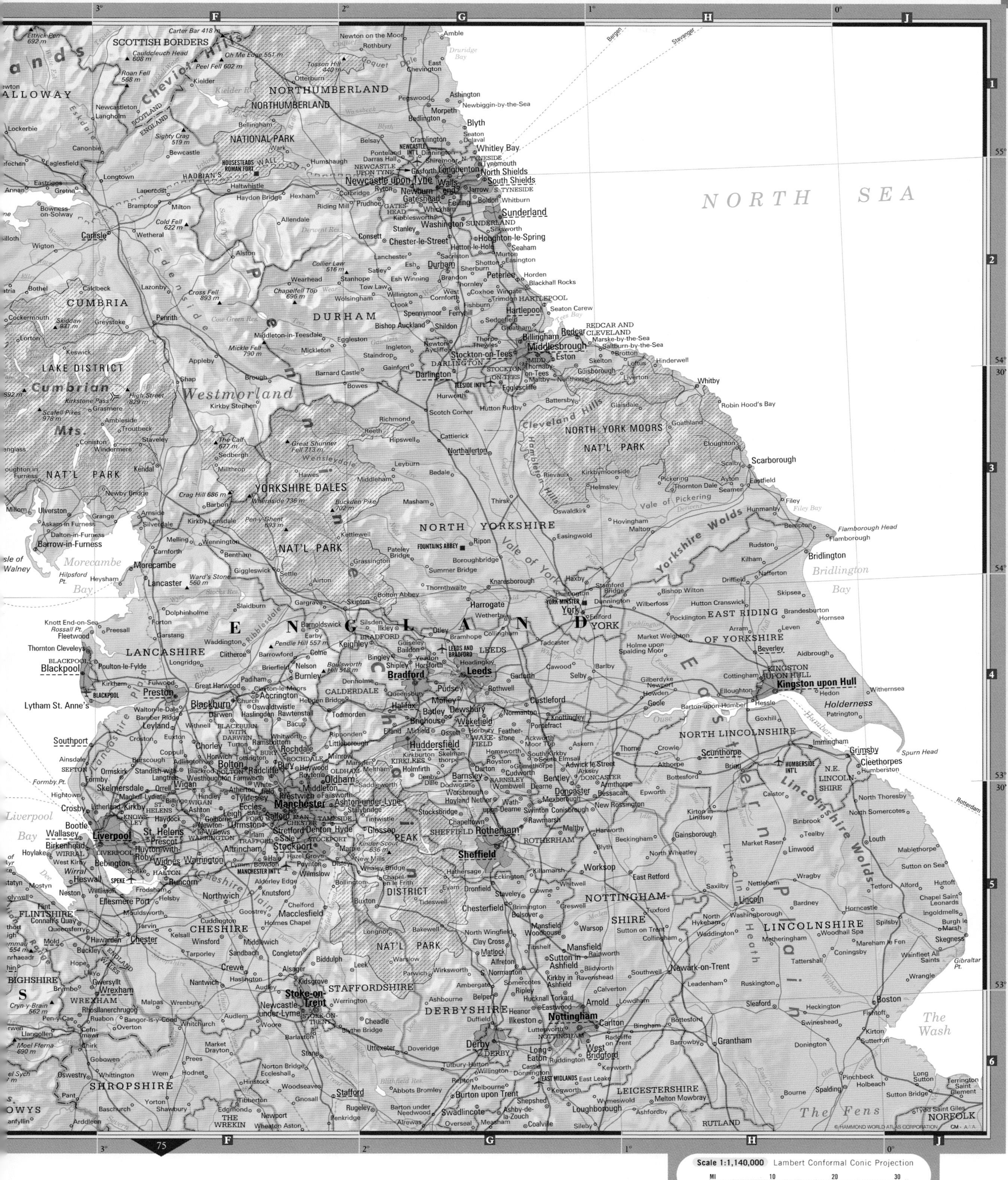

Scale 1:1,140,000 Lambert Conformal Conic Projection

MI 10 20 30

KM 10 20 30 40

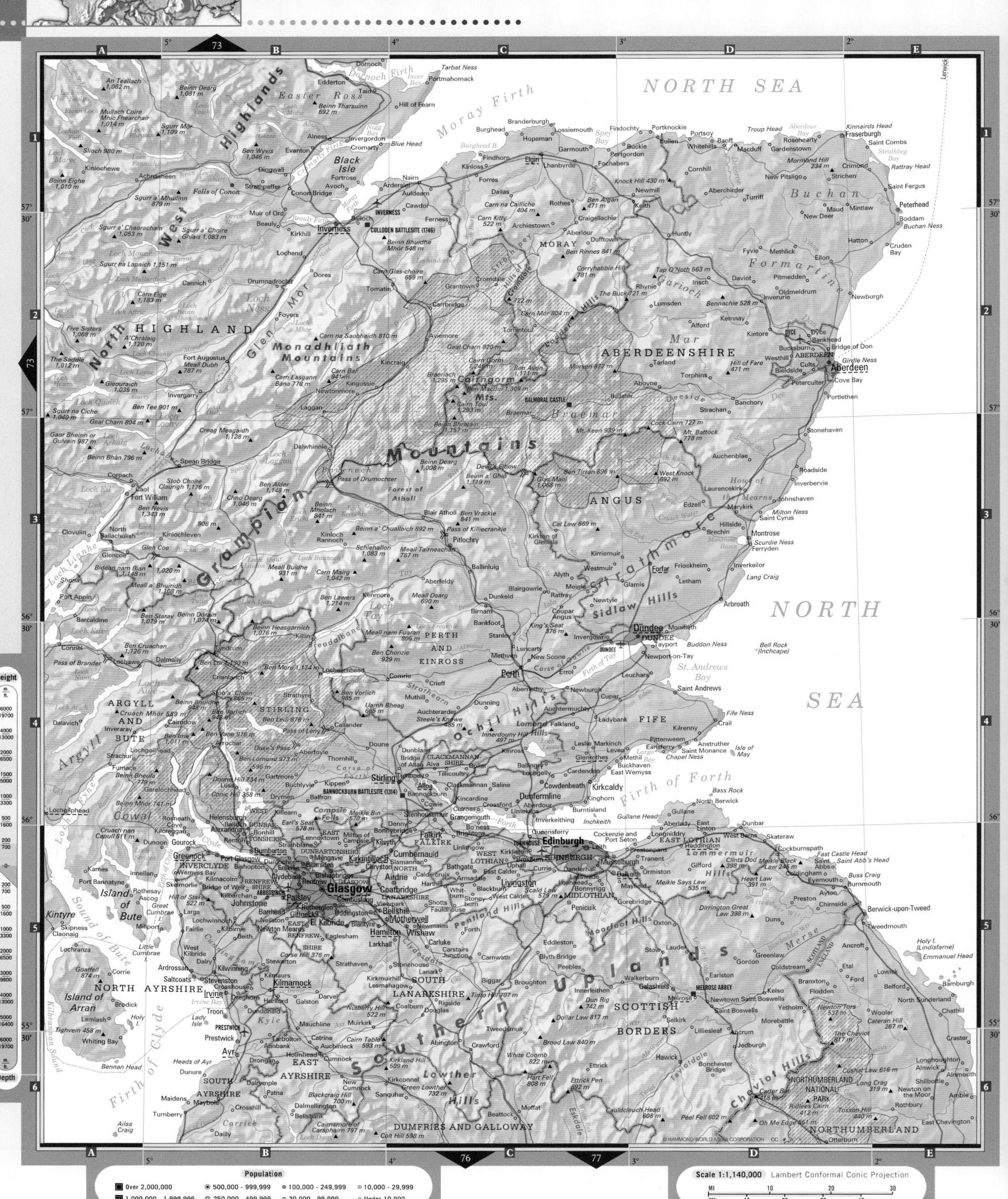

Population
- ■ Over 2,000,000
- ◉ 500,000 - 999,999
- ◉ 100,000 - 249,999
- ○ 10,000 - 29,999
- ■ 1,000,000 - 1,999,999
- ◉ 250,000 - 499,999
- ○ 30,000 - 99,999
- ○ Under 10,000

Scale 1:1,140,000   Lambert Conformal Conic Projection

MI   10   20   30
KM   10   20   30   40

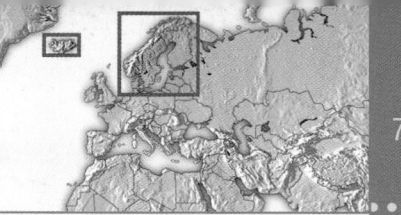

ICELAND

GREENLAND SEA

Reykjavik
Keflavik

ATLANTIC OCEAN

Arctic Circle

NORWAY

SWEDEN

FINLAND

DENMARK

Oslo

Stockholm

Helsinki

Copenhagen

Göteborg

Trondheim

Bergen

Stavanger

Turku

Tampere

ST. PETERSBURG

Murmansk

RUSSIA

ESTONIA
Tallinn

LATVIA
Riga

LITHUANIA
Klaipėda

GERMANY

NORWEGIAN SEA

BARENTS SEA

NORTH SEA

BALTIC SEA

Gulf of Bothnia

Gulf of Finland

Gulf of Riga

Skagerrak

Kattegat

Arctic Circle

FINNMARK

TROMS

NORDLAND

LAPPI

OULUN LÄÄNI

NORRBOTTEN

VÄSTERBOTTEN

JÄMTLAND

VÄSTERNORRLAND

TRØNDELAG

Scale 1:6,800,000   Lambert Conformal Conic Projection

Height
m. / ft.
6000 / 19700
4000 / 13000
2000 / 6500
1500 / 5000
1000 / 3300
500 / 1600
200 / 700
0
200 / 700
500 / 1600
1000 / 3300
2000 / 6500
3000 / 9800
4000 / 13000
5000 / 16400
6000 / 19700
Depth

© HAMMOND WORLD ATLAS CORPORATION

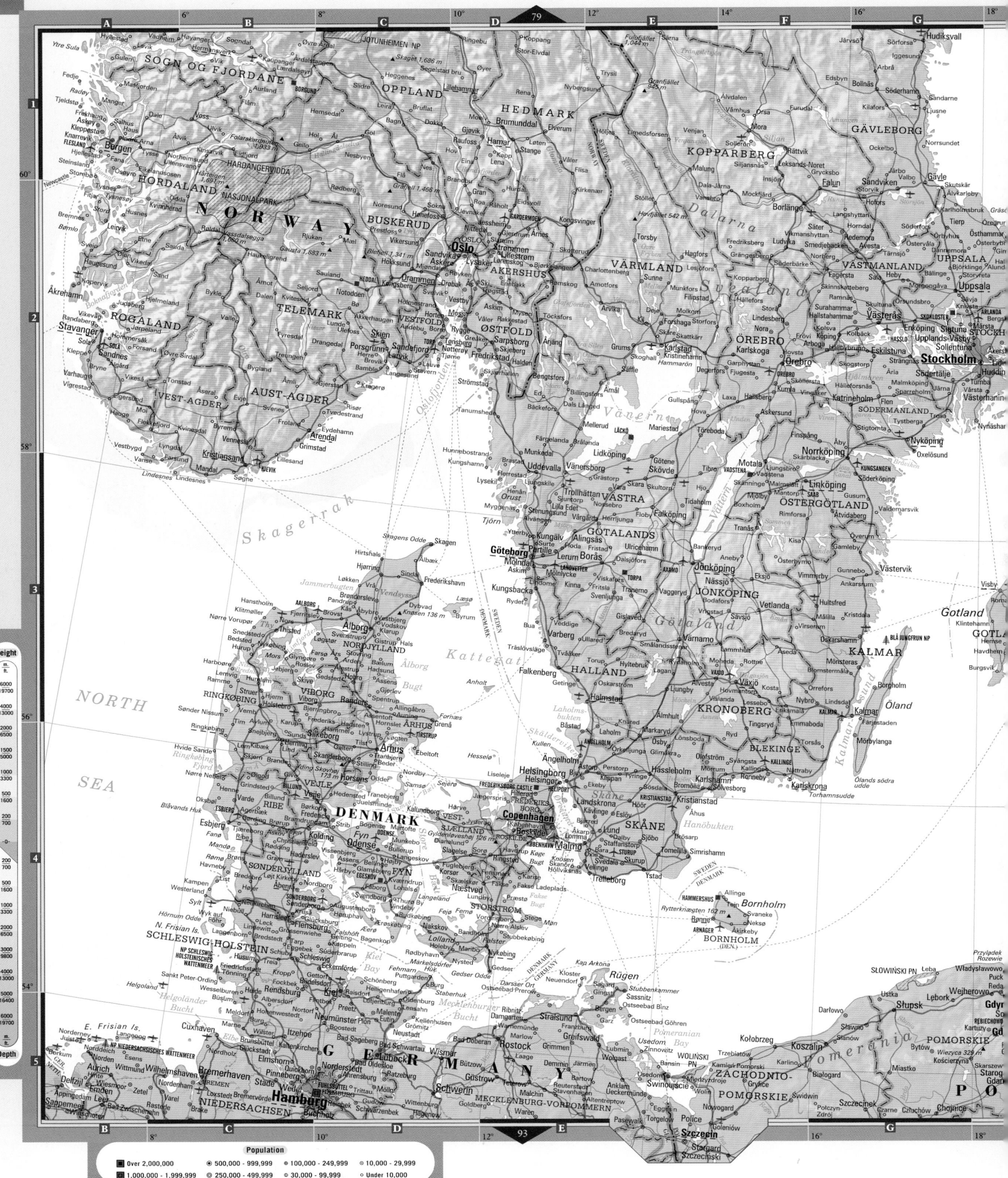

Population

- Over 2,000,000
- 1,000,000 - 1,999,999
- 500,000 - 999,999
- 250,000 - 499,999
- 100,000 - 249,999
- 30,000 - 99,999
- 10,000 - 29,999
- Under 10,000

Height

m.	ft.
6000	19700
4000	13000
2000	6500
1500	5000
1000	3300
500	1600
200	700
-0-	
200	700
500	1600
1000	3300
2000	6500
3000	9800
4000	13000
5000	16400
6000	19700

m.
ft.

Depth

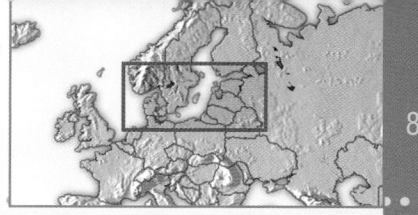
Scale 1:3,400,000   Lambert Conformal Conic Projection

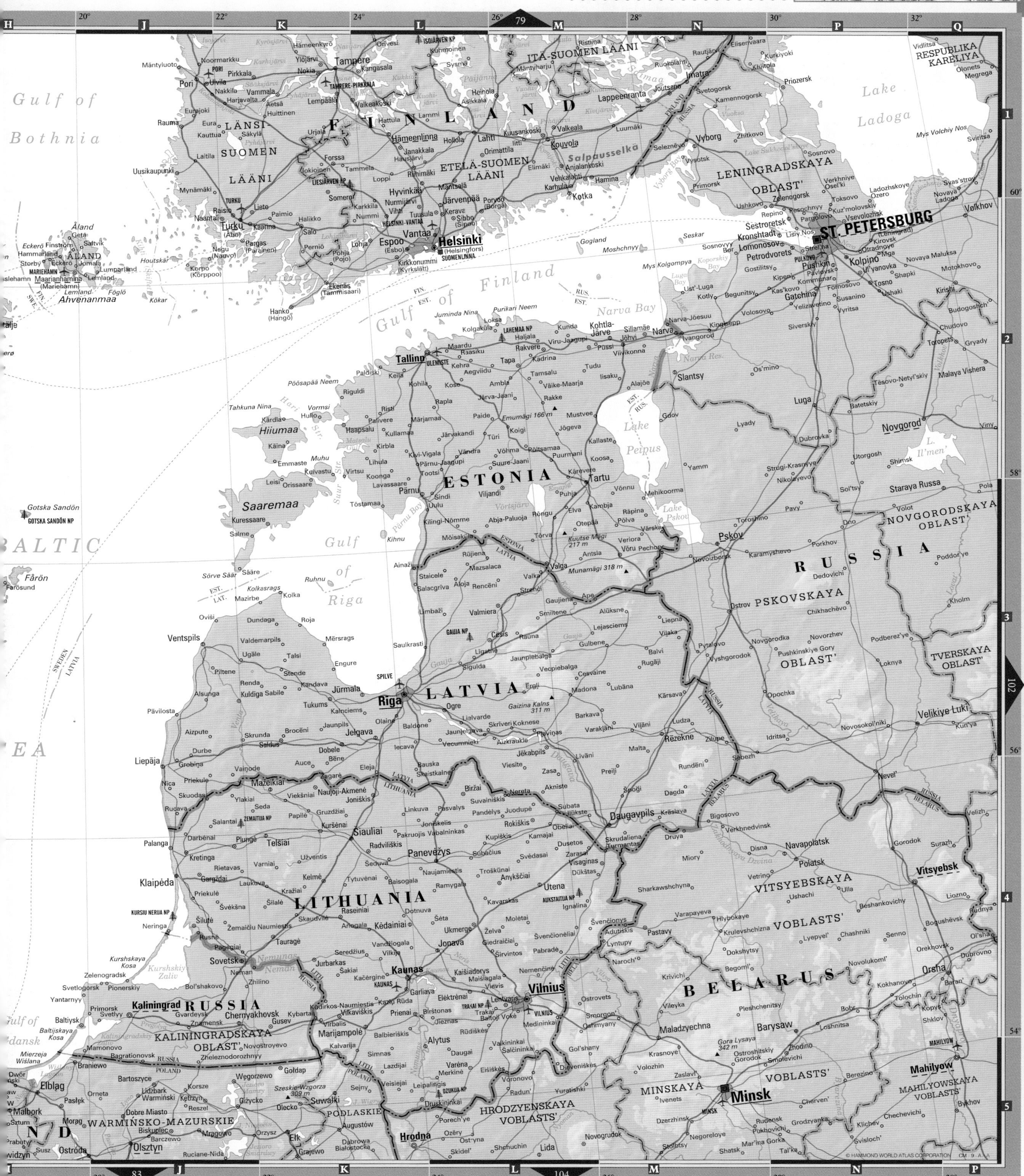

| MI | 25 | 50 | 75 | 100 |
| KM | 25 | 50 | 75 | 100 | 125 | 150 |

© Hammond World Atlas Corporation

NORTH
SEA

North

Frisian

Islands

West Frisian
Islands

Great Britain
Great Yarmouth

UNITED
Lowestoft

KINGDOM

DENMARK

Copenhagen

BRANDENBURG

BERLIN

Potsdam

Köpenick

SCHLESWIG-
HOLSTEIN

Hamburg

Bremen

NIEDERSACHSEN

NETHERLANDS

Amsterdam

The Hague

Rotterdam

Hannover

Münster

Bielefeld

Dortmund

NORDRHEIN

Duisburg Essen Bochum

Düsseldorf

Mönchengladbach

Cologne

Bonn

WESTFALEN

GERMANY

Leipzig

Halle

Magdeburg

SACHSEN-ANHALT

THÜRINGEN

BELGIUM

Brussels

HESSEN

Antwerp

NORD-PAS-
DE-CALAIS

Frankfurt am Main

Wiesbaden

RHEINLAND-PFALZ

Mainz

PICARDIE

LUXEMBOURG

Luxembourg

SAARLAND

Mannheim

BAYERN

Nürnberg

PARIS

ÎLE-DE-
FRANCE

CHAMPAGNE

LORRAINE

Nancy

Karlsruhe

Stuttgart

BADEN-

Strasbourg

ALSACE

FRANCE

ARDENNE

BOURGOGNE

WÜRTTEMBERG

Augsburg

Munich

CENTRE

FRANCHE-COMTÉ

SWITZERLAND

AUSTRIA

Scale 1:3,400,000 Lambert Conformal Conic Projection

MI	25	50	75	100
KM	25	50	75	100	125	150

© HAMMOND WORLD ATLAS CORPORATION

English Channel

Great Britain

Lyme Bay

UNITED KINGDOM

B. de Somme

Pays de Caux

Normandy

Baie de la Seine

Bay of Biscay

Golfe de St-Malo

Brittany

FRANCE

BELGIUM

Brussels (Bruxelles)

NORD-PAS DE-CALAIS

PICARDIE

HAUTE-NORMANDIE

BASSE-NORMANDIE

ILE-DE-FRANCE

PARIS

CHAMPAGNE-ARDENNE

CENTRE

BOURGOGNE

PAYS DE LA LOIRE

BRETAGNE

POITOU-CHARENTES

LIMOUSIN

AUVERGNE

RHONE-ALPES

Massif Central

AQUITAINE

MIDI-PYRÉNÉES

LANGUEDOC-ROUSSILLON

PROVENCE

Gulf of Lion

Marseille

Bordeaux

Toulouse

Lyon

Nantes

SPAIN

NAVARRA

CASTILLA y LEON

PAIS VASCO

Bilbao

CATALUNA

ANDORRA

Pyrenees

Height
m. ft.
6000 19700
4000 13000
2000 6500
1500 5000
1000 3300
500 1600
200 700
0
Depth
m. ft.
0
200 700
500 1600
1000 3300
2000 6500
3000 9800
4000 13000
5000 16400
6000 19700

Population
■ Over 2,000,000
■ 1,000,000 - 1,999,999
● 500,000 - 999,999
● 250,000 - 499,999
● 100,000 - 249,999
○ 30,000 - 99,999
○ 10,000 - 29,999
· Under 10,000

Scale 1:3,400,000 Lambert Conformal Conic Projection

MI 25 50 75 100
KM 25 50 75 100 125 150

Height
m.
ft.

6000
19700
4000
13000
2000
6500
1500
5000
1000
3300
500
1600
200
700
-0-
200
700
500
1600
1000
3300
2000
6500
3000
9800
4000
13000
5000
16400
6000
19700
m.
ft.

Depth

ATLANTIC

OCEAN

Costa Verde

Bay of Biscay

ASTURIAS

GALICIA

CANTABRIA

PAÍS VASCO

NAVARRA

La Coruña

Gijón

Santander

Bilbao

San Sebastián

Vigo

León

Oviedo

Vitoria

Logroño

LA RIOJA

Cordillera Cantábrica

CASTILLA Y LEÓN

Valladolid

Burgos

Soria

Zamora

Salamanca

Segovia

SPAIN

MADRID

Guadalajara

Alcalá de Henares

Móstoles

Getafe

Cuenca

Ávila

PORTUGAL

PORTO

Porto

AVEIRO

VISEU

GUARDA

COIMBRA

Coimbra

LEIRIA

CASTELO BRANCO

Serra da Estrela

Sierra de Gredos

Sierra de Guadalupe

CASTILLA–
LA MANCHA

Albacete

Ciudad Real

Toledo

Talavera de la
Reina

Cáceres

EXTREMADURA

Mérida

Badajoz

Montes de Toledo

SANTARÉM

PORTALEGRE

LISBOA

Lisbon

Amadora

ÉVORA

Évora

SETÚBAL

Setúbal

BEJA

FARO

Faro

Algarve

Baía de
Setúbal

Golfo de
Cádiz

Sierra Morena

Córdoba

Jaén

MURCIA

Murcia

ANDALUCIA

Sevilla

Seville

Huelva

Granada

Sierra Nevada

Cerro de Mulhacén
3,478 m

Sistema Penibético

Málaga

Almería

Cádiz

Jerez

Algeciras

Gibraltar (U.K.)

Costa del Sol

Costa de la Luz

MEDITERRANEAN SEA

Strait of Gibraltar

Tangier
(Tanger)

Tétouan

MOROCCO

Ceuta
(Sp.)

Population
- ■ Over 2,000,000
- ● 500,000 – 999,999
- ● 100,000 – 249,999
- ● 10,000 – 29,999
- ■ 1,000,000 – 1,999,999
- ● 250,000 – 499,999
- ● 30,000 – 99,999
- ● Under 10,000

Scale 1:3,400,000   Lambert Conformal Conic Projection

| MI | 25 | 50 | 75 | 100 |
| KM | 25 | 50 | 75 | 100 | 125 | 150 |

85

141

8° A 10° B 12° C 14° D 16° E

Marseille Nice
Cap Corse
Rogliano
Cap Corse
I. di Capraia
Donoratico
TOSCANA
Massa
Marittima
Sinalunga Umbertide
Gualdo Tadino
Fabriano
Macerata
Montegranaro
Civitanova Marche
Porto Sant'Epidio
Ancona

CROATIA

Genoa
L'Ile-Rousse
Calvi
San Martino-di-Lota
Bastia
PORETTA
Monte Capanne
1,018 m
Marciana Marina
Porto Azzurro
Piombino
San Vincenzo
Roccastrada
Montepulciano
Castel del Piano
Monte Amiata
1,738 m
Siena
Perugia
Monte Nerone
1,524 m
Camerino
Tolentino
Fermo
Grottammare
San Benedetto del Tronto

Hvar
Vis
Korčula
Lastovo
Palagruža Islands
(CRO.)

Isole
Tremiti

ADRIATIC

MLJET NACIONALNI PARK

42°

CORSE
Corsica
(FRANCE)

Ajaccio
Monte Cinto
2,710 m

SARDEGNA
Sardinia

Sassari

ITALY

Naples
Napoli

TYRRHENIAN

SEA

CAMPANIA

BASILICATA

Cagliari

CALABRIA

Isole Eolie
(Lipari Islands)

Palermo
Sicily
Messina

MEDITERRANEAN

Catania

Siracusa

Reggio di Calabria

MALTA

Tunis
TUNISIA

38°

36°

Gozo
Malta
MALTA

Valletta

A 10° B 12° C 14° D L 14° 30° M

Population
■ Over 2,000,000   ● 500,000 - 999,999   ⊕ 100,000 - 249,999   ⊙ 10,000 - 29,999
■ 1,000,000 - 1,999,999   ◉ 250,000 - 499,999   ⊙ 30,000 - 99,999   ○ Under 10,000

Height
m./ft.
6000 / 19700
4000 / 13000
2000 / 6500
1500 / 5000
1000 / 3300
500 / 1600
200 / 700
0
200 / 700
500 / 1600
1000 / 3300
2000 / 6500
3000 / 9800
4000 / 13000
5000 / 16400
6000 / 19700
m./ft.
Depth

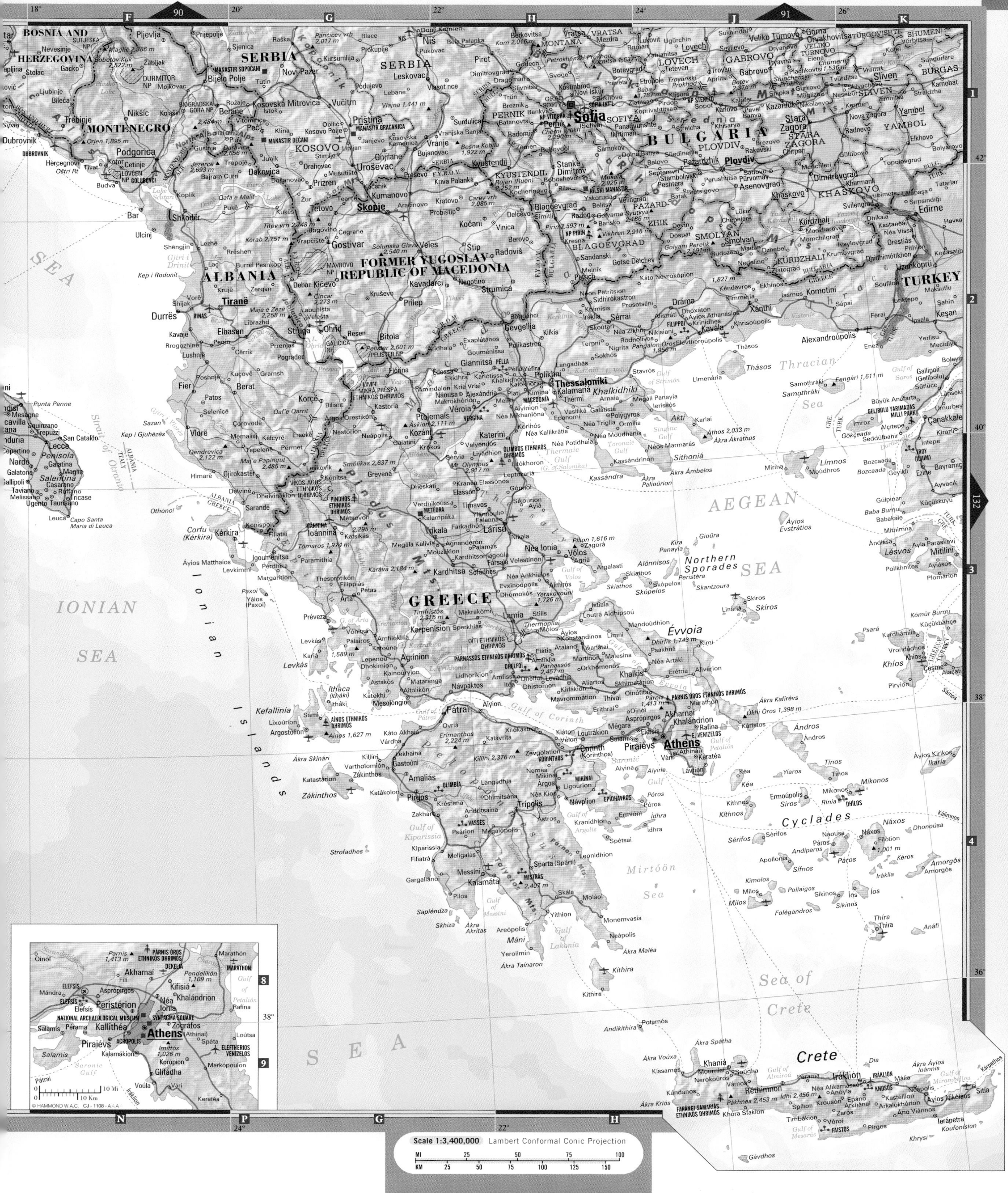

Scale 1:3,400,000   Lambert Conformal Conic Projection

| MI | 25 | 50 | 75 | 100 |

| KM | 25 | 50 | 75 | 100 | 125 | 150 |

© HAMMOND W.A.C.   CJ - 1108 - A.A.A

Height

m.
ft.

6000
19700

4000
13000

2000
6500

1500
5000

1000
3300

500
1600

200
700

0
0

200
700

500
1600

1000
3300

2000
6500

3000
9800

4000
13000

5000
16400

6000
19700

m.
ft.

Depth

Population

- ■ Over 2,000,000
- ◉ 500,000 - 999,999
- ◉ 100,000 - 249,999
- ◉ 10,000 - 29,999
- ■ 1,000,000 - 1,999,999
- ◉ 250,000 - 499,999
- Φ 30,000 - 99,999
- ◦ Under 10,000

Hungary, Northern Balkan States

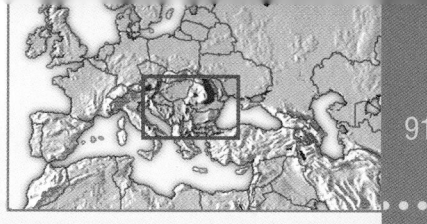

Scale 1:3,400,000   Lambert Conformal Conic Projection

MAP SECTION

Netherlands, Northwestern Germany

Population

■ Over 2,000,000 | ◉ 500,000 - 999,999 | ⊚ 100,000 - 249,999 | ○ 10,000 - 29,999
▣ 1,000,000 - 1,999,999 | ◉ 250,000 - 499,999 | ⊙ 30,000 - 99,999 | ∘ Under 10,000

GERMANY

NIEDERSACHSEN

Frisian Islands

HAMBURG
Hamburg

BREMEN
Bremen

BREMERHAVEN
Bremerhaven

Oldenburg

Hannover

Braunschweig

Wolfsburg

Bielefeld

Osnabrück

Münster

Dortmund

Bochum

Wuppertal

Hamm

Paderborn

Kassel

Göttingen

Hildesheim

Salzgitter

Goslar

NORDRHEIN-WESTFALEN

HESSEN

THÜRINGEN

SCHLESWIG-HOLSTEIN

MECKLENBURG-VORPOMMERN

SACHSEN-ANHALT

Lüneburger Heide

Ostfriesland

Münsterland

Teutoburger Wald

Wiehengebirge

Wesergebirge

HARZ

NATIONALPARK HARZ

NATIONALPARK HAINICH

Helgoländer Bucht

NP NIEDERSÄCHSISCHES WATTENMEER

NP SCHLESWIG-HOLSTEINISCHES WATTENMEER

NP HAMBURGISCHES WATTENMEER

Jadebusen

Scale 1:1,140,000   Lambert Conformal Conic Projection

MI   10   20   30
KM   10   20   30   40

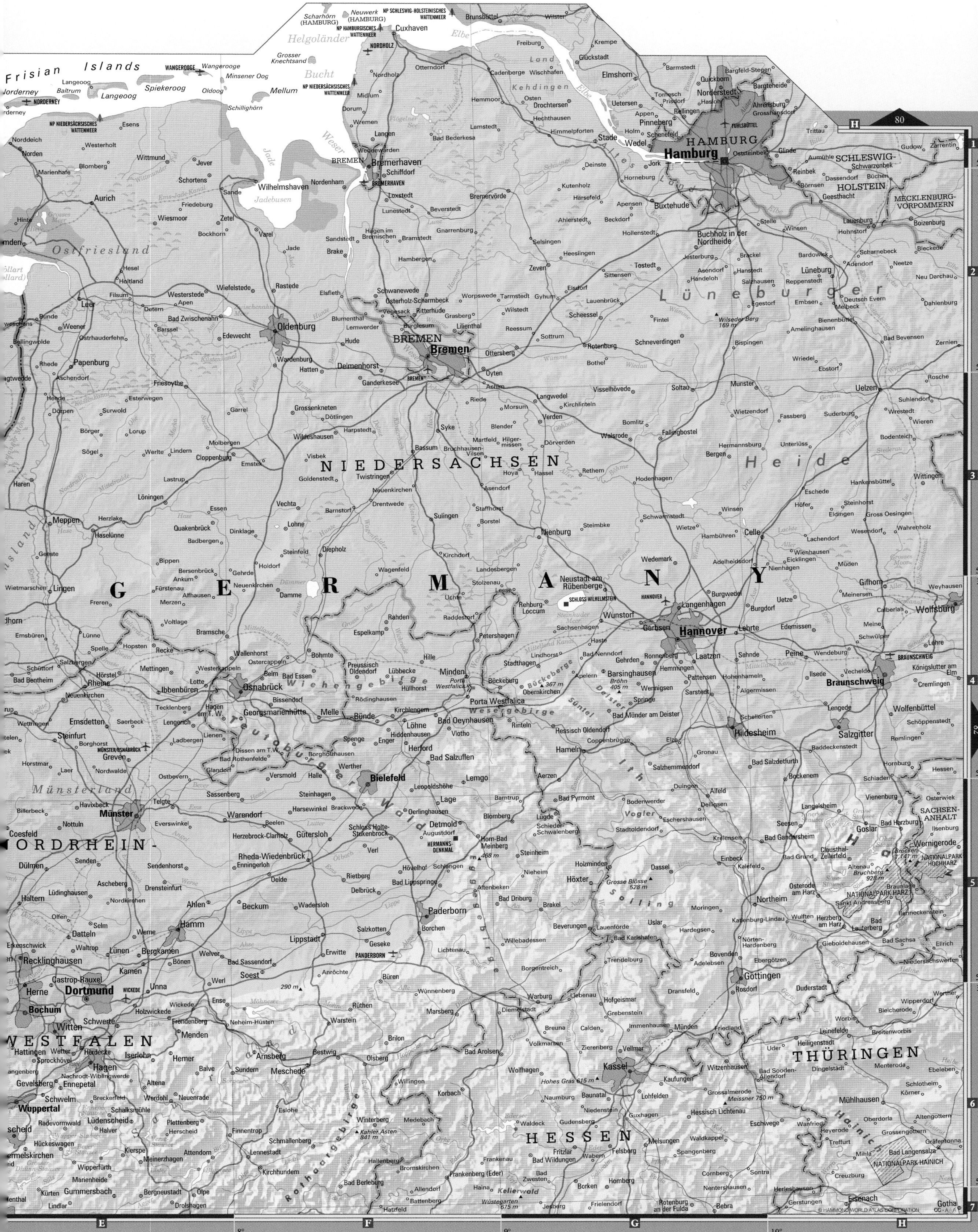

GERMANY

NIEDERSACHSEN

NORDRHEIN-WESTFALEN

HESSEN

THÜRINGEN

SACHSEN-ANHALT

SCHLESWIG-HOLSTEIN

MECKLENBURG-VORPOMMERN

HAMBURG

BREMEN

Frisian Islands

Helgoländer Bucht

Ostfriesland

Münsterland

Lüneburger Heide

Hamburg
Bremen
Bremerhaven
Oldenburg
Hannover
Braunschweig
Wolfsburg
Hildesheim
Salzgitter
Göttingen
Kassel
Osnabrück
Bielefeld
Münster
Dortmund
Bochum
Wuppertal
Paderborn
Goslar

Teutoburger Wald
Wiehengebirge
Wesergebirge
Solling
Vogler
Rothaargebirge
Hainich

NATIONALPARK HOCHHARZ
NATIONALPARK HARZ
NATIONALPARK HAINICH

Scale 1:1,140,000   Lambert Conformal Conic Projection

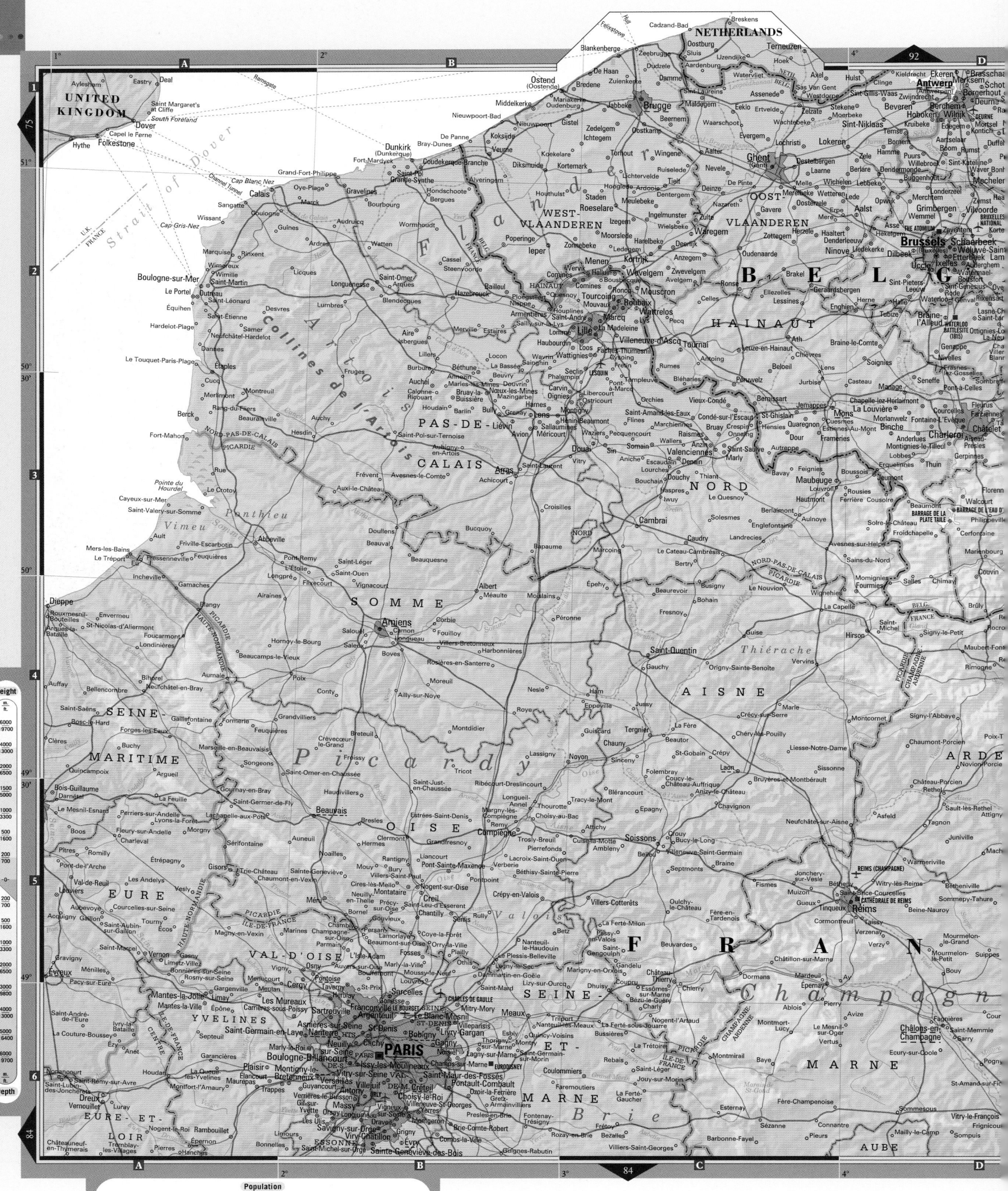

UNITED
KINGDOM

NETHERLANDS

WEST
VLAANDEREN

OOST
VLAANDEREN

Brussels

BELG

HAINAUT

Strait of Dover

PAS-DE-
CALAIS

NORD

SOMME

PICARDY

AISNE

Thiérache

ARDE

SEINE-
MARITIME

Picardy

OISE

EURE

HAUTE-NORMANDIE

PICARDIE
ÎLE-DE-FRANCE

VAL-D'OISE

FRAN

Valois

SEINE-
ET-

Champagn

YVELINES

PARIS

ET-

MARNE

CENTRE

ÎLE-DE-FRANCE

ESSONNE

MARNE

Brie

EURE-ET-
LOIR

AUBE

Belgium, Northern France, Western Germany

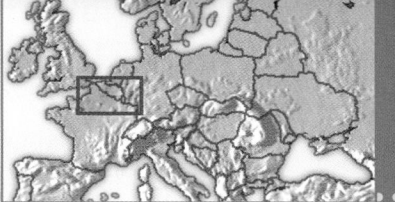

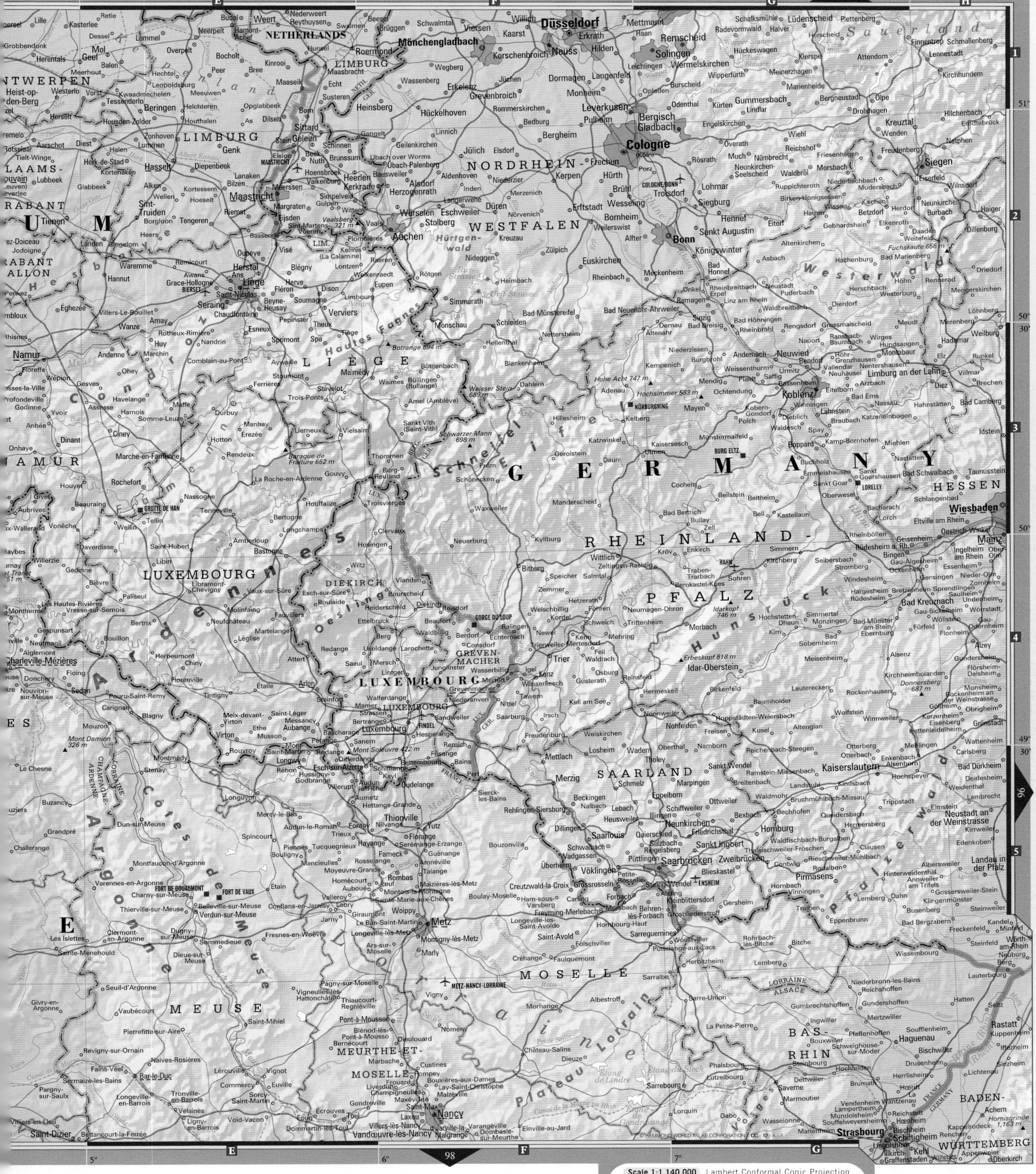

Scale 1:1,140,000 Lambert Conformal Conic Projection

MI 0 10 20 30
KM 0 10 20 30 40

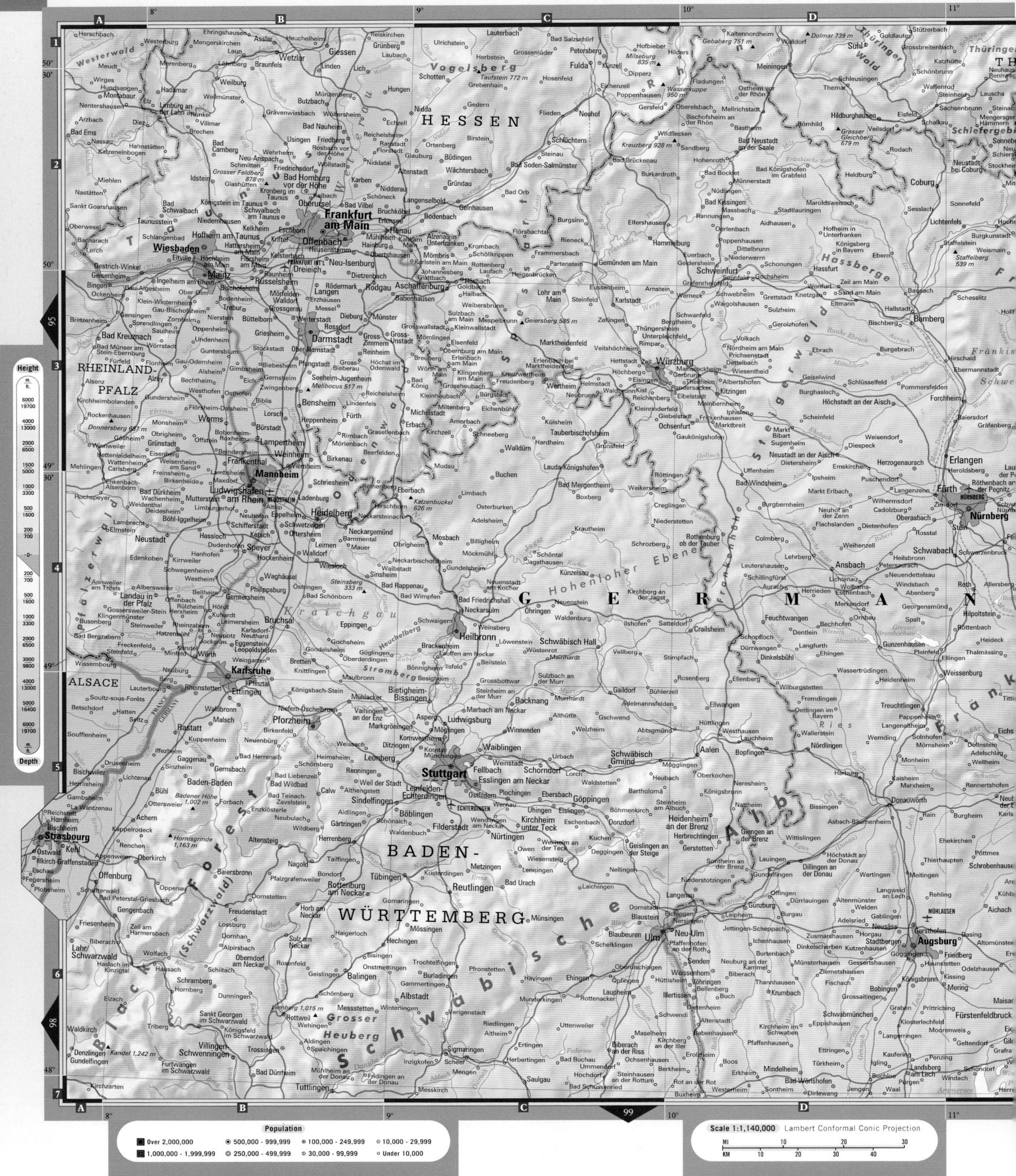

Population

- ■ Over 2,000,000
- ■ 1,000,000 - 1,999,999
- ◉ 500,000 - 999,999
- ◉ 250,000 - 499,999
- ◉ 100,000 - 249,999
- ◉ 30,000 - 99,999
- ◦ 10,000 - 29,999
- · Under 10,000

Scale 1:1,140,000   Lambert Conformal Conic Projection

| MI | | 10 | | 20 | | 30 |
| KM | 10 | | 20 | 30 | | 40 |

Southern Germany, Czech Republic, Upper Austria

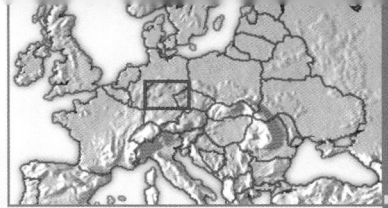

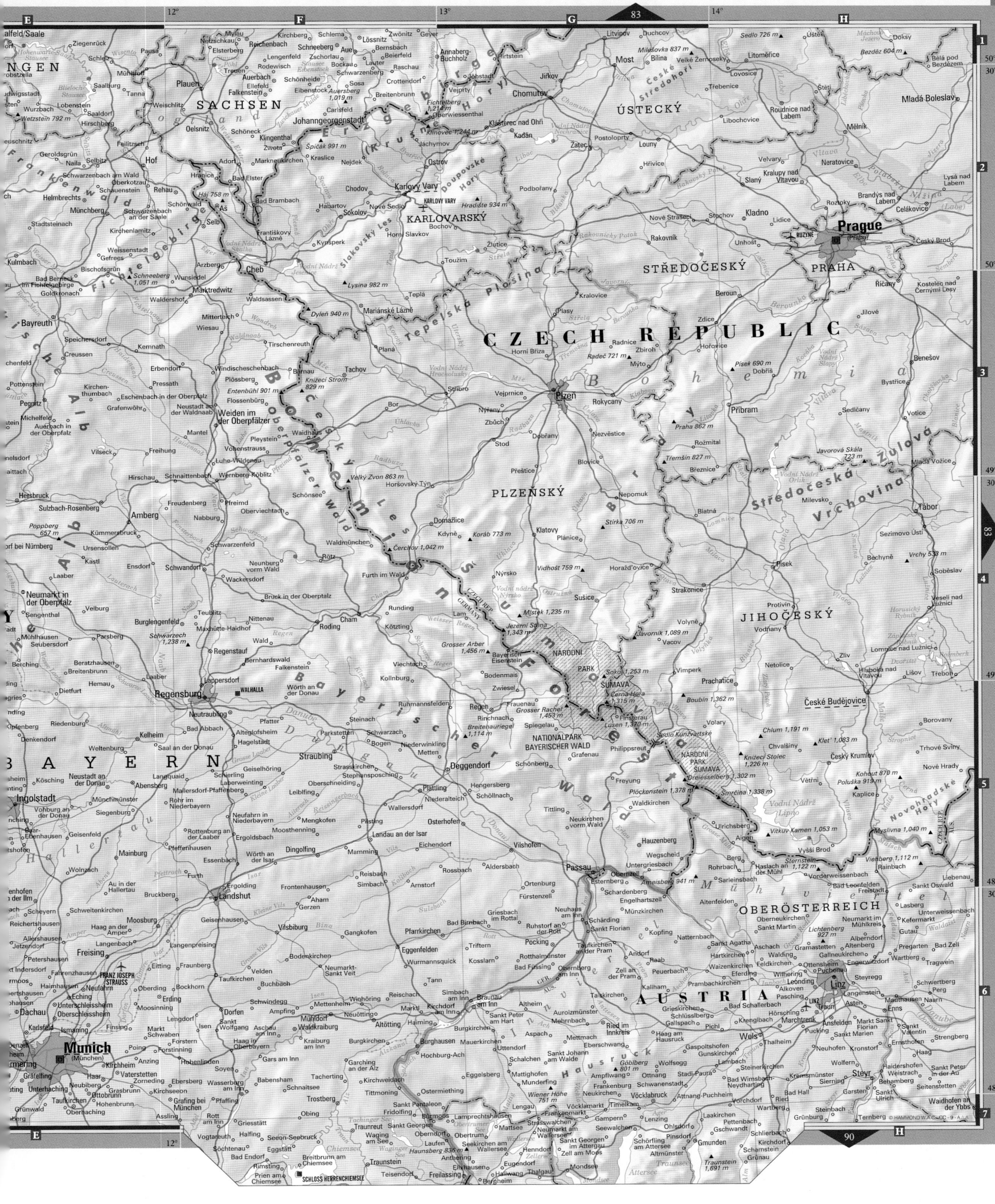

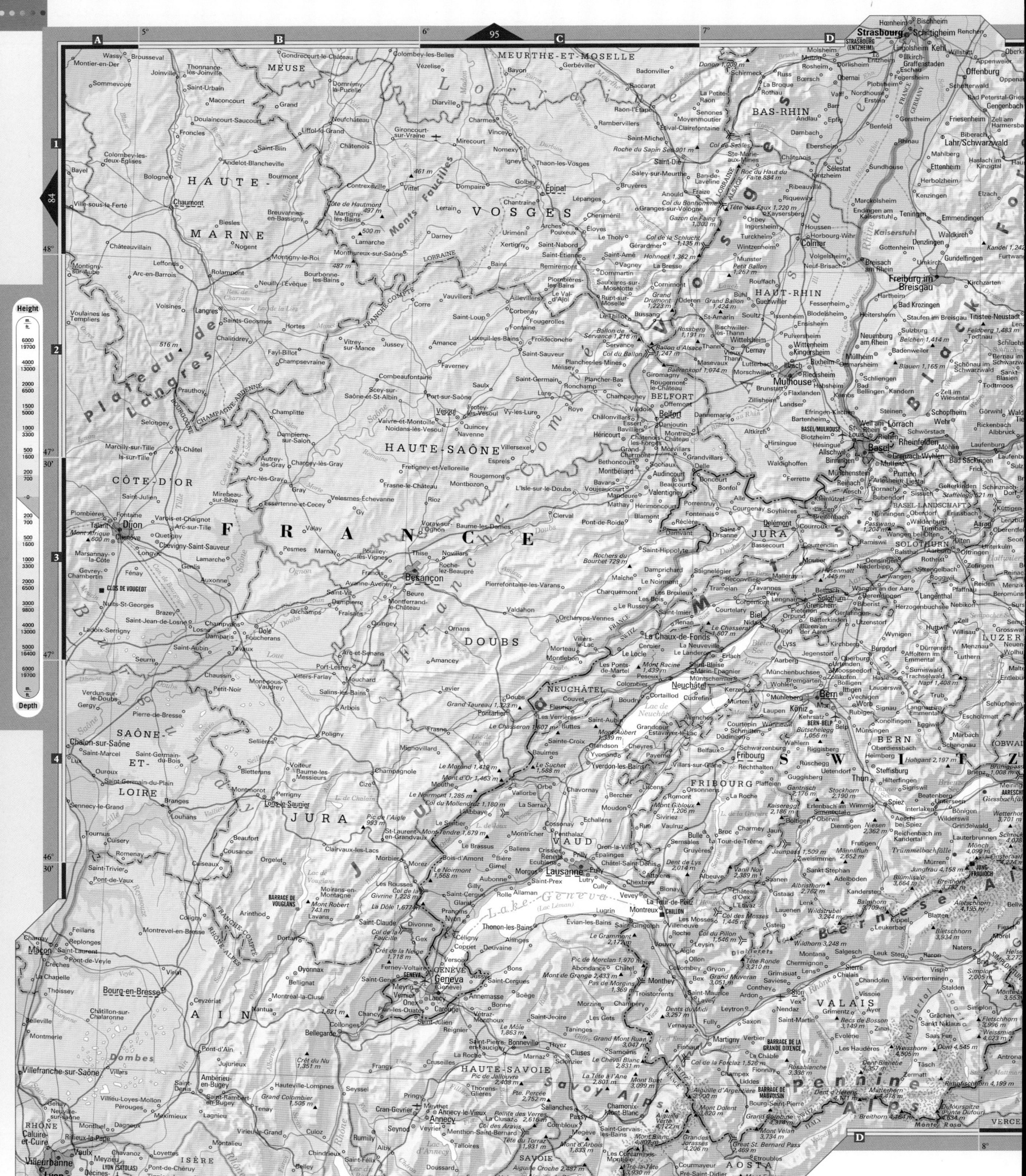

A   B   C   D

Height

m. ft.	
6000	19700
4000	13000
2000	6500
1500	5000
1000	3300
500	1600
200	700
	-0-
200	700
500	1600
1000	3300
2000	6500
3000	9800
4000	13000
5000	16400
6000	19700
m. ft.	

Depth

Central Alps Region

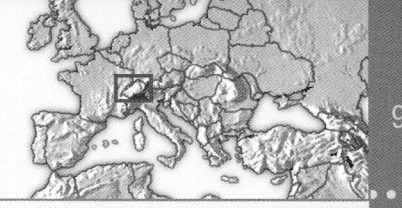

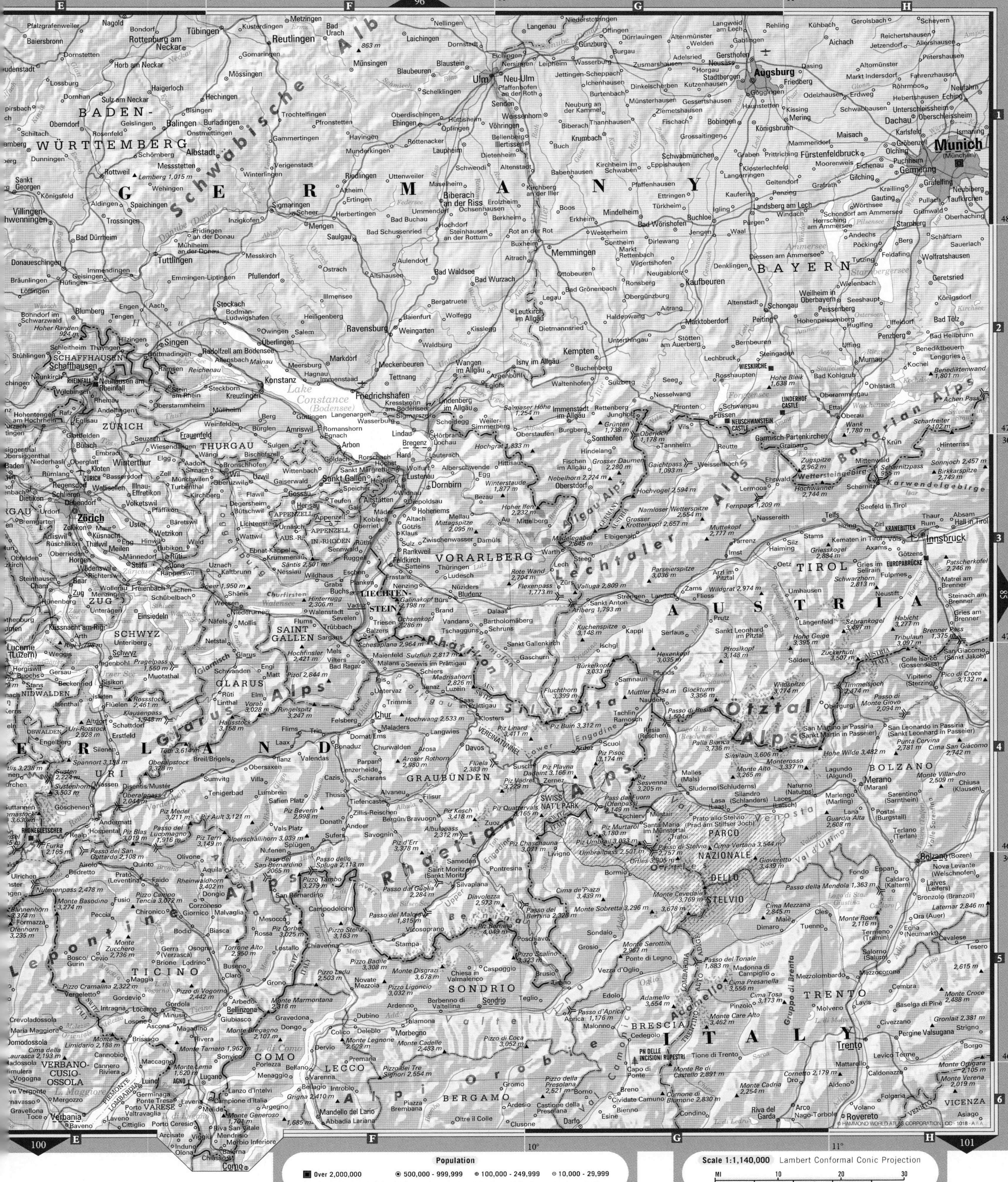

Population

- Over 2,000,000
- 1,000,000 - 1,999,999
- 500,000 - 999,999
- 250,000 - 499,999
- 100,000 - 249,999
- 30,000 - 99,999
- 10,000 - 29,999
- Under 10,000

Scale 1:1,140,000 Lambert Conformal Conic Projection

MI 0 10 20 30
KM 0 10 20 30 40

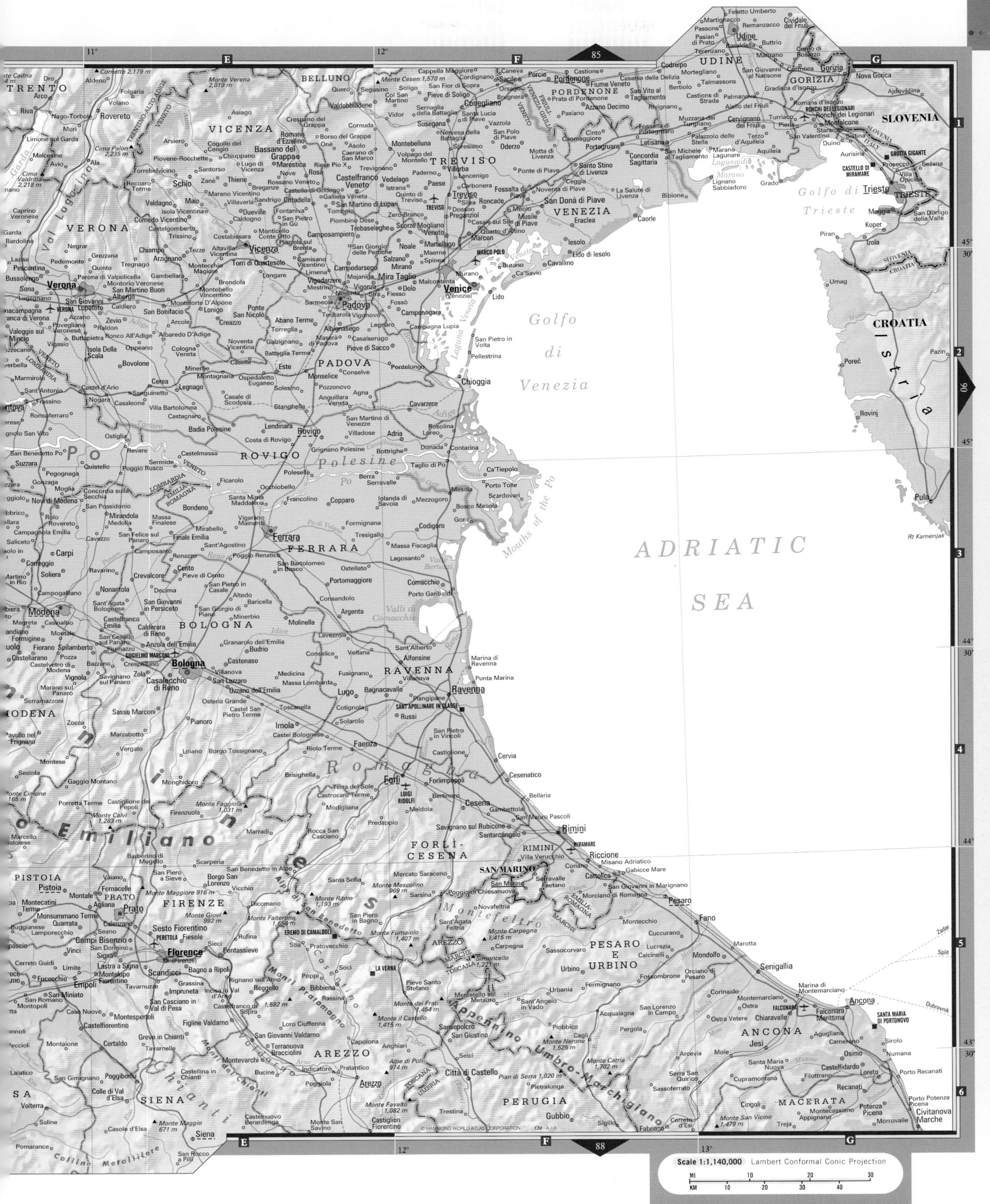

ADRIATIC

SEA

Golfo
di
Venezia

Golfo di Trieste

TRIESTE

SLOVENIA

CROATIA

Istria

UDINE

GORIZIA

BELLUNO

TREVISO

VENEZIA

PORDENONE

VICENZA

VERONA

PADOVA

ROVIGO

Polesine

FERRARA

MODENA

BOLOGNA

Romagna

RAVENNA

FORLÌ-CESENA

SAN MARINO

PESARO
E
URBINO

PISTOIA

PRATO

FIRENZE

AREZZO

SIENA

PERUGIA

MACERATA

ANCONA

Appennino Umbro-Marchigiano

Venice
(Venezia)

Verona

Vicenza

Padova

Bologna

Ferrara

Ravenna

Rimini

Florence
(Firenze)

Arezzo

Siena

Ancona

Mouths of the Po

Po

Scale 1:1,140,000   Lambert Conformal Conic Projection

MI   10   20   30

KM   10   20   30   40

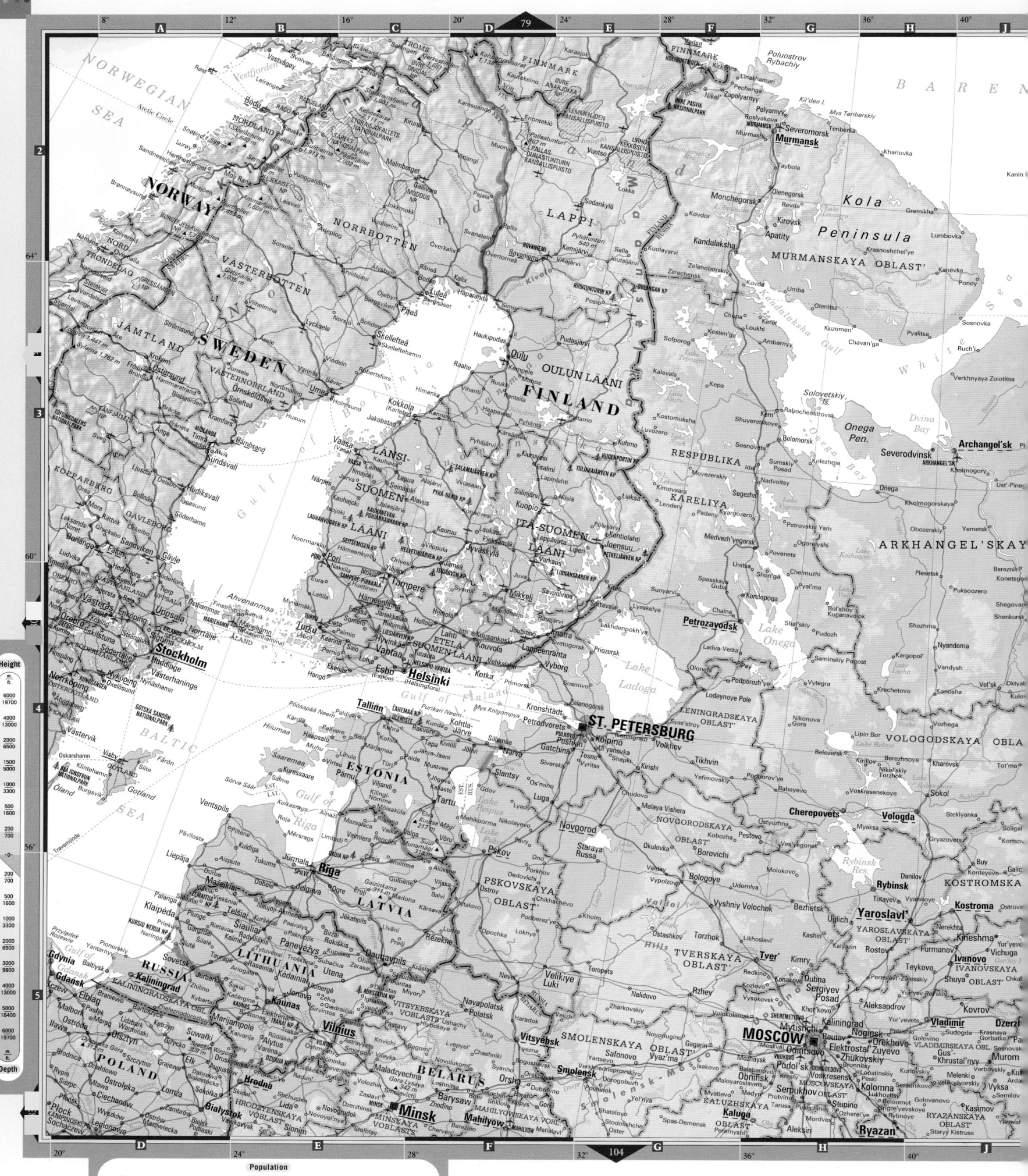

Population

Over 2,000,000
1,000,000 - 1,999,999
500,000 - 999,999
250,000 - 499,999
100,000 - 249,999
30,000 - 99,999
10,000 - 29,999
Under 10,000

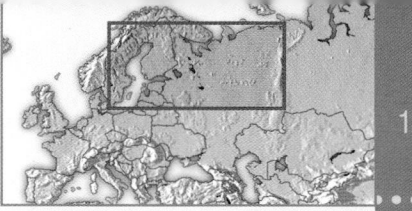

S E A

Kolguyev
Island

Kanin
Pen.

Cheshskaya
Bay

Yugorskiy
Peninsula

Pay-Khoy Mts.

NENETSKIY AVT. OKRUG

Arctic Circle

RESPUBLIKA

KOMI

OBLAST'

U S S I A

R

Syktyvkar

KOMI-
PERMYATSKIY
AVTONOMNYY
OKRUG

PERMSKAYA
OBLAST'

Solikamsk

Berezniki

SVERDLOVSKAYA OBLAST'

TYUMENSKAYA
OBLAST'

Kirov

KIROVSKAYA
OBLAST'

Perm'

Yekaterinburg

Tyumen'

**Nizhniy
Tagil**

Kurgan

KURGANSKAYA OBLAST'

RESPUBLIKA
UDMURTIYA

Izhevsk

Chelyabinsk

Zlatoust
Miass

CHELYABINSKAYA
OBLAST'

SOLTUSTIK
QAZAQSTAN

**Nizhniy
Novgorod** (Gor'kiy)

Cheboksary

RESPUBLIKA
CHUVASHIYA

Kazan'

**Naberezhnye
Chelny**

RESPUBLIKA
TATARSTAN

RESPUBLIKA
BASHKORTOSTAN

Ufa

OOSTANAY

NIZHEGORODSKAYA
OBLAST'

RESPUBLIKA
MARIY-EL
Yoshkar-Ola
Novocheboksarsk

Ul'yanovsk

KAZAKHSTAN

St. Petersburg inset

Gulf
of
Finland

Helsinki

Kronshtadt

Lake
Ladoga

ST. PETERSBURG
(Leningrad)

PETROGRAD
VYBORG
HERMITAGE
PETER AND PAUL FORTRESS

Petrodvorets

Baltic
Plain

Pushkin
GREAT PALACE
CATHERINE PALACE

Moscow inset

Smolensk-Moscow Upland

Zelenograd

SHEREMETEVO INT'L

MOSCOW

KREMLIN

Podol'sk

Domodedovo

DOMODEDOVO

© HAMMOND W.A.C.

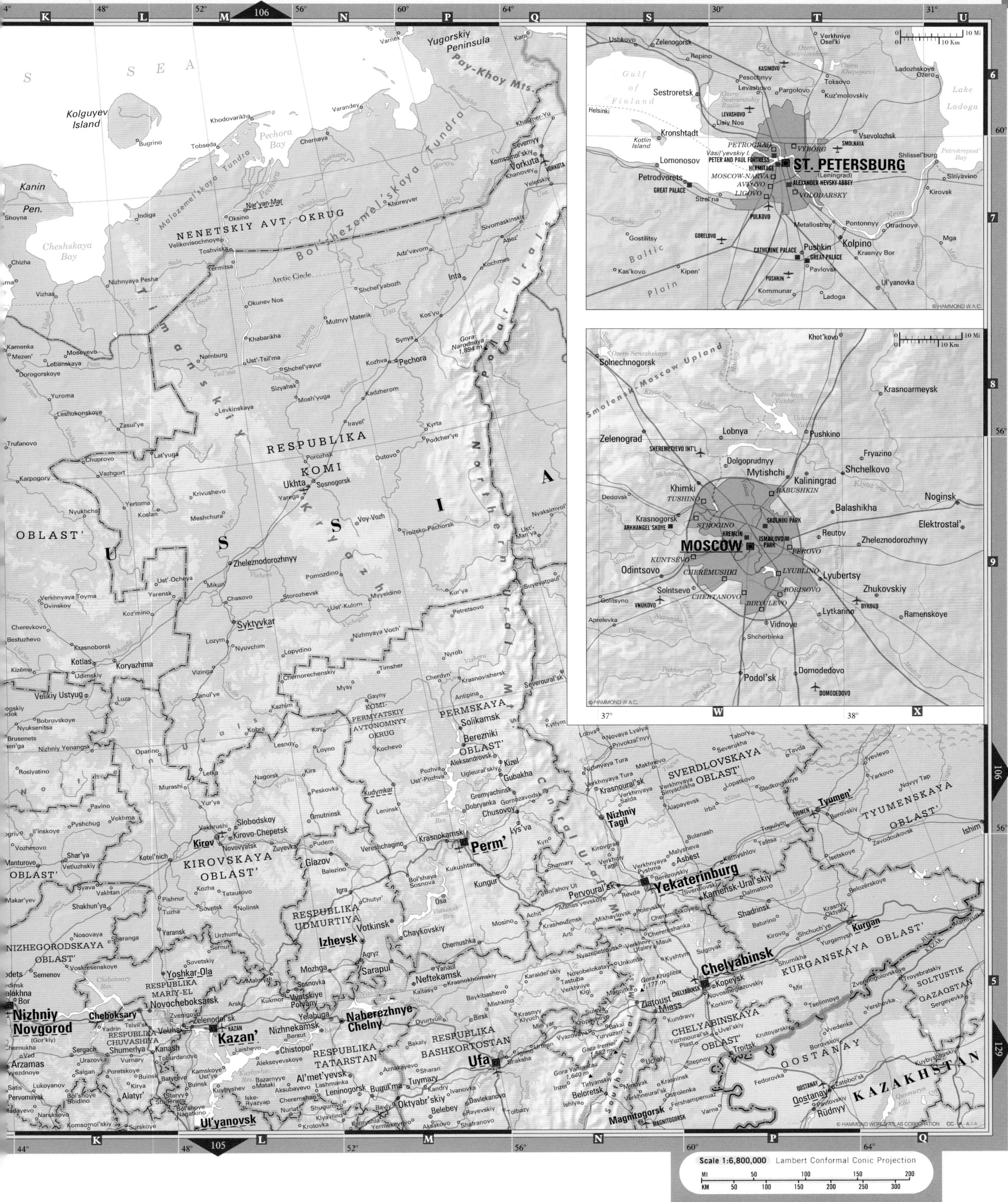

MOSCOW
Kaliningrad
Minsk
Warsaw
KIEV
Bucharest
BUCHAREST
Sofia
ISTANBUL
ANKARA
IZMIR
Athens
Odesa
Chișinău
Kharkiv
Dnipropetrovs'k
Donets'k
Rostov
Krasnodar
Sochi
POLAND
BELARUS
UKRAINE
MOLDOVA
ROMANIA
HUNGARY
SLOVAKIA
SERBIA
BULGARIA
F.Y.R.O.M.
GREECE
TURKEY
BLACK SEA
Sea of Azov
Aegean Sea
Sea of Marmara
Crimean Pen.
AVT. RESPUBLIKA KRYM
Mouths of the Danube
Height
Depth
Population
Over 2,000,000
1,000,000 - 1,999,999
500,000 - 999,999
250,000 - 499,999
100,000 - 249,999
30,000 - 99,999
10,000 - 29,999
Under 10,000

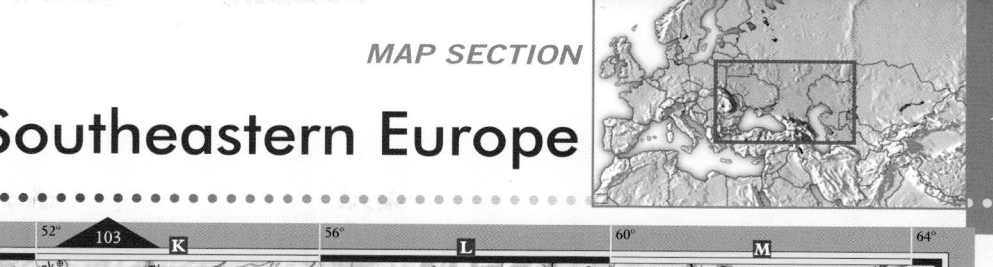
Scale 1:6,800,000   Lambert Conformal Conic Projection

© HAMMOND WORLD ATLAS CORPORATION

Population

■ Over 2,000,000	● 500,000 - 999,999	◉ 50,000 - 99,999	
■ 1,000,000 - 1,999,999	● 100,000 - 499,999	○ Under 50,000	

Height

m. / ft.
6000 / 19700
4000 / 13000
2000 / 6500
1500 / 5000
1000 / 3300
500 / 1600
200 / 700
0
200 / 700
500 / 1600
1000 / 3300
2000 / 6500
3000 / 9800
4000 / 13000
5000 / 16400
6000 / 19700
m. / ft.

Depth

Russia and Neighboring Countries

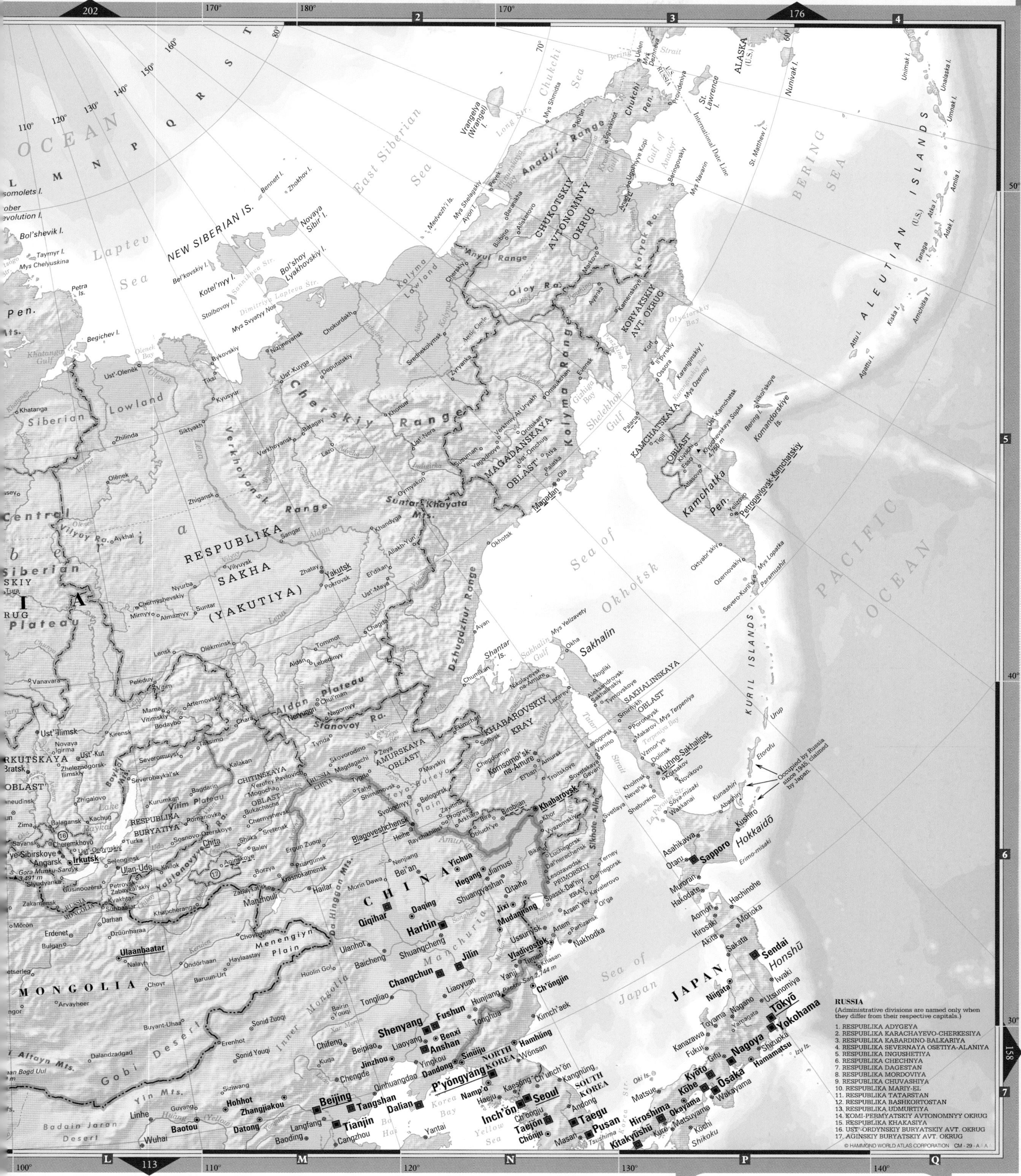

RUSSIA
(Administrative divisions are named only when they differ from their respective capitals.)

1. RESPUBLIKA ADYGEYA
2. RESPUBLIKA KARACHAYEVO-CHERKESIYA
3. RESPUBLIKA KABARDINO-BALKARIYA
4. RESPUBLIKA SEVERNAYA OSETIYA-ALANIYA
5. RESPUBLIKA INGUSHETIYA
6. RESPUBLIKA CHECHNYA
7. RESPUBLIKA DAGESTAN
8. RESPUBLIKA MORDOVIYA
9. RESPUBLIKA CHUVASHIYA
10. RESPUBLIKA MARIY-EL
11. RESPUBLIKA TATARSTAN
12. RESPUBLIKA BASHKORTOSTAN
13. RESPUBLIKA UDMURTIYA
14. KOMI-PERMYATSKIY AVTONOMNYY OKRUG
15. RESPUBLIKA KHAKASIYA
16. UST'-ORDYNSKIY BURYATSKIY AVT. OKRUG
17. AGINSKIY BURYATSKIY AVT. OKRUG

© HAMMOND WORLD ATLAS CORPORATION   CM-29-A/A

Scale 1:20,500,000   Lambert Conformal Conic Projection

MI   200   400   600
KM 200 400   600   800

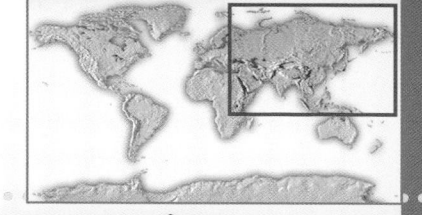

The delta of the Indus River, the longest river in southwest Asia, is the highlight of this southeast-looking, low-oblique image. Fed by snowmelt and glacial meltwater from the mountains of the Tibet Plateau, the Indus River flows nearly 1800 miles (2897 km.) before emptying into the Arabian Sea. After leaving the Tibet Plateau, the river flows onto the Punjab Plains of western Pakistan and through a vast alluvial lowland where it receives its major tributary, the Panjnad (five streams). In this severely arid landscape the rivers form precarious strips of fertile land.

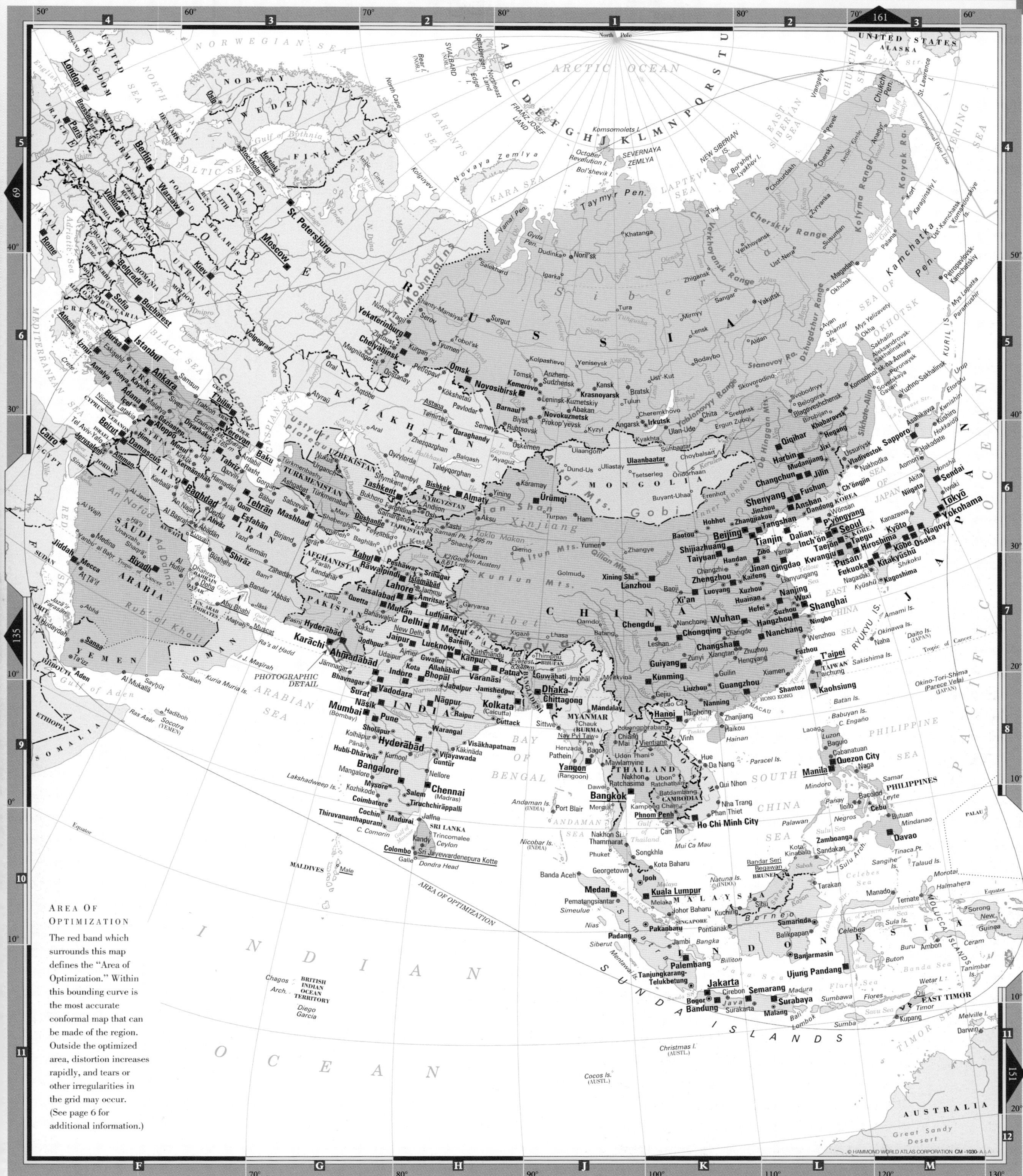

109

AREA OF OPTIMIZATION

The red band which surrounds this map defines the "Area of Optimization." Within this bounding curve is the most accurate conformal map that can be made of the region. Outside the optimized area, distortion increases rapidly, and tears or other irregularities in the grid may occur. (See page 6 for additional information.)

Population

■ Over 3,000,000	⊛ 500,000 - 999,999	∘ Under 100,000
■ 1,000,000 - 2,999,999	⊛ 100,000 - 499,999	

Scale 1:47,700,000   Hammond Optimal Conformal

MI   500   1000   1500
KM   500   1000   1500   2000

© HAMMOND WORLD ATLAS CORPORATION CM -1030- A A A

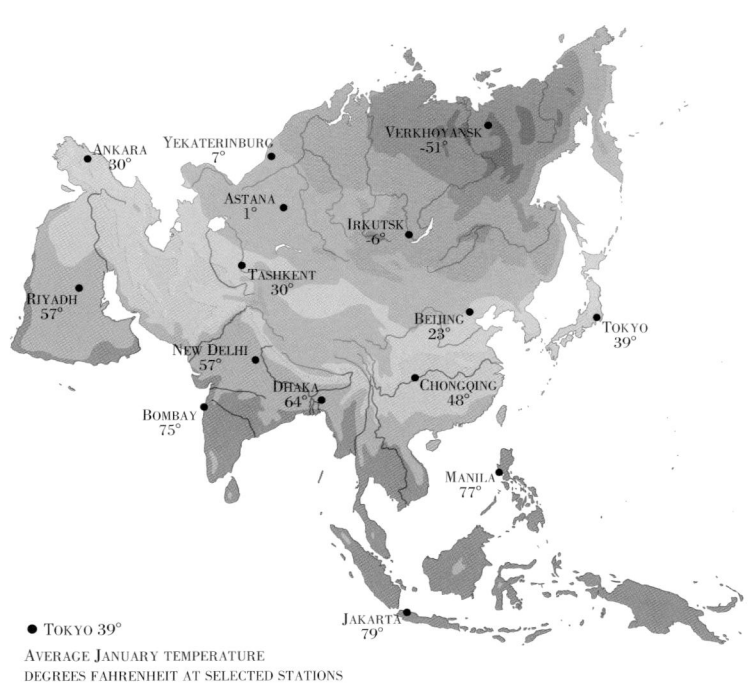

ANKARA 30° YEKATERINBURG 7° VERKHOYANSK -51° ASTANA 1° IRKUTSK -6° TASHKENT 30° BEIJING 23° TOKYO 39° RIYADH 57° NEW DELHI 57° DHAKA 64° CHONGQING 48° BOMBAY 75° MANILA 77° JAKARTA 79°

● TOKYO 39°
AVERAGE JANUARY TEMPERATURE
DEGREES FAHRENHEIT AT SELECTED STATIONS

AVERAGE JANUARY TEMPERATURE

FAHRENHEIT	CELSIUS	FAHRENHEIT	CELSIUS	FAHRENHEIT	CELSIUS
OVER 68°	OVER 20°	14° TO 32°	-10° TO 0°	-40° TO -22°	-40° TO -30°
50° TO 68°	10° TO 20°	-4° TO 14°	-20° TO -10°	UNDER -40°	UNDER -40°
32° TO 50°	0° TO 10°	-22° TO -4°	-30° TO -20°		

ANKARA 73 YEKATERINBURG 64 VERKHOYANSK 61 ASTANA 70 IRKUTSK 64 RIYADH 95 TASHKENT 81 BEIJING 79 TOKYO 77 NEW DELHI 93 DHAKA 82 CHONGQING 82 BOMBAY 81 MANILA 81 JAKARTA 79

● TOKYO 77
AVERAGE JULY TEMPERATURE
DEGREES FAHRENHEIT AT SELECTED STATIONS

AVERAGE JULY TEMPERATURE

FAHRENHEIT	CELSIUS	FAHRENHEIT	CELSIUS	FAHRENHEIT	CELSIUS
OVER 86°	OVER 30°	50° TO 68°	10° TO 20°	UNDER 32°	UNDER 0°
68° TO 86°	20° TO 30°	32° TO 50°	0° TO 10°		

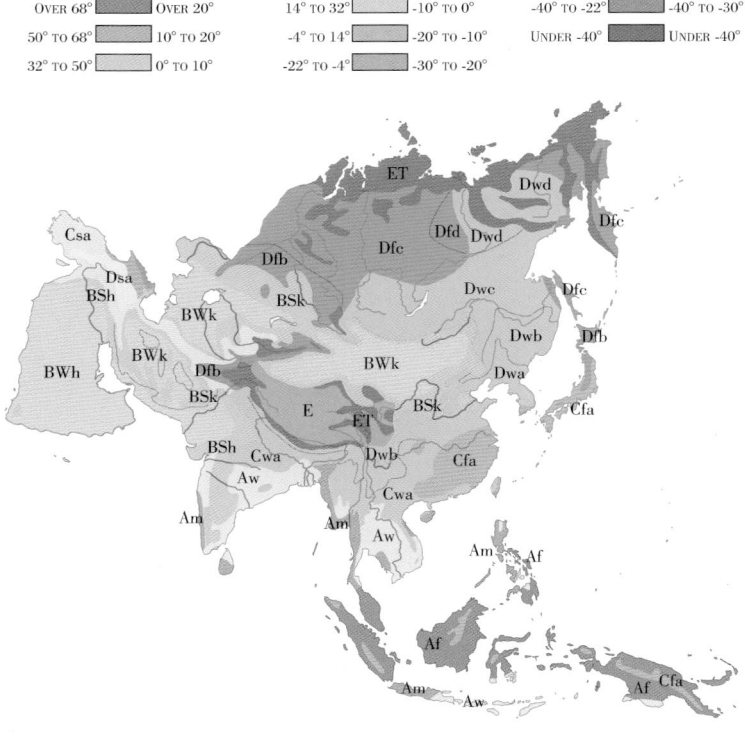

Csa Dsa BSh Dfb Dfc Dfd Dwd ET Dwd Dfc BWk BSk Dwc Dfc BWk Dwb Dfb BWk Dwa BWh BWk Dfb BSk E BSk Cfa BSh ET Cwa Dwb Cfa Aw Am Am Aw Am Af Af Am Aw Af Cfa

CLIMATE

HUMID TROPICAL
- Af NO DRY SEASON
- Am SHORT DRY SEASON
- Aw DRY WINTER

DRY
- BS SEMIARID
- BW ARID
- h HOT
- k COLD

AFTER KOEPPEN-GEIGER

HUMID WARM
- Cf NO DRY SEASON
- Cw DRY WINTER
- Cs DRY SUMMER

HUMID COLD
- Df NO DRY SEASON
- Dw DRY WINTER
- Ds DRY SUMMER

COLD POLAR
- ET SHORT COOL SUMMER, LONG COLD WINTER
- E COLD AND UNCLASSIFIED HIGHLANDS

a HOT SUMMER
b COOL SUMMER
c SHORT COOL SUMMER
d VERY COLD WINTER

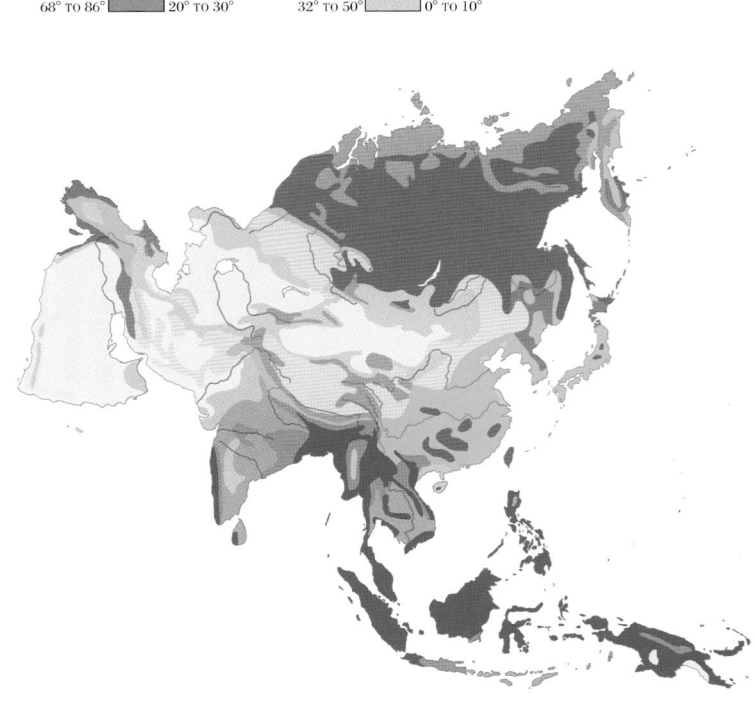

VEGETATION

TROPICAL FOREST
- TROPICAL RAINFOREST
- LIGHT TROPICAL FOREST
- WOODLAND AND SHRUB

TROPICAL GRASSLAND
- GRASS AND SHRUB (SAVANNA)
- WOODED SAVANNA

MID-LATITUDE FOREST
- NEEDLELEAF FOREST
- BROADLEAF FOREST
- MIXED NEEDLELEAF AND BROADLEAF FOREST
- WOODLAND AND SHRUB (MEDITERRANEAN)

MID-LATITUDE GRASSLAND
- SHORT GRASS (STEPPE)
- WOODED STEPPE
- DESERT AND DESERT SHRUB
- TUNDRA AND ALPINE
- UNCLASSIFIED HIGHLANDS

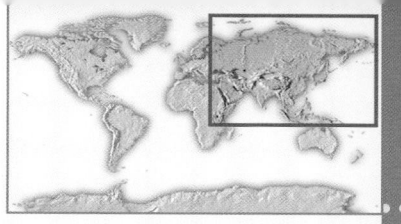

Asia - Geographical Comparisons

ANKARA 13
VERKHOYANSK 6
ASTANA 12
RIYADH 4
TEHRAN 9
TASHKENT 17
ULAANBAATR 7
BEIJING 25
TOKYO 61
NEW DELHI 28
CHONGQING 43
BOMBAY 82
CHERRAPUNJI 449
MANILA 82
PADANG 151

● TOKYO 61

AVERAGE ANNUAL RAINFALL
IN INCHES AT SELECTED STATIONS

AVERAGE ANNUAL RAINFALL

INCHES	CM	INCHES	CM	INCHES	CM
OVER 80	OVER 200	40 TO 60	100 TO 150	10 TO 20	25 TO 50
60 TO 80	150 TO 200	20 TO 40	50 TO 100	UNDER 10	UNDER 25

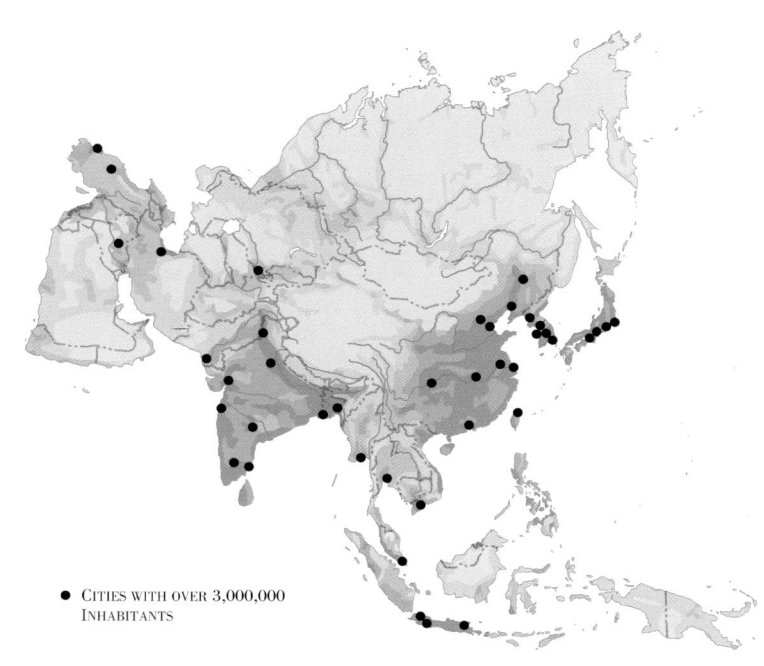

● CITIES WITH OVER 3,000,000 INHABITANTS

POPULATION DISTRIBUTION

DENSITY PER		SQ. MI.	SQ. KM.	SQ. MI.	SQ. KM.
SQ. MI.	SQ. KM.	130 TO 260	50 TO 100	3 TO 25	1 TO 10
OVER 260	OVER 100	25 TO 130	10 TO 50	UNDER 3	UNDER 1

TOBACCO
OLIVES WHEAT
FRUIT
SHEEP
DATES
SHEEP
OATS
CATTLE
WHEAT
POTATOES
OATS WHEAT
FURS
FURS
OATS
SHEEP
COTTON
SHEEP
WHEAT
SHEEP
POTATOES
SOYBEANS
WHEAT
SOYBEANS
RICE
FRUIT TEA
CORN
COTTON
RICE TEA
HOGS
CATTLE
WHEAT TEA
COTTON
RICE
RICE
JUTE
SUGARCANE
PEANUTS
CASSAVA
RICE
CORN
RUBBER
RICE
FRUIT
ABACA
DATES
RICE
TEA
RUBBER
RUBBER
COCONUTS
RUBBER
COCONUTS
SPICES
SPICES
COCONUTS
COCOA
RICE
COFFEE

LAND USE

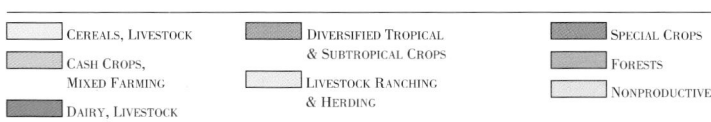

	CEREALS, LIVESTOCK		DIVERSIFIED TROPICAL & SUBTROPICAL CROPS		SPECIAL CROPS
	CASH CROPS, MIXED FARMING		LIVESTOCK RANCHING & HERDING		FORESTS
	DAIRY, LIVESTOCK				NONPRODUCTIVE

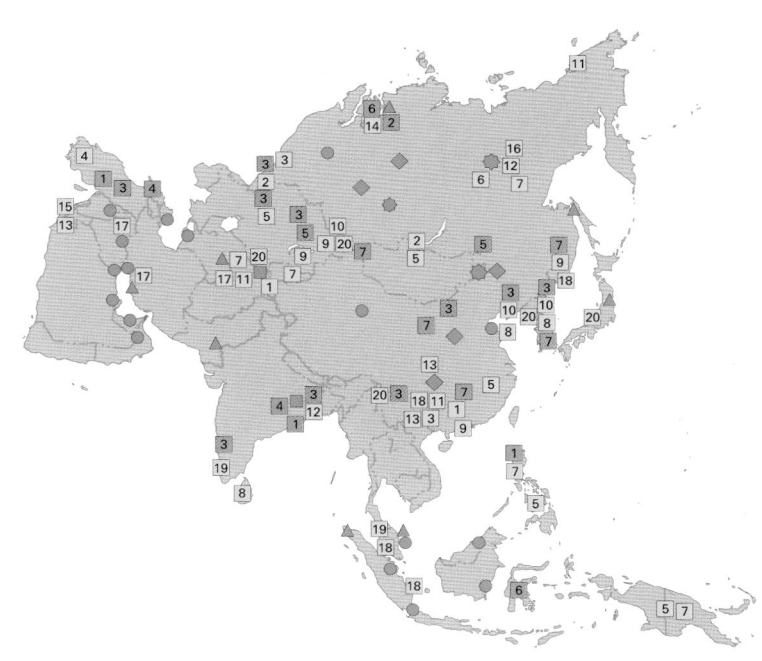

MINERAL RESOURCES

ENERGY & FUELS
◆ COAL
⬡ LIGNITE
▲ NATURAL GAS
● PETROLEUM
■ URANIUM

IRON & FERROALLOYS
1 CHROMIUM
2 COBALT
3 IRON ORE
4 MANGANESE
5 MOLYBDENUM
6 NICKEL
7 TUNGSTEN

OTHER MAJOR RESOURCES
1 ANTIMONY
2 ASBESTOS
3 BAUXITE
4 BORAX
5 COPPER
6 DIAMONDS
7 GOLD
8 GRAPHITE
9 LEAD
10 MAGNESITE
11 MERCURY
12 MICA
13 PHOSPHATES
14 PLATINUM
15 POTASH
16 SILVER
17 SULFER
18 TIN
19 TITANIUM
20 ZINC

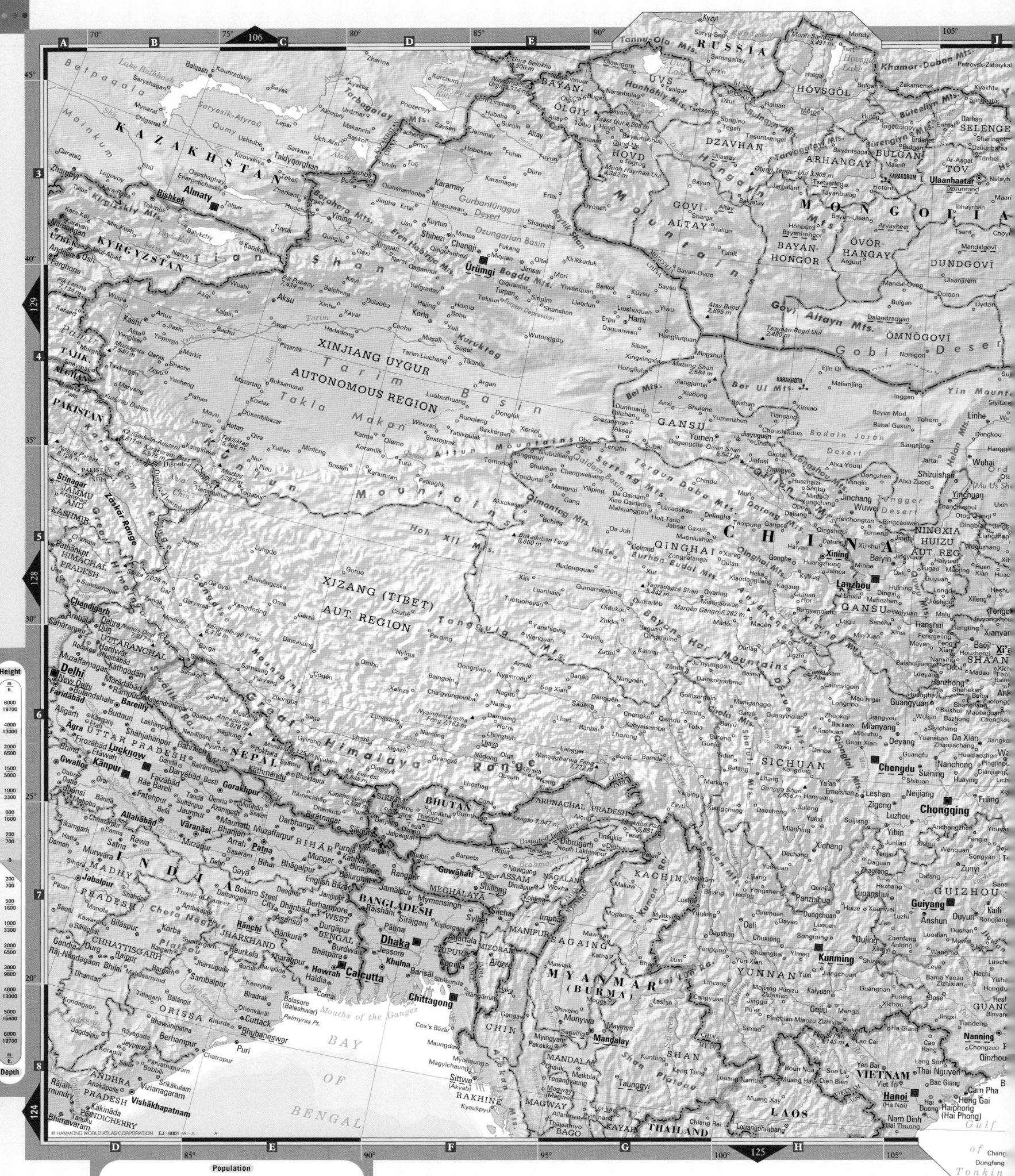

Height
m.
ft.
6000
19700
4000
13000
2000
6500
1500
5000
1000
3300
200
700
0
200
700
500
1600
1000
3300
2000
6500
3000
9800
4000
13000
5000
16400
6000
19700
m.
ft.
Depth

Population

◼ Over 2,000,000   ● 500,000 - 999,999   ◦ 50,000 - 99,999
◻ 1,000,000 - 1,999,999   ● 100,000 - 499,999   ○ Under 50,000

© HAMMOND WORLD ATLAS CORPORATION   EJ - 0001 - A - A   A

RUSSIA

SEA OF OKHOTSK

Sakhalin

Occupied by Russia since 1945, claimed by Japan.

Etorofu

Kunashiri

Hokkaidō

Sapporo

DORNOD

SÜHBAATAR

NEI MONGGOL AUT. REG.

HEILONGJIANG

Qiqihar

Daqing

Harbin

Jixi

Mudanjiang

Vladivostok

Changchun

JILIN

Jilin

SEA OF JAPAN

P

Sakata

Sendai

Niigata

LIAONING

Shenyang   Fushun

Anshan

Benxi

NORTH KOREA

Hamhŭng

P'yŏngyang

Nampʼo

Tōkyō

Chiba

Yokohama

Kanazawa

Nagoya

Kyōto   Honshū

Kōbe   Ōsaka   Sakai

Hamamatsu

NEI MONGGOL

Hohhot

Baotou

Zhangjiakou

HEBEI

BEIJING

Tangshan

Beijing

Tianjin   TIANJIN

Dalian

Korea Bay

Bo Hai
(Gulf of Chihli)

Seoul

Inchʼŏn

SOUTH
KOREA

Taejŏn

Taegu

Kwangju   Pusan

Ulsan

Hiroshima

Kitakyūshū

Fukuoka

Shikoku

SHANXI

Taiyuan

Shijiazhuang

Jinan

Zibo

SHANDONG

Qingdao

YELLOW
SEA

Cheju

Kyūshū

Kagoshima

HENAN

Zhengzhou

Luoyang

Kaifeng

Xuzhou

JIANGSU

Huainan

PACIFIC

Nanjing

ANHUI

Hefei

Changzhou
Wuxi   Suzhou

Shanghai
SHANGHAI

OCEAN

HUBEI

Wuhan

Hangzhou

ZHEJIANG

Ningbo

EAST CHINA

Amami Is.

Changsha

HUNAN

Nanchang

JIANGXI

SEA

Ryukyu Islands

Okinawa

Naha

FUJIAN

Fuzhou

Tʼaipei

Keelung

Tʼaoyüan

Tropic of Cancer

GUANGDONG

Guangzhou

Macau

Victoria

MACAU

HONG KONG

Tʼaichung

Tʼainan   TAIWAN

Pʼeng-hu
Chʼun-tao
(Pescadores)

Kaohsiung

Lan Yü
(Orchid I.)

TAIWAN

SOUTH CHINA

SEA

Bushi Channel

Babuyan I.

Babuyan Islands

Calayan I.

Hainan
Dao

Hong Kong inset

GUANGDONG

Shenzhen

GUANGDONG

Sheung Shui
Fanling

Tin Shui Wai

Yuen Long   Tai Po

Tuen Mun

Tsuen
Wan

Sha Tin

HONG KONG

New Kowloon

Kowloon
Victoria

Hong Kong

SOUTH

CHINA

SEA

Scale 1:13,600,000   Lambert Conformal Conic Projection

MI   100   200   300   400

KM   100   200   300   400   500   600

© HAMMOND W.A.C.

MAP SECTION

Northeastern China

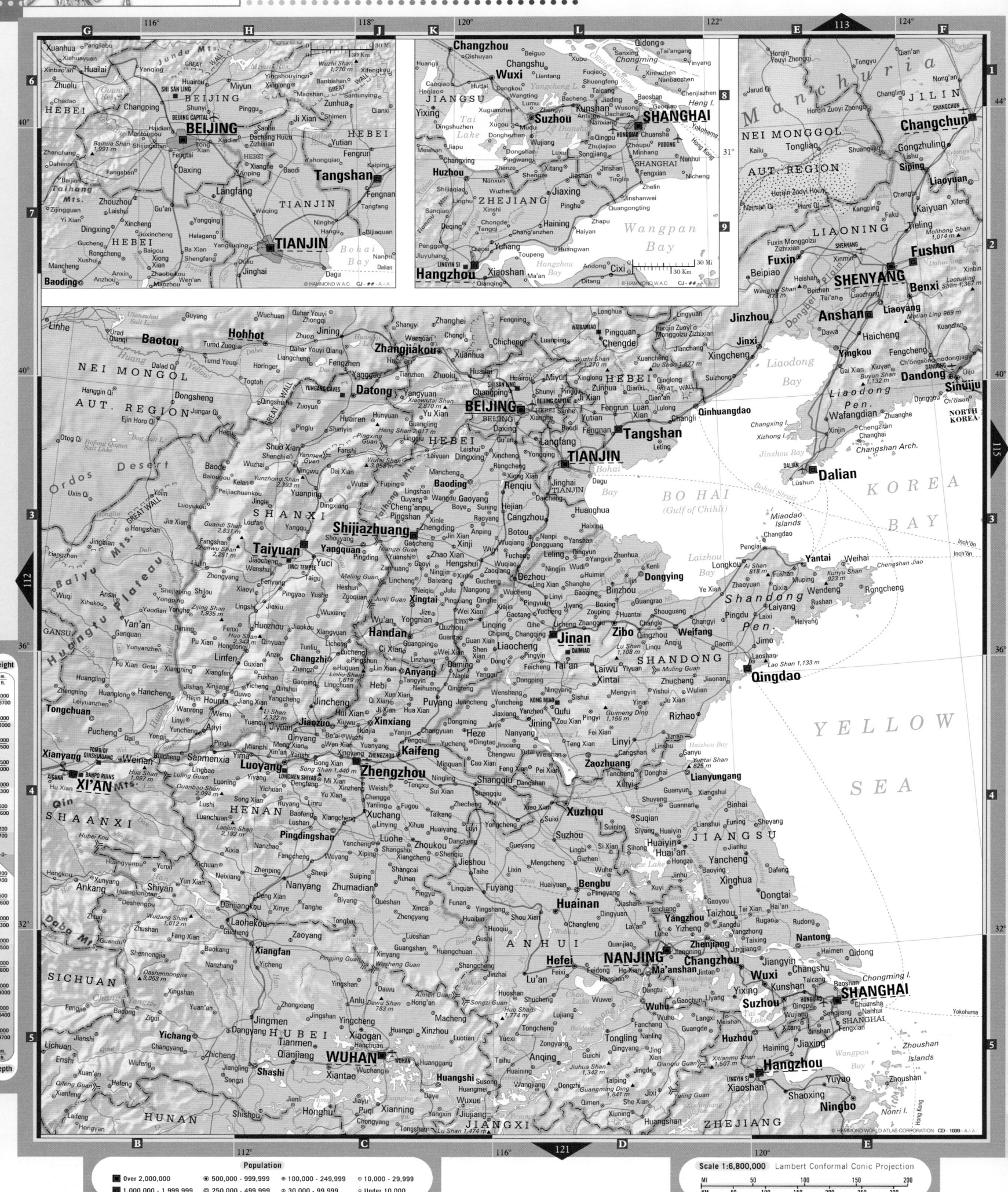

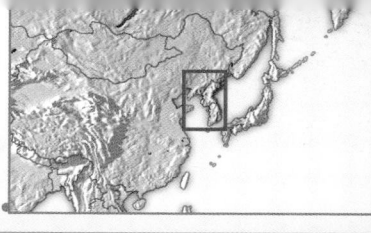
A 122° B 124° C 113 126° D 128° E 130°

1

42°

Fuxin Yemaotai Xiaotazi Tieling Daguja Jinchuan Jingyu Huayuan Fusong Quanyang Musan 1,130 m

Fuxin Monggolu Zizhixian Dafanhe Molihong Shan 1,014 m Ying'emen Wudaogou Xiatianping Pukp'ot'ae-san 2,540 m Puryŏng

SHENYANG **Fushun** Xinbin Tonghua **Hunjiang** Shirei Manjiang Paektu-san (Changbai Shan) 2,744 m Hongam-nodongjagu Yonsa **Ch'ŏngjin**

Anshan **Benxi** Jianchang Huanren Huadianzi **Tonghua** Linjiang Changbai Chaoxianzu Zizhixian 2,099 m **HAMGYŎNG BUKTO** Ŏrang Ŏdaejin

J I L I N

M A N C H U R I A C H I N A

Dandong **Sinŭiju** **P'YŎNGAN-BUKTO** **CHAGANG-DO** **YANGGANG-DO** **Kimch'aek**

L I A O N I N G

Liaodong Bay Yingkou Dawa Haicheng Qian Mts Kangnam Mts Myanglim Mts Changbai Mts Hamgyŏng Mts

40° **HAMGYŎNG-NAMDO** 40°

Liaodong Peninsula **Hamhŭng** SEA OF JAPAN

Tonghan Bay

DALIAN **Dalian** **P'YŎNGYANG** **Wŏnsan**

114 **NORTH KOREA** **KANGWŎN-DO** 3

K O R E A   B A Y **Namp'o** **HWANGHAE BUKTO** Kumgang-san 1,638 m Armistice Line, 1953

Sariwŏn **HWANGHAE-NAMDO** Demilitarized Zone SŎRAKSAN NAT'L. PK.

38° **Haeju** **Kaesŏng** Sŏraksan 1,708 m 38°

C H I N A Weihai **Uijŏngbu** ODAESAN NAT'L PK. Kangnŭng

Wendeng Rongcheng Kyŏnggi Bay **SEOUL** CH'IAK-SAN NP Samch'ŏk

S H A N D O N G **INCH'ŎN** **Sŏngnam** **KANGWŎN-DO**

4 **Suwŏn** KYŎNGGI-DO T'aebaek 4

Tŏkchŏk Arch. KOREAN FOLK VILLAGE

Asan Bay **Pyŏngt'aek** CH'UNGCH'ŎNG-BUKTO Ulchin

Ch'ŏnan **Yŏngju** P'yŏnghae

SŎSAN HAEAN NAT'L PARK **Ch'ŏngju** **SOUTH KOREA** Andong CHUWANG-SAN NP

Taejŏn KYŎNGSANG-BUKTO

6 **Kunsan** **Chŏnju** **Kimch'ŏn** **P'ohang** 6

36° Y E L L O W **Chŏnju** **TAEGU** Kyŏngju KYŎNGJU NAT'L PK.

S E A CHŎLLA-BUKTO CHIRI-SAN NAT'L PARK **Ulsan**

Kwangju **Masan** **Kimhae** **PUSAN** 5

Chinju HALLYO HAESANG NAT'L PARK

Mokp'o TADOHAE HAESANG NAT'L PARK Tsushima

Chin I. Korea Strait

F 127° **G** **C** 128° **E**

NORTH KOREA Tongduch'ŏn Hyŏndŭng-san 936 m

KYŎNGGI-DO SOUTH KOREA **Uijŏngbu** Surak-san 638 m Ch'ŏnma-san 812 m

Koyang PUK'AN-SAN NATIONAL PARK **Namyangju**

SEOUL **Hanam**

Puch'ŏn INCH'ŎN-GWANGYŎKSI **Kwangmyŏng** NAMHANSANSONG PROVINCIAL PARK

INCH'ŎN **Anyang** **Sŏngnam** **Kwangju**

Kyŏnggi Bay **Ansan** KYŎNGGI-DO **Suwŏn** KOREAN FOLK VILLAGE

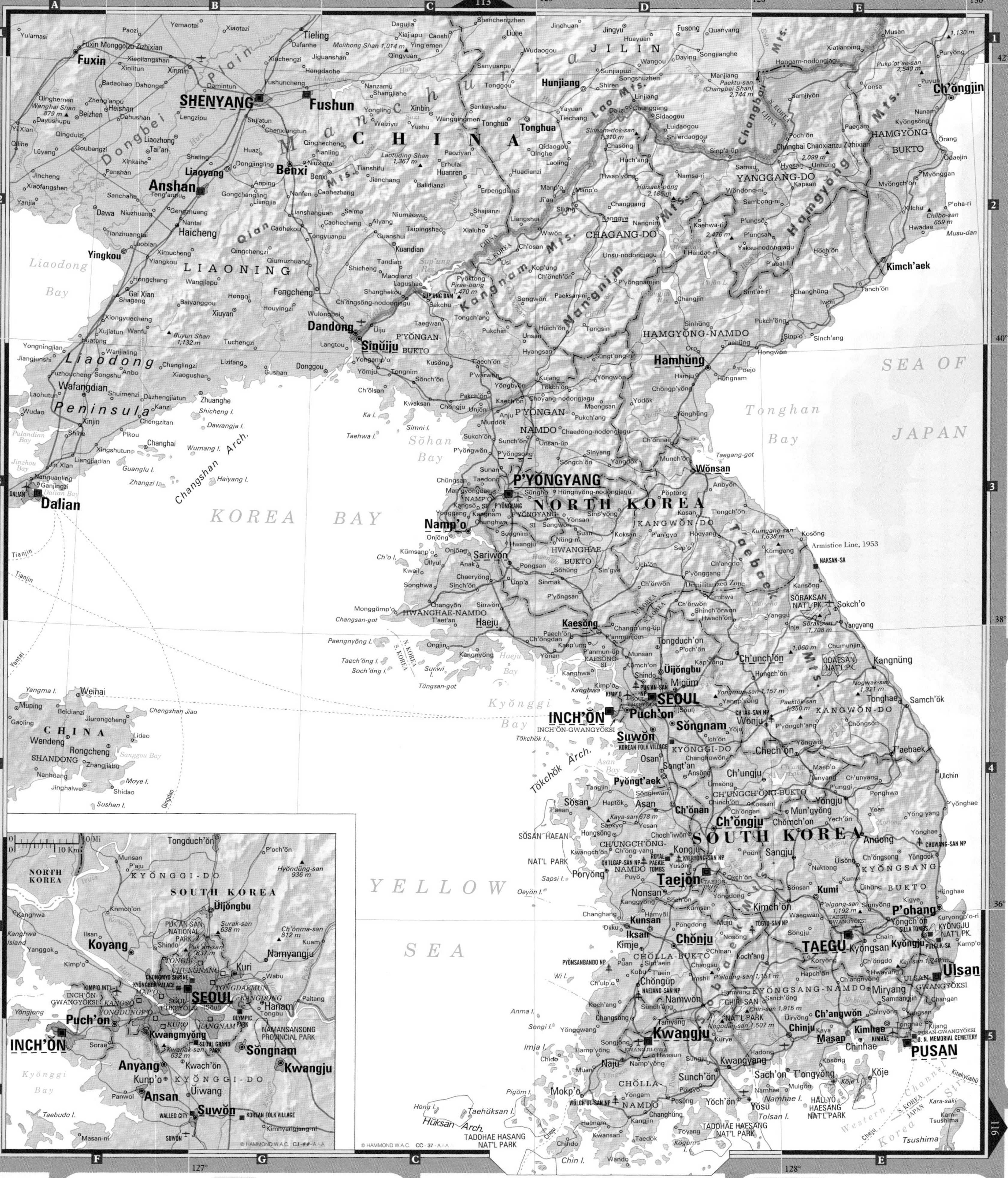

Population
Symbol	Range
■	Over 2,000,000
■	1,000,000 - 1,999,999
●	500,000 - 999,999
●	250,000 - 499,999
●	100,000 - 249,999
●	30,000 - 99,999
○	10,000 - 29,999
○	Under 10,000

Height
m. / ft.
6000 / 19700
4000 / 13000
2000 / 6500
1500 / 5000
1000 / 3300
500 / 1600
200 / 700
200 / 700
500 / 1600
1000 / 3300
2000 / 6500
3000 / 9800
4000 / 13000
5000 / 16400
6000 / 19700
Depth

Scale 1:3,400,000 Lambert Conformal Conic Projection
MI 0 25 50 75 100
KM 0 25 50 75 100 125 150

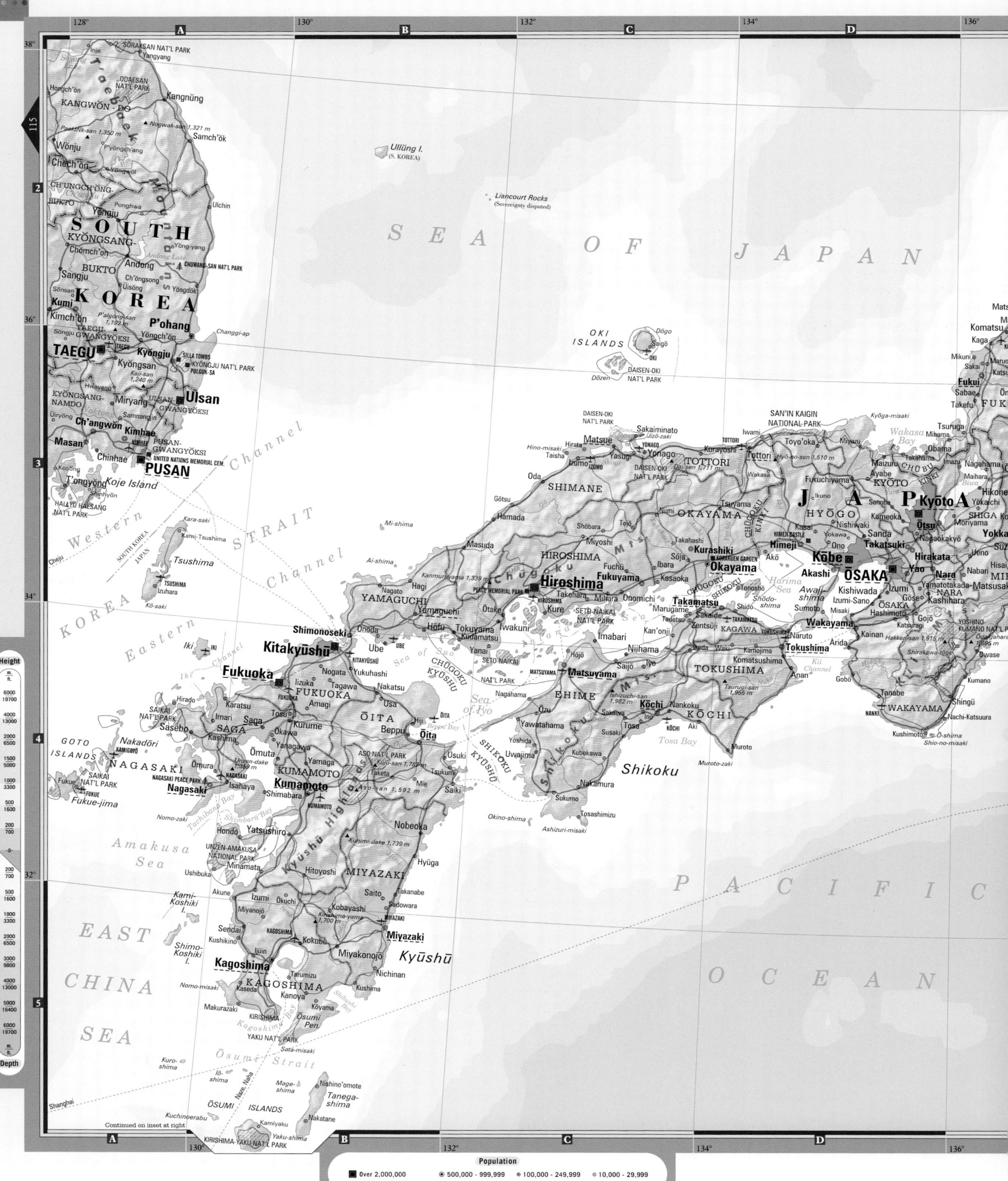
SEA OF JAPAN
SOUTH KOREA
JAPAN
PACIFIC OCEAN
EAST CHINA SEA
KOREA STRAIT
Western Channel
Eastern Channel
Kyūshū
Shikoku
OKI ISLANDS
ŌSUMI ISLANDS
GOTO ISLANDS
Ullŭng I. (S. KOREA)
Liancourt Rocks (Sovereignty disputed)
PUSAN
TAEGU
Ulsan
P'ohang
Fukuoka
Kitakyūshū
Hiroshima
Okayama
Kōbe
ŌSAKA
Kyōto
Nagasaki
Kumamoto
Kagoshima
Miyazaki
Ōita
Matsuyama
Kōchi
Tokushima
Takamatsu
Wakayama
Nara
Continued on inset at right
Population
Over 2,000,000
1,000,000 - 1,999,999
500,000 - 999,999
250,000 - 499,999
100,000 - 249,999
30,000 - 99,999
10,000 - 29,999
Under 10,000
Height
Depth

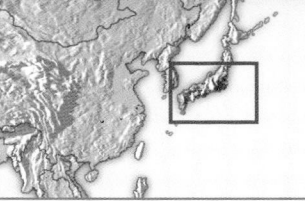

PACIFIC OCEAN

EAST CHINA SEA

Honshū

Sado

Sendai
Niigata
Fukushima
Yamagata
Kōriyama
Iwaki
Nagano
Maebashi
Utsunomiya
Toyama
Mito
Matsumoto
Takasaki
Urawa
Kawagoe
Koshigaya
Kawaguchi
Tokorozawa
Hachiōji
TŌKYŌ
Chiba
Kawasaki
YOKOHAMA
Sagamihara
Fujisawa
Yokosuka
NAGOYA
Toyota
Okazaki
Shizuoka
Hamamatsu
Toyohashi
Kagoshima
Naha

NIIGATA · FUKUSHIMA · TOHOKU · JOSHIN-ETSU · KOGEN · GUMMA · TOCHIGI · IBARAKI · SAITAMA · KANAGAWA · YAMANASHI · SHIZUOKA · AICHI · GIFU · NAGANO · TOYAMA · MIYAGI · YAMAGATA

MINAMI-ALPS NAT'L PARK · CHICHIBU-TAMA NAT'L PARK · FUJI-HAKONE-IZU NAT'L PARK · BANDAI-ASAHI NP · NIKKO NAT'L PARK · JAPANESE ALPS NAT'L PARK

Sendai Bay
Toyama Bay
Sagami Sea
Suruga Bay

Izu Islands (JAPAN)
Ō-shima
Miyake-jima
Mikura-jima
Hachijō-jima
Aoga-shima
Bōsō Pen.

FUJI-HAKONE-IZU NAT'L PARK

Fuji-san 3,776 m

Abukuma-kōchi

Kyūshū
Tokara Islands
Amami Islands
Ryukyu Islands (Nansei-Shotō)
Okinawa Is.
Sakishima Islands
Yaeyama Is.
Miyako Is.

Kagoshima

Scale 1:3,400,000   Lambert Conformal Conic Projection

© HAMMOND WORLD ATLAS CORPORATION   CD -1035-A-A-A

© HAMMOND W.A.C.   CU -1116-A-A-A

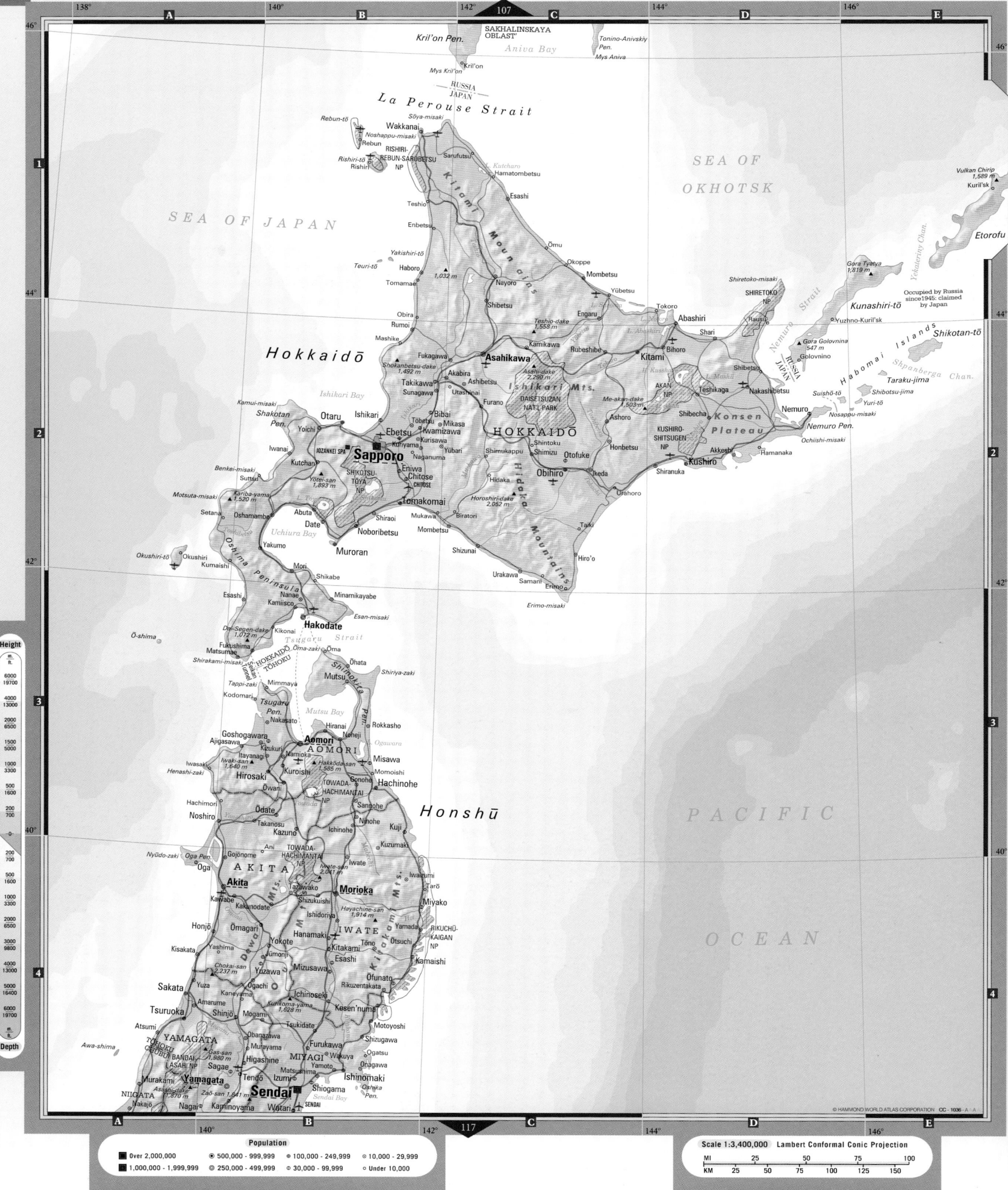

138°   140°   142°   144°   146°

| A | B | C | D | E |

46°

SAKHALINSKAYA
OBLAST'

Kril'on Pen.

Aniva Bay

Tonino-Anivskiy
Pen.

Mys Aniva

Mys Kril'on

Kril'on

RUSSIA
JAPAN

La Perouse Strait

Rebun-tō

Wakkanai

Noshappu-misaki

Sōya-misaki

Rebun

RISHIRI-
REBUN-SAROBETSU
NP

Rishiri-tō

Rishiri

Sarufutsu

SEA OF
OKHOTSK

Vulkan Chirip
1,589 m

Kuril'sk

1

SEA OF JAPAN

Teshio

Enbetsu

Esashi

L. Kutcharo

Hamatombetsu

Ōmu

Okoppe

Mombetsu

Etorofu

Yakishiri-tō

Teuri-tō

Habōro

Tomamae

1,032 m

Nayoro

Yūbetsu

Shiretoko-misaki

SHIRETOKO
NP

Gora Tyatya
1,819 m

44°

Obira

Rumoi

Mashike

Fukagawa

Akabira

Shokanbetsu-dake
1,492 m

Takikawa

Sunagawa

Ashibetsu

Teshio-dake
1,558 m

Kamikawa

Asahikawa

Asahi-dake
2,290 m

DAISETSUZAN
NAT'L PARK

Engaru

Rubeshibe

Tokoro

Kitami

Bihoro

Shintoku

Me-akan-dake
1,503 m

AKAN
NP

Teshikaga

Shibetsu

Abashiri

Shari

L. Abashiri

RUSSIA
JAPAN

Kunashiri-tō

Yuzhno-Kuril'sk

Gora Golovnina
547 m

Golovnino

Occupied by Russia
since 1945; claimed
by Japan

Habomai Islands

Shikotan-tō

44°

Hokkaidō

Kamui-misaki

Shakotan
Pen.

Otaru

Ishikari

Ishikari Bay

Yoichi

Ebetsu

JOZANKEI SPA

Sapporo

Bibai

Mikasa

Iwamizawa

Tōbetsu

Kurisawa

Yūbari

Shintoku

Shimizu

Otofuke

Honbetsu

HOKKAIDŌ

Obihiro

Shibecha

Nakashibetsu

KUSHIRO-
SHITSUGEN
NP

Kushiro

Konsen
Plateau

Nemuro

Nosappu-misaki

Nemuro Pen.

Akkeshi

Hamanaka

Shibotsu-jima

Yuri-tō

Suishō-tō

Shpanberga
Chan.

Taraku-jima

Ochiishi-misaki

2

2

Iwanai

Benkei-misaki

Kutchan

Yōtei-san
1,893 m

SHIKOTSU-
TŌYA
NP

Eniwa

Chitose

CHITOSE

Tomakomai

Naganuma

Hidaka

Horoshiri-dake
2,052 m

Hidaka
Mountains

Urahoro

42°

Motsuta-misaki

Kariba-yama
1,520 m

Setana

Oshamambe

Abuta

Date

Noboribetsu

Muroran

Shiraoi

Mukawa

Biratori

Taiki

Hiro'o

42°

Okushiri-tō

Okushiri

Kumaishi

Oshima Peninsula

Mori

Shikabe

Shizunai

Urakawa

Samani

Erimo

Esashi

Nanae

Kamiisco

Minamikayabe

Ō-shima

Dai-Segen-dake
1,072 m

Kikonai

Hakodate

Fukushima

Matsumae

Esan-misaki

Erimo-misaki

Tsugaru Strait

HOKKAIDŌ
TŌHOKU

Shirakami-misaki

Seikan Tunnel

Tappi-zaki

Ōma-zaki

Ōma

Ōhata

Shiriya-zaki

Mutsu

Shimokita

PACIFIC

3

Kodomari

Tsugaru
Pen.

Mimmaya

Mutsu Bay

Rokkasho

Ogawara

3

Goshogawara

Hiranai

Noheji

Ajigasawa

Kanagi

Itayanagi

Aomori

AOMORI

Misawa

Iwaki-san
1,640 m

Namioka

Hakkōdasan
1,585 m

Momoishi

Hachinohe

Iwasaki

Hirosaki

Kuroishi

TOWADA-
HACHIMANTAI
NP

Gonohe

Sannohe

OCEAN

Henashi-zaki

Ōwani

Odate

Hachimori

L. Towada

Ninohe

Kuji

Noshiro

Takanosu

Kazuno

Ichinohe

Kuzumaki

40°

Nyūdō-zaki

Oga Pen.

Oga

Gojōnome

Ani

TOWADA-
HACHIMANTAI
NP

Iwate-san
2,041 m

Iwate

Tarō

Honshū

40°

AKITA

Akita

Tazawako

Shizukuishi

Morioka

Hayachine-san
1,914 m

Miyako

Yamada

RIKUCHŪ-
KAIGAN
NP

Kawabe

Kakunodate

Ishidoriya

Hanamaki

Ōtsuchi

Honjō

Ōmagari

Yokote

Hanamaki

IWATE

Kamaishi

Kisakata

Yashima

Jūmonji

Mizusawa

Esashi

Tōno

Chōkai-san
2,237 m

Yuzawa

Ōgachi

Ichinoseki

Rikuzentakata

Sakata

Yuza

Kaneyama

Kurikoma-yama
1,628 m

Ichinoseki

Kesen-numa

4

Tsuruoka

Amarume

Shinjō

Mogami

Motoyoshi

4

Atsumi

YAMAGATA

Obanazawa

Furukawa

Shizugawa

Awa-shima

Gas-san
1,980 m

Murayama

Naruko

Ogatsu

TŌHOKU
CHŪBU

BANDAI-
ASAHI NP

Higashine

Sagae

Yamato

Matsushima

Ishinomaki

Murakami

Asahi-dake
1,870 m

Tendō

Izumi

MIYAGI

Wakuya

Onagawa

NIIGATA

Yamagata

Zaō-san 1,841 m

Sendai

Shiogama

Oshika
Pen.

Nagai

Kaminoyama

Watari

Sendai Bay

© HAMMOND WORLD ATLAS CORPORATION   CC - 1036 - A - A

| A | B | C | D | E |

140°   142°   144°   146°

Height
m.
ft.
6000 / 19700
4000 / 13000
2000 / 6500
1500 / 5000
1000 / 3300
500 / 1600
200 / 700
0
200 / 700
500 / 1600
1000 / 3300
2000 / 6500
3000 / 9800
4000 / 13000
5000 / 16400
6000 / 19700
m.
ft.
Depth

Population

| ■ Over 2,000,000 | ◉ 500,000 - 999,999 | ◎ 100,000 - 249,999 | ○ 10,000 - 29,999 |
| ■ 1,000,000 - 1,999,999 | ◉ 250,000 - 499,999 | ◉ 30,000 - 99,999 | ○ Under 10,000 |

Scale 1:3,400,000   Lambert Conformal Conic Projection

MI   25   50   75   100

KM   25   50   75   100   125   150

Tōkyō-Yokohama, Ōsaka-Nagoya

Population

- Over 2,000,000
- 1,000,000 - 1,999,999
- 500,000 - 999,999
- 250,000 - 499,999
- 100,000 - 249,999
- 30,000 - 99,999
- 10,000 - 29,999
- Under 10,000

Scale 1:1,140,000 Lambert Conformal Conic Projection

MI 0 10 20 30
KM 0 10 20 30 40

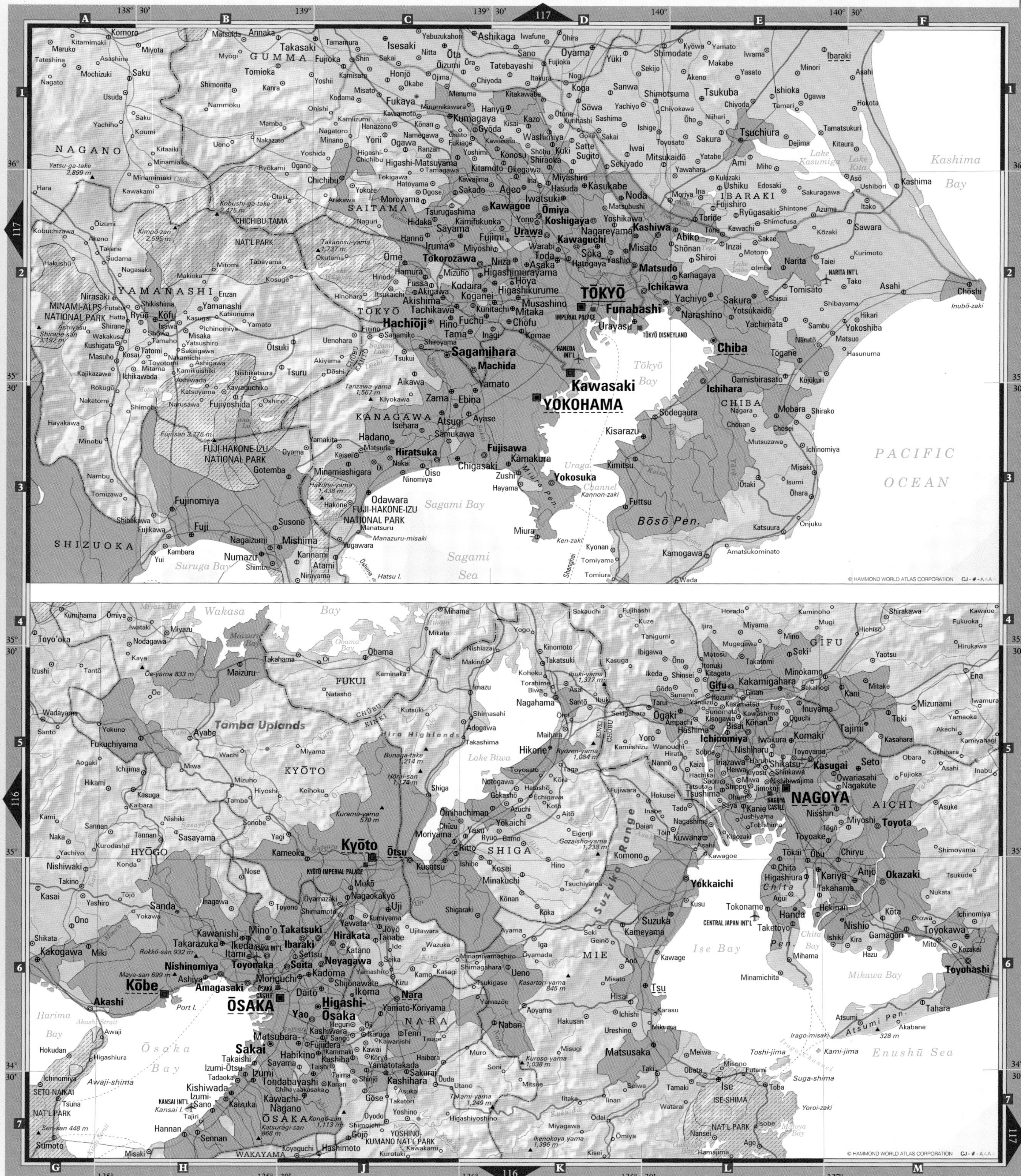

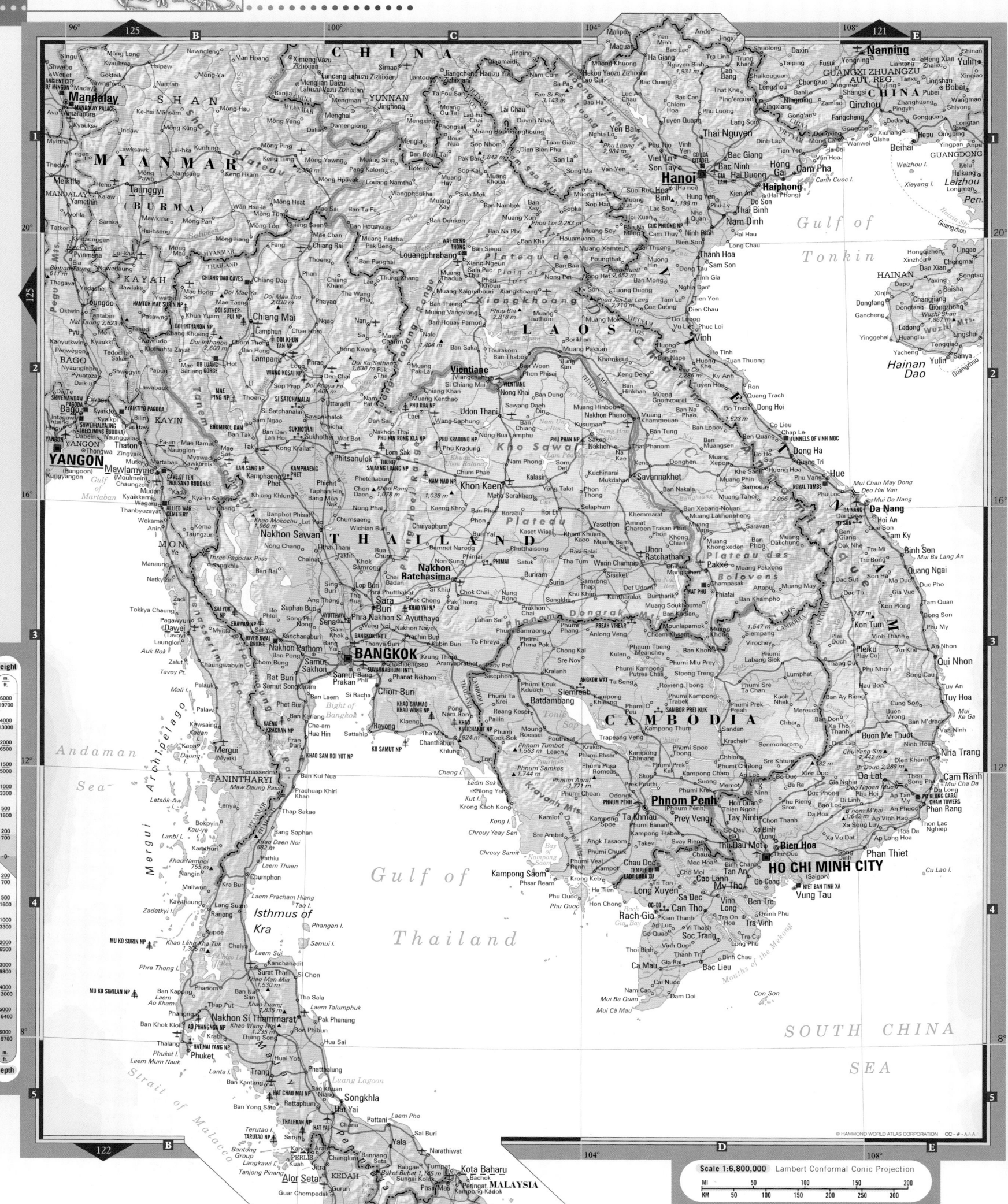

Scale 1:6,800,000   Lambert Conformal Conic Projection

© HAMMOND WORLD ATLAS CORPORATION   CC - # - A A A

Scale 1:10,200,000   Lambert Conformal Conic Projection

MI   100   200   300
KM   100   200   300   400

© HAMMOND WORLD ATLAS CORPORATION   DJ-0002-A-A-A

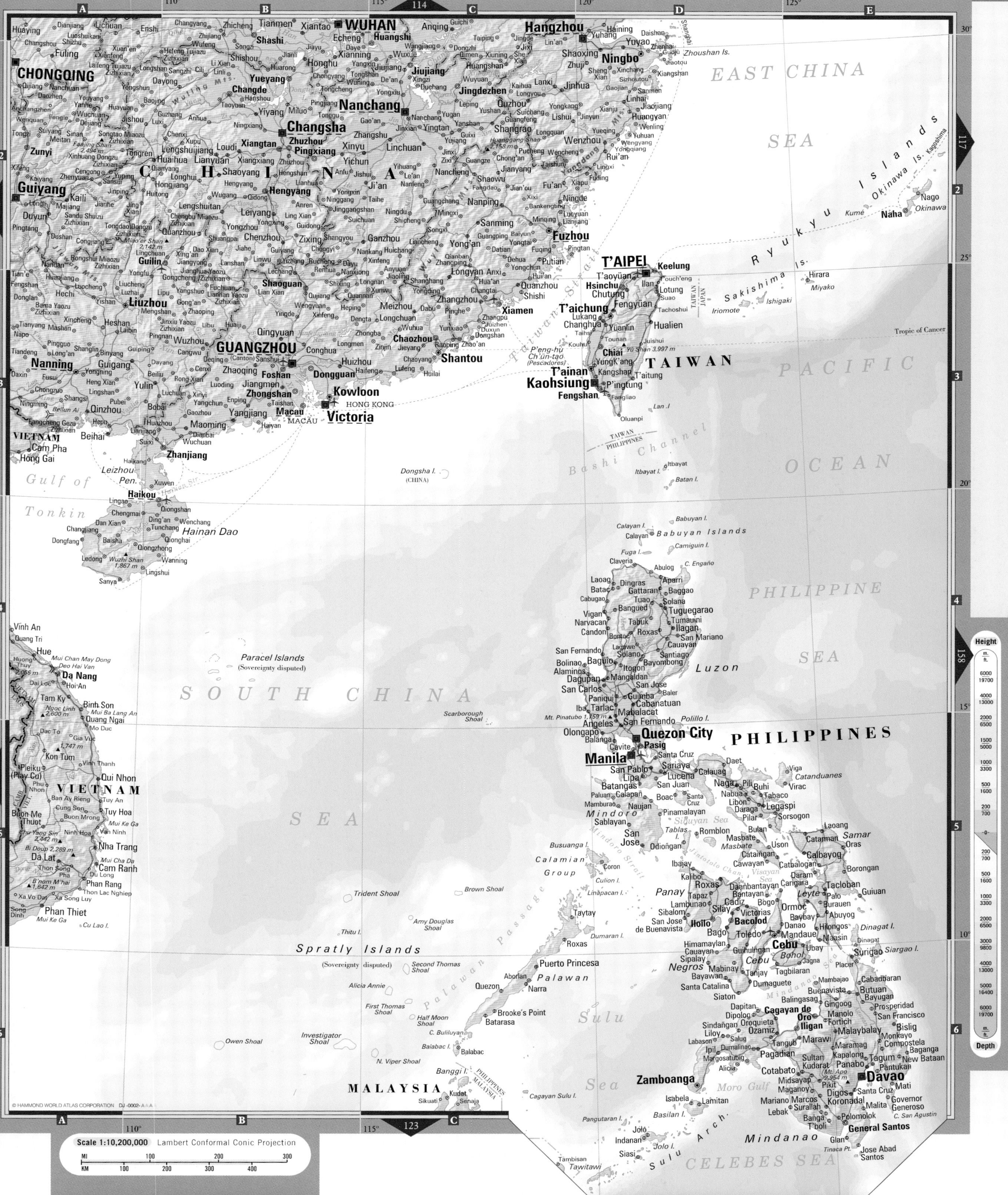

95° **A** 100° ▲120 **B** 105° **C** 110° **D**

1

Mergui
Mergui
Archipelago Meik)
MYANMAR
(BURMA)
Letsök-Aw I.

Cha-am Rayong
Sattahip
Hua Hin
Tha Mai Chanthaburi Pong Kesei Kampong Cham
Khlung Phnum Samraong Tbaeng Meanchey Senmonorom
Chang I. 1,563 m Leach Kratie
Kut I. Phnum Aoral Phumi Spoe Phumi Thmar
Krong Kaoh 1,771 m Tbong Kampong Thach
Kong **Phnom Penh** Svay Rieng
Krabi (Phnum Penh) Takeo

Tenasserim
Maw-daung
Pass
Khao Daen Noi
552 m
Kra Buri
Chumphon
THAILAND
Isthmus of
Kra

Ban Crieng
Buon Me Thuot
Ban M'drack
Dien Khanh
2,289 m
Da Lat
1,642 m
Phan Rang
Thon Lac

Tuy An
Tuy Hoa
Mui Ke Ga
Van Ninh
Nha Trang
Cam Ranh

2

Andaman
Sea

Zadetkyi I.
Khao Lang Kha Tuk
1,396 m
Phangnga
Phuket I.
Phuket
Laem Mum Nauk
Lanta I.

Ranong
Phangan I.
Surat Thani
Samui I.
Ban Na San
Nakhon Si
Thammarat
1,835 m

Gulf of
Thailand

Phu Quoc I.
Rach Gia
Kiep Thanh
Thoi Binh
Ca Mau
Bac Lieu
Mui Cà Mau

Long Xuyen
Can Tho
Ap Luc
Soc Trang

Vinh Long
Tra Vinh
Tra Cu

Con Son

Trident Shoal

SOUTH CHINA

SEA

3

Strait
of
Malacca

Pulau We Sabang
Banda Aceh
Seulimeum
Sigli
Lhokkruet Padangsidempuan
Keudeuteunom
Lhoksukon
G. Geureudong
2,885 m
Isak
Gunung Lembu
3,014 m
Langsa
Kualasimpang
Pangkalanberandan
Tanjungpura
Medan
Binjai
Tebingtinggi
Pematangsiantar
Tanjungbalai

Trang
Songkhla
Hat Yai
Terutao I. Laem Pho
Langkawi I. Satun Sai Buri
Tanjung Pinang Narathiwat
Tumpat
Alor Setar Bukit Bintang Kota Baharu
Sungai Petani 1,145 m Sungai Kampong Kuala
George Town Kolok Besut
Baling Tanah Merah
Butterworth G. Bintang Jerteh
Penang I. 1,862 m **Kuala Terengganu**
Taiping G. Chamah Marang
Lumut 2,171 m
Batu Gajah Kuala Kerai
Ipoh G. Tahan Kuala Dungun
Kampar 2,187 m
Telok Anson Kuala Lipis Kemasik
Raub Chukai
Gunung Tapis
1,512 m **Kuantan**
Bentong Temerloh Pekan
Kuala Selangor
Shah Alam Kuala Pilah
Kelang **Kuala Lumpur** *Malaya*
Putrajaya
Seremban Segamat
Port Dickson
Melaka Mersing
Muar G. Ledang
Batu Pahat 1,276 m Keluang
Rengam Tioman I.
Pekan Nanas Kulai
Johor Baharu
Tanjung Punggai
SINGAPORE
SINGAPORE

MALAYSIA
MALAY INDO.

Natuna
Is.
Ranai
Bunguran I.
Tanjung
Terempa
BRUNEI
Bandar Seri Begawan
Kuala Belait
Tanjung Baram
Seria
Miri
Lutong
MALAY
INDO.

4

Banyak
Islands
Nias I.
Lahewa
Gunungsitoli
Singkuang
Sirombu
Tuhemberua
Tuangku I.
Batangtoru
Barus
Sibolga
Singkil
Simeulue I.
Prapat
L. Toba
Tuka
Ujung Raja
G. Leuser
3,466 m

Muarasoma
Bakungan
Batanghari
Padangsidempuan
Bukittinggi
Padang
Pariaman
Payakumbuh
Sawahlunto
Padangpanjang
Solok

Pakanbaru
Bengkalis
Bengkalis I.
Buatan
Siak
Rengat
Tembilahan
Lubuksikaping
Sungailapat
Kualamandah
Tg. Datuk
KTg. Jabung

Riau Islands
Lingga
Is.

Serasan Strait
Serasan
Pamangkat
Singkawang
Sambas
Ledong
Anambas
Is.
Subi I.
Subi
Bengkayang

Tanjung Sirik
Beruit I.
Paloh
Kabong
Saratok

Batu
Bay
Oya
Kanowit
Sibu
Sarikei
Kuching
Sanggau
Ngabang

Sarawak
Bukit Batu
2,012 m
Tatau
Labang
Binatang

5

Mentawai Islands
Siberut I.
Sabulubek
Taileleo
Sipura I.
Pagai Utara I.
Pagai Selatan I.
Pasarbunga
Pulau Burung

Lubuklinggau
Curup
Bengkulu
Gunung Dempo
3,159 m
Lahat
Baturaja
Martapura
Manna
Kotabumi
Pringsewu
Kotaagung
Kalianda
Balimbing
Tanjung Rata
INDIAN
OCEAN

Enggano I.
Krul
Ngaras
Ketapang
Tg. Tua
Tg. Pujut
Serang
Merak
Depok
Bogor
Sukabumi
Ujunggenteng
Tanjung Genteng
Tanjung Cangkuang
Panaitan I.
Sunda Strait
Krakatau

Muarabungo
Jambi
Sarolangun
Muaratebo
Gunung Kerinci
3,805 m
Sungaipenuh
Surulangun
Rantauprapat
Muararupit Babat
Bangko
G. Masurai
2,933 m
Sekayu
Surulangun
Muaraenim
Prabumulih
Perabumulih
Palembang
Kayuagung
Sungsang
Pagardewa
Wiralaga
Menggala
Bandingagung
Gunung Pesagi
Tengku Tabak 2,116 m
2,232 m
Liwa
Kayuagung
Metro
Tanjungkarang-
Telukbetung

Bangka I.
Pangkalpinang
Muntok
Sungailiat
Koba
Membalong
Belitung I.
475 m
Tg. Berikat
Java
Sea
Karimunjawa
Is.

Gaspar Strait
Tanjungpandan

Bangka I.
Gunung Maras
699 m

Tanjung Samak
Karimata
Is.
Sukadana
Maya I.
Telukmelano
Karimata Strait
Pangkalanbuun
Kotawaringin
Pangkalanbuun
Sukaraja
Nangabulik
Sampit
Salabangka
Buntok
Pagatan
Tanjung Puting
Pelaihari
Martapura
Banjarmasin

Borneo
Kalimantan
Putussibau
Nanga Pinoh
Gunung Saran
1,759 m
Nangahalan
Semitau
Sintang
Bukit Raya
2,278 m
Tumbangsenamang
Schwaner Mts.
Bukit Sebayan
1,377 m
Tumbangkaman
Bawan
Kasongan
Palangkaraya
Kapuas
Gelinggang
Mandomai
Buang

Sukamara

JAKARTA
Bekasi
Karawang
Subang
Cianjur
Cirebon
Klangenan
BANDUNG
Garut
Ciamis
Tasikmalaya
Sindangbarang
Cijulang
Cilacap
Pacitan

Kudus
Pekalongan
Pati
Tegal
Kuningan
Purwokerto
Kebumen
Magelang
Yogyakarta
Gunung Muria
1,602 m
Rembang
Blora
Semarang
Madiun
Jombang
Surakarta
Kediri
Gunung Nuu
3,265 m
Gunung Slamet
3,428 m
Tuban
Bojonegoro

Madura
Sumenep
Taman
Pamekasan
SURABAYA
Pasuruan
Pare
Probolinggo
Malang
Jember
Bondowoso
3,676 m
Gunung Semeru
Genteng
Java
Muncar
Grajagan
Tg. Bantenan
Denpas

Bawean I.
Tg. Pacinan
Tg. Cand

Greater *Sunda*

6

A 100° **B** 105° **C** 110° **D**

Height
m.
ft.
6000
19700
4000
13000
2000
6500
1500
5000
1000
3300
500
1600
200
700
0
200
700
500
1600
1000
3300
2000
6500
3000
9800
4000
13000
5000
16400
6000
19700
m.
ft.
Depth

Population
■ Over 2,000,000 ● 500,000 - 999,999 ● 100,000 - 249,999 ● 10,000 - 29,999
■ 1,000,000 - 1,999,999 ● 250,000 - 499,999 ● 30,000 - 99,999 ● Under 10,000

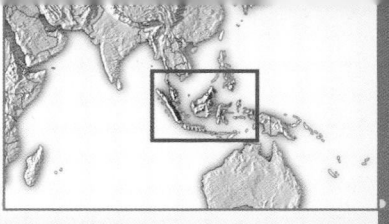

Scale 1:10,200,000   Lambert Conformal Conic Projection

© HAMMOND WORLD ATLAS CORPORATION   CD - 1047 - A-A

Population
- ■ Over 2,000,000
- ■ 1,000,000 - 1,999,999
- ⊙ 500,000 - 999,999
- ⊙ 250,000 - 499,999
- ⊙ 100,000 - 249,999
- ⊙ 30,000 - 99,999
- ⊙ 10,000 - 29,999
- ⊙ Under 10,000

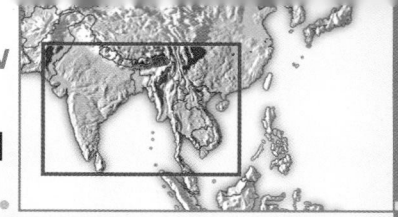
Scale 1:10,200,000   Lambert Conformal Conic Projection

MI | 100 | 200 | 300
KM | 100 | 200 | 300 | 400

© HAMMOND WORLD ATLAS CORPORATION   CM · AAA

Population

Over 2,000,000	500,000 - 999,999	100,000 - 249,999	10,000 - 29,999
1,000,000 - 1,999,999	250,000 - 499,999	30,000 - 99,999	Under 10,000

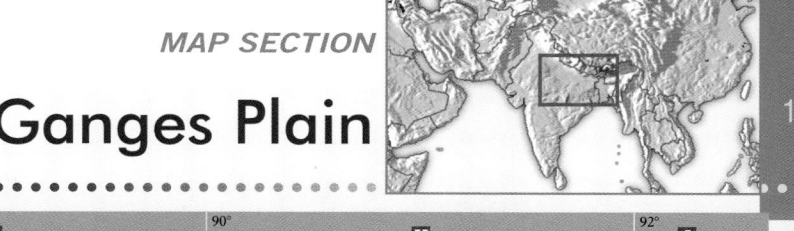

CHINA

XIZANG (TIBET) AUTONOMOUS REGION

Gangdisê Mts.

Himalaya Range

Mahābhārat Lekh

Siwalik Range

Brahmaputra (Yarlung Zangbo)

Lhasa · POTALA PALACE · SAMYE MONASTERY · YUMBU LHAKANG

Mt. Everest (Sagarmatha) 8,848 m

Kathmandu · Patan · Bhaktapur · SWAYAMBHUNATH

SAGARMATHA NAT'L PARK · LANGTANG NAT'L PARK

NEPAL · BĀGMATI · NĀRĀYANI · JANAKPUR · SAGARMATHA · MECHI · KOSI

SIKKIM · Gangtok · Darjiling · Kalimpong

BHUTAN · Thimphu · Paro · Punakha · Black Mtn. Ra.

ARUNĀCHAL PRADESH

WEST BENGAL · Siliguri · Jalpaiguri · Koch Bihār

ASSAM · Gauhāti · North Gauhāti · Barpeta

MEGHĀLAYA · Shillong · Khasi Hills

BIHĀR · Patna · Muzaffarpur · Darbhanga · Bhāgalpur · Munger · Gayā · Bodh Gaya

Ganges

Rājmahal Hills

JHARKHAND · Ranchi · Jamshedpur · Dhānbād · Bokaro Steel City · Hazāribag

WEST BENGAL · KOLKATA (Calcutta) · Howrah · Durgāpur · Asansol · Burdwān · Rājshāhi · English Bāzār

ORISSA

BANGLADESH · DHAKA (Dacca) · Tungi · Khulna · Barisāl · Mymensingh · Bogra · Rangpur · Pabna · Faridpur · Jessore

RĀJSHĀHI · DHĀKA · KHULNA

TRIPURA · Agartala

CHITTAGONG · Chittagong · S. Hātia I. · Sandwip Island

INDIA

Tropic of Cancer

Sundarbans

Mouths of the Ganges

Bay of Bengal

Hammond World Atlas Corporation

Scale 1:3,400,000 Lambert Conformal Conic Projection

MI 25 50 75 100
KM 25 50 75 100 125 150

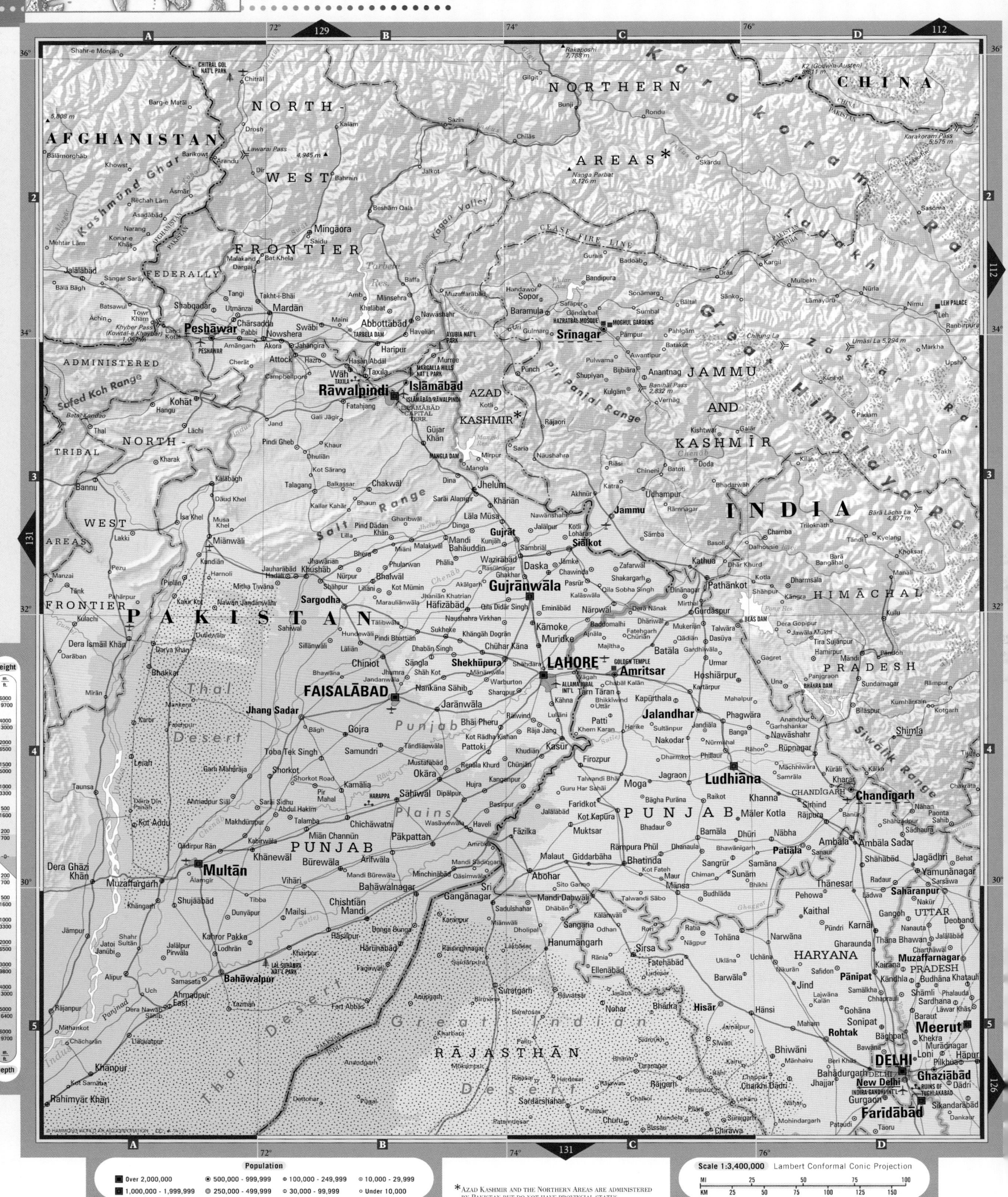

Population

■ Over 2,000,000	◉ 500,000 - 999,999	● 100,000 - 249,999	◉ 10,000 - 29,999
■ 1,000,000 - 1,999,999	◉ 250,000 - 499,999	◉ 30,000 - 99,999	○ Under 10,000

*AZAD KASHMIR AND THE NORTHERN AREAS ARE ADMINISTERED
BY PAKISTAN BUT DO NOT HAVE PROVINCIAL STATUS.

Scale 1:3,400,000 Lambert Conformal Conic Projection

MI	25		50		75		100
KM	25	50	75	100	125	150	

Central Asia

Population

- Over 2,000,000
- 1,000,000 - 1,999,999
- 500,000 - 999,999
- 250,000 - 499,999
- 100,000 - 249,999
- 30,000 - 99,999
- 10,000 - 29,999
- Under 10,000

Scale 1:10,200,000 Lambert Conformal Conic Projection

MI 100 200 300

KM 100 200 300 400

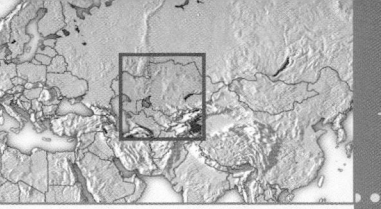

Southwestern Asia

132
143
139

Height

m.	ft.
6000	19700
4000	13000
2000	6500
1500	5000
1000	3300
500	1600
200	700
0	
200	700
500	1600
1000	3300
2000	6500
3000	9800
4000	13000
5000	16400
6000	19700

Depth

Population

- Over 2,000,000
- 1,000,000 - 1,999,999
- 500,000 - 999,999
- 250,000 - 499,999
- 100,000 - 249,999
- 30,000 - 99,999
- 10,000 - 29,999
- Under 10,000

*AZAD KASHMIR AND THE NORTHERN AREAS ARE ADMINISTER[ED] BY PAKISTAN BUT DO NOT HAVE PROVINCIAL STATUS.

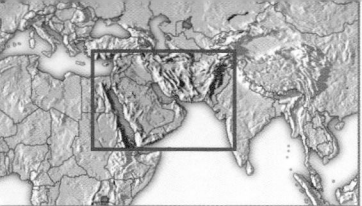

Scale 1:10,200,000   Lambert Conformal Conic Projection

© HAMMOND WORLD ATLAS CORPORATION

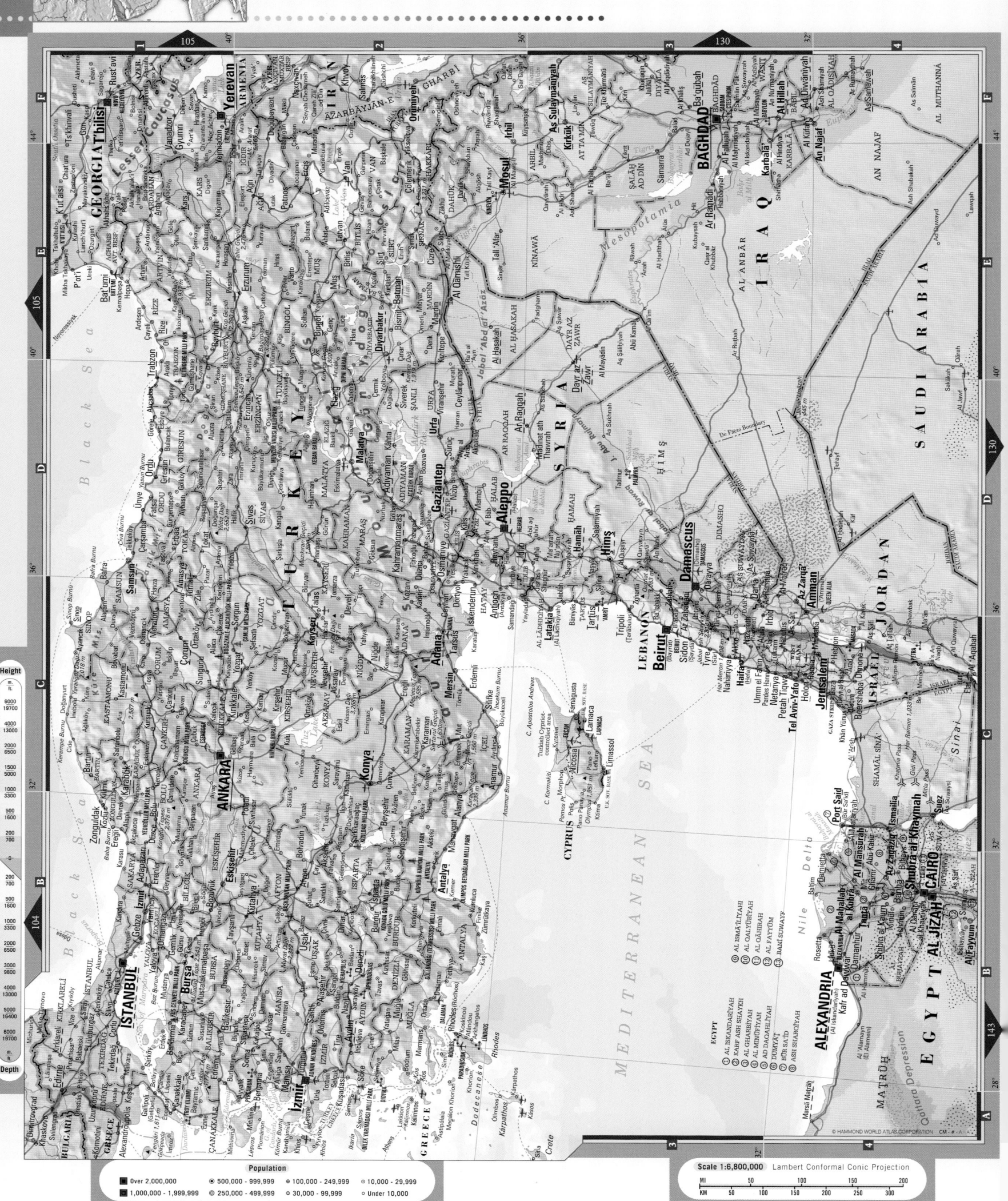

Height
m.
ft.
6000 19700
4000 13000
2000 6500
1500 5000
1000 3300
500 1600
200 700
0
200 700
1000 3300
2000 6500
3000 9800
4000 13000
5000 16400
6000 19700
m.
Depth

Population
■ Over 2,000,000
■ 1,000,000 - 1,999,999
⊛ 500,000 - 999,999
◉ 250,000 - 499,999
⊙ 100,000 - 249,999
◎ 30,000 - 99,999
○ 10,000 - 29,999
○ Under 10,000

Scale 1:6,800,000   Lambert Conformal Conic Projection
MI   50   100   150   200
KM 50 100 150 200 250 300

Eastern Mediterranean Region

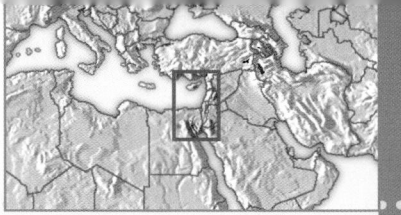

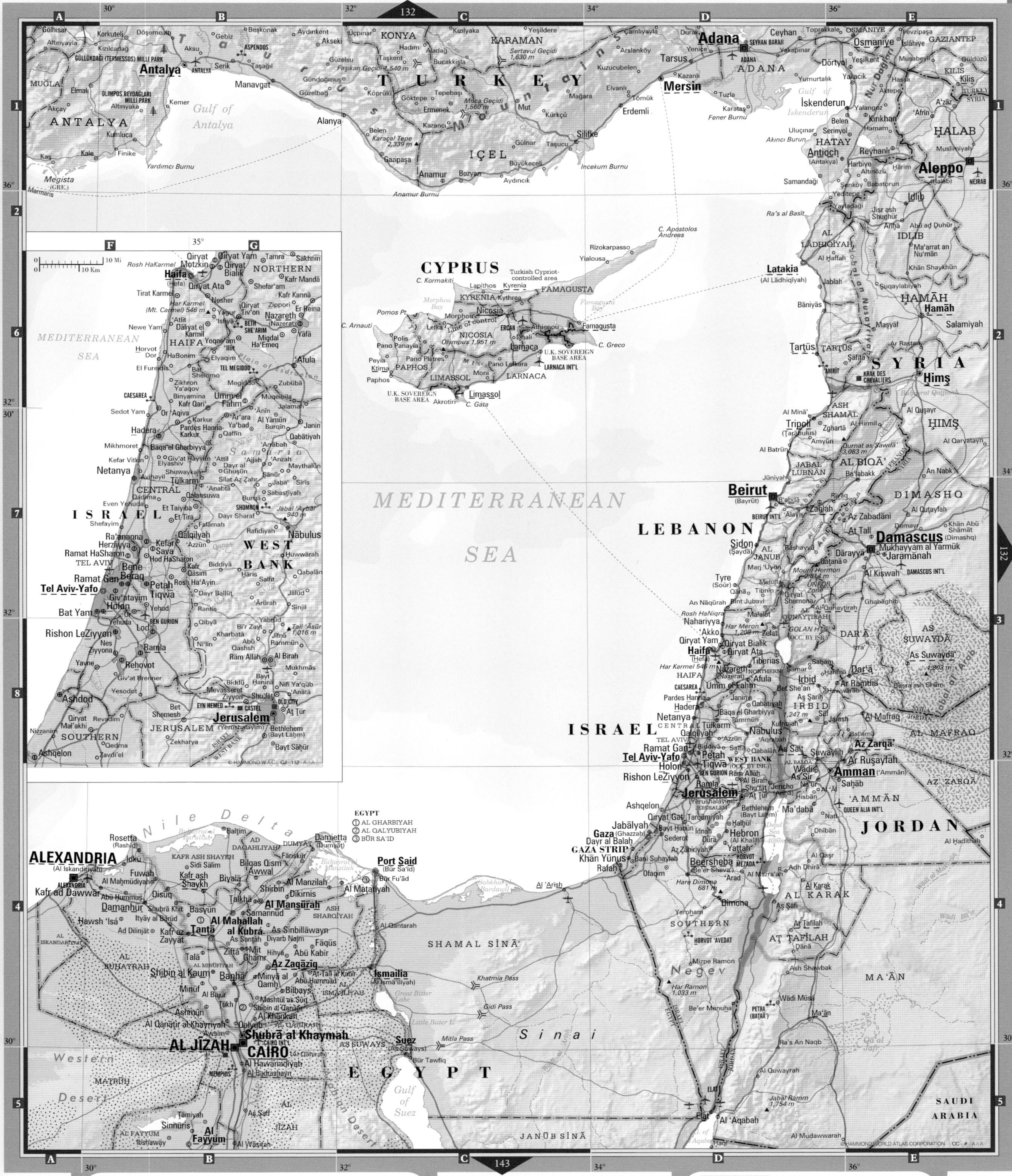

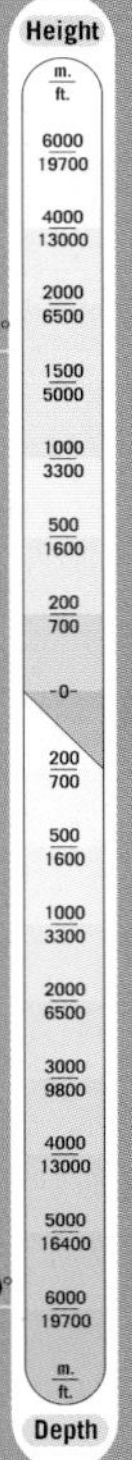

Population

■ Over 2,000,000   ◉ 500,000 - 999,999   ◎ 100,000 - 249,999   ⊙ 10,000 - 29,999
■ 1,000,000 - 1,999,999   ◉ 250,000 - 499,999   ⊙ 30,000 - 99,999   ○ Under 10,000

✳ WEST BANK AND GAZA STRIP ARE ISRAELI OCCUPIED WITH CURRENT
STATUS SUBJECT TO THE ISRAELI-PALESTINIAN INTERIM AGREEMENT
- PERMANENT STATUS TO BE DETERMINED

Scale 1:3,400,000   Lambert Conformal Conic Projection

MI   25   50   75   100
KM   25   50   75   100   125   150

Height
m.
ft.

6000
19700

4000
13000

2000
6500

1500
5000

1000
3300

500
1600

200
700

0

200
700

1000
3300

2000
6500

3000
9800

4000
13000

5000
16400

6000
19700
m.
ft.

Depth

EGYPT
① AL GHARBIYAH
② AL QALYUBIYAH
③ BŪR SA'ID

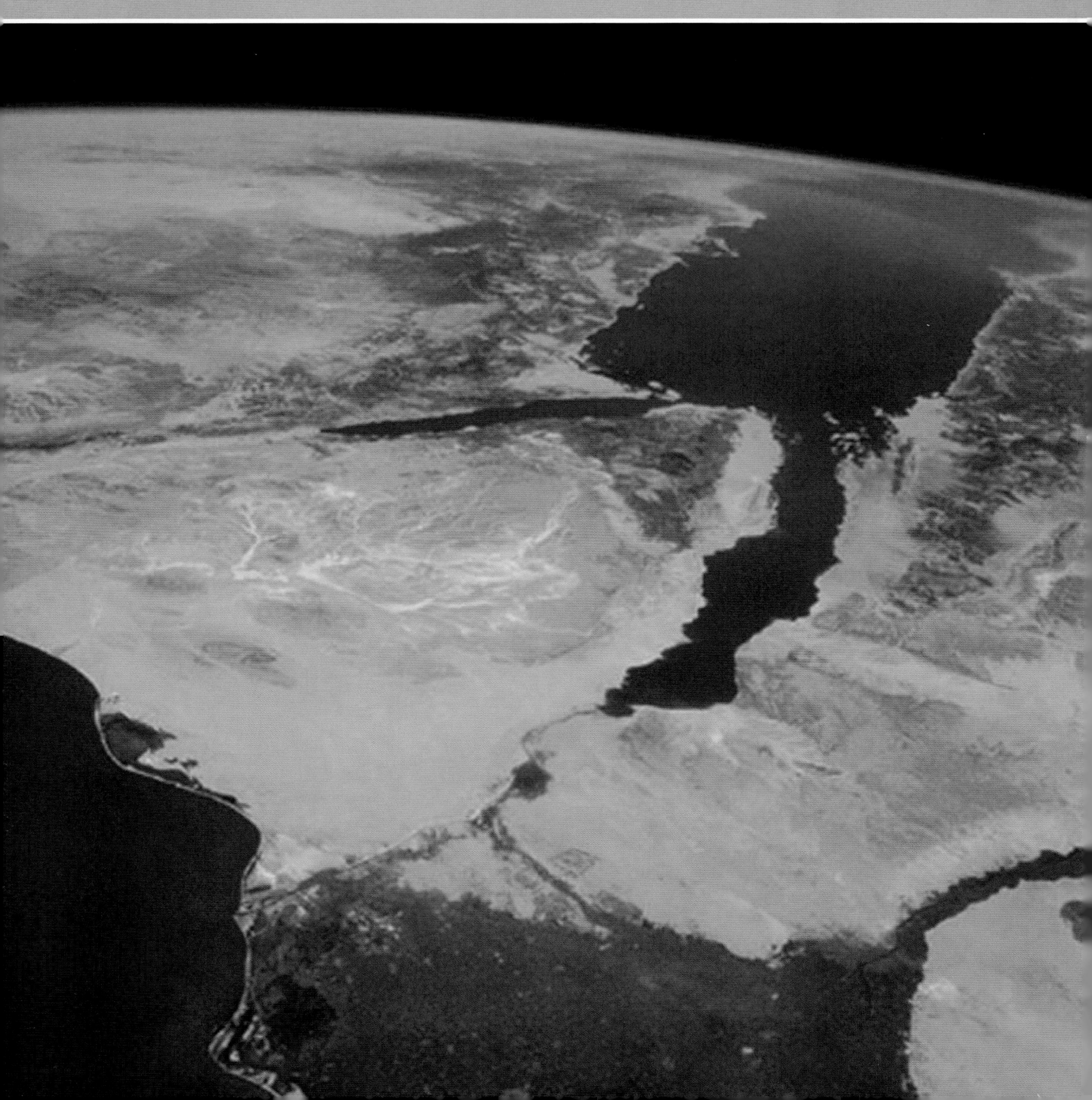

Several physiographic features are captured in this southeast-looking, high-oblique image. The Nile River Delta, the large, dark area at the bottom of the image, extends from the capital city of Cairo at the apex of the delta to the Suez Canal. The entire region is classified as desert (less than 10 inches [25 cm.] of rainfall per year). Desert-like areas are visible southwest of the delta and in the northwestern Sinai. Major rock outcrops (darker areas) are seen encircling the Red Sea. The two bodies of water flanking the southern end of the Sinai Peninsula are the Gulf of Suez and the Gulf of Aqaba.

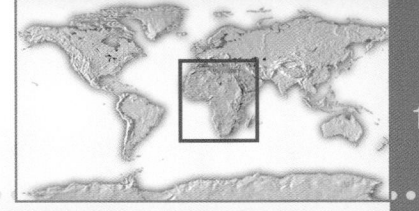

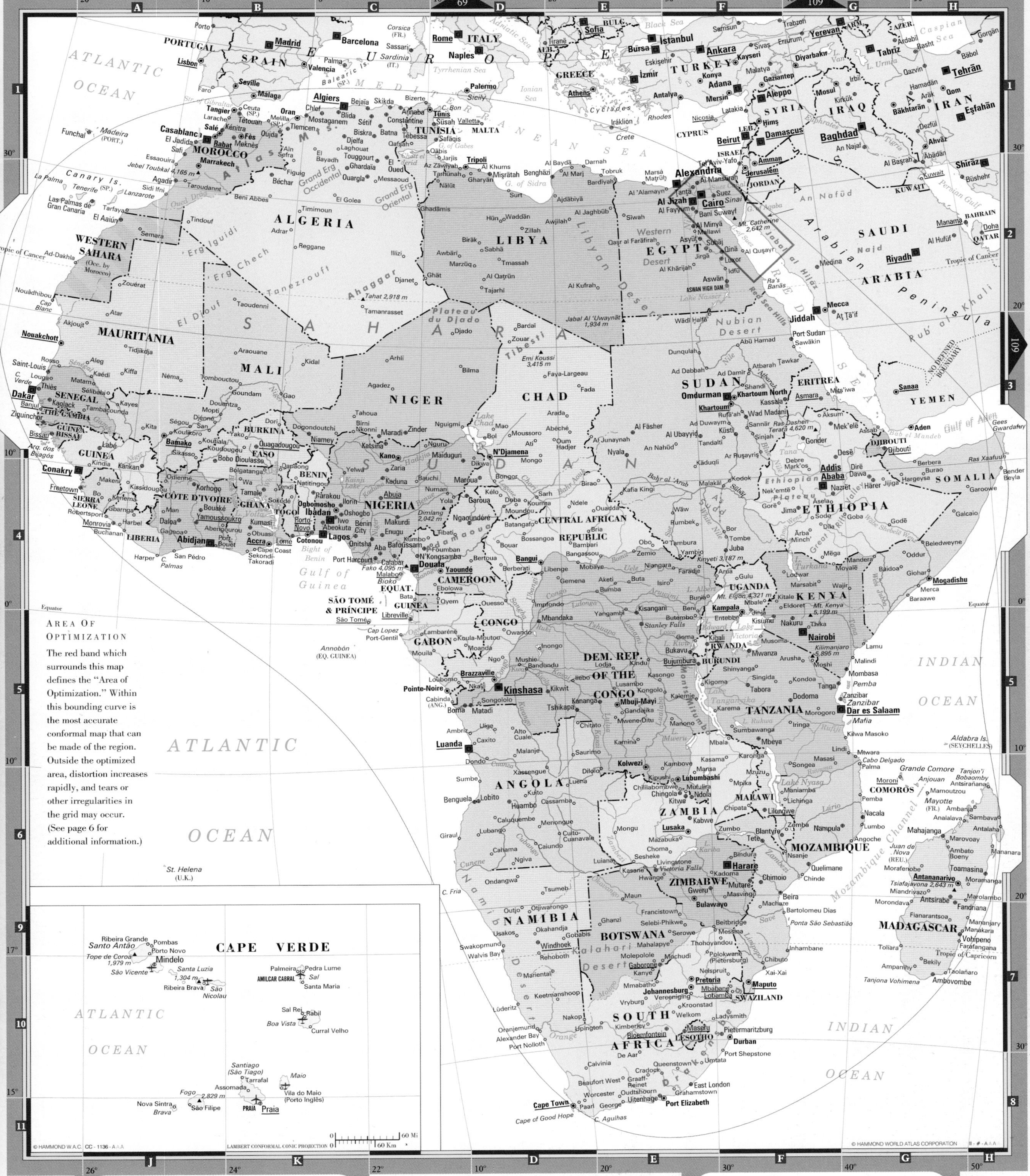

135

AREA OF OPTIMIZATION

The red band which surrounds this map defines the "Area of Optimization." Within this bounding curve is the most accurate conformal map that can be made of the region. Outside the optimized area, distortion increases rapidly, and tears or other irregularities in the grid may occur. (See page 6 for additional information.)

CAPE VERDE

Population

Symbol	Range
■ Over 3,000,000	● 500,000 - 999,999
■ 1,000,000 - 2,999,999	● 100,000 - 499,999
○ Under 100,000	

Scale 1:34,100,000   Hammond Optimal Conformal

MI   250   500   750   1000
KM 250 500 750 1000 1250 1500

0   60 Mi
0   160 Km

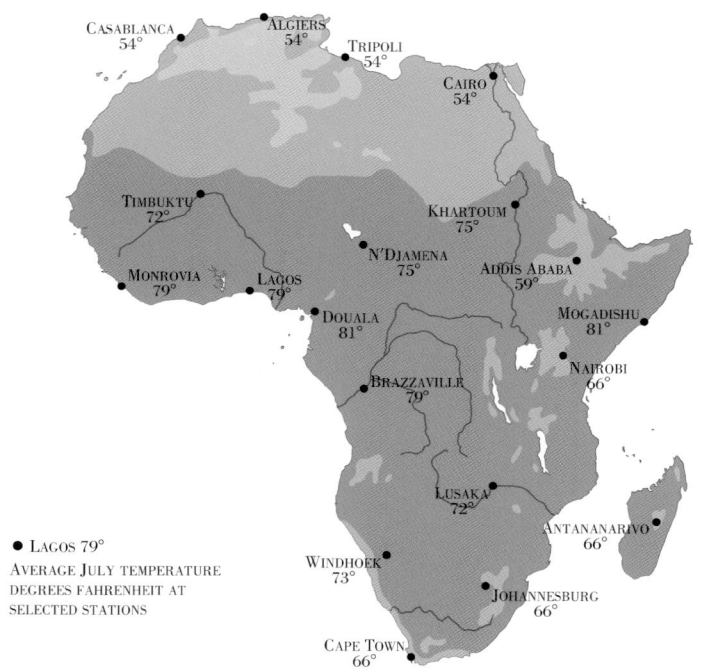

● Lagos 79°
AVERAGE JULY TEMPERATURE
DEGREES FAHRENHEIT AT
SELECTED STATIONS

AVERAGE JANUARY TEMPERATURE

FAHRENHEIT	CELSIUS		FAHRENHEIT	CELSIUS
OVER 68°	OVER 20°		32° TO 50°	0° TO 10°
50° TO 68°	10° TO 20°		UNDER 32°	UNDER 0°

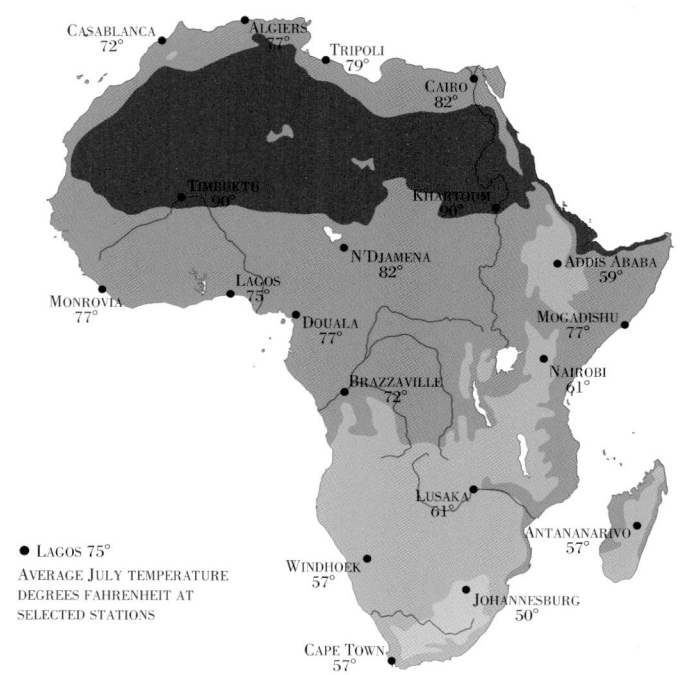

● Lagos 75°
AVERAGE JULY TEMPERATURE
DEGREES FAHRENHEIT AT
SELECTED STATIONS

AVERAGE JULY TEMPERATURE

FAHRENHEIT	CELSIUS		FAHRENHEIT	CELSIUS
OVER 86°	OVER 30°		50° TO 68°	10° TO 20°
68° TO 86°	20° TO 30°		UNDER 50°	UNDER 10°

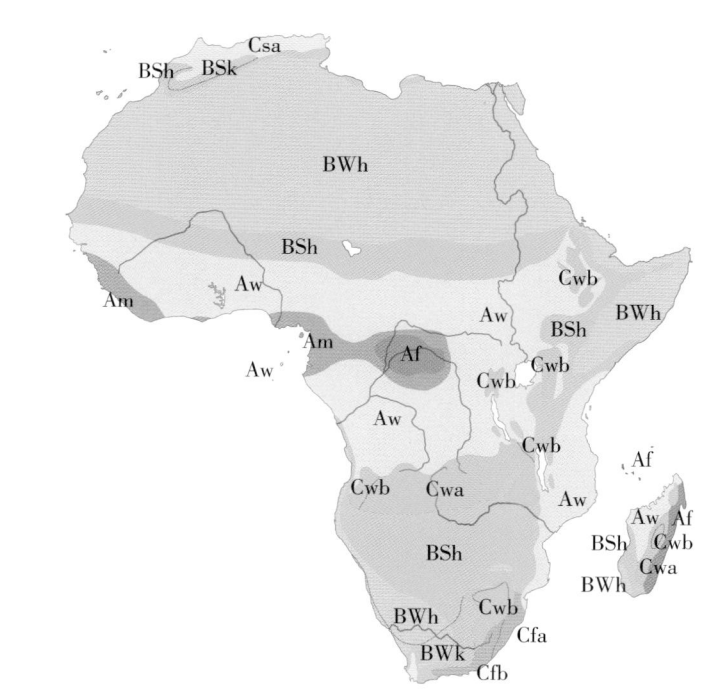

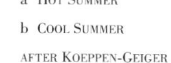

CLIMATE

HUMID TROPICAL
Af   NO DRY SEASON
Am   SHORT DRY SEASON
Aw   DRY WINTER

DRY
BS   SEMIARID   ⎱h HOT
BW   ARID   ⎰k COLD

HUMID WARM
Cf   NO DRY SEASON
Cw   DRY WINTER
Cs   DRY SUMMER

a   HOT SUMMER
b   COOL SUMMER

AFTER KOEPPEN-GEIGER

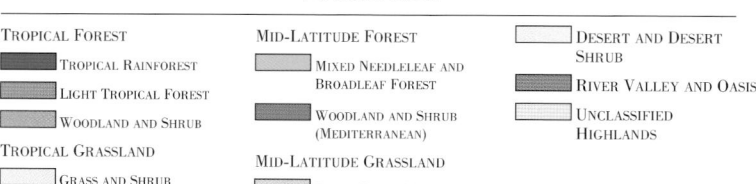

VEGETATION

TROPICAL FOREST
TROPICAL RAINFOREST
LIGHT TROPICAL FOREST
WOODLAND AND SHRUB

TROPICAL GRASSLAND
GRASS AND SHRUB (SAVANNA)
WOODED SAVANNA

MID-LATITUDE FOREST
MIXED NEEDLELEAF AND BROADLEAF FOREST
WOODLAND AND SHRUB (MEDITERRANEAN)

MID-LATITUDE GRASSLAND
SHORT GRASS (STEPPE)

DESERT AND DESERT SHRUB
RIVER VALLEY AND OASIS
UNCLASSIFIED HIGHLANDS

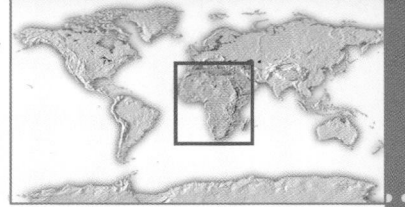
Africa - Geographical Comparisons

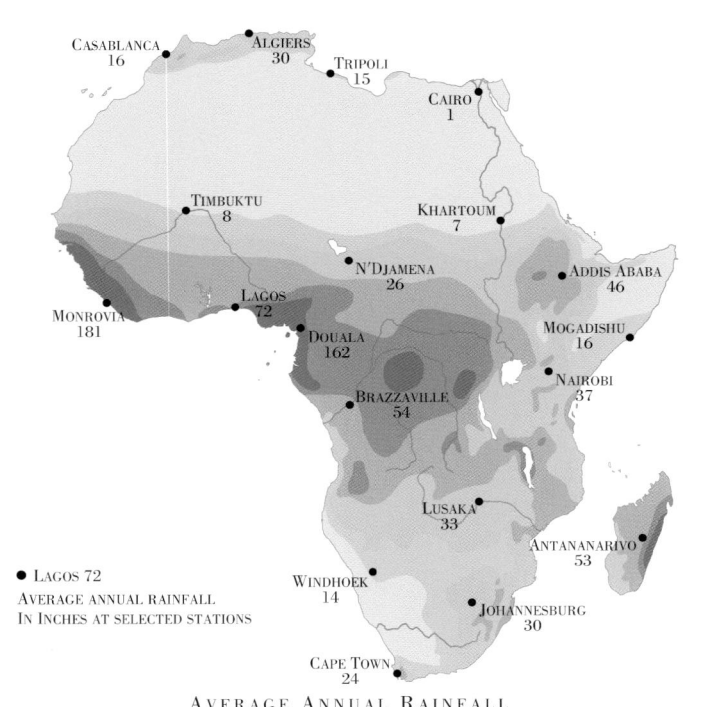

CASABLANCA
16
ALGIERS
30
TRIPOLI
15
CAIRO
1
TIMBUKTU
8
KHARTOUM
7
N'DJAMENA
26
ADDIS ABABA
46
LAGOS
72
MONROVIA
181
DOUALA
162
MOGADISHU
16
NAIROBI
37
BRAZZAVILLE
54
LUSAKA
33
ANTANANARIVO
53
WINDHOEK
14
JOHANNESBURG
30
CAPE TOWN
24

● LAGOS 72
AVERAGE ANNUAL RAINFALL
IN INCHES AT SELECTED STATIONS

AVERAGE ANNUAL RAINFALL

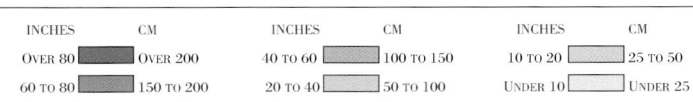

INCHES	CM	INCHES	CM	INCHES	CM
OVER 80	OVER 200	40 TO 60	100 TO 150	10 TO 20	25 TO 50
60 TO 80	150 TO 200	20 TO 40	50 TO 100	UNDER 10	UNDER 25

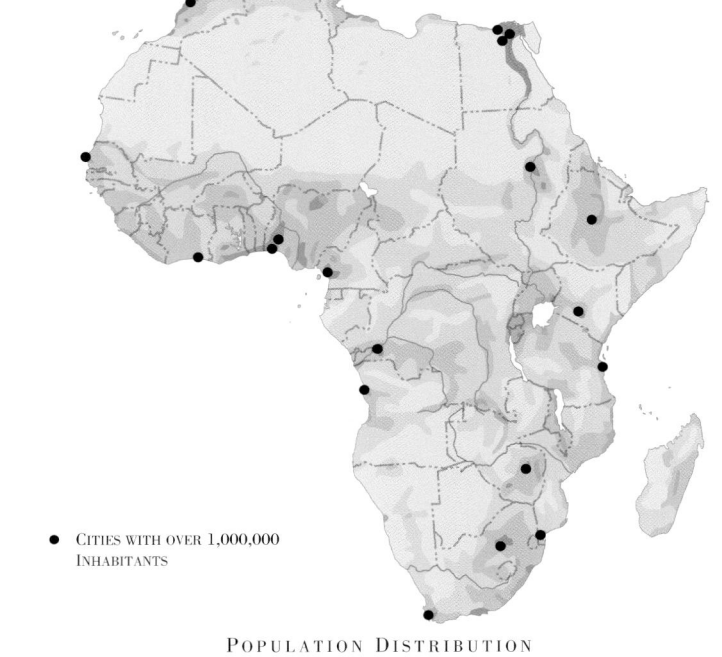

● CITIES WITH OVER 1,000,000
INHABITANTS

POPULATION DISTRIBUTION

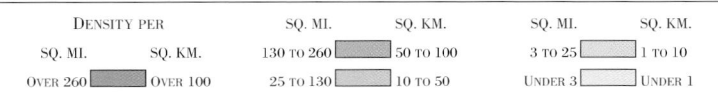

DENSITY PER		SQ. MI.	SQ. KM.	SQ. MI.	SQ. KM.
SQ. MI.	SQ. KM.	130 TO 260	50 TO 100	3 TO 25	1 TO 10
OVER 260	OVER 100	25 TO 130	10 TO 50	UNDER 3	UNDER 1

SHEEP
FRUIT
WINE
CORN
COTTON
DATES
PEANUTS
CATTLE
CATTLE
COTTON
CATTLE
PEANUTS
HOGS
COFFEE
COFFEE
COCOA
COCOA
PALM OIL
SHEEP
SHEEP
COCOA
BANANAS
COFFEE
PALM
OIL
CATTLE
SISAL
COFFEE
CORN
TOBACCO COPRA
SHEEP
CORN
CATTLE
SHEEP
SHEEP

LAND USE

	CEREALS, LIVESTOCK		SPECIAL CROPS		FORESTS
	LIVESTOCK RANCHING & HERDING		DIVERSIFIED TROPICAL & SUBTROPICAL CROPS		NONPRODUCTIVE
	CASH CROPS, MIXED FARMING				

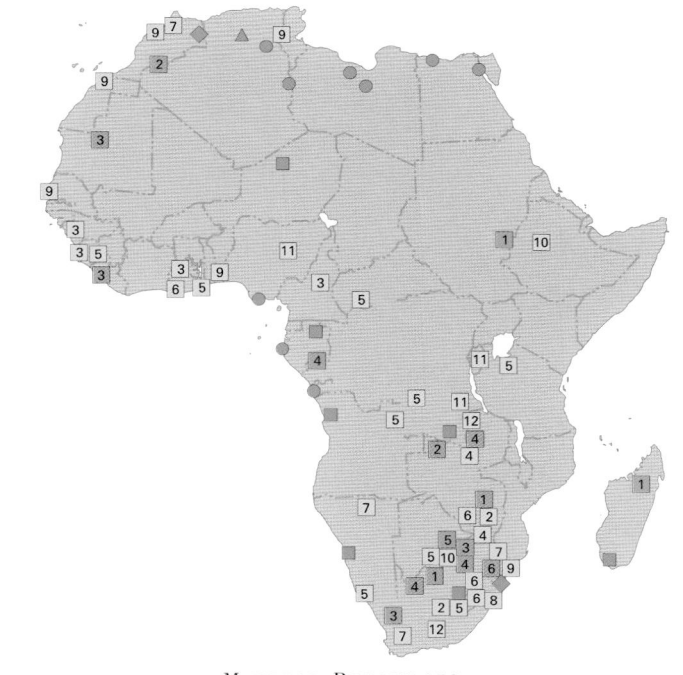

MINERAL RESOURCES

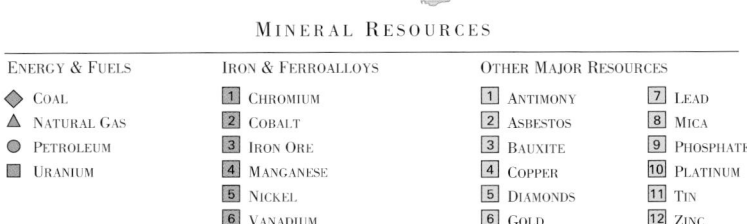

ENERGY & FUELS	IRON & FERROALLOYS	OTHER MAJOR RESOURCES	
◆ COAL	1 CHROMIUM	1 ANTIMONY	7 LEAD
▲ NATURAL GAS	2 COBALT	2 ASBESTOS	8 MICA
● PETROLEUM	3 IRON ORE	3 BAUXITE	9 PHOSPHATES
■ URANIUM	4 MANGANESE	4 COPPER	10 PLATINUM
	5 NICKEL	5 DIAMONDS	11 TIN
	6 VANADIUM	6 GOLD	12 ZINC

Height
m.
ft.

6000
19700

4000
13000

2000
6500

1500
5000

500
1600

200
700

-0-

200
700

500
1600

1000
3300

2000
6500

3000
9800

5000
16400

6000
19700
m.
ft.

Depth

Population
■ Over 2,000,000   ● 500,000 - 999,999   ◎ 50,000 - 99,999
▣ 1,000,000 - 1,999,999   ● 100,000 - 499,999   ○ Under 50,000

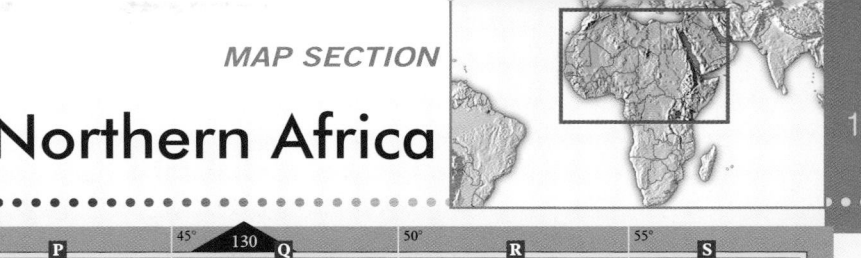

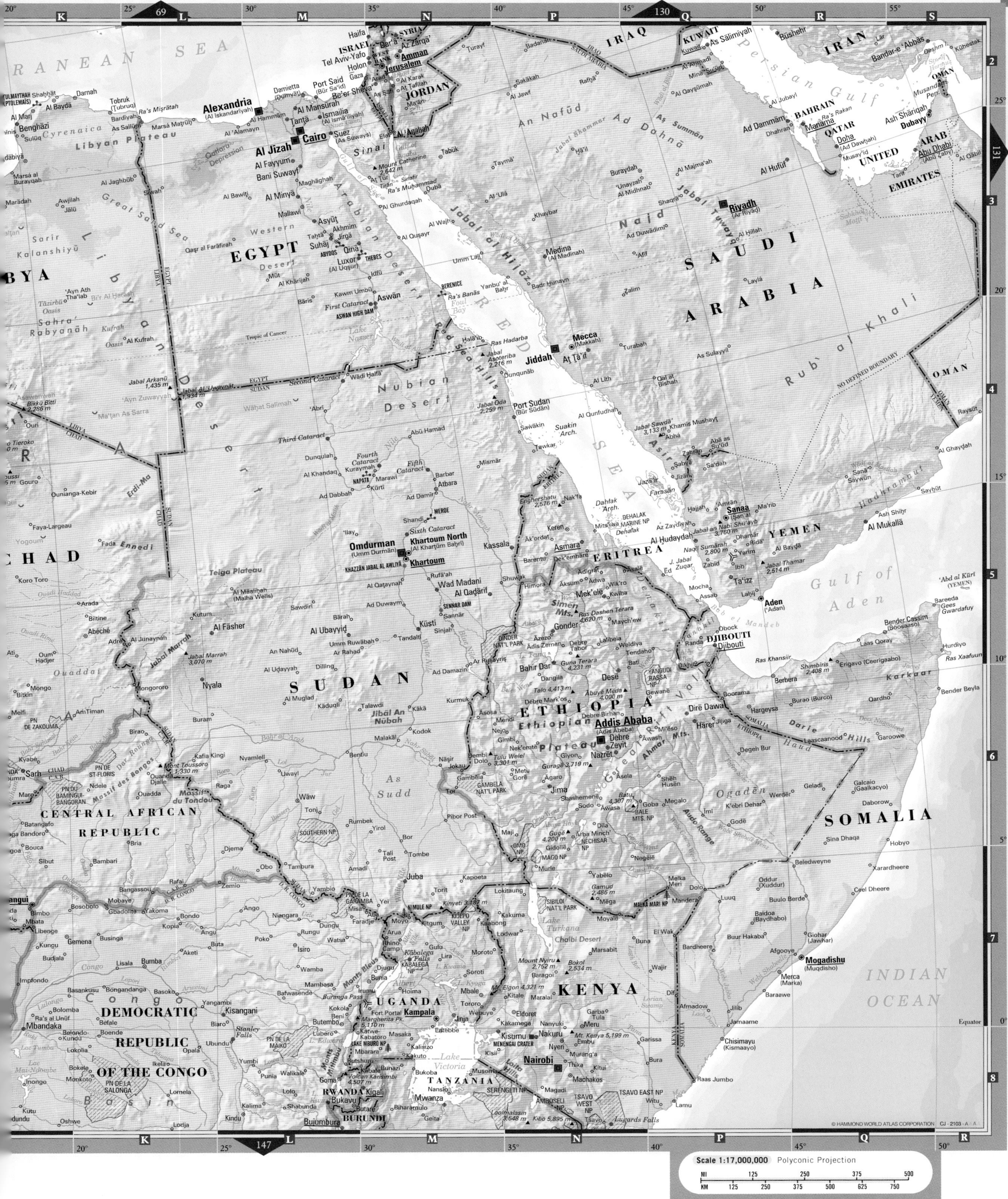

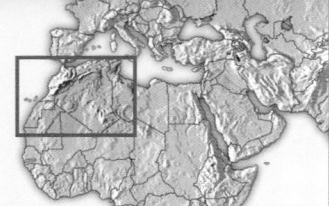

86

MOROCCO is divided into 7 non-administrative regions shown here. Scale does not permit showing the boundaries and names of Morocco's provinces and prefectures.

SPAIN
Cádiz
Chiclana de la Frontera
Barbate de Franco
Algeciras
Chefchaouene
Mijas
Marbella
La Línea de la Concepción
Gibraltar (U.K.)
Punta Almina
Ceuta (SP.)
Cap Spartel
TANGIER (IBN BATOUTA)
Tangier (Tanger)
Tétouan
Asilah
Larache
Al Hoceima
Ksar el Kebir
Souk el Arba du Rharb
Ouezzane
Kenitra
Salé
RABAT (SALE)
Sidi Kacem
Rabat
Sidi Slimane
CASABLANCA (Dar-el-Beida)
CASABLANCA (MOHAMMED V)
Mohammedia
Meknes
Fès
FEZ (SASS)
El Jadida
Azemmour
Berrechid
Benahmed
Settat
Khouribga
Oualidia
Cap Safi
El Had Harrara
Sidi Bennour
Boulaouane
Oued Zem
Khenifra
Safi
Jemaa Shim
Youssoufia
El Borouj
Boujad
CENTRE
Kasba Tadla
Beni Mellal
Midelt
Benguerir
Chemaia
El Kelaa des Srarhna
Essaouira
MOROCCO
Cap Sim
Ounara
Chichaoua
Marrakech
MARRAKECH (MENARA)
TENSIFT
Tahannout
Tamanar
Imi n'Tanout
Idelt 3.615 m
Ait Ourir
CENTRE-SUD
Er Rachidia
Erfoud
Goulmima
Tinerhir
Ouarzazate
Agadir
AGADIR (AL MASSIRA)
Taroudannt
Inezgane
Oulad Teima
Biougra
Irherm n'Ougdal
Tazenakht
ATLANTIC OCEAN

Madeira Is. (PORT.)
Porto Santo
Vila de Porto Santo
Porto Moniz
Santana
Machico
Calheta
FUNCHAL
Ribeira Brava
Ilhas Desertas
Madeira

Ilhas Selvagens (PORT.)

Canary Islands (SPAIN)
La Palma
PN LA CALDERA DE TABURIENTE
Santa Cruz de la Palma
Lanzarote
PN DE TIMANFAYA
Arrecife
LANZAROTE
Los Llanos de Aridane
Tenerife
Santa Cruz de Tenerife
La Laguna
La Orotava
Icod de los Vinos
NORTE LOS RODEOS
Puerto de la Cruz
Pico de Teide 3,718 m
PN DEL TEIDE
Antigua
Fuerteventura
Puerto del Rosario
Vallehermoso
PN DE GARAJONAY
Gomera
Arucas
Las Palmas de Gran Canaria
Granadilla SUR REINA SOFIA
Santa Lucía
Telde
Valverde
Hierro
Ingenio
GRAN CANARIA
San Bartolomé de Tirajana
Gran Canaria

Tiznit
Tafraout
Sidi Ifni
Bou Izakarn
Foum el Hassane
Guelmim
Assa
Akka
Tata
Cap Drâa
Tan-Tan
Tarfaya
Cap Juby
Oued Drâa
Jebel Ouarkziz
Hamada du Drâa
TINDOUF
Tindouf
55 m
Daora
Hagunia
El Aaiún (HASSANA)
El Aaiún
Edchera
Hasi el Farsia
Semara
Lemsid
Cabo Bojador
Bu Craa
Tifariti
Aïn Ben Tili

WESTERN SAHARA (Occupied by Morocco)
Aaglet Yeraifa
Bir Aidiat
Guelta Zemmur
Bir Moghrein
Bir Bel Guerdâne
Sebkhet Iguetti
ALGERIA MAURITANIA
El Eglab
Yetti
Erg Iguidi
El Hank

Ad Dakhla
Punta Durnford
Tropic of Cancer
El Aargub
Fuch
Aaglet Tennuaca
TIRIS ZEMMOUR
Sebkhet Oumm ed Drous Telli
Zemmel Lksat
Koret
Bir Zreig
366 m
Fderik
Zouérat
915 m
MAURITANIA
El Khatt
El Khat
El Mzereb
Erg Chech
Erg el Ahmor
Erg Iguidi

Cabo Barbas
Aguenit
Teoujli
Tichla
Zug
Galb Azefal
Guelb er Richât 519 m

NOUÂDHIBOU
Nouâdhibou
Cansado
Guera
Cabo Blanco
Levrier
DAKHLET NOUÂDHIBOU
INCHIRI
PARC NATIONAL DU BANC D'ARGUIN
Cap d'Arguin
Bou Lanuar
Chinguetti
Atar
ADRAR
TOMBOUCT
Hamada Safia
Erg Ijil
HODH ECH CHARGUI
El Djouf
MAL
Erg Aouana

144

Height
m.
ft.
6000 19700
4000 13000
2000 6500
1500 5000
1000 3300
500 1600
200 700
0
200 700
500 1600
1000 3300
2000 6500
4000 13000
5000 16400
6000 19700
m.
ft.
Depth

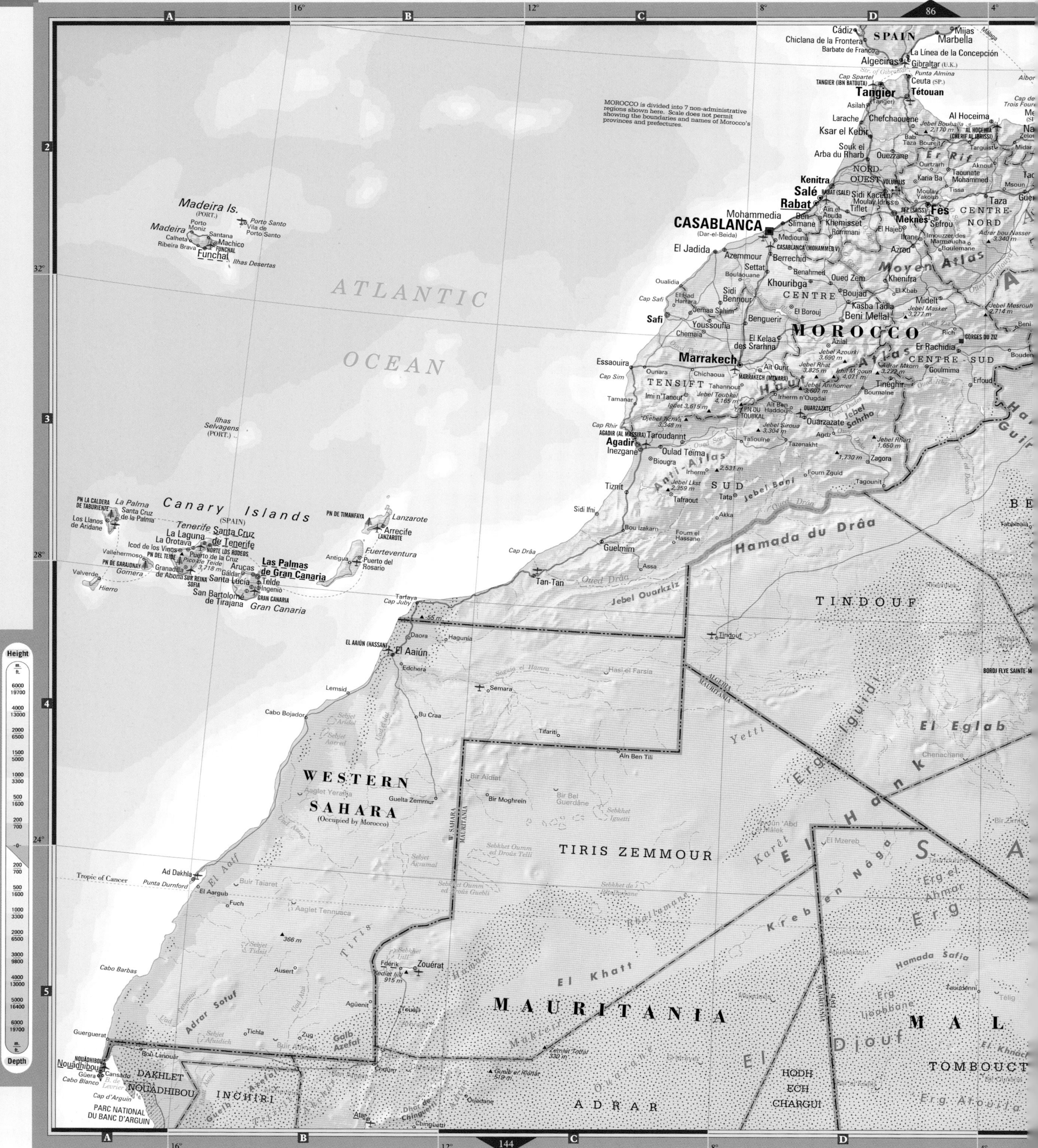

Population
- Over 2,000,000
- 1,000,000 - 1,999,999
- 500,000 - 999,999
- 250,000 - 499,999
- 100,000 - 249,999
- 30,000 - 99,999
- 10,000 - 29,999
- Under 10,000

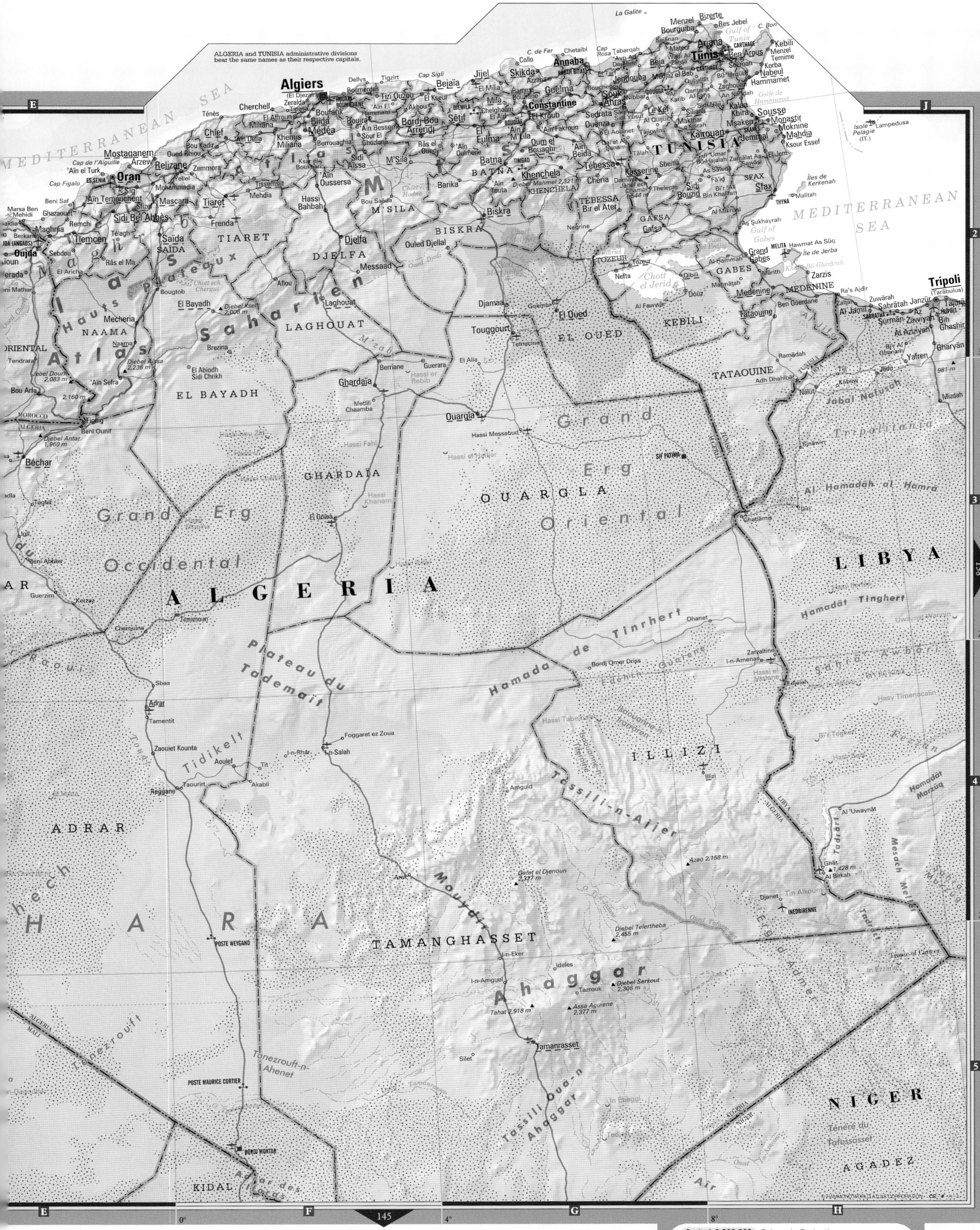

ALGERIA and TUNISIA administrative divisions bear the same names as their respective capitals.

MEDITERRANEAN SEA

Algiers (El Djezaïr)

Oran

Oujda

Tunis

Tripoli (Tarābulus)

Constantine

Annaba

Mostaganem

Arzew

Relizane

Chlef

Cherchell

Ténès

Tlemcen

Sidi Bel Abbès

Mascara

Tiaret

Saïda

SAÏDA

TIARET

DJELFA

Djelfa

Laghouat

LAGHOUAT

El Bayadh

EL BAYADH

NAAMA

Béchar

ADRAR

Adrar

Reggane

In-Salah

Aoulef

GHARDAÏA

Ghardaïa

Ouargla

OUARGLA

EL OUED

El Oued

Touggourt

Biskra

BISKRA

BATNA

Khenchela

KHENCHELA

TEBESSA

Tébessa

GAFSA

Gafsa

SFAX

Sfax

GABES

Gabès

Grand Erg Oriental

Grand Erg Occidental

Plateau du Tademaït

Hamada de Tinrhert

ALGERIA

LIBYA

TUNISIA

Hauts Plateaux

Atlas Saharien

Tamanrasset

TAMANGHASSET

Ahaggar

Tahat 2,918 m

ILLIZI

Djanet

Tassili-n-Ajjer

SAHARA

NIGER

AGADEZ

KIDAL

Bordj Moktar

Poste Maurice Cortier

Poste Weygand

Tropic of Cancer

MEDITERRANEAN SEA

Scale 1:6,800,000   Polyconic Projection

MI 50 100 150 200
KM 50 100 150 200 250 300

MAP SECTION
Northern Morocco, Algeria, Tunisia

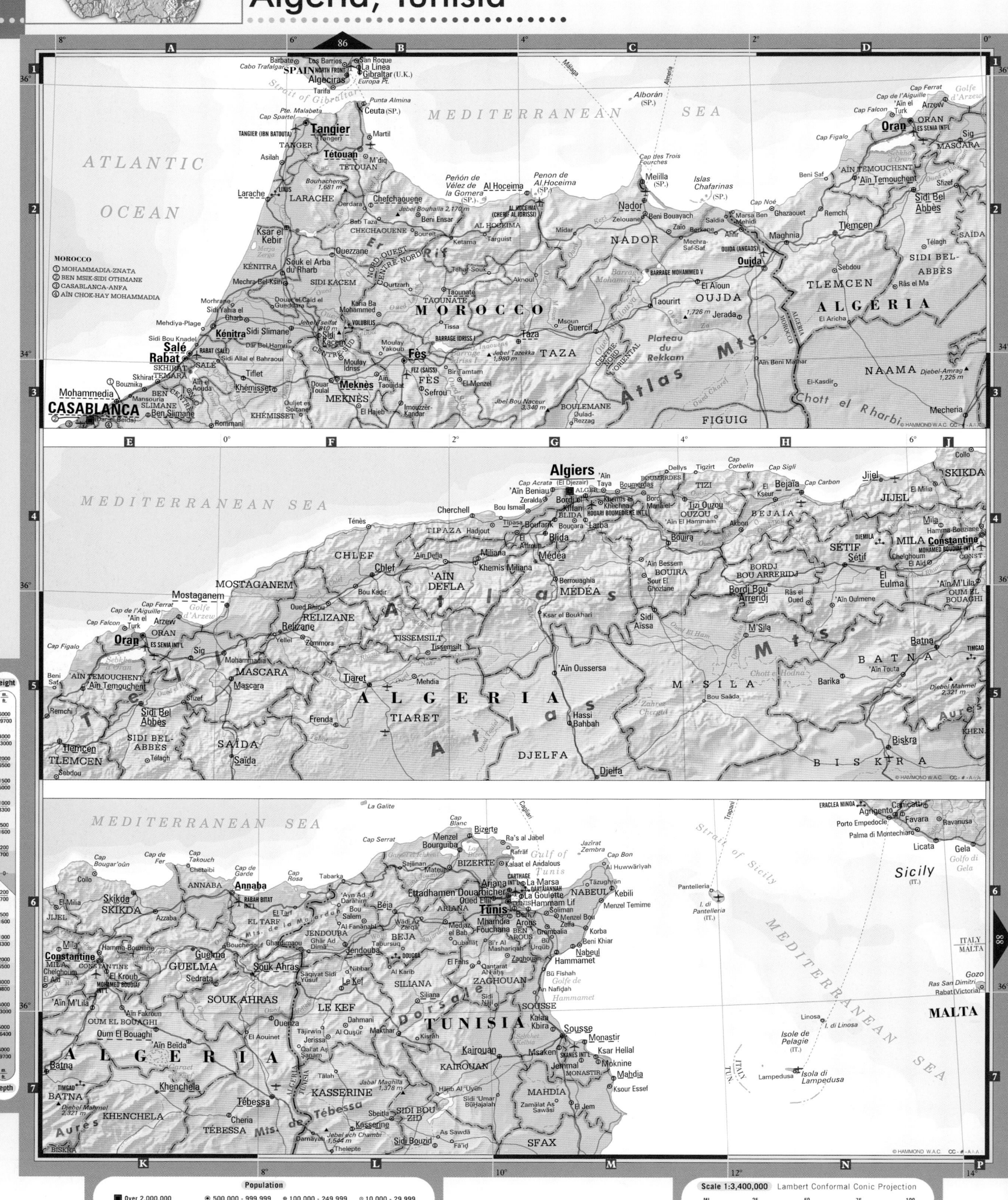

Northeastern Africa

EGYPT

1. AL ISKANDARĪYAH
2. KAFR ASH SHAYKH
3. AL GHARBĪYAH
4. AL MINŪFĪYAH
5. AD DAQAHLĪYAH
6. DUMYĀṬ
7. BŪR SAʻĪD
8. ASH SHARQĪYAH
9. AL ISMĀʻĪLĪYAH
10. AL QALYŪBĪYAH
11. AL QĀHIRAH
12. AL FAYYŪM
13. BANĪ SUWAYF

Height / Depth

m.	ft.
6000	19700
4000	13000
2000	6500
1500	5000
1000	3300
500	1600
200	700
0	
200	700
500	1600
1000	3300
2000	6500
3000	9800
4000	13000
5000	16400
6000	19700

Population

- Over 2,000,000
- 1,000,000 - 1,999,999
- 500,000 - 999,999
- 250,000 - 499,999
- 100,000 - 249,999
- 30,000 - 99,999
- 10,000 - 29,999
- Under 10,000

Scale 1:6,800,000 Polyconic Projection

MI 50 100 150 200
KM 50 100 150 200 250 300

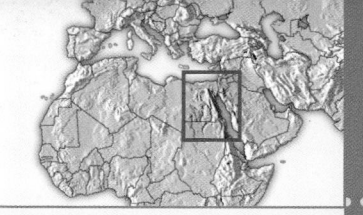

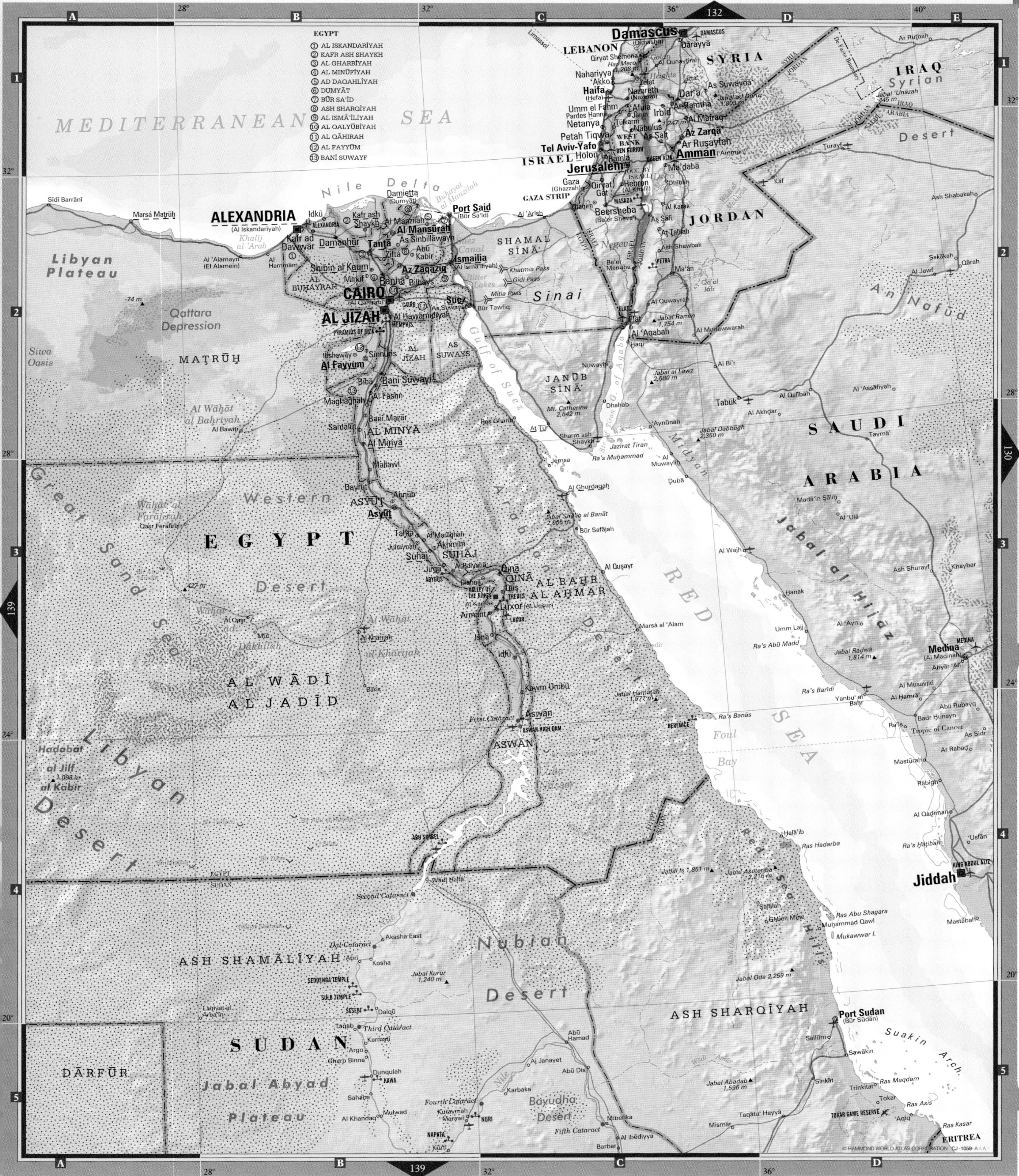

A 16° B 12° 138 C 8° D 4°

1

20°

B. d'Arguin

DAKHLET
NOUÂDHIBOU
Cap Iouik Iouik
Île Tidra
PN DU
BANC
D'ARGUIN
Cap Timiris
Nouâmghâr

INCHIRI

Akjoujt

Benichab

Tiffit

Akchâr

Adra de Chinguetti

Ouljet

Adrar

ADRAR

El Djouf

EL Mreyyé

TOMBOUCTOU

S A

2

Nouakchott

NOUAKCHOTT
Ouad Nâga

TRARZA

Tamassoumit

Tidjikdja

TAGANT

Lekhcheb

Tichit

Arhrijit

HODH
ECH
CHARGUI

Aklé Aouâna

Irigui

Arabune

Tombo
Bintagourou

16°

Saint-
Louis

Keur Massène
Rosso Tékane
Richard Toll
Dagana
Ndiago
Saint-Louis

BRAKNA

Médendra
Bogué
Bababé
Mbagne

Aleg
Magta Lahjar
M'Bagne
M'bout

Barkéwol el Abiod
Guérou
Kiffa
Bilajmick

ASSABA

Kankossa

Ayoûn el Arroûs

HODH EL
GHARBI

Tintane

Agert

Timbédra

Djigueni

Oualâta

AOUDAGHAST
Tamchakket

Hodh

Oujel
Néma

Oualâta

Néma

Koumbi Saleh

Adel Bagrou

Fassala-Néré

Niaouné
Goundam
Dire

4

SENEGAL

Dakar

DAKAR (YOFF)
Rufisque
THIÈS
M'Bour

KAOLACK

Kaolack
Fatick
FATICK

THE GAMBIA

Banjul
BANJUL

ZIGUINCHOR

Ziguinchor

GUINEA-
BISSAU

Bissau
BISSAU (BIPOINT)

Arq. dos
Bijagós

SAINT-
LOUIS

Louga
LOUGA

Linguère

Dahra

Ranérou

Namari

Matam

Kaédi
GORGOL
Sivé
Maghama

Ould Yenjé

GUIDIMAKA

Sélibabi

Hamoud

Touil

Kobenni

Yélimané

Nioro du
Sahel
Balé

Nara

Goumbou

Nampala

Boré

Sokolo

KAYES

Kayes
Lonétou

584 m

KAYES

Lakamané

Diéma

Niono

Ténenkou

Ké Macina

Macino

Mopti
MOPTI

Djénné

Sanando

Bankass

MOPTI

S

TAMBACOUNDA

Tambacounda

KOLDA

Kolda

SEGOU

Ségou
SEGOU

Sansanding

Markala

Banamba

KOULIKORO

Koulikoro
Kati
BAMAKO (SÉNOU)
Bamako

RESERVE DE
KENIEBAOULE

PN DE LA
BOUCLE DU
BAOULE

Didiéni

Kolokani

Nara

Fana

Dioïla

FORÊT CLASSÉE
DE FINA

Yanfolila
SIKASSO

Sikasso
SIKASSO
765 m

KENE-
DOUGOU

Bobo Dioulasso
HOUE

MOUHOUN

KOSSI

GUINEA

Conakry
CONAKRY

Boké

Fria

Kindia

Labé

Mamou

Dalaba

Fouta
Diallon

Dabola

Kouroussa

Kankan
KANKAN

Siguiri

Bougouni

SIKASSO

Niger

708 m

1,119 m

Faranah

KOMOÉ

Banfora

SIERRA
LEONE

FREETOWN (LUNGI INT'L)
Freetown
WESTERN
AREA
Banana Is.

Makeni
NORTHERN
Bumbuna

Loma
Mts.
1,948 m

Sankanbiriwa
1,863 m Tingi
Mts.

Kissidougou

Macenta
1,257 m

Beyla

Kouroussa

Kerouané

Korhogo
KORHOGO

Odienné

Ferkéssédougou

Boundiali

PARC NATIONAL
DE LA
KOMOÉ

8°

SOUTHERN

EASTERN
Kenema
Bo
BO

Pujehun

Zimmi

Nzérékoré
Mt. Nimba
1,752 m

Man
Mont Tonkoui
1,189 m

Danané

Touba

Séguéla

Bouaké
BOUAKÉ

CÔTE D'IVOIRE

5

ATLANTIC

OCEAN

MONTSERRADO

Monrovia
MONROVIA (ROBERTS INT'L)

GRAND
CAPE MOUNT

GRAND
BASSA

Buchanan

GRAND
GEDEH

SINOE

Greenville

MARYLAND

Harper
C. Palmas

LIBERIA

BONG

NIMBA

LOFA

Yamoussoukro
YAMOUSSOUKRO

Daloa
DALOA

Gagnoa

Divo

Abidjan
ABIDJAN
PORT BOUET
(PORT BOUET)

Grain Coast

Ivory Coast

A 16° B 12° C

Height

ft.
6000 19700
4000 13000
2000 6500
1500 5000
1000 3300
500 1600
200 700
-0-
200 700
500 1600
1000 3300
2000 6500
3000 9800
4000 13000
5000 16400
6000 19700

Depth

Population

■ Over 2,000,000
◉ 500,000 - 999,999
● 100,000 - 249,999
○ 10,000 - 29,999
■ 1,000,000 - 1,999,999
◉ 250,000 - 499,999
● 30,000 - 99,999
· Under 10,000

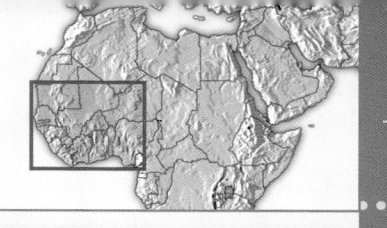
138

ALGERIA

Adrar des Iforas

KIDAL

ADRAR

TAMANGHASSET

Erg I-n-Sakane

Ténéré

Mont Gréboun 1,944 m

Aïr

Mont Tamgak 1,988 m

AGADEZ

Iferouâne

Talak

Erg de Ténéré

Monts Bagzane 2,022 m

S A H A R A

Azaouad

MALI

GAO

Gao

Falaise de Tiguidit

Agadez

NIGER

TAHOUA

ZINDER

Tahoua

Hombori Tondo 1,155 m

OUDALAN

TILLABÉRI

MARADI

DIFFA

Zinder

Maradi

SOUM

SÉNO

Niamey

NIAMEY

DOSSO

SOKOTO

Sokoto

KATSINA

Katsina

YOBE

BURKINA FASO

Ouagadougou

GOURMA

TAPOA

PN DU W DU NIGER

KEBBI

ZAMFARA

Sokoto Plains

KANO

Kano

JIGAWA

PN DU W DU BURKINA FASO

PN DU W DU BENIN

Birnin Kebbi

Gusau

KANO

Zaria

KADUNA

Kaduna

BAUCHI

GOMBE

BOULGOU

UPPER EAST

BORGOU

Kainji Lake

NIGER

Minna

Zaranda Hill 1,454 m

Jos

Shere 1,781 m

PLATEAU

YANKARI GAME RESERVE

NORTHERN

GHANA

BENIN

Parakou

KAINJI LAKE NP

Abuja

ABUJA FED. CAP. TERR.

NASSARAWA

Tamale

TOGO

ZOU

KWARA

Plateau of Yorubaland

Ilorin

KOGI

BENUE

Makurdi

TARABA

ASHANTI

Kumasi

EASTERN

VOLTA

Kpalimé

MONO

OUÉMÉ

Abeokuta

OGUN

Ibadan

OYO

Ogbomosho

Oshogbo

Iwo

Ede

OSUN

Ife

Ilesha

EKITI

Ado Ekiti

Akure

ONDO

EDO

Benin City

ENUGU

Enugu

Onitsha

ANAMBRA

EBONYI

CROSS RIVER

CAMEROON

CENTRAL

Accra

GREATER ACCRA

Lomé

Cotonou

Porto-Novo

LAGOS

Lagos

Mushin

Slave Coast

Bight of Benin

Warri

DELTA

IMO

Aba

Port Harcourt

AKWA IBOM

Calabar

RIVERS

BAYELSA

Mouths of the Niger

Bight of Biafra

Gold Coast

Cape Coast

C. Three Points

Sekondi-Takoradi

Scale 1:6,800,000   Polyconic Projection

MI   50   100   150   200

KM   50   100   150   200   250   300

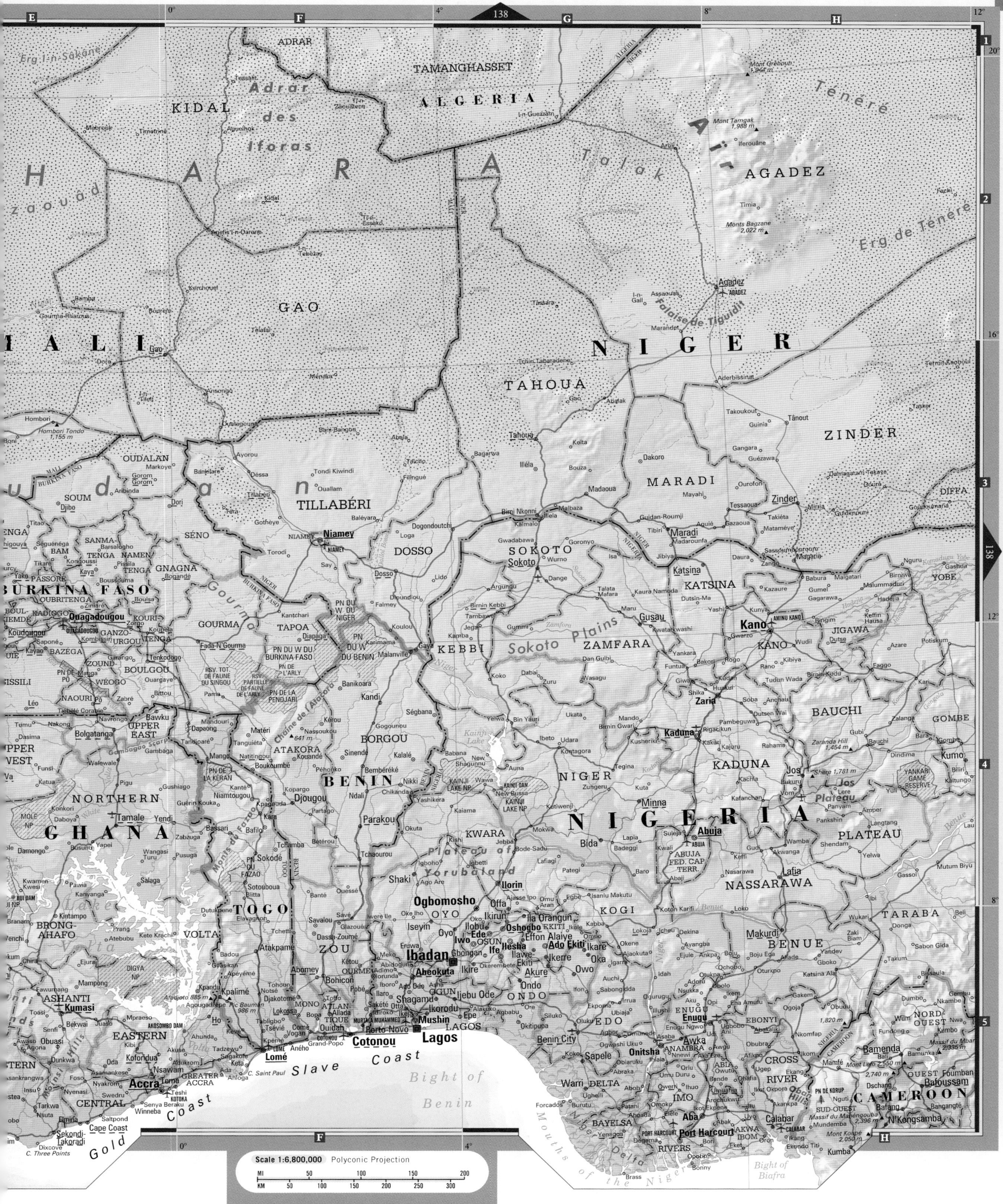

DEM. REP. OF THE CONGO

ORIENTALE

NORD KIVU

SUD KIVU

KATANGA

LUAPULA

NORTHERN

ZAMBIA

UGANDA

Kampala

Entebbe

RIFT VALLEY

WESTERN

RWANDA

Kigali

BURUNDI

Bujumbura

KAGERA

Lake Victoria

MWANZA

KIGOMA

TABORA

SHINYANGA

SINGIDA

RUKWA

MBEYA

IRINGA

TANZANIA

DODOMA

Dodoma

NORTHERN

MALAWI

NIASSA

Lake Nyasa

MOZAMBIQUE

KENYA

EASTERN

NORTH EASTERN

Nairobi

CENTRAL

NYANZA

MARA

Nakuru

SERENGETI NATIONAL PARK

NGORONGORO CONSV AREA

ARUSHA

Arusha

KILIMANJARO

Moshi

TSAVO WEST

TSAVO EAST NAT'L PARK

COAST

Mombasa

TANGA

Tanga

PEMBA

Pemba I.

ZANZIBAR NORTH

ZANZIBAR WEST

Zanzibar

Zanzibar I.

PWANI

Dar es Salaam

MOROGORO

Morogoro

SELOUS GAME RESERVE

LINDI

MTWARA

CABO DELGADO

RUVUMA

INDIAN OCEAN

Masai Steppe

Mlala Hills

SOMALIA

ETHIOPIA

Lake Turkana (L. Rudolf)

Lake Rukwa

Monts Mitumba

Population

■ Over 2,000,000	◉ 500,000 - 999,999	◎ 100,000 - 249,999	◉ 10,000 - 29,999
■ 1,000,000 - 1,999,999	◉ 250,000 - 499,999	◎ 30,000 - 99,999	• Under 10,000

Scale 1:6,800,000   Polyconic Projection

MI 50 100 150 200

KM 50 100 150 200 250 300

Height
ft.
6000 / 19700
4000 / 13000
2000 / 6500
1500 / 5000
1000 / 3300
500 / 1600
200 / 700
-0-
200 / 700
500 / 1600
1000 / 3300
2000 / 6500
3000 / 9800
4000 / 13000
5000 / 16400
6000 / 19700
ft.
Depth

Population
- Over 2,000,000
- 1,000,000 - 1,999,999
- 500,000 - 999,999
- 100,000 - 499,999
- 50,000 - 99,999
- Under 50,000

Scale 1:17,000,000   Polyconic Projection

MI   125   250   375   500
KM   125   250   375   500   625   750

Height
m / ft
6000 / 19700
4000 / 13000
2000 / 6500
1500 / 5000
1000 / 3300
500 / 1600
200 / 700
0
200 / 700
500 / 1600
1000 / 3300
2000 / 6500
3000 / 9800
4000 / 13000
5000 / 16400
6000 / 19700
m / ft
Depth

© HAMMOND WORLD ATLAS CORPORATION   CJ-2101-A-A
© HAMMOND W.A.C.   CJ-2108-A-A

SAME SCALE AS MAIN MAP

Population

- ■ Over 2,000,000
- ■ 1,000,000 - 1,999,999
- ⦿ 500,000 - 999,999
- ◎ 250,000 - 499,999
- ● 100,000 - 249,999
- ○ 30,000 - 99,999
- ◦ 10,000 - 29,999
- ○ Under 10,000

MOZAMBIQUE

INHAMBANE

GAZA

MAPUTO

Matola **Maputo**

SWAZILAND

MPUMALANGA

KWAZULU-NATAL

Durban

Richard's Bay

INDIAN OCEAN

COMOROS

MAYOTTE (FRANCE)

Îles Glorieuses (FRANCE)

Geyser Reef

ANTSIRANANA

Tsaratanana Massif

Mozambique Channel

MAHAJANGA

Mahajanga

Ikahavo Plateau

Bongolava Plateau

ANTANANARIVO

Antananarivo

TOAMASINA

Toamasina

Antsirabe

Fandriana

MADAGASCAR

FIANARANTSOA

Fianarantsoa

TOLIARA

Toliara

Betioky

Amboasary

Ambovombe

Tropic of Capricorn

INDIAN OCEAN

INDIAN OCEAN

MAURITIUS

Port Louis

RÉUNION (FRANCE)

Saint-Denis

Mascarene Islands

Scale 1:6,400,000   Polyconic Projection

MI   50   100   150   200

KM   50   100   150   200   250   300

© HAMMOND WORLD ATLAS CORPORATION

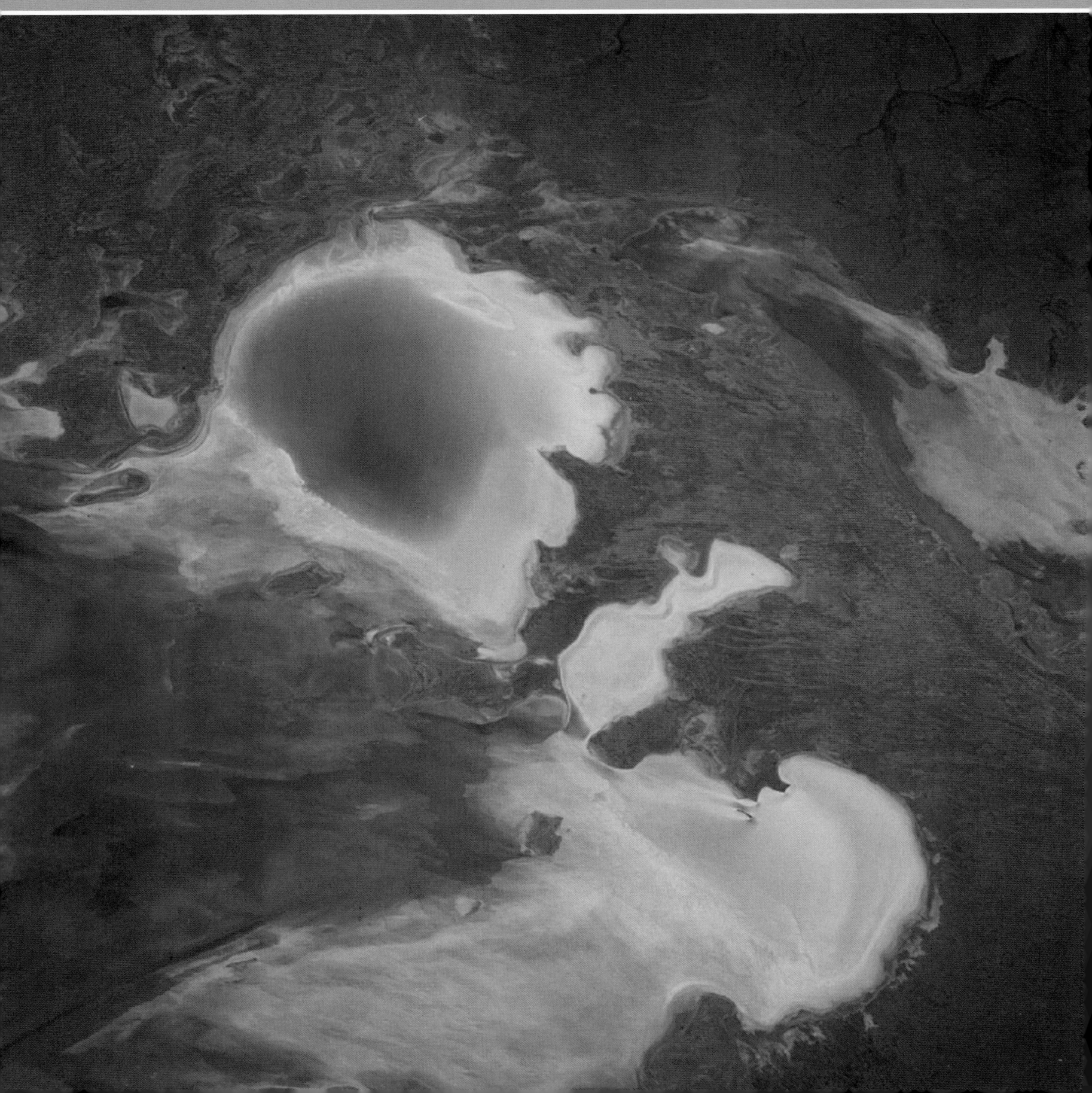

The Lake Eyre Basin is located in the arid interior of south central Australia. This basin is one of the largest areas of internal drainage in the world. It consists of two distinct, but interrelated basins: the north basin and the south basin. The much larger north basin shown here (the highly reflective areas) consists of two very large, normally dry lakebeds. The western lobe (bottom of the image) is Belt Bay, and the eastern lobe is Madigan Bay. The color change, especially in the Madigan Bay Lobe, indicates that there was some water in this lobe at the time the image was taken.

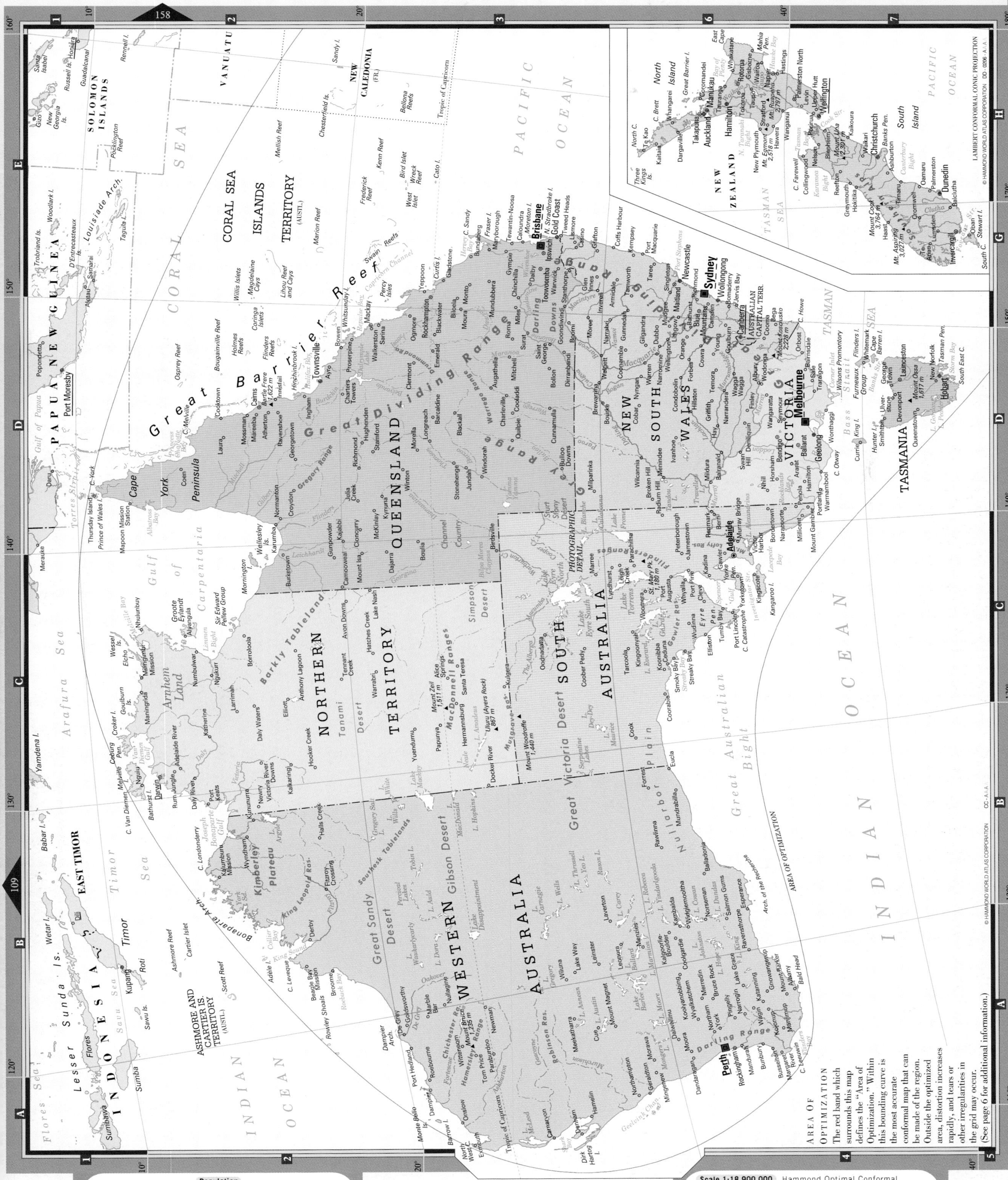

LAMBERT CONFORMAL CONIC PROJECTION

© HAMMOND WORLD ATLAS CORPORATION. DD-0806-A-A-A

PAPUA NEW GUINEA

Port Moresby

Gulf of Papua

SOLOMON ISLANDS

VANUATU

NEW CALEDONIA (FR.)

Tropic of Capricorn

CORAL SEA

CORAL SEA ISLANDS TERRITORY (AUSTL.)

PACIFIC OCEAN

NEW ZEALAND

North C.
Three Kings Is.
Cape Maria van Diemen
Auckland
Hamilton
Wellington
N. Taranaki Bight
Mt. Egmont 2,518 m
Christchurch
Mount Cook 3,764 m
Dunedin
Invercargill
South Island
Stewart I.

TASMAN SEA

Great Barrier Reef

Great Dividing Range

Cape York Peninsula

Gulf of Carpentaria

QUEENSLAND

Brisbane
Ipswich
Gold Coast
Newcastle
Sydney
Wollongong

NEW SOUTH WALES

Canberra
AUSTRALIAN CAPITAL TERR.

NORTHERN TERRITORY

Barkly Tableland

Arnhem Land

Darwin

Alice Springs
Mount Zeil 1,511 m
MacDonnell Ranges
Uluru (Ayers Rock) 867 m

Tanami Desert

Simpson Desert

SOUTH AUSTRALIA

Lake Eyre North 16 m
Lake Eyre South
Lake Torrens
Lake Gairdner
Flinders Ranges

PHOTOGRAPHIC DETAIL

Adelaide

VICTORIA

Melbourne
Geelong
Ballarat

TASMANIA

Hobart
Launceston

Bass Strait

Great Australian Bight

WESTERN AUSTRALIA

Great Sandy Desert

Gibson Desert

Great Victoria Desert

Nullarbor Plain

Kimberley Plateau

Perth

Darling Range

INDONESIA

EAST TIMOR

Timor Sea

Arafura Sea

INDIAN OCEAN

PACIFIC OCEAN

Tropic of Capricorn

Population

■ Over 2,000,000
● 1,000,000 - 1,999,999
● 500,000 - 999,999
◉ 100,000 - 499,999
○ 50,000 - 99,999
○ Under 50,000

Scale 1:18,900,000 Hammond Optimal Conformal

MI 125 250 375 500
KM 125 250 375 500 625 750

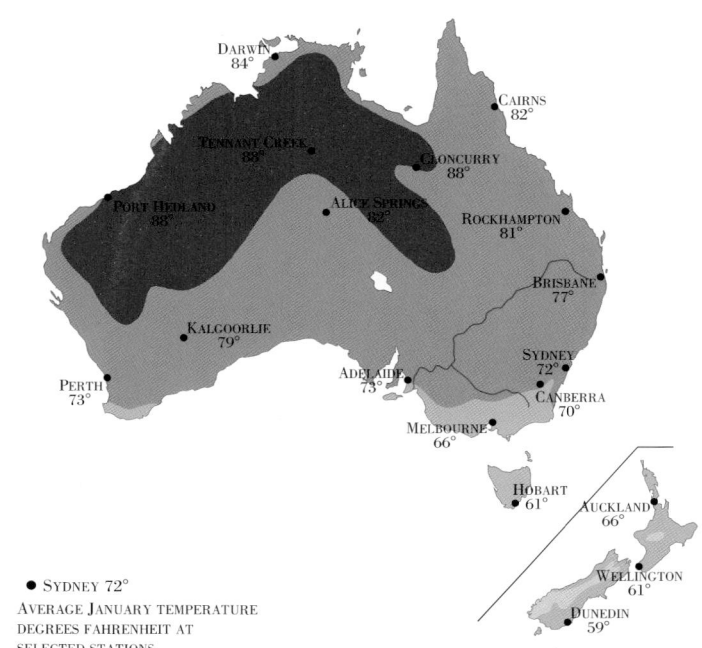

SYDNEY 72°
AVERAGE JANUARY TEMPERATURE
DEGREES FAHRENHEIT AT
SELECTED STATIONS

AVERAGE JANUARY TEMPERATURE

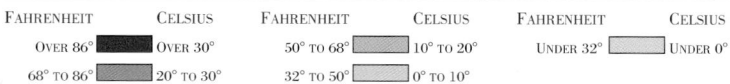

FAHRENHEIT	CELSIUS	FAHRENHEIT	CELSIUS	FAHRENHEIT	CELSIUS
OVER 86°	OVER 30°	50° TO 68°	10° TO 20°	UNDER 32°	UNDER 0°
68° TO 86°	20° TO 30°	32° TO 50°	0° TO 10°		

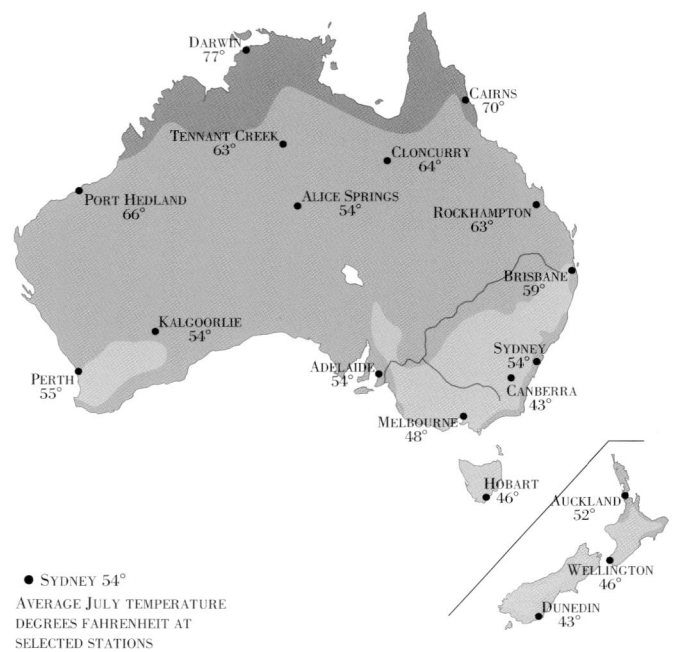

SYDNEY 54°
AVERAGE JULY TEMPERATURE
DEGREES FAHRENHEIT AT
SELECTED STATIONS

AVERAGE JULY TEMPERATURE

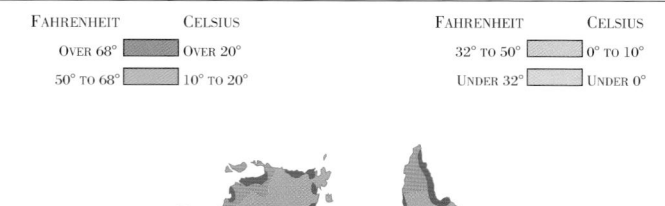

FAHRENHEIT	CELSIUS	FAHRENHEIT	CELSIUS
OVER 68°	OVER 20°	32° TO 50°	0° TO 10°
50° TO 68°	10° TO 20°	UNDER 32°	UNDER 0°

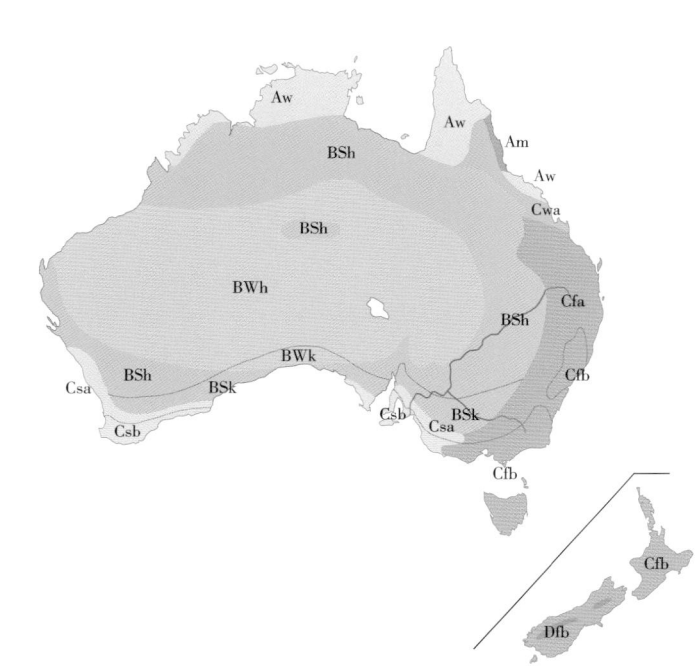

CLIMATE

HUMID TROPICAL
Am SHORT DRY SEASON
Aw DRY WINTER

DRY
BS SEMIARID h HOT
BW ARID k COLD

HUMID WARM
Cf NO DRY SEASON
Cw DRY WINTER
Cs DRY SUMMER

HUMID COLD
Df NO DRY SEASON
a HOT SUMMER
b COOL SUMMER
AFTER KOEPPEN-GEIGER

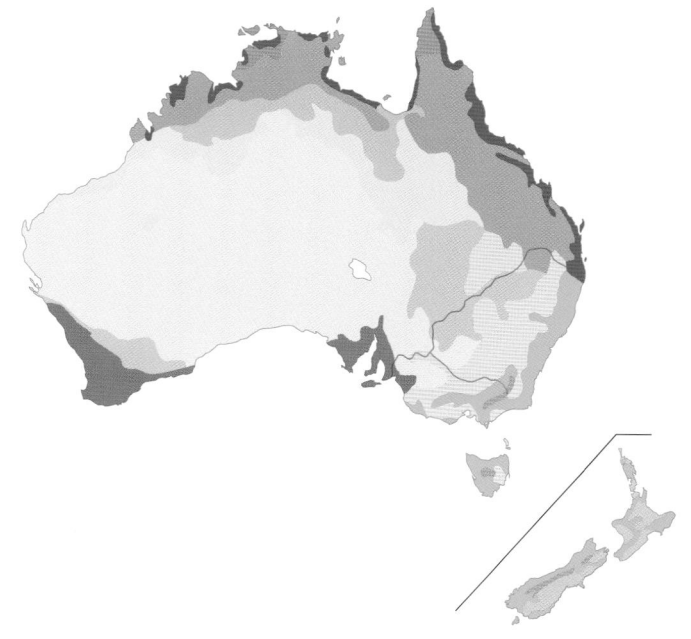

VEGETATION

TROPICAL FOREST
TROPICAL RAINFOREST
LIGHT TROPICAL FOREST
WOODLAND AND SHRUB

TROPICAL GRASSLAND
GRASS AND SHRUB (SAVANNA)
WOODED SAVANNA

MID-LATITUDE FOREST
MIXED NEEDLELEAF AND BROADLEAF FOREST
MIXED WOODLAND
WOODLAND AND SHRUB (MEDITERRANEAN)

MID-LATITUDE GRASSLAND
SCRUB AND FERNLANDS
DESERT AND DESERT SHRUB
ALPINE

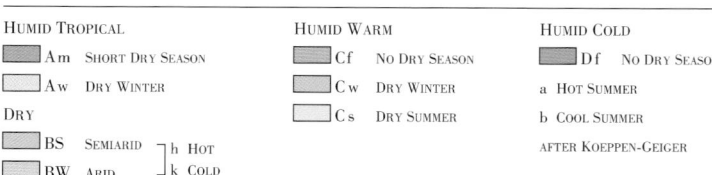
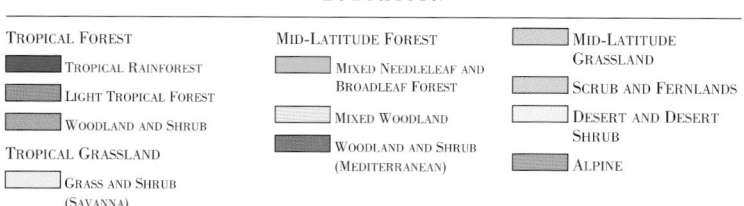

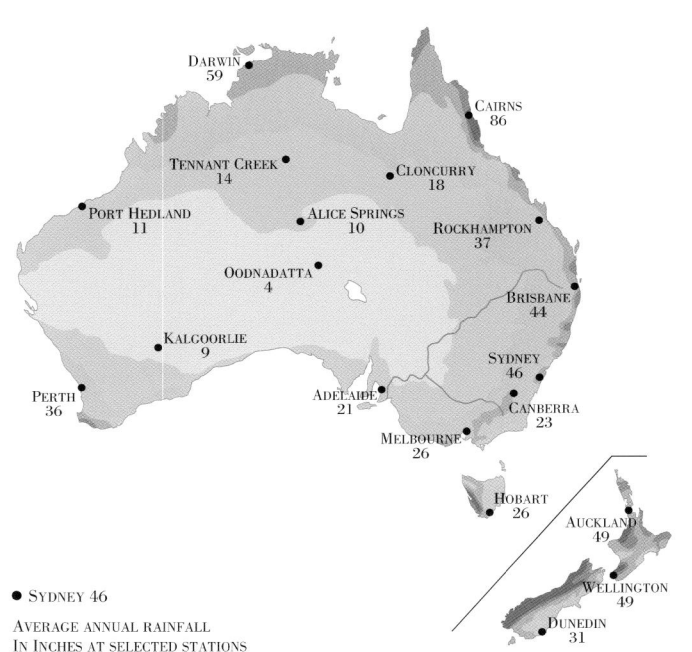

● SYDNEY 46

AVERAGE ANNUAL RAINFALL
IN INCHES AT SELECTED STATIONS

DARWIN 59
CAIRNS 86
TENNANT CREEK 14
CLONCURRY 18
PORT HEDLAND 11
ALICE SPRINGS 10
ROCKHAMPTON 37
OODNADATTA 4
BRISBANE 44
KALGOORLIE 9
SYDNEY 46
PERTH 36
ADELAIDE 21
CANBERRA 23
MELBOURNE 26
HOBART 26
AUCKLAND 49
WELLINGTON 49
DUNEDIN 31

● CITIES WITH OVER 500,000
INHABITANTS

AVERAGE ANNUAL RAINFALL

INCHES	CM	INCHES	CM	INCHES	CM
OVER 80	OVER 200	40 TO 60	100 TO 150	10 TO 20	25 TO 50
60 TO 80	150 TO 200	20 TO 40	50 TO 100	UNDER 10	UNDER 25

POPULATION DISTRIBUTION

DENSITY PER		SQ. MI.	SQ. KM.	SQ. MI.	SQ. KM.
SQ. MI.	SQ. KM.	25 TO 130	10 TO 50	UNDER 3	UNDER 1
OVER 130	OVER 50	3 TO 25	1 TO 10		

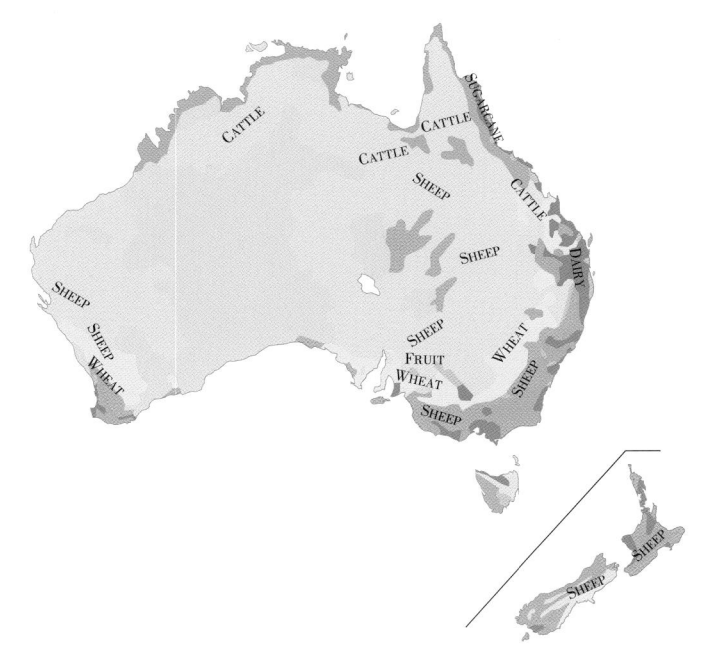

CATTLE
SUGARCANE
CATTLE
CATTLE
SHEEP
CATTLE
SHEEP
DAIRY
SHEEP
SHEEP
SHEEP
WHEAT
SHEEP
FRUIT
WHEAT
WHEAT
SHEEP
SHEEP
SHEEP
SHEEP

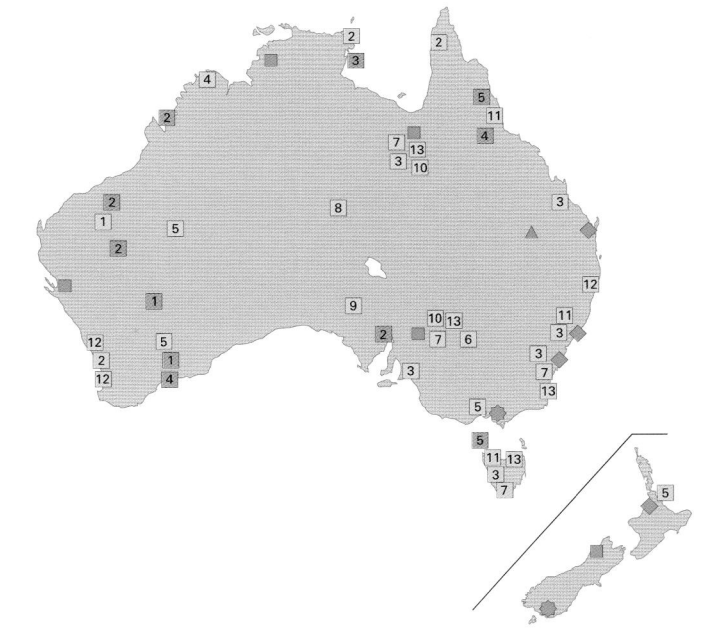

LAND USE

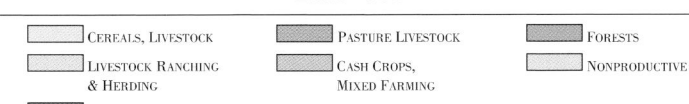

CEREALS, LIVESTOCK

LIVESTOCK RANCHING
& HERDING

DAIRY, LIVESTOCK

PASTURE LIVESTOCK

CASH CROPS,
MIXED FARMING

FORESTS

NONPRODUCTIVE

MINERAL RESOURCES

ENERGY & FUELS
◆ COAL
⬡ LIGNITE
▲ NATURAL GAS
▪ URANIUM

IRON & FERROALLOYS
1 COBALT
2 IRON ORE
3 MANGANESE
4 NICKEL
5 TUNGSTEN

OTHER MAJOR RESOURCES
1 ASBESTOS
2 BAUXITE
3 COPPER
4 DIAMONDS
5 GOLD
6 GYPSUM
7 LEAD
8 MICA
9 OPALS
10 SILVER
11 TIN
12 TITANIUM
13 ZINC

Population

- Over 2,000,000
- 1,000,000 - 1,999,999
- 500,000 - 999,999
- 250,000 - 499,999
- 100,000 - 249,999
- 30,000 - 99,999
- 10,000 - 29,999
- Under 10,000

Western and Central Australia

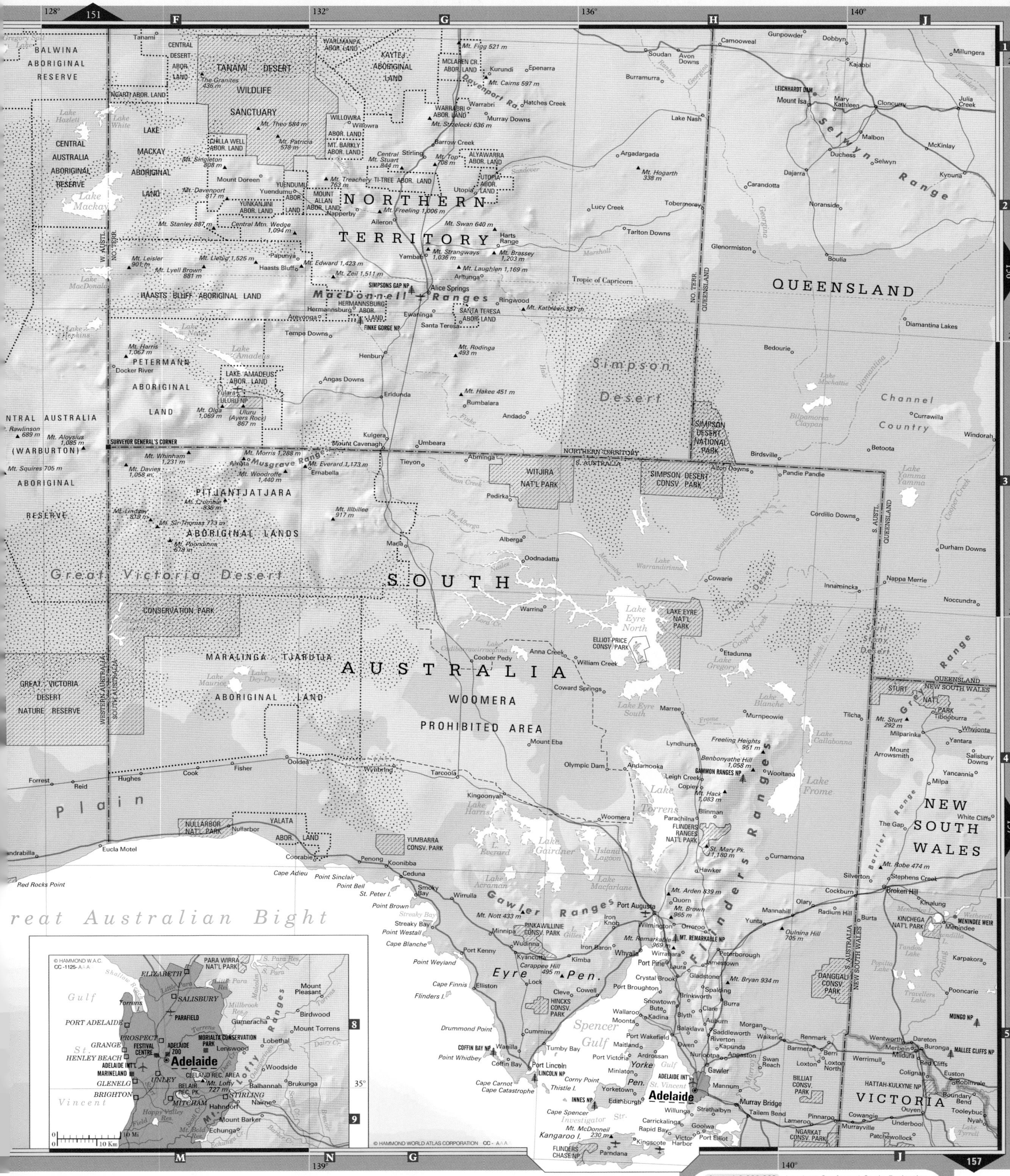

128°   **151**   132°   **F**   **G**   136°   **H**   140°   **J**

NORTHERN TERRITORY

BALWINA ABORIGINAL RESERVE

CENTRAL AUSTRALIA ABORIGINAL RESERVE

Lake Hoelett

Lake White

NGAART ABOR. LAND

Tanami
The Granites 436 m

CENTRAL DESERT ABOR. LAND

TANAMI DESERT WILDLIFE SANCTUARY

WARLMANPA ABOR. LAND

KAYTEJ ABORIGINAL LAND

Camooweal

Gunpowder   Dobbyn   Millungera

Soudan
Avon Downs

Burramurra

Mt. Figg 521 m
MCLAREN CR. ABOR. LAND   Kurundi   Epenarra

Mt. Cairns 597 m   Hatches Creek

LEICHHARDT DAM   Mount Isa   Mary Kathleen   Cloncurry   Julia Creek

Kajabbi   Malbon   McKinlay

WARRABRI ABOR. LAND   Warrabri   Murray Downs

Lake Nash   Argadargada   Noranside   Duchess   Selwyn   Kynuna

Lake Mackay

LAKE MACKAY ABORIGINAL LAND

Mt. Theo 584 m

CHILLA WELL ABOR. LAND   Mt. Patricia 578 m

Mt. Singleton 808 m

Mount Doreen

Mt. Davenport 817 m

YUNKANJINI ABOR. LAND

YUENDUMU ABOR. LAND
Yuendumu

MOUNT ALLAN ABOR. LAND   Napperby

WILLOWRA ABOR. LAND
Willowra

MT. BARKLY ABOR. LAND   Central Mt. Stuart 844 m   Stirling   Barrow Creek

Mt. Treachey 763 m   TI-TREE ABOR. LAND

Mt. Top 708 m   ALYAWARRA ABOR. LAND

UTOPIA ABOR. LAND   Utopia

Sandover

Mt. Hogarth 338 m

Lucy Creek   Tobermorey

Glenormiston   Boulia

Mt. Stanley 887 m   Central Mtn. Wedge 1,094 m

Mt. Freeling 1,006 m   Aileron

Yambah   Mt. Strangways 1,036 m   Harts Range

QUEENSLAND

Mt. Leisler 901 m

Mt. Liebig 1,525 m   Haasts Bluff

Mt. Edward 1,423 m   Papunya

Mt. Lyell Brown 881 m

HAASTS BLUFF ABORIGINAL LAND

Mt. Zeil 1,511 m

Mt. Swan 640 m

Mt. Brassey 1,203 m   Mt. Laughlen 1,169 m

Tropic of Capricorn

Tarlton Downs

Lake MacDonald

SIMPSONS GAP NP   MacDonnell Ranges   Alice Springs   Ringwood   Mt. Kathleen 387 m

Diamantina Lakes

Lake Hopkins

PETERMANN

Mt. Harris 1,067 m
Docker River

Mt. Whinham 1,231 m

Hermannsburg   HERMANNSBURG ABOR. LAND

SANTA TERESA ABOR. LAND   Santa Teresa

Ewaninga

FINKE GORGE NP

Arevonga   Tempe Downs   Henbury

Mt. Rodinga 493 m

Simpson Desert

Bedourie

Lake Amadeus

ABORIGINAL

LAKE AMADEUS ABOR. LAND

Uluru   Mt. Olga 1,069 m   ULURU NP

Angas Downs

Erldunda

Mt. Hakee 451 m

Rumbalara

Andado

Lake Machattie

Lake Caroline

Currawilla

Channel Country

Windorah

CENTRAL AUSTRALIA (WARBURTON)

Mt. Rawlinson 689 m   Mt. Aloysius 1,085 m

Mt. Squires 705 m

SURVEYOR GENERAL'S CORNER

Mt. Whinham 1,231 m   Mt. Morris 1,288 m   Aihitta

Mt. Davies 1,058 m   Mt. Woodroffe 1,440 m

Mt. Everard 1,173 m   Ernabella

(Ayers Rock) 867 m

Olga 1,069 m

Uluru

Kulgera

Mount Cavenagh   Umbeara

Tieyon

Mt. Illbillee 917 m

Abminga

Pedirka

NORTHERN TERRITORY
S. AUSTRALIA

WITJIRA NAT'L PARK

SIMPSON DESERT NATIONAL PARK

Birdsville

SIMPSON DESERT CONSV. PARK

Alton Downs

Pandie Pandie

Betoota

Lake Yamma Yamma

ABORIGINAL

Mt. Lindsay 839 m

Mt. Crombie 835 m

Mt. Sir Thomas 773 m

PITJANTJATJARA

ABORIGINAL LANDS

Mt. Poondinna 678 m

Stevenson Creek

The Alberga

Marla

Alberga

Oodnadatta

Cordillo Downs

Durham Downs

RESERVE

Great Victoria Desert

SOUTH

Warrina

Lake Warrandirinna

Cowarie

Innamincka   Noccundra

Nappa Merrie

Great Victoria Desert Nature Reserve

CONSERVATION PARK

MARALINGA TJARUTJA

ABORIGINAL LAND

Lake Dey-Dey

Lake Maurice

AUSTRALIA

WOOMERA

PROHIBITED AREA

Coober Pedy

Anna Creek   William Creek

LAKE EYRE NAT'L PARK

ELLIOT PRICE CONSV. PARK

Lake Eyre North

Etadunna

Lake Gregory

Lake Blanche   Murnpeowie

STURT NAT'L PARK

QUEENSLAND
NEW SOUTH WALES

Tilcha   Tibooburra

Mt. Sturt 292 m   Milparinka

Whyjonta

Yantara   Salisbury Downs

Coward Springs   Marree

Lake Eyre South

Lyndhurst

Freeling Heights 951 m

Benbonyathe Hill 1,058 m   Wooltana

Lake Callabonna   Mount Arrowsmith

Yancannia   Milpa

Forrest   Reid   Hughes   Cook   Fisher   Ooldea   Watson   Tarcoola

Olympic Dam

Andamooka

Leigh Creek   Copley

GAMMON RANGES NP

Mt. Hack 1,083 m   Lake Frome

The Gap   White Cliffs

Plain

NULLARBOR NAT'L PARK   Yalata   Nullarbor

YALATA ABOR. LAND

Kingoonyah

Woomera

Lake Torrens

Parachilna   Blinman

Copley

FLINDERS RANGES NAT'L PARK

Curnamona

NEW SOUTH WALES

andrabilla   Eucla Motel

Coorabie

Penong   Koonibba

Ceduna

YUMBARRA CONSV. PARK

Lake Gairdner

Island Lagoon

St. Mary Pk. 1,180 m

Hawker

Cockburn   Silverton

Mt. Robe 474 m

Broken Hill

Red Rocks Point

Cape Adieu   Point Sinclair

Point Bell   St. Peter I.

Smoky Bay

Wirrulla

Streaky Bay

Point Brown   Point Westall

Cape Blanche

Lake Acraman

Lake Everard

Gawler Ranges

Mt. Nott 433 m

Minnipa

Wudinna

PINKAWILLINIE CONSV. PARK

L. Gilles

Port Augusta

Iron Knob

Mt. Arden 839 m

Quorn

Mt. Brown 965 m

Wilmington   Orroroo

Yunta

Mannahill   Radium Hill   Burta

Oulnina Hill 705 m

Mannahill

KINCHEGA NAT'L PARK   Menindee

Menindee Weir

Great Australian Bight

Point Weyland

Iron Baron

Iron Monarch

Wirraara

Whyalla

Port Pirie

Mt. Remarkable 969 m   MT. REMARKABLE NP

Jamestown   Peterborough

Mt. Bryan 934 m

DANGGALI CONSV. PARK

Karpakora

Pinnaroo

Cape Finnis   Elliston

Flinders I.

Kimba

Cleve   Cowell

Carappee Hill 495 m

Kyancutta

Crystal Brook

Port Broughton

Snowtown

Wallaroo

Moonta

Brinkworth

Spalding

Burra

Morgan

Renmark   Paringa

Berri

Loxton

Pooncarie

Mungo NP

Drummond Point

Cummins

Eyre Pen.

Port Kenny

Lock

Spencer Gulf

Port Victoria

Maitland

Kadina

Blyth   Auburn

Balaklava

Owen

Kapunda

Riverton

Saddleworth

Waikerie

Barmera

Mildura

Wentworth   Dareton

HATTAH-KULKYNE NP

Coffin Bay

COFFIN BAY NP

Tumby Bay

Port Lincoln

LINCOLN NP

Ardrossan   Minlaton

Corny Point

Yorke Pen.

Port Wakefield

Gawler

ADELAIDE INT'L

Adelaide

BILLIAT CONSV. PARK

Swan Reach

Mannum

Murray Bridge

VICTORIA

Colignan

Red Cliffs

Point Whidbey   Cape Carnot   Cape Catastrophe

Thistle I.

Yorketown   Edithburgh

INNES NP

Cape Spencer   Investigator Str.

St. Vincent

Stansbury   Willunga

Goolwa   Port Elliot

Carrickalinga   Tailem Bend

NGARKAT CONSV. PARK

Lameroo

Murrayville

Ouyen

Nyah   Tooleybuc

© HAMMOND WORLD ATLAS CORPORATION   CC-

M   139°   **N**   **G**   136°   **J**   140°

Kangaroo I.   Mt. McDonnell 230 m   FLINDERS CHASE NP   Kingscote   Penneshaw

---

Adelaide inset map

© HAMMOND W.A.C.
CC-1125-A A A

ELIZABETH   PARA WIRRA NAT'L PARK

SALISBURY   PARAFIELD

Mount Pleasant   Gumeracha   Birdwood   Mount Torrens

PORT ADELAIDE   PROSPECT

GRANGE   FESTIVAL CENTRE

HENLEY BEACH   ADELAIDE INT'L

MARINELAND   UNLEY   BELAIR REC. PK.   MORIALTA CONSERVATION PARK   Lenswood

GLENELG

BRIGHTON

Adelaide   ADELAIDE ZOO   BELAIR   CLELAND REC. AREA

MITCHAM   STIRLING

Mt. Lofty 727 m   Aldgate   Nairne

Balhannah   Brukunga

Hahndorf

Woodside

Lobethal

Gulf

St. Vincent

Gulf

8

35°

9

Scale 1:6,800,000   Lambert Conformal Conic Projection

MI   50   100   150   200
KM   50   100   150   200   250   300

20°   **1**   **156**   **2**   24°   **3**   28°   **157**   **4**   32°   **5**   **157**

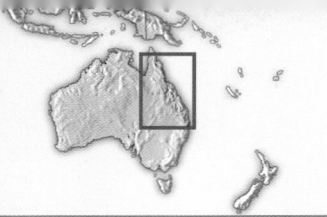

Northeastern Australia

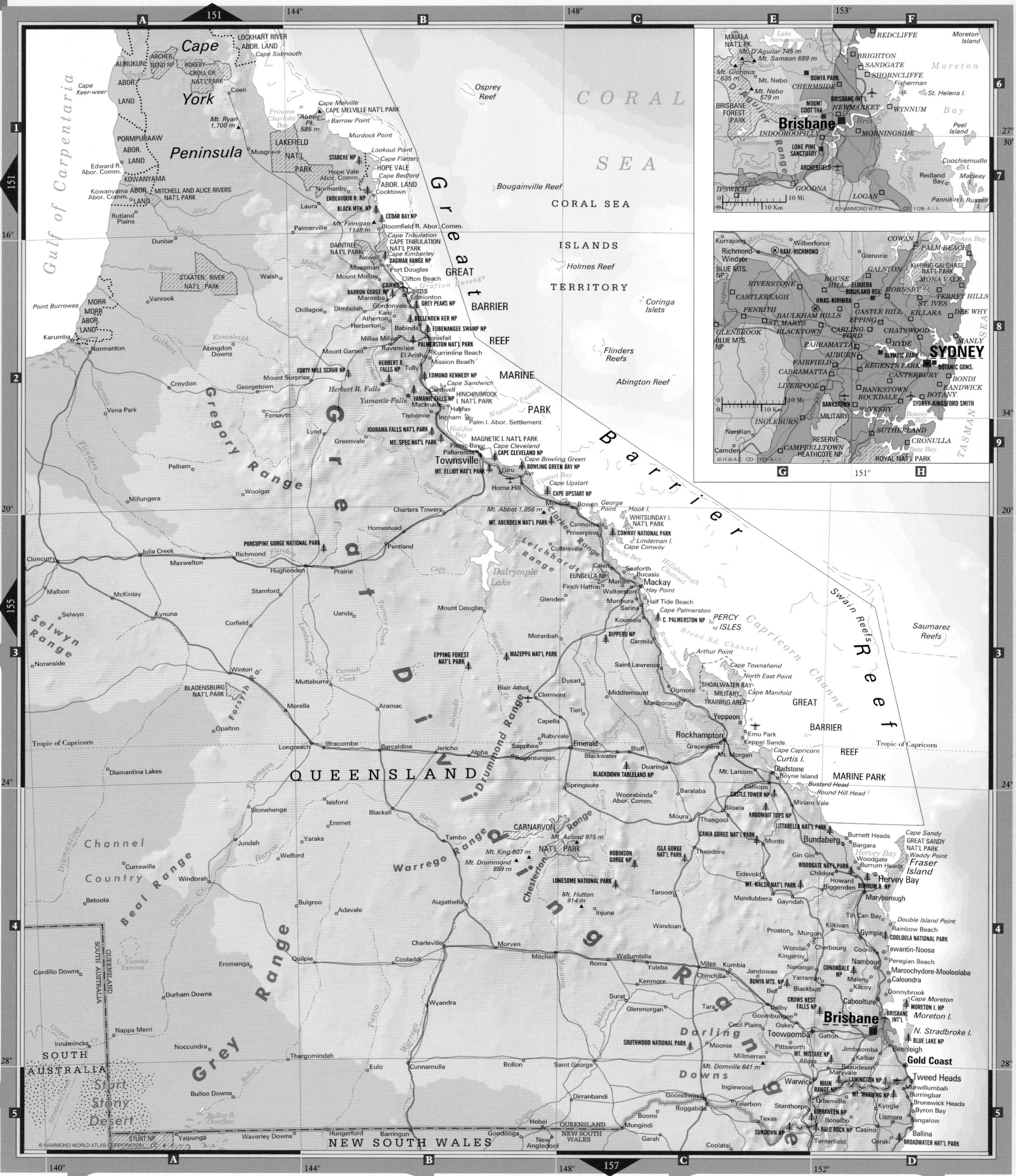

Height

m./ft.
6000 / 19700
4000 / 13000
2000 / 6500
1500 / 5000
1000 / 3300
500 / 1600
200 / 700
0
200 / 700
500 / 1600
1000 / 3300
2000 / 6500
3000 / 9800
4000 / 13000
5000 / 16400
6000 / 19700
m./ft.

Depth

Population

■	Over 2,000,000
■	1,000,000 - 1,999,999
●	500,000 - 999,999
●	250,000 - 499,999
●	100,000 - 249,999
●	30,000 - 99,999
●	10,000 - 29,999
○	Under 10,000

Scale 1:6,800,000   Lambert Conformal Conic Projection

MI 50 100 150 200
KM 50 100 150 200 250 300

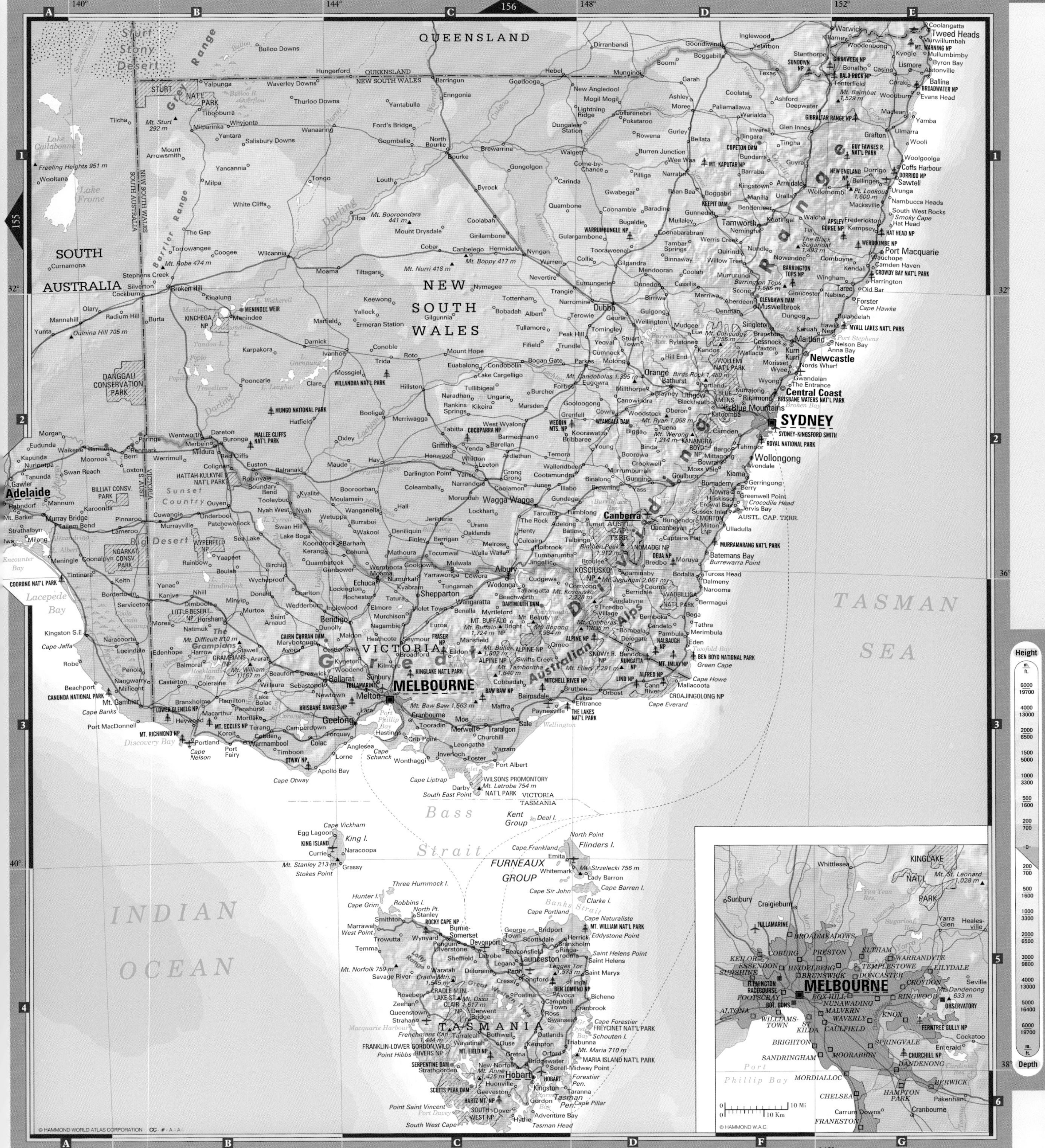

Population

■ Over 2,000,000	◉ 500,000 - 999,999	◎ 100,000 - 249,999	◦ 10,000 - 29,999
■ 1,000,000 - 1,999,999	◉ 250,000 - 499,999	◎ 30,000 - 99,999	· Under 10,000

Scale 1:6,800,000   Lambert Conformal Conic Projection

MI   50   100   150   200
KM   50   100   150   200   250   300

Height
ft.
6000 19700
4000 13000
2000 6500
1500 5000
1000 3300
500 1600
200 700
-0-
200 700
500 1600
1000 3300
2000 6500
3000 9800
4000 13000
5000 16400
6000 19700
Depth

© HAMMOND WORLD ATLAS CORPORATION
© HAMMOND W.A.C.

CHINA
JAPAN
TAIWAN
PHILIPPINES
EAST CHINA SEA
RYUKYU IS.
SOUTH CHINA SEA
PHILIPPINE SEA
NORTHERN MARIANA ISLANDS (U.S.)
Micronesia
MARSHALL ISLANDS
PALAU
CAROLINE ISLANDS
FEDERATED STATES OF MICRONESIA
NAURU
GILBERT ISLANDS
Melanesia
BISMARCK ARCHIPELAGO
INDONESIA
PAPUA NEW GUINEA
EAST TIMOR
SOLOMON ISLANDS
TUVALU
VANUATU
FIJI
WALLIS AND FUTUNA (FR.)
NEW CALEDONIA (FR.)
NEW HEBRIDES
LOYALTY IS.
CORAL SEA
Great Barrier Reef
Arafura Sea
Timor Sea
Banda Sea
Celebes Sea
Molucca Sea
Flores Sea
Savu Sea
Solomon Sea
Gulf of Carpentaria
INDIAN OCEAN
AUSTRALIA
Great Sandy Desert
Gibson Desert
Great Victoria Desert
Nullarbor Plain
Great Australian Bight
Great Dividing Range
Cape York Peninsula
Kimberley Plateau
TASMAN SEA
SOUTH
NORTH
NEW ZEALAND
KERMADEC IS. (N.Z.)
Norfolk I. (AUSTL.)
Lord Howe I. (AUSTL.)
Tropic of Cancer
Tropic of Capricorn
Equator
International Date Line
Manila
Quezon City
T'aipei
Kaohsiung
Guangzhou
Changsha
Nanchang
Davao
Ujung Pandang
Port Moresby
Honiara
Port-Vila
Nouméa
Suva
Majuro
Palikir
Koror
Tarawa
Hagåtña
Funafuti
Darwin
Brisbane
Sydney
Canberra
Adelaide
Perth
Mt. Kosciusko 2,228 m
Mt. Wilhelm 4,509 m
Puncak Jaya 5,030 m
Uluru (Ayers Rock) 867 m
Height
Depth
Population
Over 3,000,000
1,000,000 - 2,999,999
500,000 - 999,999
100,000 - 499,999
Under 100,000

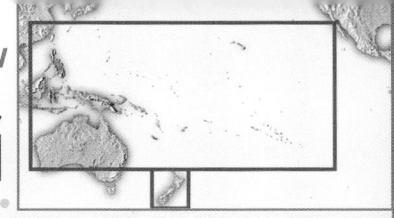

H 170° J 160° K 150° L R S 170° 175° T

9

35°

TASMAN SEA

Three Kings Is. North C.
C. Maria van Diemen Te Kao C. Kerikeri
Kaitaia C. Brett
Kaikohe Whangarei
Dargaville Great Barrier I.
Warkworth Heaurahi Gulf
Kaipara Har. Takapuna Auckland Coromandel Pen.
Manukau Thames
Huntly Te Aroha Bay of Plenty
North Island Hamilton Cambridge Tauranga Whakatane Te Araroa
Te Awamutu Kawerau Hikurangi 1,754 m
Tokoroa Rotorua East C.
Te Kuiti Murupara UREWERA NP
New Plymouth Turangi Taupo Gisborne
Waitara Mt. Ruapehu Napier
NEW ZEALAND Mt. Egmont 2,518 m 2,797 m TONGARIRO NP
C. Egmont Stratford Wanganui Mahia Pen.
Hawera Hawke Bay
South Taranaki Bight Dannevirke Hastings
Ashhurst Waipukurau
C. Farewell Palmerston North
Collingwood Levin Masterton
Tasman Bay Porirua
Karamea Motueka **Wellington** Upper Hutt
Karamea Bight Nelson Lower Hutt
Mt. Owen 1,875 m Blenheim C. Palliser
Westport Murchison NELSON
Reefton LAKES NP Mt. Una 2,301 m Ward
Greymouth Lewis Pass Clarence
Hokitika Kaikoura
Otira ARTHUR'S PASS NP
Fox Glacier Arthur's Waikari
WESTLAND NP Pass Rangiora Pegasus Bay
Mt. Cook 3,764 m MT. COOK NP Darfield Kaiapoi
Haast **Christchurch**
MT. ASPIRING NP Ashburton Banks Pen.
Mt. Aspiring 3,027 m Geraldine **South Island**
Twizel Temuka
Southern Alps Timaru
Wanaka Waimate Canterbury Bight
Cromwell Oamaru
FIORDLAND Queenstown Alexandra
Te Anau Palmerston
NAT'L PARK Lumsden Mosgiel **Dunedin**
West C. Gore Milton
Riverton Balclutha
Invercargill
Mt. Anglem 980 m Bluff
Oban
South C. Stewart I.

10

40°

11

45°

PACIFIC OCEAN

12

LAMBERT CONFORMAL CONIC PROJECTION
0 ___ 90 Mi
0 ___ 90 Km
© HAMMOND W.A.C. CJ - 1200 - A.A.A

Snares Is.

Pearl and Hermes Reef
Lisianski I. Laysan I.
Maro Reef
HAWAII (U.S.)
French Frigate Shoals
Necker I. Nihoa
Kauai
Niihau Oahu
Honolulu Molokai
Lanai Maui
Hilo
Hawaii

Johnston Atoll (U.S.)
Tropic

HAWAIIAN ISLANDS
P O L Y N E S I A

Kingman Reef (U.S.)
Palmyra Atoll (U.S.)
Teraina (Washington I.)
Tabuaeran (Fanning I.)
Kiritimati (Christmas I.)

International Date Line
LINE ISLANDS

KIRIBATI
PHOENIX IS.
Abariringa (Canton I.)
McKean Enderbury
Birnie Rawaki (Phoenix I.)
Orona (Hull I.) Manra (Sydney I.)
Jarvis I. (U.S.)

Malden I.
Starbuck I.

Vostok I.
Caroline I.
Flint I.

TOKELAU (N.Z.)
Atafu
Nukunonu Fakaofo
Swains I.

SAMOA
Mt. Silisili 1,858 m
Asau Apia Pago Pago
Savai'i Tutuila
Upolu **AMERICAN SAMOA**
Manua Is.
Rose I.

Tongareva (Penrhyn)
Rakahanga Manihiki
Pukapuka
Nassau
NORTHERN COOK IS.
Suwarrow
Bellingshausen

COOK ISLANDS (N.Z.)
Palmerston Atoll
Aitutaki Atoll Amuri
Manuae Atoll
SOUTHERN COOK IS.
Mitiaro
Atiu
Mauke
Avarua
Rarotonga
Mangaia

Niuatoputapu Group
Neiafu Vava'u Group
Alofi Niue
Pangai **NIUE** (N.Z.)
Ha'apai Group
Nuku'alofa
'Eua
TONGA

SOCIETY IS.
Îles Sous le Vent
Tupai Tikehau Rangiroa Menihi
Maupiti Bora Bora Makatea Tiputa Takaroa Tepoto Napuka Pukapuka
Huahine Kaukura Arutua Apataki Takapoto Fangatau
Raiatea Tetiaroa Toau Kauravaro
Moorea Papeete Fakahina
Faaa Uturoa Tahaa Makemo Raroia
Îles du Vent Tahiti Anaa Hikueru Amanu Tatakoto
Hereheretue Marokau Otepa Reao
FRENCH Hao Vahitahi Pukarua
Duke of Nukutavake
Gloucester Is. Vanavaro Tureia Actaeon Group
POLYNESIA Maria Moerai Mururoa Marutea
Rurutu Fangataufa
Rimatara Mataura Rikitea Mangareva
TUBUAI ISLANDS Tubuai Morane Taravai Temoe
(Austral Islands) Raivavae **GAMBIER IS.**
Rapa
Marotiri Is. (Bass Is.)

TUAMOTU ARCHIPELAGO

Nanuata Fatu Hiva
Disappointment Is.

PITCAIRN ISLANDS (U.K.)
Oeno Atoll Henderson I.
Adamstown Pitcairn I. Ducie I.

Tropic of Capricorn

Easter Island (Isla de Pascua) (CHILE)

PACIFIC OCEAN

International Date Line

H 170° J 160° K 150° L 140° M 130° N 120° P 110° Q 100°

8

10°
6
20°
7
30°

© Hammond World Atlas Corporation CC - # - A - A

Scale 1:30,700,000 Lambert Azimuthal Equal-Area
MI 300 600 900
KM 300 600 900 1200

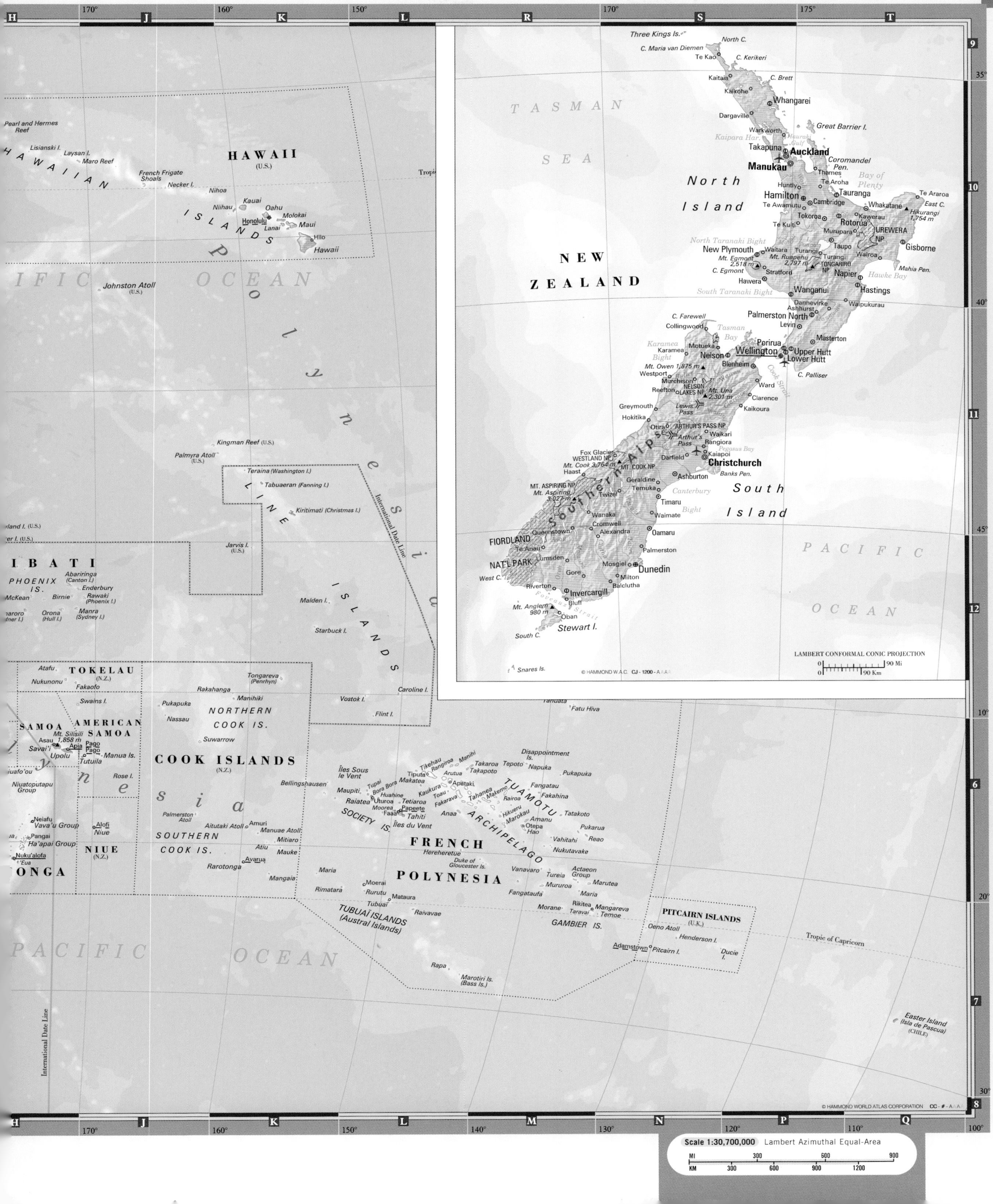

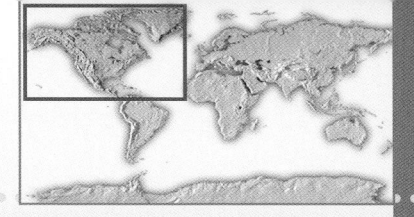

The Grand Canyon, one of the deepest canyons in the world, with a depth of 1 mile (1.6 km.), can be seen in this spectacular, west-looking, low-oblique image. The Colorado River cut through rocks billions of years old to create the canyon. The Grand Canyon is 277 miles (466 km.) long and averages nearly 10 miles (16 km.) in width. The snow-covered, forested Kaibab Plateau (north of the canyon) and the Coconino Plateau (south of the canyon) are visible. Western portions of the Painted Desert can be seen east of the canyon where the Little Colorado joins the Colorado River.

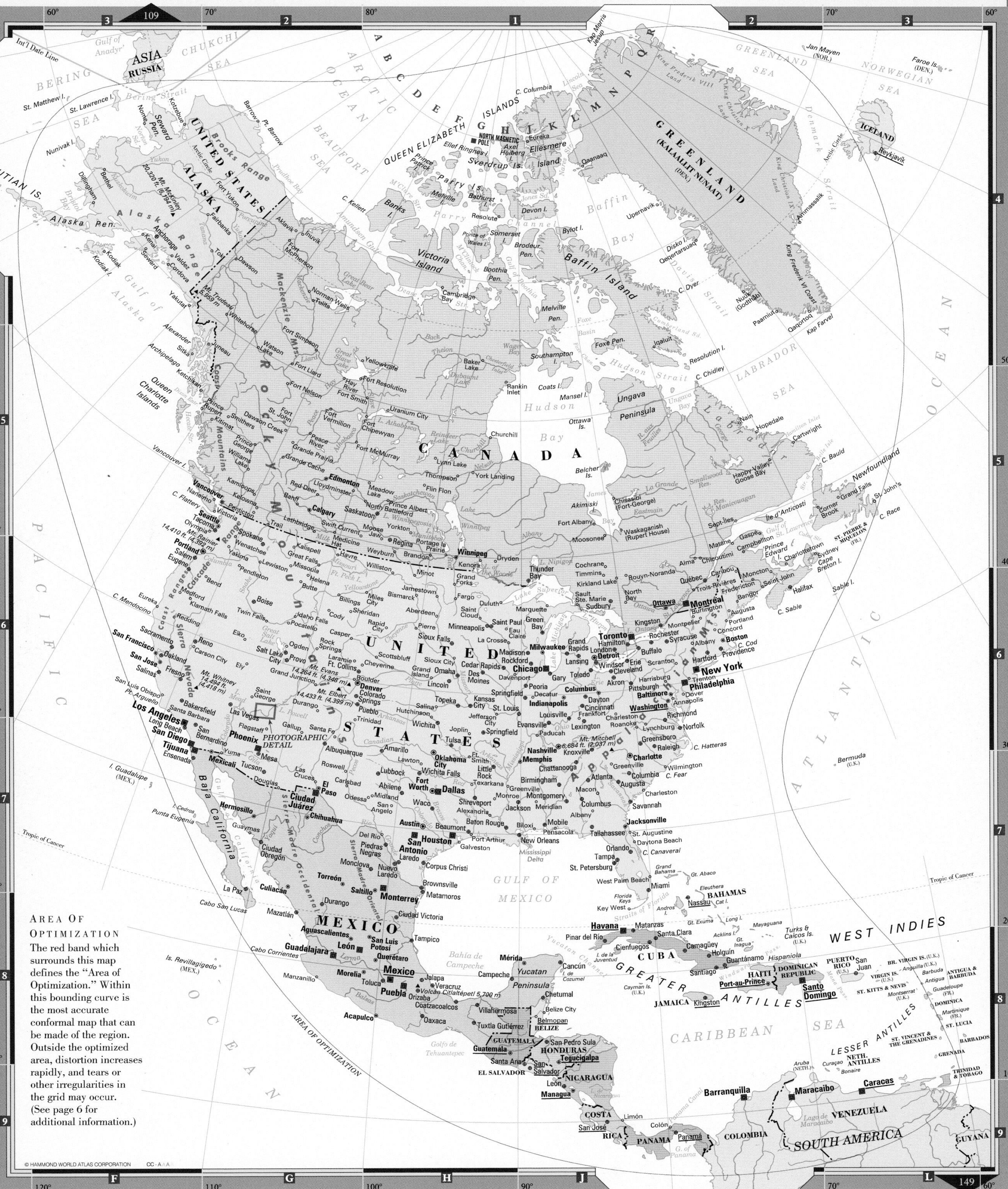

AREA OF OPTIMIZATION
The red band which surrounds this map defines the "Area of Optimization." Within this bounding curve is the most accurate conformal map that can be made of the region. Outside the optimized area, distortion increases rapidly, and tears or other irregularities in the grid may occur. (See page 6 for additional information.)

© Hammond World Atlas Corporation   CC-A-A

Population
- ■ Over 3,000,000
- ■ 1,000,000 - 2,999,999
- ● 500,000 - 999,999
- ⊕ 100,000 - 499,999
- ○ Under 100,000

Scale 1:34,100,000 Hammond Optimal Conformal

MI 250 500 750 1000
KM 250 500 750 1000 1250 1500

● New York 34°
Average January temperature
degrees Fahrenheit at
selected stations

Average January Temperature

Fahrenheit	Celsius	Fahrenheit	Celsius	Fahrenheit	Celsius
Over 68°	Over 20°	14° to 32°	-10° to 0°	-40° to -22°	-40° to -30°
50° to 68°	10° to 20°	-4° to 14°	-20° to -10°	Under -40°	Under -40°
32° to 50°	0° to 10°	-22° to -4°	-30° to -20°		

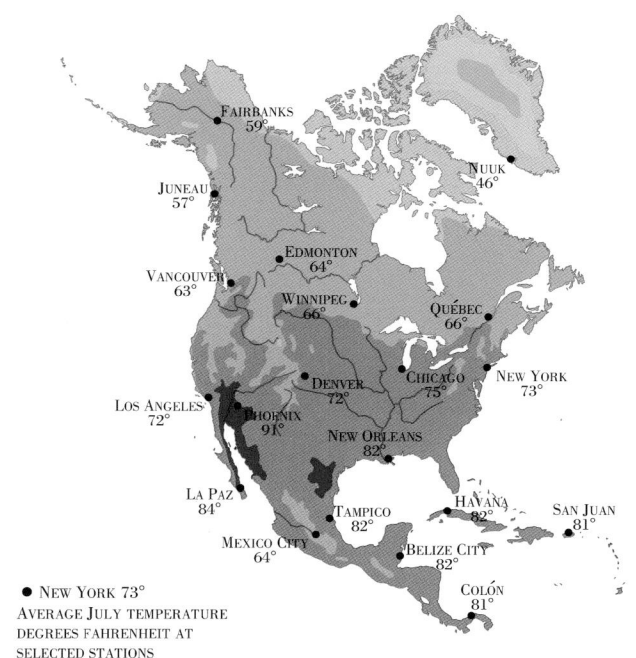

● New York 73°
Average July temperature
degrees Fahrenheit at
selected stations

Average July Temperature

Fahrenheit	Celsius	Fahrenheit	Celsius	Fahrenheit	Celsius
Over 86°	Over 30°	50° to 68°	10° to 20°	14° to 32°	-10° to 0°
68° to 86°	20° to 30°	32° to 50°	0° to 10°	Under 14°	Under -10°

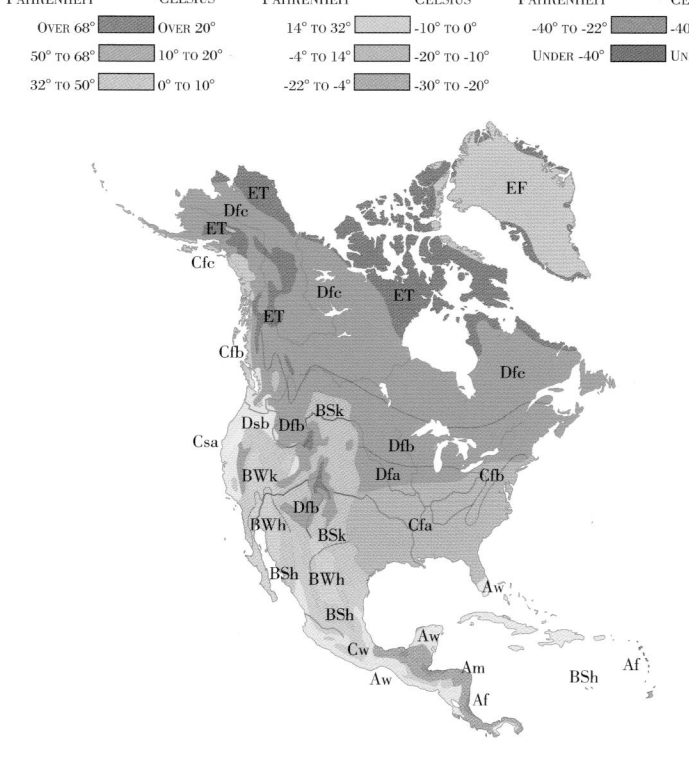

Climate

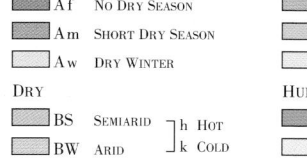

Humid Tropical
- Af No Dry Season
- Am Short Dry Season
- Aw Dry Winter

Dry
- BS Semiarid ⎤ h Hot
- BW Arid ⎦ k Cold

Humid Warm
- Cf No Dry Season
- Cw Dry Winter
- Cs Dry Summer

Humid Cold
- Df No Dry Season
- Ds Dry Summer

Cold Polar
- ET Short Cool Summer, Long Cold Winter
- EF Perpetual Frost

a Hot Summer
b Cool Summer
c Short Cool Summer

After Koeppen-Geiger

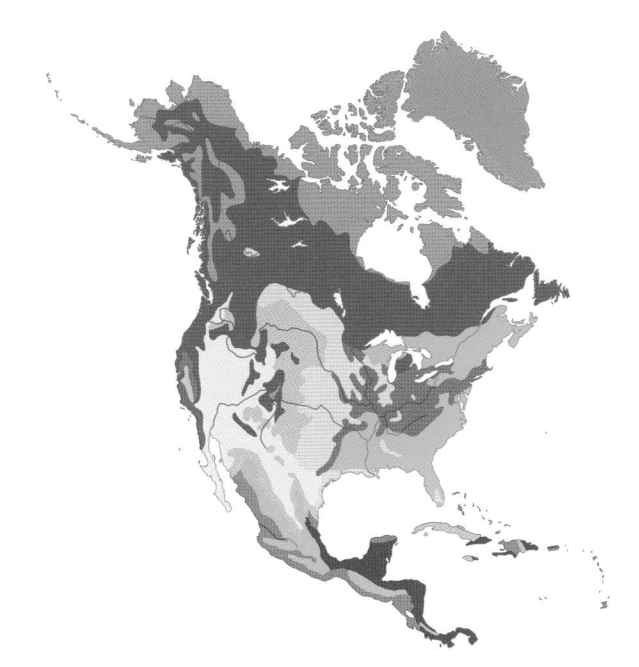

Vegetation

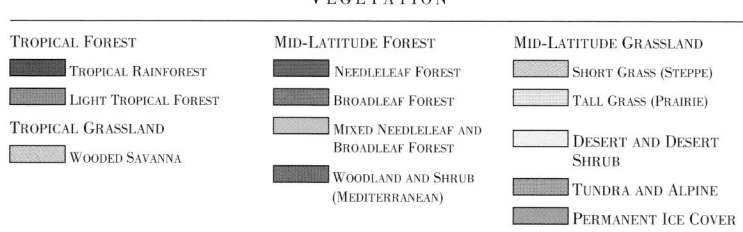

Tropical Forest
- Tropical Rainforest
- Light Tropical Forest

Tropical Grassland
- Wooded Savanna

Mid-Latitude Forest
- Needleleaf Forest
- Broadleaf Forest
- Mixed Needleleaf and Broadleaf Forest
- Woodland and Shrub (Mediterranean)

Mid-Latitude Grassland
- Short Grass (Steppe)
- Tall Grass (Prairie)
- Desert and Desert Shrub
- Tundra and Alpine
- Permanent Ice Cover

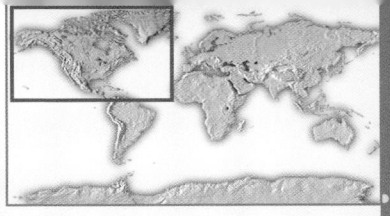

North America - Geographical Comparisons

● NEW YORK 42

AVERAGE ANNUAL RAINFALL
IN INCHES AT SELECTED STATIONS

AVERAGE ANNUAL RAINFALL

INCHES		CM		INCHES		CM		INCHES		CM	
OVER 80		OVER 200		40 TO 60		100 TO 150		10 TO 20		25 TO 50	
60 TO 80		150 TO 200		20 TO 40		50 TO 100		UNDER 10		UNDER 25	

● CITIES WITH OVER 2,000,000
INHABITANTS

POPULATION DISTRIBUTION

DENSITY PER		SQ. MI.	SQ. KM.	SQ. MI.	SQ. KM.
SQ. MI.	SQ. KM.	130 TO 260 / 50 TO 100		3 TO 25 / 1 TO 10	
OVER 260 / OVER 100		25 TO 130 / 10 TO 50		UNDER 3 / UNDER 1	

LAND USE

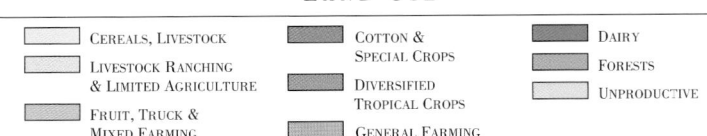

CEREALS, LIVESTOCK	COTTON & SPECIAL CROPS
LIVESTOCK RANCHING & LIMITED AGRICULTURE	DIVERSIFIED TROPICAL CROPS
FRUIT, TRUCK & MIXED FARMING	GENERAL FARMING
DAIRY	
FORESTS	
UNPRODUCTIVE	

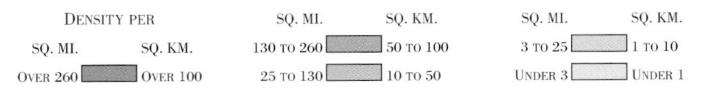

MINERAL RESOURCES

ENERGY & FUELS	IRON & FERROALLOYS	OTHER MAJOR RESOURCES	
◆ COAL	1 COBALT	1 ANTIMONY	7 GOLD	13 PLATINUM
▲ NATURAL GAS	2 IRON ORE	2 ASBESTOS	8 GRAPHITE	14 POTASH
● PETROLEUM	3 MANGANESE	3 BAUXITE	9 LEAD	15 SILVER
■ URANIUM	4 MOLYBDENUM	4 BORAX	10 MERCURY	16 SULFUR
	5 NICKEL	5 COPPER	11 MICA	17 TITANIUM
	6 TUNGSTEN	6 FLUORSPAR	12 PHOSPHATES	18 ZINC
	7 VANADIUM			

© HAMMOND WORLD ATLAS CORPORATION   CM - A-A

BEAUFORT SEA

C. Wrottesley
C. Prince Alfred

Banks Island

AULAVIK NP

Prince Albert Peninsula

Victoria Island

M'Clintock Channel

Prince of Wales Island

Somerset Island

Boothia Peninsula

Amundsen Gulf

Prince Albert Sound

Wollaston Peninsula

Coronation Gulf   Dease Str.

Queen Maud Gulf

King William I.

Gjoa Haven

Taloyoak

ALASKA
UNITED STATES

YUKON TERRITORY

Anchorage

Mount McKinley

Arctic Circle

Mackenzie R.

Franklin Mts.

NORTHWEST TERRITORIES

Yellowknife

Great Slave Lake

Hay River

Fort Smith

N U N

Baker Lake

Rankin Inlet

Whale Cove

Arviat

Gulf of Alaska

PACIFIC OCEAN

Alexander Archipelago

Queen Charlotte Islands

Hecate Strait

COAST MOUNTAINS

BRITISH COLUMBIA

Prince George

Vancouver Island

Vancouver

Victoria

Seattle
Tacoma
WASHINGTON

Portland
Salem
OREGON

Columbia Plateau

Great Basin

CALIFORNIA

San Francisco
San Jose
Sacramento

NEVADA

UTAH
Salt Lake City
Provo

IDAHO
Boise

MONTANA

Helena

Great Falls

WYOMING

ALBERTA

Edmonton

Calgary

Lethbridge

Medicine Hat

SASKATCHEWAN

Saskatoon

Regina

MANITOBA

Winnipeg

Hudson Bay

Lake Winnipeg

CANADA
UNITED STATES

U N I T E D   S T A T E S

NORTH DAKOTA

Bismarck

Fargo

SOUTH DAKOTA

Pierre

NEBRASKA

MINNESOTA

Minneapolis
Saint Paul

Duluth

WISCONSIN

IOWA

Thunder Bay

Height

m.ft.
6000 / 19700
4000 / 13000
2000 / 6500
1500 / 5000
1000 / 3300
500 / 1600
200 / 700
0
200 / 700
500 / 1600
1000 / 3300
2000 / 6500
3000 / 9800
4000 / 13000
5000 / 16400
6000 / 19700

Depth

Population
- ■ Over 2,000,000
- ■ 1,000,000 - 1,999,999
- ● 500,000 - 999,999
- ● 100,000 - 499,999
- ● 50,000 - 99,999
- ○ Under 50,000

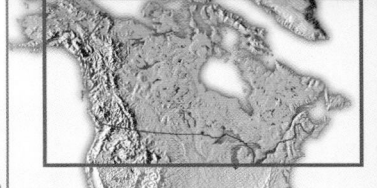
H 80° J 70° K 60° L 50° Q 140° R 120° S 100° T 80° 60°

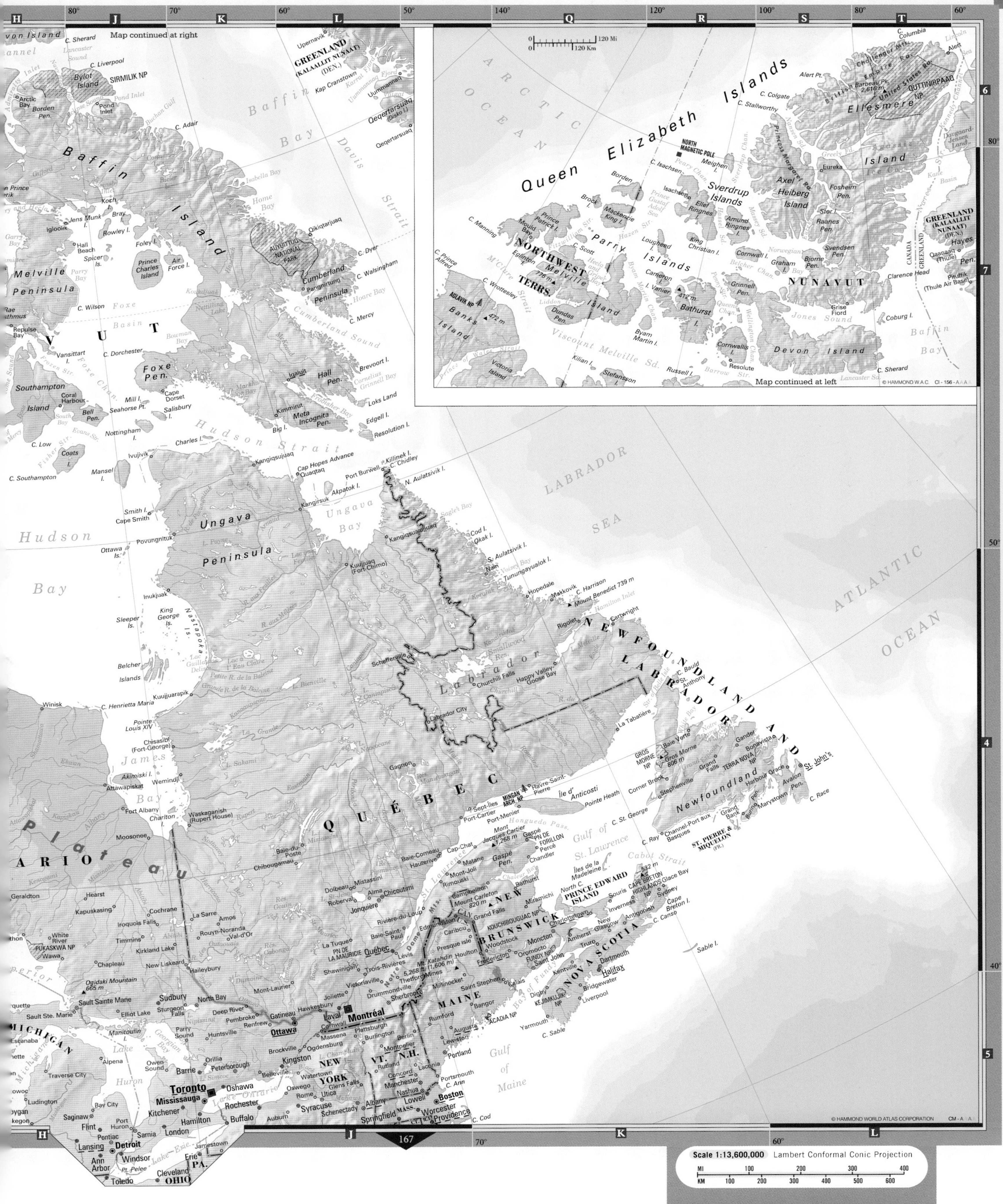

Map continued at right

0 ___ 120 Mi
0 ___ 120 Km

GREENLAND
(KALAALLIT NUNAAT)
(DEN.)

Baffin Bay

Davis Strait

SIRMILIK NP

AUYUITTUQ NATIONAL PARK

Baffin Island

Cumberland Peninsula

Cumberland Sound

Foxe Basin

NUNAVUT

Melville Peninsula

Foxe Pen.

Southampton Island

Hudson Strait

Hudson Bay

Ungava Peninsula

Ungava Bay

Queen Elizabeth Islands

North Magnetic Pole

Ellesmere Island

Ellesmere NP

GREENLAND (KALAALLIT NUNAAT) (DEN.)

Sverdrup Islands

Axel Heiberg Island

Parry Islands

NORTHWEST TERRS.

Banks Island

Melville Island

NUNAVUT

AULAVIK NP

Bathurst

Victoria Island

Devon Island

Viscount Melville Sd.

Baffin Bay

Map continued at left

© HAMMOND W.A.C.   CI-156-A-A

LABRADOR SEA

Labrador

Churchill Falls

Happy Valley-Goose Bay

Labrador City

NEWFOUNDLAND AND LABRADOR

ATLANTIC OCEAN

QUÉBEC

James Bay

Plateau

La Grande

Newfoundland

GROS MORNE NP

Gros Morne 806 m

TERRA NOVA NP

St. John's

Gulf of St. Lawrence

Anticosti

MINGAN ARCH. NP

ST. PIERRE & MIQUELON (FR.)

Cabot Strait

NEW BRUNSWICK

PRINCE EDWARD ISLAND

CAPE BRETON HIGHLANDS NP

NOVA SCOTIA

Gaspé Pen.

FORILLON NP

Bay of Fundy

Halifax

FUNDY NP

KOUCHIBOUGUAC NP

KEJIMKUJIK NP

Québec

Montréal

Ottawa

Toronto

Mississauga

Lake Ontario

MAINE

Mt. Katahdin 5,268 ft. (1,606 m)

ACADIA NP

NEW YORK

VT. N.H.

MASS.

Boston

Providence

Gulf of Maine

MICHIGAN

PUKASKWA NP

Lake Superior

Lake Huron

Detroit

Windsor

PA.

OHIO

LA MAURICIE NP

© HAMMOND WORLD ATLAS CORPORATION   CM-A-A

H J 167 K 70° L 60°

Scale 1:13,600,000   Lambert Conformal Conic Projection

MI 100 200 300 400
KM 100 200 300 400 500 600

164

184

140° 135° 130° 125° 120° 115° 110° 105° 100°

45°

3

40°

4

35°

5

30°

PACIFIC OCEAN

BRITISH COLUMBIA

Vancouver Island

Vancouver
New Westminster

Seattle
Tacoma
Olympia
WASHINGTON
Spokane
Mt. Rainier NP
14,410 ft. (4,392 m)

Portland
Salem
OREGON
Mt. Hood 11,235 ft. (3,424 m)

Eugene
Bend

Crater Lake NP
Medford

REDWOOD NP
Mt. Shasta
14,162 ft. (4,317 m)
Lassen Pk.
10,457 ft. (3,187 m)

Santa Rosa
Berkeley
San Francisco
San Mateo
Oakland
Sunnyvale
Santa Cruz
San Jose
Salinas
Monterey
Pt. Sur

CALIFORNIA

Sacramento
Stockton
Modesto
Fresno
YOSEMITE NAT'L PARK
KINGS CANYON NAT'L PARK
SEQUOIA NAT'L PARK

Bakersfield
Lancaster

Santa Barbara
Ventura
Los Angeles
Long Beach
Anaheim
Riverside
San Bernardino

San Diego
Tijuana
Mexicali

BAJA CALIFORNIA

ALBERTA
Calgary

SASKATCHEWAN

Regina

MONTANA

WYOMING

NEVADA
Great Basin
Reno
Carson City
Las Vegas
North Las Vegas
Henderson
HOOVER DAM

UTAH
Salt Lake City
Provo

IDAHO
Boise

NORTH DAKOTA

SOUTH DAKOTA

NEBRASKA

COLORADO
Denver
Aurora
Colorado Springs
Pueblo

ARIZONA
Phoenix
Tempe
Mesa
Scottsdale
Tucson

NEW MEXICO
Albuquerque
Santa Fe

El Paso
Ciudad Juárez

SONORA
CHIHUAHUA

TEXAS

COAHUILA DE ZARAGOZA

NUEVO LEÓN
Monterrey
Saltillo

MEXICO
ZACATECAS

SAN LUIS POTOSÍ

JALISCO
Guadalajara

GUANAJUATO
León

A B C D E F

Height
m. ft.
6000 19700
4000 13000
2000 6500
1500 5000
1000 3300
500 1600
200 700
0
200 700
500 1600
1000 3300
2000 6500
3000 9800
4000 13000
5000 16400
6000 19700
m. ft.
Depth

R 160° S 158° T

9
22°

10

11

H A W A I I

Kauai
Princeville
Kapaa
Lihue

Niihau

Kauai Channel

Oahu
Honolulu

Molokai

Lanai
Maui
HALEAKALA

Kahoolawe

Alenuihaha Channel

PACIFIC OCEAN

Hawaii
Mauna Kea 13,796 ft. (4,205 m)
Hilo
HAWAII VOLCANOES NAT'L PK
Mauna Loa 13,677 ft. (4,169 m)

V W T U F

Population
■ Over 2,000,000
■ 1,000,000 - 1,999,999
● 500,000 - 999,999
⊙ 100,000 - 499,999
○ 50,000 - 99,999
○ Under 50,000

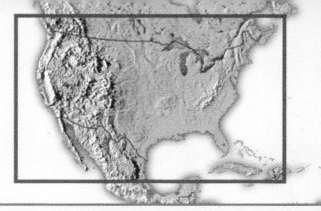
Scale 1:13,600,000   Lambert Conformal Conic Projection

| MI | | 100 | | 200 | | 300 | | 400 |
| KM | 100 | 200 | 300 | 400 | 500 | 600 | | |

© HAMMOND WORLD ATLAS CORPORATION   CM–A–A

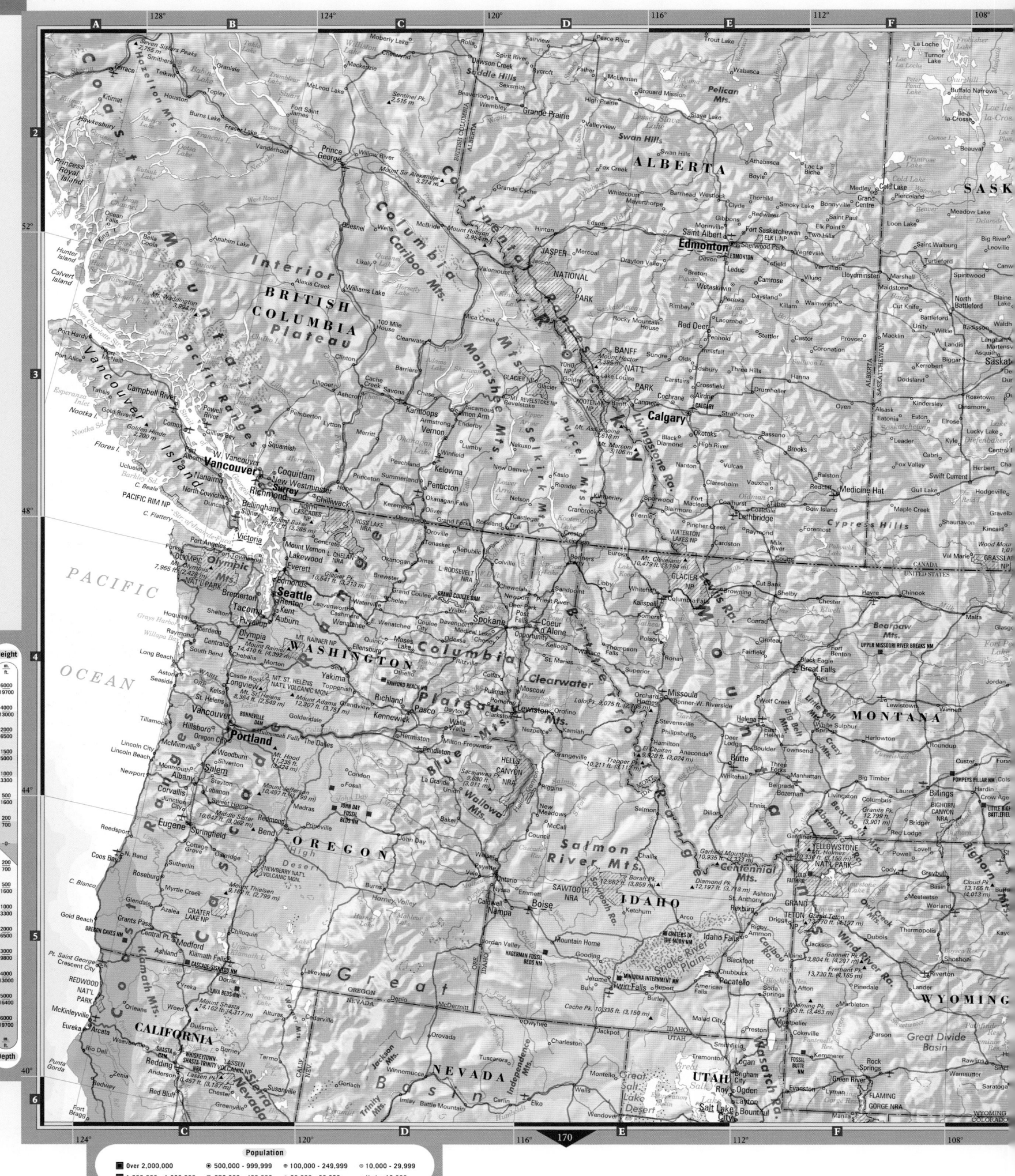

A 128° B 124° C 120° D 116° E 112° F 108°

PACIFIC

OCEAN

BRITISH
COLUMBIA

ALBERTA

SASK.

Edmonton

Calgary

Interior
Plateau

Vancouver
Island

Vancouver

Victoria

Seattle

Tacoma

Olympia

WASHINGTON

Spokane

Columbia
Plateau

MONTANA

Portland

Salem

Eugene

OREGON

Helena

Missoula

Great
Basin

IDAHO

Boise

WYOMING

CALIFORNIA

NEVADA

UTAH

Salt Lake
City

Height
m.
ft.
6000
19700
4000
13000
2000
6500
1500
5000
1000
3300
500
1600
200
700
0
200
700
500
1600
1000
3300
2000
6500
3000
9800
4000
13000
5000
16400
6000
19700
m.
ft.
Depth

A 124° C 120° D 116° 170 E 112° F 108°

Population
■ Over 2,000,000
■ 1,000,000 - 1,999,999
◉ 500,000 - 999,999
◉ 250,000 - 499,999
● 100,000 - 249,999
● 30,000 - 99,999
○ 10,000 - 29,999
○ Under 10,000

Southwestern Canada, Northwestern United States

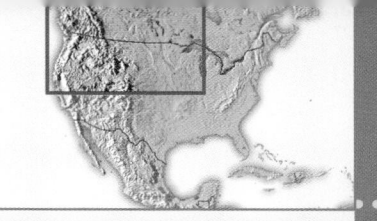

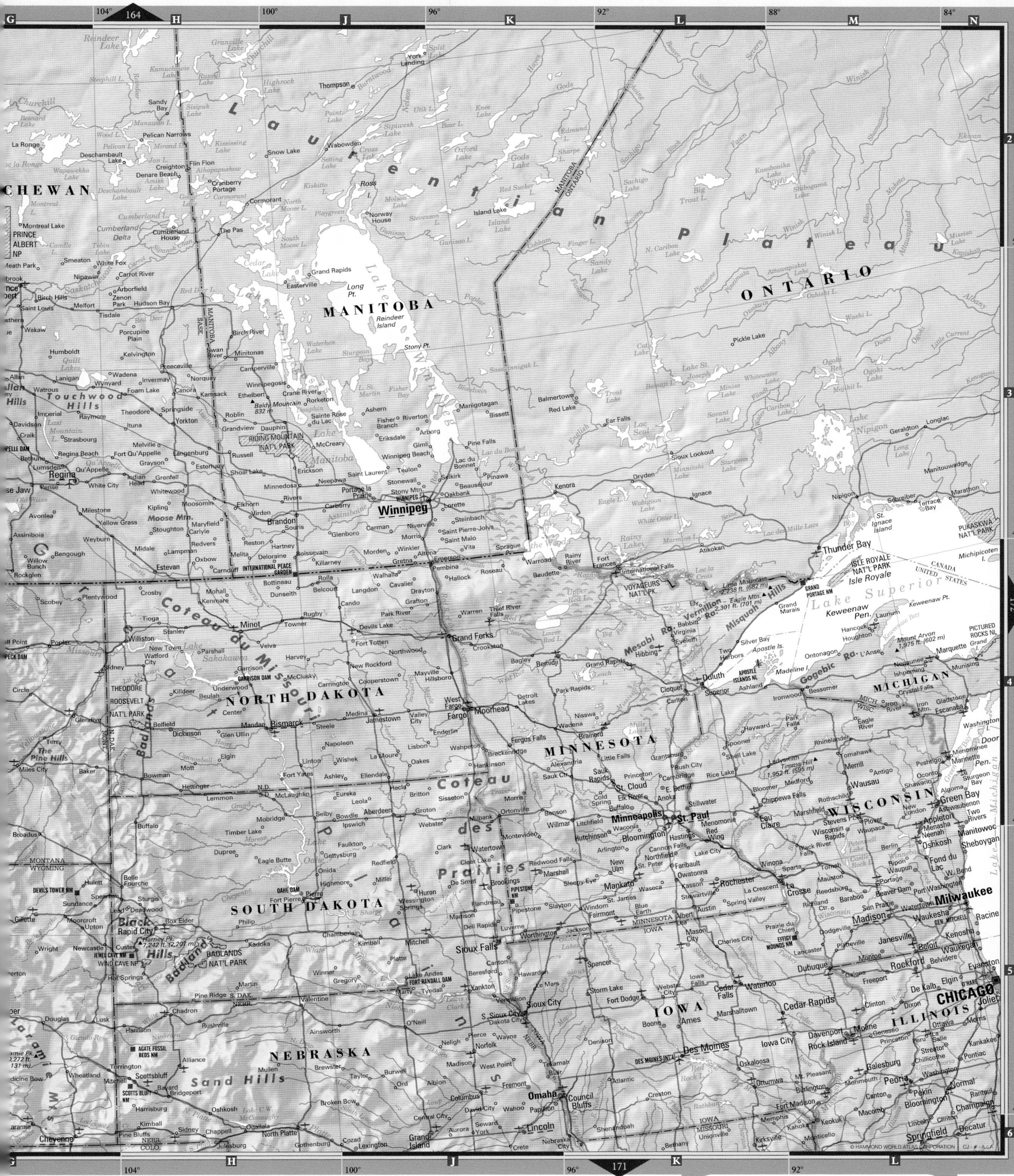

Scale 1:6,800,000 Lambert Conformal Conic Projection

MI 0 50 100 150 200
KM 0 50 100 150 200 250 300

124° 120° 116° 112° 108°

A B C D E

PACIFIC OCEAN

Height

m. ft.
6000 19700
4000 13000
2000 6500
1500 5000
1000 3300
500 1600
200 700
0
200 700
500 1600
1000 3300
2000 6500
3000 9800
4000 13000
5000 16400
6000 19700
m. ft.

Depth

OREGON

IDAHO

WYOMING

NEVADA

UTAH

CALIFORNIA

ARIZONA

COLORADO

Colorado Plateau

NEW MEXICO

BAJA CALIFORNIA

SONORA

Baja California

Gulf of California

San Francisco
Oakland
San Jose
Sacramento
Fresno
LOS ANGELES
Long Beach
Anaheim
Santa Ana
San Diego
Tijuana
Mexicali
Las Vegas
Phoenix
Mesa
Tempe
Scottsdale
Tucson
Albuquerque
Rio Rancho
Ciudad Juárez
Hermosillo

Population

■ Over 2,000,000
■ 1,000,000 - 1,999,999
● 500,000 - 999,999
● 250,000 - 499,999
● 100,000 - 249,999
● 30,000 - 99,999
○ 10,000 - 29,999
○ Under 10,000

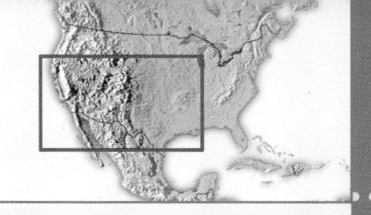

Scale 1:6,800,000 Lambert Conformal Conic Projection

MI 50 100 150 200

KM 50 100 150 200 250 300

© Hammond World Atlas Corporation

Population
- ◼ Over 2,000,000
- ◼ 1,000,000 - 1,999,999
- ● 500,000 - 999,999
- ● 250,000 - 499,999
- ● 100,000 - 249,999
- ● 30,000 - 99,999
- ○ 10,000 - 29,999
- ○ Under 10,000

Population

■ Over 2,000,000 ● 500,000 - 999,999 ● 100,000 - 249,999 ● 10,000 - 29,999
■ 1,000,000 - 1,999,999 ● 250,000 - 499,999 ● 30,000 - 99,999 ● Under 10,000

Southeastern United States

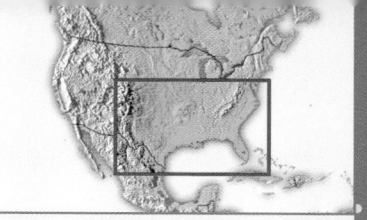

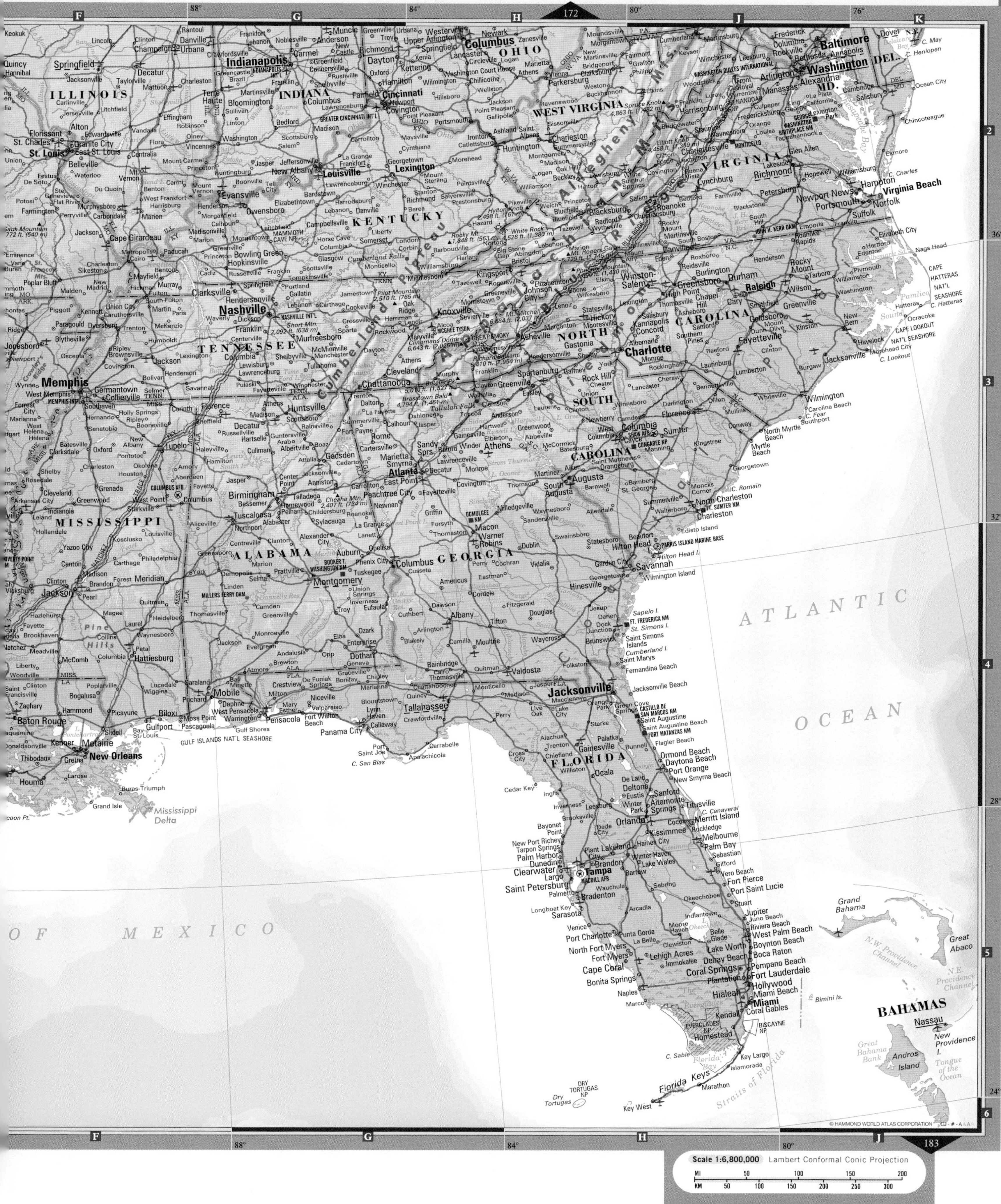

Scale 1:6,800,000   Lambert Conformal Conic Projection

MI   50   100   150   200

KM 50   100   150   200   250   300

© HAMMOND WORLD ATLAS CORPORATION

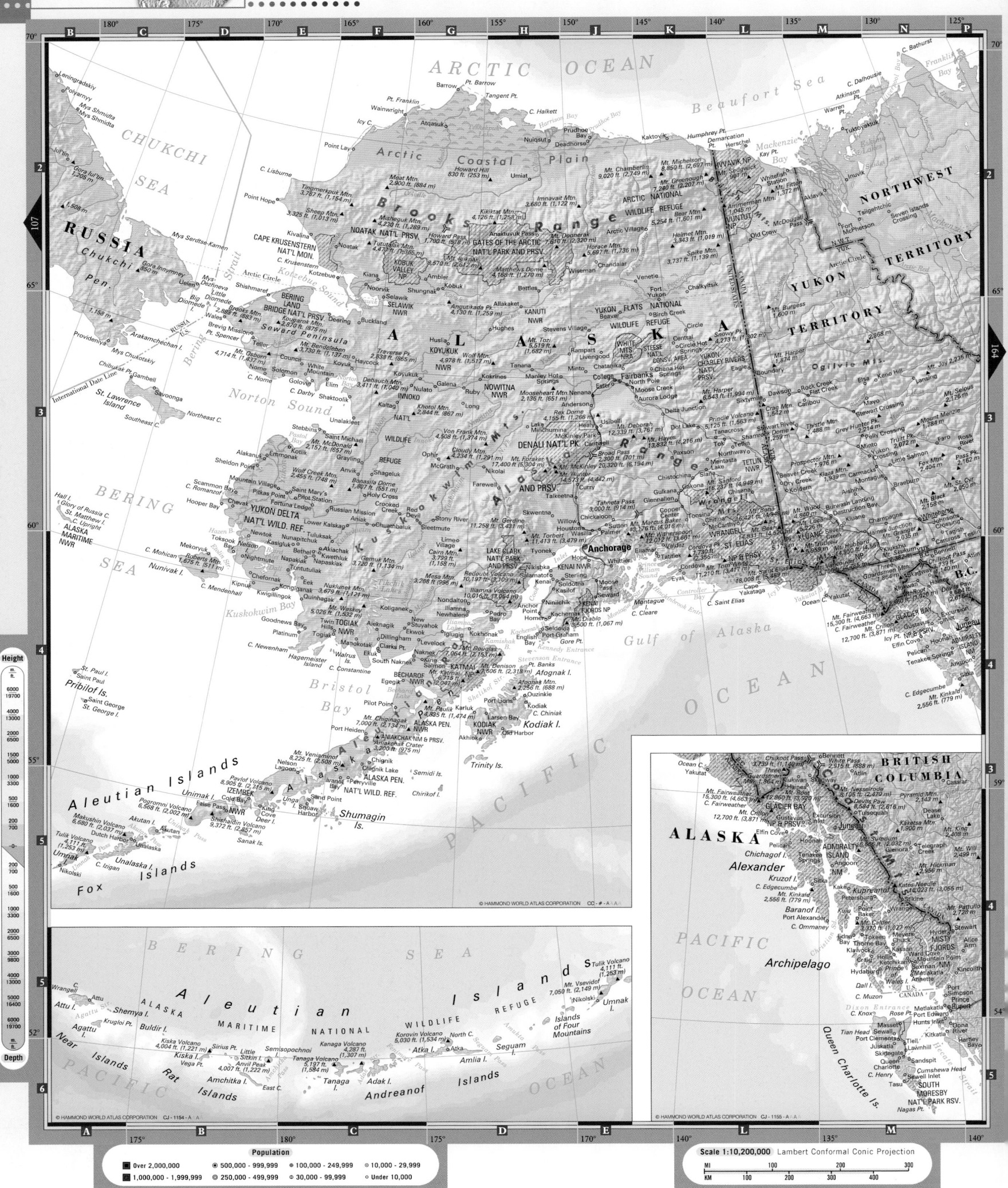

70° B 180° C 175° D 170° E 165° F 160° G 155° H 150° J 145° K 140° L 135° M 130° N 125° P 70°

ARCTIC OCEAN

Beaufort Sea

CHUKCHI SEA

RUSSIA

Chukchi Pen.

Brooks Range

Arctic Coastal Plain

NORTHWEST TERRITORIES

YUKON TERRITORY

A L A S K A

BERING SEA

Norton Sound

Seward Peninsula

Kuskokwim Mts

Alaska Range

Pribilof Is.

DENALI NAT'L PK. AND PRSV.

Anchorage

Gulf of Alaska

PACIFIC OCEAN

Bristol Bay

Kodiak I.

Aleutian Islands

Alaska Pen.

Fox Islands

Shumagin Is.

BERING SEA

Aleutian Islands

WILDLIFE REFUGE

ALASKA MARITIME NATIONAL

Near Islands   Rat Islands   Andreanof Islands

PACIFIC OCEAN

BRITISH COLUMBIA

ALASKA

Alexander Archipelago

Juneau

PACIFIC OCEAN

Queen Charlotte Is.

Height

ft. m
6000 19700
4000 13000
2000 6500
1500 5000
1000 3300
500 1600
200 700
-0-
200 700
500 1600
1000 3300
2000 6500
4000 13000
5000 16400
6000 19700

Depth

© HAMMOND WORLD ATLAS CORPORATION

Seattle, San Francisco, Detroit, Chicago

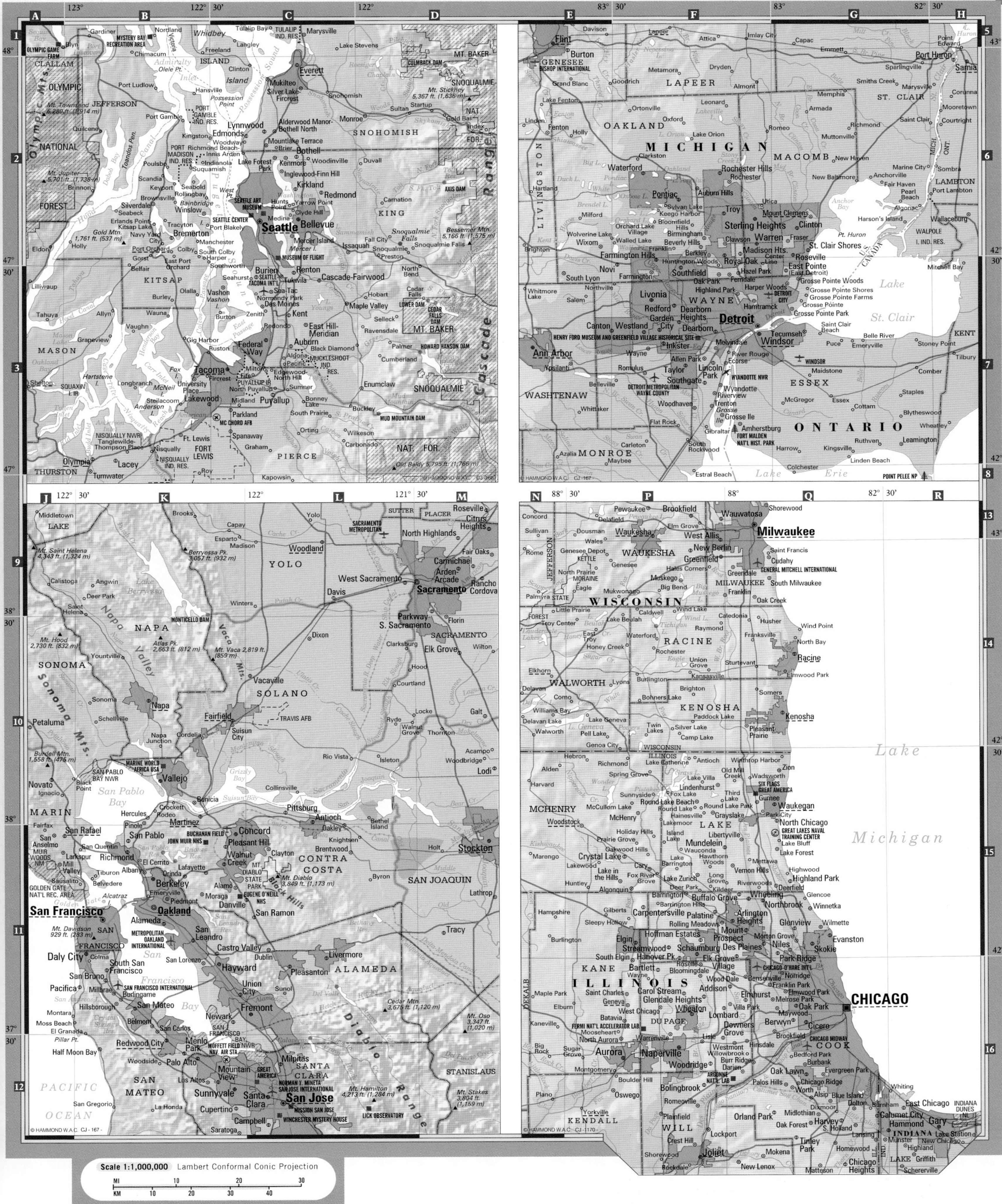

Scale 1:1,000,000   Lambert Conformal Conic Projection

MI 10   20   30
KM 10 20   30   40

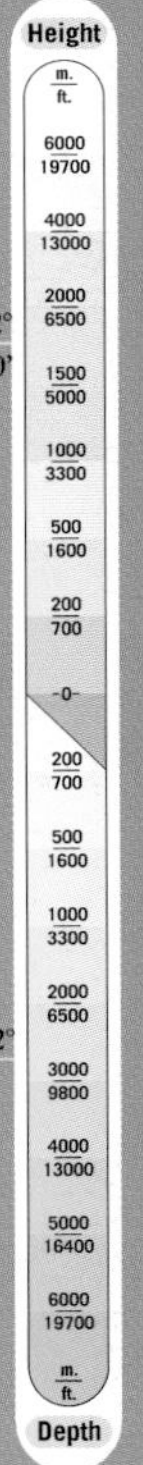

© HAMMOND W.A.C. CJ - 167
© HAMMOND W.A.C. CJ - 1170

Los Angeles-San Diego

Population
Over 2,000,000
1,000,000 - 1,999,999
500,000 - 999,999
250,000 - 499,999
100,000 - 249,999
30,000 - 99,999
10,000 - 29,999
Under 10,000

Scale 1:1,140,000 Lambert Conformal Conic Projection

Phoenix, Salt Lake City, Denver, Oklahoma City, Kansas City, St. Louis, San Antonio, New Orleans

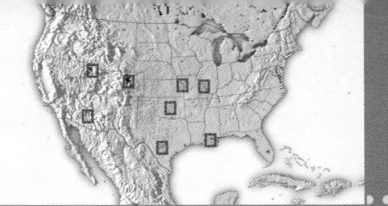

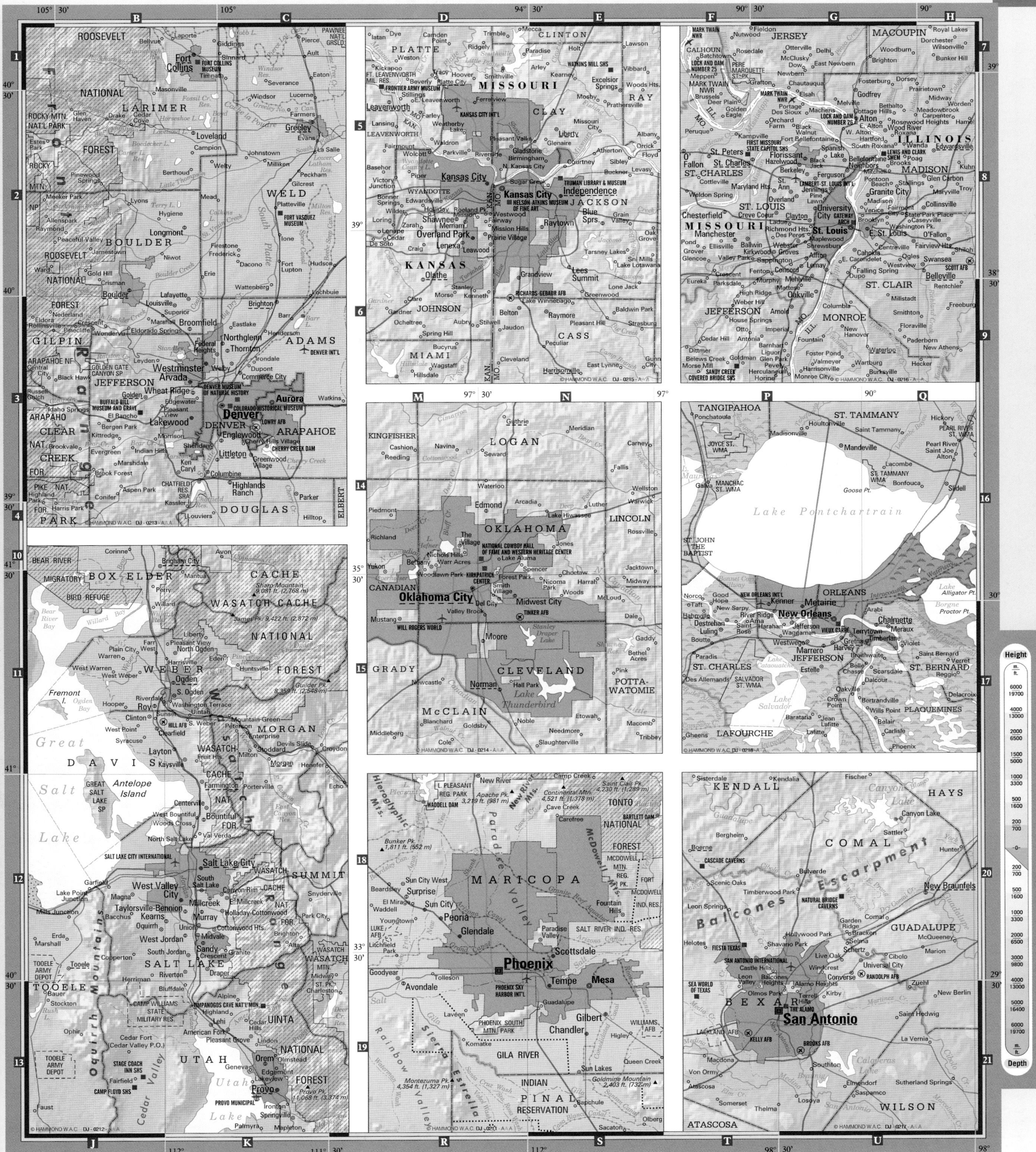

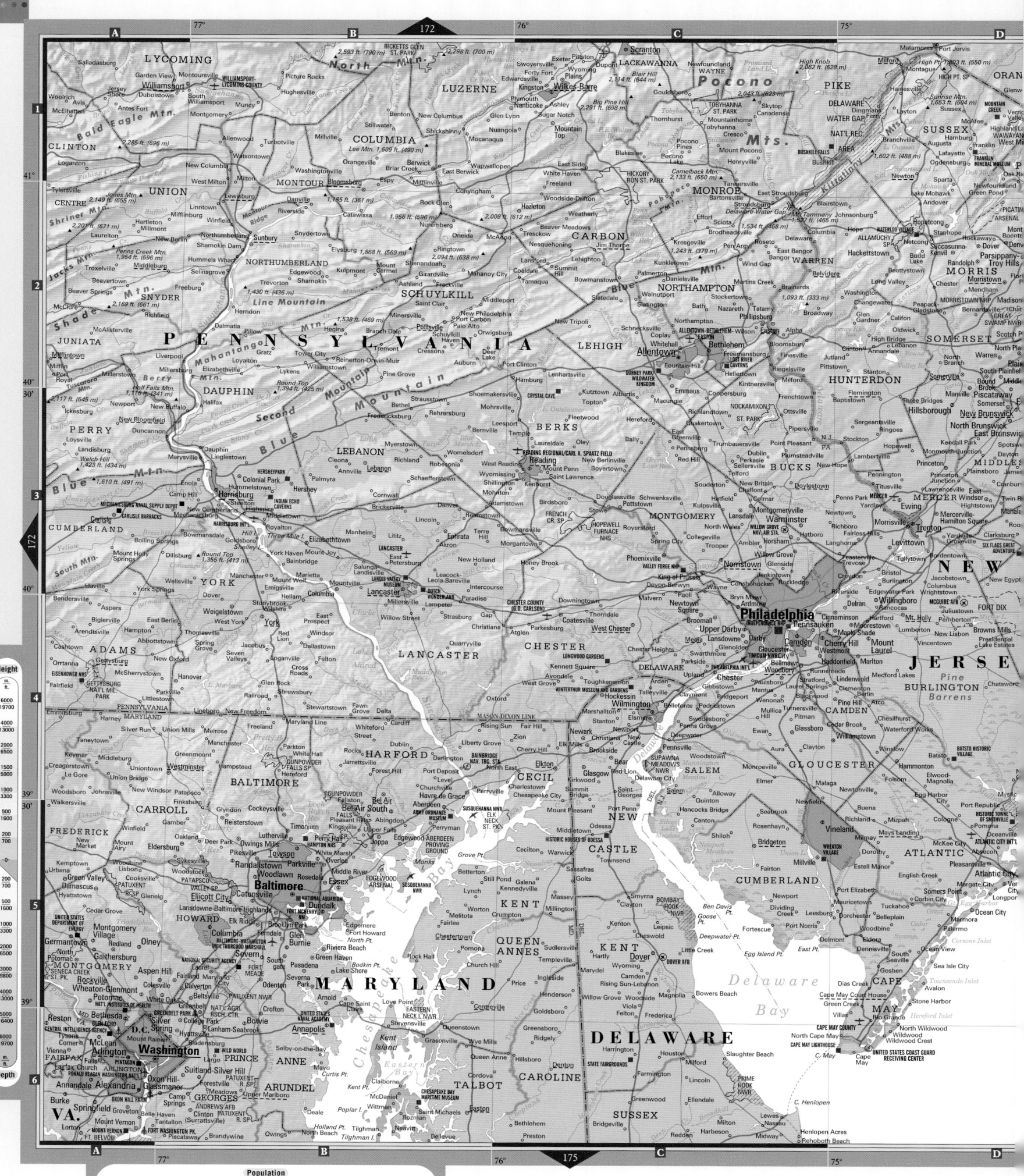

172

77°   76°   75°

A   B   C   D

LYCOMING

Salladasburg   RICKETTS GLEN   12,298 ft. (700 m)   Scranton   Matamoras   Port Jervis
Garden View   ST. PARK   Sweyowersville   Exeter Pittston   Dupont   LACKAWANNA   Newfoundland   High Knob   High Pt. 1,803 ft. (550 m)
Williamsport   Montoursville   2,593 ft. (790 m)   Forty Fort   Wyoming   WAYNE   Promised   2,062 ft. (628 m)   Milford   Montague   HIGH PT. SP.
Duboistown   South   Picture Rocks   North   Mtn.   Plains   Wilkes-Barre   Land St.   Pocono   PIKE   Sunrise Mtn.   ORAN
Woolrich   Avis   Williamsport   Muncy   Hughesville   Benton   New Columbus   Plymouth   Kingston   DELAWARE   1,653 ft. (504 m)   McAfee
McElhattan   Antes Fort   Montgomery   Glen Lyon   Nanticoke   Sugar Notch   Gouldsboro   WATER GAP   Dingmans   Layton   SUSSEX   Verno

CLINTON   Jersey   Shore   Allenwood   Turbotville   Millville   Stillwater   East Side   Blakeslee   Pocono   Mountain   NAT'L. REC.   Branchville   Highland La   West Mi
2,285 ft. (696 m)   Watsontown   **COLUMBIA**   Lee Mtn. 1,609 ft. (490 m)   White Haven   Pocono   Pines   Lake   AREA   Augusta   Franklin   MINERAL MUSEUM

Logantan   New Columbia   Washingtonville   Orangeville   Berwick   Freeland   Mount Pocono   Henryville   1,602 ft. (488 m)   Ogdensburg   P
West Milton   Milton   Bloomsburg   Espy   East Berwick   Wapwallopen   Woodside-Drifton   **MONROE**   Bartonsville   East Stroudsburg   Blairstown   Newton   Sparta   Oak Ri
CENTRE   2,149 ft. (655 m)   **MONTOUR**   Briar Creek   Hickory   RUN ST. PARK   Effort   Delaware Water Gap   Lake Mohawk   Green Pond

Shriner Mtn.   Lewisburg   Danville   1,185 ft. (361 m)   Catawissa   Rock Glen   2,133 ft. (650 m)   Scotia   Stroudsburg   Mt. Tammany   Johnsonburg
2,201 ft. (671 m)   Mifflinburg   Winfield   Riverside   2,008 ft. (612 m)   Beaver Meadows   1,534 ft. (468 m)   1,527 ft. (465 m)   Andover
UNION   Hartleton   2,094 ft. (638 m)   Weatherly   Brodheadsville   Hope   ALLAMUCHY   Rockaway   Denv

Beaverlown   Buffalo   Mifflinville   Nuremberg   Kresgeville   **WARREN**   Washington   Long Valley   Chester   Mendham
McClure   Freeburg   Shamokin Dam   NORTHUMBERLAND   Elysburg   Ringtown   Nesquehoning   Lehighton   1,243 ft. (379 m)   Pen Argyl   East Bangor   Belvidere   MORRIS   Morristown
2,168 ft. (661 m)   Edgewood   Kulpmont   Shenandoah   McAdoo   Tresckow   Jim Thorpe   Palmerton   Roseto   1,093 ft. (333 m)   Broadway   Peapack   Madison

SNYDER   Selinsgrove   Shamokin   1,430 ft. (436 m)   Mahanoy City   Coaldale   Summit   Lansford   Kunkletown   Martins Creek   Wind Gap   Changewater   MORRISTOWN NHP

Richfield   Herndon   Girardville   Frackville   Tamaqua   Bowmanstown   **NORTHAMPTON**   Bath   Nazareth   Tatamy   Gladstone   SWAMP NWR
PENNSYLVANIA   Trevorton   **SCHUYLKILL**   Saint Clair   Middleport   Bowmans   Slatedale   Stockertown   Phillipsburg   Bernardsville   GREAT
Shade   Mtn.   Dalmatia   Ashland   New Philadelphia   Palo Alto   Coplay   Northampton   Slatington   Alpha   Pohatcong   Scotch P

McAlisterville   Pillow   Herndon   Minersville   Port Carbon   New Tripoli   Whitehall   Bethlehem   Easton   North   Somerville
JUNIATA   Liverpool   Tower City   Pottsville   Schuylkill   Orwigsburg   Schnecksville   **LEHIGH**   Allentown   Freemansburg   Branch   Plain
Mifflintown   Loyalton   1,538 ft. (469 m)   Haven   Auburn   Hamburg   Emmaus   ALLENTOWN-BETHLEHEM   Hellertown   LOST RIVER   High Bridge   South Plainfield
Mifflin   Millersburg   Lykens   Williamstown   Pine Grove   Lenhartsville   Macungie   CAVERNS   Fountain Hill   Clinton   Lebanon   Bound   Piscataway

DAUPHIN   Elizabethville   Round Top   Shoemakersville   Kutztown   Alburtis   Coopersburg   Jutland   Annandale   Brook
2,117 ft. (645 m)   Halifax   1,394 ft. (425 m)   Bethel   Strausstown   Mohrsville   Topton   Richlandtown   Milford   **HUNTERDON**   East   Manville
Icksburg   Newport   New Buffalo   Fredericksburg   Rehrersburg   Leesport   Fleetwood   Bally   East   Quakertown   Flemington   Three Bridges   Somerset

PERRY   New Bloomfield   Duncannon   Myerstown   Bernville   Temple   Oley   Greenville   Pennsburg   NOCKAMIXON   Ringoes   Hillsborough   New Brunswick
Welch Hill   Marysville   Lingelstown   **LEBANON**   Cleona   Laureldale   ST. PARK   Pipersville   Baptistown   East Brunswick
1,423 ft. (434 m)   Colonial Park   Annville   Richland   Robesonia   READING REGIONAL/CARL A. SPAATZ FIELD   Trumbauersville   Point Pleasant   Kendall Park   Spotsw

Loysville   Enola   Hershey   Palmyra   Lebanon   Schaefferstown   Reading   New Berlinville   Perkasie   Dublin   Princeton   **MIDDLE**
Landisburg   HERSHEYPARK   Hummelstown   Wyomissing   Shillington   Boyertown   Sellersville   Telford   North Wales   New Hope   Junction   James
1,610 ft. (491 m)   INDIAN ECHO   Mount Penn   **BERKS**   Souderton   New Britain   Lambertville   Plainsboro   Pennington

Mechanicsburg   NAVAL SUPPLY DEPOT   CAVERNS   Mohnton   Saint Lawrence   **BUCKS**   Doylestown   Princeton   **MERCER**
Carlisle   New Cumberland   **HARRISBURG**   Middletown   Birdsboro   Douglassville   Schwenksville   Chalfont   Penns Park   East   Windsor   MERCER
CARLISLE BARRACKS   **HARRISBURG INT'L.**   Cornwall   Stowe   FRENCH   Kulpsville   Warminster   Yardley   Mercerville-Hamilton Square   Clarksbur
CUMBERLAND   Camp Hill   Brickerville   Denver   Lincoln   CR. SP.   Royersford   Lansdale   WILLOW GROVE   Hatboro   Ewing   East

South   Mtn.   Hill   Royalton   Manheim   Terre   HOPEWELL   Spring City   Collegeville   Trooper   NAV. AIR. STA.   Langhorne   TRENTON   Windsor
Mount Holly   Three Mile I.   Ephrata   Hill   FURNACE   Phoenixville   Ambler   Horsham   Feasterville   Levittown   Clarksburg
Springs   Shelley   Akron   Morgantown   NHS   VALLEY FORGE NHP   Trevose   Bristol   SIX FLAGS GREAT   New Egypt

Dillsburg   York Haven   Mount Joy   Bainbridge   Honey Brook   King of Prussia   Norristown   Jenkintown   Burlington   ADVENTURE   **N E W**
Boiling Springs   Royalton   Landisville   Intercourse   Devon Berwyn   Conshohocken   Glenside   Jacobstown   New Egypt
Goldsboro   Elizabethtown   LANDIS VALLEY   Leacock-Leola-Bareville   Wayne   Rockledge   Cinnaminson   Columbus

YORK   East Petersburg   MUSEUM   Malvern   Bryn Mawr   Ardmore   Croydon   Riverside   Delran   **JERSE**
1,355 ft. (413 m)   Mountville   DUTCH   Paradise   CHESTER COUNTY   Newtown   Bala   Levittown   Willingboro   Mount
Manchester   **LANCASTER**   WONDERLAND   Strasburg   (G. O. CARLSON)   Square   Broomall   **PHILADELPHIA**   Pennsauken   Maple Shade   Laurel

Mount Wolf   East   Lampeter   Gap   Downingtown   Upper Darby   Camden   Medford   Pine
Wrightsville   Emigsville   Willow Street   Christiana   Atglen   Thorndale   West   Cherry Hill   New Lisbon   **BURLINGTON**   Chatsworth
Dover   Hellam   Quarryville   Parkesburg   Coatesville   Chester   Lansdowne   Westmont   Marlton   Lakes   Barrens
Columbia   Swarthmore   Darby   Haddonfield   Hartford   Pemberton   Browns Mills

ADAMS   York   Red Lion   Willow Street   **CHESTER**   West Chester   Chester Heights   Glenolden   Gloucester   Presidential   Ft. Mott   FORT
Gettysburg   Windsor   Christiana   Longwood   Kennett Square   Avondale   PHILADELPHIA INT'L.   City   Beilmawr   Mount   Lake Estates   McGUIRE AFB
McSherrystown   Stonybrook-Wilshire   Red   Gardens   Toughkenamon   Chadds   Marshallton   Upland   Bellmawr   Laurel   FORT DIX
Hanover   Spring Grove   Lion   Seven   Marcus   WINTERTHUR MUSEUM AND GARDENS   Talleyville   Gibbstown   Runnemede   Clarksboro

Fairfield   New Oxford   Jacobus   Valleys   Oxford   West Grove   Claymont   Arden   Deepwater   Paulsboro   Turnersville   Pine Hill   Atco
EISENHOWER NHS   Cross   Avondale   Ardentown   Pennsville   Wenonah   Blackwood   Waterford Works
GETTYSBURG   Orrtanna   Stewartstown   Roads   Pedricktown   Swedesboro   Glassboro   **ATLANTIC**
NAT'L. MIL.   Cashtown   Felton   Fawn   Delta   MASON-DIXON LINE   Wilmington   Elsmere   **SALEM**   Pitman   Hammonton

PARK   New Freedom   Lineboro   Rising Sun   Fair Hill   Newark   New Castle   Penns Grove   Swedesboro   Cedar Brook   BATSTO HISTORIC
Fairfield   Biglerville   Stewartstown   PENNSYLVANIA   Whiteford   Cardiff   Christiana   Mullica   VILLAGE
Arendtsville   Spring   MARYLAND   Cecilton   Liberty Grove   Zion   Bear   Delaware City   SUPAWNA   Woodstown   Monroeville   Malaga   Batsto

Littlestown   Maryland Line   Whitehall   Rising Sun   Fair Hill   Elk Mills   Brookside   MEADOWS   GLOUCESTER   Folsom   Elwood-
Silver Run   Dees   Street   Rocks   Brookside   NWR   Woodstown   Magnolia
Union Mills   Freeland   Cardiff   Christiana   Glasgow   Red Lion   Swedesboro   Newfield   Egg Harbor   Atlantic

CARROLL   Melrose   Manchester   **HARFORD**   Darlington   BAINBRIDGE   Elkton   Middletown   Clayton   Williamstown   Buena   City
Taneytown   Maryland Line   Bel Air   NAV. TRG. STA.   North East   Kirkwood   Saint Georges   Aura   Winslow   ATLANTIC CITY INT'L.
Creagerstown   Harney   Union Bridge   Jarrettsville   Port Deposit   Perryville   Summit   **NEW**   Elmer   Richland

Kevmar   Silver Run   Greenmount   Forest Hill   Chesapeake City   Glasgow   Saint Georges   Clayton   Newtonville   Pleasantville
Le Gore   Middleburg   Hampstead   Bel Air South   Havre de Grace   HISTORIC HOUSES OF ODESSA   Odessa   **CASTLE**   English Creek   Northfield
Uniontown   ARMY ORDNANCE   Aberdeen   Middletown   Shiloh   Mays Landing   Margate City

Woodsboro   Johnsville   New Windsor   GUNPOWDER   MUSEUM   ABERDEEN   Chesapeake City   Canton   **CUMBERLAND**   Corbin City   Somers Point
FREDERICK   FALLS SP   Pleasant Hills   Perryman   PROVING   Cecilton   Middletown   Rosenhayn   Vineland   McKee City   Longport
New Market   Winfield   Hereford   Abingdon   GROUND   Warwick   Bridgeton   Mauricetown   Ocean

Walkersville   Woodbine   Manchester   Kingsville   Upper Falls   Joppa   Cecilton   Townsend   Fairton   Port Elizabeth   Leesburg   Ocean City
Mount Airy   Reisterstown   Timonium   EDGEWOOD   Grove Pt.   Still Pond   Galena   Golts   Millville   Dividing Creek   City

Woodsboro   Sykesville   Owings Mills   Parkville   White Marsh   ABERDEEN   SUSQUEHANNA   Lynch   Smyrna   Dorchester   Port Norris   Delmont   Woodbine   Marmora
Silver Run   Gamber   Glyndon   Lutherville   Overlea   EDGEWOOD   NWR   Massey   Clayton   Fortescue   Bellplain
BALTIMORE   Cockeysville   Rosedale   ARSENAL   Betterton   **KENT**   Kenton   Seabrook   Palermo

Germantown   Green Valley   Randallstown   Woodlawn   Essex   SUSQUEHANNA   Melitota   Crumpton   Millington   Leipsic   Port Republic   Avalon
North   Damascus   Cooksville   PATAPSCO   Dundalk   NWR   Chestertown   Millington   Kenton   **KENT**   Maurcetown   Sea Isle City
Gaithersburg   Hyattsville   VALLEY SP   Catonsville   EDGEWATER   Kennedyville   Pomona   Leipsic   Wyoming   Hartly   DOVER   Dover   Corsons Inlet

Montgomery Village   Glenelg   **BALTIMORE**   NATIONAL AQUARIUM   Sudlersville   Sudlersville   Little Creek   DOVER AFB   Dias Creek
Redland   Ellicott City   Lansdowne-Baltimore Highlands   FORT McHENRY NM   Church Hill   Templeville   Marydel   Rising Sun-Lebanon   Green Creek
MONTGOMERY   Columbia   FORT ARMISTEAD   Queenstown   **QUEEN**   Mayrel   Viola   Magnolia   Bowers Beach   CAPE MAY COUNTY   North Wildwood

Olney   SENECA   Elk Ridge   Brooklyn Park   Queen   **ANNE'S**   Frederica   Felton   CAPE MAY COURT HOUSE   Wildwood
Rockville   CREEK   Columbia   Glen   Chesterwown   Price   Woodside   Milford   **CAPE**   Wildwood Crest
UNITED STATES   ST. PK.   Ferndale   Burnie   Pomona   Ingleside   Henderson   Ellendale   Lincoln   Rio Grande   CAPE MAY LIGHTHOUSE   C. May

DEPARTMENT   Gaithersburg   Colesville   Severn   Riviera Beach   Sudlersville   Goldsboro   **MAY**   South Cape May
OF ENERGY   Wheaton-Glenmont   Laurel   Severna   Rock Hall   Pasadena   **DELAWARE**   Slaughter Beach   UNITED STATES COAST GUARD   North
North   Fairland   FORT   Park   Green Haven   Kent   Milton   Cape   RECEIVING CENTER   Cape May

Potomac   Wheaton   MEADE   Odenton   Bodkin Pt.   Island   Deepwater Pt.   Harrington   Milford   Nassau
NAT'L. INSTITUTES   NAT'L. AGRI.   Maryland   Arnold   NWR   Kent   Greensboro   Lincoln   Harbeson   Lewes
Reston   OF HEALTH   RSCH. CTR.   Crofton   City   Cape Saint   **EASTERN**   Queenstown   STATE   Farmington   Milton   Henlopen Acres

CENTRAL   Germantown   College Park   Bowie   Claire   NECK I. NWR   Wye Mills   FAIRGROUNDS   Greenwood   Ellendale   Acres
INTELLIGENCE   GREENBELT   Lanham-Seabrook   Love Point   Grasonville   **CAROLINE**   Denton   Redden   Rehoboth Beach
AGENCY   Silver   Spring   NAT'L. AGRI.   Selby-on-the-Bay   **TALBOT**   Easton   Midway

WASHINGTON   D.C.   Suitland-Silver Hill   Mayo   Kent   Cordova   Harbeson
McLean   Mount Rainier   Largo   **PRINCE**   **ANNE**   Curtis Pt.   Island   Bozman   Saint Michaels   **SUSSEX**
Vienna   Falls   PENTAGON   Oxon Hill   Lisbon   Suitland   Wild World   Deale   Eastern   McDaniel   Bridgeville
FAIRFAX   Arlington   Glassmanor   **ARUNDEL**   Bay   Wittman   Greenwood

Annandale   Alexandria   Camp   ANDREWS AFB   PATUXENT   Holland Pt.   Tilghman   Neavitt   Bethlehem   Lincoln   Milton
Burke   RONALD REAGAN WASHINGTON NAT'L.   Springs   Upper Marlboro   North Beach   Poplar I.   Preston   Harbeson
Springfield   **GEORGES**   Meadows   Tilghman I.   **CAROLINE**   Greenwood   Harbeson

VA.   OXON HILL FARM   Brandywine   Poplar I.   **TALBOT**   **DELAWARE**   Redden
Belle Haven   FORT WASHINGTON PK.   Piscataway   North Beach   Reedon   Midway
Lorton   MOUNT VERNON   Piscataway   Bellevue   Preston   Lewes

77°   76°   75°

A   B   C   D

175

Population

◼ Over 2,000,000   ⬤ 500,000 - 999,999   ⬤ 100,000 - 249,999   ⬤ 10,000 - 29,999
◼ 1,000,000 - 1,999,999   ⬤ 250,000 - 499,999   ⬤ 30,000 - 99,999   ⬤ Under 10,000

Height

ft.   m.
6000   19700
4000   13000
2000   6500
1500   5000
1000   3300
500   1600
200   700

0   0

200   700
500   1600
1000   3300
2000   6500
3000   9800
4000   13000
5000   16400
6000   19700

Depth

I
41°
40°30'
3
40°
4
39°30'
39°
5
6

New York-Philadelphia-Washington

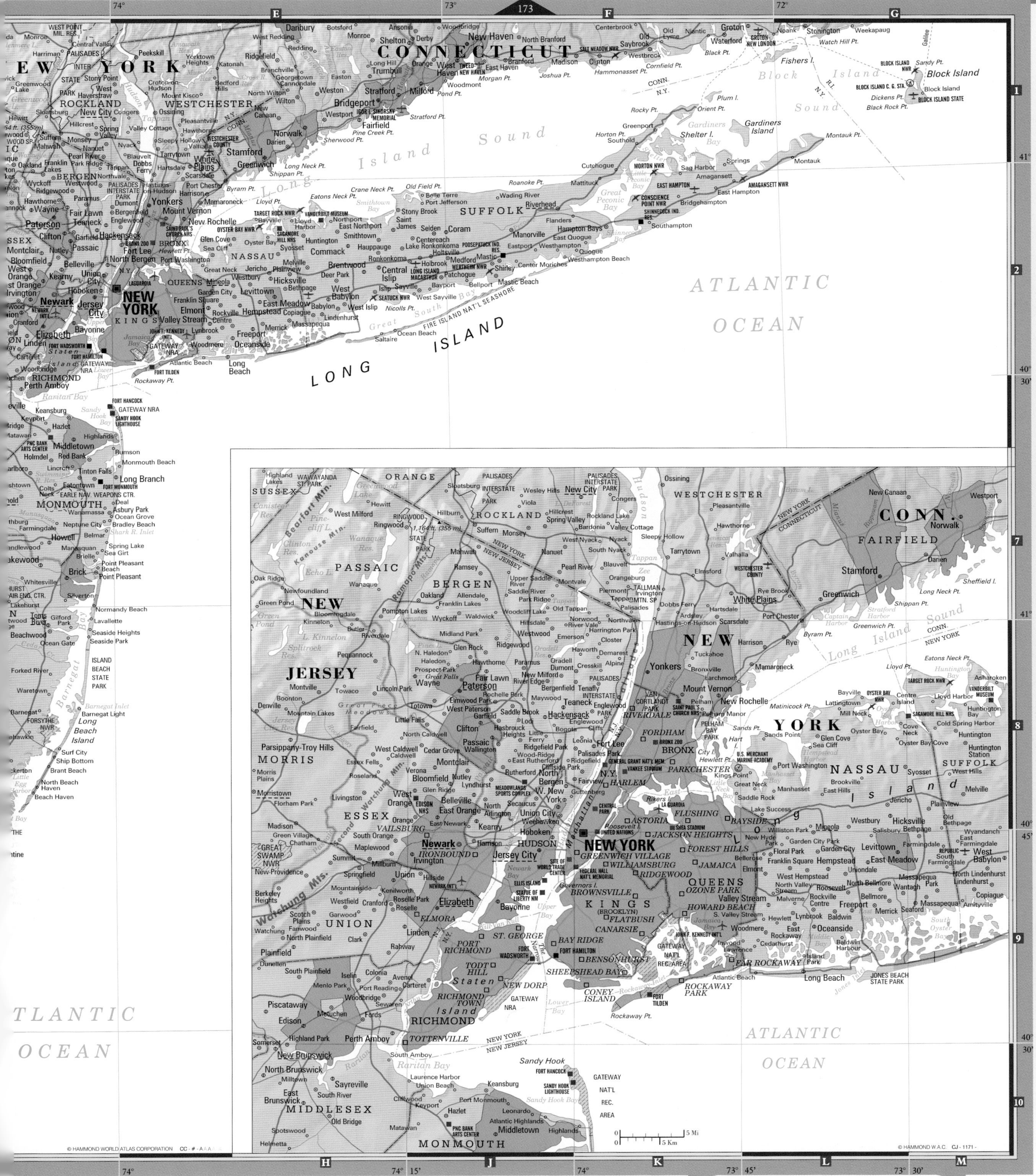

Scale 1:1,140,000 Lambert Conformal Conic Projection

© HAMMOND WORLD ATLAS CORPORATION

Height

m.	ft.
6000	19700
4000	13000
2000	6500
1500	5000
1000	3300
500	1600
200	700
-0-	
200	700
500	1600
1000	3300
2000	6500
3000	9800
4000	13000
5000	16400
6000	19700
m.	ft.

Depth

MEXICO
① DISTRITO FEDERAL
② MÉXICO
③ MORELOS
④ TLAXCALA
⑤ QUERÉTARO DE ARTEAGA
⑥ AGUASCALIENTES

Population
- ■ Over 2,000,000
- ■ 1,000,000 - 1,999,999
- ◉ 500,000 - 999,999
- ◉ 250,000 - 499,999
- ◉ 100,000 - 249,999
- ◉ 30,000 - 99,999
- ◉ 10,000 - 29,999
- ◦ Under 10,000

DOMINICAN REPUBLIC
PUERTO RICO
(U.S.)
Virgin Islands
ATLANTIC OCEAN
San Juan
Arecibo
Carolina
Bayamón
Caguas
Mayagüez
Ponce
Guayama
Aguadilla
Isabela
Fajardo
Yabucoa
Hormigueros
Yauco
I. Mona
C. Rojo
Mona Passage
Tortola I.
Virgin Gorda
Anegada
Anegada Passage
Charlotte Amalie
St. Thomas
St. John
Road Town
I. de Vieques
Frederiksted
Christiansted
St. Croix
(U.S.)
The Valley
Anguilla (U.K.)
Marigot
St-Martin (GUAD.)
Sint Maarten (N.A.)
Gustavia
St-Barthélemy (GUAD.)
Saba (N.A.)
Oranjestad
Sint Eustatius (N.A.)
St. Kitts
Basseterre
BRIMSTONE HILL NP
Charlestown
Nevis
Nevis Pk. 985 m
ST. KITTS AND NEVIS
Barbuda
Codrington
ANTIGUA AND BARBUDA
Saint John's
Falmouth
Boggy Pk. 402 m
Antigua
Montserrat (U.K.)
Plymouth
Leeward Islands
Lesser Antilles
Guadeloupe Passage
Grande-Terre
Port-Louis
Basse-Terre
GUADELOUPE NP
Guadeloupe (FRANCE)
Soufrière 1,467 m
Pointe-à-Pitre
Morne Constant 205 m
Marie-Galante
Aves I. (VEN.)
Dominica Passage
Portsmouth
Marigot
Morne Diablotin 1,447 m
DOMINICA
Roseau
Martinique Passage
Mt. Pelée 1,397 m
Sainte-Marie
Saint-Pierre
FORT DESAIX
Martinique (FRANCE)
Fort-de-France
St. Lucia Channel
Castries
Gros Islet
ST. LUCIA
Mt. Gimie 958 m
Micoud
Vieux Fort
St. Vincent Passage
Soufrière 1,234 m
Barrouallie
St. Vincent
Georgetown
Kingstown
Bequia
Windward Islands
BARBADOS
Mt. Hillaby 336 m
Bathsheba
Bridgetown
ST. VINCENT AND THE GRENADINES
Canouan
Carriacou
Sauteurs
Gouyave
Mt. St. Catherine 840 m
Saint George's
GRENADA
CARIBBEAN SEA
I. Blanquilla
Is. Los Testigos
Charlotteville
Tobago
Roxborough
Scarborough
TRINIDAD AND TOBAGO
La Asunción
NUEVA ESPARTA
Porlamar
VENEZUELA
PN PEN. DE PARIA
Port-of-Spain
El Cerro del Aripo 940 m
Galera Pt.
Arima
Sangre Grande
Cariaco
El Pilar
SUCRE
Irapa
Güiria
Chaguanas
Tabaquite
Gulf of Paria
San Fernando
Rio Claro
Point Fortin
Siparia
Carúpano
Pedernales
Fullarton
Trinidad
Dragon's Mouth
Tropic of Cancer
ATLANTIC OCEAN
Grand Bahama
Freeport
Great Abaco
BAHAMAS
Eleuthera
Nassau
New Providence I.
Great Bahama Bank
Andros I.
Berry Is.
Bimini Is.
Cat I.
Exuma Sound
San Salvador (Watling I.)
Great Guana Cay
Rum Cay
Great Exuma
Long I.
Clarence Town
Crooked I.
Northeast Pt.
Acklins I.
Salina Pt.
Mayaguana
Abraham's Bay
Turks and Caicos Is. (U.K.)
Caicos Is.
Grand Turk
Turks Is.
Little Inagua
Great Inagua
Northeast Pt.
Matthew Town
Southeast Pt.
Vero Beach
Fort Pierce
Port St. Lucie
West Palm Beach
Coral Springs
Fort Lauderdale
Hollywood
Miami
Coral Gables
BISCAYNE NP
Key Largo
Melbourne
C. Canaveral
CUBA
Sagua la Grande
Santa Clara
Caibarién
Cabaiguán
Morón
Ciego de Avila
Sancti Spíritus
Florida
Carlos M. de Céspedes
Punta Maternillos
Camagüey
Victoria de las Tunas
Nuevitas
Jesús Menéndez
Contramaestre
Holguín
Cabo Lucrecia
Jobabo
Mayarí
Sagua de Tánamo
Bayamo
Santa Cruz del Sur
Julio A. Mella
San Luis
El Salvador
Cabo Maisí
Palma Soriano
Guantánamo
Bartolomé Masó
Yara
Pico Turquino 4,131 m
Santiago de Cuba
GUANTANAMO BAY U.S. NAVAL BASE
Cabo Cruz
G. de Guacanayabo
G. de Ana María
Arch. de Camagüey
Windward Passage
Cayman Brac
Greater Antilles
WEST INDIES
JAMAICA
Montego Bay
Ocho Rios
Saint Ann's Bay
Savanna-la-Mar
Spanish Town
Port Antonio
Blue Mtn. Pk. 2,256 m
Mandeville
May Pen
Kingston
Portland Pt.
Jamaica Channel
Pedro Cays (JAM.)
Serranilla Bank (COL.)
Bajo Nuevo (COL.)
Serrana Bank (COL.)
Roncador Cay (COL.)
HAITI
Port-de-Paix
Cap-Haïtien
St-Louis du Nord
Golfe de la Gonâve
Petite Rivière de l'Artibonite
Pointe Ouest
Jérémie
Dame Marie
Anse-d'Hainault
Cap Tiburon
Chardonnière
Port-au-Prince
Pic de Macaya 2,300 m
Jacmel
Les Cayes
Pointe à Gravois
Hispaniola
Monte Cristi
Puerto Plata
Santiago
Pico Duarte 3,175 m
Mao
Sosúa
Cabo Francés Viejo
San Francisco de Macorís
Cabo Samaná
La Vega
Las Matas de Farfán
San Juan
Bonao
Hato Mayor
El Seibo
Higüey
Azua
Baní
Neiba
Barahona
SANTO DOMINGO
San Pedro de Macorís
La Romana
Pedernales
Cabo Falso
Cabo Beata
PUERTO RICO (U.S.)
Lesser Antilles
Leeward Is.
Windward Is.
CARIBBEAN SEA
Aruba (NETH.)
Oranjestad
Curaçao
Willemstad
NETH. ANTILLES
Bonaire
Kralendijk
El Roque
I. La Orchila (VEN.)
Islas Las Aves (VEN.)
Islas Los Roques (VEN.)
I. La Tortuga
I. de Margarita
Juangriego
Punta Gallinas
Cabo de la Vela
Guajira Pen.
Carrizal
Castilletes
Pen. de Paraguaná
Jadacaquiva
Santa Ana
Punta Cardón
Puerto Cumarebo
G. de Venezuela
Riohacha
Uribia
Santa Marta
Cabo de la Aguja
PN SIERRA NEVADA DE SANTA MARTA
Pico Cristóbal Colón 5,775 m
Barranquilla
Ciénaga
Soledad
Malambo
Sabanalarga
Fundación
Valledupar
Cartagena
Turbaco
Arjona
El Carmen
San Jacinto
Plato
Maracaibo
San Francisco
La Concepción
Cabimas
Ciudad Ojeda
Lago de Maracaibo
Machiques
Coro
Mitare
Cabure
Churuguara
Tucacas
Chichiriviche
Puerto Cabello
Valencia
Maracay
Caracas
Petare
Los Teques
Barquisimeto
Acarigua
Tocuyito
San Carlos
San Juan de los Morros
Turmero
Barcelona
Cumaná
Puerto La Cruz
Carúpano
San Antonio del Golfo
Maturín
Tucupita
Delta del Orinoco
VENEZUELA
COLOMBIA
Isthmus of Panama
Panamá
Colón
Sincelejo
Corozal
Mompós
Magangué
El Banco
Montería
Cereté
Sahagún
Planeta Rica
Ayapel
Turbo
Apartadó
Chinú
Gulf of Panama
PN DARIEN
PN PARAMILLO
Guanare
Barinas
Mérida
Pico Bolívar 5,007 m
El Vigía
Valera
Trujillo
Villa Bruzual
Calabozo
Valle de la Pascua
El Tigre
Anaco
Cantaura
San José de Guanipa
Ciudad Bolívar
Ciudad Guayana
Upata
El Palmar
Tumeremo
Guasipati
San Fernando de Apure
Achaguas
Bruzual
Santa Catalina
Caicara de Orinoco
Cabo San Román
Guayana
Scale 1:10,200,000
Lambert Conformal Conic Projection
MI 100 200 300
KM 100 200 300 400
194
195
© HAMMOND WORLD ATLAS CORPORATION

Height
m. ft.
6000 19700
4000 13000
2000 6500
1500 5000
1000 3300
500 1600
200 700
-0-
200 700
500 1600
1000 3300
2000 6500
3000 9800
4000 13000
5000 16400
6000 19700
ft. m.
Depth

Population

- ■ Over 2,000,000
- ◉ 500,000 - 999,999
- ◉ 100,000 - 249,999
- ◉ 10,000 - 29,999
- ■ 1,000,000 - 1,999,999
- ◉ 250,000 - 499,999
- ◉ 30,000 - 99,999
- ○ Under 10,000

Northern and Central Mexico

171

186

Scale 1:6,800,000 Lambert Conformal Conic Projection

MI 0 50 100 150 200

KM 0 50 100 150 200 250 300

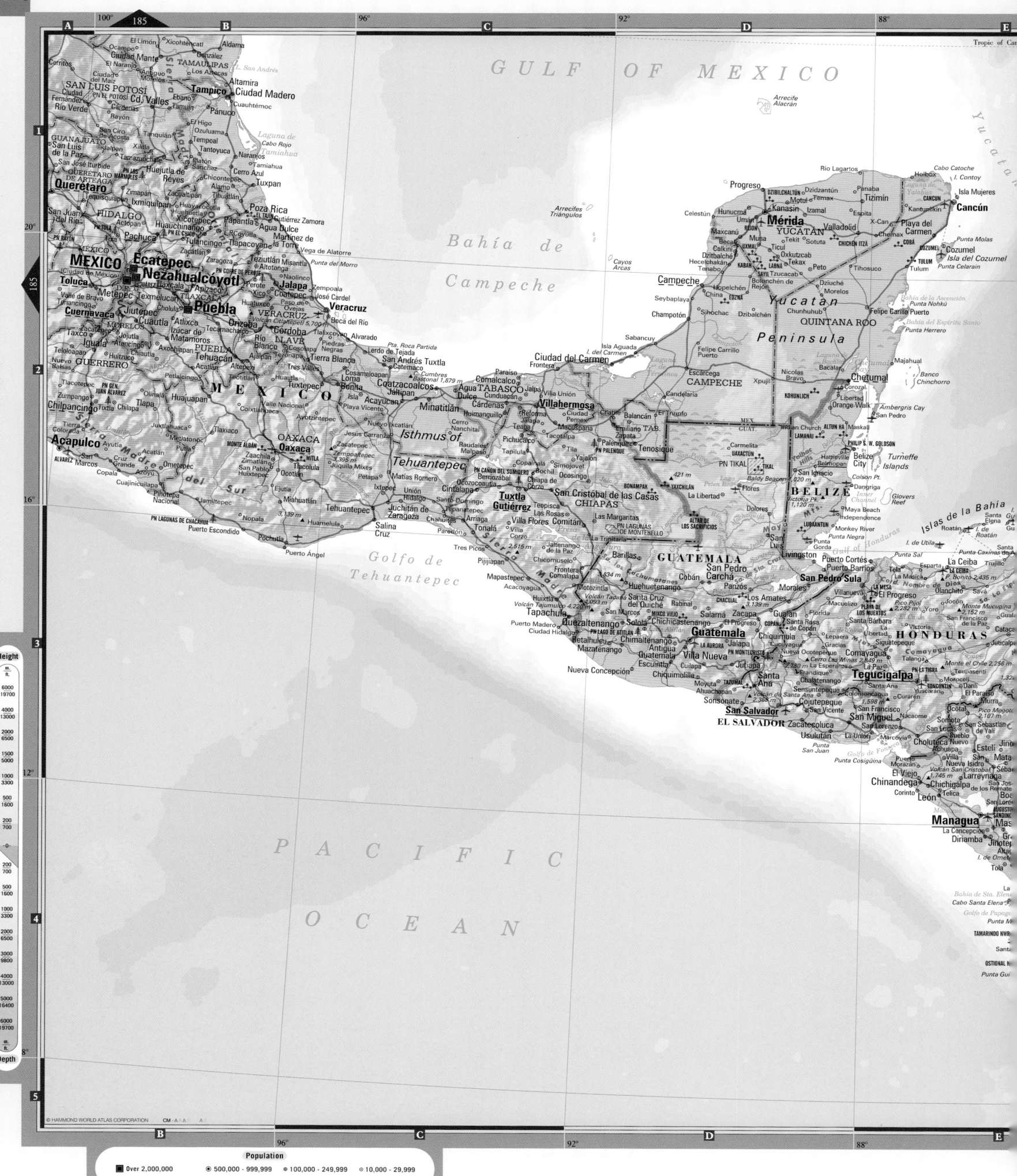
GULF OF MEXICO
Bahía de Campeche
PACIFIC OCEAN
Golfo de Tehuantepec
MEXICO
GUATEMALA
BELIZE
HONDURAS
EL SALVADOR
Yucatan Peninsula
Isthmus of Tehuantepec
Sierra Madre del Sur
Tropic of Cancer
MEXICO (Ciudad de México)
Ecatepec
Nezahualcóyotl
Puebla
Toluca
Querétaro
Tampico
Ciudad Madero
Veracruz
Acapulco
Oaxaca
Mérida
Cancún
Campeche
Ciudad del Carmen
Villahermosa
Tuxtla Gutiérrez
Chetumal
Belize City
Guatemala
San Salvador
Tegucigalpa
San Pedro Sula
Managua
León
Chinandega
Tapachula
Quezaltenango
Coatzacoalcos
Minatitlán
Salina Cruz
Tehuantepec
Juchitán de Zaragoza
San Cristóbal de las Casas
Cozumel
Isla Mujeres
Tulum
Progreso
Chilpancingo
Cuernavaca
Pachuca
Tlaxcala
Orizaba
Córdoba
Jalapa
Poza Rica
Tuxpan
TAMAULIPAS
SAN LUIS POTOSÍ
GUANAJUATO
QUERÉTARO DE ARTEAGA
HIDALGO
MÉXICO
MORELOS
GUERRERO
PUEBLA
TLAXCALA
VERACRUZ-LLAVE
OAXACA
CHIAPAS
TABASCO
CAMPECHE
YUCATÁN
QUINTANA ROO
Height
Depth
Population
Over 2,000,000
1,000,000 - 1,999,999
500,000 - 999,999
250,000 - 499,999
100,000 - 249,999
30,000 - 99,999
10,000 - 29,999
Under 10,000
© HAMMOND WORLD ATLAS CORPORATION

183

84°   F   80°   G   76°   H   72°   J

Nicholas Channel

HAVANA
(La Habana)
Marianao
Guanabacoa
Mariel   Matanzas   Cárdenas   Corralillo
Minas de   San Cristóbal   Artemisa   Guanajay   Unión de   Sagua la Grande
Matahambre   Guane   JOSÉ MARTÍ   Varadero   Reyes   Jovellanos   Cifuentes   Cayo Coco
Pinar del   Consolación del Sur   Santo Domingo   Camajuaní   Caibarién   Arch. de Camagüey
Río   Punta Gorda   Pedro   Perico   Santa Clara   Placetas   Chambas
Mantua   Pen. de Zapata   Betancourt   Cabaiguán   Morón   Cayo Guayabo
Nueva Gerona   Sancti Spíritus   Jatibonico   Ciego de   Cayo Sabinal
Cabo San   Punta   Palmillas   Condado   Ávila   Nuevitas
Antonio   Guanahacabibes   310 m   Santa Fe   La Sierpe   Guásimal   Minas   Puerto Padre
Cabo Corrientes   Golfo de   Punta Casilda   Vertientes   Camagüey   Banes
Isla de la   Batabanó   Crucero   Holguín
Juventud   Arch. de los   Contramaestre   Guáimaro   Cueto   Moa
Cabo Pepe   (I. de Pinos)   Canarreos   Cayo Largo   Santa Cruz   Río Cauto   San Germán   Mayarí   Sagua de
Cabo Frances   Golfo de   del Sur   Bayamo   Jiguaní   Julio A. Mella   Tánamo   Baracoa
Cabo   **CUBA**   Ana María   Manzanillo   Yara   San Luis   El Salvador
Camarón   Gran Piedra   Guantánamo
Golfo de   Niquero   Bartolomé   Palma   1,131 m   GUANTÁNAMO BAY
Guacanayabo   **Santiago**   Soriano   UNITED STATES NAVAL BASE
de Cuba
Cabo Cruz   Sa. Maestra   2,000 m

Little
Cayman
Cayman Islands   Cayman
(U.K.)   Brac
Grand Cayman
George Town   OWEN ROBERTS

CUBA

G r e a t e r

W E S T

Swan Islands
(HOND.)

BAHAMAS

Clarence Town   Samana
Long   Crooked I.
Island   Crooked I. Passage   Plana   Mayaguana
Long Cay   Cays
Salina Pt.   Acklins   Abraham's
Great   Providenciales   Bay   N. Caicos
Inagua   Little   W. Caicos   Middle Caicos   East Caicos
Inagua   Turks and   South   Grand
Caicos Is.   Caicos   Turk
Northeast Pt.   (U.K.)   Salt
Matthew   Southeast Pt.   Cay
Town

Môle Saint   I. de la Tortue
Nicolas   (Tortuga I.)   Monte
Fort Liberté   Cristi
Anse   Cap-Haïtien   Mao
Rouge   Port-de-Paix   Limbé   Ojabón
Pointe du   Trou du   Nord   **DOMINICAN**
Cheval Blanc   Gonaïves   Hispaniola   **REPUBLIC**
Golfe de   Desdunes   Hincha   Comendador
la   Petite Rivière   Las Matas
Gonâve   Grande Saline   de l'Artibonite   San Juan
Saint-Marc   HAITI   de Neiba
Pointe Ouest   Jérémie   Mirebalais   MAÏS GATE   Pétionville
I. de la Gonâve   Roseaux   **Port-au-Prince**   ISLA CABRITOS
Cap Dame Marie   Pic de   Petit Goâve   Miragoâne   Barahona
Dame Marie   Macaya   Anse-d'Hainault   2,300 m   Chaîne de la Selle   Belle
Coraïl   Aquin   2,680 m   Cabo
Chardonnière   Les Cayes   Jacmel   Pedernales   Beata
Torbeck   Ile à Vache   Isla Beata
Pointe à Gravois

Montego Bay   Discovery   Ocho Rios   Port Maria
Bay   Port Antonio
SANESER   Marbon Town   Ewarton   Northeast Pt.
Negrit   Christiana   Spanish   Kingston   Blue Mtn. Pk. 2,256 m
Savanna-la-Mar   Mandeville   Town   Port-   NORMAN   Morant   Southeast Pt.
Black River   May Pen   more   MANLEY   Bay
JAMAICA   Portland Pt.   Morant Pt.

Pedro Cays
(JAM.)

A n t i l l e s

I N D I E S

Cayos Cajones
(HOND.)
Cabo   Punta Patuca
Camarón   Barra Patuca
1,083 m   Cayo Cocorocuma
Laguna de   (HOND.)
Caratasca   Bancos del Cabo Falso
Puerto   Cabo Falso   (HOND.)
Lempira   Arrecifes de La Media Luna
Cabo Falso   (HOND.)
Cabo Gracias a Dios
HOND.   Cabo Gracias a Dios
Waspán   NIC.
940 m   Kuyu Tingni
Bocay   Cayos Miskitos
1,132 m   Yablis   London Reef
Cerro Saslaya   Punta Gorda
1,650 m   Kuikuina   Puerto Cabezas
Laguna Páhara
Alamikamba   Laguna Karatá
NICARAGUA   Prinzapolka
Cerro Musún   I. de Wounta
1,700 m
Wawasang   553 m
El Rama
Villa Sandino
San Pedro   Bluefields
de Lóvago   I. del Venado
710 m   de Bluefields
Pta. Mono
Barra Punta Gorda
Pta. Gorda

C A R I B B E A N

S E A

Serranilla Bank   Bajo Nuevo
(COL.)   (COL.)

Quita Sueño Bank
(COL.)

Serrana Bank
(COL.)

Roncador Cay
(COL.)

Santa Isabel
Isla de Providencia
(COL.)

San Andrés   Isla de San Andrés
ISLA DE SAN ANDRÉS   (COL.)
(COL.)   Cayos del Este Sudeste
(COL.)
Pequeña Isla del Maíz
Gran Isla del Maíz   Cayos de Albuquerque
(COL.)

Punta Gallinas
Cabo de la Vela

Carrizal   Pen. de
la Guajira

Riohacha   LA
Uribia   GUAJIRA   Maicao
Cabo de   Carraipia
la Aguja   PN TAYRONA   San Carlos
Santa Marta   Ciénaga   PN SIERRA NEVADA
PN ISLA DE   DE SANTA MARTA
SALAMANCA   Pico Cristóbal
Barranquilla   Colón 5,775 m   Valledupar
ERNESTO CORTISSOZ   Soledad   Malambo   LA CHINITA
ATLÁNTICO   La Paz
Sabanalarga   Tenerife   La Concepción
Campo de la Cruz   El Difícil   ZULIA
Cartagena   Turbaco   MAGDALENA   Machiques
San Juan Nepomuceno   Plato   Agustín   Codazzi
PN CORALES DEL ROSARIO   Mompós
Pta. San Bernardo   El Carmen   CESAR   San Antonio
Tolú   San   CÓRDOBA   El Banco   **VENEZUELA**
Sincelejo   Magangué   San Carlos
Lorica   Golfo de   del Zulia
Cereté   Morrosquillo   Caucasia   La Gloria   Encontrados
Montería   Sahagún
Planeta Rica   SUCRE   Tamalameque   Santa Bárbara
BOLÍVAR   Aguachica
Turbo   Apartadó   Ayapel   Gamarra   NORTE
ANTIOQUIA   DE
COLOMBIA   Caucasia   SANTANDER   La Fría
Cerro El Viejo   **Cúcuta**
El Bagre   2,350 m   Villa Rosario   TÁCHIRA
PN   Aguachica   Chinácota   San
PARAMILLO   Zaragoza   Antonio
Cáceres   Alto del Tamar   Rionegro   Pamplona   4,100 m
Nechí   SANTANDER

Cayos Miskitos

La Barra

Alto de Campana   (continued via grid)

Cerro   PN PORTOBELO   Pta. Grande
Cativá   Sabanita
Colón   Herrera   Narganá
PN PORTOBELO   El Llano   Ailigandí
Gatún Dam   El Porvenir
San Blas   Punta Mosquito
OMAR TORRIJOS   Puerto Escondido
La Chorrera   Tubualá
Panama   Tocumen
Arraiján   Cerro Chucanti
El Valle   1,439 m
Nueva   Chimán
Guadalupe   PN ALTOS DE CAMPANA   Yaviza   PN DARIÉN
Penonomé   Pta. Garachiné   PN LOS KATÍOS
COSTA   RICA
San José   Limón
Cartago   Cahuita
Cerro de la Muerte   GANDOCA-MANZANILLO NWR
3,491 m
PN CHIRRIPÓ   PN CAHUITA

PANAMA
Gulf   of   Panama

Scale 1:6,800,000   Lambert Conformal Conic Projection

MI   50   100   150   200
KM   50   100   150   200   250   300

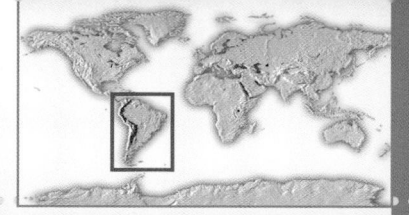

The highest mountain peak in the Americas, Mount Aconcagua, at 22,831 feet (6959 m.) above sea level, is visible in this northeast-looking, low-oblique image. Several major snow-covered peaks with summits exceeding 20,000 feet (6100 m.) rise along the north-south axis of the cohesive and massive structure of the Andes Mountains through this area of Argentina and Chile. The narrow east-west valley immediately south of Mount Aconcagua contains a section of the American Highway that connects Mendoza, Argentina, with Santiago, Chile.

Map Labels

Oceans and Seas: CARIBBEAN SEA, ATLANTIC OCEAN, PACIFIC OCEAN

Countries: COSTA RICA, PANAMA, VENEZUELA, GUYANA, SURINAME, FRENCH GUIANA, COLOMBIA, ECUADOR, PERU, BRAZIL, BOLIVIA, PARAGUAY, URUGUAY, ARGENTINA, CHILE, NETHERLANDS ANTILLES, TRINIDAD AND TOBAGO

Selected Cities: Barranquilla, Cartagena, Maracaibo, Valencia, Caracas, Medellín, Bogotá, Cali, Quito, Guayaquil, Lima, Callao, Trujillo, Arequipa, La Paz, Santa Cruz, Sucre, Asunción, Brasília, Belo Horizonte, Rio de Janeiro, São Paulo, Campinas, Nova Iguaçu, Niterói, Porto Alegre, Curitiba, Salvador, Recife, Maceió, Fortaleza, Teresina, Belém, Manaus, Goiânia, Córdoba, Rosario, Buenos Aires, La Plata, Mar del Plata, Montevideo, Santiago, Viña del Mar, Valparaíso, San José, Panamá

Physical features: Mt. Roraima 2,772 m, Pico Cristóbal Colón 5,775 m, Pico Bolívar 5,007 m, Alto Ritacuba 5,493 m, Nevado del Huila 5,750 m, Chimborazo 6,310 m, Nevado Huascarán 6,768 m, Volcán Misti 5,822 m, Nevado Ancohuma 6,550 m, Volcán Llullaillaco 6,723 m, Cerro Ojos del Salado 6,880 m, Cerro Aconcagua 6,959 m, Pico da Bandeira 2,890 m, Pico de la Neblina 3,014 m, Guiana Highlands, Brazilian Highlands, Mato Grosso, Planalto do Mato Grosso, Cordillera de los Andes, Desierto de Atacama, Altiplano, Selvas, Caatingas, Amazonas, Tierra del Fuego, Cape Horn, Falkland Islands (U.K.) (Claimed by Arg.), Tropic of Capricorn, Equator

PHOTOGRAPHIC DETAIL

AREA OF OPTIMIZATION

AREA OF OPTIMIZATION

The red band which surrounds this map defines the "Area of Optimization." Within this bounding curve is the most accurate conformal map that can be made of the region. Outside the optimized area, distortion increases rapidly, and tears or other irregularities in the grid may occur. (See page 6 for additional information.)

Population
- ■ Over 3,000,000
- ■ 1,000,000 - 2,999,999
- ● 500,000 - 999,999
- ● 100,000 - 499,999
- ○ Under 100,000

Scale 1:27,300,000   Hammond Optimal Conformal

MI   200   400   600   800
KM   200   400   600   800   1000   1200

Average January temperature, degrees Fahrenheit at selected stations:

BARRANQUILLA 79° · CARACAS 66° · PARAMARIBO 79° · QUIBDÓ 79° · BOGOTÁ 57° · QUITO 55° · MANAUS 79° · FORTALEZA 81° · LIMA 72° · LA PAZ 52° · BRASILIA 73° · ANTOFAGASTA 68° · ASUNCIÓN 84° · RÍO DE JANEIRO 79° · CURITIBA 68° · SANTIAGO 66° · BUENOS AIRES 73° · COMODORO RIVADAVIA 64° · RÍO GRANDE 48°

● LIMA 72°
AVERAGE JANUARY TEMPERATURE DEGREES FAHRENHEIT AT SELECTED STATIONS

AVERAGE JANUARY TEMPERATURE

FAHRENHEIT	CELSIUS	FAHRENHEIT	CELSIUS	FAHRENHEIT	CELSIUS
OVER 86°	OVER 30°	50° TO 68°	10° TO 20°	UNDER 32°	UNDER 0°
68° TO 86°	20° TO 30°	32° TO 50°	0° TO 10°		

Average July temperature, degrees Fahrenheit at selected stations:

BARRANQUILLA 82° · CARACAS 70° · PARAMARIBO 81° · QUIBDÓ 77° · BOGOTÁ 57° · QUITO 55° · MANAUS 81° · FORTALEZA 79° · LIMA 59° · LA PAZ 46° · BRASILIA 64° · ANTOFAGASTA 55° · ASUNCIÓN 64° · RÍO DE JANEIRO 66° · CURITIBA 55° · SANTIAGO 46° · BUENOS AIRES 52° · COMODORO RIVADAVIA 45° · RÍO GRANDE 34°

● LIMA 59°
AVERAGE JULY TEMPERATURE DEGREES FAHRENHEIT AT SELECTED STATIONS

AVERAGE JULY TEMPERATURE

FAHRENHEIT	CELSIUS	FAHRENHEIT	CELSIUS	FAHRENHEIT	CELSIUS
OVER 86°	OVER 30°	50° TO 68°	10° TO 20°	UNDER 32°	UNDER 0°
68° TO 86°	20° TO 30°	32° TO 50°	0° TO 10°		

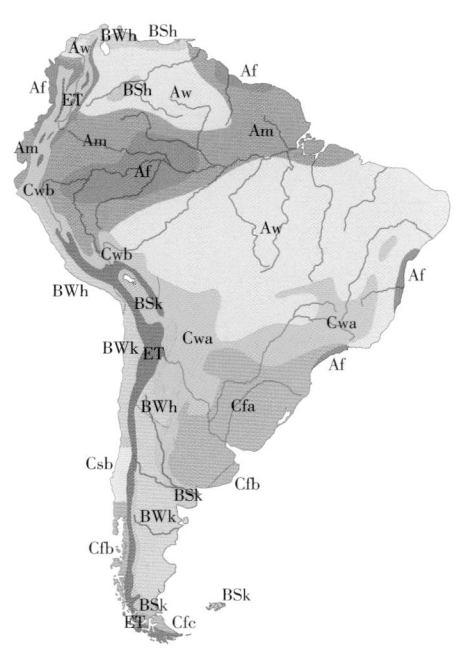

Climate zones labeled: BWh, BSh, Aw, Af, ET, BSh, Aw, Am, Am, Af, Cwb, Am, Af, Aw, BWh, BSk, Af, BWk, ET, Cwa, Cwb, Gwa, Af, BWh, Cfa, Csb, Cfb, BSk, BWk, BSk, Cfb, ET, Cfc

CLIMATE

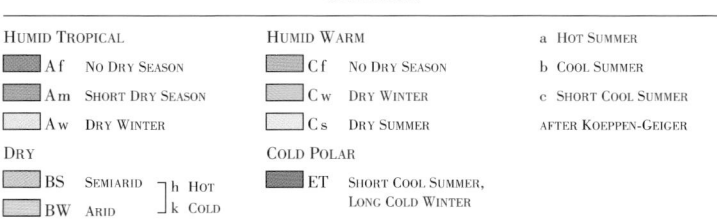

HUMID TROPICAL
Af NO DRY SEASON
Am SHORT DRY SEASON
Aw DRY WINTER

DRY
BS SEMIARID
BW ARID
h HOT
k COLD

HUMID WARM
Cf NO DRY SEASON
Cw DRY WINTER
Cs DRY SUMMER

COLD POLAR
ET SHORT COOL SUMMER, LONG COLD WINTER

a HOT SUMMER
b COOL SUMMER
c SHORT COOL SUMMER

AFTER KOEPPEN-GEIGER

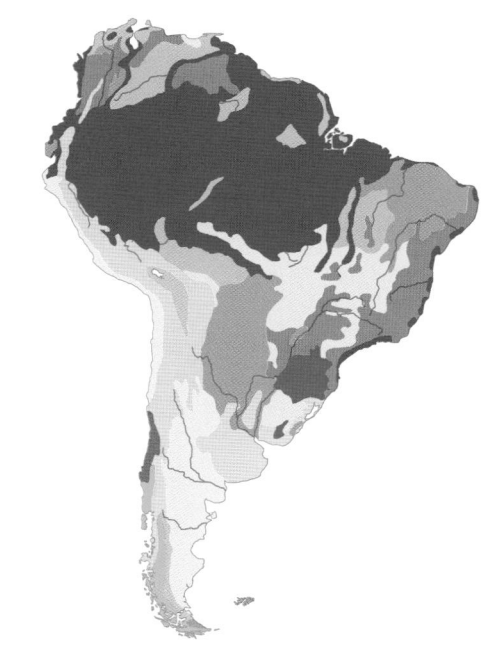

VEGETATION

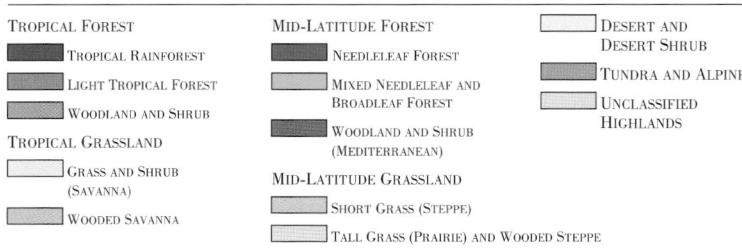

TROPICAL FOREST
TROPICAL RAINFOREST
LIGHT TROPICAL FOREST
WOODLAND AND SHRUB

TROPICAL GRASSLAND
GRASS AND SHRUB (SAVANNA)
WOODED SAVANNA

MID-LATITUDE FOREST
NEEDLELEAF FOREST
MIXED NEEDLELEAF AND BROADLEAF FOREST
WOODLAND AND SHRUB (MEDITERRANEAN)

MID-LATITUDE GRASSLAND
SHORT GRASS (STEPPE)
TALL GRASS (PRAIRIE) AND WOODED STEPPE

DESERT AND DESERT SHRUB
TUNDRA AND ALPINE
UNCLASSIFIED HIGHLANDS

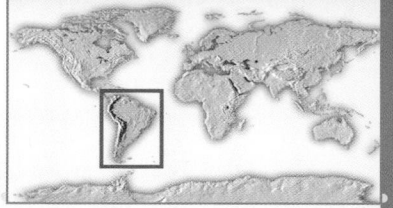

South America - Geographical Comparisons

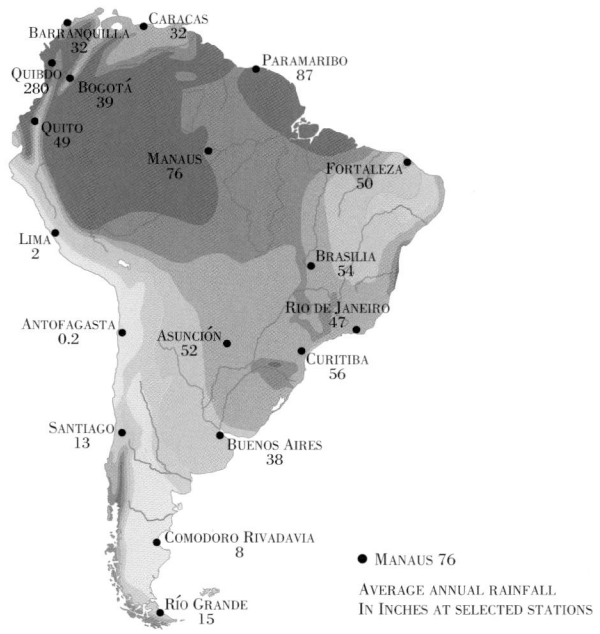

BARRANQUILLA
32
CARACAS
32
PARAMARIBO
87
QUIBDÓ
280
BOGOTÁ
39
QUITO
49
MANAUS
76
FORTALEZA
50
LIMA
2
BRASILIA
54
ANTOFAGASTA
0.2
ASUNCIÓN
52
RIO DE JANEIRO
47
CURITIBA
56
SANTIAGO
13
BUENOS AIRES
38
COMODORO RIVADAVIA
8
RÍO GRANDE
15

● MANAUS 76

AVERAGE ANNUAL RAINFALL
IN INCHES AT SELECTED STATIONS

● CITIES WITH OVER 1,000,000
INHABITANTS

AVERAGE ANNUAL RAINFALL

INCHES	CM	INCHES	CM	INCHES	CM
OVER 80	OVER 200	40 TO 60	100 TO 150	10 TO 20	25 TO 50
60 TO 80	150 TO 200	20 TO 40	50 TO 100	UNDER 10	UNDER 25

POPULATION DISTRIBUTION

DENSITY PER		SQ. MI.	SQ. KM.	SQ. MI.	SQ. KM.
SQ. MI.	SQ. KM.	130 TO 260	50 TO 100	3 TO 25	1 TO 10
OVER 260	OVER 100	25 TO 130	10 TO 50	UNDER 3	UNDER 1

RICE
HOGS
COFFEE
COCOA
CATTLE
COFFEE
CATTLE
VANILLA
BRAZIL
NUTS
BANANAS
CORN
COTTON
SISAL
BANANAS
SHEEP
WILD RUBBER
CATTLE
SHEEP
CORN
CATTLE
TOBACCO
CATTLE
HOGS
CITRUS
COCOA
SUGARCANE
COTTON
TOBACCO
COTTON
COFFEE
TEA
BANANAS
SUGARCANE
CATTLE
HOGS
TOBACCO
QUEBRACHO
SOYBEANS
CORN
SHEEP
RICE
CORN
WINE
FLAX
CORN
CATTLE
WHEAT
WINE
SHEEP
SHEEP

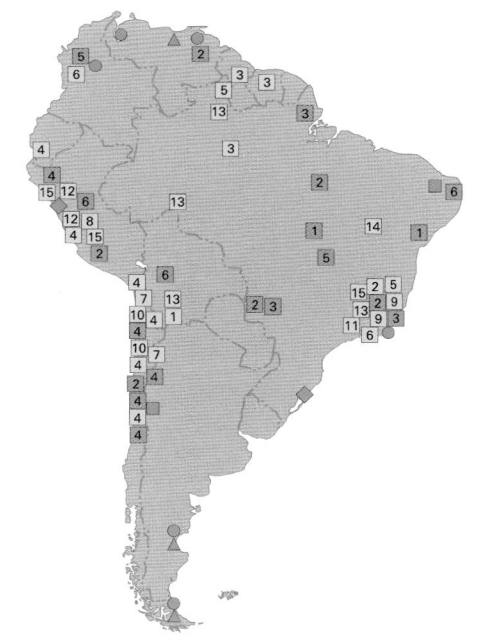

LAND USE

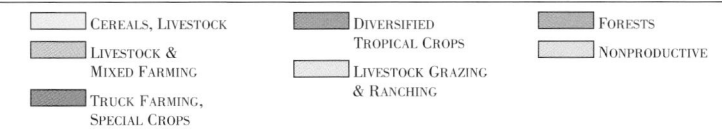

CEREALS, LIVESTOCK

LIVESTOCK &
MIXED FARMING

TRUCK FARMING,
SPECIAL CROPS

DIVERSIFIED
TROPICAL CROPS

LIVESTOCK GRAZING
& RANCHING

FORESTS

NONPRODUCTIVE

MINERAL RESOURCES

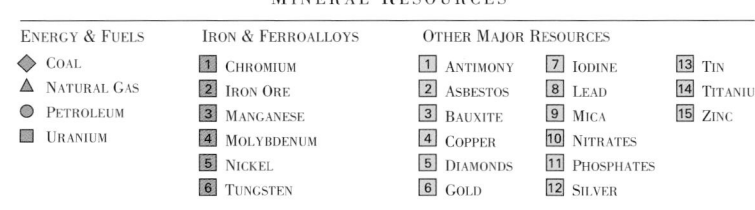

ENERGY & FUELS	IRON & FERROALLOYS	OTHER MAJOR RESOURCES		
◆ COAL	1 CHROMIUM	1 ANTIMONY	7 IODINE	13 TIN
▲ NATURAL GAS	2 IRON ORE	2 ASBESTOS	8 LEAD	14 TITANIUM
● PETROLEUM	3 MANGANESE	3 BAUXITE	9 MICA	15 ZINC
■ URANIUM	4 MOLYBDENUM	4 COPPER	10 NITRATES	
	5 NICKEL	5 DIAMONDS	11 PHOSPHATES	
	6 TUNGSTEN	6 GOLD	12 SILVER	

PACIFIC

OCEAN

CARIBBEAN SEA

COSTA
RICA

PANAMA

NICARAGUA

COLOMBIA

ECUADOR

PERU

VENEZUELA

GUYAN

BOLIVIA

CHILE

ARGENTINA

PARAGUA

B R A

Selvas

Equator

Tropic of Capricorn

Height

m.
ft.

6000
19700

4000
13000

2000
6500

1500
5000

1000
3300

500
1600

200
700

–0–

200
700

500
1600

1000
3300

2000
6500

3000
9800

4000
13000

5000
16400

6000
19700

m.
ft.

Depth

187

199

Population
■ Over 2,000,000
■ 1,000,000 - 1,999,999
⊚ 500,000 - 999,999
◉ 100,000 - 499,999
◎ 50,000 - 99,999
○ Under 50,000

ATLANTIC

OCEAN

SURINAME

FRENCH GUIANA

Tumuc-Humac Mts.

Paramaribo
Nieuw-Nickerie
Totness
Nieuw-Amsterdam
Albina
Saint-Laurent du Maroni
Sinnamary
Kourou
Cayenne
Île du Salut
Île du Diable
Pointe Béhague
Cabo Orange
Régina
Oiapoque
Saül
Ouaqui
PN DO CABO ORANGE

Juliana Top 1,230 m

Amapá
Calçoene
Cabo do Norte
Ilha de Maracá

Macapá
Mazagão
I. Janaucu
I. Caviana
I. Mexiana
I. Queimada

Soure
Salinópolis
Vigia
Bragança
Capanema
Ilhas de São João

Belém
Castanhão
Abaetetuba
Igarapé-Miri
Capitão Poço
Turiaçu
Cururupu
B. de São Marcos
PN DOS LENÇÓIS MARANHENSES

São Luís
Rosário
Parnaíba
Camocim
Fortaleza
Caucaia
Maranguape
Cascavel
Acaraú

Santarém
Altamira
Tucuruí
Marabá
Imperatriz
Teresina
Mossoró
Natal

Atol das Rocas

Fernando de Noronha (BRAZIL)

St. Peter and St. Paul Rocks (BRAZIL)

Equator

Recife
Olinda
João Pessoa
Campina Grande
Caruaru

Caatingas

Serra do Uruçuçara

Petrolina
Juazeiro
Paulo Afonso
PN DE PAULO AFONSO
Maceió
Arapiraca

Aracaju

Salvador
Feira de Santana
PN CHAPADA DIAMANTINA

Ilhéus
Itabuna
Vitória da Conquista

ATLANTIC

OCEAN

Ilha da Trindade (BRAZIL)
Ilhas Martin Vaz (BRAZIL)

Brasília
Goiânia
Planalto Central

Planalto do Mato Grosso

Belo Horizonte

Vitória

Campo Grande

Serra da Mantiqueira

Rio de Janeiro
Niterói
São Paulo
Santo André
Osasco
Campinas
Nova Iguaçu
Santos

Tropic of Capricorn

© HAMMOND WORLD ATLAS CORPORATION CJ - 2107 - A - A

Scale 1:14,800,000   Lambert Conformal Conic Projection

MI   100   200   300   400
KM   100 200 300 400 500 600

CARIBBEAN SEA
PACIFIC OCEAN
COLOMBIA
PANAMA
ECUADOR
PERU
NETH. ANTILLES
Aruba
Curaçao
Bonaire
Isthmus of Panama
Gulf of Panama
Golfo de Venezuela
Lago de Maracaibo
Golfo de Guayaquil
Barranquilla
Cartagena
Santa Marta
Medellín
Cali
BOGOTÁ
Bucaramanga
Cúcuta
Maracaibo
Barquisimeto
Valencia
Quito
Guayaquil
Panamá
Colón
ANTIOQUIA
CHOCÓ
CAUCA
NARIÑO
HUILA
TOLIMA
META
CASANARE
VICHADA
ARAUCA
GUAINÍA
GUAVIARE
VAUPÉS
CAQUETÁ
PUTUMAYO
AMAZONAS
LORETO
APURE
ZULIA
FALCÓN
LARA
BARINAS
PORTUGUESA
COJEDES
ESMERALDAS
PASTAZA
NAPO
SUCUMBÍOS
MORONA-SANTIAGO
Equator
Height
Depth
COLOMBIA
① RISARALDA
② QUINDÍO
ECUADOR
① BOLÍVAR
Population
Over 2,000,000
1,000,000 - 1,999,999
500,000 - 999,999
250,000 - 499,999
100,000 - 249,999
30,000 - 99,999
10,000 - 29,999
Under 10,000
187
198

Colombia, Venezuela, Ecuador

CARIBBEAN SEA

ATLANTIC OCEAN

GRENADA
Carriacou
Victoria
Sauteurs
Saint George's · Mt. St. Catherine 840 m
POINT SALINES

Is. Las Aves (VEN.)
DEPENDENCIAS FEDERALES (VEN.)
El Roque
I. Blanquilla (VEN.)
Is. Los Roques (VEN.)
I. La Orchila (VEN.)

Is. Los Testigos (VEN.)

Tobago
576 m · Charlotteville
Roxborough
Scarborough
CROWN POINT

NUEVA ESPARTA I. de Margarita
Juangriego · La Asunción
PN LAGUNA DE LA RESTINGA · Porlamar
GRAL. S. MARINO · PN CERRO EL COPEY
I. Cubagua · Pampatar
I. Coche
Maiquetía
BOLÍVAR
Caracas
Petare
Los Teques MIRANDA
La Victoria
acay
ARAGUA
Ocumare del Tuy
Villa de Cura
San Juan de los Morros
Francisco

Blanchisseuse
Toco · Pta. Galera
El Cerro del Aripo 940 m
Arima · Sangre Grande
TRINIDAD AND TOBAGO
Port-of-Spain
Chaguanas · PIARCO
San Fernando · Couva · Tabaquite
Point Fortin · Siparia · Rio Claro
Fullarton · Pta. Galeota
Trinidad

PN EL GUÁCHARO
Cumaná · PN MOCHIMA
San Antonio del Golfo
PN PENÍNSULA DE PARIA
Carúpano
Güiria · Irapa
El Pilar
SUCRE
Cariaco · Casanay
Pen. de Araya
Gulf of Paria
Dragon's Mouth
Serpent's Mouth
Serpent's Mouth

Barcelona · Pozuelos
Puerto La Cruz
Puerto Píritu
A. ANZOÁTEGUI
GRAL.
Guanape · San Pablo
San Mateo · Onoto
Valle de Guanape
Aragua
Quiriquire
Caripito
Pedernales

Delta del Orinoco

Zaraza
Valle de La Pascua
GUÁRICO
El Sombrero
Chaguaramas
Las Mercedes
Santa María de Ipire
Calabozo
PN AGUARO GUARIQUITO

Tucupido
ANZOÁTEGUI
Anaco · Cantaura
Aragua de Barcelona
El Tigre
San Tomé
San José de Guanipa
El Pao
La Canoa
Santa Clara

MONAGAS
Maturín
San Antonio de Tabasca
Temblador
Barrancas
Uracoa
Tucupita
DELTA AMACURO
Macareo · Santo Niño
La Horqueta
Piacoa
El Toro
Los Castillos
San José de Amacuro

VENEZUELA

Ciudad Guayana
El Pao
Soledad · Almacén
Ciudad Bolívar
PRESA GURI
Upata · El Palmar
Cerro Bolívar 802 m
Ciudad Piar
El Manteco
El Miamo
Guasipati
El Callao
El Dorado

BARIMA-WAINI
Maburuma
Mount Everard
Baramanni
Baramita
Charity
Anna Regina
POMEROON-SUPENAAM
Queenstown
Suddie

ESSEQUIBO IS.-W. DEMERARA
Vreed-en-Hoop
Georgetown
TIMEHRI
DEMERARA-MAHAICA
Mahaica
Mahaicony Village

CUYUNI-MAZARUNI
Cataratas de Kamaria
Bartica
Rockstone
Linden
UPPER DEMERARA-BERBICE
MAHAICA-BERBICE
New Amsterdam
Corriverton
E. BER. COR.
Nieuw-Nickerie
Totness
Paradise

Guiana Highlands

BOLÍVAR
Cerro Guanay 2,300 m
Cerro Yaví 2,441 m
Cerro Guaiquinima 2,100 m
Salto Pará
PARQUE Salto del Ángel (Angel Falls)
Auyán-Tepuí 2,950 m
Uruyén
NACIONAL
Urimán CANAIMA
Chimantá-Tepuí 2,342 m
Cerro Venamo 1,880 m
La Gran Sabana
Monte Roraima 2,772 m
Apaurén · Uonquén
Peraitepui
Icabarú
Santa Elena de Uairén

Cataratas de Surwakwima
Kamarang
Monte Ayanganna 2,042 m
Kangaruma
PN KAIETEUR
Cataratas de Kaieteur
POTARO-SIPARUNI
Tumatumari
Kurupukari
Mahdia
Rera
Kwakwani
Ituni
SARAMACCA
Groningen
Lelydorp
PARA
ZANDERIJ
WANICA
PARAMARIBO
COMMEWLINE
Calcutta
NICKERIE
CORONIE

SURINAME

FRENCH GUIANA
St-Laurent-du-Maroni
Mana
Apatou
St-Jean-du-Maroni
MAROWIJNE
Albina

AMAZONAS
Cerro Ovana 1,978 m
San Juan de Manapiare
Santa María de Erebato
PN JAUA SARISARIÑAMA
Yerichaña · Urirantenina
Guaína · Maniapure
PN YAPACANA
Cerro Marahuaca 2,579 m
PN DUIDA MARAHUACA
Cerro Duida 2,400 m
La Esmeralda
Platanal
Tamatama
Santa Bárbara
BOA VISTA
Boa Vista

GUYANA
Karasabai
Annai
Apoteri
Kumaka
Yupukari
Lethem
Kurupukari
Rewa
Kanuku Mts.
Wichabai
UPPER TAKUTU-UPPER ESSEQUIBO
Isherton
Biloku
Caracaraí

EAST BERBICE-CORENTYNE

SIPALIWINI
Cataratas Tonckens
Juliana Top 1,230 m
Hendrik Top 975 m
BROKOPONDO
Kayser Gebergte
Alalapadu
Majoli
Cottica
Maripasoula
Ouaqui
Intelewa

Wilhelmina Gebergte
Eilerts de Haan Gebergte
Oranje Gebergte
Tumuc-Humac Mts.

Serra Pacaraima
Sa. Parima
Serra Pacaraima
Sa. Grande

RORAIMA
1,009 m
Serra Acaraí

AMAPÁ

Parque Nacional SERRANÍA DE LA NEBLINA
Pico de la Neblina 3,014 m
PARQUE NACIONAL DO PICO DA NEBLINA
Santa Isabel
El Carmen
Sta. Rosa de Amanadona
Cucuí
VENEZUELA
BRASIL

Porto Poet

BRAZIL

PARÁ
Saulá
Equator

AMAZONAS
Barcelos
PARQUE NACIONAL DO RIO JAÚ
Catrimani
Represa de Balbina
EDUARDO GOMES
Manaus
Itacoatiara
Silves
Itapiranga
Urucurituba
Urucará
Parintins
Barreirinha
Nhamundá
Faro
Óbidos
Oriximiná
Alenquer · Monte Alegre
Santarém
L. de Erepecu
L. do Curuaí
Sa. Jauaru

Scale 1:6,800,000   Lambert Conformal Conic Projection
MI 50 100 150 200
KM 50 100 150 200 250 300

© HAMMOND WORLD ATLAS CORPORATION

MAP SECTION

Northeastern Brazil

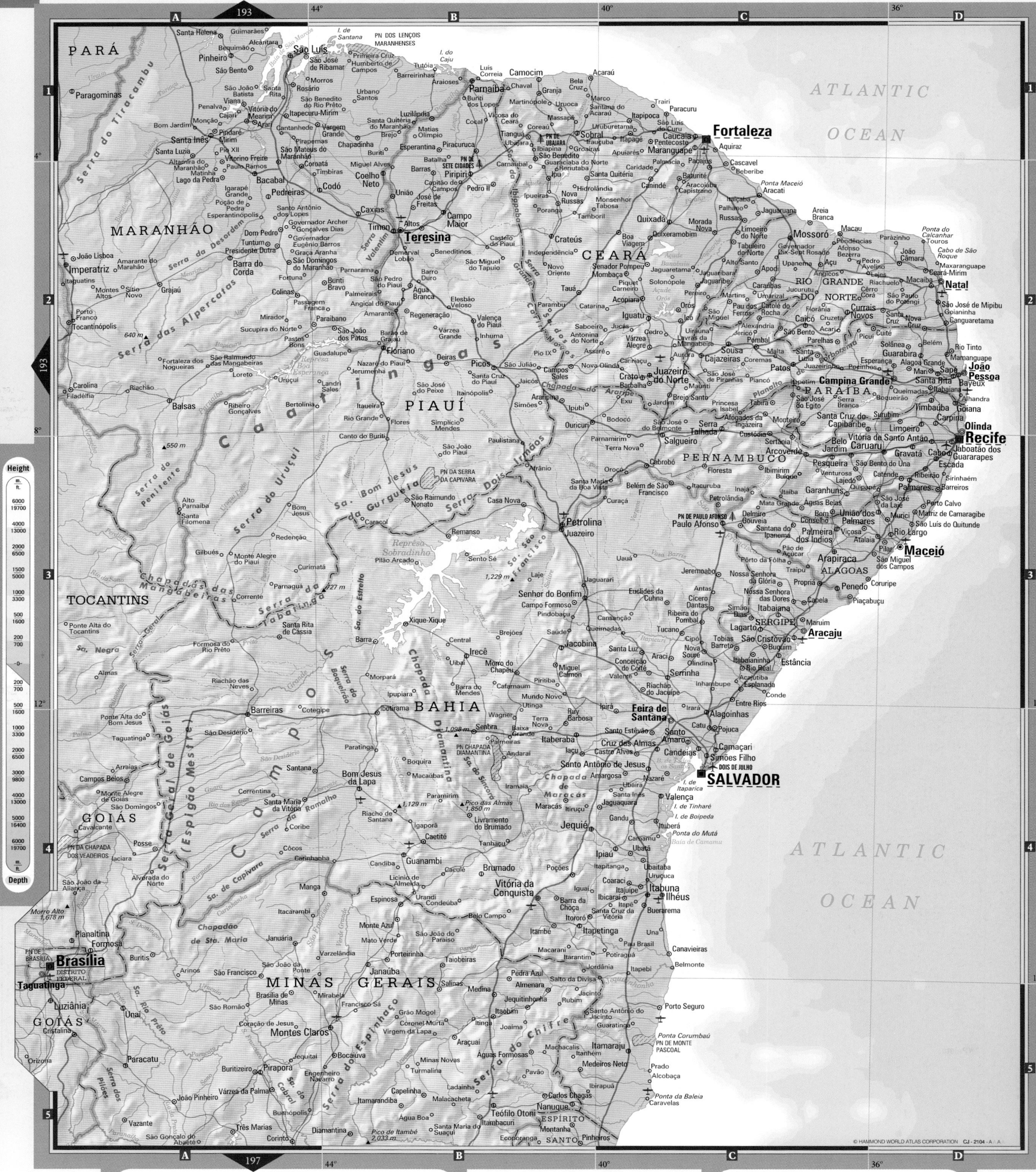

Population

- ■ Over 2,000,000
- ■ 1,000,000 - 1,999,999
- ● 500,000 - 999,999
- ● 250,000 - 499,999
- ● 100,000 - 249,999
- ● 30,000 - 99,999
- ◦ 10,000 - 29,999
- ◦ Under 10,000

Scale 1:6,800,000   Lambert Conformal Conic Projection

MI   50   100   150   200
KM   50   100   150   200   250   300

© HAMMOND WORLD ATLAS CORPORATION   CJ - 2104 - A : A

196

193

199

201

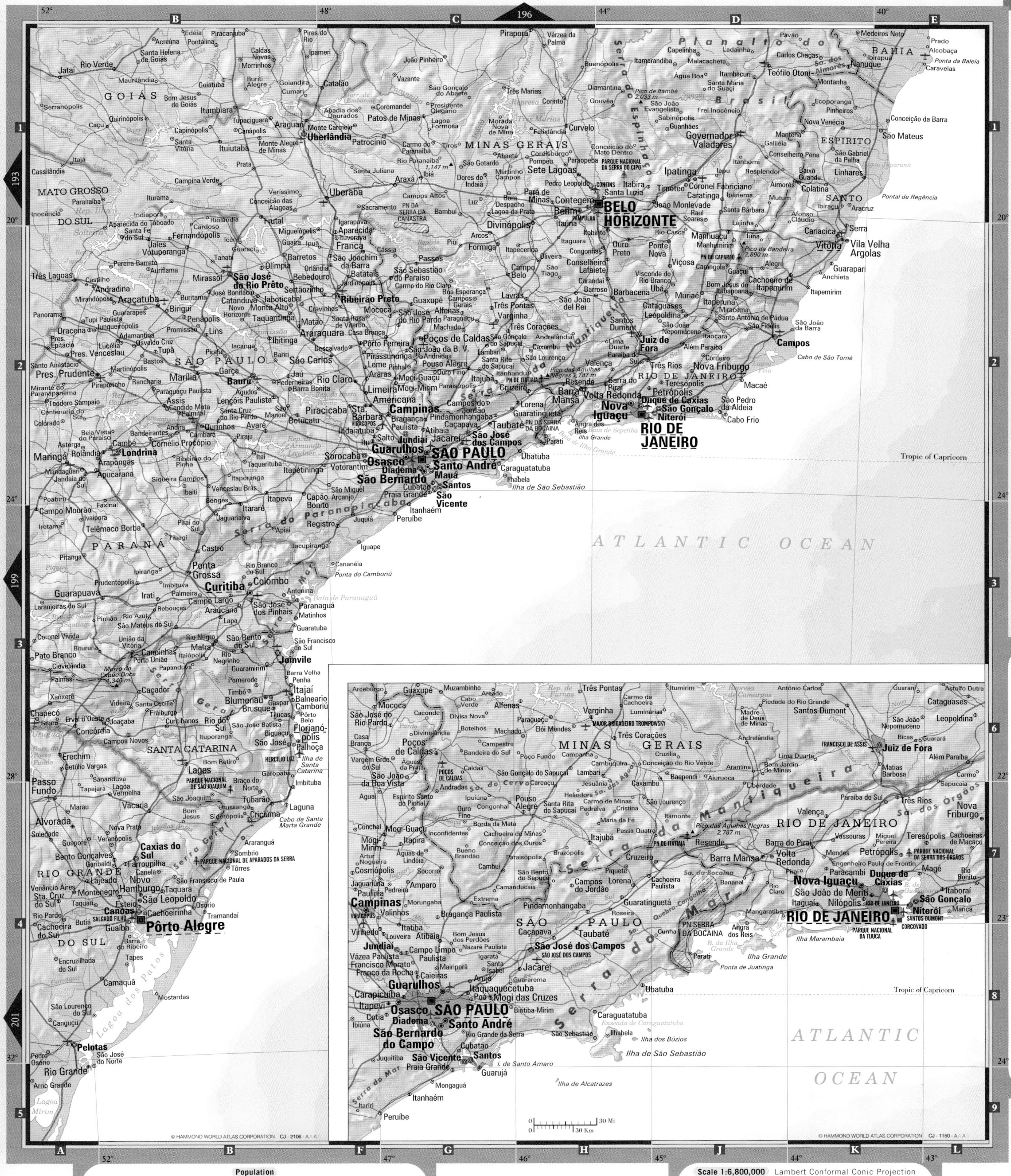

Population

- ■ Over 2,000,000
- ■ 1,000,000 - 1,999,999
- ⦿ 500,000 - 999,999
- ⦿ 250,000 - 499,999
- ⦿ 100,000 - 249,999
- ⦿ 30,000 - 99,999
- ⦿ 10,000 - 29,999
- ○ Under 10,000

Height

ft	m
6000	19700
4000	13000
2000	6500
1500	5000
1000	3300
500	1600
200	700
0	
200	700
500	1600
1000	3300
2000	6500
3000	9800
4000	13000
5000	16400
6000	19700

Depth

© HAMMOND WORLD ATLAS CORPORATION   CJ - 2106 - A - A - A

© HAMMOND WORLD ATLAS CORPORATION   CJ - 1150 - A - A - A

0   30 Mi
0   30 Km

Scale 1:6,800,000   Lambert Conformal Conic Projection

MI   50   100   150   200
KM 50 100   150   200   250   300

Peru

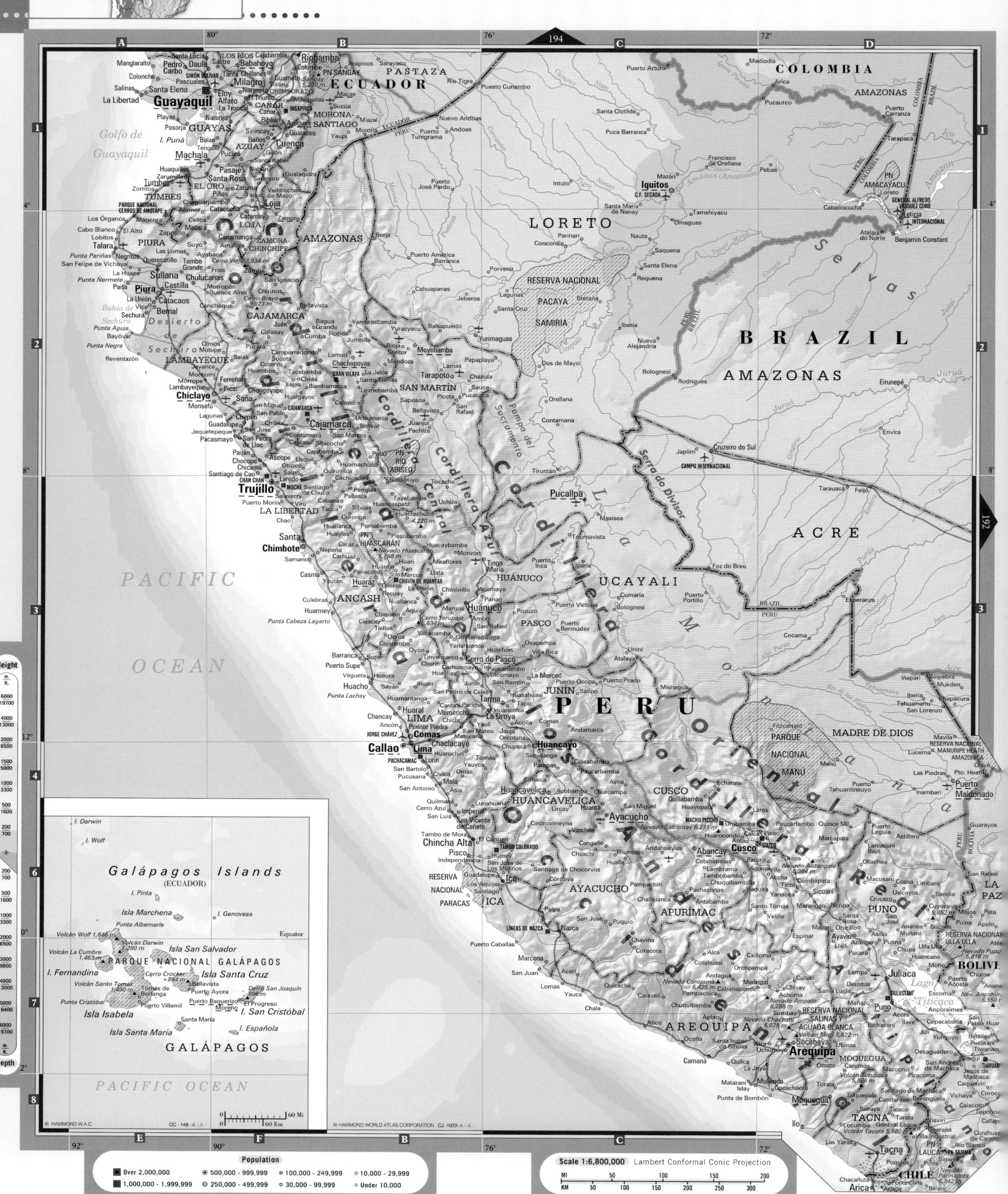
COLOMBIA
ECUADOR
LORETO
BRAZIL
AMAZONAS
ACRE
UCAYALI
PERU
PACIFIC
OCEAN
Golfo de Guayaquil
Guayaquil
Iquitos
Pucallpa
Trujillo
Chimbote
Callao
Lima
Huancayo
Ayacucho
Cusco
Arequipa
Tacna
Arica
CHILE
Galápagos Islands
(ECUADOR)
PARQUE NACIONAL GALÁPAGOS
Isla Isabela
Isla Santa Cruz
I. Fernandina
Isla San Salvador
I. San Cristóbal
I. Española
Isla Santa María
PACIFIC OCEAN
Height
Depth
Population
Over 2,000,000
1,000,000 - 1,999,999
500,000 - 999,999
250,000 - 499,999
100,000 - 249,999
30,000 - 99,999
10,000 - 29,999
Under 10,000
Scale 1:6,800,000 Lambert Conformal Conic Projection
© HAMMOND W.A.C.
© HAMMOND WORLD ATLAS CORPORATION

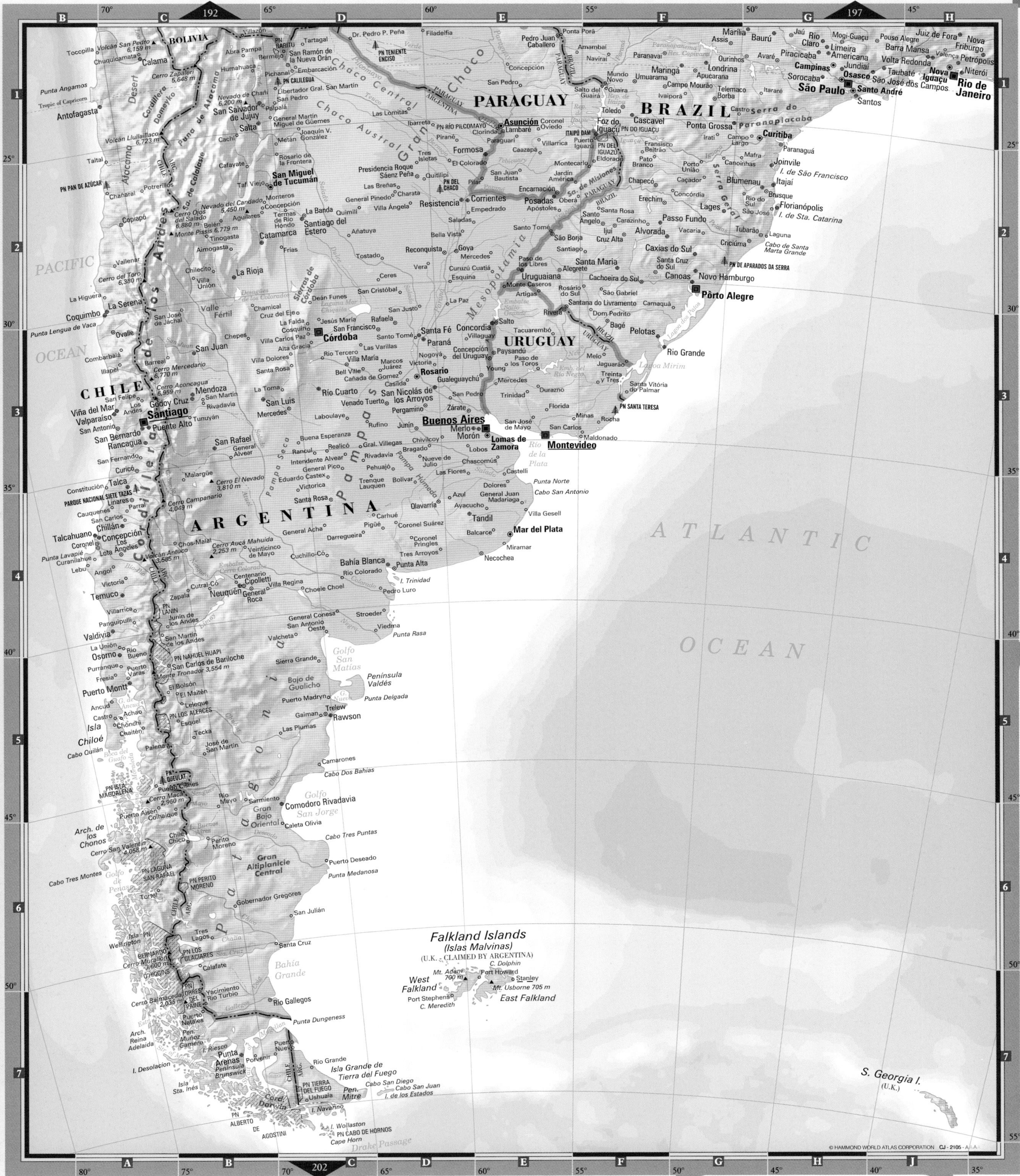

Population

- ■ Over 2,000,000
- ■ 1,000,000 - 1,999,999
- ● 500,000 - 999,999
- ● 100,000 - 499,999
- ◦ 50,000 - 99,999
- ◦ Under 50,000

Scale 1:14,800,000   Lambert Conformal Conic Projection

© HAMMOND WORLD ATLAS CORPORATION   CJ - 2105 - A - A

Population

- ■ Over 2,000,000
- ■ 1,000,000 - 1,999,999
- ◉ 500,000 - 999,999
- ◎ 250,000 - 499,999
- ⊙ 100,000 - 249,999
- ⊙ 30,000 - 99,999
- ○ 10,000 - 29,999
- ○ Under 10,000

Scale 1:6,800,000   Lambert Conformal Conic Projection

© HAMMOND WORLD ATLAS CORPORATION CJ - 153 - A-A

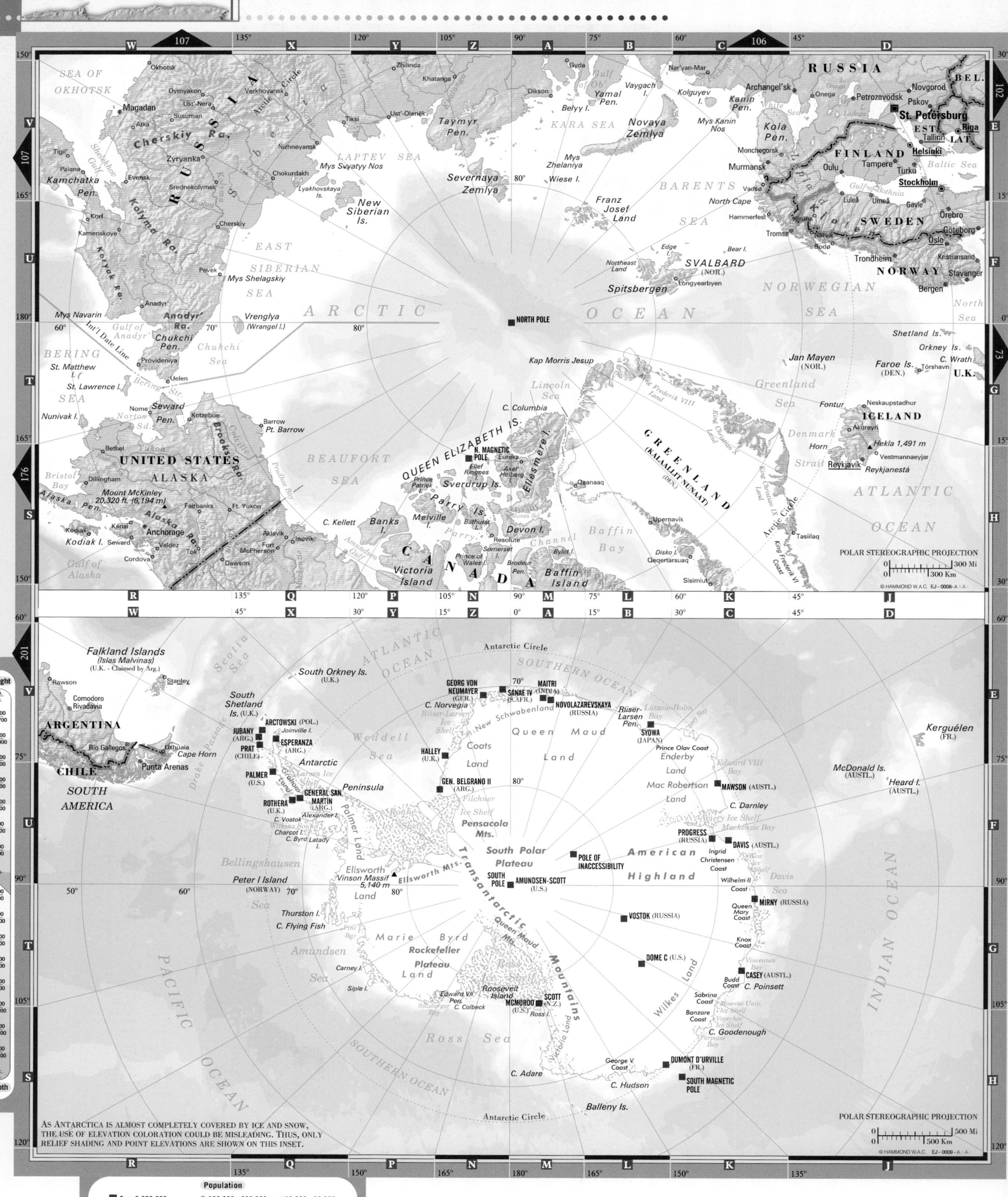

World Flags and Reference Guide

Countries of the World

Afghanistan
Page/Location: 131/H2
Area: 250,775 sq. mi.
649,507 sq. km.
Population: 29,547,078
Capital: Kabul
Largest City: Kabul
Highest Point: Noshaq
Monetary Unit: Afghani

Albania
Page/Location: 117/F2
Area: 11,110 sq. mi.
28,749 sq. km.
Population: 3,544,808
Capital: Tiranë
Largest City: Tiranë
Highest Point: Korab
Monetary Unit: lek

Algeria
Page/Location: 138/F2
Area: 919,519 sq. mi.
2,381,740 sq. km.
Population: 33,357,089
Capital: Algiers
Largest City: Algiers
Highest Point: Tahat
Monetary Unit: Algerian dinar

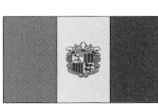

Andorra
Page/Location: 115/F1
Area: 174 sq. mi.
450 sq. km.
Population: 69,865
Capital: Andorra la Vella
Largest City: Andorra la Vella
Highest Point: Coma Pedrosa
Monetary Unit: euro

Angola
Page/Location: 147/C3
Area: 481,351 sq. mi.
1,246,700 sq. km.
Population: 10,978,552
Capital: Luanda
Largest City: Luanda
Highest Point: Morro de Môco
Monetary Unit: kwanza

Antigua and Barbuda
Page/Location: 183/N8
Area: 171 sq. mi.
443 sq. km.
Population: 68,320
Capital: St. John's
Largest City: St. John's
Highest Point: Boggy Peak
Monetary Unit: East Caribbean dollar

Argentina
Page/Location: 199/C4
Area: 1,068,296 sq. mi.
2,766,890 sq. km.
Population: 39,144,753
Capital: Buenos Aires
Largest City: Buenos Aires
Highest Point: Cerro Aconcagua
Monetary Unit: peso argentino

Armenia
Page/Location: 105/H5
Area: 11,506 sq. mi.
29,800 sq. km.
Population: 3,325,307
Capital: Yerevan
Largest City: Yerevan
Highest Point: Aragats
Monetary Unit: dram

Australia
Page/Location: 151
Area: 2,966,136 sq. mi.
7,682,300 sq. km.
Population: 19,913,144
Capital: Canberra
Largest City: Sydney
Highest Point: Mt. Kosciusko
Monetary Unit: Australian dollar

Austria*
Page/Location: 85/L3
Area: 32,375 sq. mi.
83,851 sq. km.
Population: 8,174,762
Capital: Vienna
Largest City: Vienna
Highest Point: Grossglockner
Monetary Unit: euro

Azerbaijan
Page/Location: 105/H4
Area: 33,436 sq. mi.
86,600 sq. km.
Population: 7,868,385
Capital: Baku
Largest City: Baku
Highest Point: Bazardüzü
Monetary Unit: manat

Bahamas,The
Page/Location: 183/F2
Area: 5,382 sq. mi.
13,939 sq. km.
Population: 299,697
Capital: Nassau
Largest City: Nassau
Highest Point: Mt. Alvernia
Monetary Unit: Bahamian dollar

Bahrain
Page/Location: 130/F3
Area: 240 sq. mi.
622 sq. km.
Population: 677,886
Capital: Manama
Largest City: Manama
Highest Point: Jabal Dukhān
Monetary Unit: Bahraini dinar

Bangladesh
Page/Location: 124/E3
Area: 55,598 sq. mi.
144,000 sq. km.
Population: 141,340,476
Capital: Dhākā
Largest City: Dhākā
Highest Point: Keokradong
Monetary Unit: taka

Barbados
Page/Location: 183/P9
Area: 186 sq. mi.
430 sq. km.
Population: 278,289
Capital: Bridgetown
Largest City: Bridgetown
Highest Point: Mt. Hillaby
Monetary Unit: Barbadian dollar

Belarus
Page/Location: 69/G3
Area: 80,154 sq. mi.
207,600 sq. km.
Population: 10,310,520
Capital: Minsk
Largest City: Minsk
Highest Point: Dzyarzhynskaya
Monetary Unit: Belarusian ruble

Belgium*
Page/Location: 82/C3
Area: 11,781 sq. mi.
30,513 sq. km.
Population: 10,348,276
Capital: Brussels
Largest City: Brussels
Highest Point: Botrange
Monetary Unit: euro

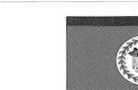

Belize
Page/Location: 186/D2
Area: 8,867 sq. mi.
22,966 sq. km.
Population: 272,945
Capital: Belmopan
Largest City: Belize City
Highest Point: Victoria Peak
Monetary Unit: Belize dollar

Benin
Page/Location: 145/F4
Area: 43,483 sq. mi.
112,620 sq. km.
Population: 7,250,033
Capital: Porto-Novo
Largest City: Cotonou
Highest Point: Sokbaro
Monetary Unit: CFA franc

Bhutan
Page/Location: 124/E2
Area: 18,147 sq. mi.
47,000 sq. km.
Population: 2,185,569
Capital: Thimphu
Largest City: Thimphu
Highest Point: Kula Kangri
Monetary Unit: ngultrum

Bolivia
Page/Location: 192/F7
Area: 424,163 sq. mi.
1,098,582 sq. km.
Population: 8,724,156
Capital: La Paz; Sucre
Largest City: La Paz
Highest Point: Nevado Sajama
Monetary Unit: boliviano

Bosnia and Herzegovina
Page/Location: 90/C3
Area: 19,940 sq. mi.
51,645 sq. km.
Population: 4,007,608
Capital: Sarajevo
Largest City: Sarajevo
Highest Point: Maglič
Monetary Unit: marka

Botswana
Page/Location: 147/D5
Area: 231,803 sq. mi.
600,370 sq. km.
Population: 1,561,973
Capital: Gaborone
Largest City: Gaborone
Highest Point: Tsodilo Hills
Monetary Unit: pula

Brazil
Page/Location: 192/F5
Area: 3,286,470 sq. mi.
8,511,965 sq. km.
Population: 184,101,109
Capital: Brasília
Largest City: São Paulo
Highest Point: Pico da Neblina
Monetary Unit: real

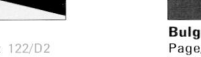

Brunei
Page/Location: 122/D2
Area: 2,226 sq. mi.
5,765 sq. km.
Population: 365,251
Capital: Bandar Seri Begawan
Largest City: Bandar Seri Begawan
Highest Point: Bukit Pagon
Monetary Unit: Brunei dollar

Bulgaria*
Page/Location: 104/C4
Area: 42,823 sq. mi.
110,912 sq. km.
Population: 7,517,973
Capital: Sofia
Largest City: Sofia
Highest Point: Musala
Monetary Unit: lev

Burkina Faso
Page/Location: 183/E3
Area: 105,869 sq. mi.
274,200 sq. km.
Population: 13,574,820
Capital: Ouagadougou
Largest City: Ouagadougou
Highest Point: Tena kourou
Monetary Unit: CFA franc

Burundi
Page/Location: 146/A3
Area: 10,747 sq. mi.
27,835 sq. km.
Population: 6,231,221
Capital: Bujumbura
Largest City: Bujumbura
Highest Point: Heha
Monetary Unit: Burundi franc

Cambodia
Page/Location: 125/H5
Area: 69,898 sq. mi.
181,036 sq. km.
Population: 13,363,421
Capital: Phnom Penh
Largest City: Phnom Penh
Highest Point: Phnum Aoral
Monetary Unit: riel

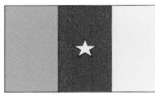

Cameroon
Page/Location: 138/H7
Area: 183,568 sq. mi.
475,441 sq. km.
Population: 16,063,678
Capital: Yaoundé
Largest City: Douala
Highest Point: Mt. Fako
Monetary Unit: CFA franc

*Member of the European Union

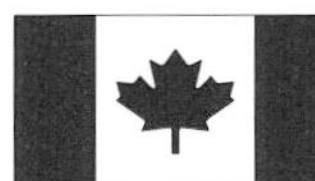

Canada
Page/Location: 164
Area: 3,851,787 sq. mi.
9,976,139 sq. km.
Population: 32,507,874
Capital: Ottawa
Largest City: Toronto
Highest Point: Mt. Trudeau
Monetary Unit: Canadian dollar

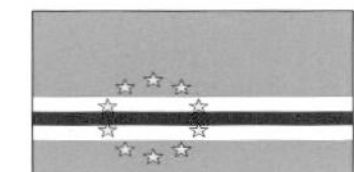

Cape Verde
Page/Location: 135/J9
Area: 1,557 sq. mi.
4,033 sq. km.
Population: 415,294
Capital: Praia
Largest City: Praia
Highest Point: Mt. Fogo
Monetary Unit: Cape Verde escudo

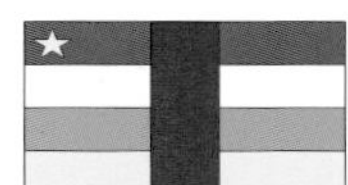

Central African Republic
Page/Location: 139/J6
Area: 240,533 sq. mi.
622,980 sq. km.
Population: 3,742,482
Capital: Bangui
Largest City: Bangui
Highest Point: Mt. Ngaoui
Monetary Unit: CFA franc

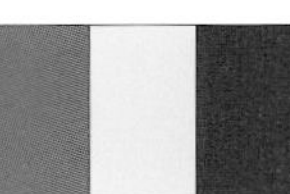

Chad
Page/Location: 139/J4
Area: 495,752 sq. mi.
1,283,998 sq. km.
Population: 9,538,544
Capital: N'Djamena
Largest City: N'Djamena
Highest Point: Emi Koussi
Monetary Unit: CFA franc

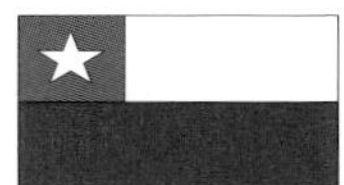

Chile
Page/Location: 199/B3
Area: 292,257 sq. mi.
756,946 sq. km.
Population: 15,827,180
Capital: Santiago
Largest City: Santiago
Highest Point: Nevado Ojos del Salado
Monetary Unit: Chilean peso

China
Page/Location: 112/G4
Area: 3,705,386 sq. mi.
9,596,960 sq. km.
Population: 1,294,629,555
Capital: Beijing
Largest City: Shangai
Highest Point: Mt. Everest
Monetary Unit: yuan

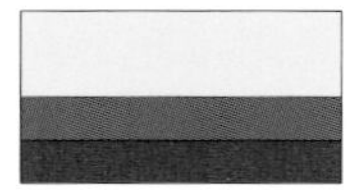

Colombia
Page/Location: 192/D3
Area: 439,513 sq. mi.
1,138,339 sq. km.
Population: 42,310,775
Capital: Bogotá
Largest City: Bogotá
Highest Point: Pico Cristóbal Colón
Monetary Unit: Colombian peso

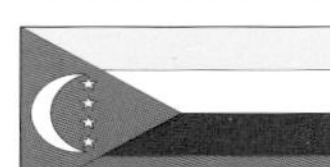

Comoros
Page/Location: 149/G5
Area: 838 sq. mi.
2,170 sq. km.
Population: 651,901
Capital: Moroni
Largest City: Moroni
Highest Point: Karthala
Monetary Unit: Comorian franc

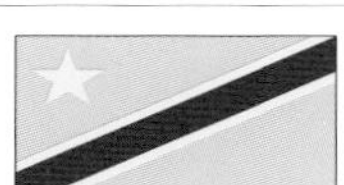

Congo, Dem. Rep. of the
Page/Location: 135/E5
Area: 905,563 sq. mi.
2,345,410 sq. km.
Population: 58,317,930
Capital: Kinshasa
Largest City: Kinshasa
Highest Point: Margherita Peak
Monetary Unit: Congolese franc

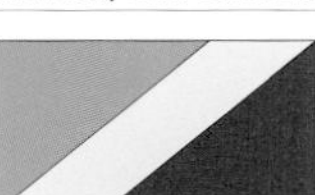

Congo, Rep. of the
Page/Location: 135/D4
Area: 132,046 sq. mi.
342,000 sq. km.
Population: 2,998,040
Capital: Brazzaville
Largest City: Brazzaville
Highest Point: Mt. Berongou
Monetary Unit: CFA franc

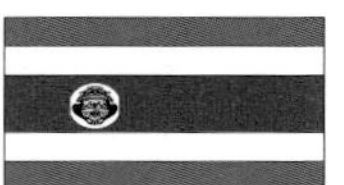

Costa Rica
Page/Location: 187/F4
Area: 19,730 sq. mi.
51,100 sq. km.
Population: 3,956,507
Capital: San José
Largest City: San José
Highest Point: Cerro Chirripó Grande
Monetary Unit: Costa Rican Colón

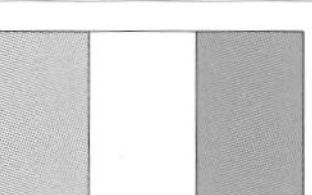

Côte d'Ivoire
Page/Location: 144/D5
Area: 124,504 sq. mi.
322,465 sq. km.
Population: 17,327,724
Capital: Yamoussoukro
Largest City: Abidjan
Highest Point: Mt. Nimba
Monetary Unit: CFA franc

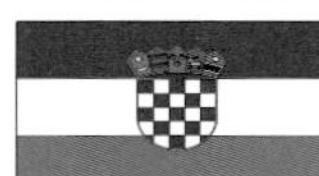

Croatia
Page/Location: 90/B3
Area: 22,050 sq. mi.
57,110 sq. km.
Population: 4,435,960
Capital: Zagreb
Largest City: Zagreb
Highest Point: Dinara
Monetary Unit: Croatian kuna

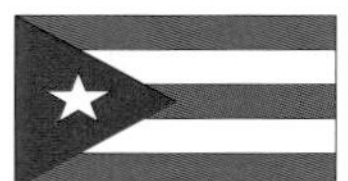

Cuba
Page/Location: 187/F1
Area: 42,803 sq. mi.
110,860 sq. km.
Population: 11,308,764
Capital: Havana
Largest City: Havana
Highest Point: Pico Turquino
Monetary Unit: Cuban peso

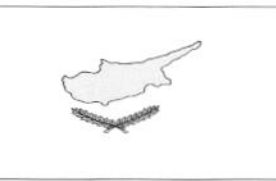

Cyprus*
Page/Location: 133/C2
Area: 3,571 sq. mi.
9,250 sq. km.
Population: 775,927
Capital: Nicosia
Largest City: Nicosia
Highest Point: Olympus
Monetary Unit: euro

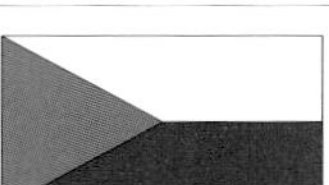

Czech Republic*
Page/Location: 83/H4
Area: 30,387 sq. mi.
78,703 sq. km.
Population: 10,246,178
Capital: Prague
Largest City: Prague
Highest Point: Sněžka
Monetary Unit: Czech koruna

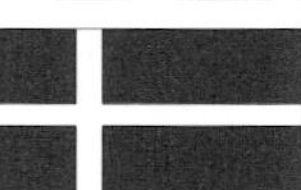

Denmark*
Page/Location: 80/C4
Area: 16,629 sq. mi.
43,069 sq. km.
Population: 5,413,392
Capital: Copenhagen
Largest City: Copenhagen
Highest Point: Yding Skovhøj
Monetary Unit: Danish krone

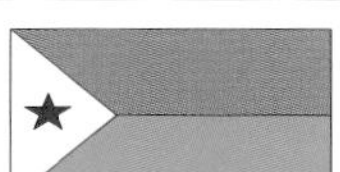

Djibouti
Page/Location: 139/P5
Area: 8,494 sq. mi.
22,000 sq. km.
Population: 466,900
Capital: Djibouti
Largest City: Djibouti
Highest Point: Moussa Ali
Monetary Unit: Djibouti franc

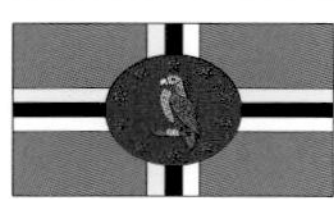

Dominica
Page/Location: 183/N9
Area: 290 sq. mi.
751 sq. km.
Population: 69,278
Capital: Roseau
Largest City: Roseau
Highest Point: Morne Diablotins
Monetary Unit: East Caribbean dollar

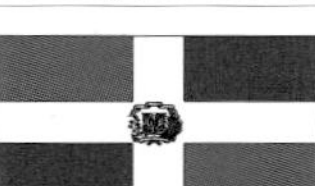

Dominican Republic
Page/Location: 183/H4
Area: 18,815 sq. mi.
48,730 sq. km.
Population: 8,833,634
Capital: Santo Domingo
Largest City: Santo Domingo
Highest Point: Pico Duarte
Monetary Unit: Dominican peso

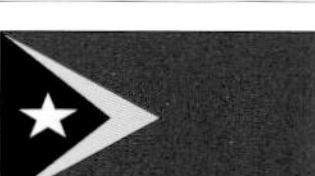

East Timor
Page/Location: 123/G5
Area: 5,743 sq. mi.
14,874 sq. km.
Population: 1,019,252
Capital: Dili
Largest City: Dili
Highest Point: Teta Mailau
Monetary Unit: U. S. dollar

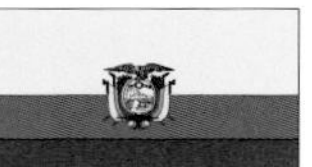

Ecuador
Page/Location: 192/C4
Area: 109,483 sq. mi.
283,561 sq. km.
Population: 13,971,798
Capital: Quito
Largest City: Guayaquil
Highest Point: Chimborazo
Monetary Unit: U.S. dollar

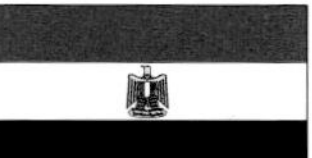
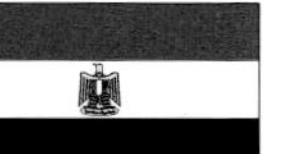

Egypt
Page/Location: 139/L2
Area: 386,659 sq. mi.
1,001,447 sq. km.
Population: 76,117,421
Capital: Cairo
Largest City: Cairo
Highest Point: Mt. Catherine
Monetary Unit: Egyptian pound

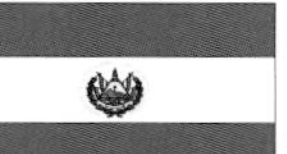

El Salvador
Page/Location: 186/D3
Area: 8,124 sq. mi.
21,040 sq. km.
Population: 6,587,541
Capital: San Salvador
Largest City: San Salvador
Highest Point: El Pital
Monetary Unit: Salvadoran colón

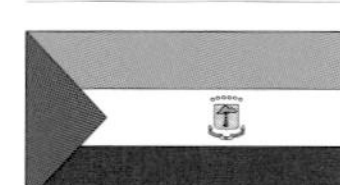

Equatorial Guinea
Page/Location: 138/G7
Area: 10,831 sq. mi.
28,052 sq. km.
Population: 523,051
Capital: Malabo
Largest City: Malabo
Highest Point: Basile
Monetary Unit: CFA franc

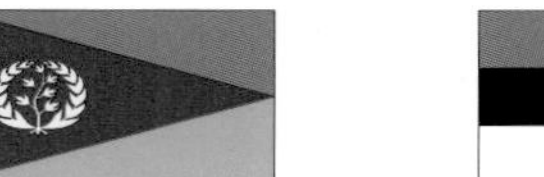

Eritrea
Page/Location: 139/N5
Area: 46,842 sq. mi.
121,320 sq. km.
Population: 4,447,307
Capital: Asmara
Largest City: Asmara
Highest Point: Soira
Monetary Unit: nafka

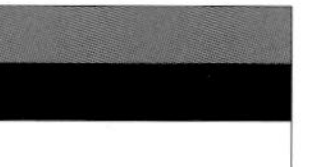

Estonia*
Page/Location: 81/L2
Area: 17,413 sq. mi.
45,100 sq. km.
Population: 1,401,945
Capital: Tallinn
Largest City: Tallinn
Highest Point: Munamägi
Monetary Unit: kroon

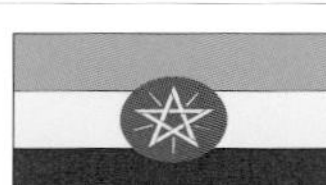

Ethiopia
Page/Location: 139/N5
Area: 435,184 sq. mi.
1,127,127 sq. km.
Population: 67,851,281
Capital: Addis Ababa
Largest City: Addis Ababa
Highest Point: Ras Dejen
Monetary Unit: birr

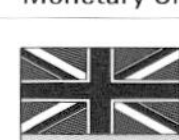

Fiji
Page/Location: 158/G6
Area: 7,055 sq. mi.
18,272 sq. km.
Population: 880,874
Capital: Suva
Largest City: Suva
Highest Point: Tomaniivi
Monetary Unit: Fijian dollar

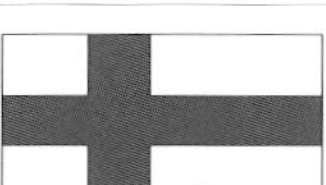

Finland*
Page/Location: 79/H2
Area: 130,128 sq. mi.
337,032 sq. km.
Population: 5,214,512
Capital: Helsinki
Largest City: Helsinki
Highest Point: Haltia
Monetary Unit: euro

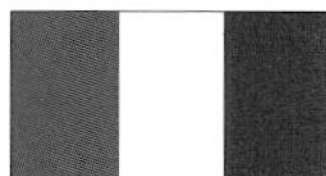

France*
Page/Location: 84/D3
Area: 211,208 sq. mi.
547,030 sq. km.
Population: 60,424,213
Capital: Paris
Largest City: Paris
Highest Point: Mont Blanc
Monetary Unit: euro

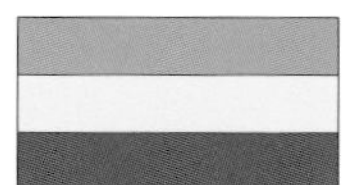

Gabon
Page/Location: 138/H7
Area: 103.346 sq. mi.
267,666 sq. km.
Population: 1,355,246
Capital: Libreville
Largest City: Libreville
Highest Point: Mt. Iboundji
Monetary Unit: CFA franc

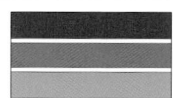

Gambia, The
Page/Location: 144/B3
Area: 4,363 sq. mi.
11,300 sq. km.
Population: 1,546,848
Capital: Banjul
Largest City: Banjul
Highest Point: 174 ft. (53 m)
Monetary Unit: dalasi

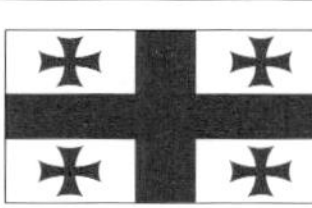

Georgia
Page/Location: 105/G4
Area: 26,911 sq. mi.
69,700 sq. km.
Population: 4,909,633
Capital: T'bilisi
Largest City: T'bilisi
Highest Point: Mt'a Shkhara
Monetary Unit: lari

Germany*
Page/Location: 82/E3
Area: 137,803 sq. mi.
356,910 sq. km.
Population: 82,424,609
Capital: Berlin
Largest City: Berlin
Highest Point: Zugspitze
Monetary Unit: euro

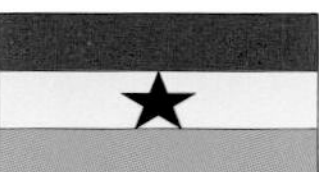

Ghana
Page/Location: 145/E4
Area: 92,099 sq. mi.
238,536 sq. km.
Population: 20,757,032
Capital: Accra
Largest City: Accra
Highest Point: Afadjato
Monetary Unit: cedi

*Member of the European Union

Greece*
Page/Location: 89/G3
Area: 50,944 sq. mi.
    131,945 sq. km.
Population: 10,647,529
Capital: Athens
Largest City: Athens
Highest Point: Mt. Olympus
Monetary Unit: euro

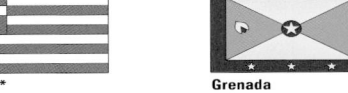

Grenada
Page/Location: 183/N10
Area: 133 sq. mi.
    344 sq. km.
Population: 89,357
Capital: St. George's
Largest City: St. George's
Highest Point: Mt. St. Catherine
Monetary Unit: East Caribbean dollar

Guatemala
Page/Location: 186/D3
Area: 42,042 sq. mi.
    108,899 sq. km.
Population: 14,280,596
Capital: Guatemala
Largest City: Guatemala
Highest Point: Tajumulco
Monetary Unit: quetzal

Guinea
Page/Location: 144/C4
Area: 94,925 sq. mi.
    245,856 sq. km.
Population: 9,246,462
Capital: Conakry
Largest City: Conakry
Highest Point: Mt. Nimba
Monetary Unit: Guinea franc

Guinea-Bissau
Page/Location: 144/B3
Area: 13,948 sq. mi.
    36,125 sq. km.
Population: 1,388,363
Capital: Bissau
Largest City: Bissau
Highest Point: 984 ft. (300 m)
Monetary Unit: CFA franc

Guyana
Page/Location: 195/G3
Area: 83,000 sq. mi.
    214,970 sq. km.
Population: 705,803
Capital: Georgetown
Largest City: Georgetown
Highest Point: Mt. Roraima
Monetary Unit: Guyana dollar

Haiti
Page/Location: 187/H2
Area: 10,694 sq. mi.
    27,697 sq. km.
Population: 7,656,166
Capital: Port-au-Prince
Largest City: Port-au-Prince
Highest Point: Pic la Selle
Monetary Unit: gourde

Honduras
Page/Location: 186/E3
Area: 43,277 sq. mi.
    112,087 sq. km.
Population: 6,823,568
Capital: Tegucigalpa
Largest City: Tegucigalpa
Highest Point: Cerro de las Minas
Monetary Unit: lempira

Hungary*
Page/Location: 90/D2
Area: 35,919 sq. mi.
    93,030 sq. km.
Population: 10,032,375
Capital: Budapest
Largest City: Budapest
Highest Point: Kékes
Monetary Unit: forint

Iceland
Page/Location: 79/N7
Area: 39,768 sq. mi.
    103,000 sq. km.
Population: 282,151
Capital: Reykjavik
Largest City: Reykjavik
Highest Point: Hvannadalshnúkúr
Monetary Unit: króna

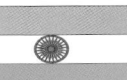

India
Page/Location: 109/G7
Area: 1,269,339 sq. mi.
    3,287,588 sq. km.
Population: 1,065,070,607
Capital: New Delhi
Largest City: Mumbai
Highest Point: Kanchenjunga
Monetary Unit: Indian rupee

Indonesia
Page/Location: 123/E4
Area: 741,096 sq. mi.
    1,919,440 sq. km.
Population: 238,452,952
Capital: Jakarta
Largest City: Jakarta
Highest Point: Puncak Jaya
Monetary Unit: rupiah

Iran
Page/Location: 109/E6
Area: 636,293 sq. mi.
    1,648,000 sq. km.
Population: 69,018,924
Capital: Tehrān
Largest City: Tehrān
Highest Point: Qolleh-ye Damāvand
Monetary Unit: Iranian rial

Iraq
Page/Location: 130/D2
Area: 168,753 sq. mi.
    437,072 sq. km.
Population: 25,374,691
Capital: Baghdad
Largest City: Baghdad
Highest Point: Haji Ibrahim
Monetary Unit: Iraqi dinar

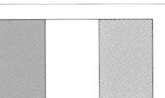

Ireland*
Page/Location: 73/P10
Area: 27,136 sq. mi.
    70,282 sq. km.
Population: 3,969,558
Capital: Dublin
Largest City: Dublin
Highest Point: Carrauntoohil
Monetary Unit: euro

Israel
Page/Location: 133/C3
Area: 8,019 sq. mi.
    20,770 sq. km.
Population: 6,199,008
Capital: Jerusalem
Largest City: Jerusalem
Highest Point: Har Meron
Monetary Unit: new Israeli shekel

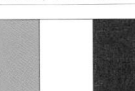

Italy*
Page/Location: 69/F4
Area: 116,303 sq. mi.
    301,225 sq. km.
Population: 58,057,477
Capital: Rome
Largest City: Rome
Highest Point: Mont Bianco
Monetary Unit: euro

Jamaica
Page/Location: 187/G2
Area: 4,243 sq. mi.
    10,990 sq. km.
Population: 2,713,130
Capital: Kingston
Largest City: Kingston
Highest Point: Blue Mountain Pk.
Monetary Unit: Jamaican dollar

Japan
Page/Location: 113/Q4
Area: 145,882 sq. mi.
    377,835 sq. km.
Population: 127,333,002
Capital: Tokyo
Largest City: Tokyo
Highest Point: Fujiyama
Monetary Unit: yen

Jordan
Page/Location: 130/C2
Area: 34,445 sq. mi.
    89,213 sq. km.
Population: 5,611,202
Capital: Ammān
Largest City: Ammān
Highest Point: Jabal Ramm
Monetary Unit: Jordanian dinar

Kazakhstan
Page/Location: 106/G5
Area: 1,049,150 sq. mi.
    2,717,300 sq. km.
Population: 16,798,552
Capital: Astana
Largest City: Almaty
Highest Point: Khan-Tengri
Monetary Unit: Kazakhstani tenge

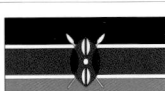

Kenya
Page/Location: 146/C2
Area: 224,960 sq. mi.
    582,646 sq. km.
Population: 32,021,856
Capital: Nairobi
Largest City: Nairobi
Highest Point: Mt. Kenya
Monetary Unit: Kenya shilling

Kiribati
Page/Location: 158/H5
Area: 277 sq. mi.
    717 sq. km.
Population: 100,798
Capital: Tarawa
Largest City: —
Highest Point: Banaba Island
Monetary Unit: Australian dollar

Korea, North
Page/Location: 115/D2
Area: 46,540 sq. mi.
    120,539 sq. km.
Population: 22,697,553
Capital: P'yŏngyang
Largest City: P'yŏngyang
Highest Point: Paektu-san
Monetary Unit: North Korean won

Korea, South
Page/Location: 115/D4
Area: 38,023 sq. mi.
    98,480 sq. km.
Population: 48,598,175
Capital: Seoul
Largest City: Seoul
Highest Point: Halla-san
Monetary Unit: South Korean won

Kuwait
Page/Location: 130/E3
Area: 6,880 sq. mi.
    17,820 sq. km.
Population: 2,257,549
Capital: Kuwait
Largest City: As Sālimiyah
Highest Point: 1,003 ft. (306 m)
Monetary Unit: Kuwaiti dinar

Kyrgyzstan
Page/Location: 129/F4
Area: 76,641 sq. mi.
    198,500 sq. km.
Population: 4,965,081
Capital: Bishkek
Largest City: Bishkek
Highest Point: Pik Pobedy
Monetary Unit: som

Laos
Page/Location: 120/C2
Area: 91,428 sq. mi.
    236,800 sq. km.
Population: 6,068,117
Capital: Vientiane
Largest City: Vientiane
Highest Point: Phou Bia
Monetary Unit: kip

Latvia*
Page/Location: 81/L3
Area: 24,749 sq. mi.
    64,100 sq. km.
Population: 2,332,078
Capital: Riga
Largest City: Riga
Highest Point: Gaizina Kalns
Monetary Unit: Latvian lat

Lebanon
Page/Location: 133/D3
Area: 4,015 sq. mi.
    10,399 sq. km.
Population: 3,777,218
Capital: Beirut
Largest City: Beirut
Highest Point: Qurnat as Sawdā'
Monetary Unit: Lebanese pound

*Member of the European Union

Lesotho
Page/Location: 148/E6
Area: 11,720 sq. mi.
30,355 sq. km.
Population: 1,865,040
Capital: Maseru
Largest City: Maseru
Highest Point: Thabana-Ntlenyana
Monetary Unit: loti

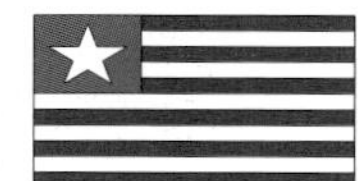

Liberia
Page/Location: 144/C5
Area: 43,000 sq. mi.
111,370 sq. km.
Population: 3,390,635
Capital: Monrovia
Largest City: Monrovia
Highest Point: Mt. Wuteve
Monetary Unit: Liberian dollar

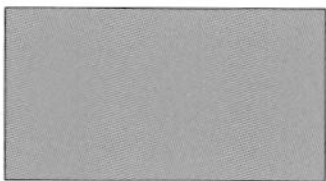

Libya
Page/Location: 139/J2
Area: 679,358 sq. mi.
1,759,537 sq. km.
Population: 5,631,585
Capital: Tripoli
Largest City: Tripoli
Highest Point: Bīkkū Bīttī
Monetary Unit: Libyan dinar

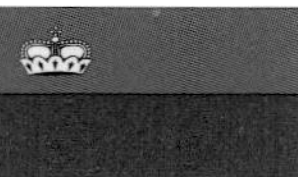

Liechtenstein
Page/Location: 99/F3
Area: 61 sq. mi.
158 sq. km.
Population: 33,436
Capital: Vaduz
Largest City: Vaduz
Highest Point: Grauspitz
Monetary Unit: Swiss franc

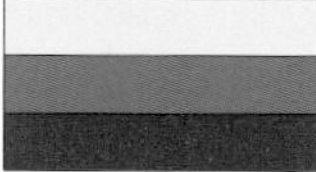

Lithuania*
Page/Location: 81/K4
Area: 25,174 sq. mi.
65,200 sq. km.
Population: 3,584,836
Capital: Vilnius
Largest City: Vilnius
Highest Point: Juozapines
Monetary Unit: litas

Luxembourg*
Page/Location: 95/E4
Area: 999 sq. mi.
2,587 sq. km.
Population: 462,690
Capital: Luxembourg
Largest City: Luxembourg
Highest Point: Buurgplaatz
Monetary Unit: euro

Macedonia (F.Y.R.O.M.)
Page/Location: 89/G2
Area: 9,781 sq. mi.
25,333 sq. km.
Population: 2,071,210
Capital: Skopje
Largest City: Skopje
Highest Point: Korab
Monetary Unit: denar

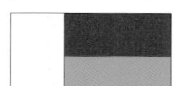

Madagascar
Page/Location: 149/H8
Area: 226,657 sq. mi.
587,041 sq. km.
Population: 17,501,871
Capital: Antananarivo
Largest City: Antananarivo
Highest Point: Maromokotro
Monetary Unit: Malagasy franc

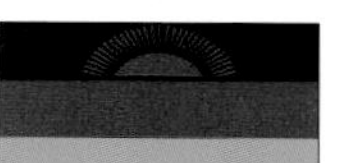

Malawi
Page/Location: 147/F3
Area: 45,747 sq. mi.
118,485 sq. km.
Population: 11,906,855
Capital: Lilongwe
Largest City: Blantyre
Highest Point: Sapitwa
Monetary Unit: Malawi kwacha

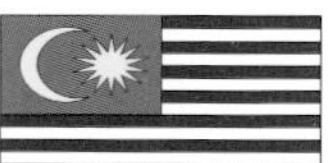

Malaysia
Page/Location: 122/C2
Area: 127,316 sq. mi.
329,750 sq. km.
Population: 23,522,482
Capital: Kuala Lumpur
Largest City: Kuala Lumpur
Highest Point: Gunung Kinabalu
Monetary Unit: ringgit

Maldives
Page/Location: 109/G9
Area: 115 sq. mi.
298 sq. km.
Population: 339,330
Capital: Male
Largest City: Male
Highest Point: 8 ft. (2.4 m)
Monetary Unit: rufiyaa

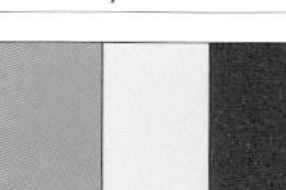

Mali
Page/Location: 138/E4
Area: 478,764 sq. mi.
1,240,000 sq. km.
Population: 11,956,788
Capital: Bamako
Largest City: Bamako
Highest Point: Hombori Tondo
Monetary Unit: CFA franc

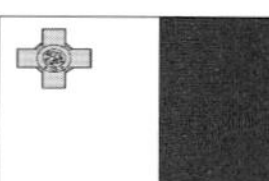

Malta*
Page/Location: 88/L7
Area: 122 sq. mi.
316 sq. km.
Population: 403,342
Capital: Valletta
Largest City: Valletta
Highest Point: Ta'Dmejrek
Monetary Unit: euro

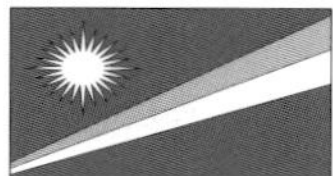

Marshall Islands
Page/Location: 158/G3
Area: 70 sq. mi.
181 sq. km.
Population: 57,738
Capital: Majuro
Largest City: —
Highest Point: 33 ft. (10 m)
Monetary Unit: U.S. dollar

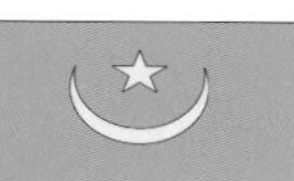

Mauritania
Page/Location: 138/C4
Area: 397.953 sq. mi.
1,030,700 sq. km.
Population: 2,998,563
Capital: Nouakchott
Largest City: Nouakchott
Highest Point: Kediet Ijill
Monetary Unit: Ouguiya

Mauritius
Page/Location: 149/T15
Area: 718 sq. mi.
1,860 sq. km.
Population: 1,220,481
Capital: Port Louis
Largest City: Port Louis
Highest Point: Mont Piton
Monetary Unit: Mauritian rupee

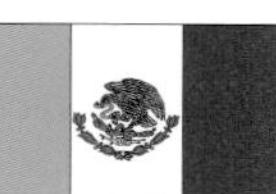

Mexico
Page/Location: 161/G7
Area: 761,601 sq. mi.
1,972,546 sq. km.
Population: 104,959,594
Capital: Mexico
Largest City: Mexico
Highest Point: Citlaltépetl
Monetary Unit: Mexican peso

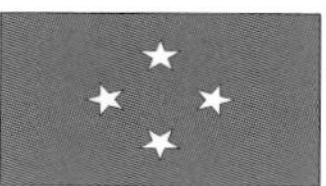

Micronesia
Page/Location: 158/D4
Area: 271 sq. mi.
702 sq. km.
Population: 108,155
Capital: Palikir
Largest City: Kolonia
Highest Point: Totolom
Monetary Unit: U.S. dollar

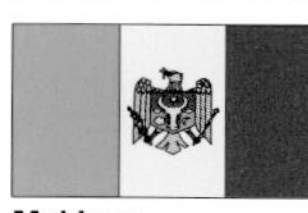

Moldova
Page/Location: 91/H2
Area: 13,012 sq. mi.
33,700 sq. km.
Population: 4,446,455
Capital: Chişinău
Largest City: Chişinău
Highest Point: Dealul Balanesti
Monetary Unit: leu

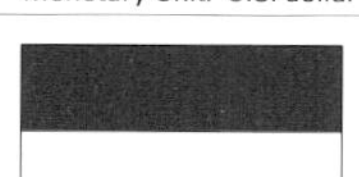

Monaco
Page/Location: 100/J8
Area: 0.7 sq. mi.
1.9 sq. km.
Population: 32,270
Capital: Monaco
Largest City: —
Highest Point: Mont Agel
Monetary Unit: euro

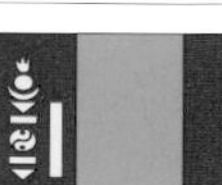

Mongolia
Page/Location: 112/G2
Area: 606,163 sq. mi.
1,569,962 sq. km.
Population: 2,751,314
Capital: Ulaanbaatar
Largest City: Ulaanbaatar
Highest Point: Nayramadlïn Orgil
Monetary Unit: tughrik

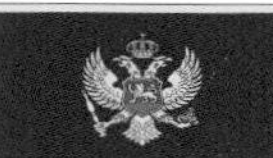

Montenegro
Page/Location: 90/D4
Area: 5,333 sq. mi.
13,812 sq. km.
Population: 620,150
Capital: Podgorica
Largest City: Podgorica
Highest Point: Bobotov Kuk
Monetary Unit: euro

Morocco
Page/Location: 140/D2
Area: 172,414 sq. mi.
446,550 sq. km.
Population: 32,209,101
Capital: Rabat
Largest City: Casablanca
Highest Point: Jebal Toubkal
Monetary Unit: Moroccan dirham

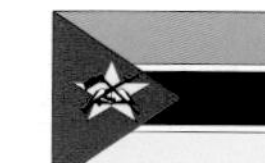

Mozambique
Page/Location: 147/G4
Area: 309,494 sq. mi.
801,590 sq. km.
Population: 18,811,731
Capital: Maputo
Largest City: Maputo
Highest Point: Monte Binga
Monetary Unit: metical

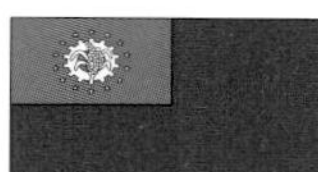

Myanmar (Burma)
Page/Location: 125/G3
Area: 261,969 sq. mi.
678,500 sq. km.
Population: 42,720,196
Capital: Yangon (Rangoon)
Largest City: Yangon (Rangoon)
Highest Point: Hkakabo Razi
Monetary Unit: kyat

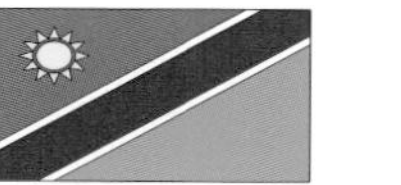

Namibia
Page/Location: 147/C5
Area: 318,694 sq. mi.
825,418 sq. km.
Population: 1,954,033
Capital: Windhoek
Largest City: Windhoek
Highest Point: Königstein
Monetary Unit: Namibian dollar

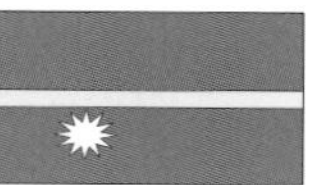

Nauru
Page/Location: 158/F5
Area: 7.7 sq. mi.
20 sq. km.
Population: 12,809
Capital: Yaren (district)
Largest City: —
Highest Point: 200 ft. (61 m)
Monetary Unit: Australian dollar

Nepal
Page/Location: 126/D1
Area: 54,663 sq. mi.
141,577 sq. km.
Population: 27,070,666
Capital: Kāthmāndu
Largest City: Kāthmāndu
Highest Point: Mt. Everest
Monetary Unit: Nepalese rupee

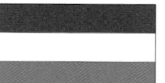

Netherlands*
Page/Location: 82/C3
Area: 14,413 sq. mi.
37,330 sq. km.
Population: 16,318,199
Capital: The Hague; Amsterdam
Largest City: Amsterdam
Highest Point: Vaalserberg
Monetary Unit: euro

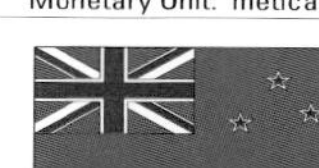

New Zealand
Page/Location: 159/R10
Area: 103,736 sq. mi.
268,676 sq. km.
Population: 3,993,817
Capital: Wellington
Largest City: Auckland
Highest Point: Mt. Cook
Monetary Unit: New Zealand dollar

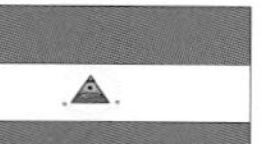

Nicaragua
Page/Location: 187/E3
Area: 49.998 sq. mi.
129,494 sq. km.
Population: 5,232,216
Capital: Managua
Largest City: Managua
Highest Point: Pico Mogotón
Monetary Unit: gold cordoba

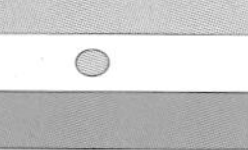

Niger
Page/Location: 138/G4
Area: 489,189 sq. mi.
1,267,000 sq. km.
Population: 11,360,538
Capital: Niamey
Largest City: Niamey
Highest Point: Bagzane
Monetary Unit: CFA franc

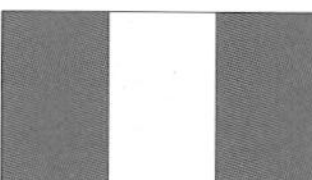

Nigeria
Page/Location: 138/G6
Area: 356,668 sq. mi.
923,770 sq. km.
Population: 137,253,133
Capital: Abuja
Largest City: Lagos
Highest Point: Chappal Waddi
Monetary Unit: naira

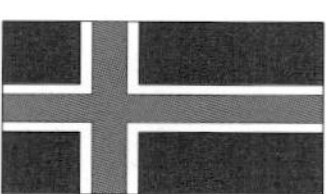

Norway
Page/Location: 79/C3
Area: 125,053 sq. mi.
323,887 sq. km.
Population: 4,574,560
Capital: Oslo
Largest City: Oslo
Highest Point: Galdhøppigen
Monetary Unit: Norwegian krone

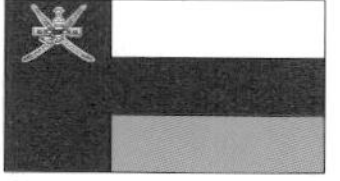

Oman
Page/Location: 131/G4
Area: 82,031 sq. mi.
212,460 sq. km.
Population: 2,903,165
Capital: Muscat
Largest City: Muscat
Highest Point: Jabal ash Shams
Monetary Unit: Omani rial

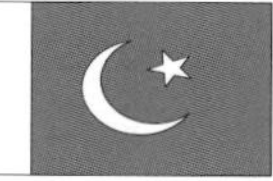

Pakistan
Page/Location: 131/H3
Area: 310,403 sq. mi.
803,944 sq. km.
Population: 153,705,278
Capital: Islāmābād
Largest City: Karāchi
Highest Point: K2 (Godwin-Austen)
Monetary Unit: Pakistani rupee

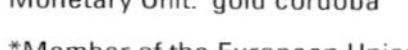

*Member of the European Union

Palau
Page/Location: 158/C4
Area: 177 sq. mi.
458 sq. km.
Population: 20,016
Capital: Koror
Largest City: Koror
Highest Point: Mt. Ngerchelchauus
Monetary Unit: U.S. dollar

Panama
Page/Location: 187/F4
Area: 30,193 sq. mi.
78,200 sq. km.
Population: 3,000,463
Capital: Panamá
Largest City: Panamá
Highest Point: Barú
Monetary Unit: balboa

Papua New Guinea
Page/Location: 158/D5
Area: 178,259 sq. mi.
461,690 sq. km.
Population: 5,420,280
Capital: Port Moresby
Largest City: Port Moresby
Highest Point: Mt. Wilhelm
Monetary Unit: kina

Paraguay
Page/Location: 189/C5
Area: 157,047 sq. mi.
406,752 sq. km.
Population: 6,191,368
Capital: Asunción
Largest City: Asunción
Highest Point: Cerro Pero
Monetary Unit: guaraní

Peru
Page/Location: 198/C3
Area: 496,222 sq. mi.
1,285,215 sq. km.
Population: 28,863,494
Capital: Lima
Largest City: Lima
Highest Point: Nevado Huascarán
Monetary Unit: nuevo sol

Philippines
Page/Location: 121/D5
Area: 115,830 sq. mi.
300,000 sq. km.
Population: 86,241,697
Capital: Manila
Largest City: Manila
Highest Point: Mt. Apo
Monetary Unit: Philippine peso

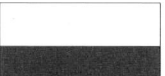

Poland*
Page/Location: 83/K2
Area: 120,725 sq. mi.
312,678 sq. km.
Population: 38,626,349
Capital: Warsaw
Largest City: Warsaw
Highest Point: Rysy
Monetary Unit: zloty

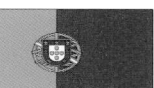

Portugal*
Page/Location: 86/A3
Area: 35,549 sq. mi.
92,072 sq. km.
Population: 10,119,250
Capital: Lisbon
Largest City: Lisbon
Highest Point: Serra da Estrela
Monetary Unit: euro

Qatar
Page/Location: 130/F3
Area: 4,247 sq. mi.
11,000 sq. km.
Population: 840,290
Capital: Doha
Largest City: Doha
Highest Point: Ṭuwayyir al Ḩamïr
Monetary Unit: Qatari riyal

Romania*
Page/Location: 91/F3
Area: 91,699 sq. mi.
237,500 sq. km.
Population: 22,355,551
Capital: Bucharest
Largest City: Bucharest
Highest Point: Moldoveanu
Monetary Unit: lei

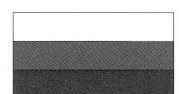

Russia
Page/Location: 106/H3
Area: 6,592,812 sq. mi.
17,075,400 sq. km.
Population: 144,112,353
Capital: Moscow
Largest City: Moscow
Highest Point: El'brus
Monetary Unit: Russian ruble

Rwanda
Page/Location: 146/A3
Area: 10,169 sq. mi.
26,337 sq. km.
Population: 7,954,013
Capital: Kigali
Largest City: Kigali
Highest Point: Karisimbi
Monetary Unit: Rwanda franc

Saint Kitts and Nevis
Page/Location: 183/N8
Area: 104 sq. mi.
269 sq. km.
Population: 38,836
Capital: Basseterre
Largest City: Basseterre
Highest Point: Mt. Liamuiga
Monetary Unit: East Caribbean dollar

Saint Lucia
Page/Location: 183/N9
Area: 238 sq. mi.
616 sq. km.
Population: 164,213
Capital: Castries
Largest City: Castries
Highest Point: Mt. Gimie
Monetary Unit: East Caribbean dollar

Saint Vincent and the Granadines
Page/Location: 183/N9
Area: 131 sq. mi.
340 sq. km.
Population: 117,193
Capital: Kingstown
Largest City: Kingstown
Highest Point: Soufière
Monetary Unit: East Caribbean dollar

Samoa
Page/Location: 159/H6
Area: 1,104 sq. mi.
2,860 sq. km.
Population: 177,714
Capital: Apia
Largest City: Apia
Highest Point: Mt. Silisili
Monetary Unit: tala

San Marino
Page/Location: 101/F5
Area: 23.4 sq. mi.
60.6 sq. km.
Population: 28,503
Capital: San Marino
Largest City: San Marino
Highest Point: Monte Titano
Monetary Unit: euro

São Tomé and Príncipe
Page/Location: 138/F7
Area: 371 sq. mi.
960 sq. km.
Population: 181,565
Capital: São Tomé
Largest City: São Tomé
Highest Point: Pico de São Tomé
Monetary Unit: dobra

Saudi Arabia
Page/Location: 130/D4
Area: 756,981 sq. mi.
1,960,582 sq. km.
Population: 25,100,425
Capital: Riyadh
Largest City: Riyadh
Highest Point: Jabal Sawdā'
Monetary Unit: Saudi riyal

Senegal
Page/Location: 144/B3
Area: 75,954 sq. mi.
196,720 sq. km.
Population: 10,852,147
Capital: Dakar
Largest City: Dakar
Highest Point: 1,906 ft, (581 m)
Monetary Unit: CFA franc

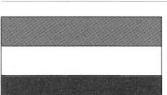

Serbia
Page/Location: 90/D3
Area: 34,185 sq. mi.
88,538 sq. km.
Population: 10,212,395
Capital: Belgrade
Largest City: Belgrade
Highest Point: Đaravica
Monetary Unit: Yugoslav new dinar

Seychelles
Page/Location: 65/M6
Area: 176 sq. mi.
455 sq. km.
Population: 80,832
Capital: Victoria
Largest City: Victoria
Highest Point: Morne Seychellois
Monetary Unit: Seychelles rupee

Sierra Leone
Page/Location: 144/B4
Area: 27,699 sq. mi.
71,740 sq. km.
Population: 5,883,889
Capital: Freetown
Largest City: Freetown
Highest Point: Loma Mansa
Monetary Unit: leone

Singapore
Page/Location: 122/B3
Area: 244 sq. mi.
632.6 sq. km.
Population: 4,767,974
Capital: Singapore
Largest City: Singapore
Highest Point: Bukit Timah
Monetary Unit: Singapore dollar

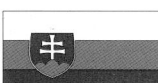

Slovakia*
Page/Location: 83/K4
Area: 18,924 sq. mi.
49,013 sq. km.
Population: 5,423,567
Capital: Bratislava
Largest City: Bratislava
Highest Point: Gerlachovský Štít
Monetary Unit: Slovak koruna

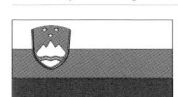

Slovenia*
Page/Location: 90/B3
Area: 7,898 sq. mi.
20,456 sq. km.
Population: 1,938,282
Capital: Ljubljana
Largest City: Ljubljana
Highest Point: Triglav
Monetary Unit: euro

Solomon Islands
Page/Location: 158/E6
Area: 11,500 sq. mi.
29,785 sq. km.
Population: 523,617
Capital: Honiara
Largest City: Honiara
Highest Point: Mt. Makarakomburu
Monetary Unit: Solomon Islands dollar

Somalia
Page/Location: 139/Q6
Area: 246,200 sq. mi.
637,658 sq. km.
Population: 8,304,601
Capital: Mogadishu
Largest City: Mogadishu
Highest Point: Shimbiris
Monetary Unit: Somali shilling

South Africa
Page/Location: 147/D6
Area: 471,008 sq. mi.
1,219,912 sq. km.
Population: 42,718,530
Capital: Cape Town; Pretoria
Largest City: Johannesburg
Highest Point: Njesuti
Monetary Unit: rand

Spain*
Page/Location: 86/C2
Area: 194,881 sq. mi.
504,742 sq. km.
Population: 40,280,780
Capital: Madrid
Largest City: Madrid
Highest Point: Pico de Teide
Monetary Unit: euro

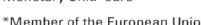

*Member of the European Union

Countries of the World

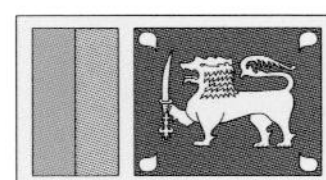

Sri Lanka
Page/Location: 124/D6
Area: 25,332 sq. mi.
65,610 sq. km.
Population: 19,905,165
Capital: Colombo
Largest City: Colombo
Highest Point: Pidurutalagala
Monetary Unit: Sri Lanka rupee

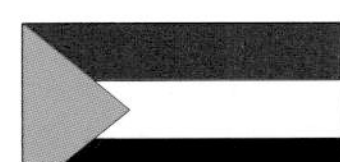

Sudan
Page/Location: 139/L5
Area: 967,494 sq. mi.
2,505,809 sq. km.
Population: 39,148,162
Capital: Khartoum
Largest City: Omdurman
Highest Point: Kinyeti
Monetary Unit: Sudanese dinar

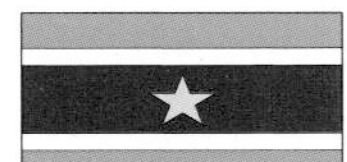

Suriname
Page/Location: 195/G3
Area: 63,039 sq. mi.
163,270 sq. km.
Population: 436,935
Capital: Paramaribo
Largest City: Paramaribo
Highest Point: Juliana Top
Monetary Unit: Surimane guilder

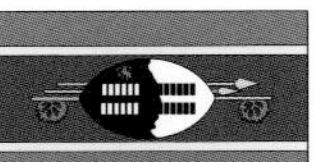

Swaziland
Page/Location: 149/E2
Area: 6,705 sq. mi.
17,366 sq. km.
Population: 1,169,241
Capital: Mbabane; Lobamba
Largest City: Mbabane
Highest Point: Emlembe
Monetary Unit: lilangeni

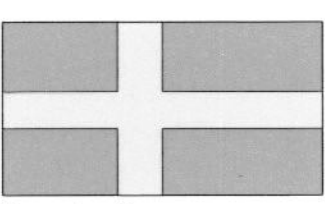

Sweden*
Page/Location: 79/E3
Area: 173,665 sq. mi.
449,792 sq. km.
Population: 8,986,400
Capital: Stockholm
Largest City: Stockholm
Highest Point: Kebnekaise
Monetary Unit: krona

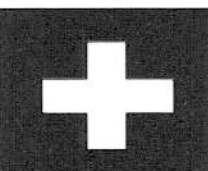

Switzerland
Page/Location: 101/D4
Area: 15,943 sq. mi.
41,292 sq. km.
Population: 7,450,867
Capital: Bern
Largest City: Zürich
Highest Point: Dufourspitze
Monetary Unit: Swiss franc

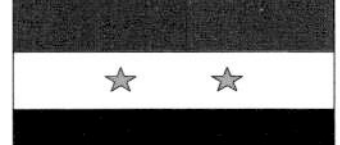

Syria
Page/Location: 132/D3
Area: 71,498 sq. mi.
185,180 sq. km.
Population: 18,016,874
Capital: Damascus
Largest City: Damascus
Highest Point: Jabal ash Shaykh
Monetary Unit: Syrian pound

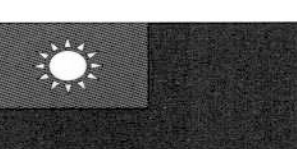

Taiwan
Page/Location: 121/D3
Area: 13,971 sq. mi.
26,185 sq. km.
Population: 22,749,838
Capital: T'aipei
Largest City: T'aipei
Highest Point: Yü Shan
Monetary Unit: new Taiwan dollar

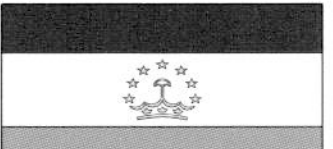

Tajikistan
Page/Location: 129/E5
Area: 55,251 sq. mi.
143,100 sq. km.
Population: 7,011,556
Capital: Dushanbe
Largest City: Dushanbe
Highest Point: Pik Imeni Ismail Samani
Monetary Unit: somoni

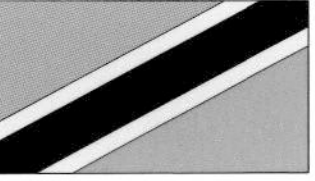

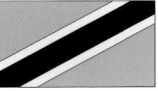

Tanzania
Page/Location: 146/B4
Area: 364,699 sq. mi.
945,090 sq. km.
Population: 36,588,225
Capital: Dar es Salaam
Largest City: Dar es Salaam
Highest Point: Kilimanjaro
Monetary Unit: Tanzanian shilling

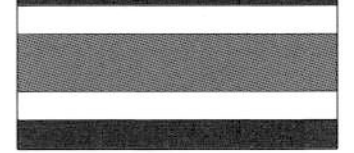

Thailand
Page/Location: 120/C3
Area: 198,455 sq. mi.
513,998 sq. km.
Population: 64,865,523
Capital: Bangkok
Largest City: Bangkok
Highest Point: Doi Inthanon
Monetary Unit: baht

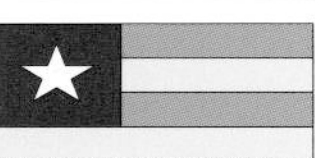

Togo
Page/Location: 145/F4
Area: 21,927 sq. mi.
56,790 sq. km.
Population: 5,556,812
Capital: Lomé
Largest City: Lomé
Highest Point: Mt. Agou
Monetary Unit: CFA franc

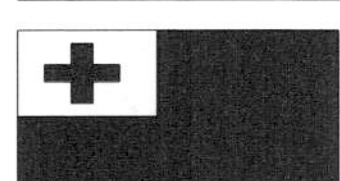

Tonga
Page/Location: 159/H7
Area: 289 sq. mi.
748 sq. km.
Population: 110,237
Capital: Nuku'alofa
Largest City: Nuku'alofa
Highest Point: Kao Island
Monetary Unit: pa'anga

Trinidad and Tobago
Page/Location: 183/N10
Area: 1,980 sq. mi.
5,128 sq. km.
Population: 1,096,585
Capital: Port-of-Spain
Largest City: Port-of-Spain
Highest Point: El Cerro del Aripo
Monetary Unit: Trin. and Tob. dollar

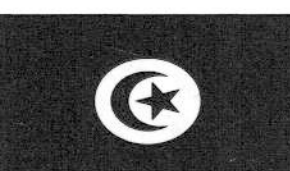

Tunisia
Page/Location: 141/H2
Area: 63,170 sq. mi.
163,610 sq. km.
Population: 10,032,050
Capital: Tūnis
Largest City: Tūnis
Highest Point: Jebel ech Chambi
Monetary Unit: Tunisian dinar

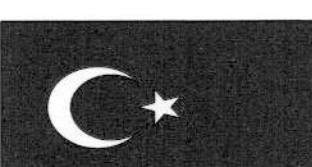

Turkey
Page/Location: 132/C2
Area: 301,382 sq. mi.
780,580 sq. km.
Population: 68,893,918
Capital: Ankara
Largest City: Istanbul
Highest Point: Mt. Ararat
Monetary Unit: Turkish lira

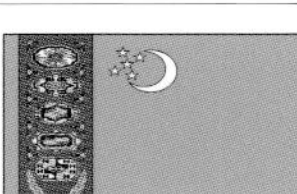

Turkmenistan
Page/Location: 129/C5
Area: 188,455 sq. mi.
488,100 sq. km.
Population: 4,863,169
Capital: Ashgabat
Largest City: Ashgabat
Highest Point: Ayrybaba
Monetary Unit: manat

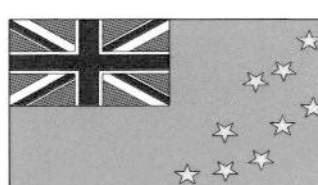

Tuvalu
Page/Location: 158/G5
Area: 9.78 sq. mi.
25.33 sq. km.
Population: 11,468
Capital: Funafuti
Largest City: —
Highest Point: 16 ft. (5 m)
Monetary Unit: Australian dollar

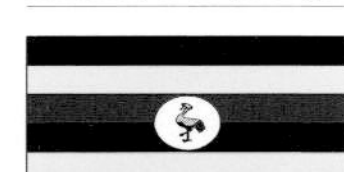

Uganda
Page/Location: 146/B2
Area: 91,076 sq. mi.
235,887 sq. km.
Population: 26,404,543
Capital: Kampala
Largest City: Kampala
Highest Point: Margherita Peak
Monetary Unit: Ugandan shilling

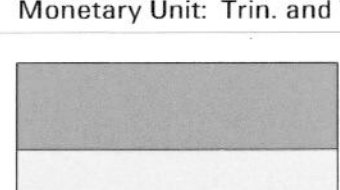

Ukraine
Page/Location: 104/D2
Area: 233,089 sq. mi.
603,700 sq. km.
Population: 47,732,079
Capital: Kiev
Largest City: Kiev
Highest Point: Hoverla
Monetary Unit: hryvnia

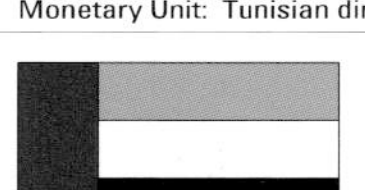

United Arab Emirates
Page/Location: 130/F4
Area: 29,182 sq. mi.
75,581 sq. km.
Population: 2,523,915
Capital: Abu Dhabi
Largest City: Dubayy
Highest Point: Jabal Yibir
Monetary Unit: Emirian dirham

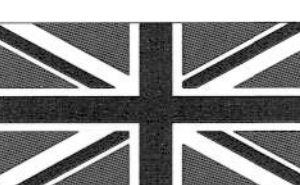

United Kingdom*
Page/Location: 73/R9
Area: 94,399 sq. mi.
244,493 sq. km.
Population: 60,270,708
Capital: London
Largest City: London
Highest Point: Ben Nevis
Monetary Unit: pound sterling

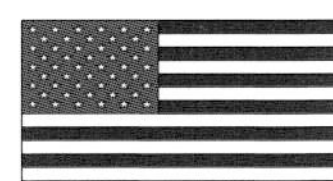

United States
Page/Location: 166
Area: 3,618,765 sq. mi.
9,372,610 sq. km.
Population: 301,139,947
Capital: Washington, D.C.
Largest City: New York
Highest Point: Mt. McKinley
Monetary Unit: U.S. dollar

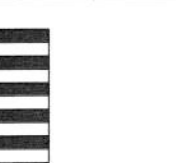

Uruguay
Page/Location: 199/E3
Area: 68,039 sq. mi.
176,220 sq. km.
Population: 3,440,205
Capital: Montevideo
Largest City: Montevideo
Highest Point: Cerro Catedral
Monetary Unit: Uruguayan peso

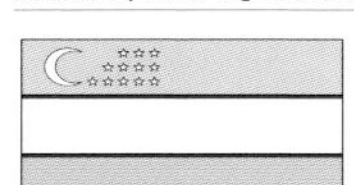

Uzbekistan
Page/Location: 129/D4
Area: 172,741 sq. mi.
447,400 sq. km.
Population: 26,410,416
Capital: Tashkent
Largest City: Tashkent
Highest Point: Adelunga Toghi
Monetary Unit: sum

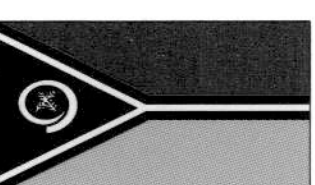

Vanuatu
Page/Location: 158/F6
Area: 5,700 sq. mi.
14,763 sq. km.
Population: 202,609
Capital: Port-Vila
Largest City: Port-Vila
Highest Point: Tabwemasana
Monetary Unit: vatu

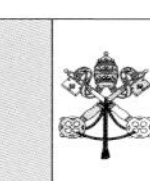

Vatican City
Page/Location: 88/C2
Area: 0.17 sq. mi.
0.44 sq. km.
Population: 911
Capital: —
Largest City: —
Highest Point: 246 ft. (75 m)
Monetary Unit: euro

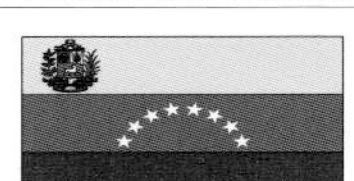

Venezuela
Page/Location: 195/E3
Area: 352,143 sq. mi.
912,050 sq. km.
Population: 25,017,387
Capital: Caracas
Largest City: Caracas
Highest Point: Pico Bolívar
Monetary Unit: bolívar

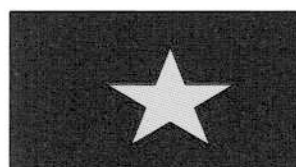

Vietnam
Page/Location: 120/D2
Area: 127,243 sq. mi.
329,560 sq. km.
Population: 82,689,518
Capital: Hanoi
Largest City: Ho Chi Minh City
Highest Point: Fan Si Pan
Monetary Unit: dong

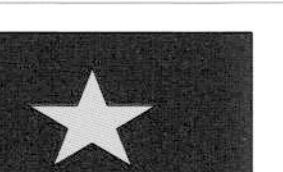

Yemen
Page/Location: 130/E5
Area: 203,849 sq. mi.
527,970 sq. km.
Population: 20,024,867
Capital: Sanaa
Largest City: Aden
Highest Point: Nabī Shu'ayb
Monetary Unit: Yemeni rial

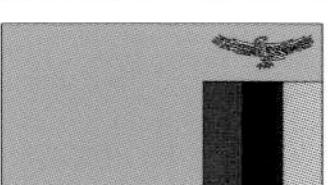
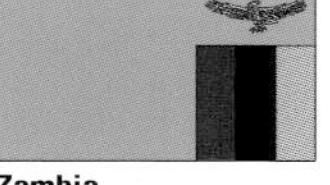

Zambia
Page/Location: 147/E3
Area: 290,568 sq. mi.
752,618 sq. km.
Population: 10,462,436
Capital: Lusaka
Largest City: Lusaka
Highest Point: Mafinga Hills
Monetary Unit: Zambian kwacha

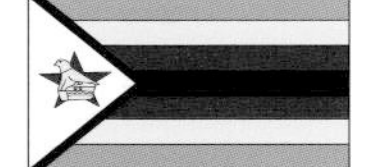

Zimbabwe
Page/Location: 147/E4
Area: 150,803 sq. mi.
390,580 sq. km.
Population: 12,671,860
Capital: Harare
Largest City: Harare
Highest Point: Inyangani
Monetary Unit: Zimbabwe dollar

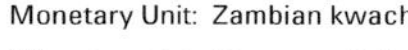

*Member of the European Union

World Statistics, Time Zones, and Index

World Statistics

ELEMENTS OF THE SOLAR SYSTEM

	Mean Distance from Sun: in Miles	in Kilometers	Period of Revolution around Sun	Period of Rotation on Axis	Equatorial Diameter in Miles	in Kilometers	Surface Gravity (Earth = 1)	Mass (Earth = 1)	Mean Density (Water = 1)	Number of Satellites
Mercury	35,990,000	57,900,000	87.97 days	58.7 days	3,032	4,880	0.38	0.055	5.4	0
Venus	67,240,000	108,200,000	224.70 days	243.7 days†	7,521	12,104	0.91	0.815	5.2	0
Earth	93,000,000	149,700,000	365.26 days	23h 56m	7,926	12,755	1.00	1.00	5.5	1
Mars	141,610,000	227,900,000	686.98 days	24h 37m	4,221	6,794	0.38	0.107	3.9	2
Jupiter	483,675,000	778,400,000	11.86 years	9h 55m	88,846	142,984	2.36	317.8	1.3	62‡
Saturn	886,572,000	1,426,800,000	29.46 years	10h 30m	74,898	120,536	0.92	95.2	0.7	59‡
Uranus	1,783,957,000	2,871,000,000	84.01 years	17h 14m†	31,763	51,118	0.89	14.5	1.3	27
Neptune	2,795,114,000	4,498,300,000	164.79 years	16h 6m	30,778	49,532	1.13	17.1	1.6	13‡
Pluto*	3,670,000,000	5,906,400,000	247.70 years	6.4 days†	1,413	2,274	0.07	0.002	2.1	3‡

† Retrograde motion ‡ Includes provisionally named satellites * Pluto is no longer considered a planet by the International Astronomical Union.

Source: NASA, National Space Science Center

DIMENSIONS OF THE EARTH

	Area in: Sq. Miles	Sq. Kilometers
Superficial area	196,939,000	510,072,000
Land surface	57,506,000	148,940,000
Water surface	139,433,000	361,132,000

	Distance in: Miles	Kilometers
Equatorial circumference	24,902	40,075
Polar circumference	24,860	40,007
Equatorial diameter	7,926.4	12,756.4
Polar diameter	7,899.8	12,713.6
Equatorial radius	3,963.2	6,378.2
Polar radius	3,949.9	6,356.8

Volume of the Earth	2.6×10^{11} cubic miles	10.84×10^{11} cubic kilometers
Mass or weight	6.6×10^{21} short tons	6.0×10^{21} metric tons
Maximum distance from Sun	94,600,000 miles	152,000,000 kilometers
Minimum distance from Sun	91,300,000 miles	147,000,000 kilometers

OCEANS AND MAJOR SEAS

	Area in: Sq. Miles	Sq. Kms.	Greatest Depth in: Feet	Meters
Pacific Ocean	63,855,000	165,384,000	36,198	11,033
Atlantic Ocean	31,744,000	82,217,000	28,374	8,648
Indian Ocean	28,417,000	73,600,000	25,344	7,725
Arctic Ocean	5,427,000	14,056,000	17,880	5,450
Caribbean Sea	970,000	2,512,300	24,720	7,535
Mediterranean Sea	969,000	2,509,700	16,896	5,150
South China Sea	895,000	2,318,000	15,000	4,600
Bering Sea	875,000	2,266,250	15,800	4,800
Gulf of Mexico	600,000	1,554,000	12,300	3,750
Sea of Okhotsk	590,000	1,528,100	11,070	3,370
East China Sea	482,000	1,248,400	9,500	2,900
Yellow Sea	480,000	1,243,200	350	107
Sea of Japan	389,000	1,007,500	12,280	3,740
Hudson Bay	317,500	822,300	846	258
North Sea	222,000	575,000	2,200	670
Black Sea	185,000	479,150	7,365	2,245
Red Sea	169,000	437,700	7,200	2,195
Baltic Sea	163,000	422,170	1,506	459

THE CONTINENTS

	Population	Total Area in: Sq. Miles	Total Area in: Sq. Kms.	Percent of World's Land
Asia	4,004,788,000	17,128,500	44,362,815	29.5
Africa	935,813,000	11,707,000	30,321,130	20.2
North America	523,686,000	9,363,000	24,250,170	16.2
South America	380,017,000	6,879,725	17,818,505	11.9
Antarctica	— — —	5,405,000	14,000,000	9.4
Europe	727,228,000	4,057,000	10,507,630	7.0
Australia	20,434,000	2,967,893	7,686,850	5.1

MAJOR SHIP CANALS

	Length in: Miles	Kms.	Minimum Depth in: Feet	Meters
Volga-Baltic, Russia	225	362	–	–
Baltic-White Sea, Russia	140	225	16	5
Suez, Egypt	100.76	162	42	13
Albert, Belgium	80	129	16.5	5
Moscow-Volga, Russia	80	129	18	6
Volga-Don, Russia	62	100	–	–
Göta, Sweden	54	87	10	3
Kiel (Nord-Ostsee), Germany	53.2	86	38	12
Panama Canal, Panama	50.72	82	41.6	13
Houston Ship, U.S.A.	50	81	36	11

LARGEST ISLANDS

	Area in: Sq. Miles	Sq. Kms.
Greenland	840,000	2,175,600
New Guinea	305,000	789,950
Borneo	286,000	740,740
Madagascar	226,656	587,040
Baffin, Canada	195,928	507,454
Sumatra, Indonesia	164,000	424,760
Honshu, Japan	88,000	227,920
Great Britain	84,400	218,896
Victoria, Canada	83,896	217,290
Ellesmere, Canada	75,767	196,236
Celebes, Indonesia	72,986	189,034
South I., New Zealand	58,393	151,238
Java, Indonesia	48,842	126,501
North I., New Zealand	44,187	114,444
Cuba	42,803	110,860
Newfoundland, Canada	42,031	108,860
Luzon, Philippines	40,420	104,688
Iceland	39,768	103,000
Mindanao, Philippines	36,537	94,631
Hokkaidō, Japan	30,436	78,829
Sakhalin, Russia	29,500	76,405
Hispaniola, Haiti & Dom. Rep.	29,399	76,143

	Area in: Sq. Miles	Sq. Kms.
Ireland	27,136	70,282
Banks, Canada	27,038	70,028
Tasmania, Australia	26,410	68,402
Ceylon, Sri Lanka	25,332	65,610
Svalbard, Norway	23,957	62,049
Devon, Canada	21,331	55,247
Novaya Zemlya (north isl.), Russia	18,600	48,200
Tierra del Fuego, Chile & Argentina	18,301	47,400
Marajó, Brazil	17,991	46,597
Alexander, Antarctica	16,700	43,250
Axel Heiberg, Canada	16,671	43,178
Melville, Canada	16,274	42,150
Southampton, Canada	15,913	41,215
New Britain, Papua New Guinea	14,100	36,519
Taiwan	13,836	35,835
Kyushu, Japan	13,770	35,664
Hainan, China	13,127	33,999
Prince of Wales, Canada	12,872	33,338
Spitsbergen, Norway	12,355	31,999
Vancouver, Canada	12,079	31,285
Timor, Indonesia	11,527	29,855
Sicily, Italy	9,926	25,708

	Area in: Sq. Miles	Sq. Kms.
Somerset, Canada	9,570	24,786
Sardinia, Italy	9,301	24,090
Shikoku, Japan	6,860	17,767
New Caledonia, France	6,530	16,913
Nordaustlandet, Norway	6,409	16,599
Samar, Philippines	5,050	13,080
Negros, Philippines	4,906	12,707
Palawan, Philippines	4,550	11,785
Panay, Philippines	4,446	11,515
Jamaica	4,232	10,961
Hawaii, United States	4,038	10,458
Viti Levu, Fiji	4,010	10,386
Cape Breton, Canada	3,981	10,311
Mindoro, Philippines	3,759	9,736
Kodiak, Alaska, U.S.A.	3,670	9,505
Cyprus	3,572	9,251
Puerto Rico, U.S.A.	3,435	8,897
Corsica, France	3,352	8,682
New Ireland, Papua New Guinea	3,340	8,651
Crete, Greece	3,218	8,335
Anticosti, Canada	3,066	7,941
Wrangel, Russia	2,819	7,301

PRINCIPAL MOUNTAINS

	Height in : Feet	Meters
Everest, Nepal-China	29,028	8,848
K2 (Godwin Austen), Pakistan-China	28,250	8,611
Kånchenjunga, Nepal-India	28,208	8,598
Lhotse, Nepal-China	27,923	8,511
Makalu, Nepal-China	27,789	8,470
Dhaulagiri, Nepal	26,810	8,172
Nanga Parbat, Pakistan	26,660	8,126
Annapurna, Nepal	26,504	8,078
Nanda Devi, India	25,645	7,817
Rakaposhi, Pakistan	25,550	7,788
Kongur Shan, China	25,325	7,719
Tirich Mir, Pakistan	25,230	7,690
Gongga Shan, China	24,790	7,556
Ismail Samani Peak, Tajikistan	24,590	7,495
Pobedy Peak, Kyrgyzstan	24,406	7,439
Chomo Lhari, Bhutan-China	23,997	7,314
Muztag, China	23,891	7,282
Cerro Aconcagua, Argentina	22,831	6,959
Ojos del Salado, Chile-Argentina	22,572	6,880
Bonete, Chile-Argentina	22,546	6,872
Tupungato, Chile-Argentina	22,310	6,800
Pissis, Argentina	22,241	6,779
Mercedario, Argentina	22,211	6,770
Huascarán, Peru	22,205	6,768
Llullaillaco, Chile-Argentina	22,057	6,723
Nevada Ancohuma, Bolivia	21,489	6,550
Chimborazo, Ecuador	20,561	6,267
McKinley, Alaska	20,320	6,194
Trudeau, Yukon, Canada	19,524	5,951
Cotopaxi, Ecuador	19,347	5,897
Kilimanjaro, Tanzania	19,340	5,895
El Misti, Peru	19,101	5,822
Pico Cristóbal Colón, Colombia	18,947	5,775
Huila, Colombia	18,865	5,750
Citlaltépetl (Orizaba), Mexico	18,700	5,700
Damavand, Iran	18,605	5,671
El'brus, Russia	18,510	5,642
St. Elias, Alaska, U.S.A.-Yukon, Canada	18,008	5,489
Dykh-tau, Russia	17,070	5,203
Batian (Kenya), Kenya	17,058	5,199
Ararat, Turkey	16,946	5,165
Vinson Massif, Antarctica	16,864	5,140
Margherita (Ruwenzori), Africa	16,795	5,119
Kazbek, Georgia-Russia	16,558	5,047
Puncak Jaya, Indonesia	16,503	5,030
Blanc, France	15,771	4,807
Klyuchevskaya Sopka, Russia	15,584	4,750
Fairweather, Br. Col., Canada	15,300	4,663
Dufourspitze (Mte. Rosa), Italy-Switzerland	15,203	4,634
Ras Dashen, Ethiopia	15,157	4,620
Matterhorn, Switzerland	14,691	4,478
Whitney, California, U.S.A.	14,494	4,418
Elbert, Colorado, U.S.A.	14,433	4,399
Rainier, Washington, U.S.A.	14,410	4,392
Shasta, California, U.S.A.	14,162	4,317
Pikes Peak, Colorado, U.S.A.	14,110	4,301
Finsteraarhorn, Switzerland	14,022	4,274
Mauna Kea, Hawaii, U.S.A.	13,796	4,205
Mauna Loa, Hawaii, U.S.A.	13,677	4,169
Jungfrau, Switzerland	13,642	4,158
Grossglockner, Austria	12,457	3,797
Fujiyama, Japan	12,389	3,776
Cook, New Zealand	12,349	3,764

LONGEST RIVERS

	Length in: Miles	Kms.
Nile, Africa	4,145	6,671
Amazon, S. America	4,007	6,448
Mississippi-Missouri-Red Rock, U.S.A.	3,710	5,971
Chang Jiang (Yangtze), China	3,500	5,633
Ob'-Irtysh, Russia-Kazakhstan	3,362	5,411
Yenisey-Angara, Russia	3,100	4,989
Huang He (Yellow), China	2,950	4,747
Congo, Africa	2,780	4,474
Amur-Shilka-Onon, Asia	2,744	4,416
Lena, Russia	2,734	4,400
Mackenzie-Peace-Finlay, Canada	2,635	4,241
Paraná-La Plata, S. America	2,630	4,232
Mekong, Asia	2,610	4,200
Niger, Africa	2,580	4,152
Missouri-Red Rock, U.S.A.	2,564	4,125
Yenisey, Russia	2,500	4,028
Mississippi, U.S.A.	2,348	3,778
Murray-Darling, Australia	2,310	3,718
Volga, Russia	2,290	3,685
Madeira, S. America	2,013	3,240
Purus, S. America	1,995	3,211
Yukon, Alaska-Canada	1,979	3,185
Zambezi, Africa	1,950	3,138
São Francisco, Brazil	1,930	3,106
St. Lawrence, Canada-U.S.A.	1,900	3,058
Rio Grande, Mexico-U.S.A.	1,885	3,034
Syrdarïya-Naryn, Asia	1,859	2,992
Indus, Asia	1,800	2,897
Danube, Europe	1,775	2,857
Brahmaputra, Asia	1,700	2,736
Tocantins, Brazil	1,677	2,699
Salween, Asia	1,675	2,696
Euphrates, Asia	1,650	2,655
Xi (Si), China	1,650	2,655
Amu Darya, Asia	1,616	2,601
Nelson-Saskatchewan, Canada	1,600	2,575
Orinoco, S. America	1,600	2,575
Paraguay, S. America	1,584	2,549
Kolyma, Russia	1,562	2,514
Ganges, Asia	1,550	2,494
Zhayyq (Ural), Kazakhstan-Russia	1,509	2,428
Japurá, S. America	1,500	2,414
Arkansas, U.S.A.	1,450	2,334
Colorado, U.S.A.-Mexico	1.450	2,334
Negro, S. America	1,400	2,253
Dnepr (Dnyapro, Dnipro), Russia-Belarus-Ukraine	1,368	2,202
Orange, Africa	1,350	2,173
Ayeyarwady, Myanmar	1,325	2,132
Brazos, U.S.A.	1,309	2,107
Ohio-Allegheny, U.S.A.	1,306	2,102
Kama, Russia	1,252	2,031
Don, Russia	1,222	1,967
Red, U.S.A.	1,222	1,966
Columbia, U.S.A.-Canada	1,214	1,953
Tigris, Asia	1,181	1,901
Darling, Australia	1,160	1,867
Angara, Russia	1,135	1,827
Sungari, Asia	1,130	1,819
Pechora, Russia	1,124	1,809
Snake, U.S.A.	1,038	1,670
Churchill, Canada	1,000	1,609
Pilcomayo, S. America	1,000	1,609
Uruguay, S. America	994	1.600
Platte-N. Platte, U.S.A.	990	1,593
Ohio, U.S.A.	981	1,578
Magdalena, Colombia	956	1,538
Pecos, U.S.A.	926	1,490
Oka, Russia	918	1,477
Canadian, U.S.A.	906	1,458
Colorado, Texas, U.S.A.	894	1,439
Dnister (Nistru), Ukraine-Moldova	876	1,410
Fraser, Canada	850	1,369
Rhine, Europe	820	1,319
Northern Dvina, Russia	809	1,302
Ottawa, Canada	790	1,271

PRINCIPAL NATURAL LAKES

	Area in: Sq. Miles	Sq. Kms.	Max. Depth in: Feet	Meters
Caspian Sea, Asia	143,243	370,999	3,264	995
Lake Superior, U.S.A.-Canada	31,820	82,414	1,329	405
Lake Victoria, Africa	26,628	69,215	270	82
Lake Huron, U.S.A.-Canada	23,010	59,596	748	228
Lake Michigan, U.S.A.	22,400	58,016	923	281
Aral Sea, Kazakhstan-Uzbekistan	15,830	41,000	213	65
Lake Tanganyika, Africa	12,650	32,764	4,700	1,433
Lake Baykal, Russia	12,162	31,500	5,316	1,620
Great Bear Lake, Canada	12,096	31,328	1,356	413
Lake Nyasa (Malawi), Africa	11,555	29,928	2,320	707
Great Slave Lake, Canada	11,031	28,570	2,015	614
Lake Erie, U.S.A.-Canada	9,940	25,745	210	64
Lake Winnipeg, Canada	9,417	24,390	60	18
Lake Ontario, U.S.A.-Canada	7,540	19,529	775	244
Lake Balkhash, Kazakhstan	7,081	18,340	87	27
Lake Chad, Africa*	7,000	18,130	25	8
Lake Ladoga, Russia	6,900	17,871	738	225
Lake Maracaibo, Venezuela	5,120	13,261	100	31
Tonle Sap, Cambodia*	3,860-965	10,000-2,500	–	–
Lake Onega, Russia	3,761	9,741	377	115
Lake Eyre, Australia*	3,500-0	9,065-0	–	–
Lake Titicaca, Peru-Bolivia	3,200	8,288	1,000	305
Lake Nicaragua, Nicaragua	3,100	8,029	230	70
Lake Athabasca, Canada	3,064	7,936	400	122
Reindeer Lake, Canada*	2,568	6,651	–	–
Lake Turkana (Rudolf), Africa	2,463	6,379	240	73
Ysyk-Köl, Kyrgyzstan	2,425	6,281	2,303	702
Lake Torrens, Australia*	2,230	5,776	–	–
Vänern, Sweden	2,156	5,584	328	100
Nettilling Lake, Canada*	2,140	5,543	–	–
Lake Winnipegosis, Canada	2,075	5,374	38	12
Lake Albert, Africa	2,075	5,374	160	49
Kariba Lake, Zambia-Zimbabwe	2,050	5,310	295	90
Lake Nipigon, Canada	1,872	4,848	540	165
Lake Mweru, Africa	1,800	4,662	60	18
Lake Manitoba, Canada	1,799	4,659	12	4
Lake Khanka, China-Russia	1,700	4,403	33	10
Lake Kioga, Uganda	1,700	4,403	25	8
Lake of the Woods, U.S.A.-Canada	1,679	4,349	70	21

* Figures subject to great seasonal variations.

Time Zones of the World

165° W	150° W	135° W	120° W	105° W	90° W	75° W	60° W	45° W	30° W	15° W	0°
1 A.M.	2 A.M.	3 A.M.	4 A.M.	5 A.M.	6 A.M.	7 A.M.	8 A.M.	9 A.M.	10 A.M.	11 A.M.	NOON

ARCTIC   OCEAN

GREENLAND

NOON

11 A.M.

3 A.M.
ALASKA

Anchorage

Whitehorse

CANADA

Nuuk

Reykjavík   ICELAND

NOR

1 A.M.

Edmonton

Winnipeg

Montréal

Halifax

NEWFOUNDLAND
8:30 A.M.

ST. PIERRE
& MIQUELON
9 A.M.

UNITED
KINGDOM

IRELAND   London   NETH.
BELG.

Seattle

Boise

Chicago   Detroit

UNITED   STATES

Denver

New York
Washington

Paris
FRANCE

San Francisco

PORTUGAL   Madrid
SPAIN   Alg

Los Angeles

Phoenix

Atlanta

BERMUDA

AZORES

MOROCCO

ATLANTIC

Houston

CANARY IS.

ALGERIA

1 A.M.

MEXICO

Miami

BAHAMAS

CUBA

HAITI DOM.
REP.

PUERTO
RICO

W. SAHARA

MAURITANIA

MALI

N

Honolulu

HAWAII

Mexico

BELIZE
GUATEMALA   HONDURAS
EL SALVADOR   NICARAGUA
COSTA RICA   PANAMA

JAMAICA

ANTIGUA & BARBUDA
DOMINICA
GRENADA   BARBADOS
TRINIDAD & TOBAGO

CAPE
VERDE   Dakar   SENEGAL
GAMBIA
GUINEA-BISSAU   GUINEA   BURKINA
FASO   BENIN
SIERRA LEONE   CÔTE   GHANA   La
D'IVOIRE   TOGO
LIBERIA

1 A.M.

MIDNIGHT

KIRIBATI

INTL. DATE LINE

PACIFIC

VENEZUELA
COLOMBIA
Bogotá

GUYANA
SURI. FR. GUIANA

OCEAN

SÃO TOMÉ
& PRÍNCIPE

FRENCH   POLYNESIA

MARQUESAS IS.
2:30 A.M.

GÁLAPAGOS IS.

ECUADOR

OCEAN

Manaus

BRAZIL

Recife

ASCENSION

Lima   PERU

La Paz
BOLIVIA

PITCAIRN IS.

EASTER I.

PARAGUAY

Rio de
Janeiro

CHILE

TRISTAN DA CUNHA

Santiago

Buenos
Aires   URUGUAY

ARGENTINA

TIME ZONES OF THE WORLD

STANDARD TIME ZONES	3 A.M.	4 A.M.	5 A.M.	6 A.M.

FALKLAND IS.

AREAS USING HALF HOUR DEVIATIONS	5:30 P.M.

S. GEORGIA

© HAMMOND WORLD ATLAS CORPORATION   HJ · A.

1 A.M.	2 A.M.	3 A.M.	4 A.M.	5 A.M.	6 A.M.	7 A.M.	8 A.M.	9 A.M.	10 A.M.	11 A.M.	NOON

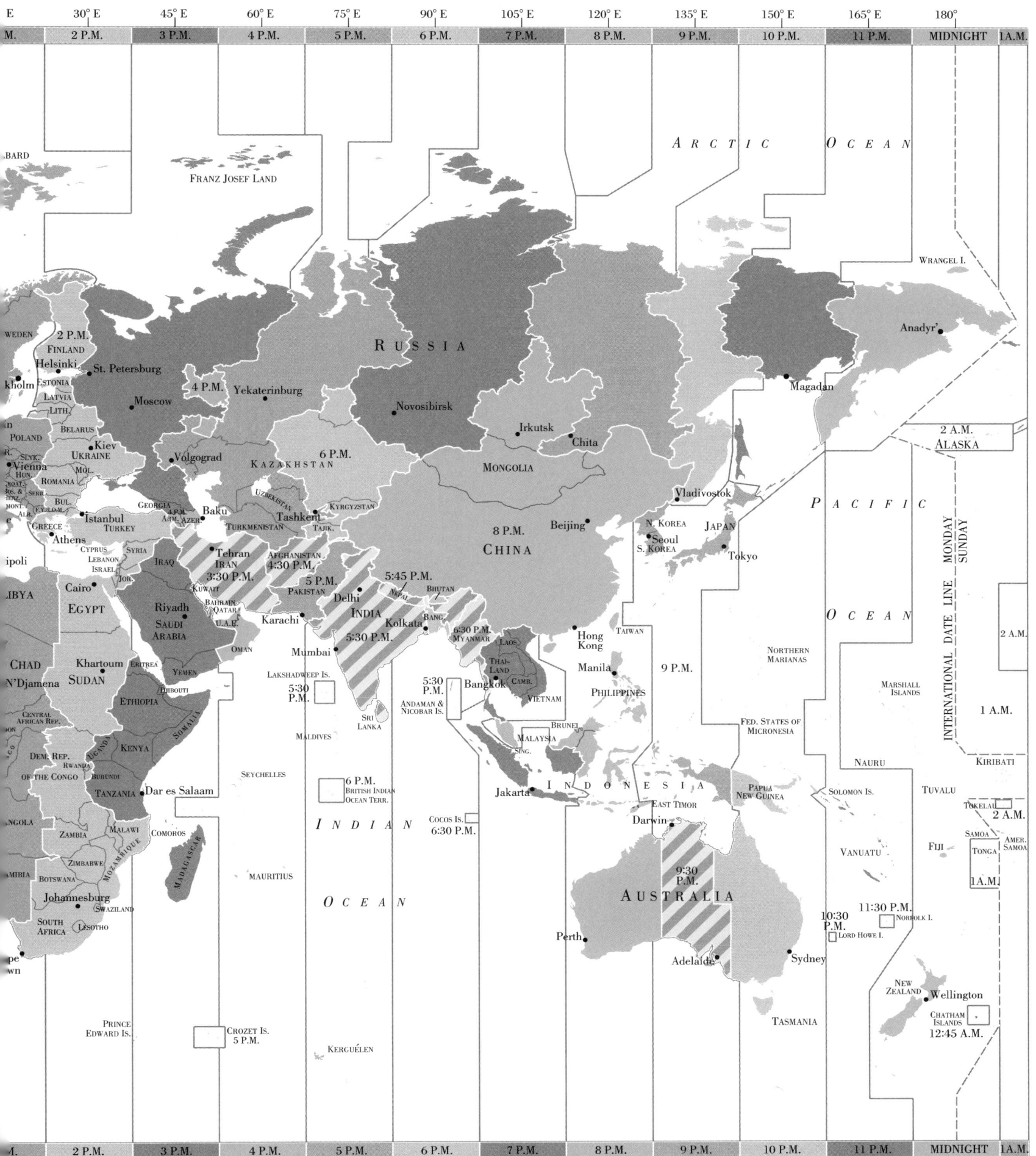

E	30° E	45° E	60° E	75° E	90° E	105° E	120° E	135° E	150° E	165° E	180°
M.	2 P.M.	3 P.M.	4 P.M.	5 P.M.	6 P.M.	7 P.M.	8 P.M.	9 P.M.	10 P.M.	11 P.M.	MIDNIGHT	1 A.M.

ARCTIC OCEAN

FRANZ JOSEF LAND

WRANGEL I.

Anadyr'

RUSSIA

2 A.M.
ALASKA

SWEDEN
2 P.M.
FINLAND
Helsinki
St. Petersburg

Magadan

ESTONIA
LATVIA
LITH.
kholm
4 P.M.
Yekaterinburg
Moscow

Novosibirsk

Irkutsk
Chita

POLAND
BELARUS
Kiev
UKRAINE

KAZAKHSTAN
6 P.M.

MONGOLIA

PACIFIC

SLVK.
Vienna
HUN.
MOL.
ROMANIA
Volgograd

Vladivostok

OCEAN

CROAT.
SERB.
BUL.
MONT.
F.Y.R.O.M.
Istanbul
GREECE
TURKEY
Athens

GEORGIA
ARM. AZER.
Baku
UZBEKISTAN
Tashkent
TURKMENISTAN
KYRGYZSTAN
TAJIK.

8 P.M.
CHINA
Beijing

N. KOREA
Seoul
S. KOREA

JAPAN
Tokyo

MONDAY
SUNDAY

ipoli
CYPRUS
LEBANON
SYRIA
ISRAEL
Tehran
IRAN
3:30 P.M.
IRAQ
JOR.
Afghanistan
4:30 P.M.
5 P.M.
PAKISTAN

5:45 P.M.
NEPAL
BHUTAN

INTERNATIONAL DATE LINE

2 A.M.

LIBYA
Cairo
EGYPT

Riyadh
SAUDI
ARABIA
KUWAIT
BAHRAIN
QATAR
U.A.E.

Karachi
Delhi
INDIA
5:30 P.M.
Kolkata
BANG.

6:30 P.M.
MYANMAR

Hong
Kong
TAIWAN

NORTHERN
MARIANAS

1 A.M.

CHAD
N'Djamena
Khartoum
SUDAN
ERITREA
YEMEN
DJIBOUTI
OMAN
Mumbai
LAKSHADWEEP IS.
5:30
P.M.

5:30
P.M.
Bangkok
THAI-
LAND
LAOS
CAMB.
VIETNAM

Manila

PHILIPPINES

MARSHALL
ISLANDS

CENTRAL
AFRICAN REP.
ETHIOPIA
SOMALIA
SRI
LANKA
MALDIVES
ANDAMAN &
NICOBAR IS.

FED. STATES OF
MICRONESIA

DEM. REP.
OF THE CONGO
RWANDA
BURUNDI
UGANDA
KENYA
SEYCHELLES

NAURU
KIRIBATI

TANZANIA
Dar es Salaam
6 P.M.
BRITISH INDIAN
OCEAN TERR.

MALAYSIA
SING.
BRUNEI

INDONESIA
Jakarta
EAST TIMOR

PAPUA
NEW GUINEA

SOLOMON IS.

TUVALU

TOKELAU
2 A.M.

ANGOLA
ZAMBIA
MALAWI
MOZAMBIQUE
COMOROS

INDIAN
Darwin

SAMOA
AMER.
SAMOA

AMIBIA
ZIMBABWE
BOTSWANA
MADAGASCAR
MAURITIUS

OCEAN
COCOS IS.
6:30 P.M.

9:30
P.M.
AUSTRALIA

VANUATU

FIJI

TONGA
1 A.M.

Johannesburg
SWAZILAND
SOUTH
AFRICA
LESOTHO

Perth

10:30
P.M.
Adelaide

NORFOLK I.
LORD HOWE I.

11:30 P.M.
Sydney

pe
wn

PRINCE
EDWARD IS.
CROZET IS.
5 P.M.

NEW
ZEALAND
Wellington
CHATHAM
ISLANDS
12:45 A.M.

KERGUÉLEN

TASMANIA

M.	2 P.M.	3 P.M.	4 P.M.	5 P.M.	6 P.M.	7 P.M.	8 P.M.	9 P.M.	10 P.M.	11 P.M.	MIDNIGHT	1 A.M.

Index of the World

This index is a comprehensive listing of the places and geographic features found in the atlas. Names are arranged in strict alphabetical order, without regard to hyphens or spaces. Every name is followed by the country or area to which it belongs. Except for cities, towns, countries and cultural areas, all entries include a reference to feature type, such as province, river, island, peak, and so on. The page number and alpha-numeric code appear in blue to the right of each listing. The page number directs you to the largest scale map on which the name can be found. The code refers to the grid squares formed by the horizontal and vertical lines of latitude and longitude on each map. Following the letters from left to right and the numbers from top to bottom helps you to quickly locate the square containing the place or feature. Inset maps have their own alpha-numeric codes. Names that are accompanied by a point symbol are indexed to the symbol's location on the map. Other names are indexed to the initial letter of the name. When a map name contains a subordinate or alternate name, both names are listed in the index. To conserve space and provide room for more entries, many abbreviations are used in this index. The primary abbreviations are listed below.

Index Abbreviations

A
Ab,Can	Alberta
Abor.	Aboriginal
Acad.	Academy
ACT	Australian Capital Territory
A.F.B.	Air Force Base
Afld.	Airfield
Afg.	Afghanistan
Afr.	Africa
Ak,US	Alaska
Al,US	Alabama
Alb.	Albania
Alg.	Algeria
Amm. Dep.	Ammunition Depot
And.	Andorra
Ang.	Angola
Angu.	Anguilla
Ant.	Antarctica
Anti.	Antigua and Barbuda
Ar,US	Arkansas
Arch.	Archipelago
Arg.	Argentina
Arm.	Armenia
Arpt.	Airport
Aru.	Aruba
ASam.	American Samoa
Ash.	Ashmore and Cartier Islands
Aus.	Austria
Austl.	Australia
Aut.	Autonomous
Az,US	Arizona
Azer.	Azerbaijan
Azor.	Azores

B
Bahm.	Bahamas, The
Bahr.	Bahrain
Bang.	Bangladesh
Bar.	Barbados
BC,Can	British Columbia
Bela.	Belarus
Belg.	Belgium
Belz.	Belize
Ben.	Benin
Berm.	Bermuda
Bfld.	Battlefield
Bhu.	Bhutan
Bol.	Bolivia
Bor.	Borough
Bosn.	Bosnia and Herzegovina
Bots.	Botswana
Braz.	Brazil
Brln.	British Indian Ocean Territory
Bru.	Brunei
Bul.	Bulgaria
Burk.	Burkina Faso
Buru.	Burundi
BVI	British Virgin Islands

C
Ca,US	California
CAfr.	Central African Republic
Camb.	Cambodia
Camr.	Cameroon
Can.	Canada
Can.	Canal
Canl.	Canary Islands
Cap.	Capital
Cap. Dist.	Capital District
Cap. Terr.	Capital Territory
Cay.	Cayman Islands
C.d'Iv.	Côte d'Ivoire
C.G.	Coast Guard
Chan.	Channel
Chl.	Channel Islands
Co.	County
Co,US	Colorado
Col.	Colombia
Com.	Comoros
Cont.	Continent
CpV.	Cape Verde Islands
CR	Costa Rica
Cr.	Creek
Cro.	Croatia
CSea.	Coral Sea Islands Territory
Ct,US	Connecticut
Ctr.	Center
Ctry.	Country
Cyp.	Cyprus
Czh.	Czech Republic

D
DC,US	District of Columbia
De,US	Delaware
Den.	Denmark
Depr.	Depression
Dept.	Department
Des.	Desert
DF	Distrito Federal
Dist.	District
Djib.	Djibouti
Dom.	Dominica
Dpcy.	Dependency
D.R.Congo	Democratic Republic of the Congo
DRep.	Dominican Republic

E
Ecu.	Ecuador
Emb.	Embankment
Eng.	Engineering
Eng,UK	England
EqG.	Equatorial Guinea
Erit.	Eritrea
ESal.	El Salvador
Est.	Estonia
Eth.	Ethiopia
ETim.	East Timor
Eur.	Europe

F
Falk.	Falkland Islands
Far.	Faroe Islands
Fed. Dist.	Federal District
Fin.	Finland
Fl,US	Florida
For.	Forest
Fr.	France
FrAnt.	French Southern and Antarctic Lands
FrG.	French Guiana
FrPol.	French Polynesia
FYROM	Former Yugoslav Rep. of Macedonia

G
Ga,US	Georgia
Galp.	Galapagos Islands
Gam.	Gambia, The
Gaza	Gaza Strip
GBis.	Guinea-Bissau
Geo.	Georgia
Ger.	Germany
Gha.	Ghana
Gib.	Gibraltar
Glac.	Glacier
Gov.	Governorate
Govt.	Government
Gre.	Greece
Grld.	Greenland
Gren.	Grenada
Grsld.	Grassland
Guad.	Guadeloupe
Guat.	Guatemala
Gui.	Guinea
Guy.	Guyana

H
Har.	Harbor
Hi,US	Hawaii
Hist.	Historic(al)
Hon.	Honduras
Hts.	Heights
Hun.	Hungary

I
Ia,US	Iowa
Ice.	Iceland
Id,US	Idaho
Il,US	Illinois
IM	Isle of Man
In,US	Indiana
Ind. Res.	Indian Reservation
Indo.	Indonesia
Int'l	International
Ire.	Ireland
Isl., Isls.	Island, Islands
Isr.	Israel
Isth.	Isthmus
It.	Italy

J
Jam.	Jamaica
Jor.	Jordan

K
Kaz.	Kazakhstan
Kiri.	Kiribati
Ks,US	Kansas
Kuw.	Kuwait
Ky,US	Kentucky
Kyr.	Kyrgyzstan

L
La,US	Louisiana
Lab.	Laboratory
Lag.	Lagoon
Lakesh.	Lakeshore
Lat.	Latvia
Lcht.	Liechtenstein
Ldg.	Landing
Leb.	Lebanon
Les.	Lesotho
Libr.	Liberia
Lith.	Lithuania
Lux.	Luxembourg

M
Ma,US	Massachusetts
Madg.	Madagascar
Madr.	Madeira
Malay.	Malaysia
Mald.	Maldives
Malw.	Malawi
Mart.	Martinique
May.	Mayotte
Mb,Can	Manitoba
Md,US	Maryland
Me,US	Maine
Mem.	Memorial
Mex.	Mexico
Mi,US	Michigan
Micr.	Micronesia, Federated States of
Mil.	Military
Mn,US	Minnesota
Mo,US	Missouri
Mol.	Moldova
Mon.	Monument
Mona.	Monaco
Mong.	Mongolia
Mont.	Montenegro
Monts.	Montserrat
Mor.	Morocco
Moz.	Mozambique
Mrsh.	Marshall Islands
Mrta.	Mauritania
Mrts.	Mauritius
Ms,US	Mississippi
Mt.	Mount
Mt,US	Montana
Mtn., Mts.	Mountain, Mountains
Mun. Arpt.	Municipal Airport
Myan.	Myanmar

N
NAm.	North America
Namb.	Namibia
NAnt.	Netherlands Antilles
Nat'l	National
Nav.	Naval
NB,Can	New Brunswick
Nbrhd.	Neighborhood
NC,US	North Carolina
NCal.	New Caledonia
ND,US	North Dakota
Ne,US	Nebraska
Neth.	Netherlands
Nf,Can	Newfoundland
Nga.	Nigeria
NH,US	New Hampshire
NI,UK	Northern Ireland
Nic.	Nicaragua
NJ,US	New Jersey
NKor.	North Korea
NM,US	New Mexico
NMar.	Northern Mariana Islands
Nor.	Norway
NS,Can	Nova Scotia
Nv,US	Nevada
Nun.,Can	Nunavut
NW,Can	Northwest Territories
NY,US	New York
NZ	New Zealand

O
Obl.	Oblast
Oh,US	Ohio
Ok,US	Oklahoma
On,Can	Ontario
Or,US	Oregon

P
Pa,US	Pennsylvania
PacUS	Pacific Islands, U.S.
Pak.	Pakistan
Pan.	Panama
Par.	Paraguay
Par.	Parish
PE,Can	Prince Edward Island
Pen.	Peninsula
Phil.	Philippines
Phys. Reg.	Physical Region
Pitc.	Pitcairn Islands
Plat.	Plateau
PNG	Papua New Guinea
Pol.	Poland
Port.	Portugal
Poss.	Possession
Pkwy.	Parkway
PR	Puerto Rico
Pref.	Prefecture
Prov.	Province
Prsv.	Preserve
Pt.	Point

Q
Qu,Can	Quebec

R
Rec.	Recreation(al)
Ref.	Refuge
Reg.	Region
Rep.	Republic
Res.	Reservoir, Reservation
Reun.	Réunion
RI,US	Rhode Island
Riv.	River
Rom.	Romania
Rsv.	Reserve
Rus.	Russia
Rvwy.	Riverway
Rwa.	Rwanda

S
SAfr.	South Africa
Sam.	Samoa
SAm.	South America
SaoT.	São Tomé and Príncipe
SAr.	Saudi Arabia
Sc,UK	Scotland
SC,US	South Carolina
SD,US	South Dakota
Seash.	Seashore
Sen.	Senegal
Serb.	Serbia
Sey.	Seychelles
SGeo.	South Georgia and Sandwich Islands
Sing.	Singapore
Sk,Can	Saskatchewan
SKor.	South Korea
SLeo.	Sierra Leone
Slov.	Slovenia
Slvk.	Slovakia
SMar.	San Marino
Sol.	Solomon Islands
Som.	Somalia
Sp.	Spain
Spr., Sprs.	Spring, Springs
SrL.	Sri Lanka
Sta.	Station
StH.	Saint Helena
Str.	Strait
StK.	Saint Kitts and Nevis
StL.	Saint Lucia
StP.	Saint Pierre and Miquelon
StV.	Saint Vincent and the Grenadines
Sur.	Suriname
Sval.	Svalbard
Swaz.	Swaziland
Swe.	Sweden
Swi.	Switzerland

T
Tah.	Tahiti
Tai.	Taiwan
Taj.	Tajikistan
Tanz.	Tanzania
Ter.	Terrace
Terr.	Territory
Thai.	Thailand
Tn,US	Tennessee
Tok.	Tokelau
Trg.	Training
Trin.	Trinidad and Tobago
Trkm.	Turkmenistan
Trks.	Turks and Caicos Islands
Tun.	Tunisia
Tun.	Tunnel
Turk.	Turkey
Tuv.	Tuvalu
Twp.	Township
Tx,US	Texas

U
UAE	United Arab Emirates
Ugan.	Uganda
UK	United Kingdom
Ukr.	Ukraine
Uru.	Uruguay
US	United States
USVI	U.S. Virgin Islands
Ut,US	Utah
Uzb.	Uzbekistan

V
Va,US	Virginia
Val.	Valley
Van.	Vanuatu
VatC.	Vatican City
Ven.	Venezuela
Viet.	Vietnam
Vill.	Village
Vol.	Volcano
Vt,US	Vermont

W
Wa,US	Washington
Wal,UK	Wales
Wall.	Wallis and Futuna
WBnk.	West Bank
Wi,US	Wisconsin
Wild.	Wildlife, Wilderness
WSah.	Western Sahara
WV,US	West Virginia
Wy,US	Wyoming

Y
Yem.	Yemen
Yk,Can	Yukon Territory

Z
Zam.	Zambia
Zim.	Zimbabwe

215
A – Al Khā

A

100 Mile House, BC, Can. 168/C3
Aa (riv.), Ger. 92/D5
Aach (riv.), Ger. 99/F2
Aach, Ger. 99/E2
Aachen, Ger. 95/F2
Aalbach (riv.), Ger. 96/C3
Aalborg (int'l arpt.), Den. 80/C3
Aalburg, Neth. 92/C5
Aalen, Ger. 96/D5
Aalsmeer, Neth. 92/B4
Aalst, Belg. 94/D2
Aalten, Neth. 92/D5
Aalter, Belg. 94/C1
Aar (riv.), Ger. 95/H3
Aarau, Swi. 98/E3
Aarberg, Swi. 98/D3
Aarburg, Swi. 98/D3
Aardenburg, Neth. 94/C1
Aare (riv.), Swi. 85/H3
Aargau (canton), Swi. 99/E3
Aarred (lake), WSah. 140/B4
Aarschot, Belg. 95/D2
Aartselaar, Belg. 95/D1
Aarwangen, Swi. 98/D3
Aba, China 112/H5
Aba, D.R. Congo 146/A2
Aba, Nga. 145/G5
Abā as Su'ūd, SAr. 130/D5
Abacaxis (riv.), Braz. 192/G5
Abadab (peak), Sudan 143/C5
Ābādān, Iran 130/E2
Ābādeh, Iran 130/F2
Abadia dos Dourados, Braz. 197/C1
Abadla, Alg. 141/E3
Abádszalók, Hun. 90/E2
Abaeté, Braz. 197/C1
Abaetetuba, Braz. 193/J4
Abaiang (isl.), Kiri. 158/G4
Abakan, Rus. 106/K4
Abancay, Peru 198/C4
Abano Terme, It. 101/E2
Abar Kūh, Iran 130/F2
Abarán, Sp. 86/E3
Abashiri (lake), Japan 118/C2
Abashiri, Japan 118/D1
Abasolo, Mex. 185/E4
Abasolo, Mex. 185/F3
Abay, Kaz. 129/F3
Ābaya Hayk (lake), Eth. 139/N6
Abbadia Lariana, It. 99/F6
Abbadia San Salvatore, It. 85/J5
Abbeville, La, US 171/J5
Abbeville, SC, US 175/H3
Abbeville, Fr. 94/A3
Abbey (peak), Austl. 156/B1
Abbeyfeale, Ire. 73/P10
Abbeyleix, Ire. 73/Q10
Abbiategrasso, It. 100/B2
Abbot (mt.), Austl. 156/B3
Abbotsinch (int'l arpt.), Sc, UK 78/B5
Abbottābād, Pak. 128/B2
Abbottstown, Pa, US 180/B4
Abcoude, Neth. 92/B4
Abdul Hakīm, Pak. 128/B4
Abdulino, Rus. 105/K1
Abéché, Chad 139/K5
Abemama (isl.), Kiri. 158/G4
Abenberg, Ger. 96/D4
Abengourou, C.d'Iv. 144/E5
Åbenrå, Den. 80/C4
Abens (riv.), Ger. 82/F4
Abensberg, Ger. 97/E5
Abeokuta, Nga. 145/F5
Abercarn, Wal, UK 74/C3
Aberchirder, Sc, UK 78/D1
Aberdare, Wal, UK 74/C3
Aberdare NP, Kenya 146/C3
Aberdeen, Austl. 157/D2
Aberdeen (lake), Nun., Can. 164/F2
Aberdeen, SAfr. 148/D4
Aberdeen, Sc, UK 78/D2
Aberdeen (pol. reg.), Sc, UK 78/D2
Aberdeen, SD, US 169/J4
Aberdeen, Ms, US 175/F3
Aberdeen, Md, US 180/B5
Aberdeen, Wa, US 168/C4
Aberdeen Proving Ground, Md, US 180/B5
Aberdeenshire, Sc, UK 78/D2
Aberdeenshire (pol. reg.), Sc, UK 78/D2
Aberdour, Sc, UK 78/C4
Aberdour (bay), Sc, UK 78/D1
Aberfeldy, Sc, UK 78/C3
Aberfoyle, Sc, UK 78/B4
Abergavenny, Wal, UK 74/C3
Abergele, Wal, UK 76/E5
Aberlour, Sc, UK 78/C2
Abernethy, Sc, UK 78/C4
Abert (lake), Or, US 168/C5
Abertillery, Wal, UK 74/C3
Aberystwyth, Wal, UK 74/B2
Abhá, SAr. 130/D5
Abhar, Iran 130/E1
Abhayāpuri, India 127/H2
Abḫe Bad (lake), Djib.,Eth. 139/P5
Abia (prov.), Nga. 145/G5
Abidjan, C.d'Iv. 144/D5
Abiko, Japan 119/E2
Abilene, Tx, US 171/H4
Abilene, Ks, US 171/H3
Abingdon, Eng, UK 75/E3
Abingdon, Md, US 180/B5
Abington (reef), Austl. 156/C2
Abington, Sc, UK 78/C6
Abino (pt.), On, Can. 173/R10
Abiquiu, NM, US 174/B2
Abitibi (lake), On,Qu, Can. 165/H4
Abitibi (riv.), On, Can. 165/H4
Abkhazia Aut. Rep., Geo. 105/G4
Ableiges, Fr. 72/H4
Abnūb, Egypt 143/B3
Åbo (Turku), Fin. 81/K1
Abohar, India 128/C4
Aboisso, C.d'Iv. 144/E5
Abomey, Ben. 145/F5
Abondance, Fr. 98/C5
Abony, Hun. 90/D2
Aboyne, Sc, UK 78/D2
Abra (riv.), Phil. 121/D4
Abra Pampa, Arg. 199/C1
Abraham Gonzalez (int'l arpt.), Mex. 184/D2
Abrantes, Port. 86/A3
Abreojos (pt.), Mex. 184/B3
Abrud, Rom. 91/F2
Abruzzi (prov.), It. 85/K5
Abruzzo, PN de, It. 88/C2
Absam, Aus. 99/H3
Absaroka (range), Mt,Wy, US 168/F4
Absecon, NJ, US 180/D5
Abtsgmünd, Ger. 96/D5
Abu Dhabi (Abū Ẓaby) (cap.), UAE 131/F4
Abu el-Husein (well), Egypt 143/B4
Abū Ḩammād, Egypt 133/B4
Abu Hashim (well), Egypt 143/C4
Abū Ḩummuş, Egypt 133/B4
Abū Kabīr, Egypt 133/B4
Abū Kamāl, Syria 132/E3
Abū Qashsh, WBnk. 133/G8
Abu Shagara (cape), Sudan 143/D4
Abu Simbel (ruin), Egypt 143/B4
Abuja (cap.), Nga. 145/G4
Abuja (int'l arpt.), Nga. 145/G4
Abuja Capital Territory, Nga. 145/G4
Abukuma (riv.), Japan 117/G2
Abukuma (plat.), Japan 117/G2
Abulog, Phil. 121/D4
Abunã (riv.), Braz. 192/E6
Abuta, Japan 118/B2
Ābuyē Mēda (peak), Eth. 139/N5
Abuyog, Phil. 121/E5
Åby, Swe. 80/G2
Åbybro, Den. 80/C3
Abydos (ruin), Egypt 143/B3
Acacías, Col. 194/C4
Acacoyagua, Mex. 186/C3
Acadia NP, Me, US 173/G2
Acadian Village, La, US 171/J5
Acajutiba, Braz. 196/C3
Acámbaro, Mex. 185/E4
Acampo, Ca, US 177/M10
Acandí, Col. 194/B2
Acaponeta (riv.), Mex. 184/D4
Acaponeta, Mex. 184/D4
Acapulco de Juárez, Mex. 182/B4
Acaraí (mts.), Braz.,Guy. 195/G4
Acarai, Serra (mts.), Braz. 192/G3
Acaraú (riv.), Braz. 196/B1
Acaraú, Braz. 196/B1
Acari, Braz. 196/C2
Acari (riv.), Braz. 192/G5
Acari, Peru 198/C4
Acarigua, Ven. 194/D2
Acatlán de Osorio, Mex. 186/B2
Acatlán de Pérez Figueroa, Mex. 185/N8
Acatzingo, Mex. 185/M7
Acayucan, Mex. 186/C2
Accha, Peru 198/D4
Acciaroli, It. 88/D2
Accra (cap.), Gha. 145/E5
Accrington, Eng, UK 77/F4
Aceuchal, Sp. 86/B3
Ach (riv.), Aus. 97/G6
Achacachi, Bol. 192/E7
Achaguas, Ven. 194/D3
Achao, Chile 200/B4
Achar, Uru. 201/K10
Achegour (well), Niger 138/H4
Achen (pass), Ger. 99/H2
Acheng, China 113/N2
Achères, Fr. 72/J5
Achhnera, India 126/A2
Achicourt, Fr. 94/B3
Achill (isl.), Ire. 72/N10
Achill Head (pt.), Ire. 72/N9
Achiltibuie, Sc, UK 73/R7
Achinsk, Rus. 106/K4
Achmîm (well), Mrta. 144/D2
Achnasheen, Sc, UK 78/A1
Achoma, Peru 198/D4
A'chràlaig (peak), Sc, UK 78/A2
Achuapa, Nic. 186/E3
Achupallas, Ecu. 198/B1
Acireale, It. 88/D4
Acklins (isl.), Bahm. 183/G3
Acland (mt.), Austl. 156/C4
Acobamba, Peru 198/C4
Acolla, Peru 198/C3
Acolman, Mex. 185/R9
Acomayo, Peru 198/D4
Acomayo, Peru 198/B3
Aconcagua (peak), Arg. 200/C2
Aconchi, Mex. 184/C2
Acopiara, Braz. 196/C2
Acora, Peru 198/D4
Acqualagna, It. 101/F5
Acquanegra sul Chiese, It. 100/D2
Acquapendente, It. 88/B1
Acqui Terme, It. 100/B3
Acraman (lake), Austl. 155/C5
Acrata (pt.), Alg. 142/G4
Acre (riv.), Braz. 192/E6
Acre (state), Braz. 198/D3
Acreúna, Braz. 197/B1
Acropolis, Gre. 89/N9
Actaeon Group (isls.), FrPol. 159/M7
Acton, Ca, US 178/B2
Actopan, Mex. 185/N7
Actopan, Mex. 185/L6
Açu, Braz. 196/C2
Açude Aratas (res.), Braz. 196/B2
Açude Banabuiu (res.), Braz. 196/C2
Acula, Mex. 185/P8
Aculeo (lag.), Chile 200/N8
Acy-en-Multien, Fr. 72/L4
Ad Dahnā' (des.), SAr. 130/D3
Ad-Dakhla, WSah. 140/B5
Ad Damazin, Sudan 139/M5
Ad Dāmir, Sudan 130/B5
Ad Dammām, SAr. 130/F3
Ad Daqahliyah (gov.), Egypt 143/B1
Ad Dilinjāt, Egypt 133/B4
Ad Dīwānīyah, Iraq 132/F4
Ad Dujayl, Iraq 132/F3
Ad Duwaym, Sudan 139/M5
Ada, Gha. 145/F5
Ada, Serb. 90/E3
Ada, Oh, US 172/D3
Ada, Ok, US 171/H4
Adainville, Fr. 72/G5
Adair (cape), Nun., Can. 165/J1
Adair, Bahia del (bay), Mex. 128/D5
Adaja (riv.), Sp. 86/C2
Adak (isl.), Ak, US 176/C6
Adak (str.), Ak, US 176/C6
Adam (mt.), Falk., UK 201/E6
Adamantina, Braz. 197/B2
Adamaoua (plat.), Camr.,Nga. 135/D4
Adamello (peak), It. 99/G5
Adaminaby, Austl. 157/D3
Adams (lake), BC, Can. 168/D3
Adams (co.), Co, US 179/C3
Adams (co.), Pa, US 180/A4
Adams (mt.), Wa, US 168/C4
Adamstown (cap.), Pitc. 159/M7
Adamstown, Pa, US 180/B3
Adamwa (plat.), Nga. 145/H5
'Adan, Yem. 130/D6
Adana, Turk. 133/D1
Adana (prov.), Turk. 132/C2
Adana (int'l arpt.), Turk. 133/D1
Adapazarı, Turk. 91/K5
Adare, Ire. 73/P10
Adare (cape), Ant. 202/M
Adarza (peak), Fr. 86/E1
Add (riv.), Sc, UK 78/A4
Adda (riv.), It. 85/H4
Addis Ababa (Ādīs Ābeba) (cap.), Eth. 139/N6
Addison, Il, US 177/P16
Addlestone, Eng, UK 72/B2
Addo Elephant NP, SAfr. 148/D4
Adekeieh (Ādī K'eyih), Erit. 130/C6
Adelaide, SAfr. 148/D4
Adelaide (pen.), Nun., Can. 164/G2
Adelaide (int'l arpt.), Austl. 155/M8
Adelaide, Austl. 155/M8
Adelaide Zoo, Austl. 155/M8
Adelanto, Ca, US 178/C1
Adelebsen, Ger. 93/G5
Adelheidsdorf, Ger. 93/H3
Adelmannsfelden, Ger. 96/D5
Adelong, Austl. 157/D2
Adelschlag, Ger. 96/E5
Adelsheim, Ger. 96/C4
Adelsried, Ger. 96/D6
Aden (gulf), Afr.,Asia 109/D8
Adenau, Ger. 95/F3
Adendorf, Ger. 93/H2
Adh Dhirā', Jor. 133/D4
Adi (isl.), Indo. 123/H4
Ādī Ugrī, Erit. 130/C6
Adieu (cape), Austl. 155/C5
Adige (riv.), It. 85/J4
Adige (Etsch) (riv.), It. 99/G4
Ādīgrat, Eth. 130/C6
Adilābād, India 124/C4
Adilcevaz, Turk. 132/E2
Adiora (well), Mali 145/E2
Adirondack (mts.), NY, US 167/L3
Ādīs Ābeba (Addis Ababa) (cap.), Eth. 139/N6
Adıyaman, Turk. 132/D2
Adıyaman (prov.), Turk. 132/D2
Adjud, Rom. 91/H2
Adjuntas, Presa de la (res.), Mex. 185/F4
Adler/Sochi (int'l arpt.), Rus. 104/F4
Adliswil, Swi. 99/E3
Admiralty (inlet), Nun., Can. 165/H1
Admiralty (isl.), Ak, US 164/C3
Admiralty Island Nat'l Mon., Ak, US 176/M4
Admiralty (isls.), PNG 158/D5
Admiralty (inlet), Wa, US 177/B2
Adnan Menderes (int'l arpt.), Turk. 132/A2
Ado (riv.), Japan 119/J5
Ado Ekiti, Nga. 145/G5
Ado Odo, Nga. 145/F5
Adogawa, Japan 119/K5
Adolfo López Mateos, Mex. 184/B3
Ādoni, India 124/C4
Adour (riv.), Fr. 84/C5
Adra, India 127/F4
Adra, Sp. 86/D4
Adrano, It. 88/D4
Adrar (phys. reg.), Mrta. 138/C3
Adrar, Alg. 141/E4
Adrar (pol. reg.), Mrta. 144/C1
Adrar (prov.), Alg. 141/E4
Adrar (reg.), Mrta. 140/C5
Adrar bou Nasser (peak), Mor. 140/E2
Adrar Sotuf (mts.), WSah. 140/B5
Adria, It. 101/F2
Adrian, Mi, US 172/C3
Adriatic (sea), Eur. 69/F4
Adro, It. 100/C1
Adulis (ruin), Erit. 130/C5
Adur (riv.), Eng, UK 75/F5
Ādwa, Eth. 130/C6
Adwick le Street, Eng, UK 77/G4
Adycha (riv.), Rus. 107/P3
Adygeya, Resp., Rus. 104/F3
Adz'va (riv.), Rus. 103/P2
Aegean (sea), Gre.,Turk. 89/J3
Aerø (isl.), Den. 80/D4
Aeron (riv.), Wal, UK 74/B2
Aesch, Swi. 98/D3
Aeschi bei Spiez, Swi. 98/D4
Äetsä, Fin. 81/K1
Afadjoto (peak), Gha. 145/F5
'Afak, Iraq 130/E2
Afándou, Gre. 132/B2
Aff (riv.), Fr. 84/B3
Affoltern im Emmental, Swi. 98/D3
Affric (lake), Sc, UK 78/A2
Affton, Mo, US 179/G8
Afghanistan (ctry.) 131/H2
Afmadow, Som. 139/P7
Afogados da Ingàzeira, Braz. 196/C2
Afognak (mtn.), Ak, US 176/H4
Afognak (isl.), Ak, US 176/H4
Afollé, Massif de (phys. reg.), Mrta. 144/C2
Afonso Bezerra, Braz. 196/C2
Afonso Cláudio, Braz. 197/D2
Afragola, It. 88/D2
Afrânio, Braz. 196/B3
Africa (cont.) 93
Afrin (riv.), Turk. 133/E1
'Afrīn, Syria 133/E1
Afrique (peak), Fr. 98/A3
Afsluitdijk (dam), Neth. 92/C2
Afte (riv.), Ger. 93/F5
Afton, Wy, US 168/F5
Afuidich (lake), WSah. 140/B5
'Afula, Isr. 133/G6
Afyon, Turk. 132/B2
Afyon (prov.), Turk. 132/B2
Afzalgarh, India 126/B1
Agades (int'l arpt.), Niger 145/G2
Agadez, Niger 145/G2
Agadez (dept.), Niger 141/H5
Agadir, Mor. 140/C3
Agago (riv.), Ugan. 146/B2
Agamor (well), Mali 145/F2
Agano (riv.), Japan 117/F2
Agassiz Ice Cap (ice field), Nun., Can. 165/T6
Agattu (isl.), Ak, US 176/A5
Agattu (str.), Ak, US 176/A5
Agbabu, Nga. 145/G5
Agboville, C.d'Iv. 144/D5
Ağdam, Azer. 105/H5
Agde, Fr. 84/E5
Agen, Fr. 84/D4
Ageo, Japan 119/D2
Ager (riv.), Aus. 97/G7
Ageræk, Den. 80/C4
Agerisee (lake), Swi. 99/E3
Agger (riv.), Ger. 95/G1
Aggteleki NP, Slvk. 90/E1
Āghā Jārī, Iran 130/E2
Aghagallon, NI, UK 76/B3
Aghagower, Ire. 73/P10
Agiabampo, Mex. 184/C3
Ağinskiy Buryatskiy Aut. Okrug, Rus. 107/Q7
Aginskoye, Rus. 113/K1
Agliana, It. 101/D5
Ağlıköy, Turk. 132/C1
Agly (riv.), Fr. 84/E5
Agna, It. 101/E2
Agnanderón, Gre. 89/G3
Agnita, Rom. 91/G3
Agno (riv.), It. 101/E1
Agno (int'l arpt.), Swi. 99/E6
Agnone, It. 88/D2
Ago, Japan 119/L7
Agogna (riv.), It. 85/H4
Agordo, It. 85/K3
Agout (riv.), Fr. 84/D5
Āgra, India 126/B2
Agraciada, Uru. 201/J10
Agrado, Col. 194/C4
Ágreda, Sp. 86/E2
Ağrı (prov.), Turk. 132/E2
Agriá, Gre. 89/H3
Agrigento, It. 88/C4
Agrihan (isl.), NMar. 158/D3
Agrínion, Gre. 89/G3
Agrio (riv.), Arg. 200/C3
Agropoli, It. 88/D2
Agryz, Rus. 103/M4
Agsumal (dry lake), WSah. 140/B4
Água Boa, Braz. 196/B5
Água Branca, Braz. 196/B2
Agua Dulce, Ca, US 178/B2
Agua Dulce, Mex. 186/C2
Agua Fria (riv.), Az, US 179/R19
Agua Fria NM, Az, US 170/E4
Agua Hedionda (lake), Ca, US 178/C4
Agua Larga, Ven. 194/D2
Agua Prieta, Mex. 184/C2
Aguachica, Col. 194/C2
Aguadilla, PR 183/M8
Aguadulce, Pan. 194/A2
Aguai, Braz. 197/G7
Agualva-Cacém, Port. 87/P10
Aguan (riv.), Hon. 182/D4
Aguanus (riv.), Qu, Can. 173/J1
Aguapeí (riv.), Braz. 197/B2
Aguarico (riv.), Peru 194/B5
Águas Belas, Braz. 196/C3
Águas Corrientes, Uru. 201/K11
Águas da Prata, Braz. 197/G6
Águas de Lindóia, Braz. 197/G7
Águas Formosas, Braz. 196/B5
Águas, Serra das (hills), Braz. 197/H7
Aguasay, Ven. 195/F2
Aguascalientes, Mex. 184/E4
Aguascalientes (state), Mex. 182/A3
Águavermelha, Represa (res.), Braz. 197/B1
Aguaytía (riv.), Peru 198/C3
Agudos, Braz. 197/B2
Agueda (riv.), Sp. 86/B2
Águeda, Port. 86/A2
Aguêraktem (well), Mali 140/D5
Agugliano, It. 101/G5
Agui, Japan 119/L6
Aguijan (isl.), NMar. 158/D3
Aguilar, Sp. 86/C4
Aguilar de Campóo, Sp. 86/C1
Aguilares, Arg. 199/C2
Aguilas, Sp. 86/E4
Aguililla, Mex. 184/E5
Aguja (pt.), Peru 198/A2
Agulhas (cape), SAfr. 148/M11
Agulhas Negras, Pico das (peak), Braz. 197/J7
Agung (vol.), Indo. 123/E5
Agusan (riv.), Phil. 121/E6
Agustín Codazzi, Col. 194/C2
Ahaggar (plat.), Arg. 138/F3
Ahaggar (mts.), Alg. 141/G5
Ahal (pol. reg.), Trkm. 129/C5
Aham, Ger. 97/F5
Ahar, Iran 105/H5
Ahaus, Ger. 92/E4
Ahfir, Mor. 142/C2
Ahırlı, Turk. 132/C2
Ahlat, Turk. 132/E2
Ahlen, Ger. 93/E5
Ahlerstedt, Ger. 93/G2
Ahmadābād, India 131/K4
Ahmadpur East, Pak. 128/A5
Ahmadpur Siāl, Pak. 128/A4
Ahmar (mts.), Eth. 139/P6
Ahmar, 'Erg el (des.), Mali 140/D4
Ahmed (well), WSah. 140/B5
Ahmeyine (well), Mrta. 140/B5
Ahoghill, NI, UK 76/B2
Ahome, Mex. 184/C3
Ahr (riv.), Ger. 85/G1
Ahraurā, India 126/D3
Ahrensburg, Ger. 93/H1
Ahse (riv.), Ger. 93/F5
Ahuacatitlán, Mex. 185/K8
Ahuacatlán, Mex. 184/D4
Ahuachapán, ESal. 186/D3
Ahualulco, Mex. 185/E4
Ahuimanu, Hi, US 166/W13
Ahumada, Mex. 184/D2
Ahun, Fr. 84/E3
Åhus, Swe. 80/F4
Ahvāz, Iran 130/E2
Ahvenanmaa (isl.), Fin. 79/F4
Ai (riv.), China 115/C2
Ai (mtn.), China 114/E3
Ai-Ais Hot Springs, Namb. 148/B2
Ai-shima (isl.), Japan 116/B3
Aibag Gol (riv.), China 114/B2
Aichach, Ger. 96/E6
Aichi (pref.), Japan 117/E3
Aidhausen, Ger. 96/D2
Aidlingen, Ger. 96/B5
Aiea, Hi, US 166/W13
Aiello del Friuli, It. 101/G1
Aiffres, Fr. 84/C3
Aigen im Mühlkreis, Aus. 97/G5
Aigle, Pic de l' (peak), Fr. 98/B4
Aiglemont, Fr. 95/D4
Aigoual (peak), Fr. 84/E4
Aiguá, Uru. 201/G2
Aigues (riv.), Fr. 84/F4
Aigües Tortes y Lago de San Mauricio, PN de, Sp. 87/F1
Aiguille, Cap de l' (cape), Alg. 142/E5
Aiguillon, Fr. 84/D4
Aikawa, Japan 117/F1
Aikawa, Japan 119/C2
Aiken, SC, US 175/H3
Ailigandí, Pan. 194/B2
Ailinglapalap (isl.), Mrsh. 158/F4
Aillevillers-et-Lyaumont, Fr. 98/C2
Ailly-sur-Noye, Fr. 94/B4
Ailsa Craig (isl.), Sc, UK 78/A6
Ailuk (isl.), Mrsh. 158/G3
Aimen (pass), China 114/C5
Aimogasta, Arg. 199/C2
Aimorés, Braz. 197/D1
Aimorés, Serra dos (mts.), Braz. 197/D1
Ain (riv.), Fr. 84/F4
'Aïn Beïda, Alg. 142/K7
'Aïn Beniau, Alg. 142/G4
'Aïn Bessem, Alg. 142/G4
Aïn Chok-Hay Mohammadia (prov.), Mor. 142/A2
'Aïn Defla, Alg. 142/F4
'Aïn Defla (prov.), Alg. 142/F4
Aïn el Aouda, Mor. 142/A3
'Aïn el Bey (int'l arpt.), Alg. 142/K6
'Aïn el Hammam, Alg. 142/H4
'Aïn el Turk, Alg. 142/D2
'Aïn Fakroun, Alg. 142/K6
'Aïn M'lila, Alg. 142/K6
'Aïn Oulmene, Alg. 142/H5
'Aïn Oussersa, Alg. 142/G5
'Aïn Sefra, Alg. 141/E2
Aïn Taoujdat, Mor. 142/B3
'Aïn Taya, Alg. 142/G4
'Aïn Temouchent, Alg. 142/D2
'Aïn Touta, Alg. 142/H5
Aina Haina, Hi, US 166/W13
Aincourt, Fr. 72/H4
Aínos (peak), Gre. 89/G3
Aínos NP, Gre. 89/G3
Aipe, Col. 194/C4
Aïr (plat.), Niger 138/G4
Air Force (isl.), Nun., Can. 165/J2
Airaines, Fr. 94/A4
Airdrie, Ab, Can. 168/E3
Airdrie, Sc, UK 78/C5
Aire (riv.), Fr. 84/F2
Aire, Canal d' (canal), Fr. 94/B2
Aire-sur-la-Lys, Fr. 94/B2
Aire-sur-l'Adour, Fr. 84/C5
Airolo, Swi. 99/E4
Airuno, It. 100/C1
Airvault, Fr. 84/C3
Aisch (riv.), Ger. 85/J2
Aiseau-Presles, Belg. 95/D3
Aisén del General Carlos Ibáñez del Campo (pol. reg.), Chile 200/B5
Aisne (riv.), Fr. 82/B4
Aïssa (peak), Alg. 141/E2
Aist (riv.), Aus. 97/H6
Aït Ourir, Mor. 140/D3
Aitape, PNG 158/D5
Aitō, Japan 119/K5
Aitolikón, Gre. 89/G3
Aitrach, Ger. 99/G2
Aitrang, Ger. 99/G2
Aitutaki Atoll (isl.), Cookls. 159/J6
Aiud, Rom. 91/F2
Aiuruoca, Braz. 197/J6
Aiuruoca (riv.), Braz. 197/J7
Aix-en-Provence, Fr. 84/F5
Aiyina, Gre. 89/H4
Aiyínion, Gre. 89/H2
Aiyion, Gre. 89/H3
Aīzawl, India 125/F3
Aizu-Wakamatsu, Japan 117/F2
Ajaccio, Fr. 88/A2
Ajaccio, Golfe d' (gulf), Fr. 88/A2
Ajaigarh, India 126/C3
Ajalpan, Mex. 185/M8
Ajaria Aut. Rep., Geo. 105/G4
Ajax, On, Can. 173/R8
Ajay (riv.), India 127/F3
Ajdābiyā, Libya 139/K1
Ajdovščina, Slov. 85/K4
Ajigasawa, Japan 118/B3
'Ajjah, WBnk. 133/G7
Ajka, Hun. 90/C2
Ajo, Az, US 170/D4
Ajo (cape), Sp. 86/D1
Ajuchitlán del Progreso, Mex. 182/A4
Ajusco (vol.), Mex. 185/Q10
Aka (riv.), Japan 117/F1
Akabane, Japan 119/M6
Akabira, Japan 118/C2
Akaishi-dake (peak), Japan 117/F3
Akaltara, India 126/D4
Akan (lake), Japan 118/D2
Akan NP, Japan 118/D2
Åkarp, Swe. 80/E4
Akarsu, Turk. 132/D2
Akashi, Japan 119/G6
Akashi (str.), Japan 119/G6
Akbarpur, India 126/D2
Akbarpur, India 126/B2
Akbaytal (pass), Taj. 129/F5
Akbou, Alg. 142/H4
Akçaabat, Turk. 132/D1
Akçakale, Turk. 132/D2
Akçakoca, Turk. 91/K5
Akçaova, Turk. 91/J5
Akçapınar, Turk. 132/D2
Akçay, Turk. 133/A1
Akchâr (riv.), Mrta. 138/B4
Akchâr (phys. reg.), Mrta. 140/B5
Akdağmadeni, Turk. 104/E5
Akechi, Japan 119/M5
Akeno, Japan 119/E1
Akeno, Japan 119/A2
Åkersberga, Swe. 80/H2
Akershus (co.), Nor. 79/D3
Aketi, D.R. Congo 139/K7
Akhalts'ikhe, Geo. 105/G4
Akharnaí, Gre. 89/N8
Akhelóos (riv.), Gre. 89/G3
Akhiok, Ak, US 176/H4
Akhisar, Turk. 132/A2
Akhnūr, India 128/C3
Akhtopol, Bul. 91/H4
Akhtuba (riv.), Rus. 105/H3
Akhtubinsk, Rus. 105/H2
Aki, Japan 116/C4
Aki (riv.), Japan 119/C2
Akiachak, Ak, US 176/F3
Akigawa, Japan 119/C2
Akimiski (isl.), On, Can. 165/H3
Akıncı (pt.), Turk. 133/D1
Akıncılar, Turk. 132/D1
Åkirkeby, Den. 80/F4
Akishima, Japan 119/C2
Akita, Japan 118/B4
Akita (pref.), Japan 118/B4
Akiyama, Japan 119/C2
Akjoujt, Mrta. 144/B2
Akka, Mor. 140/C3
Akkaraipattu, SrL. 124/D6
Akkerhaugen, Nor. 80/C2
Akkeshi, Japan 118/D2
'Akko, Isr. 133/D3
Akkrum, Neth. 92/C2
Aklavik, NW, Can. 176/L2
Akō, Japan 116/D3
Akora, Pak. 128/B2
Āk'ordat, Erit. 130/C5
Akören, Turk. 132/C2
Akosombo (dam), Gha. 145/F5
Akpatok (isl.), Qu, Can. 165/K2
Akpınar, Turk. 91/J5
Akqi, China 129/G4
Akranes, Ice. 79/M7
Åkrathos (cape), Gre. 89/J2
Åkrehamn, Nor. 80/A2
Akrítas (cape), Gre. 89/G4
Akron, Co, US 171/G2
Akron, Oh, US 172/D3
Akron, Pa, US 180/B3
Aksai Chin (reg.), China,India 112/C4
Aksaray, Turk. 132/C2
Aksaray (prov.), Turk. 132/C2
Aksay Kazakzu Zizhixian, China 112/F4
Akşehir, Turk. 132/B2
Akşehir Lake (lake), Turk. 132/B2
Akseki, Turk. 133/B1
Aksoran (peak), Kaz. 129/G3
Aksu, China 112/D3
Aksu, Turk. 133/B1
Aksu (riv.), Turk. 133/B1
Āksum, Eth. 130/C6
Aktepe, Turk. 133/E1
Aktí (pen.), Gre. 89/J2
Akto, China 129/G5
Akune, Japan 116/B4
Akure, Nga. 145/G5
Akureyri, Ice. 79/N6
Akuse, Gha. 145/F5
Akutan (isl.), Ak, US 176/E5
Akutan, Ak, US 176/E5
Akutan Pass (chan.), Ak, US 176/E5
Akwa Ibom (state), Nga. 145/G5
Akyab (Sittwe), Myan. 125/F3
Akyazı, Turk. 91/K5
Ål, Nor. 80/C1
Al 'āl, Jor. 133/D4
Al 'Amārah, Iraq 130/E2
Al Anbār (gov.), Iraq 132/E3
Al 'Aqabah, Jor. 133/D5
Al 'Arīsh, Egypt 133/C4
Al 'Ayn, UAE 131/G4
Al Azīzīyah, Libya 138/H1
Al 'Azīzīyah, Iraq 132/F3
Al Bāb, Syria 132/D2
Al Badrashayn, Egypt 133/B5
Al Baḩr Al Aḩmar (gov.), Egypt 143/C3
Al Bājūr, Egypt 133/B4
Al Balqā' (gov.), Jor. 133/D4
Al Balyanā, Egypt 143/B3
Al Başrah, Iraq 130/E2
Al Batrūn, Leb. 133/D2
Al Bayḑā, Libya 139/K1
Al Biqā' (gov.), Leb. 133/E2
Al Biqā' (valley), Leb. 133/D3
Al Bīrah, WBnk. 133/G8
Al Birkah, Libya 141/H4
Al Buḩayrah (gov.), Egypt 143/B2
Al Fāsher, Sudan 139/L5
Al Fatḩah, Iraq 132/E3
Al Fāw, Iraq 130/E3
Al Fayyum, Egypt 133/B5
Al Fayyūm (gov.), Egypt 143/B1
Al Ghurdaqah, Egypt 143/C3
Al Ḩadīthah, Iraq 132/E3
Al Ḩaḑr, Iraq 132/E3
Al Ḩaffah, Syria 133/E2
Al Ḩajar ash Sahrqī (mts.), Oman 131/G4
Al Hamādah al Hamrā (upland), Libya 138/H2
Al Ḩammāmāt, Tun. 88/B4
Al Ḩasakah, Syria 132/E2
Al Ḩasakah (prov.), Syria 132/E2
Al Hawāmidīyah, Egypt 133/B5
Al Ḩayy, Iraq 130/E2
Al Ḩillah, Iraq 132/F3
Al Hindīyah, Iraq 132/F3
Al Hirmil, Leb. 133/E2
Al Hoceima (prov.), Mor. 142/B2
Al Hoceima, Mor. 142/C2
Al Ḩudaydah, Yem. 130/D6
Al Hufūf, SAr. 130/E3
Al Iskandarīyah, Iraq 132/F3
Al Iskandarīyah (Alexandria), Egypt 133/A4
Al Iskandarīyah (gov.), Egypt 143/B1
Al Ismā'īlīyah, Egypt 133/C4
Al Ismā'īlīyah (gov.), Egypt 133/C4
Al Jabal Akaur (mts.), Oman 131/G4
Al Jaghbūb, Libya 139/K2
Al Janub (gov.), Leb. 133/D3
Al Jifārah (plain), Libya 141/H2
Al Jīzah, Egypt 133/B4
Al Junaynah, Sudan 139/K5
Al Karak (gov.), Jor. 133/D4
Al Karak, Jor. 133/D4
Al Khābūrah, Oman 131/G4
Al Khalīl (Hebron), WBnk. 133/D4
Al Khāliş, Iraq 132/F3
Al Khānkah, Egypt 133/B4
Al Khārijah, Egypt 143/B3

216

Al Kh – Ameri

Al Kharṭūm Baḥrī (Khartoum North), Sudan 139/M4
Al Khubar, SAr. 130/F3
Al Khums, Libya 138/H1
Al Kiswah, Syria 133/E3
Al Kūfah, Iraq 132/F3
Al Kufrah, Libya 139/K3
Al Lādhiqīyah (prov.), Syria 132/C3
Al Lādhiqīyah (Latakia), Syria 133/D2
Al Madīnah, SAr. 130/C4
Al Madīnah al Fikrīyah, Egypt 130/B3
Al Mafraq (gov.), Jor. 133/E3
Al Mafraq, Jor. 133/E3
Al Maghrib (reg.), Mor. 138/E1
Al Maḥallah al Kubrá, Egypt 133/B4
Al Maḥmūdīyah, Egypt 133/B4
Al Mālikīyah, Syria 132/E2
Al Manṣūrah, Egypt 133/B4
Al Manzilah, Egypt 133/B4
Al Marāghah, Egypt 143/B3
Al Marj, Libya 139/K1
Al Maṭarīyah, Egypt 133/C4
Al Mawṣil (Mosul), Iraq 132/E2
Al Mayādīn, Syria 132/E3
Al Mazra'ah, Jor. 133/D4
Al Minyā (gov.), Egypt 143/B2
Al Miqdādīyah, Iraq 132/F3
Al Mubarraz, SAr. 130/E4
Al Mudawwarah, Jor. 133/D5
Al Mukallā, Yem. 130/E6
Al Munastīr (prov.), Alg. 142/M7
Al Musayyib, Iraq 132/F3
Al Muthanná (gov.), Iraq 132/F4
Al Qābil, Oman 131/G4
Al Qaḍārif, Sudan 130/C6
Al Qādisīyah (gov.), Iraq 132/F4
Al Qāhirah (gov.), Egypt 143/B1
Al Qāhirah (Cairo) (cap.), Egypt 143/B2
Al Qā'im, Iraq 132/E3
Al Qāmishlī, Syria 132/E2
Al Qanāṭir al Khayrīyah, Egypt 133/B4
Al Qantarah, Egypt 133/C4
Al Qaṣr, Jor. 133/D4
Al Qunayṭirah (prov.), Syria 133/D3
Al Qunayṭirah, Syria 133/D3
Al Qurnah, Iraq 130/E2
Al Quṣayr, Syria 133/E2
Al Quṭayfah, Syria 133/E3
Al Quwayrah, Jor. 133/D5
Al Ubayyiḍ, Sudan 139/M5
Al 'Uwaynāt (peak), Sudan 139/L3
Al Wādī Al Jadīd (gov.), Egypt 143/B3
Al Wāḥāt al Baḥrīyah (oasis), Egypt 143/B2
Al Wāḥāt al Khārijah (oasis), Egypt 143/B3
Al Wāsiṭah, Egypt 133/B5
Al Yāmūn, WBnk. 133/G7
Ala (pt.), It. 88/B1
Ala, It. 101/E1
Alabama (riv.), Al,Ga, US 175/G4
Alabama (state), US 175/G3
Alabaster, Al, US 175/G3
Alaca, Turk. 132/C1
Alacalı, Turk. 91/J5
Alaçam, Turk. 132/C1
Alaçatı, Turk. 89/K3
Alachua, Fl, US 175/H4
Alacrán (reef), Mex. 186/D1
Alacranes (res.), Cuba 187/F1
Aladağ, Turk. 133/C1
Alaejos, Sp. 86/C2
Alagir, Rus. 105/H4
Alagna Valsesia, It. 100/A1
Alagnon (riv.), Fr. 84/E4
Alagoa Grande, Braz. 196/D2
Alagoas (state), Braz. 196/C3
Alagoinhas, Braz. 196/C4
Alagón (riv.), Sp. 86/C2
Alagón, Sp. 87/E2
Alajärvi, Fin. 102/D3
Alajuela, CR 187/E4
Alakanuk, Ak, US 176/F3
Alakol' (lake), Kaz. 112/D2
Alakol (lake), Kaz. 106/J5
Alalaú (riv.), Braz. 195/F5
Alamagan (isl.), NMar. 158/D3
'Alāmarvdasht (riv.), Iran 130/F3
Alameda, Ca, US 177/K11
Alaminos, Phil. 121/C4
Alamo (lake), Az, US 170/D4
Alamo, Mex. 186/B1
Alamo, Ca, US 177/K11
Alamo Heights, Tx, US 179/U21
Alamogordo, NM, US 171/F4
Alamor, Ecu. 198/A2
Álamos, Mex. 184/C3
Åland (isl.), Fin. 79/G3
Aland (riv.), Ger. 82/F2
Alanya, Turk. 133/C1
Alaotra (lake), Madg. 149/J7
Alapaha (riv.), Fl,Ga, US 175/H4
Alaplı, Turk. 91/K5
Alarcón, Embalse de (res.), Sp. 86/D3
Alaşehir, Turk. 132/B2
Alaska (state), US 176/G2
Alaska (range), Ak, US 176/G4
Alaska (pen.), Ak, US 176/G4
Alaska, Gulf of (gulf), Ak, US 176/J4
Alassio, It. 100/B5
Alatyr', Rus. 103/K5
Alaverdi, Arm. 105/H4
Alavus, Fin. 102/D3
Alaw (riv.), Wal, UK 76/D5
Alaw, Llyn (lake), Wal, UK 76/D5
Alayor, Sp. 86/C3
Alayskiy (mts.), Kyr. 129/F5
Alazeya (riv.), Rus. 107/R3
Alb (riv.), Ger. 96/B5
Alba, It. 85/H4
Alba (prov.), Rom. 91/F2
Alba de Tormes, Sp. 86/C2
Alba Fucens (ruin), It. 88/C1
Alba Iulia, Rom. 91/F2
Albacete, Sp. 86/E3
Albaida, Sp. 87/E3
Albairate, It. 100/B2
Ålbæk, Den. 80/D3
Albalate del Arzobispo, Sp. 87/E2
Alban, Fr. 84/E5
Albanel (lake), Qu, Can. 172/F1
Albania (ctry.) 89/F2
Albany, Austl. 154/C5
Albany (riv.), On, Can. 164/H3
Albany, Ca, US 177/K11
Albany, Ga, US 175/G4
Albany, Ky, US 172/C4
Albany, Mo, US 179/E5
Albany (cap.), NY, US 172/F3
Albany, Or, US 168/C4
Albany County (int'l arpt.), NY, US 172/F3
Albaredo d'Adige, It. 101/E2
Albarine (riv.), Fr. 98/B5
Albarracín, Sp. 86/E2
Albatross (bay), Austl. 151/D2
Albatross Rock (pt.), Namb. 148/A2
Albbruck, Ger. 98/E2
Albemarle (sound), NC, US 175/J2
Albemarle, NC, US 175/H3
Albemarle (pt.), Ecu. 198/E6
Alben (peak), It. 85/H4
Albenga, It. 100/B4
Alberche (riv.), Sp. 86/C2
Alberhill, Ca, US 178/C3
Alberndorf in der Riedmark, Aus. 97/H6
Alberschwende, Aus. 99/F3
Albersdorf, Ger. 80/C4
Albersweiler, Ger. 96/B4
Albert (lake), Austl. 157/A2
Albert (lake), D.R.Congo,Ugan. 139/M7
Albert, Fr. 94/B3
Albert Kanaal (riv.), Belg. 95/E2
Albert Nile (riv.), Ugan. 139/M7
Alberta (prov.), Can. 164/E3
Alberti, Arg. 200/E2
Albertinia, SAfr. 148/C4
Albertirsa, Hun. 90/D2
Alberto de Agostini, PN, Chile 199/B7
Alberton, SAfr. 148/Q13
Albertshofen, Ger. 96/D3
Albertville, Al, US 175/G3
Albertville, Fr. 85/G4
Albestroff, Fr. 95/F6
Albeuve, Swi. 98/D4
Albi, Fr. 84/E5
Albignasego, It. 101/E2
Albina, Sur. 193/H2
Albinea, It. 100/D3
Albino, It. 100/C1
Albion, Mi, US 172/C3
Albisola Marina, It. 100/B4
Albisola Superiore, It. 100/B4
Alblasserdam, Neth. 92/B5
Albocácer, Sp. 87/E2
Alborán (isl.), Mor. 140/E2
Ålborg (bay), Den. 80/D3
Ålborg, Den. 80/C3
Albox, Sp. 86/D4
Albright-Knox Art Gallery, NY, US 173/S10
Albristhorn (peak), Swi. 98/D5
Albufeira, Port. 86/A4
Albula (riv.), Swi. 85/H3
Albuñol, Sp. 86/D4
Albuquerque (int'l arpt.), NM, US 170/F4
Albuquerque, NM, US 170/F4
Albuquerque, Cayos de (isls.), Col. 187/F3
Alburquerque, Sp. 86/B3
Alburtis, Pa, US 180/C3
Albury, Austl. 157/C3
Alby-sur-Chéran, Fr. 98/C6
Alca, Peru 198/C4
Alcabideche, Port. 87/P10
Alcácer do Sal, Port. 86/A3
Alcalá de Chivert, Sp. 87/F2
Alcalá de Guadaira, Sp. 86/C4
Alcalá de Henares, Sp. 87/N9
Alcalá de los Gazules, Sp. 86/C4
Alcalá la Real, Sp. 86/D4
Alcamo, It. 88/C4
Alcanadre (riv.), Sp. 87/E2
Alcanar, Sp. 87/E2
Alcañices, Sp. 86/B2
Alcañiz, Sp. 87/E2
Alcântara, Braz. 196/A1
Alcántara, Sp. 86/B3
Alcántara, Embalse de (res.), Sp. 86/B3
Alcantarilla, Sp. 86/E4
Alcaraz, Sp. 86/D3
Alcaraz, Sierra de (range), Sp. 86/D3
Alcatraz (isl.), Ca, US 177/K11
Alcaudete, Sp. 86/C4
Alcázar de San Juan, Sp. 86/D3
Alcira, Sp. 87/E3
Alcira, Arg. 200/D2
Alçıtepe, Turk. 89/K2
Alcoa, Tn, US 175/H3
Alcobaça, Braz. 196/C5
Alcobaça, Port. 86/A3
Alcobendas, Sp. 87/N8
Alcochete, Port. 87/Q10
Alcora, Sp. 87/E2
Alcorcón, Sp. 87/N9
Alcorisa, Sp. 87/E2
Alcoutim, Port. 86/B4
Alcoy, Sp. 87/E3
Alcúdia, Sp. 87/G3
Aldabra (isls.), Sey. 135/G5
Aldama, Mex. 184/D2
Aldama, Mex. 185/F4
Aldan (plat.), Rus. 107/N4
Aldan, Rus. 107/N4
Aldan (riv.), Rus. 109/N3
Alde (riv.), Eng, UK 75/H2
Aldeburgh, Eng, UK 75/H2
Aldeia Nova de São Bento, Port. 86/B4
Alden, Il, US 177/N15
Aldenhoven, Ger. 95/F2
Aldeno, It. 99/H6
Aldergrove (int'l arpt.), NI, UK 76/B2
Aldergrove, NI, UK 76/B2
Alderley Edge, Eng, UK 77/F5
Alderney (isl.), Chl, UK 84/B2
Aldershot, Eng, UK 75/F4
Alderwood Manor-Bothell North, Wa, US 177/C2
Aldine, Tx, US 171/J5
Aldingen, Ger. 99/E1
Aldred (lake), Pa, US 180/B4
Aldridge, Eng, UK 75/E1
Ale Water (riv.), Sc, UK 78/D6
Aleg, Mrta. 144/B2
Alegre, Braz. 197/D2
Alegrete, Braz. 199/E2
Alejandro Gallinal, Uru. 201/G2
Alejandro Roca, Arg. 200/E2
Alejandro Selkirk (isl.), Chile 189/A6
Alejo Ledesma, Arg. 200/E2
Aleknagik, Ak, US 176/G4
Aleksandrov, Rus. 102/H4
Aleksandrovac, Serb. 90/E4
Aleksandrovsk, Rus. 103/N4
Aleksandrów Kujawski, Pol. 83/K2
Aleksandrów Łódzki, Pol. 83/K3
Alekseyevka, Kaz. 129/F2
Alekseyevka, Kaz. 129/E2
Alekseyevka, Rus. 104/F2
Aleksin, Rus. 102/H5
Aleksinac, Serb. 90/E4
Além Paraíba, Braz. 197/L6
Alençon, Fr. 84/D2
Alenquer, Braz. 193/H4
Alenuihaha (chan.), Hi, US 166/T10
Alerce Andino, PN, Chile 200/B4
Aléria, Fr. 88/A1
Alert (pt.), Nun., Can. 165/S6
Aleşd, Rom. 90/F2
Alessandria (prov.), It. 100/B3
Alessandria, It. 100/B3
Ålestrup, Den. 80/C3
Ålesund, Nor. 79/C3
Aletschhorn (peak), Swi. 98/D5
Aleutian (range), Ak, US 176/G4
Aleutian (isls.), Ak, US 176/B5
Alexander (mt.), Austl. 154/B2
Alexander (arch.), Ak, US 176/L4
Alexander (isl.), Ant. 202/V
Alexander Bay, SAfr. 148/B3
Alexander City, Al, US 175/G3
Alexander Nevsky Abbey, Rus. 103/T7
Alexandria, Braz. 196/C2
Alexandria (Al Iskandarīyah), Egypt 133/A4
Alexandria (int'l arpt.), Egypt 133/A4
Alexándria, Gre. 89/H2
Alexandria, NZ 159/R12
Alexandria, Rom. 91/G4
Alexandria, SAfr. 148/D4
Alexandria, La, US 171/J5
Alexandria, Mn, US 169/K4
Alexandria, Sc, UK 78/B5
Alexandria, Va, US 180/A6
Alexandrina (lake), Austl. 151/C4
Alexandroúpolis, Gre. 89/J2
Alexis Creek, BC, Can. 168/C2
Alfaro, Sp. 86/E1
Alfatar, Bul. 91/H4
Alfbach (riv.), Ger. 95/F3
Alfeld, Ger. 93/G5
Alfenas, Braz. 197/H6
Alfhausen, Ger. 93/E3
Alfiós (riv.), Gre. 89/G4
Alfonsine, It. 101/F3
Alfonso Bonilla Aragón (int'l arpt.), Col. 194/B4
Alfred NP, Austl. 157/D3
Alfreton, Eng, UK 77/G5
Alfter, Ger. 95/G2
Alga, Kaz. 105/L2
Ålgård, Nor. 80/A2
Algarrobo, Chile 200/N8
Algarve (reg.), Port. 86/A4
Algeciras, Sp. 86/C4
Algeciras, Col. 194/C4
Algemesí, Sp. 87/E3
Alger (prov.), Alg. 142/G4
Algeria (ctry.) 138/F2
Algermissen, Ger. 93/G4
Algete, Sp. 87/N8
Alghero, It. 88/A2
Algiers (El Djezair) (cap.), Alg. 142/G4
Algoa (bay), SAfr. 148/D4
Algodón (riv.), Peru 192/D4
Algodonales, Sp. 86/C4
Algoma, Wi, US 169/M4
Algona, Wa, US 177/C3
Algonac, Mi, US 177/G6
Algonquin, Il, US 177/P14
Algorta, Uru. 201/K10
Algueirão, Port. 87/P10
Algund (Lagundo), It. 99/H4
Alhama de Granada, Sp. 86/D4
Alhama de Murcia, Sp. 86/E4
Alhambra, Ca, US 178/F7
Alhandra, Braz. 196/D2
Alhandra, Port. 87/P10
Alhaurín el Grande, Sp. 86/C4
'Alī al Gharbī, Iraq 130/E2
'Alī ash Sharqī, Iraq 130/E2
Āli Bayramlı, Azer. 105/J5
Alia, It. 88/C4
Alía, Sp. 86/C3
Aliağa, Turk. 132/A2
Aliákmon (riv.), Gre. 89/G2
Aliákmonos (lake), Gre. 89/G2
Alíartos, Gre. 89/H3
Alibates Flint Quarries Nat'l Mon., Tx, US 171/G4
Alibey (lake), Ukr. 91/K3
Alibeyköy, Turk. 91/J5
Alicante, Sp. 87/E3
Alicante (int'l arpt.), Sp. 87/E3
Alice, Tx, US 174/D5
Alice (pt.), It. 89/E3
Alice Arm, BC, Can. 176/N4
Alice Springs, Austl. 155/G2
Aliceville, Al, US 175/F3
Alicia, Phil. 121/D6
Alicudi (isl.), It. 88/D3
Alicurá (res.), Arg. 200/C4
Alife, It. 88/D2
Alīganj, India 126/B2
Alijó, Port. 86/B2
Alima (riv.), Congo 138/J8
Alingār (riv.), Afg. 122/A1
Alingsås, Swe. 80/E3
Alīpur, Pak. 128/A5
Alīpur Duār, India 127/G2
Alirājpur, India 131/K4
Alisos (riv.), Mex. 170/E5
Alistráti, Gre. 89/H2
Alivérion, Gre. 89/J3
Aliwal North, SAfr. 148/D3
Aljezur, Port. 86/A4
Aljustrel, Port. 86/A4
Alken, Belg. 95/E2
Alkmaar, Neth. 92/B3
Alkoum (well), Alg. 141/H4
Alkoven, Aus. 97/H6
Allada, Ben. 145/F5
Allahābād, India 126/C3
Allakaket, Ak, US 176/H2
Allaman, Swi. 98/C5
Allan (hills), Sk, Can. 169/G3
Allan, Sk, Can. 169/G3
Alland, Aus. 91/N7
Allanmyo, Myan. 125/G4
Allanridge, SAfr. 148/D2
Allanson, Austl. 154/C5
'Allāq (well), Libya 138/H1
Allariz, Sp. 86/B1
Alle, Swi. 98/D3
Allegan, Mi, US 172/C3
Allegheny (mts.), US 167/K4
Allegheny (plat.), US 172/E3
Allegheny (riv.), US 172/D3
Allen (riv.), Eng, UK 74/B5
Allen, Arg. 200/D3
Allen Park, Mi, US 177/F7
Allendale, SC, US 175/H3
Allendale, NJ, US 181/J7
Allende, Mex. 185/E2
Allende, Mex. 185/E3
Allendorf, Ger. 93/F6
Allensbach, Ger. 99/F2
Allenspark, Co, US 179/A2
Allentown, Pa, US 180/C2
Allentsteig, Aus. 83/H4
Allenwood, Pa, US 180/B1
Alleppey, India 124/C6
Aller (riv.), Ger. 93/H3
Allerkanal (canal), Ger. 93/H4
Allersberg, Ger. 96/E4
Allershausen, Ger. 97/E6
Allgäu Alps (range), Aus.,Ger. 82/F5
Alliance, Ne, US 169/H5
Alliance, Oh, US 172/D3
Allied War Cemetery, Myan. 120/B2
Allier (riv.), Fr. 84/E3
Alligator (pt.), La, US 179/Q16
Allingåbro, Den. 80/D3
Allinges, Fr. 98/C5
Alloa, Sc, UK 78/C4
Allonnes, Fr. 84/D3
Allora, Austl. 156/C5
Allos, Fr. 85/G4
Alloway, NJ, US 180/C4
Allschwil, Swi. 98/D2
Alm (riv.), Aus. 97/G7
Alma, Mi, US 172/C3
Alma, Qu, Can. 173/G1
Almacelles, Sp. 87/F2
Almada, Port. 87/P10
Almadén, Sp. 86/C3
Almafuerte, Arg. 200/D2
Almagro, Sp. 86/D3
Almanor (lake), Ca, US 170/B2
Almansa, Sp. 87/E3
Almanza, Sp. 86/C1
Almanzor, Pico de (peak), Sp. 86/C2
Almanzora (riv.), Sp. 86/D4
Almas (riv.), Braz. 193/J6
Almas, Braz. 196/A3
Almas, Pico das (peak), Braz. 196/B4
Almaty (int'l arpt.), Kaz. 129/G4
Almaty, Kaz. 129/G4
Almazán, Sp. 86/D2
Almazora, Sp. 87/E3
Almeida, Port. 86/B2
Almeirim, Braz. 193/H4
Almeirim, Port. 86/A3
Almelo, Neth. 92/D4
Almenara, Braz. 196/B5
Almenara (peak), Sp. 86/D3
Almenara, Sp. 87/E3
Almendra, Embalse de (res.), Sp. 86/B2
Almendralejo, Sp. 86/B3
Almenno San Salvatore, It. 100/C1
Almere, Neth. 92/C4
Almería, Sp. 86/D4
Almería, Golfo de (gulf), Sp. 86/D4
Al'met'yevsk, Rus. 103/M5
Älmhult, Swe. 80/F3
Almina (pt.), Sp. 142/B2
Almirós, Gre. 89/H3
Almiroú (gulf), Gre. 89/J5
Almodôvar, Port. 86/A4
Almodóvar del Campo, Sp. 86/C3
Almodóvar del Río, Sp. 86/C4
Almoharín, Sp. 86/B3
Almond (riv.), Sc, UK 78/C4
Almont (riv.), Fr. 72/L6
Almonte, On, Can. 172/E2
Almonte, Sp. 86/B4
Almora, India 126/B1
Almoradí, Sp. 87/E3
Almorox, Sp. 86/C2
Almte. Montt (gulf), Chile 201/B7
Almudévar, Sp. 87/E1
Almuñécar, Sp. 86/D4
Almus, Turk. 132/D1
Alness, Sc, UK 78/B1
Alness (riv.), Sc, UK 78/B1
Alnwick, Eng, UK 78/E6
Alofi (isl.), Wall., Fr. 158/H6
Alofi, NZ 159/J6
Along, India 125/G2
Alónnisos (isl.), Gre. 89/H3
Alor (isls.), Indo. 123/F5
Alor Setar, Malay. 125/H6
Álora, Sp. 86/C4
Alotau, PNG 158/E6
Aloysius (mt.), Austl. 155/F3
Alpachiri, Arg. 200/E3
Alpe di Poti (peak), It. 101/E6
Alpedrete, Sp. 87/M8
Alpen, Ger. 92/D5
Alpena, Mi, US 172/D2
Alpercatas (riv.), Braz. 196/A2
Alpercatas, Serra das (mts.), Braz. 193/J5
Alperschällihorn (peak), Swi. 99/F4
Alpes de Provence (range), Fr. 85/G5
Alpha, Austl. 156/B3
Alpha, NJ, US 180/C2
Alphen aan de Rijn, Neth. 92/B4
Alpi Apuane (range), It. 85/J4
Alpi Dolomitiche (range), It. 85/J4
Alpi Orobie (range) It. 85/J3
Alpiarça, Port. 86/A3
Alpine, NJ, US 181/K8
Alpine, Ut, US 179/K13
Alpine, Wy, US 168/F5
Alpirsbach, Ger. 99/E1
Alpnach, Swi. 99/E4
Alps (mts.), Eur. 69/E4
Alqōsh, Iraq 132/E2
Als (isl.), Den. 82/E1
Alsace (pol. reg.), Fr. 82/D4
Alsager, Eng, UK 77/F5
Alsask, Sk, Can. 168/F3
Alsasua, Sp. 86/D1
Alsdorf, Ger. 95/F2
Alsenz (riv.), Ger. 95/G4
Alsenz, Ger. 95/G4
Alsfeld, Ger. 85/H1
Alsheim, Ger. 96/B3
Alsip, Il, US 177/Q16
Alstahaug, Nor. 79/E2
Alster (riv.), Ger. 93/H1
Alsting, Fr. 95/F5
Alstonville, Austl. 157/E1
Alt (riv.), Eng, UK 77/E4
Alta, Ut, US 179/K12
Alta, Nor. 79/G1
Alta Floresta, Braz. 193/G5
Alta Gracia, Arg. 199/D3
Altach, Aus. 99/F3
Altadena, Ca, US 178/F7
Altagracia, Nic. 186/E4
Altai (mts.), Asia 112/E2
Altamaha (riv.), Ga, US 175/H4
Altamira, Braz. 193/H4
Altamira, Mex. 186/B1
Altamira do Maranhão, Braz. 196/A2
Altamonte Springs, Fl, US 175/H4
Altamura, It. 88/E2
Altar, Mex. 184/C2
Altar (vol.), Ecu. 194/B5
Altar de los Sacrificios (ruin), Guat. 186/D2
Altar, Desierto de (des.), Mex. 170/D4
Altare, It. 100/B4
Altavilla Vicentina, It. 101/E1
Altay, China 112/E2
Altay, Mong. 112/E2
Altay, Mong. 112/G2
Altay, Resp., Rus. 106/J4
Altayskiy Kray, Rus. 129/G2
Altdorf, Swi. 99/E4
Altdorf bei Nürnberg, Ger. 97/E4
Altea, Sp. 87/E3
Altedo, It. 101/E3
Altena, Ger. 93/E6
Altenahr, Ger. 95/G2
Altenau, Ger. 93/H5
Altenau (riv.), Ger. 93/F5
Altenbeken, Ger. 93/F5
Altenberg bei Linz, Aus. 97/H6
Altenburg, Ger. 82/G3
Altenfelden, Aus. 97/G6
Altenglan, Ger. 95/G4
Altengottern, Ger. 93/H6
Altenkirchen, Ger. 95/G2
Altenmünster, Ger. 96/D6
Altenstadt, Ger. 99/G1
Altenstadt, Ger. 96/B2
Altensteig, Ger. 96/B5
Altentreptow, Ger. 80/E5
Altepexi, Mex. 185/M8
Alter Rhein (riv.), Ger. 92/D5
Altes Land (phys. reg.), Ger. 93/G1
Altheim, Aus. 97/G6
Althengstett, Ger. 96/B5
Althofen, Aus. 85/L3
Althütte, Ger. 96/C5
Altındere NP, Turk. 132/D1
Altınözü, Turk. 133/E1
Altıntaş, Turk. 132/B2
Altınyaka, Turk. 133/B1
Altınyayla, Turk. 133/A1
Altiplano (plat.), Bol.,Peru 189/C4
Altkirch, Fr. 98/D2
Altlandsberg, Ger. 82/Q6
Altmark (phys. reg.), Ger. 82/F2
Altmühl (riv.), Ger. 85/J2
Altmünster, Aus. 97/G7
Altnaharra, Sc, UK 73/R7
Alto (peak), Braz. 196/A4
Alto (peak), It. 99/G4
Alto Araguaia, Braz. 193/H7
Alto de Tamar (peak), Col. 194/C3
Alto Garças, Braz. 193/H7
Alto Lucero, Mex. 185/N7
Alto Parnaíba, Braz. 196/A3
Alto Purús (riv.), Peru 192/D6
Alto Santo, Braz. 196/C2
Alto Yuruá (riv.), Peru 198/C3
Altomünster, Ger. 96/E6
Alton, La, US 179/Q16
Alton, Il, US 179/G8
Alton, Eng, UK 75/F4
Altona, Mb, Can. 169/J3
Altoona, Pa, US 172/E3
Altopascio, It. 101/D5
Altos, Braz. 196/B2
Altos de Camapana NP, Pan. 194/B2
Altotonga, Mex. 185/M7
Altötting, Ger. 97/F6
Altrincham, Eng, UK 77/F5
Altrip, Ger. 96/B4
Altun (mts.), China 109/H6
Altun Ha (ruin), Belz. 186/D2
Alturas, Ca, US 168/C5
Altus (res.), Ok, US 171/H4
Altus, Ok, US 171/H4
Altzayanca, Mex. 185/M7
Alucra, Turk. 132/D1
Aluminé, Arg. 200/C3
Alunda, Swe. 80/H1
Ālūs, Iraq 132/E3
Alushta, Ukr. 104/E3
Alva, Ok, US 171/H3
Alva, Sc, UK 78/C4
Alvalade, Port. 86/A4
Älvängen, Swe. 80/E3
Alvarado, Mex. 185/P8
Álvarez, Arg. 200/E2
Álvaro Obregón, Presa (dam), Mex. 184/C2
Alvdal, Nor. 79/D3
Älvdalen, Swe. 80/F1
Alverca, Port. 87/P10
Alveringem, Belg. 94/B1
Alvesta, Swe. 80/F3
Ålvik, Nor. 80/B1
Alvin, Tx, US 171/J5
Alvito, Port. 86/B3
Älvkarleby, Swe. 80/G1
Alvorada, Braz. 197/A4
Alvorada do Norte, Braz. 196/A4
Älvsborg (co.), Swe. 79/E4
Älvsbyn, Swe. 79/G2
Alwen (riv.), Wal, UK 76/E5
Alxa Youqi, China 112/H4
Alxa Zuoqi, China 112/J4
Alyawarra Abor. Land, Austl. 155/G2
Alyth, Sc, UK 78/C3
Alytus, Lith. 81/L4
Alz (riv.), Ger. 85/K2
Alzano Lombardo, It. 100/C1
Alzenau in Unterfranken, Ger. 96/C2
Alzette (riv.), Lux. 95/F4
Alzey, Ger. 96/B3
Am Timan, Chad 139/K5
Ama, La, US 179/P17
Amacayacú, PN, Col. 192/D4
Amacuro (riv.), Ven. 195/F2
Amacuro (delta), Ven. 195/F2
Amacuzac (riv.), Mex. 185/K8
Amadeus (lake), Austl. 151/C3
Amadjuak (lake), Nun., Can. 165/J2
Amadora, Port. 87/P10
Amagansett, NY, US 181/F2
Amagansett NWR, NY, US 181/F2
Amagasaki, Japan 119/H6
Amagi, Japan 116/B4
Amagi-san (peak), Japan 117/F3
Amaguaña, Ecu. 194/B5
Amajac (riv.), Mex. 185/N7
Åmål, Swe. 80/E2
Amala (riv.), Kenya 146/B3
Amalfi, Col. 194/C3
Amalia, SAfr. 148/D2
Amaliás, Gre. 89/G4
Amaluza, Ecu. 198/B2
Amambaí, Braz. 199/E1
Amambaí (riv.), Braz. 193/H8
Amami (isls.), Japan 109/M7
Amami-O-Shima (isl.), Japan 117/K6
Amanā (lake), Braz. 192/F4
Amance, Fr. 98/C2
Amānganj, India 126/C3
Amāngarh, Pak. 128/A2
Amantea, It. 88/E3
Amanu (isl.), FrPol. 159/L6
Amanzimtoti, SAfr. 149/E3
Amapá, Braz. 193/H3
Amapá (state), Braz. 195/H4
Amarante, Braz. 196/B2
Amarante, Port. 86/A2
Amarante do Marahão, Braz. 196/A2
Amarapura, Myan. 125/G3
Amareleja, Port. 86/B3
Amargosa, Braz. 196/C4
Amargosa (riv.), Ca, US 170/C3
Amarillo, Tx, US 171/G4
Amaro (peak), It. 88/D1
Amarpātan, India 126/C3
Amarume, Japan 118/A4
Amarwāra, India 126/B4
Amasra, Turk. 91/L5
Amasya, Turk. 132/C1
Amasya (prov.), Turk. 132/C1
Amata, Austl. 155/F3
Amatlán de Cañas, Mex. 184/D4
Amatsukominato, Japan 119/E3
Amawalk (res.), NY, US 181/E1
Amay, Belg. 95/E2
Amayuca, Mex. 185/L8
Amazon (Amazonas) (riv.), Braz.,Peru 198/C1
Amazonas, Cuba 187/G1
Amazonas (state), Braz. 194/C5
Amazonas (Amazon) (riv.), Braz.,Peru 198/C1
Amazônia, PN da (Tapajós), Braz. 193/G4
Ambāh, India 126/B2
Ambahikily, Madg. 149/G8
Ambajogai, India 131/L5
Ambāla Sadar, India 128/D4
Ambalangoda, SrL. 124/D6
Ambalavao, Madg. 149/H8
Ambam, Camr. 138/H7
Ambanja, Madg. 149/J6
Ambaro (bay), Madg. 149/J6
Ambato, Ecu. 194/B5
Ambato Boeny, Madg. 149/H7
Ambatofinandrahana, Madg. 149/H8
Ambatolampy, Madg. 149/H7
Ambatomaidy, Madg. 149/H7
Ambatomanoina, Madg. 149/H7
Ambatondrazaka, Madg. 149/J7
Ambazac, Fr. 84/D4
Āmbelos (cape), Gre. 89/H3
Amberg, Ger. 97/E4
Ambergris Cay (isl.), Belz. 186/E2
Ambérieu-en-Bugey, Fr. 98/B6
Amberloup, Belg. 95/E3
Ambikāpur, India 126/D4
Ambilobe, Madg. 149/J6
Ambinanindrano, Madg. 149/J8
Ambinanitelo, Madg. 149/J6
Ambler, Ak, US 176/G2
Ambler, Pa, US 180/C3
Amblève (riv.), Belg. 82/C3
Amblève, Belg. 95/F3
Ambo, Peru 198/B3
Amboasary, Madg. 149/H9
Amboavory, Madg. 149/J7
Ambodifototra, Madg. 149/J7
Ambodiharina, Madg. 149/J8
Ambohidratrimo, Madg. 149/H7
Ambohijanahary, Madg. 149/J7
Ambohimahasoa, Madg. 149/H8
Ambohimandroso, Madg. 149/H7
Ambohinihaonana, Madg. 149/H8
Ambohitsilaozana, Madg. 149/J7
Ambolomoty, Madg. 149/H7
Ambon (isl.), Indo. 123/G4
Ambon, Indo. 123/G4
Ambondro, Madg. 149/H9
Amboni Caves, Tanz. 146/C4
Amborompotsy, Madg. 149/H8
Amboseli NP, Kenya 146/C3
Ambositra, Madg. 149/H8
Ambovombe, Madg. 149/H9
Ambrym (isl.), Van. 158/F6
Amchitka (isl.), Ak, US 176/B6
Amchitka Pass (chan.), Ak, US 176/B6
Amealco, Mex. 185/K6
Ameca, Mex. 184/D4
Amecameca de Juárez, Mex. 185/R10
Ameghino, Arg. 200/E2
Ameglia, It. 100/C4
Ameisberg (peak), Aus. 97/G5
Ameland (isl.), Neth. 92/C2
Amelia, It. 88/C1
Amelinghausen, Ger. 93/H2
Amer (chan.), Neth. 92/B5
American (lake), Wa, US 177/B3
American (riv.), Ca, US 177/M9

217
Ameri – Arden

American Falls (mts.), Id, US 170/D2
American Fork, Ut, US 179/K13
American, North Fork (riv.), Ca, US 170/B3
American Samoa (dpcy.), US 159/H6
American, South Fork (riv.), Ca, US 170/B3
Americana, Braz. 197/C2
Americus, Ga, US 175/G3
Ameringkogel (peak), Aus. 85/L3
Amersfoort, SAfr. 149/E2
Amersfoort, Neth. 92/C4
Amersham, Eng, UK 75/F3
Amery Ice Shelf, Ant. 202/E
Amesbury, Eng, UK 75/E4
Amet, India 131/K3
Amethi, India 126/C2
Amfíklia, Gre. 89/H3
Amfilokhía, Gre. 89/G3
Ámfissa, Gre. 89/H3
Amga (riv.), Rus. 107/N3
Amguema (riv.), Rus. 107/T3
Amgun' (riv.), Rus. 107/P4
Amherst, NS, Can. 173/H2
Amherst, NY, US 173/S10
Amherstburg, On, Can. 177/F7
Ami, Japan 119/E1
Amiata (peak), It. 85/J5
Amiens, Fr. 94/B4
Amik (lake), Turk. 132/D2
Amila (isl.), Ak, US 176/D6
Amilcar Cabral (int'l arpt.), CpV. 135/K10
Amillis, Fr. 72/M5
Amíndaion, Gre. 89/G2
Aminu Kano (int'l arpt.), Nga. 145/H3
Amisk (lake), Sk, Can. 169/H2
Amistad (res.), Mex.,US 174/C4
Amistad Nat'l Rec. Area, Tx, US 171/G5
Amite, La, US 171/K5
Amityville, NY, US 181/M9
Amla, India 126/B5
Āmlāgora, India 127/F4
Åmli, Nor. 80/C2
'Ammān (gov.), Jor. 133/E4
Amman (riv.), Wal, UK 74/C3
Amman ('Ammān) (cap.), Jor. 133/D4
Ammanford, Wal, UK 74/C3
Ammarfjället (peak), Swe. 79/E2
Ammassalik, Grld 202/J
Ammer (riv.), Ger. 96/B5
Ammerman (mtn.), Yk, Can. 176/K2
Ammersee (lake), Ger. 85/J3
Amnéville, Fr. 95/F5
Āmol, Iran 130/F1
Amora, Port. 87/P10
Amorbach, Ger. 96/C3
Amorgós, Gre. 89/J4
Amorgós (isl.), Gre. 89/J4
Amory, Ms, US 175/F3
Amos, Qu, Can. 172/E1
Åmot, Nor. 80/B2
Amotfors, Swe. 80/E2
Amozoc, Mex. 185/L7
Ampachi, Japan 119/L5
Ampanefena, Madg. 149/J6
Ampangalana (canal), Madg. 149/J8
Ampanihy, Madg. 149/H9
Amparafaravola, Madg. 149/J7
Amparai, SrL. 124/D6
Amparo, Braz. 197/G7
Ampasindava (bay), Madg. 149/H6
Ampato (peak), Peru 198/D4
Ampefy, Madg. 149/H7
Amper (riv.), Ger. 97/E6
Ampfing, Ger. 97/F6
Ampflwang im Hausruckwald, Aus. 97/G6
Ampitatafika, Madg. 149/H7
Amposta, Sp. 87/F2
Amqui, Qu, Can. 173/H1
Amravati, India 124/C3
Amreli, India 131/K4
'Amrīt (ruin), Syria 133/D2
Amritsar, India 128/C4
Amroha, India 126/B1
Amrum (isl.), Ger. 82/E1
Amstel (riv.), Neth. 92/B4
Amstelveen, Neth. 92/B4
Amsterdam, NY, US 172/F3
Amsterdam, SAfr. 149/E2
Amsterdam (cap.), Neth. 92/B4
Amsterdam (isl.), Fr. 65/N7
Amsterdam Rijnkanaal (riv.), Neth. 92/C4
Amsterdam (Schipol) (int'l arpt.), Neth. 92/B4
Amstetten, Aus. 85/L2
Amu Darya (riv.), Asia 109/F8
Amudat, Ugan. 146/B2
Amukta Pass (chan.), Ak, US 176/D5
Amuku (mts.), Guy. 195/G4
Amund Ringnes (isl.), Nun., Can. 165/S7
Amundsen (gulf), NW, Can. 164/D1
Amundsen (bay), Ant. 202/D
Amundsen (sea), Ant. 202/S
Amundsen-Scott, US, Ant. 202/A
Amunge (lake), Swe. 80/F1
Amur (riv.), Rus. 113/P2
Amurrio, Sp. 86/D1
Amurskaya Oblast, Rus. 107/N4
Amyūn, Leb. 133/D2
An Nabk, Syria 133/E2
An Nahūd, Sudan 139/L5
An Najaf, Iraq 132/F4
An Najaf (gov.),Iraq 132/E4
An Nāṣirīyah,Iraq 130/E2
An Nu'manīyah,Iraq 132/F3
An Teallach (peak), Sc, UK 78/A1
An Uaimh, Ire. 73/Q10
Ana María (gulf), Cuba 183/F3
Anaa (isl.), FrPol. 159/L6
Anabar (riv.), Rus. 107/L3
'Anabtā, WBnk. 133/G7
Anachucuna (mtn.), Pan. 194/B2
Anaco, Ven. 195/E2
Anaconda-Deer Lodge County, Mt, US 168/E4
Anadarko, Ok, US 171/H4
Anadyr' (gulf), Rus. 109/T3
Anadyr' (range), Rus. 202/U
Anadyr' (riv.), Rus. 109/S3
Anadyr', Rus. 107/T3
Anáfi (isl.), Gre. 89/J4
Anaheim, Ca, US 178/G8
Anahim Lake, BC, Can. 168/B2
Anáhuac, Mex. 174/C5
Anahuac, Tx, US 174/E4
Anahuac, Mex. 184/D2
Anak, NKor. 115/C3
Anakāpalle, India 124/D4
Anaktuvuk Pass, Ak, US 176/H2
Analalava, Madg. 149/H6
Analamaitso (plat.), Madg. 149/J7
Analavory, Madg. 149/H7
Anambas (isls.), Indo. 122/C3
Anambra (state), Nga. 145/G5
Anamur, Turk. 133/C1
Anamur (pt.), Turk. 133/C1
Anan, Japan 116/D4
Anand, India 131/K4
Ananea, Peru 198/D4
Ananea, Bol. 198/D4
Anantapur, India 124/C5
Anantnag, India 128/C3
Anapa, Rus. 104/F3
Añapi (peak), Arg. 201/C6
Anápolis, Braz. 193/J7
Anapu (riv.), Braz. 193/H4
Anār, Iran 131/G2
Anārak, Iran 130/F2
Anastácio, Braz. 193/G8
'Anātā, WBnk. 133/G8
Anathan (isl.), NMar. 158/D3
Anatolia (reg.), Turk. 132/B2
Añatuya, Arg. 199/D2
Anauá (riv.), Braz. 192/F3
Ancash (dept.), Peru 198/B3
Anchieta, Braz. 197/D2
Anchor (bay), Mi, US 177/G6
Anchor Point, Ak, US 176/H4
Anchorage, Ak, US 176/J3
Anchorville, Mi, US 177/G6
Anchovy, Jam. 187/G2
Ancient City of Oc-Eo, Viet. 120/D4
Ancoeur (riv.), Fr. 72/L6
Ancohuma (peak), Bol. 198/D4
Ancón, Peru 198/B3
Ancón de Sardinas (bay), Col. 194/B4
Ancona (prov.), It. 101/G5
Ancona, It. 101/G5
Ancoraimes, Bol. 198/D4
Ancre (riv.), Fr. 94/B3
Ancrum, Sc, UK 78/D5
Ancud, Chile 200/B4
Ancud, Golfo de (gulf), Chile 199/B5
Anda, China 113/N2
Andacollo, Arg. 200/C3
Andagua, Peru 198/C4
Andahuaylas, Peru 198/C4
Andāl, India 127/F4
Åndalsnes, Nor. 79/C3
Andalucía (aut. comm.), Sp. 86/C4
Andalusia, Al, US 175/G4
Andalusia (reg.), Sp. 86/C4
Andaman (sea), Asia 125/F5
Andaman (isls.), India 125/F5
Andaman and Nicobar (isls.), India 125/F5
Andamarca, Peru 198/C3
Andamooka, Austl. 155/H4
Andapa, Madg. 149/J6
Andaraí, Braz. 196/B4
Andau, Aus. 85/M3
Andebu, Nor. 80/D2
Andechs, Ger. 99/H2
Andeer, Swi. 99/F4
Andelfingen, Swi. 99/E2
Andelle (riv.), Fr. 94/A5
Andelot-Blancheville, Fr. 98/B1
Andelsbach (riv.), Ger. 99/F2
Andelu, Fr. 72/H5
Andemaka, Madg. 149/H8
Andenne, Belg. 95/E3
Anderlues, Belg. 95/D3
Andermatt, Swi. 99/E4
Andernach, Ger. 95/G3
Anderson (riv.), NW, Can. 164/D2
Anderson, Ak, US 176/J3
Anderson, Ca, US 170/B2
Anderson, In, US 172/C3
Anderson, SC, US 175/H3
Anderson, Tx, US 171/J5
Anderson (inlet), Wa, US 177/B3
Anderson (isl.), Wa, US 177/B3
Andes (mts.), SAm. 189/C5
Andes, Cordillera de los (mts.), SAm. 199/B4
Andevoranto, Madg. 149/J7
Andfjorden (chan.), Nor. 79/F1
Andhra Pradesh (state), India 124/C4
Andijk, Neth. 92/C3
Andijon (pol. reg.), Uzb. 129/F4
Andijon, Uzb. 129/F4
Andikíthira (isl.), Gre. 89/H5
Andilamena, Madg. 149/J7
Andilanatoby, Madg. 149/J7
Andīmeshk, Iran 130/E2
Andíparos (isl.), Gre. 89/J4
Andira, Braz. 197/B2
Ándissa, Gre. 89/J3
Andkhvoy, Afg. 129/E5
Andohajango, Madg. 149/J6
Andong, SKor. 115/E4
Andorf, Aus. 97/G6
Andorno Micca, It. 100/B1
Andorra (ctry.) 87/F1
Andorra, Sp. 87/E2
Andorra la Vella (cap.), And. 84/D5
Andover, Eng, UK 75/E4
Andover, NJ, US 180/D2
Andøy, Nor. 79/F1
Andøya (isl.), Nor. 79/E1
Andradas, Braz. 197/G7
Andradina, Braz. 197/B2
Andraitx, Sp. 87/G3
Andramasina, Madg. 149/H7
Andranolava, Madg. 149/H8
Andranomavo (riv.), Madg. 149/H7
Andranopasy, Madg. 149/G8
Andreanof (isls.), Ak, US 176/C6
Andrelândia, Braz. 197/J6
Andrespol, Pol. 83/K3
Andrésy, Fr. 72/J5
Andrezel, Fr. 72/L6
Andria, It. 88/E2
Andriba, Madg. 149/H7
Andringitra (mts.), Madg. 149/H8
Andrítsaina, Gre. 89/G4
Androka, Madg. 149/H9
Androntany (cape), Madg. 149/J6
Andros (isl.), Bahm. 183/F3
Ándros, Gre. 89/J4
Ándros (isl.), Gre. 89/J4
Androscoggin (riv.), Me,NH, US 173/G2
Andújar, Sp. 86/C3
Aneby, Swe. 80/F3
Anecón Grande (peak), Arg. 200/C4
Anegada (bay), Arg. 200/E4
Anegada (isl.), UK 183/J4
Anegada Passage (chan.), NAm. 183/J4
Aného, Togo 145/F5
Aneityum (isl.), Van. 158/F7
Añelo, Arg. 200/C3
Aneto, Pico de (peak), Sp. 87/F1
Anfu, China 125/K2
Ang Nam Ngum (res.), Laos 125/H4
Ang Thong, Thai. 120/C3
Angamos (pt.), Chile 199/B1
Angara (riv.), Rus. 109/J4
Angaston, Austl. 155/H5
Angel (riv.), Ger. 93/E5
Ángel (falls), Ven. 195/F3
Angeles, Phil. 121/D4
Angeles National Forest, Ca, US 178/B1
Ängelholm, Swe. 80/E3
Angelholm (int'l arpt.), Swe. 80/E3
Angelina (riv.), Tx, US 171/J5
Angeln (reg.), Ger. 82/E1
Angelus (lake), Mi, US 177/F6
Angera, It. 100/B1
Ångermanalven (riv.), Swe. 79/E2
Angermünde, Ger. 83/H2
Angers, Fr. 84/C3
Anghiari, It. 101/F5
Angical do Piauí, Braz. 196/B2
Angicos, Braz. 196/C2
Angkor (ruin), Camb. 120/C3
Anglem (mt.), NZ 159/R12
Anglès, Sp. 87/G2
Anglesea, Austl. 157/C3
Anglesey (isl.), Wal, UK 76/D5
Anglet, Fr. 84/C5
Angleton, Tx, US 171/J5
Anglin (riv.), Fr. 84/D3
Angoche, Moz. 147/G4
Angol, Chile 200/B3
Angola (ctry.) 147/C3
Angola, In, US 172/C3
Angoon, Ak, US 176/M4
Angostura (res.), Mex. 182/C4
Angostura, Mex. 184/C3
Angoulême, Fr. 84/D4
Angra do Heroísmo, Azor., Port. 87/S12
Angra dos Reis, Braz. 197/J7
Angren, Uzb. 129/F4
Anguilla (isl.), UK 183/N8
Anguillara Veneta, It. 101/E2
Angus (pol. reg.), Sc,UK 78/C3
Angutikada (peak), Ak, US 176/G2
Anhanduí (riv.), Braz. 193/H8
Anhée, Belg. 95/D3
Anholt (isl.), Den. 80/D3
Anhui (prov.), China 113/L5
Ani, Japan 118/B4
Aniak, Ak, US 176/G3
Aniakchak (crater), Ak, US 176/G4
Aniakchak Nat'l Mon. and Prsv., Ak, US 176/F4
Aniche, Fr. 94/C3
Animas (riv.), Co,NM, US 170/F3
Ánimas, Punta De Las (pt.), Mex. 184/B2
'Ānīn, Isr. 133/G6
Anina, Rom. 90/E3
Aniva (cape), Rus. 113/R2
Aniva (bay), Rus. 118/C1
Anivorano, Madg. 149/J7
Anizy-le-Château, Fr. 94/C4
Anjalankoski, Fin. 81/M1
Anjār, India 131/K4
Anjō, Japan 119/M6
Anjou (reg.), Fr. 84/C3
Anjou, Qu, Can. 173/N6
Anjouan (isl.), Com. 149/H6
Anjozorobe, Madg. 149/H7
Anju, NKor. 115/C3
Ankang, China 112/J5
Ankara (cap.), Turk. 132/C2
Ankara (prov.), Turk. 132/C1
Ankaramena, Madg. 149/H8
Ankaratra (mass.), Madg. 149/H7
Ankarsrum, Swe. 80/G3
Ankavandra, Madg. 149/H7
Ankazoabo, Madg. 149/H8
Ankazobe, Madg. 149/H7
Ankazomborona, Madg. 149/H7
Ankazomiriotra, Madg. 149/H7
Ankerika, Madg. 149/H6
Ankililoka, Madg. 149/G8
Ankilizato, Madg. 149/H8
Anklam, Ger. 80/E5
Ankum, Ger. 93/E3
Anlong, China 125/J2
Anloo, Neth. 92/D2
Anlu, China 114/C5
Anma (isl.), SKor. 115/D5
Ann (cape), Ma, US 173/G3
Ann Arbor, Mi, US 172/D3
Anna (lake), Va, US 172/E4
Anna Bay, Austl. 157/E2
Anna Pavlowna, Neth. 92/B3
Anna Pink (bay), Chile 200/B5
Anna Regina, Guy. 195/G3
Annaba, Alg. 142/K6
Annaba (prov.), Alg. 142/K6
Annaberg-Buchholz, Ger. 97/G1
Annaclone, NI, UK 76/B3
Annai, Guy. 195/G4
Annaka, Japan 119/B1
Annalong, NI, UK 76/C3
Annan, Sc, UK 77/E2
Annan (riv.), Sc, UK 78/C6
Annandale, Va, US 180/A6
Annandale, NJ, US 180/D2
Annapolis (cap.), Md, US 180/B6
Annapurna (peak), Nepal 126/D1
Annbank Station, Sc, UK 78/B6
Anne (mt.), Austl. 157/C4
Anne Arundel (co.), Md, US 180/B6
Annean (lake), Austl. 151/A3
Annecy, Fr. 98/C6
Annecy (lake), Fr. 98/C6
Annecy-le-Vieux, Fr. 98/C6
Annemasse, Fr. 98/C5
Annet-sur-Marne, Fr. 72/L5
Annette, Ak, US 176/M4
Annezin, Fr. 94/B2
Anniston, Al, US 175/G3
Annobón (isl.), EqG. 135/C5
Annonay, Fr. 84/F4
Annville, Pa, US 180/B3
Annweiler, Ger. 95/G5
Anō, Japan 119/K6
Áno Viánnos, Gre. 89/J5
Anoia (riv.), Sp. 87/K7
Anoka, Mn, US 169/K4
Anosibe An' Ala, Madg. 149/J7
Ânou-Zeggarene (riv.), Niger 145/G2
Anould, Fr. 98/C1
Anóyia, Gre. 89/J5
Anping, China 114/C3
Anqiu, China 114/D3
Anren, China 125/K2
Anrhomer (peak), Mor. 140/D3
Anröchte, Ger. 93/F5
Ans, Belg. 95/E2
Ansai, China 114/B3
Ansan, SKor. 115/F7
Ansbach, Ger. 96/D4
Anse-à-Galets, Haiti 187/H2
Anse-d'Hainault, Haiti 187/H2
Anse Rouge, Haiti 187/H2
Ansfelden, Aus. 97/H6
Anshan, China 115/B2
Anshun, China 125/J2
Anson, Tx, US 171/H4
Ansŏng, SKor. 115/D4
Ansongo, Mali 145/F3
Ant (riv.), Eng, UK 75/H1
Ant (isl.), Anti. 158/E4
Anta, Peru 198/C4
Antabamba, Peru 198/C4
Antakya, Turk. 133/E1
Antalaha, Madg. 149/J6
Antalya (prov.), Turk. 132/B2
Antalya (int'l arpt.), Turk. 133/B1
Antalya, Turk. 133/B1
Antalya, Gulf of (gulf), Turk. 133/B1
Antanambao Manampotsy, Madg. 149/J7
Antananarivo (prov.), Madg. 149/H7
Antananarivo (cap.), Madg. 149/H7
Antanifotsy, Madg. 149/H7
Antanimieva, Madg. 149/G8
Antanimora, Madg. 149/H9
Antar (peak), Alg. 141/E3
Antarctic (pen.), Ant. 202/W
Antarctic Circle 202/Z
Antarctica (cont.) 160
Antas, Braz. 196/C3
Antas, Rio das (riv.), Braz. 197/B4
Antella, It. 101/E5
Antelope (isl.), Ut, US 179/J12
Antelope Center, Ca, US 178/C1
Antequera, Sp. 86/C4
Antes Fort, Pa, US 180/A1
Anthering, Aus. 97/G7
Anthony, NM, US 170/F4
Anti-Atlas (mts.), Mor. 138/C2
Anti-Lebanon (mts.), Leb. 133/D3
Antibes, Fr. 85/G5
Anticosti, Île d' (isl.), Qu, Can. 165/K4
Antiesen (riv.), Aus. 97/G6
Antifer, Cap d' (cape), Fr. 84/D2
Antigo, Wi, US 169/L4
Antigonish, NS, Can. 173/J2
Antigua, Canl., Sp. 140/B3
Antigua (isl.), Anti. 183/N8
Antigua and Barbuda (ctry.) 183/N8
Antigua Guatemala, Guat. 186/D3
Antiguo Morelos, Mex. 185/F4
Antilly, Fr. 72/L4
Antioquia, Col. 194/C3
Antioquia (dept.), Col. 194/C3
Antipodes (isls.), NZ 65/T8
Antisana (vol.), Ecu. 194/B5
Antlers, Ok, US 171/J4
Antofagasta, Chile 199/B1
Antoing, Belg. 94/C2
Antokonosy Manambondro, Madg. 149/H8
Antón, Pan. 194/A2
Antón Lizardo, Mex. 185/P7
Anton Lizardo (pt.), Mex. 185/P7
Antongil (bay), Madg. 149/J7
Antonia, Mo, US 179/G9
Antonibe, Madg. 149/H6
Antoniesberg (peak), SAfr. 148/C4
Antonina, Braz. 197/B3
Antonina do Norte, Braz. 196/C2
Antônio Carlos, Braz. 197/K6
Antonito, Co, US 174/B2
Antonovo, Bul. 91/H4
Antony, Fr. 72/J5
Antrim, NI, UK 76/B2
Antrim (mts.), NI, UK 76/B1
Antrim (dist.), NI, UK 76/B2
Antronapiana, It. 98/E5
Antsalova, Madg. 149/H7
Antsambalahy, Madg. 149/J6
Antsenavolo, Madg. 149/J8
Antsirabe, Madg. 149/H7
Antsirañana, Madg. 149/J6
Antsiranana (prov.), Madg. 149/J6
Antsohihy, Madg. 149/H6
Antuco (vol.), Chile 200/C3
Antulai (mtn.), Malay. 123/E3
Antwerp (Deurne) (int'l arpt.), Belg. 92/B6
Antwerpen, Belg. 92/B6
Anūpgarh, India 128/B5
Anūpshahr, India 126/B1
Anuradhapura, SrL. 124/D6
Anvik, Ak, US 176/F3
Anvil Peak (vol.), Ak, US 176/B6
Anxi, China 121/C2
Anxi, China 112/G3
Anyang, China 114/C3
Anyang, SKor. 115/F7
A'nyêmaqên (mts.), China 112/G4
Anyi, China 114/B4
Anyuan, China 121/C2
Anza (riv.), It. 98/E6
'Anzah, WBnk. 133/G7
Anze, China 114/C3
Anzegem, Belg. 94/C2
Anzhero-Sudzhensk, Rus. 106/J4
Anzin, Fr. 94/C3
Anzing, Ger. 97/E6
Anzio, It. 88/C2
Anzoátegui, Ven. 194/D2
Anzoátegui (state), Ven. 195/E2
Anzoátegui (int'l arpt.), Ven. 195/E2
Anzola dell'Emilia, It. 101/E3
Ao Kham (pt.), Thai. 120/B4
Ao Phangnga NP, Thai. 120/B4
Aoba (isl.), Van. 158/F6
Aoga (isl.), Japan 117/F4
Aogaki, Japan 119/H5
Aoiz, Sp. 86/E1
Aomori (pref.), Japan 118/B3
Aomori, Japan 118/B3
Aonla, India 126/B1
Aoral (peak), Camb. 120/D3
Āos, Gre. 89/J4
Aosta, It. 85/G4
Aosta, Valle d' (valley), It. 100/A1
Aoudaghast (ruin), Mrta. 144/C2
Aouk, Bahr (riv.), Chad 139/K6
Aoukar (pol. reg.), Mrta. 138/D4
Aoulef, Alg. 141/F4
Aoyama, Japan 119/K6
Apache (mts.), Tx, US 174/B4
Apache (peak), Az, US 179/R18
Apalachicola, Fl, US 175/G4
Apan, Mex. 185/L7
Apaporis (riv.), Col. 192/D3
Aparados da Serra, PN de, Braz. 197/B4
Aparecida, Braz. 197/C2
Aparecida do Taboado, Braz. 197/B2
Aparición, Ven. 194/D2
Aparri, Phil. 121/D4
Apartadó, Col. 194/B3
Apátfalva, Hun. 90/E2
Apatin, Serb. 90/D3
Apatity, Rus. 102/G2
Apatzingán de la Constitución, Mex. 184/E5
Apaxco, Mex. 185/K7
Apaxtla de Castrejon, Mex. 185/F5
Apeldoorn, Neth. 92/C4
Apelern, Ger. 93/G4
Apen, Ger. 93/E2
Apennines (mts.), It. 69/F4
Apensen, Ger. 93/G2
Aphrodisias (ruin), Turk. 132/B2
Api (peak), Indo. 123/E5
Api (cape), Indo. 123/F4
Api (cape), Indo. 122/C3
Apia (cap.), Samoa 159/H6
Apiacás, Serra dos (mts.), Braz. 193/G6
Apiaí, Braz. 197/B3
Apizaco, Mex. 185/L7
Aplao, Peru 198/C5
Apo (mt.), Phil. 121/E6
Apodi, Braz. 196/C2
Apodi (riv.), Braz. 196/C2
Apollo Bay, Austl. 157/B3
Apollonía, Gre. 89/J4
Apolo, Bol. 198/D4
Aporé (riv.), Braz. 193/H7
Apore (riv.), Braz. 197/B1
Apostle (isls.), Wi, US 169/L4
Apostle Islands Nat'l Lakeshore, Wi, US 169/L4
Apóstoles, Arg. 199/E2
Apostolos Andreas (cape), Cyp. 133/D2
Apoteri, Guy. 195/G3
Appalachian (mts.), US 167/K4
Appen, Ger. 93/G1
Appennino Ligure (mts.), It. 85/H4
Appennino Tosco-Emiliano (mts.), It. 85/J4
Appennino Umbro-Marchigiano (mts.), It. 85/K5
Appenweier, Ger. 98/D1
Appenzell, Swi. 99/F3
Appenzell (canton), Swi. 99/F3
Appignano, It. 101/G6
Appingedam, Neth. 92/D2
Apple Valley, Ca, US 178/C1
Appleton, NY, US 173/S9
Aprica, It. 99/G5
Aprica, Passo dell' (pass), It. 99/G5
Aprilia, It. 88/C2
Apriltsi, Bul. 89/J1
Apsheronsk, Rus. 104/F3
Apsley Gorge NP, Austl. 157/E1
Apua (pt.), Hi, US 166/U11
Apucarana, Braz. 197/B2
Apuiarés, Braz. 196/C1
Apure (riv.), Ven. 192/E2
Apure (prov.), Ven. 194/D3
Apurímac (dept.), Peru 198/C4
Apurímac (riv.), Peru 189/B4
Aqaba (gulf), Asia 109/B7
Aqmola (obl.), Kaz. 129/E2
'Aqrabah, WBnk. 133/D3
'Aqrah, Iraq 132/E2
Aqsay, Kaz. 105/K2
Aqtaū, Kaz. 105/J4
Aqtöbe, Kaz. 129/C2
Aqtöbe (int'l arpt.), Kaz. 129/C2
Aqtöbe (obl.), Kaz. 129/C3
Aquanaval (riv.), Mex. 184/E3
Aquaro-Guariquito, PN, Ven. 192/E2
Aquia, Peru 198/B3
Aquidauana, Braz. 193/G8
Aquidauana (riv.), Braz. 193/G8
Aquila, Swi. 99/E5
Aquileia, It. 101/G1
Aquiles Serdán, Mex. 184/D2
Aquin, Haiti 187/H2
Aquiraz, Braz. 196/C1
Aquitaine (pol. reg.), Fr. 84/C4
Ar-Asgat, Mong. 112/J2
Ar Horqin Qi, China 114/E2
Ar Ramādī, Iraq 132/E3
Ar Ramthā, Jor. 133/D3
Ar Raqqah, Syria 132/D3
Ar Raqqah (prov.), Syria 132/D2
Ar Rastan, Syria 133/E2
Ar Rayyān, Qatar 130/F3
Ar Riyāḍ (Riyadh) (cap.), SAr. 130/E4
Ar Rumaythah, Iraq 132/F4
Ar Ruṣayfah, Jor. 133/E3
Ar Ruṭbah, Iraq 132/E3
Ara (riv.), Japan 117/F2
Arab, Al, US 175/G3
'Arab, Baḥr al (riv.), Sudan 139/L6
Araban, Turk. 132/D2
Arabi, La, US 179/Q17
Arabian (sea), Asia 109/F8
Arabian (des.), Egypt 139/M2
Arabian (pen.), SAr. 130/D3
Araç, Turk. 104/E4
Araç (riv.), Turk. 104/E4
Araca, Bol. 192/E7
Araça (riv.), Braz. 195/F4
Aracaju, Braz. 196/C3
Aracataca, Col. 194/C2
Aracati, Braz. 196/C2
Araçatuba, Braz. 197/B2
Aracena, Sp. 86/B4
Araci, Braz. 196/C3
Aračinovo, FYROM 89/G1
Aracoiaba, Braz. 196/C2
Aracruz, Braz. 197/D1
Araçuaí, Braz. 196/B5
Araçuaí (riv.), Braz. 196/B5
Arad, Rom. 90/E2
Arad (prov.), Rom. 90/E2
'Arad, Isr. 133/D4
Ārādān, Iran 130/F1
Arafura (sea), Austl.,Indo. 158/C5
Aragarças, Braz. 193/H7
Aragats (peak), Arm. 105/H4
Aragón (aut. comm.), Sp. 87/E2
Aragón (riv.), Sp. 87/E1
Aragua (state), Ven. 195/E2
Araguaia (riv.), Braz. 189/D3
Araguaia, PN do, Braz. 193/H6
Araguaiana, Braz. 193/H7
Araguaína, Braz. 193/J5
Araguari, Braz. 197/B1
Araguari (riv.), Braz. 193/H3
Araguatins, Braz. 193/J5
Arai, Japan 117/F2
Araioses, Braz. 196/B1
Arāk, Iran 130/E2
Arakamchechan (isl.), Rus. 176/D3
Arakan (mts.), Myan. 125/F3
Arakawa, Japan 119/C2
Arákhthos (riv.), Gre. 89/G3
Araklı, Turk. 132/D1
Aral (sea), Asia 129/C3
Aral, Kaz. 129/D3
Aral Mangy Qaraqumy (des.), Kaz. 129/D3
Aralık, Turk. 132/F2
Aralsor (lake), Kaz. 105/H2
Aramac, Austl. 156/B3
Arāmbāgh, India 127/F4
Aran (isls.), Ire. 73/P10
Aran Fawddwy (peak), Wal, UK 76/E6
Aranda de Duero, Sp. 86/D2
Arandelovac, Serb. 90/E3
Arani, India 124/C5
Aranjuez, Sp. 86/D2
Aransas Pass, Tx, US 174/D5
Arantina, Braz. 197/J6
Aranuka (isl.), Kiri. 158/G5
Arapiraca, Braz. 196/C3
Arapiuns (riv.), Braz. 195/H5
Arapongas, Braz. 197/B2
'Ar'ara, Isr. 133/G7
Araranguá, Braz. 197/B4
Araraquara, Braz. 197/B2
Araras, Braz. 197/C2
Ararat, Austl. 157/B3
Arari, Braz. 196/A1
Arāria, India 127/F2
Araripe, Chapada do (uplands), Braz. 196/B2
Araripina, Braz. 196/B2
Aras (riv.), Iran 105/H5
Aratane (well), Mrta. 144/C2
Aratoca, Col. 194/C3
Arauá (riv.), Braz. 192/F4
Arauca, Col. 194/D3
Arauca (riv.), Col.,Ven. 195/E3
Arauca (dept.), Col. 194/D3
Araucária, Braz. 197/B3
Arauco, Chile 200/B3
Arauquita, Col. 194/D3
Araure, Ven. 194/D2
Aravis, Col des (pass), Fr. 98/C6
Arawa, PNG 158/E5
Arawale Nat'l Rsv., Kenya 146/D3
Araxá, Braz. 197/C1
Araya (pen.), Ven. 195/E2
Ārba Minch', Eth. 139/N6
Arbeca, Sp. 87/F2
Arbīl (gov.), Iraq 132/E3
Arboga, Swe. 80/F2
Arbois, Fr. 98/B4
Arbois, Mont d' (peak), Fr. 98/C6
Arboletes, Col. 194/B2
Arbon, Swi. 99/F2
Arborfield, Sk, Can. 169/H2
Arborg, Mb, Can. 169/J3
Arbrå, Swe. 80/G1
Arbroath, Sc, UK 78/D3
Arc (riv.), Fr. 84/F5
Arc-en-Barrois, Fr. 98/B2
Arc-et-Senans, Fr. 98/B3
Arc-lès-Gray, Fr. 98/B3
Arc-sur-Tille, Fr. 98/B3
Arcachon, Fr. 84/C4
Arcachon, Bassin d' (lag.), Fr. 84/C4
Arcachon, Pointe d' (pt.), Fr. 84/C4
Arcadia, Ca, US 178/F7
Arcadia, Fl, US 175/H5
Arcadia, Ok, US 179/N14
Arcas, Cayos (isl.), Mex. 186/D1
Arcata, Ca, US 168/B5
Arceburgo, Braz. 197/G6
Arcelia, Mex. 185/E5
Arcene, It. 100/C1
Arceto, It. 101/D3
Archena, Sp. 86/E3
Archer City, Tx, US 171/H4
Arches, Fr. 98/C1
Arches NP, Ut, US 170/E3
Archidona, Sp. 86/C4
Archman, Trkm. 105/L5
Arcipelago Toscano (isl.), It. 85/H5
Arcisate, It. 99/E6
Arco, It. 99/G6
Arco, Paso del (pass), Arg. 200/C3
Arcola, It. 100/C4
Arcole, It. 101/E2
Arcos, Braz. 197/C2
Arcos de Jalón, Sp. 86/D2
Arcos de la Frontera, Sp. 86/C4
Arcos de Valdevez, Port. 86/A2
Arcoverde, Braz. 196/C3
Arctic (ocean) 202/U
Arctic (plain), Ak, US 176/F2
Arctic Bay, Nun., Can. 165/H1
Arctic Circle 202/J
Arctic Red (riv.), NW, Can. 176/M2
Arctic Village, Ak, US 176/J2
Arctowski, Pol., Ant. 202/W
Arda (riv.), Bul. 104/C4
Ardabīl, Iran 105/J5
Ardahan, Turk. 132/E1
Ardal, Iran 130/F2
Årdalstangen, Nor. 80/B1
Ardanuç, Turk. 132/E1
Ardèche (riv.), Fr. 84/F4
Ardee, Ire. 76/B4
Arden (mt.), Austl. 155/H5
Arden, De, US 180/C4
Arden, Den. 80/C3
Arden-Arcade, Ca, US 177/M9
Ardennes (for.), Belg. 84/F1

218
Arden – Avalo

Ardennes (dept.), Fr. 95/D4
Ardennes, Canal des (canal), Fr. 95/D4
Ardenno, It. 99/F5
Ardersier, Sc, UK 78/B1
Ardeşen, Turk. 132/E1
Ardesio, It. 99/F6
Ardestān, Iran 130/F2
Ardez, Swi. 99/G4
Ardila (riv.), Sp. 86/B3
Ardino, Bul. 91/G5
Ardivachar (pt.), Sc, UK 73/Q8
Ardle (riv.), Sc, UK 78/C3
Ardlethan, Austl. 157/C2
Ardmore, Ok, US 171/H4
Ardmore, Pa, US 180/C4
Ardnamurchan (pt.), Sc, UK 73/Q8
Ardon, Swi. 98/D5
Ardooie, Belg. 94/C2
Ardres, Fr. 94/A2
Ardrossan, Austl. 155/H5
Ardrossan, Sc, UK 78/B5
Ards (pen.), Sc, UK 76/C3
Ards (dist.), NI, UK 76/C2
Ardsley, NY, US 181/K7
Åre, Swe. 79/E3
Areado, Braz. 197/G6
Arecibo, PR 183/M8
Areia Branca, Braz. 196/C2
Arena (pt.), Ca, US 170/B3
Arena de la Ventana Punta (pt.), Mex. 184/C3
Arenal (vol.), CR 187/E4
Arenápolis, Braz. 193/G6
Arenas de San Pedro, Sp. 86/C2
Arenas, Punta de (pt.), Arg. 201/C7
Arendal, Nor. 80/C2
Arendonk, Belg. 92/C6
Arendtsville, Pa, US 180/A4
Arenig Fawr (peak), Wal, UK 76/E6
Arenys de Mar, Sp. 87/L6
Arenzano, It. 100/B4
Areo, Ven. 195/F2
Areópolis, Gre. 89/H4
Arequipa (dept.), Peru 198/C5
Arequipa, Peru 198/D5
Arequito, Arg. 200/E2
Aresing, Ger. 96/E5
Arévalo, Sp. 86/C2
Arezzo, It. 101/E6
Arezzo (prov.), It. 101/E5
Arga (riv.), Sp. 86/E1
Argalastí, Gre. 89/H3
Argamasilla de Alba, Sp. 86/D3
Argamasilla de Calatrava, Sp. 86/C3
Arganda, Sp. 87/N9
Argegno, It. 99/F6
Argelès-Gazost, Fr. 84/C5
Argelès-sur-Mer, Fr. 84/E5
Argen (riv.), Ger. 99/F2
Argenbühl, Ger. 99/F2
Argens (riv.), Fr. 85/G5
Argenta, It. 101/E3
Argentan, Fr. 84/C2
Argentat, Fr. 84/D4
Argentera (peak), It. 85/G4
Argenteuil, Fr. 72/J5
Argentière, Aiguille d' (peak), Swi. 98/D6
Argentina (ctry.), Arg. 199/C4
Argentina (riv.), It. 100/A5
Argentino (lake), Arg. 201/B6
Argenton-sur-Creuse, Fr. 84/D3
Argentona, Sp. 87/L6
Argeş (prov.), Rom. 91/G3
Argeş (riv.), Rom. 91/G3
Arghandab (riv.), Afg. 131/J2
Argıthanı, Turk. 132/B2
Argolis (gulf), Gre. 89/H4
Argonne (for.), Fr. 82/C4
Argonne National Laboratory, Il, US 177/P16
Árgos, Gre. 89/H4
Árgos Orestikón, Gre. 89/G2
Argostólion, Gre. 89/G3
Arguello (pt.), Ca, US 170/B4
Arguin, Cap d' (cape), Mrta. 140/A5
Argun' (riv.), Rus. 107/M4
Arguut, Mong. 112/H2
Argyle (lake), Austl. 151/B2
Argyll and Bute (pol. reg.), Sc, UK 78/A4
Arhangay (prov.), Mong. 112/G2
Arhreijît (well), Mrta. 140/B5
Århus, Den. 80/D3
Århus (co.), Den. 80/D3
Ariana, Tun. 142/M6
Ariano Irpino, It. 88/D2
Ariari (riv.), Col. 194/C4
Arias, Arg. 200/E2
Arica, Chile 198/D5
Arıcak, Turk. 132/E2
Arid (cape), Austl. 154/D5
Arida, Japan 116/D3
Aridhaía, Gre. 89/H2
Arido (peak), Ca, US 178/A1
Aridol (lake), WSah. 140/B4
Ariège (riv.), Fr. 84/D5
Arifiye, Turk. 91/K5
Ārifwāla, Pak. 128/B4
Arīḩā, Syria 133/E2
Arikaree (riv.), Co, US 171/G3
Arilje, Serb. 90/E4
Arima, Trin. 195/F2
Arinos (riv.), Braz. 193/G6
Arinos, Braz. 196/A4
Arinthod, Fr. 98/B5
Ario de Rosales, Mex. 185/E5
Aripao, Ven. 195/E3
Aripuanā, Braz. 192/G6
Aripuanā (riv.), Braz. 189/C3
Ariquemes, Braz. 192/F5
Arish, Austl. 156/B2
Arismendi, Ven. 194/D2
Arivechi, Mex. 184/C2
Arivonimamo, Madg. 149/H7
Ariza, Sp. 86/D2
Arizona, Arg. 200/D2
Arizona (canal), Az, US 179/R18
Arizona (state), US 170/D4
Arizpe, Mex. 184/C2
Årjäng, Swe. 80/E2
Arjeplog, Swe. 79/F2
Arjona, Sp. 86/C4
Arjona, Col. 194/C2
Arkadelphia, Ar, US 171/J4
Arkaig (lake), Sc, UK 78/A3
Arkalokhórion, Gre. 89/J5
Arkansas (riv.), US 174/E3
Arkansas (state), US 174/E3
Arkansas City, Ar, US 171/K4
Arkansas City, Ks, US 171/H3
Arkanū (peak), Libya 139/K3
Arkhángelos, Gre. 132/B2
Arkhangel'sk (int'l arpt.), Rus. 102/J2
Arkhangel'sk (Archangel), Rus. 102/J2
Arkhangel'skaya Oblast, Rus. 102/H3
Arkhangel'skoye, Rus. 103/W9
Arklow, Ire. 76/B6
Arkona (cape), Ger. 80/E4
Arkonam, India 124/C5
Arkticheskiy Institut (isls.), Rus. 106/H2
Årla, Swe. 80/G2
Arlan (peak), Trkm. 129/B5
Arlanda (int'l arpt.), Swe. 80/G2
Arlanza (riv.), Sp. 86/C1
Arlazón (riv.), Sp. 86/D1
Arlbergpass (pass), Aus. 99/G3
Arles, Fr. 84/F5
Arlesheim, Swi. 98/D3
Arley, Mo, US 179/E5
Arlington, Mn, US 169/K4
Arlington, Ga, US 175/G4
Arlington, Va, US 180/A6
Arlington Heights, Il, US 172/C3
Arló, Hun. 83/L4
Arlon, Belg. 95/E4
Arluno, It. 100/B1
Arly (riv.), Fr. 98/C6
Arly, PN de l', Burk. 145/F4
Arly, Réserve Totale de Faune de l', Burk. 145/F4
Armada, Mi, US 177/G6
Armadale, Sc, UK 78/C5
Armagh (dist.), NI, UK 76/B3
Armagh, NI, UK 76/B3
Armançon (riv.), Fr. 84/F3
Armando Laydner, Reprêsa de (res.), Braz. 197/B2
Armant, Egypt 143/C3
Armavir, Rus. 105/G3
Arme, Cap d' (cape), Fr. 85/G5
Armenia, Col. 192/C3
Armenia (ctry.) 105/H5
Armentières, Fr. 94/B2
Armentières-en-Brie, Fr. 72/M5
Armería, Mex. 184/E5
Armidale, Austl. 157/D1
Armilla, Sp. 86/D4
Armstrong, Arg. 200/E2
Armstrong, BC, Can. 168/D3
Armthorpe, Eng, UK 77/G4
Ārmūr, India 124/C4
Armutlu, Turk. 91/J5
Army Ordnance Museum, Md, US 180/B5
Arnage, Fr. 84/D3
Arnager (int'l arpt.), Den. 80/F4
Arnaía, Gre. 89/H2
Arnaud (riv.), Qu, Can. 165/J3
Arnauti (cape), Cyp. 133/C2
Arnedo, Sp. 86/D1
Arnett, Ok, US 171/H3
Arnhem, Neth. 92/C5
Arnhem Land (reg.), Austl. 151/C2
Arno (riv.), It. 85/J5
Arno (isl.), Mrsh. 158/G4
Arnold, Eng, UK 77/G6
Arnold, Md, US 180/B5
Arnold, Mo, US 179/G9
Arnoldstein, Aus. 85/K3
Arnon (riv.), Fr. 84/E3
Arnouville-lès-Gonesse, Fr. 72/K5
Arnprior, On, Can. 172/E2
Arnsberg, Ger. 93/F6
Arnstadt, Ger. 85/J1
Arnstein, Ger. 96/C3
Arnstorf, Ger. 97/F5
Aro Usu (cape), Indo. 123/H5
Aroab, Namb. 148/B2
Aroche, Sp. 86/B4
Arolsen, Ger. 93/G6
Aron (riv.), Fr. 84/E3
Arona, Canl. 87/X16
Arona, It. 100/B1
Aronde (riv.), Fr. 94/B5
Arorae (isl.), Kiri. 158/G5
Arosa, Swi. 99/F4
Aroser Rothern (peak), Swi. 99/F4
Ærøskøbing, Den. 80/D4
Arpaçay, Turk. 132/E1
Arpajon, Fr. 72/J6
Arpajon-sur-Cère, Fr. 84/E4
Arqalyq, Kaz. 129/E2
Arquata Scrivia, It. 100/B3
Arques, Fr. 94/B2
'Arrābah, WBnk. 133/G7
Arrah, India 127/E3
Arraias (riv.), Braz. 193/H6
Arraias, Braz. 196/A4
Arraiján, Pan. 194/B2
Arran (isl.), Sc, UK 73/R8
Arrancabarba (peak), Nic. 187/E4
Arras, Fr. 94/B3
Arreau, Fr. 84/D5
Arrecife, Canl., Sp. 140/B3
Arrecifes, Arg. 200/E2
Arrée, Monts d' (mts.), Fr. 84/B2
Arriaga, Mex. 186/C2
Arriondas, Sp. 86/C1
Arrochar, Sc, UK 78/B4
Arroio Grande, Braz. 197/A5
Arronville, Fr. 72/J4
Arroscia (riv.), It. 100/B4
Arroux (riv.), Fr. 84/F3
Arrow (riv.), Eng, UK 74/C2
Arrowbear Lake, Ca, US 178/C2
Arroyo de la Luz, Sp. 86/B3
Arroyo Grande, Ca, US 170/B4
Arroyo Hondo (riv.), Ca, US 177/L12
Arroyo Trabuco (riv.), Ca, US 178/C3
Års, Den. 80/C3
Ars-sur-Moselle, Fr. 95/F5
Arsen'yev, Rus. 113/P3
Arsiero, It. 101/E1
Arslanköy, Turk. 133/D1
Arta (gulf), Gre. 89/G3
Árta, Gre. 89/G3
Artá, Sp. 87/G3
Arteaga, Mex. 184/E5
Arteixo, Sp. 86/A1
Artem, Rus. 113/P3
Artemisa, Cuba 187/F1
Artesia, NM, US 171/F4
Artesia, Ca, US 178/F8
Arth, Swi. 99/E3
Arthies, Fr. 72/H4
Arthur (pt.), Austl. 156/C3
Arthur (riv.), Austl. 154/C5
Arthur Kill (riv.), NJ,NY, US 181/J9
Arthur's Pass, NZ 159/S11
Arthur's Pass NP, NZ 159/S11
Artigas, Uru. 199/E3
Artogne, It. 100/D1
Artois (reg.), Fr. 82/A3
Artova, Turk. 132/D1
Artur Nogueira, Braz. 197/F7
Arturo Merino Benitez (Santiago) (int'l arpt.), Chile 200/N8
Artux, China 129/G5
Artvin, Turk. 132/E1
Artvin (prov.), Turk. 132/E1
Aru (isls.), Indo. 123/H5
Arua, Ugan. 146/A2
Aruba (isl.), Aru., Neth. 183/H5
Arucas, Canl., Sp. 140/B3
Arudy, Fr. 84/C5
Arujá, Braz. 197/G8
Arun (riv.), China 127/F2
Arunāchal Pradesh (state), India 125/F2
Arundel, Eng, UK 75/F5
Aruppukkottai, India 124/C6
'Arūrah, WBnk. 133/G7
Arus (cape), Indo. 123/F3
Arusha, Tanz. 146/C3
Arusha (pol. reg.), Tanz. 146/C4
Arusha NP, Tanz. 146/C3
Arutua (isl.), FrPol. 159/L6
Aruwimi (riv.), D.R. Congo 139/K7
Arvada, Co, US 179/B3
Arvayheer, Mong. 112/H2
Arve (riv.), Fr. 98/C6
Arviat, Nun., Can. 164/G2
Arvidsjaur, Swe. 79/F2
Arvika, Swe. 80/E2
Arvin, Ca, US 170/C4
Arvon (mt.), Mi, US 169/L4
Arys', Kaz. 129/E4
Arz (riv.), Fr. 84/B3
Arzachena, It. 88/A2
Arzamas, Rus. 103/K5
Arzbach, Ger. 95/G3
Arzberg, Ger. 97/F2
Ärzen, Ger. 93/G4
Arzew, Alg. 142/E5
Arzignano, It. 101/E1
Arzl im Pitztal, Aus. 99/G3
Arzúa, Sp. 86/A1
Ås, Nor. 80/D2
As, Belg. 95/E1
Aš, Czh. 97/F2
As Sabkhah, Syria 132/D3
Aş Şaff, Egypt 133/B5
Aş Şāfī, Jor. 133/D4
As Sālimīyah, Kuw. 130/E3
As Sallūm, Egypt 139/L1
As Salmān, Iraq 132/F4
As Salţ, Jor. 133/D3
Aş Şanţah, Egypt 133/B4
Aş Şarīḩ, Jor. 133/D3
As Sinbillāwayn, Egypt 133/B4
As Sudd (reg.), Sudan 139/M6
As Sulaymānīyah (gov.), Iraq 132/F3
As Sulaymānīyah, Iraq 132/F3
As Suwaydā' (prov.), Syria 132/D3
As Suwaydā', Syria 133/E3
Aş Şuwayrah, Iraq 132/F3
As Suways, Egypt 143/C2
As Suways (gov.), Egypt 143/C2
Asaba, Nga. 145/G5
Asadābād, Afg. 128/A2
Asadābād, Iran 130/E2
Asagny, PN d', C.d'Iv. 144/D5
Asahan (riv.), Indo. 122/A3
Asahi, Japan 117/G3
Asahi (riv.), Japan 116/C3
Asahi, Japan 119/F1
Asahi, Japan 119/L5
Asahi, Japan 119/M5
Asahi-dake (peak), Japan 118/C2
Asahikawa, Japan 118/C2
Asai, Japan 119/K5
Asaka, Japan 119/D2
Asake (riv.), Japan 119/K5
Asama-yama (peak), Japan 117/F2
Asan (bay), SKor. 115/D4
Asansol, India 127/F4
Asashi-dake (peak), Japan 117/F1
Asashina, Japan 119/A1
Asawanwah (well), Libya 139/J3
Asbach, Ger. 95/G2
Asbach-Bäumenheim, Ger. 96/D5
Asbest, Rus. 103/P4
Asbestos (mts.), SAfr. 148/C3
Asbury Park, NJ, US 180/D3
Ascención, Bol. 192/F7
Ascención (bay), Mex. 182/D4
Ascensión, Mex. 184/D2
Ascensión, Arg. 200/E2
Aschach (riv.), Aus. 97/G6
Aschach an der Donau, Aus. 97/H6
Aschaffenburg, Ger. 96/C3
Aschau am Inn, Ger. 97/F6
Ascheberg, Ger. 93/E5
Aschendorf, Ger. 93/E2
Aschersleben, Ger. 82/F3
Ascoli Piceno, It. 85/K5
Ascoli Satriano, It. 88/D2
Ascona, Swi. 99/E5
Ascope, Peru 198/B2
Åseda, Swe. 80/F3
Āsela, Eth. 139/N6
Åsele, Swe. 79/F2
Asendorf, Ger. 93/G2
Asendorf, Ger. 93/F3
Asenovgrad, Bul. 89/J1
Åseral, Nor. 80/B2
Aserei (peak), It. 100/C3
Asfeld, Fr. 95/D5
Ash, Eng, UK 72/D3
Ash, Eng, UK 72/A3
Ash Shabakah, Iraq 132/E4
Ash Shamal (gov.), Leb. 133/E2
Ash Shāmīyah, Iraq 132/F4
Ash Shāriqah, UAE 131/G3
Ash Sharqāt, Iraq 132/E3
Ash Sharqīyah (state), Sudan 143/C5
Ash Shawbak, Jor. 133/D4
Asha, Nga. 145/F5
Ashanti (uplands), C.d'Iv. 138/E6
Ashanti (pol. reg.), Gha. 145/E5
Asharoken, NY, US 181/M8
Ashbourne, Ire. 76/B4
Ashbourne, Eng, UK 77/G5
Ashburton (riv.), Austl. 151/A3
Ashburton, NZ 159/S11
Ashby (canal), Eng, UK 75/E1
Ashby-de-la-Zouch, Eng, UK 75/E1
Ashcroft, BC, Can. 168/C3
Ashdod, Isr. 133/F8
Asheboro, NC, US 175/J3
Ashern, Mb, Can. 169/J3
Asheville, NC, US 175/H3
Asheweig (riv.), On, Can. 169/M2
Ashford, Austl. 157/D1
Ashford, Eng, UK 75/G4
Ashford, Eng, UK 72/B2
Ashford, Ire. 76/B5
Ashgabat (cap.), Trkm. 129/C5
Ashhurst, NZ 159/T11
Ashibetsu, Japan 118/C2
Ashigawa, Japan 119/B2
Ashikaga, Japan 119/C1
Ashington, Eng, UK 77/G1
Ashino (lake), Japan 119/C3
Ashiwada, Japan 119/B3
Ashiya, Japan 119/H6
Ashiyasu, Japan 119/A2
Ashizuri-misaki (cape), Japan 116/C4
Ashland, Ks, US 171/H3
Ashland, Ky, US 172/D4
Ashland, Oh, US 172/D3
Ashland, Or, US 168/C5
Ashland, Pa, US 180/B2
Ashley, ND, US 169/J4
Ashley, Pa, US 180/C1
Ashmore (reef), Austl. 151/B2
Ashmore and Cartier Islands Territory (dpcy.), Austl. 151/B2
Ashmūn, Egypt 133/B4
Ashoknagar, India 126/A3
Ashoro, Japan 118/C2
Ashqelon, Isr. 133/F8
Ashta, India 124/C3
Ashtabula, Oh, US 172/D3
Ashton, Id, US 168/F4
Ashton, SAfr. 148/M10
Ashton-in-Makerfield, Eng, UK 77/F5
Ashton-under-Lyne, Eng, UK 77/F5
Asia (cont.) 67
Asia, Peru 198/B4
Asiago, It. 99/H6
Asikkala, Fin. 81/L1
Asilah, Mor. 142/A2
Asillo, Peru 198/D4
Asinara (isl.), It. 88/A2
Asinara, Golfo dell' (gulf), It. 88/A2
Asino, Rus. 106/J4
Asipovichy, Bela. 104/D1
'Asīr (mts.), SAr. 130/D5
Asis (cape), Sudan 143/D5
Aşkale, Turk. 132/E2
Askeaton, Ire. 73/P10
Asker, Nor. 80/D2
Askersund, Swe. 80/F2
Askim, Nor. 80/D2
Askim, Swe. 80/D3
Áskion (peak), Gre. 89/G2
Askja (crater), Ice. 79/P6
Askov, Den. 80/C4
Asmara (cap.), Erit. 130/C5
Asnen (lake), Swe. 80/F3
Asnières-sur-Oise, Fr. 72/K4
Asnières-sur-Seine, Fr. 72/J5
Asō, Japan 119/E2
Aso NP, Japan 116/B4
Aso-san (peak), Japan 116/B4
Asola, It. 100/D2
Asolo, It. 101/E1
Āsosa, Eth. 139/M5
Asoteriba (peak), Sudan 143/D4
Aspach, Aus. 97/G6
Aspe, Sp. 87/E3
Aspen, Co, US 170/F3
Aspen Hill, Md, US 180/A5
Aspen Park, Co, US 179/B3
Aspendos (ruin), Turk. 133/B1
Asperg, Ger. 96/C5
Aspermont, Tx, US 171/G4
Aspers, Pa, US 180/A4
Aspetuck (riv.), Ct, US 181/E1
Aspiring (mt.), NZ 159/R11
Asprópirgos, Gre. 89/H3
Asquith, Sk, Can. 168/G2
Assa, Mor. 140/C3
Assa Aguiene (peak), Alg. 141/G5
Assab, Erit. 130/D6
Assaba (pol. reg.), Mrta. 144/C2
Assam (state), India 125/F2
Assaré, Braz. 196/C2
Asse, Belg. 95/D2
Assemini, It. 88/A3
Assen, Neth. 92/D3
Assenede, Belg. 94/C1
Assens, Den. 80/C4
Assens, Den. 80/D3
Assentoft, Den. 80/D3
Assesse, Belg. 95/E3
Assiniboia, Sk, Can. 169/G3
Assiniboine (mt.), BC, Can. 168/E3
Assiniboine (riv.), Mb,Sk, Can. 169/H3
Assinika (lake), Qu, Can. 172/F1
Assis, Braz. 197/B2
Assling, Ger. 97/F6
Asso, It. 100/C1
Assomada, CpV. 135/K10
Astakós, Gre. 89/G3
Astana (cap.), Kaz. 129/F2
Asten, Neth. 92/C6
Asten, Aus. 97/H6
Asti (prov.), It. 100/B3
Asti, It. 85/H4
Astico (riv.), It. 101/E1
Astipálaia, Gre. 132/A2
Astolfo Dutra, Braz. 197/L6
Astorga, Braz. 197/B2
Astoria, Or, US 168/C4
Åstorp, Swe. 80/E3
Astrakhan', Rus. 105/J3
Astrakhanskaya Oblast, Rus. 105/H3
Ástros, Gre. 89/H4
Astudillo, Sp. 86/C1
Asturias (aut. comm.), Sp. 86/B1
Asuka, Japan 119/J7
Asuke, Japan 119/M5
Asunción (cap.), Par. 199/E2
Asuncion (isl.), NMar. 158/D3
Asunción Ixtaltepec, Mex. 182/B4
Asunden (lake), Swe. 80/F3
Aswa (riv.), Ugan. 139/M7
Aswān (gov.), Egypt 143/C4
Aswān, Egypt 143/C3
Aswan High (dam), Egypt 143/C4
Asyūţ (gov.), Egypt 143/B3
Asyūţ, Egypt 143/B3
Aszód, Hun. 91/R9
Aţ Ţafīlah, Jor. 133/D4
Aţ Ţafīlah (gov.), Jor. 133/D4
Aţ Ţā'if, SAr. 130/D4
At Tall, Syria 133/E3
At Tall al Kabīr, Egypt 133/B4
At Ta'mīn (gov.), Iraq 132/E3
Aţ Ţūr, WBnk. 133/G8
Atabapo (riv.), Ven. 195/E4
Atacama (des.), Chile 189/B4
Atacames, Ecu. 194/B4
Atafu (isl.), Tok. 159/H5
Atakpamé, Togo 145/F5
Atalaia, Braz. 196/C3
Atalaia do Norte, Braz. 198/D2
Atalándi, Gre. 89/H3
Atalaya, Peru 198/C3
Atami, Japan 117/F3
Atar, Mrta. 138/C3
Atarfe, Sp. 86/D4
Atarra, India 126/C3
Atas Bogd (peak), Mong. 112/G3
Atascadero, Ca, US 170/B4
Atascosa (co.), Tx, US 179/T21
Atascosa, Tx, US 179/T21
Atatürk (dam), Turk. 132/D2
Atatürk (res.), Turk. 132/D2
Ataturk (int'l arpt.), Turk. 91/J5
Atbara (riv.), Eth. 139/N5
Atbara, Sudan 139/M4
Atbasar, Kaz. 129/E2
Atchafalaya (riv.), La, US 171/K5
Atchafalaya (bay), La, US 171/K5
Atchison, Ks, US 171/J3
Atco, NJ, US 180/D4
Atebubu, Gha. 145/E5
Ateca, Sp. 86/E2
Ateelva (riv.), Nor. 79/G1
Atén, Bol. 198/D4
Atencingo, Mex. 185/L8
Atenco, Mex. 185/Q10
Atenco, Mex. 185/R9
Atengo (riv.), Mex. 184/D4
Atessa, It. 88/D1
Atglen, Pa, US 180/C4
Ath, Belg. 94/C2
Athabasca, Ab, Can. 168/E2
Athabasca (riv.), Ab, Can. 164/E3
Athabasca (lake), Ab,Sk, Can. 164/E3
Athapapuskow (lake), Mb, Can. 169/H2
Āthār Ţulmaythah (Ptolemaïs) (ruin), Libya 139/K1
Athboy, Ire. 73/Q10
Athenry, Ire. 73/P10
Athens (Athínai) (cap.), Gre. 89/N9
Athens, Al, US 175/G3
Athens, Ga, US 175/H3
Athens, Tn, US 175/G3
Athens, Tx, US 171/J4
Atherstone, Eng, UK 75/E1
Atherton, Austl. 156/B2
Atherton, Eng, UK 77/F4
Atherton, Mo, US 179/E5
Athgarh, India 124/E3
Athi (riv.), Kenya 146/C3
Athínai (Athens) (cap.), Gre. 89/N9
Athis-Mons, Fr. 72/K5
Athlone, Ire. 73/Q10
Atholl (for.), Sc, UK 78/B3
Áthos (peak), Gre. 89/J2
Athy, Ire. 73/Q10
Ati, Chad 139/J5
Atibaia, Braz. 197/G8
Atibaia (riv.), Braz. 197/G7
Atico, Peru 198/C5
Atienza, Sp. 86/D2
Atikokan, On, Can. 169/L3
Atil, Mex. 184/C2
Atitlán (lake), Guat. 186/D3
Atiu (isl.), CookIs. 159/K7
Atizapan, Mex. 185/Q10
Atka, Ak, US 176/D5
Atka (isl.), Ak, US 176/C5
Atkarsk, Rus. 105/H2
Atkinson (pt.), NW, Can. 176/M2
Atlacomulco de Fabela, Mex. 185/K7
Atlanta (cap.), Ga, US 175/G3
Atlantic (ocean) 64/G3
Atlantic (co.), NJ, US 180/D4
Atlantic Beach, NY, US 181/L9
Atlantic City, NJ, US 180/D5
Atlantic Highlands, NJ, US 181/J10
Atlantico (dept.), Col. 194/C2
Atlántida, Uru. 201/L11
Atlantique (prov.), Ben. 145/F5
Atlas (mts.), Mor. 138/E1
Atlas (peak), Ca, US 177/K10
Atlas Saharien (mts.), Alg. 138/E1
Atlatlahuaca, Mex. 185/Q10
Atlin, BC, Can. 176/M3
'Atlit, Isr. 133/F6
Atlixco, Mex. 185/L8
Atmore, Al, US 175/G4
Atocha, Bol. 192/E8
Atomium, The, Belg. 95/D2
Atotonilco, Mex. 185/L6
Atouila, 'Erg (des.), Mali 140/D5
Atoyac, Mex. 185/E5
Atoyac (riv.), Mex. 186/B2
Atqasuk, Ak, US 176/G1
Atrai (riv.), Bang. 127/G3
Atrak (riv.), Iran 131/G1
Ätran (riv.), Swe. 80/E3
Atrato (riv.), Col. 192/C2
Atrauli, India 126/B1
Atsugi, Japan 119/C3
Atsumi, Japan 119/M6
Atsumi (pen.), Japan 119/M6
Attalens, Swi. 98/C4
Attalla, Al, US 175/G3
Attapu, Laos 120/D3
Attawapiskat (lake), On, Can. 169/L2
Attawapiskat (riv.), On, Can. 165/H3
Attel (riv.), Ger. 97/F7
Attendorn, Ger. 93/E6
Atteridgeville, SAfr. 148/Q12
Attersee (lake), Aus. 85/K3
Attert, Belg. 95/E4
Attica, Mi, US 177/F5
Attigny, Fr. 95/D5
'Attīl, WBnk. 133/G7
Attock, Pak. 128/B3
Attu, Ak, US 176/A5
Attu (isl.), Ak, US 176/A5
Atuel (riv.), Arg. 199/C4
Atuntaqui, Ecu. 194/B4
Åtvidaberg, Swe. 80/G2
Atwater, Ca, US 170/B3
Atyraū (obl.), Kaz. 129/B3
Atyraū, Kaz. 105/J3
Atyraū (int'l arpt.), Kaz. 105/J3
Au, Swi. 99/F3
Au, Aus. 99/F3
Au in der Hallertau, Ger. 97/E5
Au Sable (riv.), Mi, US 172/C2
Auari (riv.), Braz. 195/E3
Aubange, Belg. 95/E4
Aube (dept.), Fr. 95/D6
Aube (riv.), Fr. 82/C4
Aubenas, Fr. 84/F4
Aubepierre-Ozouer-le-Repos, Fr. 72/L6
Aubergenville, Fr. 72/H5
Aubert (peak), Swi. 98/C4
Aubervilliers, Fr. 72/K5
Aubetin (riv.), Fr. 94/C6
Aubette (riv.), Fr. 94/A5
Aubette de Magny (riv.), Fr. 72/H4
Aubigny-en-Artois, Fr. 94/B3
Aubigny-sur-Nère, Fr. 84/E3
Aubin, Fr. 84/E4
Aubonne, Swi. 98/C5
Auboué, Fr. 95/E5
Aubrac, Monts du (mts.), Fr. 84/E4
Aubrives, Fr. 95/D3
Aubry, Ks, US 179/D6
Auburn, Austl. 155/H5
Auburn, Al, US 175/G3
Auburn, Ca, US 170/B3
Auburn, In, US 172/C3
Auburn, Me, US 173/G2
Auburn, Ne, US 171/J2
Auburn, NY, US 172/E3
Auburn, Pa, US 180/B2
Auburn, Wa, US 168/C4
Auburn Hills, Mi, US 177/F6
Aubusson, Fr. 84/E4
Aucá Mahuida (peak), Arg. 200/C3
Auch, Fr. 84/D5
Auchel, Fr. 94/B3
Auchinleck, Sc, UK 78/B6
Auchterarder, Sc, UK 78/C4
Auchtermuchty, Sc, UK 78/C4
Auchy-lès-Hesdin, Fr. 94/B3
Auckland, NZ 159/S10
Auckland (int'l arpt.), NZ 159/S10
Auckland (isls.), NZ 65/T8
Aude (riv.), Fr. 84/E5
Auderghem, Belg. 95/D2
Audeux (riv.), Fr. 98/C3
Audierne (bay), Fr. 84/A3
Audincourt, Fr. 98/C3
Audo (range), Eth. 139/P6
Audruicq, Fr. 94/B2
Audun-le-Roman, Fr. 95/E5
Audun-le-Tiche, Fr. 95/E5
Aue (riv.), Ger. 93/E2
Aue, Ger. 97/F1
Auer (Ora), It. 99/H5
Auerbach, Ger. 97/F1
Auerbach in der Oberpfalz, Ger. 97/E3
Auersberg (peak), Ger. 97/F2
Aufess (riv.), Ger. 96/E3
Auffargis, Fr. 72/H5
Augathella, Austl. 156/B4
Augher, NI, UK 76/A3
Aughnacloy, NI, UK 76/B3
Aughrim, Ire. 76/B6
Augrabies Falls NP, SAfr. 148/C3
Augrabiesvalle (falls), SAfr. 148/C3
Augsburg, Ger. 96/D6
Augub (peak), Namb. 148/A2
Augusta, Ga, US 175/H3
Augusta (cap.), Me, US 173/G2
Augusta, It. 88/D4
Augusta, Austl. 154/B5
Augusta, NJ, US 180/D1
Augusta, Golfo di (gulf), It. 88/D4
Augustdorf, Ger. 93/F5
Augustenborg, Den. 80/C4
Augusto César Sandino (int'l arpt.), Nic. 186/E3
Augustów, Pol. 81/K5
Augustus (mt.), Austl. 154/C3
Auk Bok (isl.), Myan. 120/B3
Auki, Sol. 158/F5
Aukstatija NP, Lith. 81/M4
Auld (lake), Austl. 151/B3
Aulencia (riv.), Sp. 87/M9
Aulendorf, Ger. 99/F2
Aulla, It. 100/C4
Aulnay-sous-Bois, Fr. 72/K5
Aulnay-sur-Mauldre, Fr. 72/H5
Aulne (riv.), Fr. 84/A2
Aulnoy, Fr. 72/M5
Aulnoye-Aymeries, Fr. 94/C3
Aulnut (int'l arpt.), Fr. 84/E4
Ault, Co, US 179/C1
Ault (peak), Swi. 99/F4
Ault, Fr. 94/A3
Aumale, Fr. 94/A4
Aumetz, Fr. 95/E5
Aumühle, Ger. 93/H1
Aunay-sur-Odon, Fr. 84/C2
Aunette (riv.), Fr. 94/B5
Auneuil, Fr. 94/B5
Auning, Den. 80/D3
Aur (isl.), Mrsh. 158/G4
Aura, NJ, US 180/C4
Aurach, Ger. 96/D4
Aurach (riv.), Ger. 96/D3
Auraiya, India 126/B2
Aurangābād, India 127/E3
Aurangābād, India 131/L5
Auray, Fr. 84/B3
Aureilhan, Fr. 84/D5
Aurich, Ger. 93/E2
Auriflama, Braz. 197/B2
Aurillac, Fr. 84/E4
Aurisina, It. 101/G1
Aurland, Nor. 80/B1
Aurolzmünster, Aus. 97/G6
Aurora, Braz. 196/C2
Aurora, Guy. 195/G3
Aurora, Co, US 179/C3
Aurora, Il, US 171/K2
Aurora, Mo, US 171/J3
Aurora Lodge, Ak, US 176/J3
Aus, Namb. 148/B2
Ausa (riv.), It. 101/G1
Aussillon, Fr. 84/E5
Aust-Agder (co.), Nor. 79/C4
Austin, Nv, US 170/C3
Austin (lake), Austl. 151/A3
Austin (isl.), Nun., Can. 164/G2
Austral (Tubuaï Islands) (isls.), FrPol. 159/K7
Australia (cont.) 109
Australia (ctry.) 109
Australian Alps (range), Austl. 157/C3
Australian Capital Territory (cap. terr.), Austl. 157/D2
Australind, Austl. 154/B5
Austria (ctry.) 85/L3
Austurhorn (pt.), Ice. 79/P7
Auterive, Fr. 84/D5
Authie (riv.), Fr. 84/D1
Autlán de Navarro, Mex. 184/D5
Automne (riv.), Fr. 94/B5
Autreppe, Belg. 94/C3
Autun, Fr. 84/F3
Auvergne (pol. reg.), Fr. 84/E4
Auvers-sur-Oise, Fr. 72/J4
Auvézère (riv.), Fr. 84/D4
Aux Sables (riv.), On, Can. 172/D2
Auxerre, Fr. 84/E3
Auxi-le-Château, Fr. 94/B3
Auxonne, Fr. 98/B3
Auyán-Tepuí (peak), Ven. 195/F3
Auyuittuq NP, Nun., Can. 165/K2
Auzangate (peak), Peru 198/D4
Āvaj, Iran 130/E1
Avallon, Fr. 84/E3
Avalon (pen.), Nf, Can. 165/L4

Avalo – Bande
219

Avalon, Ca, US 178/B4
Avalon, NJ, US 180/D5
Avanne-Aveney, Fr. 98/B3
Avaré, Braz. 197/B2
Avarua, NZ 159/K7
Avdat (ruin), Isr. 133/D4
Avebury Stone Circle, Eng, UK 75/E4
Aveiro, Port. 86/A2
Aveiro (dist.), Port. 86/A2
Aveley, Eng, UK 72/D2
Avelgem, Belg. 94/C2
Avellaneda, Arg. 201/J11
Avellino, It. 88/D2
Avelon (riv.), Fr. 94/A5
Avenal, Ca, US 170/B3
Avenches, Swi. 98/D4
Avenel, NJ, US 181/H9
Avernes, Fr. 72/H4
Aversa, It. 88/D2
Aves (isl.), Ven. 183/J4
Avesnes-le-Comte, Fr. 94/B3
Avesnes-sur-Helpe, Fr. 94/C3
Avesta, Swe. 80/G1
Aveyron (riv.), Fr. 84/D4
Avezzano, It. 88/C1
Avich (lake), Sc, UK 78/A4
Aviemore, Sc, UK 78/C2
Avignon, Fr. 84/F5
Aviḥayil, Isr. 133/F7
Ávila de los Caballeros, Sp. 86/C2
Avilés, Sp. 86/C1
Avio, It. 101/D1
Avion, Fr. 94/B3
Avis, Pa, US 180/A1
Avisio (riv.), It. 99/H5
Avize, Fr. 94/D6
Avlum, Den. 80/C3
Avoca, Austl. 157/C4
Avoca, Austl. 157/B3
Avoca (riv.), Ire. 76/B6
Avoch, Sc, UK 78/B1
Avola, It. 88/D4
Avon (riv.), Eng, UK 74/C6
Avon (riv.), Sc, UK 78/C1
Avon, Fr. 84/E2
Avon (riv.), Fr. 72/L6
Avon Valley NP, Austl. 154/C4
Avon Water (riv.), Sc, UK 78/B5
Avonbeg (riv.), Ire. 76/B6
Avondale, Austl. 157/D2
Avondale, Az, US 179/R19
Avondale, Pa, US 180/C4
Avonlea, Sk, Can. 169/G3
Avonmore (riv.), Ire. 76/B5
Avranches, Fr. 84/C2
Avre (riv.), Fr. 82/B4
Avrillé, Fr. 84/C3
Awa-shima (isl.), Japan 118/A4
A'waj (riv.), Syria 133/E3
Awaji, Japan 119/H6
Awans, Belg. 95/E2
Āwasa, Eth. 139/N6
Āwash, Eth. 139/P6
Āwash Wenz (riv.), Eth. 139/P5
Awaso, Gha. 145/E5
Awat, China 112/D3
Awbārī, Libya 138/H2
Awbārī (des.), Libya 141/H4
Awe (lake), Sc, UK 78/A4
Awjilah, Libya 139/K2
Awka, Nga. 145/G5
Awsīm, Egypt 133/B4
Ax-les-Thermes, Fr. 84/D5
Axamo (int'l arpt.), Swe. 80/F3
Axams, Aus. 99/H3
Axarfjördhur (inlet), Ice. 79/N6
Axel, Neth. 92/A6
Axel Heiberg (isl.), Nun., Can. 165/S7
Axim, Gha. 145/E5
Axios (riv.), Gre. 89/H2
Axis (dam), Wa, US 177/D2
Axminster, Eng, UK 74/D5
Axochiapan, Mex. 185/L8
Ay (riv.), Rus. 103/N5
Ay, Fr. 94/C5
Ayabaca, Peru 198/B2
Ayabe, Japan 119/H5
Ayacucho, Peru 198/C4
Ayacucho (dept.), Peru 198/C4
Ayacucho, Arg. 200/F3
Ayagöz, Kaz. 112/D2
Ayaguz (riv.), Kaz. 112/C2
Ayama, Japan 119/K6
Ayamé I, Barrage d' (dam), C.d'Iv. 144/E5
Ayamé II, Barrage d' (dam), C.d'Iv. 144/E5
Ayamonte, Sp. 86/B4
Ayancık, Turk. 132/C1
Ayanganna (mtn.), Guy. 195/G3
Ayapel, Col. 194/C2
Ayaş, Turk. 132/C1
Ayase, Japan 119/C3
Ayaviri, Peru 198/D4
Āybak, Afg. 129/E5
'Aybāl, Jabal (peak), WBnk. 133/G7
Aybastı, Turk. 132/D1
Aydar Kŏli (lake), Trkm. 129/E4
Aydın, Turk. 132/A2
Aydın (prov.), Turk. 132/B2
Aydıncık, Turk. 132/C1
Aydıncık, Turk. 133/C1
Aydınkent, Turk. 133/B1
Ayer, Swi. 98/D5
Ayers Rock (Uluru) (peak), Austl. 155/F3
Ayeyarwady (div.), Myan. 125/F4
Ayeyarwady (Irrawaddy), (riv.) Myan. 125/G4
Ayiá, Gre. 89/H3
Ayía Paraskeví, Gre. 89/K3
Ayiásos, Gre. 89/K3
Áyios Ioánnis (cape), Gre. 89/J5
Áyios Kírikos, Gre. 89/K4
Áyios Konstandínos, Gre. 89/H3
Áyios Matthaíos, Gre. 89/F3
Áyios Nikólaos, Gre. 89/J5
Aylesbury, Eng, UK 75/F3
Aylesford, Eng, UK 75/G4
Ayllón, Sp. 86/D2
Aylmer (lake), NW, Can. 164/F2
'Ayn al 'Arab, Syria 132/D2
'Ayn Zuwayyah (well), Libya 139/K3
Ayna, Peru 198/C4
Ayon (isl.), Rus. 107/S3
Ayora, Sp. 87/E3
Ayotzintepec, Mex. 186/B2
'Ayoûn 'Abd el Mâlek (well), Mrta. 140/D4
'Ayoûn el 'Atroûs, Mrta. 144/C2
Ayr, Austl. 156/B2
Ayr, Sc, UK 78/B6
Ayr (riv.), Sc, UK 78/B5
Aytré, Fr. 84/C3
Ayubia NP, Pak. 128/B3
Ayutla, Mex. 184/D4
Ayutla de los Libres, Mex. 182/B4
Ayutthaya (ruin), Thai. 120/C3
Ayvacık, Turk. 89/K3
Ayvalık, Turk. 132/A2
Aywaille, Belg. 95/E3
Az Zabadānī, Syria 133/E3
Az Ẓāhirīyah, WBnk. 133/D4
Az Zaqāzīq, Egypt 133/B4
Az Zarqā' (gov.), Jor. 133/E3
Az Zarqā', Jor. 133/E3
Az Zāwiyah, Libya 138/H1
Az Zaydīyah, Yem. 130/D5
Azad Kashmir (terr.), Pak. 128/B3
Azahar (coast), Sp. 87/F3
Azalea, Or, US 168/C5
Azalia, Mi, US 177/E7
Azamgarh, India 126/D2
Azángaro (riv.), Peru 198/D4
Azángaro, Peru 198/D4
Azao (peak), Alg. 141/H4
Azaouâd (phys. reg.), Mali 138/E4
Āẕarān, Iran 130/E1
Āẕarbāyjān-e Gharbī (prov.), Iran 132/F2
A'zāz, Syria 133/E1
Azemmour, Mor. 140/C2
Azerbaijan (ctry.) 105/H4
Azilal, Mor. 140/D3
Azīmganj, India 127/G3
Azogues, Ecu. 194/B5
Azores (dpcy.), Port. 87/R12
Azourki (peak), Mor. 140/D3
Azov, Rus. 104/F3
Azov (sea), Rus.,Ukr. 104/E3
Azoyú, Mex. 186/B2
Azpeitia, Sp. 86/D1
Azrou, Mor. 140/D2
Aztec, NM, US 170/F3
Aztec Ruins Nat'l Mon., NM, US 170/E3
Azua de Compostela, DRep. 183/G4
Azuaga, Sp. 86/C3
Azuara, Sp. 87/E2
Azuay (dept.), Ecu. 194/B5
Azuchi, Japan 119/K5
Azuero, Peninsula de (pen.), Pan. 192/B2
Azuga, Rom. 91/G3
Azul (mtn.), CR 187/E4
Azul (riv.), Guat. 186/D2
Azul, Arg. 200/F3
Azul, Cordillera (mts.), Peru 198/B2
Azuma, Japan 119/E2
Azuma-san (peak), Japan 117/G2
Azumaya-san (peak), Japan 117/F2
Azur, Côte d' (coast), Fr. 85/G5
Azusa, Ca, US 178/C2
Azzaba, Alg. 142/K6
Azzano Decimo, It. 101/F1
Azzano San Paolo, It. 100/C1
Azzate, It. 100/B1
'Azzūn, WBnk. 133/G7

B

Ba (riv.), Viet. 120/E3
Ba Lang An (cape), Viet. 120/E3
Ba Quan (cape), Viet. 120/D4
Baar, Swi. 99/E3
Baarle-Hertog, Belg. 92/B6
Baarle-Nassau, Neth. 92/B6
Baarn, Neth. 92/C4
Bab el Mandeb (str.), Asia 130/D6
Baba (mts.), Afg. 131/J2
Baba (peak), Bul. 89/H1
Baba (pt.), Turk. 91/K5
Baba Burnu (pt.), Turk. 89/K3
Babadag, Rom. 91/J3
Babaeski, Turk. 91/H5
Babahoyo, Ecu. 194/B5
Babai Khola (riv.), Nepal 126/C1
Babakale, Turk. 89/K3
Babar (isls.), Indo. 123/G5
Babatorun, Turk. 133/E1
Babatpur (int'l arpt.), India 126/D3
Babbacombe (bay), Eng, UK 74/C6
Babbitt, Mn, US 169/L4
B'abdā, Leb. 133/D3
Babelthuap (isl.), Palau 158/C4
Babenhausen, Ger. 99/G1
Babenhausen, Ger. 96/B3
Babensham, Ger. 97/F6
Baberu, India 126/C3
Babia (peak), Pol. 104/A2
Babian (riv.), China 125/H3
Bābil (gov.), Iraq 132/F3
Bābil (Babylon) (ruin), Iraq 132/F3
Babīna, India 126/B3
Babinda, Austl. 156/B2
Babine (riv.), BC, Can. 164/D3
Babiogórski NP, Pol. 83/K4
Bābol, Iran 130/F1
Babruysk, Bela. 104/D1
Babuyan (isl.), Phil. 121/D4
Babylon, NY, US 181/E2
Bac Giang, Viet. 120/D1
Bac Lieu, Viet. 120/D4
Bac Ninh, Viet. 125/J3
Bacabal, Braz. 196/A2
Bacadéhuachi, Mex. 184/C2
Bacajá (riv.), Braz. 193/H4
Bacalar, Mex. 186/D2
Bacalar (lag.), Mex. 186/D2
Bacan (isl.), Indo. 123/G4
Bacău, Rom. 91/H2
Bacău (prov.), Rom. 91/H2
Baccarat, Fr. 98/C1
Bacchiglione (riv.), It. 101/E2
Bacchus, Ut, US 179/J12
Bacerac, Mex. 184/C2
Bacharach, Ger. 95/G3
Bachhraon, India 126/B1
Bachíniva, Mex. 184/D2
Back (riv.), Md, US 180/B5
Back (riv.), Nun., Can. 164/F2
Bačka (reg.), Serb. 90/D3
Bačka Palanka, Serb. 90/D3
Bačka Topola, Serb. 90/D3
Bäckefors, Swe. 80/E2
Backnang, Ger. 96/C5
Bacobampa, Mex. 184/C3
Bacolod, Phil. 123/F1
Bács-Kiskun (prov.), Hun. 90/D2
Bácsalmás, Hun. 90/D2
Bacup, Eng, UK 77/F4
Bad (riv.), SD, US 169/H5
Bad Abbach, Ger. 97/F5
Bad Axe, Mi, US 172/D3
Bad Bellingen, Ger. 98/D2
Bad Bergzabern, Ger. 96/A4
Bad Berneck, Ger. 97/E2
Bad Bocklet, Ger. 96/D2
Bad Brambach, Ger. 97/F2
Bad Breisig, Ger. 95/G3
Bad Brückenau, Ger. 96/C2
Bad Buchau, Ger. 99/F1
Bad Camberg, Ger. 96/B2
Bad Doberan, Ger. 80/D4
Bad Driburg, Ger. 93/G5
Bad Dürkheim, Ger. 96/B4
Bad Dürrheim, Ger. 99/E1
Bad Ems, Ger. 95/G3
Bad Endorf, Ger. 97/F7
Bad Essen, Ger. 93/F4
Bad Freienwalde, Ger. 83/H2
Bad Gandersheim, Ger. 93/H5
Bad Goisern, Aus. 85/K3
Bad Grund, Ger. 93/H5
Bad Hall, Aus. 97/H6
Bad Harzburg, Ger. 93/H5
Bad Heilbrunn, Ger. 99/H2
Bad Herrenalb, Ger. 96/B5
Bad Hersfeld, Ger. 85/H1
Bad Hofgastein, Aus. 85/K3
Bad Homburg vor der Höhe, Ger. 96/B2
Bad Honnef, Ger. 95/G2
Bad Hönningen, Ger. 95/G2
Bad Ischl, Aus. 85/K3
Bad Karlshafen, Ger. 93/G5
Bad Kissingen, Ger. 96/D2
Bad Kohlgrub, Ger. 99/H2
Bad König, Ger. 96/C3
Bad Königshofen, Ger. 96/D2
Bad Kreuznach, Ger. 95/G4
Bad Krozingen, Ger. 98/D2
Bad Langensalza, Ger. 93/H6
Bad Lauterberg, Ger. 93/H5
Bad Leonfelden, Aus. 97/H5
Bad Liebenzell, Ger. 96/B5
Bad Lippspringe, Ger. 93/F3
Bad Marienberg, Ger. 95/G2
Bad Mergentheim, Ger. 96/C4
Bad Munder am Deister, Ger. 93/G4
Bad Nauheim, Ger. 96/B2
Bad Nenndorf, Ger. 93/G4
Bad Neuenahr-Ahrweiler, Ger. 95/G2
Bad Neustadt an der Saale, Ger. 96/D2
Bad Oeynhausen, Ger. 93/F4
Bad Orb, Ger. 96/C2
Bad Peterstal-Griesbach, Ger. 98/E1
Bad Plaas, SAfr. 149/E2
Bad Pyrmont, Ger. 93/G5
Bad Ragaz, Swi. 99/F4
Bad Rappenau, Ger. 96/C4
Bad Reichenhall, Ger. 85/K3
Bad Rothenfelde, Ger. 93/F4
Bad Sachsa, Ger. 93/H5
Bad Salzdetfurth, Ger. 93/G4
Bad Salzschlirf, Ger. 96/C1
Bad Salzuflen, Ger. 93/F4
Bad Salzungen, Ger. 82/F3
Bad Sankt-Leonhard im Lavanttal, Aus. 85/L3
Bad Sassendorf, Ger. 93/F5
Bad Schallerbach, Aus. 97/G6
Bad Schwalbach, Ger. 95/H3
Bad Schwartau, Ger. 80/D5
Bad Segeberg, Ger. 80/D5
Bad Soden-Salmünster, Ger. 96/C2
Bad Sooden-Allendorf, Ger. 93/G6
Bad Tölz, Ger. 99/H2
Bad Vilbel, Ger. 96/B2
Bad Vöslau, Aus. 85/M3
Bad Waldsee, Ger. 99/F2
Bad Wildungen, Ger. 93/G6
Bad Wimpfen, Ger. 96/C4
Bad Wimsbach-Neydharting, Aus. 97/G6
Bad Windsheim, Ger. 96/D3
Bad Wörishofen, Ger. 99/G1
Bad Wurzach, Ger. 99/F2
Bad Zell, Aus. 97/H6
Bad Zwischenahn, Ger. 93/F2
Badagara, India 124/C5
Badain Jaran (des.), China 112/H3
Badajoz, Sp. 86/B3
Badalona, Sp. 87/L7
Badalucco, It. 100/A5
Badbergen, Ger. 93/E3
Baddeckenstedt, Ger. 93/H4
Baddomalhi, Pak. 128/C4
Baden, Aus. 85/M2
Baden, Swi. 99/E3
Baden-Baden, Ger. 96/B5
Baden-Württemberg (state), Ger. 85/H2
Badener (peak), Ger. 96/B5
Badenoch (reg.), Sc, UK 78/B3
Badenweiler, Ger. 98/D2
Badgastein, Aus. 85/K3
Badgingarra NP, Austl. 154/B4
Badia Polesine, It. 101/E2
Badiar, PN du, Gui. 144/B3
Badile (peak), It. 99/F5
Badīn, Pak. 131/J4
Badiraguato, Mex. 184/D3
Badlands (plat.), SD, US 169/H5
Badlands NP, SD, US 169/H5
Badonviller, Fr. 98/C1
Badou, Togo 145/F5
Badovinci, Serb. 90/D3
Bādrāh, Pak. 131/J3
Badrah, Iraq 130/E2
Badua (riv.), India 127/F3
Badulla, SrL. 124/D6
Bāduriā, India 127/G4
Baena, Sp. 86/C4
Baependi, Braz. 197/J6
Baerenkopf (peak), Fr. 98/C2
Baesweiler, Ger. 95/F2
Baeza, Sp. 86/D4
Baffa, Pak. 128/B2
Baffin (bay), Can.,Grld. 161/K2
Baffin (isl.), Nun., Can. 165/H1
Baffin (bay), Tx, US 174/D5
Bafia, Camr. 138/H7
Bafilo, Togo 145/F4
Bafing (riv.), Gui. 138/C5
Bafoulabé, Mali 144/C3
Bafoussam, Camr. 138/H6
Bāfq, Iran 131/G2
Bafra, Turk. 132/C1
Bafra (cape), Turk. 132/D1
Bāft, Iran 131/G3
Bag Salt (lake), China 114/B3
Bagaces, CR 187/E4
Bagadó, Col. 194/B3
Bagaha, India 127/E2
Bagamoyo, Tanz. 146/C4
Baganga, Phil. 121/E6
Bagda (mts.), China 112/E3
Bagé, Braz. 199/F3
Bagenkop, Den. 80/D4
Baggao, Phil. 121/D4
Baggy (pt.), Eng, UK 74/B4
Bāgh, Pak. 128/B4
Baghain (riv.), India 126/C3
Baghdād (Baghdad) (cap.), Iraq 132/F3
Bagheria, It. 88/C3
Baghlān, Afg. 131/J1
Bāghpat, India 128/D5
Bağırpaşa (peak), Turk. 132/E2
Bagley, Mn, US 169/K4
Bāgluṅ, Nepal 126/D1
Bāgmati (riv.), India 127/E2
Bāgmati (zone), Nepal 127/E2
Bagn, Nor. 80/C1
Bagnacavallo, It. 101/F4
Bagnasco, It. 100/B4
Bagnères-de-Bigorre, Fr. 84/D5
Bagnères-de-Luchon, Fr. 84/D5
Bagneux, Fr. 72/J5
Bagni di Lucca, It. 100/D4
Bagno a Ripoli, It. 101/E5
Bagnolet, Fr. 72/K5
Bagnoli Irpino, It. 88/D2
Bagnolo Cremasco, It. 100/C2
Bagnolo in Piano, It. 101/D3
Bagnolo Mella, It. 100/D2
Bagnolo San Vito, It. 101/D2
Bagnols-sur-Cèze, Fr. 84/F4
Bagnone, It. 100/C4
Bago, Phil. 121/D5
Bago (Pegu), Myan. 125/G4
Bago (div.), Myan. 125/G4
Bagoe (riv.), Mali 138/D5
Bagolino, It. 100/D1
Bagshot, Eng, UK 72/A3
Bagua Grande, Peru 198/B2
Baguio, Phil. 121/D4
Baguirmi (reg.), Chad 138/J5
Bagzane (peak), Niger 145/H2
Bāh, India 126/B2
Bahādurganj, India 127/F2
Bahādurgarh, India 128/D5
Bahamas, The (ctry.) 183/F2
Bahāwalnagar, Pak. 128/B5
Bahāwalpur, Pak. 128/A5
Bahçe, Turk. 132/D2
Bahçesaray, Turk. 132/E2
Baheri, India 126/B1
Bahi (swamp), Tanz. 146/B4
Bahia (state), Braz. 196/B4
Bahía Asunción, Mex. 184/B3
Bahía Blanca, Arg. 200/E3
Bahía de Caráquez, Ecu. 194/A5
Bahía de los Angeles, Mex. 184/B2
Bahía de Tortugas, Mex. 184/B3
Bahía, Islas de la (isls.), Hon. 182/D4
Bahía Solano, Col. 194/B3
Bahir Dar, Eth. 139/N5
Bahjoi, India 126/B1
Bahlah, Oman 131/G4
Baḩr al 'Arab (riv.), Sudan 139/L6
Baḩr al Milḩ (lake), Iraq 132/E3
Bahraich, India 126/C2
Bahrain (ctry.) 130/F3
Bahrain, Gulf of (gulf), Asia 130/F3
Baia de Aramă, Rom. 91/F3
Baia Mare, Rom. 91/F2
Baia Sprie, Rom. 91/F2
Baïbokoum, Chad 138/J6
Baicheng, China 112/D3
Baicheng, China 113/M2
Băicoi, Rom. 91/G3
Baidong (lake), China 114/D5
Baie-Comeau, Qu, Can. 173/G1
Baie-Saint-Paul, Qu, Can. 173/G2
Baienfurt, Ger. 99/F2
Baiersbronn, Ger. 96/B5
Baiersdorf, Ger. 96/E3
Baigorrita, Arg. 200/E2
Baigou (riv.), China 114/G7
Baihar, India 126/C4
Baihua (mtn.), China 114/G7
Ba'ījī, Iraq 132/E3
Baikunthpur, India 126/D4
Bailadores, Ven. 194/D2
Baildon, Eng, UK 77/G4
Băile Govora, Rom. 91/G3
Băile Herculane, Rom. 90/F3
Băile Olăneşti, Rom. 91/G3
Băile Tuşnad, Rom. 91/G2
Bailén, Sp. 86/D3
Băileşti, Rom. 91/F3
Bailieborough, Ire. 73/Q10
Bailleul, Fr. 94/B2
Bailong (riv.), China 112/H5
Bailu (riv.), China 114/C4
Baima, China 112/H5
Bain (riv.), Eng, UK 77/H5
Bainang, China 127/G1
Bainbridge, Ga, US 175/G4
Bainbridge, Pa, US 180/B3
Bainbridge (isl.), Wa, US 177/B2
Bainbridge Naval Training Sta., Md, US 180/B4
Baingoin, China 112/E5
Bains-les-Bains, Fr. 98/C2
Bairāgnia, India 127/E2
Baird (inlet), Ak, US 176/F3
Baird, Tx, US 171/H4
Bairin Youqi, China 113/L3
Bairnsdale, Austl. 157/C3
Baïse (riv.), Fr. 84/D5
Baixa da Banheira, Port. 87/P10
Baixa Grande, Braz. 196/B4
Baixiang, China 114/C3
Baixo Guandu, Braz. 197/D1
Baiyin, China 112/H4
Baiyu (mts.), China 114/B3
Baiyun (int'l arpt.), China 121/B3
Baja (pt.), Mex. 184/B2
Baja, Hun. 90/D2
Baja (pt.), Chile 201/B6
Baja California (state), Mex. 184/B2
Baja California (pen.), Mex. 184/B2
Baja California Sur (state), Mex. 184/B3
Bajánsenye, Hun. 85/M3
Bajestān, Iran 131/G2
Bājil, Yem. 130/D5
Bajina Bašta, Serb. 90/D4
Bajmbat (mt.), Austl. 157/E1
Bajmok, Serb. 90/D3
Bajo Boquete, Pan. 187/F4
Bajo de Gualicho (plain), Arg. 199/C5
Bajram Curri, Alb. 89/G1
Bakanas (riv.), Kaz. 129/G3
Bakau, Gam. 144/A3
Bakayan (peak), Indo. 123/E3
Bakel, Sen. 144/B3
Baker (lake), Nun., Can. 164/G2
Baker (riv.), Chile 201/B5
Baker (isl.), Pac., US 159/H4
Baker, La, US 171/K5
Baker, Mt, US 169/G4
Baker (mt.), Wa, US 168/C3
Baker City, Or, US 168/D4
Baker Lake, Nun., Can. 164/G2
Bakersfield, Ca, US 170/C4
Bakhchysaray, Ukr. 104/E3
Bakhmach, Ukr. 104/E2
Bākhtarān, Iran 130/E2
Bakhtiyārpur, India 127/E3
Bakhuis (mts.), Sur. 195/G4
Bakkaflói (bay), Ice. 79/P6
Baklan, Turk. 132/B2
Bakonyszombathely, Hun. 90/C2
Bakora Corridor Game Rsv., Ugan. 146/B2
Bakovský Potok (riv.), Czh. 97/G2
Bakoye (riv.), Gui. 144/C4
Baku (cap.), Azer. 105/J4
Baku (int'l arpt.), Azer. 105/J4
Balâ, Turk. 132/C2
Bala, Wal, UK 76/E6
Balabac, Phil. 123/E2
Balabac (str.), Malay.,Phil. 123/E2
Balabac (isl.), Phil. 123/E2
Ba'labakk, Leb. 133/E2
Bālāghāt, India 126/C5
Balaguer, Sp. 87/F2
Balaïtous (peak), Fr. 84/C5
Balaka, Malw. 147/F3
Balakhna, Rus. 103/J4
Balaklava, Austl. 155/H5
Balakovo, Rus. 105/H1
Bal'amā, Jor. 133/E3
Bălan, Rom. 91/G2
Balancán, Mex. 186/D2
Balanga, Phil. 121/D5
Bālāngir, India 124/D3
Balao, Ecu. 198/B1
Balarāmpur, India 127/F4
Balashikha, Rus. 103/W9
Balashov, Rus. 105/G2
Balasore (Baleshwar), India 124/E3
Balassagyarmat, Hun. 83/K4
Balaton (lake), Cro. 90/C2
Balatonföldvár, Hun. 90/C2
Balatonfüred, Hun. 90/C2
Balatonszabadi, Hun. 90/D2
Balatonszentgyörgy, Hun. 90/C2
Balbina (res.), Braz. 189/D3
Balbriggan, Ire. 76/B4
Balcarce, Arg. 200/F3
Balcary (pt.), Sc, UK 76/E2
Balchik, Bul. 91/J4
Balclutha, NZ 159/R12
Balcones Escarpment (plat.), Tx, US 179/T20
Balcones Heights, Tx, US 179/T21
Bald (pt.), Austl. 154/C5
Bald Eagle Mtn. (mtn.), Pa, US 180/A1
Bald Rock NP, Austl. 157/E1
Baldock, Eng, UK 75/F3
Baldwin, NY, US 181/L9
Baldwin Harbour, NY, US 181/L9
Baldwin Park, Mo, US 179/E6
Baldwin Park, Ca, US 178/G7
Baldy (mtn.), Mb, Can. 169/H3
Baldy Beacon (peak), Belz. 186/D2
Bale Mountains NP, Eth. 139/N6
Baleares (Balearic) (isls.), Sp. 87/G3
Baleia, Ponta da (pt.), Braz. 196/C5
Baleine, Grand Rivière de la (riv.), Qu, Can. 165/J3
Baleine, Petite Rivière de la (riv.), Qu, Can. 165/J3
Baleine, Rivière à la (riv.), Qu, Can. 165/K3
Balen, Belg. 95/E1
Baler, Phil. 121/D4
Balerna, Swi. 99/F6
Balesa (riv.), Kenya 146/C2
Baleshwar (Balasore), India 124/E3
Balfour, SAfr. 148/E2
Balfron, Sc, UK 78/B4
Balgatay, Mong. 112/G2
Balhannah, Austl. 155/M8
Bali (sea), Indo. 122/D5
Bali (isl.), Indo. 122/D5
Bāli Chak, India 127/F4
Balice (int'l arpt.), Pol. 83/K3
Baliem (riv.), Indo. 123/J4
Balıkesir, Turk. 132/A2
Balıkesir (prov.), Turk. 132/A2
Balikpapan, Indo. 123/E4
Balimbing, Phil. 123/E2
Baling, Malay. 125/H6
Balingasag, Phil. 121/D6
Balinge, Swe. 80/G2
Balingen, Ger. 99/E1
Balk, Neth. 92/C3
Balkan (pol. reg.), Trkm. 129/B4
Balkan (mts.), Bul.,Serb. 69/F3
Balkhash (lake), Kaz. 109/G5
Ballagan (pt.), Ire. 76/B4
Ballaghaderreen, Ire. 73/P10
Ballangen, Nor. 79/F1
Ballantrae, Sc, UK 76/C1
Ballarat, Austl. 157/B3
Ballard (lake), Austl. 151/B3
Ballarpur, India 124/C4
Ballater, Sc, UK 78/C2
Ballaugh, IM, UK 76/D3
Ballens, Swi. 98/C4
Balleny (isls.), Ant. 202/L
Ballia, India 127/E3
Ballina, Austl. 157/E1
Ballinamallard, NI, UK 73/Q9
Ballinasloe, Ire. 73/P10
Ballinderry (riv.), NI, UK 76/B2
Ballinger, Tx, US 171/H5
Ballingry, Sc, UK 78/C4
Ballinrobe, Ire. 73/P10
Balloch, Sc, UK 78/B2
Ballon, Col du (pass), Fr. 98/C2
Ballon d'Alsace (peak), Fr. 98/C2
Ballon de Servance (peak), Fr. 98/C2
Ballwin, Mo, US 179/F8
Bally, Pa, US 180/C3
Ballycarry, NI, UK 76/C2
Ballycastle, NI, UK 76/B1
Ballycastle, Ire. 73/P9
Ballyclare, NI, UK 76/B2
Ballyeaston, NI, UK 76/B2
Ballygawley, NI, UK 76/A3
Ballygeary, Ire. 73/Q10
Ballygowan, NI, UK 76/C3
Ballyhaunis, Ire. 73/P10
Ballyheigue, Ire. 72/P10
Ballyliffin, Ire. 76/A1
Ballymena (dist.), NI, UK 76/B2
Ballymena, NI, UK 76/B2
Ballymoney (dist.), NI, UK 76/B1
Ballymoney, NI, UK 76/B1
Ballynahinch, NI, UK 76/C3
Ballynure, NI, UK 76/C2
Ballyquintin (pt.), NI, UK 76/C3
Ballyshannon, Ire. 73/P9
Balmaceda (peak), Chile 201/B6
Balmazújváros, Hun. 83/L5
Balmhorn (peak), Swi. 98/D5
Balmoral, Austl. 157/B3
Balmoral Castle, Sc, UK 78/C2
Balneário Camboriú, Braz. 197/B3
Balneario Claromecó, Arg. 200/E3
Balneario de los Novillos, PN, Mex. 171/G5
Balochistān (reg.), Pak. 131/J3
Balonne (riv.), Austl. 151/D3
Bālotra, India 131/K3
Balqash, Kaz. 129/G3
Balrāmpur, India 126/D2
Balranald, Austl. 157/B2
Balş, Rom. 91/G3
Bálsamo (pt.), Ecu. 194/A5
Balsapuerto, Peru 198/B2
Balsas, Braz. 196/A2
Balsas (riv.), Mex. 185/F5
Balsthal, Swi. 98/D3
Baltanás, Sp. 86/C2
Bălţi, Mol. 91/H2
Baltic (sea), Swe. 79/F5
Baltic (plain), Rus. 103/S7
Baltic Spit (bar), Pol.,Rus. 81/H4
Balṭīm, Egypt 133/B4
Baltimore, Md, US 180/B5
Baltimore (co.), Md, US 180/B4
Baltimore-Washington (int'l arpt.), Md, US 180/B5
Baltiysk, Rus. 81/H4
Baltray, Ire. 76/B4
Baltrum (isl.), Ger. 93/E1
Bælum, Den. 80/D3
Bālurghāt, India 127/G3
Balve, Ger. 93/E6
Balya, Turk. 104/C5
Balykshi, Kaz. 105/J3
Balzar, Ecu. 194/B5
Balzers, Lcht. 99/F3
Bam (prov.), Burk. 145/E3
Bam, Iran 131/G3
Bama Yaozu Zizhixian, China 125/J3
Bamaji (lake), On, Can. 169/K3
Bamako (cap.), Mali 144/D3
Bamako (Senou) (int'l arpt.), Mali 144/D3
Bambamarca, Peru 198/B2
Bambana (riv.), Nic. 187/E3
Bambari, CAfr. 139/K6
Bamberg, Ger. 96/D3
Bamberg, SC, US 175/H3
Bamble, Nor. 80/C2
Bambuí, Braz. 197/C2
Bamenda, Camr. 145/H5
Bāmīān, Afg. 129/E6
Bamingui-Bangoran, PN du, CAfr. 139/J6
Bammental, Ger. 96/B4
Bampūr (riv.), Iran 131/H3
Ban Boun Tai, Laos 125/H3
Ban Chiang (ruin), Thai. 120/C2
Ban Houayxay, Laos 125/H3
Ban Kantang, Thai. 120/B5
Ban Kengkok, Laos 125/J4
Ban Pak Phanang, Thai. 120/C4
Banaba (isl.), Kiri. 158/F5
Banagher, Ire. 73/Q10
Banamba, Mali 144/D3
Banana (isls.), SLeo. 144/B4
Bananal, Braz. 197/J7
Bananal, Ilha do (isl.), Braz. 193/H6
Banar (riv.), Bang. 127/H3
Banarlı, Turk. 91/H5
Banās (pt.), Egypt 143/C4
Banās (riv.), India 131/L3
Banat (reg.), Serb. 90/E3
Banatsko Novo Selo, Serb. 90/E3
Banaz, Turk. 132/B2
Banbar, China 112/G5
Banbridge, NI, UK 76/B3
Banbridge (dist.), NI, UK 76/B3
Banbury, Eng, UK 75/E2
Banc d'Arguin, Mrta. 140/A5
Banc d'Arguin, PN du, Mrta. 138/B3
Banc d'Arguin, PN du, Mrta. 144/A2
Banchette, It. 100/A2
Banchory, Sc, UK 78/D2
Banco Chinchorro (isls.), Mex. 182/D4
Bancroft, On, Can. 172/E2
Banda (isls.), Indo. 123/H4
Bāndā, India 126/C3
Banda, India 126/B3
Banda (sea), Indo. 123/G5
Banda Aceh, Indo. 122/A2
Bandai-san (peak), Japan 117/G2
Bandama (riv.), C.d'Iv. 138/D6
Bandama Blanc (riv.), C.d'Iv. 144/D4
Bandama Rouge (riv.), C.d'Iv. 144/D4
Bandar Beheshtī, Iran 131/H3
Bandar-e 'Abbās, Iran 131/G3
Bandar-e Anzalī, Iran 130/E1
Bandar-e Deylam, Iran 130/F2
Bandar-e Lengeh, Iran 131/F3
Bandar-e Māhshahr, Iran 130/E2
Bandar-e Torkeman, Iran 130/F1
Bandar Seri Begawan (cap.), Bru. 122/D3
Bande, Sp. 86/B1
Bandeira do Sul, Braz. 197/G6
Bandeira, Pico da (peak), Braz. 197/D2
Bandeirantes, Braz. 197/B2
Bandelier Nat'l Mon., NM, US 171/F4
Bandera, Tx, US 171/H5

220
Bande – Béhou

Banderilla, Mex. 185/N7
Bandhavgarh NP, India 126/C4
Bandholm, Den. 80/D4
Bandiagara, Mali 144/E3
Bandipura, India 128/C2
Bandirma (gulf), Turk. 91/H5
Bandırma, Turk. 91/H5
Bandon, Ire. 73/P11
Bandon (riv.), Ire. 73/P11
Bandundu, D.R. Congo 147/C1
Bandung, Indo. 122/C5
Bañeres, Sp. 87/E3
Banes, Cuba 187/H1
Banff, Ab, Can. 168/E3
Banff, Sc, UK 78/D1
Banff NP, Ab, Can. 168/E3
Banfora, Burk. 144/D4
Bang Lang (res.), Thai. 120/C5
Bañga, Phil. 121/D6
Banga, India 128/C4
Bangalore, India 124/C5
Bangalow, Austl. 156/D5
Bangaon, India 127/G4
Bāngarmau, India 126/C2
Bangassou, CAfr. 139/K7
Bangau (cape), Malay. 123/E2
Banggai (isls.), Indo. 123/F4
Banghiang (riv.), Laos 120/D2
Bangka (str.), Indo. 122/B4
Bangka (isl.), Indo. 122/C4
Bangkok (Krung Thep) (cap.),Thai. 120/C3
Bangkok (int'l arpt.), Thai. 120/C3
Bangkok, Bight of (bay), Thai. 125/H5
Bangladesh (ctry.) 124/E3
Bangor, NI, UK 76/C2
Bangor (int'l arpt.), Me, US 173/G2
Bangor, Me, US 173/G2
Bangor, Pa, US 180/C2
Bangor, Wal, UK 76/D5
Bangued, Phil. 121/D4
Bangui (cap.), CAfr. 139/J7
Bangweulu (swamp), Zam. 146/A5
Bangweulu (lake), Zam. 147/E3
Banhā, Egypt 133/B4
Banhine, PN de, Moz. 147/F5
Bani (riv.), Mali 138/D5
Baní, DRep. 183/G4
Banī Mazār, Egypt 143/B2
Banī Suhaylah, Gaza 133/D4
Banī Suwayf (gov.), Egypt 143/B1
Banī Suwayf, Egypt 143/B2
Bánica, DRep. 187/J2
Banifing (riv.), Mali 144/D3
Banihāl (pass), India 128/C3
Banikoara, Ben. 145/F4
Banister (riv.), Va, US 175/J2
Bāniyās, Syria 133/D2
Banja Koviljača, Serb. 90/D3
Banja Luka, Bosn. 90/C3
Banjarmasin, Indo. 122/D4
Banjul (cap.), Gam. 144/A3
Bānka, India 127/F3
Bankas, Mali 144/E3
Bankeryd, Swe. 80/F3
Bankfoot, Sc, UK 78/C3
Bankhead, Sc, UK 78/D2
Bānki, India 127/E4
Banks (cape), Austl. 157/B3
Banks (str.), Austl. 157/C4
Banks (isl.), NW, Can. 164/D2
Banks (pen.), NZ 159/S11
Banks (pt.), Ak, US 176/H4
Banks (lake), Wa, US 168/D4
Banks (isls.), Van. 158/F6
Bānkurā, India 127/F4
Bankya, Bul. 89/H1
Banmankhi, India 127/F3
Bann (riv.), Ire. 73/Q10
Bann (riv.), NI, UK 76/B3
Banna (riv.), It. 100/A3
Bannockburn, Sc, UK 78/C4
Bannockburn Battlesite, Sc, UK 78/C4
Bannu, Pak. 128/A3
Baños, Ecu. 198/B1
Banpo Ruins, China 114/B4
Bansberia, India 127/G4
Bānsdīh, India 127/E3
Bānsi, India 126/D2
Bansin, Ger. 80/F5
Banská Bystrica, Slvk. 83/K4
Banská Štiavnica, Slvk. 90/D1
Bansko, Bul. 89/H2
Banskobystrický (pol. reg.), Slvk. 83/K4
Banstead, Eng, UK 72/C3
Bānswāra, India 131/K4
Bantayan, Phil. 121/D5
Banté, Ben. 145/F4
Bantenan (cape), Indo. 122/D5
Bantong Group (isls.), Thai. 120/B5
Bantry, Ire. 73/P11
Bañuelo (peak), Sp. 86/C3
Banyak (isls.), Indo. 122/A3
Banyoles, Sp. 87/G1
Banyuwangi, Indo. 122/D5
Banzare (coast), Ant. 202/J
Baode, China 114/B3
Baodi, China 114/H7
Baoding, China 114/G7
Baofeng, China 114/C4
Baoji, China 112/J5
Baojing, China 125/J2
Baokang, China 114/B5
Baoruco (mts.), DRep. 187/J2
Baoshan, China 125/G2
Baoshan, China 114/L8
Baotou, China 114/B2
Baoulé (riv.), Mali 138/D5
Baoying, China 114/D4
Bapaume, Fr. 94/B3
Bapchule, Az, US 179/S19
Baptistown, NJ, US 180/C2
Bāqa el Gharbiyya, Isr. 133/G7
Baqên, China 112/F5
Ba'qūbah, Iraq 132/F3
Bar, Mont. 90/D4
Bar (riv.), Fr. 82/C4
Bar Bigha, India 127/E3
Bar el Ksaïb (well), Mali 140/D5
Bar Harbor, Me, US 173/G2
Bar-le-Duc, Fr. 95/E6
Bar-sur-Aube, Fr. 84/F2
Bar-sur-Seine, Fr. 84/F2
Bara, Swe. 80/E4
Bāra Banki, India 126/C2
Bārā Lācha La (pass), India 128/D3
Barabai, Indo. 122/E4
Barabinsk, Rus. 129/G1
Baraboo, Wi, US 169/L5
Baracaldo, Sp. 86/D1
Baracoa, Cuba 187/H1
Barada (riv.), Syria 133/E3
Baradero, Arg. 201/J10
Baradine, Austl. 157/D1
Baragoi, Kenya 146/C2
Baraguá, Cuba 187/G1
Baragua, Ven. 194/D2
Barajas (int'l arpt.), Sp. 87/N9
Barajevo, Serb. 90/E3
Barākar (riv.), India 127/F3
Barakī Barak, Afg. 131/J2
Baralaba, Austl. 156/C4
Baram (cape), Malay. 122/D3
Baram (riv.), Malay. 122/D3
Barama (riv.), Guy. 192/F2
Baramanni, Guy. 195/G3
Baramula, India 128/C2
Bāran, India 131/L3
Baranagar, India 127/G4
Baranavichy, Bela. 104/C1
Barani (well), Alg. 140/E4
Baranoa, Col. 194/C2
Baranof (isl.), Ak, US 176/L4
Baranya (prov.), Hun. 90/C3
Barão de Cocais, Braz. 197/D1
Barão de Grajaú, Braz. 196/B2
Baraolt, Rom. 91/G2
Baraque de Fraiture (hill), Belg. 95/E3
Barat Daya (isls.), Indo. 123/G5
Barataria, La, US 179/P17
Barauli, India 127/E2
Baraut, India 128/D5
Baraya, Col. 194/C4
Barbacena, Braz. 197/D2
Barbacoas, Col. 194/B4
Barbados (ctry.) 183/P9
Barbalha, Braz. 196/C2
Barbaros, Turk. 91/H5
Barbas (cape), Mor. 140/A5
Barbastro, Sp. 87/F1
Barbate de Franco, Sp. 86/C4
Barbeau (peak), Nun., Can. 165/T6
Barberà del Vallès, Sp. 87/L6
Barberino di Mugello, It. 101/E5
Barbers (pt.), Hi, US 166/V13
Barberton, Oh, US 172/D3
Barberton, SAfr. 149/E2
Barbona (peak), It. 100/D5
Barbosa, Col. 194/C3
Barbourville, Ky, US 172/D4
Barbuda (isl.), Anti. 183/N8
Barcaldine, Austl. 156/B3
Barcarrota, Sp. 86/B3
Barcău (riv.), Rom. 90/F2
Barcellona Pozzo di Gotto, It. 88/D3
Barcelona, Ven. 195/E2
Barcelona, Sp. 87/L7
Barcelona (int'l arpt.), Sp. 87/L7
Barcelos, Port. 86/A2
Barcelos, Braz. 195/F5
Barcin, Pol. 83/J2
Barcoo (riv.), Austl. 151/D3
Barcs, Hun. 90/C3
Barczewo, Pol. 81/J5
Bardejov, Slvk. 83/L4
Bardi, It. 100/C3
Bardīyah, Libya 139/L1
Bārdoli, India 131/K4
Bardolino, It. 101/D1
Bardonia, NY, US 181/K7
Bardsdale, Ca, US 178/B2
Bardsey (isl.), Wal, UK 76/D6
Bardstown, Ky, US 172/C4
Bareggio, It. 100/B2
Bareli, India 126/B4
Barellan, Austl. 157/C2
Barendrecht, Neth. 92/B5
Barentin, Fr. 84/D2
Barents (seas), Eur. 106/D2
Barentu, Erit. 130/C5
Bāretswil, Swi. 99/E3
Barfleur, Pointe de (pt.), Fr. 84/C2
Barga, It. 100/D4
Bargara, Austl. 156/D4
Bargarh, India 124/D3
Bargfeld-Stegen, Ger. 93/H1
Bargi, India 126/B4
Bargo, Austl. 157/D2
Bargteheide, Ger. 93/H1
Bārh, India 127/E3
Barhaj, India 126/D2
Barhalganj, India 126/D2
Barham, Austl. 157/C2
Barhiya, India 127/F3
Bāri, India 126/A2
Bari, It. 88/E2
Bari Sardo, It. 88/A3
Bariano, It. 100/C1
Baricella, It. 101/E3
Barichara, Col. 194/C3
Barīdī (pt.), SAr. 130/C4
Barigazzo (peak), It. 100/C3
Barika, Alg. 142/H5
Barillas, Guat. 186/D3
Barima (riv.), Guy. 195/G2
Barima-Waini (pol. reg.), Guy. 195/F3
Barinas (state), Ven. 194/D2
Barinas, Ven. 194/D2
Barinitas, Ven. 194/D2
Bariri, Braz. 197/B2
Barisāl (pol. reg.), Bang. 127/H4
Barisan Mountains (mts.), Indo. 122/B4
Barito (riv.), Indo. 122/D4
Baritu, PN, Arg. 199/D1
Bark (lake), On, Can. 172/E2
Bark (riv.), Wi, US 177/N13
Barka Kāna, India 127/E4
Barker, NY, US 173/S9
Barki Saria, India 127/E3
Barking and Dagenham (bor.), Eng, UK 72/D2
Barkley (sound), BC, Can. 168/B3
Barkley (lake), Ky,Tn, US 175/G2
Barkly East, SAfr. 148/D3
Barkly Tableland (plat.), Austl. 151/C2
Barkly West, SAfr. 148/D3
Barkol Kazak Zizhixian, China 112/F3
Barlee (lake), Austl. 151/A3
Barlee (range), Austl. 154/B2
Barlee Range Nature Rsv., Austl. 154/B2
Barletta, It. 88/E2
Barlin, Fr. 94/B3
Barlinek, Pol. 83/H2
Barmedman, Austl. 157/C2
Barmera, Austl. 155/J5
Barmstedt, Ger. 93/G1
Barnāla, India 128/C4
Bärnbach, Aus. 85/L3
Barnegat (inlet), NJ, US 180/D4
Barnegat (bay), NJ, US 180/D4
Barnegat, NJ, US 180/D4
Barnegat Light, NJ, US 180/D4
Barneveld, Neth. 92/C4
Barnhart, Mo, US 179/G9
Barnoldswick, Eng, UK 77/F4
Barnsley, Eng, UK 77/G4
Barnsley (co.), Eng, UK 77/G5
Barnstaple, Eng, UK 74/B4
Barnstaple (Bideford) (bay), Eng, UK 74/B4
Barnstorf, Ger. 93/F3
Barntrup, Ger. 93/G5
Barnwell, SC, US 175/H3
Baroghil (pass), Pak. 129/F5
Baron, Fr. 72/L4
Barone (peak), It. 100/B1
Barow (riv.), Ire. 76/A5
Barowghīl (pass), Afg. 131/K1
Barquisimeto, Ven. 194/D2
Barquisimeto (int'l arpt.), Ven. 194/D2
Barr (lake), Co, US 179/C3
Barr, Co, US 179/C3
Barr, Fr. 98/D1
Barra, Braz. 196/B3
Barra (isl.), Sc, UK 73/Q8
Barra Bonita, Braz. 197/B2
Barra Bonita, Reprêsa de (res.), Braz. 197/B2
Barra da Choça, Braz. 196/B4
Barra del Colorado, PN, CR 182/E5
Barra do Bugres, Braz. 193/G7
Barra do Corda, Braz. 196/A2
Barra do Garças, Braz. 193/H7
Barra do Mendes, Braz. 196/B3
Barra do Piraí, Braz. 197/K7
Barra do Ribeiro, Braz. 197/B4
Barra Head (pt.), Sc, UK 73/Q8
Barra Mansa, Braz. 197/J7
Barra Velha, Braz. 197/B3
Barraba, Austl. 157/D1
Barrackpur, India 127/G4
Barrage de Lagdo (dam), Camr. 138/H6
Barranca, Peru 198/B3
Barranca, Peru 198/B2
Barranca de Upía, Col. 194/C3
Barranca del Cobre PN, Mex. 184/D3
Barrancabermeja, Col. 194/C3
Barrancas, Ven. 195/F2
Barrancas, Col. 194/C2
Barrancas, Chile 200/N8
Barranco de Loba, Col. 194/C2
Barrancos, Port. 86/B3
Barranquilla, Col. 194/C2
Barras, Braz. 196/B2
Barreal, Arg. 199/C3
Barreiras, Braz. 196/A4
Barreirinhas, Braz. 196/B1
Barreiro, Port. 87/P10
Barreiros, Braz. 196/D3
Barren (isl.), Madg. 149/G7
Barren, Nosy (Barren Islands) (isls.), Madg. 149/G7
Barretal, Mex. 185/F3
Barretos, Braz. 197/B2
Barrhead, Ab, Can. 168/E2
Barrhead, Sc, UK 78/B5
Barrie, On, Can. 172/E2
Barrier (range), Austl. 155/J4
Barrington, Il, US 177/P15
Barrington Hills, Il, US 177/P15
Barrington Tops (peak), Austl. 157/D1
Barrington Tops NP, Austl. 157/D1
Barro Duro, Braz. 196/B2
Barron Gorge NP, Austl. 156/B2
Barroso, Braz. 197/D2
Barrouallie, StV. 183/N9
Barrow, Ak, US 176/G1
Barrow (pt.), Ak, US 176/G1
Barrow (isl.), Austl. 151/A3
Barrow (riv.), Ire. 73/Q10
Barrow (pt.), Austl. 156/B1
Barrow (str.), Nun., Can. 164/G1
Barrow-in-Furness, Eng, UK 77/E3
Barrow Island, Austl. 154/B2
Barrowford, Eng, UK 77/F4
Barruelo de Santullán, Sp. 86/C1
Barry, Wal, UK 74/C4
Barsakel'mes (lake), Uzb. 129/C4
Barsinghausen, Ger. 93/G4
Barssel, Ger. 93/E2
Barstow, Ca, US 170/C4
Bartang (riv.), Taj. 129/F5
Bartenheim, Fr. 98/D2
Barth, Ger. 80/E4
Bartholomā, Ger. 96/C5
Bartholomäberg, Aus. 99/F3
Bartica, Guy. 195/G3
Bartın, Turk. 91/L5
Bartle Frere (peak), Austl. 151/D2
Bartlesville, Ok, US 171/J3
Bartlett, Tx, US 171/H5
Bartlett (dam), Az, US 179/S18
Bartlett (res.), Az, US 179/S18
Bartlett, Il, US 177/P16
Bartolomé Masó, Cuba 187/G1
Bartolomeu Dias, Moz. 147/G5
Bartonsville, Pa, US 180/C2
Bartoszyce, Pol. 81/J4
Bartow, Fl, US 175/H5
Bartow, Ger. 80/E5
Barú (vol.), Pan. 187/F4
Bāruipur, India 127/G4
Barumun (riv.), Indo. 122/B3
Barus, Indo. 122/A3
Baruun-Urt, Mong. 113/K2
Barwa Sāgar, India 126/B3
Barwāha, India 131/L4
Barwāla, India 128/C5
Barwon (riv.), Austl. 151/D3
Barycz (riv.), Pol. 83/J3
Barysaw, Bela. 81/N4
Barysh, Rus. 105/H1
Barzanò, It. 100/C1
Bas-Rhin (dept.), Fr. 98/D1
Basaldella, It. 101/G1
Basauri, Sp. 86/D1
Basavilbaso, Arg. 201/J10
Bascharage, Lux. 95/E4
Basehor, Ks, US 179/D5
Basel, Swi. 98/D2
Basel/Mulhouse (int'l arpt.), Fr. 98/D2
Baselga di Pinè, It. 99/H5
Baselland (canton), Swi. 98/D3
Bashee (riv.), SAfr. 148/E3
Bashi (chan.), Phil.,Tai. 121/C3
Bashkortostan, Resp., Rus. 106/G6
Bāsht, Iran 130/F2
Basilan (isl.), Phil. 123/F2
Basilan (peak), Phil. 123/F2
Basildon, Eng, UK 75/G3
Basilica di Fieschi, It. 100/C4
Basilicata (reg.), It. 88/D2
Basingstoke, Eng, UK 75/E4
Basingstoke (canal), Eng, UK 72/A3
Basīrhāt, India 127/G4
Basīrpur, Pak. 128/B4
Başkale, Turk. 132/F2
Baskatong (res.), Qu, Can. 172/F2
Baskil, Turk. 132/D2
Başkomutan NP, Turk. 132/B2
Bāsoda, India 126/A4
Basodino (peak), It. 99/E5
Basoko, D.R. Congo 139/K7
Basoli, India 128/C3
Bass (str.), Austl. 151/D4
Bass Rock (isl.), Sc, UK 78/D4
Bassae (Vassés) (ruin), Gre. 89/G4
Bassano, Ab, Can. 168/E3
Bassano del Grappa, It. 101/E1
Bassari, Togo 145/F4
Bassas da India (isl.), Reun., Fr. 147/G5
Basse-Normandie (pol. reg.), Fr. 84/C2
Basse Santa Su, Gam. 144/B3
Basse-Terre, Guad., Fr. 183/N8
Basse-Terre (isl.), Guad., Fr. 183/J4
Bassecourt, Swi. 98/D3
Bassein (riv.), Myan. 125/F4
Bassein (Vasai), India 131/K5
Bassenge, Belg. 95/E2
Bassenheim, Ger. 95/G3
Bassenthwaite (lake), Eng, UK 77/E2
Basseterre (cap.), StK. 183/N8
Bassum, Ger. 93/F3
Basswood (lake), Can.,US 172/B1
Båstad, Swe. 80/E3
Bastak, Iran 131/F3
Basṭām, Iran 131/G1
Bastelicaccia, Fr. 88/A2
Bastheim, Ger. 96/D2
Bastī, India 126/D2
Bastia, Fr. 88/A1
Bastia, It. 85/K5
Bastogne, Belg. 95/E4
Bastos, Braz. 197/B2
Bastrop, Tx, US 171/H5
Basyūn, Egypt 133/B4
Bat Shelomo, Isr. 133/F6
Bat Yam, Isr. 133/F7
Bata, EqG. 138/G7
Batabanó (gulf), Cuba 182/E3
Batac, Phil. 121/D4
Batagay, Rus. 107/P3
Batai (pass), Pak. 128/A3
Batalha, Braz. 196/B2
Batalha, Port. 86/A3
Batan (isls.), Phil. 121/D3
Batang, China 112/G6
Batangafo, CAfr. 139/J6
Batangas, Phil. 121/D5
Batarasa, Phil. 121/C6
Batatais, Braz. 197/C2
Batavia, NY, US 172/E3
Batavia, Il, US 177/P16
Bataysk, Rus. 104/F3
Batchtown, Il, US 179/F7
Bātdâmbâng, Camb. 120/C3
Bate (bay), Austl. 156/H9
Batéké (plat.), Congo 138/H8
Batemans Bay, Austl. 157/D2
Batesburg-Leesville, SC, US 175/H3
Batesville, Ms, US 171/K4
Bath, Me, US 173/G3
Bath, NY, US 172/E3
Bath, Eng, UK 74/D4
Bath, Pa, US 180/C2
Bath and Northeast Somerset (co.), Eng, UK 74/D4
Bathgate, Sc, UK 78/C5
Bathmen, Neth. 92/D4
Bathurst, Austl. 157/D2
Bathurst (cape), NW, Can. 176/N1
Bathurst, NB, Can. 173/H2
Bathurst (isl.), Nun., Can. 165/R7
Bathurst (inlet), Nun., Can. 164/F2
Bathurst Inlet, Nun., Can. 164/F2
Batian (Mt. Kenya) (peak), Kenya 146/C3
Batiquitos (lag.), Ca, US 178/C4
Batiscan (riv.), Qu, Can. 173/F2
Batley, Eng, UK 77/G4
Batlow, Austl. 157/D2
Batman, Turk. 132/E2
Batman (dam), Turk. 132/E2
Batna (prov.), Alg. 141/G2
Batna, Alg. 142/J5
Baton Rouge (cap.), La, US 171/K5
Batopilas, Mex. 184/D3
Batoti, India 128/C3
Batouri, Camr. 138/H7
Baṭrā' (Petra) (ruin), Jor. 133/D4
Båtsfjord, Nor. 79/J1
Batsto (riv.), NJ, US 180/D4
Batsto, NJ, US 180/D4
Batsto Historic Village, NJ, US 180/D4
Battaglia Terme, It. 101/E2
Battenberg, Ger. 93/F6
Bätterkinden, Swi. 98/D3
Batticaloa, SrL. 124/D6
Battipaglia, It. 88/D2
Battle, Eng, UK 75/G5
Battle (riv.), Ab,Sk, Can. 164/E3
Battle Creek, Mi, US 172/C3
Battle Mountain, Nv, US 168/D5
Battleford, Sk, Can. 168/F2
Battock (mt.), Sc, UK 78/D3
Batu (peak), Eth. 139/N6
Batu (cape), Indo. 123/E3
Batu (isls.), Indo. 122/A4
Batu (bay), Malay. 122/D3
Batu (peak), Malay. 122/D3
Batu Gajah, Malay. 122/B3
Batu Pahat, Malay. 122/B3
Batu Puteh (peak), Malay. 122/B3
Batudaka (isl.), Indo. 123/F4
Batuensambang (peak), Indo. 122/D3
Bat'umi, Geo. 105/G4
Bat'umi (int'l arpt.), Geo. 105/G4
Baturaja, Indo. 122/B4
Baturité, Braz. 196/C2
Batys Qazaqstan, Kaz. 106/E5
Bauchi (state), Nga. 145/H4
Bauchi, Nga. 145/H4
Baudette, Mn, US 169/K3
Baudó (mts.), Col. 194/B3
Baudó (riv.), Col. 194/B3
Bauer, Ut, US 179/J13
Bauld (cape), Nf, Can. 173/L1
Baulmes, Swi. 98/C4
Bauman (peak), Togo 145/F5
Baume-les-Dames, Fr. 98/C3
Baumholder, Ger. 95/G4
Baunach, Ger. 96/D3
Baunach (riv.), Ger. 96/D2
Baunatal, Ger. 93/G6
Baunei, It. 88/A2
Bauru, Braz. 197/B2
Bautzen, Ger. 83/H3
Bavans, Fr. 98/C3
Bavarian Alps (mts.), Aus.,Ger. 99/G3
Bavay, Fr. 94/C3
Båven (lake), Swe. 80/G2
Baveno, It. 99/E6
Baviácora, Mex. 184/C2
Bavilliers, Fr. 98/C2
Bavispe, Río de (riv.), Mex. 184/C2
Baw Baw (mt.), Austl. 157/C3
Baw Baw NP, Austl. 157/C3
Bawāna, India 128/D5
Bawang (cape), Indo. 122/C4
Bawean (isl.), Indo. 122/D5
Bawku, Gha. 145/E4
Baxoi, China 125/G2
Bay City, Mi, US 172/D3
Bay City, Tx, US 171/J5
Bay Minette, Al, US 175/G4
Bay Roberts, Nf, Can. 173/L2
Bay Saint Louis, Ms, US 175/F4
Bayamo, Cuba 187/G1
Bayamón, PR 183/M8
Bayan, Mong. 112/G2
Bayan Har (mts.), China 112/G5
Bayan-Hongor (prov.), Mong. 112/G2
Bayan-Ölgiy (prov.), Mong. 112/E2
Bayan-Ulaan, Mong. 112/H2
Bayanaul'skiy NP, Kaz. 129/G2
Bayanhongor, Mong. 112/H2
Bayanhushuu, Mong. 112/F2
Bayannuur, Mong. 112/F2
Bayano (lake), Pan. 187/G4
Bayanterem, Mong. 113/K2
Bayantsagaan, Mong. 112/H2
Bayard, Ne, US 169/H5
Bayat, Turk. 132/C1
Bayawan, Phil. 123/F2
Baybach (riv.), Ger. 95/G3
Baybay, Phil. 121/D5
Bayburt, Turk. 132/E1
Bayburt (prov.), Turk. 132/E1
Baydaratskaya (bay), Rus. 106/G2
Baydhabo (Baidoa), Som. 139/P7
Bayel, Fr. 98/A1
Bayerischer Wald (hills), Ger. 97/F4
Bayerischer Wald NP, Ger. 97/G5
Bayern (state), Ger. 82/F4
Bayeux, Braz. 196/D2
Bayeux, Fr. 84/C2
Baygorria (res.), Uru. 201/K10
Baykal (mts.), Rus. 107/L4
Baykal (lake), Rus. 109/L4
Baykan, Turk. 132/E2
Bayombong, Phil. 121/D4
Bayon, Fr. 98/C1
Bayona, Sp. 86/A1
Bayonet Point, Fl, US 175/H4
Bayonne, Fr. 84/C5
Bayonne, NJ, US 181/J9
Bayport, NY, US 181/E2
Bayramaly, Trkm. 131/H1
Bayramıç, Turk. 89/K3
Bayreuth, Ger. 97/E3
Bayrūt (Beirut) (cap.), Leb. 133/D3
Bays, Lake of (lake), On, Can. 172/E2
Bayşehir (lake), Turk. 132/B2
Bayt Ḥanīnā, WBnk. 133/G8
Bayt Ḥānūn, Gaza 133/D4
Bayt Laḥm (Bethlehem), WBnk. 133/G8
Bayt Sāḥūr, WBnk. 133/G8
Baytik Shan (mts.), China,Mong. 112/E2
Baytown, Tx, US 171/J5
Bayudha (des.), Sudan 143/C5
Bayugan, Phil. 121/E6
Bayville, NY, US 181/L8
Baza, Sp. 86/D4
Bazainville, Fr. 72/G5
Bazardüzü (peak), Azer. 105/H4
Bazaruto, Ilha do (isl.), Moz. 147/G5
Bazèga (prov.), Burk. 145/E4
Bazemont, Fr. 72/H5
Bazet, Fr. 84/D5
Bazhong, China 112/J5
Bazin (riv.), Qu, Can. 172/F2
Bāzpur, India 126/B1
Bazzano, It. 101/E3
Be, Nosy (isl.), Madg. 149/H6
Beach Haven, NJ, US 180/D4
Beachport, Austl. 157/B3
Beachwood, NJ, US 180/D4
Beachy Head (pt.), Eng, UK 75/G5
Beacon (peak), Wal, UK 74/C2
Beaconsfield, Austl. 157/C4
Beaconsfield, Eng, UK 75/F3
Beaconsfield, Qu, Can. 173/N7
Beal (range), Austl. 156/A4
Bealeana, Madg. 149/J6
Beale (cape), BC, Can. 168/B3
Beampingaratra (ridge), Madg. 149/H9
Bear (isl.), Nor. 202/E
Bear (riv.), US 170/E2
Bear (mt.), Ak, US 176/K3
Bear (mtn.), Ak, US 176/K2
Bear, De, US 180/C4
Bear (lake), Ut, US 170/E2
Bear Creek (lake), Co, US 179/B3
Bear River (bay), Ut, US 179/J11
Bear River Migratory Bird Refuge (nat'l wild. ref.), Ut, US 179/J10
Beardsley, Az, US 179/R18
Beardsley (canal), Az, US 179/R18
Bearfort (mtn.), NJ, US 181/H7
Bearma (riv.), India 126/B4
Bearpaw (mts.), Mt, US 168/F3
Bearsden, Sc, UK 78/B5
Beartooth (mts.), Mt,Wy, US 168/F4
Beās (riv.), India 126/B3
Beas de Segura, Sp. 86/D3
Beasain, Sp. 86/D1
Beata (isl.), DRep. 187/J2
Beata (cape), DRep. 187/J2
Beatenberg, Swi. 98/D4
Beatty, Nv, US 170/C3
Beattystown, NJ, US 180/D2
Beau Bassin-Rose Hill, Mrts. 149/T15
Beaucaire, Fr. 84/F5
Beaucamps-le-Vieux, Fr. 94/A4
Beauchamp, Fr. 72/J4
Beaucourt, Fr. 98/C3
Beaudesert, Austl. 156/D4
Beaufort, Austl. 157/B3
Beaufort (sea), Can.,US 161/C2
Beaufort, Fr. 98/B4
Beaufort, Lux. 95/F4
Beaufort, SC, US 175/H3
Beaufort West, SAfr. 148/C4
Beaugency, Fr. 84/D3
Beaujolais, Monts du (mts.), Fr. 84/F4
Beauly (riv.), Sc, UK 78/B2
Beauly, Sc, UK 78/B2
Beauly Firth (lake), Sc, UK 78/B2
Beaumaris, Wal, UK 76/D5
Beaumesnil, Fr. 84/F3
Beaumont, Tx, US 171/J5
Beaumont, Ca, US 178/D3
Beaumont, Fr. 84/E4
Beaumont, Belg. 95/D3
Beaumont-de-Lomagne, Fr. 84/D5
Beaumont-sur-Oise, Fr. 72/J4
Beaupréau, Fr. 84/C3
Beauquesne, Fr. 94/B3
Beauraing, Belg. 95/D3
Beaurainville, Fr. 94/A3
Beaurevoir, Fr. 94/C4
Beausejour, Mb, Can. 169/J3
Beautheil, Fr. 72/M5
Beautor, Fr. 94/C4
Beauvais, Fr. 94/B5
Beauval, Sk, Can. 168/G2
Beauval, Fr. 94/B3
Beauvoir, Fr. 72/L6
Beaver (lake), Ar, US 174/E2
Beaver (riv.), Yk, Can. 164/D2
Beaver, Ak, US 176/J2
Beaver (isl.), Mi, US 172/C2
Beaver (riv.), Ok, US 170/G3
Beaver (riv.), On, Can. 169/L2
Beaver, Ut, US 170/D3
Beaver Creek, Yk, Can. 176/K3
Beaver Meadows, Pa, US 180/C2
Beaver Springs, Pa, US 180/A2
Beaverhead (riv.), Mt, US 168/E4
Beaverlodge, Ab, Can. 168/D2
Beavertown, Pa, US 180/A2
Bebedouro, Braz. 197/B2
Beberibe, Braz. 196/C2
Bebington, Eng, UK 77/E5
Bebra, Ger. 93/G7
Becal, Mex. 186/D1
Beccles, Eng, UK 75/H2
Bečej, Serb. 90/E3
Becerreá, Sp. 86/B1
Bechar (prov.), Alg. 140/E3
Bechar, Alg. 141/E3
Becharof (lake), Ak, US 176/G4
Bechhofen, Ger. 95/G5
Bechtheim, Ger. 96/B3
Bechyně, Czh. 97/H4
Beckdorf, Ger. 93/G2
Beckenried, Swi. 99/E4
Beckingen, Ger. 95/F5
Beckley, WV, US 172/D4
Beckum, Ger. 93/F5
Beclean, Rom. 91/G2
Becs de Bosson (peak), Swi. 98/D5
Bédarieux, Fr. 84/E5
Bedburg, Ger. 95/F2
Bedburg-Hau, Ger. 92/D5
Beder, Den. 80/D3
Bedford (cape), Austl. 156/B1
Bedford, Qu, Can. 172/F2
Bedford, Eng, UK 75/F2
Bedford, In, US 172/C4
Bedford, SAfr. 148/D4
Bedford, Va, US 172/E4
Bedford Hills, NY, US 181/E1
Bedford Level (phys. reg.), Eng, UK 75/F2
Bedford Park, Il, US 177/Q16
Bedfordshire (co.), Eng, UK 75/F2
Bedlington, Eng, UK 77/G1
Bedonia, It. 100/C3
Bedouaram (well), Niger 138/H4
Bedretto, Swi. 99/E5
Bedsted, Den. 80/C3
Bedum, Neth. 92/D2
Bedworth, Eng, UK 75/E2
Beebe Seep (canal), Co, US 179/C2
Beechworth, Austl. 157/C3
Beek, Neth. 95/E2
Beelen, Ger. 93/F5
Beelitz, Ger. 82/P7
Beenleigh, Austl. 156/D4
Beer (pt.), Eng, UK 74/C5
Be'er Sheva', Isr. 133/D4
Beerfelden, Ger. 96/B3
Beernem, Belg. 94/C1
Beerzel, Belg. 95/D1
Beesel, Neth. 92/D6
Beeville, Tx, US 174/D4
Befandriana, Madg. 149/J6
Befandriana, Madg. 149/G8
Beforona, Madg. 149/J7
Befotaka, Madg. 149/J6
Beg (lake), NI, UK 76/B2
Bega, Austl. 157/D3
Bega (riv.), Ger. 93/F5
Bega Veche (riv.), Cro. 90/E3
Begamganj, Bang. 127/H4
Begamganj, India 126/B4
Bégard, Fr. 84/B2
Begarslan (peak), Trkm. 105/K4
Begejci, Serb. 90/E3
Begichev (isl.), Rus. 107/M2
Begna (riv.), Nor. 79/D3
Begusarai, India 127/F3
Béhague (pt.), FrG. 193/H3
Behala (str.), Indo. 122/B4
Behāla, India 124/E3
Behamberg, Aus. 97/H6
Behat, India 128/D4
Behbahān, Iran 130/F2
Behenjy-Afovany, Madg. 149/H7
Béhoust, Fr. 72/H5

Behren-lès-Forbach, Fr. 95/F5
Behri (riv.), Nepal 126/C1
Behshahr, Iran 130/F1
Bei (riv.), China 121/A2
Bei (mts.), China 112/F3
Bei'an, China 113/N2
Beierfeld, Ger. 97/F1
Beigua (peak), It. 100/B4
Beijing (mun.), China 113/L3
Beijing (cap.), China 114/H7
Beijing Capital (int'l arpt.), China 114/H6
Beilen, Neth. 92/D3
Beiliu, China 125/K3
Beilngries, Ger. 97/E4
Beilstein, Ger. 96/C4
Beilun (pass), China 121/A3
Bein Tharsuinn (peak), Sc, UK 78/B1
Beindersheim, Ger. 96/B3
Beinn a' Chuallaich (peak), Sc, UK 78/B3
Beinn a' Ghlò (peak), Sc, UK 78/C3
Beinn a' Mheadhoin (lake), Sc, UK 78/B2
Beinn Bhàn (peak), Sc, UK 78/A3
Beinn Bheula (peak), Sc, UK 78/B4
Beinn Bhrotain (peak), Sc, UK 78/C2
Beinn Bhuidhe (peak), Sc, UK 78/B4
Beinn Bhuidhe Mhór (peak),Sc, UK 78/B2
Beinn Dearg (peak), Sc, UK 78/B1
Beinn Dearg (peak), Sc, UK 78/C3
Beinn Dòrain (peak), Sc, UK 78/B4
Beinn Eighe (peak), Sc, UK 78/A1
Beinn Heasgarnich (peak), Sc, UK 78/B3
Beinn Mholach (peak), Sc, UK 78/B3
Beinn Mhór (peak), Sc, UK 78/A4
Beinwil am See, Swi. 98/E3
Beipiao, China 114/E2
Beira, Moz. 147/F4
Beiru (riv.), China 114/C4
Beirut (Bayrūt), (cap.), Leb. 133/D3
Beirut (int'l arpt.), Leb. 133/D3
Beitbridge, Zim. 147/E5
Beith, Sc, UK 78/B5
Beiuş, Rom. 90/F2
Beizhen, China 115/A2
Beja, Port. 86/B3
Beja (dist.), Port. 86/A4
Beja, Tun. 142/L6
Beja (gov.), Tun. 142/L6
Bejaïa (prov.), Alg. 142/H4
Bejaïa, Alg. 142/H4
Béjar, Sp. 86/C2
Bejhi (riv.), Pak. 131/J3
Bekabad, Uzb. 129/E4
Bekasi, Indo. 122/C5
Békés, Hun. 90/E2
Békés (prov.), Hun. 90/E2
Békéscsaba, Hun. 90/E2
Bekilli, Turk. 132/B2
Bekily, Madg. 149/H9
Bekitro, Madg. 149/H9
Bekwai, Gha. 145/E5
Bel Air, Md, US 180/B4
Bel Air South, Md, US 180/B5
Belā, India 124/D2
Bela, Pak. 131/J3
Belá, Slvk. 83/K4
Bela Crkva, Serb. 90/E3
Bela Cruz, Braz. 196/B1
Bela Palanka, Serb. 90/F4
Bělá pod Bezdězem, Czh. 97/H1
Belā Pratāpgarh, India 126/C3
Bela Vista, Braz. 193/G8
Bela Vista, Moz. 149/F2
Bela Vista do Paraíso, Braz. 197/B2
Belair, La, US 179/Q17
Belair Rec. Pk., Austl. 155/M9
Belan (riv.), India 126/D3
Belarus (ctry.) 69/G3
Belas, Port. 87/P10
Belaya (riv.), Rus. 106/F4
Belbo (riv.), It. 100/B3
Bełchatów, Pol. 83/K3
Belchen (peak), Ger. 98/D2
Belcher (chan.), Nun., Can. 165/S7
Belcher (isls.), On, Can. 165/H3
Belchite, Sp. 87/E2
Belcourt, ND, US 169/J3
Beldānga, India 127/G4
Belebey, Rus. 103/M5
Beled Weyne, Som. 139/Q7
Belém, Braz. 193/J4
Belém, Braz. 196/D2
Belém de São Francisco, Braz. 196/C3
Belem Tower, Port. 87/P10
Belén, Arg. 199/C2
Belen, NM, US 170/F4
Belén, Chile 198/D5
Belén, Nic. 182/D5
Belen, Turk. 133/E1
Belen, Turk. 133/C1
Belén de Escobar, Arg. 201/J11
Belene, Bul. 91/G4
Beles Wenz (riv.), Eth. 139/N5
Belesar, Embalse de (res.), Sp. 86/B1
Belev, Rus. 104/F1
Belews Creek, Mo, US 179/F9
Belfair, Wa, US 177/B3
Belfast (cap.), NI, UK 76/C2
Belfast (dist.), NI, UK 76/B2
Belfast, SAfr. 149/E2
Belfast, Me, US 173/G2
Belfast Lough (bay), NI, UK 76/C2
Belfaux, Swi. 98/D4
Belfield, ND, US 169/H4
Belfort (dept.), Fr. 98/C2
Belfort, Fr. 98/C2
Belgioioso, It. 100/C2
Belgium (ctry.) 82/C3
Belgorod, Rus. 104/F2
Belgorodskaya Oblast, Rus. 104/F2
Belgrade, Mt, US 168/F4
Belgrade (Beograd) (cap.),Serb. 90/E4
Beli Drim (riv.), Serb. 90/E4
Beli Manastir, Cro. 90/D3
Beli Timok (riv.), Serb. 90/F4
Belitsa, Bul. 89/H2
Belitung (isl.), Indo. 122/C4
Belize (riv.), Belz. 186/D2
Belize (ctry.) 186/D2
Belize City, Belz. 186/D2
Beljanica (peak), Serb. 90/E3
Bel'kovskiy (isl.), Rus. 107/N2
Bell, Austl. 156/C4
Bell (pt.), Austl. 155/G5
Bell (pen.), Nun., Can. 165/H2
Bell (riv.), Qu, Can. 165/J4
Bell, Ca, US 178/F8
Bell, Ger. 95/G3
Bell Gardens, Ca, US 178/F8
Bell Rock (Inchcape) (isl.), Sc, UK 78/D4
Bell Ville, Arg. 199/D3
Bella Coola, BC, Can. 168/B2
Bella Vista, Arg. 199/E2
Bellac, Fr. 84/D3
Bellaghy, NI, UK 76/B2
Bellagio, It. 99/F6
Bellano, It. 99/F5
Bellary, India 124/C4
Bellavista, Peru 198/B2
Bellavista, Peru 198/B2
Bellavista (cape), It. 88/A3
Bellavista, Ecu. 198/E7
Belle (riv.), On, Can. 177/G7
Belle-Anse, Haiti 187/H2
Belle Chasse, La, US 179/Q17
Belle Fourche (riv.), Wy, US 169/G5
Belle Glade, Fl, US 175/H5
Belle Haven, Va, US 180/A6
Belle-Île (isl.), Fr. 84/B3
Belle Isle (str.), NF, Can. 173/K1
Belle Terre, NY, US 181/E2
Belleek, NI, UK 76/B3
Bellefontaine, Oh, US 172/D3
Bellefonte, De, US 180/C4
Bellegarde-sur-Valserine, Fr. 98/B5
Bellenberg, Ger. 99/G1
Bellenden Ker NP, Austl. 156/B2
Belleplain, NJ, US 180/D5
Bellerive-sur-Allier, Fr. 84/E3
Bellerose, NY, US 181/L9
Belleu, Fr. 94/C5
Belleville, On, Can. 172/E2
Belleville, Fr. 98/A5
Belleville, Il, US 179/H8
Belleville, Mi, US 177/E7
Belleville, NJ, US 181/J8
Belleville-sur-Meuse, Fr. 95/E5
Bellevue, Md, US 180/B6
Belley, Fr. 98/B6
Bellflower, Ca, US 178/F8
Bellheim, Ger. 96/B4
Bellignat, Fr. 98/B5
Bellinge, Den. 80/D4
Bellingen, Austl. 157/E1
Bellingham, Wa, US 168/C3
Bellingshausen (isl.), FrPol. 159/K6
Bellingshausen (sea), Ant. 202/U
Bellingwolde, Neth. 93/E2
Bellinzago Novarese, It. 100/B1
Bellinzona, Swi. 99/F5
Bellmawr, NJ, US 180/C4
Bellmead, Tx, US 171/H5
Bellmore, NY, US 181/L9
Bello, Col. 192/C2
Bellona Reefs (reef), NCal., Fr. 158/E7
Bellot (str.), Nun., Can. 164/G1
Bellport, NY, US 181/F2
Bellshill, Sc, UK 78/B5
Belluno (prov.), It. 101/E1
Belluno, It. 85/K3
Bellville, Tx, US 171/H5
Bellville, SAfr. 148/L10
Bellvue, Co, US 179/B1
Bellwald, Swi. 98/E5
Belm, Ger. 93/F4
Belmar, NJ, US 180/D3
Bélmez, Sp. 86/C3
Belmont, Ca, US 177/K11
Belmonte, Braz. 196/C4
Belmonte, Sp. 86/D3
Belmonte, Port. 86/B2
Belmopan (cap.), Belz. 186/D2
Belmullet, Ire. 73/P9
Belo Campo, Braz. 196/B4
Belo Horizonte, Braz. 197/D1
Belo Jardim, Braz. 196/C3
Belo-Tsiribihina, Madg. 149/H7
Beloeil, Qu, Can. 173/P6
Beloeil, Belg. 94/C2
Belogorsk, Rus. 113/N1
Beloha, Madg. 149/H9
Beloit, Wi, US 169/L5
Beloit, Ks, US 171/H3
Belomorsk, Rus. 102/G2
Belorado, Sp. 86/D1
Belorechensk, Rus. 104/F3
Belören, Turk. 132/C2
Beloretsk, Rus. 103/N5
Beloslav, Bul. 91/H4
Belovo, Bul. 89/J1
Belovo, Rus. 106/J4
Beloye (lake), Rus. 106/D3
Belper, Eng, UK 77/G5
Belsand, India 127/E2
Belt, Mt, US 168/F4
Belterwijde (lake), Neth. 92/D3
Beltheim, Ger. 95/G3
Belton, Tx, US 171/H5
Belton, Mo, US 179/D6
Beltsville, Md, US 180/B5
Beltzville (lake), Pa, US 180/C2
Belukha (peak), Rus. 112/E2
Belvedere, Ca, US 177/K11
Belvidere, NJ, US 180/C2
Belyando (riv.), Austl. 151/D3
Belyy (isl.), Rus. 202/A
Belzig, Ger. 82/G2
Bełżyce, Pol. 83/M3
Bemaraha (plat.), Madg. 149/H7
Bemarivo (riv.), Madg. 149/H7
Bembéréké, Ben. 145/F4
Bembibre, Sp. 86/B1
Bemboka, Austl. 157/D3
Bemetāra, India 124/D3
Bemidji, Mn, US 169/K4
Bemmel, Neth. 92/C5
Ben Aigan (hill), Sc, UK 78/C1
Ben Alder (peak), Sc, UK 78/B3
Ben Améra (well), Mrta. 140/B5
Ben Avon (peak), Sc, UK 78/C2
Ben Boyd NP, Austl. 157/D3
Ben Chonzie (peak), Sc, UK 78/C4
Ben Cleuch (peak), Sc, UK 78/C4
Ben Cruachan (peak), Sc, UK 78/A4
Ben Davis (pt.), NJ, US 180/C5
Ben Gurion (int'l arpt.), Isr. 133/F7
Ben Hope (peak), Sc, UK 73/R7
Ben Ime (peak), Sc, UK 78/B4
Ben Lawers (peak), Sc, UK 78/B3
Ben Ledi (peak), Sc, UK 78/B4
Ben Lomond (peak), Sc, UK 78/B4
Ben Lomond NP, Austl. 157/C4
Ben Lui (peak), Sc, UK 78/B4
Ben Macdui (peak), Sc, UK 78/C2
Ben More (peak), Sc, UK 73/Q8
Ben More (peak), Sc, UK 78/B4
Ben More Assynt (peak), Sc, UK 73/R7
Ben Msik-Sidi Othmane (prov.), Mor. 142/A2
Ben Nevis (peak), Sc, UK 78/B3
Ben Rinnes (peak), Sc, UK 78/C2
Ben Slimane, Mor. 140/D2
Ben Slimane (prov.), Mor. 142/A3
Ben Starav (peak), Sc, UK 78/A3
Ben Tee (peak), Sc, UK 78/B2
Ben Tirran (peak), Sc, UK 78/C3
Ben Tre, Viet. 120/D4
Ben Vane (peak), Sc, UK 78/B4
Ben Vorlich (peak), Sc, UK 78/B4
Ben Vrackie (peak), Sc, UK 78/C3
Ben Wyvis (peak), Sc, UK 78/B1
Ben Zohra (well), Alg. 140/E3
Benabarre, Sp. 87/F1
Benahmed, Mor. 140/D2
Benalla, Austl. 157/C3
Benalmádena, Sp. 86/C4
Ben Arous, Tun. 142/M6
Ben Arous (gov.), Tun. 142/M6
Benavente, Sp. 86/C1
Benavides, Tx, US 174/D5
Benbane (pt.), NI, UK 76/B1
Benbecula (isl.), Sc, UK 73/Q8
Benbonyathe (peak), Austl. 155/H4
Benburb, NI, UK 76/B3
Bend, Or, US 168/C4
Bendeleben (mt.), Ak, US 176/F2
Bendemeer, Austl. 157/D1
Bendersville, Pa, US 180/A4
Bendigo, Austl. 157/C3
Bendorf, Ger. 80/C4
Bene Beraq, Isr. 133/F7
Benedict (mt.), Nf, Can. 165/L3
Benediktbeuern, Ger. 99/H2
Benediktenwand (peak), Ger. 99/H2
Beneditinos, Braz. 196/B2
Benenitra, Madg. 149/H8
Benešov, Czh. 97/H3
Benevento, It. 88/D2
Benfeld, Fr. 98/D1
Bengal, Bay of (gulf), Asia 124/E4
Bengbu, China 114/D4
Benghāzī, Libya 138/K1
Bengkalis, Indo. 122/B3
Bengkalis (isl.), Indo. 122/B3
Bengkayang, Indo. 122/C3
Bengkulu, Indo. 122/B4
Bengough, Sk, Can. 169/G3
Bengtsfors, Swe. 80/E2
Benguela, Ang. 147/B3
Benguerir, Mor. 140/D2
Beni, D.R. Congo 146/A2
Beni (riv.), Bol. 189/C4
Beni Abbes, Alg. 141/E3
Beni Bouayach, Mor. 142/C2
Beni Ensar, Mor. 142/B2
Beni Khiar, Tun. 142/M6
Beni Mellal, Mor. 140/D2
Beni Ounif, Alg. 141/E2
Benicarló, Sp. 87/F2
Benicia, Ca, US 177/K10
Benidorm, Sp. 87/E3
Benifayó, Sp. 87/E3
Benin (ctry.) 145/F4
Benin, Bight of (bay), Afr. 135/C4
Benin City, Nga. 145/G5
Benisa, Sp. 87/F3
Benito Juárez, Mex. 184/D2
Benjamin, Tx, US 171/H4
Benjamin Constant, Braz. 198/D2
Benjamín Hill, Mex. 184/C2
Benjamin, Isla (isl.), Chile 200/B5
Benkei-misaki (cape), Japan 118/B2
Benkelman, Ne, US 171/G2
Bennachie (hill), Sc, UK 78/D2
Bennan (pt.), Sc, UK 78/A6
Bennett (isl.), Rus. 107/Q2
Bennettsville, SC, US 175/J3
Bennington, Vt, US 172/F3
Bénoue, PN de la, Camr. 138/H6
Bensenville, Il, US 177/Q16
Bensheim, Ger. 96/B3
Benson, Mn, US 169/K4
Benson, Az, US 170/E5
Benta (riv.), Hun. 91/Q10
Bentheim, Ger. 93/E4
Bentley, Eng, UK 77/G4
Bento Gonçalves, Braz. 197/B4
Benton, Ar, US 171/J4
Benton, La, US 171/J4
Benton, Pa, US 180/B1
Benton Harbor, Mi, US 172/C3
Bentong, Malay. 122/B3
Benue (state), Nga. 145/H5
Benue (riv.), Nga. 138/G6
Benxi, China 115/B2
Benxi, China 115/C2
Beočin, Serb. 90/D3
Beograd (int'l arpt.), Serb. 90/E3
Beohāri, India 126/C3
Beppu (bay), Japan 116/B4
Beppu, Japan 116/B4
Bequia (isl.), StV. 183/N9
Bequimão, Braz. 196/A1
Beraber (well), Alg. 138/E1
Beragh, NI, UK 76/A2
Beraketa, Madg. 149/H8
Berane, Serb. 90/D4
Berasia, India 126/A4
Berat, Alb. 89/F2
Beratus (peak), Indo. 123/E4
Beratzhausen, Ger. 97/E4
Berau (riv.), Indo. 123/E3
Berau (bay), Indo. 123/H4
Berbenno di Valtellina, It. 99/F5
Berbera, Som. 139/Q5
Berbérati, CAfr. 138/J7
Berbice (riv.), Guy. 192/G2
Berceto, It. 100/C3
Berchem, Belg. 92/B6
Bercher, Swi. 98/C4
Berching, Ger. 97/E4
Berchtesgaden, Ger. 85/K3
Berchtesgaden, NP, Ger. 85/K3
Berck, Fr. 94/A3
Berdorf, Lux. 95/F4
Berdsk, Rus. 129/H2
Berdyans'k, Ukr. 104/F3
Berdychiv, Ukr. 104/D2
Berea, Ky, US 172/C4
Bereguardo, It. 100/C2
Berehove, Ukr. 83/M4
Berekum, Gha. 145/E5
Berenguela, Bol. 198/D5
Berenice (ruin), Egypt 143/C4
Beresford, SD, US 169/J5
Beresford, NB, Can. 173/H2
Bereşti, Rom. 91/H2
Berettyóújfalu, Hun. 90/E2
Berevo, Madg. 149/H7
Berezina (riv.), Bela. 104/D1
Berezniki, Rus. 103/N4
Berezovo, Rus. 106/G3
Berg (riv.), SAfr. 148/B4
Berg, Swi. 99/F2
Berg, Lux. 95/F4
Berg, Ger. 96/B5
Berg bei Rohrbach, Aus. 97/G5
Berga, Sp. 87/F1
Bergama, Turk. 132/A2
Bergamo, It. 100/C1
Bergamo (prov.), It. 99/F6
Bergara, Sp. 86/D1
Bergatruete, Ger. 99/F2
Bergen, Ger. 93/G3
Bergen, Ger. 80/E4
Bergen, Neth. 92/B3
Bergen, Nor. 80/A1
Bergen (co.), NJ, US 180/D2
Bergen op Zoom, Neth. 92/B5
Bergen Park, Co, US 179/B3
Bergenfield, NJ, US 181/K8
Bergerac, Fr. 84/D4
Bergeyk, Neth. 92/C6
Bergheim, Tx, US 179/T20
Bergheim, Aus. 97/G7
Bergheim, Ger. 95/F2
Bergisch Gladbach, Ger. 95/G2
Bergkamen, Ger. 93/E5
Bergnäset, Swe. 102/D2
Bergneustadt, Ger. 95/G1
Bergrheinfeld, Ger. 82/F4
Bergse Maas (riv.), Neth. 92/B5
Bergshamra, Swe. 80/H2
Bergsviken, Swe. 79/G2
Bergtheim, Ger. 96/D3
Berguent, Mor. 142/C2
Bergues, Fr. 94/B2
Bergum, Neth. 92/D2
Bergumermeer (lake), Neth. 92/D2
Bergün-Bravuogn, Swi. 99/F4
Bergviken (lake), Swe. 80/G1
Berh, Mong. 113/K2
Berikat (cape), Indo. 122/C4
Bering (isl.), Rus. 107/S4
Bering (sea), Asia,NAm. 107/U4
Bering (str.), Rus.,US 109/U3
Bering Land Bridge Nat'l Prsv., Ak, US 176/E2
Beringen, Belg. 95/E1
Beritarikap (cape), Indo. 122/B4
Berja, Sp. 86/D4
Berkel, Neth. 92/B5
Berkel (riv.), Ger. 82/D2
Berkeley, Ca, US 170/B3
Berkeley, Mo, US 179/G8
Berkeley Heights, NJ, US 181/H9
Berkhamsted, Eng, UK 72/B1
Berkheim, Ger. 99/G1
Berkhout, Neth. 92/B3
Berkley, Mi, US 177/F6
Berkovitsa, Bul. 89/H1
Berks (co.), Pa, US 180/C3
Berkshire (co.), Eng, UK 75/E3
Berkshire Downs (hills), Eng, UK 75/E3
Berlaimont, Fr. 94/C3
Berlanga de Duero, Sp. 86/D2
Berlare, Belg. 94/D1
Berleburg, Ger. 93/F6
Berlicum, Neth. 92/C5
Berlin (cap.), Ger. 82/Q6
Berlin (state), Ger. 82/Q6
Berlin, NH, US 173/G2
Berlin, NJ, US 180/D4
Berlin, Wi, US 169/L5
Bermagui, Austl. 157/D3
Bermejo, Bol. 199/D1
Bermejo (riv.), Arg. 189/D5
Bermeo, Sp. 86/D1
Bermillo de Sayago, Sp. 86/B2
Bermuda (isl.), UK 161/L6
Bern (canton), Swi. 98/D4
Bern (cap.), Swi. 98/D4
Bern-Belp (int'l arpt.), Swi. 98/D4
Bernal, Peru 198/A2
Bernalda, It. 88/E2
Bernalillo, NM, US 170/F4
Bernard (riv.), NW, Can. 164/D1
Bernardo O'Higgins, PN, Chile 199/B6
Bernardsville, NJ, US 180/D2
Bernau, Ger. 98/E2
Bernau, Ger. 82/Q6
Bernay, Fr. 84/D2
Bernbeuren, Ger. 99/G2
Bernburg, Ger. 82/F3
Berne (riv.), Ger. 93/F2
Bernes-sur-Oise, Fr. 72/J4
Bernese Alps (mtn.), Swi. 85/G3
Bernhardswald, Ger. 97/F4
Bernice, La, US 171/J4
Bernier (isl.), Austl. 154/B3
Bernier (bay), Nun., Can. 164/G1
Bernina (peak), Swi. 99/F5
Bernina (mtn.), Swi. 99/F5
Bernina, Passo del (pass), Swi. 99/G5
Bernissart, Belg. 94/C3
Bernkastel-Kues, Ger. 95/G4
Bernsbach, Ger. 97/F1
Bernville, Pa, US 180/B3
Beromünster, Swi. 98/E3
Beroroha, Madg. 149/H8
Beroun, Czh. 97/H3
Berounka (riv.), Czh. 83/G4
Berovo, FYROM 89/H2
Berra, It. 101/E3
Berre, Étang de (lake), Fr. 84/F5
Berrechid, Mor. 140/D2
Berri, Austl. 155/J5
Berriane, Alg. 141/F2
Berridale, Austl. 157/D3
Berriedale, Sc, UK 73/S7
Berrigan, Austl. 157/C2
Berriozábal, Mex. 186/C2
Berrotarán, Arg. 200/D2
Berrouaghia, Alg. 142/G4
Berry, Austl. 157/D2
Berry (isls.), Bahm. 183/F2
Berry (reg.), Fr. 84/D3
Berry (pt.), Eng, UK 74/C6
Berry (mtn.), Pa, US 180/A2
Berryessa (peak), Ca, US 177/K9
Bersenbrück, Ger. 93/E3
Berthoud, Co, US 179/B2
Bertinoro, It. 101/F4
Bertiolo, It. 101/G1
Bertogne, Belg. 95/E3
Bertolínia, Braz. 196/B2
Bertoua, Camr. 138/H7
Bertrand (peak), Arg. 201/B6
Bertrandville, La, US 179/Q17
Bertrix, Belg. 95/E4
Bertry, Fr. 94/C3
Beru (isl.), Kiri. 158/G5
Beruit (isl.), Malay. 122/D3
Bervie Water (riv.), Sc, UK 78/D3
Berwick, NS, Can. 173/H2
Berwick, Pa, US 180/B1
Berwick-upon-Tweed, Eng, UK 78/D5
Berwyn, Il, US 177/Q16
Berwyn (mts.), Wal, UK 76/E6
Berzence, Hun. 90/C2
Bès (riv.), Fr. 84/E2
Besalampy, Madg. 149/H7
Besançon, Fr. 98/C3
Besar (peak), Indo. 123/E4
Besbre (riv.), Fr. 84/E3
Beşiri, Turk. 132/E2
Beška, Serb. 90/E3
Beskids (mts.), Pol. 83/L4
Beşkonak, Turk. 133/B1
Beslan, Rus. 105/H4
Besna Kobila (peak), Serb. 90/F4
Besozzo, It. 100/B1
Bessacarr, Eng, UK 77/G5
Bessancourt, Fr. 72/J4
Bessarabia (reg.), Mol. 91/J2
Bessbrook, NI, UK 76/B3
Bessemer, Al, US 175/G3
Bessemer (mtn.), Wa, US 177/D2
Bessines-sur-Gartempe, Fr. 84/D3
Best, Neth. 92/C5
Bestensee, Ger. 82/Q7
Bestwig, Ger. 93/F6
Bet She'an, Isr. 133/D3
Bet Shemesh, Isr. 133/F8
Betanantanana, Madg. 149/H7
Betanzos, Sp. 86/A1
Beth She'arim (ruin), Isr. 133/G6
Bethal, SAfr. 148/E2
Bethalto, Il, US 179/G8
Bethanie, Namb. 148/B2
Bethany (res.), Ca, US 177/L11
Bethany, Mo, US 169/K5
Bethany, Ok, US 179/M14
Bethel, Ak, US 176/F3
Bethel, Pa, US 180/B3
Bethel Acres, Ok, US 179/N15
Bethel Island, Ca, US 177/L10
Bétheniville, Fr. 95/D5
Bétheny, Fr. 94/D5
Bethesda, Md, US 180/A6
Bethesda, Wal, UK 76/D5
Béthisy-Sainte-Pierre, Fr. 94/B5
Bethlehem, SAfr. 148/E3
Bethlehem, Pa, US 180/C2
Bethlehem, Md, US 180/C6
Bethoncourt, Fr. 98/C2
Bethpage, NY, US 181/M9
Bethulie, SAfr. 148/D3
Bethune, Sk, Can. 169/G3
Béthune (riv.), Fr. 84/D2
Béthune, Fr. 94/B2
Betim, Braz. 197/C1
Betioky, Madg. 149/H8
Betpaqala (plain), Kaz. 112/A2
Betroka, Madg. 149/H8
Betschdorf, Fr. 96/A5
Betsiamites (riv.), Qu, Can. 173/G1
Betsiboka (riv.), Madg. 149/H7
Bettancourt-la-Ferrée, Fr. 95/D6
Bette (peak), Libya 139/J3
Bettembourg, Lux. 95/F4
Betterton, Md, US 180/B5
Bettiah, India 127/E2
Bettlach, Swi. 98/D3
Bettles, Ak, US 176/H2
Betuwe (phys. reg.), Neth. 92/C5
Betwa (riv.), India 126/B3
Betz, Fr. 72/L4
Betzdorf, Ger. 95/G2
Betzenstein, Ger. 97/E3
Beulah, Austl. 157/B2
Beulah, ND, US 169/H4
Beulah (lake), Wi, US 177/P14
Beulakerwijde (lake), Neth. 92/C3
Beuningen, Neth. 92/C5
Beure, Fr. 98/C3
Beuvray (peak), Fr. 84/F3
Beuvron (riv.), Fr. 84/D3
Beuvronne (riv.), Fr. 72/L5
Beuvry, Fr. 94/B2
Bevensen, Ger. 93/H2
Bever (riv.), Ger. 93/E4
Beveren, Belg. 92/B6
Beverin (peak), Swi. 99/F4
Beverley, Austl. 154/C5
Beverley, Eng, UK 77/H4
Beverly, Mo, US 179/D5
Beverly Hills, Ca, US 178/F7
Beverly Hills, Mi, US 177/F6
Beverstedt, Ger. 93/F2
Beverungen, Ger. 93/G5
Beverwijk, Neth. 92/B4
Bewār, India 126/B3
Bewl Bridge (res.), Eng, UK 75/G4
Bex, Swi. 98/D5
Bexar (co.), Tx, US 179/T21
Bexbach, Ger. 95/G5
Bexhill, Eng, UK 75/G5
Bexley (bor.), Eng, UK 72/D2
Beyçayırı, Turk. 91/H5
Beycuma, Turk. 91/K5
Beyne-Heusay, Belg. 95/E2
Beynes, Fr. 72/H5
Beyoneisu-Retsugan (isl.), Japan 117/F5
Beypazarı, Turk. 91/K5
Beyşehir, Turk. 132/B2
Bezaha, Madg. 149/H8
Bezau, Aus. 99/F3
Bezdan, Serb. 90/D3
Bezděz (peak), Czh. 97/H1
Bezdrev (lake), Czh. 97/H4
Bezhetsk, Rus. 102/H4
Béziers, Fr. 84/E5
Bhabua, India 126/D3
Bhadarwāh, India 128/C3
Bhadaur, India 128/C4
Bhadohī, India 126/D3
Bhādra, India 128/C5
Bhadreswar, India 124/A3
Bhāgalpur, India 127/F3
Bhāi Pheru, Pak. 128/B4
Bhairab (riv.), Bang. 127/G4
Bhairab Bāzār, Bang. 127/H3
Bhakkar, Pak. 128/A4
Bhākra (dam), India 128/D4
Bhaktapur, Nepal 127/E2
Bhalwāl, Pak. 128/B3
Bhamo, Myan. 125/G3
Bhānder, India 126/B3
Bhānrer (range), India 126/B4
Bhānwad, India 124/A3
Bharatpur, Nepal 127/E2
Bhārātpur, India 126/A2
Bharthana, India 126/B2
Bharuch, India 131/K4
Bhasāwar, India 126/A2
Bhātāpāra, India 124/D3
Bhatinda, India 128/C4
Bhatkal, India 131/K6
Bhātpāra, India 127/G4
Bhavāni, India 124/C5
Bhavnagar, India 131/K4
Bhawāna, Pak. 128/B4
Bhawāni Mandi, India 131/L4
Bhera, Pak. 128/B3
Bheri (zone), Nepal 126/C1
Bhilai, India 124/D3
Bhīlwāra, India 131/K3
Bhīma (riv.), India 131/L5
Bhima (riv.), India 124/C4
Bhīmavaram, India 124/D4
Bhimunipatnam, India 124/D4
Bhinga, India 126/C2
Bhiwandi, India 131/K5
Bhiwāni, India 128/D5
Bhojpur, Nepal 127/F2
Bhokardan, India 124/C3
Bhola, Bang. 127/H4
Bhongaon, India 126/B2
Bhopāl, India 124/C3
Bhor, India 131/K5
Bhraoin (lake), Sc, UK 78/A1
Bhuban, India 124/E3
Bhumibol (dam), Thai. 120/B2
Bhusawal, India 131/L4
Bhutan (ctry.) 124/E2
Bi Doup (peak), Viet. 120/E3
Biá (riv.), Braz. 192/E4
Bia (riv.), C.d'Iv. 144/E5
Biafra, Bight of (bay), Camr. 138/G7
Biak (isl.), Indo. 123/J4
Biak (int'l arpt.), Indo. 123/J4
Biała Podlaska, Pol. 83/M2
Białobrzegi, Pol. 83/L3
Białogard, Pol. 80/G4
Białowieski NP, Pol. 83/M2
Białystok, Pol. 83/M2
Bianca (peak), It. 99/G4
Biancavilla, It. 88/D4
Biandrate, It. 100/B2
Biandronno, It. 100/B1
Bianze, It. 100/B2
Biarritz, Fr. 84/C5
Biasca, Swi. 99/E5
Bibā, Egypt 143/B2
Bibai, Japan 118/B2
Bibbiano, It. 100/D3
Bibbiena, It. 101/E5
Biberach, Ger. 98/E1
Biberach, Ger. 99/G1
Biberach an der Riss, Ger. 99/F1
Biberist, Swi. 98/D3
Bibione, It. 101/G1
Biblián, Ecu. 194/B5
Biblis, Ger. 96/B3
Bicas, Braz. 197/K6
Bicaz, Rom. 91/H2
Bicester, Eng, UK 75/E3
Bicheno, Austl. 157/D4
Bicknacre, Eng, UK 72/E1
Bicske, Hun. 90/D2
Bida, Nga. 145/G4
Bīdar, India 124/C4
Biddeford, Me, US 173/G3
Biddiyā, WBnk. 133/G7
Biddū, WBnk. 133/G8
Biddulph, Eng, UK 77/F5
Bidean nam Bian (peak), Sc, UK 78/A3
Bideford, Eng, UK 74/B4
Bidente (riv.), It. 101/F4
Bidhūna, India 126/B2
Bīdokht, Iran 131/G2
Biebesheim am Rhein, Ger. 96/B3
Biebzra (riv.), Pol. 83/M2
Biel, Swi. 98/D3
Bielawa, Pol. 83/J3
Bieldside, Sc, UK 78/D2
Bielefeld, Ger. 93/F4
Bieler (lake), Nun., Can. 165/J1
Bieler (lake), Swi. 98/D3
Biella, It. 100/B1
Biella (prov.), It. 100/B1
Bielsk Podlaski, Pol. 83/M2
Bielsko-Biała, Pol. 83/K4
Bien Hoa, Viet. 120/D4
Bienenbüttel, Ger. 93/H2
Bienne (riv.), Fr. 98/B5
Bienno, It. 99/G6
Bientina, It. 100/D5
Bienville (lake), Qu, Can. 165/J3
Bière, Swi. 98/C4
Bierset (int'l arpt.), Belg. 95/E2
Bierum, Neth. 92/D2
Bierutów, Pol. 83/J3
Biesbosch (reg.), Neth. 92/B5
Biesenthal, Ger. 82/Q6
Biesles, Fr. 98/B1
Biesme (riv.), Fr. 95/D5
Bieszczadzki NP, Pol. 83/M4
Bietigheim, Ger. 96/C5
Bietschhorn (peak), Swi. 98/D5
Bièvre (riv.), Fr. 72/J5
Bièvre, Belg. 95/E4
Bièvres, Fr. 72/J5
Big (des.), Austl. 157/B2
Big (riv.), Nun., Can. 164/D1
Big (isl.), On, Can. 164/G4
Big (lake), Mi, US 177/E6
Big (riv.), Mo, US 179/F9
Big Belt (mts.), Mt, US 168/F4
Big Bend, Swaz. 149/E2
Big Bend, Wi, US 177/P14
Big Bend NP, Tx, US 171/C5
Big Blue (riv.), Ks,Ne, US 171/H2
Big Diomede (isl.), Rus. 176/E2
Big Fork (riv.), Mn, US 169/K4
Big Hole (riv.), Mt, US 168/E4
Big Hole, SAfr. 148/D3

222
Big L – Bonav

Big Lake, Tx, US 171/G5
Big Lost (riv.), Id, US 170/D2
Big Muskego (lake), Wi, US 177/P14
Big Pine (hill), Pa, US 180/C1
Big Pines, Ca, US 178/C2
Big Rapids, Mi, US 172/C3
Big River, Sk, Can. 168/G2
Big Rock, Il, US 177/N16
Big Sandy (riv.), Wy, US 170/E2
Big Sioux (riv.), Ia,SD, US 169/J5
Big Spring, Tx, US 171/G4
Big Stone (lake), Mn,SD, US 169/J4
Big Thompson (riv.), Co, US 179/B2
Big Thompson, North Fork (riv.), Co, US 179/A2
Big Timber, Mt, US 168/F4
Big Trout (lake), On, Can. 164/H3
Big Tujunga Canyon (canyon), Ca, US 178/B2
Big Wood (riv.), Id, US 170/D2
Biga, Turk. 91/H5
Bigadiç, Turk. 132/B2
Bigbury (bay), Eng, UK 74/C6
Biggar, Sk, Can. 168/G2
Biggar, Sc, UK 78/C5
Bigge (riv.), Ger. 95/G1
Biggenden, Austl. 156/D4
Biggleswade, Eng, UK 75/F2
Bighorn (basin), Wy, US 170/E1
Bighorn (lake), Mt,Wy, US 168/F4
Bighorn (mts.), Wy, US 166/E3
Bighorn (riv.), Wy, US 168/G4
Biglerville, Pa, US 180/A4
Bignona, Sen. 144/A3
Biguaçu, Braz. 197/B3
Bihać, Bosn. 85/L4
Bīhar, India 127/E3
Biharamulo, Tanz. 146/A3
Biharamulo Game Rsv., Tanz. 146/A3
Bihārīganj, India 127/F3
Biharkeresztes, Hun. 90/E2
Bihor (co.), Rom. 83/M5
Bihorel, Fr. 84/D2
Bihoro, Japan 118/D2
Bijagós (arch.), GBis. 135/A3
Bijagós, Arquipélago do (isl.) GBis. 138/B5
Bījār, Iran 130/E1
Bijāwar, India 126/B3
Bijbiāra, India 128/C3
Bijeljina, Bosn. 90/D3
Bijelo Polje, Mont. 90/D4
Bijiang, China 125/G2
Bijie, China 125/J2
Bijni, India 127/H2
Bijnor, India 126/B1
Bīkaner, India 131/K3
Bikar (isl.), Mrsh. 158/G3
Bikin, Rus. 113/P2
Bikin (riv.), Rus. 113/Q2
Bikini (isl.), Mrsh. 158/F3
Bikramganj, India 127/E3
Bikuar, PN do, Ang. 147/C4
Bila Tserkva, Ukr. 104/D2
Bilāra, India 124/B2
Bilāri, India 126/B1
Bilāsipāra, India 127/H2
Bilāspur, India 126/D4
Bilāspur, India 126/B1
Bilāspur, India 128/D4
Bilaukraung (range), Myan. 125/G5
Bilauktaung (range), Myan.,Thai. 120/B3
Bilba Morea Claypan (lake), Austl. 151/C3
Bilbao, Sp. 86/D1
Bilbays, Egypt 133/B4
Bileća, Bosn. 89/F1
Bilecik, Turk. 132/B1
Bilecik (prov.), Turk. 132/B1
Biłgoraj, Pol. 83/M3
Bilgrām, India 126/C2
Bilhaur, India 126/C2
Bilhorod-Dnistrovs'kyy, Ukr. 91/K2
Bilibino, Rus. 107/S3
Bilin, Myan. 125/G4
Bilin (riv.), Myan. 120/B2
Bilina (riv.), Czh. 97/G2
Bílina, Czh. 97/G1
Biliu (riv.), China 115/B3
Bill of Portland (pt.), Eng, UK 74/D5
Bill Williams (riv.), Az, US 170/D4
Bille (riv.), Ger. 93/H1
Billerbeck, Ger. 93/E5
Billère, Fr. 84/C5
Billericay, Eng, UK 72/E2
Billiat Conservation Park, Austl. 157/B2
Billiat Consv. Park, Austl. 155/J5
Billigheim, Ger. 96/C4
Billinge, Eng, UK 77/F4
Billingham, Eng, UK 77/G2
Billings, Mt, US 168/F4
Billingsfors, Swe. 80/E2
Billund (int'l arpt.), Den. 80/C4
Billund, Den. 80/C4
Bilma, Niger 138/H4
Biloela, Austl. 156/C4
Biloku, Guy. 195/G4
Biloxi, Ms, US 175/F4
Bilpa Morea Claypan (lake), Austl. 155/H3
Bilqas Qism Awwal, Egypt 133/B4
Bilsi, India 126/B1
Bilthar, India 126/D2
Biltine, Chad 139/K5
Bilzen, Belg. 95/E2
Bima, Indo. 123/E5
Bimberi (peak), Austl. 157/D2
Bimbo, CAfr. 139/J7
Bimini (isls.), Bahm. 183/F2
Bina (riv.), Ger. 97/F6
Bina-Etāwa, India 126/B3
Binalong, Austl. 157/D2
Binasco, It. 100/C2
Binbrook, On, Can. 173/Q9
Binche, Belg. 95/D3
Binchuan, China 125/H2
Bindki, India 126/C2
Bindura, Zim. 147/F4
Binéfar, Sp. 87/F2
Binga (mtn.), Moz. 147/F4
Bingara, Austl. 157/D1
Bingen, Ger. 95/G4
Bingerville, C.d'Iv. 144/E5
Binghamton, NY, US 172/F3
Bingley, Eng, UK 77/G4
Bıngöl, Turk. 132/E2
Bıngöl (prov.), Turk. 132/E2
Binh Son, Viet. 120/E3
Binhai, China 114/D4
Binhon (peak), Myan. 125/G4
Binisalem, Sp. 87/G3
Binjai, Indo. 122/A3
Binkılıç, Turk. 91/J5
Binnaway, Austl. 157/D1
Binningen, Swi. 98/D2
Binongko (isl.), Indo. 123/F5
Bintang (peak), Malay. 122/B2
Binyamina, Isr. 133/F6
Bío-Bío (riv.), Chile 199/B4
Bío-Bío (pol. reg.), Chile 200/B3
Biograd, Cro. 90/B4
Biogradska NP, Mont. 90/D4
Bioko (isl.), EqG. 135/C4
Biougra, Mor. 140/C3
Bipoint (Bissau) (int'l arpt.), GBis. 144/B4
Bippen, Ger. 93/E3
Bīr, India 131/L5
Bīr Abu Minqâr (well), Egypt 143/A3
Bir Aïdiat (well), Mrta. 140/C4
Bir Bel Guerdâne (well), Mrta. 140/C4
Bi'r Ghadir (well), Egypt 143/C3
Bīr Ounâne (well), Mali 140/E5
Bi'r Zayt, WBnk. 133/G8
Birāk, Libya 138/H2
Birao, CAfr. 139/K5
Birātnagar, Nepal 127/F2
Biratori, Japan 118/C2
Birch (mts.), Ab, Can. 164/E3
Birch Creek, Ak, US 176/J2
Birch Hills, Sk, Can. 169/G2
Birch River, Mb, Can. 169/H2
Birchip, Austl. 157/B2
Bird Islet (isl.), Austl. 151/E3
Birds Rock (peak), Austl. 157/D2
Birdsboro, Pa, US 180/C3
Birdwood, Austl. 155/M8
Birecik, Turk. 132/D2
Bīrganj, Nepal 127/E2
Biritiba-Mirim, Braz. 197/G8
Bīrjand, Iran 131/G2
Birkat Qārūn (lake), Egypt 132/B4
Birken-Honigsessen, Ger. 95/G2
Birkenau, Ger. 96/B3
Birkenfeld, Ger. 95/G4
Birkenhead, Eng, UK 77/E5
Birkenheide, Ger. 96/B4
Birkenwerder, Ger. 82/Q6
Birkirkara, Malta 88/L7
Birkkarspitze (peak), Aus. 99/H3
Bîrlad, Rom. 91/H2
Birmingham, Eng, UK 75/E2
Birmingham (co.), Eng, UK 75/E2
Birmingham (int'l arpt.), Eng, UK 75/E2
Birmingham, Al, US 175/G3
Birmingham, Mi, US 177/F6
Birmingham, Mo, US 179/E5
Birmitrapur, India 127/E4
Birnam, Sc, UK 78/C3
Birnhorn (peak), Aus. 85/K3
Birni Nkonni, Niger 145/G3
Birnie (isl.), Kiri. 159/H5
Birnin Kebbi, Nga. 145/G3
Birobjian, Rus. 113/P2
Bīrpur, India 127/F2
Birr, Ire. 73/Q10
Birs (riv.), Swi. 85/G3
Birsk, Rus. 103/M5
Birstein, Ger. 96/C2
Biruaca, Ven. 195/E3
Biržai, Lith. 81/L3
Birżebbuġa, Malta 88/M7
Bis (lake), Rom. 91/F4
Bisa-Nadi Nat'l Rsv., Kenya 146/C2
Bisai, Japan 119/L5
Bīsalpur, India 126/B1
Bisamberg, Aus. 91/N7
Bisauli, India 126/B1
Biscarrosse, Fr. 84/C4
Biscarrosse,Étang de (lake), Fr. 84/C4
Biscay (bay), Fr.,Sp. 84/B4
Biscayne NP, Fl, US 175/H5
Bisceglie, It. 88/E2
Bischberg, Ger. 96/D3
Bischheim, Fr. 95/G6
Bischofsgrün, Ger. 97/E2
Bischofsheim, Ger. 96/B3
Bischofsheim an der Rhön, Ger. 96/D2
Bischofshofen, Aus. 85/K3
Bischofszell, Swi. 99/F3
Bischwiller, Fr. 98/D2
Biscubio (riv.), It. 101/F5
Biscucuy, Ven. 194/D2
Bīshah (riv.), SAr. 130/D4
Bishkek (cap.), Kyr. 129/F4
Bishnupur, India 127/F4
Bishop, Ca, US 170/C3
Bishop Auckland, Eng, UK 77/G2
Bishopbriggs, Sc, UK 78/B5
Bishop's Falls, Nf, Can. 173/L1
Bishop's Stortford, Eng, UK 75/G3
Bishopton, Sc, UK 78/B5
Bisingen, Ger. 96/B6
Biskra, Alg. 142/H5
Biskupiec, Pol. 81/J5
Bislig, Phil. 121/E6
Bismarck (cap.), ND, US 169/H4
Bismarck, On, Can. 173/Q9
Bismarck (arch.), PNG 158/D5
Bismarck (sea), PNG 158/D5
Bismil, Turk. 132/E2
Bismuna (lag.), Nic. 187/F3
Bispgarden, Swe. 79/F3
Bispingen, Ger. 93/G2
Bissau (cap.), GBis. 144/B4
Bissau, India 128/C5
Bissendorf, Ger. 93/F4
Bissett, Mb, Can. 169/K3
Bissingen, Ger. 96/D5
Bistagno, It. 100/B3
Bistrița (riv.), Rom. 91/G2
Bistrița, Rom. 91/G2
Bistrița-Năsăud (prov.), Rom. 91/G2
Biswān, India 126/C2
Bita (riv.), Col. 192/E2
Bitam, Gabon 138/H7
Bitburg, Ger. 95/F4
Bitche, Fr. 95/G5
Bitkin, Chad 139/J5
Bitlis (prov.), Turk. 132/E2
Bitlis, Turk. 132/E2
Bitola, FYROM 89/G2
Bitonto, It. 88/E2
Bitter (lakes), Egypt 143/C2
Bitterfontein, SAfr. 148/B3
Bitterroot (range), Id,Mt, US 168/E4
Bitti, It. 88/A2
Bitung, Indo. 123/G3
Bituruna, Braz. 197/B3
Biwa, Japan 119/K5
Bixby, Ok, US 174/E3
Biyalā, Egypt 133/B4
Biyang, China 114/C4
Bizard (isl.), Qu, Can. 173/M7
Bizerte, Tun. 142/L6
Bizerte (gov.), Tun. 142/L6
Bizerte (lake), Tun. 142/L6
Bjärred, Swe. 80/E4
Bjelovar, Cro. 90/C3
Bjerkvik, Nor. 79/F1
Bjerringbro, Den. 80/C3
Bjørkelangen, Nor. 80/D2
Björklinge, Swe. 80/G1
Bjørnafjorden (estu.), Nor. 80/A1
Bjorne (pen.), Nun., Can. 165/S7
Bjugn, Nor. 79/D3
Bjuv, Swe. 80/E3
Blå Jungfrun NP, Swe. 80/G3
Blace, Serb. 90/E4
Blachownia, Pol. 83/K3
Black (sea), Asia,Eur. 109/C5
Black (bay), On, Can. 169/L3
Black (riv.), On. Can. 169/L2
Black (mt.), Yk, Can. 176/M3
Black (riv.), China,Viet. 112/H7
Black (for.), Ger. 82/D5
Black (pt.), Eng, UK 74/A6
Black (pt.), NI, UK 76/C2
Black (isl.), Sc, UK 78/B1
Black (mtn.), Wal, UK 74/C3
Black (mts.), Wal, UK 74/C3
Black (mesa), Az, US 170/E3
Black (mts.), Az, US 171/D4
Black (pt.), Ct, US 181/F1
Black (range), NM, US 170/F4
Black (riv.), NY, US 172/F3
Black (hills), SD, US 166/F3
Black (riv.), Wi, US 169/L4
Black Canyon of the Gunnison Nat'l Park, Co, US 170/F3
Black Diamond, Ab, Can. 168/E3
Black Diamond, Wa, US 177/C3
Black Eagle, Mt, US 168/F4
Black Forest (Schwarzwald) (for.), Ger. 96/B6
Black Hawk, Co, US 179/B3
Black Jack, Mo, US 179/G8
Black Mountain NP, Austl. 156/B1
Black Mtn. (mtn.), Wal, UK 74/C3
Black Point, Ca, US 177/K10
Black River, Jam. 187/G2
Black River Falls, Wi, US 169/L4
Black Rock (des.), Nv, US 170/C2
Black Rock (pt.), RI, US 181/G1
Black Sea Lowland (reg.), Mol.,Ukr. 91/J3
Black Sugarloaf (peak), Austl. 157/D1
Black Volta (riv.), Burk. 138/E5
Black Walnut, Mo, US 179/G8
Black Warrior (riv.), Al, US 175/G3
Blackadder Water (riv.), Sc, UK 78/D5
Blackall, Austl. 156/B4
Blackburn, Eng, UK 77/F4
Blackburn, Sc, UK 78/C5
Blackburn with Darwen, (co.), Eng, UK 77/F4
Blackbutt, Austl. 156/D4
Blackcraig (peak), Sc, UK 78/B6
Blackdown (hills), Eng, UK 74/C5
Blackdown (hill), Eng, UK 75/F4
Blackdown Tableland NP, Austl. 156/C3
Blackfoot (res.), Id, US 168/F5
Blackheath, Austl. 157/D2
Blackmoor (upland), Eng, UK 74/B5
Blackpool, Eng, UK 77/E4
Blackpool (co.), Eng, UK 77/E4
Blackrod, Eng, UK 77/F4
Blackshear (lake), Ga, US 175/H3
Blackstone, Va, US 172/E4
Blackville, NB, Can. 173/H2
Blackwater, Austl. 156/C3
Blackwater (riv.), Ire. 73/P10
Blackwater (riv.), Eng, UK 72/A2
Blackwater (res.), Sc, UK 78/B3
Blackwater (riv.), Mo, US 171/J3
Blackwell, Ok, US 171/H3
Blackwood (riv.), Austl. 154/B5
Blackwood, NJ, US 180/C4
Bladensburg, Md, US 180/B6
Bladensburg NP, Austl. 156/A3
Bladnoch (riv.), Sc, UK 76/D2
Blaenau Gwent (co.), Wal, UK 74/C3
Blagnac, Fr. 84/D5
Blagnac (int'l arpt.), Fr. 84/D5
Blagny, Fr. 95/E4
Blagoevgrad, Bul. 89/H1
Blagoveshchensk, Rus. 113/N1
Blaine Lake, Sk, Can. 168/G2
Blainville, Qu, Can. 173/N6
Blair, Ne, US 169/J5
Blair (hill), Pa, US 180/C1
Blair Atholl, Sc, UK 78/C3
Blairstown, NJ, US 180/D2
Blaise (riv.), Fr. 84/F2
Blaj, Rom. 91/F2
Blakely, Ga, US 175/G4
Blakeslee, Pa, US 180/C1
Blamont, Fr. 98/C3
Blanc (cape), Fr. 85/G5
Blanc (peak), Fr. 98/C6
Blanc (cape), Mrta. 138/B3
Blanc, Cap (cape), Tun. 142/L6
Blanc Nez (cape), Fr. 94/A2
Blanca (peak), NM, US 171/F4
Blanca (pt.), Mex. 184/B2
Blanca (bay), Arg. 189/C6
Blanca, Cordillera (mts.), Peru 192/C5
Blanca, Costa (coast), Sp. 87/E4
Blanchard, Ok, US 179/M15
Blanche (lake), Austl. 151/D3
Blanche (peak), Swi. 98/D5
Blanche (cape), Austl. 155/G5
Blanco (cape), CR 187/E4
Blanco (cape), Mor. 140/A5
Blanco (cape), Peru 192/B4
Blanco (lake), Chile 201/C7
Blanco (riv.), Bol. 192/F6
Blanco (riv.), Tx, US 171/H5
Blanding, Ut, US 170/E3
Blandy, Fr. 72/L6
Blanes, Sp. 87/G2
Blangy-sur-Bresle, Fr. 94/A4
Blankenberge, Belg. 94/C1
Blankenfelde, Ger. 82/Q7
Blankenheim, Ger. 95/F3
Blanquilla (isl.), Ven. 192/F1
Blanquillo, Uru. 201/G2
Blansko, Czh. 83/J4
Blantyre, Malw. 147/G4
Blantyre, Sc, UK 78/B5
Blanzy, Fr. 84/F3
Blaricum, Neth. 92/C4
Blas (peak), Swi. 99/E4
Blatná, Czh. 97/G4
Blato, Cro. 88/E1
Blatten, Swi. 98/D5
Blau (riv.), Ger. 96/C6
Blaubeuren, Ger. 96/C6
Blauen (peak), Ger. 98/D2
Blaustein, Ger. 96/C6
Blauvelt, NY, US 181/K7
Blåvands (pt.), Den. 80/C4
Blavet (riv.), Fr. 84/B3
Blaye, Fr. 84/C4
Blayney, Austl. 157/D2
Bleckede, Ger. 93/H2
Bled, Slov. 85/L3
Blefjell (peak), Nor. 80/C2
Blégny, Belg. 95/E2
Bléharies, Belg. 94/C2
Bleiburg, Aus. 90/B2
Bleicherode, Ger. 93/H6
Bleik (peak), Ger. 99/G2
Bleiswijk, Neth. 92/B4
Blekinge (co.), Swe. 79/E4
Blendecques, Fr. 94/B2
Blender, Ger. 93/G3
Blenheim, NZ 159/S11
Blénod-lès-Pont-à-Mousson, Fr. 95/F6
Bléone (riv.), Fr. 85/G4
Blesberg (peak), SAfr. 148/C4
Blessington, Ire. 76/B5
Bletterans, Fr. 98/B4
Bleury, Fr. 72/H6
Bleus (mts.), D.R. Congo 139/L7
Bleus, Monts (mts.), D.R. Congo 146/A2
Blida (prov.), Alg. 142/G4
Blida, Alg. 142/G4
Blies (riv.), Ger. 95/G5
Blieskastel, Ger. 95/G5
Blik (mt.), Phil. 123/F2
Blinnenhorn (peak), Swi. 99/E5
Blithe (riv.), Eng, UK 77/F6
Blithfield (res.), Eng, UK 77/G6
Block (isl.), RI, US 173/G3
Block Island C. G. Sta., RI, US 181/G1
Block Island (New Shoreham), RI, US 181/G1
Block Island NWR, RI, US 181/G1
Blodelsheim, Fr. 98/D2
Bloemendaal, Neth. 92/B4
Bloemfontein, (cap.), SAfr. 148/D3
Bloemhof, SAfr. 148/D2
Bloemhofdam (res.), SAfr. 148/D2
Blois, Fr. 84/D3
Blomberg, Ger. 93/E1
Blomberg, Ger. 93/G5
Blomstermåla, Swe. 80/G3
Blonay, Swi. 98/C5
Blönduós, Ice. 79/N6
Bloodvein (riv.), Mb,On, Can. 164/G3
Bloody Foreland (pt.), Ire. 73/P9
Bloomfield, NJ, US 181/J8
Bloomfield, NM, US 170/F3
Bloomfield Hills, Mi, US 177/F6
Bloomingdale, NJ, US 181/H7
Bloomingdale, Il, US 177/P16
Bloomington, Mn, US 169/K4
Bloomington, Il, US 169/L5
Bloomington, Ca, US 178/C2
Bloomsburg, Pa, US 180/B2
Bloomsbury, NJ, US 180/C2
Blora, Indo. 122/D5
Blotzheim, Fr. 98/D2
Blountstown, Fl, US 175/G4
Blovice, Czh. 97/G3
Blšanka (riv.), Czh. 85/K1
Bludenz, Aus. 99/F3
Blue (mtn.), India 125/F3
Blue (riv.), Ok, US 174/D3
Blue (mts.), Or,Wa, US 166/C2
Blue Head (pt.), Sc, UK 78/C1
Blue Island, Il, US 177/Q16
Blue Lake NP, Austl. 156/D4
Blue Marsh Lake (res.), Pa, US 180/B3
Blue Mesa (res.), Co, US 170/F3
Blue Mountain (peak), Jam. 187/G2
Blue Mountain (ridge), Pa, US 180/A3
Blue Mountains, Austl. 157/D2
Blue Mountains NP, Austl. 157/D2
Blue Nile (riv.), Sudan, Eth. 139/M5
Blue Ridge (mts.), US 175/H3
Blue Ridge Parkway, US 172/D4
Blue Springs, Mo, US 179/E5
Bluefield, WV, US 172/D4
Bluefields, Nic. 187/F4
Bluefields (bay), Nic. 187/F4
Bluejoint (lake), Or, US 170/C2
Bluenose (lake), Nun., Can. 164/E2
Bluff, NZ 159/R12
Bluff (pt.), Austl. 154/B3
Bluff, Austl. 156/C3
Bluff (peak), Austl. 154/C5
Bluffdale, Ut, US 179/K13
Bluffton, In, US 172/C3
Blumberg, Ger. 99/E2
Blümlisalp (peak), Swi. 98/D5
Blyn, Wa, US 177/B1
Blyth, Austl. 155/H5
Blyth, Eng, UK 77/G1
Blythe, Ca, US 170/D4
Blytheville, Ar, US 171/K4
Bnom Mhai (peak), Viet. 120/D4
Bo, SLeo. 144/C5
Bø, Nor. 80/C2
Bo Hai (Chihli) (gulf), China 114/D3
Boa Esperança, Braz. 197/C2
Boa Esperança, Represa (res.), Braz. 193/J5
Boa Viagem, Braz. 196/C2
Boa Vista, Braz. 195/F4
Boa Vista (int'l arpt.), Braz. 195/F4
Boa Vista (isl.), CpV. 135/K10
Boac, Phil. 121/D5
Boaco, Nic. 186/E3
Boadilla del Monte, Sp. 87/N9
Bo'ai, China 114/C4
Boano (isl.), Indo. 123/G4
Boas (riv.), Nun., Can. 165/H2
Boavita, Col. 194/C3
Boaz, Al, US 175/G3
Boba, Hun. 90/C2
Bobai, China 125/J3
Bobaomby (cape), Madg. 149/J5
Bobbili, India 124/D4
Bobbio, It. 100/C3
Bobenheim-Roxheim, Ger. 96/B3
Bobigny, Fr. 72/K5
Bobingen, Ger. 99/G1
Böblingen, Ger. 96/C5
Bobo Dioulasso, Burk. 144/D4
Boboshevo, Bul. 89/H1
Bobotov Kuk (peak), Mont. 90/D4
Bobovdol, Bul. 89/H1
Bóbr (riv.), Pol. 83/H3
Bobrov, Rus. 104/G2
Bobures, Ven. 194/D2
Boby (peak), Madg. 149/H8
Boca de Aroa, Ven. 194/D2
Boca del Guafo (chan.), Chile 200/B4
Boca del Pao, Ven. 195/E2
Boca del Río, Mex. 185/N7
Bôca do Acre, Braz. 192/E5
Boca Raton, Fl, US 175/H5
Bocaina, Serra da (mts.), Braz. 197/J7
Bocairente, Sp. 87/E3
Bocas del Toro, Pan. 187/F4
Bocay (riv.), Nic. 187/E3
Bochil, Mex. 186/C2
Bochnia, Pol. 83/L4
Bocholt, Ger. 92/D5
Bocholt, Belg. 95/E1
Bochum, Ger. 93/E6
Bockau, Ger. 97/F1
Bockenem, Ger. 93/H4
Bockenheim an der Weinstrasse, Ger. 95/H4
Bockhorn, Ger. 93/F2
Bockhorn, Ger. 97/E6
Boconó, Ven. 194/D2
Bocq (riv.), Belg. 95/D3
Boda, CAfr. 139/J7
Bodafors, Swe. 80/F3
Bodalla, Austl. 157/D3
Bodaybo, Rus. 107/M4
Boddam, Sc, UK 78/E2
Boddington, Austl. 154/C5
Bode (riv.), Ger. 82/F3
Bodega (bay), Ca, US 170/B3
Bodegraven, Neth. 92/B4
Bodélé (reg.), Chad 138/J4
Bodenheim, Ger. 96/B3
Bodenkirchen, Ger. 97/F6
Bodenmais, Ger. 97/G4
Bodensee (Constance) (lake), Swi 85/H3
Bodenteich, Ger. 93/H3
Bodh Gaya, India 127/E3
Bodhan, India 124/C4
Bodināyakkanūr, India 124/C5
Bodio, Swi. 99/E5
Bodkin (pt.), Md, US 180/B5
Bodmin, Eng, UK 74/B6
Bodmin Moor (upland), Eng, UK 74/B6
Bodø, Nor. 79/E2
Bodocó, Braz. 196/C2
Bodrog (riv.), Hun.,Slvk. 83/L4
Bodrum, Turk. 132/A2
Bódvaszilas, Hun. 83/L4
Boedecker (lake), Co, US 179/B2
Boëge, Fr. 98/C5
Boegoeberg (peak), Namb. 148/A2
Boekel, Neth. 92/C5
Boende, D.R. Congo 139/K8
Boerne, Tx, US 179/T20
Boeuf (riv.), La, US 171/K4
Bog of Allen (swamp), Ire. 76/A5
Bogalusa, La, US 175/F4
Bogan (riv.), Austl. 151/D4
Bogan Gate, Austl. 157/C2
Bogandé, Burk. 145/E3
Bogatić, Serb. 90/D3
Bogatynia, Pol. 83/H3
Boğazkale-Alacahöyük NP, Turk. 132/C1
Boğazlıyan, Turk. 132/C2
Bogdanci, FYROM 89/H2
Bogen, Nor. 79/F1
Bogen, Ger. 97/F5
Bogense, Den. 80/D4
Boggabilla, Austl. 156/C5
Boggabri, Austl. 157/D1
Boggy (peak), Anti. 183/N8
Boglárlelle, Hun. 90/C2
Bogliasco, It. 100/C4
Bognor Regis, Eng, UK 75/F5
Bogny-sur-Meuse, Fr. 95/D4
Bogo, Phil. 121/D5
Bogong (mt.), Austl. 157/C3
Bogong NP, Austl. 157/C3
Bogor, Indo. 122/C5
Bogotá (cap.), Col. 192/D3
Bogota, NJ, US 181/J8
Bogovino, FYROM 89/G2
Bogra (pol. reg.), Bang. 127/G3
Bogra, Bang. 127/G3
Bogué, Mrta. 144/B2
Bohain-en-Vermandois, Fr. 94/C4
Bohemia (reg.), Czh. 83/G4
Bohemian (for.), Czh.,Ger. 82/G4
Bohicon, Ben. 145/F5
Böhl-Iggelheim, Ger. 96/B4
Böhme (riv.), Ger. 93/G3
Böhmenkirch, Ger. 96/C5
Bohmte, Ger. 93/F4
Bohners Lake, Wi, US 177/P14
Bohol (isl.), Phil. 121/D6
Böhönye, Hun. 90/C2
Bohu, China 112/E3
Boiling Springs, Pa, US 180/A3
Boipeda, Ilha de (isl.), Braz. 196/C4
Boiro, Sp. 86/A1
Bois-d'Amont, Fr. 98/C4
Bois-d'Arcy, Fr. 72/J5
Bois de Boulogne (dept.), Fr. 72/J5
Bois de Vincennes (dept.), Fr. 72/K5
Bois-des-Filion, Qu, Can. 173/N6
Bois, Rio dos (riv.), Braz. 197/B1
Boisbriand, Qu, Can. 173/N6
Boise (riv.), Id, US 168/E5
Boise City, Ok, US 171/G3
Boissevain, Mb, Can. 169/H3
Boissy-Fresnoy, Fr. 72/L4
Boissy-L'Aillerie, Fr. 72/J4
Boissy-le-Châtel, Fr. 72/M5
Boissy-Saint-Léger, Fr. 72/K5
Boissy-Sans-Avoir, Fr. 72/H5
Boizenburg, Ger. 93/H2
Bojador (cape), Mor. 138/C2
Bojano, It. 90/B5
Boji (plain), Kenya 146/C2
Bojkovice, Czh. 83/J4
Bojnūrd, Iran 131/G1
Bokaro Steel City, India 127/F4
Boké (pol. reg.), Gui. 144/B4
Boké, Gui. 144/B4
Bokhol (plain), Kenya 146/C2
Boknafjorden (estu.), Nor. 79/C4
Bokol (peak), Kenya 146/C2
Bokoro, Chad 138/J5
Bokpyin, Myan. 120/B4
Boksburg, SAfr. 148/Q13
Bokspits, Bots. 148/C2
Bol, Chad 138/H5
Bolama, GBis. 144/B4
Bolān (pass), Pak. 131/J3
Bolaños de Calatrava, Sp. 86/D3
Bolayır, Turk. 89/K2
Bolbec, Fr. 84/D2
Boldești-Scăeni, Rom. 91/H3
Boldon, Eng, UK 77/G2
Bole, China 112/D3
Bole, Gha. 145/E4
Bolesławiec, Pol. 83/H3
Bolgatanga, Gha. 145/E4
Boli, China 113/P2
Boliden, Swe. 79/G2
Bolinao, Phil. 121/C4
Bolívar, Arg. 200/E3
Bolívar, Col. 194/B3
Bolívar (dept.), Col. 194/C2
Bolívar, Ecu. 194/A4
Bolívar, Peru 198/B2
Bolivar, Mo, US 171/J3
Bolívar (peak), Ven. 194/D2
Bolivar (peak), Ven. 195/F3
Bolívar (state), Ven. 195/E3
Bolivia (ctry.), Bol. 192/F7
Bollate, It. 100/C1
Bollène, Fr. 84/F4
Bolligen, Swi. 98/D4
Bollin (riv.), Eng, UK 77/F5
Bollnäs, Swe. 80/G1
Bollullos Par del Condado, Sp. 86/B4
Bolmen (lake), Swe. 80/E3
Bolobo, D.R. Congo 138/J8
Bologna, It. 101/E4
Bologna (prov.), It. 101/E3
Bologne, Fr. 98/B1
Bolognesi, Peru 198/C3
Bologoye, Rus. 102/G4
Bolomba, D.R. Congo 139/J7
Bolonchén de Rejón, Mex. 186/D2
Bolovens (plat.), Laos 120/D3
Bolpur, India 127/F4
Bolsena, It. 88/B1
Bolsena (lake), It. 88/B1
Bol'shaya Kinel' (riv.), Rus. 105/K1
Bol'shaya Rogovaya (riv.), Rus. 103/P2
Bol'shaya Synya (riv.), Rus. 103/N2
Bol'shevik (isl.), Rus. 109/H2
Bol'shezemel'skaya (tundra), Rus. 103/M2
Bol'shoy Bolvanskiy Nos (pt.), Rus. 106/F2
Bol'shoy Irgiz (riv.), Rus. 105/J1
Bol'shoy Lyakhov (isl.), Rus. 109/P2
Bol'shoy Lyakhovskiy (isl.), Rus. 107/Q2
Bol'shoy Uzen' (riv.), Rus. 105/J2
Bolsover, Eng, UK 77/G5
Bolsward, Neth. 92/C2
Bolt (pt.), Eng, UK 74/C6
Boltaña, Sp. 87/F1
Boltigen, Swi. 98/D4
Bolton, Eng, UK 77/F4
Bolton (co.), Eng, UK 77/F4
Bolu, Turk. 91/K5
Bolu (prov.), Turk. 91/K5
Bolungavik, Ice. 79/M6
Bolus Head (pt.), Ire. 72/N11
Bolvadin, Turk. 132/B2
Bóly, Hun. 90/D3
Bolzano, It. 99/H5
Bolzano-Bozen (prov.), It. 99/H4
Bom Conselho, Braz. 196/C3
Bom Despacho, Braz. 197/C1
Bom Jardim, Braz. 196/A1
Bom Jardin de Minas, Braz. 197/J6
Bom Jesus, Braz. 197/B4
Bom Jesus, Braz. 196/A3
Bom Jesus da Gurguéia, Serra (mts.), Braz. 193/K5
Bom Jesus de Goiás, Braz. 197/B1
Bom Jesus do Itabapoana, Braz. 197/D2
Bom Jesus dos Perdões, Braz. 197/G8
Bom Retiro, Braz. 197/B3
Boma, D.R. Congo 147/B2
Bomaderry, Austl. 157/D2
Bombala, Austl. 157/D3
Bombay Hook NWR, De, US 180/C5
Bombay (Mumbai), India 131/K5
Bomberai (pen.), Indo. 123/H4
Bombo, Ugan. 146/B2
Bomi, China 125/G2
Bomlitz, Ger. 93/G3
Bømlo (isl.), Nor. 80/A2
Bomu (riv.), D.R. Congo 139/L6
Bon-Encontre, Fr. 84/D4
Bona (mt.), Ak, US 176/K3
Bonaduz, Swi. 99/F4
Bonaire (isl.), NAnt. 183/H5
Bonalbo, Austl. 157/E1
Bonampak (ruin), Mex. 186/D2
Bonao, DRep. 183/G4
Bonaparte (arch.), Austl. 151/B2
Bonaparte (isls.), Austl. 151/B2
Bonasila (mtn.), Ak, US 176/F3
Bonaventure, Qu, Can. 173/H1
Bonaventure (riv.), Qu, Can. 173/H1
Bonavista (bay) Nf, Can. 173/L1
Bonavista, Nf, Can. 173/L1

223
Bonav – Brieg

Bonavista (cape), Nf, Can. 173/L1
Boncourt, Swi. 98/D3
Bondeno, It. 101/E3
Bondo, D.R. Congo 139/K7
Bondoukou, C.d'Iv. 144/E4
Bondowoso, Indo. 122/D5
Bone (gulf), Indo. 123/F4
Bönen, Ger. 93/E5
Bonerate (isls.), Indo. 123/F5
Bonfol, Swi. 98/D3
Bonfouca, La, US 179/Q16
Bong (co.), Libr. 144/C5
Bong (range), Libr. 144/C5
Bongabong, Phil. 123/F1
Bongaigaon, India 127/H2
Bongandanga, D.R. Congo 139/K7
Bongao, Phil. 123/E3
Bonggi (isl.), Malay. 123/E2
Bongka (riv.), Indo. 123/F4
Bongo, Massif des (plat.), CAfr. 139/K6
Bongolava (uplands), Madg. 149/H7
Bongor, Chad 138/J5
Bonham, Tx, US 171/H4
Bonheiden, Belg. 95/D1
Bonhill, Sc, UK 78/B5
Bonhomme, Col du (pass), Fr. 98/D1
Boni Nat'l Rsv., Kenya 146/D3
Bonifacio, Fr. 88/A2
Bonifacio (str.), It. 88/A2
Bonifay, Fl, US 175/G4
Bönigen, Swi. 98/D4
Bonin (isls.), Japan 158/C2
Bonita, Ca, US 178/C5
Bonita Springs, Fl, US 175/H5
Bonito (peak), Hon. 186/E3
Bonn, Ger. 95/G2
Bonndorf im Schwarzwald, Ger. 99/E2
Bonne, Fr. 98/C5
Bonnelles, Fr. 72/J6
Bonner Springs, Ks, US 179/D5
Bonner-West Riverside, Mt, US 168/E4
Bonners Ferry, Id, US 168/D3
Bonnet Carré Spillway, La, US 179/P16
Bonnet, Lac du (lake), Mb, Can. 169/K3
Bonneuil-sur-Marne, Fr. 72/K5
Bonneval, Fr. 84/D2
Bonneville (dam), Wa,Or, US 168/C4
Bonneville, Fr. 98/C5
Bonney Lake, Wa, US 177/C3
Bönnigheim, Ger. 96/C4
Bonnybridge, Sc, UK 78/C5
Bonorva, It. 88/A2
Bons-en-Chablais, Fr. 98/C5
Bonsall, Ca, US 178/C4
Bontberg (peak), SAfr. 148/C4
Bontebok NP, SAfr. 148/C4
Bonthain, Indo. 123/E5
Bonthe, SLeo. 144/B5
Bontoc, Phil. 121/D4
Bonyhád, Hun. 90/D2
Booker T. Washington Nat'l Mon., Va, US 175/J2
Boom, Belg. 95/D1
Boone, Ia, US 169/K5
Boone, NC, US 172/D4
Booneville, Ms, US 175/F3
Boonton, NJ, US 181/H8
Boorabbin NP, Austl. 154/D4
Boorama, Som. 139/P6
Booroondara (mt.), Austl. 157/C1
Boorowa, Austl. 157/D2
Boos (int'l arpt.), Fr. 84/D2
Boos, Ger. 99/G1
Boosaaso (Bender Cassim), Som. 139/Q5
Boostedt, Ger. 80/D4
Boothbay Harbor, Me, US 173/G3
Boothia (pen.), Nun., Can. 164/G1
Boothia (gulf), Nun., Can. 164/G1
Bootle, Eng, UK 77/E5
Booué, Gabon 138/H8
Bopa, Ben. 145/F5
Bopfingen, Ger. 96/D5
Boppard, Ger. 95/G3
Boppy (mt.), Austl. 157/C1
Boqueirão, Braz. 196/C2
Boqueirão, Serra do (mts.), Braz. 196/B3
Boquete (peak), Arg. 200/C4
Boquilla (res.), Mex. 184/D3
Boquillas del Carmen, Mex. 174/C4
Boquira, Braz. 196/B4
Bor, Czh. 97/F3
Bor, Rus. 103/K4
Bor, Serb. 90/F3
Bor, Turk. 132/C2
Bor Ul (mts.), China 112/G3
Bora Bora (isl.), FrPol. 159/K6
Borah (peak), Id, US 168/E4
Borås, Swe. 80/E3
Borāzjān, Iran 130/F3
Borba, Braz. 192/G4
Borba, Port. 86/B3
Borbera (riv.), It. 100/B3
Borbore (riv.), It. 100/B3
Borborema, Planalto da (plat.), Braz. 193/L5
Borča, Serb. 90/E3
Borcea Branch (riv.), Rom. 91/H3
Borchen, Ger. 93/F5
Borçka, Turk. 105/G4
Borculo, Neth. 92/D4
Borda da Mata, Braz. 197/G7
Bordeaux, Fr. 84/C4
Borden (isl.), NW,Nun., Can. 165/R7
Borden (pen.), Nun., Can. 165/H1
Bordentown, NJ, US 180/D3
Bordertown, Austl. 157/B3
Bordj Bou Arreridj, Alg. 142/H4
Bordj Bou Arreridj (prov.), Alg. 142/H4
Bordj el Kiffan, Alg. 142/G4
Bordj Manaïel, Alg. 142/G4
Bordj Moktar, Alg. 141/F5
Bordj Omar Driss, Alg. 141/G3
Bordj Sainte-Marie, Alg. 140/E4
Borehamwood, Eng, UK 72/C2
Borest, Fr. 72/L4
Boretto, It. 100/D3
Borgå (Porvoo), Fin. 81/L1
Borgaretto, It. 100/A2
Borgarnes, Ice. 79/N7
Borgaro Torinese, It. 100/A2
Børgefjell NP, Nor. 79/E2
Borgentreich, Ger. 93/G5
Borger, Tx, US 171/G4
Börger, Ger. 93/E3
Borger, Neth. 92/D3
Borgerhout, Belg. 92/B6
Borges Blanques, Sp. 87/F2
Borghetto Lodigiano, It. 100/C2
Borghetto Santo Spirito, It. 100/B4
Borgholm, Swe. 80/G3
Borgholzhausen, Ger. 93/F4
Borghorst, Ger. 93/E4
Borgloon, Belg. 95/E2
Borgne (lake), La, US 179/Q17
Borgne (riv.), Swi. 98/D5
Borgo (int'l arpt.), Burk. 144/D4
Borgo, Fr. 88/A1
Borgo, It. 99/H5
Borgo a Mozzano, It. 100/D5
Borgo San Dalmazzo, It. 85/G4
Borgo San Giacomo, It. 100/C2
Borgo San Lorenzo, It. 101/E5
Borgo Tossignano, It. 101/E4
Borgo Val di Taro, It. 100/C4
Borgo Vercelli, It. 100/B2
Borgofranco d'Ivrea, It. 100/A1
Borgomanero, It. 100/B1
Borgonovo Val Tidone, It. 100/C2
Borgosatollo, It. 100/D2
Borgosesia, It. 100/B1
Borgou (prov.), Ben. 145/F4
Borgund, Nor. 80/B1
Borio, India 127/F3
Borisoglebsk, Rus. 105/G2
Borispol (int'l arpt.), Ukr. 104/D2
Borja, Peru 198/B2
Borja, Sp. 86/E2
Borken, Ger. 92/D5
Borken, Ger. 93/G6
Børkop, Den. 80/C4
Borkum, Ger. 92/D1
Borkum (isl.), Ger. 92/D1
Borlänge, Swe. 80/F1
Bormida (riv.), It. 85/H4
Bormida, It. 100/B4
Bormida di Millesimo (riv.), It. 100/B4
Bormio, It. 99/G5
Born, Neth. 95/E1
Borna, Ger. 82/G3
Borndiep (chan.), Neth. 92/C2
Borne, Neth. 92/D4
Borne (riv.), Fr. 98/C6
Bornel, Fr. 94/B5
Bornem, Belg. 95/D1
Bornemouth, Eng, UK 75/E5
Bornemouth (co.), Eng, UK 75/E5
Borneo (isl.), Indo.,Malay. 122/D3
Bornheim, Ger. 95/G2
Bornholm (co.), Den. 80/F4
Bornholm (isl.), Den. 80/F4
Bornholmsgat (chan.), Den.,Swi. 83/H1
Borno, It. 99/G6
Bornos, Sp. 86/C4
Börnsen, Ger. 93/H2
Bornu (plain), Nga. 138/H5
Boro (riv.), Sudan 139/L6
Borohoro (mts.), China 112/D3
Borongan, Phil. 121/E5
Borough Green, Eng, UK 72/D3
Borovany, Czh. 97/H5
Borovichi, Rus. 102/G4
Borovo, Bul. 91/G4
Borovo, Cro. 90/D3
Borre, Nor. 80/D2
Borrisokane, Ire. 73/P10
Borrnida (riv.), It. 100/B3
Borşa, Rom. 91/F2
Borsec, Rom. 91/G2
Borso del Grappa, It. 101/E1
Borsod-Abaúj-Zemplén (co.), Hun. 90/E1
Borssele, Neth. 92/A6
Borstel, Ger. 93/F3
Bort-les-Orgues, Fr. 84/E4
Boruca, CR 187/F4
Borūjerd, Iran 130/E2
Boryslav, Ukr. 83/M4
Borzonasca, It. 100/C4
Borzya, Rus. 113/L1
Bosa, It. 88/A2
Bosanska Dubica, Bosn. 90/C3
Bosanska Gradiška, Bosn. 90/C3
Bosanska Kostajnica, Bosn. 90/C3
Bosanska Krupa, Bosn. 90/C3
Bosanski Brod, Bosn. 90/D3
Bosanski Petrovac, Bosn. 90/C3
Bosanski Šamac, Bosn. 90/D3
Bosco Mesola, It. 101/F3
Bosconero, It. 100/A2
Bose, China 125/J3
Boshof, SAfr. 148/D3
Boskoop, Neth. 92/B4
Boskovice, Czh. 83/J4
Bosna (riv.), Bosn. 90/D3
Bosnia and Herzegovina (ctry.) 90/C3
Bošnjaci, Cro. 90/D3
Bōsō (pen.), Japan 117/G3
Bosobolo, D.R. Congo 139/J7
Bosporus (str.), Turk. 91/J5
Bosque Farms, NM, US 170/F4
Bosques Petrificados, Mon. Natural, Arg. 201/C5
Bossangoa, CAfr. 139/J6
Bossier City, La, US 171/J4
Bostān, Iran 130/E2
Bostānābād-e Bālā, Iran 130/E1
Boston (mts.), Ar, US 171/J4
Boston (cap.), Ma, US 173/G3
Boston, Eng, UK 77/H6
Bosut (riv.), Cro. 90/D3
Boswil, Swi. 99/E3
Botād, India 131/K4
Boteler (peak), NC, US 175/H3
Botelerpunt (pt.), SAfr. 149/F2
Botelhos, Braz. 197/G6
Botev (peak), Bul. 89/J1
Botevgrad, Bul. 89/H1
Bothaspas (pass), SAfr. 149/E2
Bothaville, SAfr. 148/D2
Bothel, Ger. 93/G2
Bothell, Wa, US 177/C2
Bothnia (gulf), Fin.,Swe. 202/E
Bothwell, Austl. 157/C4
Botoşani (prov.), Rom. 91/H2
Botoşani, Rom. 91/H2
Botou, China 114/D3
Botrange (peak), Belg. 95/F3
Botrivier, SAfr. 148/L11
Botsford, Ct, US 181/E1
Botswana (ctry.) 147/D5
Bottanuco, It. 100/C1
Botte Donato (peak), It. 88/E3
Botticino, It. 100/D1
Bottineau, ND, US 169/H3
Bottrighe, It. 101/F2
Bottrop, Ger. 92/D5
Botucatu, Braz. 197/B2
Botwood, Nf, Can. 173/L1
Bou (riv.), C.d'Iv. 144/D4
Bou Arfa, Mor. 141/E2
Boû Djébéha (well), Mali 144/E2
Bou Hamdane, Oued (riv.), Alg. 142/K6
Bou Ismaïl, Alg. 142/G4
Bou Izakarn, Mor. 140/C3
Bou Kadir, Alg. 142/F4
Bou Laber (well), Alg. 140/D4
Bou Naceur (peak), Mor. 142/C3
Bou Regreg (riv.), Mor. 142/A3
Bou Salem, Tun. 142/L6
Bou Sellam, Oued (riv.), Alg. 142/H4
Bouaflé, C.d'Iv. 144/D5
Bouafle, Fr. 72/H5
Bouaké, C.d'Iv. 144/D5
Bouar, CAfr. 138/J6
Boubín (peak), Czh. 97/G5
Bouca, CAfr. 139/J6
Bouchain, Fr. 94/C3
Bouchegouf, Alg. 142/K6
Boucherville, Qu, Can. 173/P6
Boucle du Baoulé, PN de la, Mali 138/D5
Boucle Du Baoulé, PN de la, Mali 144/C3
Boudry, Swi. 98/C4
Boufarik, Alg. 142/G4
Bouffémont, Fr. 72/J4
Bougainville (reef), Austl. 151/D2
Bougainville (isl.), PNG 158/E5
Bougainville (cape), Falk., UK 201/F6
Bougara, Alg. 142/G4
Bougar'oûn (cape), Alg. 142/K6
Bough Beech (res.), Eng, UK 72/D3
Bougouni, Mali 144/D4
Bougouriba (prov.), Burk. 144/E4
Bouguenais, Fr. 84/C3
Bouhachem (peak), Mor. 142/B2
Bouhalla (peak), Mor. 142/B2
Bouillancy, Fr. 72/L4
Bouillon, Belg. 95/E4
Bouira (prov.), Alg. 142/G4
Bouira, Alg. 142/G4
Boujad, Mor. 140/D2
Boukhalf (Tangier) (int'l arpt.), Mor. 142/B2
Boukoumbé, Ben. 145/F4
Boulaide, Lux. 95/E4
Boulaouane, Mor. 140/C2
Boulay-Moselle, Fr. 95/F5
Boulazac, Fr. 84/D4
Boulder, Co, US 179/B2
Boulder (co.), Co, US 179/B2
Boulder, Mt, US 168/E4
Boulder City, Nv, US 170/D4
Boulder Hill, Il, US 177/P16
Boulemane, Mor. 140/D2
Boulemane (prov.), Mor. 142/C3
Bouleurs, Fr. 72/L5
Boulgou (prov.), Burk. 145/E4
Boulia, Austl. 155/H2
Bouligny, Fr. 95/E5
Boulkiemde (prov.), Burk. 145/E3
Boullarre, Fr. 72/M4
Boulogne (riv.), Fr. 84/C3
Boulogne-Billancourt, Fr. 72/J5
Boulogne-sur-Mer, Fr. 94/A2
Boulsworth (hill), Eng, UK 77/F4
Boumaine, Mor. 140/D3
Boumerdas (prov.), Alg. 142/G4
Boumerdas, Alg. 142/G4
Boun Nua, Laos 125/H3
Bouna, C.d'Iv. 144/E4
Bound Brook, NJ, US 180/D2
Boundary (peak), Nv, US 170/C3
Boundiali, C.d'Iv. 144/D4
Bountiful, Ut, US 179/K12
Bouquet (res.), Ca, US 178/B1
Bouquet (canyon), Ca, US 178/B2
Bourbon l'Archambault, Fr. 84/E3
Bourbonnais (reg.), Fr. 84/D3
Bourbonne-les-Bains, Fr. 98/B2
Bourbourg, Fr. 94/B2
Bourdonné, Fr. 72/G5
Bourem, Mali 145/E2
Bouressa (riv.), Mali 145/F2
Bourg-en-Bresse, Fr. 98/B5
Bourg-lès-Valence, Fr. 84/F4
Bourg-Saint-Andéol, Fr. 84/F4
Bourg-Saint-Maurice, Fr. 85/G4
Bourg-Saint-Pierre, Swi. 98/D6
Bourganeuf, Fr. 84/D4
Bourges, Fr. 84/E3
Bourget (lake), Fr. 98/B6
Bourgneuf (bay), Fr. 84/B3
Bourgogne (pol. reg.), Fr. 84/F3
Bourgogne (canal), Fr. 98/B3
Bourgoin-Jallieu, Fr. 84/F4
Bourke, Austl. 157/C1
Bourmont, Fr. 98/B1
Bourne (riv.), Eng, UK 75/E4
Bourne End, Eng, UK 75/F3
Bourne, The (riv.), Eng, UK 72/B3
Bournemouth, Eng, UK 75/E5
Bourscheid, Lux. 95/F4
Bourtanger Moor (reg.), Ger. 93/E3
Bousbecque, Fr. 94/C2
Bousso, Chad 138/J5
Boussois, Fr. 94/D3
Boutilimit, Mrta. 144/B2
Boutte, La, US 179/P17
Bouvard (cape), Austl. 154/B5
Bouvet (isl.), Nor. 65/K8
Bouxières-aux-Dames, Fr. 95/F6
Bouxwiller, Fr. 95/G6
Bouznika, Mor. 142/A3
Bouzonville, Fr. 95/F5
Bovalino, It. 88/E3
Bovegno, It. 100/D1
Boven Tapanahoni (riv.), Sur. 195/H4
Bovenden, Ger. 93/G5
Bovenwijde (lake), Neth. 92/D3
Boves, Fr. 94/B4
Bovezzo, It. 100/D1
Bovingdon, Eng, UK 72/B1
Bovino, It. 90/B5
Bovolone, It. 101/E2
Bow (riv.), Ab, Can. 164/E3
Bow Island, Ab, Can. 168/F3
Bowdle, SD, US 169/J4
Bowdon, Eng, UK 77/F5
Bowen, Arg. 200/D2
Bowen, Austl. 156/C3
Bowers Beach, De, US 180/C5
Bowie, Az, US 170/E4
Bowie, Md, US 180/B6
Bowling Green (cape), Austl. 156/B2
Bowling Green, Ky, US 172/C4
Bowling Green, Mo, US 171/K3
Bowling Green, Oh, US 172/D3
Bowling Green Bay NP, Austl. 156/B2
Bowman, ND, US 169/H4
Bowman (bay), Nun., Can. 165/J2
Bowmansdale, Pa, US 180/B3
Bowmanstown, Pa, US 180/C2
Bowmansville, Pa, US 180/B3
Bowmore, Sc, UK 73/Q9
Bowokan (isls.), Indo. 123/F4
Bowral, Austl. 157/D2
Bowron (riv.), BC, Can. 168/C2
Box Elder (co.), Ut, US 179/J11
Boxberg, Ger. 96/C4
Boxholm, Swe. 80/F2
Boxing, China 114/D3
Boxmeer, Neth. 92/C5
Boxtel, Neth. 92/C5
Boyabat, Turk. 132/C1
Boyaca (dept.), Col. 194/C3
Boyanup, Austl. 154/B5
Boychinovtsi, Bul. 91/F4
Boyd (lake), Co, US 179/B2
Boye, China 114/C3
Boyer (riv.), Ia, US 169/K5
Boyertown, Pa, US 180/C3
Boyle, Ab, Can. 168/E2
Boyle, Ire. 73/P10
Boyne (riv.), Ire. 73/Q10
Boyne City, Mi, US 172/C2
Boyne Island, Austl. 156/C3
Boynton Beach, Fl, US 175/H5
Boysen (res.), Wy, US 168/F5
Boyup Brook, Austl. 154/C5
Boz (pt.), Turk. 91/J5
Bozashchy Tübegi (pen.), Kaz. 105/J3
Bozcaada (isl.), Gre. 89/J3
Bozcaada, Turk. 89/K3
Bozeman, Mt, US 168/F4
Bozkir, Turk. 132/C2
Bozkurt, Turk. 104/E4
Bozman, Md, US 180/B6
Bozoum, CAfr. 138/J6
Bozova, Turk. 132/D2
Bozüyük, Turk. 132/B2
Bozyazı, Turk. 133/C1
Bozzolo, It. 100/D2
Bra, It. 100/A3
Braan (riv.), Sc, UK 78/C3
Brač (isl.), Cro. 88/E1
Bracciano (lake), It. 88/B1
Bracebridge, On, Can. 172/E2
Brackel, Ger. 93/H2
Bracken, Tx, US 179/U20
Brackenheim, Ger. 96/C4
Brackettville, Tx, US 171/G5
Bracknell, Eng, UK 75/F4
Bracknell Forest (co.), Eng, UK 75/F4
Braço do Norte, Braz. 197/B4
Brad, Rom. 91/F2
Bradano (riv.), It. 90/B5
Bradda (pt.), IM, UK 76/D3
Bradenton, Fl, US 175/H5
Bradford, Eng, UK 77/G4
Bradford (co.), Eng, UK 77/G4
Bradford, Pa, US 172/E3
Bradley (int'l arpt.), Ct, US 173/F3
Bradley Beach, NJ, US 180/D3
Brady, Tx, US 171/H5
Braemar (reg.), Sc, UK 78/C2
Braeriach (peak), Sc, UK 78/C2
Braga (dist.), Port. 86/A2
Braga, Port. 86/A2
Bragado, Arg. 200/E2
Bragança, Braz. 193/J4
Bragança (dist.), Port. 86/B2
Bragança, Port. 86/B2
Brāhmanbāria, Bang. 127/H4
Brahmaputra (riv.), Asia 125/F2
Braich-y-Pwll (pt.), Wal, UK 76/D6
Braid (riv.), NI, UK 76/B2
Brăila (prov.), Rom. 91/H3
Brăila, Rom. 91/H3
Brainards, NJ, US 180/C2
Braine, Fr. 94/C5
Braine-l'Alleud, Belg. 95/D2
Braine-le-Comte, Belg. 95/D2
Brainerd, Mn, US 169/K4
Braintree, Eng, UK 75/G3
Braithwaite, La, US 179/Q17
Brak (riv.), SAfr. 148/C3
Brake, Ger. 93/F2
Brakel, Belg. 94/C2
Brakel, Ger. 93/G5
Brakel, Neth. 92/C5
Brakna (pol. reg.), Mrta. 144/B2
Brålanda, Swe. 80/E2
Bram, Fr. 84/E5
Bramdrupdam, Den. 80/C4
Bramley, Eng, UK 72/B3
Brampton, On, Can. 173/Q8
Bramsche, Ger. 93/F4
Bramstedt, Ger. 93/F2
Bran (riv.), Sc, UK 78/A1
Brancaleone-Marina, It. 88/E4
Branch Dale, Pa, US 180/B2
Branchville, NJ, US 180/D1
Branchville, Ct, US 181/E1
Branco (riv.), Braz. 189/C2
Brand, Aus. 99/F3
Brandberg (peak), Namb. 147/B5
Brandbu, Nor. 80/D1
Brande, Den. 80/C4
Brandenburg (state), Ger. 82/P6
Brandenburg, Ger. 82/G2
Brander, Pass of (pass), Sc, UK 78/A4
Brandfort, SAfr. 148/D3
Brandizzo, It. 100/A2
Brandon, Mb, Can. 169/J3
Brandon, Fl, US 175/H5
Brandon, Ms, US 175/F3
Brandsen, Arg. 201/J11
Brandvlei, SAfr. 148/C3
Brandýs nad Labem, Czh. 97/H2
Brandywine, Md, US 180/B6
Brandywine (riv.), Pa, US 180/C4
Branford, Ct, US 181/F1
Branges, Fr. 98/B4
Braniewo, Pol. 81/H4
Brannenburg, Ger. 85/K3
Brant Beach, NJ, US 180/D4
Branxholm, Austl. 157/C4
Branzoll (Bronzolo), It. 99/H4
Bras d'Or (lake), NS, Can. 173/J2
Brasiléia, Braz. 192/E6
Brasília (cap.), Braz. 196/A5
Brasília de Minas, Braz. 196/A5
Brasília, PN de, Braz. 193/J7
Braşov, Rom. 91/G3
Braşov (prov.), Rom. 91/G3
Brasschaat, Belg. 92/B6
Brassey (mt.), Austl. 155/G2
Brasstown Bald (peak), Ga, US 175/H3
Brastad, Swe. 80/D2
Bratislava (cap.), Slvk. 85/M2
Bratislava (Ivanka) (int'l arpt.), Slvk. 90/C1
Bratislavský (pol. reg.), Slvk. 83/J4
Bratsk, Rus. 107/L4
Brattleboro, Vt, US 173/F3
Bratunac, Bosn. 90/D3
Braubach, Ger. 95/G3
Braulio Carrillo, PN, CR 182/E5
Braunau am Inn, Aus. 97/G6
Braunfels, Ger. 96/B1
Braunig (lake), Tx, US 179/U21
Braunlage, Ger. 93/H5
Bräunlingen, Ger. 99/E2
Braunschweig, Ger. 93/H4
Brava (isl.), CpV. 135/J11
Brava (pt.), Chile 201/C7
Brava (pt.), Uru. 201/K11
Brava, Costa (coast), Sp. 87/G2
Bråviken (inlet), Swe. 80/G2
Bravo (peak), Bol. 192/F7
Bravo (peak), Peru 198/B2
Bravo del Norte (riv.), Mex. 182/A2
Brawley, Ca, US 170/D4
Bray (isl.), Nun., Can. 165/J2
Bray, Ire. 76/B5
Bray (pt.), Ire. 76/B5
Bray-Dunes, Fr. 94/B1
Braye (riv.), Fr. 84/D3
Brazey-en-Plaine, Fr. 98/B3
Brazil (ctry.) 189/D3
Brazilian Highlands (uplands), Braz. 189/E4
Brazo Casiquiare (riv.), Ven. 195/E4
Brazo Sur (riv.), Arg. 201/C6
Brazópolis, Braz. 197/H7
Brazos (riv.), Tx, US 174/D3
Brazos, Salt Fork (riv.), Tx, US 174/C3
Brazzaville (cap.), Congo 147/C1
Brčko, Bosn. 90/D3
Brda (riv.), Pol. 80/G5
Brdy (mts.), Czh. 83/G4
Brea, Ca, US 178/G8
Breadalbane (dist.), Sc, UK 78/B4
Breamish (riv.), Eng, UK 78/D6
Bréancon, Fr. 72/J4
Bréau, Fr. 72/L6
Breaza, Rom. 91/G3
Brebbia, It. 100/B1
Brêche (riv.), Fr. 94/B5
Brechen, Ger. 96/B2
Brechin, Sc, UK 78/D3
Brecht, Belg. 92/B6
Breckenridge, Mn, US 169/J4
Breckenridge, Tx, US 171/H4
Breckerfeld, Ger. 93/E6
Breckland (phys. reg.), Eng, UK 75/G2
Brecknock (pen.), Chile 201/C7
Břeclav, Czh. 85/M2
Brecon, Wal, UK 74/C3
Brecon Beacons (mts.), Wal, UK 74/C3
Breda, Neth. 92/B5
Bredaryd, Swe. 80/E3
Bredasdorp, SAfr. 148/M11
Bredebro, Den. 80/C4
Bredene, Belg. 94/B1
Bredstedt, Ger. 80/C4
Breë (riv.), SAfr. 148/B4
Bree, Belg. 95/E1
Breg (riv.), Ger. 82/E5
Bregagno (peak), It. 99/F5
Bregalnica (riv.), FYROM 89/H2
Breganze, It. 101/E1
Bregenz, Aus. 99/F3
Bregenzer Ache (riv.), Aus. 99/F3
Bregovo, Bul. 90/F3
Brégy, Fr. 72/L4
Breidhafjördhur (bay), Ice. 79/M6
Breil-Brigels, Swi. 99/F4
Breisach, Ger. 98/D1
Breitbrunn am Chiemsee, Ger. 97/F7
Breitenauriegel (peak), Ger. 97/G5
Breitenbach, Swi. 98/D3
Breitenbrunn, Ger. 97/E4
Breitenfurt bei Wien, Aus. 91/N7
Breitenworbis, Ger. 93/H6
Breithorn (peak), Swi. 98/D5
Breithorn (peak), Swi. 98/D6
Brejo, Braz. 196/B1
Brejo Santo, Braz. 196/C2
Brejões, Braz. 196/B3
Brembate di Sopra, It. 100/C1
Brembilla, It. 100/C1
Brembio, It. 100/C2
Brembo (riv.), It. 99/F6
Bremen (int'l arpt.), Ger. 93/F2
Bremen, Ger. 93/F2
Bremen (state), Ger. 80/C5
Bremer (riv.), Austl. 156/E7
Bremerhaven, Ger. 93/F1
Bremerton, Wa, US 168/C4
Bremervörde, Ger. 93/G2
Bremgarten, Ger. 99/E3
Bremgarten bei Bern, Swi. 98/D4
Bremnes, Nor. 80/A2
Brend (riv.), Ger. 96/D2
Brendel (lake), Mi, US 177/E7
Brendola, It. 101/E2
Brendon (hills), Eng, UK 74/C4
Brenig, Llyn (lake), Wal, UK 76/E5
Brenne (riv.), Fr. 82/C5
Brenner (pass), Aus. 99/H4
Brenner (riv.), Austl. 155/N9
Brenno (riv.), Swi. 99/E5
Breno, It. 99/G6
Brent (bor.), Eng, UK 72/C2
Brent (res.), Eng, UK 72/C2
Brent (riv.), Eng, UK 72/B2
Brenta (riv.), It. 85/J4
Brenta (peak), It. 99/G5
Brentwood, NY, US 181/E2
Brentwood, Ca, US 177/L11
Brentwood, Eng, UK 72/D2
Brenz (riv.), Ger. 96/D5
Brescello, It. 100/D3
Brescia, It. 100/D1
Brescia (prov.), It. 99/G6
Bresle (riv.), Fr. 84/D1
Bresles, Fr. 94/B5
Bressana, It. 100/C2
Bressanone, It. 85/J3
Bressay (isl.), Sc, UK 73/W13
Bressuire, Fr. 84/C3
Brest, Fr. 84/A2
Brest, Bela. 83/M2
Brest (int'l arpt.), Bela. 83/M2
Brestskaya Voblasts, Bela. 104/C1
Bretagne (pol. reg.), Fr. 84/B2
Bretagne, Monts de (mts.), Fr. 84/B2
Bretagne, Pointe de (pt.), Reun., Fr. 149/S15
Bretaña, Peru 198/C2
Breteuil, Fr. 94/B4
Brétigny-sur-Orge, Fr. 72/J6
Breton, Ab, Can. 168/E2
Breton (cape), NS, Can. 173/K2
Brett (cape), NZ 159/S10
Brett (riv.), Eng, UK 75/G2
Brettach (riv.), Ger. 96/C4
Bretten, Ger. 96/B4
Bretzenheim, Ger. 95/G4
Breuberg, Ger. 96/C3
Breuillet, Fr. 72/J6
Breukelen, Neth. 92/B4
Breuna, Ger. 93/G6
Breuvannes-en-Bassigny, Fr. 98/B1
Breves, Braz. 193/H4
Brevig Mission, Ak, US 176/E2
Brevik, Nor. 80/C2
Brevoort (isl.), Nun., Can. 165/K2
Brewarrina, Austl. 157/C1
Brewer, Me, US 173/G2
Brewster, Ne, US 169/J5
Brewton, Al, US 175/G4
Brey-et-Lû, Fr. 72/G4
Breyten, SAfr. 149/E2
Brežice, Slov. 85/L4
Brezina, Alg. 141/F2
Březnice, Czh. 97/G3
Breznik, Bul. 89/H1
Brezoi, Rom. 91/G3
Brezovo, Bul. 89/J1
Bria, CAfr. 139/K6
Briançon, Fr. 85/G4
Brianne, Llyn (res.), Wal, UK 74/C2
Briar Creek, Pa, US 180/B1
Briare, Fr. 84/E3
Brickerville, Pa, US 180/B3
Bricktown, NJ, US 180/D3
Bride (riv.), Ire. 73/P10
Bride, IM, UK 76/D3
Bridge City, Tx, US 174/E4
Bridge of Allan, Sc, UK 78/C4
Bridge of Don, Sc, UK 78/D2
Bridge of Weir, Sc, UK 78/B5
Bridgehampton, NY, US 181/F2
Bridgend, Wal, UK 74/C3
Bridgeport, Ca, US 170/C3
Bridgeport, Ct, US 181/E1
Bridgeport, Ne, US 169/H5
Bridgeport, NJ, US 180/C4
Bridger, Mt, US 168/F4
Bridgeton, NJ, US 180/C5
Bridgetown, Austl. 154/C5
Bridgetown (cap.), Bar. 183/P9
Bridgeville, De, US 180/C6
Bridgewater, Austl. 157/C4
Bridgewater, NS, Can. 173/H2
Bridgnorth, Eng, UK 74/D1
Bridgton, Me, US 173/G2
Bridgwater, Eng, UK 74/D4
Bridgwater (bay), Eng, UK 74/C4
Bridlington, Eng, UK 77/H3
Bridlington (bay), Eng, UK 77/H3
Bridport, Austl. 157/C4
Bridport, Eng, UK 74/D5
Brie (reg.), Fr. 82/B4
Brie-Comte-Robert, Fr. 72/K5
Brieg Brzeg, Pol. 83/J3

225
Caboo – Çarda

Caboolture, Austl. 156/D4
Cabora Bassa (lake), Moz. 147/F4
Cabora Bassa, Barragem de (dam), Moz. 147/F4
Cabot (str.), NS,NF, Can. 165/K4
Cabra, Sp. 86/C4
Cabra de Santo Cristo, Sp. 86/D4
Cabral, Serra do (range), Braz. 196/A5
Cabras, It. 88/A3
Cabrera, Isla de (isl.), Sp. 87/G3
Cabri, Sk, Can. 168/F3
Cabriel (riv.), Sp. 86/E3
Cabrillo Nat'l Mon., Ca, US 178/C5
Cabrobó, Braz. 196/C3
Cabruta, Ven. 195/E3
Cabudare, Ven. 194/D2
Cabugao, Phil. 121/D4
Cabure, Ven. 194/D2
Caçador, Braz. 197/B3
Čačak, Serb. 90/E4
Cacalotán, Mex. 184/D4
Caccia (cape), It. 88/A2
Cáceres, Braz. 192/G7
Cáceres, Sp. 86/B3
Cáceres, Col. 194/C3
Cachapoal (riv.), Chile 200/N9
Cacharí, Arg. 201/J12
Cache (peak), Id, US 168/E5
Cache (co.), Ut, US 179/K11
Cache Creek, BC, Can. 168/C3
Cache la Poudre (riv.), Co, US 179/C2
Cache Slough (riv.), Ca, US 177/L10
Cacheu, GBis. 144/A3
Cachi, Arg. 199/C2
Cachicadán, Peru 198/B3
Cachimbo, Serra do (mts.), Braz. 193/G5
Cachipo, Ven. 195/E2
Cachoeira de Minas, Braz. 197/H7
Cachoeira do Sul, Braz. 197/A4
Cachoeira Paulista, Braz. 197/H7
Cachoeiras de Macacu, Braz. 197/L7
Cachoeirinha, Braz. 197/B4
Caconde, Braz. 197/G6
Caçu, Braz. 197/B1
Caculé, Braz. 196/B4
Čadca, Slvk. 83/K4
Caddo (mts.), Ar, US 174/E3
Cadelbosco di Sopra, It. 100/D3
Cadelle (peak), It. 99/F5
Cadenberge, Ger. 93/G1
Cader Idris (peak), Wal, UK 74/C1
Cadibarrawirracanna (lake), Austl. 155/G4
Cadillac, Mi, US 172/C2
Cadiz, Phil. 123/F1
Cadiz, Ky, US 172/C4
Cádiz, Sp. 86/B4
Cádiz, Golfo de (gulf), Port.,Sp. 86/B4
Cadolzburg, Ger. 96/D4
Cadria (peak), It. 99/G6
Caen, Fr. 84/C2
Caerano di San Marco, It. 101/F1
Caernarfon (bay), Wal, UK 76/D5
Caernarfon, Wal, UK 76/D5
Caernarfon Castle, Wal, UK 76/D5
Caerphilly, Wal, UK 74/C3
Caerphilly (co.), Wal, UK 74/C3
Caesarea (ruin), Isr. 133/G6
Caesarea (ruin), Isr. 133/D3
Caetité, Braz. 196/B4
Cafarnaum, Braz. 196/B3
Cafayate, Arg. 199/C2
Cagayan Sulu (isl.), Phil. 121/C6
Cagli, It. 101/F5
Cagliari, It. 88/A3
Cagliari, Golfo di (gulf), It. 88/A3
Cagnes-sur-Mer, Fr. 85/G5
Caguán (riv.), Col. 192/D3
Caguas, PR 183/M8
Caher, Ire. 73/Q10
Cahirsiveen, Ire. 72/N11
Cahokia, Il, US 179/G8
Cahore (pt.), Ire. 73/Q10
Cahors, Fr. 84/D4
Cahuacan, Mex. 185/Q9
Cahuapanas, Peru 198/B2
Cahuinari (riv.), Col. 194/D5
Cahuita, PN, CR 187/F4
Cahul, Mol. 91/J3
Cai (riv.), Braz. 197/B4
Caia, Moz. 147/G4
Caiapó (riv.), Braz. 193/H7
Caiapó, Serra (mts.), Braz. 193/H7
Caibarién, Cuba 187/G1
Caicara, Ven. 195/F2
Caicara, Ven. 195/E3
Caicó, Braz. 196/C2
Caicos (isls.), UK 183/G3
Caicos Passage (chan.), Bahm. 187/H1
Caieiras, Braz. 197/G8
Cailloma, Peru 198/D4
Cailly (riv.), Fr. 94/A4
Caio (peak), It. 100/D4
Cairate, It. 100/B1
Cairn (mtn.), Ak, US 176/G3
Cairn Curran (dam), Austl. 157/B3
Cairn Gorm (peak), Sc, UK 78/C2
Cairn Table (peak), Sc, UK 78/B6
Cairn Toul (peak), Sc, UK 78/C2
Cairndow, Sc, UK 78/B4
Cairngorm (mts.), Sc, UK 78/B2
Cairns (int'l arpt.), Austl. 156/B2
Cairns (mt.), Austl. 155/G2
Cairns, Austl. 156/B2
Cairnsmore of Carsphairn (peak), Sc, UK 78/B6
Cairo, Ga, US 175/G4
Cairo (peak), It. 88/C2
Cairo (Al Qāhirah) (cap.), Egypt 143/B2
Cairo (int'l arpt.), Egypt 143/B2
Cairo Montenotte, It. 100/B4
Caistor Centre, On, Can. 173/Q9
Caistorville, On, Can. 173/Q9
Caizi (lake), China 114/D5
Cajabamba, Peru 198/B2
Cajabamba, Ecu. 194/B5
Cajacay, Peru 198/B3
Cajamarca (ruin), Peru 198/B2
Cajamarca, Peru 198/B2
Cajamarca (dept.), Peru 198/B2
Cajari, Braz. 196/A1
Cajatambo, Peru 198/B3
Cajazeiras, Braz. 196/C2
Cajibío, Col. 194/B4
Cajon Junction, Ca, US 178/C2
Cajones, Cayos (isl.), Hon. 182/E4
Caju (isl.), Braz. 196/B1
Çal, Turk. 132/B2
Cala d'Oliva, It. 88/A2
Calabar, Nga. 145/H5
Calabar (int'l arpt.), Nga. 145/H5
Calabasas, Ca, US 178/B2
Calabozo, Ven. 195/E2
Calabria, PN della, It. 88/D3
Calaburras (pt.), Sp. 86/C4
Calaceite, Sp. 87/F2
Calacoto, Bol. 198/D5
Calafat, Rom. 90/F4
Calahorra, Sp. 86/E1
Calais, Me, US 173/H2
Calais, Fr. 94/A2
Calais, Canal de (canal), Fr. 94/A2
Calalaste, Sierra de (mts.), Arg. 199/C2
Calama, Chile 199/C1
Calamar, Col. 194/C2
Calamian Group (isls.), Phil. 123/E1
Calamocha, Sp. 86/E2
Calamonte, Sp. 86/B3
Calañas, Sp. 86/B4
Calanda, Sp. 87/E2
Calangianus, It. 88/A2
Calapan, Phil. 121/D5
Călăraşi (prov.), Rom. 91/H3
Călăraşi, Rom. 91/H3
Calasparra, Sp. 86/E3
Calatayud, Sp. 86/E2
Calatorao, Sp. 86/E2
Calauag, Phil. 121/D5
Calaveras (lake), Tx, US 179/U21
Calaveras (res.), Ca, US 177/L12
Calayan, Phil. 121/D4
Calayan (isl.), Phil. 121/D4
Calbayog, Phil. 121/D5
Calberlah, Ger. 93/H4
Calbuco, Chile 200/B4
Calca, Peru 198/D4
Calcanhar, Ponta do (pt.), Braz. 196/D2
Calcasieu (riv.), La, US 171/J5
Calceta, Ecu. 194/A5
Calci, It. 100/D5
Calcinate, It. 100/C1
Calcinato, It. 100/D2
Calcinelli, It. 101/F5
Calcio, It. 100/C2
Calcium, NY, US 172/F2
Calçoene, Braz. 193/H3
Calcutta (Kolkata), India 127/G4
Calcutta (Kolkata) (int'l arpt.), India 127/G4
Calcutta, Sur. 195/H3
Caldaro (Kaltern), It. 85/J3
Caldas, Braz. 197/G6
Caldas (dept.), Col. 194/C3
Caldas da Rainha, Port. 86/A3
Caldas Novas, Braz. 197/B1
Calden, Ger. 93/G6
Calder (mt.), Ak, US 176/M4
Calder (riv.), Eng, UK 77/F4
Caldera de Taburiente, PN de la, Canl., Sp. 140/A3
Calderara di Reno, It. 101/E3
Calderas, Ven. 194/D2
Caldercruix, Sc, UK 78/C5
Calderdale (co.), Eng, UK 77/F4
Caldes de Montbui, Sp. 87/L6
Caldew (riv.), Eng, UK 77/F2
Caldicot, Wal, UK 74/D3
Caldiero, It. 101/E2
Çaldıran, Turk. 132/E2
Caldonazzo, It. 99/H6
Caldono, Col. 194/B4
Caldwell, NJ, US 181/H8
Caldwell, Tx, US 171/H5
Caldwell, Wi, US 177/P14
Caldy (isl.), Eng, UK 74/B3
Caledon, NI, UK 76/B3
Caledon (riv.), SAfr. 148/D3
Caledon, SAfr. 148/L11
Caledonia (hills), NB, Can. 173/H2
Caledonia, Wi, US 177/P14
Caledonian (canal), Sc, UK 78/B2
Calella, Sp. 87/G2
Calen, Austl. 156/C3
Calenzana, Fr. 88/A1
Calenzano, It. 101/E5
Calera de Tango, Chile 200/N8
Calestano, It. 100/D3
Caleta de Campos, Mex. 184/E5
Caleta Olivia, Arg. 200/D5
Calexico, Ca, US 170/D4
Calf of Man (isl.), IM, UK 76/C3
Calf, The (peak), Eng, UK 77/F3
Calgary (int'l arpt.), Ab, Can. 168/E3
Calgary, Ab, Can. 168/E3
Calheta, Azor., Port. 87/S12
Calhoun, Ga, US 175/G3
Calhoun (co.), Il, US 179/F7
Calhoun, Ky, US 172/C4
Cali, Col. 194/B4
Calicut (Kozhikode), India 124/C5
Calida, Costa (coast), Sp. 86/E4
Caliente, Nv, US 170/D3
Califon, NJ, US 180/D2
California (gulf), Mex. 184/B2
California (state), US 170/B3
California, Md, US 172/E4
California, Mo, US 171/J3
Calilegua, PN, Arg. 199/D1
Călimăneşti, Rom. 91/G3
Calimaya, Mex. 185/Q10
Calimere (pt.), India 124/C5
Calimesa, Ca, US 178/C2
Calitri, It. 88/D2
Calixa-Lavallée, Qu, Can. 173/P6
Calizzano, It. 100/B4
Calkini, Mex. 186/D1
Calkins (lake), Co, US 179/B2
Çalköy, Turk. 132/B2
Callabonna (lake), Austl. 157/A1
Callahonna (lake), Austl. 151/D3
Callalli, Peru 198/D4
Callan, Ire. 73/Q10
Callander, Sc, UK 78/B4
Callantsoog, Neth. 92/B3
Callao, Peru 198/B4
Callapa, Bol. 198/D5
Callaway, Fl, US 175/G4
Calle Larga, Chile 200/N8
Calliope, Austl. 156/C4
Callosa de Segura, Sp. 87/E3
Calne, Eng, UK 74/E4
Calolziocorte, It. 100/C1
Calonne-Ricouart, Fr. 94/B3
Calore (riv.), It. 88/D2
Caloundra, Austl. 156/D4
Calpe, Sp. 87/F3
Calpulálpan, Mex. 185/L7
Caltagirone, It. 88/D4
Caltanissetta, It. 88/D4
Caltavuturo, It. 88/C4
Caluire-et-Cuire, Fr. 84/F4
Calumet (riv.), Il, US 177/Q16
Calumet Sag (chan.), Il, US 177/Q16
Caluso, It. 100/A2
Calvello, It. 88/D2
Calvenzano, It. 100/C2
Calvert (isl.), BC, Can. 168/A3
Calvert, Tx, US 171/H5
Calverton, Md, US 180/B5
Calvi (peak), It. 101/E4
Calvi, Fr. 88/A1
Calviá, Sp. 87/G3
Calvillo, Mex. 184/E4
Calvinia, SAfr. 148/B3
Calvisano, It. 100/D2
Calvitero (peak), Sp. 86/C2
Calw, Ger. 96/B5
Calzada de Calatrava, Sp. 86/D3
Cam or Rhee (riv.), Eng, UK 75/F2
Cam Pha, Viet. 120/D1
Cam Ranh, Viet. 120/E4
Camaçari, Braz. 196/C4
Camacho, Mex. 184/E3
Camacupa, Ang. 147/C3
Camaguán, Ven. 195/E2
Camagüey (arch.), Cuba 183/F3
Camagüey, Cuba 187/G1
Camaiore, It. 100/D5
Camajuaní, Cuba 187/G1
Camalu, Mex. 184/A2
Camamu, Braz. 196/C4
Camamu, Baía de (bay), Braz. 196/C4
Camaná, Peru 198/C5
Camanducaia, Braz. 197/G7
Camaquã, Braz. 197/B4
Camaquã (riv.), Braz. 197/A4
Camargo, Sp. 86/D1
Camarillo, Ca, US 178/A2
Camariñas, Sp. 86/A1
Camarón (cape), Hon. 187/E3
Camarones (bay), Arg. 200/D5
Camarones, Arg. 200/D5
Camas, Sp. 86/B4
Cambados, Sp. 86/A1
Cambará, Braz. 197/B2
Cambay, Gulf of (gulf), India 124/B3
Cambé, Braz. 197/B2
Camberley, Eng, UK 72/A3
Cambiano, It. 100/A3
Cambodia (ctry.) 125/H5
Camboriú, Ponta do (pt.), Braz. 197/C3
Cambrai, Fr. 94/C3
Cambrian (mts.), Wal, UK 76/E5
Cambridge, Eng, UK 75/G2
Cambridge (int'l arpt.), Eng, UK 75/G2
Cambridge, NZ 159/T10
Cambridge, Ma, US 173/G3
Cambridge, Md, US 172/E4
Cambridge, Oh, US 172/D3
Cambridge, On, Can. 172/D3
Cambridge Bay, Nun., Can. 164/F2
Cambridgeshire (co.), Eng, UK 75/F2
Cambrils, Sp. 87/F2
Cambuí, Braz. 197/G7
Cambuquira, Braz. 197/H6
Cambuslang, Sc, UK 78/B5
Cambutal (mtn.), Pan. 194/A3
Camden, Austl. 156/G9
Camden (co.), Eng, UK 72/C2
Camden, Al, US 175/G4
Camden, De, US 180/C5
Camden, Me, US 173/G2
Camden, NJ, US 180/C4
Camden (co.), NJ, US 180/C4
Camden, SC, US 175/H3
Camden Haven, Austl. 157/E1
Camden Point, Mo, US 179/D5
Cameia, PN da, Ang. 147/D3
Camel (riv.), Eng, UK 74/B6
Camelback (mtn.), Pa, US 180/C1
Camerano, It. 101/G5
Cameri, It. 100/B2
Cameron (isl.), Nun., Can. 165/R7
Cameron, Mo, US 171/J3
Cameron, Tx, US 171/H5
Cameroon (ctry.) 138/H7
Cametá, Braz. 193/J4
Camicia (peak), It. 88/C1
Camiguin (isl.), Phil. 121/D4
Camilla, Ga, US 175/G4
Camilo Aldao, Arg. 200/E2
Caminha, Port. 86/A2
Camiri, Bol. 192/F8
Camisano Vicentino, It. 101/E1
Çamlıdere, Turk. 132/C1
Çamlık NP, Turk. 132/C2
Çamlıyayla, Turk. 133/D1
Camoapa, Nic. 187/E3
Camogli, It. 100/C4
Camon, Fr. 94/B4
Camorta (isl.), India 125/F6
Camp Angelus (Angelus Oaks), Ca, US 178/D2
Camp Creek, Az, US 179/S18
Camp Hill, Pa, US 180/B3
Camp Lake, Wi, US 177/P14
Camp Springs, Md, US 180/B6
Campagna Lupia, It. 101/F2
Campagnola Emilia, It. 101/D3
Campana, Arg. 201/J11
Campana (isl.), Chile 201/B6
Campana, PN de la, Chile 200/N8
Campanario, Sp. 86/C3
Campanario (peak), Arg. 200/C2
Campanella (cape), It. 88/D2
Campanha, Braz. 197/H6
Campania (prov.), It. 88/D2
Campbell, Ca, US 177/L12
Campbell (isl.), NZ 65/T8
Campbell River, BC, Can. 168/B3
Campbell Town, Austl. 157/C4
Campbellsville, Ky, US 172/C4
Campbellton, NB, Can. 173/H1
Campbeltown, Sc, UK 73/R9
Campden, On, Can. 173/R9
Campeche (state), Mex. 182/C4
Campeche, Mex. 186/D2
Campeche (bay), Mex. 185/G5
Camperdown, Austl. 157/B3
Camperville, Mb, Can. 169/H3
Campestre, Braz. 197/G6
Campi Bisenzio, It. 101/E5
Campidano (range), It. 88/A3
Campillo de Altobuey, Sp. 86/E3
Campillos, Sp. 86/C4
Campina Verde, Braz. 197/B1
Campinas, Braz. 197/F7
Campion, Co, US 179/B2
Campione d'Italia, It. 99/E6
Campo (int'l arpt.), Braz. 198/C2
Campo Belo, Braz. 197/C2
Campo de Criptana, Sp. 86/D3
Campo de la Cruz, Col. 194/C2
Campo dei Fiori (peak), It. 100/B1
Campo Grande, Braz. 193/H8
Campo Ligure, It. 100/B3
Campo Limpo Paulista, Braz. 197/G8
Campo Maior, Port. 86/B3
Campo Mourão, Braz. 197/A3
Campo Tencia (peak), Swi. 99/E5
Campo Tizzoro, It. 101/D4
Campoalegre, Col. 194/C4
Campobasso, It. 88/D2
Campodarsego, It. 101/E2
Campodolcino, It. 99/F5
Campogalliano, It. 101/D3
Campomorone, It. 100/B3
Camponogara, It. 101/F2
Camporosso, It. 100/A5
Camporredondo, Peru 198/B2
Camporredondo, Embalse de (res.), Sp. 86/C1
Campos (phys. reg.), Braz. 189/D5
Campos Altos, Braz. 197/C1
Campos Belos, Braz. 196/A4
Campos de Hielo Norte (glacier), Chile 201/B5
Campos de Hielo Sur (glacier), Chile 201/B6
Campos del Puerto, Sp. 87/G3
Campos do Jordão, Braz. 197/H7
Campos Gerais, Braz. 197/C2
Campos Novos, Braz. 197/B3
Campos Sales, Braz. 196/B2
Camposampiero, It. 101/E1
Camposanto, It. 101/E3
Campsie Fells (hills), Sc, UK 78/B4
Campti, La, US 174/E4
Camrose, Ab, Can. 168/E2
Can, Turk. 91/H5
Can (riv.), Eng, UK 72/E1
Can Tho, Viet. 120/D4
Canaçari (lake), Braz. 195/G5
Canada (ctry.) 122
Cañada de Gómez, Arg. 200/E2
Cañada Nieto, Uru. 201/J10
Cañada Rosquín, Arg. 200/E2
Canadensis, Pa, US 180/C1
Canadian (riv.), US 171/F3
Canadian (co.), Ok, US 179/M15
Canadian, Tx, US 171/G4
Canadian, North (riv.), Ok, US 171/H3
Cañadon Grande (mts.), Arg. 200/C5
Cañadón Seco, Arg. 200/D5
Canaima, PN, Ven. 192/F2
Çanakkale, Turk. 89/K2
Çanakkale (prov.), Turk. 132/A2
Canal de Moraleda (chan.), Chile 199/B6
Canalbianco (riv.), It. 101/E2
Canale, It. 100/A3
Canale Cavour (canal), It. 100/B2
Canals, Sp. 87/E3
Canals, Arg. 200/E2
Canandaigua, NY, US 172/E3
Cananea, Mex. 184/C2
Cananéia, Braz. 197/C3
Canápolis, Braz. 197/B1
Cañar, Ecu. 198/B1
Cañar (dept.), Ecu. 194/B5
Canard (riv.), On, Can. 177/G7
Canary (isls.), Canl., Sp. 140/A3
Cañas, CR 187/E4
Cañasgordas, Col. 194/B3
Canatlán de las Manzanas, Mex. 184/D3
Canaveral (cape), Fl, US 175/H4
Canberra (cap.), Austl. 157/D2
Canchaque, Peru 198/B2
Canche (riv.), Fr. 84/E1
Cancún, Mex. 186/E1
Cancun (int'l arpt.), Mex. 186/E1
Candado, Nevado del (peak), Arg. 199/C2
Candarave, Peru 198/D5
Çandarli (gulf), Gre.,Turk. 132/A2
Candás, Sp. 86/C1
Candeias, Braz. 196/C4
Candelaria, Mex. 186/D2
Candelaria (riv.), Mex. 186/D2
Candelaria, Arg. 200/D2
Candeleda, Sp. 86/C2
Candelo, Austl. 157/D3
Candelo, It. 100/B1
Candia Lomellina, It. 100/B2
Candiac, Qu, Can. 173/N7
Candiba, Braz. 196/B4
Cândido Mota, Braz. 197/B2
Canding (cape), Indo. 122/D5
Çandır, Turk. 132/C2
Candlewood, NJ, US 180/D3
Cando, ND, US 169/J3
Candon, Phil. 121/D4
Canegrate, It. 100/B1
Canela, Braz. 197/B4
Canelli, It. 100/B3
Canelones (dept.), Uru. 201/F2
Canelones, Uru. 201/K11
Cañete, Sp. 86/E2
Canete, Río de (riv.), Peru 198/B4
Cangallo, Peru 198/C4
Cangas, Sp. 86/A1
Cangas de Narcea, Sp. 86/B1
Cangas de Onís, Sp. 86/C1
Cangkuang (cape), Indo. 122/C5
Cango Caves, SAfr. 148/C4
Cangrejo (peak), Arg. 201/B6
Cangshan, China 114/D4
Canguaretama, Braz. 196/D2
Canguçu, Braz. 197/A4
Cangwu, China 125/K3
Cangyuan (Cangyuan Vazu Zizhixian), China 125/G3
Cangzhou, China 114/D3
Canh Cuoc (isl.), Viet. 120/D1
Cania Gorge NP, Austl. 156/C4
Caniapiscau (lake), Qu, Can. 165/K3
Caniapiskau (riv.), Qu, Can. 165/J3
Canicatti, It. 88/C4
Canik (mts.), Turk. 132/C1
Caniles, Sp. 86/D4
Canindé (riv.), Braz. 193/K5
Canino, It. 88/B1
Canistear (res.), NJ, US 181/H7
Cañitas de Felipe Pescador, Mex. 184/E4
Cañjáyar, Sp. 86/D4
Çankırı, Turk. 132/C1
Çankırı (prov.), Turk. 132/C1
Canlaon (vol.), Phil. 123/F1
Canmore, Ab, Can. 168/E3
Cann River, Austl. 157/D3
Canna (isl.), Sc, UK 73/Q8
Cannanore, India 124/C5
Canne (ruin), It. 88/E2
Canner (riv.), Fr. 95/F5
Cannero Riviera, It. 99/E5
Cannes, Fr. 85/G5
Canneto sull'Oglio, It. 100/D2
Canning (peak), Austl. 154/C4
Canning (dam), Austl. 154/L7
Canning (riv.), Austl. 154/K7
Cannobio, It. 99/E5
Cannock, Eng, UK 74/D1
Cannon Falls, Mn, US 169/K4
Cannonball (riv.), ND, US 169/H4
Cannondale, Ct, US 181/E1
Cannonvale, Austl. 156/C3
Caño Guaritico (riv.), Ven. 194/D3
Caño Negro NWF, CR 187/E4
Canoas, Braz. 197/B4
Canoas (riv.), Braz. 197/B3
Canobolas (mt.), Austl. 157/D2
Canoinhas, Braz. 197/B3
Cañón de Río Blanco, PN, Mex. 185/M8
Cañón del Sumidero, PN, Mex. 186/C2
Canora, Sk, Can. 169/H3
Canosa di Puglia, It. 88/E2
Canouan (isl.), StV. 183/N9
Canowindra, Austl. 157/D2
Cansanção, Braz. 196/C3
Canso (cape), NS, Can. 173/J2
Canta, Peru 198/B3
Cantabria (aut. comm.), Sp. 86/C1
Cantabria, Cordillera (mts.), Sp. 86/B1
Cantal, Massif du (mass.), Fr. 84/E4
Cantalejo, Sp. 86/D2
Cantanhede, Braz. 196/A1
Cantanhede, Port. 86/A2
Cantaura, Ven. 195/E2
Canterbury, Eng, UK 75/H4
Canterbury Bight (bay), NZ 159/S11
Canterbury Cathedral, Eng, UK 75/H4
Cantillana, Sp. 86/C4
Canto do Buriti, Braz. 196/B3
Canton, Mi, US 177/E7
Canton, Ms, US 171/K4
Canton, NJ, US 180/C5
Canton, NY, US 172/F2
Canton, Oh, US 172/D3
Canton, Ok, US 174/D2
Canton (Abariringa) (isl.), Kiri. 159/H5
Cantoria, Sp. 86/D4
Cantù, It. 100/C1
Cantwell, Ak, US 176/J3
Cañuelas, Arg. 201/J11
Canunda NP, Austl. 157/B3
Canvey (isl.), Eng, UK 72/E2
Canvey Island, Eng, UK 75/G3
Canwood, Sk, Can. 168/G2
Canyon, Tx, US 171/G4
Canyon (lake), Tx, US 179/U20
Canyon de Chelly Nat'l Mon., Az, US 170/E3
Canyon Lake, Tx, US 179/U20
Canyonlands Nat'l Park, Ut, US 170/E3
Canyon of the Ancients Nat'l Mon., Co, US 170/E3
Canzo, It. 100/C1
Cao (riv.), China 115/C2
Cao Bang, Viet. 125/J3
Cao Lanh, Viet. 120/D4
Cao Xian, China 114/C4
Caodu (riv.), China 121/A2
Caorle, It. 101/F1
Caorso, It. 100/C2
Cap-Chat, Qu, Can. 173/H1
Cap d'Agde (cape), Fr. 84/E5
Cap-de-la-Madeleine, Qu, Can. 173/F2
Cap-Haïtien, Haiti 187/H2
Cap Rock Escarpment (cliff), Tx, US 174/C3
Cap-Rouge, Qu, Can. 173/G2
Cap Roux, Pointe du (pt.), Fr. 85/G5
Capac, Mi, US 177/G5
Capanaparo (riv.), Ven. 192/E2
Capanema, Braz. 193/J4
Capanne (peak), It. 88/B1
Capannoli, It. 101/D5
Capannori, It. 100/D5
Capão Bonito, Braz. 197/B3
Capão Doce, Morro do (hill), Braz. 197/B3
Caparaó, PN do, Braz. 197/D2
Caparica, Port. 87/P10
Caparo (riv.), Ven. 194/D3
Capay, Ca, US 177/K9
Capbreton, Fr. 84/C5
Capdenac-Gare, Fr. 84/E4
Capdepera, Sp. 87/G3
Cape Arid NP, Austl. 154/D5
Cape Barren (isl.), Austl. 151/D5
Cape Breton (isl.), NS, Can. 173/J2
Cape Breton Highlands (uplands), NS, Can. 173/J2
Cape Breton Highlands NP, NS, Can. 173/J2
Cape Cleveland NP, Austl. 156/B2
Cape Coast, Gha. 145/E5
Cape Cod Nat'l Seashore, Ma, US 173/G3
Cape Coral, Fl, US 175/H5
Cape Dorset, Nun., Can. 165/J2
Cape Fear (riv.), NC, US 175/J3
Cape Hatteras Nat'l Seashore, NC, US 175/K3
Cape Krusenstern Nat'l Mon., Ak, US 176/E2
Cape Le Grand NP, Austl. 154/D5
Cape Lookout Nat'l Seashore, NC, US 175/J3
Cape May, NJ, US 180/D6
Cape May (co.), NJ, US 180/D5
Cape May Court House, NJ, US 180/D5
Cape May Lighthouse, NJ, US 180/D6
Cape Melville NP, Austl. 156/B1
Cape Palmerston NP, Austl. 156/C3
Cape Range NP, Austl. 154/B2
Cape Saint Claire, Md, US 180/B5
Cape Town (cap.), SAfr. 148/L10
Cape Town (D.F. Malan) (int'l arpt.), SAfr. 148/L10
Cape Tribulation NP, Austl. 156/B2
Cape Upstart NP, Austl. 156/B2
Cape Verde (ctry.) 135/J9
Cape Yakataga, Ak, US 176/K3
Cape York (pen.), Austl. 151/D2
Capel, Austl. 154/B5
Capela, Braz. 196/C3
Capelinha, Braz. 196/B5
Capella, Austl. 156/C3
Capellades, Sp. 87/K6
Capestang, Fr. 84/E5
Capicciola (pt.), Fr. 88/A2
Capilla del Señor, Arg. 201/J11
Capim (riv.), Braz. 193/J4
Capinópolis, Braz. 197/B1
Capirara (res.), Braz. 199/F1
Capistrano, Braz. 196/C2
Capistrello, It. 88/C2
Capitan (mts.), NM, US 174/B3
Capitão de Campos, Braz. 196/B2
Capitão Poço, Braz. 193/J4
Capitol Reef NP, Ut, US 170/E3
Capivara, Represa (res.), Braz. 193/H8
Capivara, Serra de (range), Braz. 196/A4
Capivari (riv.), Braz. 197/J6
Čapljina, Bosn. 89/E1
Caplone (peak), It. 100/D1
Capo di Ponte, It. 99/G5
Capo d'Orlando, It. 88/D3
Capodichino (int'l arpt.), It. 88/D2
Capolona, It. 101/E5
Capoterra, It. 88/A3
Cappella Maggiore, It. 101/F1
Cappoquin, Ire. 73/Q10
Capraia (isl.), It. 88/A1
Caprarola, It. 88/C1
Capreol, On, Can. 172/D2
Capricorn (chan.), Austl. 151/E3
Capricorn (cape), Austl. 156/C3
Caprino Veronese, It. 101/D1
Capriolo, It. 100/C1
Caprivi Strip (reg.), Namb. 147/D4
Captain (har.), Ct, US 181/L7
Captain Cook, Hi, US 166/U11
Captainganj, India 126/D2
Captains Flat, Austl. 157/D2
Capua, It. 90/B5
Capulhuac, Mex. 185/Q10
Capulhuac, Mex. 185/Q10
Caputh, Ger. 82/Q7
Caquetá (riv.), Col. 194/D5
Caquetá (dept.), Col. 194/C4
Caquiaviri, Bol. 198/D5
Car Nicobar (isl.), India 125/F6
Carabobo (state), Ven. 194/D2
Caracal, Rom. 91/G3
Caracaraí, Braz. 195/F4
Caracas (cap.), Ven. 192/E1
Carache, Ven. 194/D2
Caracol, Braz. 196/B3
Caracolí, Col. 194/C3
Carácuaro de Morelos, Mex. 185/E5
Caradon (hill), Eng, UK 74/B5
Caraguatatuba, Braz. 197/H8
Caraguatatuba, Enseada de (bay), Braz. 197/H8
Carahue, Chile 200/B3
Carajás, Serra dos (mts.), Braz. 193/H5
Caranavi, Bol. 192/E7
Carandaí, Braz. 197/D2
Carangola, Braz. 197/D2
Caransebeş, Rom. 90/F3
Carapicuíba, Braz. 197/G8
Carappee Hill (peak), Austl. 155/H5
Caraquet, NB, Can. 173/H2
Caraş-Severin (prov.), Rom. 90/E3
Carasco, It. 100/C4
Caratasca (lag.), Hon. 182/E4
Carate Brianza, It. 100/C1
Caratinga, Braz. 197/D1
Carauari, Braz. 192/E4
Caraúbas, Braz. 196/C2
Caravaca de la Cruz, Sp. 86/E3
Caravaggio, It. 100/C2
Caravela, Ilha (isl.), GBis. 144/A4
Caravelas, Braz. 196/C5
Caravelí, Peru 198/C4
Caraz, Peru 198/B3
Carazinho, Braz. 199/F2
Carballino, Sp. 86/A1
Carballo, Sp. 86/A1
Carberry, Mb, Can. 169/J3
Carbo, Mex. 184/C2
Carbon (cape), Alg. 142/H4
Carbon (co.), Pa, US 180/C2
Carbon (riv.), Wa, US 177/C3
Carbonara (cape), It. 88/A3
Carbonara (peak), It. 88/D4
Carbondale, Pa, US 172/F3
Carbonear, Nf, Can. 173/L2
Carbonera, It. 101/F1
Carboneras, Mex. 185/F3
Carbonia, It. 88/A3
Carbonne, Fr. 84/D5
Carbost, Sc, UK 73/Q8
Carcagente, Sp. 87/E3
Carcarañá, Arg. 200/E2
Carcare, It. 100/B4
Carcassonne, Fr. 84/E5
Carche (peak), Sp. 86/E3
Carchi (dept.), Ecu. 194/B4
Carcross, Yk, Can. 176/M3
Çardak, Turk. 91/H5

Carda – Certo

227
Cerva – Chini

Cervantes, Austl. 154/B4
Cervaro (riv.), It. 88/D2
Cervati (peak), It. 88/D2
Cervellino (peak), It. 100/D3
Cervera, Sp. 87/F2
Cervera de Pisuerga, Sp. 86/C1
Cervera del Río Alhama, Sp. 86/E1
Cervia, It. 101/F4
Cervialto (peak), It. 88/D2
Cervignano del Friuli, It. 101/G1
Cervina (peak), It. 99/H4
Cervione, Fr. 88/A1
Cervo (riv.), It. 100/B1
Cervo, Sp. 86/B1
Cervo, It. 100/B5
Cervo, Serra do (hills), Braz. 197/G7
Cesano (riv.), It. 101/F6
Cesano Boscone, It. 100/C2
Cesano Maderno, It. 100/C1
César (dept.), Col. 194/C2
César (riv.), Col. 194/C2
Cesen (peak), It. 101/F1
Cesena, It. 101/F4
Cesenatico, It. 101/F4
Cēsis, Lat. 81/L3
České Budějovice, Czh. 97/H5
České Středohoří (mts.), Czh. 97/G2
Českomoravská Vysočina (mts.), Czh. 83/H4
Český Brod, Czh. 97/H2
Český Krumlov, Czh. 97/H5
Český Les Sumava (mts.), Czh. 97/F3
Česma (riv.), Cro. 90/C3
Çeşme, Turk. 89/K3
Cesson, Fr. 72/K6
Cesson-Sévigné, Fr. 84/C2
Cestos (riv.), Libr. 144/C5
Cetinje, Mont. 90/D4
Çetinkaya, Turk. 132/D2
Ceurda del Pozo, Embalse de la (res.), Sp. 86/D2
Ceuta, Sp. 142/B2
Ceva, It. 100/B4
Cevedale (peak), It. 99/G5
Cévennes (mts.), Fr. 84/E4
Cevio, Swi. 99/E5
Ceyhan, Turk. 133/D1
Ceylânpınar, Turk. 132/E2
Ceylon (isl.), SrL. 124/D6
Ceyzériat, Fr. 98/B5
Cèze (riv.), Fr. 84/F4
Cha Da (cape), Viet. 120/E4
Chabás, Arg. 200/E2
Chabjuwardoo (bay), Austl. 154/B2
Chablé, Mex. 186/D2
Chacabuco, Arg. 200/E2
Chachani (peak), Peru 198/D5
Chachapoyas, Peru 198/B2
Chachoengsao, Thai. 120/C3
Chaclacayo, Peru 198/B3
Chaco (riv.), NM, US 170/F3
Chaco (mesa), NM, US 174/B3
Chaco Austral (plain), Arg. 199/D1
Chaco Boreal (plain), Par. 192/F8
Chaco Central (plain), Arg. 199/D1
Chaco, PN, Arg. 199/E2
Chacujal (ruin), Guat. 186/D3
Chad (lake), Niger 138/H5
Chad (ctry.) 139/J4
Chafarinas (isl.), Sp. 142/C2
Chagang-do (prov.), NKor. 115/D2
Chagda, Rus. 107/P4
Chaghcharān, Afg. 129/E6
Chagny, Fr. 84/F3
Chagos (arch.), BrIn, UK 109/G10
Chaguanas, Trin. 195/F2
Chaguarpamba, Ecu. 198/B1
Chahuites, Mex. 186/C2
Chaibāsā, India 127/E4
Chailly-en-Brie, Fr. 72/M5
Chain, SKor. 115/E5
Chainat, Thai. 120/C3
Chaîne Annamitique (mts.), Laos 125/H4
Chaine de la Selle (peak), Haiti 187/J2
Chaîne de l'Atacora (mts.), Ben. 145/F4
Chaitén, Chile 199/B5
Chaiyaphum, Thai. 120/C3
Chākdaha, India 127/G4
Chake Chake, Tanz. 146/C4
Chākia, India 126/D3
Chakradharpur, India 127/E4
Chakrāta, India 128/D3
Chakwāl, Pak. 128/B3
Chala, Peru 198/C4
Chalain (lake), Fr. 98/B4
Chalais, Swi. 98/D5
Chālakudi, India 124/C5
Chalaronne (riv.), Fr. 98/A5
Chalatenango, ESal. 186/D3
Chalbi (des.), Kenya 139/N7
Chalchihuites, Mex. 184/E4
Chalco, Mex. 185/R10
Chale (pt.), Kenya 146/C4
Chaleur (bay), NB,Qu, Can. 173/H2
Chalfont, Pa, US 180/C3
Chalfont Saint Giles, Eng, UK 72/B2
Chalfont Saint Peter, Eng, UK 72/B2
Chalhuanca, Peru 198/C4
Chalifert (canal), Fr. 72/L5
Chalindrey, Fr. 98/B2
Chalk (mts.), Tx, US 174/C4
Chalkyitsik, Ak, US 176/K2
Challans, Fr. 84/C3
Challapata, Bol. 192/E7
Challenger (mts.), Nun., Can. 165/T6
Chalmette, La, US 179/Q17
Chālna Port, Bang. 127/G4
Chalon-sur-Saône, Fr. 98/A4
Châlons-sur-Marne, Fr. 95/D6
Châlonvillars, Fr. 98/C2
Chālūs, Iran 130/F1
Cham, Ger. 97/F4
Cham (riv.), Ger. 97/F4
Cham, Swi. 99/E3
Chama, Zam. 146/B5
Chama (riv.), NM, US 170/F3
Chamah (peak), Malay. 122/B2
Chaman, Pak. 131/J2
Chamba, India 128/D3
Chambal (riv.), India 131/L3
Chambaran, Plateau de (plat.), Fr. 84/F4
Chambas, Cuba 187/G1
Chamberlain (lake), Me, US 173/G2
Chamberlin (mt.), Ak, US 176/K2
Chambersburg, Pa, US 172/E4
Chambéry, Fr. 84/F4
Chambeshi (riv.), Zam. 147/F3
Chambly, Qu, Can. 173/P7
Chambly, Fr. 72/J4
Chambourcy, Fr. 72/J5
Chambry, Fr. 72/L5
Chamchamāl, Iraq 130/D1
Chamechaude (peak), Fr. 84/F4
Chamical, Arg. 199/C3
Chamigny, Fr. 72/M5
Chamizal Nat'l Mem., Tx, US 174/B4
Chamizo, Uru. 201/L11
Chamonix-Mont-Blanc, Fr. 98/C6
Champagne, Yk, Can. 176/L3
Champagne (reg.), Fr. 82/C4
Champagne-Ardenne (pol. reg), Fr. 84/F2
Champagne-sur-Oise, Fr. 72/J4
Champagney, Fr. 98/C2
Champagnole, Fr. 98/B4
Champasak, Laos 120/D3
Champawat, India 126/C1
Champdeuil, Fr. 72/L6
Champeaux, Fr. 72/L6
Champéry, Swi. 98/C5
Champigneulles, Fr. 95/F6
Champigny-sur-Marne, Fr. 72/K5
Champlain (lake), NY,Vt, US 170/F2
Champlitte, Fr. 98/B2
Champotón, Mex. 186/D2
Champotón (riv.), Mex. 186/D2
Champs-sur-Marne, Fr. 72/K5
Champsevraine, Fr. 98/B2
Champvans, Fr. 98/B3
Chamusca, Port. 86/A3
Chan Chan (ruin), Peru 198/B3
Chan May Dong (cape), Viet. 120/E2
Chañaral, Chile 199/B2
Chança (riv.), Port. 86/B4
Chancay, Peru 198/B3
Chanco, Chile 200/B2
Chandalar, Ak, US 176/J2
Chandalar (riv.), Ak, US 176/J2
Chandalar, East Fork (riv.), Ak, US 176/J2
Chandannagar, India 127/G4
Chandausi, India 126/B1
Chanderi, India 126/B3
Chandīgarh, India 128/D4
Chandīgarh (state), India 128/D4
Chandlees (riv.), Braz. 192/D6
Chandler (riv.), Ak, US 176/H2
Chandler, Ok, US 174/D3
Chandler, Qu, Can. 173/H1
Chandler, Az, US 179/S19
Chandolin, Swi. 98/D5
Chāndpur, Bang. 127/H4
Chāndpur, India 126/B1
Chandrapur, India 124/C4
Chanduy, Ecu. 194/A5
Chang (lake), China 114/C5
Chang (riv.), China 114/B5
Changan, SKor. 115/E5
Changbai (peak), China 115/E2
Changbai Chaoxianzu Zizhixian, China 115/E2
Changchun, China 113/N3
Changdang (lake), China 114/D5
Changdao, China 114/E3
Changde, China 121/B2
Changé, Fr. 84/D3
Changewater, NJ, US 180/D2
Changfeng, China 114/D4
Changge, China 114/C4
Changgi-ap (cape), SKor. 116/A2
Changhai, China 115/B3
Changhang, SKor. 115/D4
Changhowŏn, SKor. 115/D4
Changhua, Tai. 121/D3
Changhŭng, SKor. 115/D5
Changis-sur-Marne, Fr. 72/M5
Changji, China 112/E3
Changjiang, China 125/J4
Changjin (res.), NKor. 115/D2
Changjin (lake), NKor. 115/D2
Changle, China 114/D3
Changli, China 114/D3
Changling, China 114/E1
Changning, China 125/H2
Changning, China 125/G3
Ch'angnyŏng, SKor. 115/E5
Changping, China 114/H6
Changqing, China 114/D3
Changsan-got (cape), NKor. 115/C3
Changsha, China 125/K2
Changshou, China 121/A2
Changshu, China 114/L8
Changshun, China 125/J2
Changsŏng, SKor. 115/D5
Changsu, SKor. 115/D5
Changsŭngp'o, SKor. 115/E5
Changtai, China 121/C3
Changtu, China 114/F2
Changuinola, Pan. 187/F4
Ch'angwŏn, SKor. 115/E5
Changxing, China 114/K8
Changyang, China 121/B1
Changyi, China 114/D3
Changyŏn, NKor. 115/C3
Changyuan, China 114/C4
Changzhi, China 114/C3
Changzhou, China 114/K8
Chañi, Nevado de (peak), Arg. 199/C1
Chanlers (falls), Kenya 146/C2
Channel (isls.), UK 84/B2
Channel Country (phys. reg.), Austl. 151/C3
Channel Islands NP, Ca, US 170/C4
Channel-Port aux Basques, Nf, Can. 173/K2
Channel Tunnel, Eng, Fr.,UK 75/H5
Channing, Tx, US 171/G4
Chantada, Sp. 86/B1
Chanteloup-les-Vignes, Fr. 72/J5
Chanthaburi, Thai. 120/C3
Chantilly, Fr. 94/B5
Chantraine, Fr. 98/C1
Chantrey (inlet), Nun., Can. 164/G2
Chao (lake), China 114/D5
Chao Phraya (riv.), Thai. 120/C3
Chaoyang, China 121/C3
Chaoyang, China 114/E2
Chapacura, Bol. 198/D3
Chapada Diamantina, PN, Braz. 193/K6
Chapada dos Veadeiros, PN da, Braz. 193/J6
Chapadinha, Braz. 196/B1
Chapais, Qu, Can. 172/F1
Chapala (lake), Mex. 184/E4
Chapala, Mex. 184/E4
Chaparral, Col. 194/C4
Chaparrosa, Mex. 184/E4
Chapayevsk, Rus. 105/J1
Chapel Hill, NC, US 175/J3
Chapel Ness (pt.), Sc, UK 78/D4
Chapelfell Top (peak), Eng, UK 77/F2
Chapelle-lez-Herlaimont, Belg. 95/D3
Chapeltown, Eng, UK 77/G5
Chaplain (lake), Wa, US 177/D2
Chapleau, On, Can. 172/D2
Chaplin, Sk, Can. 168/G3
Chāpra, India 127/E3
Char (well), Mrta. 140/B5
Chara (riv.), Rus. 107/M4
Charambirá (pt.), Col. 194/B3
Charaña, Bol. 198/D5
Charandra (riv.), Gre. 89/N8
Charata, Arg. 199/D2
Charcas, Mex. 185/E4
Charcot (isl.), Ant. 202/U
Chardonnière, Haiti 187/H2
Charente (riv.), Fr. 84/C4
Chari (riv.), Chad 138/J5
Chārīkār, Afg. 131/J1
Chariton (riv.), Ia,Mo, US 171/J2
Charity, Guy. 195/G3
Chärjew, Trkm. 129/D5
Charkhāri, India 126/B3
Charkhi Dādri, India 128/D5
Charlemagne, Qu, Can. 173/P6
Charlemont, NI, UK 76/B3
Charleroi, Belg. 95/D3
Charleroi à Bruxelles, Canal de (canal), Belg. 95/D2
Charles (peak), Austl. 154/D5
Charles (mt.), Austl. 154/C3
Charles (isl.), Qu, Can. 165/J2
Charles City, Ia, US 169/K5
Charles de Gaulle (int'l arpt.), Fr. 72/K4
Charleston, Ms, US 171/K4
Charleston, Nv, US 168/E5
Charleston, SC, US 175/J3
Charleston, Ut, US 179/L13
Charleston (cap.), WV, US 172/D4
Charlestown, StK. 183/N8
Charlestown, Md, US 180/C4
Charleville, Austl. 156/B4
Charleville-Mézières, Fr. 95/D4
Charlevoix, Mi, US 172/C2
Charlotte (lake), BC, Can. 168/B2
Charlotte, Mi, US 172/C3
Charlotte, NC, US 175/H3
Charlotte Amalie, USVI 183/M8
Charlotte/Douglas (int'l arpt.), NC, US 175/H3
Charlottenberg, Swe. 80/E2
Charlottenburg, Ger. 82/Q6
Charlottetown (cap.), PE, Can. 173/J2
Charlton, Austl. 157/B3
Charlton (isl.), On, Can. 165/H3
Charlton Kings, Eng, UK 74/D3
Charly, Fr. 94/C6
Charmes (res.), Fr. 98/B2
Charmes, Fr. 98/C1
Charmey, Swi. 98/D4
Charnay-lès-Mâcon, Fr. 84/F3
Charny, Fr. 72/L5
Charny-sur-Meuse, Fr. 95/E5
Charolais, Monts du (mts.), Fr. 84/F3
Charouine, Alg. 141/E3
Charquemont, Fr. 98/C3
Chars, Fr. 72/H4
Chārsadda, Pak. 128/A2
Charters Towers, Austl. 156/B3
Charthāwāl, India 128/D5
Chartres, Fr. 84/D2
Chās, India 127/F4
Chaschauna (peak), Swi. 99/G4
Chascomús, Arg. 200/F2
Chase, BC, Can. 168/D3
Chasŏng, NKor. 115/D2
Chassezac (riv.), Fr. 84/F4
Chastre-Villeroux-Blanmont, Belg. 95/D2
Chatanika, Ak, US 176/J2
Château Bougon (int'l arpt.), Fr. 84/C3
Chateau de Versailles, Fr. 72/J5
Château-d'Olonne, Fr. 84/C3
Château-du-Loir, Fr. 84/D3
Château-Porcien, Fr. 95/D4
Château-Renault, Fr. 84/D3
Château-Salins, Fr. 95/F6
Château-Thierry, Fr. 94/C5
Châteaubriant, Fr. 84/C3
Châteaudun, Fr. 84/D2
Châteauguay, Qu, Can. 173/N7
Châteauneuf-sur-Charente, Fr. 84/C4
Châteaurenard, Fr. 84/F5
Châteauroux, Fr. 84/D3
Châteauvillain, Fr. 98/A1
Châtel-Saint-Denis, Swi. 98/C4
Châtelaillon-Page, Fr. 84/C3
Châtelet, Belg. 95/D3
Châtellerault, Fr. 84/D3
Châtenay-Malabry, Fr. 72/J5
Châtenois, Fr. 98/B1
Châtenois-les-Forges, Fr. 98/C2
Chatfield (res.), Co, US 179/B3
Chatham (isls.), Chile 201/B6
Chatham, On, Can. 172/D3
Chatham, Eng, UK 75/G4
Chatham, NJ, US 181/H9
Châtillon, It. 85/G4
Châtillon, Fr. 72/J5
Châtillon-sur-Chalaronne, Fr. 98/A5
Châtillon-sur-Marne, Fr. 94/C5
Châtillon-sur-Seine, Fr. 84/F3
Chatkal (riv.), Kyr. 129/F4
Chatou, Fr. 72/J5
Chatra, India 127/E3
Chatrapur, India 124/E4
Châtres, Fr. 72/L5
Chatsworth (res.), Ca, US 178/B2
Chatsworth, NJ, US 180/D4
Chattahoochee (riv.),US 175/G4
Chattahoochee, Fl, US 175/G4
Chattanooga, Tn, US 175/G3
Chatteris, Eng, UK 75/G2
Chau Doc, Viet. 120/D4
Chaucey, Îles (isls.), Fr. 84/C2
Chauconin-Neufmontiers, Fr. 72/L5
Chaudfontaine, Belg. 95/E2
Chaudière (riv.), Qu, Can. 173/G2
Chauk, Myan. 125/F3
Chaukan (pass), India 125/G2
Chaumes-en-Brie, Fr. 72/L5
Chaumont, Fr. 98/B1
Chaumont-en-Vexin, Fr. 94/A5
Chaunskaya (bay), Rus. 107/T3
Chauny, Fr. 94/C4
Chaussin, Fr. 98/B4
Chaussy, Fr. 72/H4
Chautauqua (lake), NY, US 172/E3
Chautauqua, Il, US 179/G8
Chauvigny, Fr. 84/D3
Chaval, Braz. 196/B1
Chavanoz, Fr. 98/B6
Chaves, Port. 86/B2
Chavín de Huantar (ruin), Peru 198/B3
Chaviña, Peru 198/C4
Chavinillo, Peru 198/B3
Chavornay, Swi. 98/C4
Chawinda, Pak. 128/C3
Chay (riv.), Viet. 120/D1
Chayana (riv.), Bol. 192/E7
Chaykovskiy, Rus. 103/M4
Chazuta, Peru 198/B2
Cheadle, Eng, UK 77/G6
Cheaha (mtn.), Al, US 175/G3
Cheb, Czh. 97/F2
Cheboksary, Rus. 103/K4
Cheboksary (res.), Rus. 103/K4
Cheboygan, Mi, US 172/C2
Chechaouene, Mor. 142/B2
Chechaouene (prov.), Mor. 142/B2
Chechen' (isl.), Rus. 105/H3
Chechnya, Resp., Rus. 106/Q6
Chech'ŏn, SKor. 115/E4
Checotah, Ok, US 171/J4
Chedabucto (bay), NS, Can. 173/J2
Cheduba (isl.), Myan. 125/F4
Cheektowaga, NY, US 173/S10
Cheepash (riv.), On, Can. 172/D1
Cheepay (riv.), On, Can. 172/D1
Chefornak, Ak, US 176/F3
Chegutu, Zim. 147/F4
Chehalis, Wa, US 168/C4
Cheïkh (well), Alg. 141/F3
Cheju, SKor. 113/N5
Cheju (isl.), SKor. 113/N5
Cheju (str.), SKor. 113/N5
Cheka (peak), Rus. 129/C2
Chelan, Wa, US 168/C4
Chelan (lake), Wa, US 168/C4
Chelghoum El Aïd, Alg. 142/J4
Chelles, Fr. 72/K5
Chełm, Pol. 83/M3
Chełmno, Pol. 83/K2
Chelmsford, Eng, UK 75/G3
Chełmża, Pol. 83/K2
Cheltenham, Eng, UK 74/D3
Chelva, Sp. 87/E3
Chelyabinsk (int'l arpt.), Rus. 103/P5
Chelyabinsk, Rus. 103/P5
Chelyabinskaya Oblast, Rus. 129/D2
Chelyuskina (cape), Rus. 107/L2
Chemaïa, Mor. 140/C2
Chemax, Mex. 186/E1
Chemnitz, Ger. 82/G3
Chen (riv.), China 121/A2
Chena Hot Springs, Ak, US 176/J2
Chenāb (riv.), Pak. 131/K2
Chenachane (well), Alg. 140/D4
Cheney, Wa, US 168/D4
Cheng'anpu, China 114/C3
Chengbu Miaozu Zizhixian, China 125/K2
Chengde, China 114/D2
Chengdu, China 112/H5
Chengkou, China 112/J5
Chengmai, China 125/J4
Chengshan Jiao (cape), China 115/B4
Chengwu, China 114/C4
Cheniménil, Fr. 98/C1
Chennai (Madras), India 124/D5
Chennevières-lès-Louvres, Fr. 72/K4
Chenòve, Fr. 98/A3
Chenxi, China 125/K2
Chenzhou, China 125/K2
Chep Lak Kok (int'l arpt.), China 113/T10
Chepelare, Bul. 89/J2
Chepén, Peru 198/B2
Chepes, Arg. 199/C3
Chépica, Chile 200/C2
Chepigana, Pan. 194/B2
Chepo, Pan. 194/B2
Chepstow, Wal, UK 74/D3
Cheptsa (riv.), Rus. 103/M4
Cher (riv.), Fr. 84/E3
Chéran (riv.), Fr. 98/C6
Cherasco, It. 100/A3
Cherāt, Pak. 128/A3
Cheraw, SC, US 175/J3
Cherbourg, Fr. 84/C2
Cherbourg, Austl. 156/C4
Cherchell, Alg. 142/G4
Cherepovets, Rus. 102/H4
Cherf, Oued (riv.), Alg. 142/K6
Cheria, Alg. 142/K7
Cherkas'ka Oblasti, Ukr. 104/D2
Cherkasy, Ukr. 104/E2
Cherkessk, Rus. 105/G3
Chermignon, Swi. 98/D5
Chernaya (riv.), Rus. 103/N1
Cherni Lom (riv.), Bul. 91/H4
Cherni Vrŭkh (peak), Bul. 89/H1
Chernihiv, Ukr. 104/D2
Chernihivs'ka Oblasti, Ukr. 104/D2
Chernivets'ka Oblasti, Ukr. 104/C2
Chernivtsi, Ukr. 91/G1
Chernushka, Rus. 103/N4
Cherokee, Ok, US 171/H3
Cherry Creek (dam), Co, US 179/C3
Cherry Creek (lake), Co, US 179/C3
Cherry Hill, Md, US 180/C4
Cherry Hill, NJ, US 180/C4
Cherry Valley, Ca, US 178/D3
Cherski (range), Rus. 109/P3
Chertsey, Eng, UK 72/B2
Cherven Bryag, Bul. 91/G4
Chervonohrad, Ukr. 104/C2
Cherwell (riv.), Eng, UK 75/E3
Chesaning, Mi, US 172/C3
Chesapeake (bay), US 172/E4
Chesapeake and Delaware (canal), De,Md, US 180/C4
Chesapeake Bay Maritime Museum, Md, US 180/B6
Chesapeake City, Md, US 180/C4
Chesham, Eng, UK 75/F3
Cheshire (co.), Eng, UK 77/F5
Cheshire (plain), Eng, UK 77/F5
Cheshskaya (bay), Rus. 106/E3
Cheshunt, Eng, UK 72/C1
Chesilhurst, NJ, US 180/D4
Chester, Eng, UK 77/F5
Chester, Ca, US 168/C5
Chester (riv.), Md, US 180/B5
Chester, Mt, US 168/F3
Chester, Md, US 180/D2
Chester, Pa, US 180/C4
Chester (co.), Pa, US 180/C4
Chester, SC, US 175/H3
Chester Heights, Pa, US 180/C4
Chester-le-Street, Eng, UK 77/G2
Chester Morse (lake), Wa, US 177/D3
Chesterfield (inlet), Nun., Can. 164/G2
Chesterfield, Eng, UK 77/G5
Chesterfield, Mo, US 179/F8
Chesterfield (isls.), NCal., Fr. 158/E6
Chesterfield Inlet, Nun., Can. 164/G2
Chesterfield, Nosy (isl.), Madg. 149/G7
Chesterton (range), Austl. 156/B4
Chestertown, Md, US 180/B5
Chesuncook (lake), Me, US 173/G2
Cheswold, De, US 180/C5
Chetumal (bay), Mex. 182/D4
Chetumal, Mex. 186/D2
Chetwynd, BC, Can. 168/C2
Cheung Chau (isl.), China 113/T11
Chevak, Ak, US 176/E3
Cheval Blanc (pt.), Haiti 187/H2
Chevigny-Saint-Sauveur, Fr. 98/B3
Cheviot (hills), Sc, UK 78/D6
Cheviot, The (peak), Eng, UK 78/D6
Chevreuse, Fr. 72/J5
Chevry-Cossigny, Fr. 72/K5
Chew (riv.), Eng, UK 74/D4
Chew Valley (lake), Eng, UK 74/D4
Chewelah, Wa, US 168/D3
Chexbres, Swi. 98/C5
Cheyenne (riv.), SD,Wy, US 169/H5
Cheyenne (cap.), Wy, US 169/G5
Cheyenne, Ok, US 171/H4
Cheyenne Wells, Co, US 171/G3
Cheyres, Swi. 98/C4
Chhabra, India 126/A3
Chhaprauli, India 128/D5
Chhāta, India 126/A2
Chhatarpur, India 126/B3
Chhattisgarh (state), India 124/D3
Chhibrāmau, India 126/B2
Chhindwāra, India 126/B4
Chi (riv.), Thai. 125/H4
Chiai, Tai. 121/D3
Ch'iak-san NP, SKor. 115/E4
Chiampo, It. 101/E1
Chianciano Terme, It. 85/J5
Chiang Kai Shek (int'l arpt.), Tai. 121/D2
Chiang Mai, Thai. 125/G4
Chiang Rai, Thai. 125/G4
Chianti (reg.), It. 101/E5
Chianti, Monti del (mts.), It. 101/E5
Chiapa de Corzo, Mex. 186/C2
Chiapas (state), Mex. 182/C4
Chiappa (pt.), It. 100/C4
Chiaravalle, It. 101/G5
Chiari, It. 100/C1
Chiasso, Swi. 99/F6
Chiat'ura, Geo. 105/G4
Chiautempan, Mex. 185/L7
Chiautla, Mex. 185/R9
Chiautla de Tapia, Mex. 186/B2
Chiavari, It. 100/C4
Chiavenna, It. 99/F5
Chiba, Japan 117/G3
Chibougamau, Qu, Can. 172/F1
Chibougamau (riv.), Qu, Can. 172/F1
Chibougamau (lake), Qu, Can. 172/F1
Chibukak (pt.), Ak, US 176/D3
Chibuto, Moz. 147/F5
Chicago, Il, US 169/M5
Chicago Heights, Il, US 177/Q16
Chicago Midway (int'l arpt.), Il, US 171/L2
Chicago, North Branch (riv.), Il, US 177/Q15
Chicago-O'Hare (int'l arpt.), Il, US 169/M5
Chicago Ridge, Il, US 177/Q16
Chicago Sanitary and Ship Canal, Il, US 177/P16
Chicama, Peru 198/B2
Chichagof (isl.), Ak, US 164/C3
Chichaoua, Mor. 140/C3
Chichāwatni, Pak. 128/B4
Chichén Itzá (ruin), Mex. 186/D1
Chicheng, China 113/L3
Chichester (range), Austl. 151/A3
Chichester, Eng, UK 75/F5
Chichibu, Japan 117/F3
Chichicastenango, Guat. 186/D3
Chichigalpa, Nic. 186/E3
Chichihualco, Mex. 185/F5
Chichiriviche, Ven. 194/D2
Chichishima (isls.), Japan 158/D2
Chickaloon, Ak, US 176/J3
Chickamauga (lake), Tn, US 175/G3
Chickasaw Nat'l Rec. Area, Ok, US 171/H4
Chickasha, Ok, US 171/H4
Chicla, Peru 198/B3
Chiclana de la Frontera, Sp. 86/B4
Chiclayo, Peru 198/B2
Chico, Ca, US 170/B3
Chico (riv.), Arg. 189/B7
Chicoloapan, Mex. 185/R10
Chicomostoc (ruin), Mex. 184/E4
Chicomuselo, Mex. 186/C3
Chiconcuac, Mex. 185/R9
Chicontepec de Tejeda, Mex. 186/B1
Chicopee, Ma, US 173/F3
Chicoutimi, Qu, Can. 173/G1
Chicualacuala, Moz. 147/F5
Chidley (cape), Nf, Can. 165/K2
Chido, SKor. 115/D5
Chiefland, Fl, US 175/H4
Chiemsee (lake), Ger. 85/K3
Chieo Lan (res.), Thai. 125/G6
Chieri, It. 100/A2
Chierry, Fr. 94/C5
Chiers (riv.), Fr. 95/E5
Chiesa in Valmalenco, It. 99/F5
Chiese (riv.), It. 85/J3
Chieti, It. 88/D1
Chietla, Mex. 185/L8
Chièvres, Belg. 94/C2
Chifeng, China 113/L3
Chifre, Serra do (mts.), Braz. 193/K7
Chigasaki, Japan 117/F3
Chiginagak (mt.), Ak, US 176/G4
Chignahuapan, Mex. 185/L7
Chignecto (bay), NB,NS, Can. 173/H2
Chignik, Ak, US 176/G4
Chignik Lake, Ak, US 176/G4
Chigorodó, Col. 194/B3
Chigu (lake), China 127/H1
Chigwell, Eng, UK 72/D2
Chihayaakasaka, Japan 119/J7
Chihli (Bo Hai) (gulf), China 114/D3
Chihuahua, Mex. 184/D2
Chihuahua (state), Mex. 184/D2
Chikaskia (riv.), Ks,Ok, US 171/H3
Chikballāpur, India 124/C5
Chikhli, India 131/L4
Chikmagalūr, India 131/L6
Chikoy (riv.), Rus. 107/L5
Chikugo (riv.), Japan 116/B4
Chikuma (riv.), Japan 117/F2
Chilac, Mex. 185/M8
Chilaw, SrL. 124/C6
Chilbo-san (peak), NKor. 115/E2
Chilca, Peru 198/B4
Chilcotin (riv.), BC, Can. 164/D3
Childers, Austl. 156/D4
Childersburg, Al, US 175/G3
Childress, Tx, US 171/G4
Chile (ctry.) 199/B3
Chile Chico, Chile 200/C5
Chile, Monte el (peak), Hon. 186/E3
Chilecito, Arg. 199/C2
Chilete, Peru 198/B2
Ch'ilgap-san NP, SKor. 115/D4
Chililabombwe, Zam. 147/E3
Chilka (lake), India 124/E4
Chilko (lake), BC, Can. 164/D3
Chilkoot (pass), Can.,US 176/L4
Chilkoot (pass), Ak, US 176/L3
Chilla Well Abor. Land, Austl. 155/F2
Chillán, Chile 200/B3
Chillanes, Ecu. 198/B1
Chillicothe, Il, US 169/L5
Chilliwack, BC, Can. 168/C3
Chillon, Swi. 98/C5
Chilly-Mazarin, Fr. 72/J5
Chiloé (isl.), Chile 200/B4
Chiloé, PN, Chile 200/B4
Chiloquin, Or, US 168/C5
Chilpancingo de los Bravos, Mex. 185/F5
Chiltern (hills), Eng, UK 75/E3
Chiltern Hundreds (reg.), Eng, UK 72/A2
Chilung La (pass), India 128/D3
Chilwa (lake), Malw. 147/G4
Chimacum, Wa, US 177/B1
Chimalhuacán, Mex. 185/R10
Chimaliro (hill), Malw. 146/B5
Chimaltenango, Guat. 186/D3
Chimán, Pan. 194/B2
Chimanimani, Zim. 147/F4
Chimantá-Tepuí (peak), Ven. 195/F3
Chimay, Belg. 95/D3
Chimbay, Uzb. 129/C4
Chimborazo (dept.), Ecu. 194/B5
Chimborazo (vol.), Ecu. 194/B5
Chimbote, Peru 198/B3
Chimichaqua, Col. 194/C2
Chimoio, Moz. 147/F4
Chimtarga (peak), Taj. 129/E5
Chin (state), Myan. 125/F3
China (ctry.) 112/G4
China, Mex. 185/F3
China, Mex. 186/D2
Chinácota, Col. 194/C3
Chinan, SKor. 115/D5
Chinandega, Nic. 186/E3
Chinati (mts.), Tx, US 174/B4
Chincha Alta, Peru 198/B4
Chinchaga (riv.), Ab,BC, Can. 164/E3
Chinchilla, Sp. 86/E3
Chinchilla, Austl. 156/C4
Chinch'ŏn, SKor. 115/D4
Chinchón, Sp. 86/D2
Chincoteague, Va, US 172/E4
Chinde, Moz. 147/G4
Chindo, SKor. 115/D5
Chindrieux, Fr. 98/B6
Chindu, China 112/G4
Chindwin (riv.), Myan. 125/F3
Chingaza, PN, Col. 194/C3
Chingleput, India 124/C5
Chinguetti, Dhar de (cliff), Mrta. 140/B5
Chinhae, SKor. 115/E5
Chinhoyi, Zim. 147/F4
Chiniak (cape), Ak, US 176/H4

Chini – Colim

Colim – Cowde
229

Colima (state), Mex. 184/D5
Colima, Nevado de (peak), Mex. 184/E5
Colina, Chile 200/N8
Coliseum, Ca, US 178/F8
Coll (isl.), Sc, UK 73/Q8
Collado-Villalba, Sp. 87/N8
Collagna, It. 100/D4
Collarenebri, Austl. 157/D1
Colle di Val d'Elsa, It. 101/E6
Collecchio, It. 100/D3
College, Ak, US 176/J3
College Park, Md, US 180/B6
College Station, Tx, US 171/H5
Collegeville, Pa, US 180/C3
Collegno, It. 85/G4
Collesalvetti, It. 100/D5
Colletorto, It. 88/D2
Collie, Austl. 154/C5
Collier (bay), Austl. 151/B2
Collier (range), Austl. 154/C3
Collier Range NP, Austl. 154/C3
Collierville, Tn, US 171/K4
Colliford (res.), Eng, UK 74/B5
Collingwood, On, Can. 172/D2
Collins, Ms, US 175/F4
Collinstown (int'l arpt.), Ire. 76/B5
Collinsville, Austl. 156/B3
Collinsville, Ca, US 177/L10
Collinsville, Il, US 179/H8
Collinsville, Ok, US 174/E2
Collo, Alg. 142/K6
Collombey, Swi. 98/C5
Collon, Ire. 76/B4
Collonges, Fr. 98/B5
Colma, Ca, US 177/K11
Colmar, Fr. 98/D1
Colmar, Pa, US 180/C3
Colmberg, Ger. 96/D4
Colmenar, Sp. 86/C4
Colmenar de Oreja, Sp. 86/D2
Colmenar Viejo, Sp. 87/N8
Colmillo (cape), Chile 201/B6
Colne (riv.), Eng, UK 77/G4
Colne, Eng, UK 77/F4
Cologna Veneta, It. 101/E2
Cologne, It. 100/C1
Cologne, NJ, US 180/D5
Cologne/Bonn (int'l arpt.), Ger. 95/G2
Cologno Monzese, It. 100/C1
Colombes, Fr. 72/J5
Colombey-les-Belles, Fr. 98/B1
Colombia (ctry.) 192/D3
Colombia, Col. 194/C4
Colombier, Swi. 98/C4
Colombine (peak), It. 100/D1
Colombo, Braz. 197/B3
Colombo (cap.), SrL. 124/C6
Colomiers, Fr. 84/D5
Colomoncagua, Hon. 186/D3
Colón, Arg. 200/E2
Colón, Cuba 187/F1
Colón (mts.), Hon. 187/E3
Colón, Pan. 187/G4
Colón, Uru. 201/G2
Colonche, Ecu. 198/A1
Colonelganj, India 126/C2
Colonia, Micr. 158/C4
Colonia (dept.), Uru. 200/F2
Colonia, NJ, US 181/H9
Colonia Barón, Arg. 200/E3
Colonia del Sacramento, Uru. 201/K11
Colonia Juárez, Mex. 184/C2
Colonia Las Heras, Arg. 200/C5
Colonial Park, Pa, US 180/B3
Colonsay (isl.), Sc, UK 73/Q8
Colorado (peak), Arg. 201/C6
Colorado (riv.), Arg. 199/C4
Colorado, Braz. 197/B2
Colorado (plat.), US 170/E3
Colorado (riv.), US 170/D4
Colorado (state), US 170/F3
Colorado City, Tx, US 171/G4
Colorado Historical Museum, Co, US 179/C3
Colorado Springs, Co, US 171/F3
Colorno, It. 100/D3
Colotlán, Mex. 184/E4
Colquiri, Bol. 192/E7
Colson (pt.), Belz. 186/D2
Colstrip, Mt, US 168/G4
Colt (hill), Sc, UK 78/B6
Coltauco, Chile 200/N9
Colton, Ca, US 178/C2
Colts Neck, NJ, US 180/D3
Coluene (riv.), Braz. 189/D4
Columbe, Ecu. 198/B1
Columbia (riv.), Can.,US 168/C4
Columbia (plat.), US 168/C4
Columbia, Il, US 179/G9
Columbia, Ky, US 172/C4
Columbia, La, US 171/J4
Columbia, Md, US 180/B5
Columbia, Ms, US 175/F4
Columbia, NJ, US 180/C2
Columbia, Pa, US 180/B3
Columbia (co.), Pa, US 180/B1
Columbia (cap.), SC, US 175/H3
Columbia, Tn, US 172/C5
Columbia Falls, Mt, US 168/E3
Columbine (cape), SAfr. 148/K10
Columbus, Ga, US 175/G3
Columbus, In, US 172/C4
Columbus, Ms, US 175/F3
Columbus, Mt, US 168/F4
Columbus, Ne, US 169/J5
Columbus, NJ, US 180/D3
Columbus, NM, US 174/B4
Columbus (cap.), Oh, US 172/D4
Columbus, Tx, US 171/H5
Colunga, Sp. 86/C1
Colusa, Ca, US 170/B3
Colville (riv.), Ak, US 176/G2
Colville, Wa, US 168/D3
Colville (lake), NW, Can. 164/D2
Colvos (passg.), Wa, US 177/B3
Colwyn Bay, Wal, UK 76/E5
Comacchio, It. 101/F3
Comacchio, Valli di (lag.), It. 85/K4
Comai, China 127/H1
Comal, Tx, US 179/U20
Comal (co.), Tx, US 179/U20
Comala, Mex. 184/E5
Comalcalco, Mex. 186/C2
Comanche, Tx, US 171/H5
Comandante Luis Piedra Buena, Arg. 201/C6
Comandante Nicanor Otamendi, Arg. 200/F3
Comăneşti, Rom. 91/H2
Comarnic, Rom. 91/G3
Comas, Peru 198/C3
Comas, Peru 198/B3
Comayagua, Hon. 186/E3
Comayagua (mts.), Hon. 186/D3
Combapata, Peru 198/D4
Combarbalá, Chile 199/B3
Combeaufontaine, Fr. 98/B2
Comber, On, Can. 177/G7
Comber, NI, UK 76/C2
Comblain-au-Pont, Belg. 95/E3
Combloux, Fr. 98/C6
Combs-la-Ville, Fr. 72/K6
Comé, Ben. 145/F5
Comendador, DRep. 187/J2
Comilla (pol. reg.), Bang. 127/H4
Comines, Fr. 94/C2
Comines, Belg. 94/B2
Comino (isl.), Malta 88/L6
Comitán de Domínguez, Mex. 186/C2
Commack, NY, US 181/E2
Commentry, Fr. 84/E3
Commeny, Fr. 72/H4
Commerce, Ca, US 178/F7
Commerce City, Co, US 179/C3
Commercy, Fr. 95/E6
Commewijne (dist.), Sur. 195/H3
Committee (bay), Nun., Can. 165/H2
Como (lake), It. 85/H3
Como, It. 99/F6
Como, Wi, US 177/P14
Comodoro Rivadavia, Arg. 200/D5
Comoé (prov.), Burk. 144/D4
Comoe, PN de la, C.d'Iv. 138/E6
Comoé, PN de la, C.d'Iv. 144/D4
Comorin (cape), India 124/C6
Comoros (ctry.) 149/G5
Comox, BC, Can. 168/B3
Compiègne, Fr. 94/B5
Compostela, Phil. 121/E6
Compostela, Mex. 184/D4
Compton, Ca, US 178/F8
Comrat, Mol. 91/J2
Comrie, Sc, UK 78/C4
Comstock, Tx, US 174/C4
Con Son (isl.), Viet. 125/J6
Cona, China 125/F2
Conaica, Peru 198/C4
Conakry (pol. reg.), Gui. 144/B4
Conakry (cap.), Gui. 144/B4
Conakry (int'l arpt.), Gui. 144/B4
Conambo (riv.), Ecu. 194/B5
Conca (riv.), It. 101/F5
Concarneau, Fr. 84/B3
Conceição da Barra, Braz. 197/E1
Conceição das Alagoas, Braz. 197/B1
Conceição do Araguaia, Braz. 193/J5
Conceição do Coité, Braz. 196/C3
Conceição do Mato Dentro, Braz. 197/D1
Conceição do Rio Verde, Braz. 197/H6
Conceição dos Ouros, Braz. 197/H7
Concepción (lake), Bol. 192/F7
Concepción, Arg. 199/C2
Concepción, Bol. 192/E6
Concepción, Chile 200/B3
Concepción (pt.), Mex. 184/C3
Concepción, Par. 199/E1
Concepción, Peru 192/C6
Concepción (bay), Mex. 184/B3
Concepción de La Vega, DRep. 183/G4
Concepción del Oro, Mex. 185/E3
Concepción del Uruguay, Arg. 201/J10
Conception (pt.), Ca, US 170/B4
Concesio, It. 100/D1
Conchal, Braz. 197/F7
Conchas (lake), NM, US 171/F4
Conches, Fr. 72/L5
Conchillas, Uru. 201/J11
Concho (riv.), Tx, US 171/G5
Conchos (riv.), Mex. 184/D2
Concord, Ca, US 170/B3
Concord, NC, US 175/H3
Concord (cap.), NH, US 173/G3
Concord, Wi, US 177/N13
Concordia, Arg. 199/E3
Concórdia, Braz. 197/A3
Concordia, Mex. 184/D4
Concordia, Peru 198/C2
Concordia Sagittaria, It. 101/F1
Concordia sulla Secchia, It. 101/D3
Concrete, Wa, US 168/C3
Condado, Cuba 187/G1
Condamine (riv.), Austl. 151/E3
Condamine, Austl. 156/C3
Conde, Braz. 196/C3
Condé-sur-L'Escaut, Fr. 94/C3
Condé-sur-Noireau, Fr. 84/C2
Condé-sur-Vesgre, Fr. 72/G5
Condé-sur-Vire, Fr. 84/C2
Condécourt, Fr. 72/H4
Condeúba, Braz. 196/B4
Condino, It. 99/G6
Condobolin, Austl. 157/C2
Condom, Fr. 84/D5
Condon, Or, US 168/C4
Condroz (plat.), Belg. 82/C3
Conecuh (riv.), Al, US 175/G4
Conegliano, It. 101/F1
Conejos, Co, US 171/F3
Conesa, Arg. 200/E2
Conestoga (riv.), Pa, US 180/B3
Conewago (lake), Pa, US 180/A3
Confins (int'l arpt.), Braz. 197/D1
Conflans-en-Jarnisy, Fr. 95/E5
Conflans-Sainte-Honorine, Fr. 72/J5
Congaree Swamp Nat'l Mon., SC, US 175/H3
Congers, NY, US 181/K7
Congis-sur-Thérouanne, Fr. 72/L4
Congjiang, China 125/J2
Congleton, Eng, UK 77/F5
Congo (basin), D.R. Congo 139/K7
Congo, Rep. of the (ctry.) 135/D4
Congo (riv.), Afr. 135/D4
Congo, Democratic Republic of the (ctry.) 135/E5
Congonhal, Braz. 197/G7
Congonhas, Braz. 197/D2
Congonhas (int'l arpt.), Braz. 197/G8
Conguillío, PN, Chile 200/C3
Conic (hill), Sc, UK 78/B4
Cónico (peak), Arg. 200/C4
Conifer, Co, US 179/B3
Conil de la Frontera, Sp. 86/B4
Conisbrough, Eng, UK 77/G5
Conlig, NI, UK 76/C2
Conn (lake), Nun., Can. 165/J1
Connacht (reg.), Ire. 73/P10
Connah's Quay, Wal, UK 77/E5
Connantre, Fr. 94/C6
Conneaut, Oh, US 172/D3
Connecticut (riv.), US 173/G2
Connecticut (state), US 173/F3
Connellsville, Pa, US 172/E3
Connemara NP, Ire. 73/P10
Connersville, In, US 172/C4
Cono Grande (peak), Arg. 201/C6
Conocoto, Ecu. 194/B5
Conon, Falls of (falls), Sc, UK 78/B1
Cononbridge, Sc, UK 78/B1
Conondale NP, Austl. 156/D4
Čonoplja, Serb. 90/D3
Conrad, Mt, US 168/F3
Conroe, Tx, US 171/J5
Consandolo, It. 101/E3
Conscience Point NWR, NY, US 181/F2
Consdorf, Lux. 95/F4
Conselheiro Pena, Braz. 197/D1
Conselice, It. 101/E3
Conselve, It. 101/E2
Conservation Park, Austl. 155/F4
Consett, Eng, UK 77/G2
Conshohocken, Pa, US 180/C3
Consolación del Sur, Cuba 187/F1
Consolidated (canal), Az, US 179/S19
Constance (lake), Swi. 85/H3
Constance (Bodensee) (lake), Swi. 85/H3
Constant (mtn.), Guad., Fr. 183/N9
Constanța (prov.), Rom. 91/H3
Constanța, Rom. 91/J3
Constantí, Sp. 87/F2
Constantina, Sp. 86/C4
Constantine (cape), Ak, US 176/G4
Constantine, Alg. 142/K6
Constitución, Chile 200/B2
Constitución (res.), Uru. 201/K10
Constitución de 1857, PN, Mex. 184/B2
Consuegra, Sp. 86/D3
Contai, India 127/F5
Contamana, Peru 198/C2
Contarina, It. 101/F2
Contas, Rio de (riv.), Braz. 193/K6
Contegem, Braz. 197/C1
Contes, Fr. 85/G5
Conthey, Swi. 98/D5
Continental (range), Ab,BC, Can. 168/C2
Continental (mtn.), Az, US 179/S18
Contoy (isl.), Mex. 186/E1
Contra Costa (canal), Ca, US 177/L10
Contra Costa (co.), Ca, US 177/L11
Contramaestre, Cuba 187/G1
Contratación, Col. 194/C3
Contrecoeur, Qu, Can. 173/P6
Contreras, Embalse de (res.), Sp. 86/E3
Contrexéville, Fr. 98/B1
Controller (bay), Ak, US 176/J3
Contulmo, Chile 200/B3
Contumazá, Peru 198/B2
Contwig, Ger. 95/G5
Contwoyto (lake), Nun., Can. 164/F2
Conty, Fr. 94/B4
Convención, Col. 194/C2
Conversano, It. 89/E2
Converse, Tx, US 179/U20
Conway, Ar, US 171/J4
Conway, SC, US 175/J3
Conway, NH, US 173/G3
Conway (cape), Austl. 156/C3
Conway NP, Austl. 156/C3
Conwy (bay), Wal, UK 76/D5
Conwy (co.), Wal, UK 76/E5
Conwy (riv.), Wal, UK 76/E5
Conwy, Vale of (valley), Wal, UK 76/E5
Conyngham, Pa, US 180/B2
Coober Pedy, Austl. 155/G4
Cooch Behār, India 127/G2
Coochiemudlo (isl.), Austl. 156/F7
Cook (bay), Chile 201/C7
Cook (mt.), NZ 159/S11
Cook (str.), NZ 159/S11
Cook (inlet), Ak, US 164/A3
Cook (co.), Il, US 177/Q16
Cook Islands (dpcy.), NZ 159/J6
Cooke (mt.), Austl. 154/C5
Cookeville, Tn, US 172/C4
Cookham, Eng, UK 72/A2
Cookhouse, SAfr. 148/D4
Cookstown, NI, UK 76/B2
Cookstown (dist.), NI, UK 76/B2
Cooksville, Md, US 180/A5
Cooktown, Austl. 156/B1
Coola Coola (swamp), Austl. 157/B3
Coolah, Austl. 157/D1
Coolamon, Austl. 157/C2
Coolangatta, Austl. 157/E1
Cooley (pt.), Ire. 76/B4
Coolgardie, Austl. 154/D4
Cooloola NP, Austl. 156/D4
Cooloongup (lake), Austl. 154/K7
Cooma, Austl. 157/D3
Coonabarabran, Austl. 157/D1
Coonalpyn, Austl. 157/A2
Coonamble, Austl. 157/D1
Coonana Abor. Land, Austl. 154/D4
Coondapoor (Kundapura), India 131/K6
Coongan Abor. Land, Austl. 154/C2
Coonoor, India 124/C5
Cooper, Tx, US 171/J4
Coopersburg, Pa, US 180/C2
Cooperstown, ND, US 169/J4
Coordewandy (peak), Austl. 154/C3
Coorong NP, Austl. 157/A3
Coorow, Austl. 154/C4
Cooroy, Austl. 156/D4
Coosa (riv.), Al, US 175/G3
Cootamundra, Austl. 157/D2
Coot'tha (mt.), Austl. 156/E6
Copacabana, Bol. 198/D5
Copahué (vol.), Chile 200/C3
Copainalá, Mex. 186/C2
Copala, Mex. 182/B4
Copán (ruin), Hon. 186/D3
Cope (cape), Sp. 86/E4
Copeland (isl.), NI, UK 76/C2
Copenhagen (København) (cap.), Den. 80/E4
Copertino, It. 89/F2
Copeton (dam), Austl. 157/D1
Copiague, NY, US 181/M9
Copiapó, Chile 199/B2
Coplay, Pa, US 180/C2
Copparo, It. 101/E3
Copename (riv.), Sur. 195/H3
Coppenbrügge, Ger. 93/G4
Copper (riv.), Ak, US 164/B2
Copper Center, Ak, US 176/J3
Copperas Cove, Tx, US 171/H5
Coppermine (riv.), NW,Nun., Can. 164/E2
Copperton, Ut, US 179/J12
Coppet, Swi. 98/C5
Copşa Mică, Rom. 91/G2
Coqên, China 112/E5
Coquet (riv.), Eng, UK 78/D6
Coquet Dale (valley), Eng, UK 77/G1
Coquimbo, Chile 199/B2
Coquitlam, BC, Can. 168/C3
Corabia, Rom. 91/G4
Coração de Jesus, Braz. 196/A5
Coracora, Peru 198/C4
Corail, Haiti 187/H2
Coraki, Austl. 157/E1
Coral (sea) 158/E6
Coral Gables, Fl, US 175/H5
Coral Harbour, Nun., Can. 165/H2
Coral Sea Islands Territory (dpcy.), Austl. 151/E2
Coral Springs, Fl, US 175/H5
Corales del Rosario, PN, Col. 194/C2
Coram, NY, US 181/E2
Corato, It. 88/E2
Corbeil-Essonnes, Fr. 72/K6
Corbelin (cape), Alg. 142/H4
Corbenay, Fr. 98/C2
Corbet (peak), Swi. 99/F5
Corbett NP, India 126/B1
Corbetta, It. 100/B2
Corbie, Fr. 94/B4
Corbieres (mts.), Fr. 84/E5
Corbin, Ky, US 172/C4
Corbin City, NJ, US 180/D5
Corby, Eng, UK 75/F2
Corcovado, Braz. 197/K7
Corcovado (vol.), Chile 200/B4
Corcovado (gulf), Chile 189/B7
Corcovado, PN, CR 187/E4
Cordeiro, Braz. 197/D2
Cordele, Ga, US 175/H4
Cordelia, Ca, US 177/K10
Cordell, Ok, US 171/H4
Cordenons, It. 85/K4
Cordignano, It. 101/F1
Cordillera de Los Picachos, PN, Col. 192/D3
Cordillera Oriental (mts.), SAm. 194/B5
Cordisburgo, Braz. 197/C1
Córdoba, Arg. 199/D3
Córdoba (dept.), Col. 187/H4
Córdoba, Mex. 185/N8
Córdoba (plain), SAm. 200/E2
Córdoba, Sp. 86/C4
Córdoba, Sierra de (mts.), Arg. 199/D3
Cordova, Ak, US 176/J3
Cordova (peak), Ak, US 176/J3
Cordova, Md, US 180/C6
Coreaú, Braz. 196/B1
Corella, Sp. 86/E1
Coremas, Braz. 196/C2
Corentyne (riv.), Guy. 192/G3
Corfu (Kérika) (isl.), Gre. 89/F3
Corgémont, Swi. 98/D3
Corgo, Sp. 86/B1
Coria, Sp. 86/B3
Coria del Río, Sp. 86/B4
Coriano, It. 101/F5
Coribe, Braz. 196/A4
Coricudgy (mt.), Austl. 157/D2
Corigliano Calabro, It. 88/E3
Corinaldo, It. 101/G5
Coringa Islets (isls.), Austl. 156/C2
Corinne, Ut, US 179/J10
Corinth, Ms, US 175/F3
Corinth (gulf), Gre. 89/H3
Corinth (Kórinthos) (ruin), Gre. 89/H4
Corinto, Nic. 186/E3
Cork, Ire. 73/P11
Corleone, It. 88/C4
Corleto Perticara, It. 88/E2
Çorlu, Turk. 91/H5
Cormeilles-en-Vexin, Fr. 72/J4
Cormons, It. 101/G1
Cormontreuil, Fr. 94/D5
Cormorant, Mb, Can. 169/H2
Cormorant (lake), Mb, Can. 169/H2
Cornacchia (peak), It. 88/D2
Cornaredo, It. 100/C2
Cornberg, Ger. 93/G6
Corndon (peak), Wal, UK 74/C1
Cornedo Vicentino, It. 101/E1
Cornélio Procópio, Braz. 197/B2
Cornelius Grinnell (bay), Nun., Can. 165/K2
Cornell, Ca, US 178/B2
Cornella, Sp. 87/L7
Corner (inlet), Austl. 151/D4
Corner Brook, Nf, Can. 173/K1
Cornetto (peak), It. 99/H6
Cornfield (pt.), Ct, US 181/F1
Corniglio, It. 100/D4
Cornimont, Fr. 98/C2
Corning, NY, US 172/E3
Corno alle Scale (peak), It. 85/J4
Corno di Rosazzo, It. 101/G1
Cornone di Blumone (peak), It. 99/G6
Cornú (peak), Arg. 201/D7
Cornuda, It. 101/F1
Cornwall (isl.), Nun., Can. 165/S7
Cornwall, On, Can. 172/F2
Cornwall, PE, Can. 173/J2
Cornwall (cape), Eng, UK 74/A6
Cornwall (co.), Eng, UK 74/A6
Cornwall, Pa, US 180/B3
Cornwallis (isl.), Nun., Can. 165/S7
Corny (pt.), Austl. 155/H5
Coro, Ven. 194/D2
Coroatá, Braz. 196/A2
Corocoro, Bol. 198/D5
Coromandel, Braz. 197/C1
Coromandel (pen.), NZ 159/T10
Coromandel (coast), India 124/D5
Coron, Phil. 123/F1
Corona, Ca, US 178/C3
Coronado (bay), CR 182/E6
Coronado, Ca, US 178/C5
Coronation, Ab, Can. 168/F2
Coronation (gulf), Nun., Can. 164/E2
Coronel, Chile 200/B3
Coronel Dorrego, Arg. 200/E3
Coronel Fabriciano, Braz. 197/D1
Coronel Moldes, Arg. 200/D2
Coronel Murta, Braz. 196/B5
Coronel Oviedo, Par. 199/E2
Coronel Pringles, Arg. 200/E3
Coronel Suárez, Arg. 200/E3
Coronel Vidal, Arg. 200/F3
Coronel Vivida, Braz. 197/A3
Corongo, Peru 198/B3
Coronie (dist.), Sur. 195/G3
Coropuna (peak), Peru 198/C4
Çorovodë, Alb. 89/G2
Corozal, Col. 194/C2
Corozal, Belz. 186/D2
Corpach, Sc, UK 78/A3
Corpus Christi, Tx, US 174/D5
Corral, Chile 200/B3
Corral de Almaguer, Sp. 86/D3
Corral de Bustos, Arg. 200/E2
Corrales, Col. 194/C3
Corralillo, Cuba 187/F1
Corre, Fr. 98/C2
Correa, Arg. 200/E2
Corredor, CR 187/F4
Correggio, It. 101/D3
Corrente (riv.), Braz. 196/A4
Corrente, Braz. 196/A3
Correntina, Braz. 196/A4
Corrib (lake), Ire. 73/P10
Corrientes (riv.), Peru 192/C4
Corrientes, Arg. 199/E2
Corrientes (cape), Cuba 187/E1
Corrientes (pt.), Col. 194/B3
Corrigan, Tx, US 171/J5
Corrigin, Austl. 154/C5
Corriverton, Guy. 195/G3
Corryhabbie (peak), Sc, UK 78/C2
Corryong, Austl. 157/C3
Corse (hill), Sc, UK 78/B5
Corse (cape), Fr. 85/H5
Corse (dept.), Fr. 85/H5
Corserine (peak), Sc, UK 76/D1
Corsewall (pt.), NI, UK 76/C1
Corsham, Eng, UK 74/D4
Corsica (isl.), Fr. 88/A1
Corsicana, Tx, US 171/H4
Corsico, It. 100/C2
Corsons (inlet), NJ, US 180/D5
Cortaillod, Swi. 98/C4
Cortegana, Sp. 86/B4
Cortemaggiore, It. 100/C3
Cortemilia, It. 100/B3
Cortez, Co, US 170/E3
Cortina d'Ampezzo, It. 85/K3
Cortines, Arg. 201/J11
Cortland, NY, US 172/E3
Corubal (riv.), GBis. 144/B3
Coruche, Port. 86/A3
Çoruh (riv.), Turk. 105/G4
Çorum, Turk. 132/C1
Çorum (prov.), Turk. 132/C1
Corumbá, Braz. 192/G7
Corumbá (riv.), Braz. 193/J7
Corumbaú (pt.), Braz. 196/C5
Coruripe, Braz. 196/C3
Corvallis, Or, US 168/C4
Corve (riv.), Eng, UK 74/D2
Corvo (peak), It. 88/C1
Corvo (isl.), Azor., Port. 87/R12
Corzoneso, Swi. 99/E5
Cosalá, Mex. 184/D3
Cosamaloapan, Mex. 185/P8
Cosautlán, Mex. 185/N7
Coscomatepec, Mex. 185/M7
Cosenza, It. 88/E3
Coshocton, Oh, US 172/D3
Cosigüina (pt.), Nic. 186/E3
Coslada, Sp. 87/N9
Cosmo Newberry Abor. Rsv., Austl. 154/D3
Cosmópolis, Braz. 197/F7
Cosne-Cours-sur-Loire, Fr. 84/E3
Cosne d'Allier, Fr. 84/E3
Cosolapa, Mex. 185/N8
Cospeito, Sp. 86/B1
Cosquín, Arg. 199/D3
Cossato, It. 100/B1
Cosson (riv.), Fr. 84/D3
Cossonay, Swi. 98/C4
Costa Azul, Uru. 201/G2
Costa Brava (int'l arpt.), Sp. 87/G2
Costa da Caparica, Port. 87/P10
Costa de Mosquitos (phys. reg.), Nic. 187/E4
Costa di Rovigo, It. 101/E2
Costa Masnaga, It. 100/C1
Costa Mesa, Ca, US 178/G8
Costa Rica (ctry.) 187/F4
Costa Smeralda (int'l arpt.), It. 88/A2
Costa Volpino, It. 100/D1
Costabissara, It. 101/E1
Costeşti, Rom. 91/G3
Costigliole d'Asti, It. 100/B3
Cotabambas, Peru 198/C4
Cotabato, Phil. 123/F2
Cotacachi (peak), Ecu. 194/B4
Cotahuasi, Peru 198/C4
Cotatumbo (riv.), Col. 187/H4
Côte d'Azur (int'l arpt.), Fr. 85/G5
Côte de Hautmont (hill), Fr. 98/B1
Côte d'Ivoire (ctry.) 144/D5
Côte d'Or (uplands), Fr. 84/F3
Côte du Rif (Al Hoceima) (int'l arpt.), Mor. 142/C2
Côte-Saint-Luc, Qu, Can. 173/N7
Coteau des Prairies (plat.), SD, US 169/J4
Coteau-du-Lac, Qu, Can. 173/M7
Coteau du Missouri (plat.), ND, US 169/H3
Coteau-Landing, Qu, Can. 173/M7
Cotegipe, Braz. 196/A4
Cotentin (pen.), Fr. 84/C2
Côtes de Meuse (uplands), Fr. 84/F2
Cothi (riv.), Wal, UK 74/B3
Cotia, Braz. 197/G8
Cotignola, It. 101/E4
Cotonou, Ben. 145/F5
Cotonou (int'l arpt.), Ben. 145/F5
Cotopaxi (dept.), Ecu. 194/B5
Cotopaxi (vol.), Ecu. 194/B5
Cotopaxi, PN, Ecu. 194/B5
Cotswolds (hills), Eng, UK 74/D3
Cottage Grove, Or, US 168/C5
Cottage Hills, Il, US 179/G8
Cottam, On, Can. 177/G7
Cottbus, Ger. 83/H3
Cottian Alps (mts.), Fr. 85/G4
Cottleville, Mo, US 179/F8
Cottonport, La, US 171/J5
Cottonwood, Az, US 170/D4
Cottonwood (riv.), Tx, US 171/F5
Cotulla, Tx, US 174/D4
Coubert, Fr. 72/L6
Coubre, Pointe de la (pt.), Fr. 84/C4
Couchey, Fr. 98/A3
Coudekerque-Branche, Fr . 94/B1
Coulee City, Wa, US 168/D4
Coulee Dam Nat'l Rec. Area, Wa, US 168/D3
Coulogne, Fr. 94/A2
Coulombs-en-Valois, Fr. 72/M4
Coulommes, Fr. 72/L5
Coulommiers, Fr. 94/C6
Coulonge (riv.), Qu, Can. 172/E2
Coulounieix-Chamiers, Fr. 84/D4
Council, Ak, US 176/F3
Council, Id, US 168/D4
Council Grove, Ks, US 171/H3
Coupar Angus, Sc, UK 78/C3
Coupvray, Fr. 72/L5
Courantyne (riv.), Guy.,Sur. 195/G3
Courbevoie, Fr. 72/J5
Courcelles, Belg. 95/D3
Courcouronnes, Fr. 72/K6
Courdimanche, Fr. 72/H4
Courgenay, Swi. 98/D3
Courgent, Fr. 72/G5
Courmayeur, It. 98/C6
Cournon-d'Auvergne, Fr. 84/E4
Courpalay, Fr. 72/L6
Courrendlin, Swi. 98/D3
Courroux, Swi. 98/D3
Coursan, Fr. 84/E5
Courtelary, Swi. 98/D3
Courtepin, Swi. 98/D4
Courtice, On, Can. 173/S8
Courtisols, Fr. 95/D6
Courtland, Ca, US 177/L10
Courtmacsherry, Ire. 73/P11
Courtney, Mo, US 179/E5
Courtomer, Fr. 72/L6
Cousance, Fr. 98/B4
Coushatta, La, US 171/J4
Cousolre, Fr. 95/D3
Coutances, Fr. 84/C2
Coutevroult, Fr. 72/L5
Coutras, Fr. 84/C4
Coutts, Ab, Can. 168/F3
Couva, Trin. 195/F2
Couvet, Swi. 98/C4
Couvin, Belg. 95/D3
Couzeix, Fr. 84/D4
Covadonga NP, Sp. 86/C1
Covasna, Rom. 91/H3
Covasna (prov.), Rom. 91/G3
Cove Bay, Sc, UK 78/D2
Cove Neck, NY, US 181/L8
Coventry, Eng, UK 75/E2
Coventry (canal), Eng, UK 75/E1
Coventry (co.), Eng, UK 75/E2
Covilhã, Port. 86/B2
Covina, Ca, US 178/G7
Covington, Ga, US 175/H3
Covington, Tn, US 171/K4
Covo, It. 100/C2
Cow Green (res.), Eng, UK 77/F2
Cowal (reg.), Sc, UK 78/A4
Cowan (lake), Austl. 151/B4
Cowdenbeath, Sc, UK 78/C4

230

Cowel – Darli

Cowell, Austl. 155/H5
Cowes, Eng, UK 75/E5
Cowie, Sc, UK 78/C4
Cowlitz (riv.), Wa, US 168/C4
Cowra, Austl. 157/D2
Coxim, Braz. 193/H7
Cox's Bāzār, Bang. 125/F3
Coyame, Mex. 184/D2
Coye-la-Forêt, Fr. 72/K4
Coyotepec, Mex. 185/K7
Coyuca de Benítez, Mex. 185/E5
Coyutla, Mex. 185/M6
Cozumel, Mex. 186/E1
Cozumel (int'l arpt.), Mex. 186/E1
Cozumel (isl.), Mex. 186/E1
Cradle (mtn.), Austl. 157/C4
Cradle Mountain-Lake Saint Clair NP, Austl. 157/C4
Cradock, SAfr. 148/D4
Crag (mtn.), Yk, Can. 176/K3
Crag (peak), Eng, UK 77/F3
Craig, Co, US 170/F2
Craig, Ak, US 176/M4
Craig, Ks, US 179/D6
Craigavon (dist.), NI, UK 76/B3
Craigavon, NI, UK 76/B3
Craigieburn, Austl. 157/F5
Craik, Sk, Can. 169/G3
Crail, Sc, UK 78/D4
Crailsheim, Ger. 96/D4
Craiova, Rom. 91/F3
Cramalina (peak), Swi. 99/E5
Cramlington, Eng, UK 77/G1
Cran-Gevrier, Fr. 98/C6
Crana (riv.), Ire. 76/A1
Cranberry Portage, Mb, Can. 169/H2
Cranborne Chase (for.), Eng, UK 74/D5
Cranbourne, Austl. 157/G6
Cranbrook, BC, Can. 168/E3
Cranbrook, Austl. 154/C5
Cranbury, NJ, US 180/D3
Crane, Tx, US 174/C4
Crane Neck (pt.), NY, US 181/E2
Crane River, Mb, Can. 169/J3
Cranford, NJ, US 181/H9
Cranleigh, Eng, UK 75/F4
Craponne, Fr. 84/F4
Crasna (riv.), Rom. 90/F2
Crater (lake), Or, US 170/B2
Crater Lake NP, Or, US 170/B2
Craters of the Moon Nat'l Mon., Id, US 170/D2
Crateús, Braz. 196/B2
Crati (riv.), It. 88/E3
Crato, Port. 86/B3
Cravinhos, Braz. 197/C2
Crawfordsville, In, US 172/C3
Crawfordville, Fl, US 175/G4
Crawley, Eng, UK 75/F4
Cray (riv.), Eng, UK 72/D2
Crazy (mts.), Mt, US 168/F4
Creag Meagaidh (peak), Sc, UK 78/B3
Creagerstown, Md, US 180/A4
Creasy (Mifflinville), Pa, US 180/B1
Creazzo, It. 101/E2
Crêches-sur-Saône, Fr. 98/A5
Crécy-sur-Serre, Fr. 94/C4
Credit (riv.), On, Can. 173/Q8
Cree (lake), Sk, Can. 164/F3
Cree (riv.), Sk, Can. 164/F3
Cree (riv.), Sc, UK 76/D2
Creel, Mex. 184/D3
Creetown, Sc, UK 76/D2
Creglingen, Ger. 96/D4
Crégy-lès-Meaux, Fr. 72/L5
Créhange, Fr. 95/F5
Creighton, Sk, Can. 169/H2
Creil, Fr. 94/B5
Crema, It. 100/C2
Crémieu, Fr. 98/B6
Cremlingen, Ger. 93/H4
Cremona (prov.), It. 100/C2
Cremona, It. 100/D2
Crepaja, Serb. 90/E3
Crépy, Fr. 94/C4
Creran (lake), Sc, UK 78/A3
Cres (isl.), Cro. 90/B3
Crescent, Mo, US 179/F8
Crescent, Co, US 179/B3
Crescent, Ut, US 179/K12
Crescent City, Ca, US 168/B5
Crescentino, It. 100/B2
Cresco, Pa, US 180/C1
Crespano del Grappa, It. 101/E1
Crespellano, It. 101/E3
Crespières, Fr. 72/H5
Crespin, Fr. 94/C3
Cresskill, NJ, US 181/K8
Cressona, Pa, US 180/B2
Cressy, Austl. 157/C4
Crest, Fr. 84/F4
Crest Hill, Il, US 177/P16
Crestline, Ca, US 178/C2
Creston, Ia, US 169/K5
Creston, BC, Can. 168/D3
Crestview, Fl, US 175/G4
Crestwood Village, NJ, US 180/D4
Creswick, Austl. 157/B3
Crete (sea), Gre. 89/J4
Crete (isl.), Gre. 89/J5
Créteil, Fr. 72/K5
Creuch (hill), Sc, UK 78/B5
Creus (cape), Sp. 87/G1
Creuse (riv.), Fr. 84/D3
Creussen, Ger. 97/E3
Creussen (riv.), Ger. 97/E3
Creutzwald-la-Croix, Fr. 95/F5
Creuzburg, Ger. 93/H6
Crevacuore, It. 100/B1
Crevalcore, It. 101/E3
Creve Coeur, Mo, US 179/G8
Crèvecœur-le-Grand, Fr. 94/B4
Crevillente, Sp. 87/E3
Crevoladossola, It. 99/E5
Crewe, Eng, UK 77/F5
Crib Point, Austl. 157/C3
Criciúma, Braz. 197/B4
Crieff, Sc, UK 78/C4
Criffell (hill), Sc, UK 76/E2
Crikvenica, Cro. 90/B3
Crillon (mt.), Ak, US 176/L4
Crimean (pen.), Ukr. 91/L3
Crimeanpen (pen.), Ukr. 104/E3
Crimond, Sc, UK 78/E1
Crisenoy, Fr. 72/L6
Crisman, Co, US 179/B2
Crissier, Swi. 98/C4
Cristal, Monts de (mts.), Gabon 147/B1
Cristalina, Braz. 196/A5
Cristina, Braz. 197/H7
Cristóbal (pt.), Ecu. 198/E7
Cristóbal Colón (peak), Col. 194/C2
Cristoforo Colombo (int'l arpt.), It. 100/B4
Cristuru Secuiesc, Rom. 91/G2
Crişul Alb (riv.), Rom. 90/F2
Crişul Negru (riv.), Rom. 90/E2
Crixás-Açu (riv.), Braz. 193/H6
Crna Reka (riv.), FYROM 89/G2
Črnomelj, Slov. 85/L4
Croajingolong NP, Austl. 157/D3
Croatia (ctry.) 90/B3
Croce (peak), It. 99/H5
Croce, Pico di (peak), It. 99/H4
Croche (peak), Fr. 98/C6
Croche (riv.), Qu, Can. 173/F2
Crocker (range), Malay. 123/E3
Crocker (peak), Ecu. 198/E7
Crockett, Tx, US 171/J5
Crockett, Ca, US 177/K10
Crocodile Head (pt.), Austl. 157/D2
Crodo, It. 99/E5
Crofton, Md, US 180/B6
Croghan (mtn.), Ire. 76/B6
Croisette (cape), Fr. 84/F5
Croisilles, Fr. 94/B3
Croissy-Beaubourg, Fr. 72/K5
Croker (isl.), Austl. 151/C2
Cromarty Firth (bay), Sc, UK 78/B1
Crombie (mt.), Austl. 155/F3
Cromdale (hills), Sc, UK 78/C2
Cromwell, NZ 159/R12
Crong A Na (riv.), Viet. 120/D3
Crooked (isl.), Bahm. 183/G3
Crooked Creek, Ak, US 176/G3
Crooked Island Passage (chan.), Bahm. 187/H1
Crookston, Mn, US 169/J4
Crookwell, Austl. 157/D2
Croom, Ire. 73/P10
Crosby, ND, US 169/H3
Crosby, Eng, UK 77/E5
Crosbyton, Tx, US 171/G4
Cross (lake), Mb, Can. 169/J2
Cross City, Fl, US 175/H4
Cross Fell (peak), Eng, UK 77/F2
Cross Plains, Tx, US 171/H4
Cross River (state), Nga. 145/H5
Cross River (res.), NY, US 181/E1
Cross Roads, Pa, US 180/B4
Crossfield, Ab, Can. 168/E3
Crossford, Sc, UK 78/C4
Crosshouse, Sc, UK 78/B5
Crossroads, Ire. 73/P9
Crossville, Tn, US 175/G3
Crostolo (riv.), It. 100/D3
Croton-on-Hudson (Croton-Harmon), NY, US 181/E1
Crotone, It. 89/E3
Crottendorf, Ger. 97/F1
Croult (riv.), Fr. 72/K5
Crouy, Fr. 94/C5
Crouy-sur-Ourcq, Fr. 72/M4
Crow Agency, Mt, US 168/G4
Crowborough, Eng, UK 75/G4
Crowdy Bay NP, Austl. 157/E1
Crowe (riv.), On, Can. 172/E2
Crowley, La, US 171/J5
Crowley's (ridge), Ar, US 175/F3
Crown Point, In, US 172/C3
Crown Point, La, US 179/P17
Crown Point (int'l arpt.), Trin. 195/F2
Crown Prince Frederik (isl.), Nun., Can. 165/H1
Crownpoint, NM, US 170/E4
Crows Nest Falls NP, Austl. 156/D4
Crowthorne, Eng, UK 75/F4
Croydon, Austl. 156/A2
Croydon (bor.), Eng, UK 72/C2
Croydon, Pa, US 180/D3
Croydon, Ut, US 179/K11
Crozet (isls.), Fr. 65/M8
Crozon, Fr. 84/A2
Cruach Mhór (peak), Sc, UK 78/A4
Cruach nan Capull (peak), Sc, UK 78/A5
Crucero, Peru 198/D4
Cruden Bay, Sc, UK 78/E2
Cruick Water (riv.), Sc, UK 78/D3
Crumlin, NI, UK 76/B2
Crummock Water (lake), Eng, UK 77/E2
Crumpton, Md, US 180/C5
Cruseilles, Fr. 98/C5
Crusnes (riv.), Fr. 95/E5
Cruz (cape), Cuba 187/G2
Cruz Alta, Braz. 199/F2
Cruz Alta, Arg. 200/E2
Cruz Alta (peak), Port. 87/P10
Cruz das Almas, Braz. 196/C4
Cruz del Eje, Arg. 199/D3
Cruz Grande, Mex. 186/B2
Cruzeiro, Braz. 197/J7
Cruzeiro do Sul, Braz. 198/C2
Cruzeta, Braz. 196/C2
Cruzília, Braz. 197/J6
Crvenka, Serb. 90/D3
Cryn-y-Brain (peak), Wal, UK 77/E5
Crystal (lake), Pa, US 180/C1
Crystal Bay, Nv, US 170/C3
Crystal Brook, Austl. 155/H5
Crystal Cave, Pa, US 180/C2
Crystal City, Tx, US 174/D4
Crystal Springs, Ms, US 171/K5
Crystal Springs (res.), Ca, US 177/K11
Csenger, Hun. 83/M5
Csepreg, Hun. 85/M3
Csongrád, Hun. 90/E2
Csorna, Hun. 90/C2
Csorvás, Hun. 90/E2
Csóványos (peak), Hun. 90/D2
Csurgó, Hun. 90/C2
Cu Lao (isl.), Viet. 120/E4
Cuajinicuilapa, Mex. 186/B2
Cualedro, Sp. 86/B2
Cuamba, Moz. 147/G3
Cuando (riv.), Ang. 147/D4
Cuango (riv.), Ang. 147/C2
Cuanza (riv.), Ang. 147/B2
Cuart de Poblet, Sp. 87/E3
Cuarto (riv.), Arg. 200/D2
Cuatrociénagas de Carranza, Mex. 174/C5
Cuauhtémoc, Mex. 184/E5
Cuauhtémoc, Mex. 184/D2
Cuautepec, Mex. 185/L6
Cuautitlán, Mex. 185/Q9
Cuautitlán Izcalli, Mex. 185/Q9
Cuautla, Mex. 185/L8
Cuba, Mo, US 171/K3
Cuba, Port. 86/B3
Cuba (ctry.) 187/F1
Cubagua (isl.), Ven. 195/E2
Cuballing, Austl. 154/C5
Cubango (riv.), Ang. 147/C4
Çubuk, Turk. 132/C1
Cucamonga (Rancho Cucamonga), Ca, US 178/C2
Cuccurano, It. 101/F5
Cuchivero (riv.), Ven. 192/E2
Cuchumatanes (mts.), Guat. 186/D3
Cuckmere (riv.), Eng, UK 75/G5
Cucq, Fr. 84/D1
Cúcuta, Col. 194/C3
Cucuyagua, Hon. 186/D3
Cudahy, Ca, US 178/F8
Cuddapah, India 124/C5
Cudgewa, Austl. 157/C3
Cudillero, Sp. 86/B1
Cudrefin, Swi. 98/D4
Cudworth, Eng, UK 77/G4
Cue, Austl. 154/C3
Cuéllar, Sp. 86/C2
Cuéllar-Baza, Sp. 86/D4
Cuenca, Sp. 86/D2
Cuenca, Ecu. 194/B5
Cuenca, Sierra de (range), Sp. 86/E2
Cuencamé de Ceniceros, Mex. 184/E3
Cuernavaca, Mex. 185/K8
Cuero, Tx, US 171/H5
Cuers, Fr. 84/G5
Cueto, Cuba 187/H1
Cuetzalán, Mex. 185/M6
Cueva de los Guácharos, PN, Col. 192/C3
Cuevas de Vinromá, Sp. 87/F2
Cuevas del Almanzora, Sp. 86/E4
Cuffley, Eng, UK 72/C1
Cufré, Uru. 201/K11
Cugir, Rom. 91/F3
Cuglieri, It. 88/A2
Cugnaux, Fr. 84/D5
Cuiabá, Braz. 193/G7
Cuiabá (riv.), Braz. 193/G7
Cuicas, Ven. 194/D2
Cuijk, Neth. 92/C5
Cuilapa, Guat. 186/D3
Cuilco (riv.), Guat. 186/C3
Cuillin (sound), Sc, UK 73/Q8
Cuilo (riv.), Ang. 147/C2
Cuisance (riv.), Fr. 98/B4
Cuise-la-Motte, Fr. 94/C5
Cuiseaux, Fr. 98/B5
Cuisery, Fr. 98/A4
Cuisy, Fr. 72/L4
Cuité, Braz. 196/C2
Cuitláhuac, Mex. 185/N8
Cuito (riv.), Ang. 147/C4
Cuiuni (riv.), Braz. 192/F4
Culcairn, Austl. 157/C2
Culdaff (riv.), Ire. 76/A1
Culemborg, Neth. 92/C5
Culgoa (riv.), Austl. 151/D3
Culiacán Rosales, Mex. 184/D3
Culion (isl.), Phil. 121/D5
Cullen, Sc, UK 78/D1
Cullera, Sp. 87/E3
Culleredo, Sp. 86/A1
Cullman, Al, US 175/G3
Culloden Battlesite, Sc, UK 78/B2
Cully, Swi. 98/C5
Cullybackey, NI, UK 76/B2
Culmback (dam), Wa, US 177/D2
Culmore, NI, UK 76/A1
Culoz, Fr. 98/B6
Culpeper, Va, US 172/E4
Culross, Sc, UK 78/C4
Cults, Sc, UK 78/D2
Culver (pt.), Austl. 154/E5
Culver City, Ca, US 178/F7
Culvers (lake), NJ, US 180/D1
Cumaná, Ven. 195/E2
Cumari, Braz. 197/B1
Cumba, Peru 198/B2
Cumbal, Col. 194/B4
Cumbal, Nevado de (peak), Col. 194/B4
Cumberland (pen.), Nun., Can. 165/K2
Cumberland (sound), Nun., Can. 165/K2
Cumberland (lake), Sk, Can. 169/H2
Cumberland (plat.), US 175/G3
Cumberland (isl.), Ga, US 175/H4
Cumberland (falls), Ky, US 175/G2
Cumberland (lake), Ky, US 172/C4
Cumberland (riv.), Ky,Tn, US 167/J4
Cumberland, Md, US 172/E4
Cumberland (co.), NJ, US 180/A3
Cumberland, Wa, US 177/D3
Cumberland House, Sk, Can. 169/H2
Cumbernauld, Sc, UK 78/C5
Cumbres Bastonal, Cerro (peak), Mex. 186/C2
Cumbres de Majalca, PN, Mex. 184/D2
Cumbres de Monterrey, PN de, Mex. 185/E3
Cumbria (co.), Eng, UK 77/E2
Cumbrian (mts.), Eng, UK 77/E2
Cumbum, India 124/C4
Cummins, Austl. 155/G5
Cumnock, Austl. 157/D2
Cumpas, Mex. 184/C2
Çumra, Turk. 132/C2
Cumshewa (pt.), BC, Can. 176/M5
Cunaviche, Ven. 195/E3
Cunco, Chile 200/B3
Cundeelee Abor. Rsv., Austl. 154/D4
Cunderdin, Austl. 154/C4
Cundinamarca (dept.), Col. 194/C3
Cunduacán, Mex. 186/C2
Cunene (riv.), Ang. 147/B4
Cuneo (prov.), It. 100/A3
Cuneo, It. 85/G4
Cunha, Braz. 197/J8
Cunnamulla, Austl. 156/B5
Cunninghame (reg.), Sc, UK 78/B5
Čuokkaraš'ša (peak), Nor. 79/H1
Cuorgnè, It. 85/G4
Cupar, Sc, UK 78/C4
Cupertino, Ca, US 177/K12
Cupra Marittima, It. 85/K5
Cupramontana, It. 101/G6
Ćuprija, Serb. 90/E4
Ćuprija, Serb. 90/E4
Cuquenán (riv.), Ven. 195/F3
Curaçá, Braz. 196/C3
Curaçao (isl.), NAnt. 192/E1
Curacautín, Chile 200/C3
Curacaví, Chile 200/N8
Curahuara de Carangas, Bol. 198/D5
Curanilahue, Chile 200/B3
Curaray (riv.), Ecu. 192/C4
Curaray (riv.), Ecu.,Peru 194/C5
Curarén, Hon. 186/E3
Curaumilla (pt.), Chile 200/N8
Curcubăta (peak), Rom. 91/F2
Cure (riv.), Fr. 82/B5
Curecanti Nat'l Rec. Area, Co, US 174/B2
Curepipe, Mrts. 149/T15
Curepto, Chile 200/B2
Curicó, Chile 200/C2
Curimatá, Braz. 196/A3
Curitibanos, Braz. 197/B3
Curno, It. 100/C1
Curone (riv.), It. 100/C3
Curral Velho, CpV. 135/K10
Current (riv.), Ar,Mo, US 171/K3
Currie, Austl. 156/A3
Currie, Sc, UK 78/C5
Curry, Ak, US 176/H3
Curtea de Argeş, Rom. 91/G3
Curtici, Rom. 90/E2
Curtis (riv.), Austl. 156/D4
Curtis (isl.), NZ 158/G8
Curtis, Sp. 86/A1
Curtis (pt.), Md, US 180/B6
Curú NWR, CR 187/E4
Curuá (riv.), Braz. 193/G4
Curuá Una (riv.), Braz. 195/H5
Curuçú (riv.), Braz. 192/D5
Curup, Indo. 122/B4
Cururupu, Braz. 193/K4
Curuzú Cuatiá, Arg. 199/E2
Curvelo, Braz. 197/C1
Cusco (dept.), Peru 198/C4
Cusco, Peru 198/D4
Cusher (riv.), NI, UK 76/B3
Cushet Law (peak), Eng, UK 78/D6
Cushing, Ok, US 171/H4
Cusna (peak), It. 100/D4
Cusset, Fr. 84/E3
Cusseta, Ga, US 175/G3
Custer, Mt, US 168/G4
Custer, SD, US 169/H5
Custines, Fr. 95/F6
Custódia, Braz. 196/C3
Cut (hill), Eng, UK 74/C5
Cut Bank, Mt, US 168/E3
Cut Knife, Sk, Can. 168/F2
Cutchogue, NY, US 181/F2
Cutervo, Peru 198/B2
Cuthbert, Ga, US 175/G4
Cutral-Có, Arg. 200/C3
Cutro, It. 89/E3
Cuttack, India 124/E3
Cuvergnon, Fr. 72/L4
Cuvier (cape), Austl. 154/B3
Cuxhaven, Ger. 93/F1
Cuyabeno, Ecu. 194/C5
Cuyama (riv.), Ca, US 170/C4
Cuyo, Phil. 123/F1
Cuyo (isls.), Phil. 123/F1
Cuyocuyo, Peru 198/D4
Cuyuni (riv.), Ven. 192/F2
Cuyuni (riv.), Guy., Ven. 195/G3
Cuyuni-Mazaruni (pol. reg.), Guy. 195/F3
Cuzco (ruin), Peru 198/D4
Cwmbran, Wal, UK 74/C3
Cyangugu, Rwa. 146/A3
Cyclades (isls.), Gre. 89/J4
Cypress (hills), Ab,Sk, Can. 168/F3
Cypress, Ca, US 178/F8
Cyprus (ctry.) 133/C2
Cyrenaica (reg.), Libya 139/K1
Cysoing, Fr. 94/C2
Cywyn (riv.), Wal, UK 74/B3
Czaplinek, Pol. 83/J2
Czarna Białostocka, Pol. 83/M2
Czarnków, Pol. 83/J2
Czech Republic (ctry.) 83/H4
Częstochowa, Pol. 83/K3
Człuchów, Pol. 80/G5

D

Da (riv.), China 121/D2
Da Hinggan (mts.), China 113/M2
Da Lat, Viet. 120/E4
Da Nang (cape), Viet. 120/E2
Da Nang, Viet. 120/E2
Da Xian, China 112/J5
Daaden, Ger. 95/G2
Da'an, China 113/M2
Daanbantayan, Phil. 121/D5
Daba (mts.), China 112/J5
Dabajuro, Ven. 194/D2
Dabakala, C.d'Iv. 144/D4
Dabas, Hun. 90/D2
Dabbāgh, Jabal (peak), SAr. 130/C3
Dabeiba, Col. 194/B3
Dabo, Fr. 95/G6
Dabob (bay), Wa, US 177/B2
Dabou, C.d'Iv. 144/D5
Daboya, Gha. 145/E4
Dabra, India 126/B3
Dąbrowa Białostocka, Pol. 81/K5
Dąbrowa Górnicza, Pol. 83/K3
Dabu, China 121/C3
Dachang Huizu Zizhixian, China 114/H7
Dachau, Ger. 97/E6
Dacono, Co, US 179/C2
Dade City, Fl, US 175/H4
Dades, Oued (riv.), Mor. 140/D3
Dadi (cape), Indo. 123/H4
Dādra and Nagar Haveli (state), India 124/B4
Dādri, India 128/D5
Dādu, Pak. 131/J3
Daduru (riv.), SrL. 124/C6
Daen Noi (peak), Thai. 120/B4
Daet, Phil. 121/D5
Dafang, China 125/J2
Dafeng, China 114/E4
Dagana, Sen. 144/B2
Dağardı, Turk. 132/B2
Dağbaşı, Turk. 132/D2
Dagestan, Resp., Rus. 105/H4
Daggaboersnek (pass), SAfr. 148/D4
Daggmar Range NP, Austl. 156/B2
Dagneux, Fr. 98/B6
Dagny, Fr. 72/M5
Dagu, China 114/H7
Daguan, China 125/H2
D'Aguilar (range), Austl. 156/E6
D'Aguilar (mt.), Austl. 156/E6
Dagupan, Phil. 121/D4
Dahana (des.), SAr. 130/D3
Daharki, Pak. 124/A2
Dahei (riv.), China 114/B2
Dahlak (arch.), Erit. 139/N4
Dahlem, Ger. 95/F3
Dahlenburg, Ger. 93/H2
Dahlonega, Ga, US 175/H3
Dahmani, Tun. 142/L7
Dahme (riv.), Ger. 83/G3
Dahn, Ger. 95/G5
Dahūk, Iraq 132/E2
Dahūk (gov.), Iraq 132/E2
Dahuofang (res.), China 114/D2
Dai (lake), China 114/C2
Dai-Segen-dake (peak), Japan 118/B3
Dai-sen (peak), Japan 116/C3
Dai Xian, China 114/C3
Daian, Japan 119/L5
Daicheng, China 114/D3
Daigo, Japan 117/G2
Dailekh, Nepal 126/C1
Dailly, Sc, UK 78/B6
Daimiao, China 114/D3
Daimiel, Sp. 86/D3
Daingerfield, Tx, US 171/J4
Daiō-zaki (pt.), Japan 117/E3
Dāira Dīn Panāh, Pak. 128/A4
Daireaux, Arg. 200/E3
Daisen-Oki NP, Japan 116/C3
Daisetsuzan NP, Japan 118/C2
Daishan, China 121/D1
Daito (isl.), Japan 109/N7
Daitō, Japan 119/J6
Daiyun (peak), China 113/L6
Dajabón, DRep. 187/J2
Dakar (cap.), Sen. 144/A3
Dakar (pol. reg.), Sen. 144/A3
Dākhilah, Wāḩāt ad (oasis), Egypt 143/B3
Dakhin Shābāzpur (isl.), Bang. 127/H4
Dakhlet Nouadhibou (pol. reg.), Mrta. 140/A5
Dakoro, Niger 145/G3
Dakota City, Ne, US 169/J5
Dakovica, Serb. 90/E4
Dakovo, Cro. 90/D3
Dal (falls), Sudan 143/B4
Dala-Järna, Swe. 80/F1
Dalälven (riv.), Swe. 106/B3
Dalaas, Aus. 99/F3
Dalad Qi, China 114/B2
Dalaman, Turk. 132/B2
Dalaman (int'l arpt.), Turk. 132/B2
Dalandzadgad, Mong. 112/H3
Dalarna (reg.), Swe. 79/E3
Dalatangi (pt.), Ice. 79/Q6
Dalbeattie, Sc, UK 76/E2
Dalby, Austl. 156/C4
Dalby, Swe. 80/E4
Dalcour, La, US 179/Q17
Dalcross (int'l arpt.), Sc, UK 78/B1
Dale, Ok, US 179/N15
Dale, Nor. 80/A1
Dalen, Neth. 92/D3
Dalen, Nor. 80/C2
Dalfsen, Neth. 92/D3
Dalgaranger (mt.), Austl. 154/C3
Dalhart, Tx, US 171/G3
Dalhousie (cape), NW, Can. 176/N1
Dalhousie, NB, Can. 173/H1
Dalhousie, India 128/C3
Dali, China 125/H2
Dali, China 114/B4
Dalian (bay), China 115/A3
Dalian, China 115/A3
Dalian (int'l arpt.), China 114/E3
Dalías, Sp. 86/D4
Dalidag (peak), Azer. 105/H5
Dāliyat el Karmil, Isr. 133/G6
Dalj, Cro. 90/D3
Dalkeith, Sc, UK 78/C5
Dalkola, India 127/F3
Dall (lake), Ak, US 176/F3
Dall (isl.), Ak, US 164/C3
Dallas, Tx, US 171/H4
Dallas-Fort Worth (int'l arpt.), Tx, US 171/H4
Dallastown, Pa, US 180/B4
Dallgow, Ger. 82/Q6
Dallol Bosso (riv.), Niger,Mali 145/F3
Dalmatia (reg.), Cro. 90/B3
Dalmatia, Pa, US 180/B2
Dalmellington, Sc, UK 78/B6
Dalmeny, Austl. 157/D3
Dalmine, It. 100/C1
Dal'negorsk, Rus. 113/Q3
Dal'nerechensk, Rus. 113/P2
Daloa, C.d'Iv. 144/D5
Dalry, Sc, UK 78/B5
Dalrymple (lake), Austl. 151/D3
Dalrymple, Sc, UK 78/B6
Dals Långed, Swe. 80/E2
Dalsingh Sarai, India 127/E3
Dalsjöfors, Swe. 80/E3
Dalton, Ga, US 175/G3
Daltonganj, India 127/E3
Dalvík, Ice. 79/N6
Dalwallinu, Austl. 154/C4
Daly (riv.), Austl. 151/C2
Daly (bay), Nun., Can. 164/G2
Damak, Nepal 127/F2
Damān, India 124/B3
Damān and Diu (state), India 124/B3
Damanhūr, Egypt 133/B4
Damar (isl.), Indo. 123/G5
Damascus (int'l arpt.), Syria 133/E3
Damascus, Md, US 180/A5
Damascus (Dimashq) (cap.), Syria 133/E3
Damaturu, Nga. 138/H5
Damavānd (mtn.), Iran 130/F1
Dambach-la-Ville, Fr. 98/D1
Dambaslar, Turk. 91/H5
Dame Marie (cape), Haiti 187/H2
Dame Marie, Haiti 187/H2
Dāmghān, Iran 131/F1
Damietta (riv.), Egypt 133/B4
Damietta (Dumyāţ), Egypt 133/B4
Daming, China 114/C3
Damion (peak), Fr. 95/D4
Dammard, Fr. 72/M4
Dammartin-en-Goële, Fr. 72/L4
Dammastock (peak), Swi. 99/E4
Damme, Ger. 93/F3
Damme, Belg. 94/C1
Dāmodar (riv.), India 124/E3
Damoh, India 126/B4
Damongo, Gha. 145/E4
Damparis, Fr. 98/B3
Dampier (str.), Indo. 123/H4
Dampier (arch.), Austl. 151/A2
Dampier, Austl. 154/C2
Dampierre, Fr. 72/H5
Dampierre-sur-Salon, Fr. 98/B2
Damprichard, Fr. 98/C3
Damrei (mts.), Camb. 120/C4
Damsterdiep (riv.), Neth. 92/D2
Damvant, Swi. 98/C3
Damxung, China 112/F5
Dan (riv.), NC,Va, US 175/H2
Dan Xian, China 125/J4
Đānā, Jor. 133/D4
Dana Point, Ca, US 178/C4
Danané, C.d'Iv. 144/C5
Danao, Phil. 121/D5
Danba, China 112/H5
Danbury, Eng, UK 75/G3
Dancheng, China 114/C4
Dandaragan, Austl. 154/B4
Dandeldhurā, Nepal 126/C1
Dandenong (mt.), Austl. 157/G5
Danderhall, Sc, UK 78/C5
Dandong, China 115/C2
Dane (riv.), Eng, UK 77/F5
Danger (pt.), SAfr. 148/L11
Danggali Conservation Park, Austl. 157/B2
Dangriga, Belz. 186/D2
Dangshan, China 114/D4
Dangtu, China 114/D5
Dangyang, China 113/K5
Danielskuil, SAfr. 148/C3
Danielsville, Pa, US 180/C2
Danilov, Rus. 102/J4
Daning, China 114/B3
Danjoutin, Fr. 98/C2
Dankaur, India 128/D5
Dankov, Rus. 104/F1
Dankova (peak), Kyr. 129/G4
Danlí, Hon. 186/E3
Dannelly (res.), Al, US 175/G3
Dannemora, Swe. 80/G1
Dannenberg, Ger. 82/F2
Dannes, Fr. 94/A2
Dannevirke, NZ 159/T11
Dannhauser, SAfr. 149/E3
Danube (riv.), Eur. 69/F4
Danube, Delta of the (delta), Rom. 91/J3
Danube (Donau) (riv.), Ger. 85/H2
Danube, Mouths of the (delta), Rom.,Ukr. 91/J3
Danville, Il, US 172/C3
Danville, Ky, US 172/C4
Danville, Pa, US 180/B2
Dao Xian, China 125/K2
Daoura, Oued ed (riv.), Alg. 140/D3
Daozhen, China 125/J2
Dapaong, Togo 145/F4
Daphne, Al, US 175/G4
Dapitan, Phil. 121/D6
Daqing, China 113/N2
Daqing (riv.), China 114/H7
Dar-el-Beida (Casablanca), Mor. 140/D2
Dar es Salaam (int'l arpt.), Tanz. 146/C4
Dar es Salaam (pol. reg.), Tanz. 146/C4
Dar es Salaam (cap.), Tanz. 146/C4
Dar Rounga (reg.), CAfr. 139/K6
Dar'ā (prov.), Syria 132/C3
Dar'ā (prov.), Syria 133/E3
Dar'ā, Syria 133/E3
Dārāb, Iran 131/F3
Darabani, Rom. 91/H1
Daraga, Phil. 121/D5
Daram, Phil. 121/D5
Dārān, Iran 130/F2
Đaravica (peak), Serb. 89/G1
Dārayyā, Syria 133/E3
Darbhanga, India 127/E2
Darby (cape), Ak, US 176/F3
Darby, Pa, US 180/C4
Darda, Cro. 90/D3
Dardanelle (lake), Ar, US 171/J4
Dardanelles (str.), Turk. 132/A2
Darent (riv.), Eng, UK 72/D3
Dareton, Austl. 157/B2
Darfield, NZ 159/S11
Darfo, It. 99/G6
Dārfūr (state), Sudan 143/A5
Dargaville, NZ 159/S10
Dargle (riv.), Ire. 76/B5
D'Arguin (bay), Mrta. 144/A1
Darhan, Mong. 112/J2
Darie (hills), Som. 139/Q6
Darien, Ga, US 175/H4
Darien, Ct, US 181/M7
Darien, Il, US 177/P16
Darién, PN, Pan. 192/C2
Darién, Serranía del (mts.), Pan. 192/C2
Darkan, Austl. 154/C5
Darlag, China 112/G5
Darling (range), Austl. 151/A4
Darling (riv.), Austl. 151/D4
Darling, SAfr. 148/L10
Darling Downs (reg.), Austl. 151/D3
Darling Downs (range), Austl. 156/C3
Darlington, Eng, UK 77/G2

Darli – Distr
231

Darlington (co.), Eng, UK 77/G2
Darlington, Md, US 180/B4
Darlington, SC, US 175/J3
Darlington Point, Austl. 157/C2
Darłowo, Pol. 80/G4
Darmstadt, Ger. 96/B3
Darnah, Libya 139/K1
Darney, Fr. 98/C1
Darnley (bay), NW, Can. 164/D2
Darnley (cape), Ant. 202/E
Daroca, Sp. 86/E2
Darregueira, Arg. 200/E3
Darsser (cape), Ger. 80/E4
Dart (riv.), Eng, UK 74/C6
Dart, West (riv.), Eng, UK 74/C6
Dartford, Eng, UK 72/D2
Dartmoor (upland), Eng, UK 74/B5
Dartmoor NP, Eng, UK 74/C5
Dartmouth (dam), Austl. 157/C3
Dartmouth (res.), Austl. 157/C3
Dartmouth, NS, Can. 173/J2
Dartmouth, Eng, UK 74/C6
Darton, Eng, UK 77/G4
Dartuch (cape), Sp. 87/G3
Daruvar, Cro. 90/C3
Darvel (bay), Malay. 123/E3
Darvel, Sc, UK 78/B5
Darwen, Eng, UK 77/F4
Darwin (bay), Chile 200/B5
Darwin (isl.), Ecu. 198/E6
Darwin (vol.), Ecu. 198/E7
Darwin, Cordillera (mts.), Chile 199/B7
Darya Khan, Pak. 128/A4
Daryābād, India 126/C2
Dashennongjia (peak), China 114/B5
Dashhowuz, Trkm. 129/C4
Dashhowuz (pol. reg.), Trkm. 129/C4
Dashhowuz (int'l arpt.), Trkm. 129/C4
Dasht-e Kavīr (des.), Iran 131/F2
Dasht-e Lūt (des.), Iran 131/G2
Dasht-e Mārgow (des.), Afg. 131/H2
Dasht Kaur (riv.), Pak. 131/H3
Dasing, Ger. 96/E6
Daska, Pak. 128/C3
Dassa-Zoumé, Ben. 145/F5
Dassel, Ger. 93/G5
Dassendorf, Ger. 93/H1
Dasseneiland (isl.), SAfr. 148/B4
Dasūya, India 128/C4
Dātāganj, India 126/B1
Datchet, Eng, UK 72/B2
Date, Japan 118/B2
Datia, India 126/B3
Datian, China 121/C2
Datil, NM, US 174/B3
Datong (mts.), China 112/G4
Datong, China 112/H4
Datong, China 114/C2
Datteln, Ger. 93/E5
Datu (cape), Indo. 122/C3
Datuk (cape), Indo. 122/B3
Daugava (riv.), Lat. 81/L3
Daugavpils, Lat. 81/M4
Daule, Ecu. 194/B5
Daule (riv.), Ecu. 194/B5
Daun, Ger. 95/F3
Daund, India 131/K5
Daung (isl.), Myan. 120/B3
Dauphin, Mb, Can. 169/H3
Dauphin (lake), Mb, Can. 169/J3
Dauphin, Pa, US 180/B3
Dauphin (co.), Pa, US 180/B3
Dauphiné (reg.), Fr. 84/F4
Dauphiné, Alpes du (range), Fr. 84/F4
Dāvangere, India 131/L6
Davao, Phil. 121/E6
Davel, SAfr. 149/E2
Davenport, Wa, US 168/D4
Davenport, Ia, US 169/L5
Davenport (mt.), Austl. 155/F2
Daventry, Eng, UK 75/E2
Daverdisse, Belg. 95/E3
Daveyton, SAfr. 148/E2
Davgaard-Jensen Land (phys. reg.), Grld. 165/T6
David, Pan. 187/F4
David City, Ne, US 169/J5
Davidson, Sk, Can. 169/G3
Davidson (mt.), Ca, US 177/J11
Davies (mt.), Austl. 155/F3
Davis (sea), Ant. 202/F
Davis, Austl., Ant. 202/F
Davis, Ca, US 170/B3
Davis (mt.), Pa, US 172/E4
Davis (mts.), Tx, US 174/B4
Davis (str.), Can.,Grld. 165/L2
Davlekanovo, Rus. 103/M5
Davo (riv.), C.d'Iv. 144/D5
Davos, Swi. 99/F4
Dawa, China 115/B2
Dawa Wenz (riv.), Eth. 139/N7
Dawangja (isl.), China 115/B3
Dawson, Yk, Can. 176/L3
Dawson, Ga, US 175/G4
Dawson (riv.), Austl. 151/D3
Dawson (isl.), Chile 201/C7
Dawson Creek, BC, Can. 168/C2
Dawu, China 112/H5
Dawu (mtn.), China 114/C5
Dawu, China 114/C5
Dax, Fr. 84/C5
Daxing, China 114/H7
Daxue (mts.), China 112/H5
Dayang (riv.), China 115/B2
Dayao, China 125/H2
Daye, China 121/B1
Daying (riv.), China 125/G3
Daylesford, Austl. 157/C3
Dayong, China 121/B2
Dayr al Balaḩ, Gaza 133/D4
Dayr al Ghuşūn, WBnk. 133/G7
Dayr Az Zawr (prov.), Syria 132/E3
Dayr Ballūţ, WBnk. 133/G7
Dayr Sharaf, WBnk. 133/G7
Dayrūţ, Egypt 143/B3
Daysland, Ab, Can. 168/E2
Dayton, Wa, US 168/D4
Dayton, Tn, US 175/G3
Dayton, Oh, US 180/D3
Daytona Beach, Fl, US 175/H4
Dayu, China 125/K2
Dazhizhu Dau (isl.), China 113/T11
D.C. (fed. dist.), US 180/A6
De Aar, SAfr. 148/D3
De Bilt, Neth. 92/C4
De Doorns, SAfr. 148/L10
De Funiak Springs, Fl, US 175/G4
De Grey (riv.), Austl. 151/A3
De Haan, Belg. 94/C1
De Hart (res.), Pa, US 180/B3
De Hoge Veluwe NP, Neth. 92/C4
De Kalb (co.), Il, US 177/N16
De Land, Fl, US 175/H4
De Leijen (lake), Neth. 92/D2
De Lier, Neth. 92/B5
De Luz, Ca, US 178/C4
De Panne, Belg. 94/B1
De Peel (phys. reg.), Neth. 92/C6
De Pinte, Belg. 94/C2
De Ridder, La, US 171/J5
De Soto, Ks, US 179/D6
De Soto, Mo, US 171/K3
De Wijk, Neth. 92/D3
Dead Sea (sea), Isr.,Jor. 132/C4
Deadhorse, Ak, US 176/J1
Deadman (peak), Austl. 154/C2
Deadwood, SD, US 169/H4
Deal (isl.), Austl. 157/C3
Deal, NJ, US 180/D3
Deale, Md, US 180/B6
Dean (riv.), BC, Can. 168/B2
Dean (chan.), BC, Can. 168/B2
De'an, China 121/C2
Dean (for.), Eng, UK 74/D3
Deán Funes, Arg. 199/D3
Deanmill, Austl. 154/C5
Dearborn Heights, Mi, US 177/F7
Dearne, Eng, UK 77/G4
Dease (str.), Nun., Can. 164/F2
Dease (riv.), BC, Can. 164/D3
Dease Lake, BC, Can. 176/M4
Death Valley NP, Ca, US 170/C3
Debar, FYROM 89/G2
Debauch (mtn.), Ak, US 176/G3
Debe Habe, Nga. 138/H5
Debelets, Bul. 89/J1
Deben (riv.), Eng, UK 75/H2
Dębica, Pol. 83/L3
Dęblin, Pol. 83/L3
Dębno, Pol. 83/H2
Débo (lake), Mali 144/E3
Deborah (mt.), Ak, US 176/J3
Debre Birhan, Eth. 139/N6
Debre Mark'os, Eth. 139/N5
Debre Tabor, Eth. 139/N5
Debre Zeyit, Eth. 139/N6
Debrecen, Hun. 83/L5
Decatur, Al, US 175/G3
Decatur, Il, US 169/L6
Decatur, In, US 172/C3
Decatur, Ga, US 175/G3
Decatur, Tx, US 171/H4
Decazeville, Fr. 84/E4
Deccan (plat.), India 124/C5
Decima, It. 101/E3
Děčín, Czh. 83/H3
Décines-Charpieu, Fr. 98/A6
Decize, Fr. 84/E3
Dedemsvaart, Neth. 92/D3
Dedo (peak), Arg. 200/C5
Dédougou, Burk. 144/E3
Dedza, Malw. 147/F3
Dee (riv.), Sc, UK 78/C3
Deel (riv.), Ire. 76/A4
Deep Fork (riv.), Ok, US 179/N14
Deep River, On, Can. 172/E2
Deepcut, Eng, UK 72/F3
Deepwater, Austl. 157/D1
Deepwater, NJ, US 180/C4
Deepwater (pt.), De, US 180/C5
Deer (isl.), Ak, US 176/F5
Deer Creek (res.), Ut, US 179/L13
Deer Lake, Nf, Can. 173/K1
Deer Lake, Pa, US 180/B2
Deer Lodge, Mt, US 168/E4
Deer Park, Il, US 177/P15
Deer Park, Md, US 180/B5
Deer Park, NY, US 181/E2
Deer Park, Wa, US 168/D4
Deer Plain, Il, US 179/F8
Deerfield, Il, US 177/P15
Deering, Ak, US 176/F2
Deerlijk, Belg. 94/C2
Deeside (valley), Sc, UK 78/D2
Deex Nugaaleed (riv.), Som. 139/Q6
Defensores del Chaco, PN, Par. 192/F8
Defiance, Oh, US 172/C3
Dégelis, Qu, Can. 173/G2
Degerfors, Swe. 80/F2
Degersheim, Swi. 99/F3
Deggendorf, Ger. 97/F5
Deggingen, Ger. 96/C5
Dego, It. 100/B4
DeGrey (riv.), Austl. 154/C2
Deh Bīd, Iran 130/F2
Dehalak (isl.), Erit. 139/P4
Dehalak Marine NP, Erit. 139/P4
Deheq, Iran 130/F2
Dehra Dūn, India 131/L2
Dehri, India 127/E3
Dehua, China 121/C2
Deidesheim, Ger. 96/B4
Deinste, Ger. 93/G1
Deinze, Belg. 94/C2
Deister (mts.), Ger. 93/G4
Deiva Marina, It. 100/C4
Dej, Rom. 91/F2
Deje, Swe. 80/E2
Dejiang, China 125/J2
Dejima, Japan 119/E1
Dekemhare (**Dek'emhāre**), Erit. 130/C5
Del Campillo, Arg. 200/D2
Del Carril, Arg. 201/J11
Del City, Ok, US 179/N15
Del Dios, Ca, US 178/C4
Del Gran Paradiso, It. 100/A2
Del Mar, Ca, US 178/C5
Del Norte, Co, US 171/F3
Del Rio, Tx, US 171/G5
Del Valle, Arg. 200/E2
Del Valle (lake), Ca, US 177/L11
Delacroix, La, US 179/Q17
Delafield, Wi, US 177/P13
Delano, Ca, US 170/C4
Delareyville, SAfr. 148/D2
Delarode (lake), Sk, Can. 168/G2
Delavan, Wi, US 171/K2
Delavan (lake), Wi, US 177/P14
Delavan Lake, Wi, US 177/N14
Delaware (riv.), US 172/F3
Delaware (state), US 172/F4
Delaware, NJ, US 180/C2
Delaware (bay), NJ, US 172/F4
Delaware, Oh, US 172/D3
Delaware (co.), Pa, US 180/C4
Delaware (pass), Pa, US 180/C2
Delaware City, De, US 180/C4
Delaware Water Gap Nat'l Rec. Area, Pa, US 172/F3
Delbrück, Ger. 93/F5
Delčevo, FYROM 89/H2
Delden, Neth. 92/D4
Delebio, It. 99/F5
Delegate, Austl. 157/D3
Delémont, Swi. 98/D3
Delft, Neth. 92/B4
Delfzijl, Neth. 92/D2
Delgada (pt.), Arg. 200/E4
Delgado (cape), Moz. 146/D5
Delhi, India 128/D5
Delhi (state), India 124/C2
Delhi, Il, US 179/G7
Delhi, La, US 171/K4
Delice, Turk. 132/C2
Delice (riv.), Turk. 104/E5
Delījān, Iran 130/F2
Déljne, NW, Can. 164/D2
Delisle, Sk, Can. 168/G3
Dell Rapids, SD, US 169/J5
Delligsen, Ger. 93/G5
Delmas, SAfr. 148/Q13
Delme (riv.), Ger. 93/F3
Delmenhorst, Ger. 93/F2
Delmiro Gouveia, Braz. 196/C3
Delmont, NJ, US 180/D5
Delnice, Cro. 90/B3
Deloraine, Austl. 157/C4
Deloraine, Mb, Can. 169/H3
Delphi (Dhelfoi) (ruin), Gre. 89/H3
Delphos, Oh, US 172/C3
Delportshoop, SAfr. 148/D3
Delran, NJ, US 180/D4
Delray Beach, Fl, US 175/H5
Delson, Qu, Can. 173/N7
Delta, Ut, US 170/D3
Delta (state), Nga. 145/G5
Delta, Pa, US 180/B4
Delta del Tigre, Uru. 201/K11
Delta du Saloum, PN du, Sen. 144/A3
Delta Junction, Ak, US 176/J3
Delta-Mendota (canal), Ca, US 177/M11
Deltona, Fl, US 175/H4
Delvinë, Alb. 89/G3
Dëma (riv.), Rus. 129/C2
Demanda, Sierra de la (range), Sp. 86/D1
Demarcation (pt.), Ak, US 176/K2
Demarest, NJ, US 181/K8
Demba, D.R. Congo 147/D2
Dembī Dolo, Eth. 139/M6
Demer (riv.), Belg. 82/C3
Demerara (riv.), Guy. 195/G3
Demerara-Mahaica (pol. reg.), Guy. 195/G3
Demerval Lobão, Braz. 196/B2
Deming, NM, US 174/B3
Demini (riv.), Braz. 192/F3
Demirci, Turk. 132/B2
Demirkent, Turk. 132/C2
Demirköprü (dam), Turk. 132/B2
Demirköy, Turk. 91/H5
Demirtaş, Turk. 91/J5
Demmin, Ger. 80/E5
Democratic Republic of the Congo (ctry.) 135/E5
Demone (valley), It. 88/D4
Demopolis, Al, US 175/G3
Dempo (peak), Indo. 122/B4
Dempster (pt.), Austl. 154/D5
Den Burg, Neth. 92/B2
Den Ham, Neth. 92/D4
Den Helder, Neth. 92/B3
Den Oever, Neth. 92/C3
Denain, Fr. 94/C3
Denakil (reg.), Djib.,Eth. 139/P5
Denali NP and Prsv., Ak, US 176/H3
Denare Beach, Sk, Can. 169/H2
Denbigh, Wal, UK 77/E5
Denbighshire (co.), Wal, UK 77/E5
Dender (riv.), Belg. 82/B3
Denderleeuw, Belg. 95/D2
Dendermonde, Belg. 95/D1
Denekamp, Neth. 92/E4
Deng Xian, China 114/C4
Dengfeng, China 114/C4
Dengkou, China 112/J3
Dengta, China 121/B3
Denham (sound), Austl. 154/B3
Denham, Austl. 154/B3
Denholme, Eng, UK 77/G4
Denia, Sp. 87/F3
Deniliquin, Austl. 157/C2
Denio, Nv, US 168/D5
Denison (mt.), Ak, US 176/H4
Denison, Ia, US 169/K5
Denison, Tx, US 171/H4
Denizli, Turk. 132/B2
Denizli (prov.), Turk. 132/B2
Denkendorf, Ger. 97/E5
Denklingen, Ger. 99/G2
Denman, Austl. 157/D2
Denmark, Austl. 154/C5
Denmark (str.), Grld.,Ice. 161/R3
Denmark (ctry.) 80/C4
Dennisville, NJ, US 180/D5
Denpasar, Indo. 122/E5
Dent de Lys (peak), Swi. 98/C4
Dent d'Hérens (peak), It. 98/D6
Dentergem, Belg. 94/C2
Dentlein am Forst, Ger. 96/D4
Denton, Eng, UK 77/F5
Denton, Md, US 180/C6
Denton, Tx, US 174/D3
Denton, Tx, US 171/H4
D'Entrecasteaux (isls.), PNG 158/D5
D'Entrecasteaux (pt.), Austl. 154/B5
Dents du Midi (peak), Swi. 98/C5
Denver (cap.), Co, US 179/C3
Denver (co.), Co, US 179/B3
Denver, Pa, US 180/B3
Denver International (int'l arpt.), Co, US 179/C3
Denver Museum of Natural History, Co, US 179/C3
Denville, NJ, US 180/D2
Denzlingen, Ger. 98/D1
Deoband, India 128/D5
Deogarh, India 124/D3
Deoghar, India 127/F3
Deohā (riv.), India 126/B1
Deolāli, India 131/K5
Deoli, India 124/C3
Déols, Fr. 84/D3
Deorī, India 126/B4
Deoria, India 126/D2
Dependencias Federales (state), Ven. 195/E1
Depew, NY, US 173/S10
Depok, Indo. 122/C5
Deqing, China 121/B3
Deqing, China 114/L9
Dera Ghāzi Khān, Pak. 128/A4
Dera Gopipur, India 128/D4
Dera Ismāīl Khān, Pak. 128/A4
Derbent, Rus. 105/J4
Derby, Eng, UK 77/G6
Derby (co.), Eng, UK 77/G6
Derby, Ct, US 181/E1
Derbyshire (co.), Eng, UK 77/G6
Derdap NP, Serb. 90/F3
Derecske, Hun. 90/E2
Dereköy, Turk. 91/H5
Derendingen, Swi. 98/D3
Derg, Lough (lake), Ire. 73/P10
Derik, Turk. 132/E2
Derinkuyu, Turk. 132/C2
Dernau, Ger. 95/G2
Déroute, Passage de la (chan.), Fr. 84/B2
Derrevaragh (lake), Ire. 76/A4
Derry, NH, US 173/G3
Derryboy, NI, UK 76/C3
Dervaig, Sc, UK 73/Q8
Derventa, Bosn. 90/C3
Dervio, It. 99/F5
Derwent (riv.), Austl. 157/C4
Derwent (riv.), Eng, UK 77/E2
Derwent (res.), Eng, UK 77/F2
Derwent Water (lake), Eng, UK 77/E2
Des Allemands, La, US 179/P17
Des Moines (cap.), Ia, US 169/K5
Des Moines (riv.), Ia,Mn, US 169/J2
Des Peres, Mo, US 179/G8
Desaguadero (riv.), Bol. 192/E7
Desaguadero, Peru 198/D5
Desagües de los Colorados (dry lake), Arg. 199/C2
Desana, It. 100/B2
Descabezado Grande (vol.), Chile 200/C2
Descalvado, Braz. 197/C2
Descartes, Fr. 84/D3
Deschambault (lake), Sk, Can. 169/H2
Deschambault Lake, Sk, Can. 169/H2
Deschutes (riv.), Or, US 168/C4
Desdunes, Haiti 187/H2
Desē, Eth. 139/N5
Dese (riv.), It. 101/F2
Deseado (riv.), Arg. 189/C7
Deseado (cape), Chile 201/B7
Desengaño (pt.), Arg. 201/D6
Desenzano del Garda, It. 100/D2
Désertines, Fr. 84/E3
Desio, It. 100/C1
Desna (riv.), Ukr. 104/D2
Desolación (isl.), Chile 199/A7
Desordem, Serra da (range), Braz. 196/A2
Despatch, SAfr. 148/D4
Dessau, Ger. 82/G3
Dessel, Belg. 92/C6
Dessoubre (riv.), Fr. 98/C3
Destelbergen, Belg. 94/C1
Destrehan, La, US 179/P17
Destruction Bay, Yk, Can. 176/L3
Desulo, It. 88/A2
Desvres, Fr. 94/A2
Deta, Rom. 90/E3
Detern, Ger. 93/E2
Detmold, Ger. 93/F5
Detroit (riv.), Can.,US 177/F7
Detroit Lakes, Mn, US 169/K4
Detroit Metropolitan Wayne County (int'l arpt.), Mi, US 172/D3
Dettelbach, Ger. 96/D3
Dettifoss (falls), Ice. 79/P6
Dettwiller, Fr. 95/G6
Deua NP, Austl. 157/D2
Deuil-la-Barre, Fr. 72/J5
Deûle (riv.), Fr. 94/B2
Deurne, Belg. 92/B6
Deurne, Neth. 92/C6
Deustua, Peru 198/D4
Deutsch Evern, Ger. 93/H2
Deutsch Wagram, Aus. 91/P7
Deutschkreutz, Aus. 85/M3
Deutschlandsberg, Aus. 85/L3
Deux-Montagnes, Qu, Can. 173/N6
Deux-Montagnes (co.), Qu, Can. 173/M6
Deux-Montagnes, Lac des (lake), Qu, Can. 173/M7
Deva, Rom. 90/F3
Dévaványa, Hun. 90/E2
Develi, Turk. 132/C2
Deventer, Neth. 92/D4
Deveron (riv.), Sc, UK 78/D2
Deville, Fr. 95/D4
Devil's (isl.), FrG. 193/H2
Devils (riv.), Mex. 185/E2
Devil's Elbow (pass), Sc, UK 78/C3
Devils Lake, ND, US 169/J3
Devils Paw (peak), Ak, US 176/M4
Devils Postpile Nat'l Mon., Ca, US 170/C3
Devils Slide, Ut, US 179/K11
Devine, Tx, US 171/H5
Devizes, Eng, UK 74/E4
Devnya, Bul. 91/H4
Devoll (riv.), Alb.,Gre. 90/E5
Devon, Ab, Can. 168/E2
Devon (isl.), Nun., Can. 165/S7
Devon (co.), Eng, UK 74/C5
Devon (riv.), Sc, UK 78/C4
Devon-Berwyn, Pa, US 180/C3
Devonport, Austl. 157/C4
Devore, Ca, US 178/C2
Devrek, Turk. 91/K5
Devrek (riv.), Turk. 91/K5
Devrez (riv.), Turk. 104/E4
Dewa (pt.), Indo. 122/A3
Dewa (mts.), Japan 118/B4
Dewās, India 131/L4
Dewetsdorp, SAfr. 148/D3
Dewsbury, Eng, UK 77/G4
Dexter, Me, US 173/G2
Dey-Dey (lake), Austl. 151/C3
Deyang, China 112/H5
Dez (riv.), Iran 106/E6
Dezfūl, Iran 130/E2
Dezhneva (cape), Rus. 176/E2
Dezhou, China 114/D3
Dhabān Singh, Pak. 128/B4
Dhaka (cap.), Bang. 127/H4
Dhākā (div.), Bang. 127/H4
Dhāka, India 127/E2
Dhaleswari (riv.), Bang. 127/H4
Dhali, Cyp. 133/C2
Dhāmpur, India 126/B1
Dhamtari, India 124/D3
Dhanaula, India 128/C4
Dhanaura, India 126/B1
Dhānbād, India 127/F4
Dhangadhī, Nepal 126/C1
Dhankutā, Nepal 127/F2
Dhār, India 131/L4
Dharampur, India 131/K4
Dharān, Nepal 127/F2
Dhāri, India 131/K4
Dhāriwāl, India 128/C4
Dharmapuri, India 124/C5
Dharmavaram, India 124/C5
Dharmjaygarh, India 126/D4
Dharmsāla, India 128/D3
Dhasan (riv.), India 126/B3
Dhaulāgiri (peak), Nepal 126/D1
Dhaulāgiri (zone), Nepal 126/D1
Dhaurahra, India 126/C1
Dhelfoí, Gre. 89/H3
Dhelvinákion, Gre. 89/G3
Dheskáti, Gre. 89/G3
Dheune (riv.), Fr. 98/A4
Dhībān, Jor. 133/D4
Dhidhimótikhon, Gre. 89/K2
Dhíkaia, Gre. 89/K2
Dhílos (ruin), Gre. 89/J4
Dhimitsána, Gre. 89/H4
Dhírfis (peak), Gre. 89/H3
Dhístomon, Gre. 89/H3
Dhofar (reg.), Oman 130/F5
Dhokímion, Gre. 89/G3
Dholka, India 131/K4
Dhomokós, Gre. 89/H3
Dhonoúsa (isl.), Gre. 89/J4
Dhorāji, India 131/K4
Dhronbach (riv.), Ger. 95/F4
Dhūlia, India 131/K4
Dhuliān, India 127/F3
Dhulikhel, Nepal 127/E2
Dhupgāri, India 127/G2
Dhūri, India 128/C4
Di Linh, Viet. 120/E4
Dia (isl.), Gre. 89/J5
Diablo (mt.), Ak, US 176/H4
Diablo (range), Ca, US 170/B3
Diablo (plat.), Tx, US 174/B4
Diablo, Punta del (pt.), Uru. 201/G2
Diablotin (peak), Dom. 183/N9
Diadema, Braz. 197/G8
Diadema Argentina, Arg. 200/D5
Diamante (riv.), Arg. 200/D2
Diamantina, Braz. 196/B5
Diamantina (riv.), Austl. 151/D3
Diamantina, Chapada (hills), Braz. 193/K6
Diamantino, Braz. 193/G6
Diamond Bar, Ca, US 178/G8
Diamond Harbour, India 127/G4
Diamond Head (pt.), Hi, US 166/W13
Dianalund, Den. 80/D4
Dianbai, China 125/K3
Dianjiang, China 121/A1
Diano Marina, It. 100/B5
Dianshan (lake), China 114/L8
Diapaga, Burk. 145/F3
Dias Creek, NJ, US 180/D5
Diavolezza (peak), Swi. 99/F5
Dibai, India 126/B1
Dibeng, SAfr. 148/C2
Dibiāpur, India 126/B2
Dibis (well), Egypt 143/B4
Dibs, Iraq 132/F3
Dickens, Tx, US 171/G4
Dickens (pt.), RI, US 181/G1
Dickinson, ND, US 169/H4
Dickson, Tn, US 172/C4
Dicle (dam), Turk. 132/E2
Dicomano, It. 101/E5
Didam, Neth. 92/D5
Didcot, Eng, UK 75/E3
Didsbury, Ab, Can. 168/E3
Dīdwāna, India 131/K3
Didyma (ruin), Turk. 132/A2
Die Berg (peak), SAfr. 147/F6
Dieblich, Ger. 95/G3
Diébougou, Burk. 144/E4
Dieburg, Ger. 96/B3
Diedersdorf, Ger. 82/Q7
Diefenbaker (lake), Sk, Can. 168/G3
Diego de Almagro (isl.), Chile 201/B6
Diego Garcia (isl.), UK 109/G10
Diekirch (dist.), Lux. 95/E4
Diekirch, Lux. 95/F4
Diemen, Neth. 92/B4
Diemtigen, Swi. 98/D4
Diepenbeek, Belg. 95/E2
Diepenveen, Neth. 92/D4
Diepholz, Ger. 93/F3
Diepoldsau, Swi. 99/F3
Dieppe, Fr. 84/D2
Dierdorf, Ger. 95/G2
Diespeck, Ger. 96/D3
Diessen am Ammersee, Ger. 99/H2
Diest, Belg. 95/E2
Dietenheim, Ger. 99/G1
Dietenhofen, Ger. 96/D4
Dietersheim, Ger. 96/D3
Dietfurt an der Altmühl, Ger. 97/E4
Dietikon, Swi. 99/E3
Dietmannsried, Ger. 99/G2
Dietzenbach, Ger. 96/B2
Dieue-sur-Meuse, Fr. 95/E5
Dieulouard, Fr. 95/F6
Dieuze, Fr. 95/F6
Diever, Neth. 92/D3
Diez, Ger. 96/B2
Diffa, Niger 138/H5
Diffa (dept.), Niger 145/H3
Differdange, Lux. 95/E4
Difficult (mt.), Austl. 157/B3
Dīg, India 126/A2
Digboi, India 125/G2
Digby, NS, Can. 173/H2
Dighwāra, India 127/E3
Digne-les-Bains, Fr. 85/G4
Digoin, Fr. 84/E3
Digor, Turk. 132/E1
Digul (riv.), Indo. 123/K4
Digya NP, Gha. 145/E5
Dijon, Fr. 98/A3
Dikirnis, Egypt 133/B4
Diklosmta (peak), Geo. 105/H4
Diksmuide, Belg. 94/B1
Dīla, Eth. 139/N6
Dilbeek, Belg. 95/D2
Dilek Yarımadası NP, Turk. 132/A2
Dili (cap.), ETim. 123/G5
Dillenburg, Ger. 95/H2
Dillingen, Ger. 95/F5
Dillingen an der Donau, Ger. 96/D5
Dillingham, Ak, US 176/G4
Dillon, Mt, US 168/E4
Dillon, SC, US 175/J3
Dillsburg, Pa, US 180/A3
Dilolo, D.R. Congo 147/D3
Dilsen, Belg. 95/E1
Dimāpur, India 125/F2
Dimaro, It. 99/G5
Dimas, Mex. 184/D4
Dimashq (prov.), Syria 132/D3
Dimbokro, C.d'Iv. 144/D5
Dimboola, Austl. 157/B3
Dîmbovița (prov.), Rom. 91/G3
Dimbulah, Austl. 156/B2
Dimitriya Lapteva (str.), Rus. 107/P2
Dimitrovgrad, Bul. 89/J1
Dimitrovgrad, Rus. 105/J1
Dimitrovgrad, Serb. 90/F4
Dimlang (peak), Nga. 138/H6
Dimmitt, Tx, US 171/G4
Dimona, Isr. 133/D4
Dimovo, Bul. 91/F4
Dina, Pak. 128/B3
Dinagat (isl.), Phil. 121/E5
Dinagat, Phil. 121/E6
Dinājpur (pol. reg.), Bang. 127/G3
Dinan, Fr. 84/B2
Dīnānagar, India 128/C3
Dinant, Belg. 95/D3
Dinar, Turk. 132/B2
Dinard, Fr. 84/B2
Dinaric Alps (mts.), Cro. 90/C3
Dinas (pt.), Wal, UK 74/B2
Dinder NP, Sudan 139/N5
Dindigul, India 124/C5
Dindori, India 126/C4
Dinga, Pak. 128/B3
Ding'an, China 125/K4
Dingbian, China 112/J4
Dingelstädt, Ger. 93/H6
Dinggyê, China 127/F1
Dingle, Ire. 72/F10
Dingle (bay), Ire. 72/N10
Dingmans Ferry, Pa, US 180/D1
Dingnan, China 121/C3
Dingolfing, Ger. 97/F5
Dingras, Phil. 121/D4
Dingtao, China 114/C4
Dingwall, Sc, UK 78/B1
Dingxi, China 112/H4
Dingxiang, China 114/C3
Dingxing, China 114/G7
Dingyuan, China 114/D4
Dinkel (riv.), Ger. 93/E4
Dinkelsbühl, Ger. 96/D4
Dinkelscherben, Ger. 96/D6
Dinklage, Ger. 93/F3
Dinosaur Nat'l Mon., US 170/E2
Dinslaken, Ger. 92/D5
Dinsmore, Sk, Can. 168/G3
Dintel Mark (riv.), Neth. 92/B5
Dinuba, Ca, US 170/C3
Dinxperlo, Neth. 92/D5
Dioïla, Mali 144/D3
Dion (riv.), Gui. 144/C4
Diósd, Hun. 91/Q10
Diourbel (pol. reg.), Sen. 144/A3
Diourbel, Sen. 144/A3
Dīpālpur, Pak. 128/B4
Diphu, India 125/F2
Diplo, Pak. 131/J4
Dipni (dam), Turk. 132/E2
Dipperu NP, Austl. 156/C3
Dipperz, Ger. 96/C1
Dique (canal), Col. 187/H4
Diré, Mali 144/E2
Dirē Dawa, Eth. 139/P6
Diriamba, Nic. 186/E4
Dirj, Libya 141/H3
Dirk Hartog (isl.), Austl. 151/A3
Dirksland, Neth. 92/B5
Dirlewang, Ger. 99/G2
Dirranbandi, Austl. 156/C5
Dirrington Great Law (hill), Sc, UK 78/D5
Dirty Devil (riv.), Ut, US 170/E3
Disappointment (lake), Austl. 151/B3
Disappointment (isls.), FrPol. 159/L6
Discovery (bay), Austl. 157/B3
Discovery Bay, Jam. 187/G2
Disentis-Mustér, Swi. 99/E4
Disgrazi (peak), It. 99/F5
Disko (isl.), Grld. 161/M3
Disko (Qeqertarsuaq) (isl.), Grld. 165/L2
Disneyland, Ca, US 178/G8
Dison, Belg. 95/E2
Dispur, India 125/F2
Disraëli, Qu, Can. 173/G2
Dissen am Teutoburger Wald, Ger. 93/F4
District of Columbia (fed. dist.), US 180/A6
Distrito Federal (fed. dist.), Braz. 196/A4

232
Distr – Dziba

Distrito Federal (fed. dist.), Col. 194/C3
Distrito Federal (fed. dist.), Mex. 185/Q10
Distrito Federal (fed. dist.), Ven. 195/E2
Disūq, Egypt 133/B4
Ditchling Beacon (hill), Eng, UK 75/F5
Dittaino (riv.), It. 88/D4
Dittelbrunn, Ger. 96/D2
Dittmer, Mo, US 179/F9
Ditzingen, Ger. 96/C5
Diu, India 124/B3
Dive (riv.), Fr. 84/D3
Dividing Creek, NJ, US 180/C5
Divinolândia, Braz. 197/G6
Divinópolis, Braz. 197/C2
Divisa Nova, Braz. 197/G6
Divisor, Serra do (mts.), Braz. 192/D5
Divo, C.d'Iv. 144/D5
Divonne-les-Bains, Fr. 98/C5
Divriği, Turk. 132/D2
Dix (lake), Swi. 98/D5
Dixmoor, Il, US 177/Q16
Dixon, Il, US 169/L5
Dixon Entrance (chan.), Can.,US 176/M4
Diyadin, Turk. 132/E2
Diyāla (gov.), Iraq 132/F3
Diyarb Najm, Egypt 133/B4
Diyarbakir (prov.), Turk. 132/E2
Diyarbakır, Turk. 132/E2
Djado (plat.), Niger 135/D2
Djakotomé, Ben. 145/F5
Djamaa, Alg. 141/G2
Djambala, Congo 138/H8
Djanet, Alg. 141/H4
Djebel-Amrag (mtn.), Alg. 142/D3
Djebel Tichka (peak), Mor. 140/C3
Djedi, Oued (riv.), Alg. 141/G2
Djelfa, Alg. 138/F1
Djema, CAfr. 139/L6
Djemila (ruin), Alg. 142/H4
Djénné, Mali 144/D3
Djibo, Burk. 145/E3
Djibouti (ctry.) 139/P5
Djibouti (cap.), Djib. 139/P5
Djougou, Ben. 145/F4
Djúpivogur, Ice. 79/P7
Dnepr (riv.), Rus. 104/D1
Dnipro (riv.), Ukr. 69/H3
Dniprodzerzhyns'k, Ukr. 104/E2
Dnipropetrovs'k, Ukr. 104/E2
Dnipropetrovs'ka Oblasti, Ukr. 104/E2
Dniprovs'kyy Lyman (estu.), Ukr. 91/K2
Dnister (riv.), Ukr. 82/M4
Dnistrovs'kyy Lyman (estu.), Ukr. 91/K2
Dnyapro (riv.), Bela. 81/P4
Do (lake), Mali 145/E3
Do Rāh (pass), Afg. 131/K1
Do Son, Viet. 120/D1
Doany, Madg. 149/J6
Doba, Chad 138/J6
Dobbs Ferry, NY, US 181/K7
Dobele, Lat. 81/K3
Döbeln, Ger. 82/G3
Doberai (pen.), Indo. 123/H4
Dobiegniew, Pol. 83/H2
Dobogo-kó (peak), Hun. 91/Q9
Doboj, Bosn. 90/D3
Dobřany, Czh. 97/G3
Dobre Miasto, Pol. 81/J5
Dobrich, Bul. 91/H4
Dobříš, Czh. 97/H3
Dobruja (reg.), Bul. 91/H4
Dobrush, Bela. 104/D1
Dobryanka, Rus. 103/N4
Doce (riv.), Braz. 193/K7
Dochart (riv.), Sc, UK 78/B4
Dock Junction, Ga, US 175/H4
Docker River, Austl. 155/F3
Doctor Arroyo, Mex. 185/E4
Doctor Pedro P. Peña, Par. 199/D1
Doctor Petru Groza, Rom. 90/F2
Doda (lake), Qu, Can. 172/F1
Doda, India 128/C3
Doda (riv.), India 128/D3
Dodder (riv.), Ire. 76/B5
Doddinghurst, Eng, UK 72/D2
Dodecanese (isl.), Gre. 132/A2
Dodge City, Ks, US 171/G3
Dodger Stadium, Ca, US 178/F7
Dodgeville, Wi, US 169/L5
Dodman (pt.), Eng, UK 74/B6
Dodoma, Tanz. 146/B4
Dodoma (pol. reg.), Tanz. 146/B4
Dodori Nat'l Rsv., Kenya 146/D3
Dodsland, Sk, Can. 168/F3
Dodworth, Eng, UK 77/G4
Doesburg, Neth. 92/D4
Doetinchem, Neth. 92/D5
Doğanhisar, Turk. 132/B2
Doğankent (riv.), Turk. 132/D1
Doğanşar, Turk. 132/D1
Doğanşehir, Turk. 132/D2
Doğanyurt, Turk. 132/C1
Döğer, Turk. 132/B2
Dogliani, It. 100/A3
Dogondoutchi, Niger 145/G3
Doğubayazıt, Turk. 132/F2
Doğukaradeniz (mts.), Turk. 132/D1
Doha (cap.), Qatar 130/F3
Dohad, India 131/K4
Dohrīghāt, India 126/D2
Doi Khun Tan NP, Thai. 120/B2
Doilungdêqên, China 124/F2
Doiras, Embalse de (res.), Sp. 86/B1
Dois de Julho (int'l arpt.), Braz. 196/C4
Dois Irmãos, Serra (mts.), Braz. 193/K5
Doische, Belg. 95/D3
Dokka, Nor. 80/D1
Dokkum, Neth. 92/D2
Dokkumer Ee (riv.), Neth. 92/C2
Doksy, Czh. 97/H1
Dolbeau, Qu, Can. 173/F1
Dolcedorme (peak), It. 88/E3
Dole, Fr. 98/B3
Dolent (peak), Swi. 98/D6
Dolgellau, Wal, UK 74/C1
Dolgoprudnyy, Rus. 103/W9
Dolianova, It. 88/A3
Dolinsk, Rus. 113/R2
Dolj (prov.), Rom. 91/F3
Dollar, Sc, UK 78/C4
Dollar Law (peak), Sc, UK 78/C5
Dollard-des-Ormeaux, Qu, Can. 173/N7
Dollard (Dollart) (bay), Ger.,Neth. 93/E2
Doller (riv.), Fr. 82/D5
Dollnstein, Ger. 96/E5
Dolmar (peak), Ger. 96/D1
Dolmen (ruin), It. 88/E2
Dolna Banya, Bul. 89/H1
Dolni Dŭbnik, Bul. 91/G4
Dolnośląskie (prov.), Pol. 83/J3
Dolo, Eth. 139/P7
Dolo, It. 101/F2
Dolo (riv.), It. 100/D4
Doloon, Mong. 112/J3
Dolores, Arg. 200/F3
Dolores, Guat. 186/D2
Dolores (riv.), Co, US 170/E3
Dolores, Co, US 174/A2
Dolores, Uru. 201/J10
Dolores, Ven. 194/D2
Dolphin (cape), UK 201/F6
Dolphin and Union (str.), Nun., Can. 164/E2
Dölsach, Aus. 85/K3
Dolton, Il, US 177/Q16
Dom (peak), Swi. 98/D5
Dom (peak), Indo. 123/J4
Dom Noi (res.), Thai. 120/D3
Dom Pedrito, Braz. 199/F3
Dom Pedro, Braz. 196/A2
Domat-Ems, Swi. 99/F4
Domažlice, Czh. 97/F4
Dombasle-sur-Meurthe, Fr. 95/F6
Dombay-Ul'gen (peak), Geo. 105/G4
Dombes (lake), Fr. 98/B5
Dombóvár, Hun. 90/D2
Dombrád, Hun. 90/E1
Domburg, Neth. 92/A5
Dome C, US, Ant. 202/J
Domérat, Fr. 84/E3
Domeyko, Cordillera (mts.), Chile 199/C1
Dominica (ctry.) 183/N9
Dominica Passage (chan.), Dom.,Guad. 183/N9
Dominican Republic (ctry.) 183/H4
Dommartin-lès-Remiremont, Fr. 98/C2
Dommartin-lès-Toul, Fr. 95/E6
Dommel (riv.), Belg. 95/E1
Domodedovo (int'l arpt.), Rus. 103/W9
Domodossola, It. 99/E5
Domohāni, India 127/G2
Domont, Fr. 72/J4
Dompu, Indo. 123/E5
Domrémy-la-Pucelle, Fr. 98/B1
Dömsöd, Hun. 90/D2
Domusnovas, It. 88/A3
Domuyo (vol.), Arg. 200/C3
Domville (mt.), Austl. 156/C5
Domžale, Slov. 85/L3
Don (riv.), Eng, UK 77/G5
Don (ridge), Rus. 106/E5
Don (riv.), Rus. 69/J4
Don Benito, Sp. 86/C3
Donabate, Ire. 76/B5
Donada, It. 101/F2
Donaghadee, NI, UK 76/C2
Donaghmore, NI, UK 76/B2
Donald, Austl. 157/B3
Donaldsonville, La, US 171/K5
Doñana NP, Sp. 86/B4
Donath, Swi. 99/F4
Donau (Danube) (riv.), Ger. 85/H2
Donaueschingen, Ger. 99/E2
Donauwörth, Ger. 96/D5
Doncaster, Eng, UK 77/G4
Doncaster (co.), Eng, UK 77/G4
Donchery, Fr. 95/D4
Dondra Head (pt.), SrL. 124/D6
Donegal, Ire. 73/P9
Donegal (dist.), Ire. 76/A1
Donegal (bay), Ire. 73/P9
Donets (riv.), Rus., Ukr. 105/G2
Donets'k, Ukr. 104/F2
Donets'k (int'l arpt.), Ukr. 104/F2
Donets'ka Oblasti, Ukr. 104/F3
Dong (riv.), Viet. 125/J5
Dong Ha, Viet. 120/D2
Dong Hoi, Viet. 120/D2
Dong Noi (riv.), Viet. 120/D4
Donga (riv.), Nga. 145/H4
Dongar Parāsia, India 126/B4
Dongara, Austl. 154/B4
Dongbei (plain), China 114/E2
Dongchuan, China 125/H2
Dong'e, China 114/D3
Dongen, Neth. 92/B5
Dongfang, China 125/J4
Donggou, China 115/C3
Dongguan, China 125/K3
Dongguang, China 114/D3
Donghai, China 114/D4
Dongio, Swi. 99/E5
Dongkya (pass), China 127/G2
Donglan, China 121/A3
Dongliao (riv.), China 114/F2
Dongming, China 114/C4
Dongo, It. 99/F5
Dongping, China 114/D4
Dongsha (isl.), China 121/C3
Dongshan, China 121/C3
Dongtai, China 114/E4
Dongtiao (riv.), China 114/L9
Dongting (lake), China 121/B2
Dongzhi, China 121/C1
Donihue, Chile 200/N9
Donjek (riv.), Yk, Can. 164/C2
Donji Komren, Serb. 90/E4
Donji Vakuf, Bosn. 90/C3
Donnas, It. 100/A1
Donnersberg (peak), Ger. 95/G4
Donnybrook, Austl. 156/D4
Donnybrook, Austl. 154/B5
Donon (peak), Fr. 98/D1
Donoratico, It. 85/J5
Donzdorf, Ger. 96/C5
Donzy, Fr. 84/E3
Dooleena (peak), Austl. 154/C2
Doon (riv.), Sc, UK 78/B6
Doon (lake), Sc, UK 78/B6
Doonbeg, Ire. 73/P10
Doonerak (mt.), Ak, US 176/H2
Door (pen.), Wi, US 169/M4
Doorn (riv.), SAfr. 148/B3
Doorn, Neth. 92/C4
Doppo (peak), It. 100/D1
Doqên (lake), China 127/G1
Dora (lake), Austl. 151/B3
Dora Riparia (riv.), It. 85/G4
Dorada (coast), Sp. 87/F2
Dorchester, NB, Can. 173/H2
Dorchester, Il, US 179/H7
Dorchester, Eng, UK 74/D5
Dorchester (cape), Nun., Can. 165/J2
Dorchester, NJ, US 180/D5
Dordogne (riv.), Fr. 84/D4
Dordrecht, SAfr. 148/D3
Dordrecht, Neth. 92/B5
Dore (lake), Sk, Can. 168/G2
Dore, Monts (mts.), Fr. 84/E4
Dores do Indaiá, Braz. 197/C1
Dorfen, Ger. 97/F6
Dorfen (riv.), Ger. 97/E6
Dorgali, It. 88/A2
Dori, Burk. 145/E3
Dorion, Qu, Can. 173/M7
Dorking, Eng, UK 72/C3
Dorlisheim, Fr. 98/D1
Dormagen, Ger. 95/F1
Dormans, Fr. 94/C5
Dornach, Swi. 98/D3
Dornbirn, Aus. 99/F3
Dorney Park/ Wildwater Kingdom, Pa, US 180/C2
Dornhan, Ger. 99/E1
Dorno, It. 100/B2
Dornoch Firth (inlet), Sc, UK 78/B1
Dornod (prov.), Mong. 113/K2
Dornogovĭ (prov.), Mong. 113/J3
Dornstadt, Ger. 96/C6
Dornstetten, Ger. 96/B6
Dorog, Hun. 91/Q9
Dorothy, NJ, US 180/D5
Dörpen, Ger. 93/E3
Dorre (isl.), Austl. 154/B3
Dorrigo, Austl. 157/E1
Dorrigo NP, Austl. 157/E1
Dorsale (mts.), Tun. 142/L7
Dorsbach (riv.), Ger. 96/B2
Dorset (co.), Eng, UK 74/D5
Dorsey, Il, US 179/G8
Dorsten, Ger. 92/D5
Dortan, Fr. 98/B5
Dortmund, Ger. 93/E5
Dortmund-Ems (canal), Ger. 93/E4
Dortmund (Wickede) (int'l arpt.), Ger. 93/E5
Dörtyol, Turk. 133/E1
Dorum, Ger. 93/F1
Dorval, Qu, Can. 173/N7
Dörverden, Ger. 93/G3
Dos Bahias (cape), Arg. 200/D5
Dos de Mayo, Peru 198/C2
Dos Hermanas, Sp. 86/C4
Döşemealtı, Turk. 133/B1
Dosewallips (riv.), Wa, US 177/A2
Dōshi, Japan 119/C2
Dōshi (riv.), Japan 119/C2
Dosse (riv.), Ger. 82/G2
Dosso, Niger 145/F3
Dosso (dept.), Niger 145/F3
Dosson, It. 101/F1
Dossor, Kaz. 105/K3
Dot Lake, Ak, US 176/K3
Dothan, Al, US 175/G4
Dötlingen, Ger. 93/F3
Döttingen, Swi. 99/E2
Douai, Fr. 94/C3
Douala, Camr. 138/G7
Douar el Cäid el Gueddara, Mor. 142/A2
Douar Toulal, Mor. 142/B3
Douarnenez, Fr. 84/A2
Douarnenez, Baie de (bay), Fr. 84/A2
Double Island (pt.), Austl. 156/D4
Double Mountain Fork Brazos (riv.), Tx, US 171/G4
Doubs (riv.), Fr. 84/F3
Doubs (dept.), Fr. 98/C3
Doubs, Fr. 98/C4
Doubtful Island (bay), Austl. 154/C5
Douchy-les-Mines, Fr. 94/C3
Doue, Fr. 72/M5
Doué-la-Fontaine, Fr. 84/C3
Douentza, Mali 144/E3
Dougga (ruin), Tun. 142/L6
Douglas, SAfr. 148/C3
Douglas (cap.), IM, UK 76/D3
Douglas, Sc, UK 78/C5
Douglas (mt.), Ak, US 176/H4
Douglas (co.), Co, US 179/C4
Douglas, Ga, US 175/H4
Douglas, Wy, US 169/G5
Douglassville, Pa, US 180/C3
Doulaincourt-Saucourt, Fr. 98/B1
Doullens, Fr. 94/B3
Doune, Sc, UK 78/B4
Doune (peak), Sc, UK 78/B4
Doupovské Hory (mts.), Czh. 85/K1
Dour, Belg. 95/D3
Dourados, Braz. 193/H8
Dourdan, Fr. 72/J6
Dourdou (riv.), Fr. 84/E4
Dourh (peak), Mor. 141/E2
Douro (riv.), Port. 86/B2
Dousman, Wi, US 177/P13
Doussard, Fr. 98/C6
Douvaine, Fr. 98/C5
Douvrin, Fr. 94/B2
Doux (riv.), Fr. 84/F4
Douze (riv.), Fr. 84/C4
Dove Creek, Co, US 170/E3
Dover, Austl. 157/C4
Dover (pt.), Austl. 154/E5
Dover, Eng, UK 75/H4
Dover (cap.), De, US 180/C5
Dover, NJ, US 180/D2
Dover, Pa, US 180/B4
Dover-Foxcroft, Me, US 173/G2
Dover, Strait of (str.), Fr.,UK 75/H5
Dovrefjell NP, Nor. 79/D3
Dow, Il, US 179/G7
Dowerin, Austl. 154/C4
Dowlatābād, Iran 131/G3
Down (dist.), NI, UK 76/C3
Downers Grove, Il, US 177/P16
Downey, Ca, US 178/F8
Downieville, Ca, US 170/B3
Downingtown, Pa, US 180/C4
Downpatrick, NI, UK 76/C3
Doylestown, Pa, US 180/C3
Dōzen (isl.), Japan 116/C3
Dozois (res.), Qu, Can. 172/E2
Drâa (cape), Mor. 140/C3
Drâa, Oued (riv.), Mor. 140/C3
Drac (riv.), Fr. 84/F4
Dracena, Braz. 197/B2
Drachten, Neth. 92/D2
Drăgăneşti-Olt, Rom. 91/G3
Dragoman, Bul. 89/H1
Dragon's Mouth (str.), Trin.,Ven. 195/F2
Draguignan, Fr. 85/G5
Drake (passg.) 199/C8
Drake, Co, US 179/B2
Drake (passg.), SAm. 201/D8
Drakensberg (mts.), SAfr. 148/D3
Dráma, Gre. 89/J2
Drammen, Nor. 80/D2
Drance (riv.), Swi. 98/D5
Drancy, Fr. 72/K5
Drangedal, Nor. 80/C2
Dranse (riv.), Fr. 98/C5
Dransfeld, Ger. 93/G5
Draper, Ut, US 179/K12
Drau (riv.), Aus. 85/K3
Dráva (riv.), Aus. 90/C3
Drava (riv.), Slov. 85/L3
Draveil, Fr. 72/K5
Drawa (riv.), Pol. 83/H2
Drawienski NP, Pol. 83/H2
Drawsko Pomorskie, Pol. 83/H2
Drayton, ND, US 169/J3
Drayton Valley, Ab, Can. 168/E2
Dreghorn, Sc, UK 78/B5
Drei Zinnen (peak), PNG 123/K4
Dreiesselberg (peak), Ger. 97/G5
Dreisam (riv.), Ger. 98/D2
Drensteinfurt, Ger. 93/E5
Drenthe (prov.), Neth. 92/D3
Drentse Hoofdvaart (riv.), Neth. 92/D3
Drentwede, Ger. 93/F3
Dresano, It. 100/C2
Dresden, Ger. 83/G3
Drezdenko, Pol. 83/H2
Driebergen, Neth. 92/C4
Driedorf, Ger. 95/H2
Drigh Road, Pak. 131/J4
Drimoleague, Ire. 73/P11
Drina (riv.), Bosn., Serb. 90/D4
Drinit (gulf), Alb. 89/F2
Drinit (riv.), Alb. 89/F1
Drniš, Cro. 90/C4
Dro, It. 99/G6
Drøbak, Nor. 80/D2
Drobeta-Turnu Severin, Rom. 90/F3
Drochtersen, Ger. 93/G1
Drocourt, Fr. 72/H4
Drogheda, Ire. 76/B5
Drohobych, Ukr. 104/B2
Droitwich, Eng, UK 74/D2
Drolshagen, Ger. 95/G1
Dromiskin, Ire. 76/B4
Dromore (riv.), Ire. 76/A3
Dromore, NI, UK 76/B3
Dronero, It. 85/G4
Dronfield, Eng, UK 77/G5
Drongan, Sc, UK 78/B6
Dronne (riv.), Fr. 84/D4
Dronten, Neth. 92/C3
Dropt (riv.), Fr. 84/D4
Drouette (riv.), Fr. 94/A6
Drowning (riv.), On, Can. 172/C1
Drumbeg, NI, UK 76/C2
Drumcar, Ire. 76/B4
Drumheller, Ab, Can. 168/E3
Drumleck (pt.), Ire. 76/B5
Drummond (range), Austl. 151/D3
Drummond (pt.), Austl. 155/G5
Drummond (mt.), Austl. 156/B4
Drummondville, Qu, Can. 173/F2
Drumochter, Pass of (pass), Sc, UK 78/B3
Drunen, Neth. 92/C5
Druridge (bay), Eng, UK 77/G1
Drusenheim, Fr. 95/G6
Druskininkai, Lith. 81/K4
Druten, Neth. 92/C5
Drvar, Bosn. 90/C3
Drwęca (riv.), Pol. 83/K2
Dry Fork Cheyenne (riv.), Wy, US 171/F2
Dry Tortugas (isl.), Fl, US 175/H5
Dry Tortugas NP, Fl, US 175/H5
Dryanovo, Bul. 89/J1
Dryden, On, Can. 169/K3
Dryden, Tx, US 174/C4
Dryden, Mi, US 177/F6
Drygarn Fawr (peak), Wal, UK 74/C2
Du Bois, Pa, US 172/E3
Du Page (co.), Il, US 177/P16
Du Page (riv.), Il, US 177/P16
Du Page, East Br. (riv.), Il, US 177/P16
Du Quoin, Il, US 171/K3
Duaringa, Austl. 156/C3
Duarte (peak), DRep. 183/G4
Duarte, Ca, US 178/G7
Dubawnt (riv.), NW, Can. 164/F2
Dubawnt (lake), Nun., Can. 164/F2
Dubayy, UAE 131/G3
Dubbo, Austl. 157/D2
Dübendorf, Swi. 99/E3
Dübener Heide (phys. reg.), Ger. 82/G3
Dubino, It. 99/F5
Dublin (cap.), Ire. 76/B5
Dublin (co.), Ire. 76/B5
Dublin, Ca, US 177/L11
Dublin, Ga, US 175/H3
Dublin, Md, US 180/B4
Dublin, Pa, US 180/C3
Dubna, Rus. 102/H4
Dubnica nad Váhom, Slvk. 83/K4
Dubno, Ukr. 104/C2
Dubois, Wy, US 168/F5
Duboistown, Pa, US 180/A1
Dubossary (res.), Mol. 91/J2
Dubrājpur, India 127/F4
Dubrovnik, Cro. 89/F1
Dubrovnik (int'l arpt.), Cro. 89/F1
Dubuque, Ia, US 169/L5
Duchang, China 121/C2
Duchcov, Czh. 97/G1
Duchesne (riv.), Ut, US 170/E2
Duchesne, Ut, US 170/E2
Ducie (isl.), Pitc. 159/N7
Duck (riv.), Tn, US 172/C5
Duck (lake), Mi, US 177/E7
Duckabush (riv.), Wa, US 177/A2
Duda (riv.), Col. 194/C4
Duddon (riv.), Eng, UK 77/E3
Dudelange, Lux. 95/F5
Dudenhofen, Ger. 96/B4
Duderstadt, Ger. 93/H5
Dudh Kosi (riv.), Nepal 127/F2
Dūdhi, India 126/D3
Dudhwa NP, India 126/C1
Dudignac, Arg. 200/E2
Düdingen, Swi. 98/D4
Dudinka, Rus. 106/J3
Dudley, Eng, UK 74/D1
Dudley (co.), Eng, UK 74/D2
Dueñas, Sp. 86/C2
Duero (riv.), Sp. 86/C2
Dueville, It. 101/E1
Dufaja (riv.), Kenya 146/C3
Duff (isls.), Sol. 158/F5
Duffel, Belg. 95/D1
Dufftown, Sc, UK 78/C2
Dufour (Dufourspitze) (peak), Swi. 100/A1
Dufourspitze (peak), Swi. 85/G4
Dugi Otok (isl.), Cro. 90/B3
Dugny-sur-Meuse, Fr. 95/E5
Dugo Selo, Cro. 90/C3
Dugway, Ut, US 170/D2
Duich (lake), Sc, UK 78/A2
Duida (peak), Ven. 195/E4
Duida Marahuaca, PN, Ven. 192/E3
Duingen, Ger. 93/G4
Duisburg, Ger. 92/D6
Duitama, Col. 194/C3
Duiven, Neth. 92/D5
Duke of Gloucester (isls.), FrPol. 159/L7
Duke's (pass), Sc, UK 78/B4
Dukielska (Dukla Pass) (pass), Pol. 83/L4
Dulan, China 112/G4
Dulce (riv.), Arg. 199/D2
Dulce, NM, US 170/F3
Dulce (gulf), Pan. 187/F4
Dulce Nombre de Culmí, Hon. 187/E3
Duleek, Ire. 76/B4
Dŭlgopol, Bul. 91/H4
Duliu (riv.), China 125/J2
Dullewāla, Pak. 128/A4
Dülmen, Ger. 93/E5
Dulnain (riv.), Sc, UK 78/C2
Dulovo, Bul. 91/H4
Dumalinao, Phil. 121/D6
Dumaran (isl.), Phil. 123/E1
Dumaresq (riv.), Austl. 157/D1
Dumas, Ar, US 171/K4
Dumas, Tx, US 171/G4
Dumbarton, Sc, UK 78/B5
Ďumbier (peak), Slvk. 83/K4
Dumbleyung, Austl. 154/C5
Dumbrăveni, Rom. 91/G2
Dume (pt.), Ca, US 178/B2
Dumfries, Sc, UK 76/E1
Dumfries and Galloway (pol. reg.), Sc, UK 78/C6
Dumka, India 127/F3
Dumlu, Turk. 105/G4
Dümmer (lake), Ger. 93/F3
Dumoine (riv.), Qu, Can. 172/E2
Dumoine (lake), Qu, Can. 165/J4
Dumont, NJ, US 181/K8
Dumont d'Urville, Fr., Ant. 202/K
Dumraon, India 127/E3
Dumyāt (gov.), Egypt 143/B1
Dún Laoghaire, Ire. 76/B5
Dun Rig (peak), Sc, UK 78/C5
Dunaföldvár, Hun. 90/D2
Dunaharaszti, Hun. 91/R10
Dunajec (riv.), Pol. 83/L4
Dunakeszi, Hun. 91/R9
Dunany (pt.), Ire. 76/B4
Dunaszekcso, Hun. 90/D2
Dunaújváros, Hun. 90/D2
Dunavecse, Hun. 90/D2
Dunavtsi, Bul. 90/F4
Dunbar, Sc, UK 78/D5
Dunblane, Sc, UK 78/C4
Dunboyne, Ire. 76/B5
Duncan, BC, Can. 168/C3
Duncan, Ok, US 171/H4
Duncannon, Pa, US 180/A3
Duncansby Head (pt.), Sc, UK 73/V14
Duncanville, Tx, US 174/D3
Dund-Us, Mong. 112/F2
Dundalk (bay), Ire. 73/Q10
Dundalk, Md, US 180/B5
Dundalk, Ire. 76/B4
Dundas (lake), Austl. 151/B4
Dundas, On, Can. 173/Q9
Dundas (pen.), NW, Can. 165/R7
Dundee, SAfr. 149/E3
Dundee, Sc, UK 78/D4
Dundee (pol. reg.), Sc, UK 78/D4
Dundgovi (prov.), Mong. 112/J2
Dundonald, Sc, UK 78/B5
Dundrum, NI, UK 76/C3
Dundrum (bay), NI, UK 76/C3
Dundurn, Sk, Can. 168/G3
Dundwa (range), Nepal 126/D2
Dundwārāganj, India 126/B2
Dunedin, Fl, US 175/H4
Dunedin, NZ 159/S12
Dunedoo, Austl. 157/D2
Dunellen, NJ, US 181/H9
Dunfanaghy, Ire. 73/Q9
Dunfermline, Sc, UK 78/C4
Dunga Bunga, Pak. 128/B5
Dungannon, NI, UK 76/B3
Dungannon (co.), NI, UK 76/B3
Dungarpur, India 131/K4
Dungarvan, Ire. 73/Q10
Dungau (reg.), Ger. 97/F5
Dungeness (pt.), Eng, UK 75/G5
Dungeness (pt.), Arg. 201/C7
Dungiven, NI, UK 76/B2
Dunglow, Ire. 73/P9
Dungog, Austl. 157/D2
Dungu, D.R. Congo 146/A2
Dungu (riv.), D.R. Congo 146/A2
Dunhua, China 113/N3
Dunhuang, China 112/F3
Dunkeld, Sc, UK 78/C3
Dunkerque (Dunkirk), Fr. 84/E1
Dunkery (hill), Eng, UK 74/C4
Dunkirk (Dunkerque), Fr. 84/E1
Dunkwa, Gha. 145/E5
Dunleer, Ire. 76/B4
Dunloy, NI, UK 76/B2
Dunmanway, Ire. 73/P11
Dunmurry, NI, UK 76/B2
Dunn, NC, US 175/J3
Dunnamanagh, NI, UK 76/A2
Dünnern (riv.), Swi. 98/D3
Dunnet Head (pt.), Sc, UK 73/V14
Dunningen, Ger. 99/E1
Dunnville, On, Can. 173/Q10
Dunolly, Austl. 157/B3
Dunoon, Sc, UK 78/B5
Dunqulah, Sudan 143/B5
Duns, Sc, UK 78/D5
Dunsborough, Austl. 154/B5
Dunseith, ND, US 169/H3
Dunshaughlin, Ire. 76/B4
Dunsmuir, Ca, US 170/B2
Dunstable, Eng, UK 75/F3
Dunyāpur, Pak. 128/A5
Duolun, China 113/L3
Dupo, Il, US 179/G8
Dupont, Pa, US 180/C1
Dupree, SD, US 169/H4
Dupuy (cape), Austl. 154/B2
Duque de Caxias, Braz. 197/K7
Duque de York (isl.), Chile 201/A6
Dūrā, WBnk. 133/D4
Durağan, Turk. 132/C1
Durak, Turk. 133/D1
Durance (riv.), Fr. 84/F5
Durango (state), Mex. 182/A3
Durango, Sp. 86/D1
Durango de Victoria, Mex. 184/D3
Durant, Ok, US 171/H4
Durazno (dept.), Uru. 201/F2
Durazno, Uru. 201/K10
Durban, SAfr. 149/E3
Durbanville, SAfr. 148/L10
Durbion (riv.), Fr. 98/C1
Durbuy, Belg. 95/E3
Dúrcal, Sp. 86/D4
Durdevac, Cro. 90/C2
Durdevo, Serb. 90/E3
Düren, Ger. 95/F2
Durg, India 124/D3
Durgāpur, India 127/F4
Durham, NH, US 173/G3
Durham, NC, US 175/J3
Durham, Eng, UK 77/G2
Durham (co.), Eng, UK 77/F2
Durlston (pt.), Eng, UK 74/E5
Durmitor NP, Mont. 90/D4
Durnford (pt.), WSah. 140/B5
Dürrenroth, Swi. 98/D3
Durrës, Alb. 89/F2
Dürrlauingen, Ger. 96/D6
Dürrwangen, Ger. 96/D4
Dursunbey, Turk. 132/B2
Durūz (peak), Syria 133/E3
D'Urville (cape), Indo. 123/J4
Dusanovac, Serb. 90/E4
Dusey (riv.), On, Can. 169/M3
Dushan, China 125/J2
Dushanbe (cap.), Taj. 129/E5
Dushanbe (int'l arpt.), Taj. 129/E5
Düsseldorf (int'l arpt.), Ger. 92/D6
Düsseldorf, Ger. 92/D6
Duszniki-Zdrój, Pol. 83/J3
Dutch (riv.), Eng, UK 77/H4
Dutch Harbor, Ak, US 176/E5
Dutch Wonderland, Pa, US 180/B3
Dutoitspiek (peak), SAfr. 148/L10
Dutse, Nga. 145/H4
Duvall, Wa, US 177/D2
Duvno, Bosn. 90/C4
Duyun, China 125/J2
Düzce, Turk. 91/K5
Düzici, Turk. 132/D2
Dve Mogili, Bul. 91/G4
Dvina (bay), Rus. 102/H2
Dvořiště (lake), Czh. 97/H4
Dwārka, India 131/J4
Dwārkeswar (riv.), India 127/F4
Dworshak (res.), Id, US 168/D4
Dwyfor (riv.), Wal, UK 76/D6
Dwyka (riv.), SAfr. 148/C4
Dyat'kovo, Rus. 104/E1
Dybvad, Den. 80/D3
Dyce (int'l arpt.), Sc, UK 78/D2
Dyce, Sc, UK 78/D2
Dye, Mo, US 179/D5
Dyer (cape), Nun., Can. 165/K2
Dyer (cape), Chile 201/B6
Dyer, In, US 172/C3
Dyfi (riv.), Wal, UK 74/C1
Dyje (riv.), Czh. 83/J4
Dykh-tau (peak), Rus. 105/G4
Dyle (riv.), Belg. 82/C3
Dyleň (peak), Czh. 97/F3
Dylewska (peak), Pol. 83/K2
Dysart, Austl. 156/C3
Dysselsdorp, SAfr. 148/C4
Dyul'tydag (peak), Rus. 105/H4
Dzaoudzi (cap.), May. 149/H6
Dzaoudzi (int'l arpt.), May. 149/H6
Dzavhan (prov.), Mong. 112/G2
Dzavhan (riv.), Mong. 112/F2
Dzenzik (pt.), Ukr. 104/F3
Dzerzhinsk, Rus. 102/J4
Dzhankoy, Ukr. 104/E3
Dzharylgach (gulf), Ukr. 91/L2
Dzhebel, Bul. 89/J2
Dzhugdzhur (range), Rus. 109/N4
Działdowo, Pol. 83/L2
Dzibalchén, Mex. 186/D2

Dzibi – Elsme
233

Dzibilchaltún (ruin), Mex. 186/D1
Dzidzantún, Mex. 186/D1
Dzierżoniów, Pol. 83/J3
Dzitbalché, Mex. 186/D1
Dziuché, Mex. 186/D2
Dzukija NP, Lith. 81/L4
Dzungarian (basin), China 112/E3
Dzur, Mong. 112/G2
Dzüünbayan, Mong. 113/K3
Dzüünbulag, Mong. 113/K2
Dzüünharaa, Mong. 112/J2
Dzuunmod, Mong. 112/J2

E

Eads, Co, US 171/G3
Eagle (riv.), Nf, Can. 165/L3
Eagle (lake), On, Can. 172/A1
Eagle, Ak, US 176/K3
Eagle (lake), Ca, US 168/C5
Eagle, Co, US 170/F3
Eagle (mtn.), Mn, US 169/L4
Eagle, Wi, US 177/P14
Eagle (lake), Wi, US 169/K3
Eagle Butte, SD, US 169/H4
Eagle Pass, Tx, US 174/C4
Eagle River, Wi, US 169/L4
Eaglesham, Sc, UK 78/B5
Ealing (bor.), Eng, UK 72/B2
Ear Falls, On, Can. 169/K3
Earle Naval Weapons Center, NJ, US 180/D3
Earlimart, Ca, US 170/C4
Earl's Seat (peak), Sc, UK 78/B4
Earlston, Sc, UK 78/D5
Earn (riv.), Sc, UK 78/C4
Earn (lake), Sc, UK 78/B4
Easley, SC, US 175/H3
East (mt.), Austl. 154/D4
East (cape), NZ 159/T10
East (cape), Ak, US 176/B6
East (pt.), NJ, US 180/C5
East (riv.), NY, US 181/K8
East (passg.), Wa, US 177/C3
East Alton, Il, US 179/G8
East Anglia (reg.), Eng, UK 75/H2
East Angus, Qu, Can. 173/G2
East Ayrshire (pol. reg.), Sc, UK 78/B6
East Bangor, Pa, US 180/C2
East Berbice-Corentyne (pol. reg.), Guy. 195/G3
East Berlin, Pa, US 180/B4
East Berwick, Pa, US 180/B1
East Brunswick, NJ, US 181/H10
East Caicos (isl.), UK 187/J1
East Canyon (res.), Ut, US 179/K12
East Carondelet, Il, US 179/G8
East China (sea), Asia 109/M6
East Dart (riv.), Eng, UK 74/C5
East Dereham, Eng, UK 75/G1
East Dunbartonshire (pol. reg.), Sc, UK 78/B5
East Falkland (isl.), UK 201/F7
East Farmingdale, NY, US 181/M9
East Frisian (isls.), Ger. 82/D2
East Glen (riv.), Eng, UK 77/H6
East Greenville, Pa, US 180/C3
East Grinstead, Eng, UK 75/F4
East Hampton, NY, US 181/F2
East Haven, Ct, US 181/F1
East Helena, Mt, US 168/F4
East Hill-Meridian, Wa, US 177/C3
East Hills, NY, US 181/L8
East Jordan, Mi, US 172/C2
East Kilbride, Sc, UK 78/B5
East Lamma (chan.), China 113/U11
East Lansing, Mi, US 172/C3
East Leavenworth, Mo, US 179/D5
East Linton, Sc, UK 78/D5
East Liverpool, Oh, US 172/D3
East London, SAfr. 148/D4
East Los Angeles, Ca, US 178/F7
East Lothian (pol. reg.), Sc, UK 78/D5
East Lynne, Mo, US 179/E6
East Meadow, NY, US 181/L9
East Midlands (int'l arpt.), Eng, UK 77/G6
East Millcreek, Ut, US 179/K12
East Millinocket, Me, US 173/G2
East Newark, NJ, US 181/J9
East Newbern, Il, US 179/G7
East Nishnabotna (riv.), Ia, US 171/J2
East Northport, NY, US 181/E2
East Orange, NJ, US 181/J8
East Peckham, Eng, UK 72/E3
East Petersburg, Pa, US 180/B3
East Point, Ga, US 175/G3
East Pointe (East Detroit), Mi, US 177/G7
East Port Orchard, Wa, US 177/B2
East Prospect, Pa, US 180/B4
East Quogue, NY, US 181/F2
East Renfrewshire (pol. reg.), Sc, UK 78/B5
East Retford, Eng, UK 77/H5
East Riding of Yorkshire (co.), Eng, UK 77/H4
East Rockaway, NY, US 181/L9
East Rutherford, NJ, US 181/J8
East Saint Louis, Il, US 179/G8
East Siberian (sea), Rus. 107/S2
East Side, Pa, US 180/C1
East Stroudsburg, Pa, US 180/C2
East Sussex (co.), Eng, UK 75/G5
East Tawas, Mi, US 172/D2
East Timor (ctry.) 123/G5
East Troy, Wi, US 177/P14
East Wemyss, Sc, UK 78/C4
East Wenatchee, Wa, US 168/C4
East Windsor, NJ, US 180/D3
East York, Can. 173/R8
Eastbourne, Eng, UK 75/G5
Eastern (plain), Eng, UK 77/H4
Eastern (pol. reg.), Gha. 145/E5
Eastern (chan.), Japan 116/A4
Eastern (prov.), SLeo. 144/C4
Eastern (bay), Md, US 180/B6
Eastern (prov.), Zam. 146/B5
Eastern Ghats (mts.), India 124/C5
Eastern Neck Island NWR, Md, US 180/B5
Eastern Sayans (mts.), Rus. 106/K4
Easterville, Mb, Can. 169/J2
Eastlake, Co, US 179/C3
Eastleigh (int'l arpt.), Eng, UK 75/E5
Eastleigh, Eng, UK 75/E5
Eastmain (riv.), Qu, Can. 165/J3
Eastman, Ga, US 175/H3
Easton, Ct, US 181/E1
Easton (res.), Ct, US 181/E1
Easton, Pa, US 180/C2
Eastport, Me, US 173/H2
Eastport, NY, US 181/F2
Eastriggs, Sc, UK 77/E2
Eastwood, Eng, UK 77/G6
Eaton, Co, US 179/C1
Eatonia, Sk, Can. 168/F3
Eatons Neck (pt.), NY, US 181/M8
Eatontown, NJ, US 180/D3
Eau (riv.), Eng, UK 77/H5
Eau Claire (lake), Qu, Can. 165/J3
Eau d'Heure (riv.), Belg. 95/D3
Eau d'Heure, Barrage de l' (dam), Belg. 95/D3
Eaubonne, Fr. 72/J5
Eaulne (riv.), Fr. 94/A4
Eauripik (isl.), Micr. 158/D4
Eauze, Fr. 84/D5
Ebano, Mex. 186/B1
Ebble (riv.), Eng, UK 75/E4
Ebbw Vale, Wal, UK 74/C3
Ebebiyín, EqG. 138/H7
Ebeggi (well), Alg. 141/G5
Ebeleben, Ger. 93/H6
Ebeltoft, Den. 80/D3
Ebensee, Aus. 85/K3
Eberbach, Ger. 96/B4
Ebergassing, Aus. 91/P7
Ebergötzen, Ger. 93/H5
Ebermannstadt, Ger. 96/E3
Ebern, Ger. 96/D2
Ebersbach an der Fils, Ger. 96/C5
Ebersberg, Ger. 97/E6
Eberschwang, Aus. 97/G6
Ebersheim, Fr. 98/D1
Eberswalde-Finow, Ger. 83/G2
Ebetsu, Japan 118/B2
Ebian, China 125/H2
Ebina, Japan 119/C3
Ebnat-Kappel, Swi. 99/F3
Eboli, It. 88/D2
Ebolowa, Camr. 138/H7
Ebon (isl.), Mrsh. 158/F4
Ebonyi (state), Nga. 145/H5
Ebrach, Ger. 96/D3
Ebreichsdorf, Aus. 91/N8
Ebro (riv.), Sp. 87/F2
Ebstorf, Ger. 93/H2
Ecatepec, Mex. 185/Q9
Ecclefechan, Sc, UK 77/E1
Eccles, Eng, UK 77/F5
Eceabat, Turk. 91/H5
Echallens, Swi. 98/C4
Echarate, Peru 198/C4
Echaz (riv.), Ger. 96/C6
Éché Fadadinga (riv.), Niger 145/H3
Echigawa, Japan 119/K5
Eching, Ger. 97/E6
Échirolles, Fr. 84/F4
Echo (lake), NJ, US 180/D1
Echo, Ut, US 179/L12
Echoing (riv.), Mb,On, Can. 169/L2
Echt, Neth. 95/E1
Echterdingen (int'l arpt.), Ger. 96/C5
Echternach, Lux. 95/F4
Echuca, Austl. 157/C3
Echunga, Austl. 155/M9
Echzell, Ger. 96/B2
Écija, Sp. 86/C4
Ečka, Serb. 90/E3
Eckernförde, Ger. 80/C4
Eckerö (isl.), Fin. 81/H1
Eckerö, Fin. 81/H1
Eclipse Sound (bay), Nun., Can. 165/H1
Écommoy, Fr. 84/D3
Ecoporanga, Braz. 196/B5
Ecorse (riv.), Mi, US 177/F7
Ecorse, Mi, US 177/F7
Écouen, Fr. 72/K4
Ecquevilly, Fr. 72/H5
Ecrins, PN des, Fr. 85/G4
Ecrosnes, Fr. 72/H6
Écrouves, Fr. 95/E6
Ecuador (ctry.) 192/C4
Ecublens, Swi. 98/C4
Ed, Swe. 80/D2
Eday (isl.), Sc, UK 73/V14
Eddystone (pt.), Austl. 157/D4
Eddystone Rocks (isls.), Eng, UK 74/B6
Ede, Nga. 145/G5
Ede, Neth. 92/C4
Edéa, Camr. 138/H7
Edegem, Belg. 95/D1
Edehin Ouarene (des.), Alg. 141/G4
Edéia, Braz. 197/B1
Edelény, Hun. 83/L4
Edemissen, Ger. 93/H4
Eden, Austl. 157/D3
Eden (riv.), Sc, UK 78/D4
Eden, NC, US 172/E4
Eden, Ut, US 179/K11
Edenbridge, Eng, UK 72/D3
Edenburg, SAfr. 148/D3
Edendale, SAfr. 149/E3
Edenhope, Austl. 157/B3
Edenkoben, Ger. 96/B4
Edenside (valley), Eng, UK 77/F2
Edenton, NC, US 175/J2
Eder (riv.), Ger. 82/E3
Eder-Stausee (lake), Ger. 93/F6
Edewecht, Ger. 93/E2
Edgar (mt.), Austl. 154/D2
Edge (isl.), Sval. 202/E
Edgecumbe (cape), Ak, US 176/L4
Edgell (isl.), Nun., Can. 165/K2
Edgemere, Md, US 180/B5
Edgemont, Ut, US 179/K13
Edgerton, Wy, US 169/G5
Edgewater, Co, US 179/B3
Edgewater Park, NJ, US 180/D3
Edgewood, Pa, US 180/B2
Edgewood, Md, US 180/B5
Edgewood Arsenal, Md, US 180/B5
Edgewood-North Hill, Wa, US 177/C3
Édhessa, Gre. 89/H2
Edinboro, Pa, US 172/D3
Edinburg, Tx, US 174/D5
Edinburgh (cap.), Sc, UK 78/C5
Edinburgh (pol. reg.), Sc, UK 78/C5
Edirne (prov.), Turk. 91/H5
Edirne, Turk. 91/H5
Edison, NJ, US 181/H9
Edison International Field, Ca, US 178/G8
Edison Nat'l Hist. Site, NJ, US 181/J8
Edisto Island, SC, US 175/H3
Edisto, South Fork (riv.), SC, US 175/H3
Edithburgh, Austl. 155/H5
Édjérir (riv.), Mali 145/F2
Edmond, Ok, US 179/N14
Edmonds, Wa, US 168/C4
Edmonton (int'l arpt.), Ab, Can. 168/E2
Edmonton (cap.), Ab, Can. 168/E2
Edmund Kennedy NP, Austl. 156/B2
Edmundston, NB, Can. 173/G2
Edna, Tx, US 171/H5
Edna Bay, Ak, US 176/M4
Edo (state), Nga. 145/G5
Edo (riv.), Japan 119/D2
Edolo, It. 99/G5
Edosaki, Japan 119/E2
Edremit, Turk. 132/A2
Edremit (gulf), Gre.,Turk. 132/A2
Edsbyn, Swe. 80/F1
Edson, Ab, Can. 168/D2
Eduardo Castex, Arg. 200/D2
Edward (mt.), Austl. 155/F2
Edward (lake), D.R. Congo 146/A3
Edward River Aboriginal Community, Austl. 156/A1
Edward VII (pen.), Ant. 202/P
Edward VIII (bay), Ant. 202/D
Edwards (riv.), Il, US 171/K2
Edwards (plat.), Tx, US 171/G5
Edwardsville, Il, US 179/H8
Edwardsville, Ks, US 179/D5
Edwardsville, Pa, US 180/C1
Edzell, Sc, UK 78/D3
Edzná (ruin), Mex. 186/D2
Eek, Ak, US 176/F3
Eeklo, Belg. 94/C1
Eel (riv.), Ca, US 170/B3
Eelde-Paterswolde, Neth. 92/D2
Eem (riv.), Neth. 92/C4
Eemnes, Neth. 92/C4
Eems (Ems) (riv.), Ger., Neth 92/D2
Eemshaven (har.), Neth. 92/D2
Eemskanaal (riv.), Neth. 92/D2
Eersel, Neth. 92/C6
Efate (isl.), Van. 158/F6
Eferding, Aus. 97/H6
Effigy Mounds Nat'l Mon., Ia, US 169/L5
Effingham, Il, US 171/K3
Effingham, On, Can. 173/R9
Effon Alaiye, Nga. 145/G5
Effort, Pa, US 180/C2
Eforie, Rom. 91/J3
Efringen-Kirchen, Ger. 98/D2
Efyrnwy, Llyn (lake), Wal, UK 76/E6
Egadi (isls.), It. 88/B3
Egan (range), Nv, US 170/D3
Egan (riv.), Ger. 96/D5
Egaña, Uru. 201/K10
Egegik, Ak, US 176/G4
Eger (riv.), Ger. 82/G3
Eger, Hun. 83/L5
Egeskov, Den. 80/D4
Egestorf, Ger. 93/H2
Egg, Aus. 99/F3
Egg, Swi. 99/E3
Egg Harbor City, NJ, US 180/D4
Egg Island (pt.), NJ, US 180/C5
Eggebek, Ger. 80/C4
Eggegebirge (ridge), Ger. 93/F5
Eggelsberg, Aus. 97/F6
Eggenburg, Aus. 85/L2
Eggenfelden, Ger. 97/F6
Eggenstein-Leopoldshafen, Ger. 96/B4
Eggesin, Ger. 80/F5
Eggiwil, Swi. 98/D4
Egglescliffe, Eng, UK 77/G3
Eggstätt, Ger. 97/F7
Egham, Eng, UK 72/B2
Éghezée, Belg. 95/D2
Egilsstadhir, Ice. 79/P6
Égletons, Fr. 84/E4
Eglinton (isl.), NW, Can. 165/R7
Eglinton, NI, UK 76/A1
Eglisau, Swi. 99/E2
Égly, Fr. 72/J6
Egmond aan Zee, Neth. 92/B3
Egmont (cape), NZ 159/S10
Egmont (mt.), NZ 159/S10
Egna (Neumarkt), It. 99/H5
Egnach, Swi. 99/F2
Eğridir, Turk. 132/B2
Eğridir (lake), Turk. 132/B2
Éguas, Rio das (riv.), Braz. 196/A4
Egypt (ctry.) 139/L2
Ehebach (riv.), Ger. 96/D3
Ehekirchen, Ger. 96/D5
Ehime (pref.), Japan 116/C4
Ehingen, Ger. 99/F1
Ehingen, Ger. 96/D4
Ehringshausen, Ger. 96/B1
Ehrwald, Aus. 99/G3
Eibar, Sp. 86/D1
Eibelstadt, Ger. 96/C3
Eibenstock, Ger. 97/F1
Eibergen, Neth. 92/D4
Eich, Ger. 96/B3
Eichel (riv.), Fr. 95/G6
Eichenau, Ger. 96/E6
Eichenbühl, Ger. 96/C3
Eichendorf, Ger. 97/F5
Eichenzell, Ger. 96/C2
Eichstätt, Ger. 96/E5
Eichwalde, Ger. 82/Q7
Eicklingen, Ger. 93/H3
Eid, Nor. 79/C3
Eidfjord, Nor. 80/B1
Eidsvold, Austl. 156/C4
Eidsvoll, Nor. 80/D1
Eifel (plat.), Ger. 82/D3
Eiffel Tower, Fr. 72/J5
Eigenji, Japan 119/K5
Eiger (peak), Swi. 98/D4
Eigersund, Nor. 80/A2
Eigg (isl.), Sc, UK 73/Q8
Eight Degree (chan.), India,Mald. 124/B6
Eijerlandse Gat (chan.), Neth. 92/B2
Eijsden, Neth. 95/E2
Eikelandsosen, Nor. 80/A1
Eil, Loch (inlet), Sc, UK 78/A3
Eildon (lake), Austl. 157/C3
Eildon, Austl. 157/C3
Eilerts de Haan (mts.), Sur. 195/G4
Einbeck, Ger. 93/G5
Eindhoven (int'l arpt.), Neth. 92/C6
Eindhoven, Neth. 92/C6
Einsiedeln, Swi. 99/E3
Einville-au-Jard, Fr. 95/F6
Eirunepé, Braz. 198/D2
Eisch (riv.), Lux. 95/E4
Eisenach, Ger. 93/H7
Eisenberg, Ger. 96/B3
Eisenhower Nat'l Hist. Site, Pa, US 180/A4
Eisenhüttenstadt, Ger. 83/H2
Eiserfeld, Ger. 95/G2
Eisfeld, Ger. 96/D2
Eisingen, Ger. 96/C3
Eislingen, Ger. 96/C5
Eitelborn, Ger. 95/G3
Eiter (riv.), Ger. 93/F3
Eitorf, Ger. 95/G2
Eitting, Ger. 97/E6
Ejea de los Caballeros, Sp. 87/E1
Ejeda, Madg. 149/H9
Ejido, Ven. 194/D2
Ejin Horo Qi, China 114/B3
Ejin Qi, China 112/H3
Ejutla de Crespo, Mex. 186/B2
Ekeby, Swe. 80/E3
Ekenäs (Tammisaari), Fin. 81/K2
Ekeren, Belg. 92/B6
Ekhínos, Gre. 89/J2
Ekibastuz, Kaz. 129/G2
Eksjö, Swe. 80/F3
Ekuk, Ak, US 176/G4
Ekwan (riv.), On, Can. 165/H3
Ekwok, Ak, US 176/G4
El Aaiún, WSah. 140/B4
El Aatf (reg.), WSah. 140/B5
El Abiodh Sidi Chrikh, Alg. 141/F2
El 'Açâba (mass.), Mrta. 144/C2
El Affroun, Alg. 142/G4
El Águila, Mex. 174/B5
El Aïoun, Mor. 142/C2
El Alto, Peru 198/A2
El Amparo de Apure, Ven. 194/D3
El Anegado, Ecu. 194/A5
El Aouinet, Alg. 142/K7
El Arahal, Sp. 86/C4
El Arhlaf (well), Mrta. 144/D2
El Astillero, Sp. 86/D1
El Bagre, Col. 194/C3
El Banco, Col. 194/C2
El Barco, Sp. 86/B1
El Barco de Ávila, Sp. 86/C2
El Baúl, Ven. 194/D2
El Bayadh (prov.), Alg. 141/F2
El Bayadh, Alg. 141/F2
El Bolsón, Arg. 200/C4
El Bonillo, Sp. 86/D3
El Borouj, Mor. 140/D2
El Burgo de Osma, Sp. 86/D2
El Cajon, Ca, US 178/D5
El Cajón (res.), Hon. 186/E3
El Calafate, Arg. 201/B6
El Callao, Ven. 195/F3
El Capitan (peak), Mt, US 168/E4
El Carmen, Chile 200/B3
El Carmen, Col. 194/B3
El Carmen, Peru 198/B4
El Carmen de Bolívar, Col. 194/C2
El Casar de Talamanca, Sp. 87/N8
El Centro, Ca, US 170/D4
El Cerrito, Col. 194/B4
El Cerrito, Ca, US 177/K11
El Cerro del Aripo (peak), Trin. 195/F2
El Cerrón (peak), Ven. 194/D2
El Chico, PN, Mex. 185/L6
El Cocuy, Col. 194/C3
El Cocuy, PN, Col. 192/D2
El Colorado, Arg. 199/E2
El Difícil, Col. 194/C2
El Djouf (des.), Mrta. 138/D3
El Dorado, Mex. 184/D3
El Dorado, Ar, US 171/J4
El Dorado, Ks, US 171/H3
El Dorado, Ven. 195/F3
El Eglab (plat.), Alg. 138/D2
El Empedrado, Ven. 194/D2
El Escorial, Sp. 87/M8
El Espinar, Sp. 86/C2
El Eulma, Alg. 142/H4
El Fahs, Tun. 142/L6
El Ferrol, Sp. 86/A1
El Fuerte, Mex. 184/C3
El Fureidîs, Isr. 133/F6
El Gogorrón, PN, Mex. 182/A3
El Golea, Alg. 141/F3
El Golfete (lake), Guat. 186/D3
El Granada, Ca, US 177/K11
El Grullo, Mex. 184/D5
El Guachara, PN, Ven. 195/F2
El Hajeb, Mor. 142/B3
El Hank (cliff), Mali 140/D4
El Harino, Pan. 194/A2
El Harta (well), Alg. 141/E4
El Higo, Mex. 186/B1
El Indio, Tx, US 174/C4
El Jadida, Mor. 140/C2
El Jem, Tun. 142/M7
El Kelaâ des Srarhna, Mor. 140/D2
El Khatt (cliff), Mrta. 138/C3
El Khatt (depr.), Mrta. 144/C2
El Khnâchîch (cliff), Mali 140/E5
El Kroub, Alg. 142/K6
El Kseur, Alg. 142/H4
El Libertador General Bernardo O'Higgins (pol. reg.), Chile 200/N8
El Limón, Mex. 185/F4
El Mahia (phys. reg.), Mali 141/E5
El Maitén, Arg. 200/C4
El Malpais Nat'l Mon., NM, US 170/F4
El Manteco, Ven. 195/F3
El-Menzel, Mor. 142/B3
El Miamo, Ven. 195/F3
El Milia, Alg. 142/J4
El Mirage, Az, US 179/R18
El Mirage, Ca, US 178/C1
El Montcau (peak), Sp. 87/K6
El Monte, Ca, US 178/F7
El Morrito (pt.), Chile 200/C1
El Mrâyer (well), Mrta. 140/C5
El Mreyyé (phys. reg.), Mrta. 144/C2
El Mzereb (well), Mali 140/D4
El Naranjo de Carlos Sarabia, Mex. 185/F4
El Nayar, Mex. 184/D4
El Nevado (peak), Arg. 200/C2
El Nido, Phil. 123/E1
El Olivar Alto, Chile 200/N9
El Oro (prov.), Ecu. 198/A1
El Oued (prov.), Alg. 141/G2
El Oued, Alg. 141/G2
El Palmar, Ven. 195/F3
El Pao, Ven. 195/F2
El Pao, Ven. 195/E2
El Paraíso, Mex. 185/E5
El Paraíso, Hon. 186/E3
El Paso, Tx, US 170/F5
El Paso International (int'l arpt.), Tx, US 171/F5
El Pilar, Ven. 195/F2
El Porvenir, Mex. 184/D2
El Porvenir, Pan. 194/B2
El Potosí, Mex. 185/E3
El Potosí, PN, Mex. 182/B3
El Prat de Llobregat, Sp. 87/L7
El Progreso, Ecu. 198/F7
El Progreso, Guat. 186/D3
El Progreso, Hon. 186/E3
El Progreso Industrial, Mex. 185/Q9
El Puerto de Santa María, Sp. 86/B4
El Quelite, Mex. 184/D4
El Quisco, Chile 200/N8
El Rama, Nic. 187/E3
El Rancho, Co, US 179/B3
El Reno, Ok, US 171/H4
El Rio, Ca, US 178/A2
El Roble, Pan. 194/A2
El Rosario de Arriba, Mex. 184/B2
El Sacromonte, PN, Mex. 185/L7
El Salto, Mex. 184/D4
El Salvador (ctry.) 186/D3
El Salvador, Mex. 185/E3
El Salvador, Cuba 187/H1
El Salvador (int'l arpt.), ESal. 186/D3
El Samán de Apure, Ven. 194/D3
El Sauz, Mex. 184/D2
El Sauzal, Mex. 184/A2
El Segundo, Ca, US 178/F8
El Shab (well), Egypt 143/B4
El Tabo, Chile 200/N8
El Tajín (ruin), Mex. 185/M6
El Tama, PN, Ven. 194/C3
El Tambo, Ecu. 194/B5
El Tarf (prov.), Alg. 142/K6
El Tarf, Alg. 142/L6
El Teleno (peak), Sp. 86/B1
El Tepozteco, PN, Mex. 185/R10
El Tiemblo, Sp. 86/C2
El Tigre, Ven. 195/E2
El Tocuyo, Ven. 194/D2
El Toro, Ca, US 178/C3
El Triunfo, Ecu. 194/B5
El Triunfo, Mex. 186/D2
El Tucuche (peak), Trin. 195/F2
El Tuito, Mex. 184/D4
El Tuparro, PN, Col. 192/E3
El Valle, Pan. 194/A2
El Venado (isl.), Nic. 187/F4
El Viejo (peak), Col. 194/C3
El Viejo, Nic. 186/E3
El Vigía, Ven. 194/D2
El Yagual, Ven. 194/D3
El Yunque (peak), PR 183/M8
El Zacatón, Mex. 184/E4
Elan (riv.), Wal, UK 74/C2
Élancourt, Fr. 72/H5
Elandsrivier (riv.), SAfr. 148/Q12
Elassón, Gre. 89/H3
Elat (int'l arpt.), Isr. 133/D5
Elat, Isr. 133/D5
Eláteia, Gre. 89/H3
Elato (isl.), Micr. 158/D4
Elazığ, Turk. 132/D2
Elazig (prov.), Turk. 132/D2
Elba, Al, US 175/G4
Elba (isl.), It. 85/H5
Elbasan, Alb. 89/G2
Elbbach (riv.), Ger. 95/G2
Elbe (riv.), Ger. 82/F2
Elbe (Labe) (riv.), Czh.,Ger. 83/H2
Elbe-Seitenkanaal (canal), Ger. 93/H2
Elbert (co.), Co, US 179/C4
Elberton, Ga, US 175/H3
Elbeuf, Fr. 84/D2
Elbigenalp, Aus. 99/G3
Elbląg, Pol. 81/H4
Elbow, Sk, Can. 168/G3
El'brus (peak), Rus. 105/G4
Elburg, Neth. 92/C4
Elburn, Il, US 177/N16
Elburz (mts.), Iran 130/E1
Elche, Sp. 87/E3
Elche de la Sierra, Sp. 86/D3
Elchingen, Ger. 96/D6
Elcho (isl.), Austl. 151/C2
Eld (inlet), Wa, US 177/A3
Elda, Sp. 87/E3
Elde (riv.), Ger. 82/G2
Eldersburg, Md, US 180/B5
Eldivan, Turk. 132/C1
Eldon, Wa, US 177/A2
Eldora, Co, US 179/A3
Eldora, NJ, US 180/D5
Eldorado, Arg. 199/F2
Eldorado, Tx, US 171/G5
Eldorado Springs, Co, US 179/B3
Eldoret, Kenya 146/B2
Eleao (peak), Hi, US 166/W13
Elefsís, Gre. 89/H3
Elek, Hun. 90/E2
Elektrostal', Rus. 103/X9
Elena, Arg. 200/D2
Elesbão Veloso, Braz. 196/B2
Eleşkirt, Turk. 132/E2
Eleuthera (isl.), Bahm. 183/F2
Eleven Point (riv.), Mo, US 171/K3
Elevsís (ruin), Gre. 89/N8
Elevtheroúpolis, Gre. 89/J2
Elfershausen, Ger. 96/C2
Elgg, Swi. 99/E3
Elgin, ND, US 169/H4
Elgin, Il, US 169/L5
Elgin, Tx, US 171/H5
Elgin, Sc, UK 78/C1
Elgóibar, Sp. 86/D1
Elgon (Wagagai) (peak), Ugan. 146/B2
Elida, NM, US 174/C3
Elim, Ak, US 176/F3
Elimäki, Fin. 81/M1
Elista, Rus. 105/H3
Elixhausen, Aus. 97/G7
Elizabeth (bay), Namb. 148/A2
Elizabeth, NJ, US 181/J9
Elizabeth City, NC, US 175/J2
Elizabethan Village Hist. Site, Austl. 154/L7
Elizabethton, Tn, US 172/D4
Elizabethtown, Pa, US 180/B3
Elizabethville, Pa, US 180/B2
Elk (mts.), Co, US 174/B2
Elk (riv.), WV, US 175/H2
Ełk, Pol. 81/K5
Elk City, Ok, US 171/H4
Elk Grove, Ca, US 177/M10
Elk Grove Village, Il, US 177/P16
Elk Island NP, Ab, Can. 168/E2
Elk Mills, Md, US 180/C4
Elk Point, Ab, Can. 168/F2
Elk Rapids, Mi, US 172/C2
Elk Ridge, Md, US 180/B5
Elk River, Mn, US 169/K4
Elk Slough (riv.), Ca, US 177/L10
Elkenroth, Ger. 95/G2
Elkhart, In, US 172/C3
Elkhart, Ks, US 171/G3
Elkhart, Tx, US 171/J5
Elkhorn, Mb, Can. 169/H3
Elkhorn, Wi, US 172/B3
Elkhorn (riv.), Ne, US 169/H2
Elkhovo, Bul. 89/K1
Elkin, NC, US 172/D4
Elko, Nv, US 168/E5
Elkton, Md, US 180/C4
Ellamar, Ak, US 176/J3
Elland, Eng, UK 77/G4
Elle (riv.), Ger. 95/F2
Ellef Ringnes (isl.), Nun., Can. 165/R7
Ellefeld, Ger. 97/F2
Ellen (riv.), Eng, UK 77/E2
Ellenberg, Ger. 96/D4
Ellendale, ND, US 169/J4
Ellendale, De, US 180/C6
Ellensburg, Wa, US 168/C4
Eller (riv.), Ger. 93/H5
Ellerbach (riv.), Ger. 95/G4
Ellero (riv.), It. 100/A4
Ellery (mt.), Austl. 157/D3
Ellesmere (isl.), Nun., Can. 165/S6
Ilesmere Port, Eng, UK 77/F5
Ellezelles, Belg. 94/C2
Ellice (riv.), Nun., Can. 164/F2
Ellicott City, Md, US 180/B5
Ellinikón (int'l arpt.), Gre. 89/N9
Elliot, SAfr. 148/D3
Elliot Lake, On, Can. 172/D2
Elliot Price Consv. Park, Austl. 155/H4
Elliott (peak), Va, US 175/J2
Ellis Island, NJ,NY, US 181/J9
Ellisras, SAfr. 147/E5
Elliston, Austl. 155/G5
Ellisville, Mo, US 179/F8
Ellon, Sc, UK 78/D2
Ellrich, Ger. 93/H5
Ellsworth (mts.), Ant. 202/U
Ellsworth, Ks, US 171/H3
Ellsworth, Me, US 173/G2
Ellsworth, Wi, US 172/A2
Ellsworth Land (phys. reg.), Ant. 202/U
Ellwangen, Ger. 96/D5
Elm, Swi. 99/F4
Elm Grove, Wi, US 177/P13
Elma, NY, US 173/S10
Elmadağ, Turk. 104/E5
Elmalı, Turk. 133/A1
Elmas (int'l arpt.), It. 88/A3
Elmendorf, Tx, US 179/U21
Elmer, NJ, US 180/C4
Elmhurst, Il, US 177/Q16
Elmina, Gha. 145/E5
Elmira, NY, US 172/E3
Elmont, NY, US 181/L9
Elmore, Austl. 157/C3
Elmsford, NY, US 181/K7
Elmshorn, Ger. 93/G1
Elmstein, Ger. 95/G5
Elmwood Park, Wi, US 177/Q14
Elmwood Park, NJ, US 181/J8
Elmwood Park, Il, US 177/Q16
Elne, Fr. 84/E5
Elói Mendes, Braz. 197/H6
Élorn (riv.), Fr. 84/A2
Elortondo, Arg. 200/E2
Elorza, Ven. 194/D3
Elouera Nat'l Rsv., Austl. 156/H8
Eloy, Az, US 170/E4
Eloy Alfaro, Ecu. 194/B5
Éloyes, Fr. 98/C1
Elpitiya, SrL. 124/D6
Elrose, Sk, Can. 168/F3
Elsa, Yk, Can. 176/L3
Elsa (riv.), It. 85/J5
Elsa, Embalse de (res.), Sp. 86/B2
Elsah, Il, US 179/G8
Elsdorf, Ger. 93/G2
Elsdorf, Ger. 95/F2
Else (riv.), Ger. 93/F4
Elsenfeld, Ger. 96/C3
Elsenz (riv.), Ger. 96/B4
Elsfleth, Ger. 93/F2
Elsinore (lake), Ca, US 178/C3
Elsmere, De, US 180/C4

234

Elst – Fajar

Elst, Neth. 92/C5
Elstal, Ger. 82/Q6
Elstead, Eng, UK 75/F4
Elsterberg, Ger. 97/F1
Eltmann, Ger. 96/D3
El'ton (lake), Rus. 105/H2
Eltville am Rhein, Ger. 96/B2
Elūrū, India 124/D4
Elvanlı, Turk. 133/D1
Elvas, Port. 86/B3
Elverum, Nor. 80/D1
Elvire (mt.), Austl. 154/C2
Elvo (riv.), It. 100/B2
Elwell (lake), Mt, US 168/F3
Elwood, In, US 172/C3
Elwood-Magnolia, NJ, US 180/D4
Elwy (riv.), Wal, UK 76/E5
Ely, Nv, US 170/D3
Ely, Eng, UK 75/G2
Elyaqim, Isr. 133/G6
Elyashiv, Isr. 133/F7
Elyria, Oh, US 172/D3
Elysburg, Pa, US 180/B2
Elysian Park, Ca, US 178/F7
Elz (riv.), Ger. 96/B6
Elz, Ger. 96/B2
Elzach, Ger. 98/E1
Elzbach (riv.), Ger. 95/G3
Elze, Ger. 93/G4
Emajõgi (riv.), Est. 81/M2
Emāmshahr (Shāhrūd), Iran 131/F1
Emån (riv.), Swe. 80/F3
Emancé, Fr. 72/H6
Emas, PN das, Braz. 193/H7
Emba (riv.), Kaz. 104/K3
Embarcación, Arg. 199/D1
Embarras (riv.), Il, US 175/F2
Embi, Kaz. 105/L2
Embi (riv.), Kaz. 106/F5
Embira (riv.), Braz. 192/D5
Emborcação, Barragem de (res.), Braz. 197/C1
Embrach, Swi. 99/E3
Embrun, Fr. 85/G4
Embsen, Ger. 93/H2
Embu, Kenya 146/C3
Emden, Ger. 93/E2
Emeishan, China 125/H2
Emerald, Austl. 156/C3
Emerald, Austl. 157/G5
Emerson, Mb, Can. 169/J3
Emerson, NJ, US 181/J8
Emeryville, Ca, US 177/K11
Emet, Turk. 132/B2
Emigsville, Pa, US 180/B3
Emilia-Romagna (pol. reg.), It. 85/J4
Emiliano Zapata, Mex. 186/D2
Emin, China 112/D2
Eminābād, Pak. 128/C3
Eminence, Mo, US 171/K3
Emir Pasha (gulf), Tanz. 146/A3
Emirdağ, Turk. 132/B2
Emirgazi, Turk. 132/C2
Emlembe (peak), Swaz. 149/E2
Emlichheim, Ger. 92/D3
Emma (riv.), Sur. 195/H4
Emmaboda, Swe. 80/F3
Emmanuel Head (pt.), Eng, UK 78/E5
Emmaus, Pa, US 180/C2
Emme (riv.), Swi. 98/D4
Emmeloord, Neth. 92/C3
Emmen, Neth. 92/D3
Emmendingen, Ger. 98/D1
Emmental (valley), Swi. 98/D3
Emmer (riv.), Ger. 93/G4
Emmerbach (riv.), Ger. 93/E5
Emmerich, Ger. 92/D5
Emmett, Mi, US 177/G6
Emmingen-Liptingen, Ger. 99/E2
Emmitsburg, Md, US 180/A4
Emmonak, Ak, US 176/F3
Emneth, Eng, UK 75/G1
Emőd, Hun. 90/E2
Emory, Tx, US 171/J4
Emosson (lake), Swi. 98/C5
Empalme, Mex. 184/C3
Empangeni, SAfr. 149/E3
Empedrado, Arg. 199/E2
Empedrado, Chile 200/B2
Empoli, It. 101/D5
Emporia, Ks, US 171/H3
'Emrānī, Iran 131/G2
Ems (Eems) (riv.), Ger.,Neth. 92/D2
Ems-Jade (canal), Ger. 93/E2
Emsbüren, Ger. 93/E4
Emsdetten, Ger. 93/E4
Emskirchen, Ger. 96/D3
Emsland (reg.), Ger. 82/D2
Emstek, Ger. 93/F3
Emu Park, Austl. 156/C3
Emumägi (hill), Est. 81/M2
Emyvale, Ire. 76/B3
Ena, Japan 117/E3
Enbetsu, Japan 118/B1
Encantada, Cerro (peak), Mex. 184/B3
Encantada, Cerro de la (peak), Mex. 184/B2
Encarnación, Par. 199/E2
Encarnación de Díaz, Mex. 184/E4
Enchi, Gha. 144/E5
Encinitas, Ca, US 178/C4
Enciso, Col. 194/C3
Encontrados, Ven. 194/C2
Encounter (bay), Austl. 157/A2
Encruzilhada do Sul, Braz. 197/A4
Encs, Hun. 83/L4
Endau (peak), Kenya 146/C3
Ende, Indo. 123/F5
Endeavour River NP, Austl. 156/B1
Enderbury (isl.), Kiri. 159/H5
Enderby, BC, Can. 168/D3
Enderby Land (phys. reg.), Ant. 202/D
Enderlin, ND, US 169/J4
Endicott, NY, US 172/E3
Endingen, Ger. 98/D1
Ene (riv.), Peru 192/D6
Eneabba, Austl. 154/B4
Enebakk, Nor. 80/D2
Enewetak (isl.), Mrsh. 158/F3
Enez, Turk. 89/K2
Enfield (bor.), Eng, UK 72/C2
Engaño (cape), Phil. 121/D4
Engaru, Japan 118/C1
Engaruka (basin), Tanz. 146/B3
Engelberg, Swi. 99/E4
Engelhartszell, Aus. 97/G5
Engelskirchen, Ger. 95/G2
Engelsmanplaat (isl.), Neth. 92/D2
Engen, Ger. 99/E2
Engenheiro Navarro, Braz. 196/B5
Engenheiro Paulo de Frontin, Braz. 197/K7
Enger, Ger. 93/F4
Engerwitzdorf, Aus. 97/H6
Enggano (isl.), Indo. 122/B5
Enghershatu (peak), Erit. 130/C5
Enghien, Belg. 94/D2
Engi, Swi. 99/F4
England, UK 74/D2
Englefontaine, Fr. 94/C3
Englehart, On, Can. 172/E2
Englewood, Co, US 179/C3
Englewood, NJ, US 181/K8
Englewood Cliffs, NJ, US 181/K8
English (riv.), On, Can. 169/K3
English (chan.), Fr.,UK 84/B2
English Bay, Ak, US 176/H4
English Bāzār, India 127/G3
English Creek, NJ, US 180/D5
Englishtown, NJ, US 180/D3
Énguera, Sp. 87/E3
Enguri (riv.), Geo. 105/G4
Enhtal, Mong. 112/J2
Enid, Ok, US 171/H3
Eniwa, Japan 118/B2
Enkenbach-Alsenborn, Ger. 95/G5
Enkhuizen, Neth. 92/C3
Enkirch, Ger. 95/G4
Enköping, Swe. 80/G2
Enna, It. 88/D4
Ennedi (plat.), Chad 139/K4
Ennepe (riv.), Ger. 93/E6
Ennepetal, Ger. 93/E6
Ennery, Fr. 72/J4
Enningerloh, Ger. 93/F5
Ennis, Mt, US 168/F4
Ennis, Tx, US 171/H4
Ennis, Ire. 73/P10
Enniscorthy, Ire. 73/Q10
Enniskerry, Ire. 76/B5
Enniskillen, NI, UK 73/Q9
Ennistimon, Ire. 73/P10
Enns, Aus. 97/H6
Enns (riv.), Aus. 83/H5
Enogger (res.), Austl. 156/E6
Enola, Pa, US 180/B3
Enontekiö, Fin. 79/G1
Enoree (riv.), SC, US 175/H3
Enping, China 125/K3
Enrick (riv.), Sc, UK 78/B2
Enrique Carbó, Arg. 201/J10
Enriquillo, DRep. 187/J2
Enschede, Neth. 92/D4
Ensdorf, Ger. 97/E4
Ense, Ger. 93/E5
Enseleni, SAfr. 149/F3
Ensenada, Mex. 184/A2
Ensenada, Arg. 201/K11
Enshi, China 121/A1
Ensisheim, Fr. 98/D2
Entebbe (int'l arpt.), Ugan. 146/B2
Entebbe, Ugan. 146/B2
Entenbühl (peak), Ger. 97/F3
Enterprise, Al, US 175/G4
Enterprise, Ut, US 179/K11
Entlebuch, Swi. 98/E4
Entre Rios, Braz. 196/C3
Entre Rios (mts.), Hon. 187/E3
Entroncamento, Port. 86/A3
Entzheim, Fr. 98/D1
Enugu, Nga. 145/G5
Enugu (state), Nga. 145/G5
Enumclaw, Wa, US 177/D3
Enushū (sea), Japan 119/M6
Envira, Braz. 198/D2
Enz (riv.), Ger. 85/H2
Enza (riv.), It. 100/D4
Enzan, Japan 117/F3
Enzbach (riv.), Ger. 95/F4
Enzersdorf an der Fischa, Aus. 91/P7
Enzklösterle, Ger. 96/B5
Epalinges, Swi. 98/C4
Epáno Arkhánai, Gre. 89/J5
Epanomí, Gre. 89/H2
Epe, Nga. 145/F5
Epe, Neth. 92/C4
Épehy, Fr. 94/C3
Épernay, Fr. 94/C5
Epfig, Fr. 98/D1
Ephrata, Pa, US 180/B3
Epi (isl.), Van. 158/F6
Épiais-Rhus, Fr. 72/J4
Epidhavros (Epidaurus) (ruin), Gre. 89/H4
Épinal, Fr. 98/C1
Épinay-sur-Orge, Fr. 72/J6
Épinay-sur-Seine, Fr. 72/J5
Epira, Guy. 195/G3
Epirus (reg.), Gre. 89/G3
Épône, Fr. 94/A6
Eppelborn, Ger. 95/F5
Eppelheim, Ger. 96/B4
Eppenbrunn, Ger. 95/G5
Eppeville, Fr. 94/C4
Epping (for.), Eng, UK 72/D2
Epping, Eng, UK 72/D1
Epping Forest NP, Austl. 156/B3
Eppingen, Ger. 96/B4
Eppishausen, Ger. 99/G1
Epsom, Eng, UK 72/C3
Epsom and Ewell, Eng, UK 75/F4
Epte (riv.), Fr. 94/A4
Equator (fall), Ecu. 194/A4
Equatorial Guinea (ctry.) 138/G7
Équihen-Plage, Fr. 94/A2
Er (lake), China 125/H2
Er Rachidia, Mor. 140/D3
Er Reina, Isr. 133/G6
Er Rif (mts.), Mor. 138/D1
Era (riv.), It. 101/D6
Eraclea, It. 101/F1
Eraclea (ruin), It. 88/E2
Eraclea Minoa (ruin), It. 88/C4
Éragny, Fr. 72/J4
Erandique, Hon. 186/D3
Eravur, SrL. 124/D6
Erawan NP, Thai. 120/B3
Erba, It. 100/C1
Erbaa, Turk. 132/D1
Erbach, Ger. 96/B3
Erbendorf, Ger. 97/F3
Erbeskopf (peak), Ger. 95/G4
Ercan (int'l arpt.), Cyp. 133/C2
Erçek, Turk. 132/E2
Erçek (lake), Turk. 132/E2
Ercilla, Chile 200/B3
Erciş, Turk. 132/E2
Erciyes (peak), Turk. 132/C2
Erclin (riv.), Fr. 94/C3
Érd, Hun. 91/Q10
Erda, Ut, US 179/J12
Erdek (gulf), Turk. 91/H5
Erdek, Turk. 91/H5
Erdemli, Turk. 133/D1
Erdenet, Mong. 112/H2
Erdi-Ma (plat.), Chad 139/K4
Erding, Ger. 97/E6
Erdre (riv.), Fr. 84/C3
Erdweg, Ger. 96/E6
Erechim, Braz. 197/A3
Ereen Davaanī (mts.), Mong. 113/K2
Ereğli, Turk. 132/C2
Ereğli, Turk. 91/K5
Eremo di Camaldoli, It. 101/E5
Erenhaberga (mts.), China 112/D3
Erenhot, China 113/K3
Erenler, Turk. 91/K5
Erentepe, Turk. 132/E2
Erepecu, Lago do (lake), Braz. 193/G4
Eresma (riv.), Sp. 86/C2
Erétria, Gre. 89/H3
Ereymentaū, Kaz. 129/F2
Érezée, Belg. 95/E3
Erfa (riv.), Ger. 96/C3
Erfoud, Mor. 140/D3
Erft (riv.), Ger. 82/D3
Erftstadt, Ger. 95/F2
Erfurt, Ger. 82/F3
'Erg Chech (des.), Mali,Alg. 138/E3
'Erg Iguidi (des.), Alg.,Mrta. 140/D4
Ergene Nehri (riv.), Turk. 91/H5
Erguig (riv.), Chad 138/J5
Ergun Youqi, China 113/M1
Ergun Zuoqi, China 113/M1
Ericeira, Port. 87/P10
Ericht (lake), Sc, UK 78/B3
Ericht (riv.), Sc, UK 78/B3
Erickson, Mb, Can. 169/J3
Erickson, BC, Can. 168/D3
Erie (lake), Can.,US 172/D3
Erie, Co, US 179/B2
Erie (canal), NY, US 173/S9
Erie (co.), NY, US 173/S10
Erie, Pa, US 172/D3
Erie (int'l arpt.), Pa, US 172/D3
Eriksdale, Mb, Can. 169/J3
Eriksmalä, Swe. 80/F3
Erikub (isl.), Mrsh. 158/F4
Erímanthos (peak), Gre. 89/G4
Erimo, Japan 118/C2
Erimo-misaki (cape), Japan 118/C3
Erithraí, Gre. 89/H3
Eritrea (ctry.) 139/N5
Erkelenz, Ger. 95/F1
Erken (isl.), Swe. 81/H1
Erkheim, Ger. 99/G1
Erkner, Ger. 82/Q7
Erkrath, Ger. 92/D6
Erlach, Swi. 98/D3
Erlands Point-Kitsap Lake, Wa, US 177/B2
Erlangen, Ger. 96/E3
Erlau (riv.), Ger. 97/G5
Erlenbach (riv.), Ger. 96/B4
Erlenbach am Main, Ger. 96/C3
Erlenbach bei Marktheidenfeld, Ger. 96/C3
Erlenbach im Simmental, Swi. 98/D4
Erlinsbach, Swi. 98/E3
Erlongshan (res.), China 114/F2
Erme (riv.), Eng, UK 74/C6
Ermelo, SAfr. 149/E2
Ermelo, Neth. 92/C4
Ermenek (riv.), Turk. 133/C1
Ermenek, Turk. 133/C1
Ermenonville, Fr. 72/L4
Ermióni, Gre. 89/H4
Ermont, Fr. 72/J5
Ermoúpolis, Gre. 89/J4
Erms (riv.), Ger. 96/C6
Erndtebrück, Ger. 95/H2
Ernée (riv.), Fr. 84/C2
Ernée, Fr. 84/C2
Ernesto Cortissoz (int'l arpt.), Col. 194/C2
Ernsthofen, Aus. 97/H6
Erode, India 124/C5
Erolzheim, Ger. 99/G1
Erowal Bay, Austl. 157/D2
Erpel, Ger. 95/G2
Erquelinnes, Belg. 95/D3
Errigal (mtn.), Ire. 73/P9
Erris Head (pt.), Ire. 73/P9
Erro (riv.), It. 100/B4
Errochty (lake), Sc, UK 78/B3
Erromango (isl.), Van. 158/F6
Erse (riv.), Ger. 93/H4
Ersekë, Alb. 89/G2
Erstein, Fr. 98/D1
Erstfeld, Swi. 99/E4
Ertingen, Ger. 99/F1
Ertis (riv.), Kaz. 106/H4
Ertix (riv.), China 112/E2
Eruh, Turk. 132/E2
Eruwa, Nga. 145/F5
Erwin, Tn, US 172/D4
Erwitte, Ger. 93/F5
Eryuan, China 125/G2
Erzegebirge (Krušné Hory) (mts.), Czh.,Ger. 85/K1
Erzen (riv.), Alb. 89/F2
Erzhausen, Ger. 96/B3
Erzincan, Turk. 132/D2
Erzurum, Turk. 132/E2
Erzurum (prov.), Turk. 132/E1
Es Senia (int'l arpt.), Alg. 142/E5
Esan-misaki (cape), Japan 118/B3
Esashi, Japan 118/C1
Esashi, Japan 118/B3
Esashi, Japan 118/B4
Esbiye, Turk. 132/D1
Esbjerg, Den. 80/C4
Esbjerg (int'l arpt.), Den. 80/C4
Esbly, Fr. 72/L5
Esbo (Espoo), Fin. 81/L1
Escada, Braz. 196/D3
Escalante (riv.), Ut, US 170/E3
Escalón, Mex. 184/D3
Escalona, Sp. 86/C2
Escambia (riv.), Fl, US 175/G4
Escaudain, Fr. 94/C3
Escaut (riv.), Fr. 82/B3
Esch (riv.), Fr. 95/E6
Esch-sur-Alzette, Lux. 95/E4
Esch-sur-Sure, Lux. 95/E4
Eschach (riv.), Ger. 99/E1
Eschau, Fr. 98/D1
Eschborn, Ger. 96/B2
Eschede, Ger. 93/H3
Eschen, Lcht. 99/F3
Eschenbach, Ger. 96/C5
Eschenbach in der Oberpfalz, Ger. 97/E3
Eschershausen, Ger. 93/G5
Esches (riv.), Fr. 94/B5
Escholzmatt, Swi. 98/D4
Eschwege, Ger. 93/H6
Eschweiler, Ger. 95/F2
Escobedo (int'l arpt.), Mex. 185/E3
Escoma, Bol. 198/D4
Escondido, Ca, US 178/C4
Escuinapa de Hidalgo, Mex. 184/D4
Escuintla, Guat. 186/D3
Esdraelon, Plain of (plain), Isr. 133/G6
Eséka, Camr. 138/H7
Esenboga (int'l arpt.), Turk. 132/C1
Esence (peak), Turk. 132/D2
Esens, Ger. 93/E1
Esera (riv.), Sp. 87/F1
Eşfahān, Iran 130/F2
Esfandak, Iran 131/H3
Esgair Ddu (peak), Wal, UK 74/C1
Esha Ness (cape), Sc, UK 73/W13
Esher, Eng, UK 72/B2
Eshowe, SAfr. 149/E3
Esil, Kaz. 129/E2
Esil (riv.), Kaz. 129/E2
Esine, It. 99/G6
Esino (riv.), It. 101/G6
Esk (riv.), Eng, UK 77/E2
Eskdale (valley), Sc, UK 78/C6
Eskifjördhur, Ice. 79/Q6
Eskil, Turk. 132/C2
Eskilstuna, Swe. 80/G2
Eskimalatya, Turk. 132/D2
Eskimo (lakes), NW, Can. 164/C2
Eskipazar, Turk. 132/C1
Eskişehir, Turk. 132/B2
Eskişehir (prov.), Turk. 132/B2
Esla (riv.), Sp. 86/C1
Eslāmābād, Iran 130/E2
Eslohe, Ger. 93/F6
Eslöv, Swe. 80/E4
Eşme, Turk. 132/B2
Esmeralda, Cuba 187/G1
Esmeraldas, Ecu. 194/B4
Esmeraldas (dept.), Ecu. 194/B4
Esneux, Belg. 95/E2
Espada (pt.), Col. 194/D1
Espalion, Fr. 84/E4
Española, NM, US 171/F4
Española, On, Can. 172/D2
Española (isl.), Ecu. 198/F7
Esparraguera, Sp. 87/K6
Esparta, Hon. 186/E3
Esparto, Ca, US 177/K9
Espejo, Sp. 86/C4
Espelkamp, Ger. 93/F4
Esperança, Braz. 196/D2
Esperance (bay), Austl. 154/D5
Esperance, Austl. 154/D5
Esperantina, Braz. 196/B1
Esperantinópolis, Braz. 196/A2
Esperanza, Arg., Ant. 202/W
Esperanza (inlet), BC, Can. 168/B3
Esperanza (mts.), Hon. 186/E3
Esperanza, Mex. 184/C3
Esperanza, Mex. 185/M8
Esperanza, Peru 198/D3
Espichel (cape), Port. 87/P11
Espinal, Mex. 185/M6
Espinal, Col. 194/C3
Espinar, Peru 198/D4
Espinhaço, Serra do (mts.), Braz. 193/K7
Espinho, Port. 86/A2
Espinillo (pt.), Uru. 201/F2
Espinosa, Braz. 196/B4
Espírito Santo (state), Braz. 197/D2
Espiritu Santo (isl.), Van. 158/F6
Espíritu Santo (bay), Mex. 186/E2
Espita, Mex. 186/D1
Esplanada, Braz. 196/C3
Espluga de Francolí, Sp. 87/E2
Espluges, Sp. 87/L7
Esposende, Port. 86/A2
Espungabera, Moz. 147/F5
Espy, Pa, US 180/B1
Esqueda, Mex. 184/C2
Esquel, Arg. 200/C4
Esquina, Arg. 199/E3
Essaouira, Mor. 140/C3
Esse (riv.), Ger. 93/G5
Essen, Belg. 92/B6
Essen, Ger. 92/E6
Essen, Ger. 93/E3
Essenbach, Ger. 97/F5
Essendon (mt.), Austl. 154/D3
Essenheim, Ger. 95/H4
Essequibo (riv.), Guy. 189/D2
Essequibo Island-West Demerara (pol. reg.), Guy. 195/G3
Essex, On, Can. 177/G7
Essex (co.), On, Can. 177/G7
Essex (co.), Eng, UK 72/E1
Essex, Md, US 180/B5
Essex (co.), NJ, US 180/D2
Essex Fells, NJ, US 181/H8
Esslingen, Ger. 96/C5
Essômes-sur-Marne, Fr. 94/C5
Essonne (riv.), Fr. 84/E2
Est, Canal de l' (canal), Fr. 95/E5
Estaca de Bares, Punta de la (cape), Sp. 86/B1
Estación Santa Engracia, Mex. 185/F3
Estados, Isla de los (isl.), Arg. 199/D7
Eştahbān, Iran 130/F3
Estaires, Fr. 94/B2
Estância, Braz. 196/C3
Estats, Pico de (peak), Sp. 87/F1
Estavayer-le-Lac, Swi. 98/C4
Estcourt, SAfr. 149/E3
Este, It. 101/E2
Este, Punta del (pt.), Cuba 182/E3
Este Sudeste, Cayos del (isls.), Col. 187/F3
Esteio, Braz. 197/B4
Estelí, Nic. 186/E3
Estell Manor (Risley), NJ, US 180/D5
Estella, Sp. 86/D1
Estelle (mtn.), Ca, US 178/C3
Estelle, La, US 179/P17
Estepa, Sp. 86/C4
Estepona, Sp. 86/C4
Ester, Ak, US 176/J3
Esterhazy, Sk, Can. 169/H3
Esterias (cape), Gabon 138/G7
Esternay, Fr. 94/C6
Estero de Agiabampo (lag.), Mex. 184/C3
Estéron (riv.), Fr. 85/G5
Esterwegen, Ger. 93/E3
Estes Park, Co, US 179/A2
Estevan, Sk, Can. 169/H3
Estinnes-au-Mont, Belg. 95/D3
Eston, Sk, Can. 168/F3
Eston and South Bank, Eng, UK 77/G2
Estonia (ctry.) 81/L2
Estoril, Port. 87/P10
Estral Beach, Mi, US 177/F8
Estrées-Saint-Denis, Fr. 94/B5
Estrela, Serra da (mts.), Port. 86/A3
Estrela, Serra da (peak), Port. 86/B2
Estrella (pt.), Mex. 184/B2
Estrelto, Serra do (range), Braz. 196/B3
Estremoz, Port. 86/B3
Estrondo, Serra do (mts.), Braz. 193/J5
Esztergom, Hun. 90/D2
Et Taiyiba, Isr. 133/G7
Et Tīra, Isr. 133/F7
Etah, India 126/B2
Étain, Fr. 95/E5
Etal (isl.), Micr. 158/E4
Étalle, Belg. 95/E4
Étaples, Fr. 94/A2
Etāwah, India 126/B2
Etāwah Branch (riv.), India 126/B2
Etchojoa, Mex. 184/C3
Ethelbert, Mb, Can. 169/H3
Ethiopia (ctry.) 139/N5
Ethiopian (plat.), Eth. 139/N6
Eti (riv.), Japan 119/K5
Etili, Turk. 91/H6
Étival-Clairefontaine, Fr. 98/C1
Etive, Loch (inlet), Sc, UK 78/A4
Etna (peak), It. 88/D4
Etna, Monte (Mount Etna) (vol.), It. 88/D4
Etne, Nor. 80/A2
Etobicoke, Can. 173/Q8
Etolin (str.), Ak, US 176/E3
Eton, Eng, UK 72/B2
Etorofu (isl.), Rus. 113/S2
Etosha (salt pan), Namb. 147/C4
Etosha NP, Namb. 147/C4
Etowah, Ok, US 179/N15
Étrépilly, Fr. 72/L4
Etropole, Bul. 89/J1
Etroubles, It. 98/D6
Ettadhamen Douarhicher, Tun. 142/M6
Ettelbruck, Lux. 95/E4
Etten-Leur, Neth. 92/B5
Ettenheim, Ger. 98/D1
Etterbeek, Belg. 95/D2
Etters (Goldsboro), Pa, US 180/B3
Ettlingen, Ger. 96/B5
Ettrick Pen (peak), Sc, UK 78/C6
Ettrick Water (riv.), Sc, UK 78/C5
Ettringen, Ger. 99/G1
Eu, Fr. 94/A3
'Eua (isl.), Tonga 159/H7
Eubenangee Swamp NP, Austl. 156/B2
Euclid, Oh, US 172/D3
Euclides da Cunha, Braz. 196/C3
Eudora, Ar, US 171/K4
Eudunda, Austl. 157/A2
Euerbach, Ger. 96/D2
Eufaula, Al, US 175/G4
Eufaula (lake), Ok, US 169/J4
Eugendorf, Aus. 97/G7
Eugene, Or, US 168/C4
Eugene O'Neill NHS, Ca, US 177/L11
Eugenia (pt.), Mex. 184/B3
Eugowra, Austl. 157/D2
Eume, Embalse de (res.), Sp. 86/B1
Eungella NP, Austl. 156/C3
Eunice, La, US 171/J5
Eunice, NM, US 171/G4
Eupen, Belg. 95/F2
Euphrates (riv.), Iraq,Syria 132/E3
Eura, Fin. 81/K1
Eurajoki, Fin. 81/J1
Eure (riv.), Fr. 84/D2
Eure (dept.), Fr. 94/A5
Eure-et-Loir (dept.), Fr. 94/A6
Eureka (sound), Nun., Can. 165/S7
Eureka, Ca, US 168/B5
Eureka, Mo, US 179/F9
Eureka, Mt, US 168/E3
Eureka, Nv, US 170/D3
Eureka, SD, US 169/J4
Euroa, Austl. 157/C3
Eurodisney, Fr. 72/L5
Euron (riv.), Fr. 98/C1
Europa (pt.), Gib. 86/C4
Europabrücke, Aus. 99/H3
Europe (cont.) 27
Europoort, Neth. 92/B5
Euskirchen, Ger. 95/F2
Eussenheim, Ger. 96/C3
Eustis, Fl, US 175/H4
Euston, Austl. 157/B2
Eutin, Ger. 80/D4
Eutini, Malw. 146/B5
Eutsuk (lake), BC, Can. 168/B2
Euville, Fr. 95/E6
Évain, Qu, Can. 172/E1
Evander, SAfr. 148/E2
Evans (mt.), Co, US 171/F3
Evans (lake), Qu, Can. 172/E1
Evans, Co, US 179/C2
Evans (str.), Nun., Can. 165/H2
Evans Head, Austl. 157/E1
Evanston, Wy, US 168/F5
Evansville, In, US 172/C4
Evansville, Wy, US 171/F2
Evaporation (basin), Ut, US 168/E5
Evart, Mi, US 172/C3
Evaton, SAfr. 148/D2
Evaz, Iran 130/F3
Ève, Fr. 72/L4
Even Yehuda, Isr. 133/F7
Evenlode (riv.), Eng, UK 75/E3
Evenkiyskiy Aut. Okrug, Rus. 106/K3
Everard (cape), Austl. 157/D3
Everard (lake), Austl. 151/C4
Everard (mt.), Austl. 155/G3
Everest (peak), China,Nepal 124/E2
Everest (Sagarmatha) (mtn.), China,Nepal 127/F2
Everett, Wa, US 168/C4
Evergem, Belg. 94/C1
Everglades (swamp), Fl, US 175/H5
Everglades NP, Fl, US 175/H5
Evergreen, Al, US 175/G4
Evergreen, Co, US 179/B3
Evergreen Park, Il, US 177/Q16
Everswinkel, Ger. 93/E5
Evesham, Eng, UK 75/E2
Evesham, Vale of (valley), Eng, UK 74/D2
Évian-les-Bains, Fr. 98/C5
Évinos (riv.), Gre. 89/G3
Evje, Nor. 80/B2
Evolène, Swi. 98/D5
Évora, Port. 86/B3
Évora (dist.), Port. 86/A3
Évreux, Fr. 84/D2
Évron, Fr. 84/C2
Evrótas (riv.), Gre. 89/H4
Évry, Fr. 72/K6
Évvoia (gulf), Gre. 89/H3
Évvoia (isl.), Gre. 89/H3
Evxinoúpolis, Gre. 89/H3
Ewa Beach, Hi, US 166/V13
Ewa Villages, Hi, US 166/V13
Ewan, NJ, US 180/C4
Ewarton, Jam. 187/G2
Ewaso Ng'iro (riv.), Kenya 146/C2
Ewell, Eng, UK 72/C3
Ewing, NJ, US 180/D3
Exaplátanos, Gre. 89/H2
Excelsior Springs, Mo, US 179/E5
Excursion Inlet, Ak, US 176/L4
Exe (riv.), Eng, UK 74/C4
Exeter, NH, US 173/G3
Exmoor (upland), Eng, UK 74/C4
Exmoor NP, Eng, UK 74/C4
Exmore, Va, US 175/K2
Exmouth, Austl. 154/B2
Exmouth (gulf), Austl. 154/B2
Exmouth (pen.), Chile 201/B6
Extrema, Braz. 197/G7
Extremadura (reg.), Sp. 86/B3
Exu, Braz. 196/C2
Exuma (sound), Bahm. 183/F3
Eyach (riv.), Ger. 96/B6
Eyak, Ak, US 176/J3
Eyasi (lake), Tanz. 147/F1
Eyb (riv.), Ger. 96/C5
Eydehamn, Nor. 80/C2
Eyemouth, Sc, UK 78/D5
Eyguières, Fr. 84/F5
Eyn Hemed (ruin), Isr. 133/G8
Eyre (pen.), Austl. 151/C4
Eyre North (lake), Austl. 151/C3
Eyre South (lake), Austl. 151/C3
Ézanville, Fr. 72/K4
Ezequiel Ramos Mexía (res.), Arg. 200/C3
Ezhou, China 121/B1
Ezine, Turk. 89/K3
Ezzane (well), Alg. 138/H3

F

F.E. Walter (res.), Pa, US 180/C1
Fabbrico, It. 101/D3
Fabens, Tx, US 174/B4
Fabero, Sp. 86/B1
Fåborg, Den. 80/D4
Fabriano, It. 85/K5
Facatativá, Col. 192/D3
Faches-Thumesnil, Fr. 94/C2
Fada (lake), Sc, UK 78/A1
Fada-N'Gourma, Burk. 145/F3
Faenza, It. 101/E4
Fafa (riv.), CAfr. 139/J6
Fafe, Port. 86/A2
Fafen Shet' (riv.), Eth. 139/P6
Făgăraş, Rom. 91/G3
Fagersta, Swe. 80/F2
Faggiola (peak), It. 101/E4
Fagnano (lake), Arg. 201/D7
Fagnano Olona, It. 100/B1
Fagnières, Fr. 95/D6
Faguibine (lake), Mali 138/D4
Fahl (well), Alg. 141/F3
Fahrenzhausen, Ger. 97/E6
Faial (isl.), Azor., Port. 87/S12
Faido, Swi. 99/E5
Failsworth, Eng, UK 77/F4
Fains-Véel, Fr. 95/E6
Fair Haven, Mi, US 177/G6
Fair Haven, Vt, US 172/F3
Fair Hill, Md, US 180/C4
Fair Isle (isl.), Sc, UK 73/W14
Fair Lawn, NJ, US 181/J8
Fair Oaks, Ca, US 177/M9
Fairbanks, Ak, US 176/J3
Fairfax, Ca, US 177/J11
Fairfax, Va, US 180/A6
Fairfax (co.), Va, US 180/A6
Fairfield, Ca, US 170/B3
Fairfield, Ct, US 181/E1
Fairfield (co.), Ct, US 181/L7
Fairfield, Mt, US 168/F4
Fairfield, NJ, US 181/H8
Fairfield, Pa, US 180/A4
Fairfield, Tx, US 171/H5
Fairfield, Ut, US 179/J13
Fairland, Md, US 180/B5
Fairlee, Md, US 180/B5
Fairless Hills, Pa, US 180/D3
Fairlie, Sc, UK 78/B5
Fairmont, WV, US 172/D4
Fairmont City, Il, US 179/G8
Fairmount, Ks, US 179/D5
Fairplay, Co, US 174/B2
Fairton, NJ, US 180/C5
Fairview, NJ, US 181/K8
Fairview, Ok, US 171/H3
Fairview Heights, Il, US 179/G8
Fairway, Ks, US 179/D5
Fairweather (mt.), Ak, US 176/L4
Fairweather (cape), Ak, US 176/L4
Fairweather (mt.), BC, Can. 164/C3
Faisalābād, Pak. 128/B4
Faistós (ruin), Gre. 89/J5
Faizābād, India 126/D2
Fajardo, PR 183/M8

235
Fakah – Fort L

Fakahina (isl.), FrPol. 159/M6
Fakaofo (isl.), Tok. 159/H5
Fakarava (isl.), FrPol. 159/L6
Fako (peak), Camr. 138/G7
Fakse, Den. 80/E4
Fakse Ladeplads, Den. 80/E4
Faku, China 114/E2
Fal (riv.), Eng, UK 74/B6
Fālākāta, India 127/G2
Falāmah, WBnk. 133/G7
Fálanna, Gre. 89/H3
Falcon (res.), Mex.,US 174/D5
Falcon (cape), Alg. 142/D2
Falcón (state), Ven. 194/D2
Falconara Marittima, It. 101/G5
Falémé (riv.), Mali 138/C5
Falfurrias, Tx, US 174/D5
Falher, Ab, Can. 168/D2
Falkenberg, Swe. 80/E3
Falkensee, Ger. 82/Q6
Falkenstein, Ger. 97/F4
Falkenstein, Ger. 97/F2
Falkirk, Sc, UK 78/C5
Falkirk (pol. reg.), Sc, UK 78/C5
Falkland (isls.), UK 201/E7
Falkland, Sc, UK 78/C4
Falkland Sound (str.), UK 201/E7
Falköping, Swe. 80/E2
Fall City, Wa, US 177/D2
Fall River, Ma, US 173/G3
Fallbrook, Ca, US 178/C4
Fallere (peak), It. 98/D6
Falling Spring, Il, US 179/G8
Fallingbostel, Ger. 93/G3
Fallis, Ok, US 179/N14
Fallon, Nv, US 170/C3
Falls Church, Va, US 180/A6
Fallston, Md, US 180/B4
Falmouth, Anti. 183/N8
Falmouth, Eng, UK 74/A6
Falmouth (bay), Eng, UK 74/A6
False Pass, Ak, US 176/F5
Falshöft (pt.), Ger. 80/C4
Falso (cape), Hon. 187/F3
Falso, Cabo (cape), Mex. 184/C4
Falso Cabo de Hornos (cape), Chile 201/C7
Falster (isl.), Den. 79/E5
Falterona (peak), It. 101/E5
Fălticeni, Rom. 91/H2
Falun, Swe. 80/F1
Famagusta (bay), Cyp. 133/C2
Famagusta (dist.), Cyp. 133/C2
Famagusta, Cyp. 133/C2
Fameck, Fr. 95/F5
Famenne (reg.), Belg. 95/E3
Fammau, Moel (peak), Wal, UK 77/E5
Fan Si Pan (peak), Viet. 125/H3
Fana, Nor. 80/A1
Fanchang, China 114/D5
Fandriana, Madg. 149/H8
Fang Xian, China 114/B4
Fangatau (isl.), FrPol. 159/L6
Fangataufa (isl.), FrPol. 159/L7
Fangcheng, China 114/C4
Fangcheng Gezu Zizhixian, China 125/J3
Fangshan, China 114/B3
Fanjing (peak), China 125/J2
Fannich (lake), Sc, UK 78/A1
Fanning (Tabuaeran) (isl.), Kiri. 159/K4
Fano, It. 101/G5
Fanø (isl.), Den. 80/C4
Fanshi, China 114/C3
Fanwood, NJ, US 181/H9
Faqīrwāli, Pak. 128/B5
Fāqūs, Egypt 133/B4
Fara Novarese, It. 100/B1
Faradje, D.R. Congo 146/A2
Farafangana, Madg. 149/H8
Farāfirah, Wāḩāt al (oasis), Egypt 143/A3
Farāh, Afg. 131/H2
Farāh (riv.), Afg. 131/H2
Farallon (isls.), Ca, US 170/B3
Farallon de Medinilla (isl.), NMar. 158/D3
Farallon de Pajaros (isl.), NMar. 158/D2
Farallones de Cali, PN, Col. 192/C3
Faranah (pol. reg.), Gui. 144/C4
Faranah, Gui. 144/C4
Farángi Samariás NP, Gre. 89/H5
Faraony (riv.), Madg. 149/H8
Faraulep (isl.), Micr. 158/D4
Farciennes, Belg. 95/D3
Fareham, Eng, UK 75/E5
Faremoutiers, Fr. 94/C6
Farewell, Ak, US 176/H3
Farewell (cape), NZ 159/S11
Färgelanda, Swe. 80/D2
Farghona (pol. reg.), Uzb. 129/F4
Farghona, Uzb. 129/F4
Fargo, ND, US 169/J4
Faribault, Mn, US 169/K4
Farīdābād, India 128/D5
Farīdkot, India 128/C4
Farīdpur, Bang. 127/G4
Farīdpur (pol. reg.), Bang. 127/G4
Farīdpur, India 126/B1
Fāriskūr, Egypt 133/B4
Färjestaden, Swe. 80/G3
Farkadhón, Gre. 89/H3
Farkasgyepü, Hun. 90/C2
Farley, Mo, US 179/D5
Farmers, Co, US 179/C2
Farmingdale, NJ, US 180/D3
Farmingdale, NY, US 181/M9
Farmington, De, US 180/C6
Farmington, Me, US 173/G2
Farmington, Mi, US 177/F7
Farmington, Mo, US 171/K3
Farmington, NM, US 170/E3
Farmington, Ut, US 179/K12
Farmington Hills, Mi, US 177/E6
Farnborough, Eng, UK 75/F4
Farnham, Eng, UK 75/F4
Farnham Royal, Eng, UK 72/B2
Farnworth, Eng, UK 77/F4
Faro, Yk, Can. 176/M3
Faro (dist.), Port. 86/A4
Faro, Port. 86/B4
Faro (int'l arpt.), Port. 86/B4
Faro, PN du, Camr. 138/H6
Faroe (isls.), Den. 202/G
Fåron (isl.), Swe. 81/H3
Farösund, Swe. 81/H3
Farquhar (cape), Austl. 154/B2
Farr West, Ut, US 179/J11
Farroupilha, Braz. 197/B4
Farrukhābād, India 126/B2
Fársala, Gre. 89/H3
Farsø, Den. 80/C3
Farson, Wy, US 168/F5
Farsund, Nor. 80/B2
Fartak, Ras (pt.), Yem. 130/F5
Farwell, Tx, US 171/G4
Fasā, Iran 130/F3
Fasano, It. 89/E2
Faşıkan (pass), Turk. 133/C1
Fassberg, Ger. 93/H3
Fast Castle (pt.), Sc, UK 78/D5
Fastiv, Ukr. 104/D2
Fatagar Tuting (cape), Indo. 123/H4
Fatahjang, Pak. 128/B3
Fatehābād, India 128/C5
Fatehpur, India 126/C3
Fatehpur, India 126/C2
Fatehpur, India 131/K3
Fatick (pol. reg.), Sen. 144/A3
Fatick, Sen. 144/A3
Fátima, Port. 86/A3
Fatsa, Turk. 132/D1
Fatu Hiva (isl.), FrPol. 159/M6
Faucille, Col de la (pass), Fr. 98/C5
Faucilles (mts.), Fr. 82/C4
Faughan (riv.), NI, UK 76/A2
Fauglia, It. 100/D5
Fauldhouse, Sc, UK 78/C5
Faulkton, SD, US 169/J4
Faulquemont, Fr. 95/F5
Faure (isl.), Austl. 154/B3
Făurei, Rom. 91/H3
Fauske, Nor. 79/E2
Faust, Ut, US 179/J13
Fauvillers, Belg. 95/E4
Faux, Tête de (peak), Fr. 98/D1
Favalto (peak), It. 101/F6
Favara, It. 88/C4
Fave (riv.), Fr. 98/C1
Faverges, Fr. 98/C6
Faverney, Fr. 98/C2
Faversham, Eng, UK 75/G4
Favières, Fr. 72/L5
Favignana, It. 88/C4
Favria, It. 100/A2
Favrieux, Fr. 72/G5
Fawn (riv.), On, Can. 169/L2
Fawn Grove, Pa, US 180/B4
Faxaflói (bay), Ice. 79/M7
Faxinal, Braz. 197/B2
Faya-Largeau, Chad 139/J4
Fayette, Al, US 175/G3
Fayette, Ms, US 171/K5
Fayetteville, Tn, US 175/G3
Fayetteville, Ga, US 175/G3
Fayetteville, NC, US 175/J3
Fayl-la-Forêt, Fr. 98/B2
Fazao, Monts du (mts.), Togo 145/F4
Fazao, PN du, Togo 145/F4
Fdérik, Mrta. 140/B5
Feale (riv.), Ire. 73/P10
Fear (cape), NC, US 175/J3
Feasterville-Trevose, Pa, US 180/D3
Feather (riv.), Ca, US 170/B3
Featherstone, Eng, UK 77/G4
Fécamp, Fr. 82/D4
Fecht (riv.), Fr. 98/D1
Federal Hall Nat'l Mem., NY, US 181/K9
Federal Heights, Co, US 179/B3
Federally Admin. Tribal Areas, Pak. 128/A2
Federsee (lake), Ger. 96/C6
Fedje, Nor. 80/A1
Feeny, NI, UK 76/A2
Fegersheim, Fr. 96/A6
Fehérgyarmat, Hun. 90/F2
Fehmarn (isl.), Den. 80/D4
Fehmarn Belt (str.), Den. 82/F1
Fei Huang (riv.), China 114/D4
Fei Xian, China 114/D4
Feia, Lagoa (lake), Braz. 197/D2
Feicheng, China 114/D3
Feidong, China 114/D5
Feignies, Fr. 94/C3
Feijó, Braz. 198/D3
Feillans, Fr. 98/A5
Feira, Port. 86/A2
Feira de Santana, Braz. 196/C4
Feistritz (riv.), Aus. 85/L3
Feixi, China 114/D5
Fejér (co.), Hun. 90/D2
Fejø (isl.), Ger. 80/D4
Feke, Turk. 132/C2
Feketić, Serb. 90/D3
Felanitx, Sp. 87/G3
Feldafing, Ger. 99/H2
Feldaist (riv.), Aus. 97/H6
Feldberg (peak), Ger. 98/E2
Feldkirch, Aus. 99/F3
Feldkirchen an der Donau, Aus. 97/H6
Feldkirchen bei Graz, Aus. 90/B2
Feldkirchen in Kärnten, Aus. 85/L3
Feletto, It. 100/A2
Feletto Umberto, It. 101/G1
Felino, It. 100/D3
Felipe Carillo Puerto, Mex. 186/D2
Felixdorf, Aus. 90/C2
Felixlândia, Braz. 197/C1
Felixstowe, Eng, UK 75/H3
Felizzano, It. 100/B3
Fell, Ger. 95/F4
Fellbach, Ger. 96/C5
Felling, Eng, UK 77/G2
Felsberg, Ger. 93/G6
Felsberg, Swi. 99/F4
Felton, Pa, US 180/B4
Felton, De, US 180/C5
Fema (peak), It. 85/K5
Femø (isl.), Den. 80/D4
Femundsmarka NP, Nor. 79/D3
Fénay, Fr. 98/B3
Fene, Sp. 86/A1
Fener (pt.), Turk. 133/D1
Fénérive, Madg. 147/K10
Feng Xian, China 114/D4
Fengári (peak), Gre. 89/J2
Fengcheng, China 113/L6
Fengcheng, China 115/C2
Fenghuang, China 125/J2
Fengle (riv.), China 114/D5
Fengnan, China 114/J7
Fengning, China 114/D2
Fengqing, China 125/G3
Fengqiu, China 114/C4
Fengrun, China 114/J7
Fengshan, Tai. 121/D3
Fengtai, China 114/H7
Fengxian, China 114/L9
Fengyang, China 114/D4
Fengyüan, Tai. 121/D3
Fengzhen, China 114/C2
Fenimore Pass (chan.), Ak, US 176/C5
Fenoarivo Atsinanana, Madg. 149/J7
Fens (phys. reg.), Eng, UK 75/G1
Fensmark, Den. 80/D4
Fensterbach (riv.), Ger. 97/F4
Fenton, Mi, US 172/D3
Fenton, Mo, US 179/G8
Fenton (lake), Mi, US 177/E7
Fenxi, China 114/B3
Feodosiya, Ukr. 104/E3
Fer, Cap de (cape), Alg. 142/K6
Ferbane, Ire. 73/Q10
Ferdinandshof, Ger. 83/G2
Fère-Champenoise, Fr. 94/C6
Fère-en-Tardenois, Fr. 94/C5
Ferentino, It. 88/C2
Ferento (ruin), It. 88/C1
Fergus Falls, Mn, US 169/J4
Ferguson, Mo, US 179/G8
Ferguson (lake), Nun., Can. 164/F2
Ferihegy (int'l arpt.), Hun. 90/D2
Ferkéssédougou, C.d'Iv. 144/D4
Ferlach, Aus. 85/L3
Fermanagh (dist.), NI, UK 76/A3
Fermi National Accelerator Laboratory, Il, US 177/P16
Fermignano, It. 101/F5
Fermin (pt.), Ca, US 178/F8
Fermo, It. 85/K5
Fermoselle, Sp. 86/B2
Fermoy, Ire. 73/P10
Fernán-Núñez, Sp. 86/C4
Fernandina (isl.), Ecu. 198/E7
Fernandina Beach, Fl, US 175/H4
Fernando de Noronha (isl.), Braz. 189/F3
Fernandópolis, Braz. 197/B2
Ferndale, Md, US 180/B5
Ferndale, Mi, US 177/F7
Ferney-Voltaire, Fr. 98/C5
Fernie, BC, Can. 168/E3
Fernpass (pass), Aus. 99/G3
Ferntree Gully NP, Austl. 157/G5
Ferrandina, It. 88/E2
Ferrara (prov.), It. 101/E3
Ferrara, It. 101/E3
Ferrat (cape), Alg. 142/E5
Ferreira do Alentejo, Port. 86/A3
Ferrelview, Mo, US 179/D5
Ferreñafe, Peru 198/B2
Ferret (cape), Fr. 84/C4
Ferrette, Fr. 98/D3
Ferriday, La, US 171/K5
Ferriere, It. 100/C3
Ferrière-la-Grande, Fr. 94/D3
Ferrières, Belg. 95/E3
Ferryden, Sc, UK 78/D3
Ferryfield (int'l arpt.), Eng, UK 75/G5
Ferryhill, Eng, UK 77/G2
Fertő (Neusiedler See) (lake), Aus. 85/M3
Ferté-Bernard, Fr. 84/D2
Fértil (valley), Arg. 199/C3
Ferwerd, Neth. 92/C2
Fès, Mor. 142/B2
Fès (prov.), Mor. 142/B3
Fesches-le-Châtel, Fr. 98/C2
Feshie (riv.), Sc, UK 78/C2
Fessenheim, Fr. 98/D2
Festival Centre, Austl. 155/M8
Feteşti, Rom. 91/H3
Fethaland (pt.), Sc, UK 73/W13
Fethiye, Turk. 132/B2
Feucherolles, Fr. 72/H5
Feucht, Ger. 96/E4
Feuchtwangen, Ger. 96/D4
Feuilles (lake), Qu, Can. 165/J3
Feuilles, Rivière aux (riv.), Qu, Can. 165/J3
Feuquières, Fr. 94/A4
Feuquières-en-Vimeu, Fr. 94/A3
Feurs, Fr. 84/F4
Fevzipaşa, Turk. 133/E1
Feyẕābād, Afg. 131/K1
Fez (Saïss) (int'l arpt.), Mor. 142/B3
Fezzan (reg.), Libya 138/H2
Fferna, Moel (peak), Wal, UK 77/E6
Ffestiniog, Wal, UK 76/E6
Fianarantsoa (prov.), Madg. 149/H8
Fianarantsoa, Madg. 149/H8
Fianga, Chad 138/J6
Ficarolo, It. 101/E3
Fichtelberg (peak), Ger. 97/F2
Fichtelgebirge (mts.), Ger. 82/F3
Fichtelnaab (riv.), Ger. 97/E3
Ficksburg, SAfr. 148/D3
Fidenza, It. 100/D3
Fié (riv.), Gui. 144/C4
Field (riv.), Austl. 155/M9
Fieldon, Il, US 179/G7
Fieni, Rom. 91/G3
Fier (riv.), Fr. 98/B6
Fierzë (lake), Alb. 89/G1
Fiesch, Swi. 98/E5
Fiesole, It. 101/E5
Fiesso, It. 101/F2
Fiesso Umbertiano, It. 101/E3
Fiesta Texas, Tx, US 179/T20
Fife, Wa, US 177/C3
Fife (pol. reg.), Sc, UK 78/D4
Fife Ness (pt.), Sc, UK 78/D4
Fifth Cataract (falls), Sudan 143/C5
Figalo (cape), Alg. 142/D2
Figari, Fr. 88/A2
Figeac, Fr. 84/E4
Figline Valdarno, It. 101/E5
Figueira da Foz, Port. 86/A2
Figueres, Sp. 87/G1
Figuig, Mor. 141/E2
Figuig (prov.), Mor. 142/C3
Fiherenana (riv.), Madg. 149/G8
Fiji (ctry.) 158/G6
Filadelfia, Par. 199/D1
Filadélfia, Braz. 196/A2
Filattiera, It. 100/C4
Filchner Ice Shelf, Ant. 202/Y
Filey (bay), Eng, UK 77/H3
Fili, Gre. 89/N8
Filiaşi, Rom. 91/F3
Filiatái, Gre. 89/G3
Filiatrá, Gre. 89/G4
Filicudi (isl.), It. 88/D3
Filingué, Niger 145/F3
Filippiás, Gre. 89/G3
Filippoi (ruin), Gre. 89/J2
Filipstad, Swe. 80/F2
Filisur, Swi. 99/F4
Fillière (riv.), Fr. 98/C6
Fillmore, Ca, US 178/B2
Fillmore, Ut, US 170/D3
Filomeno Mata, Mex. 185/M6
Filótion, Gre. 89/J4
Filottrano, It. 101/G6
Fils (riv.), Ger. 96/C5
Filsum, Ger. 93/E2
Fimi (riv.), D.R. Congo 139/J8
Fina, Forêt Classée de, Mali 144/C3
Finale Emilia, It. 101/E3
Finale Ligure, It. 100/B4
Fiñana, Sp. 86/D4
Finch Hatton, Austl. 156/C3
Findel (int'l arpt.), Lux. 95/F4
Findhorn, Sc, UK 78/C1
Findhorn (riv.), Sc, UK 78/B2
Findlay, Oh, US 172/D3
Findochty, Sc, UK 78/D1
Finesville, NJ, US 180/C2
Fingal, Austl. 157/C4
Finger (lake), On, Can. 169/K2
Finhaut, Swi. 98/C5
Finike, Turk. 133/B1
Finisterre, Sp. 86/A1
Finisterre (cape), Sp. 86/A1
Finke (riv.), Austl. 155/G3
Finke Gorge NP, Austl. 155/G3
Finkenstein, Aus. 85/K3
Finksburg, Md, US 180/B5
Finland (ctry.) 79/H2
Finland (gulf), Eur. 79/H2
Finlay (riv.), BC, Can. 164/D3
Finlay (mts.), Tx, US 174/B4
Finley, Austl. 157/C2
Finn (riv.), Ire. 73/Q9
Finnentrop, Ger. 93/E6
Finnigan (mt.), Austl. 156/B1
Finnis (cape), Austl. 155/G5
Finnmark (co.), Nor. 79/G1
Fino Mornasco, It. 100/C1
Finsing, Ger. 97/E6
Finspång, Swe. 80/F2
Finsteraarhorn (peak), Swi. 98/E4
Finström, Fin. 81/H1
Fintel, Ger. 93/G2
Fintona, NI, UK 76/A3
Fionn Loch (lake), Sc, UK 78/A1
Fiora (riv.), It. 85/J5
Fiorano, It. 101/D3
Fiordland NP, NZ 159/R12
Fiorenzuola d'Arda, It. 100/C3
Fircrest, Wa, US 177/C3
Fire Island Nat'l Seashore, NY, US 181/E2
Firenze (prov.), It. 101/E5
Firenze (Florence), It. 101/E5
Firenzuola, It. 101/E4
Firestone, Co, US 179/C2
Firmat, Arg. 200/E2
Firmi, Fr. 84/E4
Firminy, Fr. 84/F4
Fīrozābād, India 126/B2
Firozpur, India 128/C4
First Cataract (falls), Egypt 143/C3
Fīrūz Kūh, Iran 130/F1
Fīrūzābād, Iran 130/F3
Fischa (riv.), Aus. 91/P7
Fischach, Ger. 99/G1
Fischamend Markt, Aus. 91/P7
Fischbacher Alpen (mts.), Aus. 85/L3
Fischen im Allgäu, Ger. 99/G3
Fischer, Tx, US 179/U20
Fish (riv.), Namb. 147/C5
Fisher (bay), Mb, Can. 169/J3
Fisher (str.), Nun., Can. 165/H2
Fisher Branch, Mb, Can. 169/J3
Fisherman (isl.), Austl. 156/F6
Fishers (isl.), NY, US 181/G1
Fishguard, Wal, UK 74/B3
Fisht (peak), Rus. 104/F4
Fismes, Fr. 94/C5
Fitful Head (pt.), Sc, UK 73/W14
Fitjar, Nor. 80/A2
Fitton (mt.), Yk, Can. 176/L2
Fitzgerald, Ga, US 175/H4
Fitzgerald River NP, Austl. 154/C5
Fitzroy (peak), Arg. 201/B6
Fitzroy (riv.), Austl. 151/B2
Fitzwilliam (str.), NW, Can. 165/R7
Fiume Veneto, It. 101/F1
Fiumicino, It. 88/C2
Five Sisters (peak), Sc, UK 78/A2
Fivemiletown, NI, UK 76/A3
Fivizzano, It. 100/D4
Fjell, Nor. 80/A1
Fjerritslev, Den. 80/C3
Fjugesta, Swe. 80/F2
Flå, Nor. 80/C1
Flachslanden, Ger. 96/D4
Fladungen, Ger. 96/D1
Flagler, Co, US 174/C2
Flagler Beach, Fl, US 175/H4
Flagstaff, Az, US 170/E4
Flambeau (riv.), Wi, US 169/L4
Flamborough, On, Can. 173/Q9
Flamborough Head (pt.), Eng, UK 77/H3
Fläming (hills), Ger. 82/G2
Flaming Gorge (res.), Ut,Wy, US 168/F5
Flaming Gorge Nat'l Rec. Area, Ut,Wy, US 170/E2
Flamingo Field (int'l arpt.), NAnt. 194/D1
Flanagan (riv.), On, Can. 169/K2
Flanders (reg.), Fr. 84/E1
Flanders, NY, US 181/F2
Flat Holm (isl.), Eng, UK 74/C4
Flat River, Mo, US 171/K3
Flathead (riv.), Mt, US 168/E4
Flathead (lake), Mt, US 168/E4
Flathead, South Fork (riv.), Mt, US 168/E3
Flattery (cape), Austl. 156/B1
Flattery (cape), Wa, US 168/B3
Flavio Alfaro, Ecu. 194/B5
Flawil, Swi. 99/F3
Flaxlanden, Fr. 98/D2
Fleet, Eng, UK 75/F4
Fleetwood, Pa, US 180/C3
Fleetwood, Eng, UK 77/E4
Flekkefjord, Nor. 80/B2
Flemington, NJ, US 180/D2
Flemington Racecourse, Austl. 157/F5
Flemish Brabant (prov.), Belg. 95/D2
Flen, Swe. 80/G2
Flensburg, Ger. 80/C4
Flero, It. 100/D2
Fleron, Belg. 95/E2
Flers, Fr. 84/C2
Flesland (int'l arpt.), Nor. 80/A1
Fletschhorn (peak), Swi. 98/D5
Fleurance, Fr. 84/D5
Fleurier, Swi. 98/C4
Fleurus, Belg. 95/D3
Fleury-les-Aubrais, Fr. 84/D3
Flevoland (prov.), Neth. 92/C4
Flevoland (isl.), Neth. 82/C2
Flexenpass (pass), Aus. 99/G3
Flieden, Ger. 96/C2
Flieden (riv.), Ger. 96/C2
Fliess, Aus. 99/G3
Flims, Swi. 99/F4
Flin Flon, Mb, Can. 169/H2
Flinders (bay), Austl. 154/B5
Flinders (ranges), Austl. 155/H5
Flinders (reef), Austl. 151/D2
Flinders (reefs), Austl. 151/D4
Flinders (riv.), Austl. 151/D2
Flinders Chase NP, Austl. 155/H5
Flinders Ranges NP, Austl. 155/H4
Flinders Reefs (isls.), Austl. 156/C2
Flines-lez-Raches, Fr. 94/C3
Flint (lake), Nun., Can. 165/J2
Flint (isl.), Kiri. 159/K6
Flint, Wal, UK 77/E5
Flint (hills), Ks, US 171/H3
Flint (riv.), Ga, US 175/G4
Flint, Mi, US 172/D3
Flint, South Branch (riv.), Mi, US 177/F5
Flintbek, Ger. 80/D4
Flintshire (co.), Wal, UK 77/E5
Flisa, Nor. 80/E1
Flix, Sp. 87/F2
Flixecourt, Fr. 94/B3
Flize, Fr. 95/D4
Floby, Swe. 80/E2
Floda, Swe. 80/E3
Flögelner See (riv.), Ger. 93/F1
Flöha (riv.), Ger. 83/G3
Floing, Fr. 95/D4
Flonheim, Ger. 96/B3
Flora (mt.), Austl. 154/C2
Flora, Nor. 79/C3
Flora, Il, US 171/K3
Floral Park, NY, US 181/L9
Florange, Fr. 95/F5
Florânia, Braz. 196/C2
Floraville, Il, US 179/G9
Floreffe, Belg. 95/D3
Florence, Al, US 175/G3
Florence, Az, US 170/E4
Florence, SC, US 175/J3
Florence (Firenze), It. 85/J5
Florence-Graham, Ca, US 178/F8
Florencia, Col. 194/C4
Florennes, Belg. 95/D3
Florenville, Belg. 95/E4
Flores (isl.), Indo. 123/F5
Flores (sea), Indo. 123/E5
Flores, Guat. 186/D2
Flores (dept.), Uru. 201/F2
Flores do Piauí, Braz. 196/B2
Floresta, Braz. 196/C3
Florham Park, NJ, US 181/H8
Floriano, Braz. 196/B2
Florianópolis, Braz. 197/B3
Florida, Col. 194/B4
Florida, Cuba 187/G1
Florida (str.), Cuba,US 167/K7
Florida, Hon. 186/D3
Florida, Peru 198/B2
Florida, Uru. 201/K11
Florida (dept.), Uru. 201/F2
Florida (state), US 175/H4
Florida (bay), Fl, US 175/H5
Florida, NY, US 180/D1
Florida Keys (isls.), Fl, US 175/H5
Floridablanca, Col. 194/C3
Floridia, It. 88/D4
Florin, Ca, US 177/M10
Flórina, Gre. 89/G2
Florissant, Mo, US 179/G8
Florissant Fossil Beds Nat'l Mon., Co, US 174/B2
Flörsbachtal, Ger. 96/C2
Flörsheim am Main, Ger. 96/B2
Flörsheim-Dalsheim, Ger. 96/B3
Florstadt, Ger. 96/B2
Flossenbürg, Ger. 97/F3
Floyd, Mo, US 179/E5
Floydada, Tx, US 171/G4
Fluchthorn (peak), Aus. 99/G4
Flüelapass (pass), Swi. 99/F4
Flüelen, Swi. 99/E4
Fluessen (lake), Neth. 92/C3
Flums, Swi. 99/F3
Flushing, Mi, US 172/D3
Fly (riv.), PNG 158/D5
Flying Fish (cape), Ant. 202/T
Fnjóská (riv.), Ice. 79/P6
Foam Lake, Sk, Can. 169/H3
Foča, Bosn. 90/D4
Fochabers, Sc, UK 78/C1
Fochville, SAfr. 148/P13
Fockbek, Ger. 80/C4
Focşani, Rom. 91/H3
Fogang, China 125/K3
Foggia, It. 88/D2
Foglia (riv.), It. 101/F5
Foglizzo, It. 100/A2
Föglö (isl.), Fin. 81/J3
Fogo (isl.), CpV. 135/J10
Fohnsdorf, Aus. 85/L3
Föhren, Ger. 95/F4
Foix, Fr. 84/D5
Folarskardnuten (peak), Nor. 80/B1
Folda (inlet), Nor. 79/E2
Földeák, Hun. 90/E2
Folégandros (isl.), Gre. 89/J4
Folembray, Fr. 94/C4
Foley (isl.), Nun., Can. 165/J2
Folgaria, It. 99/H6
Foligno, It. 85/K5
Folkestone, Eng, UK 75/H4
Folkston, Ga, US 175/H4
Follainville-Dennemont, Fr. 72/H4
Follonica, Golfo di (gulf), It. 85/J5
Folschviller, Fr. 95/F5
Folsom, NJ, US 180/D4
Fomboni, Com. 149/G6
Fond du Lac, Wi, US 169/L5
Fond du Lac, Sk, Can. 164/F3
Fond du Lac (riv.), Sk, Can. 164/F3
Fondi, It. 88/C2
Fondo, It. 99/H5
Fongen (peak), Nor. 79/D3
Fonni, It. 88/A2
Fonsagrada, Sp. 86/B1
Fonseca, Col. 194/C2
Fonseca (gulf), Nic. 182/D5
Font Sancte, Pic de la (peak), Fr. 85/G4
Fontaine, Fr. 84/F4
Fontaine-Châalis, Fr. 72/L4
Fontaine-lès-Dijon, Fr. 98/A3
Fontaine-lès-Luxeuil, Fr. 98/C2
Fontaine-L'Evêque, Belg. 95/D3
Fontainebleau, Fr. 84/E2
Fontana, Ca, US 178/C2
Fontanarossa (int'l arpt.), It. 88/D4
Fontanella, It. 100/C2
Fontanellato, It. 100/D3
Fontaniva, It. 101/E1
Fonte Boa, Braz. 195/E5
Fontenailles, Fr. 72/L6
Fontenais, Swi. 98/D3
Fontenay-en-Parisis, Fr. 72/K4
Fontenay-le-Comte, Fr. 84/C3
Fontenay-le-Fleury, Fr. 72/J5
Fontenay-les-Briis, Fr. 72/J6
Fontenay-Saint-Père, Fr. 72/H4
Fontenay-sous-Bois, Fr. 72/K5
Fontenay-Trésigny, Fr. 72/L5
Fontenelle (res.), Wy, US 168/F5
Fontoy, Fr. 95/F5
Fontur (pt.), Ice. 79/P6
Foping, China 112/J5
Foraker (mt.), Ak, US 176/H3
Forbach, Fr. 95/F5
Forbach, Ger. 96/B5
Forbes, Austl. 157/D2
Forbesganj, India 127/F2
Forcarey, Sp. 86/A1
Forchheim, Ger. 96/E3
Forclaz, Col de la (pass), Swi. 98/D5
Førde, Nor. 79/C3
Fords, NJ, US 181/H9
Foreland (pt.), Eng, UK 74/C4
Foreland, The (pt.), Eng, UK 75/E5
Foremost, Ab, Can. 168/F3
Foreness (pt.), Eng, UK 75/H4
Forest, Ms, US 175/F3
Forest Hill, Md, US 180/B4
Forest Park, Ok, US 179/N14
Forestier (pen.), Austl. 157/D4
Forestier (cape), Austl. 157/D4
Forestville, Qu, Can. 173/G1
Forestville, Md, US 180/B6
Forez, Monts du (mts.), Fr. 84/E4
Forfar, Sc, UK 78/D3
Forges-les-Bains, Fr. 72/J6
Forggensee (lake), Ger. 99/G2
Forillon NP, Qu, Can. 173/H1
Forked River, NJ, US 180/D4
Forkill, NI, UK 76/B3
Forks, Wa, US 168/B4
Forlì, It. 101/F4
Forlì-Cesena (prov.), It. 101/F4
Forlimpopoli, It. 101/F4
Formartine (reg.), Sc, UK 78/D2
Formby, Eng, UK 77/E4
Formby (pt.), Eng, UK 77/E4
Formentera, Isla de (isl.), Sp. 87/F3
Formentor (cape), Sp. 87/G3
Former Yugoslav Republic of Macedonia (Macedonia) (ctry.) 89/G2
Formerie, Fr. 94/A4
Formia, It. 88/C2
Formiga, Braz. 197/C2
Formigine, It. 101/D3
Formignana, It. 101/E3
Formosa, Arg. 199/E2
Formosa, Braz. 196/A4
Formosa (peak), SAfr. 148/C4
Formosa (isl.), GBis. 144/B4
Formosa do Rio Prêto, Braz. 196/A3
Formosa, Serra (mts.), Braz. 193/G6
Formoso (riv.), Braz. 193/J6
Fornacelle, It. 101/E5
Fornaci di Barga, It. 100/D4
Fornæs (cape), Den. 80/D3
Fornebu (int'l arpt.), Nor. 80/D2
Fornovo di Taro, It. 100/D3
Forres, Sc, UK 78/C1
Forrest City, Ar, US 171/K4
Forsand, Nor. 80/B2
Forshaga, Swe. 80/E2
Forssa, Fin. 81/K1
Forstern, Ger. 97/E6
Forstinning, Ger. 97/E6
Forsyth, Mt, US 168/G4
Forsyth, Ga, US 175/H3
Forsyth (range), Austl. 156/A3
Forsythe NWR, NJ, US 180/D5
Fort Abbās, Pak. 128/B5
Fort Augustus, Sc, UK 78/B2
Fort Beaufort, SAfr. 148/D4
Fort Belvoir, Va, US 180/A6
Fort Benton, Mt, US 168/F4
Fort Bragg, Ca, US 168/C6
Fort Chambly Nat'l Hist. Park, Qu, Can. 173/P7
Fort Chipewyan, Ab, Can. 164/E3
Fort Cobb (res.), Ok, US 171/H4
Fort Collins, Co, US 179/B1
Fort Collins Museum, Co, US 179/B1
Fort Davis, Tx, US 171/G5
Fort de Douaumont, Fr. 95/E5
Fort-de-France, Guad. 183/N9
Fort de Vaux, Fr. 95/E5
Fort Desaix Mil. Res., Mart., Fr. 183/N9
Fort Dodge, Ia, US 169/K5
Fort Erie, On, Can. 173/S10
Fort Frances, On, Can. 169/K3
Fort Frederica Nat'l Mon., Ga, US 175/H4
Fort George Nat'l Hist. Park, On, Can. 173/R9
Fort Gibson (lake), Ok, US 174/E3
Fort Good Hope, NW, Can. 164/D2
Fort Hancock, NJ, US 181/J10
Fort Howard, Md, US 180/B5
Fort Kent, Me, US 173/G2
Fort Lauderdale, Fl, US 175/H5
Fort Lauderdale-Hollywood (int'l arpt.), Fl, US 175/H5
Fort Lee, NJ, US 181/K8
Fort Lewis, Wa, US 177/B3
Fort Liard, NW, Can. 164/D2
Fort Liberté, Haiti 187/J2

236
Fort L – Garça

Fort Lupton, Co, US 179/C2
Fort Macleod, Ab, Can. 168/E3
Fort Madison, Ia, US 169/L5
Fort-Mahon-Plage, Fr. 94/A3
Fort Malden Nat'l Hist. Park, On, Can. 177/F7
Fort-Mardyck, Fr. 94/B1
Fort Matanzas Nat'l Mon., Fl, US 175/H4
Fort McDowell Ind. Res., Az, US 179/S18
Fort McHenry Nat'l Mon., Md, US 180/B5
Fort McMurray, Ab, Can. 164/E3
Fort McPherson, NW, Can. 176/M2
Fort Meade, Md, US 180/B5
Fort Morgan, Co, US 171/G2
Fort Myers, Fl, US 175/H5
Fort Nelson, BC, Can. 164/D3
Fort Nelson (riv.), BC, Can. 164/D3
Fort Nottingham, SAfr. 149/E3
Fort Payne, Al, US 175/G3
Fort Peck (dam), Mt, US 169/G4
Fort Peck (lake), Mt, US 168/G4
Fort Pierce, Fl, US 175/H5
Fort Portal, Ugan. 146/A2
Fort Providence, NW, Can. 164/E2
Fort Qu'Appelle, Sk, Can. 169/H3
Fort Randall (dam), SD, US 169/J5
Fort Resolution, NW, Can. 164/E2
Fort Saint James, BC, Can. 168/B2
Fort Saint John, BC, Can. 164/D3
Fort Saskatchewan, Ab, Can. 168/E2
Fort Scott, Ks, US 171/J3
Fort-Shevchenko, Kaz. 105/J3
Fort Simpson, NW, Can. 164/D2
Fort Smith, Ar, US 171/J4
Fort Smith, NW, Can. 164/E2
Fort Stanwix Nat'l Mon., NY, US 172/F3
Fort Stockton, Tx, US 171/G5
Fort Sumner, NM, US 171/F4
Fort Sumter, SC, US 175/J3
Fort Tilden, NY, US 181/K9
Fort Totten, ND, US 169/J4
Fort Vasquez Museum, Co, US 179/C2
Fort Vermilion, Ab, Can. 164/E3
Fort Wadsworth, NY, US 181/J9
Fort Walton Beach, Fl, US 175/G4
Fort Wayne, In, US 172/C3
Fort Wellington Nat'l Hist. Park, Can. 172/F2
Fort William, Sc, UK 78/A3
Fort Yates, ND, US 169/H4
Fort Yukon, Ak, US 176/J2
Fortaleza, Braz. 196/C1
Fortaleza dos Nogueiras, Braz. 196/A2
Fortaleza Santa Teresa, Uru. 201/G2
Forte dei Marmi, It. 100/D5
Fortescue (riv.), Austl. 154/C2
Fortescue, NJ, US 180/C5
Forth, Sc, UK 78/C5
Forth (riv.), Sc, UK 78/B4
Forth, Firth of (inlet), Sc, UK 78/C4
Fortín, Mex. 185/N8
Fortore (riv.), It. 88/D2
Fortrose, Sc, UK 78/B1
Fortuna, Braz. 196/A2
Fortuna, Arg. 200/D2
Fortuna Ledge, Ak, US 176/F3
Fortune (bay), Nf, Can. 173/L2
Fortune, Nf, Can. 173/L2
Forty Fort, Pa, US 180/C1
Forty Mile Scrub NP, Austl. 156/B2
Foshan, China 125/K3
Fosheim (pen.), Nun., Can. 165/S7
Foss (riv.), Eng, UK 77/G3
Fossalta di Piave, It. 101/F1
Fossalta di Portogruaro, It. 101/F1
Fossano, It. 100/A3
Fosses, Fr. 72/K4
Fosses-la-Ville, Belg. 95/D3
Fossil, Or, US 168/C4
Fossil Creek (res.), Co, US 179/B2
Fossò, It. 101/F2
Fossombrone, It. 101/F5
Foster, Austl. 157/C3
Foster Pond, Il, US 179/G9
Fosterburg, Il, US 179/G8
Fostoria, Oh, US 172/D3
Fót, Hun. 91/R9
Foucarmont, Fr. 94/A4
Foucherans, Fr. 98/B3
Foug, Fr. 95/E6
Fougères, Fr. 84/C2
Fougerolles, Fr. 98/C2
Fouilloy, Fr. 94/B4
Foul (bay), Egypt, Sudan 139/N3
Foula (isl.), Sc, UK 73/V13
Foulness (pt.), Eng, UK 75/G3
Foulness (isl.), Eng, UK 75/G3
Foulness (riv.), Eng, UK 77/H4
Foum Zguid, Mor. 140/D3
Foumban, Camr. 138/H6
Foundiougne, Sen. 144/A3
Fountain, Il, US 179/G9
Fountain Hill, Pa, US 180/C2
Fountain Hills, Az, US 179/S18
Fountain Valley, Ca, US 178/G8
Fountains Abbey, Eng, UK 77/G3
Fourchambault, Fr. 84/E3
Fourche La Fave (riv.), Ar, US 171/J4
Fourges, Fr. 72/G4
Fourmies, Fr. 94/D4
Fourth Cataract (falls), Sudan 143/C5
Fouta Djallon (phys. reg.), Gui. 138/C5
Foveaux (str.), NZ 159/R12
Fowey (riv.), Eng, UK 74/B6
Fowman, Iran 130/E1
Fox (isls.), Ak, US 176/E5
Fox (mtn.), Yk, Can. 176/M3
Fox (riv.), Il,Wi, US 169/L5
Fox (isl.), Wa, US 177/B3
Fox Creek, Ab, Can. 168/D2
Fox Glacier, NZ 159/S11
Fox Lake, Il, US 177/P15
Fox River Grove, Il, US 177/P15
Fox Valley, Sk, Can. 168/F3
Foxe (pen.), Nun., Can. 165/J2
Foxe (chan.), Nun., Can. 165/H2
Foxe Basin (chan.), Nun., Can. 165/J2
Foxen (lake), Swe. 80/D2
Foyle (riv.), NI, UK 76/A2
Foz, Sp. 86/B1
Foz do Iguaçu, Braz. 199/F2
Frackville, Pa, US 180/B2
Fraga, Sp. 87/F2
Fragosa, Cayo (isl.), Cuba 187/G1
Fraiburgo, Braz. 197/B3
Frailes, Cordillera de los (mts.), Ven. 192/E7
Fraisans, Fr. 98/B3
Fraize, Fr. 98/D1
Frameries, Belg. 94/C3
Framlingham, Eng, UK 75/H2
Frammersbach, Ger. 96/C2
Franca, Braz. 197/C2
Francavilla al Mare, It. 88/D1
Francavilla Fontana, It. 89/E2
Francavilla in Sinni, It. 88/E2
France (ctry.) 84/D3
Frances (cape), Cuba 187/F1
Frances (lake), Yk, Can. 164/C2
Francés Viejo (cape), DRep. 183/H4
Franceville, Gabon 138/H8
Franche-Comté (pol. reg.), Fr. 98/B5
Franche-Comteé (pol. reg.), Fr. 85/G3
Francis Case (lake), SD, US 169/J5
Francisco de Orellana, Peru 198/C1
Francisco Escárcega, Mex. 186/D2
Francisco Javier Mina, Mex. 184/C3
Francisco Sá, Braz. 196/B5
Francisco Zarco, Mex. 184/A1
Francistown, Bots. 147/E5
Franco da Rocha, Braz. 197/G8
Francolino, It. 101/E3
Franconville, Fr. 72/J5
Franeker, Neth. 92/C2
Frangy, Fr. 98/B5
Frank Hahn NP, Austl. 154/C5
Franken Wald (for.), Ger. 97/E2
Frankenau, Ger. 93/F6
Frankenberg-Eder, Ger. 93/F6
Frankenburg am Hausruck, Aus. 97/G6
Frankenhöhe (mts.), Ger. 82/F4
Frankenmarkt, Aus. 97/G7
Frankenmuth, Mi, US 172/D3
Frankenthal, Ger. 96/B3
Frankfort (cap.), Ky, US 172/C4
Frankfort, SAfr. 148/E2
Frankfurt, Ger. 83/H2
Frankfurt (int'l arpt.), Ger. 96/B2
Frankfurt am Main, Ger. 96/B2
Fränkische Alb (mts.), Ger. 82/F4
Fränkische Rezat (riv.), Ger. 96/D4
Fränkische Saale (riv.), Ger. 82/E3
Fränkische Schweiz (reg.), Ger. 85/J2
Fränkische Schweiz (reg.), Ger. 82/F4
Frankland (cape), Austl. 157/C3
Franklin (pt.), Ak, US 176/G1
Franklin, NC, US 175/H3
Franklin, La, US 171/K5
Franklin, Ky, US 172/C4
Franklin, In, US 172/C4
Franklin, Tn, US 172/C5
Franklin, WV, US 172/E4
Franklin, NJ, US 180/D1
Franklin (mts.), NW, Can. 164/D2
Franklin (bay), NW, Can. 164/D2
Franklin, Mi, US 177/F6
Franklin D. Roosevelt (lake), Wa, US 168/D3
Franklin Lakes, NJ, US 181/J7
Franklin-Lower Gordon Wild Rivers NP, Austl. 157/C4
Franklin Mineral Museum, NJ, US 180/D1
Franklin Park, Il, US 177/Q16
Franklin Square, NY, US 181/L9
Franksville, Wi, US 177/Q14
Franois, Fr. 98/B3
Franschhoek, SAfr. 148/L10
Fransisco Beltrão, Braz. 199/F2
Fransisco Morato, Braz. 197/G8
Františkovy Lázně, Czh. 97/F2
Franz Josef Land (isls.), Rus. 202/C
Franz Joseph Strauss (int'l arpt.), Ger. 97/E6
Franzburg, Ger. 80/E4
Fraser (isl.), Austl. 151/E3
Fraser (mt.), Austl. 154/C3
Fraser (riv.), BC, Can. 168/C2
Fraser, Mi, US 177/G6
Fraser Lake, BC, Can. 168/B2
Fraser NP, Austl. 157/C3
Fraserburg, SAfr. 148/C3
Fraserburgh, Sc, UK 78/D1
Frasne, Fr. 98/C4
Frassine (riv.), It. 101/E2
Frassino, It. 101/D2
Frastanz, Aus. 99/F3
Frati, Monte dei (peak), It. 101/F5
Frauenfeld, Swi. 99/E2
Fraunberg, Ger. 97/E6
Fray Bentos, Uru. 201/J10
Fray Marcos, Uru. 201/L11
Frazier Park, Ca, US 170/C4
Frechen, Ger. 95/F2
Freckenfeld, Ger. 96/B4
Fred (mt.), Les. 148/E3
Frederica, De, US 180/C6
Fredericia, Den. 80/C4
Frederick (reef), Austl. 151/E3
Frederick, Co, US 179/C2
Frederick, Md, US 172/E4
Frederick (co.), Md, US 180/A5
Frederick, Ok, US 171/H4
Fredericksburg, Pa, US 180/B3
Fredericksburg, Tx, US 171/H5
Frederickton, Austl. 157/E1
Fredericton (cap.), NB, Can. 173/H2
Frederik Willem IV (falls), Sur. 195/G4
Frederiks, Den. 80/C3
Frederiksborg (co.), Den. 80/E4
Frederiksborg Slot (Frederiksborg Castle), Den. 80/E4
Frederikshavn, Den. 80/D3
Frederiksted, USVI 183/M8
Fredersdorf bei Berlin, Ger. 82/Q7
Fredonia, Az, US 170/D3
Fredonia, NY, US 172/E3
Fredriksberg, Swe. 80/F1
Fredrikstad, Nor. 80/D2
Free State (prov.), SAfr. 148/P13
Freeburg, Il, US 179/H9
Freeburg, Pa, US 180/B2
Freedom, Ok, US 174/D2
Freehold, NJ, US 180/D3
Freeland, Pa, US 180/C1
Freeland, Md, US 180/B4
Freeland, Wa, US 177/B1
Freeling (mt.), Austl. 155/G2
Freeling Heights (peak), Austl. 155/H4
Freemansburg, Pa, US 180/C2
Freeport, Bahm. 183/F2
Freeport, Il, US 169/L5
Freeport, NY, US 181/L9
Freeport, Tx, US 171/J5
Freer, Tx, US 174/D5
Freetown (cap.), SLeo. 144/B4
Fregenal de la Sierra, Sp. 86/B3
Fréhel (cape), Fr. 84/B2
Frei Inocêncio, Braz. 197/D1
Freib Mulde (riv.), Ger. 82/G3
Freiberg, Ger. 83/G3
Freiburg, Ger. 93/G1
Freiburg, Ger. 98/D2
Freienbach, Swi. 99/E3
Freihung, Ger. 97/E3
Freilassing, Ger. 97/F7
Freinsheim, Ger. 96/B3
Freire, Chile 200/B3
Freisen, Ger. 95/G4
Freising, Ger. 97/E6
Freistadt, Aus. 97/H5
Freital, Ger. 83/G3
Freixo de Espada à Cinta, Port. 86/B2
Frejorgues (int'l arpt.), Fr. 84/E5
Fréjus, Fr. 85/G5
Frekhaug, Nor. 80/A1
Frémainfille, Fr. 72/H4
Fremdingen, Ger. 96/D5
Frémécourt, Fr. 72/J4
Fremont (riv.), Ut, US 170/E3
Fremont, Oh, US 172/D3
Fremont, Mi, US 172/C3
Fremont, Ca, US 170/B3
Fremont (isl.), Ut, US 179/J11
French (riv.), On, Can. 172/D2
French Creek State Park, Pa, US 180/C3
French Frigate Shoals (bar), Hi, US 159/J2
French Guiana (dpcy.), Fr. 193/H3
French Polynesia (terr.), Fr. 159/L6
Frenchman (riv.), Can.,US 164/F4
Frenchman's (bay), On, Can. 173/R8
Frenchmans Cap (peak), Austl. 157/C4
Frenchtown, NJ, US 180/C2
Frenda, Alg. 142/F5
Frépillon, Fr. 72/J4
Freren, Ger. 93/E4
Fresco (riv.), Braz. 193/H5
Fresco, C.d'Iv. 144/D5
Fresia, Chile 200/B4
Fresnes, Fr. 72/J5
Fresnes-en-Woëvre, Fr. 95/E5
Fresnillo, Mex. 184/E4
Fresno, Ca, US 170/C3
Fresnoy-le-Grand, Fr. 94/C4
Fresse-sur-Moselle, Fr. 98/C2
Fressenneville, Fr. 94/A3
Fretin, Fr. 94/C2
Freuchie (lake), Sc, UK 78/C3
Freudenberg, Ger. 97/E4
Freudenberg, Ger. 95/G2
Freudenberg, Ger. 95/F4
Freudenstadt, Ger. 99/E1
Frévent, Fr. 94/B3
Freycinet (har.), Austl. 154/B3
Freycinet NP, Austl. 157/D4
Freyming-Merlebach, Fr. 95/F5
Freystadt, Ger. 97/E4
Freyung, Ger. 97/G5
Fria (cape), Namb. 147/B4
Frías, Arg. 199/C2
Frías, Peru 198/B2
Fribourg, Swi. 98/D4
Fribourg (canton), Swi. 98/D4
Frick, Swi. 98/E3
Frickenhausen am Main, Ger. 96/D3
Fridingen an der Donau, Ger. 99/E1
Fridolfing, Ger. 97/F6
Friedberg, Ger. 96/B2
Friedberg, Ger. 96/D6
Friedeburg, Ger. 93/E2
Friedrichsdorf, Ger. 96/B2
Friedrichshafen, Ger. 99/F2
Friedrichstadt, Ger. 80/C4
Friedrichsthal, Ger. 95/G5
Frielendorf, Ger. 93/G7
Friesenhagen, Ger. 95/G2
Friesenheim, Ger. 98/D1
Friesland (prov.), Neth. 92/C2
Friesoythe, Ger. 93/E2
Frignicourt, Fr. 95/D6
Frio (riv.), Tx, US 171/H5
Friockheim, Sc, UK 78/D3
Friol, Sp. 86/B1
Frisange, Lux. 95/F4
Fristad, Swe. 80/E3
Fritsla, Swe. 80/E3
Fritzlar, Ger. 93/G6
Friuli-Venezia Giula (prov.), It. 85/K3
Friville-Escarbotin, Fr. 94/A3
Frobisher (bay), Nun., Can. 165/K2
Frogmore, Eng, UK 72/A3
Frohavel (inlet), Nor. 79/D3
Frohnleiten, Aus. 85/L3
Froid-Chapelle, Belg. 95/D3
Froideconche, Fr. 98/C2
Froissy, Fr. 94/B4
Froland, Nor. 80/C2
Frolovo, Rus. 105/G2
Frome (lake), Austl. 151/D4
Frome (riv.), Austl. 155/H4
Frome, Eng, UK 74/D4
Frome (riv.), Eng, UK 74/D5
Froncles, Fr. 98/B1
Front (range), Co, US 171/F2
Fronteira, Port. 86/B3
Frontenhausen, Ger. 97/F5
Frontera, Mex. 186/C2
Frontera Comalapa, Mex. 186/C3
Frontier Army Museum, Ks, US 179/D5
Frontignan, Fr. 84/E5
Fronton, Fr. 84/D5
Frosinone, It. 88/C2
Frösö, Swe. 79/E3
Frotey-lès-Vesoul, Fr. 98/C2
Frouard, Fr. 95/F6
Frövi, Swe. 80/F2
Frøya (isl.), Nor. 79/D3
Frozen (str.), Nun., Can. 165/H2
Fruges, Fr. 94/B2
Fruit Heights, Ut, US 179/K11
Fruška Gora NP, Cro. 90/D3
Frutal, Braz. 197/B1
Frutigen, Swi. 98/D4
Frutillar, Chile 200/B4
Fryazino, Rus. 103/X9
Frýdek-Místek, Czh. 83/K4
Fu Xian, China 114/B4
Fu'an, China 121/C2
Fucecchio, It. 101/D5
Fucheng, China 114/D3
Fuchskaute (peak), Ger. 85/H1
Fuchū, Japan 116/C3
Fuchū, Japan 119/C2
Fuchuan, China 121/B3
Fuchun (riv.), China 114/D5
Fuding, China 121/D2
Fuengirola, Sp. 86/C4
Fuenlabrada, Sp. 87/N9
Fuensalida, Sp. 86/C2
Fuente, Sp. 87/N8
Fuente de Cantos, Sp. 86/B3
Fuente del Maestre, Sp. 86/B3
Fuente Obejuna, Sp. 86/C3
Fuentelapeña, Sp. 86/C2
Fuentes de Oñoro, Sp. 86/B2
Fuentesaúco, Sp. 86/C2
Fuerte (riv.), Mex. 184/C3
Fuerte Olimpo, Par. 192/G8
Fuerteventura (isl.) Canl., Sp. 140/B3
Fuga (isl.), Phil. 121/D4
Fuglebjerg, Den. 80/D4
Fugong, China 125/G2
Fugou, China 114/C4
Fuhai, China 112/E2
Fuhne (riv.), Ger. 82/F3
Fuhse (riv.), Ger. 93/H4
Fuji, Japan 117/F3
Fuji (riv.), Japan 117/F3
Fuji-san (peak), Japan 117/F3
Fuji-Hakone-Izu NP, Japan 117/F3
Fujian (prov.), China 113/L6
Fujieda, Japan 117/F3
Fujihashi, Japan 119/K4
Fujiidera, Japan 119/J6
Fujikawa, Japan 119/B3
Fujimi, Japan 119/D2
Fujino, Japan 119/C2
Fujinomiya, Japan 119/B3
Fujioka, Japan 117/F2
Fujioka, Japan 119/D1
Fujioka, Japan 119/M5
Fujisawa, Japan 117/F3
Fujishiro, Japan 119/E2
Fujiwara, Japan 119/K5
Fujiyoshida, Japan 117/F3
Fukagawa, Japan 118/C2
Fukang, China 112/E3
Fukaya, Japan 119/C1
Fukiage, Japan 119/C1
Fukuchiyama, Japan 119/H5
Fukue, Japan 116/A4
Fukui (pref.), Japan 116/E3
Fukui, Japan 116/E2
Fukuoka, Japan 116/B4
Fukuoka, Japan 119/M4
Fukuoka (int'l arpt.), Japan 116/B4
Fukuoka (pref.), Japan 116/B4
Fukuroi, Japan 117/E3
Fukushima, Japan 117/G2
Fukushima (pref.), Japan 117/F2
Fukushima, Japan 118/B3
Fukuyama, Japan 116/C3
Fūlādī (mtn.), Afg. 131/J2
Fulda (riv.), Ger. 82/E3
Fulda, Ger. 96/C1
Fullerton, Ca, US 178/G8
Fullerton (Whitehall), Pa, US 180/C2
Fully, Swi. 98/D5
Fulpmes, Aus. 99/H3
Fulton, Mo, US 171/K3
Fulton, NY, US 172/E3
Fulton, Ky, US 172/B4
Fulufjället (peak), Swe. 80/E1
Fumaiolo (peak), It. 101/F5
Fumay, Fr. 95/D4
Fumel, Fr. 84/D4
Fumin, China 125/H2
Funabashi, Japan 119/D2
Funafuti (cap.), Tuv. 158/G5
Funafuti (isl.), Tuv. 158/G5
Funan, China 114/C4
Funchal, Port. 140/A2
Funchal (int'l arpt.), Port. 140/A2
Fundación, Col. 194/C2
Fundão, Port. 86/B2
Fundy (bay), US,Can. 173/H2
Fundy NP, NB, Can. 173/H2
Funhalouro, Moz. 147/F5
Funing, China 125/J3
Funing, China 114/D4
Fuorn, Pass dal (Ofenpass) (pass), Swi. 99/G4
Fuping, China 114/C3
Fuqing, China 121/C2
Fuquan, China 125/J2
Fur (riv.), China 115/C2
Furan (riv.), Fr. 98/B6
Furano, Japan 118/C2
Fürfeld, Ger. 95/G4
Furmanov, Rus. 102/J4
Furnas (res.), Braz. 193/J8
Furneaux Group (isls.), Austl. 151/D4
Fürstenau, Ger. 93/E3
Fürstenfeld, Aus. 85/M3
Fürstenfeldbruck, Ger. 96/E6
Fürstenwalde, Ger. 83/H2
Fürth, Ger. 96/B3
Fürth, Ger. 96/D4
Furth, Ger. 97/F5
Furth im Wald, Ger. 97/F4
Furtwangen im Schwarzwald, Ger. 98/E1
Furudal, Swe. 80/F1
Furukawa, Japan 118/B4
Fury and Hecla (str.), Nun., Can. 165/H2
Fushan, China 114/B4
Fushan, China 114/E3
Fushun, China 115/B2
Fushun, China 125/J2
Fusignano, It. 101/E4
Fusio, Swi. 99/E5
Fuso, Japan 119/L5
Fussa, Japan 119/C2
Füssen, Ger. 99/G2
Fusui, China 120/D1
Futaba, Japan 119/A2
Futaleufú, Chile 200/C4
Futami, Japan 119/L7
Futog, Serb. 90/D3
Futrono, Chile 200/B4
Futtsu, Japan 117/F3
Futuna (isl.), Wall., Fr. 158/H6
Fuwah, Egypt 133/B4
Fuxian (lake), China 125/H3
Fuxin, China 114/E2
Fuxin Monggolzu Zizhixian, China 114/E2
Fuyang, China 114/C4
Fuyi (riv.), China 121/B2
Fuyu, China 113/M2
Fuyu, China 113/M2
Fuyuan, China 125/H2
Fuyun, China 112/E2
Füzesabony, Hun. 90/E2
Fuzhou, China 121/C2
Fyn (co.), Den. 80/D4
Fyn (isl.), Den. 79/D5
Fyne, Loch (inlet), Sc, UK 78/A5
Fyresdal, Nor. 80/C2

G

Ga Vache (isl.), Haiti 187/H2
Gaast, Neth. 92/C2
Gabas (riv.), Fr. 84/C5
Gabela, Ang. 147/B3
Gabes (gov.), Tun. 141/H2
Gabes (gulf), Tun. 141/H2
Gabicce Mare, It. 101/F5
Gablingen, Ger. 96/D6
Gablitz, Aus. 91/N7
Gabon (ctry.) 138/H7
Gaborone (cap.), Bots. 147/E5
Gabriel Leyva Solano, Mex. 184/C3
Gabrovo, Bul. 89/J1
Gaby, It. 100/A1
Gacko, Bosn. 89/F1
Gādarwāra, India 126/B4
Gaddy, Ok, US 179/N15
Gadmen, Swi. 99/E4
Gadsden, Al, US 175/G3
Găeşti, Rom. 91/G3
Gaeta, It. 88/C2
Gaeta, Golfo di (gulf), It. 88/C2
Gaferut (isl.), Micr. 158/D4
Gaffney, SC, US 175/H3
Gafsa, Tun. 141/H2
Gafsa (gov.), Tun. 141/H2
Gagarin, Rus. 102/G5
Gaggenau, Ger. 96/B5
Gaggio Montano, It. 101/D4
Gaglianico, It. 100/B1
Gagnoa, C.d'Iv. 144/D5
Gagny, Fr. 72/K5
Gagra, Geo. 104/G4
Gagret, India 128/D4
Gai Xian, China 115/B2
Gaichtpass (pass), Aus. 99/G3
Gail (riv.), Aus. 85/K3
Gaildorf, Ger. 96/C5
Gaillac, Fr. 84/D5
Gailtaler (mts.), Aus. 85/K3
Gaiman, Arg. 200/D4
Gaimersheim, Ger. 97/E5
Gainesville, Tx, US 171/H4
Gainesville, Ga, US 175/H3
Gainesville, Fl, US 175/H4
Gainsborough, Eng, UK 77/H5
Gairdner (lake), Austl. 151/C4
Gairn (riv.), Sc, UK 78/C2
Gais, Swi. 99/F3
Gaiserwald, Swi. 99/F3
Gaizina (peak), Lat. 81/L3
Gakarosa (peak), SAfr. 148/C2
Gakona, Ak, US 176/J3
Galana (riv.), Kenya 146/C3
Galand, Iran 131/G1
Galapagar, Sp. 87/M8
Galápagos (isls.), Ecu. 198/E6
Galápagos (dept.), Ecu. 198/E7
Galápagos, PN, Ecu. 198/E7
Galashiels, Sc, UK 78/D5
Galaţi (prov.), Rom. 91/H3
Galaţi, Rom. 91/J3
Galatina, It. 89/F2
Galatiní, Gre. 89/G2
Galátista, Gre. 89/H2
Galatone, It. 89/F2
Galb Azefal (hill), WSah. 140/B5
Galbiate, It. 100/C1
Galdácano, Sp. 86/D1
Gáldar, Canl., Sp. 140/B3
Galeana, Mex. 185/E3
Galela, Indo. 123/G3
Galena, Ak, US 176/G3
Galena, Md, US 180/C5
Galeota (pt.), Trin. 195/F2
Galera (pt.), Ecu. 194/A4
Galera (pt.), Trin. 195/F2
Galera (pt.), Chile 200/B3
Galesburg, Il, US 169/L5
Galey (riv.), Ire. 73/P10
Galga (riv.), Hun. 91/R9
Galgamácsa, Hun. 91/R9
Galgorm, NI, UK 76/B2
Galich, Rus. 102/J4
Galicia (aut. comm.), Sp. 86/A1
Galičica NP, FYROM 89/G2
Galiléia, Braz. 197/D1
Galileo Galilei (int'l arpt.), It. 100/D5
Galinakopf (peak), Aus. 99/F3
Galion, Oh, US 172/D3
Gallan Head (pt.), Sc, UK 73/Q7
Gallarate, It. 100/B1
Gallatin, Tn, US 172/C4
Galle, SrL. 124/D6
Gallegos (riv.), Arg. 199/B7
Galliate, It. 100/B2
Gallicano, It. 100/D4
Galliera Veneta, It. 101/E1
Gallinas (mts.), NM, US 174/B3
Gallinas (pt.), Col. 194/D1
Gallipoli, It. 89/E2
Gallipoli (pen.), Turk. 91/H5
Gällivare, Swe. 79/G2
Gallneukirchen, Aus. 97/H6
Gallo (cape), It. 88/C3
Gallo (lake), It. 99/G4
Gallspach, Aus. 97/G6
Gallus, Fr. 72/H5
Gallup, NM, US 170/E4
Gallur, Sp. 86/E2
Gally (riv.), Fr. 72/H5
Galston, Sc, UK 78/B5
Galten, Den. 80/C3
Galtymore (peak), Ire. 73/P10
Galva, La, US 179/P16
Galvarino, Chile 200/B3
Galveston, Tx, US 171/J5
Galveston (bay), Tx, US 171/J5
Galveston (isl.), Tx, US 171/J5
Gálvez, Sp. 86/C3
Galway, Ire. 73/P10
Galway (bay), Ire. 73/P10
Galzignano, It. 101/E2
Gam (riv.), Viet. 125/J3
Gamaches, Fr. 94/A4
Gamagara (riv.), SAfr. 148/C2
Gamagōri, Japan 119/M6
Gamarra, Col. 194/C2
Gamba, China 127/G1
Gambaga, Gha. 145/E4
Gambaga Scarp (cliff), Gha. 145/E4
Gambais, Fr. 72/H5
Gambara, It. 100/D2
Gambat, Pak. 124/A2
Gambela NP, Eth. 139/M6
Gambell, Ak, US 176/D3
Gambellara, It. 101/E2
Gamber, Md, US 180/B5
Gambettola, It. 101/F4
Gambia, The (ctry.) 144/B3
Gambia (riv.), Gam. 144/A3
Gambier (isls.), FrPol. 159/M7
Gámbita, Col. 194/C3
Gambo, Nf, Can. 173/L1
Gambolò, It. 100/B2
Gambsheim, Fr. 96/A5
Gaming, Aus. 85/L3
Gamka (riv.), SAfr. 148/C4
Gamkab (riv.), Namb. 148/B3
Gamleby, Swe. 80/G3
Gammelstad, Swe. 79/G2
Gammertingen, Ger. 99/F1
Gammon Ranges NP, Austl. 155/H4
Gamo, Japan 119/K5
Gampern, Aus. 97/G7
Gamud (peak), Eth. 146/C1
Gan (riv.), China 113/L6
Gan, Fr. 84/C5
Gananoque, On, Can. 172/E2
Gäncä, Azer. 105/H4
Ganda, Ang. 147/B3
Gandajika, D.R. Congo 147/D2
Gandak (riv.), India 127/E2
Gandaki (zone), Nepal 126/D1
Gander (lake), Nf, Can. 173/L1
Gander, Nf, Can. 173/L1
Ganderkesee, Ger. 93/F2
Gandesa, Sp. 87/F2
Gāndhi Sāgar (res.), India 124/B3
Gāndhīdhām, India 131/K4
Gandhinagar, India 131/K4
Gandia, Sp. 87/E3
Gandino, It. 100/C1
Gandoca-Manzanillo NWR, CR 187/F4
Gandu, Braz. 196/C4
Ganeb (well), Mrta. 144/C2
Ganesh (mtn.), China 127/E1
Gangāpur, India 131/L3
Gangārāmpur, India 127/G3
Gangaw, Myan. 125/F3
Gangca, China 112/H4
Gangdisê (mts.), China 112/D5
Gangelt, Ger. 95/F2
Ganges, Fr. 84/E5
Ganges (riv.), Asia 112/E7
Ganges (Ganga) (riv.), India 126/B1
Ganges, Mouths of the (delta), Bang. 127/G5
Gangi, It. 88/D4
Gangkofen, Ger. 97/F6
Gangoh, India 128/D5
Gangtok, India 127/G2
Ganluo, China 125/H2
Gannat, Fr. 84/E3
Ganquan, China 114/B3
Gansbaai, SAfr. 148/L11
Gänserndorf, Aus. 91/P7
Gansu (prov.), China 112/H4
Gantrisch (peak), Swi. 98/D4
Ganyu, China 114/D4
Ganzhou, China 121/B2
Ganzlin, Ger. 82/G2
Ganzourgou (prov.), Burk. 145/E3
Gao (pol. reg.), Mali 145/F2
Gao, Mali 145/E2
Gao'an, China 121/C2
Gaocheng, China 114/C3
Gaochun, China 114/D5
Gaomi, China 114/D3
Gaoping, China 114/C4
Gaoqing, China 114/D3
Gaor Bheinn (Gulvain) (peak), Sc, UK 78/A3
Gaotai, China 112/G4
Gaotang, China 114/D3
Gaoua, Burk. 144/E4
Gaoyang, China 114/C3
Gaoyi, China 114/C3
Gaoyou, China 114/D4
Gaozhou, China 125/K3
Gap, Fr. 85/G4
Gap, Pa, US 180/B4
Gar, China 112/C5
Garabogazköl Aylagy (gulf), Trrkm. 105/K4
Garachiné, Pan. 187/G4
Garachiné (pt.), Pan. 187/G4
Garai (riv.), Bang. 124/E3
Garajonay, PN de, Canl., Sp. 140/A3
Garamba, PN de la, D.R. Congo 139/L7
Garancières, Fr. 94/A6
Garanhuns, Braz. 196/C3
Garbsen, Ger. 93/G4
Garça, Braz. 197/B2

237
Garça – Gober

Garças (riv.), Braz. 193/H7
Garching an der Alz, Ger. 97/F6
Garcia de Sota, Embalse de (res.), Sp. 86/C3
Gard (riv.), Fr. 84/F4
Garda (lake), It. 85/J4
Garda, It. 101/D1
Garde, Cap de (cape), Alg. 142/K6
Gardelegen, Ger. 82/F2
Garden (isl.), Austl. 154/K7
Garden City, Ga, US 175/H3
Garden City, NY, US 181/L9
Garden City, Mi, US 177/F7
Garden City Park, NY, US 181/L9
Garden Grove, Ca, US 178/G8
Garden Ridge, Tx, US 179/U20
Garden View, Pa, US 180/A1
Gardena, Ca, US 178/F8
Gardenstown, Sc, UK 78/D1
Gardēz, Afg. 131/J2
Gardiner, Mt, US 168/F4
Gardiner, Me, US 173/G2
Gardiner, Wa, US 177/B1
Gardiners (isl.), NY, US 181/F1
Gardiners (bay), NY, US 181/F1
Gardner (lake), Ks, US 179/D6
Gardner, Ks, US 179/D6
Gardone val Trompia, It. 100/D1
Gare Loch (inlet), Sc, UK 78/B4
Gareat el Tarf (salt pan), Alg. 142/K7
Garelochhead, Sc, UK 78/B4
Garessio, It. 100/B4
Garet el Djenoun (peak), Alg. 141/G4
Garfield (mtn.), Mt, US 168/E4
Garfield, Ut, US 179/J12
Garfield, NJ, US 181/J8
Garforth, Eng, UK 77/G4
Gargaliánoi, Gre. 89/G4
Gargan (peak), Fr. 84/D4
Gargenville, Fr. 94/A6
Garges-lès-Gonesse, Fr. 72/K5
Gargnano, It. 101/D1
Garh Mahārāja, Pak. 128/A4
Garhākotā, India 126/B4
Garhbeta, India 127/F4
Garhmuktesar, India 126/B1
Garibaldi, Braz. 197/B4
Garies, SAfr. 148/B3
Garioch (reg.), Sc, UK 78/D2
Garissa, Kenya 146/C3
Garland, Tx, US 171/H4
Garlasco, It. 100/B2
Garmisch-Partenkirchen, Ger. 99/H3
Garmsār, Iran 130/F1
Garnpung (lake), Austl. 157/B2
Garonne (riv.), Fr. 84/D4
Garopaba, Braz. 197/B4
Garou (lake), Mali 145/E2
Garoua, Camr. 138/H6
Garphyttan, Swe. 80/F2
Garraf (mts.), Sp. 87/K7
Garrel, Ger. 93/F3
Garrison (dam), ND, US 169/H4
Garrison, ND, US 169/H4
Garron (pt.), NI, UK 76/C1
Garrovillas, Sp. 86/B3
Garry (bay), Nun., Can. 165/H2
Garry (lake), Nun., Can. 164/F2
Garry (lake), Sc, UK 78/B2
Garry (riv.), Sc, UK 78/A2
Gars am Inn, Ger. 97/F6
Garsten, Aus. 97/H6
Garte (riv.), Ger. 93/H6
Gartempe (riv.), Fr. 84/D3
Gärtringen, Ger. 96/B5
Garut, Indo. 122/C5
Garvagh, NI, UK 76/B2
Garwa, India 126/D3
Garwolin, Pol. 83/L3
Garwood, NJ, US 181/H9
Gary, In, US 172/C3
Garza García, Mex. 185/E3
Garzê, China 112/H5
Garzón, Col. 194/C4
Gas, Fr. 72/G6
Gas City, In, US 172/C3
Gas-san (peak), Japan 118/B4
Gæsafjöll (peak), Ice. 79/P6
Gaschurn, Aus. 99/G4
Gasconade (riv.), Mo, US 171/J3
Gascony (reg.), Fr. 84/C5
Gascoyne (riv.), Austl. 151/A3
Gascoyne (mt.), Austl. 154/C3
Gaspar (str.), Indo. 122/C4
Gaspar, Braz. 197/B3
Gaspé, Qu, Can. 173/H1
Gaspé (pen.), Qu, Can. 173/H1
Gaspé, Cap de (cape), Qu, Can. 173/H1
Gaspoltshofen, Aus. 97/G6
Gasport, NY, US 173/S9
Gassino Torinese, It. 100/A2
Gastins, Fr. 72/M6
Gaston (lake), NC, US 175/J2
Gastonia, NC, US 175/H3
Gastoúni, Gre. 89/G4
Gata (cape), Sp. 86/D4
Gata (cape), Cyp. 133/C2
Gata de Gorgos, Sp. 87/F3
Gata, Sierra de (mts.), Sp. 86/B2
Gatchina, Rus. 81/P2
Gatehouse-of-Fleet, Sc, UK 76/D2
Gates of the Arctic NP and Prsv., Ak, US 176/G2
Gateshead (isl.), Nun., Can. 164/F1
Gateshead, Eng, UK 77/G2
Gateshead (co.), Eng, UK 77/G2
Gatesville, Tx, US 174/D4
Gateway Arch (arch), Mo, US 179/G8
Gateway NRA, NJ,NY, US 181/K9
Gatineau, Qu, Can. 172/F2
Gatineau (riv.), Qu, Can. 165/J4
Gatow, Ger. 82/Q7
Gattaran, Phil. 121/D4
Gattendorf, Aus. 85/M2
Gattinara, It. 100/B1
Gatton, Austl. 156/D4
Gatún (dam), Pan. 187/G4
Gatún (lake), Pan. 187/G4
Gatwick (int'l arpt.), Eng, UK 72/C3
Gau Algesheim, Ger. 96/B3
Gau Bischofsheim, Ger. 96/B3
Gau Odernheim, Ger. 96/B3
Gaubickelheim, Ger. 95/H4
Gauchy, Fr. 94/C4
Gaucín, Sp. 86/C4
Gauja (riv.), Est.,Lat. 81/L3
Gauja NP, Lat. 81/L3
Gaukönigshofen, Ger. 96/C3
Gauless (riv.), Eng, UK 77/G2
Gaupne, Nor. 79/C3
Gaur (riv.), Sc, UK 78/B3
Gauri Sankar (peak), Nepal 127/F2
Gauripur, India 127/G2
Gausta (peak), Nor. 80/C2
Gauting, Ger. 97/E6
Gavà, Sp. 87/L7
Gávdhos (isl.), Gre. 89/J5
Gavere, Belg. 94/C2
Gavi, It. 100/B3
Gavião, Port. 86/B3
Gavirate, It. 100/B1
Gävle, Swe. 80/G1
Gävleborg (co.), Swe. 79/E3
Gawler (ranges), Austl. 151/C4
Gawler, Austl. 155/H5
Gay (peak), WV, US 172/D4
Gay, Rus. 105/L2
Gaya, Niger 145/F4
Gayaza, Ugan. 146/A3
Gaylord, Mi, US 172/C2
Gayndah, Austl. 156/C4
Gaza Strip, Isr. 132/C4
Gazeran, Fr. 72/H6
Gaziantep (prov.), Turk. 132/D2
Gaziantep, Turk. 132/D2
Gaziköy, Turk. 91/H5
Gazipaşa, Turk. 133/C1
Gazon de Faing (peak), Fr. 98/D1
Gazzaniga, It. 100/C1
Gbadolite, D.R. Congo 139/K7
Gbarnga, Libr. 144/C5
Gbongan, Nga. 145/G5
Gdansk (gulf), Pol. 83/K1
Gdańsk, Pol. 80/H4
Gdynia, Pol. 80/H4
Ge (lake), China 114/D5
Geal Charn (peak), Sc, UK 78/C2
Geal Charn (peak), Sc, UK 78/A3
Gebaberg (peak), Ger. 96/D1
Gebe (isl.), Indo. 123/G3
Gebhardshain, Ger. 95/G2
Gebiz, Turk. 133/B1
Gebze, Turk. 91/J5
Gede (peak), Indo. 122/C5
Gedern, Ger. 96/C2
Gedi Ruins Nat'l Mon., Kenya 146/D3
Gedikbulak, Turk. 132/E2
Gedinne, Belg. 95/D4
Gediz, Turk. 132/B2
Gediz (riv.), Turk. 132/B2
Gedser (cape), Den. 80/D4
Gedser, Den. 80/D4
Gedsted, Den. 80/C3
Geel, Belg. 95/E1
Geelong, Austl. 157/C3
Geelvink (chan.), Austl. 151/A3
Geertruidenberg, Neth. 92/B5
Geeste (riv.), Ger. 93/F1
Geeste, Ger. 93/E3
Geesthacht, Ger. 93/H2
Geeveston, Austl. 157/C4
Gefrees, Ger. 97/E2
Gê'gyai, China 112/D5
Gehrde, Ger. 93/F3
Gehrden, Ger. 93/G4
Geifas (peak), Wal, UK 74/C2
Geikie (riv.), Sk, Can. 164/F3
Geilenkirchen, Ger. 95/F2
Geilo, Nor. 80/C1
Geinō, Japan 119/K6
Geiselhöring, Ger. 97/F5
Geiselwind, Ger. 96/D3
Geisenfeld, Ger. 97/E5
Geisenhausen, Ger. 97/F6
Geisenheim, Ger. 95/G4
Geislingen, Ger. 99/E1
Geislingen an der Steige, Ger. 96/C5
Geita, Tanz. 146/B3
Gejiu, China 125/H3
Gela, It. 88/D4
Gela, Golfo di (gulf), It. 88/D4
Gelai (peak), Tanz. 146/C3
Gelderland (prov.), Neth. 92/C4
Geldermalsen, Neth. 92/C5
Geldern, Ger. 92/D5
Geldersheim, Ger. 96/D2
Geldrop, Neth. 92/C6
Geleen, Neth. 95/E2
Gelendost, Turk. 132/B2
Gelendzhik, Rus. 104/F3
Gelibolu (Gallipoli), Turk. 89/K2
Gelibolu Yarımadas NP, Turk. 89/K2
Gelincik (peak), Turk. 132/E2
Gelligaer, Wal, UK 74/C3
Gelnhausen, Ger. 96/C2
Gelsenkirchen, Ger. 92/E5
Geltendorf, Ger. 99/H1
Gelterkinden, Swi. 98/D3
Gelting, Ger. 80/C4
Gemas, Malay. 122/B3
Gembloux, Belg. 95/D2
Gemena, D.R. Congo 139/J7
Gemert, Neth. 92/C5
Gemlik (gulf), Turk. 91/J5
Gemlik, Turk. 91/J5
Gemona del Friuli, It. 85/K3
Gemsbok NP, Bots. 147/D6
Gemuk (mtn.), Ak, US 176/G3
Gemünden am Main, Ger. 96/C2
Genalē Wenz (riv.), Eth. 139/N6
Genappe, Belg. 95/D2
Genay, Fr. 98/A6
Genç, Turk. 132/E2
Gendringen, Neth. 92/D5
Gendt, Neth. 92/C5
Genemuiden, Neth. 92/D3
General Abelardo L. Rodriguez (int'l arpt.), Mex. 184/A1
General Acha, Arg. 200/D3
General Alfredo Vasquez Cobo (int'l arpt.), Col. 198/D2
General Alvear, Arg. 200/D2
General Alvear, Arg. 200/E3
General Arenales, Arg. 200/E2
General Belgrano, Arg. 200/F2
General Belgrano II, Arg., Ant. 202/X
General Cabrera, Arg. 200/E2
General Carrera (lake), Chile 199/B6
General Cepeda, Mex. 185/E3
General Conesa, Arg. 200/D4
General Deheza, Arg. 200/E2
General Edward Lawrence Logan (Logan Int'l) (int'l arpt.), Ma, US 173/G3
General Enrique Godoy, Arg. 200/D3
General Francisco Villa, Mex. 185/F3
General Galarza, Arg. 201/J10
General Grant Nat'l Mem., NY, US 181/K8
General Juan Álvarez, PN, Mex. 185/F5
General Juan José Rios, Mex. 184/C3
General Juan Madariaga, Arg. 201/F3
General La Madrid, Arg. 200/E3
General Lagos, Chile 198/D5
General Las Heras, Arg. 201/J11
General Lavalle, Arg. 201/K12
General Martín Miguel de Güemes, Arg. 199/C1
General Pico, Arg. 200/E2
General Pinedo, Arg. 199/D2
General Pinto, Arg. 200/E2
General Roca, Arg. 200/D3
General San Martín, Arg. 200/E3
General San Martín, Arg. 201/J11
General San Martín, Arg., Ant. 202/V
General Santiago Marino (int'l arpt.),Ven. 195/F2
General Terán, Mex. 185/F3
General-Toshevo, Bul. 91/J4
General Viamonte, Arg. 200/E2
General Villalobas (int'l arpt.), Mex. 184/D2
General Villegas, Arg. 200/E2
General Zaragoza, Mex. 185/F4
Generoso (peak), Swi. 99/F6
Genesee (co.), Mi, US 177/E6
Genesee (riv.), NY, US 172/E3
Genesee, Wi, US 177/P14
Genesee Depot, Wi, US 177/P14
Geneseo, Il, US 169/L5
Geneseo, NY, US 172/E3
Geneva (Léman) (lake), Fr. 85/G3
Geneva (Genève), Swi. 85/G3
Geneva (int'l arpt.), Swi. 98/C5
Geneva, Al, US 175/G4
Geneva, Ne, US 171/H2
Geneva, NY, US 172/E3
Geneva, Ut, US 179/K13
Genève (canton), Swi. 98/C5
Genève, Swi. 98/C5
Gengenbach, Ger. 98/E1
Génicourt, Fr. 72/J4
Genk, Belg. 95/E2
Genlis, Fr. 98/B3
Gennach (riv.), Ger. 99/G2
Gennargentu (mts.), It. 88/A2
Gennep, Neth. 92/C5
Gennevilliers, Fr. 72/J5
Genoa (Genova), It. 85/H4
Genoa City, Wi, US 177/P14
Genova (prov.), It. 100/C4
Genova (Genoa), It. 100/B4
Genova, Golfo di (gulf), It. 85/H4
Genovesa (isl.), Ecu. 198/F6
Gensingen, Ger. 95/G4
Gent-Brugge Kanaal (canal), Belg. 94/C1
Gent (Ghent), Belg. 94/C1
Genteng (cape), Indo. 122/C5
Genteng, Indo. 122/D5
Geographe (bay), Austl. 154/B5
Geographe (chan.), Austl. 154/B3
Georg von Neumayer, Ger., Ant. 202/Z
George (lake), Austl. 155/D2
George (pt.), Austl. 156/C3
George (riv.), Qu, Can. 165/K3
George, SAfr. 148/C4
George (lake), Ugan. 146/A3
George (lake), Fl, US 175/H4
George Land (isl.), Rus. 106/E2
George Town, Austl. 157/C4
George Town (cap.), Cay. 187/F2
George Town, Malay. 122/B2
George V (coast), Ant. 202/L
George Washington Birthplace Nat'l Mon., Va, US 175/J2
George West, Tx, US 174/D4
Georgensmünd, Ger. 96/E4
Georges (riv.), Austl. 156/G9
Georgetown, Austl. 156/A2
Georgetown, Gam. 144/B3
Georgetown (cap.), Guy. 195/G3
Georgetown, StV. 183/N9
Georgetown, Ct, US 181/E1
Georgetown, Ga, US 175/H4
Georgetown, Ky, US 172/C4
Georgetown, SC, US 175/J3
Georgetown, Tx, US 171/H5
Georgi Traykov, Bul. 91/H4
Georgia (ctry.) 105/G4
Georgia, Strait of (str.), BC, Can. 168/B3
Georgia (state), US 175/G3
Georgian (bay), On, Can. 165/H4
Georgian Bay Islands NP, On, Can. 172/D2
Georgina (riv.), Austl. 151/C3
Georgsmarienhütte, Ger. 93/F4
Gepatsch (lake), Aus. 99/G4
Gera, Ger. 82/G3
Geraardsbergen, Belg. 94/C2
Geral de Goiás, Serra (mts.), Braz. 193/J6
Geral, Serra (mts.), Braz. 199/F2
Geraldine, NZ 159/S11
Geraldton, Austl. 154/B4
Gérardmer, Fr. 98/C1
Gerasdorf bei Wien, Aus. 91/N7
Gerbéviller, Fr. 98/C1
Gerbier de Jonc (peak), Fr. 84/F4
Gerbrunn, Ger. 96/C3
Gerdau (riv.), Ger. 93/H3
Gerdine (mt.), Ak, US 176/H3
Gerede, Turk. 91/L5
Geretsried, Ger. 99/H2
Gérgal, Sp. 86/D4
Gerger, Turk. 132/D2
Gerlach, Nv, US 168/D5
Gerlachovský Štít (peak), Slvk. 83/L4
Gerlafingen, Swi. 98/D3
Germantown, Tn, US 171/K4
Germantown, Md, US 180/A5
Germany (ctry.) 82/E3
Germering, Ger. 97/E6
Germersheim, Ger. 96/B4
Germigny-l'Evêque, Fr. 72/L5
Germinaga, It. 99/E6
Germiston, SAfr. 148/E2
Gernsbach, Ger. 96/B5
Geroldsgrün, Ger. 97/E2
Gerolsbach, Ger. 97/E5
Gerolstein, Ger. 95/F3
Gerolzhofen, Ger. 96/D3
Gerpinnes, Belg. 95/D3
Gerra (Verzasca), Swi. 99/E5
Gerringong, Austl. 157/D2
Gers (riv.), Fr. 84/D5
Gersau, Swi. 99/E4
Gersfeld, Ger. 96/C2
Gersheim, Ger. 95/G5
Gerspenz (riv.), Ger. 96/B3
Gerstetten, Ger. 96/E5
Gerstheim, Fr. 98/D1
Gersthofen, Ger. 96/D6
Gerstungen, Ger. 93/H7
Gêrzê, China 112/D5
Gerze, Turk. 104/E4
Gescher, Ger. 92/E5
Geseke, Ger. 93/F5
Gespunsart, Fr. 95/D4
Gessertshausen, Ger. 96/D6
Gestro Wenz (riv.), Eth. 139/P6
Gesves, Belg. 95/E3
Geta, Fin. 81/H1
Getafe, Sp. 87/N9
Gete (riv.), Belg. 95/E2
Getinge, Swe. 80/E3
Gettorf, Ger. 80/C4
Gettysburg, SD, US 169/J4
Gettysburg, Pa, US 172/E4
Gettysburg Nat'l Mil. Park, Pa, US 180/A4
Getúlio Vargas, Braz. 197/A3
Geul (riv.), Neth. 95/E2
Geureudong (peak), Indo. 122/A3
Geurie, Austl. 157/D2
Gevaş, Turk. 132/E2
Gevelsberg, Ger. 93/E6
Gevgelija, FYROM 89/H2
Gex, Fr. 98/C5
Geyer, Ger. 97/F1
Geyersberg (peak), Ger. 96/C3
Geyikli, Turk. 89/K3
Geyser (reef), Madg. 149/H6
Geyve, Turk. 91/K5
Gez (riv.), China 129/F5
Ghadāmis, Libya 141/H3
Ghaggar (riv.), India 128/C5
Ghaghara (riv.), India 126/C2
Ghakhar, Pak. 128/C3
Ghana (ctry.) 145/E4
Ghanzi, Bots. 147/D5
Gharaunda, India 128/D5
Ghardaïa, Alg. 141/F2
Ghardaïa (prov.), Alg. 141/F3
Ghardimaou, Tun. 142/L6
Gharghoda, India 126/D4
Gharyān, Libya 138/H1
Ghāt, Libya 141/H4
Ghātāl, India 127/F4
Ghātampur, India 126/C2
Ghātsīla, India 127/F4
Ghazal, Bahr el (riv.), Chad 138/J5
Ghazaouet, Alg. 142/D2
Ghāzīpur, India 126/D3
Ghaznī, Afg. 131/J2
Ghedi, It. 100/D2
Gheens, La, US 179/P17
Ghemme, It. 100/B1
Ghenghis Khan, Wall of, Mong. 113/K2
Gheorghe Gheorghiu-Dej, Rom. 91/H2
Gheorgheni, Rom. 91/G2
Gherla, Rom. 91/F2
Ghilarza, It. 88/A2
Ghinda (Gīnda), Erit. 130/C5
Ghio (lake), Arg. 200/C5
Ghirārah (gulf), Tun. 141/H2
Ghisalba, It. 100/C1
Ghisonaccia, Fr. 88/A1
Ghotki, Pak. 124/A2
Ghugri (riv.), India 127/F3
Ghūrīān, Afg. 131/H2
Ghuzayyil, Bi'r al (well), Libya 138/H2
Giannutri (isl.), It. 88/B1
Giant's Castle (peak), SAfr. 148/E3
Giant's Causeway, NI, UK 76/B1
Giant Sequoia Nat'l Mon., Ca, US 170/C4
Giarre, It. 88/D4
Gibbons, Ab, Can. 168/E2
Gibbstown, NJ, US 180/C4
Gibloux (peak), Swi. 98/D4
Gibraleón, Sp. 86/B4
Gibraltar (pt.), Eng, UK 77/J5
Gibraltar (cap.), Gib. 86/C4
Gibraltar (str.), Mor.,Sp. 86/B5
Gibraltar (res.), Ca, US 178/A1
Gibraltar, Mi, US 177/F7
Gibraltar, Ven. 183/G6
Gibraltar Range NP, Austl. 157/E1
Gibson (des.), Austl. 151/B3
Gibson Desert Nature Reserve, Austl. 154/E3
Giddarbāha, India 128/C4
Giddings, Tx, US 171/H5
Giddings, Co, US 179/B1
Gidi (pass), Egypt 133/C4
Giebelstadt, Ger. 96/C3
Gieboldehausen, Ger. 93/H5
Gien, Fr. 84/E3
Giengen an der Brenz, Ger. 96/D5
Gier (riv.), Fr. 84/F4
Giessbachfälle (falls), Swi. 98/E4
Giessen (riv.), Fr.,Ger. 98/D1
Giessen, Ger. 96/B1
Giessendam, Neth. 92/B5
Gieten, Neth. 92/D2
Gif-sur-Yvette, Fr. 72/J5
Gīfān, Iran 105/L5
Gifford, Fl, US 175/H5
Gifford (riv.), Nun., Can. 165/H1
Giffre (riv.), Fr. 98/C5
Gifhorn, Ger. 93/H4
Gifu, Japan 119/L5
Giganta, Sierra de la (mts.), Mex. 184/C3
Gigante, Col. 194/C4
Giglio (isl.), It. 88/B1
Gijón, Sp. 86/C1
Gil de Vilches, PN, Chile 200/C2
Gila (riv.), Az, US 170/D4
Gila Bend, Az, US 170/D4
Gila Cliff Dwellings Nat'l Mon., NM, US 170/E4
Gila River Ind. Res., Az, US 179/R19
Gilbert, Mn, US 172/A2
Gilbert (riv.), Austl. 151/D2
Gilbert, Az, US 179/S19
Gilbert (isls.), Kiri. 158/G5
Gilberts, Il, US 177/P15
Gilbués, Braz. 196/A3
Gilching, Ger. 96/E6
Gilcrest, Co, US 179/C2
Gilford, NI, UK 76/B3
Gilford Park, NJ, US 180/D4
Gilgandra, Austl. 157/D1
Gilgil, Kenya 146/C3
Gilgit (riv.), Pak. 129/F5
Gilles (lake), Austl. 155/H5
Gillette, Wy, US 169/G4
Gillies Bay, BC, Can. 168/B3
Gillingham, Eng, UK 75/G4
Gillot (int'l arpt.), Reun., Fr. 149/S15
Gilly, Swi. 98/C5
Gilman Hot Springs, Ca, US 178/D3
Gilmer, Tx, US 171/J4
Gilpin, Co, US 179/A3
Gilgit (riv.), Pak. 131/K1
Gilze, Neth. 92/B5
Gīmbī, Eth. 139/N6
Gimbsheim, Ger. 96/B3
Gimel, Swi. 98/C4
Gimie (mt.), StL. 183/N9
Gimli, Mb, Can. 169/J3
Gimo, Swe. 80/H1
Gin Gin, Austl. 156/C4
Ginan, Japan 119/L5
Gingelom, Belg. 95/E2
Gingin, Austl. 154/B4
Gingindlovu, SAfr. 149/E3
Gingoog, Phil. 121/E6
Gingst, Ger. 80/E4
Ginosa, It. 88/E2
Ginowan, Japan 117/J7
Gioia (gulf), It. 88/D3
Gioia del Colle, It. 88/E2
Gioia Tauro, It. 88/D3
Giornico, Swi. 99/E5
Gioúra (isl.), Gre. 89/J3
Gioveretto (peak), It. 99/G5
Giovi (peak), It. 101/E5
Gipping (riv.), Eng, UK 75/G2
Girardot, Col. 192/D3
Girardville, Pa, US 180/B2
Giraumont, Fr. 95/E5
Girdle Ness (pt.), Sc, UK 78/D2
Giresun (prov.), Turk. 132/D1
Giresun, Turk. 132/D1
Girgnasco, It. 100/B1
Girīdīh, India 127/F3
Girifalco, It. 88/E3
Girling (res.), Eng, UK 72/C2
Giromagny, Fr. 98/C2
Girón, Ecu. 194/B5
Girón, Col. 194/C3
Girona, Sp. 87/G2
Gironcourt-sur-Vraine, Fr. 98/B1
Gironde (riv.), Fr. 84/C4
Gironella, Sp. 87/F1
Girraween NP, Austl. 157/D1
Giru, Austl. 156/B2
Girvan, Sc, UK 76/D1
Gisborne, NZ 159/T10
Gisenyi, Rwa. 146/A3
Gislaved, Swe. 80/E3
Gisors, Fr. 94/A5
Gistel, Belg. 94/B1
Gistrup, Den. 80/D3
Gitega, Buru. 146/A3
Gittsfjället (peak), Swe. 79/E2
Giubiasco, Swi. 99/F5
Giugliano in Campania, It. 90/B5
Giulianova, It. 85/K5
Giurgiu (prov.), Rom. 91/G3
Giurgiu, Rom. 91/G4
Giussano, It. 100/C1
Giv'at Brenner, Isr. 133/F8
Giv'at Hayyim, Isr. 133/F7
Giv'atayim, Isr. 133/F7
Give, Den. 80/C4
Givet, Fr. 95/D3
Givors, Fr. 84/F4
Givrine, Col de la (pass), Swi. 98/C5
Giyani, SAfr. 147/F5
Gizhiga (bay), Rus. 107/R3
Gizo, Sol. 158/E5
Giżycko, Pol. 81/J4
Gjerdrum, Nor. 80/D1
Gjerlev, Den. 80/D3
Gjerstad, Nor. 80/C2
Gjirokastër, Alb. 89/G2
Gjoa Haven, Nun., Can. 164/G2
Gjøvik, Nor. 80/D1
Glabbeek, Belg. 95/E2
Glace Bay, NS, Can. 173/K2
Glacier (peak), Wa, US 168/C3
Glacier Bay NP and Prsv., Ak, US 176/L4
Glacier NP, BC, Can. 168/D3
Gladbeck, Ger. 92/D5
Gladewater, Tx, US 171/J4
Gladstone, Mo, US 179/D5
Gladstone, Austl. 156/C3
Gladstone, Austl. 155/H5
Gladwin, Mi, US 172/C3
Glafsfjorden (lake), Swe. 80/D2
Glåma (riv.), Nor. 79/D3
Glamis, Sc, UK 78/D3
Glamsbjerg, Den. 80/D4
Glan, Phil. 121/E6
Glan (riv.), Ger. 82/D4
Glanamman, Wal, UK 74/C3
Gland, Swi. 98/C5
Gland (riv.), Fr. 95/D4
Glandorf, Ger. 93/F4
Glärnisch (range), Swi. 99/E3
Glarus, Swi. 99/F3
Glarus (canton), Swi. 99/E4
Glarus Alps (range), Swi. 85/H3
Glas Maol (peak), Sc, UK 78/C3
Glasgow, Mt, US 168/G3
Glasgow, Ky, US 172/C4
Glasgow, De, US 180/C4
Glasgow, Sc, UK 78/B5
Glashütten, Ger. 96/B2
Glaslyn (riv.), Wal, UK 76/D6
Glass (mts.), Ok, US 174/D2
Glass (lake), Sc, UK 78/B1
Glass (riv.), Sc, UK 78/B2
Glassboro, NJ, US 180/C4
Glastonbury, Eng, UK 74/D4
Glatt (riv.), Ger. 96/B6
Glattbach, Ger. 96/C3
Glattfelden, Swi. 99/E2
Glavinitsa, Bul. 91/H4
Glazoué, Ben. 145/F5
Glazov, Rus. 103/M4
Glems (riv.), Ger. 96/C5
Glen (riv.), Eng, UK 77/H6
Glen Burnie, Md, US 180/B5
Glen Canyon (dam), Az, US 170/E3
Glen Canyon Nat'l Rec. Area, US 170/E3
Glen Carbon, Il, US 179/H8
Glen Coe (pass), Sc, UK 78/B3
Glen Cove, NY, US 181/L8
Glen Gardner, NJ, US 180/D2
Glen Haven, Co, US 179/B2
Glen Innes, Austl. 157/D1
Glen Lyon, Pa, US 180/B1
Glen Mòr (valley), Sc, UK 78/B2
Glen Park, Mo, US 179/G9
Glen Ridge, NJ, US 181/J8
Glen Rock, Pa, US 180/B4
Glen Rock, NJ, US 181/J8
Glen Ullin, ND, US 169/H4
Glenaire, Mo, US 179/E5
Glenan, Îles de (isls.), Fr. 84/A3
Glenarm, NI, UK 76/C2
Glenarm (riv.), NI, UK 76/C2
Glenavy, NI, UK 76/B2
Glenbawn (dam), Austl. 157/D2
Glenboro, Mb, Can. 169/J3
Glencoe, SAfr. 149/E3
Glencoe, Mo, US 179/F8
Glencoe, Il, US 177/Q15
Glencoe, Sc, UK 78/A3
Glendale, Or, US 168/C5
Glendale, Az, US 179/R18
Glendale, Ca, US 178/F7
Glendale Heights, Il, US 177/P16
Glenden, Austl. 156/C3
Glendive, Mt, US 169/G4
Glendo (res.), Wy, US 169/G5
Glendora, Ca, US 178/C2
Glendun (riv.), NI, UK 76/B1
Glenealy, Ire. 76/B6
Glenelg (riv.), Austl. 157/B3
Glenelg, Md, US 180/B5
Glenelg, Sc, UK 73/R8
Glenelly (riv.), NI, UK 76/A2
Glengarry (range), Austl. 154/C3
Glenluce, Sc, UK 76/D2
Glenmere (lake), NY, US 180/D1
Glennallen, Ak, US 176/J3
Glenolden, Pa, US 180/C4
Glenorie, Austl. 156/H8
Glenpool, Ok, US 171/H4
Glenrothes, Sc, UK 78/C4
Glens Falls, NY, US 172/F3
Glenshane (pass), NI, UK 76/B2
Glenside, Pa, US 180/C3
Glenties, Ire. 73/P9
Glenveagh NP, Ire. 73/Q9
Glenview, Il, US 177/Q15
Glenwood, NJ, US 180/D1
Glenwood Springs, Co, US 170/F3
Gleouraich (peak), Sc, UK 78/A2
Glifádha, Gre. 89/N9
Glimåkra, Swe. 80/F3
Glina, Cro. 90/C3
Glinde, Ger. 93/H1
Glindow, Ger. 82/P7
Gliwice, Pol. 83/K3
Globe, Az, US 170/E4
Glockturm (peak), Aus. 99/G4
Gloggnitz, Aus. 83/H5
Głogów, Pol. 83/J3
Głogówek, Pol. 83/J3
Glonn (riv.), Ger. 96/E6
Gloria (bay), Cuba 187/G1
Glorieuses, Îles (isls.), Reun., Fr. 149/H5
Glorious (mt.), Austl. 156/E6
Glory of Russia (cape), Ak, US 176/D3
Glossop, Eng, UK 77/G5
Gloster, Ms, US 171/K5
Gloucester, Austl. 157/D1
Gloucester, On, Can. 172/F2
Gloucester, Eng, UK 74/D3
Gloucester (co.), NJ, US 180/C4
Gloucester City, NJ, US 180/C4
Gloucestershire (co.), Eng, UK 74/D3
Glovers (reef), Belz. 186/E2
Glovertown, Nf, Can. 173/L1
Głowno, Pol. 83/K3
Głubczyce, Pol. 83/J3
Głuchołazy, Pol. 83/J3
Glücksburg, Ger. 80/C4
Glückstadt, Ger. 93/G1
Glyndon, Md, US 180/B5
Glyngøre, Den. 80/C3
Glynn, NI, UK 76/C2
Gmünd, Aus. 83/H4
Gmunden, Aus. 97/G7
Gnagna (prov.), Burk. 145/E3
Gnarrenburg, Ger. 93/G2
Gniew, Pol. 81/H5
Gniezno, Pol. 83/J2
Gnjilane, Serb. 90/E4
Gnowangerup, Austl. 154/C5
Gō (riv.), Japan 116/C3
Go Cong, Viet. 120/D4
Goa (state), India 124/B4
Goālpāra, India 127/H2
Goat Fell (peak), Sc, UK 78/A5
Goba, Eth. 139/N6
Gobabis, Namb. 147/C5
Gobardānga, India 127/G4
Gobernador Castro, Arg. 200/F2

238
Gober – Green

Gobernador Costa, Arg. 200/C5
Gobernador Gregores, Arg. 201/C6
Gobernador Mansilla, Arg. 201/J10
Gobi (des.), China,Mong. 112/H4
Göblberg (peak), Aus. 97/G6
Gobō, Japan 116/D4
Goch, Ger. 92/D5
Gochsheim, Ger. 96/D2
Godalming, Eng, UK 75/F4
Godāvari (riv.), India 124/C4
Goddā, India 127/F3
Godeanu (peak), Rom. 90/F3
Godech, Bul. 89/H1
Goderich, On, Can. 172/D3
Godfrey, Il, US 179/G8
Gōdo, Japan 119/L5
Gödöllő, Hun. 83/K5
Godoy Cruz, Arg. 200/C2
Gods (riv.), Mb, Can. 164/G3
Gods (lake), Mb, Can. 164/G3
Gods Mercy (bay), Nun., Can. 165/H2
Godthåb (Nuuk), Grld. 161/M3
Godwin Austen (K2) (peak), Pak. 128/D2
Goéland (lake), Qu, Can. 172/E1
Goeree (isl.), Neth. 92/A5
Goes, Neth. 92/A5
Gogebic (range), Mi, US 169/L4
Göggingen, Ger. 96/D6
Gogland (isl.), Rus. 81/M1
Gogōme, Japan 118/B4
Gogounou, Ben. 145/F4
Gogra (riv.), India 124/D2
Gohad, India 126/B2
Gohāna, India 128/D5
Gohbach (riv.), Ger. 93/G3
Goiana, Braz. 196/D2
Goiandira, Braz. 197/B1
Goiânia, Braz. 193/J7
Goianinha, Braz. 196/D2
Goiás, Braz. 193/H7
Goiás (state), Braz. 196/A5
Goiatuba, Braz. 197/B1
Goil (lake), Sc, UK 78/B4
Goirle, Neth. 92/C5
Góis, Port. 86/A2
Goito, It. 101/D2
Gojō, Japan 116/D3
Gojra, Pak. 128/B4
Gok (riv.), Turk. 104/E4
Goka, Japan 119/D1
Gokase (riv.), Japan 116/B4
Gokashō, Japan 119/K5
Gokasho (bay), Japan 119/L7
Gökçeada (isl.), Turk. 132/A1
Gökçebey, Turk. 91/L5
Gökçekaya (dam), Turk. 132/B1
Göksu (riv.), Turk. 132/D2
Göksun, Turk. 132/D2
Göktepe, Turk. 133/C1
Gol, Nor. 80/C1
Gola Gokarannāth, India 126/C1
Golan Hts. (reg.), Syria 133/D3
Golasecca, It. 100/B1
Gölbaşı, Turk. 132/D2
Golbey, Fr. 98/C1
Golborne, Eng, UK 77/F5
Gölcük, Turk. 91/J5
Gold (coast), Gha. 138/E7
Gold (mtn.), Wa, US 177/B2
Gold Bar, Wa, US 177/D2
Gold Beach, Or, US 168/B5
Gold Coast, Austl. 156/D5
Gold Hill, Co, US 179/B2
Gold River, BC, Can. 168/B3
Goldach, Swi. 99/F3
Gołdap, Pol. 81/K4
Goldbach, Ger. 96/C3
Goldberg, Ger. 80/E5
Golden, BC, Can. 168/D3
Golden, Co, US 179/B3
Golden Eagle, Il, US 179/F8
Golden Gate (chan.), Ca, US 177/J11
Golden Gate Highlands NP, SAfr. 148/D3
Golden Hinde (peak), BC, Can. 168/B3
Golden Temple, India 128/C4
Goldendale, Wa, US 168/C4
Goldene Aue (reg.), Ger. 82/F3
Goldenstedt, Ger. 93/F3
Goldkronach, Ger. 97/E2
Goldman, Mo, US 179/F9
Goldmine (mtn.), Az, US 179/S19
Goldsboro, NC, US 175/J3
Goldsboro, Md, US 180/C5
Goldsby, Ok, US 179/N15
Goldsworthy, Austl. 154/C2
Goldthwaite, Tx, US 174/D4
Göle, Turk. 132/E1
Goleniów, Pol. 80/F5
Golfito NWR, CR 187/F4
Golfo Aranci, It. 88/A2
Golfo de Santa Clara, Mex. 184/B2
Gölhısar, Turk. 133/A1
Goliad, Tx, US 171/H5
Gölköy, Turk. 132/D1
Gollach (riv.), Ger. 96/D3
Göllheim, Ger. 96/B3
Gölmarmara, Turk. 132/A2
Golmud, China 112/F4
Golovin, Ak, US 176/F3
Golovnina (peak), Rus. 118/D2
Golpāyegān, Iran 130/F2
Gölpazarı, Turk. 91/K5
Gols, Aus. 85/M3
Golts, Md, US 180/C5
Golub-Dobrzyń, Pol. 83/K2
Golubovci (int'l arpt.), Mont. 90/D4
Golyam Perelik (peak), Bul. 89/J2
Golyama Kamchiya (riv.), Bul. 91/H4
Golyama Syutkya (peak), Bul. 89/J2
Goma, D.R. Congo 146/A3
Goma (int'l arpt.), D.R. Congo 146/A3
Gomaringen, Ger. 96/C6
Gomati (riv.), India 126/C2
Gombe (state), Nga. 145/H4
Gombe (riv.), Tanz. 146/A4
Gombe NP, Tanz. 146/A4
Gomera (isl.), Canl., Sp. 140/A4
Gómez Farías, Mex. 184/D2
Gómez Palacio, Mex. 184/E3
Gomīshān, Iran 130/F1
Gommern, Ger. 82/F2
Gomoh, India 127/F4
Goms (valley), Swi. 98/E5
Gonābād, Iran 131/G2
Gonaïves, Haiti 187/H2
Gonarezhou NP, Zim. 147/F5
Gonâve (gulf), Haiti 183/G4
Gonâve (isl.), Haiti 187/H2
Gonbad-e Qābūs, Iran 131/G1
Gonbadlī, Iran 129/D5
Gönc, Hun. 83/L4
Gonçalves Dias, Braz. 196/A2
Gondelsheim, Ger. 96/B4
Gonder, Eth. 139/N5
Gondia, India 124/D3
Gondomar, Sp. 86/A1
Gondomar, Port. 86/A2
Gondrecourt-le-Château, Fr. 98/B1
Gondreville, Fr. 95/E6
Gondrexange (lake), Fr. 95/F6
Gönen, Turk. 91/H5
Gonesse, Fr. 72/K5
Gong Xian, China 125/H2
Gong Xian, China 114/C4
Gong'an, China 125/K3
Gongbo'gyamda, China 125/F2
Gongcheng, China 121/B3
Gongga (peak), China 125/H2
Gonggar, China 127/H1
Gonghe, China 112/H4
Gongliu, China 112/D3
Gongola (riv.), Nga. 138/H5
Gongshan Drungzu Nuzu Zizhixian, China 125/G2
Gongzhuling, China 114/F2
Goñi, Uru. 201/K10
Gonjo, China 112/G5
Gónnoi, Gre. 89/H3
Gonohe, Japan 118/B3
Gonubie, SAfr. 148/D4
Gönyű, Hun. 90/C2
Gonzaga, It. 101/D3
Gonzales, Tx, US 171/H5
González, Mex. 185/F4
Good Hope, La, US 179/P17
Good Hope, Cape of (cape), SAfr. 148/L11
Goodenough (cape), Ant. 202/J
Goodnews Bay, Ak, US 176/F4
Goodooga, Austl. 157/C1
Goodrich, Mi, US 177/F6
Goodwick, Wal, UK 74/B2
Goodwood, SAfr. 148/L10
Goodyear, Az, US 179/R19
Gooimeer (lake), Neth. 92/C4
Goole, Eng, UK 77/H4
Goolgowi, Austl. 157/C2
Gooloogong, Austl. 157/D2
Goolwa, Austl. 155/H5
Goomalling, Austl. 154/C4
Goombungee, Austl. 156/C4
Goondiwindi, Austl. 156/C5
Goongarrie NP, Austl. 154/D4
Goor, Neth. 92/D4
Goose (lake), Mb, Can. 169/H2
Goose (lake), Ca,Or, US 168/C5
Goose (pt.), De, US 180/C5
Goose (pt.), La, US 179/Q16
Gopālganj, India 127/E2
Gopālpur, Bang. 127/G3
Gopat (riv.), India 126/D3
Göppingen, Ger. 96/C5
Góra, Pol. 83/J3
Góra Kalwaria, Pol. 83/L3
Goražde, Bosn. 90/D4
Gorczański NP, Pol. 83/L4
Gorda (pt.), Cuba 187/F1
Gorda (pt.), Nic. 187/F3
Gorda (pt.), Nic. 187/F4
Gordevio, Swi. 99/E5
Gørding, Den. 80/C4
Gordola, Swi. 99/E5
Gordon, Austl. 157/C4
Gordon (lake), Austl. 151/D5
Gordonsbaai, SAfr. 148/L11
Gordonvale, Austl. 156/B2
Gore (pt.), Ak, US 176/H4
Goré, Chad 138/J6
Gorē, Eth. 139/N6
Gore, NZ 159/R12
Gorebridge, Sc, UK 78/C5
Görele, Turk. 132/D1
Goresbridge, Ire. 73/Q10
Gorey, Chl, UK 84/B2
Gorey, Ire. 73/Q10
Gorgān, Iran 131/F1
Gorge du Loup, Lux. 95/F4
Gorges du Ziz, Mor. 140/D2
Gorgol (pol. reg.), Mrta. 144/B3
Gorgol (riv.), Mrta. 144/B2
Gorgona, Isola di (isl.), It. 100/C6
Gorgonzola, It. 100/C1
Gori, Geo. 105/H4
Gorinchem, Neth. 92/B5
Gorizia, It. 101/G1
Gorizia (prov.), It. 101/G1
Gorj (prov.), Rom. 91/F3
Gorki, Bela. 104/D1
Gor'kiy (res.), Rus. 102/J4
Gorlice, Pol. 83/L4
Görlitz, Ger. 83/H3
Gorllwyn (peak), Wal, UK 74/C2
Gorman, Tx, US 171/H4
Gormanstown, Ire. 76/B4
Gormī, India 126/B2
Gorner (glacier), Swi. 98/D6
Gornji Milanovac, Serb. 90/E3
Gornji Vakuf, Bosn. 90/C4
Gorno-Altay Aut. Rep., Rus. 106/J4
Goro, It. 101/F3
Gorodets, Rus. 103/J4
Gorom Gorom, Burk. 145/E3
Gorong (isl.), Indo. 123/H4
Gorongoza, Moz. 147/F4
Gorontalo, Indo. 123/F3
Gorssel, Neth. 92/D4
Gorst, Wa, US 177/B2
Gortin, NI, UK 76/A2
Görwihl, Ger. 98/E2
Goryn' (riv.), Ukr. 104/C2
Gorzano (peak), It. 85/K5
Gorzów Wielkopolski, Pol. 83/H2
Gosainganj, India 126/D2
Göschenen, Swi. 99/E4
Gōse, Japan 119/J7
Gosen, Japan 117/F2
Gosford, Austl. 157/D2
Gosforth, Eng, UK 77/G2
Goshen, NJ, US 180/D5
Goshogawara, Japan 118/B3
Goslar, Ger. 93/H5
Gospić, Cro. 90/B3
Gosport, Eng, UK 75/E5
Gossas, Sen. 144/A3
Gossau, Swi. 99/F3
Gossersweiler-Stein, Ger. 95/G5
Gostivar, FYROM 89/G2
Gostyń, Pol. 83/J3
Gostynin, Pol. 83/K2
Göta (riv.), Swe. 80/G2
Götaland (reg.), Swe. 80/E3
Göteborg, Swe. 80/D3
Göteborg Och Bohus (co.), Swe. 79/D4
Gotel (mts.), Nga. 138/H6
Gotemba, Japan 117/F3
Götene, Swe. 80/E2
Gotha, Ger. 93/H7
Gotland (co.), Swe. 79/F4
Gotland (isl.), Swe. 79/F4
Gotse Delchev, Bul. 89/H2
Gotska Sandön (isl.), Swe. 81/H2
Gotska Sandön NP, Swe. 81/H2
Gōtsu, Japan 116/C3
Gottenheim, Ger. 98/D1
Göttingen, Ger. 93/G5
Gottmadingen, Ger. 99/E2
Gottolengo, It. 100/D2
Götzis, Aus. 99/F3
Gouda, Neth. 92/B4
Gouda, SAfr. 148/L10
Gough (isl.), StH 64/J7
Gouin (res.), Qu, Can. 165/J4
Goulais (riv.), On, Can. 172/C2
Goulburn (riv.), Austl. 157/D2
Goulburn, Austl. 157/D2
Goulburn (isls.), Austl. 151/C2
Gould, Ar, US 174/F3
Gould (mt.), Austl. 154/C3
Gouldsboro, Pa, US 180/C1
Goulimine, Mor. 140/C3
Goulmima, Mor. 140/D3
Goundam, Mali 144/E2
Goupillières, Fr. 72/H5
Gourdon, Fr. 84/D4
Gouré, Niger 145/H3
Gourin, Fr. 84/B2
Gourits (riv.), SAfr. 148/C4
Gourma (phys. reg.), Burk. 145/F3
Gourma (prov.), Burk. 145/F3
Gourma Rharous, Mali 145/E2
Gournay-en-Bray, Fr. 94/A5
Gourock, Sc, UK 78/B5
Goussainville, Fr. 72/K4
Gouvêa, Braz. 197/D1
Gouveia, Port. 86/B2
Gouvieux, Fr. 72/K4
Gouvy, Belg. 95/E3
Gouyave, Gren. 183/N9
Govardhan, India 126/A2
Goverla (peak), Ukr. 91/G1
Governador Archer, Braz. 196/A2
Governador Dix-Sept Rosado, Braz. 196/C2
Governador Eugênio Barros, Braz. 196/A2
Governador Valadares, Braz. 197/D1
Governor Generoso, Phil. 121/E6
Governors (isl.), NY, US 181/J9
Govi-Altay (prov.), Mong. 112/F2
Govĭ Altayn (mts.), Mong. 112/G3
Govind Sāgar (res.), India 128/D4
Govindgarh, India 126/C3
Gower (pen.), Wal, UK 74/B3
Goya, Arg. 199/E2
Goyllarisquizga, Peru 198/B3
Göynük, Turk. 91/K5
Goyt (riv.), Eng, UK 77/F5
Gozaisho-yama (peak), Japan 119/K5
Gözeli, Turk. 132/D2
Gozo (isl.), Malta 88/D4
Gozzano, It. 100/B1
Graaff-Reinet, SAfr. 148/D4
Graafschap (phys. reg.), Neth. 92/D4
Graben, Ger. 99/G1
Graberberg (peak), Namb. 148/B2
Grabouw, SAfr. 148/L11
Grabow, Ger. 82/F2
Graça Aranha, Braz. 196/A2
Gračac, Cro. 90/B3
Gračanica, Bosn. 90/D3
Gracemere, Austl. 156/C3
Graceville, Fl, US 175/G4
Grächen, Swi. 98/D5
Gracias, Hon. 186/D3
Gracias a Dios (cape), Hon. 187/F3
Graciosa (isl.), Azor., Port. 87/S12
Grad Sofiya (prov.), Bul. 89/H1
Gradačac, Bosn. 90/D3
Gradisca d'Isonzo, It. 101/G1
Grado, It. 101/G1
Grado, Sp. 86/B1
Grady (co.), Ok, US 179/M15
Gräfelfing, Ger. 97/E6
Grafenau, Ger. 97/G5
Gräfenberg, Ger. 96/E3
Grafenrheinfeld, Ger. 96/D3
Gräfentonna, Ger. 93/H6
Grafenwöhr, Ger. 97/E3
Graffignana, It. 100/C2
Grafing bei München, Ger. 97/E6
Gråfjell (peak), Nor. 80/C1
Grafrath, Ger. 99/H1
Grafton, Austl. 157/E1
Grafton, ND, US 169/J3
Grafton, WV, US 172/D4
Grafton, Il, US 179/G8
Grafton Passage, Austl. 156/B2
Graham, Tx, US 171/H4
Graham (isl.), Nun., Can. 165/S7
Graham (isl.), BC, Can. 164/C3
Graham Bell (isl.), Rus. 106/G1
Graham Land (phys. reg.), Ant. 202/V
Grahamstown, SAfr. 148/D4
Graian Alps (range), It. 85/G4
Grain (coast), Libr. 138/D6
Grain Valley, Mo, US 179/E5
Grainau, Ger. 99/H3
Grajaú (riv.), Braz. 193/J5
Grajaú, Braz. 196/A2
Grajewo, Pol. 81/K5
Gram, Den. 80/C4
Gramada, Bul. 90/F4
Gramastetten, Aus. 97/H6
Gramat, Fr. 84/D4
Gramat, Causse de (plat.), Fr. 84/D4
Gramatneusiedl, Aus. 91/N7
Grampian (pol. reg.), Sc, UK 78/C2
Grampian (mts.), Sc, UK 78/B3
Grampians NP, Austl. 157/B3
Grampians, The (phys. reg.), Austl. 157/B3
Gramsbergen, Neth. 92/D3
Gramsh, Alb. 89/G2
Gran, Nor. 80/D1
Gran Altiplanicie Central (plat.), Arg. 199/C6
Gran Bajo de San Julián (plain),Arg. 201/C6
Gran Bajo Oriental (plain), Arg. 199/C6
Gran Canaria (isl.), Canl., Sp. 140/B4
Gran Canaria (int'l arpt.), Canl., Sp. 140/B4
Gran Chaco (plain), SAm. 189/C5
Gran Isla del Maíz (isl.), Nic. 187/F3
Gran Laguna Salada (lag.), Arg. 200/D5
Gran Paradiso, PN del, It. 85/G4
Gran Piedra (hill), Cuba 187/H2
Gran Pilastro (peak), It. 85/J3
Gran Vilaya (ruin), Peru 198/B2
Granada, Col. 194/C4
Granada, Nic. 186/E4
Granada, Sp. 86/D4
Granadilla de Abona, Canl., Sp. 140/A3
Granados, Mex. 184/C2
Granard, Ire. 73/Q10
Granarolo dell'Emilia, It. 101/E3
Granbury, Tx, US 171/H4
Grand (lake), Nf, Can. 165/L4
Grand (canal), China 114/D4
Grand (falls), Kenya 146/C3
Grand (canal), Az, US 179/R18
Grand (isl.), NY, US 169/M4
Grand (isl.), Mi, US 172/C2
Grand (riv.), Mo, US 174/E2
Grand (riv.), SD, US 169/H4
Grand Bahama (isl.), Bahm. 183/F2
Grand Bank, Nf, Can. 173/L2
Grand Bassa (co.), Libr. 144/C5
Grand-Bassam, C.d'Iv. 144/E5
Grand Bay, NB, Can. 173/H2
Grand Canal d'Alsace (canal), Fr. 98/D2
Grand Canyon, Az, US 170/D3
Grand Canyon Nat'l Park, Az, US 170/D3
Grand Canyon-Parashant Nat'l Mon., Az, US 170/D3
Grand Cape Mount (co.), Libr. 144/C5
Grand Cayman (isl.), Cay. 182/E4
Grand Centre, Ab, Can. 168/F2
Grand-Charmont, Fr. 98/C2
Grand Colombier (peak), Fr. 98/B6
Grand Combine (peak), Swi. 98/D6
Grand Coulee, Wa, US 168/D4
Grand Coulee (dam), Wa, US 168/D4
Grand Drumont (peak), Fr. 98/C2
Grand Erg de Bilma (des.), Niger 138/H4
Grand Erg Occidental (des.), Alg. 141/E3
Grand Erg Oriental (des.), Alg. 141/G3
Grand Falls, NB, Can. 173/H2
Grand Falls, Nf, Can. 173/L1
Grand Forks, ND, US 169/J4
Grand Forks, BC, Can. 168/D3
Grand-Fort-Philippe, Fr. 94/B2
Grand Gabes, Tun. 141/H2
Grand Goâve, Haiti 187/H2
Grand Haven, Mi, US 172/C3
Grand Isle, La, US 175/F4
Grand Jide (co.), Libr. 144/D5
Grand Junction, Co, US 170/E3
Grand-lahou, C.d'Iv. 144/D5
Grand Lake o' the Cherokees (lake), Ok, US 171/J3
Grand Manan (isl.), NB, Can. 173/H2
Grand-Mère, Qu, Can. 173/F2
Grand Mont Ruan (peak), Fr. 98/C5
Grand Muveran (peak), Swi. 98/D5
Grand-Popo, Ben. 145/F5
Grand Portage Nat'l Mon., Mn, US 169/L4
Grand Rapids, Mb, Can. 169/J2
Grand Rapids, Mi, US 172/C3
Grand Rhône (riv.), Fr. 84/F5
Grand Saint-Bernard, Col du (pass), Swi. 98/D6
Grand Staircase-Escalante Nat'l Mon., Ut, US 170/E3
Grand Taureau (peak), Fr. 98/C4
Grand Teton NP, Wy, US 170/E2
Grandcour, Swi. 98/C4
Grande (bay), Arg. 201/C6
Grande (isl.), Braz. 197/C2
Grande (lake), Braz. 195/H5
Grande (riv.), Braz. 192/J7
Grande (peak), It. 88/C1
Grande (peak), It. 88/C4
Grande (pt.), Pan. 187/G4
Grande Cache, Ab, Can. 168/D2
Grande Comore (isl.), Com. 149/G5
Grande de Gurupá, Ilha (isl.), Braz. 193/H4
Grande de Manacapuru, Lago (lake), Braz. 192/F4
Grande de Matagalpa (riv.), Nic. 182/D5
Grande de Santiago (riv.), Mex. 184/D4
Grande de Tierra del Fuego (isl.), Arg.,Chile 199/C7
Grande Dixence, Barrage de la (dam), Swi. 98/D5
Grande do Curuaí (lake), Braz. 195/H5
Grande Miquelon (isl.), StP., Fr. 173/K2
Grande Prairie, Ab, Can. 168/D2
Grande Saline, Haiti 187/H2
Grande, Serra (mts.), Braz. 195/F4
Grande-Synthe, Fr. 94/B1
Grande-Terre (isl.), Guad. 183/J4
Grandes Jorasses (peak), It. 98/D6
Grandfresnoy, Fr. 94/B5
Grândola, Port. 86/A3
Grandpuits-Bailly-Carrois, Fr. 72/L6
Grandson, Swi. 98/C4
Grandview, Wa, US 168/D4
Grandview, Mb, Can. 169/H3
Grandview, Tx, US 171/H4
Grandview, Mo, US 179/D6
Grandvillars, Fr. 98/C2
Grandvilliers, Fr. 94/A4
Graneros, Chile 200/N9
Granfjället (peak), Swe. 80/E1
Grange, Mont de (peak), Fr. 98/C5
Grangemouth, Sc, UK 78/C4
Granger (mt.), Yk, Can. 176/L3
Granges-sur-Vologne, Fr. 98/C1
Grängesberg, Swe. 80/F1
Grangeville, Id, US 168/D4
Granisle, BC, Can. 168/B2
Granite (peak), Mt, US 168/F4
Granite, Ut, US 179/K12
Granite City, Il, US 179/G8
Granite Reef Aqueduct, Az, US 179/S18
Granites, The (peak), Austl. 155/F2
Granja, Braz. 196/B1
Granollers, Sp. 87/L6
Grantham, Eng, UK 77/H6
Grantown-on-Spey, Sc, UK 78/C2
Grants, NM, US 170/F4
Grants Pass, Or, US 168/C5
Granville, Fr. 84/C2
Granville (lake), Mb, Can. 164/F3
Grão Mogol, Braz. 196/B5
Grapeview, Wa, US 177/B3
Gras-Ellenbach, Ger. 96/B3
Grasberg, Ger. 93/F2
Grasbrunn, Ger. 97/E6
Grasø (isl.), Swe. 80/H1
Grasonville, Md, US 180/B6
Grass (lake), Il, US 177/P15
Grasse, Fr. 85/G5
Grassie, On, Can. 173/Q9
Grasslands NP, Sk, Can. 168/G3
Grassy, Austl. 157/C4
Grassy Park, SAfr. 148/L11
Grästorp, Swe. 80/E2
Gratkorn, Aus. 85/L3
Gratz, Pa, US 180/B2
Graubünden (canton), Swi. 99/F4
Graulhet, Fr. 84/E5
Graus, Sp. 87/F1
Gravatá, Braz. 196/D3
Grave, Neth. 92/C5
Gravedona, It. 99/F5
Gravelbourg, Sk, Can. 168/G3
Gravelines, Fr. 94/B2
Gravellona Toce, It. 99/E6
Gravenhurst, On, Can. 172/E2
Grävenwiesbach, Ger. 96/B2
Gravesend, Eng, UK 72/E2
Gravina di Puglia, It. 88/E2
Gravois (pt.), Haiti 187/H2
Gray, Fr. 98/B3
Grayling, Ak, US 176/F3
Grayling, Mi, US 172/C2
Grays (har.), Wa, US 168/B4
Grays (lake), Id, US 168/F5
Grays, Eng, UK 72/E2
Grayslake, Il, US 177/P15
Grayson, Sk, Can. 169/H3
Graz, Aus. 85/L3
Grazalema, Sp. 86/C4
Great (lake), Austl. 157/C4
Great (plain), Can.,US 169/G3
Great (basin), Nv, US 166/C4
Great (falls), NJ, US 181/J8
Great Abaco (isl.), Bahm. 183/F2
Great Alfold (plain), Serb. 90/D2
Great America, Ca, US 177/L12
Great Australian Bight (bay), Austl. 151/B4
Great Barrier (reef), Austl. 151/D2
Great Barrier (isl.), NZ 159/T10
Great Basin NP, Nv, US 170/D3
Great Bear (lake), NW, Can. 164/D2
Great Bend, Ks, US 171/H3
Great Bitter (lake), Egypt 133/C4
Great Brak (riv.), SAfr. 148/C3
Great Britain (isl.), UK 73/T9
Great Cedar (swamp), NJ, US 180/D5
Great Coco (isl.), Myan. 125/F5
Great Cumbrae (isl.), Sc, UK 78/B5
Great Divide (basin), Wy, US 168/F5
Great Dividing (range), Austl. 151/D2
Great Egg (har.), NJ, US 180/D5
Great Egg Harbor (riv.), NJ, US 180/D4
Great Exuma (isl.), Bahm. 183/F3
Great Falls, Mt, US 168/F4
Great Fish (riv.), SAfr. 148/D4
Great Fish (pt.), SAfr. 148/D4
Great Guana Cay (isl.), Bahm. 183/F3
Great Harwood, Eng, UK 77/F4
Great Himalaya (range), Asia 112/D6
Great Inagua (isl.), Bahm. 183/G3
Great Indian (des.), India, Pak. 124/B2
Great Karoo (plat.), SAfr. 147/D7
Great Kei (riv.), SAfr. 148/D4
Great Mis Tor (hill), Eng, UK 74/B5
Great Missenden, Eng, UK 75/F3
Great Neck, NY, US 181/L8
Great Nicobar (isl.), India 125/F6
Great Ouse (riv.), Eng, UK 75/E2
Great Oyster (bay), Austl. 157/D4
Great Palace, Rus. 103/S7
Great Palace, Rus. 103/T7
Great Peconic (bay), NY, US 181/F2
Great Pee Dee (riv.), SC, US 175/J3
Great Piece Meadows (swamp), NJ, US 181/H8
Great Rift (valley), Afr. 147/F1
Great Ruaha (riv.), Tanz. 147/F2
Great Salt (lake), Ut, US 170/D2
Great Salt Lake (des.), Ut, US 170/D2
Great Sand Dunes Nat'l Park Co, US 171/F3
Great Sand Sea (des.), Egypt, Li 139/K2
Great Sandy (des.), Austl. 151/B2
Great Scarcies (riv.), SLeo. 144/B4
Great Shunner Fell (peak), Eng, UK 77/F3
Great Slave (lake), NW, Can. 164/E2
Great Smoky Mountains NP, NC,Tn, US 175/H3
Great South (bay), NY, US 181/E2
Great Stour (riv.), Eng, UK 75/G4
Great. Tenasserim (riv.), Myan. 120/B3
Great Victoria (des.), Austl. 151/B3
Great Victoria Desert Nature Rsv., Austl. 155/E4
Great Wall, China 112/J4
Great Western Tiers (mts.),Austl. 157/C4
Great Winterhoek (peak), SAfr. 148/L10
Great Yarmouth, Eng, UK 75/H1
Great Zab (riv.), Iraq 132/E2
Great Zimbabwe (ruin), Zim. 147/F5
Greater Accra (pol. reg.), Gha. 145/F5
Greater Antilles (isls.), NAm. 183/F3
Greater Buffalo (int'l arpt.), NY, US 173/S10
Greater Cincinnati (int'l arpt.), Ky, US 172/C4
Greater London (co.), Eng, UK 72/D2
Greater Manchester (co.), Eng, UK 77/F4
Greater Pittsburgh (int'l arpt.), Pa, US 172/D3
Greater Rochester (int'l arpt.), NY, US 172/E3
Greater Sunda (isls.), Indo. 122/C4
Grebenhain, Ger. 96/C2
Grebenstein, Ger. 93/G6
Grébon (peak), Niger 145/H2
Grecco, Uru. 201/K10
Greco (peak), It. 88/C2
Greco (cape), Cyp. 133/D2
Greding, Ger. 97/E4
Gredos, Sierra de (mts.), Sp. 86/C2
Greece (ctry.) 89/G3
Greeley, Co, US 179/C2
Greeley Number 2 (canal), Co, US 179/C2
Greely (fjord), Nun., Can. 165/S6
Green (cape), Austl. 157/D3
Green (riv.), Ky, US 172/C4
Green (bay), Mi,Wi, US 169/M4
Green (riv.), Ut,Wy, US 170/E3
Green (mts.), Vt, US 172/F3
Green Cove Springs, Fl, US 175/H4
Green Creek, NJ, US 180/D5
Green Haven, Md, US 180/B5
Green Lane (res.), Pa, US 180/C3
Green Lowther (peak), Sc, UK 78/C6
Green Pond, NJ, US 180/D1
Green River, Wy, US 168/F5
Green Valley, Az, US 170/E5
Green Valley, Ca, US 178/B1
Green Valley Lake, Ca, US 178/C2
Green Village, NJ, US 181/H9
Greenbelt, Md, US 180/B6
Greenbushes, Austl. 154/C5
Greencastle, In, US 172/C4
Greencastle, Ire. 76/B1
Greendale, Wi, US 177/Q14
Greeneville, Tn, US 172/D4
Greenfield, In, US 172/C4
Greenfield, Ma, US 173/F3
Greenfield, Wi, US 177/P14
Greenfield Park, Qu, Can. 173/P7
Greenisland, NI, UK 76/C2
Greenland (sea) 161/R2
Greenmount, Md, US 180/B4
Greenock, Sc, UK 78/B5
Greenough (riv.), Austl. 154/B4
Greenough (mt.), Ak, US 176/K2
Greenport, NY, US 181/F1
Greensboro, Al, US 175/G3
Greensboro, Md, US 180/C6
Greensboro, NC, US 175/J2
Greensburg, In, US 172/C4
Greensburg, Pa, US 172/E3
Greenvale, Austl. 156/B2
Greenville, Libr. 144/C5
Greenville, Al, US 175/G4
Greenville, Ca, US 168/C5
Greenville, Mi, US 172/C3
Greenville, Ms, US 171/K4
Greenville, NC, US 175/J3
Greenville, Oh, US 172/C3
Greenville, SC, US 175/H3
Greenville, Tx, US 171/H4
Greenwater (riv.), Wa, US 177/D3
Greenwell Point, Austl. 157/D2
Greenwich, Ct, US 181/L7
Greenwich (bor.), Eng, UK 72/D2
Greenwich (pt.), Ct, US 181/L8
Greenwich Observatory, Eng, UK 72/D2
Greenwood (lake), SC, US 175/H3
Greenwood, SC, US 175/H3
Greenwood, Ms, US 171/K4
Greenwood, Mo, US 179/E6
Greenwood, De, US 180/C6
Greenwood Lake, NY, US 180/D1

239

Greer – Haich

Greers Ferry (lake), Ar, US 171/J4
Grefrath, Ger. 92/D6
Gregório (riv.), Braz. 192/D5
Gregory, SD, US 169/J5
Gregory (range), Austl. 151/D2
Gregory (lake), Austl. 151/B3
Greifswald, Ger. 80/E4
Greifswalder Bodden (bay), Ger. 83/G1
Greimberg (peak), Aus. 85/L3
Greiz, Ger. 85/K1
Gremyachinsk, Rus. 103/N4
Grenå, Den. 80/D3
Grenada, Ms, US 171/K4
Grenada (ctry.) 183/N10
Grenade, Fr. 84/D5
Grenay, Fr. 94/B3
Grenchen, Swi. 98/D3
Grenfell, Austl. 157/D2
Grenfell, Sk, Can. 169/H3
Grennach (riv.), Ger. 96/D6
Grenoble, Fr. 84/F4
Grenzach-Wyhlen, Ger. 98/D2
Gressåmoen NP, Nor. 79/E2
Greta (riv.), Eng, UK 77/E2
Gretna, Mb, Can. 169/J3
Gretna, La, US 179/P17
Gretna, Sc, UK 77/E2
Grettstadt, Ger. 96/D3
Gretz-Armainvilliers, Fr. 72/L5
Greve (riv.), It. 101/E5
Greve in Chianti, It. 101/E5
Grevelingendam (dam), Neth. 92/B5
Greven, Ger. 93/E4
Grevená, Gre. 89/G2
Grevenbroich, Ger. 95/F1
Grevenmacher (dist.), Lux. 95/F4
Grevenmacher, Lux. 95/F4
Grevesmühlen, Ger. 82/F2
Grevlingen (chan.), Neth. 92/A5
Grey (range), Austl. 151/D3
Grey (riv.), Nf, Can. 173/K2
Grey (pt.), NI, UK 76/C2
Grey Abbey, NI, UK 76/C2
Grey Hunter (peak), Yk, Can. 176/L3
Grey Peaks NP, Austl. 156/B2
Greybull, Wy, US 168/F4
Greylingstad, SAfr. 148/E2
Greymouth, NZ 159/S11
Greystones, Ire. 76/B5
Greytown, SAfr. 149/E3
Grez-Doiceau, Belg. 95/D2
Grezzana, It. 101/E1
Gribbin (pt.), Eng, UK 74/B6
Griefensee (lake), Swi. 99/E3
Griekwastad, SAfr. 148/C3
Griend (isl.), Neth. 92/C2
Gries am Brenner, Aus. 99/H3
Griesheim, Ger. 96/B3
Grieskirchen, Aus. 97/G6
Griesskogel (peak), Aus. 99/H3
Griesstätt, Ger. 97/F7
Griffin, Ga, US 175/G3
Griffith, Austl. 157/C2
Griffith, In, US 177/R16
Griffith Park, Ca, US 178/F7
Grigna (peak), It. 99/F6
Grignano Polesine, It. 101/E2
Grigny, Fr. 72/K6
Grijalva (riv.), Mex. 186/C2
Grijpskerk, Neth. 92/D2
Grim (cape), Austl. 157/C4
Grimbergen, Belg. 95/D2
Grimisuat, Swi. 98/D5
Grimmen, Ger. 80/E4
Grimsby, On, Can. 173/Q9
Grimsby, Eng, UK 77/H4
Grimselpass (pass), Swi. 99/E4
Grimsey (isl.), Ice. 79/N6
Grimstad, Nor. 80/C2
Grindavík, Ice. 79/M7
Grindelwald, Swi. 98/E4
Grindsted, Den. 80/C4
Grinnell (pen.), Nun., Can. 165/S7
Grintavec (peak), Slov. 85/L3
Griqualand East (reg.), SAfr. 148/E3
Griqualand West (reg.), SAfr. 148/C3
Gris-Nez (cape), Fr. 94/A2
Grise Fiord, Nun., Can. 165/S7
Grisslehamn, Swe. 81/H1
Grisy-les-Plâtres, Fr. 72/J4
Grisy-Suisnes, Fr. 72/L5
Grivette (riv.), Fr. 72/L4
Grizzly (bay), Ca, US 177/K10
Grmeč (mts.), Bosn. 90/C3
Groaíras, Braz. 196/B1
Grobbendonk, Belg. 92/B6
Gröbenzell, Ger. 97/E6
Groblershoop, SAfr. 148/C3
Grodków, Pol. 83/J3
Grodzisk Wielkopolski, Pol. 83/J2
Groenlo, Neth. 92/D4
Groesbeck, Tx, US 174/D4
Groesbeek, Neth. 92/C5
Groix (isl.), Fr. 84/B3
Grójec, Pol. 83/L3
Grombalia, Tun. 142/M6
Grömitz, Ger. 80/D4
Gromo, It. 99/F6
Gronau, Ger. 92/E4
Gronau, Ger. 93/G4
Groningen, Neth. 92/D2
Groningen (prov.), Neth. 92/D2
Gronlait (peak), It. 99/H5
Grono, Swi. 99/F5
Groot (riv.), SAfr. 147/D7
Groot-Marico (riv.), SAfr. 148/D2
Grootdraaidam (res.), SAfr. 148/Q13
Groote Eylandt (isl.), Austl. 151/C2
Grootegast, Neth. 92/D2
Grootfontein, Namb. 147/C4
Grootvloer (salt pan), SAfr. 148/C3
Gropello Cairoli, It. 100/B2
Gros Islet, StL. 183/N9
Gros Morne (peak), Nf, Can. 173/K1
Gros Morne NP, Nf, Can. 173/K1
Grosbliederstroff, Fr. 95/G5
Grosio, It. 99/G5
Grosne (riv.), Fr. 84/F3
Grosrouvre, Fr. 72/H5
Gross Bieberau, Ger. 96/B3
Gross-Enzersdorf, Aus. 91/P7
Gross-Gerungs, Aus. 83/H4
Gross Oesingen, Ger. 93/H3
Gross Unstadt, Ger. 96/B3
Gross-Zimmern, Ger. 96/B3
Grossaitingen, Ger. 99/G1
Grossalmerode, Ger. 93/G6
Grossbeeren, Ger. 82/Q7
Grossbottwar, Ger. 96/C5
Grossbreitenbach, Ger. 96/D1
Grosse (isl.), Mi, US 177/F7
Grosse Aue (riv.), Ger. 93/F4
Grosse Ile, Mi, US 177/F7
Grosse Laber (riv.), Ger. 97/F5
Grosse Mühl (riv.), Aus. 97/G6
Grosse Münzenberg (peak), Namb. 148/A2
Grosse Nister (riv.), Ger. 95/G2
Grosse Pointe, Mi, US 177/G7
Grosse Pointe Farms, Mi, US 177/G7
Grosse Pointe Park, Mi, US 177/G7
Grosse Pointe Shores, Mi, US 177/G7
Grosse Pointe Woods, Mi, US 177/G7
Grosse Rodl (riv.), Aus. 97/H6
Grossengottern, Ger. 93/H6
Grossenkneten, Ger. 93/F3
Grossenlüder, Ger. 96/C1
Grossenwiehe, Ger. 80/C4
Grosser Ahrensberg (peak), Ger. 93/G5
Grosser Aletsch (glacier), Swi. 98/D5
Grosser Arber (peak), Ger. 97/G4
Grosser Beer-Berg (peak), Ger. 85/J1
Grosser Bösenstein (peak), Aus. 85/L3
Grosser Daumen (peak), Ger. 99/G3
Grosser Feldberg (peak), Ger. 96/B2
Grosser Gleichberg (peak), Ger. 96/D2
Grosser Heuberg (mts.), Ger. 96/B6
Grosser Knechtsand (isl.), Ger. 93/F1
Grosser Peilstein (peak), Aus. 83/H4
Grosser Plessower (lake), Ger. 82/P7
Grosser Priel (peak), Aus. 85/L3
Grosser Rachel (peak), Ger. 97/G5
Grosser Seddiner (lake), Ger. 82/P7
Grosser Selchower (lake), Ger. 82/Q7
Grosses Meer (lake), Ger. 93/E2
Grosses Moor (swamp), Ger. 93/H3
Grosseto, It. 85/J5
Grossgerau, Ger. 96/B3
Grossglienicke, Ger. 82/Q7
Grossglockner (peak), Aus. 85/K3
Grosshansdorf, Ger. 93/H1
Grossheubach, Ger. 96/C3
Grosskrotzenburg, Ger. 96/B2
Grossmaischeid, Ger. 95/G3
Grosso (cape), Fr. 85/H5
Grossrosseln, Ger. 95/F5
Grosssiegharts, Aus. 83/H4
Grosswallstadt, Ger. 96/C3
Grosswangen, Swi. 98/E3
Grosuplje, Slov. 85/L4
Grote Gete (riv.), Belg. 95/D2
Groton, SD, US 169/J4
Grotta Gigante, It. 101/G1
Grottaglie, It. 88/E2
Grottammare, It. 85/K5
Grotte de Han, Belg. 95/E3
Grouard Mission, Ab, Can. 168/D2
Groundhog (riv.), On, Can. 172/D1
Grouw, Neth. 92/C2
Grovdageaidnu-Kautokeino, Nor. 79/G1
Grove, Ok, US 171/J3
Grove (pt.), Md, US 180/B5
Grover, Mo, US 179/F8
Grover City, Ca, US 170/B4
Groves, Tx, US 171/J5
Groveton, Va, US 180/A6
Groznyy, Rus. 105/H4
Grudovo, Bul. 91/H4
Grudziądz, Pol. 83/K2
Grumeti (riv.), Tanz. 146/B3
Grums, Swe. 80/E2
Grünau im Almtal, Aus. 97/G7
Grünburg, Aus. 97/H7
Gründau, Ger. 96/C2
Grune (pt.), Eng, UK 77/E2
Grünsfeld, Ger. 96/C3
Grünstadt, Ger. 96/B3
Grünwald, Ger. 97/E6
Gruyères, Swi. 98/D4
Gryazi, Rus. 104/F1
Gryckbo, Swe. 80/F1
Gryfice, Pol. 80/F5
Gryfino, Pol. 83/H2
Gryon, Swi. 98/D5
Gschwandt, Aus. 97/G7
Gschwend, Ger. 96/C5
Gsteig, Swi. 98/D5
Gua, India 127/E4
Guabún (pt.), Chile 200/B4
Guaca, Col. 194/C3
Guacanayabo (gulf), Cuba 183/F3
Guacarí, Col. 194/B4
Guachochi, Mex. 184/D3
Guácimo, CR 187/F4
Guaçuí, Braz. 197/D2
Guadalajara, Mex. 184/E4
Guadalajara, Sp. 86/D2
Guadalcanal, Sp. 86/C3
Guadalcanal (isl.), Sol. 158/E6
Guadalentín (riv.), Sp. 86/D4
Guadalimar (riv.), Sp. 86/D3
Guadalix (riv.), Sp. 87/N8
Guadalope (riv.), Sp. 87/E2
Guadalquivir (riv.), Sp. 86/D4
Guadalupe, Braz. 196/B2
Guadalupe, Col. 194/C4
Guadalupe, Mex. 184/E4
Guadalupe, Mex. 185/E3
Guadalupe (isl.), Mex. 161/E7
Guadalupe, Pan. 187/G4
Guadalupe, Peru 198/C4
Guadalupe, Peru 198/B2
Guadalupe, Sp. 86/C3
Guadalupe (mts.), NM,Tx, US 174/B3
Guadalupe (co.), Tx, US 179/U20
Guadalupe (peak), Tx, US 171/F5
Guadalupe (riv.), Tx, US 174/D4
Guadalupe Mountains NP, Tx, US 171/F5
Guadalupe, Sierra de (mts.), Sp. 86/C3
Guadalupe Victoria, Mex. 184/B1
Guadalupe Victoria, Mex. 184/D3
Guadalupe Victoria, Mex. 185/M7
Guadarrama (riv.), Sp. 86/C3
Guadarrama, Ven. 194/D2
Guadarrama, Sp. 87/M8
Guadarrama, Sierra de (mts.), Sp. 86/C2
Guadeloupe (isl.), Guad., Fr. 183/N8
Guadeloupe NP, Guad., Fr. 183/N8
Guadeloupe Passage (chan.), Guad., Fr. 183/J4
Guadiana (riv.), Port.,Sp. 86/B3
Guadiana Menor (riv.), Sp. 86/D4
Guadix, Sp. 86/D4
Guafo (isl.), Chile 200/B4
Guafo, Boca del (mouth), Chile 200/B4
Guagua Pichincha (peak), Ecu. 194/B5
Guaíba, Braz. 197/B4
Guaíba (riv.), Braz. 197/B4
Guáimaro, Cuba 187/G1
Guainía (riv.), Col. 192/E3
Guainía (dept.), Col. 194/D4
Guaiquinima (peak), Ven. 195/F3
Guaíra, Braz. 199/F1
Guaíra, Braz. 197/B2
Guaiteca (isl.), Chile 200/B4
Guajará-Mirim, Braz. 192/E6
Guajira (pen.), Col. 194/D1
Gualaceo, Ecu. 194/B5
Gualaco, Hon. 186/E3
Gualán, Guat. 186/D3
Gualaquiza, Ecu. 198/B1
Gualeguay, Arg. 201/J10
Gualeguaychú, Arg. 201/J10
Gualtieri, It. 100/D3
Guam (isl.), Pac., US 158/D3
Guamal, Col. 194/C2
Guamblin, Isla (isl.), Chile 200/A5
Guamote, Ecu. 198/B1
Guamúchil, Mex. 184/C3
Gu'an, China 114/H7
Guan Xian, China 112/H5
Guan Xian, China 114/C3
Guanabacoa, Cuba 187/F1
Guanabara (bay), Braz. 197/K7
Guanahacabibes (gulf), Cuba 187/E1
Guanahacabibes (pen.), Cuba 187/E1
Guanaja, Hon. 186/E2
Guanaja (isl.), Hon. 186/E2
Guanajay, Cuba 187/F1
Guanajuato, Mex. 185/E4
Guanajuato (state), Mex. 182/A3
Guanambi, Braz. 196/B4
Guanape, Ven. 195/E2
Guanare, Ven. 194/D2
Guanare (riv.), Ven. 192/E2
Guanarito, Ven. 194/D2
Guanay (peak), Ven. 195/E3
Guandi (mtn.), China 114/B3
Guane, Cuba 187/E1
Guangchang, China 121/C2
Guangde, China 114/D5
Guangdong (prov.), China 113/K7
Guangfeng, China 121/C2
Guangling, China 114/C3
Guanglu (isl.), China 115/B3
Guangnan, China 125/J3
Guangping, China 121/C2
Guangping, China 114/C3
Guangrao, China 114/D3
Guangshan, China 114/C4
Guangxi Zhuangzu (aut. reg.), China 112/J7
Guangyuan, China 112/J5
Guangze, China 121/C2
Guangzhou, China 125/K3
Guanhães, Braz. 197/D1
Guanipa (riv.), Ven. 192/F2
Guannan, China 114/D4
Guantánamo, Cuba 187/H1
Guantánamo Bay U.S. Naval Base, Cuba 187/H2
Guantao, China 114/C3
Guanting (res.), China 114/G6
Guanujo, Ecu. 194/B5
Guanyun, China 114/D4
Guapí, Col. 194/B4
Guaporé, Braz. 197/B4
Guaporé (riv.), Braz. 189/C4
Guaqui, Bol. 198/D5
Guarabira, Braz. 196/D2
Guaraci, Braz. 197/B2
Guaraciaba do Norte, Braz. 196/B2
Guaraí, Braz. 193/J5
Guaramirim, Braz. 197/B3
Guaranda, Ecu. 194/B5
Guarani, Braz. 197/K6
Guarapari, Braz. 197/D2
Guarapuava, Braz. 197/B3
Guarará, Braz. 197/K6
Guararapes (int'l arpt.), Braz. 196/D3
Guararapes, Braz. 197/B2
Guaratinga, Braz. 196/C5
Guaratinguetá, Braz. 197/H7
Guaratuba, Braz. 197/B3
Guarda (dist.), Port. 86/B2
Guarda, Port. 86/B2
Guardamar, Sp. 87/E3
Guardamiglio, It. 101/C2
Guardarrama (riv.), Sp. 87/N8
Guardia Alta (peak), It. 99/H4
Guardia Mitre, Arg. 200/E4
Guardia Sanframondi, It. 90/B5
Guardiagrele, It. 88/D1
Guareña, Sp. 86/B3
Guarico (pt.), Cuba 187/H1
Guárico (riv.), Ven. 195/E2
Guárico (state), Ven. 195/E2
Guárico, Embalse de (res.), Ven. 195/E2
Guarujá, Braz. 197/G9
Guarulhos, Braz. 197/G8
Guarulhos (int'l arpt.), Braz. 197/G8
Guarumal, Pan. 187/F5
Guasave, Mex. 184/C3
Guasdualito, Ven. 194/D3
Guasimal, Cuba 187/G1
Guasipati, Ven. 195/F3
Guastalla, It. 100/D3
Guatemala (ctry.) 186/D3
Guatemala (cap.), Guat. 186/D3
Guateque, Col. 194/C3
Guaviare (dept.), Col. 194/C4
Guaviare (riv.), Col. 192/E3
Guaxupé, Braz. 197/G6
Guayabero (riv.), Col. 194/C4
Guayabo, Cayo (isl.), Cuba 187/G1
Guayalejo (riv.), Mex. 185/F4
Guayama, PR 183/M8
Guayape (riv.), Hon. 186/E3
Guayaquil (gulf), Ecu.,Peru 189/A3
Guayaquil, Ecu. 194/B5
Guayaquil, Gulf of (gulf), Ecu.,Peru 198/A1
Guayaramerín, Bol. 192/E6
Guayas, Ecu. 194/B5
Guayas (prov.), Ecu. 194/A5
Guayas (riv.), Col. 194/C4
Guaymas, Mex. 184/C3
Gubakha, Rus. 103/N4
Gubbio, It. 101/F6
Guben, Ger. 83/H3
Gubin, Pol. 83/H3
Gubkin, Rus. 104/F2
Gucheng, China 114/B4
Gucheng, China 114/C3
Gúdar, Sierra de (range), Sp. 87/E2
Gudenå (riv.), Den. 80/D3
Gudensberg, Ger. 93/G6
Gudermes, Rus. 105/H4
Gudivāda, India 124/D4
Gudow, Ger. 93/H1
Güdül, Turk. 91/L5
Gūdūr, India 124/C5
Guebli (lake), Mrta. 140/B5
Guebwiller, Fr. 98/D2
Guecho, Sp. 86/D1
Guelb Azefal (hill), Mrta. 140/B5
Guelb er Rîchât (peak), Mrta. 140/C5
Guelma, Alg. 142/K6
Guelma (prov.), Alg. 142/K6
Guelph, On, Can. 172/D3
Guémené-Penfao, Fr. 84/C3
Guénange, Fr. 95/F5
Guérande, Fr. 84/B3
Guerara, Alg. 141/G2
Guérard, Fr. 72/L5
Guercif, Mor. 142/C2
Guéret, Fr. 84/D3
Guernes, Fr. 72/G4
Guernsey (int'l arpt.), Chl, UK 84/B2
Guernsey (isl.), Chl, UK 84/B2
Guerrero (state), Mex. 182/B4
Guerrero, Mex. 184/D2
Guerrero Negro, Mex. 184/B3
Guerville, Fr. 72/H5
Guesle (riv.), Fr. 72/H6
Gueugnon, Fr. 84/F3
Gueux, Fr. 94/C5
Gugē (peak), Eth. 139/N6
Guggisberg, Swi. 98/D4
Gugielmo Marconi (int'l arpt.), It. 101/E3
Güglingen, Ger. 96/B4
Guguan (isl.), NMar. 158/D3
Guguletu, SAfr. 148/L11
Gui (riv.), China 121/B3
Guiana Highlands (uplands), SAm. 189/C2
Guichen, Fr. 84/C3
Guichón, Uru. 201/K10
Guidder, Camr. 138/H6
Guidimaka (pol. reg.), Mrta. 144/B3
Guiding, China 125/J2
Guidizzolo, It. 100/D2
Guidong, China 125/K2
Guidonia, It. 88/C2
Guiglo, C.d'Iv. 144/D5
Guignes-Rabutin, Fr. 72/L6
Guihulngan, Phil. 123/F1
Guija, Moz. 147/F5
Guijuelo, Sp. 86/C2
Guilder (peak), Ut, US 179/L11
Guilderton, Austl. 154/B4
Guildford, Eng, UK 72/B3
Guilherand, Fr. 84/F4
Guilin (int'l arpt.), China 121/B2
Guilin, China 125/K2
Guillaume-Delisle (lake), Qu, Can. 165/J3
Guillena, Sp. 86/B4
Guimarães, Braz. 196/A1
Guimarães, Port. 86/A2
Guimba, Phil. 121/D4
Guimeng (mtn.), China 114/D4
Guinan, China 112/H4
Guinard (riv.), Sc, UK 78/A1
Guinea (ctry.) 144/C4
Guinea (gulf), Afr. 135/C4
Guinea-Bissau (ctry.) 144/B3
Guînes, Fr. 94/A2
Guingamp, Fr. 84/B2
Guinguinéo, Sen. 144/B3
Guiones (pt.), CR 186/E4
Guipavas, Fr. 84/A2
Guipavas (int'l arpt.), Fr. 84/A2
Guir, Oued (riv.), Alg. 140/E2
Guiratinga, Braz. 193/H7
Güiria, Ven. 195/F2
Guisborough, Eng, UK 77/G2
Guiscard, Fr. 94/C4
Guise, Fr. 94/C4
Guitiriz, Sp. 86/B1
Guitrancourt, Fr. 72/H4
Guiuan, Phil. 121/E5
Güiza (riv.), Col. 194/B4
Guizhou (prov.), China 112/J6
Gujan-Mestras, Fr. 84/C4
Gūjar Khān, Pak. 128/B3
Gujarāt (state), India 124/B3
Gujrānwāla, Pak. 128/C3
Gujrāt, Pak. 128/C3
Gukovo, Rus. 104/F2
Gulaothi, India 126/A1
Gulargambone, Austl. 157/D1
Gulbarga, India 124/C4
Guldenbach (riv.), Ger. 95/G3
Güldüzü, Turk. 133/E1
Gulen, Nor. 80/A1
Gulf Coastal (plain), Tx, US 174/D5
Gulf Islands Nat'l Seashore, US 175/F4
Gulf Shores, Al, US 175/G4
Gulfport, Ms, US 175/F4
Gulgong, Austl. 157/D2
Guliston, Uzb. 129/E4
Gulkana, Ak, US 176/J3
Gull Lake, Sk, Can. 168/F3
Gulladuff, NI, UK 76/B2
Gullane, Sc, UK 78/D4
Gullane (pt.), Sc, UK 78/D4
Gullspång, Swe. 80/F2
Güllükdağı (Termessos) NP, Turk. 133/B1
Gulmarg, India 128/C2
Gülnar, Turk. 133/C1
Gulpen, Neth. 95/E2
Gülpınar, Turk. 89/K3
Gulu, Ugan. 146/B2
Gulyantsi, Bul. 91/G4
Gumal (riv.), Pak. 128/A4
Gumare, Bots. 147/D4
Gumbrechtshoffen, Fr. 95/G6
Gumdag, Trkm. 105/K5
Gumeracha, Austl. 155/M8
Gumia, India 127/E4
Gumla, India 127/E4
Gumma (pref.), Japan 117/F2
Gummersbach, Ger. 95/G1
Gumpoldskirchen, Aus. 91/N7
Gumti (riv.), India 127/H4
Gümüşhacıköy, Turk. 104/E4
Gümüşhane, Turk. 132/D1
Gümüşhane (prov.), Turk. 132/D1
Guna (peak), Eth. 139/N5
Gunbower, Austl. 157/C2
Gundagai, Austl. 157/D2
Gundelfingen, Ger. 98/D1
Gundelfingen an der Donau, Ger. 96/D5
Gundelsheim, Ger. 96/C4
Gundersheim, Ger. 96/B3
Gundershoffen, Fr. 95/G6
Gündoğmuş, Turk. 133/C1
Güneydogu Toroslar (mts.), Turk. 132/D2
Gunisao (riv.), Mb, Can. 169/J2
Gunisao (lake), Mb, Can. 169/J2
Gunja, Cro. 90/D3
Gunn City, Mo, US 179/E6
Gunnaur, India 126/B1
Gunnebo, Swe. 80/G3
Gunnedah, Austl. 157/D1
Gunning, Austl. 157/D2
Gunnison (riv.), Co, US 170/F3
Gunnison, Ut, US 170/E3
Gunpowder (riv.), Md, US 180/B5
Gunpowder Falls State Park, Md, US 180/B4
Gunskirchen, Aus. 97/G6
Guntersblum, Ger. 96/B3
Guntersville, Al, US 175/G3
Guntersville (lake), Al, US 175/G3
Guntramsdorf, Aus. 91/N7
Guntūr, India 124/D4
Günz (riv.), Ger. 82/F4
Günzburg, Ger. 96/D6
Gunzenhausen, Ger. 96/D4
Guoyang, China 114/D4
Gura Humorului, Rom. 91/G2
Gurage (peak), Eth. 139/N6
Gurbantünggut (des.), China 112/E2
Gurdāspur, India 128/C3
Gurgaon, India 128/D5
Gürgentepe, Turk. 132/D1
Gurguéia (riv.), Braz. 193/K6
Guri (dam), Ven. 195/F3
Guri (res.), Ven. 195/F3
Gurk (riv.), Aus. 85/L3
Gurkthaler Alpen (mts.), Aus. 85/K3
Gurnee, Il, US 177/Q15
Guro, Moz. 147/F4
Gürpınar, Turk. 132/E2
Gursarai, India 126/B3
Gürsu, Turk. 132/B1
Guru Sikhar (peak), India 131/K4
Gürün, Turk. 132/D2
Gurupi, Braz. 193/J6
Gurupi (riv.), Braz. 193/J4
Gurupi, Serra do (mts.), Braz. 193/J4
Gus'-Khrustal'nyy, Rus. 102/J5
Gusau, Nga. 145/G3
Gushi, China 114/C4
Gushikawa, Japan 117/J7
Gusinje, Serb. 90/D4
Guskhara, India 127/F4
Guspini, It. 88/A3
Gussola, It. 100/D3
Gustavo Díaz Ordaz, Mex. 184/C3
Gustavo Díaz Ordaz, Mex. 184/B3
Gusterath, Ger. 95/F4
Güstrow, Ger. 80/E5
Gusum, Swe. 80/G2
Gutau, Aus. 97/H6
Gütersloh, Ger. 93/F5
Guthrie, Tx, US 171/G4
Guthrie, Ok, US 179/N14
Gutiérrez Zamora, Mex. 185/M6
Guttannen, Swi. 99/E4
Guttenberg, NJ, US 181/K8
Guttingen, Swi. 99/F2
Gutulia NP, Nor. 79/E3
Guwāhāti, India 125/F2
Guxhagen, Ger. 93/G6
Guxian, China 114/B3
Guy Fawkes River NP, Austl. 157/E1
Guyana (ctry.) 195/G3
Guyancourt, Fr. 72/J5
Guyandotte (riv.), WV, US 175/H2
Guyang, China 114/B2
Guyenne (reg.), Fr. 84/C4
Guymon, Ok, US 171/G3
Guyra, Austl. 157/D1
Guyuan, China 112/J4
Güzelbağ, Turk. 133/B1
Güzelsu, Turk. 133/B1
Guzhang, China 125/J2
Guzhen, China 114/D4
Guzmán (lake), Mex. 184/D2
Gwādar, Pak. 131/H3
Gwaii Haanas NP, BC, Can. 164/C3
Gwalior, India 126/B2
Gwanda, Zim. 147/E5
Gwandalan, Austl. 157/D2
Gwash (riv.), Eng, UK 75/F1
Gwaunceste (peak), Wal, UK 74/C2
Gwda (riv.), Pol. 83/J2
Gwersyllt, Wal, UK 77/E5
Gweru, Zim. 147/E4
Gwydir (riv.), Austl. 157/D1
Gwynedd (co.), Wal, UK 76/D5
Gwyrfai (riv.), Wal, UK 76/D5
Gy, Fr. 98/B3
Gya (pass), China 127/E1
Gyaca, China 125/F2
Gyál, Hun. 91/R10
Gyasikan, Gha. 145/F5
Gyda (pen.), Rus. 109/G2
Gyhum, Ger. 93/G2
Gyirong, China 127/E1
Gyldenløveshøj (peak), Den. 80/D4
Gympie, Austl. 156/D4
Gyōda, Japan 119/C1
Gyoma, Hun. 90/E2
Gyömró, Hun. 91/R10
Győr, Hun. 90/C2
Győr-Moson-Sopron (co.), Hun. 83/J5
Győrújbarát, Hun. 90/C2
Gyumri, Arm. 105/G4
Gyzylarbat, Trkm. 105/L5
Gžira, Malta 88/L7

H

Hå, Nor. 80/A2
Ha Giang, Viet. 125/H3
Ha Noi (Hanoi) (cap.), Viet. 125/J3
Haacht, Belg. 95/D2
Haag, Aus. 97/H6
Haag am Hausruck, Aus. 97/G6
Haag an der Amper, Ger. 97/E6
Haag in Oberbayern, Ger. 97/F6
Haaksbergen, Neth. 92/D4
Haaltert, Belg. 94/D2
Haamstede, Neth. 92/A5
Haan, Ger. 92/E6
Ha'apai Group (isl.), Tonga 159/H7
Haapavesi, Fin. 79/H2
Haapsalu, Est. 81/K2
Haar, Ger. 97/E6
Haardt (mts.), Ger. 85/G2
Haarlem, Neth. 92/B4
Haast, NZ 159/R11
Haasts Bluff Abor. Land, Austl. 155/F2
Hab (riv.), Pak. 131/J3
Habahe, China 112/E2
Habartov, Czh. 97/F2
Habbānīyah, Iraq 132/E3
Habicht (peak), Aus. 99/H3
Habiganj, Bang. 127/H3
Habikino, Japan 119/J6
Habomai (isls.), Rus. 118/D2
HaBonim, Isr. 133/F6
Haboro, Japan 118/B1
Hābra, India 127/G4
Habsheim, Fr. 98/D2
Hacha (falls), Ven. 195/F3
Hache (riv.), Ger. 93/F3
Hachenburg, Ger. 95/G2
Hachijō, Japan 117/F4
Hachikai, Japan 119/L5
Hachimori, Japan 118/B3
Hachinohe, Japan 118/B3
Hachiōji, Japan 117/F3
Hacıbektaş, Turk. 132/C2
Hacienda Heights, Ca, US 178/G8
Hacılar, Turk. 132/C2
Hack (mt.), Austl. 155/H4
Hackensack, NJ, US 181/J8
Hackensack (riv.), NJ, US 181/J8
Hackettstown, NJ, US 180/D2
Hackney (bor.), Eng, UK 72/C2
Ḩaḑabat al Jilf al Kabīr (plat.), Egypt 143/A4
Hadāli, Pak. 128/B3
Hadamar, Ger. 96/B2
Hadano, Japan 117/F3
Hadarba (cape), Sudan 143/D4
Ḩadd, Ra's al (pt.), Oman 131/G4
Haddenham, Eng, UK 75/F3
Haddington, Sc, UK 78/D5
Haddonfield, NJ, US 180/C4
Hadejia (riv.), Nga. 145/H3
Hadelner (canal), Ger. 93/F1
Ḩadera, Isr. 133/F7
Haderslev, Den. 80/C4
Hadhramaut (reg.), Yem. 130/E6
Hadım, Turk. 133/C1
Hadjout, Alg. 142/G4
Hadleigh, Eng, UK 72/E2
Hadley (bay), Nun., Can. 164/F1
Hadlow, Eng, UK 72/E3
Hadrian's Wall, Eng, UK 77/F1
Hadselfjorden (inlet), Nor. 79/E1
Hadsten, Den. 80/D3
Hadsund, Den. 80/D3
Haeju (bay), NKor. 115/C4
Haeju, NKor. 115/C3
Haena (pt.), Hi, US 166/S9
Haenam, SKor. 115/D5
Hafik, Turk. 132/D2
Hāfizābād, Pak. 128/B3
Hāflong, India 125/F2
Hafnarfjördhur, Ice. 79/N7
Hafnarhreppur, Ice. 79/P7
Haft Gel, Iran 130/E2
Hafun (pt.), Som. 139/R5
Hagåtña (cap.), Guam 158/D3
Hagelstadt, Ger. 97/F5
Hagemeister (isl.), Ak, US 176/F4
Hagen, Ger. 93/E6
Hagen am Teutoburger Wald, Ger. 93/E4
Hagen im Bremischen, Ger. 93/F2
Hagenow, Ger. 80/D5
Hagerman, NM, US 174/B3
Hagerstown, Md, US 172/E4
Hagetmau, Fr. 84/C5
Hagfors, Swe. 80/E1
Hagi, Japan 116/B3
Hagnau am Bodensee, Ger. 99/F2
Hags (pt.), Ire. 73/P10
Hague, Sk, Can. 169/G2
Hague, Cap de la (cape), Fr. 84/C2
Haguenau, Fr. 95/G6
Hahashima (isls.), Japan 158/D2
Hahaya (int'l arpt.), Com. 149/G5
Hahle (riv.), Ger. 93/H5
Hahndorf, Austl. 155/M9
Hahnenbach (riv.), Ger. 95/G4
Hahnstätten, Ger. 96/B2
Hahnville, La, US 179/P17
Ḩahrā Awbārī (des.), Libya 138/H2
Hai (riv.), China 114/D3
Hai Duong, Viet. 120/D1
Hai Phong, Viet. 125/J3
Hai Van (pass), Viet. 120/E2
Hai'an, China 114/E4
Haibach, Ger. 96/C3
Haibara, Japan 119/J6
Haicheng, China 115/B2

Haide – Heike

241
Heilb – Hopki

Heilbron, SAfr. 148/D2
Heilbronn, Ger. 96/C4
Heilbronn, Ger. 96/D4
Heiligenberg, Ger. 99/F2
Heiligenblut, Aus. 85/K3
Heiligenhafen, Ger. 80/D4
Heiligenhaus, Ger. 92/D6
Heiligenstadt, Ger. 93/H6
Heilong (Amur) (riv.), China, Rus. 107/N5
Heilongjiang (prov.), China 113/N2
Heiloo, Neth. 92/B3
Heimaey (isl.), Ice. 79/N7
Heimbach, Ger. 95/F2
Heimberg, Swi. 98/D4
Heimsheim, Ger. 96/B5
Heino, Neth. 92/D4
Heinola, Fin. 81/M1
Heinsberg, Ger. 95/F1
Heishan, China 115/B2
Heist-op-den-Berg, Belg. 95/D1
Heitersheim, Ger. 98/D2
Heiwa, Japan 119/L5
Hejian, China 114/D3
Hejin, China 114/B4
Hejing, China 112/E3
Hekimhan, Turk. 132/D2
Hekinan, Japan 119/L6
Hekla (vol.), Ice. 79/N7
Hekou, China 125/H3
Hel, Pol. 81/H4
Helan (mts.), China 112/J4
Helbe (riv.), Ger. 93/H6
Helden, Neth. 92/D6
Helena (cap.), Mt, US 168/E4
Helena (riv.), Austl. 154/L6
Helensburgh, Sc, UK 78/B4
Helgasjön (lake), Swe. 80/F3
Helgoland (isl.), Ger. 80/B4
Helgoländer (bay), Wa, US 177/B3
Helgoländer (bay), Ger. 80/C5
Heliodora, Braz. 197/H7
Heliport (int'l arpt.), Swe. 80/E3
Hellas (see Greece) 89/G3
Ḩelleh (riv.), Iran 130/F3
Hellendoorn, Neth. 92/D4
Hellenthal, Ger. 95/F3
Hellertown, Pa, US 180/C2
Hellevoetsluis, Neth. 92/B5
Hellín, Sp. 86/E3
Hells (canyon), Id, US 168/D4
Hells Canyon Nat'l Rec. Area, US 168/D4
Hell's Gate NP, Kenya 146/C3
Helmand (riv.), Afg. 131/H2
Helmbrechts, Ger. 97/E2
Helmet (mtn.), Ak, US 176/K2
Helmetta, NJ, US 181/H10
Helmond, Neth. 92/C6
Helmstadt, Ger. 96/C3
Helmstedt, Ger. 82/F2
Helong, China 113/N3
Helotes, Tx, US 179/T20
Helper, Ut, US 170/E3
Helsenhorn (peak), Swi. 98/E5
Helsingør, Den. 80/E3
Helsinki (Helsingfors) (cap.), Fin. 79/H3
Helsinki-Vantaa (int'l arpt.), Fin. 81/L1
Hem (riv.), Fr. 94/B2
Hemau, Ger. 97/E4
Hemel Hempstead, Eng, UK 72/B1
Hemer, Ger. 93/E6
Hemet, Ca, US 178/D3
Hemmingen, Ger. 93/G4
Hemmoor, Ger. 93/G1
Hemphill, Tx, US 174/E4
Hempstead, Tx, US 171/H5
Hempstead (har.), NY, US 181/L8
Hempstead, NY, US 181/L9
Hemse, Swe. 80/H3
Hemsedal, Nor. 80/C1
Hemsworth, Eng, UK 77/G4
Henan (prov.), China 113/K5
Henån, Swe. 80/D2
Henares (riv.), Sp. 86/D2
Henashi-zaki (pt.), Japan 118/A3
Hendaye, Fr. 84/C5
Hendek, Turk. 91/K5
Henderson, NC, US 172/E4
Henderson, Nv, US 170/D3
Henderson, Tn, US 172/B5
Henderson, Ky, US 172/C4
Henderson, Co, US 179/C3
Henderson (isl.), Pitc. 159/N7
Henderson, Arg. 200/E3
Henderson, Md, US 180/C5
Hendersonville, Tn, US 172/C4
Hendersonville, NC, US 175/H3
Hendrik-Ido-Ambacht, Neth. 92/B5
Hendrik Verwoerdam (res.), SAfr. 148/D3
Hendrina, SAfr. 149/E2
Henefer, Ut, US 179/L11
Heng (mtn.), China 114/C3
Heng (isl.), China 114/L8
Heng Xian, China 125/J3
Hengduan (mts.), China 112/G6
Hengelo, Neth. 92/D4
Hengersberg, Ger. 97/G5
Hengoed, Wal, UK 74/C3
Hengshan, China 121/B2
Hengshan, China 114/B3
Hengshui, China 114/C3
Hengyang, China 121/B2
Heniches'k, Ukr. 104/E3
Hénin-Beaumont, Fr. 94/B3
Henley-on-Thames, Eng, UK 75/F3
Henlopen (cape), De, US 180/C6
Henlopen Acres, De, US 180/C6
Henndorf am Wallersee, Aus. 97/G7
Henne, Den. 80/C4
Hennebont, Fr. 84/B3
Hennef, Ger. 95/G2
Hennenman, SAfr. 148/D2
Hennigsdorf, Ger. 82/D6
Henrietta, Tx, US 171/H4
Henrietta Maria (cape), On, Can. 165/H3
Henry (cape), BC, Can. 176/M5
Henry (mts.), Ut, US 170/E3
Henry Ford Museum and Greenfield Village Historical Site, Mi, US 177/E7
Henryetta, Ok, US 171/J4
Henryville, Pa, US 180/C1
Hensies, Belg. 94/C3
Hentiy (prov.), Mong. 113/J2
Hentiyn (mts.), Mong. 112/J2
Henty, Austl. 157/C2
Henzada, Myan. 125/G4
Heping, China 121/B3
Heppenheim an der Bergstrasse, Ger. 96/B3
Hepu, China 125/J3
Heqing, China 125/H2
Hequ, China 114/B3
Heradhsvötn (riv.), Ice. 79/N6
Herāt, Afg. 131/H2
Herbert, Sk, Can. 168/G3
Herbert River (falls), Austl. 156/B2
Herbert River Falls NP, Austl. 156/B2
Herberton, Austl. 156/B2
Herbeumont, Belg. 95/E4
Herblay, Fr. 72/J5
Herbolzheim, Ger. 98/D1
Herbrechtingen, Ger. 96/D5
Herbstein, Ger. 96/C1
Hercegnovi, Mont. 90/D4
Hercílio Luz (int'l arpt.), Braz. 197/B3
Herculaneum, Mo, US 179/G9
Herculaneum (ruin), It. 88/D2
Hercules, Ca, US 177/K10
Herdecke, Ger. 93/E6
Herdorf, Ger. 95/G2
Hereford, Eng, UK 74/D2
Hereford, Md, US 180/B4
Hereford (inlet), NJ, US 180/D5
Hereford, Pa, US 180/C3
Hereford, Tx, US 171/G4
Herefordshire (co.), Eng, UK 74/D2
Hereheretue (isl.), FrPol. 159/L7
Hereke, Turk. 91/J5
Herencia, Sp. 86/C3
Herentals, Belg. 92/B6
Herford, Ger. 93/F4
Hergiswil, Swi. 99/E4
Héricourt, Fr. 98/C2
Hérimoncourt, Fr. 98/C3
Herington, Ks, US 171/H3
Herisau, Swi. 99/F3
Herk (riv.), Belg. 95/E2
Herk-de-Stad, Belg. 95/E2
Herlen Gol (Kerulen) (riv.), Mong. 113/K2
Herleshausen, Ger. 93/H6
Herma Ness (cape), Sc, UK 73/W13
Hermann, Mo, US 171/K3
Hermannsburg, Ger. 93/H3
Hermannsburg, Austl. 155/G2
Hermannsburg Abor. Land, Austl. 155/G2
Hermansverk, Nor. 80/B1
Hermanus, SAfr. 148/L11
Hermeray, Fr. 72/G6
Hermersberg, Ger. 95/G5
Hermes, Fr. 94/B5
Hermeskeil, Ger. 95/F4
Hermiston, Or, US 168/D4
Hermitage, Rus. 103/T7
Hermosa Beach, Ca, US 178/F8
Hermosillo, Mex. 184/C2
Hermsdorf, Ger. 82/G6
Hernández, Mex. 184/E4
Hernando, Ms, US 171/K4
Hernani, Sp. 86/E1
Herndon, Pa, US 180/B2
Herne, Ger. 93/E5
Herne, Belg. 94/D2
Herne Bay, Eng, UK 75/H4
Herning, Den. 80/C3
Heroes de la Independencia, Mex. 184/B2
Heroica Caborca, Mex. 184/B2
Heroica Ciudad de Tlaxiaco, Mex. 186/B2
Heroica Nogales, Mex. 184/C2
Heroldsberg, Ger. 96/E3
Hérouville, Fr. 72/J4
Hérouville-Saint-Clair, Fr. 84/C2
Herøy, Nor. 79/C3
Herpf (riv.), Ger. 96/D1
Herre, Nor. 80/C2
Herrenberg, Ger. 96/B5
Herrera, Sp. 86/C4
Herrera de Pisuerga, Sp. 86/C1
Herrera del Duque, Sp. 86/C3
Herrero (pt.), Mex. 186/E2
Herrestad, Swe. 80/D2
Herrieden, Ger. 96/D4
Herriman, Ut, US 179/J12
Herrlisheim, Fr. 95/G6
Herrljunga, Swe. 80/E2
Herrsching am Ammersee, Ger. 99/H2
Hers (riv.), Fr. 84/D5
Hersbruck, Ger. 97/E3
Herschbach, Ger. 95/G2
Herscheid, Ger. 93/E6
Herselt, Belg. 95/D1
Hershey, Pa, US 180/B3
Hersheypark, Pa, US 180/B3
Herstal, Belg. 95/E2
Herten, Ger. 93/E5
Hertford, NC, US 175/J2
Hertford, Eng, UK 75/F3
Herval d'Oeste, Braz. 197/B3
Hervás, Sp. 86/C2
Herve, Belg. 95/E2
Hervey (bay), Austl. 151/E3
Hervey Bay, Austl. 156/D4
Hervey Bay (reef), Austl. 156/D3
Herxheim bei Landau, Ger. 96/B4
Herzberg am Harz, Ger. 93/H5
Herzebrock-Clarholz, Ger. 93/F5
Herzele, Belg. 94/C2
Herzliyya, Isr. 133/F7
Herzogenaurach, Ger. 96/D3
Herzogenbuchsee, Swi. 98/D3
Herzogenburg, Aus. 90/B1
Herzogenrath, Ger. 95/F2
Hesbaye (plat.), Belg. 82/C3
Hesdin, Fr. 94/B3
Hesel, Ger. 93/E2
Heshui, China 112/J4
Heshun, China 114/C3
Hésingue, Fr. 98/D2
Hesperange, Lux. 95/F4
Hesperia, Ca, US 178/C2
Hess (riv.), Yk, Can. 164/C2
Hessel (riv.), Ger. 93/F5
Hesselø (isl.), Den. 80/D3
Hessen (state), Ger. 85/H1
Hessen, Ger. 93/H4
Hessisch Lichtenau, Ger. 93/G6
Hessisch Oldendorf, Ger. 93/G4
Hetauḍā, Nepal 127/E2
Heteren, Neth. 92/C5
Hettenleidelheim, Ger. 96/B3
Hettinger, ND, US 169/H4
Hetton-le-Hole, Eng, UK 77/G2
Hettstadt, Ger. 96/C3
Hetzerath, Ger. 95/F4
Heubach (riv.), Ger. 93/E5
Heubach, Ger. 96/C5
Heuchelheim, Ger. 96/B1
Heukuppe (peak), Aus. 83/H5
Heusden, Neth. 92/C5
Heusden-Zolder, Belg. 95/E1
Heusenstamm, Ger. 96/B2
Heusweiler, Ger. 95/F5
Hève, Cap de la (cape), Fr. 84/D2
Heves, Hun. 90/E2
Heves (co.), Hun. 83/L5
Hewitt, NJ, US 181/H7
Hewlett (pt.), NY, US 181/L8
Hewlett, NY, US 181/L9
Hex River (mts.), SAfr. 148/L10
Hex River (pass), SAfr. 148/L10
Hexenkopf (peak), Aus. 99/G3
Heyerode, Ger. 93/H6
Heythuysen, Neth. 92/C6
Heywood, Austl. 157/B3
Heywood, Eng, UK 77/F4
Heze, China 114/C4
Hialeah, Fl, US 175/H5
Hiawatha, Ks, US 171/J3
Hibbing, Mn, US 169/K4
Hibbs (pt.), Austl. 157/C4
Hicacos (pt.), Cuba 187/F1
Hichisō, Japan 119/M4
Hickman (mt.), BC, Can. 176/M4
Hickory, NC, US 175/H3
Hickory, La, US 179/Q16
Hickory Run State Park, Pa, US 180/C1
Hicksville, NY, US 181/L8
Hico, Tx, US 171/H5
Hida (riv.), Japan 117/E3
Hidaka (riv.), Japan 116/D4
Hidaka, Japan 118/C2
Hidaka (mts.), Japan 118/C2
Hidaka, Japan 119/C2
Hidalgo, Mex. 185/F3
Hidalgo (state), Mex. 182/B3
Hidalgo del Parral, Mex. 184/D3
Hidden Hills, Ca, US 178/B2
Hiddenhausen, Ger. 93/F4
Hidrolândia, Braz. 196/B2
Hierapolis (ruin), Turk. 132/B2
Hieroglyphic (mts.), Az, US 179/R18
Hierro (isl.), Canl., Sp. 140/A4
Hieve (lake), Ger. 93/E2
Higashi-Chichibu, Japan 119/C1
Higashi-Matsuyama, Japan 119/C1
Higashi-Ōsaka, Japan 119/J6
Higashikurume, Japan 119/D2
Higashimurayama, Japan 119/C2
Higashine, Japan 118/B4
Higashiura, Japan 119/G6
Higashiura, Japan 119/L6
Higashiyoshino, Japan 119/J7
High (des.), Or, US 168/C5
High (hill), Pa, US 180/C1
High (isl.), China 113/V10
High Bridge, NJ, US 180/D2
High Island, Tx, US 174/E4
High Level, Ab, Can. 164/E3
High Point, NC, US 175/H3
High Ridge, Mo, US 179/F9
High River, Ab, Can. 168/E3
High Street (peak), Eng, UK 77/F3
High Willhays (hill), Eng, UK 74/B5
High Wycombe, Eng, UK 75/F3
Higham, Eng, UK 72/E2
Higham Ferrers, Eng, UK 75/F2
Highland, Ca, US 178/C2
Highland, Ut, US 179/K13
Highland, In, US 177/R16
Highland (pol. reg.), Sc, US 78/A2
Highland Lakes, NJ, US 180/D1
Highland Park, Co, US 179/A4
Highland Park, Mi, US 177/F7
Highland Park, NJ, US 181/H10
Highlands, NJ, US 181/K10
Highrock (lake), Mb, Can. 169/H2
Highspire, Pa, US 180/B3
Hightstown, NJ, US 180/D3
Highwood, Il, US 177/Q15
Higley, Az, US 179/S19
Higuera de Zaragoza, Mex. 184/C3
Hihyā, Egypt 133/B4
Hiidenportin NP, Fin. 79/J3
Hiiumaa (isl.), Est. 81/K2
Híjar, Sp. 87/E2
Hijāz, Jabal al (mts.), SAr. 130/C3
Hiji, Japan 116/B4
Hijuelas de Conchali, Chile 200/N8
Hikami, Japan 119/H5
Hikari, Japan 119/F2
Hikone, Japan 119/K5
Hikueru (isl.), FrPol. 159/L6
Hikurangi (peak), NZ 159/T10
Hildburghausen, Ger. 96/D2
Hilden, Ger. 95/F1
Hilders, Ger. 96/C1
Hildesheim, Ger. 93/G4
Hilgermissen, Ger. 93/G3
Hill (isl.), Pa, US 180/B3
Hill City, Ks, US 171/H3
Hill of Fare (hill), Sc, UK 78/D2
Hill of Stake (hill), Sc, UK 78/B5
Hillaby (mt.), Bar. 183/P9
Hillburn, NY, US 181/J7
Hillcrest, NY, US 181/J7
Hille, Ger. 93/F4
Hillegom, Neth. 92/B4
Hillerød, Den. 80/E4
Hillesheim, Ger. 95/F3
Hillingdon (bor.), Eng, UK 72/B2
Hillsboro, Md, US 180/C6
Hillsboro, ND, US 169/J4
Hillsboro, Oh, US 172/D4
Hillsboro, Or, US 168/C4
Hillsboro, Tx, US 171/H4
Hillsborough (chan.), Austl. 156/C3
Hillsborough, Ca, US 177/K11
Hillsborough, NJ, US 180/D3
Hillsdale, Mi, US 172/C3
Hillsdale, Ks, US 179/D6
Hillsdale (lake), Ks, US 179/D6
Hillsdale, NJ, US 181/J7
Hillside, NJ, US 181/J9
Hillside, Sc, UK 78/D3
Hillston, Austl. 157/C2
Hillswick, Sc, UK 73/W13
Hilltop, Co, US 179/C4
Hilltown, NI, UK 76/B3
Hilo, Hi, US 166/U11
Hilongos, Phil. 121/D5
Hilpoltstein, Ger. 96/E4
Hilpsford (pt.), Eng, UK 77/E3
Hilsa, India 127/E3
Hilterfingen, Swi. 98/D4
Hilton Head (isl.), SC, US 175/H3
Hilton Head Island, SC, US 175/H3
Hilvarenbeek, Neth. 92/C6
Hilversum, Neth. 92/C4
Hilzingen, Ger. 99/E2
Himāchal Pradesh (state), India 128/D3
Himalaya (range), Asia 109/G6
Himālchuli (peak), Nepal 127/E1
Himamaylan, Phil. 121/D5
Himanka, Fin. 79/G2
Himberg, Aus. 91/N7
Himeji, Japan 116/D3
Himeji Castle, Japan 116/D3
Himi, Japan 117/E2
Himmelpforten, Ger. 93/G1
Ḩimş (prov.), Syria 132/D3
Ḩimş, Syria 133/E2
Hinche, Haiti 187/H2
Hinchinbrook (isl.), Austl. 151/D2
Hinchinbrook Entrance (chan.), Ak., US 176/J3
Hinchinbrook Island NP, Austl. 156/B2
Hinckley, Eng, UK 75/E1
Hincks Conservation Park, Austl. 155/H5
Hindan (riv.), India 126/A1
Hindaun, India 126/A2
Hindelang, Ger. 99/G3
Hindeloopen, Neth. 92/C3
Hindley, Eng, UK 77/F4
Hindmarsh (lake), Austl. 157/B3
Hindu Kush (mts.), Asia 109/F6
Hindupur, India 124/C5
Hinesville, Ga, US 175/H4
Hinganghāt, India 124/C3
Hingol (riv.), Pak. 131/J3
Hingoli, India 124/C4
Hingorja, Pak. 131/J3
Hınıs, Turk. 132/E2
Hino, Japan 119/K5
Hino, Japan 119/C2
Hino (riv.), Japan 119/K5
Hino-misaki (cape), Japan 116/C3
Hinode, Japan 119/C2
Hinohara, Japan 119/C2
Hinojosa del Duque, Sp. 86/C3
Hinsdale, Il, US 177/Q16
Hinte, Ger. 93/E2
Hinterbrühl, Aus. 91/N7
Hinterrhein (riv.), Swi. 99/F4
Hinterrugg (peak), Swi. 99/F3
Hinterweidenthal, Ger. 95/G5
Hinton, Ab, Can. 168/D2
Hinton, WV, US 172/D4
Hinwil, Swi. 99/E3
Hipólito Bouchard, Arg. 200/E2
Hippolytushoef, Neth. 92/B3
Hipswell, Eng, UK 77/G3
Hira Highlands (uplands), Japan 119/J5
Hirado, Japan 116/A4
Hirakata, Japan 119/J6
Hirakud (res.), India 124/D3
Hiraman (riv.), Kenya 146/C3
Hiran (riv.), India 126/B4
Hiranai, Japan 118/B3
Hirara, Japan 117/H8
Hirata, Japan 116/C3
Hirata, Japan 119/L5
Hiratsuka, Japan 119/C3
Hirfanli (dam), Turk. 132/C2
Hîrlău, Rom. 91/H2
Hiro'o, Japan 118/C2
Hirosaki, Japan 118/B3
Hiroshima, Japan 116/C3
Hiroshima (pref.), Japan 116/C3
Hirschaid, Ger. 96/D3
Hirschau, Ger. 97/E3
Hirschhorn, Ger. 96/B4
Hirson, Fr. 95/D4
Hîrşova, Rom. 91/H3
Hirtshals, Den. 80/C3
Hirukawa, Japan 119/M4
Hisai, Japan 119/K6
Hisarcık, Turk. 132/B2
Ḩisbān, Jor. 133/D4
Ḩişn al 'Abr, Yem. 130/E5
Hispaniola (isl.), DRep.,Haiti 183/G4
Historic Houses of Odessa, De, US 180/C5
Historic Towne of Smithville, NJ, US 180/D5
Hisua, India 127/E3
Hīt, Iraq 132/E3
Hitachi, Japan 117/G2
Hitachi-Ōta, Japan 117/G2
Hitchin, Eng, UK 75/F3
Hitoyoshi, Japan 116/B4
Hitra (isl.), Nor. 79/C3
Hittisau, Aus. 99/F3
Hitzacker, Ger. 82/F2
Hitzkirch, Swi. 99/E3
Hiyoshi, Japan 119/J5
Hizan, Turk. 132/E2
Hjålmaren (lake), Swe. 80/G2
Hjartfjellet (peak), Nor. 79/E2
Hjelmeland, Nor. 80/B2
Hjerm, Den. 80/C3
Hjo, Swe. 80/F2
Hjørring, Den. 80/C3
Hka (riv.), Myan. 120/B1
Hkakabo (peak), Myan. 125/G2
Hlabisa, SAfr. 149/E3
Hlohovec, Slvk. 90/C1
Hluboká nad Vltava, Czh. 97/H4
Hluhluwe, SAfr. 149/F3
Hlukhiv, Ukr. 104/E2
Hmawbi, Myan. 125/G4
Ho, Gha. 145/F5
Hoa Binh, Viet. 120/D1
Hoare (bay), Nun., Can. 165/K2
Hobara, Japan 117/G2
Hobart, Austl. 157/C4
Hobart (int'l arpt.), Austl. 157/C4
Hobart, Wa, US 177/D3
Hobbs, NM, US 171/G4
Hoboken, Belg. 92/B6
Hoboken, NJ, US 181/J9
Hoboksar Monggol Zizhixian, China 112/E2
Hobro, Den. 80/C3
Hochalmspitze (peak), Aus. 85/K3
Höchberg, Ger. 96/C3
Hochdorf, Ger. 99/F1
Hochfelden, Fr. 95/G6
Hochfinsler (peak), Swi. 99/F3
Hochgrat (peak), Ger. 99/G3
Hochheim am Main, Ger. 96/B2
Hochkönig (peak), Aus. 85/K3
Höch'ŏn (riv.), NKor. 115/D2
Hochschwab (peak), Aus. 85/L3
Hochsimmer (peak), Ger. 95/G3
Hochspeyer, Ger. 95/G5
Höchst, Aus. 99/F3
Höchst im Odenwald, Ger. 96/B3
Hochstadt am Main, Ger. 96/E2
Höchstadt an der Aisch, Ger. 96/D3
Hochstädt an der Donau, Ger. 96/D5
Hochstetten-Dhaun, Ger. 95/G4
Hochvogel (peak), Aus. 99/G3
Hochwang (peak), Swi. 99/F4
Hockenheim, Ger. 96/B4
Hockessin, De, US 180/C4
Hockley, Eng, UK 72/F2
Hod Hasharon, Isr. 133/F7
Hodal, India 126/A2
Hodder (riv.), Eng, UK 77/F4
Hoddesdon, Eng, UK 72/D1
Hodenhagen, Ger. 93/G3
Hodges (lake), Ca, US 178/C4
Hodgeville, Sk, Can. 168/G3
Hodh (phys. reg.), Mrta. 144/C2
Hodh El Gharbi (pol. reg.), Mrta. 144/C2
Hódmezővásárhely, Hun. 90/E2
Hodonín, Czh. 83/J4
Hoekse Waard (isl.), Neth. 92/B5
Hoensbroek, Neth. 95/E2
Hoeselt, Belg. 95/E2
Hoevelaken, Neth. 92/C4
Hoeven, Neth. 92/B5
Hoeybuktmoen (int'l arpt.), Nor. 79/J1
Hof, Ger. 97/E2
Hofbieber, Ger. 96/C1
Höfdhakaupstadhur, Ice. 79/N6
Hoffman Estates, Il, US 177/P15
Hofgeismar, Ger. 93/G6
Hofheim am Taunus, Ger. 96/B2
Hofheim in Unterfranken, Ger. 96/D2
Hofmeyr, SAfr. 148/D3
Hofong Qagan Salt (lake), China 114/B3
Hofors, Swe. 80/G1
Hofsá (riv.), Ice. 79/P6
Hofsjökull (glacier), Ice. 79/N7
Hōfu, Japan 116/B3
Hogarth (mt.), Austl. 155/H2
Hogyész, Hun. 90/D2
Hoh Xil (mts.), China 112/E4
Höhbürd, Mong. 112/H2
Hohe Acht (peak), Ger. 95/G3
Hohe Geige (peak), Aus. 99/G4
Hohe Tauern (mts.), Aus. 85/K3
Hohe Tauern NP, Aus. 85/K3
Hohegrass (peak), Ger. 93/G6
Hohen Neuendorf, Ger. 82/Q6
Hohenbrunn, Ger. 97/E6
Hohenems, Aus. 99/F3
Hohenhameln, Ger. 93/H4
Hohenlinden, Ger. 97/F6
Hohenlockstedt, Ger. 82/E2
Hohenloher Ebene (plain), Ger. 82/E4
Hohenpeissenberg, Ger. 99/G2
Hohenroth, Ger. 96/D2
Hoher Dachstein (peak), Aus. 85/K3
Hoher Ifen (peak), Ger. 99/G3
Hoher Randen (peak), Ger. 99/E2
Hohgant (peak), Swi. 98/D4
Hohhot, China 113/K3
Höhn, Ger. 95/G2
Hohneck (peak), Fr. 98/D1
Hohnstorf, Ger. 93/H2
Hohokam Pima Nat'l Mon., Az, US 170/E4
Höhr-Grenzhausen, Ger. 95/G3
Hoi An, Viet. 120/E3
Hoima, Ugan. 146/A2
Hoisington, Ks, US 171/H3
Højby, Den. 80/D4
Højer, Den. 80/C4
Hōjō, Japan 116/C4
Hokitika, NZ 159/S11
Hokkaidō (isl.), Japan 118/B2
Hokksund, Nor. 80/C2
Hokota, Japan 117/G2
Hokudan, Japan 119/G6
Hokusei, Japan 119/L5
Hol, Nor. 80/C1
Holbox, Mex. 186/E1
Holbrook, Austl. 157/C2
Holbrook, Az, US 170/E4
Holbrook, NY, US 181/E2
Holderness (pen.), Eng, UK 77/H4
Holdorf, Ger. 93/F3
Holdrege, Ne, US 171/H2
Holeby, Den. 80/D4
Holguín, Cuba 187/G1
Holiday Hills, Il, US 177/P15
Holitna (riv.), Ak, US 176/G3
Höljes, Swe. 80/E1
Holladay-Cottonwood, Ut, US 179/K12
Holland, Mi, US 172/C3
Holland (pt.), Md, US 180/B6
Hollandale, Ms, US 171/K4
Hollandse IJssel (riv.), Neth. 92/B5
Hollandstoun, Sc, UK 73/V14
Hollenstedt, Ger. 93/G2
Hollfeld, Ger. 96/E3
Holliday, Ks, US 179/D5
Hollis, Ok, US 171/H4
Hollis, Ak, US 176/M4
Hollister, Ca, US 170/B3
Hollister (mt.), Austl. 154/B2
Hollogne-aux-Pierres, Belg. 95/E2
Hollola, Fin. 81/L1
Höllviksnäs, Swe. 80/E4
Holly, Wa, US 177/B2
Holly Springs, Ms, US 175/F3
Hollywood, Fl, US 175/H5
Hollywood Bowl, Ca, US 178/F7
Hollywood Park, Tx, US 179/U20
Holm, Ger. 93/G1
Holman, NW, Can. 164/E1
Hólmavík, Ice. 79/N6
Holmdel, NJ, US 180/D3
Holmes (reefs), Austl. 151/D2
Holmesdale (valley), Eng, UK 72/C3
Holmestrand, Nor. 80/D2
Holmfirth, Eng, UK 77/G4
Holmsjön (lake), Swe. 79/F3
Holmsund, Swe. 79/G3
Ḩolon, Isr. 133/F7
Holstebro, Den. 80/C3
Holston (riv.), Tn, US 175/H2
Holt, Mo, US 179/E5
Holt, Ca, US 177/M11
Holtålen, Nor. 79/D3
Holten, Neth. 92/D4
Holtland, Ger. 93/E2
Holton, Ks, US 171/J3
Holtsville, NY, US 181/E2
Holy (isl.), Sc, UK 78/A5
Holy Cross, Ak, US 176/G3
Holyhead, Wal, UK 76/D5
Holyoke, Co, US 171/G2
Holyoke, Ma, US 173/F3
Holywell, Wal, UK 77/E5
Holywood, NI, UK 76/C2
Holzkirchen, Ger. 85/J3
Holzminden, Ger. 93/G5
Holzwickede, Ger. 93/E5
Hom (riv.), Namb. 148/B3
Homberg, Ger. 93/G6
Homberg, Ger. 92/D6
Hombori Tondo (peak), Mali 145/E3
Hombourg-Haut, Fr. 95/F5
Homburg, Ger. 95/G5
Home (bay), Nun., Can. 165/K2
Home Hill, Austl. 156/B2
Homécourt, Fr. 95/E5
Homeland, Ca, US 178/C3
Homer, Ak, US 176/H4
Homer, La, US 171/J4
Homestead, Fl, US 175/H5
Homestead Nat'l Mon. of America, Ne, US 171/H2
Homewood, Al, US 175/G3
Homewood, Il, US 177/Q16
Homib (riv.), Erit. 130/C5
Hommersåk, Nor. 80/A2
Homochitto (riv.), Ms, US 174/F4
Homyel', Bela. 104/D1
Homyel'skaya Voblasts, Bela. 104/D1
Hon Quan, Viet. 120/D4
Honaunau-Napoopoo, Hi, US 166/U11
Honbetsu, Japan 118/C2
Honddu (riv.), Wal, UK 74/C2
Hondeklipbaai, SAfr. 148/B3
Hondo (riv.), Belz. 186/D2
Hondo, Japan 116/B4
Hondo, Tx, US 171/H5
Hondschoote, Fr. 94/B2
Hondsrug (reg.), Neth. 92/D3
Hondsrug (hills), Neth. 82/D2
Honduras (gulf), NAm. 186/E2
Honduras (ctry.) 186/E3
Honey (lake), Ca, US 168/C5
Honey Brook, Pa, US 180/C3
Honey Creek, Wi, US 177/P14
Hong (isl.), SKor. 115/C5
Hong (lake), China 114/C5
Hong (riv.), China 114/C4
Hong Gai, Viet. 125/J3
Hong Kong (dpcy.), China 121/B3
Hong Kong (isl.), China 121/B3
Hong'an, China 114/C5
Hongch'ŏn, SKor. 115/D4
Hongdu (riv.), China 125/J2
Honghu, China 121/B2
Hongjiang, China 125/J2
Hongqiao (int'l arpt.), China 114/L8
Hongshui (riv.), China 112/J6
Hongsŏng, SKor. 115/D4
Hongtong, China 114/B3
Honguedo (passg.), Qu, Can. 173/H1
Hongwŏn, NKor. 115/D2
Hongze, China 114/D4
Hœnheim, Fr. 95/G6
Honiara (cap.), Sol. 158/E5
Honjō, Japan 118/B4
Honjō, Japan 119/C1
Honolulu (cap.), Hi, US 166/T10
Honolulu (co.), Hi, US 166/V13
Honolulu (int'l arpt.), Hi, US 166/W13
Honouliuli, Hi, US 166/V13
Hönow, Ger. 82/Q6
Honshū (isl.), Japan 113/Q5
Hood (pt.), Austl. 154/C5
Hood, Ca, US 177/L10
Hood (mt.), Ca, US 177/J10
Hood (mt.), Or, US 168/C4
Hood Canal (str.), Wa, US 168/C4
Hoofddorp, Neth. 92/B4
Hoogeloon, Neth. 92/C6
Hoogeveen, Neth. 92/D3
Hoogeveense Vaart (canal), Neth. 92/D3
Hoogezand, Neth. 92/D2
Hooghly (riv.), India 127/F5
Hooghly-Chinsura, India 127/G4
Hoogkarspel, Neth. 92/C3
Hooglede, Belg. 94/C2
Hoogstraten, Belg. 92/B6
Hook (pt.), Ire. 73/Q10
Hook (sound), Austl. 156/C3
Hookena, Hi, US 166/U11
Hoonah, Ak, US 176/L4
Hooper, Ut, US 179/J11
Hooper Bay, Ak, US 176/E3
Hoopeston, Il, US 172/C3
Hoopstad, SAfr. 148/D2
Höör, Swe. 80/E4
Hoorn, Neth. 92/C3
Hoornse Hop (bay), Neth. 92/C3
Hoover (dam), Az, US 170/D3
Hoover, Mo, US 179/D5
Hopa, Turk. 132/E1
Hopatcong, NJ, US 180/D2
Hopatcong (lake), NJ, US 180/D2
Hope (lake), Austl. 151/A4
Hope, BC, Can. 168/C3
Hope, Ak, US 176/J3
Hope, NJ, US 180/D2
Hope Vale Aboriginal Community, Austl. 156/B1
Hopedale, Nf, Can. 165/K3
Hopelchén, Mex. 186/D2
Hopeman, Sc, UK 78/C1
Hopes Advance (cape), Qu, Can. 165/K2
Hope's Nose (pt.), Eng, UK 74/C6
Hopetown, SAfr. 148/D3
Hopewell, NJ, US 180/D3
Hopewell Furnace NHS, Pa, US 180/C3
Hopkins (riv.), Austl. 157/B3
Hopkins (lake), Austl. 151/B3
Hopkinsville, Ky, US 172/C4

242

Hoppe – Ilych

Hoppecke (riv.), Ger. 93/F6
Hoppegarten, Ger. 82/Q6
Hoppstädten-Weiersbach, Ger. 95/G4
Hopsten, Ger. 93/E4
Hoquiam, Wa, US 168/C4
Horace (mtn.), Ak, US 176/J2
Horado, Japan 119/L4
Hōrai-san (peak), Japan 119/J5
Horasan, Turk. 132/E1
Horažďovice, Czh. 97/G4
Horb am Neckar, Ger. 96/B6
Horbourg-Wihr, Fr. 98/D1
Hörbranz, Aus. 99/F2
Horche, Sp. 86/D2
Horconcitos, Pan. 187/F4
Hordaland (co.), Nor. 79/C3
Hördt, Ger. 96/B4
Hœrdt, Fr. 95/G6
Horezu, Rom. 91/G3
Horgau, Ger. 96/D6
Horgen, Swi. 99/E3
Horine, Mo, US 179/G9
Horinger, China 114/B2
Horley, Eng, UK 72/C3
Horlivka, Ukr. 104/F2
Hormigüeros, PR 183/M8
Hormuz (str.), Oman 131/G3
Horn, Aus. 85/L2
Horn (pt.), Ice. 202/H
Horn-Bad Meinberg, Ger. 93/F5
Hornachuelos, Sp. 86/C4
Hornád (riv.), Slvk. 83/L4
Hornavan (lake), Swe. 79/F2
Hornbach, Ger. 95/G5
Hornberg, Ger. 99/E1
Horndal, Swe. 80/G1
Horneburg, Ger. 93/G1
Hornell, NY, US 172/E3
Horní Bříza, Czh. 97/G3
Horní Slavkov, Czh. 97/F2
Hornisgrinde (peak), Ger. 96/B5
Hornos (cape), Chile 201/D7
Hornoy-le-Bourg, Fr. 94/A4
Hornslet, Den. 80/D3
Hörnum (cape), Ger. 80/C4
Horoshiri-dake (peak), Japan 118/C2
Hořovice, Czh. 97/G3
Horqin Zuoyi Houqi, China 114/E2
Horqin Zuoyi Zhongqi, China 114/E1
Hörsching, Aus. 97/H6
Horse Cave, Ky, US 172/C4
Horsefly (lake), BC, Can. 168/C2
Horsens, Den. 80/C4
Horseshoe (lake), Il, US 179/G8
Horseshoe (lake), Co, US 179/B2
Horsetooth (res.), Co, US 179/B1
Horsey (isl.), Eng, UK 75/H3
Horsforth, Eng, UK 77/G4
Horsham, Austl. 157/B3
Horsham, Eng, UK 75/F4
Horsham, Pa, US 180/C3
Horšovský Týn, Czh. 97/F3
Horst, Neth. 92/D6
Hörstel, Ger. 93/E4
Horstmar, Ger. 93/E4
Horta, Azor., Port. 87/S12
Horten, Nor. 80/D2
Hortes, Fr. 98/B2
Hortobágyi NP, Hun. 90/E2
Horton (pt.), NY, US 181/F1
Horton (riv.), NW, Can. 164/D2
Høruphav, Den. 80/C4
Horusický Rybník (lake), Czh. 97/H4
Hørve, Den. 80/D4
Horvot Dor, Isr. 133/F6
Horw, Swi. 99/E3
Horwich, Eng, UK 77/F4
Horwood (lake), On, Can. 172/D2
Hösbach, Ger. 96/C2
Hosenfeld, Ger. 96/C1
Hoshiārpur, India 128/C4
Hosingen, Lux. 95/F3
Hospental, Swi. 99/E4
Hosszúpereszteg, Hun. 90/C2
Hoste (isl.), Chile 201/C7
Hot Springs, SD, US 169/H5
Hot Springs NP, Ar, US 171/J4
Hotaka, Japan 117/E2
Hotaka-dake (peak), Japan 117/E2
Hotan, China 112/C4
Hotan (riv.), China 112/D4
Hotazel, SAfr. 148/C2
Hotont, Mong. 112/H2
Hottah (lake), NW, Can. 164/E2
Hottentot (bay), Namb. 148/A2
Hotton, Belg. 95/E3
Houari Boumedienne (int'l arpt.), Alg. 142/G4
Houdain, Fr. 94/B3
Houdan, Fr. 72/G5
Houet (prov.), Burk. 144/D4
Houffalize, Belg. 95/E3
Houghton Lake, Mi, US 172/C2
Houghton-le-Spring, Eng, UK 77/G2
Houilles, Fr. 72/J5
Houlton, Me, US 173/H2
Houma, China 114/B4
Houplines, Fr. 94/B2
Hourdel (pt.), Fr. 94/A3
Hourn, Loch (inlet), Sc, UK 78/A2
Hourtin, Fr. 84/C4
Housatonic (riv.), Ct, US 181/E1
House (range), Ut, US 170/D3
House Springs, Mo, US 179/F9
Housesteads Roman Fort, Eng, UK 77/F1
Houssen, Fr. 98/D1
Houston, BC, Can. 168/B2
Houston, Ak, US 176/J3
Houston, De, US 180/C6
Houston, Mo, US 171/K3
Houston, Ms, US 175/F3
Houston, Tx, US 171/J5
Houtbaai, SAfr. 148/L11
Houten, Neth. 92/C4
Houthulst, Belg. 94/B2
Houtman Abrolhos (isl.), Austl. 154/B4
Houtribdijk (dam), Neth. 92/C3
Houtskär (isl.), Fin. 81/J1
Houyet, Belg. 95/E3
Hov, Nor. 80/D1
Hova, Swe. 80/F2
Hovd, Mong. 112/F2
Hovd (prov.), Mong. 112/F2
Hövelhof, Ger. 93/F5
Hovenweep Nat'l Mon., Ut, US 170/E3
Hovfjället (peak), Swe. 80/E1
Hovmantorp, Swe. 80/F3
Hövsgöl (prov.), Mong. 112/G1
Hovsta, Swe. 80/F2
Howard, Austl. 156/D4
Howard (hill), Ak, US 176/H2
Howard (pass), Ak, US 176/G2
Howard (co.), Md, US 180/B5
Howard Hanson (res.), Wa, US 177/D3
Howard Hanson (dam), Wa, US 177/D3
Howe (cape), Austl. 157/D3
Howe of the Mearns (reg.), Sc, UK 78/D3
Howell, Mi, US 172/D3
Howell, NJ, US 180/D3
Howick, SAfr. 149/E3
Howland (isl.), Pac., US 159/H4
Höxter, Ger. 93/G5
Hoxud, China 112/E3
Hoy (isl.), Sc, UK 73/V14
Hoya, Ger. 93/G3
Hōya, Japan 119/D2
Høyanger, Nor. 80/B1
Hoyerswerda, Ger. 83/H3
Hoylake, Eng, UK 77/E5
Hoyland Nether, Eng, UK 77/G4
Hoyo de Manzanares, Sp. 87/N8
Hoyos, Sp. 86/B2
Hoyoux (riv.), Belg. 95/E3
Hozumi, Japan 119/L5
Hracholusky (res.), Czh. 97/F3
Hradec Králové, Czh. 83/H3
Hradiště (peak), Czh. 97/G2
Hrasnica, Bosn. 90/D4
Hrastnik, Slov. 85/L3
Hrazdan, Arm. 105/H4
Hrodna, Bela. 81/K5
Hrodzyenskaya Voblasts, Bela. 102/E5
Hrolleifsborg (peak), Ice. 79/M6
Hron (riv.), Slvk. 83/K4
Hronov, Czh. 83/J3
Hrubieszów, Pol. 83/M3
Hrubý Jeseník (mts.), Czh.,Pol. 83/J3
Hrútafjöll (peak), Ice. 79/P6
Hsinchu, Tai. 121/D3
Hua (peak), China 114/B4
Hua Hin, Thai. 120/B3
Hua Xian, China 114/C4
Hua'an, China 121/C2
Huacaybamba, Peru 198/B3
Huachi, China 112/J4
Huacho, Peru 198/B3
Huachón, Peru 198/C3
Huachuca City, Az, US 170/E5
Huacrachuco, Peru 198/B3
Huade, China 113/K3
Huahine (isl.), FrPol. 159/K6
Huai (riv.), China 114/C4
Huai'an, China 114/C2
Huai'an, China 114/D4
Huaibei, China 113/L5
Huaibin, China 114/C4
Huaiji, China 125/K3
Huailai, China 114/G6
Huainan, China 114/D4
Huaining, China 114/C3
Huairou, China 114/H6
Huaiyang, China 114/C4
Huaiyin, China 114/D4
Huaiyin, China 114/D4
Huaiyuan, China 114/D4
Huajicori, Mex. 184/D4
Huajuapan de León, Mex. 186/B2
Hualahuises, Mex. 185/F3
Hualañé, Chile 200/C2
Hualgayoc, Peru 198/B2
Hualien, Tai. 121/D3
Hualla, Peru 198/C4
Huallaga (riv.), Peru 198/B3
Huallanca, Peru 198/B3
Huallanca, Peru 198/B3
Huamachuco, Peru 198/B3
Huamantanga, Peru 198/B3
Huamantla, Mex. 185/M7
Huambo, Ang. 147/C3
Huambos, Peru 198/B2
Huan (riv.), China 114/C5
Huan Xian, China 112/J4
Huancané, Peru 198/D4
Huancapi, Peru 198/C4
Huancaspata, Peru 198/B3
Huancavelica (dept.), Peru 198/C4
Huancavelica, Peru 198/C4
Huancayo, Peru 198/C4
Huanchaca (peak), Bol. 192/E8
Huang (riv.), China 109/L6
Huangchuan, China 114/C4
Huanggang (peak), China 121/C2
Huanghua, China 114/D3
Huangling, China 114/B4
Huanglong, China 114/B4
Huangping, China 125/J2
Huangqi (lake), China 114/C2
Huangshan, China 121/C2
Huangtang (lake), China 114/C5
Huangtu (plat.), China 114/B4
Huanguelén, Arg. 200/E3
Huangyan, China 121/D2
Huangzhong, China 112/H4
Huanren, China 115/C2
Huanta, Peru 198/C4
Huantai, China 114/D3
Huántar, Peru 198/B3
Huánuco (dept.), Peru 198/C3
Huánuco, Peru 198/B3
Huanuni, Bol. 192/E7
Huapi (mts.), Nic. 187/E3
Huaquechula, Mex. 185/L8
Huaquillas, Ecu. 198/A1
Huaral, Peru 198/B3
Huaraz, Peru 198/B3
Huari, Peru 198/B3
Huaricolca, Peru 198/C3
Huarina, Bol. 198/D5
Huarmey, Peru 198/B3
Huarochirí, Peru 198/B4
Huarocondo, Peru 198/C4
Huarong, China 121/B2
Huásabas, Mex. 184/C2
Huasahuasi, Peru 198/C3
Huascarán (peak), Peru 198/B3
Huatabampo, Mex. 184/C3
Huatunas (lake), Bol. 192/E6
Huatuxco, Mex. 185/N7
Huauchinango, Mex. 185/L6
Huaura, Peru 198/B3
Huautla de Jiménez, Mex. 186/B2
Huayacocotla, Mex. 185/L6
Huaying, China 121/A1
Huaylas, Peru 198/B3
Huayllay, Peru 198/B3
Huayopata, Peru 198/C4
Huayuan, China 125/J2
Huazhou, China 125/K3
Hubbard (mt.), Ak, US 176/L3
Hubbard Creek (res.), Tx, US 171/H4
Hubei (prov.), China 113/K5
Hubei (pass), China 114/B4
Hubli-Dhārwār, India 131/L5
Huch'ang, NKor. 115/D2
Hückelhoven, Ger. 95/F1
Hückeswagen, Ger. 95/G1
Hucknall, Eng, UK 77/G5
Huddersfield, Eng, UK 77/G4
Huddinge, Swe. 80/G2
Hude, Ger. 93/F2
Hudiksvall, Swe. 80/G1
Hudson (cape), Ant. 202/L
Hudson (bay), Can. 165/H2
Hudson (str.), Nun.,Qu, Can. 165/J2
Hudson, Qu, Can. 173/M7
Hudson, Co, US 179/C2
Hudson (co.), NJ, US 181/J9
Hudson (riv.), NJ,NY, US 172/F3
Hudson, NY, US 172/F3
Hudson Bay, Sk, Can. 169/H2
Hudson's Hope, BC, Can. 164/D3
Hue, Viet. 120/D2
Huedin, Rom. 91/F2
Huehuetenango, Guat. 186/D3
Huehuetla, Mex. 185/L6
Huehuetlán, Mex. 185/L8
Huejotzingo, Mex. 185/L7
Huejuquilla el Alto, Mex. 184/E4
Huejutla de Reyes, Mex. 186/B1
Huelma, Sp. 86/D4
Huelva, Sp. 86/B4
Huelva (riv.), Sp. 86/B4
Huequi (vol.), Chile 200/B4
Huercal-Overa, Sp. 86/E4
Huerfano (riv.), Co, US 171/F3
Huesca, Sp. 87/E1
Huéscar, Sp. 86/D4
Huetamo de Nuñez, Mex. 185/E5
Huete, Sp. 86/D2
Huexoculco, Mex. 185/R10
Hüfingen, Ger. 99/E2
Hugh Town, Eng, UK 73/Q12
Hughenden, Austl. 156/B3
Hughenden Valley, Eng, UK 72/A2
Hughes, Ak, US 176/H2
Hughes, Arg. 200/E2
Hughesville, Pa, US 180/B1
Huglfing, Ger. 99/H2
Hugli (riv.), India 124/E3
Hugo, Ok, US 171/J4
Huguan, China 114/C3
Hui Xian, China 114/C4
Hui'an, China 121/C2
Huib-Hock (plat.), Namb. 148/B2
Huichang, China 121/C2
Huichapan, Mex. 185/K6
Hŭich'ŏn, NKor. 115/D2
Huila (dept.), Col. 194/C4
Huila, Nevado del (peak), Col. 194/C4
Huilai, China 121/C3
Huilango, Mex. 185/Q9
Huili, China 125/H2
Huimanguillo, Mex. 186/C2
Huimin, China 114/D3
Huinca Renancó, Arg. 200/D2
Huining, China 112/J4
Hŭisaek-pong (peak), NKor. 115/D2
Huishui, China 125/J2
Huisne (riv.), Fr. 84/D2
Huissen, Neth. 92/C5
Huitong, China 125/J2
Huittinen, Fin. 81/K1
Huitzilan, Mex. 185/M7
Huitzuco, Mex. 185/K8
Huixcolotla, Mex. 185/M8
Huixquilucan, Mex. 185/Q10
Huixtla, Mex. 186/C3
Huize, China 125/H2
Huizen, Neth. 92/C4
Hujra, Pak. 128/B4
Hulan, China 113/N2
Hulett, Wy, US 169/G4
Hull (riv.), Eng, UK 77/H4
Hullbridge, Eng, UK 72/E2
Hüllhorst, Ger. 93/F4
Hulst, Neth. 92/B6
Hultsfred, Swe. 80/F3
Huma, China 113/N1
Huma (riv.), China 113/M1
Humahuaca, Arg. 199/C1
Humaitá, Braz. 192/F5
Humansdorp, SAfr. 148/D4
Humay, Peru 198/C4
Humber (riv.), Nf, Can. 173/K1
Humber (bay), On, Can. 173/R8
Humber (riv.), Eng, UK 77/H4
Humberto de Campos, Braz. 196/B1
Humble, Tx, US 171/J5
Humboldt, Sk, Can. 169/G2
Humboldt (bay), Col. 187/G5
Humboldt (range), Nv, US 170/C2
Humboldt (riv.), Nv, US 170/C2
Humboldt, Tn, US 172/B5
Hume (lake), Austl. 157/C2
Húmeda, Pampa (plain), Arg. 200/E2
Humenné, Slvk. 83/L4
Humida, Pampa (plain), Arg. 199/D4
Humlum, Den. 80/C3
Hummels Wharf, Pa, US 180/B2
Hummelstown, Pa, US 180/B3
Humphrey (pt.), Ak, US 176/K2
Humphreys (peak), Az, US 170/E4
Hūn, Libya 138/J2
Húnaflói (bay), Ice. 79/N6
Hunan (prov.), China 113/K6
Hundsangen, Ger. 95/G3
Hunedoara, Rom. 90/F3
Hunedoara (prov.), Rom. 90/F3
Hünenberg, Swi. 99/E3
Hünfeld, Ger. 85/H1
Hung Yen, Viet. 120/D1
Hungaroring, Hun. 91/R9
Hungary (ctry.) 90/D2
Hungen, Ger. 96/B2
Hŭngnam, NKor. 115/D3
Hunjiang, China 115/D2
Hunnebostrand, Swe. 80/D2
Hunsel, Neth. 92/C6
Hunsrück (mts.), Ger. 82/D4
Hunte (riv.), Ger. 82/E2
Hunter (isl.), Austl. 151/D5
Hunter (riv.), Austl. 157/D2
Hunter (mt.), Ak, US 176/H3
Hunter, Tx, US 179/U20
Hunterdon (co.), NJ, US 180/C2
Huntingburg, In, US 172/C4
Huntingdon, Eng, UK 75/F2
Huntington, In, US 172/C3
Huntington, NY, US 181/M8
Huntington (bay), NY, US 181/M8
Huntington, WV, US 172/D4
Huntington Bay, NY, US 181/M8
Huntington Beach, Ca, US 178/G8
Huntington Park, Ca, US 178/F8
Huntington Station, NY, US 181/M8
Huntington Woods, Mi, US 177/F7
Huntley, Il, US 177/P15
Huntly, NZ 159/T10
Huntly, Sc, UK 78/D2
Hunts Inlet, BC, Can. 176/M4
Hunts Point, Wa, US 177/C2
Huntsville, Al, US 175/G3
Huntsville, On, Can. 172/E2
Huntsville, Ut, US 179/K11
Huntsville (res.), Pa, US 180/B1
Hunucmá, Mex. 186/D1
Hünxe, Ger. 92/D5
Hunyuan, China 114/C3
Huo (mtn.), China 114/B3
Huo (mtn.), China 114/D5
Huocheng, China 112/D3
Huojia, China 114/C4
Huolin Gol, China 113/L2
Huoqiu, China 114/D4
Huoshan, China 114/D5
Huozhou, China 114/B3
Hurdal, Nor. 80/D1
Hure Qi, China 114/E2
Hurepoix (reg.), Fr. 72/H6
Hurley, NM, US 170/E4
Hurley, Eng, UK 72/A2
Hurley (riv.), Ire. 76/B4
Hurlford, Sc, UK 78/B5
Huron (lake), Can.,US 172/D2
Huron (mts.), Mi, US 172/B2
Huron (pt.), Mi, US 177/G6
Huron (riv.), Mi, US 177/E7
Hurricane, WV, US 172/D4
Hurtaut (riv.), Fr. 94/D4
Hürtgenwald (reg.), Ger. 95/F2
Hürth, Ger. 95/F2
Hurup, Den. 80/C3
Husainābād, India 127/E3
Húsavík, Ice. 79/P6
Huscarán, PN, Peru 198/B3
Husher, Wi, US 177/Q14
Huși, Rom. 91/J2
Huskisson, Austl. 157/D2
Huslia, Ak, US 176/G2
Husnes, Nor. 80/A2
Hussigny-Godbrange, Fr. 95/E5
Husum, Ger. 80/C4
Husum, Swe. 79/F3
Hutag, Mong. 112/H2
Hutchinson, Mn, US 169/K4
Hutchinson, Ks, US 171/H3
Hüttisheim, Ger. 99/F1
Hüttlingen, Ger. 96/D5
Hutton (mt.), Austl. 156/C4
Hutton, Eng, UK 72/E2
Huttwil, Swi. 98/D3
Hutuo (riv.), China 114/C3
Ḩuwwārah, WBnk. 133/G7
Huy, Belg. 95/E2
Huyton-with-Roby, Eng, UK 77/F5
Huzhou, China 114/L9
Hvammstangi, Ice. 79/N6
Hvannadalshnúkur (peak), Ice. 79/P7
Hvar (isl.), Cro. 88/E1
Hvide Sande, Den. 80/C4
Hvítá (riv.), Ice. 79/N7
Hvolsvöllur, Ice. 79/N7
Hwange, Zim. 147/E4
Hwange (Wankie) NP, Zim. 147/E4
Hwanghae-bukto (prov.), NKor. 115/D3
Hwanghae-namdo (prov.), NKor. 115/C3
Hwangju, NKor. 115/C3
Hwangju (riv.), NKor. 115/C3
Hwasun, SKor. 115/D5
Hyades (peak), Chile 200/B5
Hyattstown, Md, US 180/A5
Hyattsville, Md, US 180/B6
Hydaburg, Ak, US 176/M4
Hyde, Eng, UK 77/F5
Hyder, Ak, US 176/M4
Hyderābād, India 124/C4
Hyderābād, Pak. 131/J3
Hyères, Fr. 85/G5
Hyères, Îles d' (isls.), Fr 85/G5
Hyesan, NKor. 115/E2
Hygiene, Co, US 179/B2
Hyland (riv.), Yk, Can. 164/D2
Hyllestad, Nor. 80/A1
Hyltebruk, Swe. 80/E3
Hylton (hill), Ky, US 172/D4
Hyō-no-sen (peak), Japan 116/D3
Hyōgo (pref.), Japan 116/D3
Hyŏndŭng-san (peak), SKor. 115/G6
Hyrum, Ut, US 170/E2
Hythe, Eng, UK 75/H4
Hyūga, Japan 116/B4
Hyvinkää, Fin. 81/L1
Hywel, Moel (peak), Wal, UK 74/C2

I

I-n-Amenas, Alg. 141/H3
I-n-Azaoua, Oued (riv.), Niger 141/H5
I-n-Dagouber (well), Mali 141/E5
I-n-Échaï (well), Mali 145/E1
I-n-Gall, Niger 145/G2
I-n-Guezzâm, Alg. 145/G2
I-n-Milach (well), Mali 145/E2
I-n-Sâkâne, 'Erg (des.), Mali 145/E1
I-n-Salah, Alg. 141/F4
I-n-Tassik (well), Mali 145/F2
Iacanga, Braz. 197/B2
Iaciara, Braz. 196/A4
Iaco (riv.), Braz. 192/E6
Iaçu, Braz. 196/B4
Iâf di Montasio (peak), It. 85/K3
Iakora, Madg. 149/H8
Ialomița (prov.), Rom. 91/H3
Ialomița (riv.), Rom. 91/H3
Ianapera, Madg. 149/H8
Iapu, Braz. 197/D1
Iași, Rom. 91/H2
Iași (prov.), Rom. 91/H2
Iasmos, Gre. 89/J2
Iatan, Mo, US 179/D5
Iba, Phil. 121/C4
Ibadan, Nga. 145/F5
Ibagué, Col. 192/C3
Ibaiti, Braz. 197/B2
Ibajay, Phil. 121/D5
Ibanda, Ugan. 146/A3
Ibans (lake), Hon. 187/E3
Ibapaba, Serra da (range), Braz. 196/B1
Ibar (riv.), Serb. 90/E4
Ibara, Japan 116/C3
Ibaraki (pref.), Japan 117/F2
Ibaraki, Japan 119/J6
Ibaraki, Japan 119/E1
Ibarra, Ecu. 194/B4
Ibarreta, Arg. 199/E2
Ibb, Yem. 130/D6
Ibba (riv.), Sudan 139/L6
Ibbenbüren, Ger. 93/E4
Ibdekkene (riv.), Mali 145/F2
Iberia, Peru 198/D3
Iberia, Peru 198/C2
Ibérico, Sistema (range), Sp. 86/D2
Iberville, Qu, Can. 173/P7
Ibi, Sp. 87/E3
Ibiá, Braz. 197/C1
Ibiapina, Braz. 196/B1
Ibicaraí, Braz. 196/C4
Ibicuy, Arg. 201/J10
Ibigawa, Japan 119/L5
Ibimirim, Braz. 196/C3
Ibiraçu, Braz. 197/D1
Ibirapuã, Braz. 196/B5
Ibitinga, Braz. 197/B2
Ibiúna, Braz. 197/F8
Ibiza (isl.), Sp. 87/F3
Ibiza, Sp. 87/F3
Ibo, Moz. 147/H3
Ibo (riv.), Japan 116/D3
Iboro, Nga. 145/F5
Ibotirama, Braz. 196/B4
Iboundji (peak), Gabon 138/H8
Ibrány, Hun. 83/L4
Ibshawāy, Egypt 133/B5
Ibuki, Japan 119/K5
Ibuki-yama (peak), Japan 119/K5
Ica (dept.), Peru 198/C4
Ica, Peru 198/C4
Iça (riv.), SAm. 192/E4
Içana (riv.), Braz. 192/E3
Icel (prov.), Turk. 132/C2
Iceland (ctry.) 79/N7
Icém, Braz. 197/B2
Ichalkaranji, India 131/K5
Ichāmati (riv.), Bang. 127/G3
Ichchāpuram, India 124/D4
Ichenhausen, Ger. 96/D6
Ichhāwar, India 126/A4
Ichihara, Japan 119/E3
Ichijima, Japan 119/H5
Ichikawa, Japan 119/D2
Ichikawada, Japan 119/B2
Ichinohe, Japan 118/B3
Ichinomiya, Japan 119/B2
Ichinomiya, Japan 119/E3
Ichinomiya, Japan 119/G7
Ichinomiya, Japan 119/M6
Ichinomiya, Japan 119/L5
Ichinoseki, Japan 118/B4
Ichishi, Japan 119/K6
Ichkeul (lake), Tun. 142/L6
Ich'ŏn, SKor. 115/D4
Ichtegem, Belg. 94/C1
Ickesburg, Pa, US 180/A3
Icó, Braz. 196/C2
Icod de los Vinos, Canl., Sp. 140/A3
Icy (bay), Ak, US 176/K4
Icy (cape), Ak, US 176/F1
Icy (pt.), Ak, US 176/L4
Icy (str.), Ak, US 176/L4
Idabel, Ok, US 171/J4
Idaho (state), US 168/E5
Idaho Springs, Co, US 179/A3
Idanha-a-Nova, Port. 86/B3
Idar, India 124/B3
Idar-Oberstein, Ger. 95/G4
Idarkopf (peak), Ger. 95/G4
Idaville, Pa, US 180/A3
Ide, Japan 119/J6
Ideles, Alg. 141/G5
Idfū, Egypt 143/C3
Ídhi (peak), Gre. 89/J5
Ídhra, Gre. 89/H4
Idice (riv.), It. 101/E4
Idjwe, Île (isl.), D.R. Congo 146/A3
Idkū, Egypt 133/B4
Idle (riv.), Eng, UK 77/H5
Idlib (prov.), Syria 132/D3
Idlib, Syria 133/E2
Idnah, WBnk. 133/D4
Idrija, Slov. 85/L4
Idriss I (dam), Mor. 142/B2
Idriss I, Barrage (res.), Mor. 142/B2
Idro, Lago d' (lake), It. 100/D1
Idstein, Ger. 96/B2
Ie (isl.), Japan 117/J7
Ieper, Belg. 94/B2
Ierápetra, Gre. 89/J5
Ierissós, Gre. 89/H2
Iesolo, It. 101/F1
Ifalik (isl.), Micr. 158/D4
Ifanadiana, Madg. 149/H8
Ife, Nga. 145/G5
Iferfes (well), Libya 141/H3
Iffeldorf, Ger. 99/H2
Iffezheim, Ger. 96/B5
Iforas, Adrar des (upland), Alg.,Mali 138/F4
Ifrane, Mor. 140/D2
Iga (riv.), Japan 119/K6
Iga, Japan 119/K6
Igal, Hun. 90/C2
Iganga, Ugan. 146/B2
Igaporã, Braz. 196/B4
Igara Paraná (riv.), Col. 194/C5
Igarapava, Braz. 197/C2
Igarapé Grande, Braz. 196/A2
Igarapé-Miri, Braz. 193/J4
Igaratá, Braz. 197/G8
Igarka, Rus. 106/J3
Igatpuri, India 124/B4
Igdet (peak), Mor. 140/C3
Iğdır, Turk. 132/F2
Igel, Ger. 95/F4
Iggesund, Swe. 80/G1
Ightham, Eng, UK 72/D3
Igikpak (mt.), Ak, US 176/H2
Igis, Swi. 99/F4
Igiugig, Ak, US 176/G4
Iglesias, It. 88/A3
Igli, Alg. 141/E3
Igling, Ger. 99/G1
Igloolik, Nun., Can. 165/H2
Ignace, On, Can. 169/L3
Ignacio, Ca, US 177/J10
Ignacio de la Llave, Mex. 185/P8
Ignacio Zaragoza, Mex. 184/D2
Iğneada Burnu (cape), Turk. 91/J5
Igney, Fr. 98/C1
Ignon (riv.), Fr. 98/A2
Igny, Fr. 72/J5
Igombe (riv.), Tanz. 146/B4
Igora Paraná (riv.), Col. 198/C1
Igoumenítsa, Gre. 89/G3
Igra, Rus. 103/M4
Igreja, Morro da (peak), Braz. 197/B4
Iguaçu (riv.), Braz. 189/D5
Iguaçu, PN do, Braz. 199/F2
Iguaí, Braz. 196/B4
Iguala, Mex. 185/K8
Igualada, Sp. 87/F2
Iguape, Braz. 197/C3
Iguape (riv.), Braz. 197/B3
Iguatu, Braz. 196/C2
Iguazú, PN del, Arg. 199/F2
Iguetti (lake), Mrta. 140/C4
Iheya (isl.), Japan 117/J7
Ihhayrhan, Mong. 112/J2
Ihosy, Madg. 149/H8
Ihotry (lake), Madg. 149/G8
Ihuari, Peru 198/B3
Ii, Fin. 79/H2
Iida, Japan 117/E3
Iide-san (peak), Japan 117/F2
Iijoki (riv.), Fin. 79/H2
Iinan, Japan 119/K7
Iisalmi, Fin. 79/H2
Iitaka, Japan 119/K7
Iitti, Fin. 81/M1
Iiyama, Japan 117/F2
Iizuka, Japan 116/B4
Ijebu Ode, Nga. 145/F5
Ijill (peak), Mrta. 140/B5
Ijill (lake), Mrta. 140/B5
Ijira, Japan 119/L4
IJmeer (bay), Neth. 92/C4
IJmuiden, Neth. 92/B4
Ijnaoun (well), Mrta. 144/B2
Ijoki (riv.), Fin. 79/H2
Ijoubbane, 'Erg (des.), Mali 140/D5
IJssel (riv.), Neth. 92/C3
IJsselmeer (lake), Neth. 82/C2
IJsselmuiden, Neth. 92/C3
IJsselstein, Neth. 92/C4
Ijuí, Braz. 199/F2
Ijūin, Japan 116/B5
Ijzer (riv.), Belg. 82/B3
Ik (riv.), Rus. 103/M5
Ikahavo (plat.), Madg. 149/H7
Ikalamavony, Madg. 149/H8
Ikare, Nga. 145/G5
Ikaría, Gre. 132/A2
Ikaría (isl.), Gre. 89/J4
Ikaruga, Japan 119/J6
Ikeda, Japan 116/C3
Ikeda, Japan 118/C2
Ikeda, Japan 119/H6
Ikeda, Japan 119/L5
Ikeja, Nga. 145/F5
Ikenokoya-yama (peak), Japan 119/K7
Ikerre, Nga. 145/G5
Ikhtiman, Bul. 89/H1
Iki (isl.), Japan 116/A4
Iki (chan.), Japan 116/A4
Ikire, Nga. 145/G5
Ikirun, Nga. 145/G5
İkizce, Turk. 132/C2
İkizdere, Turk. 132/E1
Ikoma, Japan 119/J6
Ikongo, Madg. 149/H8
Ikopa (riv.), Madg. 149/H7
Ikorodu, Nga. 145/F5
Ikuno, Japan 116/D3
Ila Orangun, Nga. 145/G4
Ilabaya, Peru 198/D5
Ilagan, Phil. 121/D4
Ilam, Nepal 127/F2
Īlām, Iran 130/E2
Ilan, Tai. 121/D3
Ilanz, Swi. 99/F4
Ilaro, Nga. 145/F5
Ilave, Peru 198/D5
Iława, Pol. 83/K2
Ilawe-Ekiti, Nga. 145/G5
Ile (riv.), China.,Kaz. 112/C3
Île-à-la-Crosse, Sk, Can. 168/G2
Île-a-la-Crosse (lake), Sk, Can. 168/G2
Île-de-France (pol. reg.), Fr. 94/A6
Ilebo, D.R. Congo 147/D1
Ilek (riv.), Rus. 105/K2
Îles Ehotilés, PN des, C.d'Iv. 144/E5
Iles Tristao, Îles (isls.), Gui. 144/B4
Ilesha, Nga. 145/G5
Ilfis (riv.), Swi. 98/D4
Ilgaz, Turk. 104/E4
Ilgın, Turk. 132/B2
Ilha Grande (bay), Braz. 197/J8
Ilha Grande, Baía de (bay), Braz. 197/C2
Ilha Solteira, Represa (res.), Braz. 193/H7
Ilhabela, Braz. 197/H8
Ílhavo, Port. 86/A2
Ilhéus, Braz. 196/C4
Iliamna, Ak, US 176/H4
Iliamna (lake), Ak, US 176/G4
Iliamna (vol.), Ak, US 176/H3
Iliç, Turk. 132/D2
Ilıca, Turk. 105/G5
Ilijaš, Bosn. 90/D4
Iliniza (peak), Ecu. 194/B5
Ilirska Bistrica, Slov. 85/L4
Ilısu (dam), Turk. 132/E2
Ilısu (res.), Turk. 132/E2
Ilium (Troy) (ruin), Turk. 89/K3
Ilkeston, Eng, UK 77/G6
Ilkley, Eng, UK 77/G4
Ill (riv.), Aus. 85/H3
Ill (riv.), Fr. 85/G3
Illana, Sp. 86/D2
Illapel, Chile 199/B3
Illasi (riv.), It. 101/E1
Illbillee (mt.), Austl. 155/G3
Illéla, Niger 145/G3
Iller (riv.), Ger. 85/J2
Illertissen, Ger. 99/G1
Illescas, Sp. 86/D2
Illiers-Combray, Fr. 84/D2
Illimani (peak), Bol. 192/E7
Illingen, Ger. 95/G5
Illinois (riv.), Il, US 172/B3
Illinois (state), US 172/B4
Illizi, Alg. 141/H4
Illizi (prov.), Alg. 141/G4
Illkirch-Graffenstaden, Fr. 98/D1
Illmensee, Ger. 99/F2
Illnau, Swi. 99/E3
Illora, Sp. 86/D4
Illovo, SAfr. 149/E3
Illzach, Fr. 98/D2
Ilm (riv.), Ger. 82/F4
Ilmajoki, Fin. 79/G3
Ilme (riv.), Ger. 93/G5
Il'men (lake), Rus. 106/D4
Ilmenau, Ger. 85/J1
Ilmenau (riv.), Ger. 93/H2
Ilo, Peru 198/D5
Ilobu, Nga. 145/G5
Ilorin, Nga. 145/G4
Ilovlya (riv.), Rus. 105/H2
Ilpendam, Neth. 92/B4
Ilse (riv.), Ger. 93/H5
Ilsede, Ger. 93/H4
Ilsenburg, Ger. 93/H5
Ilsfeld, Ger. 96/C4
Ilshofen, Ger. 96/C4
Ilyas Burnu (pt.), Turk. 91/H5
Ilych (riv.), Rus. 103/N3

243
Ilz – Jagna

Ilz (riv.), Ger. 83/G4
Imabari, Japan 116/C3
Imaichi, Japan 117/F2
Imaloto (riv.), Madg. 149/H8
İmamoğlu, Turk. 132/C2
Imandra (lake), Rus. 79/J2
Imari, Japan 116/A4
Imatra, Fin. 81/N1
Imazu, Japan 119/K5
Imba (lake), Japan 119/E2
Imba, Japan 119/E2
Imbabura (prov.), Ecu. 194/B4
Imbituba, Braz. 197/B4
Imbituva, Braz. 197/B3
Imeni Moskvy (canal), Rus. 103/W9
Imerimandroso, Madg. 149/J7
Imi n'tanout, Mor. 140/C3
İmişli, Azer. 105/J5
Imittós (peak), Gre. 89/N9
Imja (isl.), SKor. 115/C5
Imlay, Nv, US 168/D5
Immendingen, Ger. 99/E2
Immenhausen, Ger. 93/G6
Immenstaad am Bodensee, Ger. 99/F2
Immenstadt im Allgäu, Ger. 99/G2
Immingham, Eng, UK 77/H4
Immokalee, Fl, US 175/H5
Imnavait (mtn.), Ak, US 176/J2
Imo (state), Nga. 145/G5
Imola, It. 101/E4
Imouzzèr-Kandar, Mor. 142/B3
Imperatriz, Braz. 196/A2
Imperia, It. 100/B5
Imperial, Sk, Can. 169/G3
Imperial, Peru 198/B4
Imperial, Ne, US 171/G2
Imperial, Mo, US 179/G9
Imperial Beach, Ca, US 178/C5
Imperial Palace, Japan 119/D2
Impero (riv.), It. 100/B5
Impfondo, Congo 139/J7
Imphāl, India 125/F3
Imphy, Fr. 84/E3
Impruneta, It. 101/E5
İmrali (isl.), Turk. 91/J5
İmranlı, Turk. 132/D2
İmroz, Gre. 89/J2
Imshil, SKor. 115/D5
Imst, Aus. 99/G3
Imuris, Mex. 184/C2
Ina, Japan 117/E3
Ina, Japan 119/E2
Ina, Japan 119/D2
Ina (riv.), Pol. 80/F5
Inabe, Japan 119/L5
Inabu, Japan 119/M5
Inagawa, Japan 119/H6
Inagi, Japan 119/D2
Inajá, Braz. 196/C3
Inambari (riv.), Peru 198/D4
Inami, Japan 119/G6
Inaouene (riv.), Mor. 142/B2
Iñapari, Peru 198/D3
Inarjärvi (lake), Fin. 79/H1
Inău (peak), Rom. 91/G2
Inawashīro (lake), Japan 117/F2
Inazawa, Japan 119/L5
Inca, Sp. 87/G3
Incekum (pt.), Turk. 133/C1
Incheville, Fr. 94/A3
Inchinnan, Sc, UK 78/B5
Inchkeith (isl.), Sc, UK 78/C4
Inchnadamph, Sc, UK 73/R7
Inch'ŏn, SKor. 115/F7
Inch'on-Gwangyŏksi (prov.), SKor. 115/D4
İncirliova, Turk. 132/A2
Incisa in Val d'Arno, It. 101/E5
Inconfidentes, Braz. 197/G7
Incudine, Mont l' (peak), Fr. 88/A2
Indaiá (riv.), Braz. 197/C1
Indaiatuba, Braz. 197/C2
Indalsälven (riv.), Swe. 79/E3
Indanan, Phil. 123/F2
Inde (riv.), Ger. 95/F2
Inden, Ger. 95/F2
Independence (mts.), Nv, US 168/E5
Independence, Ks, US 171/J3
Independence, Ca, US 170/C3
Independence, Mo, US 179/E5
Independence, Belz. 186/D2
Independence Nat'l Hist. Park, Pa, US 180/C4
Independência, Braz. 196/B2
Independencia, Peru 198/B4
Index, Wa, US 177/D2
India (ctry.) 109/G7
Indian (ocean) 65/N6
Indian Echo Caverns, Pa, US 180/B3
Indian Head, Sk, Can. 169/H3
Indian Hills, Co, US 179/B3
Indian Peaks Wilderness Area, Co, US 179/A2
Indiana (state), US 172/C3
Indiana, Pa, US 172/E3
Indianapolis (int'l arpt.), In, US 172/C4
Indianapolis (cap.), In, US 172/C4
Indianola, Ms, US 171/K4
Indianola, Wa, US 177/B2
Indiantown, Fl, US 175/H5
Indiaporã, Braz. 197/B1
Indigirka (riv.), Rus. 109/P3
Indija, Serb. 90/E3
Indio, Ca, US 170/C4
Indira Gandhi (int'l arpt.), India 128/D5
Indochina (reg.), Laos 125/H4
Indonesia (ctry.) 123/E4
Indore, India 131/L4
Indragiri (riv.), Indo. 122/B4
Indramayu (cape), Indo. 122/C5
Indrāvati (riv.), India 124/D4
Indre (riv.), Fr. 84/D3
Indre Arna, Nor. 80/A1
Indrois (riv.), Fr. 84/D3
Induno Olona, It. 99/E6
Indus (riv.), Asia 131/J4
Industry, Ca, US 178/G7
İnebolu, Turk. 132/C1
İnece, Turk. 91/H5
İnecik, Turk. 91/H5
Inedbirenne (int'l arpt.), Alg. 141/H4
İnegöl, Turk. 132/B1
Iner (riv.), Ger. 96/C3
Ineu, Rom. 90/E2
Inezgane, Mor. 140/C3
Inezgane (Agadir) (int'l arpt.), Mor. 140/C3
Infanta (cape), SAfr. 148/C4
Infiernillo (res.), Mex. 182/A4
Infiernillo, Presa del (dam), Mex. 184/E5
Infiesto, Sp. 86/C1
Ingapirca (ruin), Ecu. 194/B5
Ingatestone, Eng, UK 72/E2
Ingelmunster, Belg. 94/C2
Ingeniero Jacobacci, Arg. 200/C4
Ingeniero Luiggi, Arg. 200/D2
Ingenio, Canl., Sp. 140/B4
Ingersheim, Fr. 98/D1
Ingettolgoy, Mong. 112/H2
Ingham, Austl. 156/B2
Ingleside, Md, US 180/C5
Inglewood, Austl. 157/B3
Inglewood, Austl. 156/C5
Inglewood, Ca, US 178/F8
Inglewood-Finn Hill, Wa, US 177/C2
Inglis, Fl, US 175/H4
Ingoda (riv.), Rus. 107/M4
Ingolstadt, Ger. 97/E5
Ingrid Christianson (coast), Ant. 202/F
Ingushetia, Resp., Rus. 105/H4
Ingwavuma, SAfr. 149/E2
Ingwiller, Fr. 95/G6
Inhambane, Moz. 147/G5
Inhambupe, Braz. 196/C3
Inharrime, Moz. 147/G5
Inhuma, Braz. 196/B2
Inhumas, Braz. 193/J7
Iniesta, Sp. 86/E3
Inifel (well), Alg. 141/F3
Inini (riv.), FrG. 195/H4
Inírida (riv.), Col. 192/E3
Inishbofin (isl.), Ire. 72/N10
Inishowen (pen.), Ire. 76/A1
Inishowen (pt.), Ire. 76/B1
Inje, SKor. 115/E3
Injune, Austl. 156/C4
Inkster, Mi, US 177/F7
Inland (sea), Japan 116/C4
Inle (lake), Myan. 125/G3
Inn (riv.), Aus. 85/J3
Inn (riv.), Ger. 85/K2
Inn (riv.), Swi. 85/J3
Innbach (riv.), Aus. 97/H6
Innellan, Sc, UK 78/B5
Inner (chan.), Belz. 186/D2
Inner (sound), Sc, UK 73/R8
Inner Hebrides (isls.), Sc, UK 73/Q8
Inner Mongolia (reg.), China 109/L5
Innerdouny (hill), Sc, UK 78/C4
Innerleithen, Sc, UK 78/C5
Innerste (riv.), Ger. 93/G4
Innertkirchen, Swi. 99/E4
Innes NP, Austl. 155/H5
Innichen (San Candito), It. 85/K3
Innisfail, Ab, Can. 168/E2
Innisfail, Austl. 156/B2
Innoko (riv.), Ak, US 176/G3
Innsbruck, Aus. 99/H3
Innviertel (reg.), Aus. 97/G6
Inny (riv.), Eng, UK 74/B5
Ino, Japan 116/C4
Inocência, Braz. 197/B1
Inongo, D.R. Congo 139/J8
İnönü, Turk. 132/B2
Inowrocław, Pol. 83/K2
Insch, Sc, UK 78/D2
Inscription (cape), Austl. 154/B3
Insein, Myan. 125/G4
Inside (passg.), BC, Can. 168/A2
Insjön, Swe. 80/F1
Inta, Rus. 103/N2
Intendente Alvear, Arg. 200/E2
İntepe, Turk. 89/K2
Intercourse, Pa, US 180/B3
Interior (plat.), BC, Can. 168/B2
Interlaken, Swi. 98/D4
Internacional (int'l arpt.), Braz. 198/D2
Internacional (int'l arpt.), Mex. 185/E5
International Peace Garden, ND, US 169/H3
Inthanon (peak), Thai. 125/G4
Întorsura Buzăului, Rom. 91/H3
Intracoastal Waterway, La, US 179/P17
Intragna, Swi. 99/E5
Introbio, It. 99/F6
Inubō-zaki (pt.), Japan 117/G3
Inukjuak, Qu, Can. 165/J3
Inutil (bay), Chile 201/C7
Inuvik, NW, Can. 176/M2
Inuyama, Japan 119/L5
Inver (bay), Sc, UK 78/C1
Inveraray, Sc, UK 78/A4
Inverbervie, Sc, UK 78/D3
Invercargill, NZ 159/R12
Inverclyde (pol. reg.), Sc, UK 78/B5
Inverell, Austl. 157/D1
Invergordon, Sc, UK 78/B1
Inverie, Sc, UK 73/R8
Inverigo, It. 100/C1
Inverkeithing, Sc, UK 78/C4
Inverloch, Austl. 157/C3
Invermay, Sk, Can. 169/H3
Inverness, Sc, UK 78/B2
Inverness, Al, US 175/G3
Inverness, Fl, US 175/H4
Inveruno, It. 100/B1
Inverurie, Sc, UK 78/D2
Investigator (str.), Austl. 151/C4
Invorio, It. 100/B1
Inwood, NY, US 181/L9
Inyanga, Zim. 147/F4
Inyangani (peak), Zim. 147/F4
Inymney (peak), Rus. 176/D2
Inyo (mts.), Ca, US 170/C3
Inza, Rus. 105/H1
Inzai, Japan 119/E2
Inzigkofen, Ger. 99/F1
Inzing, Aus. 99/H3
Iō-shima (isl.), Japan 116/B5
Ioánnina (int'l arpt.), Gre. 89/G3
Ioánnina, Gre. 89/G3
Iolotan', Trkm. 131/H1
Iona (isl.), Sc, UK 73/Q8
Iona, PN da, Ang. 147/B4
Ione, Ca, US 179/C2
Ionia, Mi, US 172/C3
Ionian (sea), Gre. 89/F3
Ionian (isls.), Gre. 89/F3
Íos (isl.), Gre. 89/J4
Iouîk (cape), Mrta. 144/A2
Iowa (state), US 171/J2
Iowa (riv.), Ia, US 169/K5
Iowa Falls, Ia, US 169/K5
Ipameri, Braz. 197/B1
Ipanema, Braz. 197/D1
Iparia, Peru 198/C3
Ipatinga, Braz. 197/D1
Ipel' (riv.), Slvk. 83/K4
Iphofen, Ger. 96/D3
Ipiales, Col. 194/B4
Ipiaú, Braz. 196/C4
Ipil, Phil. 121/D6
Ipirá, Braz. 196/C4
Ipiranga, Braz. 197/B3
Ipoh, Malay. 122/B3
Ipoly (riv.), Hun. 83/K4
Iporá, Braz. 193/H7
İpsala, Turk. 89/K2
Ipsheim, Ger. 96/D3
Ipswich, SD, US 169/J4
Ipswich, Eng, UK 75/H2
Ipu, Braz. 196/B2
Ipuã, Braz. 197/B2
Ipubi, Braz. 196/B2
Ipueiras, Braz. 196/B2
Ipuiúna, Braz. 197/G7
Ipumba (hill), Tanz. 146/A4
Ipun, Isla (isl.), Chile 200/B5
Ipupiara, Braz. 196/B3
Iqaluit (cap.), Nun, Can. 165/K2
Iquique, Chile 192/D8
Iquitos, Peru 198/C1
Irago (chan.), Japan 119/L6
Irago-misaki (cape), Japan 119/M6
Iráklia, Gre. 89/H2
Iráklia (isl.), Gre. 89/J4
Iráklion, Gre. 89/J5
Iráklion (int'l arpt.), Gre. 88/D2
Iramaia, Braz. 196/B4
Iran (mts.), Indo.,Malay. 122/D3
Iran (ctry.) 109/E6
Irapa, Ven. 195/F2
Irapuato, Mex. 185/E4
Iraq (ctry.) 130/D2
Irará, Braz. 196/C4
Irati, Braz. 197/B3
Irauçuba, Braz. 196/C1
Irbid (gov.), Jor. 133/D3
Irbid, Jor. 133/D3
Irbīl, Iraq 132/F2
Irecê, Braz. 196/B3
Ireland (ctry.) 73/P10
Ireland's Eye (isl.), Ire. 76/B5
Iremel' (peak), Rus. 103/N5
Iretama, Braz. 197/A3
Irfon (riv.), Wal, UK 74/C2
Irharhar, Oued (riv.), Alg. 141/G4
Irhazer Oua-n-Agadez (riv.), Niger 145/G2
Iri, SKor. 115/D5
Irian Jaya (reg.), Indo. 123/H4
Iricoume (mts.), Braz. 195/G4
Irig, Serb. 90/D3
Irigui (phys. reg.), Mali 144/D2
Iriklinskiy (res.), Rus. 105/L2
Iringa (prov.), Tanz. 146/B5
Iringa, Tanz. 146/B4
Iriomote (isl.), Japan 121/D3
Iriri (riv.), Braz. 193/H4
Irish (sea), Ire.,UK 76/C4
Irlam, Eng, UK 77/F5
Irō-zaki (pt.), Japan 117/F3
Iroise (bay), Fr. 84/A2
Iron Baron, Austl. 155/H5
Iron Knob, Austl. 155/H5
Iron Mountain, Mi, US 169/L4
Irondale, Co, US 179/C3
Ironton, Oh, US 172/D4
Ironton, Ut, US 179/K13
Ironwood, Mi, US 169/L4
Ironwood Forest Nat'l Mon., Az, US 170/E4
Irput' (riv.), Rus. 104/E1
Irrawaddy (Ayeyarwady) (riv.), Myan. 125/G4
Irrawaddy, Mouths of the (delta), Myan. 125/F4
Irsch, Ger. 95/F4
Irsen (riv.), Ger. 95/F3
Irsina, It. 88/E2
Irt (riv.), Eng, UK 77/E3
Irthing (riv.), Eng, UK 77/F1
Irthlingborough, Eng, UK 75/F2
Irtysh (riv.), Rus. 109/G4
Iruma, Japan 119/C2
Irumu, D.R. Congo 146/A2
Irún, Sp. 86/E1
Irvine, Ca, US 178/G8
Irvine, Sc, UK 78/B5
Irvine (bay), Sc, UK 78/B5
Irvine (riv.), Sc, UK 78/B5
Irving, Tx, US 174/D3
Irvington, NJ, US 181/J9
Irvington, NY, US 181/K7
Is (peak), Sudan 143/C4
Is-sur-Tille, Fr. 98/B2
Īsa Khel, Pak. 128/A3
Isaac (riv.), Austl. 151/D3
Isabela (isl.), Ecu. 198/E7
Isabela, Phil. 123/F2
Isabela, PR 183/M8
Isabelia (mts.), Nic. 186/E3
Isabella (bay), Nun., Can. 165/K2
Isaccea, Rom. 91/J3
Isachsen (cape), Nun., Can. 165/R7
Ísafjardhardjúp (inlet), Ice. 79/M6
Ísafjördhur, Ice. 79/M6
Isahaya, Japan 116/B4
Isalo, PN de l', Madg. 149/H8
Isalo Ruiniform (mass.), Madg. 149/H8
Isana (riv.), Col. 194/D4
Isandhlwana Battlesite, SAfr. 149/E3
Isangano NP, Zam. 146/A5
Isaouanne-n-Irarraren (des.), Alg. 141/G4
Isaouanne-n-Tifernine (des.), Alg. 141/G4
Isarco (riv.), It. 85/J3
Isarco (Eisack) (riv.), It. 99/H4
Isaszeg, Hun. 91/R9
Isawa, Japan 117/G3
Isbergues, Fr. 94/B2
Iscar, Sp. 86/C2
Ischgl, Aus. 99/G3
Ischia, It. 90/A5
Ise (bay), Japan 117/E3
Ise (riv.), Eng, UK 75/F2
Ise, Japan 119/L7
Ise-Shima NP, Japan 117/E3
Isehara, Japan 117/F3
Iselin, NJ, US 181/H9
Isen, Ger. 97/F6
Isen (riv.), Ger. 82/G4
Isenthal, Swi. 99/E4
Iseo (lake), It. 85/J4
Iseo, It. 100/D1
Iseo, Lago d' (lake), It. 100/C1
Isère (riv.), Fr. 84/F4
Isère (dept.), Fr. 98/B6
Iserlohn, Ger. 93/E6
Isernia, It. 88/D2
Isesaki, Japan 117/F2
Iset' (riv.), Rus. 129/D1
Iseyin, Nga. 145/F5
'Isfiyā, Isr. 133/G6
Ishi (riv.), Japan 119/J7
Ishibashi, Japan 117/F2
Ishibe, Japan 119/K5
Ishidoriya, Japan 118/B4
Ishigaki (isl.), Japan 121/D3
Ishige, Japan 117/F2
Ishikari, Japan 118/B2
Ishikari (bay), Japan 118/B2
Ishikari (mts.), Japan 118/C2
Ishikari (riv.), Japan 118/B2
Ishikawa (pref.), Japan 117/E2
Ishikawa, Japan 117/G2
Ishiki, Japan 119/M6
Ishim (riv.), Rus. 106/H4
Ishim, Rus. 103/R4
Ishimbay, Rus. 105/L1
Ishinomaki, Japan 118/B4
Ishioka, Japan 117/G2
Ishizuchi-san (peak), Japan 116/C4
Isiboro Sécure, PN, Bol. 192/E7
Isigny-sur-Mer, Fr. 84/C2
Isil'kul', Rus. 129/F2
Isiolo, Kenya 146/C2
Isiro, D.R. Congo 139/L7
Isisford, Austl. 156/B4
İskenderun, Turk. 133/E1
İskenderun, Gulf of (gulf), Turk. 133/D1
İskilip, Turk. 132/C1
Iskŭr (riv.), Aus. 91/G4
Iskŭr (res.), Bul. 91/F4
Iskŭr (riv.), Bul. 89/H1
Isla, Mex. 186/C2
Isla (riv.), Sc, UK 78/C3
Isla Aguada, Mex. 186/D2
Isla Cabritos, PN, DRep. 187/J2
Isla Cedros, Mex. 184/B2
Isla Cristina, Sp. 86/B4
Isla de Maipo, Chile 200/N8
Isla de Salamanca, PN, Col. 194/C2
Isla de San Andrés (int'l arpt.), Col. 187/F3
Isla Gorge NP, Austl. 156/C4
Isla Guamblin, PN, Chile 200/B5
Isla Isabela, PN, Mex. 184/D4
Isla Magdalena, PN, Chile 199/B5
Isla Mujeres, Mex. 186/E1
İslâhiye, Turk. 133/E1
Islām Kot, Pak. 131/K4
Islāmābād (cap. terr.), Pak. 128/B3
Islāmābād (cap.), Pak. 128/B3
Islāmābād/Rāwalpindi (int'l arpt.), Pak. 128/B3
Islāmnagar, India 126/B1
Islamorada, Fl, US 175/H5
Islāmpur, India 127/G2
Islāmpur, India 127/E3
Island (lake), Mb, Can. 164/G3
Island (co.), Wa, US 177/B2
Island Beach State Park, NJ, US 180/D4
Island Lagoon (lake), Austl. 155/H4
Island Lake, Mb, Can. 169/K2
Island Lake, Il, US 177/P15
Island Park, NY, US 181/L9
Islands (bay), Nf, Can. 173/K1
Islay, Peru 198/C5
Islay (isl.), Sc, UK 73/Q9
Isle (riv.), Fr. 84/D4
Isle of Anglesey (co.), Wal, UK 76/D5
Isle of Ely (phys. reg.), Eng, UK 75/G2
Isle of Portland (pen.), Eng, UK 74/D5
Isle of Thanet (phys. reg.), Eng, UK 75/H4
Isle of Wight (co.), Eng, UK 75/E5
Isle Royale NP, Mi, US 172/B2
Isleton, Ca, US 177/L10
Islington (bor.), Eng, UK 72/A1
Islip, NY, US 181/E2
Ismailovo Park, Rus. 103/W9
Ismaning, Ger. 97/E6
Isny, Ger. 99/G2
Isoanala, Madg. 149/H8
Isobe, Japan 119/L7
Isojärven NP, Fin. 81/L1
Isojärvi (lake), Fin. 81/J1
Isoka, Zam. 146/B5
Isola del Liri, It. 88/C2
Isola della Scala, It. 101/D2
Isola di Capo Rizzuto, It. 88/E3
Isola Vicentina, It. 101/E1
Isonzo (riv.), It. 101/G1
Isorella, It. 100/D2
Isparta, Turk. 132/B2
Isparta (prov.), Turk. 132/B2
Isperikh, Bul. 91/H4
İspir, Turk. 105/G4
Israel (ctry.) 133/C3
Issaquah, Wa, US 177/C2
Issel (riv.), Ger. 92/D5
Isselburg, Ger. 92/D5
Issenheim, Fr. 98/D2
Issia, C.d'Iv. 144/D5
Issoire, Fr. 84/E4
Issou, Fr. 72/H5
Issoudun, Fr. 84/E3
Issum, Ger. 92/D5
Issy-les-Moulineaux, Fr. 72/J5
Istállós-kó (peak), Hun. 90/E1
İstanbul (prov.), Turk. 91/J5
İstanbul, Turk. 91/J5
Istead Rise, Eng, UK 72/E2
Istiaía, Gre. 89/H3
Istmina, Col. 194/B3
Istok, Serb. 90/E4
Istra (riv.), Rus. 103/W9
Istrana, It. 101/F1
Istranca (mts.), Turk. 91/H5
Istres, Fr. 84/F5
Istria (pen.), Cro. 90/A3
Isulan, Phil. 123/F2
Isumi, Japan 119/E3
Itabaiana, Braz. 196/C3
Itabaiana, Braz. 196/D2
Itabaianinha, Braz. 196/C3
Itabapoana (riv.), Braz. 197/D2
Itaberaba, Braz. 196/B4
Itabira, Braz. 197/D1
Itabirito, Braz. 197/D2
Itaboraí, Braz. 197/L7
Itabuna, Braz. 196/C4
Itacaiunas (riv.), Braz. 193/H5
Itacarambi, Braz. 196/A4
Itacoatiara, Braz. 192/G4
Itacuaí (riv.), Braz. 192/D5
Itacuruba, Braz. 196/C3
Itaguaí, Braz. 197/K7
Itaguara, Braz. 197/C2
Itaguatins, Braz. 196/A2
Itagüí, Col. 192/C2
Itaí, Braz. 197/B2
Itaíba, Braz. 196/C3
Itaiçaba, Braz. 196/C2
Itainópolis, Braz. 196/B2
Itaiópolis, Braz. 197/B3
Itaipu (dam), Par. 199/F2
Itaipu (res.), Braz.,Par. 199/F1
Itaituba, Braz. 193/G4
Itajá, Braz. 197/B1
Itajaí, Braz. 197/B3
Itajaí (riv.), Braz. 197/B3
Itajubá, Braz. 197/H7
Itajuípe, Braz. 196/C4
Itako, Japan 117/G3
Itakura, Japan 119/D1
Italy (ctry.) 69/F4
Italy, Tx, US 171/H4
Itamaraju, Braz. 196/C5
Itamarandiba, Braz. 196/B5
Itambacuri, Braz. 196/B5
Itambé, Braz. 196/B4
Itambé, Pico de (peak), Braz. 196/B5
Itami, Japan 119/H6
Itamonte, Braz. 197/J7
Itampolo, Madg. 149/G9
Itanhaém, Braz. 197/G9
Itanhandu, Braz. 197/C2
Itanhém, Braz. 196/B5
Itanhém (riv.), Braz. 197/D1
Itanhomi, Braz. 197/D1
Itaobim, Braz. 196/B5
Itaocara, Braz. 197/D2
Itapagé, Braz. 196/C1
Itaparica (isl.), Braz. 196/C4
Itapé, Braz. 196/C4
Itapebi, Braz. 196/C4
Itapecerica, Braz. 197/C2
Itapecuru-Mirim, Braz. 196/A1
Itapemirim, Braz. 197/D2
Itaperuna, Braz. 197/D2
Itapetim, Braz. 196/C2
Itapetinga, Braz. 196/B4
Itapetininga, Braz. 197/B2
Itapeva, Braz. 197/B2
Itapevi, Braz. 197/G8
Itapicuru (riv.), Braz. 196/C3
Itapicuru (riv.), Braz. 193/K5
Itapipoca, Braz. 196/C1
Itapira, Braz. 197/G7
Itapitanga, Braz. 196/C4
Itaporanga, Braz. 197/B2
Itaquaquecetuba, Braz. 197/G8
Itarantim, Braz. 196/B4
Itararé, Braz. 197/B3
Itariri, Braz. 197/F9
Itārsi, India 126/A4
Itatiaia, PN de, Braz. 197/J7
Itatiba, Braz. 197/G7
Itaueira (riv.), Braz. 193/K5
Itaueira, Braz. 196/B2
Itaúna, Braz. 197/C2
Itayanagi, Japan 118/B3
Itbayat, Phil. 121/D3
Itbayat (isl.), Phil. 121/D3
Itchen (riv.), Eng, UK 75/E4
Itéa, Gre. 89/H3
Iténez (riv.), Bol. 189/C4
Itezhi-Tezhi (dam), Zam. 147/E4
Ith (hills), Ger. 93/G4
Ithaca, NY, US 172/E3
Ithaca, (Itháki) (isl.), Gre. 89/G3
Itháki, Gre. 89/G3
Ithon (riv.), Wal, UK 74/C2
Itimbiri (riv.), D.R. Congo 139/K7
Itinga, Braz. 196/B5
Itiruçu, Braz. 196/B4
Itō, Japan 117/F3
Itogon, Phil. 121/D4
Itoigawa, Japan 117/E2
Itoman, Japan 117/J7
Iton (riv.), Fr. 84/D2
Itonuki, Japan 119/L5
Itororó, Braz. 196/B4
Itsukaichi, Japan 119/C2
Itter (riv.), Ger. 93/F6
Itterbeck, Ger. 92/D3
Ittiri, It. 88/A2
Itu, Braz. 197/C2
Ituango, Col. 194/C3
Ituberá, Braz. 196/C4
Ituí (riv.), Braz. 192/D5
Ituiutaba, Braz. 197/B1
Itumbiara, Braz. 197/B1
Itumbiara, Barragem (res.), Braz. 197/B1
Itumirim, Braz. 197/J6
Ituna, Sk, Can. 169/H3
Itupiranga, Braz. 193/J5
Ituporanga, Braz. 197/B3
Iturama, Braz. 197/B1
Ituri (riv.), D.R. Congo 146/A2
Itutinga, Represa de (res.), Braz. 197/C2
Ituverava, Braz. 197/C2
Ituxi (riv.), Braz. 192/E5
Ituzaingó, Uru. 201/K11
Ityāy al Bārūd, Egypt 133/B4
Itz (riv.), Ger. 82/F3
Iul'tin (peak), Rus. 176/C2
Iúna, Braz. 197/D2
Ivaí (riv.), Braz. 197/B3
Ivaiporã, Braz. 197/B3
Ivalojoki (riv.), Fin. 79/H1
Ivančice, Czh. 85/M2
Ivanec, Cro. 85/M3
Ivanhoe, Austl. 157/C2
Ivanhoe (riv.), On, Can. 172/D1
Ivanjica, Serb. 90/E4
Ivanjska, Bosn. 90/C3
Ivankovo, Cro. 90/D3
Ivano-Frankivs'k, Ukr. 104/C2
Ivano-Frankivs'ka Oblasti, Ukr. 104/C2
Ivanof Bay, Ak, US 176/G4
Ivanovo, Rus. 102/J4
Ivanovovskaya Oblast, Rus. 102/J4
Ivato, Madg. 149/H8
Ivato (int'l arpt.), Madg. 149/H7
Ivaylovgrad (res.), Bul. 89/J2
Ivaylovgrad, Bul. 89/J2
Ivdel, Rus. 106/G3
Iveragh (pen.), Ire. 72/P11
Iverny, Fr. 72/L5
Ivindo (riv.), Gabon 138/H7
Ivohibe, Madg. 149/H8
Ivondro (riv.), Madg. 149/J7
Ivory (coast), C.d'Iv. 138/D7
Ivösjön (lake), Swe. 80/F3
Ivrea, It. 100/A2
İvrindi, Turk. 132/A2
Ivry-sur-Seine, Fr. 72/K5
Ivujivik, Qu, Can. 165/J2
Ivvavik NP, Yk, Can. 164/B2
Iwafune, Japan 119/D1
Iwai, Japan 117/F2
Iwaizumi, Japan 118/B4
Iwaki, Japan 117/G2
Iwaki-san (peak), Japan 118/B3
Iwakuni, Japan 116/C3
Iwakura, Japan 119/L5
Iwama, Japan 119/E1
Iwami, Japan 116/D3
Iwamizawa, Japan 118/B2
Iwamura, Japan 119/M5
Iwanai, Japan 118/B2
Iwanuma, Japan 117/G1
Iwasaki, Japan 118/A3
Iwata, Japan 117/E3
Iwataki, Japan 119/H4
Iwate (pref.), Japan 118/B4
Iwate, Japan 118/B4
Iwate-san (peak), Japan 118/B4
Iwatsuki, Japan 119/D2
Iwere Ile, Nga. 145/F5
Iwo, Nga. 145/G5
Iwo Jima (isl.), Japan 158/D2
Iwŏn, NKor. 115/E2
Iwuy, Fr. 94/C3
Ixcán (riv.), Guat. 186/D3
Ixelles, Belg. 95/D2
Ixmiquilpan, Mex. 185/K6
Ixopo, SAfr. 149/E3
Ixtapa, Mex. 185/L7
Ixtapan de la Sal, Mex. 185/K8
Ixtlán del Río, Mex. 184/D4
Iyo (sea), Japan 116/B4
Iyo, Japan 116/C4
Izabal (lake), Guat. 182/D4
Īzad Khvāst, Iran 130/F2
Izamal, Mex. 186/D1
Izberbash, Rus. 105/H4
Izegem, Belg. 94/C2
Izhevsk, Rus. 103/M4
Izhma (riv.), Rus. 103/M2
Izhora (riv.), Rus. 103/T7
Izi (well), Alg. 141/F3
Izigan (cape), Ak, US 176/E5
Izkī, Oman 131/G4
İzmayil, Ukr. 91/J3
İzmir, Turk. 132/A2
İzmir (prov.), Turk. 132/A2
İzmit (gulf), Turk. 91/J5
İzmit, Turk. 91/J5
Iznájar, Sp. 86/C4
İznik, Turk. 91/J5
İznik (lake), Turk. 91/J5
Izola, Slov. 101/G1
Izra', Syria 133/E3
Izsák, Hun. 90/D2
Iztaccíhuatl-Popocatépetl, PN, Mex. 185/L7
Izu (pen.), Japan 117/F3
Izu (isls.), Japan 117/F4
Izúcar de Matamoros, Mex. 185/L8
Izuhara, Japan 116/A3
Izumi, Japan 116/B4
Izumi, Japan 118/B4
Izumi, Japan 119/H7
Izumi-Ōtsu, Japan 119/H7
Izumi-Sano, Japan 119/H7
Izumo, Japan 116/C3
Izunagaoka, Japan 119/B3
Izushi, Japan 119/G5
Izyum, Ukr. 104/F2

J

J. Paul Getty Museum, Ca, US 178/E7
Jääsjärvi (lake), Fin. 81/M1
Jaba', WBnk. 133/G7
Jabal 'Abd al 'Azīz (mts.), Syria 132/D2
Jabal Abu Rujmayn (mts.), Syria 132/D3
Jabal Abyad (plat.), Sudan 143/B5
Jabal al 'Arab (mts.), Syria 133/E3
Jabal an Nusayriyah (mts.), Syria 133/E2
Jabal ar Ruwaq (mts.), Syria 132/D3
Jabal as Sawdā' (hills), Libya 138/H2
Jabal ash Shaykh (peak), Leb. 133/D3
Jabal Lubnān (gov.), Leb. 133/D2
Jabal Ramm (peak), Jor. 133/D5
Jabal 'Unāzah (peak), SAr. 132/D3
Jabalí (pt.), Pan. 187/F5
Jabalón (riv.), Sp. 86/D3
Jabalpur, India 126/B4
Jabālyah, Gaza 133/D4
Jabbeke, Belg. 94/C1
Jablah, Syria 133/D2
Jablanica (mts.), Alb. 89/G2
Jablonec nad Nisou, Czh. 83/H3
Jaboatão dos Guararapes, Braz. 196/D3
Jaboticabal, Braz. 197/B2
Jabuka, Serb. 90/E3
Jabung (cape), Indo. 122/B4
Jaca, Sp. 87/E1
Jacaré (riv.), Braz. 196/B3
Jacareí, Braz. 197/H8
Jaceel (riv.), Som. 139/Q5
Jáchymov, Czh. 97/F2
Jacinto, Braz. 196/B5
Jacinto Arauz, Arg. 200/E3
Jackman, Me, US 173/G2
Jackpot, Nv, US 168/E5
Jacks Mountain (ridge), Pa, US 180/A2
Jacksboro, Tx, US 171/H4
Jackson, Al, US 175/G4
Jackson, Ca, US 170/B3
Jackson, La, US 171/K5
Jackson, Mi, US 172/C3
Jackson, Mo, US 171/K3
Jackson (co.), Mo, US 179/E5
Jackson (cap.), Ms, US 171/K4
Jackson (mts.), Nv, US 168/D5
Jackson, Tn, US 172/B5
Jackson, Wy, US 168/F5
Jackson (lake), Wy, US 170/E2
Jacksonville, Al, US 175/G3
Jacksonville, Ar, US 171/J4
Jacksonville, Fl, US 175/H4
Jacksonville (int'l arpt.), Fl, US 175/H4
Jacksonville, Il, US 171/K3
Jacksonville, NC, US 175/J3
Jacksonville Beach, Fl, US 175/H4
Jacktown, Ok, US 179/N14
Jacmel, Haiti 187/H2
Jacobābād, Pak. 131/J3
Jacobina, Braz. 196/B3
Jacobsdal, SAfr. 148/D3
Jacobstown, NJ, US 180/D3
Jacobus, Pa, US 180/B4
Jacomo (lake), Mo, US 179/E6
Jacona de Plancarte, Mex. 184/E5
Jacques-Cartier (riv.), Qu, Can. 173/G2
Jacques Cartier (peak), Qu, Can. 173/H1
Jacuí (riv.), Braz. 199/F2
Jacuípe (riv.), Braz. 193/L6
Jacupiranga, Braz. 197/B3
Jacura, Ven. 194/D2
Jadacaquiva, Ven. 194/D2
Jaddi (pt.), Pak. 131/H3
Jade, Ger. 93/F2
Jade (riv.), Ger. 93/F1
Jade (bay), Ger. 82/E2
Jadebusen (bay), Ger. 93/F2
Jaén, Peru 198/B2
Jaén, Sp. 86/D4
Jaffa (cape), Austl. 157/A3
Jaffna, SrL. 124/C6
Jagādhri, India 128/D4
Jagdīspur, India 127/E3
Jagersfontein, SAfr. 148/D3
Jægerspris, Den. 80/D4
Jagna, Phil. 121/D6

Jagra – Kaesŏ

Kafar – Kayen 245

Kafar Jar Ghar (mts.), Afg. 131/J2
Kaffraria (reg.), SAfr. 148/D4
Kaffrine, Sen. 144/B3
Kafirévs (cape), Gre. 89/J3
Kafr Ash Shaykh (gov.), Egypt 143/B1
Kafr ash Shaykh, Egypt 133/B4
Kafr az Zayyāt, Egypt 133/B4
Kafr Kannā, Isr. 133/G6
Kafr Mandā, Isr. 133/G6
Kafr Qari', Isr. 133/G6
Kafr Qāsim, Isr. 133/F7
Kafu (riv.), Ugan. 146/A2
Kafue (riv.), Zam. 147/E4
Kafue, Zam. 147/E4
Kafue NP, Zam. 147/E3
Kaga, Japan 116/E2
Kaga Bandoro, CAfr. 139/J6
Kagan, Uzb. 129/D5
Kāgān (valley), Pak. 128/B2
Kagawa (pref.), Japan 116/D3
Kagera (riv.), Tanz. 146/A3
Kağızman, Turk. 132/E1
Kagoshima (int'l arpt.), Japan 116/B5
Kagoshima, Japan 116/B5
Kagoshima (bay), Japan 116/B5
Kagoshima (dept.), Japan 117/L5
Kahaluu, Hi, US 166/W13
Kahama, Tanz. 146/B3
Kahayan (riv.), Indo. 122/D4
Kahiu (pt.), Hi, US 166/T10
Kahl am Main, Ger. 96/C2
Kāhna, Pak. 128/C4
Kahoka, Mo, US 169/L5
Kahoolawe (isl.), Hi, US 166/T10
Kahperusvaara (peak), Fin. 79/G1
Kahraman Maraş (prov.), Turk. 132/D2
Kahramanmaraş, Turk. 132/D2
Kahror Pakka, Pak. 128/A5
Kāhta, Turk. 132/D2
Kahuku, Hi, US 166/W12
Kahuku (pt.), Hi, US 166/W12
Kahului, Hi, US 166/T10
Kahuzi-Biega, PN de, D.R. Congo 147/E1
Kai (isls.), Indo. 123/H5
Kai Besar (isl.), Indo. 123/H5
Kai Kecil (isl.), Indo. 123/H5
Kaiapoi, NZ 159/S11
Kaibab (plat.), Az, US 170/D3
Kaibara, Japan 119/H5
Kaieteur (falls), Guy. 195/G3
Kaieteur NP, Guy. 195/G3
Kaifeng, China 113/K5
Kaifeng, China 114/C4
Kaihua, China 121/C2
Kaikohe, NZ 159/S10
Kaikoura, NZ 159/S11
Kaili, China 125/J2
Kailu, China 114/E2
Kailua, Hi, US 166/U11
Kailua, Hi, US 166/W13
Kaimganj, India 126/B2
Kaimur (range), India 126/C3
Kainab (riv.), Namb. 148/B2
Kainach (riv.), Aus. 90/B2
Kainan, Japan 116/D3
Kainji (dam), Nga. 145/G4
Kainji (lake), Nga. 145/G4
Kainji Lake NP, Nga. 145/F4
Kainoúryion, Gre. 89/G3
Kaipara (har.), NZ 159/S10
Kairāna, India 128/D5
Kairi, Austl. 156/B2
Kairouan, Tun. 142/L7
Kairouan (gov.), Tun. 142/L7
Kaisei, Japan 119/C3
Kaiseregg (peak), Swi. 98/D4
Kaisersesch, Ger. 95/G3
Kaiserslautern, Ger. 95/G5
Kaisheim, Ger. 96/D5
Kaitaia, NZ 159/S10
Kaithal, India 128/D5
Kaiwi (chan.), Hi, US 166/T10
Kaiyang, China 125/J2
Kaiyuan, China 125/H3
Kaiyuan, China 114/F2
Kaizu, Japan 119/L5
Kaizuka, Japan 119/H7
Kajaani, Fin. 79/H2
Kaji-san (peak), SKor. 115/E5
Kajiado, Kenya 146/C3
Kajikazawa, Japan 119/A2
Kakamas, SAfr. 148/C3
Kakamega, Kenya 146/B2
Kakamigahara, Japan 119/L5
Kakanj, Bosn. 90/D3
Kake, Ak, US 176/M4
Kaketsa (mtn.), BC, Can. 176/M4
Kakhovka, Ukr. 91/L2
Kakhovs'ke Vodoskhovyshche (res.), Ukr. 104/E3
Kākināda, India 124/D4
Kakiri, Ugan. 146/B2
Kako (riv.), Japan 119/G6
Kakogawa, Japan 119/G6
Kākori, India 126/C2
Kakrāla, India 126/B2
Kakrima (riv.), Gui. 144/B4
Kaktovik, Ak, US 176/K1
Kakuda, Japan 117/G2
Kakunodate, Japan 118/B4
Kalaa Kbira, Tun. 142/M7
Kalaat El Andalous, Tun. 142/M6
Kālābāgh, Pak. 128/A3
Kalabo, Zam. 147/D3
Kalach, Rus. 105/G2
Kalach-na-Donu, Rus. 105/G2
Kalachinsk, Rus. 129/F1
Kaladan (riv.), Myan. 125/F3
Kālāgarh, India 126/B1
Kalahari (des.), Namb. 148/C2
Kalahari-Gemsbok NP, SAfr. 147/C6
Kalaheo, Hi, US 166/S10
Kalaiya, Nepal 127/E2
Kalalé, Ben. 145/F4
Kalamákion, Gre. 89/N8
Kalamaloué, PN de, Camr. 138/H5
Kalamariá, Gre. 89/H2
Kalamáta, Gre. 89/H4
Kalamazoo, Mi, US 172/C3
Kalampáka, Gre. 89/G3
Kalandy, Madg. 149/J6
Kalaoa, Hi, US 166/U11
Kalasin, Thai. 120/C2
Kalāswāla, Pak. 128/C3
Kalāt, Pak. 131/J3
Kalaupapa, Hi, US 166/T10
Kalávrita, Gre. 89/H3
Kalbach, Ger. 96/B2
Kalbar, Austl. 156/D4
Kalbarri, Austl. 154/B3
Kalbarri NP, Austl. 154/B3
Kaldakvísl (riv.), Ice. 79/N7
Kale, Turk. 104/F4
Kale, Turk. 133/A1
Kalecik, Turk. 132/C1
Kalefeld, Ger. 93/H5
Kalemie (int'l arpt.), D.R. Congo 146/A4
Kalemie, D.R. Congo 146/A4
Kalemyo, Myan. 125/F3
Kalety, Pol. 83/K3
Kalewa, Myan. 125/F3
Kaleya, Zam. 147/E4
Kalgoorlie-Boulder, Austl. 154/D4
Kāli (riv.), India 126/B1
Kāli (riv.), India 126/B2
Kāli (riv.), Nepal 126/D2
Kalianda, Indo. 122/C5
Kalima, D.R. Congo 139/L8
Kalimantan (reg.), Indo. 122/D4
Kálimnos, Gre. 132/A2
Kálimnos (isl.), Gre. 132/A2
Kālimpong, India 127/G2
Kaliningrad, Rus. 103/W9
Kaliningrad, Rus. 81/J4
Kaliningradskaya Oblast, Rus. 102/D5
Kalininsk, Rus. 105/H2
Kalinkavichy, Bela. 104/D1
Kaliro, Ugan. 146/B2
Kalisizo, Ugan. 146/A3
Kalispell, Mt, US 168/E3
Kalisz, Pol. 83/K3
Kalix, Swe. 79/G2
Kalixälven (riv.), Swe. 79/G2
Kāliyāganj, India 127/G3
Kalkaska, Mi, US 172/C2
Kallham, Aus. 97/G6
Kallinge, Swe. 80/F3
Kallinge (int'l arpt.), Swe. 80/F3
Kallithéa, Gre. 89/N9
Kallsjön (lake), Swe. 79/E3
Kalmar, Swe. 80/G3
Kalmar (co.), Swe. 79/F4
Kalmar (int'l arpt.), Swe. 80/G3
Kalmarsund (sound), Swe. 80/G3
Kalmthout, Belg. 92/B6
Kalmykia, Resp., Rus. 106/E5
Kālna, India 127/G4
Kalni (riv.), Bang. 127/H3
Kalocsa, Hun. 90/D2
Kalofer, Bul. 89/J1
Kalohi (chan.), Hi, US 166/T10
Kalokhórion, Gre. 89/H2
Kālol, India 131/K4
Kalomo, Zam. 147/E4
Kalongo, Ugan. 146/B2
Kālpi, India 126/B2
Kalpin, China 112/C3
Kalsdorf bei Graz, Aus. 85/L3
Kaltag, Ak, US 176/G3
Kaltbrunn, Swi. 99/F3
Kaltenleutgeben, Aus. 91/N7
Kaltennordheim, Ger. 96/D1
Kaltern (Caldaro), It. 85/J3
Kalu (riv.), SrL. 124/D6
Kaluga, Rus. 102/H5
Kalundborg, Den. 80/D4
Kalungu, Ugan. 146/A3
Kalungwishi (riv.), Zam. 146/A5
Kalūr Kot, Pak. 128/A3
Kalush, Ukr. 104/C2
Kalutara, SrL. 124/C6
Kaluzhskaya Oblast, Rus. 102/G5
Kalyān, India 131/K5
Kama, D.R. Congo 147/E1
Kama (res.), Rus. 103/M4
Kama (riv.), Rus. 103/M4
Kamagaya, Japan 119/E2
Kamaishi, Japan 118/B4
Kamakou (peak), Hi, US 166/T10
Kamakura, Japan 119/D3
Kamālia, Pak. 128/B4
Kamalo, Hi, US 166/T10
Kāman, India 126/A2
Kaman, Turk. 132/C2
Kamango (lake), Mali 144/E2
Kamanjab, Namb. 147/B4
Kamarang, Guy. 195/F3
Kāmāreddi, India 124/C4
Kāmārhāti, India 124/E3
Kamaria (falls), Guy. 195/G3
Kambalda, Austl. 154/D4
Kambar, Pak. 124/A2
Kambara, Japan 119/B3
Kambia, SLeo. 144/B4
Kambove, D.R. Congo 147/E3
Kambuno (peak), Indo. 123/F4
Kamchatka (pen.), Rus. 109/Q4
Kamchatskaya Oblast, Rus. 107/R4
Kamchiya (riv.), Bul. 91/H4
Kamen, Ger. 93/E5
Kamen'-na-Obi, Rus. 129/H2
Kamenka, Rus. 105/H1
Kameno, Bul. 91/H4
Kamensk-Shakhtinskiy, Rus. 104/G2
Kamensk-Ural'skiy, Rus. 103/P4
Kameoka, Japan 119/J5
Kameyama, Japan 119/K6
Kami, Japan 119/G5
Kami (isl.), Japan 119/M6
Kami-koshiki (isl.), Japan 116/A5
Kamiah, Id, US 168/D4
Kamień Pomorski, Pol. 80/F5
Kamieskroon, SAfr. 148/B3
Kamifukuoka, Japan 119/D2
Kamiisco, Japan 118/B3
Kamiishizu, Japan 119/K5
Kamiizumi, Japan 119/C1
Kamikawa, Japan 118/C2
Kamikuishiki, Japan 119/B2
Kamilo (pt.), Hi, US 166/U11
Kamina, D.R. Congo 147/E2
Kaminaka, Japan 119/J5
Kaminoho, Japan 119/M4
Kaminoyama, Japan 117/G1
Kamisato, Japan 119/C1
Kamishak (bay), Ak, US 176/H4
Kamiyahagi, Japan 119/M5
Kamiyaku, Japan 117/L5
Kamla (riv.), India 127/F3
Kamloops, BC, Can. 168/C3
Kammaki, Japan 119/J6
Kamnik, Slov. 85/L3
Kamo, Japan 117/F2
Kamo, Japan 119/J5
Kamo (riv.), Japan 119/J5
Kamogawa, Japan 117/G3
Kamojima, Japan 116/D3
Kāmoke, Pak. 128/C4
Kamp (riv.), Aus. 83/H4
Kamp-Bornhofen, Ger. 95/G3
Kamp-Lintfort, Ger. 92/D5
Kampala (cap.), Ugan. 146/B2
Kampar, Malay. 122/B3
Kampar (riv.), Indo. 122/B3
Kampen, Neth. 92/C3
Kampen, Ger. 80/C4
Kamphaeng Phet, Thai. 120/C5
Kamphaeng Phet (ruin), Thai. 120/B2
Kampinoski NP, Pol. 83/L2
Kamp'o, SKor. 115/E5
Kampong Kuala Besut, Malay. 122/B2
Kampong Saom (bay), Camb. 122/B1
Kampong Saom, Camb. 120/C4
Kampville, Mo, US 179/F8
Kamsack, Sk, Can. 169/H3
Kamsdorf, Ger. 97/E1
Kamuchawie (lake), Mb,Sk, Can. 169/H1
Kamui-misaki (cape), Japan 118/B2
Kámuk (mtn.), CR 187/F4
Kamuli, Ugan. 146/B2
Kam'yanets'-Podil's'kyy, Ukr. 104/C2
Kamyshin, Rus. 105/H2
Kanaaupscow (riv.), Qu, Can. 165/J3
Kanab, Ut, US 170/D3
Kanab (wash), Az, US 170/C6
Kanairiktok (riv.), Nf, Can. 165/K3
Kanan, Japan 119/J7
Kananga, D.R. Congo 147/D2
Kanangra-Boyd NP, Austl. 157/D2
Kanash, Rus. 103/K5
Kanasin, Mex. 186/D1
Kanawaki Ind. Res., Qu, Can. 173/N7
Kanawha (riv.), WV, US 175/H2
Kanazawa, Japan 117/E2
Kanchanaburi, Thai. 120/B3
Kānchenjunga (peak), Nepal 124/E2
Kānchīpuram, India 124/C5
Kandahār, Afg. 131/J2
Kandalaksha, Rus. 102/G2
Kandalaksha (gulf), Rus. 79/K2
Kándanos, Gre. 89/H5
Kandé, Togo 145/F4
Kandel (peak), Ger. 98/E1
Kandel, Ger. 96/B4
Kander (riv.), Swi. 98/D4
Kandern, Ger. 98/D2
Kandersteg, Swi. 98/D5
Kandhkot, Pak. 131/J3
Kāndhla, India 128/D5
Kandi, Ben. 145/F4
Kāndi, India 127/G4
Kandi (cape), Indo. 123/F3
Kandıra, Turk. 91/K5
Kandos, Austl. 157/D2
Kandukūr, India 124/C4
Kandy, SrL. 124/D6
Kane (basin), Grld. 165/T7
Kane (co.), Il, US 177/P16
Kanem (reg.), Chad 138/H5
Kaneohe, Hi, US 166/W13
Kaneohe (bay), Hi, US 166/W13
Kaneohe Marine Air Corps Station, Hi, US 166/W13
Kaneville, Il, US 177/N16
Kaneyama, Japan 118/B4
Kang, Bots. 147/D5
Kanga (riv.), Bang. 127/G5
Kangaba, Mali 144/C4
Kangal, Turk. 132/D2
Kangān, Iran 130/F3
Kangan Abor. Land, Austl. 154/C2
Kanganpur, Pak. 128/C4
Kangar, Malay. 120/C5
Kangaroo (isl.), Austl. 151/C4
Kangasala, Fin. 81/L1
Kangāvar, Iran 130/E2
Kangbao, China 113/K3
Kangding, China 112/H5
Kangean (isls.), Indo. 123/E5
Kangeq, NKor. 115/D2
Kanggyŏng, SKor. 115/D4
Kanghwa, SKor. 115/F6
Kangiqsualujjuaq, Qu, Can. 165/K3
Kangiqsujuaq, Qu, Can. 165/J2
Kangirsuk, Qu, Can. 165/J2
Kangjin, SKor. 115/D5
Kangmar, China 127/G1
Kangnam (mts.), NKor. 115/C2
Kangnŭng, SKor. 115/E4
Kangping, China 114/E2
Kāngra, India 128/D3
Kangrinboqê (peak), China 112/D5
Kangshan, Tai. 121/D3
Kangto (peak), China 125/F2
Kangwŏn-do (prov.), SKor. 115/E4
Kanha NP, India 126/C4
Kanhān (riv.), India 124/C3
Kani, Japan 119/M5
Kanie, Japan 119/L5
Kanin (pen.), Rus. 202/C
Kanin Nos (pt.), Rus. 106/E3
Kaniva, Austl. 157/B3
Kanjiža, Serb. 90/E2
Kankakee (riv.), Il,In, US 172/C3
Kankan (pol. reg.), Gui. 144/C4
Kankan, Gui. 144/C4
Kanmuri-yama (peak), Japan 116/C3
Kannami, Japan 119/B3
Kannapolis, NC, US 175/H3
Kannauj, India 126/B2
Kannon-zaki (pt.), Japan 119/D3
Kannus, Fin. 79/G3
Kano, Nga. 145/H4
Kano (state), Nga. 145/H4
Kan'onji, Japan 116/C3
Kanouse (mtn.), NJ, US 181/H7
Kanoya, Japan 116/B5
Kanra, Japan 119/B1
Kansai (int'l arpt.), Japan 119/H7
Kansai (isl.), Japan 119/H7
Kansas (state), US 171/H3
Kansas (riv.), Ks, US 171/H3
Kansas City (int'l arpt.), Mo, US 171/J3
Kansas City, Ks, US 179/D5
Kansas City, Mo, US 179/D5
Kansasville, Wi, US 177/P14
Kansk, Rus. 106/K4
Kansŏng, SKor. 115/E3
Kantābānji, India 124/D3
Kānth, India 126/B1
Kantō (prov.), Japan 117/F2
Kantunilkin, Mex. 186/E1
Kanuku (mts.), Guy. 192/G3
Kanuma, Japan 117/F2
Kanye, Bots. 147/E5
Kaohsiung, Tai. 121/D3
Kaohsiung (int'l arpt.), Tai. 121/D3
Kaokoveld (mts.), Namb. 147/B4
Kaolack, Sen. 144/A3
Kaolack (pol. reg.), Sen. 144/B3
Kaolinovo, Bul. 91/H4
Kaoma, Zam. 147/D3
Kapaa, Hi, US 166/S9
Kapaahu, Hi, US 166/U11
Kapaau, Hi, US 166/U10
Kapalong, Phil. 121/E6
Kapan, Arm. 105/H5
Kapchorwa, Ugan. 146/B2
Kapellen, Belg. 92/B6
Kapenguria, Kenya 146/B2
Kapidaği (pen.), Turk. 91/H5
Kapingamarangi (isl.), Micr. 158/E4
Kapiri Mposhi, Zam. 147/E3
Kapiskau (riv.), On, Can. 165/H3
Kaplice, Czh. 97/H5
Kapos (riv.), Hun. 90/C2
Kaposvár, Hun. 90/C2
Kappl, Aus. 99/G3
Kapsan, NKor. 115/E2
Kapuas (riv.), Indo. 122/C4
Kapuas Hulu (mts.), Indo.,Malay. 122/D3
Kapunda, Austl. 155/H5
Kapūrthala, India 128/C4
Kapuskasing, On, Can. 172/D1
Kapuskasing (riv.), On, Can. 172/D1
Kapuvár, Hun. 85/M3
Kapydzhik (peak), Azer. 105/H5
Kap'yŏng, SKor. 115/D4
Kara (riv.), Rus. 103/Q1
Kara (sea), Rus. 202/A
Kara, Togo 145/F4
Kara-saki (pt.), Japan 116/A3
Karaali, Turk. 132/C2
Karabiğa, Turk. 91/H5
Karabük, Turk. 132/C1
Karaburun, Turk. 91/J5
Karaca (peak), Turk. 132/D2
Karacabey, Turk. 132/B1
Karacaköy, Turk. 91/J5
Karaçal (peak), Turk. 133/C1
Karacaoğlan, Turk. 91/H5
Karachayevo-Cherkesiya, Resp., Rus. 105/G4
Karachev, Rus. 104/E1
Karāchi, Pak. 131/J4
Karadere, Turk. 91/K5
Karaginskiy (isl.), Rus. 109/R4
Karaj, Iran 130/F1
Karakax (riv.), China 131/L1
Karakaya (dam), Turk. 132/D2
Karakelong (isl.), Indo. 123/G3
Karakhoto (ruin), China 112/H3
Karakol, Kyr. 129/G4
Karakoram (range), India 112/C4
Karakoram (pass), India 128/D2
Karakoro (riv.), Mali 144/C3
Karakorum (ruin), Mong. 112/H2
Karakorum (ruin), Mong. 129/G5
Karakorum (pass), China 131/L1
Karaköse, Turk. 132/E2
Karaköy, Turk. 132/E2
Karakul' (lake), Taj. 129/F5
Karakumy (des.), Trkm. 106/F5
Karakyon (peak), Trkm. 129/B4
Karakyr (peak), Trkm. 131/H1
Karam (riv.), Indo. 123/E4
Karaman (prov.), Turk. 132/C2
Karaman, Turk. 132/C2
Karamay, China 112/D2
Karamea Bight (bay), NZ 159/S11
Karamoja (prov.), Ugan. 146/B2
Karamürsel, Turk. 91/J5
Karangasem, Indo. 123/E5
Karanginskiy (isl.), Rus. 107/S4
Karanginskiy (bay), Rus. 107/S4
Kāranja, India 124/C3
Karanpur, India 128/B5
Karapınar, Turk. 132/C2
Karasabai, Guy. 195/G3
Karaşar, Turk. 91/L5
Karasburg, Namb. 148/B3
Karasjohka-Karasjok, Nor. 79/H1
Karasu, Turk. 91/K5
Karasu, Japan 119/L6
Karasuk, Rus. 129/G2
Karatá (lag.), Nic. 187/F3
Karataş, Turk. 133/D1
Karatoya (riv.), Bang. 127/G3
Karatsu, Japan 116/A4
Karauli, India 126/A2
Karaurgan, Turk. 132/E1
Karáva (peak), Gre. 89/G3
Karawang, Indo. 122/C5
Karayaka, Turk. 104/F4
Karayazı, Turk. 132/E2
Karazhal, Kaz. 129/F3
Karbalā' (gov.), Iraq 132/E3
Karbalā', Iraq 132/E3
Karben, Ger. 96/B2
Karcag, Hun. 90/E2
Kardhámila, Gre. 89/K3
Kardhítsa, Gre. 89/G3
Kardhitsomagoúla, Gre. 89/G3
Kareha (riv.), India 127/E3
Karelī, India 126/B4
Karelia (reg.), Rus. 79/J2
Karelia, Resp., Rus. 106/D3
Karera, India 126/B3
Karesuando, Swe. 79/G1
Karêt (reg.), Mrta. 140/D4
Karf Ash Shaykh (gov.) 132/B4
Kargı, Turk. 132/C1
Kargil, India 128/D2
Karhal, India 126/B2
Karhijärvi (lake), Fin. 81/K1
Karhula, Fin. 81/M1
Kariá, Gre. 89/G3
Karia Ba Mohammed, Mor. 142/B2
Kariai, Gre. 89/J2
Karianga, Madg. 149/H8
Kariba (dam), Zam. 147/E4
Kariba (lake), Zam., Zim. 135/E6
Kariba, Zim. 147/E4
Kariba-yama (peak), Japan 118/A2
Karibib, Namb. 147/C5
Karimama, Ben. 145/F3
Karimata (isl.), Indo. 122/D4
Karimata (str.), Indo. 122/C4
Karīmnagar, India 124/C4
Karimunjawa (isls.), Indo. 122/D5
Kariótissa, Gre. 89/H2
Karise, Den. 80/E4
Karisimbi (vol.), D.R. Congo 146/A3
Karisimbi (vol.), Rwa. 147/E1
Káristos, Gre. 89/J3
Kariya, Japan 119/L6
Karkaar (mts.), Som. 139/Q6
Kārkal, India 124/B5
Karkar (isl.), PNG 158/D5
Karkinits'ka Zatoka (gulf), Ukr. 104/D3
Karkkila, Fin. 81/L1
Karkonski NP, Pol. 83/H3
Karla Marksa (peak), Taj. 131/K1
Karlholmsbruk, Swe. 80/G1
Karlino, Pol. 80/F4
Karlovac, Cro. 90/B3
Karlovarský (pol. reg.), Czh. 97/F2
Karlovo, Bul. 89/J1
Karlovy Vary, Czh. 97/F2
Karlsdorf-Neuthard, Ger. 96/B4
Karlsfeld, Ger. 97/E6
Karlshamn, Swe. 80/F3
Karlshuld, Ger. 96/E5
Karlskoga, Swe. 80/E1
Karlskron, Ger. 97/E5
Karlskrona, Swe. 80/F3
Karlsruhe, Ger. 96/B4
Karlstad, Swe. 80/E2
Karlstadt, Ger. 96/C3
Karlstein am Main, Ger. 96/C2
Karluk, Ak, US 176/H4
Karmāla, India 131/L5
Karnali (riv.), Nepal 126/C1
Karnali (zone), Nepal 126/C1
Karnaphuli (res.), Bang. 127/H4
Karnataka (state), India 124/C4
Karnes City, Tx, US 171/H5
Karnobat, Bul. 89/K1
Kärnten (prov.), Aus. 85/K3
Karonga, Malw. 146/B5
Karoo NP, SAfr. 148/D4
Karoo NP, SAfr. 148/C4
Karoonda, Austl. 157/A2
Karor, Pak. 128/A4
Karoso (cape), Indo. 123/E5
Kárpathos, Gre. 132/A3
Kárpathos (isl.), Gre. 132/A3
Karpatskiy NP, Ukr. 91/G1
Karpenísion, Gre. 89/G3
Karratha, Austl. 154/C2
Kars, Turk. 132/E1
Kars (prov.), Turk. 132/E1
Kars (riv.), Turk. 105/G4
Kärsämäki, Fin. 102/E3
Karsantı, Turk. 132/C2
Karshi (int'l arpt.), Uzb. 129/E5
Kartaly, Rus. 105/M1
Kartārpur, India 128/C4
Kartuzy, Pol. 80/H4
Karuah, Austl. 157/D2
Karuma (falls), Ugan. 146/B2
Karumba, Austl. 156/A2
Karūn (riv.), Iran 130/E2
Karup, Den. 80/C3
Karviná, Czh. 83/K4
Kaş, Turk. 133/A1
Kås, Den. 80/C3
Kasaan, Ak, US 176/M4
Kasabonika (lake), On, Can. 169/L2
Kasagi, Japan 119/J6
Kasahara, Japan 119/M5
Kāsai (riv.), India 127/F4
Kasai, Japan 119/G6
Kasai (riv.), D.R. Congo 147/C1
Kasama, Zam. 146/A5
Kasama, Japan 117/G2
Kasamatsu, Japan 119/L5
Kasane, Bots. 147/E4
Kasaoka, Japan 116/C3
Kasar (cape), Sudan 143/D5
Kāsaragod, India 124/C5
Kasartori-yama (peak), Japan 119/K6
Kasba (lake), NW,Nun., Can. 164/F2
Kasba Tadla, Mor. 140/D2
Kaseda, Japan 116/B5
Kasese, Ugan. 146/A2
Kashaf (riv.), Iran 131/H1
Kāshān, Iran 130/F2
Kashi, China 129/G5
Kashiba, Japan 119/J6
Kashihara, Japan 119/J6
Kashima, Japan 116/B4
Kashima, Japan 117/G3
Kashima (bay), Japan 119/F1
Kashin, Rus. 102/H4
Kāshīpur, India 126/B1
Kashiwa, Japan 119/D2
Kashiwara, Japan 119/J6
Kashiwazaki, Japan 117/F2
Kāshmar, Iran 131/G1
Kashmir (reg.), India,Pak. 129/G5
Kashmūnd Ghar (range), Afg. 128/A2
Kasigau (peak), Kenya 146/C3
Kasigluk, Ak, US 176/F3
Kasilof, Ak, US 176/H3
Kasimov, Rus. 102/J5
Kasiruta (isl.), Indo. 123/G4
Kasiui (isl.), Indo. 123/H4
Kaskaskia (riv.), Il, US 171/K3
Kaslo, BC, Can. 168/D3
Kasongo, D.R. Congo 147/E1
Kásos (isl.), Gre. 132/A3
Kaspichan, Bul. 91/H4
Kaspiysk, Rus. 105/H4
Kassala, Sudan 130/C5
Kassándria, Gre. 89/H2
Kassándra (pen.), Gre. 89/H3
Kassel, Ger. 93/G6
Kasserine, Tun. 142/L7
Kasserine (gov.), Tun. 142/L7
Kassikaityu (riv.), Guy. 195/G4
Kassler, Co, US 179/B4
Kasson, Mn, US 169/K4
Kastamonu, Turk. 132/C1
Kastamonu (prov.), Turk. 132/C1
Kastanéai, Gre. 89/K2
Kaštel Stari, Cro. 90/C4
Kaštel Sućurac, Cro. 90/C4
Kastellaun, Ger. 95/G3
Kastéllion, Gre. 89/J5
Kasterlee, Belg. 92/B6
Kastl, Ger. 97/E4
Kastoría, Gre. 89/G2
Kastrakíou (lake), Gre. 89/G3
Kasuga, Japan 119/H5
Kasuga, Japan 119/K5
Kasugai, Japan 119/B2
Kasugai, Japan 119/L5
Kasukabe, Japan 117/F3
Kasumiga (lake), Japan 117/G2
Kasungu, Malw. 147/F3
Kasūr, Pak. 128/C4
Kat O Chau (isl.), China 113/V9
Katahdin (mt.), Me, US 173/G2
Katákolon, Gre. 89/G4
Katanga (reg.), D.R. Congo 147/D2
Katanga (pol. reg.), D.R. Congo 146/A5
Katangi, India 126/B4
Katanning, Austl. 154/C5
Katano, Japan 119/J6
Katastárion, Gre. 89/G4
Katavi NP, Tanz. 146/A4
Katchall (isl.), India 125/F6
Kateríni, Gre. 89/H2
Kates Needle (peak), Ak, US 176/M4
Katete, Zam. 147/F3
Katghora, India 126/D4
Kāthgodām, India 126/B1
Kathiawar (pen.), India 131/K4
Kathleen (mt.), Austl. 155/G2
Kāthmāndu (cap.), Nepal 127/E2
Kathua, India 128/C3
Kati, Mali 144/C3
Katiola, C.d'Iv. 144/D4
Katlehong, SAfr. 148/E2
Katlenburg-Lindau, Ger. 93/H5
Katmai (vol.), Ak, US 176/H4
Katmai NP, Ak, US 176/G4
Káto Akhaía, Gre. 89/G3
Katokhí, Gre. 89/G3
Katonah, NY, US 181/E1
Katonga (riv.), Ugan. 146/A2
Katoúna, Gre. 89/G3
Katowice, Pol. 83/K3
Katra, India 128/C3
Kātrās, India 127/F4
Katrine (lake), Sc, UK 78/B4
Katrineholm, Swe. 80/G2
Katsikás, Gre. 89/G3
Katsina (state), Nga. 145/G3
Katsina, Nga. 145/G3
Katsina Ala (riv.), Nga. 145/H5
Katsunuma, Japan 119/B2
Katsura (riv.), Japan 119/J5
Katsuragi, Japan 116/D3
Katsuragi-san (peak), Japan 119/H7
Katsuta, Japan 117/G2
Katsuura, Japan 117/G3
Katsuyama, Japan 116/E2
Katsuyama, Japan 119/B3
Kattakurgan, Uzb. 129/E5
Kattegat (str.), Den. 80/D3
Katumbi, Malw. 146/B5
Kātwa, India 127/G4
Katwe-Kabatooro, Ugan. 146/A3
Katwijk aan Zee, Neth. 92/B4
Katy, Tx, US 171/J5
Katzenbach (riv.), Ger. 96/B4
Katzenbuckel (peak), Ger. 96/C4
Katzenelnbogen, Ger. 95/G3
Katzhütte, Ger. 96/D1
Katzwinkel, Ger. 95/F3
Kau-ye (isl.), Myan. 120/B4
Kauai (chan.), Hi, US 166/S10
Kauai (isl.), Hi, US 166/S9
Kaufbeuren, Ger. 99/G2
Kaufering, Ger. 99/G1
Kaufungen, Ger. 93/G6
Kauhava, Fin. 102/D3
Kauhola (pt.), Hi, US 166/U10
Kauiki (pt.), Hi, US 166/U10
Kaukaveld (uplands), Namb. 147/C5
Kaukura (isl.), FrPol. 159/L6
Kaulakahi (chan.), Hi, US 166/R9
Kaulsdorf, Ger. 97/E1
Kaumalapau, Hi, US 166/T10
Kauna (pt.), Hi, US 166/U11
Kaunakakai, Hi, US 166/T10
Kaunas (int'l arpt.), Lith. 81/K4
Kaunas (res.), Lith. 81/L4
Kaunas, Lith. 81/K4
Kaupanger, Nor. 80/B1
Kauttua, Fin. 81/K1
Kavadarci, FYROM 89/H2
Kavajë, Alb. 89/F2
Kavála, Gre. 89/J2
Kavalerovo, Rus. 113/Q3
Kāvali, India 124/C5
Kavangel (isls.), Palau 158/C4
Kavaratti, India 124/B5
Kavarna, Bul. 91/J4
Kavgolovskoye (lake), Rus. 103/T6
Kavieng, PNG 158/E5
Kavīr-e Namak (dry lake), Iran 129/C6
Kävlinge, Swe. 80/E4
Kaw (lake), Ok, US 171/H3
Kawa (ruin), Sudan 143/B5
Kawabe, Japan 118/B4
Kawachi, Japan 119/E2
Kawachi-Nagano, Japan 119/J7
Kawage, Japan 119/L6
Kawagoe, Japan 117/F3
Kawagoe, Japan 119/L5
Kawaguchi, Japan 117/F3
Kawaguchiko, Japan 119/B3
Kawai, Japan 119/J6
Kawaihoa (pt.), Hi, US 166/R10
Kawaikini (peak), Hi, US 166/S9
Kawajima, Japan 119/C2
Kawakami, Japan 119/B2
Kawakami, Japan 119/J7
Kawamata, Japan 117/G2
Kawambwa, Zam. 146/A5
Kawamoto, Japan 119/C1
Kawanishi, Japan 119/H6
Kawanishi, Japan 119/J6
Kawardha, India 126/C4
Kawartha (lakes), On, Can. 172/E2
Kawasaki, Japan 117/F3
Kawasato, Japan 119/D1
Kawashima, Japan 119/L5
Kawaue, Japan 119/M4
Kawela (Kawela Bay), Hi, US 166/V12
Kawerau, NZ 159/T10
Kawlin, Myan. 125/G3
Kawthaung, Myan. 120/B4
Kax (riv.), China 112/D3
Kay (pt.), Yk, Can. 176/L2
Kaya, SKor. 115/E5
Kaya, Japan 119/H5
Kaya-san (peak), SKor. 115/D4
Kayadibi, Turk. 132/C2
Kayagangiri (peak), CAfr. 138/J6
Kayah (state), Myan. 125/G4
Kayan (riv.), Indo. 123/E3
Kayanga (riv.), Sen. 144/B3
Kaycee, Wy, US 168/G5
Kayenta, Az, US 170/E3

246
Kayes – Kirov

Kayes, Mali 144/C3
Kayes (pol. reg.), Mali 144/C3
Kayin (state), Myan. 125/G4
Kayl, Lux. 95/F5
Kaymaz, Turk. 91/K5
Kaynarca, Turk. 91/J5
Kaynaşlı, Turk. 91/K5
Kayoa (isl.), Indo. 123/G3
Kayser (mts.), Sur. 195/G4
Kayseri, Turk. 132/C2
Kayseri (prov.), Turk. 132/C2
Kaysersberg, Fr. 98/D1
Kaysville, Ut, US 179/K11
Kayuagung, Indo. 122/B4
Kazakhstan (ctry.) 106/G5
Kazan', Rus. 103/L5
Kazan (int'l arpt.), Rus. 103/L5
Kazan (riv.), Nun., Can. 164/F2
Kazancı, Turk. 133/C1
Kazanlı, Turk. 133/D1
Kazanlŭk, Bul. 89/J1
Kazbek (peak), Geo. 105/H4
Kāzerūn, Iran 130/F3
Kazgar (riv.), China 112/C4
Kazimierza Wielka, Pol. 83/L3
Kâzımkarabekir, Turk. 132/C2
Kazincbarcika, Hun. 83/L4
Kazo, Japan 119/D1
Kazuno, Japan 118/B3
Ke Ga (cape), Viet. 120/E3
Ké Macina, Mali 144/D3
Kéa (isl.), Gre. 89/J4
Kéa, Gre. 89/J4
Keaau, Hi, US 166/U11
Keady, NI, UK 76/B3
Keahole (pt.), Hi, US 166/T11
Keanapapa (pt.), Hi, US 166/T10
Keansburg, NJ, US 181/J10
Kearney, Ne, US 171/H2
Kearney, Mo, US 179/E5
Kearns, Ut, US 179/K12
Kearny, NJ, US 181/J8
Kearny (pt.), NI, UK 76/C3
Keawakapu, Hi, US 166/T10
Keawekaheka (pt.), Hi, US 166/U11
Keban (dam), Turk. 132/D2
Kebbi (state), Nga. 145/G4
Kébémer, Sen. 144/A3
Kebili, Tun. 142/M6
Kebnekaise (peak), Swe. 79/F2
Kebumen, Indo. 122/C5
Kecel, Hun. 90/D2
Keçiborlu, Turk. 132/B2
Kecskemét, Hun. 90/D2
Kedah (state), Malay. 120/C5
Kėdainiai, Lith. 81/K4
Kediri, Indo. 122/D5
Kédougou, Sen. 144/B3
Kędzierzyn-Koźle, Pol. 83/K3
Keego Harbor, Mi, US 177/F6
Keele (riv.), NW, Can. 164/D2
Keele (peak), Yk, Can. 164/C2
Keelung, Tai. 121/D2
Keelung, Japan 117/G8
Keen (mt.), Sc, UK 78/D3
Keene, NH, US 173/F3
Keepit (dam), Austl. 157/D1
Keer-Weer (cape), Austl. 156/A1
Keetmanshoop, Namb. 148/B2
Kefallinía (isl.), Gre. 89/G3
Kefar Sava, Isr. 133/F7
Kefar Vitkin, Isr. 133/F7
Keflavík, Ice. 79/M7
Keflavík (int'l arpt.), Ice. 79/M7
Kehl, Ger. 98/D1
Kehrsatz, Swi. 98/D4
Keighley, Eng, UK 77/G4
Keihoku, Japan 119/J5
Keimoes, SAfr. 148/C3
Kéita (riv.), Chad 139/J6
Keith, Austl. 157/B3
Keith, Sc, UK 78/D1
Kejimkujik NP, NS, Can. 173/H2
Kekaha, Hi, US 166/S10
Kékes (peak), Hun. 83/K5
Kelan, China 114/B3
Kelang (isl.), Indo. 123/G4
Kelang, Malay. 122/B3
Kelberg, Ger. 95/F3
Kelbia, Sebkhet (swamp), Tun. 142/M7
Keles, Turk. 104/D5
Kelheim, Ger. 97/E5
Kelkheim, Ger. 96/B2
Kelkıt, Turk. 104/F4
Kelkıt (riv.), Turk. 132/D1
Kell, Ger. 95/F4
Kellenhusen, Ger. 80/D4
Keller (peak), Ca, US 178/C2
Keller (lake), NW, Can. 164/D2
Kellerberrin, Austl. 154/C4
Kellogg, Id, US 168/D4
Kells, NI, UK 76/B2
Kélo, Chad 138/J6
Kelowna, BC, Can. 168/D3
Kelsey (pt.), Eng, UK 74/A6
Kelso, Wa, US 168/C4
Kelso, Sc, UK 78/D5
Kelsterbach, Ger. 96/B2
Keluang, Malay. 122/B3
Kelvington, Sk, Can. 169/H2
Kem', Rus. 102/G2
Kem' (riv.), Rus. 106/D3
Kemah, Turk. 104/F5
Kemaliye, Turk. 132/D2
Kemalpaşa, Turk. 132/E1
Kemasik, Malay. 122/B3
Kematen an der Ybbs, Aus. 97/H6
Kematen in Tirol, Aus. 99/H3
Kembs, Fr. 98/D2
Kemecse, Hun. 83/L4
Kemena (riv.), Malay. 122/D3
Kemence, Hun. 83/K4
Kemer, Turk. 133/B1
Kemer (dam), Turk. 132/B2
Kemerhisar, Turk. 132/C2
Kemerovo, Rus. 106/J4
Kemerovskaya Oblast, Rus. 106/J4
Kemi, Fin. 79/H2
Kemijärvi, Fin. 102/E2
Kemijoki (riv.), Fin. 79/H2
Kemmerer, Wy, US 168/F5
Kemnath, Ger. 97/E3
Kemnay, Sc, UK 78/D2
Kemp (lake), Tx, US 171/H4
Kempele, Fin. 102/E2
Kempen, Ger. 92/D6
Kempenich, Ger. 95/G3
Kempenland (phys. reg.), Belg. 92/C6
Kempisch Kanaal (canal), Belg. 95/E1
Kempsey, Austl. 157/E1
Kempston, Eng, UK 75/F2
Kempt (res.), Qu, Can. 172/F2
Kempten, Ger. 99/G2
Kempton, Austl. 157/C4
Kempton Park, SAfr. 148/Q13
Kemptown, Md, US 180/A5
Kemri, India 126/B1
Kemul (peak), Indo. 123/E3
Ken (riv.), India 126/C3
Ken (lake), Sc, UK 76/D1
Ken-zaki (pt.), Japan 119/D3
Kenadsa, Alg. 141/E3
Kenai, Ak, US 176/H3
Kenai Fjords NP, Ak, US 176/H4
Kendal, Eng, UK 77/F3
Kendalia, Tx, US 179/T20
Kendall, Austl. 157/E1
Kendall, Fl, US 175/H5
Kendall (co.), Il, US 177/P16
Kendall (co.), Tx, US 179/T20
Kendall Park, NJ, US 180/D3
Kendallville, In, US 172/C3
Kendari, Indo. 123/F4
Kéndavros, Gre. 89/J2
Kendel (riv.), Ger. 92/D5
Kendrāpāra, India 124/E3
Kénédougou (prov.), Burk. 144/D4
Kenema, SLeo. 144/C5
Kenge, D.R. Congo 147/C1
Kenhardt, SAfr. 148/C3
Kenhorst, Pa, US 180/C3
Kenié-Baoulé, Réserve de, Mali 144/C3
Kenilworth, Eng, UK 75/E2
Kenilworth, NJ, US 181/H9
Kénitra, Mor. 142/A2
Kénitra (prov.), Mor. 142/A2
Kenli, China 114/D3
Kenmare, ND, US 169/H3
Kenmare, Ire. 73/P11
Kenmore, NY, US 173/S10
Kenmore, Wa, US 177/C2
Kenn (reef), Austl. 151/E3
Kenn, Ger. 95/F4
Kennebec (riv.), Me, US 173/G2
Kennebunk, Me, US 173/G3
Kennedy (chan.), Grld.,Nun., Can. 165/T6
Kennedy (range), Austl. 154/B3
Kennedy Entrance (chan.) 176/H4
Kennedyville, Md, US 180/C5
Kennelbach, Aus. 99/F3
Kennemerduinen, NP de, Neth. 92/B4
Kenner, La, US 179/P17
Kennet (riv.), Eng, UK 75/E4
Kennet and Avon (canal), Eng, UK 74/D4
Kenneth, Ks, US 179/D6
Kennett, Mo, US 171/K3
Kennett Square, Pa, US 180/C4
Kennewick, Wa, US 168/D4
Keno Hill, Yk, Can. 176/L3
Kenogami (riv.), On, Can. 165/H3
Kenora, On, Can. 169/K3
Kenosha, Wi, US 177/Q14
Kenosha (co.), Wi, US 177/P14
Kensico (res.), NY, US 181/K7
Kensington and Chelsea (bor.), Eng, UK 72/A1
Kent (pen.), Nun., Can. 164/F2
Kent (co.), On, Can. 177/G6
Kent (riv.), Eng, UK 77/F3
Kent (isl.), Md, US 180/B6
Kent (pt.), Md, US 180/B6
Kent (lake), Mi, US 177/E7
Kent, Oh, US 172/D3
Kent, Wa, US 168/C4
Kent County (int'l arpt.), Mi, US 172/C3
Kent Group (isls.), Austl. 157/C3
Kentau, Kaz. 129/E4
Kenton, De, US 180/C5
Kenton, Oh, US 172/D3
Kentucky (state), US 175/G2
Kentucky (riv.), Ky, US 172/C4
Kentucky (lake), Ky, US 175/F2
Kentville, NS, Can. 173/H2
Kenya (ctry.) 146/C2
Kenzingen, Ger. 98/D1
Keonjhar, India 124/E3
Kep i Gjuhëzës (cape), Alb. 89/F2
Kep i Rodonit (cape), Alb. 89/F2
Kępno, Pol. 83/J3
Keppel Sands, Austl. 156/C3
Kerala (state), India 124/C5
Kéran, PN de la, Togo 145/F4
Kerang, Austl. 157/B2
Keratéa, Gre. 89/N9
Kerava, Fin. 81/L1
Kerch' (str.), Rus.,Ukr. 104/F3
Kerch, Ukr. 104/F3
Keremeos, BC, Can. 168/D3
Kerempe Burnu (cape), Turk. 132/C1
Keren, Erit. 130/C5
Kerepestarcsa, Hun. 91/R9
Keret' (lake), Rus. 79/K2
Kerguélen (isl.), Fr. 65/N8
Kericho, Kenya 146/B3
Kerikeri (cape), NZ 159/S9
Kerinci (peak), Indo. 122/B4
Kerio (riv.), Kenya 146/C2
Kerio Valley Nat'l Rsv., Kenya 146/B2
Kerkdriel, Neth. 92/C5
Kerken, Ger. 92/D6
Kerkenah (isl.), Tun. 141/H2
Kerki, Trkm. 129/E5
Kerkínis (lake), Gre. 89/H2
Kérkira, Gre. 89/F3
Kerkrade, Neth. 95/F2
Kerkwijk, Neth. 92/C5
Kermadec (isls.), NZ 158/G8
Kermān, Iran 131/G2
Kern (riv.), Ca, US 170/C4
Kern, South Kern (riv.), Ca, US 170/C4
Kerns, Swi. 99/E4
Kéros (isl.), Gre. 89/J4
Kérou, Ben. 145/F4
Kerr (lake), Ok, US 171/J4
Kerr (res.), NC,Va, US 175/J2
Kerrobert, Sk, Can. 168/F3
Kerrville, Tx, US 171/H5
Kert (riv.), Mor. 142/C2
Kerulen (riv.), Mong. 113/K3
Kerzaz, Alg. 141/E3
Kerzenheim, Ger. 95/H4
Kerzers, Swi. 98/D4
Kesagami (riv.), On, Can. 172/D1
Keşan, Turk. 89/K2
Kesch (peak), Swi. 99/F4
Kesen'numa, Japan 118/B4
Keshan, China 113/N2
Keshod, India 124/B3
Keski-Suomi (prov.), Fin. 79/H3
Keskin, Turk. 132/C2
Kesselbach (riv.), Ger. 96/D5
Kestel, Turk. 132/B1
Kesteren, Neth. 92/C5
Keszthely, Hun. 90/C2
Ket' (riv.), Rus. 106/J4
Keta, Gha. 145/F5
Keta (riv.), Rus. 106/K3
Ketchikan, Ak, US 176/M4
Kete Krachi, Gha. 145/E5
Ketelmeer (lake), Neth. 92/C3
Kétou, Ben. 145/F5
Kętrzyn, Pol. 81/J4
Ketsch, Ger. 96/B4
Kettering, Eng, UK 75/F2
Kettle (riv.), Mn, US 168/D3
Kettle Moraine State Forest, Wi, US 177/P14
Ketzin, Ger. 82/P7
Keukenhof, Neth. 92/B4
Kevelaer, Ger. 92/D5
Kewaunee, Wi, US 172/C2
Keweenaw (pen.), Mi, US 169/L4
Keweenaw (pt.), Mi, US 169/M4
Keweenaw (bay), Mi, US 169/L4
Key Largo, Fl, US 175/H5
Key West, Fl, US 175/H5
Keymar, Md, US 180/A4
Keyport, NJ, US 181/J10
Keyport, Wa, US 177/B2
Keystone (lake), Ok, US 171/H3
Kežmarok, Slvk. 83/L4
Khaanziir (cape), Som. 139/Q5
Khabarovsk, Rus. 113/Q2
Khabarovskiy Kray, Rus. 107/P4
Khagaria, India 127/F3
Khair, India 126/A2
Khairābād, India 126/C2
Khairpur, Pak. 128/B5
Khairpur, Pak. 131/J3
Khakasiya, Resp., Rus. 107/P6
Khalándrion, Gre. 89/N8
Khalīlābād, India 126/D2
Khalkhāl, Iran 130/E1
Khalkhidhikhi (pen.), Gre. 89/H2
Khalkidhón, Gre. 89/H2
Khalkís, Gre. 89/H3
Khamar-Daban (mts.), Rus. 112/H1
Khambhāliya, India 131/J4
Khambhat, India 131/K4
Khamīs Mushayţ, SAr. 130/D5
Khammam, India 124/D4
Khamr, Yem. 130/D5
Khān Yūnus, Gaza 133/D4
Khānābād, Afg. 131/J1
Khānaqīn, Iraq 132/F3
Khandwa, India 131/L4
Khanem (well), Alg. 141/F3
Khānewāl, Pak. 128/A4
Khāngāh Dogrān, Pak. 128/B4
Khāngarh, Pak. 128/A5
Khaniá, Gre. 89/J5
Khanka (lake), China,Rus. 113/P3
Khanna, India 128/D4
Khānpur, Pak. 128/A5
Khanty-Mansiysk, Rus. 106/G3
Khanty-Mansiyskiy Aut. Okrug, Rus. 106/G3
Khao Chamao-Khao Wong NP, Thai. 120/C3
Khao Khitchakut NP, Thai. 120/C3
Khao Laem (res.), Thai. 125/G4
Khao Sam Roi Yot NP, Thai. 120/B3
Khao Yai NP, Thai. 120/C3
Kharagpur, India 127/F4
Kharagpur, India 127/F3
Kharak, Pak. 128/A3
Khārān, Pak. 131/J3
Kharar, India 127/F4
Kharar, India 128/D4
Kharbatā, Isr. 133/G8
Khargon, India 131/L4
Khāriān, Pak. 128/B3
Kharkiv, Ukr. 104/F2
Kharkiv (int'l arpt.), Ukr. 104/F2
Kharkivs'ka Oblasti, Ukr. 104/F2
Kharmanli, Bul. 89/J2
Kharovsk, Rus. 102/J4
Kharrour (riv.), Mor. 142/B2
Kharsia, India 126/D5
Khartoum (Kharţūm) (cap.), Sudan 130/B5
Khasavyurt, Rus. 105/H4
Khāsh (riv.), Afg. 131/H2
Khashuri, Geo. 105/G4
Khasi (hills), India 127/H3
Khaskovo (pol. reg.), Bul. 89/J2
Khaskovo (prov.), Bul. 91/G5
Khatanga (riv.), Rus. 202/Z
Khatanga (gulf), Rus. 107/L2
Khatauli, India 128/D5
Khātegaon, India 126/A4
Khatīma, India 126/B1
Khatlon (obl.), Taj. 129/E5
Khatmia (pass), Egypt 133/C4
Khātra, India 127/F4
Khatt Atoui (riv.), Mrta. 138/B3
Khaur, Pak. 128/B3
Khaybar (pass), Afg. 128/A2
Khazzān Dūkān (res.), Iraq 132/F3
Khazzān Jabal Al Awliyā (dam), Sudan 139/M4
Khekra, India 128/D5
Khemis el Khechna, Alg. 142/G4
Khemis Miliana, Alg. 142/G4
Khémisset (prov.), Mor. 142/A3
Khémisset, Mor. 142/A3
Khenchela (prov.), Alg. 141/G2
Khenchela, Alg. 142/K7
Khénifra, Mor. 140/D2
Khepoyarvi (lake), Rus. 103/T6
Kheri, India 126/C2
Khersān (riv.), Iran 130/F2
Kherson, Ukr. 91/L2
Kherson (int'l arpt.), Ukr. 91/L2
Khersons'ka Oblasti, Ukr. 104/E3
Khilok, Rus. 113/K1
Khimki, Rus. 103/W9
Khíos, Gre. 89/K3
Khíos (isl.), Gre. 89/J3
Khirpai, India 127/F4
Khisarya, Bul. 89/J1
Khiva, Uzb. 129/D4
Khlebarovo, Bul. 91/H4
Khmel'nyts'ka Oblasti, Ukr. 104/C2
Khmel'nytskyy, Ukr. 104/C2
Kho Sawai (plat.), Thai. 125/H4
Khodzheyli, Uzb. 129/C4
Khojak (pass), Pak. 131/J2
Kholm, Afg. 131/J1
Kholmsk, Rus. 113/R2
Khomeynīshahr, Iran 130/F2
Khon Kaen, Thai. 120/C2
Khoper (riv.), Rus. 106/E4
Khor (riv.), Rus. 107/P5
Khóra Sfakíon, Gre. 89/J5
Khorazm (pol. reg.), Uzb. 129/D4
Khoríon, Gre. 132/A2
Khorramābād, Iran 130/E2
Khorramshahr, Iran 130/E2
Khorugh, Taj. 131/K1
Khotol (mtn.), Ak, US 176/G3
Khouribga, Mor. 140/D2
Khowai, India 125/F3
Khrisoúpolis, Gre. 89/J2
Khromtaū, Kaz. 105/L2
Khrysí (isl.), Gre. 89/J5
Khuan Ubon Ratana (lake), Thai. 120/C2
Khudiān, Pak. 128/C4
Khuis, Bots. 148/C2
Khujand, Taj. 129/E4
Khulna (pol. div.), Bang. 127/G4
Khūnjerāb (pass), Pak. 131/L1
Khunjerab NP, Pak. 129/G5
Khunti, India 127/E4
Khurai, India 126/B3
Khurda, India 124/E3
Khurja, India 126/A1
Khushāb, Pak. 128/B3
Khust, Ukr. 83/M4
Khūtār, India 126/C1
Khuzdār, Pak. 131/J3
Khvalynka, Rus. 113/P3
Khvonsār, Iran 130/F2
Khvor, Iran 131/G2
Khvoy, Iran 105/H5
Khwaja Rawash (int'l arpt.), Afg. 129/E6
Khyber (pass), Pak. 128/A2
Kia, Sol. 158/E5
Kiama, Austl. 157/D2
Kiamichi (mts.), Ok, US 174/E3
Kiana, Ak, US 176/F2
Kibæk, Den. 80/C3
Kibali (riv.), D.R. Congo 146/A2
Kibergneset (pt.), Nor. 79/J1
Kibo (Kilimanjaro) (peak), Tanz. 146/C3
Kiboga, Ugan. 146/A2
Kıbrısçık, Turk. 91/K5
Kibwezi, Kenya 146/C3
Kičevo, FYROM 89/G2
Kichha, India 126/B1
Kickapoo, Ks, US 179/D5
Kidal, Mali 145/F2
Kidal (pol. reg.), Mali 145/F2
Kidapawan, Phil. 123/G2
Kidderminster, Eng, UK 74/D2
Kidepo Valley NP, Ugan. 139/M7
Kidsgrove, Eng, UK 77/F5
Kiel (bay), Den. 79/D5
Kiel, Ger. 80/D4
Kielce, Pol. 83/L3
Kielder (res.), Eng, UK 77/F1
Kien An, Viet. 120/D1
Kierspe, Ger. 95/G1
Kiev (Kyyiv) (cap.), Ukr. 104/D2
Kiffa, Mrta. 144/C2
Kifisiá, Gre. 89/N8
Kigali (cap.), Rwa. 146/A3
Kigali (Gregoire Kayibanda) (int'l arpt.), Rwa. 146/A3
Kiği, Turk. 132/E2
Kigoma (pol. reg.), Tanz. 146/A4
Kigoma, Tanz. 146/A4
Kigye, SKor. 115/E4
Kihei, Hi, US 166/T10
Kihnu (isl.), Est. 81/L2
Kiholo, Hi, US 166/U11
Kihti (str.), Fin. 81/J1
Kii (chan.), Japan 116/D4
Kii (mts.), Japan 116/D4
Kijang, SKor. 115/E5
Kikai (isl.), Japan 117/L6
Kikepa (pt.), Hi, US 166/R9
Kikiktat (mtn.), Ak, US 176/H2
Kikinda, Serb. 90/E3
Kikonai, Japan 118/B3
Kikwit, D.R. Congo 147/C2
Kil, Swe. 80/E2
Kilafors, Swe. 80/G1
Kilauea, Hi, US 166/S9
Kilbarchan, Sc, UK 78/B5
Kilberry, Ire. 73/Q10
Kilbirnie, Sc, UK 78/B5
Kilbrannan (sound), Sc, UK 78/A5
Kilchoan, Sc, UK 73/Q8
Kilchu, NKor. 115/E2
Kilcoole, Ire. 76/B5
Kilcormac, Ire. 73/Q10
Kilcoy, Austl. 156/D4
Kildare, Ire. 73/Q10
Kildeer, Il, US 177/P15
Kil'den (isl.), Rus. 102/G1
Kilembe Estates, Ugan. 146/A2
Kilgarvan, Ire. 73/P11
Kilgore, Tx, US 171/J4
Kilian (isl.), Nun., Can. 164/E1
Kilifi, Kenya 146/C3
Kilimanjaro (pol. reg.), Tanz. 146/C3
Kilimanjaro (int'l arpt.), Tanz. 146/C3
Kilimanjaro NP, Tanz. 146/C3
Kilimli, Turk. 91/K5
Kilinochchi, SrL. 124/D6
Kilis, Turk. 133/E1
Kiliya, Ukr. 91/J3
Kilkee, Ire. 73/P10
Kilkeel, NI, UK 76/B3
Kilkenny, Ire. 73/Q10
Kilkenny (co.), Ire. 76/A6
Kilkís, Gre. 89/H2
Kilkivan, Austl. 156/D4
Kill, Ire. 73/Q10
Kill Van Kull (riv.), NJ,NY, US 181/J9
Killam, Ab, Can. 168/F2
Killarney, Austl. 157/E1
Killarney, Mb, Can. 169/J3
Killarney, Ire. 73/P10
Killarney NP, Ire. 73/P10
Killdeer, ND, US 169/H4
Killearn, Sc, UK 78/B4
Killeen, Tx, US 171/H5
Killenaule, Ire. 73/Q10
Killiecrankie, Pass of (pass), Sc, UK 78/C3
Killin, Sc, UK 78/B4
Killinchy, NI, UK 76/C3
Killinek (isl.), Nun., Can. 165/K2
Killíni (peak), Gre. 89/H4
Killíni, Gre. 89/G4
Killough, NI, UK 76/C3
Killybegs, Ire. 73/P9
Killyclogher, NI, UK 76/A2
Killyleagh, NI, UK 76/C3
Kilmacanogue, Ire. 76/B5
Kilmacolm, Sc, UK 78/B5
Kilmacow, Ire. 73/Q10
Kilmallock, Ire. 73/P10
Kilmar Tor (hill), Eng, UK 74/B5
Kilmarnock, Sc, UK 78/B5
Kilmaurs, Sc, UK 78/B5
Kilmichael (pt.), Ire. 76/B6
Kilmore, Austl. 157/C3
Kilmore Quay, Ire. 73/Q10
Kilombero (riv.), Tanz. 146/C5
Kilosa, Tanz. 146/C4
Kilraghts, NI, UK 76/B1
Kilrea, NI, UK 76/B2
Kilrush, Ire. 73/P10
Kilsyth, Sc, UK 78/B5
Kilwa Kivinje, Tanz. 146/C5
Kilwinning, Sc, UK 78/B5
Kimba, Austl. 155/H5
Kimball, SD, US 169/J5
Kimbe, PNG 158/E5
Kimberley (cape), Austl. 156/B2
Kimberley (plat.), Austl. 151/B2
Kimberley, BC, Can. 168/E3
Kimberley, SAfr. 148/D3
Kimch'aek, NKor. 115/E2
Kimch'ŏn, SKor. 115/E4
Kimhae, SKor. 115/E5
Kimhae (int'l arpt.), SKor. 115/E5
Kími, Gre. 89/J3
Kímina, Gre. 89/H2
Kimitsu, Japan 117/F3
Kimje, SKor. 115/D5
Kimméria, Gre. 89/J2
Kimmirut, Nun., Can. 165/K2
Kímolos (isl.), Gre. 89/J4
Kimovsk, Rus. 104/F1
Kimp'o, SKor. 115/F6
Kimp'o (int'l arpt.), SKor. 115/F6
Kimpō-zan (peak), Japan 119/B2
Kimry, Rus. 102/H4
Kinabalu (peak), Malay. 123/E2
Kinabatangan (riv.), Malay. 123/E2
Kinango, Kenya 146/C4
Kinbasket (lake), BC, Can. 168/D2
Kinbrace, Sc, UK 73/S7
Kincaid, Sk, Can. 168/G3
Kincardine, On, Can. 172/D2
Kincardine, Sc, UK 78/C4
Kinchega NP, Austl. 157/B2
Kinder Scout (peak), Eng, UK 77/G5
Kindersley, Sk, Can. 168/F3
Kindia, Gui. 144/B4
Kindia (pol. reg.), Gui. 144/B4
Kinding, Ger. 97/E5
Kindsbach, Ger. 95/G5
Kindu, D.R. Congo 147/E1
Kinel', Rus. 105/J1
Kineshma, Rus. 102/J4
King (lake), Austl. 154/C5
King (mt.), Austl. 156/B4
King (sound), Austl. 151/B2
King (isl.), BC, Can. 168/B2
King (mt.), BC, Can. 176/N4
King (peak), Yk, Can. 176/K3
King (co.), Wa, US 177/D2
King Christian (isl.), Nun., Can. 165/R7
King Christian IX Land (reg.), Grld. 161/P3
King Christian X Land (reg.),Grld. 161/Q2
King City, Ca, US 170/B3
King Cove, Ak, US 176/F4
King Frederik VI Coast (reg.), Grld. 161/N3
King Frederik VIII Land (reg.), Grld. 161/Q2
King George (isls.), FrPol. 159/L6
King George Is. (isls.), Qu, Can. 165/J3
King George's (res.), Eng, UK 72/C2
King Leopold (ranges), Austl. 151/B2
King of Prussia, Pa, US 180/C3
King Salmon, Ak, US 176/G4
King William (isl.), Nun., Can. 164/G2
King William's Town, SAfr. 148/D4
Kingaroy, Austl. 156/C4
Kingfisher, Ok, US 171/H4
Kingfisher (co.), Ok, US 179/M14
Kinghorn, Sc, UK 78/C4
Kinglake NP, Austl. 157/G5
Kingman, Ks, US 171/H3
Kingman, Az, US 170/D4
Kingman (reef), Pac., US 159/J4
Kings (riv.), Ca, US 170/C3
Kings (co.), NY, US 181/K9
Kings (peak), Ut, US 170/E2
Kings Canyon NP, Ca, US 170/C3
Kings Langley, Eng, UK 72/B1
King's Lynn, Eng, UK 75/G1
Kings Park, Austl. 154/K6
Kings Point, NY, US 181/L8
King's Seat (hill), Sc, UK 78/C4
Kingsbridge, Eng, UK 74/C6
Kingscote, Austl. 155/H5
Kingscourt, Ire. 73/Q10
Kingsford, Mi, US 172/B2
Kingsport, Tn, US 172/D4
Kingston, Austl. 157/C4
Kingston, Austl. 158/F7
Kingston, On, Can. 172/E2
Kingston, NY, US 172/F3
Kingston (cap.), Jam. 187/G2
Kingston, Pa, US 180/C1
Kingston, Wa, US 177/B2
Kingston S.E., Austl. 157/A3
Kingston upon Hull, Eng, UK 77/H4
Kingston upon Hull (co.), Eng, UK 77/H4
Kingston upon Thames, Eng, UK 72/C2
Kingston upon Thames (bor.), Eng, UK 72/C2
Kingstown (cap.), StV. 183/N9
Kingstree, SC, US 175/J3
Kingsville, Tx, US 174/D5
Kingsville, Md, US 180/B5
Kingswood, Eng, UK 74/D4
Kingussie, Sc, UK 78/B2
Kınık, Turk. 132/A2
Kinkaid (mt.), Ak, US 176/L4
Kinkala, Congo 147/B1
Kinki (prov.), Japan 116/D3
Kinlochewe, Sc, UK 78/A1
Kinlochleven, Sc, UK 78/B3
Kinloss, Sc, UK 78/C1
Kinna, Swe. 80/E3
Kinnairds (pt.), Sc, UK 78/D1
Kinnelon, NJ, US 181/H8
Kinnelon (lake), NJ, US 181/H8
Kinnitty, Ire. 73/Q10
Kino (riv.), Japan 116/D3
Kinoje (riv.), On, Can. 172/D1
Kinomoto, Japan 119/K5
Kinrooi, Belg. 95/E1
Kinross, Sc, UK 78/C4
Kinsach (riv.), Ger. 97/F4
Kinsale, Ire. 73/P11
Kinsarvik, Nor. 80/B1
Kinshasa (cap.), D.R. Congo 147/C1
Kinston, NC, US 175/J3
Kintampo, Gha. 145/E4
Kintnersville, Pa, US 180/C2
Kintore, Sc, UK 78/D2
Kintyre (isl.), Sc, UK 73/R8
Kintzheim, Fr. 98/D1
Kinu (riv.), Japan 117/F2
Kinvarra, Ire. 73/P10
Kinyeti (peak), Sudan 139/M7
Kinzig (riv.), Ger. 82/E4
Kipahulu, Hi, US 166/T10
Kiparissía (gulf), Gre. 89/G4
Kiparissía, Gre. 89/G4
Kipawa (lake), Qu, Can. 172/E2
Kipkarren (riv.), Kenya 146/B2
Kipling, Sk, Can. 169/H3
Kipnuk, Ak, US 176/F4
Kippel, Swi. 98/D5
Kippen, Sc, UK 78/B4
Kippure (peak), Ire. 76/B5
Kipushi, D.R. Congo 147/E3
Kira, Japan 119/M6
Kira Panayía (isl.), Gre. 89/H3
Kirakira, Sol. 158/F6
Kiranomena, Madg. 149/H7
Kīratpur, India 126/B1
Kirazlı, Turk. 89/K2
Kirby, Tx, US 179/U21
Kırcasalih, Turk. 89/K2
Kirchberg, Swi. 98/D3
Kirchberg, Swi. 99/F3
Kirchberg, Ger. 95/G4
Kirchberg, Ger. 97/F1
Kirchberg an der Iller, Ger. 99/G1
Kirchberg an der Jagst, Ger. 96/C4
Kirchdorf, Ger. 93/F3
Kirchdorf an der Krems, Aus. 97/H7
Kirchenlamitz, Ger. 97/E2
Kirchenthumbach, Ger. 97/E3
Kirchheim, Ger. 99/G1
Kirchheim bei München, Ger. 97/E6
Kirchheim unter Teck, Ger. 96/C5
Kirchheimbolanden, Ger. 96/B3
Kirchhundem, Ger. 93/F6
Kirchlengern, Ger. 93/F4
Kirchlinteln, Ger. 93/G3
Kirchsee (lake), Ger. 99/H2
Kirchseeon, Ger. 97/E6
Kirchweidach, Ger. 97/F6
Kirchzarten, Ger. 98/D2
Kirchzell, Ger. 96/C3
Kircudbright (bay), Sc, UK 76/D2
Kirensk, Rus. 107/L4
Kirgiz Steppe (upland), Kaz. 106/F5
Kirgizskiy (mts.), Kyr. 112/B3
Kiriákion, Gre. 89/H3
Kiribati (ctry.) 158/H5
Kırık, Turk. 132/E1
Kırıkhan, Turk. 133/E1
Kırıkkale, Turk. 132/C2
Kırıkkale (prov.), Turk. 132/C2
Kirishi, Rus. 81/Q2
Kirishima-Yaku NP, Japan 116/B5
Kirishima-yama (peak), Japan 116/B5
Kiritimati (Christmas) (isl.), Kiri. 159/K4
Kırkağaç, Turk. 132/A2
Kirkby, Eng, UK 77/F5
Kirkby in Ashfield, Eng, UK 77/G5
Kirkcaldy, Sc, UK 78/C4
Kirkconnel, Sc, UK 78/C6
Kirkcudbright, Sc, UK 76/D2
Kirkee, India 131/K5
Kirkenær, Nor. 80/E1
Kirkintilloch, Sc, UK 78/B5
Kirklees (co.), Eng, UK 77/G4
Kirkkonummi (Kyrkslätt), Fin. 81/L1
Kirkland, Qu, Can. 173/N7
Kirkland (hill), Sc, UK 78/C6
Kirkland Lake, On, Can. 172/D1
Kırklar (peak), Turk. 132/A2
Kirklareli, Turk. 91/H5
Kirklareli (prov.), Turk. 91/H5
Kirkliston, Sc, UK 78/C5
Kirkstone (pass), Eng, UK 77/F3
Kirkūk, Iraq 132/F3
Kirkwall, Sc, UK 73/V14
Kirkwood, SAfr. 148/D4
Kirkwood, De, US 180/C4
Kirn, Ger. 95/G4
Kirov, Rus. 104/E1
Kirov, Rus. 103/L4
Kirovskaya Oblast, Rus. 103/L4

Kirov – Kroko
247

Kirovo-Chepetsk, Rus. 103/L4
Kirovohrad, Ukr. 104/E2
Kirovohrads'ka Oblasti, Ukr. 104/D2
Kirovsk, Rus. 102/G2
Kirriemuir, Sc, UK 78/D3
Kirrweiler, Ger. 96/B4
Kirsanov, Rus. 105/G1
Kirşehir (prov.), Turk. 132/C2
Kırşehir, Turk. 132/C2
Kiruna, Swe. 79/G2
Kiryū, Japan 117/F2
Kisa, Swe. 80/F3
Kisai, Japan 119/D1
Kisakata, Japan 118/A4
Kisangani, D.R. Congo 139/L7
Kisarazu, Japan 117/F3
Kisber, Hun. 83/K5
Kisei, Japan 119/K7
Kiselevsk, Rus. 106/J4
Kishanganj, India 127/F2
Kishangarh, India 131/K3
Kishiwada, Japan 119/H7
Kishorganj, Bang. 127/H3
Kishtwar, India 128/C3
Kishwaukee (riv.), Il, US 177/N15
Kisigo (riv.), Tanz. 146/B4
Kisii, Kenya 146/B3
Kiska (vol.), Ak, US 176/B5
Kiska (isl.), Ak, US 176/B6
Kiskatinnaw (riv.), BC, Can. 168/C2
Kiskitto (lake), Mb, Can. 169/J2
Kiskőrös, Hun. 90/D2
Kiskunfélegyháza, Hun. 90/D2
Kiskunhalas, Hun. 90/D2
Kiskunmajsa, Hun. 90/D2
Kiskunsági Nemzeti NP, Hun. 90/D2
Kislovodsk, Rus. 105/G4
Kismaayo (Chisimayu), Som. 139/P8
Kiso (riv.), Japan 117/E3
Kisogawa, Japan 119/L5
Kisozaki, Japan 119/L5
Kíssamos, Gre. 89/H5
Kissimmee (lake), Fl, US 175/H4
Kissimmee, Fl, US 175/H4
Kissing, Ger. 96/D6
Kississing (lake), Mb, Can. 169/H2
Kisslegg, Ger. 99/F2
Kist, Ger. 96/C3
Kisújszállás, Hun. 90/E2
Kisumu, Kenya 146/B3
Kisvárda, Hun. 83/M4
Kita, Mali 144/C3
Kita (lake), Japan 117/G2
Kita-Ibaraki, Japan 117/G2
Kitaaiki, Japan 119/B1
Kitadaitō (isl.), Japan 117/L8
Kitagata, Japan 119/L5
Kitakami (mts.), Japan 118/B4
Kitakami (riv.), Japan 118/B4
Kitakami, Japan 118/B4
Kitakata, Japan 117/F2
Kitakawabe, Japan 119/D1
Kitakyūshū, Japan 116/B4
Kitale, Kenya 146/B2
Kitami, Japan 118/C2
Kitamimaki, Japan 119/A1
Kitamoto, Japan 119/D1
Kitan (str.), Japan 119/G7
Kitangiri (lake), Tanz. 146/B4
Kitaura, Japan 119/F1
Kitchener, On, Can. 172/D3
Kitgum, Ugan. 146/B2
Kíthira, Gre. 89/H4
Kíthira (isl.), Gre. 89/H4
Kíthnos, Gre. 89/J4
Kíthnos (isl.), Gre. 89/J4
Kitimat Arm (lake), BC, Can. 168/A2
Kitsap (co.), Wa, US 177/B3
Kittatinny (mts.), NJ, US 180/C1
Kittery, Me, US 173/G3
Kittredge, Co, US 179/B3
Kitui, Kenya 146/C3
Kitumbeine (peak), Tanz. 146/C3
Kitwe, Zam. 147/E3
Kitzbühel, Aus. 85/K3
Kitzingen, Ger. 96/D3
Kiunga Marine Nat'l Rsv., Kenya 146/D3
Kiuruvesi, Fin. 102/E3
Kiuyu (pt.), Tanz. 146/C4
Kivalina, Ak, US 176/F2
Kivalo (mts.), Fin. 79/H2
Kivijärvi (lake), Fin. 81/M1
Kiviõli, Est. 81/M2
Kivu (lake), D.R. Congo 146/A3
Kıyıköy, Turk. 91/J5
Kiyokawa, Japan 119/C3
Kiyosu, Japan 119/L5
Kizel, Rus. 103/N4
Kizil (riv.), China 106/H6
Kızılcadağ, Turk. 133/A1
Kızılcahamam, Turk. 132/C1
Kızıldag NP, Turk. 132/B2
Kızılhisar, Turk. 132/B2
Kızılırmak (riv.), Turk. 132/C1
Kızıltepe, Turk. 132/E2
Kızılyaka, Turk. 133/C1
Kizlyar, Rus. 105/H4
Kizu (riv.), Japan 116/E3
Kizu, Japan 119/J6
Kizukuri, Japan 118/B3
Kjerkestinden (peak), Nor. 79/F1
Kjevik (int'l arpt.), Nor. 80/C2
Kjølen (mts.), Nor. 79/E2
Klabava (riv.), Czh. 97/G3
Kladanj, Bosn. 90/D3
Kladno, Czh. 97/H2
Kladovo, Serb. 90/F3
Klagenfurt, Aus. 85/L3
Klaipėda, Lith. 81/J4
Klamath (mts.), Ca,Or, US 168/C5
Klamath (riv.), Ca,Or, US 168/C5
Klamath Falls, Or, US 168/C5
Klangenan, Indo. 122/C5
Klarälven (riv.), Swe. 79/E3
Klarup, Den. 80/D3
Klášterec nad Ohří, Czh. 97/G2
Klatovy, Czh. 97/G4
Klaus, Aus. 99/F3
Klausen (Chiusa), It. 99/H4
Klausenpass (pass), Swi. 99/E4
Klawock, Ak, US 176/M4
Klaza (mtn.), Yk, Can. 176/L3
Klazienaveen, Neth. 92/E3
Kleinblittersdorf, Ger. 95/G5
Kleine Elster (riv.), Ger. 83/G3
Kleine Emme (riv.), Swi. 98/E4
Kleine Gete (riv.), Belg. 95/D2
Kleine Laber (riv.), Ger. 97/F5
Kleine Nete (riv.), Belg. 95/D1
Kleinheubach, Ger. 96/C3
Kleinlützel, Swi. 98/D3
Kleinmachnow, Ger. 82/Q7
Kleinmond, SAfr. 148/L11
Kleinolifants (riv.), SAfr. 148/Q12
Kleinrinderfeld, Ger. 96/C3
Kleinsee, SAfr. 148/B3
Kleinwallstadt, Ger. 96/C3
Kleinwinternheim, Ger. 96/B3
Kleppe, Nor. 80/A2
Kleppestø, Nor. 80/A1
Klerksdorp, SAfr. 148/D2
Klet' (peak), Czh. 97/H5
Kleve, Ger. 92/D5
Klina, Serb. 90/E4
Klingenberg am Main, Ger. 96/C3
Klingenmünster, Ger. 96/B4
Klingenthal, Ger. 97/F2
Klínovec (peak), Czh. 97/F2
Klintehamn, Swe. 80/H3
Klintsy, Rus. 104/E1
Klip (riv.), SAfr. 148/E2
Klippan, Swe. 80/E3
Klipplaat, SAfr. 148/D4
Klisura, Bul. 89/J1
Klitmøller, Den. 80/C3
Kljajićevo, Serb. 90/D3
Ključ, Bosn. 90/C3
Kłodawa, Pol. 83/K2
Kłodzko, Pol. 83/J3
Klöntaler-See (lake), Swi. 99/E3
Klosterbach (riv.), Ger. 93/F3
Klosterlechfeld, Ger. 99/G1
Klosterneuburg, Aus. 91/N7
Klosters, Swi. 99/F4
Klosterwappen (peak), Aus. 83/H5
Kloten, Swi. 99/E3
Klötze, Ger. 82/F2
Kluane NP, Yk, Can. 176/K3
Kluczbork, Pol. 83/K3
Klukwan, Ak, US 176/L3
Klundert, Neth. 92/B5
Klyaz'ma (riv.), Rus. 102/J4
Klyuchevskaya (peak), Rus. 107/S4
Knäred, Swe. 80/E3
Knaresborough, Eng, UK 77/G3
Knee (lake), Mb, Can. 169/K2
Knetzgau, Ger. 96/D3
Knezha, Bul. 91/G4
Knight (inlet), BC, Can. 168/B3
Knighton, Wal, UK 74/C2
Knightsen, Ca, US 177/L11
Knin, Cro. 90/C3
Knittelfeld, Aus. 85/L3
Knittlingen, Ger. 96/B4
Knivsta, Swe. 80/G2
Knížecí Stolec (peak), Czh. 97/H5
Knížecí Strom (peak), Czh. 97/F3
Knjaževac, Serb. 90/F4
Knob (cape), Austl. 154/C5
Knob (peak), Phil. 123/F1
Knobby (pt.), Austl. 154/B4
Knoch (hill), Sc, UK 78/D1
Knockcloghrim, NI, UK 76/B2
Knösen (pt.), Swe. 80/E4
Knøsen (peak), Den. 80/D3
Knosós (Knossos) (ruin), Gre. 89/J5
Knottingley, Eng, UK 77/G4
Knott's Berry Farm, Ca, US 178/G8
Knowsley (co.), Eng, UK 77/F5
Knox (coast), Ant. 202/G
Knox (cape), BC, Can. 176/M4
Knox City, Tx, US 171/H4
Knoxville, Tn, US 172/D5
Knutsford, Eng, UK 77/F5
Knysna, SAfr. 148/C4
Ko (riv.), Sen. 144/B3
Ko-saki (pt.), Japan 116/A3
Ko Samut NP, Thai. 120/C3
Koali, Hi, US 166/T10
Koani, Tanz. 146/C4
Koāth, India 127/E3
Kobayashi, Japan 116/B5
Kōbe, Japan 119/H6
København (int'l arpt.), Den. 80/E4
Kobern-Gondorf, Ger. 95/G3
Kobipato (peak), Indo. 123/G4
Koblach, Aus. 99/F3
Koblenz, Swi. 99/E2
Koblenz, Ger. 95/G3
Kobryn, Bela. 83/N2
Kobuchizawa, Japan 119/A2
Kobuk (riv.), Ak, US 176/G2
Kobuk, Ak, US 176/G2
Kobuk Valley NP, Ak, US 176/G2
Kobushi-ga-take (peak), Japan 117/F3
Kocába (riv.), Czh. 97/H3
Kocaeli (prov.), Turk. 91/J5
Koçalı, Turk. 132/D2
Kočani, FYROM 89/H2
Kocapınar, Turk. 132/E2
Kočevje, Slov. 85/L4
Koch (isl.), Nun., Can. 165/J2
Koch'ang, SKor. 115/D5
Koch'ang, SKor. 115/D5
Kochel am See, Ger. 99/H2
Kochelsee (lake), Ger. 99/H2
Kocher (riv.), Ger. 85/H2
Kocherinovo, Bul. 89/H1
Kōchi, Japan 116/C4
Kōchi (pref.), Japan 116/C4
Kodaira, Japan 119/C2
Kodala, India 124/E4
Kodama, Japan 119/C1
Kodarmā, India 127/E3
Kodiak, Ak, US 176/H4
Kodiak (isl.), Ak, US 176/H4
Kodinār, India 131/K4
Kodomari, Japan 118/B3
Kodry (hills), Mol. 91/H2
Koekelare, Belg. 94/B1
Koel (riv.), India 124/D3
Koes, Namb. 148/B2
Koesan, SKor. 115/D4
Koetari (riv.), Sur. 195/G4
Kofa (mts.), Az, US 170/D4
Kofarnihon (riv.), Taj. 129/E5
Kofçaz, Turk. 91/H5
Koffiefontein, SAfr. 148/D3
Kofiau (isl.), Indo. 123/G4
Koforidua, Gha. 145/E5
Kōfu, Japan 117/F3
Koga, Japan 117/F2
Koganei, Japan 119/D2
Køge (bay), Den. 80/E4
Kogi, Nga. 145/G4
Kogon (riv.), Gui. 138/C5
Kōgum (isl.), SKor. 115/D5
Kohāt, Pak. 128/A3
Kohīma, India 125/F2
Kohoku, Japan 119/K5
Kohout (peak), Czh. 97/H5
Kohtla-Järve, Est. 81/M2
Kohŭng, SKor. 115/D5
Kohunlich (ruin), Mex. 186/D2
Koímisis, Gre. 89/H2
Koito (riv.), Japan 119/D3
Koiva (riv.), Lat. 81/M3
Kōje (isl.), SKor. 115/E5
Kojonup, Austl. 154/C5
Kojšovská (peak), Slvk. 83/L4
Kok (riv.), Myan. 120/B1
Kōka, Japan 119/K6
Kokai (riv.), Japan 119/E2
Kōkar (isl.), Fin. 81/J3
Kokemäenjoki (riv.), Fin. 81/J1
Kokhonak, Ak, US 176/H4
Kokkola (Karleby), Fin. 102/D3
Koko Head (pt.), Hi, US 166/W13
Kokomo, In, US 172/C3
Kokrajhar, India 127/H2
Kokrines, Ak, US 176/H3
Koksan, NKor. 115/D3
Kökshetaū, Kaz. 129/E2
Kökshetaū (obl.), Kaz. 129/E2
Koksijde, Belg. 94/B1
Koksoak (riv.), Qu, Can. 165/K3
Kokstad, SAfr. 148/E3
Kokubu, Japan 116/B5
Kola (pen.), Rus. 202/D
Kola (riv.), Rus. 102/G1
Kolaka, Indo. 123/F4
Kolār, India 124/C5
Kolāras, India 126/A3
Kolašin, Mont. 90/D4
Kolbäck, Swe. 80/G2
Kol'bay (peak), Kaz. 129/B4
Kolbermoor, Ger. 85/K3
Kolbuszowa, Pol. 83/L3
Kolda, Sen. 144/B3
Kolda (pol. reg.), Sen. 144/B3
Kolding, Den. 80/C4
Kölen (mts.), Swe. 79/E2
Kolgompya (cape), Rus. 81/N2
Kolguyev (isl.), Rus. 202/C
Kolhāpur, India 131/K5
Koliba (riv.), Gui. 144/B3
Koliganek, Ak, US 176/G4
Kolín, Czh. 83/H3
Kolkasrags (pt.), Lat. 81/K3
Kolkata (Calcutta), India 127/G4
Kolkata (Calcutta) (int'l arpt.), India 127/G4
Kollbach (riv.), Ger. 97/F5
Kollnburg, Ger. 97/F4
Kollum, Neth. 92/D2
Köln (Cologne), Ger. 95/F2
Kolno, Pol. 83/L2
Koło, Pol. 104/A1
Koloa, Hi, US 166/S10
Kołobrzeg, Pol. 80/F4
Kolokani, Mali 144/C3
Kolomna, Rus. 102/H5
Kolomyya, Ukr. 91/G1
Kolondiéba, Mali 144/D4
Kolossa (riv.), Mali 144/D3
Kolpashevo, Rus. 106/J4
Kolpino, Rus. 103/T7
Kolsva, Swe. 80/F2
Kolubara (riv.), Serb. 90/D3
Koluszki, Pol. 83/K3
Kolva (riv.), Rus. 103/N2
Kolwezi, D.R. Congo 147/E3
Kolyma (riv.), Rus. 109/Q3
Kolyma (range), Rus. 109/Q3
Kolyma Lowland (plain), Rus. 107/R2
Kom (peak), Bul. 89/H1
Koma (riv.), Japan 119/C2
Komádi, Hun. 90/E2
Komadugu Gana (riv.), Niger.,Nga. 138/H5
Komadugu Yobe (riv.), Nga. 145/H3
Komae, Japan 119/D2
Komagane, Japan 117/E3
Komaki, Japan 119/L5
Komandorskiye (isls.), Rus. 109/R4
Komárno, Slvk. 90/D2
Komárom, Hun. 90/D2
Komárom-Esztergom (prov.), Hun. 90/D2
Komatirivier (riv.), SAfr. 148/Q13
Komatke, Az, US 179/R19
Komatsu, Japan 116/E2
Komatsu (int'l arpt.), Japan 116/E2
Komatsushima, Japan 116/D3
Kombissiri, Burk. 145/E3
Kome (isl.), Tanz. 146/B3
Komi, Resp., Rus. 103/M2
Komi-Permyatskiy Aut. Okrug, Rus. 103/M2
Komló, Hun. 90/D2
Kommetjie, SAfr. 148/L11
Kommunizma (peak), Taj. 129/F5
Komodo (isl.), Indo. 123/E5
Komodo Island NP, Indo. 123/E5
Komoé (riv.), C.d'Iv. 138/E6
Komono, Japan 119/L5
Komoran (isl.), Indo. 123/J5
Komoro, Japan 119/A1
Komotiní, Gre. 89/J2
Kompasberg (peak), SAfr. 148/D3
Komsomolets (isl.), Rus. 109/J1
Komsomol'skiy, Rus. 103/P2
Kömür (pt.), Turk. 89/K3
Kon Tum, Viet. 120/D3
Konakovo, Rus. 102/H4
Konan, Japan 119/C1
Kōnan, Japan 119/L5
Kōnan, Japan 119/K6
Konār (riv.), India 127/E4
Konār (res.), India 127/E4
Konar (riv.), Afg. 128/A2
Konaweha (riv.), Indo. 123/F4
Konda, Japan 119/H6
Kondagaon, India 124/D4
Kondinin, Austl. 154/C5
Kondoa, Tanz. 146/B4
Kondopoga, Rus. 102/G3
Kondūz, Afg. 129/E5
Kong, C.d'Iv. 144/D4
Kong (riv.), Laos 120/D3
Kong (isl.), Camb. 120/C4
Kong Miao, China 114/D4
Kongiganak, Ak, US 176/F4
Kongju, SKor. 115/D4
Kongō-zan (peak), Japan 119/J7
Kongolo, D.R. Congo 147/E2
Kongoussi, Burk. 145/E3
Kongsberg, Nor. 80/C2
Kongsvinger, Nor. 80/E1
Kongur (peak), China 129/G5
Koniecpol, Pol. 83/K3
Königs Wusterhausen, Ger. 82/Q7
Königsberg in Bayern, Ger. 96/D2
Königsberg-Stein, Ger. 96/B5
Königsbronn, Ger. 96/D5
Königsbrunn, Ger. 99/G1
Königsdorf, Ger. 99/H2
Königsfeld im Schwarzwald, Ger. 99/E1
Königslutter am Elm, Ger. 93/H4
Königstein im Taunus, Ger. 96/B2
Königswinter, Ger. 95/G2
Konin, Pol. 83/K2
Kónitsa, Gre. 89/G2
Köniz, Swi. 98/D4
Konjic, Bosn. 90/C4
Könkämäeno (riv.), Fin. 102/D1
Konkouré (riv.), Gui. 144/B4
Konnevesi, Fin. 102/E3
Konolfingen, Swi. 98/D4
Kōnosu, Japan 119/D1
Konotop, Ukr. 104/E2
Konqi (riv.), China 106/J5
Konsen (plat.), Japan 118/D2
Końskie, Pol. 83/L3
Konstancin-Jeziorna, Pol. 83/L2
Konstantynów Łódzki, Pol. 83/K3
Konstanz, Ger. 99/F2
Kontich, Belg. 95/D1
Kontiolahti, Fin. 102/F3
Konuralp, Turk. 91/K5
Kóny, Hun. 90/C2
Konya, Turk. 132/C2
Konya (prov.), Turk. 132/C2
Konz, Ger. 95/F4
Koondrook, Austl. 157/C2
Koorawatha, Austl. 157/D2
Koorda, Austl. 154/C4
Kootenai (riv.), Id, US 168/D3
Kootenay (lake), BC, Can. 164/E3
Kootenay NP, BC, Can. 168/D3
Kootingal, Austl. 157/D1
Kop-Geçidi (pass), Turk. 132/E2
Kopāganj, India 126/D2
Kopargaon, India 131/K5
Kópavogur, Ice. 79/N7
Kope (peak), C.d'Iv. 144/D5
Köpenick, Ger. 82/Q7
Koper, Slov. 85/K4
Kopervik, Nor. 80/A2
Kopeysk, Rus. 103/P5
Kopfing im Innkreis, Aus. 97/G6
Köping, Swe. 80/G2
Kopondei (cape), Indo. 123/F5
Koporskiy (bay), Rus. 81/N2
Koppang, Nor. 80/D1
Kopparberg, Swe. 80/F2
Kopparberg (co.), Swe. 79/E3
Koppies, SAfr. 148/D2
Koprivnica, Cro. 90/C2
Koprivshtitsa, Bul. 89/J1
Köprü (riv.), Turk. 133/B1
Köprülü, Turk. 133/C1
Köprülü Kanyon NP, Turk. 132/B2
Kor (riv.), Iran 130/F2
Kora, India 126/C2
Kōra, Japan 119/K5
Kora NP, Kenya 146/C3
Korab (peak), Alb. 89/G2
Koráb (peak), Czh. 97/G4
Korakuen Garden, Japan 116/C3
Koraluk (riv.), Nf, Can. 165/K3
Korana (riv.), Cro. 85/L4
Koraput, India 124/D4
Korba, India 126/D4
Korba, Tun. 142/M6
Korbach, Ger. 93/F6
Korçë, Alb. 89/G2
Korčula (isl.), Cro. 88/E1
Korčulanski Kanal (chan.), Cro. 88/E1
Kord Kūy, Iran 130/F1
Kordel, Ger. 95/F4
Korea (bay), China,NKor. 115/B3
Korea (str.), Japan,SKor. 116/A4
Korea, North (ctry.) 115/D2
Korea, South (ctry.) 115/D4
Korean Folk Village, SKor. 115/G7
Korenovsk, Rus. 104/F3
Korhogo, C.d'Iv. 144/D4
Korinós, Gre. 89/H2
Kórinthos (Corinth), Gre. 89/H4
Kőris-hegy (peak), Hun. 90/C2
Kōriyama, Japan 117/G2
Korizo, Passe de (pass), Chad 138/J3
Korkodon (riv.), Rus. 107/R3
Korkuteli, Turk. 133/B1
Korla, China 112/E3
Kormakiti (cape), Cyp. 133/C2
Körmend, Hun. 85/M3
Kornat (isl.), Cro. 90/B4
Körner, Ger. 93/H6
Korneuburg, Aus. 91/N7
Korntal-Münchingen, Ger. 96/C5
Kornwestheim, Ger. 96/C5
Koro (sea), Fiji 158/G6
Köroğlu (peak), Turk. 91/K5
Korogwe, Tanz. 146/C4
Koroit, Austl. 157/B3
Koronadal, Phil. 121/D6
Korónia (lake), Gre. 89/H2
Koronowo, Pol. 83/J2
Koropion, Gre. 89/N9
Koror (cap.), Palau 158/C4
Körös (riv.), Hun. 90/E2
Korosten', Ukr. 104/D2
Korostyshiv, Ukr. 104/D2
Korotaikha (riv.), Rus. 103/P1
Korovin (vol.), Ak, US 176/D5
Korpo (Korppoo), Fin. 81/J1
Korsakov, Rus. 113/R2
Korschenbroich, Ger. 92/D6
Korsør, Den. 80/D4
Korsze, Pol. 81/J4
Kortemark, Belg. 94/C1
Kortenaken, Belg. 95/E2
Kortenberg, Belg. 95/D2
Kortessem, Belg. 95/E2
Kortrijk, Belg. 94/C2
Korup, PN de, Camr. 145/H5
Koryak (range), Rus. 109/R3
Koryakskiy Aut. Okrug, Rus. 107/S3
Koryazhma, Rus. 103/K3
Kōryō, Japan 119/J6
Koryŏng, SKor. 115/E5
Kós (isl.), Gre. 132/A2
Kós, Gre. 132/A2
Kosai, Japan 117/E3
Kosai, Japan 119/A2
Kösching, Ger. 97/E5
Kościan, Pol. 83/J2
Kościerzyna, Pol. 80/G4
Kosciusko (mt.), Austl. 157/D3
Kosciusko, Ms, US 175/F3
Kosciusko NP, Austl. 157/D3
Köse, Turk. 132/D1
Kosei, Japan 119/K6
Koshigaya, Japan 117/F3
Köshim (riv.), Kaz. 129/B3
Koshiki (isls.), Japan 117/K5
Kosi, India 126/A2
Kosi (zone), Nepal 127/F2
Kosi (riv.), India 124/E2
Košice, Slvk. 83/L4
Košický (pol. reg.), Slvk. 83/L4
Koskinoú, Gre. 132/B2
Kosoba (peak), Kaz. 129/G3
Kosŏng, SKor. 115/E5
Kosŏng, NKor. 115/E3
Kosovo (prov.), Serb. 90/E4
Kosovo Polje, Serb. 90/E4
Kosovska Kamenica, Serb. 90/E4
Kosovska Mitrovica, Serb. 90/E4
Kosový (riv.), Czh. 97/F3
Kosrae (isl.), Micr. 158/F4
Kossi (prov.), Burk. 144/D3
Kossou, Barrage de (dam), C.d'Iv. 144/D5
Kossou, Lac de (lake), C.d'Iv. 138/D6
Kosta, Swe. 80/F3
Kostelec nad Černými Lesy, Czh. 97/H3
Koster, SAfr. 148/D2
Kostinbrod, Bul. 89/H1
Kostopil', Ukr. 104/C2
Kostroma (riv.), Rus. 102/J4
Kostroma, Rus. 102/J4
Kostromskaya Oblast, Rus. 102/J4
Kostrzyn, Pol. 83/H2
Kostrzyn, Pol. 83/J2
Kostyantynivka, Ukr. 104/F2
Kosuge, Japan 119/B2
Kos'va (riv.), Rus. 103/N4
Kos'yu (riv.), Rus. 103/N2
Koszalin, Pol. 80/G4
Kőszeg, Hun. 85/M3
Kot Addu, Pak. 128/A4
Kot Kapūra, India 128/C4
Kot Mūmin, Pak. 128/B4
Kot Rādha Kishan, Pak. 128/C4
Kot Samāba, Pak. 128/A5
Kota, India 126/D4
Kota, India 131/L3
Kōta, Japan 119/M6
Kota Baharu, Malay. 125/H6
Kota Kinabalu, Malay. 123/E2
Kotaagung, Indo. 122/B5
Kotabaru, Indo. 123/E4
Kotabumi, Indo. 122/B4
Kotapād, India 124/D4
Kotdwāra, India 126/B1
Kotel, Bul. 89/K1
Kotel'nich, Rus. 103/L4
Kotel'nikovo, Rus. 105/G3
Kotel'nyy (isl.), Rus. 107/P2
Kothagūdem, India 124/D4
Köthen, Ger. 82/F3
Kotido, Ugan. 146/B2
Kotka, Fin. 81/M1
Kotlas, Rus. 103/K3
Kotli Lohārān, Pak. 128/C3
Kotlik, Ak, US 176/F3
Kotlin (isl.), Rus. 103/S7
Kotō, Japan 119/K5
Kotoka (int'l arpt.), Gha. 145/E5
Kotor, Mont. 90/D4
Kotor Varoš, Bosn. 90/C3
Kotovo, Rus. 105/H2
Kotovsk, Rus. 105/G1
Kotri, Pak. 131/J3
Kottayam, India 124/C6
Kotto (riv.), CAfr. 139/K6
Kotuy (riv.), Rus. 109/K3
Kotzebue, Ak, US 176/F2
Kotzebue (sound), Ak, US 176/E2
Kötzting, Ger. 97/F4
Kouandé, Ben. 145/F4
Kouchibouguac NP, NB, Can. 173/H2
Koudougou, Burk. 145/E3
Koufonísion (isl.), Gre. 89/J5
Kougarok (mtn.), Ak, US 176/E2
Koukdjuak (riv.), Nun., Can. 165/J2
Koula-Moutou, Gabon 138/H8
Koulikoro, Mali 144/D3
Koulikoro (pol. reg.), Mali 144/C3
Koulountou (riv.), Sen. 144/B3
Koumbi Saleh (ruin), Mrta. 144/D3
Koumi, Japan 119/A1
Koumra, Chad 139/J6
Koundara, Gui. 144/B3
Kounradskiy, Kaz. 129/G3
Kountze, Tx, US 171/J5
Koupela, Burk. 145/E3
Kouritenga (prov.), Burk. 145/E3
Kourou, FrG. 193/H2
Koussi (peak), Chad 139/J4
Koutiala, Mali 144/D3
Kouvola, Fin. 81/M1
Kovačica, Serb. 90/E3
Kovada Gölü NP, Turk. 132/B2
Kovashi (riv.), Rus. 103/S7
Kovdozero (lake), Rus. 79/J2
Kovel', Ukr. 104/C2
Kovilj, Serb. 90/E3
Kovilpatti, India 124/C6
Kovrov, Rus. 102/J4
Kovūr, India 124/C5
Kovylkino, Rus. 105/G1
Kowanyama Aboriginal Community, Austl. 156/A1
Kowkcheh (riv.), Afg. 131/J1
Kowl-e Namaksār (lake), Afg. 129/D6
Kowloon, China 121/B3
Kowt-e 'Ashrow, Afg. 131/J2
Kōyaguchi, Japan 119/J7
Kōyama, Japan 116/B5
Koynare, Bul. 91/G4
Koyuk, Ak, US 176/F3
Koyukuk (riv.), Ak, US 176/H2
Koyukuk, Ak, US 176/G3
Koyukuk, South Fork (riv.), Ak, US 176/H2
Kozakai, Japan 119/M6
Kōzaki, Japan 119/E2
Kozaklı, Turk. 132/C2
Kozan, Turk. 132/C2
Kozáni, Gre. 89/G2
Kozara NP, Aus. 90/C3
Kozhikode (Calicut), India 124/C5
Kozhozero (lake), Rus. 102/H3
Kozhva (riv.), Rus. 103/M2
Kozienice, Pol. 83/L3
Kozloduy, Bul. 91/F4
Kozlu, Turk. 91/K5
Kozluk, Turk. 132/E2
Koźmin, Pol. 83/J3
Koznitsa (peak), Bul. 89/H1
Kōzu (isl.), Japan 117/F3
Kożuchów, Pol. 83/H3
Kozyatyn, Ukr. 104/D2
Kpalimé, Togo 145/F5
Kpandu, Gha. 145/F5
Kpémé, Togo 145/F5
Kra (isth.), Myan. 125/G6
Kraai (riv.), SAfr. 148/D3
Kraaifontein, SAfr. 148/L10
Krabi, Thai. 120/B4
Kragerø, Nor. 80/C2
Kragujevac, Serb. 90/E3
Kraiburg am Inn, Ger. 97/F6
Kraichbach (riv.), Ger. 96/B4
Kraichgau (reg.), Ger. 85/H2
Krailling, Ger. 97/E6
Krakatau (vol.), Indo. 122/C5
Kraków, Pol. 83/K3
Kralendijk, NAnt. 194/D1
Kraljevo, Serb. 90/E4
Kralkızı (dam), Turk. 132/E2
Královéhradecký (pol. reg.), Czh. 83/H3
Kralovice, Czh. 97/G3
Kralupy nad Vltavou, Czh. 97/H2
Kramators'k, Ukr. 104/F2
Kramfors, Swe. 79/F3
Krammer (chan.), Neth. 92/B5
Kranéa Elassónos, Gre. 89/G3
Kranebitten (int'l arpt.), Aus. 99/H3
Kranenburg, Ger. 92/D5
Kranídhion, Gre. 89/H4
Kranj, Slov. 85/L3
Kranskop, SAfr. 149/E3
Krapkowice, Pol. 83/J3
Kraslice, Czh. 97/F2
Kraśnik, Pol. 83/M3
Kraśnik Fabryczny, Pol. 83/M3
Krasnoarmeysk, Rus. 105/H2
Krasnodar, Rus. 104/F3
Krasnodar (int'l arpt.), Rus. 104/F3
Krasnodarskiy Kray, Rus. 106/D5
Krasnogorsk, Rus. 103/W9
Krasnohrad, Ukr. 104/E2
Krasnokamensk, Rus. 113/L1
Krasnokamsk, Rus. 103/M4
Krasnoslobodsk, Rus. 105/H2
Krasnotur'insk, Rus. 106/G4
Krasnoural'sk, Rus. 103/P4
Krasnowodsk (int'l arpt.), Trkm. 105/K4
Krasnowodsk (Türkmenbashi), Trkm. 105/K5
Krasnoyarsk, Rus. 106/K4
Krasnoyarskiy Kray, Rus. 106/J4
Krasnyy Kut, Rus. 105/H2
Krasnyy Luch, Ukr. 104/F2
Krasnyy Sulin, Rus. 104/G3
Kratovo, FYROM 89/H1
Krautheim, Ger. 96/C4
Kravanh (mts.), Camb. 125/H5
Kreb en Nâga (cliff), Mali 140/D5
Kreck (riv.), Ger. 96/D2
Krefeld, Ger. 92/D6
Kreiensen, Ger. 93/G5
Kremastón (lake), Gre. 89/G3
Křemelna (riv.), Czh. 97/G4
Kremenchuk, Ukr. 104/E2
Kremenchuts'ke Vodoskhovyshche (res.), Ukr. 104/E2
Kremlin, Rus. 103/W9
Kremmen, Ger. 82/Q6
Kremmling, Co, US 170/F2
Krempe, Ger. 93/G1
Krems an der Donau, Aus. 83/H4
Kremsmünster, Aus. 97/H6
Krenglbach, Aus. 97/G6
Kresgeville, Pa, US 180/C2
Kresna, Bul. 89/H2
Kressbronn am Bodensee, Ger. 99/F2
Kresta (gulf), Rus. 107/T3
Kréstena, Gre. 89/G4
Kretinga, Lith. 81/J4
Kreuzau, Ger. 95/F2
Kreuzberg (peak), Ger. 96/C2
Kreuzlingen, Swi. 99/F2
Kreuztal, Ger. 95/G2
Kreuzwertheim, Ger. 96/C3
Kría Vrísi, Gre. 89/H2
Kribi, Camr. 138/G7
Krieglach, Aus. 85/L3
Kriens, Swi. 99/E3
Kriftel, Ger. 96/B2
Kril'on (pen.), Rus. 118/B1
Kril'on (cape), Rus. 118/C1
Krimpen aan de IJssel, Neth. 92/B5
Krinídhes, Gre. 89/J2
Kriós (cape), Gre. 89/H5
Krishna (riv.), India 124/D4
Krishnagiri, India 124/C5
Krishnanagar, India 127/G4
Kristdala, Swe. 80/G3
Kristiansand, Nor. 80/B2
Kristianstad, Swe. 80/F3
Kristianstad (co.), Swe. 79/E4
Kristianstad (int'l arpt.), Swe. 80/F4
Kristiansund, Nor. 79/C3
Kristinehamn, Swe. 80/F2
Kriva Palanka, FYROM 89/H1
Krk (isl.), Cro. 90/B3
Krk, Cro. 90/B3
Krnov, Czh. 83/J3
Krokom, Swe. 79/E3

248

Króko – Lagho

Krókos, Gre. 89/G2
Krolevets', Ukr. 104/E2
Krombach, Ger. 96/C2
Kroměříž, Czh. 83/J4
Kronach, Ger. 97/E2
Kronberg im Taunus, Ger. 96/B2
Kronoberg (co.), Swe. 79/E4
Kronshtadt, Rus. 103/S6
Kronstorf, Aus. 97/H6
Kroombit Tops NP, Austl. 156/C4
Kroonstad, SAfr. 148/D2
Kropotkin, Rus. 105/G3
Kropp, Ger. 80/C4
Krosno, Pol. 83/L4
Krosno Odrzańskie, Pol. 83/H2
Krotoszyn, Pol. 83/J3
Krottenkopf (peak), Aus. 99/G3
Krousón, Gre. 89/J5
Kröv, Ger. 95/G4
Krško, Slov. 85/L4
Kruckau (riv.), Ger. 93/G1
Kruger NP, SAfr. 149/E2
Krugersdorp, SAfr. 148/P13
Kruglitsa (peak), Rus. 103/N5
Kruibeke, Belg. 92/B6
Kruisfontein, SAfr. 148/D4
Krujë, Alb. 89/F2
Krumbach, Ger. 99/G1
Krummenau, Swi. 99/F3
Krumovgrad, Bul. 89/J2
Krün, Ger. 99/H3
Krupina, Slvk. 90/D1
Kruså, Den. 80/C4
Krusenstern (cape), Ak, US 176/F2
Kruševac, Serb. 90/E4
Kruševo, FYROM 89/G2
Krušné Hory (Erzgebirge) (mts.), Czh.,Ger. 85/K1
Kruszwica, Pol. 83/K2
Kruzof (isl.), Ak, US 176/L4
Krychaw, Bela. 104/D1
Krym, Aut. Rep., Ukr. 104/E3
Krymsk, Rus. 104/F3
Krynica, Pol. 83/L4
Kryvyy Rih, Ukr. 91/L2
Krzna (riv.), Pol. 83/M3
Krzyż, Pol. 83/J2
Ksar el Kebir, Mor. 142/B2
Ksar Hellal, Tun. 142/M7
Ksel (peak), Alg. 141/F2
Ksour Essef, Tun. 142/M7
Ktima, Cyp. 133/C2
Ku-Ring-Gai NP, Austl. 156/H8
Ku Sathan (peak), Thai. 120/C2
Kuah, Malay. 120/B5
Kuala Belait, Bru. 122/D3
Kuala Dungun, Malay. 122/B3
Kuala Kerai, Malay. 125/H6
Kuala Lipis, Malay. 122/B3
Kuala Lumpur (cap.), Malay. 122/B3
Kuala Pilah, Malay. 122/B3
Kuala Selangor, Malay. 122/B3
Kuala Terengganu, Malay. 125/H6
Kualapuu, Hi, US 166/T10
Kuancheng, China 114/D2
Kuandian, China 115/C2
Kuantan, Malay. 122/B3
Kuban' (riv.), Rus. 106/D5
Kubaysah, Iraq 132/E3
Kubenskoye (lake), Rus. 102/H4
Kubokawa, Japan 116/C4
Kubrat, Bul. 91/H4
Kučevo, Serb. 90/E3
Kuchen (peak), Aus. 99/G3
Kuchen, Ger. 96/C5
Kuching, Malay. 122/D3
Kuchino (isl.), Japan 117/K6
Kuchinoerabu (isl.), Japan 116/A5
Kuchl, Aus. 85/K3
Küçükbahçe, Turk. 89/K3
Küçükkuyu, Turk. 89/K3
Kudamatsu, Japan 116/B3
Kudat, Malay. 123/E2
Kudus, Indo. 122/D5
Kudymkar, Rus. 103/M4
Kufrah (oasis), Libya 139/K3
Kufrinjah, Jor. 133/D3
Kufstein, Aus. 85/K3
Kugluktuk, Nun., Can. 164/E2
Kuhardt, Ger. 96/B4
Kühbach, Ger. 96/E6
Kuhmo, Fin. 102/F2
Kuhmoinen, Fin. 81/L1
Kuhn, Il, US 179/H8
Kūhpāyeh, Iran 130/F2
Kuinder of Tjonger (riv.), Neth. 92/C3
Kuito, Ang. 147/C3
Kuiu (isl.), Ak, US 164/C3
Kujawsko-Pomorskie (prov.), Pol. 83/K2
Kujawy (reg.), Pol. 83/K2
Kuji, Japan 118/B3
Kujū-san (peak), Japan 116/B4
Kujūkuri, Japan 119/E2
Kukalaya (riv.), Nic. 187/E3
Kuki, Japan 117/F2
Kukizaki, Japan 119/E2
Kukkia (lake), Fin. 81/L1
Kūl (riv.), Iran 130/G3
Kula, Bul. 90/F4
Kula, Serb. 90/D3
Kula Kangri (peak), Bhu. 127/H1
Kulachi, Pak. 128/A4
Kulai, Malay. 122/B3
Kulal (mt.), Kenya 146/C2
Kulaly (isl.), Kaz. 105/J3
Kulandag (mts.), Kaz. 129/B4
Kuldīga, Lat. 81/J3
Kulebaki, Rus. 102/J5
Kulgām, India 128/C3
Kulin, Austl. 154/C5
Kullen (cape), Swe. 80/E3
Kullu, India 128/D4
Kulmbach, Ger. 97/E2
Kŭlob, Taj. 131/J1
Kuloy (riv.), Rus. 103/J2
Kulpahār, India 126/B3
Kulpmont, Pa, US 180/B2
Kulpsville, Pa, US 180/C3
Kul'sary, Kaz. 105/K3
Külsheim, Ger. 96/C3
Kulsi (riv.), India 127/H2
Kulti, India 127/F4
Kulunda (lake), Rus. 129/G2
Kulunda, Rus. 129/G2
Kum (riv.), SKor. 115/D4
Kuma (riv.), Rus. 106/E5
Kumagaya, Japan 117/F2
Kumaishi, Japan 118/A2
Kumamoto, Japan 116/B4
Kumamoto (int'l arpt.), Japan 116/B4
Kumamoto (pref.), Japan 116/B4
Kumano (riv.), Japan 116/D4
Kumano, Japan 116/E4
Kumanovo, FYROM 89/G1
Kumār (riv.), Bang. 127/G4
Kumasi, Gha. 145/E5
Kumatori, Japan 119/H7
Kumba, Camr. 138/G7
Kumbia, Austl. 156/C4
Kumbo, Camr. 138/H6
Kŭmch'on, SKor. 115/F6
Kumé (isl.), Japan 121/E2
Kumertau, Rus. 105/K1
Kumgang-san (peak), NKor. 115/E3
Kŭmho (riv.), SKor. 115/E5
Kumi, Ugan. 146/B2
Kumi, SKor. 115/E4
Kumihama, Japan 119/G4
Kumiyama, Japan 119/J6
Kumkale, Turk. 91/H6
Kumköy, Turk. 91/J5
Kumla, Swe. 80/F2
Kumluca, Turk. 133/B1
Kümmersbruck, Ger. 97/E4
Kumo, Nga. 138/H5
Kumon (range), Myan. 125/G2
Kŭmsan, SKor. 115/D4
Kumta, India 131/K6
Kunashiri (isl.), Rus. 107/Q5
Kūnch, India 126/B3
Kunda, India 126/C3
Kundapura (Coondapoor), India 131/K6
Kundarkhi, India 126/B1
Kundelungu, PN de, D.R. Congo 147/E3
Kundiān, Pak. 128/A3
Kundla, India 131/K4
Kungälv, Swe. 80/D3
Kungsangen (int'l arpt.), Swe. 80/G2
Kungsbacka, Swe. 80/E3
Kungshamn, Swe. 80/D2
Kungur, Rus. 103/N4
Kunhegyes, Hun. 90/E2
Kunimi-dake (peak), Japan 116/B4
Kuningan, Indo. 122/C5
Kunishiri (isl.), Rus. 109/P5
Kunitachi, Japan 119/C2
Kunjāh, Pak. 128/B3
Kunjirap (pass), China 131/L1
Kunkletown, Pa, US 180/C2
Kunlun (mts.), China 112/C4
Kunmadaras, Hun. 83/L5
Kunming, China 125/H2
Kunsan, SKor. 115/D5
Kunshan, China 114/L8
Kunszentmárton, Hun. 90/E2
Kunu (riv.), India 131/L3
Kunwāri (riv.), India 126/A2
Kunwi, SKor. 115/E4
Kunyu (mtn.), China 114/E3
Künzell, Ger. 96/C1
Kunžvartské (pass), Czh. 97/G5
Kuocang (peak), China 113/M6
Kuohijärvi (lake), Fin. 81/L1
Kuolimo (lake), Fin. 81/M1
Kuopio, Fin. 102/E3
Kuopio (prov.), Fin. 79/H3
Kupa (riv.), Cro. 90/B3
Kupang, Indo. 123/F6
Kupino, Rus. 129/G2
Kuppenheim, Ger. 96/B5
Kupreanof (isl.), Ak, US 164/C3
Kup'yans'k, Ukr. 104/F2
Kuqa, China 113/L3
Kür (riv.), Azer. 105/J5
Kūrālī, India 128/D4
Kurama-yama (peak), Japan 119/J5
Kurashiki, Japan 116/C3
Kurayoshi, Japan 116/C3
Kurdistan (reg.), Asia 106/E6
Kŭrdzhali, Bul. 89/J2
Kŭrdzhali (res.), Bul. 89/J2
Küre (mts.), Turk. 132/C1
Kure, Japan 116/C3
Küre, Turk. 132/C1
Kure (isl.), Hi, US 158/H2
Kuressaare, Est. 81/K2
Kureyka (riv.), Rus. 106/K3
Kurgan, Rus. 103/Q5
Kurganskaya Oblast, Rus. 129/D1
Kuri, SKor. 115/G6
Kuria (isl.), Kiri. 158/G4
Kuria Muria (isls.), Oman 131/G5
Kurīgrām, Bang. 127/G3
Kurihashi, Japan 119/D1
Kurikoma-yama (peak), Japan 118/B4
Kuril (isls.), Rus. 109/Q5
Kurimoto, Japan 119/F2
Kurinwas (riv.), Nic. 187/E3
Kurisawa, Japan 118/B2
Kuriyama, Japan 118/B2
Kürkçü, Turk. 133/C1
Kurla, India 124/B4
Kurnool, India 124/C4
Kuro-shima (isl.), Japan 116/A5
Kurodashō, Japan 119/G5
Kuroishi, Japan 118/B3
Kuroiso, Japan 117/G2
Kuroso-yama (peak), Japan 119/K6
Kurotaki, Japan 119/J7
Kurrajong, Austl. 156/G8
Kurram (riv.), Afg.,Pak. 131/K2
Kurrimine Beach, Austl. 156/B2
Kuršėnai, Lith. 81/K3
Kurseong, India 127/G2
Kursiu Nerija NP, Lith. 81/J4
Kursk, Rus. 104/F2
Kurskskaya Oblast, Rus. 104/E2
Kurskaya Spit (bar), Lith.,Rus. 81/J4
Kurskiy (lag.), Lith.,Rus. 81/J4
Kuršumlija, Serb. 90/E4
Kurşunlu, Turk. 132/C1
Kurtalan, Turk. 132/E2
Kürten, Ger. 95/G1
Kuru (riv.), Sudan 139/L6
Kuruca (pass), Turk. 132/E2
Kuruçay, Turk. 132/D2
Kuruçay (riv.), Turk. 105/G4
Kuruktag (mts.), China 112/E3
Kuruman, SAfr. 148/C2
Kurumansrivier (riv.), SAfr. 148/C2
Kurume, Japan 116/B4
Kurunegala, SrL. 124/D6
Kurupukari, Guy. 195/G3
Kurur (peak), Sudan 143/B4
Kurwongbah (lake), Austl. 156/E6
Kurye, SKor. 115/D5
Kuryong (riv.), NKor. 115/C3
Kuş Cenneti NP, Turk. 132/B1
Kuşadası, Turk. 132/A2
Kusatsu, Japan 119/J5
Kusel, Ger. 95/G4
Kushālgarh, India 131/K4
Kushida (riv.), Japan 119/K7
Kushigata, Japan 119/A2
Kushihara, Japan 119/M5
Kushikino, Japan 116/B5
Kushima, Japan 116/B5
Kushimoto, Japan 116/D4
Kushiro, Japan 118/D2
Kushiro (riv.), Japan 118/D2
Kushiro-Shitsugen NP, Japan 118/D2
Kushtia (pol. reg.), Bang. 127/G4
Kushtia, Bang. 127/G4
Kusiyana (riv.), Bang. 127/H3
Kuskokwim (bay), Ak, US 176/F4
Kuskokwim (mts.), Ak, US 176/G3
Kuskokwim (riv.), Ak, US 176/F3
Kuskokwim, North Fork (riv.), Ak, US 176/H3
Kuskokwim, South Fork (riv.), Ak, US 176/H3
Küsnacht, Swi. 99/E3
Kusŏng, NKor. 115/C3
Kussharo (lake), Japan 118/C2
Küssnacht am Rigi, Swi. 99/E3
Küstenkanal (canal), Ger. 93/E3
Kusterdingen, Ger. 96/C5
Kūstī, Sudan 139/M5
Kusu, Japan 119/L6
Kut (isl.), Thai. 125/H5
Kütahya, Turk. 132/B2
K'ut'aisi (int'l arpt.), Geo. 105/G4
K'ut'aisi, Geo. 105/G4
Kutch (reg.), India 131/J4
Kutch, Gulf of (gulf), India 131/J4
Kutchan, Japan 118/B1
Kutcharo (lake), Japan 118/C1
Kutenholz, Ger. 93/G2
Kutná Hora, Czh. 83/H4
Kutno, Pol. 83/K2
Kutsuki, Japan 119/J5
Küttigen, Swi. 98/E3
Kutu, D.R. Congo 139/J8
Kutzenhausen, Ger. 96/D6
Kutztown, Pa, US 180/C2
Kuujjua (riv.), NW, Can. 164/E1
Kuujjuaq, Qu, Can. 165/K3
Kuusamo, Fin. 79/J2
Kuusankoski, Fin. 81/M1
Kuutse (hill), Est. 81/M2
Kuvandyk, Rus. 105/L2
Kuwait (ctry.) 130/E3
Kuwait (cap.), Kuw. 130/E3
Kuwānā (riv.), India 124/D2
Kuwana, Japan 119/L5
Kuybyshev (res.), Rus. 106/E4
Kuyto (lake), Rus. 79/J2
Kuytun, China 112/E3
Kuyuwini (riv.), Guy. 195/G4
Kuze, Japan 119/K4
Kuzitrin (riv.), Ak, US 176/E2
Kuznetsk, Rus. 105/H1
Kuzucubelen, Turk. 133/D1
Kuzumaki, Japan 118/B3
Kvaløy (isl.), Nor. 79/F1
Kværndrup, Den. 80/D4
Kvarner (gulf), Cro. 90/B3
Kvarnerić (chan.), Cro. 90/B3
Kvigtinden (peak), Nor. 79/E2
Kvinesdal, Nor. 80/B2
Kvinnherad, Nor. 80/B2
Kviteseid, Nor. 80/C2
Kwa (riv.), D.R. Congo 147/C1
Kwach'ŏn, SKor. 115/F7
Kwajalein (isl.), Mrsh. 158/F4
Kwale, Kenya 146/C4
KwaMashu, SAfr. 149/E3
Kwanak-san (peak), SKor. 115/F7
Kwangch'ŏn, SKor. 115/D4
Kwangju, SKor. 115/D5
Kwangju, SKor. 115/G7
Kwangju-Gwangyŏksi (prov.), SKor. 115/D5
Kwangmyŏng, SKor. 115/F7
Kwango (riv.), D.R. Congo 147/C2
Kwangyang, SKor. 115/D5
Kwania (lake), Ugan. 139/M7
Kwansan, SKor. 115/D5
Kwara (state), Nga. 145/G4
Kwaraha (peak), Tanz. 146/B4
Kwataboahegan (riv.), On, Can. 172/D1
Kwazulu Natal (prov.), SAfr. 149/E3
Kwekwe, Zim. 147/E4
Kwethluk, Ak, US 176/F3
Kwidzyn, Pol. 81/H5
Kwigillingok, Ak, US 176/F4
Kwili (riv.), D.R. Congo 147/C1
Kwilu (riv.), D.R. Congo 147/C1
Kwinana, Austl. 154/K7
Kyabé, Chad 139/J6
Kyabram, Austl. 157/C3
Kyaiktiyo Pagoda, Myan. 120/B2
Kyaikto, Myan. 125/G4
Kyakhta, Rus. 112/J1
Kyan-zaki (cape), Japan 117/J7
Kyangin, Myan. 125/G4
Kyaukpadaung, Myan. 125/G3
Kyaukpyu, Myan. 125/F4
Kyaukse, Myan. 125/G3
Kyenjojo, Ugan. 146/A2
Kyeryong-san NP, SKor. 115/D4
Kyjov, Czh. 83/J4
Kyle, Sk, Can. 168/F3
Kyle (reg.), Sc, UK 78/B5
Kyll (riv.), Ger. 82/D3
Kym (riv.), Eng, UK 75/F2
Kymi (prov.), Fin. 79/H3
Kymijoki (riv.), Fin. 81/M1
Kymore, India 126/B4
Kyneton, Austl. 157/C3
Kynšperk nad Ohří, Czh. 97/F2
Kyoga (lake), Ugan. 139/M7
Kyōga-misaki (cape), Japan 116/D3
Kyogle, Austl. 156/D5
Kyonan, Japan 117/F3
Kyŏngbok Palace, SKor. 115/F6
Kyŏnggi (bay), SKor. 115/C4
Kyŏnggi-do (prov.), SKor. 115/D4
Kyŏngju, SKor. 115/E5
Kyŏngju NP, SKor. 115/E5
Kyŏngsan, SKor. 115/E5
Kyŏngsang-bukto (prov.), SKor. 115/E4
Kyŏngsang-namdo (prov.), SKor. 115/E5
Kyōto (pref.), Japan 116/D3
Kyōto, Japan 119/J5
Kyōtō Imperial Palace, Japan 119/J6
Kyōwa, Japan 119/E1
Kyrenia (dist.), Cyp. 133/C2
Kyrenia, Cyp. 133/C2
Kyrgyzstan (ctry.) 129/F4
Kyritz, Ger. 82/G2
Kyrösjärvi (lake), Fin. 81/K1
Kythrea, Cyp. 133/C2
Kyūshū (isl.), Japan 116/B5
Kyūshū Highlands (uplands), Japan 116/B4
Kyustendil, Bul. 89/H1
Kywebwe, Myan. 125/F4
Kyyivs'ka Oblasti, Ukr. 104/D2
Kyyivs'ke Vodoskhovyshche (res.), Ukr. 104/D2
Kyzyl, Rus. 112/F1

L

La Algaba, Sp. 86/B4
La Almunia de Doña Godina, Sp. 86/E2
La Amistad Int'l Park, CR 182/E6
La Araucanía (pol. reg.), Chile 200/B3
La Ascensión, Mex. 185/F3
La Asunción, Ven. 195/F2
La Aurora (int'l arpt.), Guat. 186/D3
La Babia, Mex. 174/C4
La Baie, Qu, Can. 173/G1
La Banda, Arg. 199/D2
La Bañeza, Sp. 86/C1
La Bassée, Fr. 94/B2
La Baule-Escoublac, Fr. 84/B3
La Belle, Fl, US 175/H5
La Birse (riv.), Swi. 98/D3
La Blanquilla (isl.), Ven. 195/E2
La Bocana, Mex. 184/B3
La Bresse, Fr. 98/C2
La Broque, Fr. 98/D1
La Calera, Chile 200/N8
La Campana, Sp. 86/C4
La Cañada (peak), Cuba 187/F1
La Canada-Flintridge, Ca, US 178/F7
La Capelle, Fr. 94/C4
La Carlota, Sp. 86/C4
La Carlota, Arg. 200/E2
La Carolina, Sp. 86/D3
La Catedral (peak), Mex. 185/Q9
La Ceiba, Hon. 186/E3
La Ceiba (int'l arpt.), Hon. 186/E3
La Celle-les-Bordes, Fr. 72/H6
La Celle-Saint-Cloud, Fr. 72/J5
La Celle-sur-Morin, Fr. 72/L5
La Chapelle-de-Guinchay, Fr. 98/A5
La Chapelle-Saint-Luc, Fr. 84/F2
La Chaux-de-Bonds, Swi. 98/C3
La Chinita (int'l arpt.), Ven. 194/D2
La Chorrera, Pan. 187/G4
La Cienega, NM, US 171/F4
La Ciotat, Fr. 84/F5
La Clusaz, Fr. 98/C6
La Concepción, Nic. 186/E4
La Concepción, Pan. 187/F4
La Concepcion, Ven. 194/D2
La Coronilla, Uru. 201/G2
La Coruña, Sp. 86/A1
La Couronne, Fr. 84/D4
La Crèche, Fr. 84/C3
La Crescenta-Montrose, Ca, US 178/F7
La Croix-en-Brie, Fr. 72/M6
La Croix, Lac (lake), On, Can. 169/L3
La Cruz, Uru. 200/N8
La Cruz, Col. 194/B4
La Cruz, CR 186/E4
La Cruz, Mex. 184/D4
La Cruz, Uru. 201/K10
La Cumbre (vol.), Ecu. 198/E7
La Dôle (peak), Swi. 98/C5
La Dorada, Col. 192/D2
La Dormida, Arg. 200/D2
La Esperanza, Hon. 186/D3
La Estrada, Sp. 86/A1
La Estrella, Chile 200/N9
La Falda, Arg. 199/D3
La Fayette, Ga, US 175/G3
La Fère, Fr. 94/C4
La Ferté-Gaucher, Fr. 94/C6
La Ferté-Macé, Fr. 84/C2
La Ferté-Milon, Fr. 72/M7
La Ferté-Sous-Jouarre, Fr. 94/C6
La Flèche, Fr. 84/C3
La Fría, Ven. 194/C2
La Galite (isl.), Tun. 142/L6
La Garamba NP, D.R. Congo 146/A2
La Garita (mts.), Co, US 174/B2
La Garriga, Sp. 87/L6
La Gineta, Sp. 86/E3
La Gloria, Col. 194/C2
La Goulette, Tun. 142/M6
La Gran Sabana (plain), Ven. 192/F2
La Grande, Or, US 168/D4
La Grande (riv.), Qu, Can. 165/J3
La Grande Ruine (peak), Fr. 85/G4
La Grange, Ga, US 175/G3
La Grange, Tx, US 171/H5
La Grita, Ven. 187/J4
La Gruyère (lake), Swi. 98/D4
La Guajira (dept.), Col. 194/C2
La Guajira (pen.), Col. 194/D1
La Guardia, Sp. 86/A2
La Guardia (int'l arpt.), NY, US 181/K8
La Habana (Havana) (cap.), Cuba 182/E3
La Habra, Ca, US 178/G8
La Have (riv.), NS, Can. 173/H2
La Higuera, Chile 199/B2
La Honda, Ca, US 177/K12
La Houssaye-en-Brie, Fr. 72/L5
La Huaca, Peru 198/A2
La Huacana, Mex. 185/E5
La Huerta, Mex. 184/D5
La Isla, Mex. 185/Q10
La Jalca, Peru 198/B2
La Joya, Peru 198/D5
La Joya de los Sachas, Ecu. 194/B5
La Junta, Co, US 171/G3
La Junta, Mex. 184/D2
La Laguna, Canl., Sp. 140/A3
La Libertad, Ecu. 194/A5
La Libertad, Guat. 186/D2
La Libertad, Hon. 186/E3
La Libertad (dept.), Peru 198/B3
La Ligua, Chile 200/C2
La Línea de la Concepción, Sp. 86/C4
La Llagosta, Sp. 87/L6
La Loche, Sk, Can. 168/F1
La Loggia, It. 100/A3
La Louvière, Belg. 95/D3
La Luisiana, Sp. 86/C4
La Luz, NM, US 171/F4
La Machine, Fr. 84/E3
La Maddalena, It. 88/A2
La Madeleine, Fr. 94/C2
La Malbaie, Qu, Can. 173/G2
La Marsá, Tun. 142/M6
La Martre (lake), NW, Can. 164/E2
La Masica, Hon. 186/E3
La Mauricie NP, Qu, Can. 172/F2
La Mensura (peak), Col. 194/C4
La Merca, Sp. 86/B1
La Merced, Peru 198/C3
La Mesa, Ca, US 178/C5
La Mesa (int'l arpt.), Hon. 186/E3
La Mesa, Ven. 194/D2
La Mira, Mex. 184/E5
La Mirada, Ca, US 178/F8
La Moine (riv.), Il, US 172/B3
La Montaña (phys. reg.), Peru 198/C3
La Moure, ND, US 169/J4
La Neuveville, Swi. 98/D3
La Norville, Fr. 72/J6
La Orchila (isl.), Ven. 183/H5
La Orotava, Canl., Sp. 140/A3
La Oroya, Peru 198/C3
La Palma, Pan. 187/G4
La Palma (isl.), Sp. 140/A3
La Paloma, Uru. 201/G2
La Pampa (prov.), Arg. 200/D3
La Paz, Arg. 199/E3
La Paz, Arg. 200/C3
La Paz (cap.), Bol. 192/E7
La Paz (dept.), Bol. 198/D4
La Paz, Col. 194/C2
La Paz, Col. 194/C3
La Paz, Hon. 186/E3
La Paz, Mex. 184/C3
La Paz (bay), Mex. 184/C3
La Paz, Uru. 201/K11
La Pêche, Qu, Can. 172/F2
La Peña, Pan. 182/E6
La Perla, Mex. 184/D2
La Pérouse (str.), Japan,Rus 113/R2
La Perouse (str.), Japan,Rus. 109/P5
La Petite-Raon, Fr. 98/C1
La Piedad Cavadas, Mex. 184/E4
La Plata, Md, US 172/E4
La Plata, Col. 194/C4
La Plata, Arg. 201/K11
La Pobla de Lillet, Sp. 87/F1
La Pocatière, Qu, Can. 173/G2
La Pola de Gordón, Sp. 86/C1
La Ponge (lake), Sk, Can. 168/G2
La Porte, In, US 172/C3
La Prairie, Qu, Can. 173/P7
La Pryor, Tx, US 171/H5
La Puebla, Sp. 87/G3
La Puebla de Almoradiel, Sp. 86/D3
La Puebla de Cazalla, Sp. 86/C4
La Puebla de Montalbán, Sp. 86/C3
La Puente, Ca, US 178/G7
La Puntilla (pt.), Ecu. 194/A5
La Quebrada, Ven. 194/D2
La Queue-les-Yvelines, Fr. 94/A6
La Quiaca, Arg. 192/E8
La Rambla, Sp. 86/C4
La Reforma, Mex. 184/C3
La Rinconada, Sp. 86/C4
La Rioja, Arg. 199/C2
La Rioja (aut. comm.), Sp. 86/D1
La Rioja (prov.), Sp. 86/D1
La Robla, Sp. 86/C1
La Roche (lake), Sk, Can. 168/F1
La Roche, Swi. 98/D4
La Roche-en-Ardenne, Belg. 95/E3
La Roche-sur-Foron, Fr. 98/C5
La Roche-sur-Yon, Fr. 84/C3
La Rochelle, Fr. 84/C3
La Roda, Sp. 86/D3
La Romana, DRep. 183/H4
La Ronge, Sk, Can. 169/G2
La Rúa, Sp. 86/B1
La Salle, Co, US 179/C2
La Sarraz, Swi. 98/C4
La Sarre, Qu, Can. 172/E1
La Sauvette (peak), Fr. 85/G5
La Scie, Nf, Can. 173/L1
La Serena, Chile 199/B2
La Seu d'Urgell, Sp. 87/F1
La Seyne-sur-Mer, Fr. 84/F5
La Sierpe, Cuba 187/G1
La Sila (mts.), It. 88/E3
La Silueta (peak), Chile 201/B7
La Solana, Sp. 86/D3
La Souterraine, Fr. 84/D3
La Spezia (prov.), It. 100/C4
La Spezia, It. 100/C4
La Tabatière, Qu, Can. 173/K1
La Teste, Fr. 84/C4
La Tête à l'Ane (peak), Fr. 98/C6
La Tigra, PN, Hon. 186/E3
La Toma, Arg. 200/D2
La Tortue (isl.), Haiti 187/H1
La Tortuga (isl.), Ven. 195/E2
La Tortuga, Isla (isl.), Ven. 192/E1
La Tour-de-Peilz, Swi. 98/C5
La Tour-de-Trême, Swi. 98/D4
La Tremblade, Fr. 84/C4
La Trinitaria, Mex. 186/C2
La Troncal, Ecu. 194/B5
La Tuque, Qu, Can. 173/F2
La Turbie, Fr. 100/H8
La Unión, Chile 200/B4
La Unión, Col. 194/B4
La Unión, ESal. 186/E3
La Unión, Mex. 185/E5
La Unión, Peru 198/A2
La Unión, Peru 198/B3
La Unión, Sp. 87/E4
La Unión, Ven. 194/E2
La Vecilla, Sp. 86/C1
La Verna, It. 101/E5
La Verne, Ca, US 178/C2
La Vernia, Tx, US 179/U21
La Verrière, Fr. 72/H5
La Víbora, Mex. 174/C5
La Victoria, Ven. 192/E1
La Victoria, Ven. 194/D3
La Wantzenau, Fr. 95/G6
Laa an der Thaya, Aus. 85/M2
Laaber, Ger. 97/E4
Laage, Ger. 80/E5
Laakirchen, Aus. 97/G7
Laarne, Belg. 94/C1
Laas Caanood, Som. 139/Q6
Laas Qoray, Som. 139/Q5
Laatzen, Ger. 93/G4
Laax, Swi. 99/F4
Labasan, Phil. 121/D6
L'Abbaye, Swi. 98/C4
Labdah (Leptis Magna) (ruin), Libya 138/H1
Labé, Gui. 144/B4
Labé (pol. reg.), Gui. 144/B4
Labe (Elbe) (riv.), Czh. 85/L1
Laberweinting, Ger. 97/F5
Labian (cape), Malay. 123/E2
Labin, Cro. 90/B3
Labinsk, Rus. 105/G3
Labná (ruin), Mex. 186/D1
Laborde, Arg. 200/E2
Laborec (riv.), Slvk. 83/L4
Laboulaye, Arg. 200/E2
Labrador (reg.), Nf, Can. 165/K3
Labrador (sea), Can.,Grld. 161/M4
Labrador City, Nf, Can. 165/K3
Lábrea, Braz. 192/F5
Labruguière, Fr. 84/E5
Labry, Fr. 95/E5
Labuk (riv.), Malay. 123/E2
Labuk (bay), Malay. 123/E2
Labuništa, FYROM 89/G2
Labutta, Myan. 125/F4
Laç, Alb. 89/F2
Lac Afwein (riv.), Kenya 146/C2
Lac du Bonnet, Mb, Can. 169/J3
Lac La Biche, Ab, Can. 168/F2
Lac-Mégantic, Qu, Can. 173/G2
L'Acadie, Qu, Can. 173/P7
Lacantum (riv.), Mex. 186/D2
Lacaune, Fr. 84/E5
Laccadive (sea), India 124/B5
Lacchiarella, It. 100/C2
Lacepede (bay), Austl. 157/A3
Lach Dera (riv.), Som. 139/P7
Lacha (lake), Rus. 102/H3
Lachapelle-aux-Pots, Fr. 94/A5
Lachay (pt.), Peru 198/B3
Lachen, Swi. 99/E3
Lachenaie, Qu, Can. 173/N6
Lachendorf, Ger. 93/H3
Lāchi, Pak. 128/A3
L'Achigan (riv.), Qu, Can. 173/N6
Lachine, Qu, Can. 173/N7
Lachlan (riv.), Austl. 157/C2
Lachte (riv.), Ger. 93/H3
Lackawanna, NY, US 173/S10
Lackawanna (co.), Pa, US 180/C1
Läckö, Swe. 80/E2
Lacombe, Ab, Can. 168/E2
Lacombe, La, US 179/Q16
Laconia, NH, US 173/G3
Lacroix-Saint-Ouen, Fr. 94/B5
Ladainha, Braz. 196/B5
Ladakh (mts.), India 131/L2
Ladbergen, Ger. 93/E4
Ladder (hills), Sc, UK 78/C2
Lądek-Zdrój, Pol. 83/J3
Ladenburg, Ger. 96/B4
Ladera Heights, Ca, US 178/F8
Ladismith, SAfr. 148/C4
Ladispoli, It. 88/C2
Ladoga (lake), Rus. 202/D
Ladoix-Serrigny, Fr. 98/A3
Ladrillero (mtn.), Chile 201/B7
Ladue, Mo, US 179/G8
Lādwa, India 128/D5
Lady Isle (isl.), Sc, UK 78/B5
Ladybank, Sc, UK 78/C4
Ladybower (res.), Eng, UK 77/G5
Ladybrand, SAfr. 148/D3
Ladysmith, SAfr. 149/E3
Lae (isl.), Mrsh. 158/F4
Laer, Ger. 93/E4
Lafayette, Ca, US 177/K11
Lafayette, Co, US 179/B3
Lafayette, In, US 172/C3
Lafayette, La, US 171/J5
Lafayette, NJ, US 180/D1
Lafia, Nga. 145/H4
Lafitte, La, US 179/P17
Laflamme (riv.), Qu, Can. 172/E1
Lafnitz (riv.), Aus. 85/L3
Lafontaine, Qu, Can. 173/M6
Lafourche (parish), La, US 179/T17
Laga Balal (riv.), Kenya 146/C2
Laga Mado Gali (riv.), Kenya 146/C2
Laga Merille (riv.), Kenya 146/C2
Lagan, Swe. 80/E3
Lagan (riv.), Swe. 80/E3
Lagarto, Braz. 196/C3
Lagawe, Phil. 121/D4
Lagdo, Lac de (lake), Camr. 138/H6
Lage, Ger. 93/F5
Lage Vaart (canal), Neth. 92/C4
Lågen (riv.), Nor. 80/C1
Lages, Braz. 197/B3
Laggan (lake), Sc, UK 78/B3
Lagh Bogal (riv.), Kenya 146/C2
Lagh Bor (riv.), Kenya 139/N7
Lagh Kutulo (riv.), Kenya 146/D2
Laghouat (prov.), Alg. 141/F2
Laghouat, Alg. 141/F2

249
Lagni – Lecco

Lagnieu, Fr. 98/B6
Lagny-le-Sec, Fr. 72/L4
Lagny-sur-Marne, Fr. 72/L5
Lago da Pedra, Braz. 196/A2
Lago de Atitlán, PN, Guat. 186/D3
Lago Puelo, PN, Arg. 200/C4
Lago Verde, Chile 200/C5
Lagoa, Port. 86/A4
Lagoa da Prata, Braz. 197/C2
Lagoa Formosa, Braz. 197/C1
Lagoa Vermelha, Braz. 197/B4
Lagoda (lake), Rus. 79/J3
Lagonegro, It. 88/D2
Lagord, Fr. 84/C3
Lagos, Nga. 145/F5
Lagos (state), Nga. 145/F5
Lagos, Port. 86/A4
Lagos de Moreno, Mex. 184/E4
Lagosanto, It. 101/F3
Laguardia, Sp. 86/D1
Laguna, Braz. 197/B4
Laguna Beach, Ca, US 178/C3
Laguna Blanca, PN, Arg. 200/C3
Laguna de Duero, Sp. 86/C2
Laguna de la Restinga, PN, Ven. 195/E2
Laguna del Laja, PN, Chile 200/C3
Laguna del Rey, Mex. 184/E3
Laguna Hills, Ca, US 178/C3
Laguna San Rafael, PN, Chile 199/B6
Lagunas, Peru 198/C2
Lagunas, Peru 198/B2
Lagunas de Chacahua, PN, Mex. 186/B2
Lagunas de Montebello, Mex. 182/C4
Lagunas de Zempoala, PN, Mex. 185/Q10
Lagunillas, Ven. 194/D2
Laguntara (lag.), Hon. 187/E3
Lahad Datu, Malay. 123/E2
Lahār, India 126/B2
Lāharpur, India 126/C2
Lahat, Indo. 122/B4
Lāhījān, Iran 130/F1
Lahn (riv.), Ger. 82/E3
Lahnstein, Ger. 95/G3
Laholm, Swe. 80/E3
Laholms (bay), Den. 80/F3
Lahore, Pak. 128/C4
Lahore (int'l arpt.), Pak. 128/C4
Lahr, Ger. 98/D1
Lahti, Fin. 81/L1
Laï, Chad 138/J6
Lai Chau, Viet. 120/C1
Lai'an, China 114/D4
Laibin, China 121/A3
Laichingen, Ger. 96/C5
Laidon (lake), Sc, UK 78/B3
Laie, Hi, US 166/W12
Laifeng Tujiazu Zizhixian, China 121/A2
L'Aigle, Fr. 84/D2
Laigueglia, It. 100/B5
Laihia, Fin. 79/G3
Lainate, It. 100/C1
Laingsburg, SAfr. 148/C4
Lainioälven (riv.), Swe. 79/G1
Laishui, China 114/G7
Laisvall, Swe. 79/F2
Laitila, Fin. 81/J1
Laives (Leifers), It. 99/H5
Laiwu, China 114/D3
Laixi, China 114/E3
Laiyuan, China 114/C3
Laizhou (bay), China 114/D3
Laja (lake), Chile 200/C3
Lajas, Peru 198/B2
Laje, Braz. 196/B3
Lajeado, Braz. 197/B4
Lajedo, Braz. 196/C3
Lajes, Braz. 196/C2
Lajes, Azor., Port. 87/S12
Lajes (int'l arpt.), Azor., Port. 87/S12
Lajing (pass), Nepal 127/E1
Lajinha, Braz. 197/D2
Lajosmizse, Hun. 90/D2
L'Akagera, PN de, Rwa. 146/A3
Lakato, Madg. 149/J7
Lake (co.), Il, US 177/P15
Lake Aluma, Ok, US 179/N14
Lake Amadeus Abor. Land, Austl. 155/F3
Lake Arrowhead, Ca, US 178/C2
Lake Barrington, Il, US 177/P15
Lake Beulah, Wi, US 177/P14
Lake Bluff, Il, US 177/Q15
Lake Boga, Austl. 157/B2
Lake Bogoria Nat'l Rsv., Kenya 146/C2
Lake Bolac, Austl. 157/B3
Lake Cargelligo, Austl. 157/C2
Lake Catherine, Il, US 177/P15
Lake Chany (lake), Rus. 129/G2
Lake Charles, La, US 171/J5
Lake Chelan Nat'l Rec. Area, Wa, US 168/C3
Lake City, Fl, US 175/H4
Lake Clark NP and Prsv., Ak, US 176/G3
Lake District NP, Eng, UK 77/E2
Lake Elsinore, Ca, US 178/C3
Lake Forest, Il, US 177/Q15
Lake Forest Park, Wa, US 177/C2
Lake Fork (res.), Tx, US 174/E3
Lake Grace, Austl. 154/C5
Lake Havasu City, Az, US 170/D4
Lake Hiwassee, Ok, US 179/N14
Lake in the Hills, Il, US 177/P15
Lake Jackson, Tx, US 171/J5
Lake Lotawana, Mo, US 179/E6
Lake Louise, Ab, Can. 168/D3
Lake Malawi NP, Malw. 147/F3
Lake Manyara NP, Tanz. 146/B3
Lake Mburo NP, Ugan. 146/A3
Lake Mead Nat'l Rec. Area, US 170/D4
Lake Meredith Nat'l Rec. Area, Tx, US 174/C3
Lake Minchumina, Ak, US 176/H3
Lake Mohawk, NJ, US 180/D1
Lake Nakuru NP, Kenya 146/C3
Lake of the Woods (lake), US,Can. 169/K3
Lake Orion, Mi, US 177/F6
Lake Point Junction, Ut, US 179/J12
Lake Providence, La, US 171/K4
Lake Ronkonkoma, NY, US 181/E2
Lake Shore, Md, US 180/B5
Lake Station, In, US 177/R16
Lake Success, NY, US 181/L8
Lake Villa, Il, US 177/P15
Lake Wales, Fl, US 175/H5
Lake Winnebago, Mo, US 179/E6
Lake Worth, Fl, US 175/H5
Lake Zurich, Il, US 177/P15
Lakehurst, NJ, US 180/D3
Lakehurst Naval Air Eng. Ctr., NJ, US 180/D3
Lakeland, Fl, US 175/H4
Lakeland Village, Ca, US 178/C3
Lakemoor, Il, US 177/P15
Lakeport, Ca, US 170/B3
Lakes Entrance, Austl. 157/D3
Lakes NP, The, Austl. 157/C3
Lakesfjorden (inlet), Nor. 79/H1
Lakeside, Ca, US 178/D5
Lakeview, Or, US 168/C5
Lakeview, Ut, US 179/K13
Lakeview, Ca, US 178/C3
Lakeville (lake), Mi, US 177/F6
Lakeway, Tx, US 171/H5
Lakewood, Wa, US 168/C3
Lakewood, Co, US 179/B3
Lakewood, NJ, US 180/D3
Lakewood, Ca, US 178/F8
Lakewood, Il, US 177/P15
Lakhemaa NP, Est. 81/L2
Lakhīmpur, India 126/C2
Lakhnādon, India 126/B4
Laki (vol.), Ice. 79/N7
Lakki, Pak. 128/A3
Lakkíon, Gre. 132/A2
Lakonía (gulf), Gre. 89/H4
Lakshadweep (isls.), India 124/B5
Lakshadweep (terr.), India 124/B6
Lal Suhanra NP, Pak. 128/B5
Lāla Mūsa, Pak. 128/B3
Lalana (riv.), Madg. 149/H8
Lalang (riv.), Indo. 122/B4
Lālganj, India 127/E3
Lālgola, India 127/G3
Lāliān, Pak. 128/B4
Lalín, Sp. 86/A1
Lalinde, Fr. 84/D4
Lalitpur, India 126/B3
Lalitpur (Pāṭan), Nepal 127/E2
Lalla Rookh Abor. Land, Austl. 154/C2
Lamachan (peak), Sc, UK 76/D1
Lamadrid, Mex. 174/C5
Lamanai (ruin), Belz. 186/D2
Lamandau (riv.), Indo. 122/D4
Lamar, Co, US 171/G3
Lamarche, Fr. 98/B1
Lamarche-sur-Saône, Fr. 98/B3
Lamarque, Arg. 200/D3
Lamas, Peru 198/B2
Lambach, Aus. 97/G6
Lamballe, Fr. 84/B2
Lambaré, Par. 199/E2
Lambaréné, Gabon 138/H8
Lambari, Braz. 197/H6
Lambay (isl.), Ire. 73/Q10
Lambayeque (dept.), Peru 198/A2
Lambayeque, Peru 198/B2
Lambé Coba (riv.), Mali 144/C3
Lambert-St. Louis (int'l arpt.), Mo, US 171/K3
Lambert's Bay, SAfr. 148/B4
Lambertville, Mi, US 172/D3
Lambertville, NJ, US 180/D3
Lambesc, Fr. 84/F5
Lambeth (bor.), Eng, UK 72/C2
Lambrama, Peru 198/C4
Lambrecht, Ger. 96/B4
Lambro (riv.), It. 100/C2
Lambsheim, Ger. 96/B3
Lambton (co.), On, Can. 177/H6
Lambunao, Phil. 121/D5
Lamego, Port. 86/B2
Lamèque (isl.), NB, Can. 173/H2
Lameroo, Austl. 155/J5
Lamesa, Tx, US 171/G4
Lamía, Gre. 89/H3
Lamington (riv.), NJ, US 180/D2
Lamington NP, Austl. 156/D5
Lamitan, Phil. 121/D6
Lamlash, Sc, UK 78/A5
Lamma (isl.), China 113/U11
Lammermuir (hills), Sc, UK 78/D5
Lammhult, Swe. 80/F3
Lammi, Fin. 81/L1
Lamone (riv.), It. 85/J4
Lamont, Ca, US 170/C4
Lamorlaye, Fr. 72/K4
Lamotrek (isl.), Micr. 158/D4
Lampa, Chile 200/N8
Lampa, Peru 198/D4
Lampang, Thai. 120/B2
Lampasas, Tx, US 171/H5
Lampasas (riv.), Tx, US 174/D4
Lampazos de Naranjo, Mex. 185/E3
Lampedusa, It. 88/C5
Lampedusa (isl.), It. 88/C5
Lampertheim, Ger. 96/B3
Lampeter, Pa, US 180/B4
Lamphun, Thai. 120/B2
Lampman, Sk, Can. 169/H3
Lamporecchio, It. 101/D5
Lamstedt, Ger. 93/G1
Lamu, Kenya 146/D3
Lamud, Peru 198/B2
Lamwa (peak), Ugan. 146/B2
Lan Sang NP, Thai. 120/B2
Lana, It. 99/H4
Lana, Río de la (riv.), Mex. 186/C2
Lanai (isl.), Hi, US 166/T10
Lanaihale (peak), Hi, US 166/T10
Lanaken, Belg. 95/E2
Lanark, Sc, UK 78/C5
Lanbi (isl.), Myan. 125/G5
Lancang Lahuzu Zizhixian, China 125/G3
Lancashire (co.), Eng, UK 77/F4
Lancashire (plain), Eng, UK 77/E4
Lancaster (sound), Nun., Can. 165/H1
Lancaster, Eng, UK 77/F3
Lancaster, Ca, US 170/C4
Lancaster, NY, US 173/S10
Lancaster, Pa, US 180/B3
Lancaster (co.), Pa, US 180/B4
Lancaster, SC, US 175/H3
Lancelin, Austl. 154/B4
Lanciano, It. 88/D1
L'Ancienne-Lorette, Qu, Can. 173/G2
Lanco, Chile 200/B3
Łańcut, Pol. 83/M3
Lancy, Swi. 98/C5
Land Kehdingen (reg.), Ger. 93/G1
Landau an der Isar, Ger. 97/F5
Landau in der Pfalz, Ger. 96/B4
Landeck, Aus. 99/G3
Landen, Belg. 95/E2
Lander, Wy, US 168/F5
Landerneau, Fr. 84/A2
Landes (reg.), Fr. 84/C4
Landes de Lanvaux (mts.), Fr. 84/B3
Landesbergen, Ger. 93/G3
Landis, Sk, Can. 168/F2
Landis Valley Museum, Pa, US 180/B3
Landisburg, Pa, US 180/A3
Landivisiau, Fr. 84/A2
Landrecies, Fr. 94/C3
Landri Sales, Braz. 196/B2
Landriano, It. 100/C2
Land's End (pt.), Eng, UK 74/A6
Landsberg, Ger. 99/G1
Landser, Fr. 98/D2
Landshut, Ger. 97/F5
Landskrona, Swe. 80/E4
Landsmeer, Neth. 92/B4
Landstuhl, Ger. 95/G5
Landvetter (int'l arpt.), Swe. 80/E3
Lane End, Eng, UK 72/A2
Lanester, Fr. 84/B3
Lanett, Al, US 175/G3
Lang Craig (pt.), Sc, UK 78/D3
Lang Kha Tuk (peak), Thai. 120/B4
Lang Son, Viet. 125/J3
Lang Suan, Thai. 120/B4
Langadhás, Gre. 89/H2
Langdon, ND, US 169/J3
Langeac, Fr. 84/E4
Langebaanweg, SAfr. 148/L10
Langeberg (mts.), SAfr. 148/L10
Langeland (isl.), Ger. 80/D4
Langelsheim, Ger. 93/H5
Langen, Ger. 93/F1
Langen, Ger. 96/B3
Langenaltheim, Ger. 96/D5
Langenargen, Ger. 99/F2
Langenau, Ger. 96/D5
Langenbach, Ger. 97/E6
Langenberg, Ger. 93/E6
Langenburg, Sk, Can. 169/H3
Längenfeld, Aus. 99/G3
Langenfeld, Ger. 95/F1
Langenhagen, Ger. 93/G4
Langenhorn, Ger. 80/C4
Langenlois, Aus. 83/H4
Langenpreising, Ger. 97/E6
Langenselbold, Ger. 96/C2
Langenstein, Aus. 97/H6
Langenthal, Swi. 98/D3
Langenzenn, Ger. 96/D3
Langenzersdorf, Aus. 91/N7
Langeoog, Ger. 93/E1
Langeoog (isl.), Ger. 93/E1
Langerringen, Ger. 99/G1
Langeskov, Den. 80/D4
Langesund, Nor. 80/C2
Langeten (riv.), Swi. 98/D3
Langfang, China 114/H7
Langfurth, Ger. 96/D4
Langham, Sk, Can. 168/G2
Langhirano, It. 100/D3
Langholm, Sc, UK 77/F1
Langhorne, Pa, US 180/D3
Langjökull (glacier), Ice. 79/N7
Langkawi (isl.), Malay. 125/G6
Langley, Wa, US 177/C1
Langnau im Emmental, Swi. 98/D4
Langney (pt.), Eng, UK 75/G5
Langogne, Fr. 84/E4
Langon, Fr. 84/C4
Langøya (isl.), Nor. 79/E1
Langquaid, Ger. 97/F5
Langres, Fr. 98/B2
Langres, Plateau de (plat.), Fr. 84/F3
Langsa, Indo. 122/A3
Langshyttan, Swe. 80/G1
Langtang Lirung (peak), Nepal 127/E1
Langtang NP, Nepal 127/E1
Langtry, Tx, US 174/C4
Languedoc (reg.), Fr. 84/E5
Languedoc-Roussillon (pol. reg.), Fr. 84/E5
Langwedel, Ger. 93/G3
Langweid an Lech, Ger. 96/E6
Langwies, Swi. 99/F4
Langxi, China 114/D5
Lanham-Seabrook, Md, US 180/B6
Lanigan, Sk, Can. 169/G3
Laniloa (pt.), Hi, US 166/W12
Lanín (vol.), Arg. 200/C3
Lanín, PN, Arg. 199/B4
Länkäran, Azer. 105/J5
Lanlacuni Bajo, Peru 198/D4
Lannemezan (plat.), Fr. 84/D5
Lannion (bay), Fr. 84/B2
Lannion, Fr. 84/B2
Lansdale, Pa, US 180/C3
Lansdowne, India 126/B1
Lansdowne, Pa, US 180/C4
Lansdowne-Baltimore Highlands, Md, US 180/B5
Lansford, Pa, US 180/C2
Lanshan, China 125/K2
Lansing (cap.), Mi, US 172/C3
Lansing, Ks, US 179/D5
Lansing, Il, US 177/Q16
Lanta (isl.), Thai. 125/G6
Lantau (chan.), China 113/T11
Lantau (peak), China 113/T11
Lantau (isl.), China 113/T10
Lanterne (riv.), Fr. 98/C2
Lanús, Arg. 201/J11
Lanusei, It. 88/A3
Lanxi, China 121/C2
Lanzarote (int'l arpt.), Canl., Sp. 140/B3
Lanzarote (isl.), Canl., Sp. 140/B3
Lanžhot, Czh. 83/J4
Lanzhou, China 112/H4
Lao (mts.), China 115/D2
Lao (peak), China 114/E3
Lao Cai, Viet. 120/C1
Laoag, Phil. 121/D4
Laoang, Phil. 121/E5
Laohekou, China 114/B4
Laojun (mtn.), China 114/B4
Laon, Fr. 94/C4
Laos (ctry.) 120/C2
Laoshan, China 114/E3
Laotuding (peak), China 115/C2
Laou (riv.), Mor. 142/B2
Lapa, Braz. 197/B3
Lapeer, Mi, US 172/D3
Lapeer (co.), Mi, US 177/F6
Lapinlahti, Fin. 102/E3
Lapithos, Cyp. 133/C2
Lapland (reg.), Swe. 202/D
Laporte, Co, US 179/B1
Lappeenranta, Fin. 81/N1
Lappersdorf, Ger. 97/F4
Lappi (prov.), Fin. 79/H2
Laptev (sea), Rus. 109/M2
Lapua, Fin. 102/D3
Łapy, Pol. 83/M2
L'Aquila, It. 88/C1
Lār, Iran 131/F3
Lara, Austl. 157/C3
Lara (state), Ven. 194/D2
Laracha, Sp. 86/A1
Larache (prov.), Mor. 142/B2
Larache, Mor. 142/A2
Laragne-Montéglin, Fr. 84/F4
Laramie, Wy, US 169/G5
Laramie (riv.), Wy, US 169/G5
Laramie (mts.), Wy, US 169/G5
Laranjeiras do Sul, Braz. 197/A3
Larat (isl.), Indo. 123/H5
Larba, Alg. 142/G4
Larchmont, NY, US 181/K8
Lærdalsøyri, Nor. 80/B1
Laredo, Peru 198/B3
Laredo (int'l arpt.), Tx, US 174/D5
Laredo, Tx, US 174/D5
Laredo, Sp. 86/D1
Laren, Neth. 92/C4
Lares, Peru 198/C4
Largo, Fl, US 175/H5
Largo, Md, US 180/B6
Largo (bay), Sc, UK 78/D4
Largo, Cayo (isl.), Cuba 187/F1
Largs, Sc, UK 78/B5
Largue (riv.), Fr. 98/D2
Lariang (riv.), Indo. 123/E4
Larino, It. 88/D2
Lárisa, Gre. 89/H3
Lark (riv.), Eng, UK 75/G2
Lārkāna, Pak. 131/J3
Larkhall, Sc, UK 78/C5
Larkspur, Ca, US 177/J11
Larmor-Plage, Fr. 84/B3
Larnaca (int'l arpt.), Cyp. 133/C2
Larnaca (dist.), Cyp. 133/C2
Larnaca, Cyp. 133/C2
Larne, NI, UK 76/C2
Larne (dist.), NI, UK 76/C2
Larne Lough (inlet), NI, UK 76/C2
Larned, Ks, US 171/H3
Larochette, Lux. 95/F4
Laroque-d'Olmes, Fr. 84/D5
Larose, La, US 175/F4
Larreynaga, Nic. 186/E3
Larroque, Arg. 201/J10
Larsen Bay, Ak, US 176/H4
Larsen Ice Shelf, Ant. 202/V
Larsen Sound (bay), Nun., Can. 164/G1
L'Artois, Collines de (hills), Fr. 82/A3
Laruns, Fr. 84/C5
Larvik, Nor. 80/D2
Las Animas, Co, US 171/G3
Las Aves (isls.), Ven. 183/H5
Las Breñas, Arg. 199/D2
Las Cabezas de San Juan, Sp. 86/C4
Las Cabras, Chile 200/N9
Las Cruces, NM, US 170/F4
Las Delicias, Ven. 194/C3
Las Eutimias, Mex. 174/C4
Las Flores, Arg. 200/F3
Las Guacamayas, Mex. 184/E5
Las Hermosas, PN, Col. 194/C4
Las Higueras, Arg. 200/D2
Las Lajas, Arg. 200/C3
Las Lajas (peak), Arg. 200/C3
Las Lomas, Peru 198/A2
Las Lomitas, Arg. 199/D1
Las Margaritas, Mex. 186/D2
Las Martinas, Cuba 187/E1
Las Mercedes, Ven. 195/E2
Las Minas (peak), Hon. 186/D3
Las Nieves, Mex. 184/D3
Las Orquídeas, PN, Col. 194/B3
Las Palmas, Pan. 187/F4
Las Palmas de Cocalán, PN, Chile 200/N9
Las Palmas de Gran Canaria, Canl., Sp. 140/B3
Las Pedroñeras, Sp. 86/D3
Las Perdices, Arg. 200/E2
Las Perlas (arch.), Pan. 187/G4
Las Piedras, Peru 198/D4
Las Piedras, Ven. 194/C2
Las Piedras, Uru. 201/K11
Las Pipinas, Arg. 201/F2
Las Rosas, Mex. 186/C2
Las Rozas de Madrid, Sp. 87/N9
Las Tablas, Pan. 187/F5
Las Varas, Mex. 184/D4
Las Varillas, Arg. 199/D3
Las Vegas, NM, US 171/F4
Las Vegas, Nv, US 170/D3
Lasalle, Qu, Can. 173/N7
Lasberg, Aus. 97/H6
Lascano, Uru. 201/G2
Lashio, Myan. 125/G3
Lashkar Gāh, Afg. 131/H2
Lasne-Chapelle-Saint-Lambert, Belg. 95/D2
Læsø (isl.), Den. 80/D3
Lasolo (riv.), Indo. 123/F4
Lassen (peak), Ca, US 168/C5
Lassen Volcanic NP, Ca, US 170/B2
L'Assomption, Qu, Can. 173/P6
L'Assomption (co.), Qu, Can. 173/N6
L'Assomption (riv.), Qu, Can. 173/P6
Last Mountain (lake), Sk, Can. 169/G3
Lastovo (isl.), Cro. 88/E1
Lastovski (chan.), Cro. 90/C4
Lastovski Kanal (chan.), Cro. 88/E1
Lastra a Signa, It. 101/E5
Lastrup, Ger. 93/E3
Lata, Sol. 158/F6
Latacunga, Ecu. 194/B5
Latady (isl.), Ant. 202/U
L'Atakora (prov.), Ben. 145/F4
Lātehār, India 127/E4
Latemar (peak), It. 99/H5
Laterza, It. 88/E2
Lathan (riv.), Fr. 84/C3
Lathrop, Ca, US 177/M11
Latina, It. 88/C2
Latisana, It. 101/G1
Latorica (riv.), Slvk.,Ukr. 83/M4
Latrobe, Austl. 157/C4
Latrobe (mt.), Austl. 157/C3
Latrobe (riv.), Austl. 157/C3
Lattes, Fr. 84/E5
Lattingtown, NY, US 181/L8
Lātūr, India 131/L5
Latvia (ctry.) 81/L3
Lau Group (isl.), Fiji 158/H6
Laubach, Ger. 96/B1
Lauca, PN, Chile 192/D7
Lauch (riv.), Fr. 85/G3
Lauchert (riv.), Ger. 96/C6
Lauchheim, Ger. 96/D5
Lauda-Königshofen, Ger. 96/C3
Lauder, Sc, UK 78/D5
Lauderdale (lakes), Wi, US 177/N14
Lauenbrück, Ger. 93/G2
Lauenburg, Ger. 93/H2
Lauenen, Swi. 98/D5
Lauenförde, Ger. 93/H5
Lauer (riv.), Ger. 96/D2
Lauf, Ger. 96/E3
Laufach, Ger. 96/C2
Laufen, Swi. 98/D3
Laufen, Ger. 97/F7
Laufenburg, Swi. 98/E2
Lauffen am Neckar, Ger. 96/C4
Laughlen (mt.), Austl. 155/G2
Lauhanvuoren NP, Fin. 102/D3
Lauingen, Ger. 96/D5
Launceston, Austl. 157/C4
Launette (riv.), Fr. 72/L4
Laupahoehoe, Hi, US 166/U11
Laupen, Swi. 98/D4
Lauperswil, Swi. 98/D4
Laupheim, Ger. 99/F1
Laura, Austl. 155/H5
Laureana di Borrello, It. 88/E3
Laurel, Mt, US 168/F4
Laurel, Ms, US 175/F4
Laurel, Md, US 180/B5
Laurel Springs, NJ, US 180/C4
Laureldale, Pa, US 180/C3
Laurelton, Pa, US 180/A2
Laurence Harbor, NJ, US 181/J10
Laurencekirk, Sc, UK 78/D3
Laurens, SC, US 175/H3
Laurentian (plat.), On, Can. 164/G3
Laurentides, Qu, Can. 173/N6
Laurinburg, NC, US 175/J3
Laurium, Mi, US 169/L4
Lausanne, Swi. 98/C4
Lauscha, Ger. 96/E2
Laut (isl.), Indo. 123/E4
Lautaro, Chile 200/B3
Lauter, Ger. 97/F1
Lauter (riv.), Ger. 82/E3
Lauterach (riv.), Ger. 97/E4
Lauterbach (riv.), Ger. 96/E2
Lauterbach, Ger. 96/C1
Lauterbourg, Fr. 96/B5
Lauterbrunnen, Swi. 98/D4
Lauterecken, Ger. 95/G4
Lauve, Nor. 80/D2
Lauwers (chan.), Neth. 92/D1
Lauwersmeer (lake), Neth. 92/D2
Lava Beds Nat'l Mon., Ca, US 168/C5
Lavagna (riv.), It. 100/C4
Lavagna, It. 100/C4
Laval, Fr. 84/C2
Laval, Qu, Can. 173/N6
Lavalleja (dept.), Uru. 201/G2
Lavallette, NJ, US 180/D4
Lavans-lès-Saint-Claude, Fr. 98/B5
Lavant (riv.), Aus. 85/L3
Lavapié (pt.), Chile 200/B3
Lavaur, Fr. 84/D5
Laveen, Az, US 179/R19
Lavelanet, Fr. 84/D5
Lavello, It. 88/D2
Laveno, It. 99/E6
Laverton, Austl. 154/D4
Lavey, Swi. 98/D5
Lavezzola, It. 101/E3
Lavino (riv.), It. 101/E4
Lavis, It. 99/H5
Lavos, Port. 86/A2
Lavras, Braz. 197/C2
Lavras da Mangabeira, Braz. 196/C2
Lávrion, Gre. 89/J4
Lawa (riv.), FrG. 195/H4
Lāwar Khās, India 126/A1
Lawarai (pass), Pak. 128/A2
Lawit (mtn.), Indo. 122/D3
Lawit (peak), Malay. 125/H6
Lawndale, Ca, US 178/F8
Lawnhill, BC, Can. 176/M5
Lawra, Gha. 144/E4
Lawrence, Ks, US 171/J3
Lawrence, Ma, US 173/G3
Lawrence, NY, US 181/L9
Lawrenceburg, In, US 172/C4
Lawrenceburg, Ky, US 175/G2
Lawrenceburg, Tn, US 175/G3
Lawrencetown, NI, UK 76/B3
Lawrenceville, Ga, US 175/H3
Lawrenceville, NJ, US 180/D3
Lawson, Mo, US 179/E5
Lawu (peak), Indo. 122/D5
Lawz, Jabal al (peak), SAr. 130/C3
Laxå, Swe. 80/F2
Laxey, IM, UK 76/D3
Laxou, Fr. 95/F6
Lay (riv.), Fr. 84/C3
Lay-Saint-Christophe, Fr. 95/F6
Laya (riv.), Rus. 103/N2
Layar (cape), Indo. 123/E4
Laylān, Iraq 132/F3
Layon (riv.), Fr. 84/C3
Laysan (isl.), Hi, US 159/H2
Layton, NJ, US 180/D1
Layton, Ut, US 179/K11
Lazarevac, Serb. 90/E3
Lázaro Cárdenas, Mex. 184/B2
Lázaro Cárdenas, Mex. 184/E5
Lazio (prov.), It. 85/J5
Lbiriktepe, Turk. 89/K2
Le Ban-Saint-Martin, Fr. 95/F5
Le Blanc, Fr. 84/D3
Le Blanc-Mesnil, Fr. 72/K5
Le Breuil, Fr. 84/F3
Le Cannet, Fr. 85/G5
Le Cateau-Cambrésis, Fr. 94/C3
Le Chasseral (peak), Swi. 98/D3
Le Chasseron (peak), Swi. 98/C4
Le Chesnay, Fr. 72/J5
Le Chesne, Fr. 95/D4
Le Cheval Blanc (peak), Fr. 98/C5
Le Cheylard, Fr. 84/F4
Le Cornate (peak), It. 85/J5
Le Creusot, Fr. 84/F3
Le Crotoy, Fr. 94/A3
Le Gore, Md, US 180/A4
Le Grammont (peak), Swi. 98/C5
Le Grand (cape), Austl. 154/D5
Le Grand Ballon (peak), Fr. 98/D2
Le Grau-du-Roi, Fr. 84/F5
Le Grazie, It. 100/C4
Le Havre, Fr. 84/D2
Le Landeron, Swi. 98/D3
Le Lavandou, Fr. 85/G5
Le Locle, Swi. 98/C3
Le Luc, Fr. 85/G5
Le Mans, Fr. 84/D2
Le Mée-sur-Seine, Fr. 72/K6
Le Mesnil-Amelot, Fr. 72/K4
Le Mesnil-Aubry, Fr. 72/K4
Le Mesnil-Esnard, Fr. 94/A5
Le Mesnil-le-Roi, Fr. 72/J5
Le Mesnil-Saint-Denis, Fr. 72/H5
Le Mesnil-sur-Oger, Fr. 94/D6
Le Môle (peak), Fr. 98/C5
Le Morond (peak), Fr. 98/C4
Le Moure de la Gardille (peak), Fr. 84/E4
Le Murge (mts.), It. 88/E2
Le Noirmont (peak), Fr. 98/C4
Le Noirmont (peak), Swi. 98/C5
Le Noirmont, Swi. 98/C3
Le Nouvion-en-Thiérache, Fr. 52/C3
Le Palais, Fr. 84/B3
Le Palais-sur-Vienne, Fr. 84/D4
Le Passage, Fr. 84/D4
Le Perray-en-Yvelines, Fr. 72/H5
Le Petit Ballon (peak), Fr. 98/D2
Le Plessis-Belleville, Fr. 72/L4
Le Plessis-Feu-Aussoux, Fr. 72/M5
Le Plessis-Placy, Fr. 72/L4
Le Port, Reun., Fr. 149/S15
Le Portel, Fr. 94/A2
Le Puy-en-Velay, Fr. 84/E4
Le Quesnoy, Fr. 94/C3
Le Russey, Fr. 98/C3
Le Suchet (peak), Swi. 98/C4
Le Tampon, Reun., Fr. 149/S15
Le Teil, Fr. 84/F4
Le Tholy, Fr. 98/C1
Le Touquet-Paris-Plage, Fr. 94/A2
Le Tréport, Fr. 94/A3
Le Val-d'Ajol, Fr. 98/C2
Le Vésinet, Fr. 72/J5
Le Vigan, Fr. 84/E5
Lea (riv.), Eng, UK 75/F3
Leach (lake), Ca, US 169/K4
Leach (riv.), Eng, UK 75/E3
Leacock-Leola-Bareville, Pa, US 180/B3
Lead, SD, US 169/H4
Leader, Sk, Can. 168/F3
Leader Water (riv.), Sc, UK 78/D5
Leadon (riv.), Eng, UK 74/D3
Leadville, Co, US 174/B2
Leaf (riv.), Ms, US 175/F4
Leaghur (lake), Austl. 157/B2
League City, Tx, US 171/J5
Leakey, Tx, US 171/H5
Leam (riv.), Eng, UK 75/E2
Leamington, On, Can. 172/D3
Le'an, China 121/C2
Leander (pt.), Austl. 154/B4
Leaota (peak), Rom. 91/G3
Learmonth, Austl. 154/B2
Leatherhead, Eng, UK 72/C3
Leavenworth, Ks, US 179/D5
Leavenworth (co.), Ks, US 179/D5
Leavenworth, Wa, US 168/C4
Leawood, Ks, US 179/D6
Łeba, Pol. 80/G4
Lebach, Ger. 95/F5
Lebak, Phil. 121/D6
Lebane, Serb. 90/E4
Lebanon (ctry.) 133/D3
Lebanon (mts.), Leb. 133/D3
Lebanon, In, US 172/C3
Lebanon, Ky, US 172/C4
Lebanon, Mo, US 171/J3
Lebanon, NH, US 173/F3
Lebanon, NJ, US 180/D2
Lebanon, Or, US 168/C4
Lebanon, Pa, US 180/B3
Lebanon, Tn, US 172/C4
Lebbeke, Belg. 95/D2
Lebedyn, Ukr. 104/E2
Lebel-sur-Quévillon, Qu, Can. 172/E1
Lebene (riv.), Mor. 142/B2
Lébény, Hun. 90/C2
Lębork, Pol. 80/G4
Lebrija, Sp. 86/B4
Lebu, Chile 199/B4
Lebu, Chile 200/B3
Leça da Palmeira, Port. 86/A2
Lecce, It. 89/F2
Lecco, It. 100/C1
Lecco (prov.), It. 100/C1

250
Lecco – Littl

Lecco, Lago di (lake), It. 100/C1
Lech, Aus. 99/G3
Lech (riv.), Ger. 85/K2
Lechang, China 125/K2
Lechbruck, Ger. 99/G2
Leche (lake), Cuba 187/G1
Lechtaler Alps (mts.), Aus. 99/G3
Leck, Ger. 80/C4
Lectoure, Fr. 84/D5
Łęczna, Pol. 83/M3
Leda (riv.), Ger. 93/E2
Ledang (peak), Malay. 122/B3
Lede, Belg. 94/C2
Ledegem, Belg. 94/C2
Ledesma, Sp. 86/B2
Ledge Point, Austl. 154/B4
Ledong, China 125/J4
Ledro (lake), It. 99/G6
Ledu (peak), It. 99/F5
Leduc, Ab, Can. 168/E2
Lee (riv.), Ire. 73/P11
Lee (mtn.), Pa, US 180/B1
Leech (lake), Mn, US 169/K4
Leeds, Eng, UK 77/G4
Leeds (co.), Eng, UK 77/G4
Leeds and Bradford (int'l arpt.), Eng, UK 77/G4
Leeds and Liverpool (canal), Eng, UK 77/G4
Leeds Point, NJ, US 180/D5
Leegebruch, Ger. 82/Q6
Leek, Neth. 92/D2
Leek, Eng, UK 77/F5
Leeman, Austl. 154/B4
Leer, Ger. 93/E2
Leerdam, Neth. 92/C5
Leersum, Neth. 92/C4
Lees Summit, Mo, US 179/E6
Leesburg, Fl, US 175/H4
Leesburg, NJ, US 180/D5
Leese, Ger. 93/G3
Leesport, Pa, US 180/C3
Leesville, La, US 171/J5
Leeton, Austl. 157/C2
Leeu (riv.), SAfr. 148/L10
Leeudoringstad, SAfr. 148/D2
Leeuwarden, Neth. 92/C2
Leeuwin (cape), Austl. 154/B5
Leeuwin-Naturaliste NP, Austl. 154/B5
Leeward (isls.), NAm. 183/J4
Leff (riv.), Fr. 84/B2
Lefka, Cyp. 133/C2
Lefo (peak), Camr. 145/H5
Lefroy (lake), Austl. 154/D4
Legana, Austl. 157/C4
Leganés, Sp. 87/N9
Legaspi, Phil. 121/D5
Legau, Ger. 99/G2
Legazpia, Sp. 86/D1
Legges Tor (peak), Austl. 157/C4
Legionowo, Pol. 83/L2
Léglise, Belg. 95/E4
Legnago, It. 101/E2
Legnano, It. 85/H4
Legnaro, It. 101/E2
Legnica, Pol. 83/J3
Legnone (peak), It. 99/F5
Leh, India 128/D2
Leh Palace, India 128/D2
Lehi, Ut, US 179/K13
Lehigh (co.), Pa, US 180/C2
Lehigh Acres, Fl, US 175/H5
Lehighton, Pa, US 180/C2
Lehinch, Ire. 73/P10
Lehrberg, Ger. 96/D4
Lehrte, Ger. 93/G4
Lei (riv.), China 125/K2
Leiah, Pak. 128/A4
Leiblfing, Ger. 97/F5
Leibo, China 125/H2
Leicester, Eng, UK 75/E1
Leicester (co.), Eng, UK 75/E1
Leicestershire (co.), Eng, UK 77/H6
Leichhardt (dam), Austl. 155/H2
Leichhardt (riv.), Austl. 151/C2
Leichlingen, Ger. 95/G1
Leiden, Neth. 92/B4
Leiderdorp, Neth. 92/B4
Leidschendam, Neth. 92/B4
Leie (riv.), Belg. 84/E1
Leifers (Laives), It. 85/J3
Leigh, Eng, UK 77/F5
Leigh Creek, Austl. 155/H4
Leimebamba, Peru 198/B2
Leimen, Ger. 96/B4
Leimersheim, Ger. 96/B4
Leine (riv.), Ger. 82/D3
Leinefelde, Ger. 93/H6
Leinfelden-Echterdingen, Ger. 96/C5
Leinster (mt.), Ire. 73/Q10
Leinster, Austl. 154/D3
Leinster (reg.), Ire. 76/A5
Leipheim, Ger. 96/D6
Leipsic, De, US 180/C5
Leipsic (riv.), De, US 180/C5
Leipzig, Ger. 82/G3
Leira, Nor. 80/C1
Leiria, Port. 86/A3
Leiria (dist.), Port. 86/A3
Leisler (mt.), Austl. 155/F2
Leith (hill), Eng, UK 72/B3
Leitha (riv.), Aus. 83/J5
Leixlip, Ire. 76/B5
Leizhou (pen.), China 125/J3
Lek (riv.), Neth. 82/C3
Le Kef, Tun. 142/L6
Le Kef (gov.), Tun. 142/L6
Lekhainá, Gre. 89/G4
Lekkerkerk, Neth. 92/B5
Lekki (lag.), Nga. 145/G5
Leksands-Noret, Swe. 80/F1
Leksozero (lake), Rus. 79/J3
Lelai (cape), Indo. 123/G3
Leland, Ms, US 171/K4
Leläng (lake), Swe. 80/E2
Leling, China 114/D3
Lelystad, Neth. 92/C3
Lem, Den. 80/C3
Lema (peak), It. 99/E5
Léman (Geneva) (lake), Fr. 85/G3
Lemberg (peak), Ger. 99/E1
Lemberg, Ger. 95/G5
Lembu (peak), Indo. 122/A3
Leme, Braz. 197/C2
Lemenjoen NP, Fin. 79/H1
Lemgo, Ger. 93/F4
Lemland (isl.), Fin. 81/H2
Lemland, Fin. 81/J1
Lemmer, Neth. 92/C3
Lemmon, SD, US 169/H4
Lemon Grove, Ca, US 178/C5
Lempa (riv.), ESal. 186/D3
Lempäälä, Fin. 81/K1
Lempdes, Fr. 84/E4
Lemva (riv.), Rus. 103/P2
Lemvig, Den. 80/C3
Lemwerder, Ger. 93/F2
Lena (riv.), Rus. 109/M3
Lena, Nor. 80/D1
Lenape, Ks, US 179/D6
Lenape (lake), NJ, US 180/D5
Lençóis Maranhenses, PN dos, Braz. 193/K4
Lençóis Paulista, Braz. 197/B2
Lendinara, It. 101/E2
Lenexa, Ks, US 179/D6
Lengau, Aus. 97/G6
Lengdorf, Ger. 97/F6
Lengede, Ger. 93/H4
Lengenfeld, Ger. 97/F1
Lengerich, Ger. 93/E4
Lenggries, Ger. 99/H2
Lengnau, Swi. 98/D3
Lengshuitan, China 125/K2
Lengua de Vaca (pt.), Chile 199/B3
Lenhartsville, Pa, US 180/C2
Lenina (peak), Taj. 129/F5
Leninabad (int'l arpt.), Taj. 129/E4
Leningradskaya Oblast, Rus. 102/G3
Leninobod (obl.), Taj. 129/E5
Leninogorsk, Rus. 103/M5
Leninsk-Kuznetskiy, Rus. 106/J4
Leninváros, Hun. 83/L5
Lenk, Swi. 98/D5
Lenne (riv.), Ger. 95/G1
Lennestadt, Ger. 93/F6
Lenningen, Ger. 96/C5
Lennox (isl.), Chile 201/D7
Lennox, Ca, US 178/F8
Lennox (hills), Sc, UK 78/B5
Lennoxtown, Sc, UK 78/B5
Leno, It. 100/D2
Lenoir, NC, US 175/H3
Lenoir City, Tn, US 175/G3
Lens, Swi. 98/D5
Lens, Fr. 94/B3
Lens, Belg. 94/C2
Lensahn, Ger. 80/D4
Lensk, Rus. 107/M3
Lenting, Ger. 97/E5
Lentini, It. 88/D4
Lenvik, Nor. 79/F1
Leny, Pass of (pass), Sc, UK 78/B4
Lenzburg, Swi. 98/E3
Lenzing, Aus. 97/G7
Lenzkirch, Ger. 99/E2
Léo, Burk. 145/E4
Leoben, Aus. 85/L3
Leográ (riv.), It. 101/E1
Leola, SD, US 169/J4
León, Mex. 185/E4
Leon (int'l arpt.), Mex. 184/C3
León, Nic. 186/E3
León, Sp. 86/C1
Leon (riv.), Tx, US 174/D3
Leon, Étang de (lake), Fr. 84/C4
Leon-Guanajuato (int'l arpt.), Mex. 185/E4
Leon Springs, Tx, US 179/T20
Leon Valley, Tx, US 179/T21
Leona Valley, Ca, US 178/B1
Leonard, Mi, US 177/F6
Leonard, Tx, US 171/H4
Leonardo, NJ, US 181/J10
Leonardo da Vinci (int'l arpt.), It. 88/C2
Leonberg, Ger. 96/C5
Leonding, Aus. 97/H6
Leone (peak), It. 98/E5
Leones, Arg. 200/E2
Leonforte, It. 88/D4
Leongatha, Austl. 157/C3
Leonia, NJ, US 181/K8
Leonídhion, Gre. 89/H4
Leonora, Austl. 154/D4
Leopoldina, Braz. 197/L6
Leopoldkanaal (riv.), Belg. 94/C1
Leopoldsburg, Belg. 95/E1
Leopoldsdorf, Aus. 91/N7
Leopoldsdorf im Marchfelde, Aus. 91/P7
Leopoldshöhe, Ger. 93/F4
Leoville, Sk, Can. 168/G2
Lepaera, Hon. 186/D3
Lépanges-sur-Vologne, Fr. 98/C1
Lepe, Sp. 86/B4
Lepenoú, Gre. 89/G3
L'Épiphanie, Qu, Can. 173/P6
Lepontine Alps (mts.), Swi 85/H3
Leptokariá, Gre. 89/H2
Léraba (riv.), Burk. 144/D4
Lercara Friddi, It. 88/C4
Lerdo de Tejada, Mex. 186/C2
Leribe, Les. 148/E3
Lerici, It. 100/C4
Lerín, Sp. 86/E1
Lerma, Sp. 86/D1
Lerma, Mex. 185/Q10
Lerma (riv.), Mex. 185/K7
Lermoos, Aus. 99/G3
Lérouville, Fr. 95/E6
Lerum, Swe. 80/E3
Lerwick, Sc, UK 73/W13
Lery (lake), La, US 179/Q17
Léry, Qu, Can. 173/N7
Les Alluets-le-Roi, Fr. 72/H5
Les Bois, Swi. 98/C3
Les Breuleux, Swi. 98/D3
Les Bréviaires, Fr. 72/H5
Les Cayes, Haiti 187/H2
Les Cèdres, Qu, Can. 173/M7
Les Clayes-sous-Bois, Fr. 72/H5
Les Contamines-Montjoie, Fr. 98/C6
Les Diablerets (range), Swi. 98/D5
Les Essarts-le-Roi, Fr. 72/H5
Les Gets, Fr. 98/C5
Les Hautes-Rivières, Fr. 95/D4
Les Herbiers, Fr. 84/C3
Les Islettes, Fr. 95/E5
Les Mesnuls, Fr. 72/H5
Les Molières, Fr. 72/J6
Les Mureaux, Fr. 94/A6
Les Ponts-de-Martel, Swi. 98/C4
Les Rousses, Fr. 98/C5
Les Sables-d'Olonne, Fr. 84/C3
Les Salines (int'l arpt.), Alg. 142/K6
Les Ulis, Fr. 72/J6
Les Verrières, Swi. 98/C4
Lesa, It. 100/B1
Leshan, China 125/H2
Lésigny, Fr. 72/K5
Lesima (peak), It. 100/C3
Lesja, Nor. 79/D3
Lesjöfors, Swe. 80/F2
Lesko, Pol. 83/M4
Leskovac, Serb. 90/E4
Leslie, Sc, UK 78/C4
Lesmahagow, Sc, UK 78/C5
Lesneven, Fr. 84/A2
Lešnica, Serb. 90/D3
Lesotho (ctry.) 148/E6
Lesozavodsk, Rus. 113/P2
Lesparre-Médoc, Fr. 84/C4
Lesquin (int'l arpt.), Fr. 94/C2
Lesse (riv.), Belg. 82/C3
Lessebo, Swe. 80/F3
Lesser Antilles (isls.), NAm. 183/M8
Lesser Caucasus (mts.), Asia 105/G4
Lesser Slave (lake), Ab, Can. 164/E3
Lesser Sunda (isls.), Indo. 123/E5
Lessines, Belg. 94/C2
Lesung (peak), Indo. 122/D3
Lésvos (isl.), Gre. 89/J3
Leszno, Pol. 83/J3
Létavértes, Hun. 90/E2
Letchworth, Eng, UK 75/F3
Letham, Sc, UK 78/D3
Lethbridge, Ab, Can. 168/E3
Lethe (riv.), Ger. 93/F2
Lethem, Guy. 195/G4
Leti (isls.), Indo. 123/G5
Leticia, Col. 198/D2
Leting, China 114/D3
Letlhakane, Bots. 147/E5
Letlhakeng, Bots. 147/D5
Letnitsa, Bul. 91/G4
L'Étoile, Fr. 94/B3
Letpadan, Myan. 125/G4
Letschin, Ger. 83/H2
Letsök-Aw (isl.), Myan. 122/A1
Letterkenny, Ire. 73/Q9
Leucate, Fr. 84/E5
Leuchars, Sc, UK 78/D4
Leuk, Swi. 98/D5
Leukerbad, Swi. 98/D5
Leun, Ger. 96/B1
Leusden-Zuid, Neth. 92/C4
Leuser (peak), Indo. 122/A3
Leuterhausen, Ger. 96/D4
Leutkirch im Allgäu, Ger. 99/G2
Leuze-en-Hainaut, Belg. 94/C2
Levádhia, Gre. 89/H3
Levallois-Perret, Fr. 72/J5
Levanger, Nor. 79/D3
Levante, Riviera di (coast), It. 100/C4
Levanto, It. 100/C4
Levasy, Mo, US 179/E5
Level (isl.), Chile 200/B5
Level, Md, US 180/B4
Levelland, Tx, US 171/G4
Levelock, Ak, US 176/G4
Leven (pt.), SAfr. 149/F2
Leven, Sc, UK 78/D4
Leven (lake), Sc, UK 78/A3
Leven (riv.), Sc, UK 78/C4
Leveque (cape), Austl. 151/B2
Leverburgh, Sc, UK 73/Q8
Leverkusen, Ger. 95/F1
Levice, Slvk. 90/D1
Levico Terme, It. 99/H5
Levier, Fr. 98/C4
Levin, NZ 159/T11
Lévis, Qu, Can. 173/G2
Lévis-Saint-Nom, Fr. 72/H5
Levittown, Pa, US 180/D3
Levittown, NY, US 181/L9
Levkás, Gre. 89/G3
Levkás (isl.), Gre. 89/G3
Levkímmi, Gre. 89/G3
Levoča, Slvk. 83/L4
Levrier (bay), Mrta. 140/A5
Levski, Bul. 91/G4
Lewes, Eng, UK 75/G5
Lewin Brzeski, Pol. 83/J3
Lewis (riv.), Wa, US 168/C4
Lewis (range), Mt, US 168/E3
Lewis (hills), Nf, Can. 173/K1
Lewis (pass), NZ 159/S11
Lewis (isl.), Sc, UK 73/Q7
Lewis and Clark (lake), Ne,SD, US 169/J5
Lewis Smith (lake), Al, US 175/G3
Lewisburg, Tn, US 175/G3
Lewisburg, WV, US 172/D4
Lewisburg, Pa, US 180/B2
Lewisham (bor.), Eng, UK 72/C2
Lewisporte, Nf, Can. 173/L1
Lewiston, Id, US 168/D4
Lewiston, Me, US 173/G2
Lewiston, NY, US 173/R9
Lewistown, Mt, US 168/F4
Lewistown, Pa, US 172/E3
Lewotobi (peak), Indo. 123/F5
Lexington, Ky, US 172/C4
Lexington, NC, US 175/H3
Lexington, Ne, US 169/J5
Lexington, Tn, US 172/B5
Lexington Park, Md, US 172/E4
Leyburn, Eng, UK 77/G3
Leyden, Co, US 179/B3
Leye, China 125/J3
Leyland, Eng, UK 77/F4
Leysin, Swi. 98/D5
Leyte (isl.), Phil. 121/D5
Leytron, Swi. 98/D5
Lez (riv.), Fr. 84/F4
Leżajsk, Pol. 83/M3
Lezhë, Alb. 89/F2
Lézignan-Corbières, Fr. 84/E5
Lezuza, Sp. 86/D3
L'gov, Rus. 104/E2
Lhanbyrd, Sc, UK 78/C1
Lhari, China 112/F5
Lhasa, China 124/F2
Lhazê, China 127/F1
L'Hongrin (lake), Swi. 98/D5
Lhorong, China 112/G5
L'Hospitalet de Llobregat, Sp. 87/L7
Lhozhag, China 127/H1
Lhünzê, China 125/G2
Li (riv.), China 121/B2
Li (riv.), China 125/K2
Li (mtn.), China 114/B4
Li Xian, China 121/B2
Lian (riv.), China 121/B3
Lian Xian, China 125/K3
Liancheng, China 121/C2
Liancourt, Fr. 94/B5
Liancourt Rocks (isl.), Asia 116/B2
Liangcheng, China 114/C2
Liangpran (peak), Indo. 122/D3
Liangzi (lake), China 114/C5
Lianhua, China 125/K2
Lianjiang, China 121/C2
Lianjiang, China 125/K3
Liannan Yaozu Zizhixian, China 121/B3
Lianshui, China 114/D4
Lianyuan, China 121/B2
Lianyungang, China 114/D4
Liao (riv.), China 109/M5
Liaocheng, China 114/C3
Liaodong (pen.), China 115/A3
Liaodong (isls.), China 114/E3
Liaodong, Gulf of (gulf), China 113/M3
Liaoning (prov.), China 113/M3
Liaoyang, China 115/B2
Liaoyuan, China 113/N3
Liaozhong, China 115/B2
Liāquatpur, Pak. 128/A5
Liard (riv.), NW, Can. 164/D2
Libby, Mt, US 168/E3
Liběchovka (riv.), Czh. 97/H2
Libenge, D.R. Congo 139/J7
Libercourt, Fr. 94/C3
Liberdade (riv.), Braz. 193/H6
Liberdade, Braz. 197/J7
Liberec, Czh. 83/H3
Liberecký (pol. reg.), Czh. 83/H3
Liberia, CR 187/E4
Liberia (ctry.) 144/C5
Libertad, Belz. 186/D2
Libertad, Ven. 194/D2
Libertad, Uru. 201/K11
Libertador General San Martín, Arg. 199/D1
Liberty, Ky, US 172/C4
Liberty (res.), Md, US 180/B5
Liberty, Ms, US 171/K5
Liberty, Mo, US 179/E5
Liberty, Tx, US 171/J5
Liberty, Ut, US 179/K11
Liberty Grove, Md, US 180/B4
Libertyville, Il, US 177/P15
Libin, Belg. 95/E4
Libo, China 125/J2
Libobo (cape), Indo. 123/G4
Liboc (riv.), Czh. 83/G3
Libochovice, Czh. 97/H2
Libon, Phil. 121/D5
Librazhd, Alb. 89/G2
Libres, Mex. 185/M7
Libreville (cap.), Gabon 138/G7
Libya (ctry.) 138/J2
Libyan (plat.), Libya 139/K1
Libyan (des.), Egypt,Libya 139/K2
Licantén, Chile 200/B2
Licata, It. 88/C4
Lice, Turk. 132/E2
Lich, Ger. 96/B1
Licheng, China 114/C3
Licheng, China 114/D3
Lichfield, Eng, UK 75/E1
Lichinga, Moz. 147/G3
Lichtenau, Ger. 93/F5
Lichtenau, Ger. 96/D4
Lichtenau, Ger. 96/B5
Lichtenburg, SAfr. 148/D2
Lichtenfels, Ger. 96/D2
Lichtenrade, Ger. 82/Q7
Lichtensteig, Swi. 99/F3
Lichtenvoorde, Neth. 92/D5
Lichtervelde, Belg. 94/C1
Lichuan, China 121/A1
Licinio de Almeida, Braz. 196/B4
Lick Observatory, Ca, US 177/L12
Licking (riv.), Ky, US 172/C4
Licosa (cape), It. 88/D2
Licques, Fr. 94/A2
Lida, Bela. 81/L5
Liddell Water (riv.), Sc, UK 77/F1
Liddes, Swi. 98/D6
Liddon (gulf), NW, Can. 165/R7
Lidhorikion, Gre. 89/H3
Lidingö, Swe. 80/H2
Lidköping, Swe. 80/E2
Lido, It. 101/F2
Lido di Iesolo, It. 101/F1
Lido di Ostia, It. 88/C2
Lidzbark, Pol. 83/K2
Lidzbark Warmiński, Pol. 81/J4
Liebenau, Aus. 97/H5
Liebenbergsvlei (riv.), SAfr. 148/E2
Liebig (mt.), Austl. 155/F2
Liechtenstein (ctry.) 99/F3
Liedekerke, Belg. 95/D2
Liège, Belg. 95/E2
Liège (prov.), Belg. 95/E3
Lieksa, Fin. 102/F3
Lienden, Neth. 92/C5
Lienen, Ger. 93/E4
Lienz, Aus. 85/K3
Liepāja, Lat. 81/J3
Lier, Belg. 95/D1
Lierneux, Belg. 95/E3
Lieser (riv.), Ger. 95/F3
Liesjärven NP, Fin. 81/K1
Liesse-Notre-Dame, Fr. 94/C4
Liestal, Swi. 98/D3
Lieto, Fin. 81/K1
Liévin, Fr. 94/B3
Lièvre (riv.), Qu, Can. 172/F2
Liez (lake), Fr. 98/B2
Liezen, Aus. 85/L3
Liffey (riv.), Ire. 76/B5
Liffol-le-Grand, Fr. 98/B1
Lifford, Ire. 73/Q9
Ligao, Phil. 123/F1
Lightning Ridge, Austl. 157/C1
Lightwater, Eng, UK 72/B3
Lignano Sabbiadoro, It. 101/G1
Ligny-en-Barrois, Fr. 95/E6
Ligoncio (peak), It. 99/F5
Ligoúrion, Gre. 89/H4
Liguori, Mo, US 179/G9
Liguria (pol. reg.), It. 100/B4
Liguria (prov), It. 85/H4
Ligurian (sea), Fr.,It. 85/H5
Lihou (reefs), Austl. 151/E2
Lihue, Hi, US 166/S10
Lijiang Naxizu Zizhixian, China 125/H2
Lijin, China 114/D3
Likasi, D.R. Congo 147/E3
Likely, BC, Can. 168/C2
Likoma (isl.), Malw. 147/F3
Likouala (riv.), Congo 138/H7
Likova (riv.), Rus. 103/W9
L'Île-Perrot, Qu, Can. 173/N7
L'Île-Rousse, Fr. 88/A1
Liliāni, Pak. 128/B3
Lilienthal, Ger. 93/F2
Liling, China 125/K2
Lilla Edet, Swe. 80/E2
Lille, Belg. 92/B6
Lille, Fr. 94/C2
Lille Bælt (chan.), Ger. 80/C4
Lillehammer, Nor. 80/D1
Lillers, Fr. 94/B2
Lillesand, Nor. 80/C2
Lillestrøm, Nor. 80/D2
Lilliwaup, Wa, US 177/A3
Lillo, Sp. 86/D3
Lillooet, BC, Can. 168/C3
Lillooet (riv.), BC, Can. 168/C3
Lilongwe (cap.), Malw. 147/F3
Liloy, Phil. 121/D6
Lim (riv.), Serb. 90/D4
Lima, Peru 201/J11
Lima (riv.), It. 101/D4
Lima (cap.), Peru 198/B4
Lima (dept.), Peru 198/B3
Lima (riv.), Port. 87/A2
Lima, Oh, US 172/C3
Lima Duarte, Braz. 197/K6
Limache, Chile 200/N8
Limanowa, Pol. 83/L4
Limassol, Cyp. 133/C2
Limassol (dist.), Cyp. 133/C2
Limavady (dist.), NI, UK 76/A2
Limavady, NI, UK 76/B1
Limay (riv.), Arg. 200/C4
Limbach, Ger. 96/C4
Limbani, Peru 198/D4
Limbara (peak), It. 88/A2
Limbdi, India 131/K4
Limbé, Haiti 187/H2
Limbiate, It. 100/C1
Limbourg, Belg. 95/E2
Limburg (prov.), Belg. 95/E1
Limburg an der Lahn, Ger. 96/B2
Limburgerhof, Ger. 96/B4
Lime Village, Ak, US 176/G3
Limedsforsen, Swe. 80/E1
Limeira, Braz. 197/C2
Limekilns, Sc, UK 78/C4
Limena, It. 101/E2
Limenária, Gre. 89/J2
Limerick, Ire. 73/P10
Limfjorden (chan.), Den. 80/C3
Limidario (peak), It. 99/E5
Limite, It. 101/D5
Limmat (riv.), Swi. 99/E3
Limmen Bight (bay), Austl. 151/C2
Límni, Gre. 89/H3
Límnos (isl.), Gre. 89/J3
Limoeiro, Braz. 196/D2
Limoeiro do Norte, Braz. 196/C2
Limoges, Fr. 84/D4
Limogne, Causse de (plat.), Fr. 84/D4
Limón, CR 187/F4
Limón, Hon. 187/E3
Limours, Fr. 72/J6
Limousin (mts.), Fr. 84/D4
Limousin (pol. reg.), Fr. 84/D4
Limoux, Fr. 84/E5
Limpopo (riv.), Moz. 147/F5
Lin Xian, China 114/C3
Lin'an, China 121/C1
Linapacan (isl.), Phil. 121/C5
Linard (peak), Swi. 99/G4
Linares, Mex. 185/F3
Linares, Sp. 86/D3
Linares, Chile 200/C2
Linariá, Gre. 89/J3
Linate (int'l arpt.), It. 100/C2
Lincang, China 125/H3
Lincheng, China 114/C3
Linchuan, China 121/C2
Lincoln, Arg. 200/E2
Lincoln (sea), Can.,Grld. 161/L1
Lincoln, On, Can. 173/R9
Lincoln, Eng, UK 77/H5
Lincoln, De, US 180/C6
Lincoln, Il, US 169/L5
Lincoln, Me, US 173/G2
Lincoln (cap.), Ne, US 169/J5
Lincoln (co.), Ok, US 179/N14
Lincoln, Pa, US 180/B3
Lincoln Beach, Or, US 168/B4
Lincoln City, Or, US 168/B4
Lincoln Heath (woodld.), Eng, UK 77/H5
Lincoln NP, Austl. 155/G5
Lincoln Park, Mi, US 177/F7
Lincoln Park, NJ, US 181/H8
Lincolnshire (co.), Eng, UK 77/H5
Lincolnshire Wolds (grsld.), Eng, UK 77/H4
Lincroft, NJ, US 180/D3
Lind, Den. 80/C3
Lind NP, Austl. 157/D3
Lindau, Ger. 99/F2
Lindau, Swi. 99/E3
Linde (riv.), Neth. 92/D3
Lindeman (chan.), Austl. 156/C3
Linden, Ger. 96/B1
Linden, Guy. 195/G3
Linden, Al, US 175/G3
Linden, NJ, US 181/J9
Linden, Mi, US 177/E6
Linden, Tx, US 171/J4
Linden Beach, On, Can. 177/G7
Lindenberg im Allgäu, Ger. 99/F2
Lindenfels, Ger. 96/B3
Lindenhurst, NY, US 181/E2
Lindenhurst, Il, US 177/P15
Lindenwold, NJ, US 180/D4
Lindern, Ger. 93/E3
Lindesberg, Swe. 80/F2
Lindesnes (cape), Nor. 80/B3
Lindewitt, Ger. 80/C4
Lindhorst, Ger. 93/E5
Líndhos (ruin), Gre. 132/B2
Lindi (pol. reg.), Tanz. 146/C5
Lindi, Tanz. 146/C5
Lindlar, Ger. 95/G1
Lindley, SAfr. 148/D2
Lindome, Swe. 80/E3
Lindon, Ut, US 179/K13
Lindre (lake), Fr. 95/F6
Lindsay, Ca, US 170/C3
Lindsay, On, Can. 172/E2
Lindsay (mt.), Austl. 154/C5
Lindsay (mt.), Austl. 155/F3
Lindsdal, Swe. 80/G3
Line (isls.), Kiri. 159/J4
Line Mountain (mtn.), Pa, US 180/B2
Líneas de Nazca, Peru 198/C4
Lineboro, Md, US 180/B4
Linfen, China 114/B3
Ling (riv.), Sc, UK 78/A2
Ling Xian, China 125/K2
Ling Xian, China 114/D3
Lingbao, China 114/B4
Lingbi, China 114/D4
Lingchuan, China 125/K2
Lingchuan, China 114/C4
Linge (riv.), Neth. 92/C5
Lingen, Ger. 93/E3
Lingfield, Eng, UK 72/C3
Lingga (isls.), Indo. 122/B3
Linglestown, Pa, US 180/B3
Lingolsheim, Fr. 98/D1
Lingqiu, China 114/C3
Lingshan, China 125/J3
Lingshan, China 114/C3
Lingshi, China 114/B3
Lingshui, China 125/K4
Linguère, Sen. 144/B3
Lingyin Si, China 114/L9
Lingyuan, China 114/D2
Lingyun, China 125/J3
Linhai, China 121/D2
Linhares, Braz. 197/D1
Linhe, China 112/J3
Linköping, Swe. 80/F2
Linli, China 121/B2
Linlithgow, Sc, UK 78/C5
Linliu (mtn.), China 114/C3
Linney (pt.), Wal, UK 74/A3
Linnhe (lake), Sc, UK 78/A3
Linnich, Ger. 95/F2
Linntown, Pa, US 180/B2
Linosa (isl.), It. 142/N7
Linqing, China 114/C3
Linqu, China 114/D3
Linquan, China 114/C4
Linru, China 114/C4
Lins, Braz. 197/B2
Linschoten, Neth. 92/B4
Linshu, China 114/D4
Linta (riv.), Madg. 149/H9
Linth (riv.), Swi. 99/F3
Linthal, Swi. 99/F4
Linton, ND, US 169/H4
Linwood, Eng, UK 77/H5
Linwu, China 125/K2
Linxi, China 114/C3
Linyi, China 114/B4
Linyi, China 114/D3
Linyi, China 114/D4
Linying, China 114/C4
Linz (int'l arpt.), Aus. 97/H6
Linz, Aus. 97/H6
Linz am Rhein, Ger. 95/G2
Linzhang, China 114/C3
Lion (gulf), Fr.,Sp. 87/G1
Lipa, Phil. 121/D5
Lipari (isl.), It. 88/D3
Lipari (isls.), It. 88/D3
Lipari, It. 88/D3
Liperi, Fin. 102/F3
Lipetsk, Rus. 104/F1
Lipetsk (int'l arpt.), Rus. 104/F1
Lipetskaya Oblast, Rus. 104/F1
Lipez (riv.), Bol. 192/E8
Lipez, Cordillera de (mts.), Bol. 192/E8
Liping, China 125/J2
Lipljan, Serb. 90/E4
Lipno (res.), Czh. 97/H5
Lipno, Pol. 83/K2
Lipno, Údolní nádrž (lake), Czh. 85/L2
Lipova, Rom. 90/E2
Lippe (riv.), Ger. 82/D3
Lippstadt, Ger. 93/F5
Liptovský Svätý Mikuláš, Slvk. 83/K4
Liptrap (cape), Austl. 157/C3
Lira, Ugan. 146/B2
Lircay, Peru 198/C4
Liri (riv.), It. 88/C2
Liria, Sp. 87/E3
Liro (riv.), It. 99/F5
Lisboa (dist.), Port. 86/A3
Lisboa (int'l arpt.), Port. 87/P10
Lisbon (Lisboa) (cap.), Port. 87/P10
Lisbon, ND, US 169/J4
Lisbon, Me, US 173/G2
Lisbon, Md, US 180/A5
Lisburn, NI, UK 76/B2
Lisburn (dist.), NI, UK 76/B3
Lisburne (cape), Ak, US 176/E2
Lisdoonvarna, Ire. 73/P10
Liseleje, Den. 80/D3
Lishi (riv.), China 125/H2
Lishu, China 114/F2
Lishui, China 121/C2
Lisianski (isl.), Hi, US 159/H2
Lisieux, Fr. 84/D2
Liski, Rus. 104/F2
Lisle, Il, US 177/P16
L'Isle-Adam, Fr. 72/J4
L'Isle-en-Dodon, Fr. 84/D5
L'Isle-sur-la-Sorgue, Fr. 84/F5
L'Isle-sur-le-Doubs, Fr. 98/C3
Lisle-sur-Tarn, Fr. 84/D5
Lismore, Austl. 157/E1
Lisnacree, NI, UK 76/B3
Lišov, Czh. 97/H4
Lispeszentadorján, Hun. 90/C2
Lisse, Neth. 92/B4
Lisses, Fr. 72/K6
List, Ger. 80/C4
Lister (riv.), Ger. 93/E6
Listowel, On, Can. 172/D3
Listowel, Ire. 73/P10
Lit. Scarcies (riv.), SLeo. 144/B4
Litang, China 112/H6
Litang (riv.), China 125/H2
Līṭānī (riv.), Leb. 133/D3
Litavka (riv.), Czh. 97/G3
Litchfield, Mn, US 169/K4
Litchfield, Il, US 171/K3
Litchfield Park, Az, US 179/R19
Lith, Neth. 92/C5
Litherland, Eng, UK 77/F5
Lithgow, Austl. 157/D2
Lithuania (ctry.) 81/K4
Litija, Slov. 85/L3
Lititz, Pa, US 180/B3
Litókhoron, Gre. 89/H2
Litoměřice, Czh. 97/H1
Littabella NP, Austl. 156/D4
Littau, Swi. 99/E3
Little (riv.), Ar, US 171/J4
Little (riv.), Ga, US 175/H4
Little (riv.), Tx, US 174/D4
Little (riv.), NC, US 175/J3
Little (riv.), Ok, US 179/N15
Little Abitibi (riv.), On, Can. 172/D1
Little Andaman (isl.), India 125/F5
Little Belt (mts.), Mt, US 168/F4
Little Bighorn Battlefield Nat'l Mon., Mt, US 168/G4
Little Bitter (lake), Egypt 133/C4
Little Blue (riv.), Ks,Ne, US 171/H2
Little Calumet (riv.), Il, US 177/Q16
Little Cayman (isl.), Cay. 183/E4
Little Colorado (riv.), Az, US 170/E4
Little Creek, De, US 180/C5
Little Cumbrae (isl.), Sc, UK 78/A5
Little Current (riv.), On, Can. 169/M3
Little Current, On, Can. 172/D2

Lukov – Mallā

Malla – Martí
253

Mallasvesi (lake), Fin. 81/K1
Mallee Cliffs NP, Austl. 157/B2
Mallén, Sp. 86/E2
Malleray, Swi. 98/D3
Mallero (riv.), It. 99/F5
Mallersdorf-Pfaffenberg, Ger. 97/F5
Malles (Mals), It. 99/G4
Malloa, Chile 200/N9
Mallow, Ire. 73/P10
Malmberget, Swe. 79/G2
Malmédy, Belg. 95/F3
Malmesbury, SAfr. 148/L10
Malmköping, Swe. 80/G2
Malmö, Swe. 80/E4
Malmöhus (co.), Swe. 79/E5
Malmslätt, Swe. 80/F2
Malnate, It. 100/B1
Malo, It. 101/E1
Maloelap (isl.), Mrsh. 158/G4
Malone, NY, US 172/F2
Malong, China 125/H2
Malonje (peak), Tanz. 146/A5
Malonno, It. 99/G5
Małopolska (uplands), Pol. 83/K3
Małopolskie (prov.), Pol. 83/K4
Malpartida de Cáceres, Sp. 86/B3
Malpartida de Plasencia, Sp. 86/B3
Malpelo (isl.), Col. 192/B3
Malpensa (int'l arpt.), It. 100/B1
Malpica, Sp. 86/A1
Malsch (riv.), Aus. 97/H5
Malsch, Ger. 96/B5
Malše (riv.), Czh. 83/H4
Mälstek (peak), Czh. 97/G4
Malta, Mt, US 168/G3
Malta, Braz. 196/C2
Malta (chan.), Malta 88/C4
Malta (ctry.) 88/L7
Maltahöhe, Namb. 147/C5
Maltby, Eng, UK 77/G5
Malters, Swi. 98/E3
Maltorne (riv.), Fr. 72/G6
Malung, Swe. 80/E1
Malvaglia, Swi. 99/E5
Malvan, India 131/K5
Malveira, Port. 87/P10
Malvern, Pa, US 180/C3
Malverne, NY, US 181/L9
Malvinas (Falkland) (isls.), UK 202/W
Malvy Uzen' (riv.), Rus. 105/H2
Malyn, Ukr. 104/D2
Malyy Yenisey (riv.), Rus. 112/G1
Malzéville, Fr. 95/F6
Mamanguape, Braz. 196/D2
Mamaroneck, NY, US 181/L8
Mamba, Zam. 147/E4
Mamba, Japan 119/B1
Mambajao, Phil. 121/D6
Mambasa, D.R. Congo 146/A2
Mamberamo (riv.), Indo. 123/J4
Mambéré (riv.), CAfr. 138/J7
Mambij, Syria 132/D2
Mamburao, Phil. 121/D5
Mamer, Lux. 95/F4
Mamers, Fr. 84/D2
Mamfé, Camr. 145/H5
Mammendorf, Ger. 99/H1
Mamming, Ger. 97/F5
Mammoth, Az, US 170/E4
Mammoth Cave NP, Ky, US 175/G2
Mamoré (riv.), Braz. 192/E6
Mamou, La, US 171/J5
Mamoutzou, May. 149/H6
Mampikony, Madg. 149/H7
Mampong, Gha. 145/E5
Mamry (lake), Pol. 81/J4
Mamuju, Indo. 123/E4
Mamuru (riv.), Braz. 193/G4
Mamwera (peak), Tanz. 146/C4
Man, C.d'Iv. 144/D5
Man, Isle of (isl.), IM, UK 76/D3
Man Mia (peak), Thai. 120/B4
Mana (riv.), FrG. 195/H3
Manabl (prov.), Ecu. 194/A5
Manacapuru, Braz. 192/F4
Manacle (pt.), Eng, UK 74/A6
Manacor, Sp. 87/G3
Manado, Indo. 123/F3
Manage, Belg. 95/D3
Managua (cap.), Nic. 186/E3
Managua (lake), Nic. 186/E3
Manahawkin, NJ, US 180/D4
Manakambahiny, Madg. 149/J7
Manakara, Madg. 149/J8
Manalapan, NJ, US 180/D3
Manāli, India 128/D3
Manama (cap.), Bahr. 130/F3
Manambaho (riv.), Madg. 149/H7
Manambolo (riv.), Madg. 149/H7
Manantantanana (riv.), Madg. 149/H8
Mananara, Madg. 149/J7
Mananara (riv.), Madg. 149/H8
Mananjary, Madg. 149/J8
Mananjary (riv.), Madg. 149/H8
Manara (pt.), It. 100/C4
Manaratsandry, Madg. 149/H7
Manas, China 112/E3
Manas (int'l arpt.), Kyr. 129/F4
Manas (peak), Kyr. 129/F4
Manās (riv.), India 127/H2
Manas (riv.), China 112/E2
Manāslu (peak), Nepal 127/E1
Manasquan, NJ, US 180/D3
Manasquan (riv.), NJ, US 180/D3
Manassa, Co, US 174/B2
Manastir Dečani, Serb. 89/G1
Manastir Gračanica, Serb. 90/E4
Manastir Sopoćani, Serb. 90/E4
Manatsuru, Japan 119/C3
Manaus, Braz. 192/F4
Manawatu (riv.), NZ 159/T11
Mañazo, Peru 198/D4
Manazuru-misaki (cape), Japan 119/C3
Mance (riv.), Fr. 98/B2
Mancha Real, Sp. 86/D4
Mancheng, China 114/G7
Mancherāl, India 124/C4
Manchester (lake), Austl. 156/E7
Manchester, Eng, UK 77/F5
Manchester (co.), Eng, UK 77/F5
Manchester (Ringway) (int'l arpt.), Eng, UK 77/F5
Manchester, Ky, US 172/D4
Manchester, Mo, US 179/F8
Manchester, Md, US 180/B4
Manchester, NH, US 173/G3
Manchester, Pa, US 180/B3
Manchester, Tn, US 175/G3
Manchester, Wa, US 177/B2
Manchuria (reg.), China 113/M3
Mancieulles, Fr. 95/E5
Máncora, Peru 198/A2
Mand (riv.), Iran 131/F3
Manda, PN de, Chad 139/J6
Mandabe, Madg. 149/H8
Mandaguari, Braz. 197/B2
Mandal, India 124/B3
Mandal, Nor. 80/B2
Mandal-Ovoo, Mong. 112/H3
Mandala (peak), Indo. 123/K4
Mandalay, Myan. 125/G3
Mandalay (div.), Myan. 125/G3
Mandalgovĭ, Mong. 112/J2
Mandalī, Iraq 130/E2
Mandan, ND, US 169/H4
Mandasavu (peak), Indo. 123/F5
Mandaue, Phil. 121/D5
Mandeb (str.), Afr.,Asia 135/G3
Mandello del Lario, It. 99/F6
Mandera, Kenya 139/P7
Mandeure, Fr. 98/C3
Mandeville, La, US 179/P16
Mandeville, Jam. 187/G2
Mandi Bahāuddīn, Pak. 128/B3
Mandi Dabwāli, India 128/C5
Mandi Sādiqganj, Pak. 128/B4
Mandié, Moz. 147/F4
Mandiola (isl.), Indo. 123/G4
Mandira (res.), India 127/E4
Mandla, India 126/C4
Mandø (isl.), Den. 80/C4
Mándok, Hun. 83/M4
Mandoto, Madg. 149/H7
Mandoúdhion, Gre. 89/H3
Mándra, Gre. 89/N8
Mandrare (riv.), Madg. 149/H9
Mandritsara, Madg. 149/J6
Mandsaur, India 131/L4
Mandurah, Austl. 154/B5
Manduria, It. 89/E2
Māndvi, India 131/J4
Mandya, India 124/C5
Mane (pass), Nepal 126/D1
Manéngouba, Massif du (peak), Camr. 145/H5
Maner, India 127/E3
Manerbio, It. 100/D2
Manfalūt, Egypt 130/B3
Manfredonia, It. 88/D2
Manfredonia, Golfo di (gulf), It. 88/D2
Mang (riv.), China 114/B4
Manga, Braz. 196/B4
Manga, Burk. 145/E4
Mangabeiras, Chapada das (hills), Braz. 193/J6
Mangai, D.R. Congo 147/C1
Mangaia (isl.), Cookls. 159/K7
Mangaldai, India 125/F2
Mangalia, Rom. 91/J4
Mangalisa (peak), Tanz. 146/C4
Mangalore, India 124/B5
Mangaratiba, Braz. 197/J7
Mangareva (isl.), FrPol. 159/M7
Manger, Nor. 80/A1
Mangghystaū (obl.), Kaz. 106/F5
Mangghystaū Tübegi (pen.), Kaz. 105/J3
Mangghystaū Üstirti (plat.), Kaz. 105/K4
Mangkalihat (cape), Indo. 123/E3
Mangla (dam), Pak. 128/B3
Mangla, Pak. 128/B3
Mangla (res.), Pak. 128/B3
Manglaralto, Ecu. 198/A1
Manglares (pt.), Col. 194/B4
Manglaur, India 126/A1
Mangles (bay), Austl. 154/K7
Mango, Togo 145/F4
Mangoche, Malw. 147/G3
Mangoky (riv.), Madg. 147/J11
Mangole (isl.), Indo. 123/G4
Mangoro (riv.), Madg. 149/J7
Mangotsfield, Eng, UK 74/D4
Māngrol, India 131/K4
Mangualde, Port. 86/B2
Mangueira (lake), Braz. 201/G2
Mangum, Ok, US 171/H4
Manhasset, NY, US 181/L8
Manhasset (bay), NY, US 181/L8
Manhattan, Mt, US 168/F4
Manhattan (isl.),NY, US 181/K9
Manhattan Beach, Ca, US 178/F8
Manhay, Belg. 95/E3
Manheim, Pa, US 180/B3
Manhiça, Moz. 147/F6
Manhuaçu, Braz. 197/D2
Manhumirim, Braz. 197/D2
Mania (riv.), Madg. 149/H7
Maniamba, Moz. 147/G3
Maniāri (riv.), India 126/C4
Manicoré (riv.), Braz. 192/F5
Manicoré, Braz. 192/F5
Manicouagan (riv.), Qu, Can. 165/K3
Manicouagan (res.), Qu, Can. 173/G1
Manifold (cape), Austl. 156/C3
Manigotagan, Mb, Can. 169/J3
Manihāri, India 127/F3
Manihi (isl.), FrPol. 159/L6
Manihiki (isl.), Cookls. 159/J6
Manikarchar, India 127/G3
Manila (cap.), Phil. 121/D5
Manilla, Austl. 157/D1
Maningory (riv.), Madg. 149/J7
Manipa (str.), Indo. 123/G4
Manipat (hills), India 126/D4
Manipur (state), India 125/F3
Manisa (prov.), Turk. 132/B2
Manistee (riv.), Mi, US 172/C2
Manistee, Mi, US 172/C2
Manistique, Mi, US 172/C2
Manitoba (prov.), Can. 164/G3
Manitoba (lake), Mb, Can. 169/J3
Manitou (riv.), Qu, Can. 173/H1
Manitou Springs, Co, US 171/F3
Manitoulin (isl.), On, Can. 172/D2
Manitowoc, Wi, US 169/M4
Maniwaki, Qu, Can. 172/F2
Manizales, Col. 192/C2
Manja, Madg. 149/H8
Manjakandriana, Madg. 149/J7
Manjimup, Austl. 154/C5
Mankono, C.d'Iv. 144/D4
Manley Hot Springs, Ak, US 176/H2
Manlleu, Sp. 86/D1
Manlyutka, Rus. 103/R4
Manmād, India 131/K4
Mannar, SrL. 124/C6
Mannar (gulf), India,SrL. 124/C6
Männedorf, Swi. 99/E3
Mannetjiesberg (peak), SAfr. 148/C4
Mannheim, Ger. 96/B4
Manning, SC, US 175/H3
Manning (cape), NW, Can. 165/Q7
Manning, Ab, Can. 164/E3
Mannington Meadow (lake), NJ, US 180/C4
Männlifluh (peak), Swi. 98/D4
Mannum, Austl. 155/H5
Mano (riv.), Libr. 138/C6
Manokotak, Ak, US 176/G4
Manolo Fortich, Phil. 121/D6
Manombo, Madg. 149/G8
Manono, D.R. Congo 147/E2
Manorville, NY, US 181/F2
Manosque, Fr. 84/F5
Manouane (riv.), Qu, Can. 173/G1
Manouane (lake), Qu, Can. 173/G1
Manp'o, NKor. 115/D2
Manra (Sydney) (isl.), Kiri. 159/H5
Manresa, Sp. 87/K6
Mansa, Zam. 146/A5
Mānsa, India 128/C5
Mansa Konko, Gam. 144/B3
Mansalay, Phil. 123/F1
Mānsehra, Pak. 128/B2
Mansel (isl.), Nun., Can. 165/H2
Mansfield, Austl. 157/C3
Mansfield, Eng, UK 77/G5
Mansfield, La, US 171/J4
Mansfield, Oh, US 172/D3
Mansfield Woodhouse, Eng, UK 77/G5
Mansilla de las Mulas, Sp. 86/C1
Manta, Ecu. 194/A5
Mantalingajan (mt.), Phil. 123/E2
Mantaro (riv.), Peru 192/C6
Manteca, Ca, US 170/B3
Mantecal, Ven. 194/D3
Manteigas, Port. 86/B2
Mantena, Braz. 197/D1
Manthani, India 124/C4
Manti, Ut, US 170/E3
Mantiqueira, Serra da (mts.), Braz. 193/K8
Mantorp, Swe. 80/F2
Mantova (prov.), It. 100/D2
Mantova, It. 101/D2
Mäntsälä, Fin. 81/L1
Mantua, Cuba 187/E1
Mantua, NJ, US 180/C4
Mantua, Ut, US 179/K11
Manturovo, Rus. 103/K4
Mäntyharju, Fin. 81/M1
Manu (riv.), India 192/D6
Manú, Peru 198/D4
Manú, PN, Peru 192/D6
Manua (isls.), ASam. 159/J6
Manuae Atoll (atoll), Cookls. 159/K6
Manuel Alves da Natividade (riv.), Braz. 193/J6
Manuel Benavides, Mex. 174/C4
Manuel J. Cobo, Arg. 201/K11
Manui (isl.), Indo. 123/F4
Manuk (riv.), Indo. 122/C5
Manukau, NZ 159/S10
Manumuskin (riv.), NJ, US 180/D5
Manuripe (riv.), Bol. 192/E6
Manuripe Heath Amazonica, Reserva Nacional, Bol. 198/D4
Manus (isl.), PNG 158/D5
Manville, NJ, US 180/D2
Many, La, US 171/J5
Many Farms, Az, US 170/E3
Manyara (lake), Tanz. 146/B3
Manych (riv.), Rus. 106/E5
Manych-Gudilo (lake), Rus. 105/G3
Manzanares, Sp. 86/D3
Manzanares (riv.), Sp. 87/N8
Manzanares el Real, Sp. 87/N8
Manzanillo, Mex. 184/D5
Manzanillo (int'l arpt.), Mex. 184/D5
Manzanillo, Cuba 187/G1
Manzano (mts.), NM, US 174/B3
Manzano, It. 101/G1
Manzhouli, China 113/L2
Manzilah, Buḩayrat al (lake), Egypt 133/B4
Manzini, Swaz. 149/E2
Mao, Chad 138/J5
Maoke (mts.), Indo. 123/J4
Maoming, China 125/K3
Mapastepec, Mex. 186/C3
Mapi (riv.), Indo. 123/J5
Mapimí, Bolsón de (depr.), Mex. 184/D3
Mapire, Ven. 195/E3
Maple (riv.), ND, US 169/J4
Maple Creek, Sk, Can. 168/F3
Maple Grove, Qu, Can. 173/N7
Maple Park, Il, US 177/N16
Maple Shade, NJ, US 180/D4
Maple Valley, Wa, US 177/C3
Mapleton, Ut, US 179/K13
Maplewood, Mo, US 179/G8
Maplewood, NJ, US 181/H9
Maporal, Ven. 194/D3
Mapuera (riv.), Braz. 192/G3
Maputo (int'l arpt.), Moz. 149/F2
Maputo (cap.), Moz. 149/F2
Maqdam (cape), Sudan 143/D5
Maqên Gangri (peak), China 112/G5
Maquan (Damqog) (riv.), China 126/E1
Maquinchao, Arg. 200/C4
Maquoketa (riv.), Ia, US 171/K2
Mar (mts.), Braz. 189/E5
Mar (reg.), Sc, UK 78/D2
Mar Chiquita (lake), Arg. 199/D3
Mar de Ajó, Arg. 201/F3
Mar del Plata, Arg. 200/F3
Mar del Tuyú, Arg. 201/F3
Mara (pol. reg.), Tanz. 146/B3
Mara (riv.), Tanz. 146/B3
Marabá, Braz. 193/J5
Maracá, Ilha de (isl.), Braz. 193/H3
Maracaibo, Ven. 194/D2
Maracaibo (lake), Ven. 194/D2
Maracaju, Serra de (mts.), Braz. 193/G8
Maracás, Braz. 196/B4
Maracás, Chapada de (hills), Braz. 196/B4
Maracay, Ven. 192/E1
Maracena, Sp. 86/D4
Marādah, Libya 138/J2
Maradi, Niger 145/G3
Maradi (dept.), Niger 145/G3
Marāgheh, Iran 130/E1
Mārahra, India 126/B2
Marahuaca (peak), Ven. 195/E4
Marais de St-Gond (swamp), Fr. 94/C6
Marais des Cygnes (riv.), Ks,Mo, US 171/J3
Marajó (bay), Braz. 193/J4
Marajó, Ilha de (isl.), Braz. 193/H4
Maralal, Kenya 146/C2
Maralinga-Tjarutja Abor. Land, Austl. 155/F4
Maramag, Phil. 121/E6
Marambaia, Ilha (isl.), Braz. 197/K8
Maramureş (co.), Rom. 83/M5
Marana, Az, US 170/E4
Marana (lag.), Cro. 101/G1
Marand, Iran 105/H5
Marang, Malay. 122/B2
Marangani, Peru 198/D4
Maranguape, Braz. 196/C1
Maranhão (riv.), Braz. 193/J6
Maranhão (state), Braz. 196/A2
Marano Lagunare, It. 101/G1
Marano sul Panaro, It. 101/D4
Marano Vicentino, It. 101/E1
Maranoa (riv.), Austl. 151/D3
Marañón (riv.), Peru 198/B2
Marans, Fr. 84/C3
Maraoue, PN de la, C.d'Iv. 144/D5
Marapi (peak), Indo. 122/B4
Maras (peak), Indo. 122/C4
Mărăşeşti, Rom. 91/H3
Marathon, On, Can. 169/M3
Marathon, Fl, US 175/H5
Marathon, Tx, US 174/C4
Marathón, Gre. 89/N8
Marau, Braz. 197/A4
Maraulīānwāla, Pak. 128/B3
Maravatio de Ocampo, Mex. 185/E5
Marawi, Phil. 121/D6
Marbach, Swi. 98/D4
Marbach am Neckar, Ger. 96/C5
Marbache, Fr. 95/F6
Marbella, Sp. 86/C4
Marble Bar, Austl. 154/C2
Marbleton, Wy, US 168/F5
Marburg, Ger. 85/H1
Marburg (lake), Pa, US 180/B4
Marca, Ponta da (pt.), Ang. 147/B4
Marcali, Hun. 90/C2
Marcallo, It. 100/B2
Marcapata, Peru 198/D4
March, Eng, UK 75/G1
Marche (prov.), It. 85/K5
Marche (mts.), Fr. 84/D3
Marche-en-Famenne, Belg. 95/E3
Marchémoret, Fr. 72/L4
Marchena, Sp. 86/C4
Marchena (isl.), Ecu. 198/E6
Marcheno, It. 100/D1
Marchiennes, Fr. 94/C3
Marchin, Belg. 95/E3
Marchtrenk, Aus. 97/H6
Marciana Marina, It. 88/B1
Marcilly, Fr. 72/L4
Marcilly-sur-Tille, Fr. 98/B2
Marck, Fr. 94/A2
Marckolsheim, Fr. 98/D1
Marco, Braz. 196/B1
Marco, Fl, US 175/H5
Marco Polo (int'l arpt.), It. 101/F2
Marcoing, Fr. 94/C3
Marcon, It. 101/F1
Marcona, Peru 198/C4
Marconi (mt.), BC, Can. 168/E3
Marcos Juárez, Arg. 200/E2
Marcoussis, Fr. 72/J6
Marcovia, Hon. 186/E3
Marcq-en-Barœul, Fr. 94/C2
Marcus Baker (mt.), Ak, US 176/J3
Marcy (mt.), NY, US 172/F2
Mardān, Pak. 128/B2
Marden, Eng, UK 72/E3
Mardeuil, Fr. 94/C5
Mardin (town), Turk. 132/E2
Marecchia (riv.), It. 101/F5
Maree (lake), Sc, UK 73/R8
Mareeba, Austl. 156/B2
Mareil-sur-Mauldre, Fr. 72/H5
Marengo, Il, US 177/N15
Marennes, Fr. 84/C4
Mareuil-sur-Ourcq, Fr. 72/M4
Marfa, Tx, US 171/F5
Margalla Hills NP, Pak. 128/B3
Marganets', Ukr. 104/E3
Margao (Madgaon), India 131/K5
Margaret (mt.), Austl. 154/C2
Margaret River, Austl. 154/B5
Margarita (peak), Ca, US 178/C4
Margarita, Isla de (isl.), Ven. 192/F1
Margarition, Gre. 89/G3
Margate, SAfr. 149/E3
Margate, Eng, UK 75/H4
Margate City, NJ, US 180/D5
Margeride, Monts de la (mts.), Fr. 84/E4
Margherita (peak), Ugan. 146/A2
Marghilon, Uzb. 129/F4
Marghita, Rom. 90/F2
Margny-lès-Compiègne, Fr. 94/B5
Margos, Peru 198/B3
Margosatubig, Phil. 121/D6
Margraten, Neth. 95/E2
Mari, Braz. 196/D2
Maria (mt.), Austl. 157/D4
Maria Cleófas (isl.), Mex. 184/D4
Maria da Fé, Braz. 197/H7
Maria Island NP, Austl. 157/D4
María Madre (isl.), Mex. 184/D4
María Magdalena (isl.), Mex. 184/D4
Maria van Diemen (cape), NZ 159/S9
Mariāhū, India 126/D3
Marian, Austl. 156/C3
Marianao, Cuba 187/F1
Marianna, Fl, US 175/G4
Marianna, Ar, US 171/K4
Mariano Comense, It. 100/C1
Mariano Marcos, Phil. 121/D6
Mariánské Lázně, Czh. 97/F3
Marias (riv.), Mt, US 168/F3
Mariato (pt.), Pan. 187/F5
Maribo, Den. 80/D4
Maribor, Slov. 85/L3
Maricá, Braz. 197/L7
Maricopa (co.), Az, US 179/R18
Marié (riv.), Braz. 192/E4
Marie Byrd Land (phys. reg.), Ant. 202/S
Marie-Galante (isl.), Dom. 183/J4
Mariehamn (int'l arpt.), Fin. 81/H1
Mariel, Cuba 187/F1
Marienhafe, Ger. 93/E1
Marienheide, Ger. 95/G1
Mariental, Namb. 147/C5
Mariestad, Swe. 80/E2
Marietta, Ok, US 171/H4
Marietta, Ga, US 175/G3
Marietta, Pa, US 180/B3
Marignane, Fr. 84/F5
Marigot, Dom. 183/N9
Marijampolė, Lith. 81/K4
Marília, Braz. 197/B2
Marín, Sp. 86/A1
Marin (co.), Ca, US 177/J10
Marin-Epagnier, Swi. 98/D3
Marina, It. 88/D3
Marina del Rey, Ca, US 178/F8
Marina del Rey (har.), Ca, US 178/F8
Marina di Andora, It. 100/B5
Marina di Montemarciano, It. 101/G5
Marina di Ravenna, It. 101/F4
Marine Nat'l Rsv., Kenya 146/D3
Marine World Africa USA, Ca, US 177/K10
Marineland, Austl. 155/M8
Marines, Fr. 72/H4
Marinette, Wi, US 169/M4
Maringá, Braz. 197/B2
Marinha Grande, Port. 86/A3
Marinhas, Port. 86/A2
Marion (reef), Austl. 151/E2
Marion, Al, US 175/G3
Marion, In, US 172/C3
Marion, Ky, US 172/B4
Marion, Mi, US 172/C2
Marion, Oh, US 172/D3
Marion (lake), SC, US 175/H3
Maripa, Ven. 195/E3
Mariposa, Ca, US 170/C3
Mariscal Estigarribia, Par. 192/F8
Mariscal Sucre (int'l arpt.), Ecu. 194/B5
Maritime Alps (mts.), Fr. 85/G4
Maritsa (riv.), Bul. 91/H5
Mariupol', Ukr. 104/F3
Mariupol' (int'l arpt.), Ukr. 104/F3
Mariy-El, Resp., Rus. 106/Q6
Marj 'Uyūn, Leb. 133/D3
Mark (riv.), Belg. 92/B6
Mark Twain NWR, Il, US 179/F7
Mark Twain (lake), Mo, US 171/J3
Mark Twain NWR, Mo, US 179/G8
Marka (riv.), Ger. 93/E3
Marka (Merca), Som. 139/P7
Markam, China 125/G2
Markaryd, Swe. 80/E3
Markdorf, Ger. 99/F2
Markelsdorfer (pt.), Ger. 80/D4
Marken (isl.), Neth. 92/C4
Markerwaard (polder), Neth. 92/C3
Market Harborough, Eng, UK 75/F2
Markgroningen, Ger. 96/C5
Markham, On, Can. 173/R8
Markham (bay), Nun., Can. 165/J2
Marki, Pol. 83/L2
Markinch, Sc, UK 78/C4
Markit, China 129/G5
Markleeville, Ca, US 170/C3
Markneukirchen, Ger. 97/F2
Markópoulon, Gre. 89/N9
Markovac, Serb. 90/E3
Marks, Rus. 105/H2
Marksville, La, US 171/J5
Markt Bibart, Ger. 96/D3
Markt Erlbach, Ger. 96/D4
Markt Indersdorf, Ger. 97/E6
Markt Rettenbach, Ger. 99/G2
Markt Sankt Florian, Aus. 97/H6
Markt Schwaben, Ger. 97/E6
Marktbreit, Ger. 96/D3
Marktheidenfeld, Ger. 96/C3
Marktl, Ger. 97/F6
Marktoberdorf, Ger. 99/G2
Marktredwitz, Ger. 97/F3
Marl, Ger. 93/E5
Marla, Austl. 155/G3
Marlboro, NJ, US 180/D3
Marlboro (Upper Marlboro), Md, US 180/B6
Marle, Fr. 94/C4
Marlengo (Marling), It. 99/H4
Marlenheim, Fr. 95/G6
Marles-en-Brie, Fr. 72/L5
Marles-les-Mines, Fr. 94/B3
Marlow, Eng, UK 75/F3
Marlow, Ger. 80/E4
Marlton, NJ, US 180/D4
Marly, Fr. 95/F5
Marly, Fr. 94/C3
Marly-la-Ville, Fr. 72/K4
Marly-le-Roi, Fr. 72/J5
Marmagão, India 131/K5
Marmande, Fr. 84/D4
Marmara, Turk. 91/H5
Marmara (isl.), Turk. 91/H5
Marmara (sea), Turk. 91/J5
Marmaraereğlisi, Turk. 91/H5
Marmaris, Turk. 132/B2
Marmelos (riv.), Braz. 192/F5
Marmion (lake), Austl. 154/D4
Marmirolo, It. 101/D2
Marmolada (peak), It. 85/J3
Marmolejo, Sp. 86/C3
Marmontana (peak), It. 99/F5
Marmora, NJ, US 180/D5
Marmoutier, Fr. 95/G6
Marnay, Fr. 98/B3
Marnaz, Fr. 98/C5
Marne (riv.), Fr. 84/F2
Marne, Ger. 80/C5
Marne (dept.), Fr. 94/C6
Marne au Rhin, Canal de la (canal), Fr. 95/D6
Maro (reef), Hi, US 159/H2
Maroa, Ven. 195/E4
Maroantsetra, Madg. 149/J6
Marokau (isl.), FrPol. 159/L6
Marolambo, Madg. 149/J8
Maroldsweisach, Ger. 96/D2
Marolles-en-Brie, Fr. 72/M5
Marolles-en-Hurepoix, Fr. 72/J6
Maromokotro (peak), Madg. 149/J6
Marondera, Zim. 147/F4
Marone, It. 100/D1
Maroni (riv.), FrG.,Sur. 193/H3
Maroochydore-Mooloolaba, Austl. 156/D4
Maroon Town, Jam. 187/G2
Marostica, It. 101/E1
Marotandrano, Madg. 149/J7
Marotiri (Bass Is.) (isls.), FrPol. 159/L7
Marotta, It. 101/G5
Maroua, Camr. 138/H5
Marouini (riv.), FrG. 195/H4
Marovato, Madg. 149/J6
Marovoay, Madg. 149/H7
Marowijne (dist.), Sur. 195/H3
Marpingen, Ger. 95/G5
Marple, Eng, UK 77/F5
Marquan (riv.), China 124/E2
Marquard, SAfr. 148/D3
Marquarie (riv.), Austl. 157/C1
Marquesas (isls.), FrPol. 159/M5
Marquise, Fr. 94/A2
Marracuene, Moz. 149/F2
Marradi, It. 101/E4
Marrah (mts.), Sudan 139/K5
Marrah (peak), Sudan 139/K5
Marrakech, Mor. 140/D3
Marrero, La, US 179/P17
Marromeu, Moz. 147/G4
Marrupa, Moz. 147/G3
Mars (peak), It. 100/A1
Marsá al Burayqah, Libya 139/J1
Marsá Maţrūḩ, Egypt 143/A2
Marsabit, Kenya 146/C2
Marsabit Nat'l Rsv., Kenya 146/C2
Marsala, It. 88/C4
Marsange (riv.), Fr. 72/L5
Marsannay, Fr. 98/A3
Marsberg, Ger. 93/F6
Marsciano, It. 85/K5
Marsdiep Texelstroom (chan.), Neth. 92/B3
Marseille, Fr. 84/F5
Marseille-en-Beauvaisis, Fr. 94/A4
Marsh (isl.), La, US 174/E4
Marshall (riv.), Austl. 155/H2
Marshall, Sk, Can. 168/F2
Marshall, Co, US 179/B3
Marshall, Mn, US 169/K4
Marshall, Mo, US 171/J3
Marshall, Tx, US 171/J4
Marshall, Ut, US 179/J12
Marshall Islands (ctry.) 158/G3
Marshallton, De, US 180/C4
Marshalltown, Ia, US 169/K5
Marshdale, Co, US 179/B3
Marshfield, Mo, US 171/J3
Märsta, Swe. 80/G2
Marston (lake), Co, US 179/B3
Marsyandi (riv.), Nepal 127/E1
Marta, It. 88/B1
Martaban, Myan. 120/B2
Martaban (gulf), Myan. 120/B2
Martapura, Indo. 122/D4
Marte R. Gomez, Mex. 184/C3
Martelange, Belg. 95/E4
Martellago, It. 101/F1
Martensville, Sk, Can. 168/G2
Martfeld, Ger. 93/G3
Martha's Vineyard (isl.), Ma, US 173/G3
Martignacco, It. 101/G1
Martigny, Swi. 98/D5
Martigny-les-Bains, Fr. 98/B1
Martigues, Fr. 84/F5
Martil, Mor. 142/B2
Martin, Tn, US 172/B4
Martin (lake), Al, US 175/G3
Martin Vaz (isls.), Braz. 193/N8
Martina Franca, It. 89/E2
Martinengo, It. 100/C1
Martinez, Ga, US 175/H3
Martínez de la Torre, Mex. 185/M6

254
Marti – Menta

Martinho Campos, Braz. 197/C1
Martinique (isl.), Fr. 183/N9
Martinique Passage (chan.), Dom.,Mart. 183/J4
Martinon, Gre. 89/H3
Martinópole, Braz. 196/B1
Martinópolis, Braz. 197/B2
Martins, Braz. 196/C2
Martins Creek, Pa, US 180/C2
Martinsburg, WV, US 172/E4
Martinsville, Va, US 172/E4
Martorell, Sp. 87/K7
Martos, Sp. 86/D4
Martre (riv.), Qu, Can. 172/F1
Martres-Tolosane, Fr. 84/D5
Marty, SD, US 169/J5
Marugame, Japan 116/C3
Maruim, Braz. 196/C3
Maruko, Japan 117/F2
Marum, Neth. 92/D2
Maruoka, Japan 116/E2
Marutea (isl.), FrPol. 159/M7
Marv Dasht, Iran 130/F3
Marxheim, Ger. 96/D5
Mary, Trkm. 131/H1
Mary Anne Passage, Austl. 154/B2
Mary Esther, Fl, US 175/G4
Mary-sur-Marne, Fr. 72/M4
Maryborough, Austl. 157/B3
Maryborough, Austl. 156/D4
Marydale, SAfr. 148/C3
Marydel, Md, US 180/C5
Maryfield, Sk, Can. 169/H3
Maryland (co.), Libr. 144/C5
Maryland (state), US 172/E4
Maryland City, Md, US 180/B5
Maryland Heights, Mo, US 179/G8
Maryland Line, Md, US 180/B4
Marystown, Nf, Can. 173/L2
Marysville, Ks, US 171/H3
Marysville, Pa, US 180/B3
Maryville, Tn, US 175/H3
Maryville, Il, US 179/H8
Marzabotto, It. 101/E4
Marzano (peak), It. 88/D2
Marzo (pt.), Col. 194/B3
Marzūq, Libya 138/H2
Masada (ruin), Isr. 133/D4
Masai Mara Nat'l Rsv., Kenya 147/F1
Masai Steppe (grsld.), Tanz. 146/C4
Masaka, Ugan. 146/A3
Masamagrell, Sp. 87/E3
Masamba, Indo. 123/F4
Masan, SKor. 115/E5
Masangwe (hill), Tanz. 146/A4
Masaya, Nic. 186/E4
Masbate (isl.), Phil. 121/D5
Mascara, Alg. 142/F5
Mascarene (isls.), Mrts 149/T15
Mascota, Mex. 184/D4
Mascouche, Qu, Can. 173/N6
Maselheim, Ger. 99/F1
Maserà di Padova, It. 101/E2
Maseru (cap.), Les. 148/D3
Masevaux, Fr. 98/D2
Masfjorden, Nor. 80/A1
Mashan, China 121/A3
Mashhad (int'l arpt.), Iran 129/C5
Mashike, Japan 118/B2
Māshkīd (riv.), Iran 131/H3
Mashtūl as Sūq, Egypt 133/B4
Mashū (lake), Japan 118/D2
Masiaca, Mex. 184/C3
Maside, Sp. 86/A1
Masim (peak), Rus. 105/L1
Masindi, Ugan. 146/A2
Maşīrah, Jazīrat (isl.), Oman 131/G4
Masisea, Peru 198/C3
Masjed-e Soleymān, Iran 130/E2
Mask (lake), Ire. 73/P10
Masker (peak), Mor. 140/D2
Masnou, Sp. 87/L7
Masoala (cape), Madg. 149/J6
Masoala (pen.), Madg. 147/L10
Masoarivo, Madg. 149/H7
Mason, Mi, US 172/C3
Mason, Tx, US 171/H5
Mason (co.), Wa, US 177/A3
Mason (lake), Wa, US 177/B3
Mason and Dixon Line, Pa, US 180/B4
Masone, It. 100/B4
Masonville, Co, US 179/B2
Masquefa, Sp. 87/K6
Massa, It. 100/D4
Massa-Carrara (prov.), It. 100/C4
Massa Finalese, It. 101/E3
Massa Fiscaglia, It. 101/F3
Massa Lombarda, It. 101/E4
Massa Marittima, It. 85/J5
Massa Martana, It. 85/K5
Massachusetts (state), US 173/F3
Massachusetts (bay), Ma, US 173/G3
Massaciuccoli, Lago di (lake), It. 100/D5
Massafra, It. 89/E2
Massangena, Moz. 147/F5
Massapê, Braz. 196/B1
Massapequa, NY, US 181/M9
Massapequa Park, NY, US 181/M9
Massarosa, It. 100/D5
Massbach, Ger. 96/D2
Massena, NY, US 172/F2
Masset, BC, Can. 176/M4
Massey (sound), Nun., Can. 165/S7
Massey, Md, US 180/C5
Massillon, Oh, US 172/D3
Massy, Fr. 72/J5
Masterton, NZ 159/T11
Mastgat (chan.), Neth. 92/B5
Mastic, NY, US 181/F2
Mastic Beach, NY, US 181/F2
Mastník (riv.), Czh. 97/H3
Mastūj (riv.), Pak. 128/A2
Mastung, Pak. 131/J3
Masuda, Japan 116/B3
Masuho, Japan 119/A2
Masurai (peak), Indo. 122/B4
Masvingo, Zim. 147/F5
Maswa Game Rsv., Tanz. 146/B3
Maşyāf, Syria 133/E2
Mat (riv.), Alb. 89/F2
Mata Grande, Braz. 196/C3
Mata Utu, Fr. 159/H6
Mātābhānga, India 127/G2
Matadi, D.R. Congo 147/B2
Matador, Tx, US 171/G4
Matagalpa, Nic. 186/E3
Matagami (lake), Qu, Can. 172/E1
Matagorda (bay), Tx, US 174/D4
Matagorda (isl.), Tx, US 174/D4
Matale, SrL. 124/D6
Matam, Sen. 144/B3
Matamoras, Pa, US 180/D1
Matamoros, Mex. 184/E3
Ma'ţan as Sarra (well), Libya 139/K3
Matandu (riv.), Tanz. 146/C5
Matane (riv.), Qu, Can. 173/H1
Matane, Qu, Can. 173/H1
Matanga, Madg. 149/H8
Matanzas, Cuba 182/E3
Matão, Braz. 197/B2
Matape (riv.), Mex. 184/C2
Matapedia (riv.), Qu, Can. 173/H1
Mataquito (riv.), Chile 200/C2
Matara (ruin), Erit. 130/C6
Matara, SrL. 124/D6
Mataram, Indo. 123/E5
Mataránga, Gre. 89/G3
Mataró, Sp. 87/L6
Matatiele, SAfr. 148/E3
Mataura (riv.), NZ 159/R12
Matawan, NJ, US 181/J10
Matehuala, Mex. 185/E4
Matéri, Ben. 145/F4
Maternillos (pt.), Cuba 183/F3
Mátészalka, Hun. 83/M5
Mateur, Tun. 142/L6
Mathay, Fr. 98/C3
Matheniko Game Rsv., Ugan. 146/B2
Mathew's (peak), Kenya 146/C2
Mathews (lake), Ca, US 178/C3
Mathis, Tx, US 174/D4
Mathoura, Austl. 157/C2
Mathurā, India 126/A2
Mati, Phil. 121/E6
Matias Barbosa, Braz. 197/K6
Matias Olímpio, Braz. 196/B1
Matías Romero, Mex. 186/C2
Matiguás, Nic. 187/E3
Matilija (dam), Ca, US 178/A2
Matinha, Braz. 196/A2
Matinhos, Braz. 197/B3
Matinicock (pt.), NY, US 181/L8
Matiyuri (riv.), Ven. 194/D3
Mātla (riv.), India 127/G5
Matlock, Eng, UK 77/G5
Mato Grosso (plat.), Braz. 193/G6
Mato Grosso do Sul (state), Braz. 197/A1
Mato Grosso, Planalto do (plat.), Braz. 193/H6
Mato Verde, Braz. 196/B4
Matopos, Zim. 147/E5
Matosinhos, Port. 86/A2
Matoya (bay), Japan 119/L7
Maţraḩ, Oman 131/G4
Matrei am Brenner, Aus. 99/H3
Matrei in Osttirol, Aus. 85/K3
Matriz de Camaragibe, Braz. 196/D3
Matroosberg (peak), SAfr. 148/L10
Matsalu (gulf), Est. 81/K2
Matsapa (Manzini) (int'l arpt.), Swaz. 149/E2
Matsiatra (riv.), Madg. 149/H8
Matsoandakana, Madg. 149/J6
Matsubara, Japan 119/J6
Matsubushi, Japan 119/D2
Matsuda, Japan 119/C3
Matsudo, Japan 119/D2
Matsue, Japan 116/C3
Matsuida, Japan 119/B1
Matsumae, Japan 118/B3
Matsumoto, Japan 117/E2
Matsuo, Japan 119/E2
Matsusaka, Japan 119/L6
Matsushima, Japan 118/B4
Matsutō, Japan 116/E2
Matsuyama, Japan 116/C4
Matt, Swi. 99/F4
Mattagami (riv.), On, Can. 172/D1
Mattarello, It. 99/H6
Mattawa, On, Can. 172/E2
Matterhorn (peak), It.,Swi. 98/D6
Mattertal (valley), Swi. 98/D5
Mattese, Mo, US 179/G9
Matthews (mtn.), Ak, US 176/H2
Mattig (riv.), Aus. 97/G6
Mattighofen, Aus. 97/G6
Mattituck, NY, US 181/F2
Mattmarksee (lake), Swi. 98/D5
Mattō, Japan 116/E2
Mattock (riv.), Ire. 76/B4
Mattsee, Aus. 97/G7
Matucana, Peru 198/B3
Maturín, Ven. 195/F2
Matusadona NP, Zim. 147/E4
Matzen, Aus. 91/P7
Maú (riv.), Guy. 192/G3
Mau (peak), Kenya 146/B3
Mau Aimma, India 126/C3
Mau Rānīpur, India 126/B3
Mauá, Braz. 197/C2
Maubert-Fontaine, Fr. 95/D4
Maubeuge, Fr. 94/C3
Maubourguet, Fr. 84/D5
Mauchline, Sc, UK 78/B5
Maud (pt.), Austl. 154/B2
Maud, Sc, UK 78/D1
Maudaha, India 126/C3
Mauerbach, Aus. 91/N7
Mauerkirchen, Aus. 97/G6
Maués, Braz. 192/G4
Maués Açu (riv.), Braz. 192/G4
Maug (isls.), NMar. 158/D2
Mauganj, India 126/C3
Maughold, IM, UK 76/D3
Maughold (pt.), IM, UK 76/D3
Mauguio, Fr. 84/F5
Maui (isl.), Hi, US 166/T10
Mauke (isl.), Cookls. 159/K7
Maulbronn, Ger. 96/B5
Mauldre (riv.), Fr. 94/A6
Maule (pol. reg.), Chile 200/B2
Maule (riv.), Chile 200/C2
Maule, Fr. 72/H5
Mauléon, Fr. 84/C3
Maullín, Chile 200/B4
Maumee (riv.), In,Oh, US 172/C3
Maun, Bots. 147/D4
Mauna Kea (peak), Hi, US 166/U11
Mauna Loa (peak), Hi, US 166/U11
Maunath Bhanjan, India 126/D3
Maungdaw, Myan. 125/F3
Mauperthuis, Fr. 72/M5
Maupertus (int'l arpt.), Fr. 84/C2
Maupiti (isl.), FrPol. 159/K6
Maur, Swi. 99/E3
Maurāwān, India 126/C2
Maurecourt, Fr. 72/J5
Maurepas (lake), La, US 179/P16
Maurepas, Fr. 94/A6
Mauriac, Fr. 84/E4
Maurice (lake), Austl. 155/F4
Maurice (riv.), NJ, US 180/C5
Mauricetown, NJ, US 180/D5
Maurienne (valley), Fr. 85/G4
Maurilândia, Braz. 197/B1
Mauritania (ctry.) 138/C4
Mauriti, Braz. 196/C2
Mauritius (ctry.) 149/T15
Mauston, Wi, US 169/L5
Mauthausen, Aus. 97/H6
Mauvoisin, Barrage de (dam), Swi. 98/D6
Mavrommátion, Gre. 89/H3
Mavrovo NP, FYROM 89/G2
Maw Daung (pass), Thai. 120/B4
Mawāna, India 126/A1
Mawlaik, Myan. 125/F3
Mawlamyine (Moulmein), Myan. 120/B2
Mawson, Austl., Ant. 202/E
Maxaranguape, Braz. 196/D2
Maxcanú, Mex. 186/D1
Maxdorf, Ger. 96/B4
Maxéville, Fr. 95/F6
Maxhütte-Haidhof, Ger. 97/F4
May (cape), NJ, US 180/D5
May-en-Multien, Fr. 72/M4
May, Isle of (isl.), Sc, UK 78/D4
May Pen, Jam. 187/G2
Maya (isl.), Indo. 122/C4
Maya (riv.), Rus. 109/N4
Maya (mts.), Guat. 186/D2
Maya-san (peak), Japan 119/H6
Mayaguana (isl.), Bahm. 183/G3
Mayaguana Passage (chan.), Bahm. 187/H1
Mayagüez, PR 183/M8
Mayakovskogo (peak), Taj. 131/K1
Mayang, China 125/J2
Mayarí, Cuba 187/H1
Maybee, Mi, US 177/E8
Maybole, Sc, UK 78/B6
Maydān, Iraq 130/E2
Mayen, Ger. 95/G3
Mayenne, Fr. 84/C2
Mayenne (riv.), Fr. 84/C3
Mayerthorpe, Ab, Can. 168/E2
Mayfield, Ky, US 172/B4
Mayfield, Sc, UK 78/C5
Maykop, Rus. 104/G3
Maymyo, Myan. 125/G3
Maynooth, Ire. 73/Q10
Mayo (riv.), Arg. 199/B6
Mayo, Yk, Can. 176/L3
Mayo, Md, US 180/B6
Mayotte (isl.), May. 149/H6
Mays Landing, NJ, US 180/D5
Maysville, Ky, US 172/D4
Maythalūn, WBnk. 133/G7
Mayville, ND, US 169/J4
Maywood, NJ, US 181/J8
Maywood, Il, US 177/Q16
Maywood, Ca, US 178/F8
Mazabuka, Zam. 147/E4
Mazagão, Braz. 193/H4
Mazamet, Fr. 84/E5
Mazán, Peru 198/C1
Mazār-e Sharīf, Afg. 131/J1
Mazara del Vallo, It. 88/C4
Mazara, Val di (valley), It. 88/C4
Mazarrón, Sp. 86/E4
Mazaruni (riv.), Guy. 192/G2
Mazatán, Mex. 184/C2
Mazatenango, Guat. 186/D3
Mazatlán, Mex. 184/D4
Mažeikiai, Lith. 81/K3
Mazeppa NP, Austl. 156/B3
Mazgirt, Turk. 132/D2
Mazıkıran (pass), Turk. 132/D2
Mazingarbe, Fr. 94/B3
Mazocruz, Peru 198/D5
Mazong (peak), China 112/G3
Mazowieckie (prov.), Pol. 83/L2
Mazury (reg.), Pol. 83/L2
Mazyr, Bela. 104/D1
Mbabala (isl.), Zam. 146/A5
Mbabane (cap.), Swaz. 149/E2
Mbabo (peak), Camr. 138/H6
Mbacké, Sen. 144/B3
Mbaïki, CAfr. 139/J7
Mbakaou, Lac de (lake), Camr. 138/H6
Mbala, Zam. 146/A5
Mbale, Ugan. 146/B2
Mbalmayo, Camr. 138/H7
Mbandaka, D.R. Congo 139/J7
Mbarangandu (riv.), Tanz. 146/C5
Mbarara, Ugan. 146/A3
Mbata, CAfr. 139/J7
Mbeya (peak), Tanz. 146/B5
Mbeya (range), Tanz. 147/F2
Mbeya, Tanz. 146/B5
Mbeya (pol. reg.), Tanz. 146/B5
Mbini, EqG. 138/G7
Mbini (riv.), EqG.,Gabon 138/H7
Mbirizi, Ugan. 146/A3
Mbomou (riv.), CAfr. 139/L6
M'Bour, Sen. 144/A3
Mbuji-Mayi, D.R. Congo 147/D2
Mbwemburu (riv.), Tanz. 146/C5
McAdoo, Pa, US 180/C2
McAfee, NJ, US 180/D1
McAlester, Ok, US 171/J4
McAlisterville, Pa, US 180/A2
McAllen, Tx, US 174/D5
McBride, BC, Can. 168/C2
McCall, Id, US 168/D4
McCarran (int'l arpt.), Nv, US 170/D3
McCarthy, Ak, US 176/K3
McClain (co.), Ok, US 179/M15
McClure, Pa, US 180/A2
McClusky, Il, US 179/G7
McClusky, ND, US 169/H4
McComb, Ms, US 171/K5
McConaughy (lake), Ne, US 169/H5
McCook, Ne, US 171/G2
McCormick, SC, US 175/H3
McCreary, Mb, Can. 169/J3
McCullom Lake, Il, US 177/P15
McDaniel, Md, US 180/B6
McDermitt, Nv, US 168/D5
McDonald (mt.), Ak, US 176/F3
McDonald (isls.), Austl. 65/N8
McDonnell (mt.), Austl. 155/H5
McDougall (pass), NW,Yk, Can. 176/L2
McDowell (mts.), Az, US 179/S18
McElhattan, Pa, US 180/A1
McGhee Tyson (int'l arpt.), Tn, US 175/H3
McGrath, Ak, US 176/G3
McGregor (riv.), BC, Can. 168/C2
McGregor, On, Can. 177/G7
McHenry (co.), Il, US 177/N15
McKean (isl.), Kiri. 159/H5
McKeand (riv.), Nun., Can. 165/K2
McKee City, NJ, US 180/D5
McKeesport, Pa, US 172/E3
McKenzie, Tn, US 172/B4
McKinlay, Austl. 156/A3
McKinley (mt.), Ak, US 176/H3
McKinleyville, Ca, US 168/B5
McLaughlin, SD, US 169/H4
McLean, Va, US 180/A6
McLennan, Ab, Can. 168/D2
McLeod (lake), Austl. 154/B3
McLeod (riv.), BC, Can. 168/D2
McLeod (bay), NW, Can. 164/E2
McLeod Lake, BC, Can. 168/C2
M'Clintock (chan.), Nun., Can. 164/F1
McLoud, Ok, US 179/N15
M'Clure (str.), NW, Can. 165/Q7
McMinnville, Or, US 168/C4
McMinnville, Tn, US 172/C5
McMurdo, US, Ant. 202/M
McNeil (isl.), Wa, US 177/B3
McPherson, Ks, US 171/H3
McQueeney, Tx, US 179/U20
Mdantsane, SAfr. 148/D4
M'diq, Mor. 142/B2
Me-akan-dake (peak), Japan 118/C2
Mead, Co, US 179/C2
Mead (lake), Az,Nv, US 170/D3
Meade (riv.), Ak, US 176/G2
Meadow Lake, Sk, Can. 168/F2
Meadow Valley Wash (riv.), Nv, US 170/D3
Meadowbrook, Il, US 179/G8
Meadowlands Sports Complex, NJ, US 181/J8
Meadows, Md, US 180/B6
Meadville, Ms, US 175/F4
Meadville, Pa, US 172/D3
Mealhada, Port. 86/A2
Meall a' Bhuiridh (peak), Sc, UK 78/B3
Meall Buidhe (peak), Sc, UK 78/B3
Meall Dearg (peak), Sc, UK 78/C3
Meall Dubh (peak), Sc, UK 78/B2
Meall nam Fuaran (peak), Sc, UK 78/C4
Meall Tairneachan (peak), Sc, UK 78/C3
Mearim (riv.), Braz. 193/J5
Meat (mtn.), Ak, US 176/F2
Meath (co.), Ire. 76/B4
Meath Park, Sk, Can. 169/G2
Méaulte, Fr. 94/B4
Meaux, Fr. 72/L5
Mecapalapa, Mex. 185/M6
Mécatina,Rivière du Petit (riv.), Nf,Qu, Can. 165/K3
Mecca, Mo, US 179/D5
Mechanicsburg, Pa, US 180/A3
Mechanicsburg Naval Rsv., Pa, US 180/B3
Mechelen, Belg. 95/D1
Mecheria, Alg. 141/E2
Mechi (zone), Nepal 127/F2
Mechra-Bel-Ksiri, Mor. 142/B2
Mecidiye, Turk. 89/K2
Mecitözü, Turk. 132/C1
Meckenbeuren, Ger. 99/F2
Meckenheim, Ger. 95/G2
Mecklenburg-Vorpommern (state), Ger. 80/E5
Mecklenburger (bay), Ger. 82/F1
Mecuia (peak), Moz. 147/G3
Meda, It. 100/C1
Medak, India 124/C4
Medan, Indo. 122/A3
Médanos, Arg. 200/E3
Médanos de Coro, PN, Ven. 194/D2
Medanosa (pt.), Arg. 201/D6
Mede Lomellina, It. 100/B2
Médéa, Alg. 142/G4
Médéa (prov.), Alg. 142/G4
Medebach, Ger. 93/F6
Medeiros Neto, Braz. 196/B5
Medel (peak), Swi. 99/E4
Medellín, Col. 192/C2
Medemblik, Neth. 92/C3
Meden (riv.), Eng, UK 77/G5
Medenine, Tun. 141/H2
Medenine (gov.), Tun. 141/H2
Medesano, It. 100/D3
Medetsiz (peak), Turk. 132/C2
Medford, Or, US 168/C5
Medford, NY, US 181/E2
Medford Lakes, NJ, US 180/D4
Medgidia, Rom. 91/J3
Media, Pa, US 180/C4
Media Luna, La (isls.), Hon. 187/F3
Mediaş, Rom. 91/G2
Medical Lake, Wa, US 168/D4
Medicine Bow, Wy, US 169/G5
Medicine Bow (range), Wy, US 170/F2
Medicine Hat, Ab, Can. 168/F3
Medina (riv.), Tx, US 171/H5
Medina, Braz. 196/B5
Medina, Col. 194/C3
Medina, ND, US 169/J4
Medina, Oh, US 172/D3
Medina, Wa, US 177/C2
Medina de Pomar, Sp. 86/D1
Medina de Rioseco, Sp. 86/C2
Medina del Campo, Sp. 86/C2
Medina-Sidonia, Sp. 86/C4
Medinaceli, Sp. 86/D2
Medinipur, India 127/F4
Mediouna, Mor. 140/D2
Mediterranean (sea) 69/E5
Mednogorsk, Rus. 105/L2
Medole, It. 100/D2
Medolla, It. 101/E3
Međugorje, Bosn. 90/C4
Medveditsa (riv.), Rus. 106/E5
Medvezh'i (isls.), Rus. 107/S2
Medvezh'yegorsk, Rus. 102/G3
Medvode, Slov. 85/L3
Medway (co.), Eng, UK 75/G4
Meekatharra, Austl. 154/C3
Meeker, Co, US 170/F2
Meeker Park, Co, US 179/A2
Meerbusch, Ger. 92/D6
Meerhout, Belg. 95/E1
Meersburg, Ger. 99/F2
Meerssen, Neth. 95/E2
Meerut, India 126/A1
Meeteetse, Wy, US 168/F4
Megá Kalívia, Gre. 89/G3
Megáli Panayía, Gre. 89/H2
Megálon Khoríon, Gre. 132/A2
Megalópolis, Gre. 89/H4
Megantic (peak), Qu, Can. 173/G2
Mégara, Gre. 89/H3
Megève, Fr. 98/C6
Meghālaya (state), India 125/F2
Meghna (riv.), Bang. 127/H4
Megiddo, Isr. 133/G6
Mégiscane (lake), Qu, Can. 172/E1
Mégiscane (riv.), Qu, Can. 172/E1
Megisti (isl.), Greece 133/A1
Mehaigne (riv.), Belg. 95/E2
Mehamn, Nor. 79/H1
Meharry (mt.), Austl. 154/C2
Mehdia, Alg. 142/F5
Mehdiya-Plage, Mor. 142/A2
Mehe (riv.), Ger. 93/G1
Mehedinţi (prov.), Rom. 90/F3
Mehlingen, Ger. 95/G4
Mehlville, Mo, US 179/G9
Mehndāwal, India 126/D2
Mehrān (riv.), Iran 131/F3
Mehring, Ger. 95/F4
Mehrnbach, Aus. 97/G6
Mehtar Lām, Afg. 128/A2
Mei (riv.), China 121/C3
Meia Ponte (riv.), Braz. 197/B1
Meiganga, Camr. 138/H6
Meighen (isl.), Nun., Can. 165/R7
Meigu, China 125/H2
Meihekou, China 113/N3
Meikle Bin (peak), Sc, UK 78/B4
Meikle Black Law (hill), Sc, UK 78/D5
Meikle Says Law (peak), Sc, UK 78/D5
Meiktila, Myan. 125/G3
Meilen, Swi. 99/E3
Meine, Ger. 93/H4
Meiners Oaks, Ca, US 178/A2
Meinersen, Ger. 93/H4
Meinerzhagen, Ger. 95/G1
Meiningen, Ger. 96/D1
Meiringen, Swi. 98/E4
Meisenheim, Ger. 95/G4
Meishan (res.), China 114/C5
Meissen, Ger. 83/G3
Meissner (peak), Ger. 93/G6
Meitan, China 121/A2
Meitingen, Ger. 96/D5
Meiwa, Japan 119/L6
Meix-devant-Virton, Belg. 95/E4
Meizhou, China 121/C3
Mejaniga, It. 101/E2
Mejaouda (well), Mrta. 140/D5
Mejorada del Campo, Sp. 87/N9
Mek'elē, Eth. 139/N5
Meknès (prov.), Mor. 142/B3
Meknès, Mor. 142/B3
Mekong (riv.), Asia 112/G5
Mekong, Mouths of the (delta), Viet. 125/J6
Mekongga (peak), Indo. 123/F4
Mekoryuk, Ak, US 176/E3
Melaka, Malay. 122/B3
Melanesia (reg.) 158/E5
Melappālaiyam, India 124/C6
Melawi (riv.), Indo. 122/D4
Melbeck, Ger. 93/H2
Melbourne, Fl, US 175/H4
Melbourne (isl.), Nun., Can. 164/F2
Melbourne, Austl. 157/G5
Melbu, Nor. 79/E1
Melchor (isl.), Chile 200/B5
Melchor Múzquiz, Mex. 174/C5
Melchor Ocampo, Mex. 185/Q9
Meldola, It. 101/F4
Meldorf, Ger. 80/C4
Mele (cape), It. 100/B5
Melegnano, It. 100/C2
Melenci, Serb. 90/E3
Melenki, Rus. 102/J5
Melesse, Fr. 84/C2
Meleuz, Rus. 105/K1
Mélèzes (riv.), Qu, Can. 165/J3
Melezza (riv.), It. 99/E5
Melfi, It. 88/D2
Melfort, Sk, Can. 169/G2
Melgar de Fernamental, Sp. 86/C1
Melhus, Nor. 79/D3
Melibocus (peak), Ger. 96/B3
Melide, Swi. 99/E6
Meligalás, Gre. 89/G4
Melíki, Gre. 89/H2
Melili (peak), Kenya 146/C3
Melilla, Sp. 142/C2
Melimoyu (peak), Chile 200/B5
Melipilla, Chile 200/N8
Mélisey, Fr. 98/C2
Melissano, It. 89/F3
Melita, Mb, Can. 169/H3
Melito di Porto Salvo, It. 88/D4
Melitopol', Ukr. 104/E3
Melitota, Md, US 180/B5
Melkbosstrand, SAfr. 148/L10
Melksham, Eng, UK 74/D4
Mella (riv.), It. 100/D2
Mellan Fryken (lake), Swe. 80/E2
Melle, Ger. 93/F4
Melle, Belg. 94/C2
Mellea (riv.), It. 100/A3
Mellègue, Oued (riv.), Alg. 142/K7
Mellerud, Swe. 80/E2
Mellid, Sp. 86/A1
Mellieħa, Malta 88/L7
Mellingen, Swi. 99/E3
Mellizo Sur (peak), Chile 201/B6
Mellrichstadt, Ger. 96/D2
Mellum (isl.), Ger. 93/F1
Melmoth, SAfr. 149/E3
Melnik, Bul. 89/H2
Mělník, Czh. 97/H2
Melo, Uru. 199/F3
Melocheville, Qu, Can. 173/N7
Melrose, Md, US 180/B4
Melrose, Sc, UK 78/D5
Melrose Abbey, Sc, UK 78/D5
Melrose Park, Il, US 177/Q16
Mels, Swi. 99/F3
Melsungen, Ger. 93/G6
Meltham, Eng, UK 77/G4
Melton, Austl. 157/C3
Melton Mowbray, Eng, UK 75/F1
Melun, Fr. 72/K6
Melville (cape), Phil. 123/E2
Melville, Sk, Can. 169/H3
Melville (isl.), Austl. 151/C2
Melville (bay), Austl. 151/C2
Melville, Il, US 179/G8
Melville (cape), Austl. 156/B1
Melville (lake), Nf, Can. 165/L3
Melville (pen.), Nun., Can. 165/H2
Melville, NY, US 181/M8
Melvindale, Mi, US 177/F7
Mélykút, Hun. 90/D2
Melzo, It. 100/C2
Memāri, India 127/G4
Memmert (isl.), Ger. 92/D1
Memmingen, Ger. 99/G2
Memphis, Mo, US 169/K5
Memphis (int'l arpt.), Tn, US 171/K4
Memphis, Tx, US 171/G4
Memphis, Tn, US 171/K4
Memphis (ruin), Egypt 133/B5
Memphis, Mi, US 177/G6
Mena, Ar, US 171/J4
Menaggio, It. 99/F5
Menai (str.), Wal, UK 76/D5
Menai Bridge, Wal, UK 76/D5
Ménaka, Mali 145/F3
Menaldum, Neth. 92/C2
Menarandra (riv.), Madg. 149/H9
Menard, Tx, US 171/H5
Menasalbas, Sp. 86/C3
Menavava (riv.), Madg. 149/H7
Mendawai (riv.), Indo. 122/D4
Mende, Fr. 84/E4
Menden, Ger. 93/E6
Mendenhall (cape), Ak, US 176/E4
Mendes, Braz. 197/K7
Méndez, Mex. 185/F3
Mendham, NJ, US 180/D2
Mendig, Ger. 95/G3
Mendip (hills), Eng, UK 74/D4
Mendocino, Ca, US 170/B3
Mendocino (cape), Ca, US 124/A3
Mendooran, Austl. 157/D1
Mendoza, Arg. 200/C2
Mendoza (prov.), Arg. 200/C2
Mendoza, Cuba 187/E1
Mendoza, Peru 198/B2
Mendoza (El Plumerillo) (int'l arpt.), Arg. 200/C2
Mendrisio, Swi. 99/E6
Mene Grande, Ven. 194/D2
Menegosa (peak), It. 100/C3
Menemen, Turk. 104/C5
Menen, Belg. 94/C2
Menengai Crater, Kenya 146/C3
Menengiyn (plain), Mong. 113/L2
Menfi, It. 88/C4
Meng Xian, China 114/C4
Mengcheng, China 114/D4
Mengen, Ger. 99/F1
Mengersgereuth-Hämmern, Ger. 96/D2
Mengerskirchen, Ger. 96/B1
Mengeš, Slov. 85/L3
Menggala, Indo. 122/C4
Menghai, China 120/C1
Mengibar, Sp. 86/D4
Mengkofen, Ger. 97/F5
Mengla, China 120/C1
Menglian Daizu Lahuzu Vazu Zizhixian, China 125/G3
Mengyin, China 114/D4
Mengzi, China 125/H3
Menindee, Austl. 157/B2
Menindee (dam), Austl. 157/B2
Menindee (lake), Austl. 155/J5
Meningie, Austl. 157/A2
Menlo Park, Ca, US 177/K12
Menlo Park, NJ, US 181/H9
Menlolat (peak), Chile 200/B5
Mennecy, Fr. 72/K6
Menomonee Falls, Wi, US 172/B3
Menomonie, Wi, US 169/L4
Menongue, Ang. 147/C3
Menorca (int'l arpt.), Sp. 87/H3
Menorca (Minorca) (isl.), Sp. 87/H2
Mentasta Lake, Ak, US 176/K3
Mentawai (isls.), Indo. 122/A4

Menta – Mito
255

Mentawai (str.), Indo. 122/A4
Menteroda, Ger. 93/H6
Menthon-Saint-Bernard, Fr. 98/C6
Mentone, Tx, US 171/G5
Mentone, Ca, US 178/C2
Mentor, Oh, US 172/D3
Mentue (riv.), Swi. 98/C4
Menucourt, Fr. 72/H4
Menuma, Japan 119/C1
Menyapa (peak), Indo. 123/E3
Menzel Bou Zelafa, Tun. 142/M6
Menzel Bourguiba, Tun. 142/L6
Menzel Temime, Tun. 142/M6
Menzie (mt.), Yk, Can. 176/M3
Menzies, Austl. 154/D4
Menziken, Swi. 98/E3
Menzingen, Swi. 99/E3
Menznau, Swi. 98/E3
Meolo, It. 101/F1
Meon (riv.), Eng, UK 75/E5
Meoqui, Mex. 184/D2
Mepistskaro (peak), Geo. 105/G4
Meppel, Neth. 92/D3
Meppen, Ger. 93/E3
Meppen, Il, US 179/F8
Mequinenzo, Embalse de (res.), Sp. 87/E2
Mer, Fr. 84/D3
Mera (riv.), It. 99/F5
Meramec (riv.), Mo, US 171/K3
Merano, It. 99/H4
Merate, It. 100/C1
Meratus (mts.), Indo. 122/D4
Meraux, La, US 179/Q17
Merbein, Austl. 157/B2
Mercaderes, Col. 194/B4
Mercantour, PN du, Fr. 85/G4
Mercatello sul Metauro, It. 101/F5
Mercato Saraceno, It. 101/F5
Merced (riv.), Ca, US 170/B3
Merced, Ca, US 170/B3
Mercedario (peak), Arg. 199/B3
Mercedes, Arg. 199/E2
Mercedes, Arg. 200/D2
Mercedes, Arg. 201/J11
Mercedes, Uru. 201/J10
Mercer (co.), NJ, US 180/D3
Mercer (isl.), Wa, US 177/C2
Mercer Island, Wa, US 177/C2
Mercerville-Hamilton Square, NJ, US 180/D3
Merchtem, Belg. 95/D2
Mercier, Qu, Can. 173/N7
Mercoal, Ab, Can. 168/D2
Mercy (cape), Nun., Can. 165/K2
Mercy-le-Bas, Fr. 95/E5
Méré, Fr. 72/H5
Meredith (lake), Tx, US 171/G4
Meredith (cape), UK 201/E7
Merefa, Ukr. 104/F2
Merelbeke, Belg. 94/C2
Merenberg, Ger. 96/B1
Mergozzo, It. 99/E6
Mergui (arch.), Myan. 125/G5
Mergui (Myeik), Myan. 120/B3
Meriç, Turk. 91/H5
Méricourt, Fr. 72/G4
Méricourt, Fr. 94/B3
Mérida, Sp. 86/B3
Mérida, Ven. 194/D2
Mérida (state), Ven. 194/D2
Mérida, Mex. 186/D1
Mérida, Cordillera de (mts.), Ven. 192/D2
Meridian, Ms, US 175/F3
Meridian, Ok, US 179/N14
Mérignac, Fr. 84/C4
Merignac (int'l arpt.), Fr. 84/C4
Merimbula, Austl. 157/D3
Merinda, Austl. 156/C3
Mering, Ger. 96/D6
Merinos, Uru. 201/K10
Merja Zerga (lake), Mor. 142/A2
Mérk, Hun. 90/F2
Merkendorf, Ger. 96/D4
Merksem, Belg. 92/B6
Merksplas, Belg. 92/B6
Merlimont, Fr. 94/A3
Merlo, Arg. 201/J11
Meroe (ruin), Sudan 130/B5
Merone, It. 100/C1
Merredin, Austl. 154/C4
Merriam, Ks, US 179/D5
Merrick, NY, US 181/L9
Merrick (peak), Sc, UK 76/D1
Merrill, Wi, US 169/L4
Merrill Creek (res.), NJ, US 180/C2
Merrimack, NH, US 173/G3
Merritt, BC, Can. 168/C3
Merritt Island, Fl, US 175/H4
Merriwa, Austl. 157/D2
Mers-les-Bains, Fr. 94/A3
Mersch, Lux. 95/F4
Merse (reg.), Sc, UK 78/D5
Mersey (riv.), Eng, UK 77/F5
Merseyside (co.), Eng, UK 77/F5
Mersing, Malay. 122/B3
Mertert, Lux. 95/F4
Mertesdorf, Ger. 95/F4
Merthyr Tydfil, Wal, UK 74/C3
Merthyr Tydfil (co.), Wal, UK 74/C3
Mértola, Port. 86/B4
Merton (bor.), Eng, UK 72/C2
Mertzon, Tx, US 171/G5
Mertzwiller, Fr. 95/G6
Meru (mt.), Tanz. 146/C3
Meru, Kenya 146/C2
Méru, Fr. 94/B5
Meru NP, Kenya 146/C2
Merville, Fr. 94/B2
Merwedekanaal (riv.), Neth. 92/C5
Méry-sur-Oise, Fr. 72/J4
Merzen, Ger. 93/E4
Merzenich, Ger. 95/F2
Merzifon, Turk. 132/C1
Merzig, Ger. 95/F5
Mesa (mtn.), Ak, US 176/G3
Mesa, Az, US 179/S19
Mesa (peak), Arg. 201/C6
Mesa Verde NP, Co, US 170/E3
Mesabi (range), Mn, US 169/K4
Mesach Mellet (hills), Libya 141/H4
Mesagne, It. 89/E2
Mesarás (gulf), Gre. 89/J5
Mescalero (ridge), NM, US 174/C3
Meschede, Ger. 93/F6
Mesco, Punta di (pt.), It. 100/C4
Mesolcina (peak), It. 101/F5
Meseta de Montemayor (plat.), Arg. 200/D5
Mesgouez (lake), Qu, Can. 172/F1
Mesola, It. 101/F3
Mesolóngion, Gre. 89/G3
Mesomeloka, Madg. 149/J8
Mesopotamia (reg.), Arg. 199/E3
Mesoraca, It. 88/E3
Mespelbrunn, Ger. 96/C3
Mesquite, Tx, US 171/H4
Mesrouh (peak), Mor. 140/E2
Messaad, Alg. 138/F1
Messancy, Belg. 95/E4
Messel, Ger. 96/B3
Messina, SAfr. 147/F5
Messina (str.), It. 88/D4
Messina, It. 88/D3
Messini (gulf), Gre. 89/H4
Messíni, Gre. 89/H4
Messkirch, Ger. 99/F2
Messstetten, Ger. 99/E1
Messy, Fr. 72/L5
Mesta (riv.), Bul. 91/F5
Mestre, It. 101/F2
Mestrino, It. 101/E2
Mesudiye, Turk. 104/F4
Mesumba (peak), Tanz. 146/C4
Mesurado (cape), Libr. 144/C5
Meta (dept.), Col. 194/C4
Meta (riv.), Col.,Ven. 194/D3
Meta Incognita (pen.), Nun., Can. 165/K2
Metabetchouan, Qu, Can. 173/G1
Métabetchouane (riv.), Qu, Can. 173/F1
Metairie, La, US 179/P17
Metallifere, Colline (mts.), It. 101/D6
Metamora, Mi, US 177/F6
Metán, Arg. 199/D2
Metapontum (ruin), It. 88/E2
Metauro (riv.), It. 85/K5
Metelen, Ger. 93/E4
Metéora, Gre. 89/G3
Metepec, Mex. 185/Q10
Methven, Sc, UK 78/C4
Metica (riv.), Col. 194/C4
Metković, Cro. 89/E1
Metlakatla, Ak, US 176/M4
Metlatonoc, Mex. 186/B2
Metlili Chaamba, Alg. 141/F2
Metnitz, Aus. 85/L3
Metro Toronto Zoo, On, Can. 173/R8
Metropolis, Il, US 172/B4
Metropolitan Oakland (int'l arpt.), Ca, US 170/B3
Metropolitana de Santiago (pol. reg.), Chile 200/N8
Métsovon, Gre. 89/G3
Mettawa, Il, US 177/Q15
Mettenheim, Ger. 97/F6
Mettet, Belg. 95/D3
Mettingen, Ger. 93/E4
Mettlach, Ger. 95/F4
Mettmach, Aus. 97/G6
Mettmann, Ger. 92/D6
Metu, Eth. 139/N6
Metuchen, NJ, US 181/H9
Metulla, Isr. 133/D3
Metz, Fr. 95/F5
Metz-Nancy-Lorraine (int'l arpt.), Fr. 95/F6
Metzingen, Ger. 96/C5
Metztitlán, Mex. 185/L6
Meudon, Fr. 72/J5
Meudt, Ger. 95/G3
Meulan, Fr. 72/H4
Meulebeke, Belg. 94/C2
Meurthe (riv.), Fr. 98/C1
Meurthe-et-Moselle (dept.), Fr. 95/E6
Meuse (dept.), Fr. 95/E6
Meuse (riv.), Fr. 82/C4
Meuzin (riv.), Fr. 98/A3
Mevasseret Ẕiyyon, Isr. 133/G8
Mexborough, Eng, UK 77/G5
Mexia, Tx, US 171/H5
Mexiana, Ilha (isl.), Braz. 193/J3
Mexicalcingo, Mex. 185/Q10
Mexicali, Mex. 184/B1
Mexico (ctry.) 161/G7
Mexico (cap.), Mex. 185/Q10
México (state), Mex. 182/A5
Mexico (gulf), NAm. 182/C2
Mexico, Mo, US 171/K3
Meximieux, Fr. 98/B6
Meybod, Iran 130/F2
Meyers Chuck, Ak, US 176/M4
Meyerton, SAfr. 148/Q13
Meymaneh, Afg. 131/H1
Meyrin, Swi. 98/C5
Meythet, Fr. 98/C6
Meyzieu, Fr. 98/A6
Mezdra, Bul. 89/H1
Mèze, Fr. 84/E5
Mezen' (riv.), Rus. 106/E3
Mezen' (bay), Rus. 103/J2
Mezha (riv.), Bela. 81/P4
Mezhdurechensk, Rus. 106/J4
Mezhdusharskiy (isl.), Rus. 106/E2
Mézières-sur-Seine, Fr. 72/H5
Mezőberény, Hun. 90/E2
Mezőkovácsháza, Hun. 90/E2
Mezőkövesd, Hun. 83/L5
Mezőtúr, Hun. 90/E2
Mezquital (riv.), Mex. 184/D4
Mezzana (peak), It. 99/G5
Mezzocorona, It. 99/H5
Mezzogoro, It. 101/F3
Mezzolombardo, It. 99/H5
Mfangano (isl.), Kenya 146/B3
Mga (riv.), Rus. 103/U7
M'goun (peak), Mor. 140/D3
Mhamdia Fouchana, Tun. 142/M6
Mhòr (lake), Sc, UK 78/B2
Mhow, India 131/L4
Mi (riv.), China 121/B2
Mi-shima (isl.), Japan 116/B3
Mi Xian, China 114/C4
Miahuatlán de Porfirio Díaz, Mex. 186/B2
Miajadas, Sp. 86/C3
Miami, Az, US 170/E4
Miami, Fl, US 175/H5
Miami (int'l arpt.), Fl, US 175/H5
Miami (co.), In, US 179/D6
Miami, Ok, US 171/J3
Miami Beach, Fl, US 175/H5
Miān Channūn, Pak. 128/B4
Mianchi, China 114/B4
Mīāndoāb, Iran 130/E1
Miandrivazo, Madg. 149/H7
Mīāneh, Iran 130/E1
Miāni, Pak. 128/B3
Mianning, China 125/H2
Mianus (riv.), Ct, US 181/E1
Miānwāli, Pak. 128/A3
Mianyang, China 112/D5
Mianzhu, China 112/H5
Miao'er (peak), China 121/B2
Miarinarivo, Madg. 149/H7
Miary, Madg. 149/G8
Miass, Rus. 103/P5
Miass (riv.), Rus. 103/P5
Miastko, Pol. 80/G4
Mica Creek, BC, Can. 168/D2
Michalovce, Slvk. 83/L4
Michelfeld, Ger. 97/E3
Michelson (mt.), Ak, US 176/K2
Michelstadt, Ger. 96/C3
Michendorf, Ger. 82/Q7
Michigan (state), US 172/C2
Michigan (lake), US 172/C2
Michigan City, In, US 172/C3
Michipicoten (isl.), On, Can. 172/C2
Michoacán de Ocampo (state), Mex. 182/A4
Michurin, Bul. 91/H4
Michurinsk, Rus. 105/G1
Mickle Fell (peak), Eng, UK 77/F2
Mico (riv.), Nic. 182/E5
Micoud, StL. 183/N9
Micronesia (reg.) 158/E3
Micronesia, Federated States of (ctry.) 158/D4
Mid Yell, Sc, UK 73/W13
Midal (well), Niger 145/G2
Midale, Sk, Can. 169/H3
Middelburg, SAfr. 148/D3
Middelburg, SAfr. 149/E2
Middelburg, Neth. 92/A5
Middelharnis, Neth. 92/B5
Middelkerke, Belg. 94/B1
Middle (bay), NY, US 181/L9
Middle Alkali (lake), Ca, US 170/C2
Middle Andaman (isl.), India 125/F5
Middle Caicos (isl.), UK 187/J1
Middle Concho (riv.), Tx, US 174/C4
Middle Raccoon (riv.), Ia, US 171/J2
Middle River, Md, US 180/B5
Middle Sister (peak), Or, US 168/C4
Middleburg, Md, US 180/A4
Middleberg, Ok, US 179/M15
Middleburg, Pa, US 180/A2
Middlebury, Vt, US 172/F2
Middlemount, Austl. 156/C3
Middleport, Pa, US 180/B2
Middlesboro, Ky, US 172/D4
Middlesbrough, Eng, UK 77/G2
Middlesbrough (co.), Eng, UK 77/G2
Middlesex (co.), Eng, UK 75/F4
Middlesex, NJ, US 180/D2
Middleton, Eng, UK 77/F4
Middletown, De, US 180/C5
Middletown, NJ, US 181/J10
Middletown, Pa, US 180/B3
Midelt, Mor. 140/D2
Midi (canal), Fr. 84/D5
Midi-Pyrénées (pol. reg.), Fr. 84/D4
Midland, On, Can. 172/E2
Midland, Mi, US 172/C3
Midland, Tx, US 171/G5
Midland, Wa, US 177/C3
Midland Park, NJ, US 181/J8
Midleton, Ire. 73/P11
Midlothian, Il, US 177/Q16
Midlothian (pol. reg.), Sc, UK 78/C5
Midlum, Ger. 93/F1
Midongy Atsimo, Madg. 149/H8
Midou (riv.), Fr. 84/C5
Midsayap, Phil. 121/D6
Midu, China 125/H2
Midvale, Ut, US 179/K12
Midway (isls.), Pac., US 158/H2
Midway, De, US 180/C6
Midway, Il, US 179/H8
Midway, Ok, US 179/N15
Midway, Ut, US 179/L12
Midyan (reg.), SAr. 130/C3
Midyat, Turk. 132/E2
Midžor (peak), Serb. 91/F4
Mie, Japan 116/B4
Mie (pref.), Japan 116/E3
Miechów, Pol. 104/B2
Międzychód, Pol. 83/H2
Międzylesie, Pol. 83/J3
Międzyrzec Podlaski, Pol. 83/M3
Międzyrzecz, Pol. 83/H2
Międzyzdroje, Pol. 80/F5
Miehlen, Ger. 95/G3
Mielec, Pol. 83/L3
Miercurea Ciuc, Rom. 91/G2
Mieres, Sp. 86/C1
Miesbach, Ger. 85/J3
Mifflin, Pa, US 180/A2
Mifflinburg, Pa, US 180/A2
Migdal Ha'emeq, Isr. 133/G6
Migennes, Fr. 84/E3
Migliarino, It. 100/D5
Mignanego, It. 100/B3
Mignovillard, Fr. 98/C4
Migori (riv.), Kenya 146/B3
Migori, Kenya 146/B3
Miguel Alemán, Mex. 184/C2
Miguel Aleman, Presa (dam), Mex. 185/M8
Miguel Alves, Braz. 196/B2
Miguel Auza, Mex. 184/E3
Miguel Calmon, Braz. 196/B3
Miguel Hidalgo (int'l arpt.), Mex. 184/E4
Miguel Hidalgo (res.), Mex. 184/C3
Miguel Pereira, Braz. 197/K7
Miguel Riglos, Arg. 200/E3
Miguelete, Uru. 201/K11
Miguelópolis, Braz. 197/B2
Miguelturra, Sp. 86/D3
Migŭm, SKor. 115/G6
Mihama, Japan 116/D3
Mihama, Japan 119/L6
Mihara, Japan 116/C3
Mihara, Japan 119/J6
Miharu, Japan 117/G2
Mihla, Ger. 93/H6
Miho, Japan 119/E2
Mihrābpur, Pak. 131/J3
Mijares (riv.), Sp. 87/E2
Mijas, Sp. 86/C4
Mijdrecht, Neth. 92/B4
Mikasa, Japan 118/B2
Mikata, Japan 119/J4
Mikata (lake), Japan 119/J4
Mikawa (bay), Japan 119/M6
Mikhaylovka, Rus. 105/G2
Mikhmoret, Isr. 133/F7
Miki, Japan 119/G6
Míkínai, Gre. 89/H4
Míkínai (Mycenae) (ruin), Gre. 89/H4
Mikkeli (prov.), Fin. 79/H3
Míkonos, Gre. 89/J4
Míkonos (isl.), Gre. 89/J4
Mikri Prespa (lake), Alb.,Gre. 89/G2
Mikri Prespa NP, Gre. 89/G2
Mikuma, Japan 119/L6
Mikumi NP, Tanz. 147/G2
Mikuni, Japan 116/E2
Mikuni-tōge (pass), Japan 117/F2
Mikura (isl.), Japan 117/F4
Mila (prov.), Alg. 142/H4
Milagro, Ecu. 194/B5
Milak, India 126/B1
Milan (Milano), It. 85/H4
Milang, Austl. 157/A2
Milano (prov.), It. 100/C2
Milano (Milan), It. 85/H4
Milas, Turk. 132/A2
Milazzo, It. 88/D3
Milbank, SD, US 169/J4
Mildura, Austl. 157/B2
Miles, Tx, US 174/C4
Miles, Austl. 156/C4
Miles City, Mt, US 169/G4
Milešovka (peak), Czh. 97/G1
Milestone, Sk, Can. 169/G3
Miletto (peak), It. 88/D2
Milevsko, Czh. 97/H4
Milford, Ct, US 181/E1
Milford, De, US 180/C6
Milford (lake), Ks, US 174/D2
Milford, Mi, US 177/E6
Milford, NJ, US 180/C2
Milford, Ut, US 170/D3
Milford Haven, Wal, UK 74/A3
Milford Haven (inlet), Wal., UK 74/A3
Milgis (riv.), Kenya 146/C2
Mili (isl.), Mrsh. 158/G4
Miliana, Alg. 142/G4
Milicz, Pol. 83/J3
Mililani Town, Hi, US 166/V13
Milk (hill), Eng, UK 75/E4
Milk (riv.), Can.,US 164/F4
Milk River, Ab, Can. 168/E3
Mill (isl.), Nun., Can. 165/J2
Mill (riv.), Ct, US 181/E1
Mill Neck, NY, US 181/L8
Millaa Millaa, Austl. 156/B2
Millau, Fr. 84/E4
Millbrae, Ca, US 177/K11
Millbrook (res.), Austl. 155/M8
Millburn, NJ, US 181/H9
Millcreek, Ut, US 179/K12
Mille Îles (riv.), Qu, Can. 173/N6
Mille Lacs (lake), Mn, US 169/K4
Milledgeville, Ga, US 175/H3
Miller, SD, US 169/J4
Millerovo, Rus. 105/G2
Millers Ferry (dam), Al, US 175/G3
Millersburg, Pa, US 180/B2
Millerstown, Pa, US 180/A2
Millersville, Pa, US 180/B4
Millesimo, It. 100/B4
Milleur (pt.), Sc, UK 76/C1
Millevaches (plat.), Fr. 84/D4
Millgrove, On, Can. 173/Q9
Millicent, Austl. 157/B3
Milliken, Co, US 179/C2
Millingen aan de Rijn, Neth. 92/D5
Millington, Md, US 180/C5
Millinocket, Me, US 173/G2
Millisle, NI, UK 76/C2
Millmerran, Austl. 156/C4
Millmont, Pa, US 180/A2
Millport, Sc, UK 78/B5
Mills Junction, Ut, US 179/J12
Millstadt, Il, US 179/G9
Millstone (riv.), NJ, US 180/D3
Millstream-Chichester NP, Austl. 154/C2
Millthorpe, Austl. 157/D2
Milltown Malbay, Ire. 73/P10
Millville, Pa, US 180/B1
Millville, NJ, US 180/C5
Millwood (lake), Ar, US 174/E3
Milmay, NJ, US 180/D5
Milnathort, Wal, UK 77/E5
Milne (bay), PNG 158/E5
Milngavie, Sc, UK 78/B5
Milnrow, Eng, UK 77/F4
Milo, Me, US 173/G2
Milo (riv.), Gui. 144/C4
Milolii, Hi, US 166/U11
Milos (isl.), Gre. 89/J4
Mílos, Gre. 89/J4
Milseburg (peak), Ger. 96/C1
Miltenberg, Ger. 96/C3
Milton, Austl. 157/D2
Milton, On, Can. 173/Q8
Milton, NZ 159/R12
Milton (res.), Co, US 179/C2
Milton, Fl, US 175/G4
Milton, NH, US 173/G3
Milton, Pa, US 180/B1
Milton, Ut, US 179/K11
Milton, Wa, US 177/C3
Milton-Freewater, Or, US 168/D4
Milton Keynes, Eng, UK 75/F2
Milton Keynes (co.), Eng, UK 75/F2
Milton Ness (pt.), Sc, UK 78/D3
Milton of Campsie, Sc, UK 78/B5
Milwaukee, Wi, US 169/M5
Milwaukee (co.), Wi, US 177/P14
Milz (riv.), Ger. 96/D2
Mimi (riv.), Japan 116/B4
Mimizan, Fr. 84/C4
Mimmaya, Japan 118/B3
Min (riv.), China 112/H5
Min Xian, China 112/H5
Mina (riv.), Alg. 142/F5
Mīnāb, Iran 131/G3
Minahasa (pen), Indo. 123/F3
Minakuchi, Japan 119/K6
Minamata, Japan 116/B4
Minami Alps NP, Japan 117/F3
Minami-tori-shima (isl.), Japan 158/E2
Minamiaiki, Japan 119/B1
Minamiashigara, Japan 119/G3
Minamichita, Japan 119/L6
Minamidaitō (isl.), Japan 117/L8
Minamiiō (isl.), Japan 158/D2
Minamikawara, Japan 119/C1
Minamimaki, Japan 119/A2
Minamiyamashiro, Japan 119/J6
Minano, Japan 119/C1
Minas, Cuba 187/G1
Minas (peak), Ecu. 194/B5
Minas, Uru. 201/G2
Minas de Matahambre, Cuba 187/F1
Minas de Ríotinto, Sp. 86/B4
Minas Gerais (state), Braz. 196/A5
Minas Novas, Braz. 196/B5
Minatitlán, Mex. 186/C2
Minbu, Myan. 125/F3
Minbya, Myan. 125/F3
Minch, The (North Minch) (str.), Sc, UK 73/Q8
Minchinābād, Pak. 128/B4
Minchinmávida (vol.), Chile 200/B4
Mincio (riv.), It. 101/D2
Mindanao (isl.), Phil. 121/D6
Mindanao (sea), Phil. 123/F2
Mindel (riv.), Ger. 82/F4
Mindelheim, Ger. 99/G1
Mindelo, CpV. 135/J10
Minden, Ger. 93/F4
Minden, La, US 171/J4
Minden, Ne, US 171/H2
Mindoro (isl.), Phil. 121/D5
Mindoro (str.), Phil. 121/C5
Mine (pt.), Ire. 73/Q10
Mineiros, Braz. 193/H7
Mineola, Tx, US 171/J4
Mineola, NY, US 181/L8
Mineral del Monte, Mex. 185/L6
Mineral Wells, Tx, US 171/H4
Mineral'nye Vody (int'l arpt.), Rus. 105/G3
Mineral'nye Vody, Rus. 105/G3
Minerbe, It. 101/E2
Minerbio, It. 101/E3
Minerbio (pt.), Fr. 85/H5
Minersville, Pa, US 180/B2
Minfeld, Ger. 96/B4
Minfeng, China 112/D4
Ming (riv.), China 125/J3
Mingäçevir, Azer. 105/H4
Mingäçevir Su Anbari (res.), Azer. 105/H4
Mingan (riv.), Qu, Can. 173/J1
Mingāora, Pak. 128/B2
Mingenew, Austl. 154/B4
Minglanilla, Sp. 86/E3
Mingshui, China 113/N2
Mingxi, China 121/C2
Minhe, China 112/H4
Minhla, Myan. 125/G4
Minho (riv.), Sp. 86/A1
Minidoka Internment Nat'l Mon., Id, US 168/E6
Minigwal (lake), Austl. 154/D4
Minitonas, Mb, Can. 169/H2
Minlaton, Austl. 155/H5
Minle, China 112/H4
Minna, Nga. 145/G4
Minneapolis, Mn, US 169/K4
Minneapolis-St. Paul (Wold-Chamberlain) (int'l arpt.), Mn, US 169/K4
Minnedosa, Mb, Can. 169/J3
Minnesota (state), US 169/K4
Minnesota (riv.), Mn, US 169/K4
Minnigaff, Sc, UK 76/D2
Minnis (lake), On, Can. 172/B1
Minnitaki (lake), On, Can. 169/K3
Miño (riv.), Port.,Sp. 86/A1
Mino, Japan 119/L4
Minobu, Japan 117/F3
Minokamo, Japan 119/M5
Mino'o, Japan 119/H6
Mino'o (riv.), Japan 119/H6
Minori, Japan 119/E1
Minot, ND, US 169/H3
Minqin, China 112/H4
Minqing, China 121/C2
Minquan, China 114/C4
Minsener Oog (isl.), Ger. 93/F1
Minsk (cap.), Bela. 81/M5
Minsk (int'l arpt.), Bela. 81/M5
Mińsk Mazowiecki, Pol. 83/L2
Minskaya Voblasts Bela. 104/C1
Mintaka (pass), China 131/K1
Mintaka (pass), Pak. 129/F5
Mintlaw, Sc, UK 78/E1
Minto, Ak, US 176/J2
Minto, NB, Can. 173/H2
Minto (inlet), NW, Can. 164/E1
Minūf, Egypt 133/B4
Minusinsk, Rus. 106/K4
Minusio, Swi. 99/E5
Minyā al Qamḩ, Egypt 133/B4
Minyip, Austl. 157/B3
Miquan, China 112/E3
Mira, Port. 86/A2
Mira (riv.), Col. 194/B4
Mira Loma, Ca, US 178/C2
Mira Monte, Ca, US 178/A2
Mira Taglio, It. 101/F2
Mirabel (int'l arpt.), Qu, Can. 173/M6
Mirabel, Qu, Can. 173/M6
Mirabela, Braz. 196/A5
Mirabello, It. 101/E3
Miracema, Braz. 197/D2
Miracema do Norte, Braz. 193/J5
Miradolo Terme, It. 100/C2
Mirador, Braz. 196/A2
Mirador (pass), Chile 200/C4
Miraflores, Col. 194/C4
Miraflores, Col. 194/C3
Miraflores, Mex. 184/C4
Miraflores, Peru 198/B3
Miragoâne, Haiti 187/H2
Miraj, India 131/K5
Miramar, Ca, US 178/C5
Miramar, Arg. 200/F3
Miramar Naval Air Station, Ca, US 178/C5
Mirambéllou (gulf), Gre. 89/J5
Miramichi, NB, Can. 173/H2
Miramont-de-Guyenne, Fr. 84/D4
Miranda (riv.), Braz. 193/G8
Miranda de Ebro, Sp. 86/D1
Miranda do Corvo, Port. 86/A2
Miranda do Douro, Port. 86/B2
Mirande, Fr. 84/D5
Mirandela, Port. 86/B2
Mirandola, It. 85/J4
Mirandópolis, Braz. 197/B2
Mirano, It. 101/F2
Mīrānpur, India 126/A1
Mirante do Paranapanema, Braz. 197/B2
Mirassol, Braz. 197/B2
Miravalles (peak), Sp. 86/B1
Miravalles (vol.), CR 187/E4
Mirebalais, Haiti 187/H2
Mirebeau, Fr. 98/B3
Mirecourt, Fr. 98/C1
Mirfield, Eng, UK 77/G4
Miri, Malay. 122/D3
Miriam Vale, Austl. 156/C4
Mirim (lake), Braz. 199/F3
Mirimire, Ven. 194/D2
Mírina, Gre. 89/J3
Miritiparaná (riv.), Col. 194/D5
Mirna (riv.), Cro. 101/G2
Mirnyy, Rus. 107/M3
Mirnyy, Rus., Ant. 202/G
Mirond (lake), Sk, Can. 169/H2
Mirow, Ger. 82/G2
Mirror (lake), NJ, US 180/D4
Mirtóön (sea), Gre. 89/H4
Miryang, SKor. 115/E5
Mirzāpur, India 126/D3
Misa (riv.), It. 101/G5
Misāha (well), Egypt 143/A4
Misaka, Japan 119/B2
Misaki, Japan 116/D3
Misaki, Japan 119/E3
Misano Adriatico, It. 101/F5
Misantla, Mex. 185/N7
Misato, Japan 119/C1
Misato, Japan 119/D2
Misato, Japan 119/K6
Misawa, Japan 118/B3
Mishan, China 113/P2
Mishawaka, In, US 172/C3
Misheguk (mtn.), Ak, US 176/F2
Mishima, Japan 117/F3
Misilmeri, It. 88/C3
Misiones, Sierra de (mts.), Arg. 199/E2
Miskitos, Cayos (isls.), Nic. 182/E5
Miskolc, Hun. 83/L4
Misono, Japan 119/L6
Misool (isl.), Indo. 123/H4
Misquah (hills), Mn, US 169/L4
Mişrātah, Libya 138/J1
Mişrātah (pt.), Libya 139/L1
Missinaibi (lake), On, Can. 172/D1
Missinaibi (riv.), On, Can. 165/H3
Mission, Tx, US 174/D5
Mission (bay), Ca, US 178/C5
Mission, Ks, US 179/D5
Mission Beach, Austl. 156/B2
Mission Hills, Ks, US 179/D5
Mission Ind. Res., Ca, US 178/C4
Mission San Buenaventura, Ca, US 178/A2
Mission San Jose, Ca, US 177/L12
Mission San Juan Capistrano, Ca, US 178/C3
Mission Viejo, Ca, US 178/C3
Missisa (lake), On, Can. 169/M2
Missisicabi (riv.), Qu, Can. 172/E1
Mississauga, On, Can. 173/Q8
Mississippi (pt.), Austl. 154/D5
Mississippi (riv.), US 167/H5
Mississippi (state), US 175/F3
Mississippi (delta), La, US 175/F4
Mississippi River Gulf Outlet (canal), La, US 179/Q17
Missoula, Mt, US 168/E4
Missouri (riv.), US 167/G3
Missouri (state), US 171/J3
Missouri City, Mo, US 179/E5
Missouri City, Tx, US 171/J5
Mistaken (pt.), Nf, Can. 173/L2
Mistassibi (riv.), Qu, Can. 173/F1
Mistassibi Nord-Est (riv.), Qu, Can. 173/G1
Mistassini, Qu, Can. 173/F1
Mistassini (riv.), Qu, Can. 173/F1
Mistassini (lake), Qu, Can. 165/J3
Mistelbach an der Zaya, Aus. 85/M2
Misti (vol.), Peru 198/D5
Mistissini, Qu, Can. 172/F1
Mistrás (ruin), Gre. 89/H4
Mistretta, It. 88/D4
Misty Fjords Nat'l Mon., Ak, US 176/M4
Misugi, Japan 119/K6
Mita, Punta de (pt.), Mex. 184/D4
Mitaka, Japan 119/D2
Mitake, Japan 119/M5
Mitama, Japan 119/B2
Mitare, Ven. 194/D2
Mitchell, Austl. 156/B4
Mitchell (riv.), Austl. 156/A1
Mitchell, Il, US 179/G8
Mitchell (mt.), NC, US 175/H3
Mitchell, SD, US 169/J5
Mitchell River NP, Austl. 157/C3
Mitha Tiwāna, Pak. 128/B3
Mithankot, Pak. 128/A5
Mithi, Pak. 131/J4
Mithimna, Gre. 89/K3
Mitiaro (isl.), Cookls. 159/K6
Mitilíni, Gre. 89/K3
Mitla (pass), Egypt 133/C4
Mitla (ruin), Mex. 186/B2
Mito, Japan 117/G2
Mito, Japan 119/M6

256
Mitom – Morga

Mitomi, Japan 119/B2
Mitra (peak), EqG. 138/G7
Mitre (pen.), Arg. 199/C7
Mitry-Mory, Fr. 72/K5
Mitsamiouli, Com. 149/G5
Mitsinjo, Madg. 149/H7
Mitsio, Nosy (isl.), Madg. 149/J6
Mits'iwa, Erit. 139/N4
Mitsue, Japan 119/K7
Mitsukaidō, Japan 117/F2
Mitsuke, Japan 117/F2
Mittagong, Austl. 157/D2
Mittagspitze (peak), Aus. 99/F3
Mittainville, Fr. 72/G5
Mittelberg, Aus. 99/G3
Mittelland (canal), Ger. 93/F4
Mittelradde (riv.), Ger. 93/E3
Mittenwald, Ger. 99/H3
Mittersill, Aus. 85/K3
Mitterteich, Ger. 97/F3
Mittlere-Isar (canal), Ger. 97/E6
Mittweida, Ger. 82/G3
Mitú, Col. 194/D4
Mitumba, Monts (mts.), D.R. Congo 147/E1
Mitwitz, Ger. 96/E2
Miura (pen.), Japan 119/D3
Miura, Japan 119/D3
Miwa, Japan 119/H5
Miwa, Japan 119/L5
Mixco Viejo (ruin), Guat. 186/D3
Mixquiahuala, Mex. 185/K6
Mixteco (riv.), Mex. 186/B2
Miya (riv.), Japan 119/K7
Miyagawa, Japan 119/K7
Miyagi (pref.), Japan 118/B4
Miyake (isl.), Japan 117/F3
Miyako, Japan 118/B4
Miyako (isls.), Japan 117/H8
Miyakonojō, Japan 116/B5
Miyama, Japan 119/J5
Miyama, Japan 119/L4
Miyanojō, Japan 116/B5
Miyashiro, Japan 119/D2
Miyazaki (pref.), Japan 116/B4
Miyazaki, Japan 116/B5
Miyazu, Japan 119/H4
Miyazu (bay), Japan 119/H4
Miyi, China 125/H2
Miyoshi, Japan 116/C3
Miyoshi, Japan 119/D2
Miyoshi, Japan 119/D3
Miyoshi, Japan 119/M5
Miyota, Japan 119/B1
Miyun, China 114/H6
Miyun (res.), China 114/H6
Mizen (pt.), Ire. 76/B6
Miziya, Bul. 91/F4
Mizoram (state), India 125/F3
Mizpah, NJ, US 180/D5
Mizpe Ramon, Isr. 133/D4
Mizuho, Japan 119/C2
Mizuho, Japan 119/H5
Mizunami, Japan 119/M5
Mizusawa, Japan 118/B4
Mjölby, Swe. 80/F2
Mjøndalen, Nor. 80/D2
Mjörn (lake), Swe. 80/E3
Mjøsa (lake), Nor. 79/D3
Mkata (plain), Tanz. 146/C4
Mkokotoni, Tanz. 146/C4
Mkomazi Game Rsv., Tanz. 146/C4
Mkombo (riv.), Tanz. 146/A4
Mkondoa (riv.), Tanz. 146/C4
Mkorn (peak), Mor. 140/D3
Mkumbi (pt.), Tanz. 146/C4
Mkushi, Zam. 147/E3
Mkuze (riv.), SAfr. 149/F2
Mladá Boleslav, Czh. 97/H2
Mladá Vožice, Czh. 97/H3
Mladenovac, Serb. 90/E3
Mlala (hills), Tanz. 146/A4
Mława, Pol. 83/L2
Mljet (isl.), Cro. 89/E1
Mljet NP, Cro. 89/E1
Mmabatho, SAfr. 148/D2
Mnyera (riv.), Tanz. 146/B5
Mo Duc, Viet. 120/E3
Moa, Cuba 187/H1
Moa (isl.), Indo. 123/G5
Moa (riv.), SLeo. 144/C5
Moab, Ut, US 170/E3
Moala Group (isl.), Fiji 158/G6
Moama, Austl. 157/C1
Moamba, Moz. 149/F2
Moaña, Sp. 86/A1
Moanda, Gabon 138/H8
Moate, Ire. 73/Q10
Mobara, Japan 119/E3
Mobaye, CAfr. 139/K7
Moberly, Mo, US 171/J3
Moberly Lake, BC, Can. 168/C2
Mobile, Al, US 175/F4
Mobridge, SD, US 169/H4
Moca (pass), Turk. 133/C1
Mocache, Ecu. 194/B5
Mocajuba, Braz. 193/J4
Moçambique, Moz. 147/H4
Mocanaqua, Pa, US 180/B1
Mocha (riv.), Rus. 103/W9
Moche (ruin), Peru 198/B3
Mochima, PN, Ven. 195/E2
Mochizuki, Japan 119/A1
Mochudi, Bots. 147/E5
Mochumí, Peru 198/B2
Mocímboa da Praia, Moz. 146/D5
Möckeln (lake), Swe. 80/E3
Mockfjärd, Swe. 80/F1
Möckmühl, Ger. 96/C4
Moclín, Sp. 86/D4
Mocoa, Col. 194/B4
Mococa, Braz. 197/F6
Mocorito, Mex. 184/D3
Moctezuma, Mex. 185/E4
Moctezuma, Mex. 184/C2
Mocuba, Moz. 147/G4
Modāsa, India 131/K4
Modderrivier (riv.), SAfr. 148/D3
Modena (prov.), It. 101/D3
Modena, It. 101/D3
Moder (riv.), Fr. 85/G2
Modesto, Ca, US 170/B3
Modica, It. 88/D4
Modigliana, It. 101/E4
Modjeska, Ca, US 178/C3
Modjigo (reg.), Niger 138/H4
Mödling, Aus. 91/N7
Modot, Mong. 113/J2
Modriča, Bosn. 90/D3
Modugno, It. 88/E2
Moe, Austl. 157/C3
Moeb (bay), Namb. 148/A2
Moel-y-Llyn (peak), Wal, UK 74/C2
Moëlan-sur-Mer, Fr. 84/B3
Moelfre (peak), Wal, UK 74/C1
Moen, Nor. 79/F1
Moenkopi (riv.), US 170/E3
Moerai (isl.), FrPol. 159/K7
Moerbeke, Belg. 94/C1
Moers, Ger. 92/D6
Moervaart (riv.), Belg. 94/C1
Moesa (riv.), Swi. 99/F5
Moffat, Sc, UK 78/C6
Moffett Field Naval Air Sta., Ca, US 177/K12
Moga, India 128/C4
Mogadishu (Muqdisho) (cap.), Som. 139/Q7
Mogadouro, Port. 86/B2
Mogami (riv.), Japan 118/B4
Mogami, Japan 118/B4
Mogaung, Myan. 125/G2
Mogent (riv.), Sp. 87/L6
Mogglingen, Ger. 96/C5
Moghul Gardens, India 128/C3
Mogi das Cruzes, Braz. 197/G8
Mogi-Guaçu, Braz. 197/G7
Mogi-Guaçu (riv.), Braz. 197/G7
Mogi-Mirim, Braz. 197/G7
Mogilno, Pol. 83/J2
Moglia, It. 101/D3
Mogliano Veneto, It. 101/F1
Möglingen, Ger. 96/C5
Mogoro, It. 88/A3
Mogotes (pt.), Arg. 200/F3
Mogotón (peak), Nic. 186/E3
Moguer, Sp. 86/B4
Mohács, Hun. 90/D3
Mohaeli (isl.), Com. 149/G6
Mohales Hoek, Les. 148/D3
Mohall, ND, US 169/H3
Mohamed V (dam), Mor. 142/C2
Mohamed V, Barrage (res.), Mor. 142/C2
Mohamed V (Casablanca) (int'l arpt.), Mor. 140/D2
Mohammadia, Alg. 142/F5
Mohammadia-Znata (prov.), Mor. 142/A2
Mohammedia, Mor. 142/A3
Mohawk (lake), NJ, US 180/D1
Moheda, Swe. 80/F3
Mohembo, Bots. 147/D4
Mohican (cape), Ak, US 176/E3
Möhlin, Swi. 98/D2
Möhne (riv.), Ger. 93/F6
Möhnestausee (lake), Ger. 93/F5
Mohnton, Pa, US 180/C3
Moho, Peru 198/D4
Mohrsville, Pa, US 180/C3
Mohyliv-Podil's'kyy, Ukr. 91/H1
Moi (int'l arpt.), Kenya 146/C4
Moi, Nor. 80/B2
Moie, It. 101/G5
Moineşti, Rom. 91/H2
Moinkum (des.), Kaz. 106/H5
Moinsi (hills), Gha. 145/E5
Moira (riv.), On, Can. 172/E2
Moirans, Fr. 84/F4
Moirans-en-Montagne, Fr. 98/B5
Moisie (riv.), Qu, Can. 165/K3
Moislains, Fr. 94/B4
Moissac, Fr. 84/D4
Moisselles, Fr. 72/K4
Moisson, Fr. 72/G4
Moita, Port. 87/Q10
Moitaco, Ven. 195/E3
Mojácar, Sp. 86/E4
Mojave (riv.), Ca, US 170/C4
Mojave (des.), Ca, US 170/C4
Mojiang Hanizu Zizhixian, China 125/H3
Mojikit (lake), On, Can. 169/L3
Mojkovac, Mont. 90/D4
Mojos, Llanos de (plain), Bol. 192/E6
Moju (riv.), Braz. 193/J4
Mōka, Japan 117/F2
Mokameh, India 127/E3
Mokapu (pt.), Hi, US 166/W13
Mokau (riv.), NZ 159/S10
Mokelumne (riv.), Ca, US 170/B3
Mokelumne (aqueduct), Ca, US 177/M11
Mokena, Il, US 177/Q16
Mokil (isl.), Micr. 158/E4
Moknine, Tun. 142/M7
Mokochu (peak), Thai. 120/B3
Mokokchūng, India 125/F2
Mokolo, Camr. 138/H5
Mokp'o, SKor. 115/D5
Mokrin, Serb. 90/E3
Moksha (riv.), Rus. 105/G1
Mokuleia, Hi, US 166/V12
Mol, Serb. 90/E3
Mol, Belg. 92/C6
Moláoi, Gre. 89/H4
Molare, It. 100/B3
Molas, Punta (pt.), Mex. 186/E1
Molat (isl.), Cro. 90/B3
Molatón (peak), Sp. 86/E3
Molbergen, Ger. 93/E3
Mold, Wal, UK 77/E5
Moldavia (reg.), Rom. 91/H2
Moldavian Carpathians (range), Rom. 91/G2
Molde, Nor. 79/C3
Moldova (ctry.) 91/H2
Moldova (riv.), Rom. 91/G2
Moldova Nouă, Rom. 90/E3
Moldoveanu (peak), Rom. 91/G3
Mole (riv.), Eng, UK 74/C5
Mole NP, Gha. 145/E4
Môle Saint-Nicolas, Haiti 187/H2
Molepolole, Bots. 147/E5
Molina, Sp. 86/E2
Molina, Chile 200/C2
Molina de Segura, Sp. 86/E3
Moline, Il, US 169/L5
Molinella, It. 101/E3
Molinicos, Sp. 86/D3
Molino de Flores, PN, Mex. 185/R9
Molins de Rei, Sp. 87/L7
Molise (reg.), It. 88/D2
Molkom, Swe. 80/E2
Möll (riv.), Aus. 85/K3
Møllebjerg (peak), Den. 79/D5
Mollendo, Peru 198/C5
Mollendruz, Col du (pass), Swi. 98/C4
Mollerussa, Sp. 87/F2
Molles (pt.), Chile 200/C2
Molles, Uru. 201/K10
Mollet del Vallès, Sp. 87/L6
Mollis, Swi. 99/E3
Mölndal, Swe. 80/E3
Mölnlycke, Swe. 80/E3
Molodezhnaya, Rus., Ant. 202/D
Mologa (riv.), Rus. 102/G4
Molokai (isl.), Hi, US 166/T10
Moloma (riv.), Rus. 103/L4
Molong, Austl. 157/D2
Molopo (riv.), Bots. 148/C5
Mólos, Gre. 89/H3
Molsheim, Fr. 98/D1
Molteno, SAfr. 148/D3
Molu (isl.), Indo. 123/H5
Molucca (sea), Asia 123/G4
Molucca Islands (arch.), Indo. 123/G3
Molveno (lake), It. 99/G5
Molveno, It. 99/G5
Mombaça, Braz. 196/C2
Mombasa, Kenya 146/C4
Mombetsu, Japan 118/C1
Mombetsu, Japan 118/C2
Mömbris, Ger. 96/C2
Momchilgrad, Bul. 91/G5
Momfafa (cape), Indo. 123/H4
Momignies, Belg. 95/D3
Mömlingen, Ger. 96/C3
Momo, It. 100/B1
Momoishi, Japan 118/B3
Mompós, Col. 194/C2
Mon (state), Myan. 125/G4
Mon (riv.), Myan. 125/F3
Møn (isl.), Den. 79/E5
Mona (isl.), PR 183/M8
Mona (passg.), NAm. 183/L8
Monaco (ctry.) 100/J8
Monaco (cap.), Mona. 100/J8
Monaco, Port of (har.), Mona. 100/J8
Monadhliath (mts.), Sc, UK 78/B2
Monagas (state), Ven. 195/F2
Monaghan (co.), Ire. 76/A3
Monagrillo, Pan. 187/F4
Monagrillo (ruin), Pan. 187/F4
Monar (lake), Sc, UK 78/A2
Monashee (mts.), BC, Can. 168/D3
Monastir, Tun. 142/M7
Moncada, Sp. 87/E3
Moncalieri, It. 85/G4
Moncalvo, It. 100/B2
Monção, Braz. 196/A1
Moncayo, Sierra del (range), Sp. 86/E2
Mönch (peak), Swi. 98/D4
Monchegorsk, Rus. 102/G2
Mönchengladbach, Ger. 92/D6
Monchigue, Serra de (mts.), Port. 86/A4
Monchique, Port. 86/A4
Moncks Corner, SC, US 175/H3
Monclova, Mex. 185/E3
Moncton, NB, Can. 173/H2
Mondego (cape), Port. 86/A2
Mondego (riv.), Port. 86/A2
Mondéjar, Sp. 86/D2
Mondolfo, It. 101/G5
Mondoñedo, Sp. 86/B1
Mondorf-les- Bains, Lux. 95/F4
Mondovì, It. 100/A4
Mondragón, Sp. 86/D1
Mondragone, It. 88/C2
Mondsee (lake), Aus. 97/G7
Mondsee, Aus. 97/G7
Moneglia, It. 100/C4
Monemvasía, Gre. 89/H4
Mones Cazón, Arg. 200/E3
Monesterio, Sp. 86/B3
Money (pt.), Sc, UK 76/C2
Moneyreagh, NI, UK 76/C2
Monferrato (reg.), It. 85/H4
Monforte, Sp. 86/B1
Monforte, Port. 86/B3
Mongaguá, Braz. 197/G9
Mongers (lake), Austl. 154/C4
Monghidoro, It. 101/E4
Mongo, Chad 139/J5
Mongo (riv.), Gui. 144/C4
Mongolia (ctry.) 112/G2
Mongu, Zam. 147/D4
Mönh Hayrhan (peak), Mong. 112/F2
Mönh Sarĭdag (peak), Mong. 112/H1
Monheim, Ger. 96/D5
Monheim, Ger. 95/F1
Monifieth, Sc, UK 78/D4
Moniquirá, Col. 194/C3
Monistrol de Montserrat, Sp. 87/K6
Monistrol-sur-Loire, Fr. 84/F4
Monitor (range), Nv, US 170/C3
Monkayo, Phil. 121/E6
Monkey (pt.), Nic. 187/F4
Monkey River Town, Belz. 186/D2
Mońki, Pol. 83/M2
Monks (isl.), Md, US 180/B5
Monmouth, Il, US 169/L5
Monmouth, Or, US 168/C4
Monmouth Beach, NJ, US 180/E3
Monmouth Junction, NJ, US 180/D3
Monmouth Mil. Res., NJ, US 180/D3
Monmouthshire (co.), Wal, UK 74/D3
Monmow (riv.), Eng, UK 74/C2
Monnickendam, Neth. 92/C4
Mono (riv.), Togo 138/F6
Mono (lake), Ca, US 170/C3
Mono (prov.), Ben. 145/F5
Monocacy (riv.), Md, US 180/A4
Monor, Hun. 90/D2
Monóvar, Sp. 87/E3
Monreal del Campo, Sp. 86/E2
Monreale, It. 88/C3
Monroe, Ct, US 181/E1
Monroe (lake), Fl, US 175/G2
Monroe, Ga, US 175/H3
Monroe, La, US 171/J4
Monroe, Mi, US 172/D3
Monroe, NC, US 175/H3
Monroe, NY, US 180/D1
Monroe, Ut, US 170/D3
Monroe, Wa, US 177/C2
Monroe, Wi, US 169/L5
Monroe City, Il, US 179/G9
Monroeville, Al, US 175/G4
Monroeville, NJ, US 180/C4
Monrovia (cap.), Libr. 144/C5
Monrovia, Ca, US 178/G7
Mons, Belg. 94/C3
Monsanto, Port. 86/B2
Monschau, Ger. 95/F2
Monsefú, Peru 198/B2
Monselice, It. 85/J4
Monsenhor Tabosa, Braz. 196/B2
Monsey, NY, US 181/J7
Monsheim, Ger. 96/B3
Monster, Neth. 92/B4
Mönsteras, Swe. 80/G3
Monsummano Terme, It. 101/D5
Mont-de-Marsan, Fr. 84/C5
Mont-Joli, Qu, Can. 173/G1
Mont-Laurier, Qu, Can. 172/F2
Mont Peko, PN du, C.d'Iv. 144/D5
Mont-Royal, Qu, Can. 173/N6
Mont-Saint-Martin, Fr. 95/E4
Mont-Saint-Michel, Qu, Can. 172/F2
Mont Sangbé, PN du, C.d'Iv. 144/D4
Mont-Sous-Vaudrey, Fr. 98/B4
Montà, It. 100/A3
Monta Fon (mts.), Aus. 99/F3
Montabaur, Ger. 95/G3
Montagnana, It. 101/E2
Montagne d'Ambre NP, Madg. 149/J6
Montagny-Sainte-Félicité, Fr. 72/L4
Montagu, SAfr. 148/M10
Montague (str.), Ak, US 176/J4
Montague, Tx, US 171/H4
Montague, PE, Can. 173/J2
Montague, NJ, US 180/D1
Montague (isl.), Ak, US 176/J4
Montaigu, Fr. 84/C3
Montaione, It. 101/D5
Montalbán, Sp. 87/E2
Montalbano Jonico, It. 88/E2
Montale, It. 101/E5
Montale, It. 101/D3
Montalieu-Vercieu, Fr. 98/B6
Montalvão, Port. 86/B3
Montalvo, Ca, US 178/A2
Montana, Bul. 91/F4
Montana (prov.), Bul. 90/F4
Montana, Swi. 98/D5
Montana (state), US 168/F4
Montanaro, It. 100/A2
Montanha, Braz. 196/B5
Montara, Ca, US 177/J11
Montargis, Fr. 84/E2
Montataire, Fr. 94/B5
Montauban, Fr. 84/D4
Montauk, NY, US 181/G1
Montauk (pt.), NY, US 181/G1
Montbard, Fr. 84/F3
Montbéliard, Fr. 98/C2
Montblanc, Sp. 87/F2
Montcada i Reixac, Sp. 87/L7
Montceau-les-Mines, Fr. 84/F3
Montclair, Ca, US 178/C2
Montclair, NJ, US 181/J8
Montcornet, Fr. 94/D4
Montdidier, Fr. 94/B4
Monte Albán (ruin), Mex. 186/B2
Monte Alegre, Braz. 193/H4
Monte Alegre de Goiás, Braz. 196/A4
Monte Alegre de Minas, Braz. 197/B1
Monte Alegre do Piauí, Braz. 196/A3
Monte Alto, Braz. 197/B2
Monte Azul, Braz. 196/B4
Monte Carmelo, Braz. 197/C1
Monte Carmelo, Ven. 194/D2
Monte Caseros, Arg. 199/E3
Monte Comán, Arg. 200/D2
Monte Escobedo, Mex. 184/E4
Monte Maíz, Arg. 200/E2
Monte Pascoal, PN de, Braz. 193/L7
Monte Pascoal, PN de, Braz. 196/C5
Monte Rosa (mts.), It. 98/D6
Monte San Savino, It. 101/E6
Montealegre, Sp. 86/E3
Montebello (isls.), Austl. 154/B2
Montebello, Ca, US 178/F7
Montebello Vicentino, It. 101/E2
Montebelluna, It. 101/F1
Montebruno, It. 100/C3
Montecarlo, Arg. 199/F2
Montecassiano, It. 101/G6
Montecatini Terme, It. 101/D5
Montecavolo, It. 100/D3
Montecchio, It. 101/F5
Montechiaro d'Asti, It. 100/B2
Montecito, Ca, US 178/A2
Montecristo (isl.), It. 88/B1
Montecristo, PN, ESal. 186/D3
Montefeltro (reg.), It. 101/F5
Monteforte d'Alpone, It. 101/E2
Montefrío, Sp. 86/C4
Montego Bay, Jam. 187/G2
Montegranaro, It. 85/K5
Montegrotto Terme, It. 101/E2
Montehermoso, Sp. 86/B2
Monteiro, Braz. 196/C2
Montelavar, Port. 87/P10
Montélimar, Fr. 84/F4
Montellano, Sp. 86/C4
Montello, Nv, US 168/E5
Montelupo Fiorentino, It. 101/E5
Montemagno, It. 100/B3
Montemarciano, It. 101/G5
Montemor-o-Novo, Port. 86/A3
Montemor-o-Velho, Port. 86/A2
Montemorelos, Mex. 185/F3
Montemuro (peak), Port. 86/A2
Montendre, Fr. 84/C4
Montenegro (ctry.) 90/D4
Montenegro, Braz. 197/B4
Montenero di Bisaccia, It. 88/D2
Montepulciano, It. 85/J5
Montereau-Faut-Yonne, Fr. 84/E2
Montereau-sur-le-Jard, Fr. 72/L6
Monterey, Ca, US 170/B3
Monterey (bay), Ca, US 170/B3
Monterey Park, Ca, US 178/F7
Montería, Col. 194/C2
Montero, Bol. 192/F7
Monteros, Arg. 199/C2
Monterosso (peak), It. 99/G4
Monterosso al Mare, It. 100/C4
Monterotondo, It. 88/C1
Monterrey, Mex. 185/E3
Monterrey, Sp. 86/B2
Montes (pt.), Arg. 201/C6
Montes Altos, Braz. 196/A2
Montes Claros, Braz. 196/B5
Montescaglioso, It. 88/E2
Montese, It. 101/D4
Montespertoli, It. 101/E5
Montesson, Fr. 72/J5
Monteux, Fr. 84/F4
Montevarchi, It. 101/E5
Montevideo, Mn, US 169/K4
Montevideo (cap.), Uru. 201/K11
Montevideo (dept.), Uru. 201/K11
Montévrain, Fr. 72/L5
Montezuma (peak), Az, US 179/R19
Montezuma Castle Nat'l Mon., Az, US 170/E4
Montfermeil, Fr. 72/K5
Montferrand-le-Château, Fr. 98/B3
Montfoort, Neth. 92/B4
Montfort-L'Amaury, Fr. 94/A6
Montgeron, Fr. 72/K5
Montgomery, Wal, UK 74/C1
Montgomery (cap.), Al, US 175/G3
Montgomery, Il, US 177/P16
Montgomery (co.), Md, US 180/A5
Montgomery, Pa, US 180/B1
Montgomery, WV, US 172/D4
Montgomery Village, Md, US 180/A5
Montgomeryville, Pa, US 180/C3
Montgrand (peak), Fr. 84/E5
Monthermé, Fr. 95/D4
Monthey, Swi. 98/C5
Monthureux-sur-Saône, Fr. 98/B1
Monthyon, Fr. 72/L4
Monti Sabini (mts.), It. 88/C1
Monticelli d'Ongina, It. 100/C2
Monticelli Terme, It. 100/D3
Monticello, Mo, US 169/L5
Monticello, Ky, US 172/C4
Monticello, In, US 172/C3
Monticello, La, US 171/K4
Monticello, Fl, US 175/H4
Monticello, Va, US 175/J2
Monticello Conte Otto, It. 101/E1
Montichiari, It. 100/D2
Montier-en-Der, Fr. 98/A1
Montignies-le-Tilleul, Belg. 95/D3
Montigny-en-Gohelle, Fr. 52/B3
Montigny-le-Bretonneux, Fr. 30/J5
Montigny-le-Roi, Fr. 98/B2
Montijo, Sp. 86/B3
Montijo, Port. 87/Q10
Montilla, Sp. 86/C4
Montivilliers, Fr. 84/D2
Montlebon, Fr. 98/C3
Montlhéry, Fr. 72/J6
Montluçon, Fr. 84/E3
Montluel, Fr. 98/B6
Montmagny, Qu, Can. 173/G2
Montmédy, Fr. 95/E4
Montmerle-sur-Saône, Fr. 98/A5
Montmirail, Fr. 94/C6
Montmorency, Fr. 72/J5
Montmorillon, Fr. 84/D3
Montmorot, Fr. 98/B4
Monto, Austl. 156/C4
Montodine, It. 100/C2
Montoir-de-Bretagne, Fr. 42/B3
Montois-la-Montagne, Fr. 95/F5
Montone (riv.), It. 101/E4
Montopoli, It. 101/D5
Montorio Veronese, It. 101/E2
Montoro, Sp. 86/C3
Montour (ridge), Pa, US 180/B2
Montour, Pa, US 180/B1
Montoursville, Pa, US 180/B1
Montpelier (cap.), Vt, US 173/F2
Montpellier, Fr. 84/E5
Montreal (lake), Sk, Can. 169/G2
Montreal (riv.), On, Can. 172/C2
Montréal, Qu, Can. 173/N6
Montréal-Est, Qu, Can. 173/N6
Montréal-la-Cluse, Fr. 98/B5
Montréal-Nord, Qu, Can. 173/N6
Montréjeau, Fr. 84/D5
Montreuil, Fr. 72/K5
Montreuil, Fr. 94/A3
Montreuil-Bellay, Fr. 84/C3
Montreuil-sur-Epte, Fr. 72/G4
Montreux, Swi. 98/C5
Montreux-Château, Fr. 98/C2
Montrevel-en-Bresse, Fr. 98/B5
Montricher, Swi. 98/C4
Montrose, Co, US 170/F3
Montrose (basin), Sc, UK 78/D3
Montrose, Sc, UK 78/D3
Montrouge, Fr. 72/J5
Montry, Fr. 72/L5
Monts, Fr. 84/D3
Montseny, PN, Sp. 87/L6
Montserrado (co.), Libr. 144/C5
Montserrat (peak), Sp. 87/F2
Montserrat (dpcy.), UK 183/N8
Montsoult, Fr. 72/J4
Montvale, NJ, US 181/J7
Montville, NJ, US 181/H8
Monywa, Myan. 125/G3
Monza, It. 100/C1
Monze, Zam. 147/E4
Monzingen, Ger. 95/G4
Monzón, Peru 198/B3
Monzón, Sp. 87/F2
Mooirivier, SAfr. 149/E3
Mool (riv.), SAfr. 148/P13
Moonta, Austl. 155/H5
Moora, Austl. 154/C4
Moorcroft, Wy, US 169/G4
Moordrecht, Neth. 92/B5
Moore (lake), Austl. 154/C4
Moore, Ok, US 179/N15
Moore Haven, Fl, US 175/H5
Moore River NP, Austl. 154/B4
Moorea (isl.), FrPol. 159/K6
Moorenweis, Ger. 99/H1
Moorestown, NJ, US 180/D4
Mooresville, NC, US 175/H3
Mooretown, On, Can. 177/H6
Moorfoot (hills), Sc, UK 78/C5
Moorhead, Mn, US 169/J4
Moorook, Austl. 157/B2
Moorpark, Ca, US 178/B2
Moorreesburg, SAfr. 148/L10
Moorslede, Belg. 94/C2
Moosburg, Ger. 97/E6
Moose (mtn.), Sk, Can. 169/H3
Moose (riv.), On, Can. 172/D1
Moose Creek, Ak, US 176/J3
Moose Jaw, Sk, Can. 169/G3
Moose Pass, Ak, US 176/J3
Moosehead (lake), Me, US 173/G2
Mooseheart (mtn.), Ak, US 176/H3
Mooseheart, Il, US 177/P16
Moosinning, Ger. 97/E6
Moosomin, Sk, Can. 169/H3
Moosonee, On, Can. 172/D1
Moosseedorf, Swi. 98/D3
Moosthenning, Ger. 97/F5
Mopti (pol. reg.), Mali 144/E3
Mopti, Mali 144/D3
Moquegua (dept.), Peru 198/D5
Moquegua, Peru 198/D5
Moquehuá, Arg. 201/J11
Mor (riv.), India 127/F4
Mór, Hun. 90/D2
Mora, Camr. 138/H5
Mora (riv.), NM, US 171/F4
Mora, NM, US 171/F4
Mora, Sp. 86/D3
Mora, Port. 86/A3
Mora, Swe. 80/F1
Mora de Rubielos, Sp. 87/E2
Morača (riv.), Mont. 90/D4
Morada Nova, Braz. 196/C2
Morada Nova de Minas, Braz. 197/C1
Morādābād, India 126/B1
Morado, PN, Chile 200/P8
Morafenobe, Madg. 149/H7
Morąg, Pol. 81/H5
Moraga, Ca, US 177/K11
Mórahalom, Hun. 90/D2
Morainvilliers, Fr. 72/H5
Moral de Calatrava, Sp. 86/D3
Moraleja, Sp. 86/B2
Morales, Guat. 186/D3
Moramanga, Madg. 149/J7
Moranbah, Austl. 156/C3
Morane (isl.), FrPol. 159/M7
Morangis, Fr. 72/K5
Morano Calabro, It. 88/E3
Morant Bay, Jam. 187/G2
Morar (lake), Sc, UK 73/R8
Morarano Chrome, Madg. 149/J7
Morat (lake), Swi. 98/D4
Morata de Tajuña, Sp. 87/N9
Moratalla, Sp. 86/E3
Moratuwa, SrL. 124/C6
Morava (riv.), Czh. 83/J4
Moravia (reg.), Czh. 83/J4
Moravská Třebová, Czh. 83/J4
Moravské Budějovice, Czh. 83/H4
Morawa, Austl. 154/C4
Morawhanna, Guy. 192/G2
Moray (pol. reg.), Sc, UK 78/E2
Moray Firth (inlet), Sc, UK 78/B1
Morbach, Ger. 95/G4
Morbegno, It. 99/F5
Morbier, Fr. 98/C4
Morbio Inferiore, Swi. 99/F6
Morbras (riv.), Fr. 72/K5
Mörbylanga, Swe. 80/G3
Morcenx, Fr. 84/C4
Morciano di Romagna, It. 101/F5
Morclan, Pic de (peak), Fr. 98/C5
Morden, Mb, Can. 169/J3
Mordoviya, Resp., Rus. 106/Q6
Møre Og Romsdal (co.), Nor. 79/C3
Moreau (riv.), SD, US 169/H4
Morecambe (bay), Eng, UK 77/E3
Moree, Austl. 157/D1
Morehead, Ky, US 172/D4
Morehead City, NC, US 175/J3
Mörel, Swi. 98/E5
Morelia, Mex. 185/E5
Morella, Sp. 87/E2
Morelos (state), Mex. 182/A5
Morena, Sierra (range), Sp. 86/C4
Moreni, Rom. 91/G3
Moreno Valley, Ca, US 178/C3
Moresby (isl.), BC, Can. 164/C3
Moreton (bay), Austl. 156/F6
Moreton (cape), Austl. 156/D4
Moreton (isl.), Austl. 156/D4
Moreton Island NP, Austl. 156/D4
Moreuil, Fr. 94/B4
Moreyu (riv.), Rus. 103/P2
Morez, Fr. 98/C4
Morgan, Austl. 155/H5
Morgan (pt.), Ct, US 181/F1
Morgan, Ut, US 179/K11
Morgan (co.), Ut, US 179/K11
Morgan City, La, US 171/K5
Morganfield, Ky, US 172/C4
Morgantina (ruin), It. 88/D4
Morganton, NC, US 175/H3

257
Morga – Mut

Morgantown, Ky, US 172/C4
Morgantown, Pa, US 180/C3
Morge (riv.), Fr. 84/E3
Morgenzon, SAfr. 149/E2
Morges, Swi. 98/C4
Morgex, It. 98/D6
Morghāb (riv.), Afg. 131/H1
Morgongåva, Swe. 80/G2
Morguilla (pt.), Chile 200/B3
Morhange, Fr. 95/F6
Morhar (riv.), India 127/E3
Mori, It. 85/J4
Mori, Japan 118/B2
Mori Kazak Zizhixian, China 112/F3
Morialta Conservation Park, Austl. 155/M8
Moriarty, NM, US 171/F4
Morice (lake), BC, Can. 168/B2
Morie (lake), Sc, UK 78/B1
Moriguchi, Japan 119/J6
Morin Dawa Daurzu Zizhiqi, China 113/M2
Moringen, Ger. 93/G5
Morinville, Ab, Can. 168/E2
Morioka, Japan 118/B4
Morisset, Austl. 157/D2
Moriston (riv.), Sc, UK 78/B2
Moriya, Japan 119/D2
Moriyama, Japan 119/J5
Morlaix, Fr. 84/B2
Morlanwelz, Belg. 95/D3
Mörlenbach, Ger. 96/B3
Morley, Eng, UK 77/G4
Mormant, Fr. 72/L6
Mormond (hill), Sc, UK 78/D1
Mornaguia, Tun. 46/B4
Mornington (isl.), Austl. 151/C2
Mörnsheim, Ger. 96/D5
Moro, Pak. 131/J3
Moro (gulf), Phil. 121/D6
Morocco (ctry.) 140/D2
Morocelí, Hon. 186/E3
Morococha, Peru 198/B3
Morogoro (pol. reg.), Tanz. 146/C4
Morogoro, Tanz. 146/C4
Morombe, Madg. 149/G8
Mörön, Mong. 112/H2
Morón, Ven. 194/D2
Morón, Cuba 187/G1
Morón, Arg. 201/J11
Morón de la Frontera, Sp. 86/C4
Morona (riv.), Peru 192/C4
Morona-Santiago (dept.), Ecu. 194/B5
Morondara (riv.), Madg. 149/H8
Morondava, Madg. 149/H8
Moroni (cap.), Com. 149/G5
Morotai (isl.), Indo. 123/G3
Morotai (str.), Indo. 123/G3
Moroto, Ugan. 146/B2
Moroto (mt.), Ugan. 146/B2
Moroyama, Japan 119/C2
Morpará, Braz. 196/B3
Morpeth, Eng, UK 77/G1
Morphou, Cyp. 133/C2
Morphou (bay), Cyp. 133/C2
Morra (lake), Neth. 92/C3
Morrinhos, Braz. 197/B1
Morris (mt.), Austl. 155/F3
Morris, Mb, Can. 169/J3
Morris (res.), Ca, US 178/C2
Morris, Mn, US 169/K4
Morris (co.), NJ, US 180/D2
Morris Jesup (cape), Grld 202/J
Morris Plains, NJ, US 181/H8
Morrison, Co, US 179/B3
Morristown, NJ, US 180/D2
Morristown NHP, NJ, US 180/D2
Morrisville, Pa, US 180/D3
Morro Bay, Ca, US 170/B4
Morro de Môco (peak), Ang. 147/C3
Morro de Puercos (pt.), Pan. 187/F5
Morro do Chapéu, Braz. 196/B3
Morro, Punta del (pt.), Mex. 185/N7
Morrocoy, PN, Ven. 194/D2
Mórrope, Peru 198/A2
Morropón, Peru 198/B2
Morros, Braz. 196/A1
Morrosquillo (gulf), Col. 187/G4
Mörrum, Swe. 80/F3
Mørs (isl.), Den. 80/C3
Morsang-sur-Orge, Fr. 72/K6
Morsbach, Ger. 95/G2
Morsbach, Fr. 95/F5
Morschwiller-le-Bas, Fr. 98/D2
Morse, Ks, US 179/D6
Morse Mill, Mo, US 179/F9
Morshansk, Rus. 105/G1
Morskoy (isl.), Kaz. 105/J3
Morsum, Ger. 93/G3
Mortagne (riv.), Fr. 98/C1
Mortagne-sur-Sèvre, Fr. 84/C3
Mortara, It. 100/B2
Mortcerf, Fr. 72/L5
Morte (pt.), Eng, UK 74/B4
Morte (riv.), Fr. 98/B3
Morteau, Fr. 98/C3
Mortefontaine, Fr. 72/K4
Mortegliano, It. 101/G1
Mortes, Rio das (riv.), Braz. 193/H6
Mortlake, Austl. 157/B3
Morton, Wa, US 168/C4
Morton, Il, US 171/K2
Morton Grove, Il, US 177/Q15
Morton NP, Austl. 157/D2
Morton NWR, NY, US 181/F2
Mortsel, Belg. 92/B6
Morungaba, Braz. 197/G7
Moruya, Austl. 157/D2
Morvan (plat.), Fr. 84/E3
Morven, Austl. 156/B4
Morven (peak), Sc, UK 78/C2
Morvi, India 131/K4
Morvillars, Fr. 98/C2
Morwell, Austl. 157/C3
Morzine, Fr. 98/C5
Mos, Sp. 86/A1
Mosbach, Ger. 96/C4
Mosby, Mo, US 179/E5
Moscavide, Port. 87/P10
Moscow (Moskva) (cap.), Rus. 103/W9
Moscow (upland), Rus. 102/F5
Moscow, Id, US 168/D4
Moscow University Ice Shelf, Ant. 202/J
Moselle (riv.), Fr. 85/G2
Moselle (dept.), Fr. 95/F5
Moselotte (riv.), Fr. 98/C2
Moses Lake, Wa, US 168/D4
Mosfellsbær, Ice. 79/N7
Mosgiel, NZ 159/S12
Moshaweng (riv.), SAfr. 148/C2
Moshchnyy (isl.), Rus. 81/M2
Moshi, Tanz. 146/C3
Moshoeshoe (Maseru) (int'l arpt.), Les. 148/D3
Mosina, Pol. 83/J2
Moskovskaya Oblast, Rus. 102/H5
Moskva (riv.), Rus. 102/G5
Moskva (Moscow) (cap.), Rus. 104/F1
Mosonmagyaróvár, Hun. 90/C2
Mosquera, Col. 194/B4
Mosquero, NM, US 171/G4
Mosquitia (phys. reg.), Hon. 187/E3
Mosquito (pt.), Pan. 187/G4
Mosquitos, Golfo de los (gulf), Pan. 187/F4
Moss, Nor. 80/D2
Moss Beach, Ca, US 177/J11
Moss Bluff, La, US 171/J5
Moss Point, Ms, US 175/F4
Moss-Side, NI, UK 76/B1
Moss Vale, Austl. 157/D2
Mosselbaai, SAfr. 148/C4
Mosses, Col des (pass), Swi. 98/D5
Mossi Highlands (uplands), Burk. 144/E4
Mössingen, Ger. 96/C6
Mossman, Austl. 156/B2
Mossoró, Braz. 196/C2
Most, Czh. 97/G1
Mostaganem (prov.), Alg. 142/F4
Mostaganem, Alg. 142/F5
Mostar, Bosn. 89/E1
Mostardas, Braz. 197/B4
Móstoles, Sp. 87/N9
Mota del Cuervo, Sp. 86/D3
Motagua (riv.), Guat. 182/D4
Motala, Swe. 80/F2
Motherwell, Sc, UK 78/C5
Motian (mtn.), China 114/E2
Motīhāri, India 127/E2
Motilla del Palancar, Sp. 86/E3
Motobu, Japan 117/J7
Motomiya, Japan 117/G2
Motono, Japan 119/E2
Motosu (lake), Japan 119/B3
Motosu, Japan 119/L5
Motovskiy (gulf), Rus. 79/K1
Motoyoshi, Japan 118/B4
Motozintla de Mendoza, Mex. 186/C3
Motril, Sp. 86/D4
Motsuta-misaki (cape), Japan 118/A2
Mott, ND, US 169/H4
Motta di Livenza, It. 101/F1
Motta Visconti, It. 100/B2
Mottarone (peak), It. 100/B1
Motueka, NZ 159/S11
Motul de Carrillo Puerto, Mex. 186/D1
Motupe, Peru 198/B2
Motygino, Rus. 106/K4
Mouchard, Fr. 98/B4
Mouchoir Passage (chan.), UK 187/J1
Moúdhros, Gre. 89/J3
Moudon, Swi. 98/C4
Mougris (well), Mrta. 144/B2
Mouhoun (prov.), Burk. 144/E3
Mouila, Gabon 138/H8
Mouïna (well), Alg. 141/F3
Moul (well), Niger 138/H4
Moulamein (riv.), Austl. 157/C2
Moulamein, Austl. 157/C2
Moulay Idriss, Mor. 142/B2
Moulins, Fr. 84/E3
Moulouya (riv.), Mor. 142/C2
Moultrie, Ga, US 175/H4
Moultrie (lake), SC, US 175/J3
Moundou, Chad 138/J6
Moundsville, WV, US 172/D4
Mount Aberdeen NP, Austl. 156/B3
Mount Abu, India 131/K4
Mount Airy, NC, US 172/D4
Mount Airy, Md, US 180/A5
Mount Allan Abor. Land, Austl. 155/G2
Mount Aspiring NP, NZ 159/R11
Mount Baker-Snoqualmie, Wa, US 177/D1
Mount Baker-Snoqualmie Nat'l For., Wa, US 177/D3
Mount Baldy, Ca, US 178/C2
Mount Barker, Austl. 154/C5
Mount Barker, Austl. 155/M9
Mount Barkly Abor. Land, Austl. 155/G2
Mount Beauty, Austl. 157/C3
Mount Bold (res.), Austl. 155/M9
Mount Buffalo NP, Austl. 157/C3
Mount Carmel, Il, US 172/C4
Mount Carmel, Pa, US 180/B2
Mount Darwin, Zim. 147/F4
Mount Diablo State Park, Ca, US 177/L11
Mount Eccles NP, Austl. 157/B3
Mount Elgon NP, Ugan. 146/B2
Mount Elliot NP, Austl. 156/B2
Mount Everard, Guy. 195/G3
Mount Field NP, Austl. 157/C4
Mount Gambier, Austl. 157/B3
Mount Garnet, Austl. 156/B2
Mount Holly, NJ, US 180/D4
Mount Holly Springs, Pa, US 180/A3
Mount Imlay NP, Austl. 157/D3
Mount Isa, Austl. 155/H2
Mount Joy, Pa, US 180/B3
Mount Kaputar NP, Austl. 157/D1
Mount Kenya NP, Kenya 146/C3
Mount Kisco, NY, US 181/E1
Mount Larcom, Austl. 156/C3
Mount Laurel, NJ, US 180/D4
Mount Lofty (ranges), Austl. 155/M9
Mount Magnet, Austl. 154/C4
Mount Mistake NP, Austl. 156/D4
Mount Morgan, Austl. 156/C3
Mount Morris, Mi, US 172/D3
Mount Nebo, Austl. 156/E6
Mount Olive, NC, US 175/J3
Mount Pearl, Nf, Can. 173/L2
Mount Penn, Pa, US 180/C3
Mount Pleasant, Ia, US 169/L5
Mount Pleasant, Mi, US 172/C3
Mount Pleasant, Ut, US 170/E3
Mount Pleasant, De, US 180/C4
Mount Pleasant (int'l arpt.), UK 201/F6
Mount Pleasant, Austl. 155/N8
Mount Pocono, Pa, US 180/C1
Mount Prospect, Il, US 177/P15
Mount Rainier, Md, US 180/B6
Mount Rainier NP, Wa, US 168/C4
Mount Remarkable NP, Austl. 155/H5
Mount Revelstoke NP, BC, Can. 168/D3
Mount Richmond NP, Austl. 157/B3
Mount Rushmore Nat'l Mem., SD, US 171/G2
Mount Spec NP, Austl. 156/B2
Mount St. Helens Nat'l Volcanic Mon., Wa, US 168/C4
Mount Sterling, Ky, US 172/D4
Mount Torrens, Austl. 155/M8
Mount Vernon, Il, US 171/K3
Mount Vernon, NY, US 181/K8
Mount Vernon, Oh, US 172/D3
Mount Vernon, Tx, US 171/J4
Mount Vernon, Va, US 180/A6
Mount Vernon, Wa, US 168/C3
Mount Walsh NP, Austl. 156/C4
Mount Warning NP, Austl. 156/D5
Mount Welcome Abor. Land, Austl. 154/C2
Mount William NP, Austl. 157/D4
Mount Wolf, Pa, US 180/B3
Mountain (riv.), NW, Can. 164/D2
Mountain Ash, Wal, UK 74/C3
Mountain Green, Ut, US 179/K11
Mountain Grove, Mo, US 171/J3
Mountain Home, Id, US 168/E5
Mountain Lakes, NJ, US 181/H8
Mountain Point, Ak, US 176/M4
Mountain Top, Pa, US 180/C1
Mountain View, Ar, US 171/J4
Mountain View, Ca, US 177/K12
Mountain View, Hi, US 166/U11
Mountain Village, Ak, US 176/F3
Mountain Zebra NP, SAfr. 148/D4
Mountainhome, Pa, US 180/C1
Mountainside, NJ, US 181/H9
Mountlake Terrace, Wa, US 177/C2
Mountmellick, Ire. 73/Q10
Mountrath, Ire. 73/Q10
Mount's (bay), Eng, UK 74/A6
Mountville, Pa, US 180/B3
Moura, Port. 86/B3
Moura, Austl. 156/C4
Mourão, Port. 86/B3
Mourenx, Fr. 84/C5
Mourmelon-le-Grand, Fr. 95/D5
Mourmelon-le-Petit, Fr. 95/D5
Mourne (mts.), NI, UK 76/B3
Mourniaí, Gre. 89/J5
Mouroux, Fr. 72/M5
Mouscron, Belg. 94/C2
Mousseaux-sur-Seine, Fr. 72/G4
Moussoro, Chad 138/J5
Moussy-le-Neuf, Fr. 72/K4
Moussy-le-Vieux, Fr. 72/K4
Mouths of the Niger, Nga. 138/G6
Moutier, Swi. 98/D3
Mouvaux, Fr. 94/C2
Mouy, Fr. 94/B5
Mouydir (plat.), Alg. 141/G4
Mouzákion, Gre. 89/G3
Mouzon (riv.), Fr. 98/B1
Mouzon, Fr. 95/E4
Moville, Ire. 76/A1
Moxotó (riv.), Braz. 196/C3
Moy, NI, UK 76/B3
Moyamba, SLeo. 144/B4
Moye (isl.), China 115/B4
Moyen Atlas (mts.), Mor. 138/D1
Moyenmoutier, Fr. 98/C1
Moyeuvre-Grande, Fr. 95/F5
Moyle (dist.), NI, UK 76/B1
Moyo (isl.), Indo. 123/E5
Moyo, Ugan. 146/A2
Moyobamba, Peru 198/B2
Moyowosi (riv.), Tanz. 146/A3
Moyu, China 112/C4
Moyuta, Guat. 186/D3
Mozambique (ctry.) 147/G4
Mozambique (chan.), Afr. 147/G5
Mozhaysk, Rus. 102/H5
Mozhga, Rus. 103/M4
Mozzanica, It. 100/C2
Mozzecane, It. 101/D2
Mpanda, Tanz. 146/A4
Mpigi, Ugan. 146/B2
Mpika, Zam. 146/A5
Mporokoso, Zam. 146/A5
Mpraeso, Gha. 145/E5
Mpulungu, Zam. 146/A5
Mpumalanga (prov.), SAfr. 149/E2
Mpwapwa, Tanz. 146/C4
Mrągowo, Pol. 81/J5
Mrkonjić Grad, Bosn. 90/C3
Msaken, Tun. 142/M7
M'Sila (prov.), Alg. 141/F2
M'sila, Alg. 142/H5
M'sila (riv.), Alg. 142/H5
Msoun (riv.), Mor. 142/C2
Msta (riv.), Rus. 102/G4
Mszana Dolna, Pol. 83/L4
Mtorwi (peak), Tanz. 146/B5
Mtsensk, Rus. 104/F1
Mtubatuba, SAfr. 149/F3
Mtunzini, SAfr. 149/E3
Mtwara, Tanz. 146/D5
Mtwara (pol. reg.), Tanz. 146/C5
Mu-kawa (riv.), Japan 118/C2
Mu Ko Similan NP, Thai. 120/B4
Mu Ko Surin NP, Thai. 120/B4
Mualama, Moz. 147/G4
Muan, SKor. 115/D5
Muang Hinboun, Laos 120/D2
Muang Khammouan, Laos 120/D2
Muang Khong, Laos 120/D3
Muang Khongxedon, Laos 120/D3
Muang Pak-lay, Laos 120/C2
Muang Pakxan, Laos 120/C2
Muang Sing, Laos 125/H3
Muang Vangviang, Laos 120/C2
Muang Xaignabouri, Laos 120/C2
Muang Xay, Laos 125/H3
Muar, Malay. 122/B3
Muarabungo, Indo. 122/B4
Muāri (pt.), Pak. 131/J4
Mubārakpur, India 126/D2
Mubende, Ugan. 146/A2
Mucajaí (riv.), Braz. 192/F3
Much, Ger. 95/G2
Muchinga (mts.), Zam. 147/F3
Muck (isl.), Sc, UK 73/G8
Muckleshoot Ind. Res., Wa, US 177/C3
Mucojo, Moz. 147/H3
Mucupina (mtn.), Hon. 186/E3
Mucur, Turk. 132/C2
Mucuri (riv.), Braz. 193/K7
Mud Mountain (dam), Wa, US 177/D3
Mud Mountain (lake), Wa, US 177/D3
Mudanjiang, China 113/N3
Mudanya, Turk. 91/J5
Mudau, Ger. 96/C3
Mudbach (riv.), Ger. 96/C3
Muddan (riv.), China 113/N2
Muddas NP, Swe. 79/G2
Muddy Run (res.), Pa, US 180/B4
Müden, Ger. 93/H3
Mudersbach, Ger. 95/G2
Mudgee, Austl. 157/D2
Mudjatik (riv.), Sk, Can. 164/F3
Mudon, Myan. 120/B2
Mudurnu, Turk. 91/K5
Muela (peak), Chile 201/B7
Muerte, Cerro de la (peak), CR 187/F4
Muff, Ire. 76/A1
Mufulira, Zam. 147/E3
Mugardos, Sp. 86/A1
Mugegawa, Japan 119/L4
Mughal Sarai, India 126/D3
Mugi, Japan 119/L4
Mugia, Sp. 86/A1
Muğla, Turk. 132/B2
Muğla (prov.), Turk. 132/B2
Mughalzhar Taūy (mts.), Kaz. 129/C3
Muhamdi, India 126/C2
Muḩammad (pt.), Egypt 143/C3
Muhammadābad, India 126/D3
Muhavura (vol.), Rwa. 146/A3
Muhila, Monts (mts.), D.R. Congo 147/E3
Mühlacker, Ger. 96/B5
Mühlbach (riv.), Ger. 96/A2
Mühldorf, Ger. 97/F6
Mühleberg, Swi. 98/D4
Mühlenbeck, Ger. 82/Q6
Mühlhausen, Ger. 97/E4
Mühlheim am Main, Ger. 96/B2
Mühlheim an der Donau, Ger. 99/E1
Mühltroff, Ger. 97/E1
Mühlviertel (reg.), Aus. 83/G4
Muhos, Fin. 102/E2
Muhu (isl.), Est. 81/K2
Muiden, Neth. 92/C4
Muir of Ord, Sc, UK 78/B1
Muir Woods Nat'l Mon., Ca, US 177/J11
Muirkirk, Sc, UK 78/B5
Muizon, Fr. 94/C5
Muju, SKor. 115/D4
Mukacheve, Ukr. 83/M4
Mukawa, Japan 118/B2
Mukawwar (isl.), Sudan 143/D4
Mukden, Bol. 198/D3
Mukeriān, India 128/C4
Mukhayyam al Yarmūk, Syria 133/E3
Mukhmās, Isr. 133/G8
Mukinbudin, Austl. 154/C4
Mukō, Japan 119/J6
Mukono, Ugan. 146/B2
Mukoshima (isls.), Japan 158/D2
Muktsar, India 128/C4
Mukwonago, Wi, US 177/P14
Mula, Sp. 86/E3
Mulanje, Malw. 147/G4
Mulchatna (riv.), Ak, US 176/G4
Mulchén, Chile 200/B3
Mulde (riv.), Ger. 82/G3
Mulegé, Mex. 184/C3
Muleshoe, Tx, US 171/G4
Mulhacén, Cerro de (peak), Sp. 86/D4
Mülhausen, Ger. 93/H6
Mülheim an der Ruhr, Ger. 92/D6
Mulhouse, Fr. 98/D2
Muli (riv.), Indo. 123/J5
Muli Zangzu Zizhixian, China 125/H2
Muling (pass), China 114/D3
Mull (isl.), Sc, UK 73/R8
Mull of Galloway (pt.), Sc, UK 76/D2
Mull of Kintyre (pt.), Sc, UK 76/C1
Mull of Logan (pt.), Sc, UK 76/D2
Mullach Coire Mhic Fhearchair (peak), Sc, UK 78/A1
Mullaghcleevaun (peak), Ire. 76/B5
Mullaghmore (peak), NI, UK 76/B2
Mullaittivu, SrL. 124/D6
Mullardoch (lake), Sc, UK 78/A2
Muller (mts.), Indo. 122/D4
Mullewa, Austl. 154/B4
Müllheim, Ger. 98/D2
Müllheim, Swi. 99/F2
Mullica (riv.), NJ, US 180/D4
Mullica Hill, NJ, US 180/C4
Mullingar, Ire. 73/Q10
Mullins, SC, US 175/J3
Mullumbimby, Austl. 157/E1
Mulobezi, Zam. 147/E4
Multai, India 126/B5
Multān, Pak. 128/A4
Multnomah (falls), Or, US 168/C4
Mulu (peak), Malay. 122/D3
Mulwala, Austl. 157/C2
Mum Nauk (pt.), Thai. 120/B5
Mumbai (Bombay), India 131/K5
Mumbwa, Zam. 147/E3
Mümling (riv.), Ger. 96/B3
Mumoni (peak), Kenya 146/C3
Mun (riv.), Thai. 125/H4
Muna (isl.), Indo. 123/F4
Muna, Mex. 186/D1
Munamägi (hill), Est. 81/M3
Muñani, Peru 198/D4
Muncar, Indo. 122/D5
Münchberg, Ger. 97/E2
München (Munich), Ger. 97/E6
Münchenstein, Swi. 98/D2
Munchique (peak), Col. 194/B4
Munchique, PN, Col. 194/B4
Münchmünster, Ger. 97/E5
Muncie, In, US 172/C3
Muncy, Pa, US 180/B1
Mundaring, Austl. 154/L6
Munday, Tx, US 171/H4
Mundelein, Il, US 177/Q15
Mundemba, Camr. 145/H5
Münden, Ger. 93/G6
Munderfing, Aus. 97/G6
Munderkingen, Ger. 99/F1
Mundo Novo, Braz. 199/F1
Mundo Novo, Braz. 196/B3
Mundubbera, Austl. 156/C4
Munera, Sp. 86/D3
Mungaolī, India 126/B3
Mungeli, India 126/C4
Munger, India 127/F3
Mungo NP, Austl. 157/B2
Mun'gyŏng, SKor. 115/E4
Munising, Mi, US 169/M4
Munkebo, Den. 80/D4
Munkedal, Swe. 80/D2
Munkfors, Swe. 80/E2
Munku-Sardyk (peak), Rus. 112/H1
Münnerstadt, Ger. 96/D2
Muñoz Gamero (pen.), Chile 199/B7
Munsan, SKor. 115/F6
Münsingen, Swi. 98/D4
Münsingen, Ger. 96/C6
Munster (reg.), Ire. 73/P10
Münster, Ger. 93/E5
Munster, Ger. 93/H3
Munster, Fr. 98/D1
Münster, Swi. 99/E5
Munster, In, US 177/R16
Münster, Ger. 96/B3
Münster/Osnabrück (int'l arpt.), Ger. 93/E4
Münstereifel, Ger. 95/F2
Münsterhausen, Ger. 96/D6
Münsterland (reg.), Ger. 82/D2
Münstermaifeld, Ger. 95/G3
Muntele Mare (peak), Rom. 91/F2
Muntendam, Neth. 92/D2
Muntok, Indo. 122/C4
Müntschemier, Swi. 98/D4
Münzenberg, Ger. 96/B2
Münzkirchen, Aus. 97/G6
Munzur Vadisi NP, Turk. 132/D2
Muonio, Fin. 79/G2
Muonioälven (riv.), Swe. 79/G1
Muotathal, Swi. 99/E4
Mupa, PN da, Ang. 147/C4
Muping, China 114/E3
Muqdisho (Mogadishu) (cap.), Som. 139/Q7
Muqeibila, Isr. 133/G6
Mur (riv.), Aus. 85/L3
Mura (riv.), Hun.,Slov. 90/C2
Muradiye, Turk. 132/E2
Murādnagar, India 128/D5
Murakami, Japan 117/F1
Murallón (peak), Chile 201/B6
Murano, It. 101/F2
Murat (peak), Turk. 132/B2
Muratlı, Turk. 132/E2
Muratlı, Turk. 91/H5
Murayama, Japan 118/B4
Murchison, Austl. 157/C3
Murchison (riv.), Austl. 154/C3
Murchison (mt.), Austl. 154/C3
Murchison, NZ 159/S11
Murcia, Sp. 87/E4
Murcia (aut. comm.), Sp. 86/E4
Murderkill (riv.), De, US 180/C6
Murdochville, Qu, Can. 173/H1
Murdock (pt.), Austl. 156/B1
Mürefte, Turk. 91/H5
Mureş (prov.), Rom. 91/G2
Mureş (riv.), Rom. 91/G2
Muret, Fr. 84/D5
Murfreesboro, Ar, US 171/J4
Murg (riv.), Ger. 95/H6
Murgab (riv.), Turk. 129/D5
Murgap (riv.), Trkm. 106/G6
Murgon, Austl. 156/C4
Muri, Swi. 99/E3
Muri bei Bern, Swi. 98/D4
Muria (peak), Indo. 122/D5
Muriaé, Braz. 197/D2
Murias de Paredes, Sp. 86/B1
Murici, Braz. 196/D3
Murīdke, Pak. 128/C4
Müritz (lake), Ger. 82/G2
Murlīganj, India 127/F3
Murmansk, Rus. 102/G1
Murmansk (int'l arpt.), Rus. 102/G1
Murmanskaya Oblast, Rus. 79/J1
Murnau, Ger. 99/H2
Muro, Sp. 87/G3
Muro, Japan 119/K6
Muro Lucano, It. 88/D2
Murom, Rus. 102/J5
Muroran, Japan 118/B2
Muros, Sp. 86/A1
Muroto, Japan 116/D4
Muroto-zaki (pt.), Japan 116/D4
Murowana Goślina, Pol. 83/J2
Murphy, NC, US 175/G3
Murphy, Mo, US 179/G9
Murr (riv.), Ger. 96/C5
Murra, Nic. 186/E3
Murramarang NP, Austl. 157/D2
Murray (riv.), Austl. 157/B2
Murray, Ky, US 172/B4
Murray (lake), SC, US 175/H3
Murray, Ut, US 179/K12
Murray Bridge, Austl. 155/H5
Murraysburg, SAfr. 148/C3
Murrayville, Austl. 157/B2
Murree, Pak. 128/B3
Murrieta, Ca, US 178/C3
Murrieta Hot Springs, Ca, US 178/C3
Murrumbidgee (riv.), Austl. 157/C2
Murrumburrah, Austl. 157/D2
Murrurundi, Austl. 157/D1
Murshidābād, India 127/G3
Murtala Muhammed (int'l arpt.), Nga. 145/F5
Murtaröl (peak), Swi. 99/G4
Murten, Swi. 98/D4
Murtoa, Austl. 157/B3
Murud (peak), Malay. 122/E3
Murupara, NZ 159/T10
Mururoa (isl.), FrPol. 159/M7
Murwāra, India 126/C4
Murwillumbah, Austl. 156/D5
Mürz (riv.), Aus. 83/H5
Mürzzuschlag, Aus. 83/H5
Muş (prov.), Turk. 132/E2
Muş, Turk. 132/E2
Musabeyli, Turk. 133/E1
Musāfirkhāna, India 126/C2
Musala (peak), Bul. 91/F4
Musan, NKor. 115/E1
Musashino, Japan 119/D2
Muscat (cap.), Oman 131/G4
Musconetcong (riv.), NJ, US 180/C2
Muscoot (res.), NY, US 181/E1
Muscoy, Ca, US 178/C2
Musekwapoort (pass), SAfr. 147/E5
Museum of Flight, Wa, US 177/C2
Musgrave (ranges), Austl. 155/F3
Musgrave Harbour, Nf, Can. 173/L1
Mushābani, India 127/F4
Mushie, D.R. Congo 138/J8
Mushin, Nga. 145/F5
Musi (riv.), Indo. 122/B4
Musile di Piave, It. 101/F1
Musinga (peak), Col. 194/B3
Muskego, Wi, US 177/P14
Muskegon, Mi, US 172/C3
Muskegon (riv.), Mi, US 172/C3
Muskingum (riv.), Oh, US 172/D4
Muskoka (lake), On, Can. 172/E2
Musoma, Tanz. 146/B3
Musone (riv.), It. 101/G6
Musquaro (riv.), Qu, Can. 173/J1
Mussau (isl.), PNG 158/D5
Musselburgh, Sc, UK 78/C5
Musselshell (riv.), Mt, US 168/F4
Mussomeli, It. 88/C4
Musson, Belg. 95/E4
Mustafābād, Pak. 128/B4
Mustafakemalpaşa, Turk. 132/B1
Müstair, Swi. 99/G4
Mustang, Ok, US 179/M15
Musters (lake), Arg. 200/C5
Musu-dan (pt.), NKor. 115/E2
Musún (mtn.), Nic. 187/E3
Mušutište, Serb. 90/E4
Muswellbrook, Austl. 157/D2
Mūt, Egypt 143/B3
Mut, Turk. 133/C1

Mutá, Ponta do (pt.), Braz. 196/C4
Mutare, Zim. 147/F4
Muthill, Sc, UK 78/C4
Mutis (peak), Indo. 123/F5
Mutsamudu, Com. 149/H6
Mutsu (bay), Japan 118/B3
Mutsu, Japan 118/B3
Mutsuzawa, Japan 119/E3
Muttekopf (peak), Aus. 99/G3
Muttenz, Swi. 98/D2
Mutters, Aus. 99/H3
Mutterstadt, Ger. 96/B4
Muttler (peak), Swi. 99/G4
Muttonville, Mi, US 177/G6
Mutum, Braz. 197/D1
Mutzig, Fr. 98/D1
Müynoq, Uzb. 105/L4
Muzaffargarh, Pak. 128/A4
Muzaffarnagar, India 128/D5
Muzaffarpur, India 127/E2
Muzambinho, Braz. 197/G6
Muzon (cape), Ak, US 176/M4
Muztag (peak), China 112/D4
Muztagata (peak), China 129/G5
Muzzana del Turgnano, It. 101/G1
Mwadui, Tanz. 146/B3
Mwana (cape), Kenya 146/D3
Mwanza (pol. reg.), Tanz. 146/B3
Mwanza, Tanz. 146/B3
Mweelrea (peak), Ire. 73/P10
Mweka, D.R. Congo 147/D1
Mwene-Ditu, D.R. Congo 147/D2
Mwense, Zam. 146/A5
Mweru (lake), D.R. Congo 147/E2
Mweru-Wantipa NP, Zam. 146/A5
Mwesi (mtn.), Tanz. 146/A4
Mwinilunga, Zam. 147/D3
My Son Temples (ruin), Viet. 120/E3
My Tho, Viet. 120/D4
Myall Lakes NP, Austl. 157/E2
Myanaung, Myan. 125/G4
Myanmar (Burma) (ctry.) 125/G3
Myebon, Myan. 125/F3
Myerstown, Pa, US 180/B3
Myggenäs, Swe. 80/D2
Myingyan, Myan. 125/G3
Myitkyinā, Myan. 125/G2
Myjava, Slvk. 83/J4
Mykolayiv, Ukr. 91/L2
Mykolayiv (int'l arpt.), Ukr. 91/L2
Mykolayivs'ka Oblasti, Ukr. 104/D3
Mylau, Ger. 97/F1
Mymensingh (pol. reg.), Bang. 127/H3
Mynämäki, Fin. 81/J1
Mynydd Eppynt (mts.), Wal, UK 74/C2
Mynydd Pencarreg (peak), Wal, UK 74/B2
Mynydd Preseli (mtn.), Wal, UK 74/B3
Myōgi, Japan 119/B1
Myohaung, Myan. 125/F3
Myōkō-san (peak), Japan 117/F2
Myŏngch'ŏn, NKor. 115/E2
Myrhorod, Ukr. 104/E2
Myrtle Beach, SC, US 175/J3
Myrtle Creek, Or, US 168/C5
Myrtleford, Austl. 157/C3
Mysen, Nor. 80/D2
Myślenice, Pol. 83/K4
Myślibórz, Pol. 83/H2
Myslivna (peak), Czh. 97/H5
Mysore, India 124/C5
Mystery Bay Rec. Area, Wa, US 177/B1
Mystic Island, NJ, US 180/D4
Myszków, Pol. 83/K3
Mytishchi, Rus. 103/W9
Mže (riv.), Czh. 82/G4
Mzimba, Malw. 146/B5
Mzuzu, Malw. 146/B5

N

Na (riv.), Viet. 120/C1
Naab (riv.), Ger. 85/J2
Naaldwijk, Neth. 92/B4
Naalehu, Hi, US 166/U11
Naama, Alg. 141/E2
Naantali, Fin. 81/K1
Naarden, Neth. 92/C4
Naarn im Machlande, Aus. 97/H6
Naas, Ire. 73/Q10
Nababeep, SAfr. 148/B3
Nabari, Japan 119/K6
Nabari (riv.), Japan 119/K6
Nabberu (lake), Austl. 154/D3
Nabburg, Ger. 97/F4
Naberezhnye Chelny, Rus. 103/M5
Nabeul, Tun. 88/B4
Nabeul (gov.), Tun. 88/B4
Nābha, India 128/D4
Nabiac, Austl. 157/E2
Nabisipi (riv.), Qu, Can. 173/J1
Nabón, Ecu. 198/B1
Nabua, Phil. 121/D5
Nacala, Moz. 147/H3
Nacaome, Hon. 186/E3
Nachi-Katsuura, Japan 116/D4
Nachingwea, Tanz. 146/C5
Náchod, Czh. 83/J3
Nachrodt-Wiblingwerde, Ger. 93/E6
Nacimiento, Chile 200/B3
Naco, Mex. 184/C2
Nacogdoches, Tx, US 171/J5
Nácori Chico, Mex. 184/C2
Nacozari de García, Mex. 184/C2
Nādbai, India 126/A2
Nadder (riv.), Eng, UK 74/D4
Nadiād, India 131/K4
Nădlac, Rom. 90/E2
Nador (prov.), Mor. 142/C2
Nador, Mor. 142/C2
Nadur, Malta 88/L6
Naejang-san NP, SKor. 115/D5
Näfels, Swi. 99/F3
Nafūsah, Jabal (mts.), Libya 141/H3
Naga, Phil. 121/D5
Nagagami (riv.), On, Can. 172/C1
Nagahama, Japan 116/C4
Nagahama, Japan 119/K5
Nagai, Japan 117/G1
Nagaizumi, Japan 119/B3
Nagakute, Japan 119/M5
Nāgāland (state), India 125/F2
Nagambie, Austl. 157/C3
Nagano, Japan 117/F2
Nagano (pref.), Japan 117/E3
Naganuma, Japan 118/B2
Nagaoka, Japan 117/F2
Nagaokakyō, Japan 119/J6
Nagaon (Nowgong), India 125/F2
Nagar, India 126/A2
Nagara (riv.), Japan 117/E3
Nagara, Japan 119/E3
Nagareyama, Japan 119/D2
Nāgārjuna Sāgar (res.), India 124/C4
Nagarote, Nic. 182/D5
Nagarzê, China 127/H1
Nagas (pt.), BC, Can. 176/M5
Nagasaka, Japan 119/A2
Nagasaki, Japan 116/A4
Nagasaki (int'l arpt.), Japan 116/A4
Nagasaki (pref.), Japan 116/A4
Nagasaki Peace, Japan 116/A4
Nagashima, Japan 119/L5
Nagato, Japan 116/B3
Nagato, Japan 119/A1
Nagatoro, Japan 119/C1
Nāgaur, India 131/K3
Nāgda, India 131/L4
Nāgercoil, India 124/C6
Nagīna, India 126/B1
Nago, Japan 117/J7
Nago-Torbole, It. 99/G6
Nāgod, India 126/C3
Nagold (riv.), Ger. 96/B5
Nagold, Ger. 96/B5
Nagorno-Karabakh (prov.), Azer. 105/H5
Nagoya, Japan 119/L5
Nagoya Castle, Japan 119/L5
Nagpula (pass), China 127/F1
Nāgpur, India 124/C3
Nags Head, NC, US 175/K3
Naguri, Japan 119/C2
Nagy-Milic (peak), Hun. 83/L4
Nagyatád, Hun. 90/C2
Nagyecsed, Hun. 83/M5
Nagyhalász, Hun. 90/E1
Nagykanizsa, Hun. 90/C2
Nagykáta, Hun. 90/D2
Nagykőrös, Hun. 90/D2
Naha, Japan 117/J7
Naḥal Shillo (riv.), Isr.,WBnk. 133/G7
Nāhan, India 128/D4
Nahanni NP, NW, Can. 164/D2
Nahariyya, Isr. 133/D3
Nahāvand, Iran 130/E2
Nahe (riv.), Ger. 85/G2
Naḥel Soreq (riv.), Isr.,WBnk. 133/F8
Nahouri (prov.), Burk. 145/E4
Nahr 'Atbarah (riv.), Sudan 139/M4
Nahr Mufjir (riv.), Isr.,WBnk. 133/G7
Nahr Ouassel (riv.), Alg. 142/F5
Nahuel Huapi (lake), Arg. 200/C4
Nahuel Huapi, PN, Arg. 200/C4
Nahuelbuta, PN, Chile 200/B3
Naica, Mex. 184/D3
Naihāti, India 127/G4
Naila, Ger. 97/E2
Naiman Qi, China 114/E2
Nā'īn, Iran 130/F2
Nain, Nf, Can. 165/K3
Nainital, India 126/B1
Nainpur, India 126/C4
Naintré, Fr. 84/D3
Nairn (riv.), Sc, UK 78/B2
Nairn, Sc, UK 78/C1
Nairne, Austl. 155/M9
Nairobi (cap.), Kenya 146/C3
Nairobi NP, Kenya 146/C3
Naivasha, Kenya 146/C3
Naives-Rosières, Fr. 95/E6
Najafābād, Iran 130/F2
Nájera, Sp. 86/D1
Najin, NKor. 113/P3
Naju, SKor. 115/D5
Naka, Japan 119/G5
Naka (riv.), Japan 116/D4
Nakadōri (isl.), Japan 116/A4
Nakai, Japan 119/C3
Nakajō, Japan 117/F1
Nakalele (pt.), Hi, US 166/T10
Nakamichi, Japan 119/B2
Nakaminato, Japan 117/G2
Nakamura, Japan 116/C4
Nakano, Japan 117/F2
Nakano (lag.), Japan 116/C3
Nakasato, Japan 118/B3
Nakashibetsu, Japan 118/D2
Nakasongola, Ugan. 146/B2
Nakatane, Japan 117/L5
Nakatomi, Japan 119/A3
Nakatsu, Japan 116/B4
Nakatsugawa, Japan 117/E3
Nakazato, Japan 119/B1
Nakhodka, Rus. 113/P3
Nakhon Nayok, Thai. 120/C3
Nakhon Pathom, Thai. 120/C3
Nakhon Phanom, Thai. 120/D2
Nakhon Ratchasima, Thai. 120/C3
Nakhon Sawan, Thai. 120/C3
Nakhon Si Thammarat, Thai. 120/B4
Nakkila, Fin. 81/J1
Nakło nad Notecią, Pol. 83/J2
Naknek, Ak, US 176/G4
Nakodar, India 128/C4
Nakonde, Zam. 146/B5
Naksan-sa, SKor. 115/E3
Nakskov, Den. 80/D4
Naktong, SKor. 115/E4
Naktong (riv.), SKor. 115/E4
Nakūr, India 128/D5
Nakuru, Kenya 146/C3
Nakusp, BC, Can. 168/D3
Nāl (riv.), Pak. 131/J3
Nalayh, Mong. 112/J2
Nalbach, Ger. 95/F5
Nalbāri, India 127/H2
Nalbaugh NP, Austl. 157/D3
Nal'chik (int'l arpt.), Rus. 105/G4
Nal'chik, Rus. 105/G4
Nalgonda, India 124/C4
Nalhāti, India 127/F3
Naliya, India 131/J4
Nallıhan, Turk. 91/K5
Nalón (riv.), Sp. 86/B1
Nālūt, Libya 141/H3
Nam (riv.), NKor. 115/D3
Nam Dinh, Viet. 125/J3
Nam Nao NP, Thai. 120/C2
Nam Un (res.), Thai. 120/C2
Namakzār-e Shadād (salt pan), Iran 131/G2
Namangan (pol. reg.), Uzb. 129/F4
Namangan, Uzb. 129/F4
Namanunga (isl.), Tuv. 158/G5
Namaqualand (reg.), SAfr. 148/B3
Namaripi (cape), Indo. 123/J4
Namasagali, Ugan. 146/B2
Namatanai, PNG 158/E5
Namborn, Ger. 95/G4
Nambour, Austl. 156/D4
Nambu, Japan 119/A3
Nambucca Heads, Austl. 157/E1
Nambung NP, Austl. 154/B4
Namdae (riv.), NKor. 115/E2
Namdalseid, Nor. 79/D2
Namegawa, Japan 119/C1
Namekagon (riv.), Wi, US 169/L4
Namentenga (prov.), Burk. 145/E3
Namerikawa, Japan 117/E2
Nametil, Moz. 147/G4
Namhae (isl.), SKor. 115/D5
Namhae, SKor. 115/D5
Namib (des.), Namb. 147/B5
Namibe, Ang. 147/B4
Namibia (ctry.) 147/C5
Namie, Japan 117/G2
Namioka, Japan 118/B3
Namja (pass), Nepal 124/D2
Namjagbarwa (peak), China 125/G2
Namling, China 124/E2
Namloser Wetterspitze (peak), Aus. 99/G3
Nammoku, Japan 119/B1
Namnoi (peak), Myan. 120/B4
Namoi (riv.), Austl. 157/D1
Namonuito (isl.), Micr. 158/D4
Namorik (isl.), Mrsh. 158/F4
Namp'o, NKor. 115/C3
Nampula, Moz. 147/G4
Namsê (pass), China 124/D2
Namsos, Nor. 79/D2
Namu (isl.), Mrsh. 158/F4
Namur (prov.), Belg. 95/D3
Namur, Belg. 95/D3
Namwŏn, SKor. 115/D5
Namysłów, Pol. 83/J3
Nan (riv.), Thai. 125/H4
Nan, Thai. 120/C2
Nanae, Japan 118/B3
Nanaimo, BC, Can. 168/C3
Nanakuli, Hi, US 166/V13
Nanam, NKor. 115/E2
Nanango, Austl. 156/D4
Nanao, Japan 117/E2
Nanauta, India 128/D5
Nanay (riv.), Peru 192/D4
Nancagua, Chile 200/C2
Nanchang, China 121/C2
Nanchang, China 121/C2
Nancheng, China 121/C2
Nanchong, China 112/J5
Nancy, Fr. 95/F6
Nanda Devi (peak), India 112/C5
Nandan, China 125/J3
Nānded, India 124/C4
Nanding (riv.), China 125/G3
Nandrin, Belg. 95/E3
Nandu (riv.), China 121/A4
Nandurbār, India 131/K4
Nandy, Fr. 72/K6
Nandyāl, India 124/C4
Nanfeng, China 121/C2
Nang Xian, China 125/F2
Nanga Parbat (peak), Pak. 128/C2
Nangapinoh, Indo. 122/D4
Nangis, Fr. 72/M6
Nangnim (mts.), NKor. 115/D2
Nangong, China 114/C3
Nangtud (mt.), Phil. 123/F1
Nangwarry, Austl. 157/B3
Nanhui, China 114/L8
Nanjian Yizu Zizhixian, China 125/H2
Nanjing, China 114/D4
Nankāna Sāhib, Pak. 128/B4
Nankang, China 121/B2
Nankoku, Japan 116/C4
Nanle, China 114/C3
Nanliu (riv.), China 125/J3
Nannestad, Nor. 80/D1
Nanning, China 125/J3
Nannō, Japan 119/L5
Nannup, Austl. 154/B5
Nanny (riv.), Ire. 76/B4
Nānpāra, India 126/C2
Nanpi, China 114/D3
Nanping, China 121/C2
Nansei, Japan 119/L7
Nansen (sound), Nun., Can. 165/S6
Nant (lake), Sc, UK 78/A4
Nantai-san (peak), Japan 117/F2
Nanterre, Fr. 72/J5
Nantes, Fr. 84/C3
Nanteuil-le-Haudouin, Fr. 72/L4
Nanteuil-lès-Meaux, Fr. 94/B6
Nanticoke, On, Can. 172/D3
Nanticoke, Pa, US 180/B1
Nanton, Ab, Can. 168/E3
Nantong, China 114/E4
Nantua, Fr. 98/B5
Nantucket (isl.), Ma, US 173/G3
Nantwich, Eng, UK 77/F5
Nanuet, NY, US 181/J7
Nanumanga (isl.), Tuv. 158/G5
Nanumea (isl.), Tuv. 158/G5
Nanuque, Braz. 196/B5
Nanwon (res.), China 114/C4
Nanxi, China 125/H2
Nanxiong, China 121/B2
Nanyang, China 114/C4
Nanyang, China 114/C4
Nanyuki, Kenya 146/C2
Nanzhang, China 114/B5
Nanzhao, China 114/C4
Nao, Cabo de la (cape), Sp. 87/F3
Naococane (lake), Qu, Can. 165/J3
Naogaon, Bang. 127/G3
Naokot, Pak. 124/A3
Naolinco, Mex. 185/N7
Naoua (falls), C.d'Iv. 144/D5
Náousa, Gre. 89/J4
Náousa, Gre. 89/H2
Napa, Ca, US 177/K10
Napa (co.), Ca, US 177/K10
Napa (riv.), Ca, US 177/K10
Napa (valley), Ca, US 177/K9
Napa Junction, Ca, US 177/K10
Napak (peak), Ugan. 146/B2
Napakiak, Ak, US 176/F3
Napanee, On, Can. 172/E2
Napaskiak, Ak, US 176/F3
Napata (ruin), Sudan 143/B5
Naperville, Il, US 172/B3
Napf (peak), Swi. 98/D4
Napier, NZ 159/T10
Napier, SAfr. 148/L11
Naples, Fl, US 175/H5
Naples (Napoli), It. 88/D2
Napo (prov.), Ecu. 194/B5
Napo (riv.), Ecu.,Peru 194/C5
Napoleon, ND, US 169/J4
Napoleonville, La, US 171/K5
Napoli, Golfo di (gulf), It. 88/C2
Napuka (isl.), FrPol. 159/L6
Naqīl Sumārah (pass), Yem. 130/D6
Nara, Mali 144/D3
Nāra (riv.), Pak. 131/J4
Nara, Japan 119/J6
Naracoorte, Austl. 157/B3
Naraini, India 126/C3
Naranbulag, Mong. 112/F2
Naranjal, Ecu. 194/B5
Naranjito, Ecu. 198/B1
Naranjos, Mex. 186/B1
Narāq, Iran 130/F2
Narasannapeta, India 124/D4
Narashino, Japan 119/E2
Narathiwat, Thai. 120/C5
Nārāyanganj, Bang. 127/H4
Nārāyani (zone), Nepal 127/E2
Narayani (riv.), Nepal 127/E2
Nārāyanpet, India 124/C4
Narbonne, Fr. 84/E5
Narceo (riv.), Sp. 86/B1
Nardò, It. 89/F2
Nare (pt.), Eng, UK 74/B6
Narellan, Austl. 156/G9
Narembeen, Austl. 154/C5
Nares (str.), Can.,Grld. 165/T6
Narew (riv.), Pol. 102/D5
Narganá, Pan. 187/G4
Narinda (bay), Madg. 149/H6
Nariño (dept.), Col. 194/B4
Narita (int'l arpt.), Japan 117/G3
Narita, Japan 119/E2
Nariz (peak), Chile 201/C7
Narkatiāganj, India 127/E2
Narmada (riv.), India 124/C3
Narman, Turk. 105/G4
Narni, It. 88/C1
Narodnaya (peak), Rus. 103/P2
Narok, Kenya 146/B3
Narón, Sp. 86/A1
Narooma, Austl. 157/D3
Nārowāl, Pak. 128/C3
Nærøy, Nor. 79/D2
Narra, Phil. 123/E2
Narrabri, Austl. 157/D1
Narrandera, Austl. 157/C2
Narrogin, Austl. 154/C5
Narromine, Austl. 157/D2
Narrows (riv.), NY, US 181/J9
Narsimhapur, India 126/B4
Narsinghgarh, India 131/L4
Narsinghdi, Bang. 127/H4
Narusawa, Japan 119/B3
Naruto, Japan 116/D3
Narutō, Japan 119/E2
Narva (res.), Rus. 102/F4
Narva (riv.), Est.,Rus. 102/E4
Narva (bay), Est.,Rus. 81/M2
Narva, Est. 81/N2
Narvacan, Phil. 121/D4
Narvik, Nor. 79/F1
Narwāna, India 128/D5
Nar'yan-Mar, Rus. 103/M2
Naryn, Kyr. 129/G4
Naryn (obl.), Kyr. 129/G4
Naryn (riv.), Kyr. 106/H5
Naryn Qum (plain), Kaz. 105/J2
Narzole, It. 100/A3
Năsăud, Rom. 91/G2
Naschel, Arg. 200/D2
Nash (pt.), Wal, UK 74/C4
Nashua, NH, US 173/G3
Nashville (int'l arpt.), Tn, US 172/C4
Nashville (cap.), Tn, US 172/C4
Našice, Cro. 90/D3
Nasielsk, Pol. 83/L2
Nasijärvi (lake), Fin. 81/K1
Nāsik, India 131/K5
Nasīrābād, India 131/K3
Naso (pt.), Phil. 123/F1
Nāsriganj, India 127/E3
Nass (riv.), BC, Can. 176/N4
Nassach (riv.), Ger. 96/D2
Nassarawa (state), Nga. 145/G4
Nassau (cap.), Bahm. 183/F2
Nassau (bay), Chile 201/D7
Nassau (isl.), Cookls. 159/J6
Nassau, Ger. 95/G3
Nassau, De, US 180/C6
Nassau (co.), NY, US 181/E2
Nasser (lake), Egypt 143/C4
Nassereith, Aus. 99/G3
Nässjö, Swe. 80/F3
Nassogne, Belg. 95/E3
Nastapoka (isls.), Qu, Can. 165/J3
Nastätten, Ger. 95/G3
Næstved, Den. 80/D4
Nasu-dake (peak), Japan 117/F2
Nat (peak), Myan. 125/G4
Nata, Bots. 147/E5
Natá, Pan. 194/A2
Natagaima, Col. 194/C4
Natal, Braz. 196/D2
Naṭanz, Iran 130/F2
Natashō, Japan 119/J5
Natashquan (riv.), Qu, Can. 165/K3
Natchez, Ms, US 171/K5
Natchez Trace Nat'l Parkway, US 172/C5
Natchitoches, La, US 171/J5
Naters, Swi. 98/D5
Nāthdwāra, India 131/K4
Natimuk, Austl. 157/B3
Nation (riv.), BC, Can. 182/F2
National Agriculture Research Center, Md, US 180/B6
National Aquarium, Md, US 180/B5
National Archaeological Museum, Gre. 89/N8
National City, Ca, US 178/C5
National Cowboy Hall of Fame and Western Heritage Center, Ok, US 179/N14
National Exhibition Centre, Eng, UK 75/E2
National Institutes of Health, Md, US 180/A6
National Museum, Mona. 100/J8
National Security Agency, Md, US 180/B5
Natitingou, Ben. 145/F4
Natl, Jor. 133/D4
Natron (lake), Tanz. 146/B3
Natternbach, Aus. 97/G6
Nattheim, Ger. 96/D5
Nättraby, Swe. 80/F3
Natuna (isls.), Indo. 122/C3
Natural Bridge Caverns, Tx, US 179/U20
Natural Bridges Nat'l Mon., Ut, US 170/E3
Naturaliste (cape), Austl. 157/D4
Naturaliste (chan.), Austl. 154/B3
Naturaliste (cape), Austl. 154/B5
Naturno (Naturns), It. 99/G4
Naucalpan, Mex. 185/Q10
Naucelle, Fr. 84/E4
Nauders, Aus. 99/G4
Naudesnek (pass), SAfr. 148/E3
Nauen, Ger. 82/F6
Naugachhia, India 127/F3
Naugaon Sādāt, India 126/B1
Nauhcampatépetl (vol.), Mex. 185/M7
Nauheim, Ger. 96/B3
Naujan, Phil. 121/D5
Naujoji-Akmenė, Lith. 81/K3
Naumburg, Ger. 93/G6
Naumburg, Ger. 82/F3
Nauort, Ger. 95/G3
Nā'ūr, Jor. 133/D4
Nauru (ctry.) 158/F5
Naushahra, India 128/C3
Naushahra Virkhan, Pak. 128/B4
Nauta, Peru 198/C2
Nautla, Mex. 185/N6
Nauvo (Nagu), Fin. 81/J1
Nava, Mex. 185/E2
Nava, Colle di (pass), It. 100/A4
Nava del Rey, Sp. 86/C2
Navajo (res.), NM, US 170/F3
Navajo Nat'l Mon., Az, US 170/E3
Navalcarnero, Sp. 87/M9
Navalmoral de la Mata, Sp. 86/C3
Navalvillar de Pela, Sp. 86/C3
Navapolatsk, Bela. 81/N4
Navarin (cape), Rus. 107/T3
Navarino (isl.), Chile 199/C8
Navarra (aut. comm.), Sp. 86/D1
Navarro, Arg. 201/J11
Navàs, Sp. 87/F2
Navas de San Juan, Sp. 86/D3
Navasota (riv.), Tx, US 185/F2
Navassa (isl.), Myan. 187/H2
Navax (pt.), Eng, UK 74/A6
Nave, It. 100/D1
Navenne, Fr. 98/C2
Navia, Sp. 86/B1
Navia (riv.), Sp. 86/B1
Navidad, Chile 200/N8
Navina, Ok, US 179/M14
Naviraí, Braz. 199/F1
Návodari, Rom. 91/J3
Navojoa, Mex. 184/C3
Navolato, Mex. 184/D3
Návpaktos, Gre. 89/G3
Návplion, Gre. 89/H4
Navsāri, India 131/K4
Navy Board (inlet), Nun., Can. 165/H1
Navy Yard City, Wa, US 177/B2
Nawābganj, India 126/B1
Nawābganj, India 126/C2
Nawābganj, Bang. 127/G3
Nawābshāh, Pak. 131/J3
Nawāda, India 127/E3
Nawān Jandānwāla, Pak. 128/A3
Nawāshahr, India 128/D4
Nawāshahr, Pak. 128/B2
Nawoiy, Uzb. 129/E4
Nawoiy (pol. reg.), Uzb. 129/D4
Nawṣ, Ra's (pt.), Oman 131/G5
Naxçıvan, Azer. 105/H5
Naxçivan Aut. Rep., Azer. 105/H5
Naxi, China 125/J2
Náxos, Gre. 89/J4
Náxos (isl.), Gre. 89/J4
Nay Pyi Taw (cap.), Myan. 125/G4
Nayarit (state), Mex. 184/D4
Nayong, China 125/J2
Nayoro, Japan 118/C1
Nayramadlïn (peak), Mong. 112/E2
Nayzatash (pass), Taj. 129/F5
Nazaré, Braz. 196/C4
Nazaré, Port. 86/A3
Nazaré do Piauí, Braz. 196/B2
Nazaré Paulista, Braz. 197/G8
Nazareth, Pa, US 180/C2
Nazareth, Belg. 94/C2
Nazas (riv.), Mex. 184/D3
Nazas, Mex. 184/D3
Nazca, Peru 198/C4
Naze, Japan 117/K6
Naze, The (pt.), Eng, UK 75/H3
Naẕerat (Nazareth), Isr. 133/G6
Nazilli, Turk. 132/B2
Nazrēt, Eth. 139/N6
Nazyvayevsk, Rus. 129/F1
Nchelenge, Zam. 146/A5
Ncheu, Malw. 147/F3
Ndalatando, Ang. 147/B2
Ndali, Ben. 145/F4
Ndele, CAfr. 139/K6
Ndende (isl.), Sol. 158/F6
N'Djamena (cap.), Chad 138/J5
Ndola, Zam. 147/E3
Ndrhamcha (lake), Mrta. 144/B2
Né (riv.), Fr. 84/C4
Néa Alikarnassós, Gre. 89/J5
Néa Ankhíalos, Gre. 89/H3
Néa Artáki, Gre. 89/H3
Néa Ionía, Gre. 89/H3
Néa Ionía, Gre. 89/N8
Néa Kallikrátia, Gre. 89/H2
Néa Kíos, Gre. 89/H4
Néa Mikhanióna, Gre. 89/H2
Néa Moudhaniá, Gre. 89/H2
Néa Potídhaia, Gre. 89/H2
Néa Tríglia, Gre. 89/H2
Néa Zíkhni, Gre. 89/H2
Neagh (lake), NI, UK 76/B2
Neale (lake), Austl. 155/F3
Neales (riv.), Austl. 155/G3
Neamț (prov.), Rom. 91/H2
Neaophli-le-Château, Fr. 72/H5
Neápolis, Gre. 89/H4
Neápolis, Gre. 89/G2
Neápolis, Gre. 89/J5
Near (isls.), Ak, US 176/A5
Neath, Wal, UK 74/C3
Neath (riv.), Wal, UK 74/C3
Neath Port Talbot (co.), Wal, UK 74/C3
Neavitt, Md, US 180/B6
Nebbi, Ugan. 146/A2
Nebel-Horn (peak), Ger. 99/G3
Nebikon, Swi. 98/D3
Nebitdag, Trkm. 105/K5
Neblina (peak), Braz. 195/E4
Nebo (mt.), Austl. 156/E6
Nebraska (state), US 171/G2
Nebrodi (mts.), It. 88/C4
Nechako (riv.), BC, Can. 164/D3
Neches (riv.), Tx, US 174/E4
Nechisar NP, Eth. 139/N6
Nechranice (res.), Czh. 97/G2
Neckar (riv.), Ger. 82/D4
Neckarbischofsheim, Ger. 96/B4
Neckargemünd, Ger. 96/B4
Neckarsteinach, Ger. 96/B4
Neckarsulm, Ger. 96/C4
Necker (isl.), Hi, US 159/J2
Necochea, Arg. 200/F3
Necoclí, Col. 194/B2
Necropoli (ruin), It. 88/C1
Neda, Sp. 86/A1
Nedelino, Bul. 91/G5
Nedelišće, Cro. 85/M3
Nederland, Tx, US 171/J5
Nederland, Co, US 179/A3
Nederweert, Neth. 92/C6
Neede, Neth. 92/D4
Needles, Ca, US 170/D4
Needles, The, Eng, UK 75/E5
Needmore, Ok, US 179/N15
Neepawa, Mb, Can. 169/J3
Neerabup NP, Austl. 154/K6
Neerpelt, Belg. 92/C6
Neetze (riv.), Ger. 93/H2
Neetze, Ger. 93/H2
Neffelbach (riv.), Ger. 95/F2
Neftekamsk, Rus. 103/M4
Nefud (des.), SAfr. 130/D3
Nefyn, Wal, UK 76/D6
Negēlē, Eth. 139/N6
Negev (reg.), Isr. 132/C4
Negoiu (peak), Rom. 91/G3
Negombo, SrL. 124/C6
Negotin, Serb. 90/F3
Negotino, FYROM 89/H2
Negra (pt.), Peru 198/A2
Negra (range), Braz. 196/A3
Negra (pt.), Belz. 186/D2
Negrais (cape), Myan. 125/F4
Negrar, It. 101/D1
Negreira, Sp. 86/A1
Negrești, Rom. 91/H2
Negritos, Peru 198/A2
Negro (riv.), Arg. 199/D5
Negro (peak), Arg. 200/C3
Negro (riv.), Uru. 199/E3
Negros (isl.), Phil. 121/D6
Nehbandān, Iran 131/H2
Nei Monggol (aut. reg.), China 113/K3
Nei Monggol (plat.), China 113/K3
Neiafu, Tonga 159/H6
Neiba, DRep. 183/G4
Neiba (mts.), DRep. 187/J2
Neiderösterreich (prov.), Aus. 85/L2
Neige, Crêt de la (peak), Fr. 98/B5
Neihuang, China 114/C4
Neijiang, China 112/J6
Neilston, Sc, UK 78/B5
Neiqiu, China 114/C3
Neisse (riv.), Ger. 83/H3
Neiva, Col. 194/C4
Neixiang, China 114/B4
Nejanilini (lake), Mb, Can. 164/G3
Nejdek, Czh. 97/F2
Nejrab (int'l arpt.), Syria 133/E1
Nek'emtē, Eth. 139/N6
Neksø, Den. 80/F4
Nelas, Port. 86/B2
Nelidovo, Rus. 102/G4
Nellingen, Ger. 96/C5
Nellore, India 124/C5
Nelson (cape), Austl. 157/B3
Nelson (isl.), Ak, US 176/E3
Nelson (str.), Chile 199/A7
Nelson, BC, Can. 168/D3
Nelson, NZ 159/S11
Nelson (riv.), Mb, Can. 164/G3
Nelson, Eng, UK 77/F4
Nelson-Atkins Museum of Fine Art, Mo, US 179/D5
Nelson Bay, Austl. 157/E2
Nelson Lagoon, Ak, US 176/F4
Nelson Lakes NP, NZ 159/S11
Nelspruit, SAfr. 147/F6
Néma, Mrta. 144/D2
Néma, Dhar (cliff), Mrta. 144/D2
Neman (riv.), Rus. 83/M1
Nembro, It. 100/C1
Neméa, Gre. 89/H4
Nemingha, Austl. 157/D1
Nemira (peak), Rom. 91/H2
Nemours, Fr. 84/E2
Nemunas (riv.), Lith. 81/K4
Nemuro, Japan 118/D2
Nemuro (pen.), Japan 118/D2
Nen (riv.), China 113/M2
Nenagh, Ire. 73/P10
Nenana, Ak, US 176/J3
Nendaz, Swi. 98/D5
Nene (riv.), Eng, UK 77/J6
Nenetskiy Aut. Okrug, Rus. 103/L2
Nenjiang, China 113/N2
Nentershausen, Ger. 93/G6
Nentershausen, Ger. 95/G3
Nenzing, Aus. 99/F3

Neo Volcanica, Cordillera (mts.), Mex. 185/Q10
Néon Petritsion, Gre. 89/H2
Neoria Husainpur, India 126/B1
Néos Marmarás, Gre. 89/H2
Neosho (riv.), Ks,Ok, US 171/J3
Nepal (ctry.) 126/D1
Nepālganj, Nepal 126/C1
Nepanagar, India 131/L4
Nepean, On, Can. 172/F2
Nepean (riv.), Austl. 156/G8
Nepeña, Peru 198/B3
Nepessina (lake), Mi, US 177/F6
Nephi, Ut, US 170/E3
Nepisiguit (riv.), NB, Can. 173/H2
Nepomuk, Czh. 97/G4
Neptune City, NJ, US 180/D3
Nera (riv.), It. 85/K5
Nérac, Fr. 84/D4
Neratovice, Czh. 97/H2
Nerekhta, Rus. 102/J4
Neresheim, Ger. 96/D5
Neretva (riv.), Bosn. 90/D4
Neris (riv.), Lith. 81/L4
Nerja, Sp. 86/D4
Nermete (pt.), Peru 198/A2
Nerokoúros, Gre. 89/J5
Nerone (peak), It. 101/F5
Nerpio, Sp. 86/D3
Nersingen, Ger. 96/D6
Nerva, Sp. 86/B4
Nervesa della Battaglia, It. 101/F1
Nerviano, It. 100/B1
Nes, Neth. 92/C2
Nes, Nor. 80/D1
Nes Ziyyona, Isr. 133/F8
Nesbyen, Nor. 80/C1
Nesebŭr, Bul. 89/K1
Nesher, Isr. 133/G6
Neskaupstadhur, Ice. 79/Q6
Nesle, Fr. 94/B4
Nesles-la-Vallée, Fr. 72/J4
Nesquehoning, Pa, US 180/C2
Ness (lake), Sc, UK 78/B2
Ness (riv.), Sc, UK 78/B2
Nesselrode (mt.), Ak, US 176/M4
Nesselwang, Ger. 99/G2
Nesslau, Swi. 99/F3
Neston, Eng, UK 77/E5
Nestórion, Gre. 89/G2
Néstos (riv.), Gre. 91/G5
Netanya, Isr. 133/F7
Netarhāt, India 127/E4
Netcong, NJ, US 180/D2
Nethe (riv.), Ger. 93/G5
Netherlands (ctry.) 82/C3
Netherlands Antilles (dpcy.), Neth. 183/H5
Netolice, Czh. 97/H4
Netphen, Ger. 95/H2
Netstal, Swi. 99/F3
Nette (riv.), Ger. 92/D6
Nettebach (riv.), Ger. 95/G3
Nettersheim, Ger. 95/F3
Nettetal, Ger. 92/D6
Nettilling (lake), Nun., Can. 165/J2
Nettuno, It. 88/C2
Netzschkau, Ger. 97/F1
Neu Darchau, Ger. 93/H2
Neu-Isenburg, Ger. 96/B2
Neu-Ulm, Ger. 96/D6
Neu Zittau, Ger. 82/Q7
Neubiberg, Ger. 97/E6
Neubrandenburg, Ger. 83/G2
Neubulach, Ger. 96/B5
Neuburg, Ger. 96/B5
Neuburg an der Donau, Ger. 96/E5
Neuburg an der Kammel, Ger. 99/G1
Neuchâtel, Swi. 98/C4
Neuchâtel (canton), Swi. 98/C4
Neuchâtel, Lac de (lake), Swi. 85/G3
Neuenbürg, Ger. 96/B5
Neuenburg am Rhein, Ger. 98/D2
Neuendettelsau, Ger. 96/D4
Neuenhagen, Ger. 82/Q6
Neuenhaus, Ger. 92/D3
Neuenkirchen, Ger. 93/F3
Neuenkirchen, Ger. 93/F3
Neuenkirchen, Ger. 93/E4
Neuenrade, Ger. 93/E6
Neuenstadt am Kocher, Ger. 96/C4
Neuenstein, Ger. 96/C4
Neuerburg, Ger. 95/F3
Neuf-Brisach, Fr. 98/D1
Neufahrn bei Freising, Ger. 97/E6
Neufchâteau, Fr. 98/B1
Neufchâteau, Belg. 95/E4
Neufchâtel-en-Bray, Fr. 84/D2
Neufchâtel-Hardelot, Fr. 94/A2
Neufchelles, Fr. 72/M4
Neufmanil, Fr. 95/D4
Neufmoutiers-en-Brie, Fr. 72/L5
Neuhaus am Inn, Ger. 97/G6
Neuhaus am Rennweg, Ger. 96/E1
Neuhaus-Schierschnitz, Ger. 96/E2
Neuhäusel, Ger. 95/G3
Neuhausen am Rheinfall, Swi. 99/E2
Neuhof, Ger. 96/C2
Neuhof an der Zenn, Ger. 96/D4
Neuhofen, Ger. 96/B4
Neuhofen an der Krems, Aus. 97/H6
Neuilly-en-Thelle, Fr. 94/B5
Neuilly-L'Évêque, Fr. 98/B2
Neuilly-sur-Marne, Fr. 72/K5
Neuilly-sur-Seine, Fr. 72/J5
Neukirchen, Ger. 80/C4
Neukirchen an der Vöckla, Aus. 97/G6
Neukirchen vorm Wald, Ger. 97/G5
Neumarkt am Wallersee, Aus. 97/G7
Neumarkt (Enga), It. 99/H5
Neumarkt im Mühlkreis, Aus. 97/H6
Neumarkt in der Oberpfalz, Ger. 97/E4
Neumarkt-Sankt Veit, Ger. 97/F6
Neumünster, Ger. 80/C4
Neunkirch, Swi. 99/E2
Neunkirchen, Aus. 85/M3
Neunkirchen, Ger. 95/H2
Neunkirchen, Ger. 95/G5
Neunkirchen-Seelscheid, Ger. 95/G2
Neupotz, Ger. 96/B4
Neuquén (riv.), Arg. 199/C4
Neuquén (prov.), Arg. 200/C3
Neuquén, Arg. 200/C3
Neuruppin, Ger. 82/G2
Neusäss, Ger. 96/D6
Neuse (riv.), NC, US 175/J3
Neusiedl am See, Aus. 85/M3
Neusiedler (lake), Aus. 83/J5
Neusiedler See (lake), Aus. 90/C2
Neuss, Ger. 92/D6
Neustadt, Ger. 95/G2
Neustadt am Rübenberge, Ger. 93/G3
Neustadt an der Aisch, Ger. 96/D3
Neustadt an der Donau, Ger. 97/E5
Neustadt an der Waldnaab, Ger. 97/F3
Neustadt an der Weinstrasse, Ger. 96/B4
Neustadt bei Coburg, Ger. 96/E2
Neustadt in Holstein, Ger. 80/D4
Neustift im Stubaital, Aus. 99/H3
Neustrelitz, Ger. 82/G2
Neutraubling, Ger. 97/F5
Neuves-Maisons, Fr. 84/F2
Neuvic, Fr. 84/E4
Neuville-sur-Saône, Fr. 98/A6
Neuwied, Ger. 95/G3
Neuzelle, Ger. 83/H2
Neva (riv.), Rus. 81/P2
Nevada (state), US 170/C3
Nevada, Mo, US 171/J3
Nevada (mts.), Col. 194/C2
Nevada, Sierra (mts.), Sp. 86/D4
Nevado de Colima PN, Mex. 184/D5
Nevado de Toluca, PN, Mex. 185/K7
Nevado del Huila, PN, Col. 192/C3
Nevado, Sierra del (mts.), Arg. 200/C3
Nevel', Rus. 81/N3
Nevele, Belg. 94/C1
Nevel'sk, Rus. 113/R2
Nevers, Fr. 84/E3
Nevesinje, Bosn. 89/F1
Nevinnomyssk, Rus. 105/G3
Nevis (isl.), StK. 183/N8
Nevis (peak), StK. 183/N8
Nevola (riv.), It. 101/G5
Nevşehir (prov.), Turk. 132/C2
Nevşehir, Turk. 132/C2
New (riv.), Guy. 192/G3
New (riv.), WV, US 172/D4
New Albany, In, US 172/C4
New Albany, Ms, US 175/F3
New Amsterdam, Guy. 195/G3
New Ancholme (riv.), Eng, UK 77/H4
New Athens, Il, US 179/H9
New Baltimore, Mi, US 177/G6
New Bataan, Phil. 121/E6
New Bedford, Ma, US 173/G3
New Berlin, Tx, US 179/U21
New Berlin, Pa, US 180/B2
New Berlin, Wi, US 177/P14
New Berlinville, Pa, US 180/C3
New Bern, NC, US 175/J3
New Braunfels, Tx, US 179/U20
New Britain, Ct, US 173/F3
New Britain (isl.), PNG 158/D5
New Britain, Pa, US 180/C3
New Brunswick (prov.), Can. 173/H2
New Brunswick, NJ, US 181/H10
New Buffalo, Pa, US 180/B3
New Buildings, NI, UK 76/A2
New Caledonia (isl.), NCal., Fr. 158/F7
New Caledonia (terr.), NCal., Fr. 158/F6
New Canaan, Ct, US 181/M7
New Castle, De, US 180/C4
New Castle (co.), De, US 180/C5
New Castle, In, US 172/C4
New Castle, Pa, US 172/D3
New Chicago, In, US 177/R16
New City, NY, US 181/K7
New Columbia, Pa, US 180/B1
New Columbus, Pa, US 180/B1
New Cumberland, Pa, US 180/B3
New Cumnock, Sc, UK 78/B6
New Delhi (cap.), India 128/D5
New Denver, BC, Can. 168/D3
New Egypt, NJ, US 180/D3
New England NP, Austl. 157/E1
New Freedom, Pa, US 180/B4
New Galloway, Sc, UK 76/D1
New Georgia (isls.), Sol. 158/E5
New Georgia (sound), Sol. 158/E5
New Glasgow, NS, Can. 173/J2
New Glasgow, Qu, Can. 173/N6
New Gretna, NJ, US 180/D4
New Guinea (isl.), Indo.,PNG 158/C5
New Hampshire (state), US 173/G3
New Hanover, SAfr. 149/E3
New Hanover, Il, US 179/G9
New Hanover (isl.), PNG 158/D5
New Haven, Ct, US 173/F3
New Haven, Mi, US 177/G6
New Hebrides (isls.), Van. 158/F6
New Holland, Pa, US 180/B3
New Hope, Pa, US 180/D3
New Hyde Park, NY, US 181/L9
New Iberia, La, US 171/K5
New Ireland (isl.), PNG 158/E5
New Jersey (state), US 180/D3
New Kensington, Pa, US 172/E3
New Kowloon, China 113/U10
New Lenox, Il, US 177/Q16
New Lisbon, NJ, US 180/D4
New Liskeard, On, Can. 172/E2
New London, Ct, US 173/F3
New Madrid, Mo, US 171/K3
New Market, Md, US 180/A5
New Meadows, Id, US 168/D4
New Mexico (state), US 170/G4
New Milford, NJ, US 181/J8
New Mills, Eng, UK 77/F5
New Norfolk, Austl. 157/C4
New Orleans, La, US 179/P17
New Orleans (Moisant Field), La, US 179/P17
New Oxford, Pa, US 180/A4
New Philadelphia, Oh, US 172/D3
New Philadelphia, Pa, US 180/B2
New Pitsligo, Sc, UK 78/D1
New Plymouth, NZ 159/S10
New Port Richey, Fl, US 175/H4
New Providence (isl.), Bahm. 183/F3
New Providence, NJ, US 181/H9
New Richmond, Qu, Can. 173/H1
New River (mts.), Az, US 179/R18
New River, Az, US 179/R18
New Rochelle, NY, US 181/K8
New Rockford, ND, US 169/J4
New Romney, Eng, UK 75/G5
New Ross, Ire. 73/Q10
New Rossington, Eng, UK 77/G5
New Sarpy, La, US 179/P17
New Schwabenland (phys. reg.), Ant. 202/Z
New Scone, Sc, UK 78/C4
New Siberian (isls.), Rus. 109/N2
New Smyrna Beach, Fl, US 175/H4
New South Wales, Austl. 157/D1
New South Wales (state), Austl. 157/C2
New Stuyahok, Ak, US 176/G4
New Town, ND, US 169/H4
New Tripoli, Pa, US 180/C2
New Ulm, Mn, US 169/K4
New Waterford, NS, Can. 173/J2
New Westminster, BC, Can. 168/C3
New Windsor, Md, US 180/A4
New York (state), US 172/G3
New York, NY, US 181/K9
New Zealand (ctry.) 159/R10
Newark, Oh, US 172/D3
Newark, De, US 180/C4
Newark (int'l arpt.), NJ, US 181/J9
Newark, NJ, US 181/J9
Newark, Ca, US 177/K11
Newark (bay), NJ, US 181/J9
Newark-on-Trent, Eng, UK 77/H5
Newbern, Il, US 179/G8
Newberry, SC, US 175/H3
Newberry, Mi, US 172/C2
Newberry Nat'l Volcanic Mon., Or, US 168/C5
Newburgh, Sc, UK 78/C4
Newburn, Eng, UK 77/G2
Newbury, Eng, UK 75/E4
Newcastle, Austl. 157/D2
Newcastle, SAfr. 149/E2
Newcastle, Ire. 73/P10
Newcastle, Ire. 76/B5
Newcastle, Ok, US 179/M15
Newcastle, NI, UK 76/C3
Newcastle (int'l arpt.), Eng, UK 77/G1
Newcastle, Wy, US 169/G5
Newcastle-under-Lyme, Eng, UK 77/F6
Newcastle upon Tyne, Eng, UK 77/G2
Newcastle upon Tyne (co.), Eng, UK 77/G1
Newcastleton, Sc, UK 77/F1
Newe Yam, Isr. 133/F6
Newel, Ger. 95/F4
Newell, Austl. 156/B2
Newellton, La, US 171/K4
Newenham (cape), Ak, US 176/F4
Newfane, NY, US 173/S9
Newfield, NJ, US 180/C4
Newfoundland (isl.), Can. 173/L1
Newfoundland, NJ, US 181/H7
Newfoundland, Pa, US 180/C1
Newfoundland and Labrador (prov.), Can. 165/K3
Newhalen, Ak, US 176/H4
Newham (bor.), Eng, UK 72/D2
Newhaven, Eng, UK 75/F5
Newington, Eng, UK 72/F3
Newkirk, Ok, US 171/H3
Newllano, La, US 171/J5
Newmains, Sc, UK 78/C5
Newman (mt.), Austl. 154/C2
Newman, Austl. 154/C2
Newmarket, On, Can. 172/E2
Newmarket, Eng, UK 75/G2
Newmill, Sc, UK 78/D1
Newnan, Ga, US 175/G3
Newport, Eng, UK 74/D1
Newport, Eng, UK 75/E5
Newport, Wal, UK 74/D3
Newport (co.), Wal, UK 74/C3
Newport, Ar, US 171/K4
Newport (bay), Ca, US 178/C3
Newport, De, US 180/C4
Newport, Ky, US 172/C4
Newport, NJ, US 180/C5
Newport, Or, US 168/B4
Newport, Pa, US 180/A3
Newport, RI, US 173/G3
Newport, Tn, US 172/D5
Newport, Vt, US 173/F2
Newport, Wa, US 168/D3
Newport Beach, Ca, US 178/G8
Newport Meadows (lake), NJ, US 180/C5
Newport-on-Tay, Sc, UK 78/D4
Newport Pagnell, Eng, UK 75/F2
Newquay, Eng, UK 74/A6
Newry, NI, UK 76/B3
Newry (dist.), NI, UK 76/B3
Newry (canal), NI, UK 76/B3
Newtok, Ak, US 176/F3
Newton, Tx, US 171/J5
Newton, Ma, US 173/G3
Newton, NJ, US 180/D1
Newton Abbot, Eng, UK 74/C5
Newton-le-Willows, Eng, UK 77/F5
Newton Mearns, Sc, UK 78/B5
Newton Stewart, Sc, UK 76/D2
Newton Tors (hill), Eng, UK 78/D5
Newtonmore, Sc, UK 78/B2
Newtonville, NJ, US 180/D4
Newtown, Austl. 157/B3
Newtown, Wal, UK 74/C1
Newtown, Pa, US 180/D3
Newtown Mount Kennedy, Ire. 76/B5
Newtown Saint Boswells, Sc, UK 78/D5
Newtown Square, Pa, US 180/C4
Newtownabbey, NI, UK 76/C2
Newtownards, NI, UK 76/C2
Newtownhamilton, NI, UK 76/B3
Newtownstewart, NI, UK 76/A2
Newtyle, Sc, UK 78/C3
Nextlalpan, Mex. 185/Q9
Neyagawa, Japan 119/J6
Neyrīz, Iran 131/F3
Neyshābūr, Iran 131/G1
Neyva (riv.), Rus. 103/P4
Neyveli, India 124/C5
Neyyāttinkara, India 124/C6
Nezahualcóyotl, Mex. 185/Q10
Neznayka (riv.), Rus. 103/W9
Nezperce, Id, US 168/D4
Ngabang, Indo. 122/C3
Ngabordamlu (cape), Indo. 123/H5
Ngabu, Malw. 147/F4
Ngai-Ndethya Nat'l Rsv., Kenya 146/C3
Ngamring, China 127/F1
Nganda (peak), Malw. 146/B5
Ngangerabeli (plain), Kenya 146/C3
Ngaoundéré, Camr. 138/H6
Ngarkat Conservation Park, Austl. 155/J5
Ngatik (isl.), Micr. 158/E4
Ngoan Muc (pass), Viet. 120/E4
Ngoc Linh (peak), Viet. 125/J4
Ngomeni (cape), Kenya 146/D3
Ngong, Kenya 146/C3
Ngonye (falls), Zam. 147/D4
Ngorongoro Consv. Area, Tanz. 146/B3
Ngounié (riv.), Gabon 138/H8
Nguigmi, Niger 138/H5
Ngulu (isl.), Micr. 158/C4
Ngumbe Sukani (pt.), Tanz. 146/C5
Nguru (mts.), Tanz. 146/C4
Ngwenya (peak), Swaz. 149/E2
Nha Trang, Viet. 120/E3
Nhamunda (riv.), Braz. 189/D3
Nhill, Austl. 157/B3
Nhlangano, Swaz. 149/E2
Niagara (falls), Can.,US 173/R9
Niagara (riv.), Can.,US 173/R9
Niagara (co.), On, Can. 173/R9
Niagara Falls, On, Can. 173/R9
Niagara Falls, NY, US 173/R9
Niagara-on-the-Lake, On, Can. 173/R9
Niamey (dept.), Niger 145/F3
Niamey (cap.), Niger 145/F3
Niamey (int'l arpt.), Niger 145/F3
Niamtougou, Togo 145/F4
Niandan (riv.), Afr. 145/G5
Niangara, D.R. Congo 139/L7
Niangay (lake), Mali 138/E4
Niangzi (pass), China 114/C3
Nias (isl.), Indo. 122/A3
Niassa (prov.), Moz. 146/B5
Nicaragua (ctry.) 187/E3
Nicaragua (lake), Nic. 187/E4
Nicastro-Sambiase, It. 88/E3
Nice, Fr. 85/G5
Niceville, Fl, US 175/G4
Nichinan, Japan 116/B5
Nichlaul, India 126/D2
Nicholas (chan.), Bang. 187/F1
Nichols Hills, Ok, US 179/M14
Nicholson (range), Austl. 154/C3
Nickerie (dist.), Sur. 195/G3
Nickerie (riv.), Sur. 195/G3
Nickol (bay), Austl. 154/C2
Nicobar (isls.), India 125/F6
Nicolás Bravo, Mex. 186/D2
Nicolás Romero, Mex. 185/Q9
Nicolet, Qu, Can. 173/F2
Nicolls (pt.), NY, US 181/E2
Nicoma Park, Ok, US 179/N15
Nicosia, It. 88/D4
Nicosia (cap.), Cyp. 133/C2
Nicosia (dist.), Cyp. 133/C2
Nicotera, It. 88/D3
Nicoya, CR 187/E4
Nicoya (gulf), CR 187/E4
Nicoya, Peninsula de (pen.), CR 187/E4
Nidau, Swi. 98/D3
Nidd (riv.), Eng, UK 77/G3
Nidda, Ger. 96/B2
Nidda (riv.), Ger. 82/E3
Niddatal, Ger. 96/B2
Nidder (riv.), Ger. 96/C2
Nideggen, Ger. 95/F2
Nidge (prov.), Turk. 132/C2
Nidwalden (canton), Swi. 99/E4
Nidzica, Pol. 83/L2
Niebüll, Ger. 80/C4
Nied (riv.), Fr. 85/G2
Niedenstein, Ger. 93/G6
Nieder-Olm, Ger. 95/H4
Niederanven, Lux. 95/F4
Niederbipp, Swi. 98/D3
Niederbronn-les-Bains, Fr. 95/G6
Niedere Tauern (mts.), Aus. 85/K3
Niederfischbach, Ger. 95/G2
Niederlausitz (reg.), Ger. 83/G3
Niedernhausen, Ger. 96/B2
Niederösterreich (prov.), Aus. 90/B2
Niedersachsen (state), Ger. 80/C5
Niedersächsisches Wattenmeer NP, Ger. 93/E1
Niedersachswerfen, Ger. 93/H5
Niederstetten, Ger. 96/C4
Niederstotzingen, Ger. 96/D5
Niederurnen, Swi. 99/F3
Niederwerrn, Ger. 96/D2
Niederwinkling, Ger. 97/F5
Niederzier, Ger. 95/F2
Niederzissen, Ger. 95/G3
Niefern-Öschelbronn, Ger. 96/B5
Niegocin (lake), Pol. 81/J5
Nieheim, Ger. 93/G5
Niemodlin, Pol. 83/J3
Nienburg, Ger. 93/G3
Nienhagen, Ger. 93/H3
Niénokoué (peak), C.d'Iv. 144/D5
Nieppe, Fr. 94/B2
Niéri (riv.), Sen. 144/B3
Niers (riv.), Ger. 95/F1
Nierstein, Ger. 96/B3
Niet Ban Tinh Xa, Viet. 120/D4
Nieuw-Amsterdam, Sur. 193/G2
Nieuw-Bergen, Neth. 92/D5
Nieuw-Loosdrecht, Neth. 92/C4
Nieuw-Nickerie, Sur. 195/G3
Nieuw-Schoonebeek, Neth. 92/D3
Nieuw-Vossemeer, Neth. 92/B5
Nieuwe Pekela, Neth. 92/D2
Nieuwegein, Neth. 92/C4
Nieuwerkerk aan de IJssel, Neth. 92/B5
Nieuweschans, Neth. 93/E2
Nieuwkoop, Neth. 92/B4
Nieuwleusen, Neth. 92/D3
Nieuwoudtville, SAfr. 148/B3
Nieuwpoort, Belg. 94/B1
Nieves, Mex. 184/E3
Niğde, Turk. 132/C2
Nigel, SAfr. 148/E2
Niger (ctry.) 138/G4
Niger (delta), Nga. 145/G5
Niger (riv.), Afr. 138/F5
Nigeria (ctry.) 138/G6
Nigg (bay), Sc, UK 78/B1
Nighthawk (lake), On, Can. 172/D1
Nightmute, Ak, US 176/F3
Nigrán, Sp. 86/A1
Nigrita, Gre. 89/H2
Nihoa (isl.), Hi, US 159/J2
Nihonmatsu, Japan 117/G2
Nihtaur, India 126/B1
Nii (isl.), Japan 117/F3
Niigata (int'l arpt.), Japan 117/F2
Niigata, Japan 117/F2
Niigata (pref.), Japan 118/A4
Niihama, Japan 116/C4
Niihari, Japan 119/E1
Niihau (isl.), Hi, US 166/R10
Niimi, Japan 116/C3
Niitsu, Japan 117/F2
Niiza, Japan 119/D2
Níjar, Sp. 86/D4
Nijkerk, Neth. 92/C4
Nijlen, Belg. 95/D1
Nijmegen, Neth. 92/C5
Nikaia, Gre. 89/H3
Nikel', Rus. 79/J1
Nikishka, Ak, US 176/H3
Nikísiani, Gre. 89/J2
Nikki, Ben. 145/F4
Nikkō, Japan 117/F2
Nikkō NP, Japan 117/F2
Niklasdorf, Aus. 85/L3
Nikolai, Ak, US 176/H3
Nikolayevsk-na-Amure, Rus. 107/Q4
Nikol'sk, Rus. 105/H1
Nikolski, Ak, US 176/E5
Nikonga (riv.), Tanz. 146/A3
Nikopol', Ukr. 104/E3
Nikopol, Bul. 91/G4
Niksar, Turk. 104/F4
Nīkshahr, Iran 131/H3
Nikšić, Mont. 90/D4
Nikumaroro (Gardner) (isl.), Kiri. 159/H5
Nikunau (isl.), Kiri. 158/G5
Nile (delta), Egypt 133/B4
Nile (riv.), Afr. 139/M2
Niles, Mi, US 172/C3
Niles, Oh, US 172/D3
Niles, Il, US 177/Q15
Ni'līn, Isr. 133/G8
Nilópolis, Braz. 197/K7
Nilsiä, Fin. 102/F3
Nilvange, Fr. 95/F5
Nīmāj, India 124/B2
Nimba (peak), C.d'Iv. 144/C5
Nimba (co.), Libr. 144/C5
Nîmes, Fr. 84/F5
Nimsbach (riv.), Ger. 95/F4
Nimule NP, Sudan 146/A2
Nin, Cro. 90/B3
Nīnawā (gov.), Iraq 132/E3
Nīnawá (Nineveh) (ruin), Iraq 132/E2
Ninepin Group (isls.), China 113/V11
Ninfas (pt.), Arg. 200/D4
Ning'an, China 113/N3
Ningbo, China 114/E5
Ningde, China 121/C2
Ningdu, China 121/C2
Ninggang, China 125/K2
Ninghua, China 121/C2
Ningjin, China 114/C3
Ningjin, China 114/D3
Ninglang Yizu Zizhixian, China 125/H2
Ningling, China 114/C4
Ningming, China 125/J3
Ningwu, China 114/C3
Ningxia Huizu (aut. reg.), China 112/J4
Ningxiang, China 121/B2
Ningyang, China 114/D4
Ningyuan, China 125/K2
Ninh Binh, Viet. 120/D1
Ninilchik, Ak, US 176/H3
Niningo (isls.), PNG 158/D5
Ninohe, Japan 118/B3
Ninomiya, Japan 119/C3
Ninove, Belg. 94/D2
Ninoy Aquino (int'l arpt.), Phil. 121/D5
Niobara (riv.), Ne, US 166/F3
Niobrara (riv.), Ne, US 169/H5
Niokolo-Koba, PN du, Sen. 144/B3
Niono, Mali 144/D3
Nioro-du-Rip, Sen. 144/B3
Nioro du Sahel, Mali 144/C3
Niort, Fr. 84/C3
Nipawin, Sk, Can. 169/H2
Nipe (bay), Cuba 187/H1
Nipigon, On, Can. 169/L3
Nipigon (lake), On, Can. 164/G3
Nipissing (lake), On, Can. 165/J4
Ñiquén, Chile 200/C3
Niquero, Cuba 187/G1
Nirasaki, Japan 117/F3
Nirayama, Japan 119/B3
Nirimba Army Afld., Austl. 156/G8
Nirmal, India 124/C4
Nirmāli, India 127/F2
Niš, Serb. 90/E4
Niš (int'l arpt.), Serb. 90/E4
Nišava (riv.), Serb. 89/H1
Niscemi, It. 88/D4
Nishiazai, Japan 119/K5
Nishibiwajima, Japan 119/L5
Nishiharu, Japan 119/L5
Nishikatsura, Japan 119/B2
Nishiki (riv.), Japan 116/B3
Nishiki, Japan 119/H5
Nishinomiya, Japan 119/H6
Nishino'omote, Japan 116/B5
Nishio, Japan 119/M6
Nishiwaki, Japan 119/G6
Nisko, Pol. 83/M3
Nisqually, Wa, US 177/B3
Nisqually (riv.), Wa, US 177/B3
Nisqually Ind. Res., Wa, US 177/B3
Nisqually Reach (str.), Wa, US 177/B3
Nissan (isl.), PNG 158/E5
Nisser (lake), Nor. 80/C2
Nisshin, Japan 119/M5
Nissum (bay), Den. 80/C3
Nisswa, Mn, US 169/K4
Nistru (riv.), Mol. 91/H1
Niterói, Braz. 197/K7
Nith (riv.), Sc, UK 78/C6
Nith (riv.), Sc, UK 76/E1
Nithsdale (valley), Sc, UK 76/E1
Nitra, Slvk. 90/D1
Nitra (riv.), Slvk. 83/K4
Nitriansky (pol. reg.), Slvk. 83/K4
Nitsa (riv.), Rus. 103/P4
Nitta, Japan 119/C1
Nittedal, Nor. 80/D1
Nittel, Ger. 95/F4
Nittenau, Ger. 97/F4
Niuafo'ou (isl.), Tonga 159/H6
Niuatoputapu Group (isls.), Tonga 159/H6
Niue (terr.), NZ 159/H7
Niue (isl.), Niue 159/J6
Niulakita (isl.), Tuv. 158/G6
Niulan (riv.), China 125/H2
Niut (peak), Indo. 122/C3
Niutao (isl.), Tuv. 158/G5
Nivelles, Belg. 95/D2
Nivernais, Collines de (hills), Fr. 84/E3
Niverville, Mb, Can. 169/J3
Niwot, Co, US 179/B2
Niyazov (int'l arpt.), Trkm. 129/C5
Niyodo (riv.), Japan 116/C4
Nizāmābād, India 124/C4
Nizhegorodskaya Oblast, Rus. 105/G1
Nizhnekama (res.), Rus. 103/M4
Nizhnekamsk, Rus. 103/L5
Nizhneudinsk, Rus. 107/K4
Nizhnevartovsk, Rus. 106/H3
Nizhniy Lomov, Rus. 105/G1
Nizhniy Novgorod, Rus. 103/K4
Nizhniy Tagil, Rus. 103/N4
Nizhyn, Ukr. 104/D2
Nizip, Turk. 132/D2
Nízke Tatry NP, Slvk. 104/A2
Nizza Monferrato, It. 100/B3
Nizzanim, Isr. 133/F8
Njardhvik, Ice. 79/M7
Njombe (riv.), Tanz. 146/B4
Nkandla, SAfr. 149/E3
Nkayi, Congo 147/B1
Nkhata Bay, Malw. 146/B5
N'kongsamba, Camr. 138/G7
Nkululu (riv.), Tanz. 146/B4
Nkusi (riv.), Ugan. 146/A2
Nmai (riv.), Myan. 125/G2
Noailles, Fr. 94/B5
Noākhāli (pol. reg.), Bang. 127/H4
Noale, It. 101/F1
Noāmundi, India 127/E4
Noank, Ct, US 181/F1
Noatak, Ak, US 176/F2
Noatak (riv.), Ak, US 176/F2
Noatak Nat'l Prsv., Ak, US 176/F2
Nobeoka, Japan 116/B4
Noble, Ok, US 179/N15
Noboa, Ecu. 194/A5
Noboribetsu, Japan 118/B2
Noce (riv.), It. 99/G5
Noceto, It. 100/D3
Noci, It. 89/E2
Nockamixon State Park, Pa, US 180/C3
Noda, Japan 119/D2
Nodagawa, Japan 119/H4
Noé (cape), Alg. 142/D2
Nogales, Az, US 170/E5
Nogales, Mex. 185/M8
Nogara, It. 101/E2
Nogaro, Fr. 84/C5
Nogat (riv.), Pol. 81/H4
Nogata, Japan 116/B4

260

Nogen – Ober

Nogent, Fr. 98/B1
Nogent-l'Artaud, Fr. 94/C6
Nogent-le-Rotrou, Fr. 84/D2
Nogent-sur-Oise, Fr. 94/B5
Nogent-sur-Seine, Fr. 84/E2
Nogi, Japan 119/D1
Noginsk, Rus. 103/X9
Nogoa (riv.), Austl. 156/B4
Nogodan-san (peak), SKor. 115/D5
Nogoonnuur, Mong. 112/F2
Nogoyá, Arg. 199/E3
Nógrád (co.), Hun. 83/K5
Nogwak-san (peak), SKor. 115/E4
Nohar, India 128/C5
Noheji, Japan 118/B3
Nohfelden, Ger. 95/G4
Nohkú (pt.), Mex. 186/E2
Noi (riv.), Viet. 125/J5
Noidans-lès-Vesoul, Fr. 98/C2
Noire (riv.), Qu, Can. 172/E2
Noires, Montagnes (mts.), Fr. 84/B2
Noirmoutier, Île de (isl.), Fr. 84/B3
Noisiel, Fr. 94/B6
Noisy-le-Grand, Fr. 72/K5
Noisy-le-Mec, Fr. 72/K5
Noisy-le-Roi, Fr. 72/J5
Nojima-zaki (pt.), Japan 117/F3
Nokia, Fin. 81/K1
Nokilalaki (peak), Indo. 123/F4
Nola, CAfr. 138/J7
Noli, It. 100/B4
Noli, Capo di (cape), It. 100/B4
Nomadgi NP, Austl. 157/D2
Nombre de Dios, Mex. 184/D4
Nombre de Dios (mts.), Hon. 186/E3
Nome, Ak, US 176/E3
Nome (cape), Ak, US 176/F3
Nomény, Fr. 95/F6
Nomexy, Fr. 98/C1
Nomo-misaki (cape), Japan 116/B5
Nomo-zaki (pt.), Japan 116/A4
Nonacho (lake), NW, Can. 164/F2
Nonantola, It. 101/E3
Nondalton, Ak, US 176/H4
None, It. 85/G4
Nonette (riv.), Fr. 94/B5
Nong Han (res.), Thai. 120/D2
Nong Khai, Thai. 120/C2
Nong'an, China 113/N3
Nongoma, SAfr. 149/E2
Nongstoin, India 127/H3
Nonnweiler, Ger. 95/F4
Nonoava, Mex. 184/D3
Nonouti (isl.), Kiri. 158/G5
Nonri (isl.), China 114/E5
Nonsan, SKor. 115/D4
Nontron, Fr. 84/D4
Noord-Brabant (prov.), Neth. 92/C5
Noord Holland (prov.), Neth. 92/B3
Noordbeveland (isl.), Neth. 92/A5
Noorderhaaks (isl.), Neth. 92/B3
Noordhollandsch Kanaal (riv.), Neth. 92/B3
Noordostpolder (polder), Neth. 92/C3
Noordwijk aan Zee, Neth. 92/B4
Noordwijkerhout, Neth. 92/B4
Noordzeekanaal (canal), Neth. 92/B4
Noormarkku, Fin. 81/J1
Noorvik, Ak, US 176/F2
Nootka (isl.), BC, Can. 168/B3
Nora, Swe. 80/F2
Norala, Phil. 123/F2
Norberg, Swe. 80/F1
Norberto de la Riestra, Arg. 201/J11
Norchia (ruin), It. 88/B1
Norco, Ca, US 178/C3
Norco, La, US 179/P16
Nord (riv.), Qu, Can. 173/M6
Nord (canal), Fr. 94/B4
Nord (prov.), Fr. 94/C3
Nord-Kivu (pol. reg.), D.R. Congo 146/A3
Nord-Ostsee (Kiel) (canal), Ger. 93/G1
Nord-Ouest (prov.), Camr. 145/H5
Nord-Ouest (pol. reg.), Mor. 142/B2
Nord-Pas-de-Calais (pol. reg.), Fr. 84/D1
Nord-Radde (riv.), Ger. 93/E3
Nord-Sud Kanal (canal), Ger. 93/E3
Nord-Trøndelag (co.), Nor. 79/E2
Nordborg, Den. 80/C4
Nordby, Den. 80/D4
Norddeich, Ger. 93/E1
Nordela (int'l arpt.), Azor., Port. 87/T13
Norden, Ger. 93/E1
Nordenham, Ger. 93/F1
Nordenskjöld (arch.), Rus. 106/J2
Norderney, Ger. 93/E1
Norderney (isl.), Neth. 93/E1
Norderstedt, Ger. 93/G1
Nordhausen, Ger. 82/F3
Nordholz, Ger. 93/F1
Nordhorn, Ger. 93/E4
Nordhouse, Fr. 98/D1
Nordjylland (co.), Den. 80/C3
Nordkapp (cape), Nor. 79/H1
Nordkapp, Nor. 79/H1
Nordkinn (pt.), Nor. 79/H1
Nordkirchen, Ger. 93/E5
Nordland (co.), Nor. 79/E2
Nördlingen, Ger. 96/D5
Nordmaling, Swe. 79/F3
Nordreisa, Nor. 79/G1
Nordrhein-Westfalen (state), Ger. 82/E3
Nords Wharf, Austl. 157/D2
Nordwalde, Ger. 93/E4
Nore (riv.), Ire. 73/Q10
Noresund, Nor. 80/C1
Norfolk (mt.), Austl. 157/C4
Norfolk (lake), Ar,Mo, US 171/J3
Norfolk, Ne, US 169/J5
Norfolk (isl.), Austl. 158/F7
Norfolk Broads (swamp), Eng, UK 75/H1
Norg, Neth. 92/D2
Norheimsund, Nor. 80/B1
Norikura-dake (peak), Japan 117/E2
Noril'sk, Rus. 106/J3
Normal, Il, US 169/L5
Norman, Ok, US 179/N15
Norman Manley (int'l arpt.), Jam. 187/G2
Norman Wells, NW, Can. 164/D2
Normanby (isl.), PNG 158/E6
Normandie, Collines de (hills), Fr. 84/C2
Normandy (reg.), Fr. 84/C2
Normandy Beach, NJ, US 180/D4
Normandy Park, Wa, US 177/C3
Normanton, Austl. 156/A2
Normanton South, Eng, UK 77/G4
Norotshama (peak), Namb. 148/B3
Norquay, Sk, Can. 169/H3
Ñorquinco, Arg. 200/C4
Norrbotten (co.), Swe. 79/F2
Nørre Alslev, Den. 80/D4
Nørre Nebel, Den. 80/C4
Nørre Vorupør, Den. 80/C3
Norridge, Il, US 177/Q16
Norris (lake), Tn, US 175/G2
Norristown, Pa, US 180/C3
Norrköping, Swe. 80/G2
Norrland (reg.), Swe. 79/F2
Norrsundet, Swe. 80/G1
Norrtälje, Swe. 81/H2
Nors, Den. 80/C3
Norseman, Austl. 154/D5
Norsjö, Swe. 79/F2
Norte (pt.), Arg. 201/F3
Norte (pt.), Arg. 200/E4
Norte, Cabo do (cape), Braz. 193/J3
Norte de Santander (dept.), Col. 194/C2
Norte Los Rodeos (int'l arpt.), Sp. 140/A3
Norte, Serra do (mts.), Braz. 192/G6
Nortelândia, Braz. 193/G6
Nörten-Hardenberg, Ger. 93/G5
North (pt.), Austl. 157/C3
North (pt.), Austl. 157/C4
North (pt.), Austl. 154/B4
North (cape), PE, Can. 173/J2
North (sea), Eur. 78/D4
North (cape), NZ 159/S9
North (isl.), NZ 159/S10
North (sound), Sc, UK 73/V14
North (chan.), UK 76/C1
North (cape), Ak, US 176/D5
North (pt.), Md, US 180/B5
North Albanian Alps (mts.), Alb.,Mont. 90/D4
North America (cont.) 119
North Andaman (isl.), India 125/F5
North Arlington, NJ, US 181/J8
North Aulatsivik (isl.), Nf, Can. 165/K3
North Aurora, Il, US 177/P16
North Ayrshire (pol. reg.), Sc, UK 78/A5
North Battleford, Sk, Can. 168/F2
North Bay, On, Can. 172/E2
North Bay, Wi, US 177/Q14
North Beach, Md, US 180/B6
North Beach Haven, NJ, US 180/D4
North Bellmore, NY, US 181/L9
North Bend, Or, US 168/B5
North Bend, Wa, US 177/D3
North Bergen, NJ, US 181/J8
North Berwick, Sc, UK 78/D4
North Branch (riv.), Md, US 180/B5
North Branch, NJ, US 180/D2
North Branford, Ct, US 181/F1
North Brunswick, NJ, US 180/D3
North Buganda (prov.), Ugan. 146/B2
North Caicos (isl.), UK 187/J1
North Caldwell, NJ, US 181/J8
North Canadian (riv.), Ok, US 171/H3
North Cape May, NJ, US 180/D6
North Caribou (lake), On, Can. 169/L2
North Carolina (state), US 175/H3
North Cascades NP, Wa, US 168/C3
North Central (plain), Tx, US 185/F1
North Charleston, SC, US 175/J3
North Cowichan, BC, Can. 168/C3
North Dakota (state), US 169/H4
North Dorset Downs (uplands), Eng, UK 74/D5
North Down (dist.), NI, UK 76/C2
North East, Pa, US 172/E3
North East (pt.), Austl. 156/C3
North East, Md, US 180/C4
North Eastern (prov.), Kenya 146/C2
North Esk (riv.), Sc, UK 78/C5
North Foreland (pt.), Eng, UK 75/H4
North Fork Crow (riv.), Mn, US 169/K4
North Fort Myers, Fl, US 175/H5
North French (riv.), On, Can. 172/D1
North Frisian (isls.), Ger. 82/D1
North Front (int'l arpt.), UK 140/D1
North Gauhāti, India 127/H2
North Haledon, NJ, US 181/J8
North Hero, Vt, US 172/F2
North Highlands, Ca, US 177/L9
North Kansas City, Mo, US 179/D5
North Kitui Nat'l Rsv., Kenya 146/C3
North Korea (ctry.) 115/D2
North Lakhimpur, India 125/F2
North Lanarkshire (pol. reg.), Sc, UK 78/C5
North Las Vegas, Nv, US 170/D3
North Lincolnshire (co.), Eng, UK 77/H4
North Lindenhurst, NY, US 181/M9
North Little Rock, Ar, US 171/J4
North Luangwa NP, Zam. 147/F3
North Magnetic Pole 165/R7
North Minch (The Minch) (str.), Sc, UK 73/Q8
North Moose (lake), Mb, Can. 169/J2
North Mountain (mtn.), Pa, US 180/B1
North Myrtle Beach, SC, US 175/J3
North Ogden, Ut, US 179/K11
North Ossetian Aut. Rep., Rus. 105/G4
North Pacific (ocean) 64/A4
North Pine (riv.), Austl. 156/E6
North Plainfield, NJ, US 181/H9
North Platte, Ne, US 169/H5
North Platte (riv.), Ne,Wy, US 171/G2
North Pole, Ak, US 176/J3
North Pole 202/G
North Potomac, Md, US 180/A5
North Prairie, Wi, US 177/P14
North Puyallup, Wa, US 177/C3
North Raccoon (riv.), Ia, US 169/K5
North Ronaldsay (isl.), Sc, UK 73/V14
North Salt Lake, Ut, US 179/K12
North Saskatchewan (riv.), Ab,Sk, Can. 164/E3
North Shields, Eng, UK 77/G2
North Siberian Lowland (plain), Rus. 106/K2
North Skunk (riv.), Ia, US 171/J2
North Somerset (co.), Eng, UK 74/D4
North Stadbroke (isl.), Austl. 156/D4
North Taranaki Bight (bay), NZ 159/S10
North Thompson (riv.), BC, Can. 168/D3
North Tolsta, Sc, UK 73/Q7
North Tonawanda, NY, US 173/S9
North Tyne (riv.), Eng, UK 77/F1
North Tyneside (co.), Eng, UK 77/G1
North Uist (isl.), Sc, UK 73/Q8
North Umpqua (riv.), Or, US 170/B2
North Valley Stream, NY, US 181/L9
North Vancouver, BC, Can. 164/D4
North Wales, Pa, US 180/C3
North Weald Bassett, Eng, UK 72/D1
North West (cape), Austl. 154/B2
North-West Frontier (co.), India 128/A3
North West Highlands (uplands), Sc, UK 73/R8
North Wildwood, NJ, US 180/D6
North Wilton, Ct, US 181/E1
North York, Can. 173/Q8
North York Moors NP, Eng, UK 77/G3
North Yorkshire (co.), Eng, UK 77/G3
Northallerton, Eng, UK 77/G3
Northam, Austl. 154/C4
Northampton, Austl. 154/B4
Northampton, Eng, UK 75/F2
Northampton, Ma, US 173/F3
Northampton, Pa, US 180/C2
Northampton (co.), Pa, US 180/C2
Northampton Uplands (uplands), Eng, UK 75/E2
Northamptonshire (co.), Eng, UK 75/E2
Northbrook, Il, US 177/Q15
Northeast (cape), Ak, US 176/E3
Northeast (pt.), Bahm. 187/H1
Northeast (pt.), Jam. 187/G2
Northeast Land (isl.), Sval. 202/E
Northeast Lincolnshire (co.), Eng, UK 77/H4
Northeim, Ger. 93/G5
Northern (pol. reg.), Gha. 145/E4
Northern (dist.), Isr. 133/D3
Northern (pol. reg.), Malw. 146/B5
Northern (prov.), SLeo. 144/B4
Northern (prov.), Ugan. 146/B2
Northern Areas (terr.), Pak. 129/F5
Northern Cape (prov.), SAfr. 148/C3
Northern Cook (isls.), CookIs. 159/J6
Northern Dvina (riv.), Rus. 69/J2
Northern Light (lake), On, Can. 172/B1
Northern Mariana Islands (dpcy.), US 158/D3
Northern Province (prov.), SAfr. 148/E2
Northern Sporades (isls.), Gre. 89/J3
Northern Territory (terr.), Austl. 151/C2
Northern Ural (mts.), Rus. 103/N3
Northern Uvals (hills), Rus. 103/K4
Northfield, Mn, US 169/K4
Northfleet, Eng, UK 72/D2
Northglenn, Co, US 179/C3
Northport, Al, US 175/G3
Northport (Old Northport), NY, US 181/E2
Northumberland (str.), Can. 173/J2
Northumberland, Pa, US 180/B2
Northumberland NP, Eng, UK 78/D6
Northvale, NJ, US 181/K7
Northville, Mi, US 177/E7
Northway, Ak, US 176/K3
Northwest Gander (riv.), Nf, Can. 173/L1
Northwest Territories (terr.), Can. 164/D2
Northwich, Eng, UK 77/F5
Northwood, ND, US 169/J4
Norton (bay), Ak, US 176/F3
Norton (sound), Ak, US 176/E3
Norton Shores, Mi, US 172/C3
Nortorf, Ger. 80/C4
Norvegia (cape), Ant. 202/Y
Nörvenich, Ger. 95/F2
Norwalk, Oh, US 172/D3
Norwalk, Ca, US 178/F8
Norwalk, Ct, US 181/M7
Norwalk (riv.), Ct, US 181/M7
Norway (ctry.) 79/C3
Norwegian (bay), Nun., Can. 165/S7
Norwegian (sea), Eur. 69/D2
Norwich, NY, US 172/F3
Norwich, Eng, UK 75/H1
Norwich (int'l arpt.), Eng, UK 75/H1
Norwood, NJ, US 181/K8
Nos Emine (cape), Bul. 91/H4
Nos Kaliakra (pt.), Bul. 91/J4
Nos Maslen Nos (pt.), Bul. 91/H4
Nosappu-misaki (cape), Japan 118/D2
Nose, Japan 119/H6
Noshappu-misaki (cape), Japan 118/B1
Noshaq (peak), Afg. 131/K1
Noshiro, Japan 118/B3
Nosivka, Ukr. 104/D2
Nosong (cape), Malay. 123/E2
Noşratābād, Iran 131/G3
Noss Head (pt.), Sc, UK 73/S7
Nossa Senhora da Glória, Braz. 196/C3
Nossa Senhora das Dores, Braz. 196/C3
Nossebro, Swe. 80/E2
Nosy-Varika, Madg. 149/J8
Notch (cape), Chile 201/B6
Notec (riv.), Pol. 83/J2
Noto (pen.), Japan 117/E2
Noto, It. 88/D4
Noto Antica (ruin), It. 88/D4
Noto, Golfo di (gulf), It. 88/D4
Noto, Val di (valley), It. 88/D4
Notodden, Nor. 80/C2
Notogawa, Japan 119/K5
Notoro (lake), Japan 118/C1
Notre Dame (mts.), On, Can. 165/J4
Notre Dame (bay), Nf, Can. 165/L4
Notre Dame, Fr. 72/K5
Notre-Dame-de-l'Île-Perrot, Qu, Can. 173/N7
Notsé, Togo 145/F5
Nott (mt.), Austl. 155/G5
Nottaway (riv.), Qu, Can. 165/J3
Nøtterøy, Nor. 80/D2
Nottingham (isl.), Nun., Can. 165/H2
Nottingham, Eng, UK 77/G6
Nottingham (co.), Eng, UK 77/G6
Nottinghamshire (co.), Eng, UK 77/G5
Nottuln, Ger. 93/E5
Nouâdhibou, Mrta. 140/A5
Nouâdhibou (int'l arpt.), Mrta. 140/A5
Nouakchott (cap.), Mrta. 144/B2
Nouakchott (int'l arpt.), Mrta. 144/B2
Nouna, Burk. 144/E3
Noupoort, SAfr. 148/D3
Nouvion-sur-Meuse, Fr. 95/D4
Nœux-les-Mines, Fr. 94/B3
Nouzonville, Fr. 95/D4
Nova Andradina, Braz. 193/H8
Nova Cruz, Braz. 196/D2
Nová Dubnica, Slvk. 83/K4
Nova Friburgo, Braz. 197/D2
Nova Gorica, Slov. 101/G1
Nova Gradiška, Cro. 90/C3
Nova Iguaçu, Braz. 197/K7
Nova Kakhovka, Ukr. 91/L2
Nova Olinda, Braz. 196/C2
Nova Olinda do Norte, Braz. 192/G4
Nova Pazova, Serb. 90/E3
Nova Prata, Braz. 197/B4
Nova Russas, Braz. 196/B2
Nova Scotia (prov.), Can. 173/J2
Nova Sintra, CpV. 135/J11
Nova Soure, Braz. 196/C3
Nova Varoš, Serb. 90/D4
Nova Venécia, Braz. 197/D1
Nova Xavantina, Braz. 193/H6
Nova Zagora, Bul. 91/H4
Novaci, Rom. 91/F3
Novafeltria, It. 101/F5
Novara, It. 100/B2
Novate Mezzola, It. 99/F5
Novaya Sibir' (isl.), Rus. 107/R2
Novaya Zemlya (isl.), Rus. 202/C
Nove, It. 101/E1
Nové Hrady, Czh. 97/H5
Nové Město nad Váhom, Slvk. 83/J4
Nové Strašecí, Czh. 97/G2
Nové Zámky, Slvk. 90/D2
Novelda, Sp. 87/E3
Novellara, It. 101/D3
Noventa, It. 101/E2
Noventa di Piave, It. 101/F1
Noventa Vicentina, It. 101/E2
Novgorod, Rus. 81/P2
Novgorodskaya Oblast, Rus. 102/G4
Novi, Mi, US 177/E7
Novi Bečej, Serb. 90/E3
Novi di Modena, It. 101/D3
Novi Iskŭr, Bul. 91/F4
Novi Ligure, It. 85/H4
Novi Pazar, Serb. 90/E4
Novi Pazar, Bul. 91/H4
Novi Sad, Serb. 90/D3
Novi Vinodolski, Cro. 90/B3
Novillars, Fr. 98/C3
Nóvita, Col. 194/B3
Novo (riv.), Braz. 197/K6
Novo Alexeyevka (int'l arpt.), Geo. 105/H4
Novo Aripuanã, Braz. 192/F5
Novo Hamburgo, Braz. 197/B4
Novo Horizonte, Braz. 197/B2
Novo Miloševo, Serb. 90/E3
Novo Oriente, Braz. 196/B2
Novoanninskiy, Rus. 105/G2
Novocheboksarsk, Rus. 103/K4
Novocherkassk, Rus. 104/G3
Novogrudok, Bela. 81/L5
Novohrad-Volyns'kyy, Ukr. 104/C2
Novohradské Hory (mts.), Czh. 97/H5
Novokuybyshevsk, Rus. 105/J1
Novokuznetsk, Rus. 106/J4
Novolazarevskaya, Rus., Ant. 202/A
Novomoskovsk, Rus. 104/F1
Novorossiysk, Rus. 104/F3
Novoshakhtinsk, Rus. 104/F3
Novosibirsk (res.), Rus. 129/H2
Novosibirsk, Rus. 129/H1
Novosibirsk (Tolmachevo) (int'l arpt.), Rus. 129/H1
Novosibirskaya Oblast, Rus. 129/G1
Novotroitsk, Rus. 105/L2
Novoukrayinka, Ukr. 104/D2
Novovolyns'k, Ukr. 104/C2
Novovyatsk, Rus. 103/L4
Novozybkov, Rus. 104/D1
Novska, Cro. 90/C3
Nový Jičín, Czh. 83/K4
Nowa Dęba, Pol. 83/L3
Nowa Ruda, Pol. 83/J3
Nowa Sarzyna, Pol. 83/M3
Nowa Sól, Pol. 83/H3
Nowata, Ok, US 171/J3
Nowe, Pol. 83/K2
Nowe Miasto Lubawskie, Pol. 83/K2
Nowgong, India 126/B3
Nowitna (riv.), Ak, US 176/G3
Nowogard, Pol. 80/F5
Nowood (riv.), Wy, US 170/F1
Nowshāk (peak), Afg. 129/F5
Nowshera, Pak. 128/A2
Nowy Dwór Gdański, Pol. 81/H4
Nowy Sącz, Pol. 83/L4
Nowy Staw, Pol. 81/H4
Nowy Targ, Pol. 83/L4
Nowy Tomyśl, Pol. 83/J2
Noya, Sp. 86/A1
Noye (riv.), Fr. 94/B4
Noyon, Fr. 94/C4
Nsanje, Malw. 147/G4
Nsawam, Gha. 145/E5
Nsumbu NP, Zam. 146/A5
Nsuta, Gha. 145/E5
Ntoroko, Ugan. 146/A2
Ntungamo, Ugan. 146/A3
Ntusi, Ugan. 146/A2
Nu, Crêt du (peak), Fr. 98/B5
Nuangola, Pa, US 180/C1
Nūbah, Jibāl an (mts.), Sudan 139/M5
Nubian (des.), Sudan 143/C4
Nucet, Rom. 90/F2
Nucla, Co, US 174/A2
Nucourt, Fr. 72/H4
Nüdlingen, Ger. 96/D2
Nueces (riv.), Tx, US 174/D4
Nueltin (lake), Mb,Nun., Can. 164/G2
Nuenen, Neth. 92/C6
Nueva Alejandría, Peru 198/C2
Nueva Concepción, Guat. 186/D3
Nueva Esparta (state), Ven. 195/E2
Nueva Florida, Ven. 194/D2
Nueva Gerona, Cuba 187/F1
Nueva Helvecia, Uru. 201/K11
Nueva Imperial, Chile 200/B3
Nueva Italia de Ruiz, Mex. 184/E5
Nueva Loja, Ecu. 194/B4
Nueva Ocotepéque, Hon. 186/D3
Nueva Palmira, Uru. 201/J10
Nueva Rosita, Mex. 185/E3
Nueva Villa de Padilla, Mex. 185/F3
Nueve de Julio, Arg. 200/E2
Nuevitas, Cuba 187/G1
Nuevo, Ca, US 178/C3
Nuevo Balsas, Mex. 185/F5
Nuevo Berlín, Uru. 201/J10
Nuevo Casas Grandes, Mex. 184/D2
Nuevo Chagres, Pan. 187/F4
Nuevo, Gulfo (gulf), Arg. 199/D5
Nuevo Ideal, Mex. 184/D3
Nuevo Ixcatlán, Mex. 186/C2
Nuevo Laredo, Mex. 185/F3
Nuevo Leon (state), Mex. 182/A2
Nuevo Rocafuerte, Ecu. 194/C5
Nufenen, Swi. 99/F4
Nufenenpass (pass), Swi. 99/E5
Nuguria (isls.), PNG 158/E5
Nuhne (riv.), Ger. 93/F6
Nui (isl.), Tuv. 158/G5
Nuiqsut, Ak, US 176/H1
Nuits-Saint-Georges, Fr. 98/A3
Nukata, Japan 119/M6
Nuklunek (mtn.), Ak, US 176/F4
Nuku'alofa (cap.), Tonga 159/H7
Nukufetau (isl.), Tuv. 158/G5
Nukulaelae (isl.), Tuv. 158/H5
Nukumanu (atoll), PNG 158/E5
Nukunonu (isl.), Tok. 159/H5
Nukuoro (isl.), Micr. 158/E4
Nukus (int'l arpt.), Uzb. 129/C4
Nukus, Uzb. 129/C4
Nukutavake (isl.), FrPol. 159/M6
Nulato, Ak, US 176/G3
Nules, Sp. 87/E3
Nullarbor (plain), Austl. 154/E5
Nullarbor NP, Austl. 155/F4
Numana, It. 101/G5
Numansdorp, Neth. 92/B5
Numata, Japan 117/F2
Numazu, Japan 117/F3
Nümbrecht, Ger. 95/G2
Numfoor (isl.), Indo. 123/H4
Nummi, Fin. 81/K1
Numurkah, Austl. 157/C3
Nunapitchuk, Ak, US 176/F3
Nunchía, Col. 194/C3
Nundle, Austl. 157/D1
Nuneaton, Eng, UK 75/E1
Nungarin, Austl. 154/C4
Nungatta NP,Austl. 157/D3
Nunivak (isl.), Ak, US 176/E4
Nunningen, Swi. 98/D3
Nuñoa, Peru 198/D4
Nunspeet, Neth. 92/C4
Nuon (riv.), Libr. 144/C5
Nuoro, It. 88/A2
Nuquí, Col. 194/B3
Nur (mts.), Turk. 133/E1
Nura (riv.), Kaz. 129/F2
Nürburgring, Ger. 95/F3
Nure (riv.), It. 100/C3
Nuremberg, Pa, US 180/B2
Nurhak, Turk. 132/D2
Nuri (ruin), Sudan 143/B5
Nuriootpa, Austl. 155/H5
Nurmijärvi, Fin. 81/L1
Nürnberg (int'l arpt.), Ger. 96/E3
Nürnberg, Ger. 96/E4
Nurpur, Pak. 128/B3
Nurri (mt.), Austl. 157/C1
Nürtingen, Ger. 96/C5
Nushagak (riv.), Ak, US 176/G4
Nushki, Pak. 131/J3
Nutberry (hill), Sc, UK 78/C5
Nuth, Neth. 95/E2
Nuthe-Graben (riv.), Ger. 82/Q7
Nutley, NJ, US 181/J8
Nutwood, Il, US 179/F7
Nuuk (Godthåb), Grld. 161/M3
Nuvolento, It. 100/D1
Nuy (riv.), SAfr. 148/L10
Nüziders, Aus. 99/F3
Nxai Pan NP, Bots. 147/D4
Nyabisindu, Rwa. 146/A3
Nyack, NY, US 181/K7
Nyah, Austl. 157/B2
Nyah West, Austl. 157/B2
Nyainqêntanglha (peak), China 112/F5
Nyaki NP, Malw. 146/B5
Nyala, Sudan 139/K5
Nyalam, China 127/E1
Nyandoma, Rus. 102/J3
Nyanza (prov.), Kenya 146/B3
Nyasa (lake), Malw. 147/F3
Nybro, Swe. 80/F3
Nyêmo, China 127/H1
Nyeri, Kenya 146/C3
Nyima, China 112/E5
Nyírábrány, Hun. 90/F2
Nyíradony, Hun. 83/L5
Nyírbátor, Hun. 83/M5
Nyíregyháza, Hun. 83/L5
Nyírmada, Hun. 83/M4
Nyiru (mt.), Kenya 146/C2
Nykøbing, Den. 80/C3
Nykøbing, Den. 80/D4
Nyköping, Swe. 80/G2
Nylstroom, SAfr. 147/E5
Nynäshamn, Swe. 80/G2
Nyngan, Austl. 157/C1
Nyoman (riv.), Bela. 104/B1
Nyon, Swi. 98/C5
Nyons, Fr. 84/F4
Nýřany, Czh. 97/G3
Nýrsko, Czh. 97/G4
Nýrsko (res.), Czh. 97/G4
Nysa, Pol. 83/J3
Nyssa, Or, US 168/D5
Nysted, Den. 80/D4
Nyūdo-zaki (pt.), Japan 118/A4
Nyuk (lake), Rus. 102/F2
Nyúl, Hun. 90/C2
Nyunzu, D.R. Congo 147/E2
Nyūzen, Japan 117/E2
Nzega, Tanz. 146/B4
Nzérékoré (pol. reg.), Gui. 144/C4
Nzérékoré, Gui. 144/C5
Nzi (riv.), C.d'Iv. 138/E6

O

Ō-shima (isl.), Japan 118/A3
Oa, Mull of (pt.), Sc, UK 73/Q9
Oahe (dam), SD, US 169/H4
Oahe (lake), ND,SD, US 169/H4
Oahu (isl.), Hi, US 166/V13
Oak Forest, Il, US 177/Q16
Oak Grove, Mo, US 179/E6
Oak Hill, WV, US 172/D4
Oak Park, Il, US 177/Q16
Oak Park, Mi, US 177/F7
Oak Ridge, Tn, US 172/C4
Oak Ridge, NJ, US 180/D1
Oak View, Ca, US 178/A2
Oakbank, Mb, Can. 169/J3
Oakdale, La, US 171/J5
Oakes, ND, US 169/J4
Oakey, Austl. 156/C4
Oakham, Eng, UK 75/F1
Oakhurst, Ca, US 170/C3
Oakland, Ca, US 170/B3
Oakland, Md, US 180/B5
Oakland (co.), Mi, US 177/E6
Oakland (lake), Mi, US 177/F6
Oakland, NJ, US 181/J7
Oakland (bay), Wa, US 177/A3
Oaklands, Austl. 157/C2
Oakley, Ca, US 177/L10
Oakover (riv.), Austl. 154/D2
Oakridge, Or, US 168/C5
Oakville, La, US 179/P17
Oakville, Mo, US 179/G9
Oakville, On, Can. 173/Q9
Oakwood Hills, Il, US 177/P15
Oamaru, NZ 159/S12
Ōamishirasato, Japan 119/E2
Oat (mtn.), Ca, US 178/B2
Oatlands, Austl. 157/C4
Oaxaca (state), Mex. 182/B4
Oaxaca de Juárez, Mex. 186/B2
Ob' (gulf), Rus. 109/G3
Ob' (riv.), Rus. 109/F3
Ob Luang Gorge, Thai. 120/B2
Obama, Japan 119/J5
Obama (bay), Japan 119/J4
Oban (hills), Nga. 145/H5
Oban, Sc, UK 73/R8
Obanazawa, Japan 118/B4
Obara, Japan 119/M5
Obata, Japan 119/L7
Ober-Olm, Ger. 96/B3
Ober Ramstadt, Ger. 96/B3

261
Oberá – Orlân

Oberá, Arg. 199/E2
Oberalppass (pass), Swi. 99/E4
Oberalpstock (peak), Swi. 99/E4
Oberammergau, Ger. 99/H2
Oberasbach, Ger. 96/D4
Oberau, Ger. 99/H2
Oberburg, Swi. 98/D3
Oberderdingen, Ger. 96/B4
Oberdiessbach, Swi. 98/D4
Oberding, Ger. 97/E6
Oberdorf, Swi. 98/D3
Oberdorla, Ger. 93/H6
Oberelsbach, Ger. 96/D2
Oberentfelden, Swi. 98/E3
Oberglatt, Swi. 99/E3
Obergünzburg, Ger. 99/G2
Oberhaching, Ger. 97/E6
Oberhausen, Ger. 92/D6
Oberkirch, Ger. 98/E1
Oberkochen, Ger. 96/D5
Oberkotzau, Ger. 97/E2
Oberlausitz (reg.), Ger. 83/H3
Oberlin, Ks, US 171/G3
Obernai, Fr. 98/D1
Obernburg am Main, Ger. 96/C3
Oberndorf am Neckar, Ger. 99/E1
Oberndorf bei Salzburg, Aus. 97/F7
Oberneukirchen, Aus. 97/H6
Obernkirchen, Ger. 93/G4
Oberon, Austl. 157/D2
Oberösterreich (prov.), Aus. 83/G4
Oberpfälzer Wald (for.), Ger. 97/F3
Oberrieden, Swi. 99/E3
Oberriet, Swi. 99/F3
Obersaxen, Swi. 99/F4
Oberschleissheim, Ger. 97/E6
Oberschneiding, Ger. 97/F5
Obersiggenthal, Swi. 99/E3
Oberstammheim, Swi. 99/E2
Oberstaufen, Ger. 99/G2
Oberstdorf, Ger. 99/G3
Oberthal, Ger. 95/G4
Obertrum am See, Aus. 97/G7
Obertshausen, Ger. 96/B2
Oberursel, Ger. 96/B2
Oberuzwil, Swi. 99/F3
Oberviechtach, Ger. 97/F4
Oberwald, Swi. 99/E4
Oberwart, Aus. 90/C2
Oberwesel, Ger. 95/G3
Oberwil, Swi. 98/D4
Obfelden, Swi. 99/E3
Obi (str.), Indo. 123/G4
Obi (isls.), Indo. 123/G4
Óbidos, Braz. 193/G4
Óbidos, Port. 86/A3
Obihiro, Japan 118/C2
Obilić, Serb. 90/E4
Obing, Ger. 97/F6
Obira, Japan 118/B1
Obitsu (riv.), Japan 119/D3
Obluch'ye, Rus. 113/P2
Obninsk, Rus. 102/H5
Obo, CAfr. 139/L6
Oborniki, Pol. 83/J2
Oborniki Śląskie, Pol. 83/J3
Obra (riv.), Pol. 83/J2
Obrenovac, Serb. 90/E3
Obrež, Serb. 90/E4
Obrigheim, Ger. 96/C4
Obrigheim, Ger. 96/B3
Observatory, Austl. 157/G5
Obtrumer (lake), Aus. 97/F7
Ōbu, Japan 119/L6
Obuasi, Gha. 145/E5
Obw. (canton), Swi. 99/E4
Obzor, Bul. 91/H4
Ocala, Fl, US 175/H4
Ocampo, Mex. 184/E3
Ocaña, Sp. 86/D3
Ocaña, Col. 194/C2
Occhieppo Inferiore, It. 100/B1
Occhieppo Superiore, It. 100/A1
Occhiobello, It. 101/E3
Occidental, Cordillera (mts.), Ecu. 192/C3
Occimiano, It. 100/B2
Ocean (cape), Ak, US 176/L3
Ocean (co.), NJ, US 180/D4
Ocean Beach, NY, US 181/E2
Ocean City, Md, US 172/F4
Ocean City, NJ, US 180/D5
Ocean Falls, BC, Can. 168/B2
Ocean Gate, NJ, US 180/D4
Ocean Grove, NJ, US 180/D3
Ocean View, NJ, US 180/D5
Oceanographic Museum, Mona. 100/J8
Oceanside, Ca, US 178/C4
Oceanside, NY, US 181/L9
Oceanville, NJ, US 180/D5
Och'amch'ire, Geo. 105/G4
Ocheltree, Ks, US 179/D6
Ochiishi-misaki (cape), Japan 118/D2
Ochil (hills), Sc, UK 78/C4
Ocho Rios, Jam. 187/G2
Ochsenfurt, Ger. 96/D3
Ochsenhausen, Ger. 99/F1
Ochsenkopf (peak), Aus. 99/F3
Ochtendung, Ger. 95/G3
Ochtrup, Ger. 93/E4
Ochtum (riv.), Ger. 93/F2
Ockelbo, Swe. 80/G1
Ockenheim, Ger. 95/G4
Ocmulgee (riv.), Ga, US 175/H3
Ocmulgee Nat'l Mon., Ga, US 175/H3
Ocna Mureş, Rom. 91/F2
Ocna Sibiului, Rom. 91/G3
Ocoña (riv.), Peru 192/D6
Ocoña, Peru 198/C5
Oconee (lake), Ga, US 175/H3
Oconee (riv.), Ga, US 175/H3
Oconto, Wi, US 169/M4
Ocosingo, Mex. 186/C2
Ocotal, Nic. 186/E3
Ocotlán, Mex. 184/E4
Ocotlán de Morelos, Mex. 186/B2
Ocoyoacac, Mex. 185/Q10
Ocozocoautla de Espinosa, Mex. 186/C2
Ocracoke, NC, US 175/K3
Ocros, Peru 198/B3
Octeville, Fr. 84/C2
October Revolution (isl.), Rus. 109/H2
Oda (peak), Sudan 143/D4
Oda, Japan 116/C3
Oda, Gha. 145/E5
Odaesan NP, SKor. 115/E4
Ōdai, Japan 119/K7
Ōdaigahara-san (peak), Japan 116/E3
Ōdate, Japan 118/B3
Odawara, Japan 117/F3
Odda, Nor. 80/B1
Odder, Den. 80/D4
Odeborn (riv.), Ger. 93/F6
Odelzhausen, Ger. 96/E6
Odemira, Port. 86/A4
Ödemiş, Turk. 132/A2
Odendaalsrus, SAfr. 148/D2
Odense, Den. 80/D4
Odense (int'l arpt.), Den. 80/D4
Odenthal, Ger. 95/G1
Odenton, Md, US 180/B5
Odenwald (reg.), Ger. 96/B3
Oder (Odra) (riv.), Ger.,Pol. 83/H2
Oder-Spree Kanal (canal), Ger. 82/Q7
Oderen, Fr. 98/C2
Oderhaff (lag.), Ger. 83/H2
Oderzo, It. 101/F1
Odesa, Turk. 132/B1
Odesa, Ukr. 91/K2
Odes'ka Oblasti, Ukr. 104/D3
Odessa, De, US 180/C5
Odessa, Tx, US 171/G5
Odessa, Wa, US 168/D4
Odet (riv.), Fr. 84/B2
Odienné, C.d'Iv. 144/D4
Odintsovo, Rus. 103/W9
Odiongan, Phil. 121/D5
Odivelas, Port. 87/P10
Odobeşti, Rom. 91/H3
Odon (riv.), Fr. 84/C2
Odoorn, Neth. 92/D3
Odorheiu Secuiesc, Rom. 91/G2
Odžaci, Serb. 90/D3
Odzala, PN d', Congo 138/J7
Ōe, Japan 119/H5
Ōe-yama (peak), Japan 119/H5
Oegstgeest, Neth. 92/B4
Oeiras, Braz. 196/B2
Oelde, Ger. 93/F5
Oelsnitz, Ger. 97/F2
Oeno (isl.), Pitc. 159/M7
Oensingen, Swi. 98/D3
Oer-Erkenschwick, Ger. 93/E5
Oesling (mts.), Lux. 95/E4
Oesterdam (dam), Neth. 92/B6
Oestrich-Winkel, Ger. 96/B3
Oeta NP, Gre. 89/H3
Oetz, Aus. 99/G3
Oey'ŏn (isl.), SKor. 115/D3
Of, Turk. 132/E1
O'Fallon, Mo, US 179/F8
O'Fallon, Il, US 179/H8
Ofanto (riv.), It. 88/D2
Ofaqim, Isr. 133/D4
Ofenhorn (peak), Swi. 99/E5
Offa, Nga. 145/G4
Offaly (co.), Ire. 76/A5
Offanengo, It. 100/C2
Offement, Fr. 98/C2
Offenbach, Ger. 96/B2
Offenbach an der Queich, Ger. 96/B4
Offenburg, Ger. 98/D1
Offingen, Ger. 96/D6
Offstein, Ger. 96/B3
Oftersheim, Ger. 96/B4
Oftringen, Swi. 98/D3
Ōfunato, Japan 118/B4
Oga, Japan 118/A4
Oga (pen.), Japan 118/A4
Ogachi, Japan 118/B4
Ogadēn (reg.), Eth. 139/P6
Ōgaki, Japan 119/L5
Ogano, Japan 119/C2
Ogasawara, Japan 158/D2
Ogatsu, Japan 118/B4
Ogawa, Japan 119/E1
Ogawa, Japan 119/C1
Ogawara (lake), Japan 118/B3
Ogbomosho, Nga. 145/G4
Ogden, Ut, US 179/K11
Ogden Bay (bay), Ut, US 179/J11
Ogden, South Fork (riv.), Ut, US 179/K11
Ogdensburg, NY, US 172/F2
Ogdensburg, NJ, US 180/D1
Ogeechee (riv.), Ga, US 175/H3
Oggiono, It. 100/C1
Ogi, Japan 117/F2
Ogidaki (mtn.), On, Can. 172/D2
Ogies, SAfr. 148/E2
Ogilvie (mts.), Yk, Can. 164/C2
Ogilvie (riv.), Yk, Can. 164/C2
Ogles, Il, US 179/G8
Oglesby, Tx, US 185/F2
Oglio (riv.), It. 85/J4
Ognon (riv.), Fr. 82/C5
Ogoamas (peak), Indo. 123/F3
Ogoki (lake), On, Can. 169/M3
Ogoki (res.), On, Can. 169/L3
Ogoki (riv.), On, Can. 169/M3
Ogooué (riv.), Gabon 138/H8
Ogose, Japan 119/C2
Ogosta (riv.), Bul. 91/F4
Ogre, Lat. 81/L3
Oguchi, Japan 119/L5
Ogulin, Cro. 90/B3
Ogun (riv.), Nga. 138/F6
Ogun (state), Nga. 145/F5
Ogurjaly (isl.), Trkm. 129/B5
Oğuz, Turk. 132/D2
Oh Me Edge (hill), Eng, UK 78/D6
Ōhara, Japan 119/E3
Oharu, Japan 119/L5
Ōhata, Japan 118/B3
Ohey, Belg. 95/E3
O'Higgins (pol. reg.), Chile 200/B1
O'Higgins (lake), Chile 201/B6
Ohio (riv.), US 172/B4
Ohio (state), US 172/D3
Ōhira, Japan 119/D1
Ohlsdorf, Aus. 97/G7
Ohlstadt, Ger. 99/H2
Ohm (riv.), Ger. 96/C1
Ōho, Japan 119/E1
Ohoopee (riv.), Ga, US 175/H3
Ohře (riv.), Czh. 82/H3
Ohre (riv.), Ger. 82/F2
Ohrid, FYROM 89/G2
Ohrid (lake), Alb., Mac 89/G2
Oi (riv.), China 125/G2
Ōi, Japan 119/J5
Ōi, Japan 119/C3
Ōi, Japan 119/D2
Oiapoque (riv.), Braz. 193/H3
Oiapoque, Braz. 193/H3
Oich (lake), Sc, UK 78/B2
Oieras, Port. 87/P10
Oignies, Fr. 94/B3
Oignin (riv.), Fr. 98/B5
Oil City, Pa, US 172/E3
Oinófita, Gre. 89/H3
Oinóï, Gre. 89/N8
Oirschot, Neth. 92/C5
Oise (dept.), Fr. 94/B5
Oise (riv.), Fr. 82/B4
Oise à l'Aisne, Canal de l' (canal), Fr. 94/C4
Oiseaux du Djoudj, PN des, Sen. 144/A2
Ōiso, Japan 119/C3
Oissery, Fr. 72/L4
Oisterwijk, Neth. 92/C5
Ōita (riv.), Japan 116/B4
Ōita (pref.), Japan 116/B4
Ōita, Japan 116/B4
Ōizumi, Japan 119/C1
Ōizumi, Japan 119/A2
Ojai, Ca, US 178/A2
Ojcowski NP, Pol. 83/K3
Öjebyn, Swe. 79/G2
Ōji, Japan 119/J6
Ojima, Japan 119/C1
Ojinaga, Mex. 184/D2
Ojiya, Japan 117/F2
Ojo de Agua, Mex. 185/Q9
Ojo de Liebre (lag.), Mex. 184/B3
Ojocaliente, Mex. 184/E4
Ojos del Salado (peak), Chile 199/C2
Ojos Negros, Sp. 86/E2
Ojuelos de Jalisco, Mex. 185/E4
Oka, Qu, Can. 173/M7
Oka, Nga. 145/G5
Oka (riv.), Rus. 107/L4
Okabe, Japan 119/C1
Okahandja, Namb. 147/C5
Okak (isl.), Nf, Can. 165/K3
Okanagan (lake), BC, Can. 164/D4
Okanagan Falls, BC, Can. 168/D3
Okanda, PN de l', Gabon 147/B1
Okanogan, Wa, US 168/D3
Okanogan (riv.), Wa, US 168/D3
Okāra, Pak. 128/B4
Okavango (delta), Bots. 147/D4
Ōkawa, Japan 116/B4
Okaya, Japan 117/F2
Okayama (pref.), Japan 116/C3
Okayama, Japan 116/C3
Okazaki, Japan 119/M6
Okch'ŏn, SKor. 115/D4
Okęcie (int'l arpt.), Pol. 83/L2
Okeechobee, Fl, US 175/H5
Okeechobee (lake), Fl, US 175/H5
Okegawa, Japan 119/D2
Okement (riv.), Eng, UK 74/B5
Okha, Rus. 107/Q4
Ókhi Óros (peak), Gre. 89/J3
Okhotsk, Sea of (sea), Japan,Rus. 109/P4
Okhta (riv.), Rus. 103/T6
Okhtyrka, Ukr. 104/E2
Oki (isls.), Japan 116/C2
Okidaitō (isl.), Japan 117/L8
Okiep, SAfr. 148/B3
Okinawa (isl.), Japan 117/J7
Okinawa (pref.), Japan 117/J8
Okino-shima (isl.), Japan 116/C4
Okinoerabu (isl.), Japan 117/K7
Okitipupa, Nga. 145/G5
Okkan, Myan. 125/G4
Okku, SKor. 115/D5
Oklahoma (state), US 171/H4
Oklahoma City (cap.), Ok, US 179/M15
Okmulgee, Ok, US 171/J4
Oko, Nga. 145/G5
Okobaji (lakes), Ia, US 169/K5
Okok (riv.), Ugan. 146/B2
Okolona, Ms, US 175/F3
Okoppe, Japan 118/C1
Okotoks, Ab, Can. 168/E3
Okovango (riv.), Namb. 135/E6
Oksbøl, Den. 80/C4
Oksskolten (peak), Nor. 79/E2
Oktyabr'sk, Rus. 105/J1
Oktyabr'skiy, Rus. 103/M5
Ōkuchi, Japan 116/B4
Okulovka, Rus. 102/G4
Okushiri, Japan 118/A2
Okutama (lake), Japan 119/C2
Okutama, Japan 119/C2
Okwa (riv.), Bots. 147/D5
Ol Doinyo Sabuk NP, Kenya 146/C3
Ólafsfjördhur, Ice. 79/N6
Ólafsvík, Ice. 79/M7
Olalla, Wa, US 177/B3
Olan, Pic d' (peak), Fr. 85/G4
Olanchito, Hon. 186/E3
Öland (isl.), Swe. 79/F4
Ölands södra udde (pt.), Swe. 80/G3
Olathe, Ks, US 179/D6
Olavarría, Arg. 200/E3
Oława, Pol. 83/J3
Ölbach (riv.), Ger. 93/F5
Olberg, Az, US 179/S19
Olbia, It. 88/A2
Olching, Ger. 97/E6
Olcott, NY, US 173/S9
Old (riv.), Ca, US 177/L11
Old Bahama (chan.), Cuba 187/G1
Old Bar, Austl. 157/E1
Old Bedford (canal), Eng, UK 75/G2
Old Bethpage, NY, US 181/M9
Old Bridge, NJ, US 181/H10
Old City, Isr. 133/G8
Old Crow, Yk, Can. 176/L2
Old Faithful Geyser, Wy, US 168/F4
Old Field (pt.), NY, US 181/E2
Old Fort Niagara, NY, US 173/R9
Old Harbor, Ak, US 176/H4
Old Man of Hoy, Sc, UK 73/V14
Old Mill Creek, Il, US 177/Q15
Old Nene (riv.), Eng, UK 75/F2
Old Rhine (riv.), Neth. 92/B4
Old Saybrook, Ct, US 181/F1
Old Tappan, NJ, US 181/K8
Old Town, Me, US 173/G2
Old Windsor, Eng, UK 72/B2
Old Wives (lake), Sk, Can. 169/G3
Oldeani (peak), Tanz. 146/B3
Oldebroek, Neth. 92/C4
Oldemarkt, Neth. 92/C3
Oldenburg, Ger. 93/F2
Oldenburg, Ger. 80/D4
Oldenzaal, Neth. 92/D4
Oldham, Eng, UK 77/F4
Oldham (co.), Eng, UK 77/F4
Oldman (riv.), Ab, Can. 168/E3
Oldmeldrum, Sc, UK 78/D2
Oldoog (isl.), Ger. 93/E1
Olds, Ab, Can. 168/E3
Olduvai Gorge, Tanz. 146/B3
Oldwick, NJ, US 180/D2
Olean, NY, US 172/E3
Olecko, Pol. 81/K4
Oleggio, It. 100/B1
Oleiros, Port. 86/B3
Oleiros, Sp. 86/A1
Olekma (riv.), Rus. 107/N4
Oleksandriya, Ukr. 104/E2
Olele (pt.), Wa, US 177/B2
Olemari (riv.), Sur. 195/H4
Ølen, Nor. 80/A2
Olenegorsk, Rus. 102/G1
Olenëk (riv.), Rus. 107/L3
Olenek (bay), Rus. 107/M2
Oléron, île (isl.), Fr. 84/C4
Olesa de Montserrat, Sp. 87/K6
Oleśnica, Pol. 83/J3
Olesno, Pol. 83/K3
Oley, Pa, US 180/C3
Olfen, Ger. 93/E5
Olga (mt.), Austl. 155/F3
Olginate, It. 100/C1
Ölgiy, Mong. 112/E2
Ølgod, Den. 80/C4
Olhão, Port. 86/B4
Öli Qoltyq Sory (swamp), Kaz. 129/B3
Oliena, It. 88/A2
Olifantshoek, SAfr. 148/P12
Olifantsrivier (riv.), SAfr. 147/E5
Olimarao (isl.), Micr. 158/D4
Olimbía (Olympia) (ruin), Gre. 89/G4
Ólimbos, Gre. 132/A3
Ólimbos NP (Olympos NP), Gre. 89/H2
Olímpia, Braz. 197/B2
Olimpos Beydağları NP, Turk. 133/B1
Olinalá, Mex. 186/B2
Olinda, Braz. 196/D3
Olindina, Braz. 196/C3
Oliva, Sp. 87/E3
Oliva de la Frontera, Sp. 86/B3
Olivais, Port. 86/A3
Oliveira, Braz. 197/C2
Olivenza, Sp. 86/B3
Oliver, BC, Can. 168/D3
Olivet, Fr. 84/D3
Olivone, Swi. 99/E4
Olla, La, US 171/J5
Ollachea, Peru 198/D4
Ollagüe (vol.) 192/E8
Ollainville, Fr. 72/J6
Ollería, Sp. 87/E3
Olleros, Peru 198/B3
Ollon, Swi. 98/D5
Ollūr, India 124/C5
Olmaliq, Uzb. 129/E4
Olmedo, Sp. 86/C2
Olmos, Peru 198/B2
Olmos Park, Tx, US 179/U21
Olmstead, Ut, US 179/K13
Olmué, Chile 200/N8
Olney, Tx, US 171/H4
Olney, Md, US 180/A5
Olofström, Swe. 80/F3
Olomane (riv.), Qu, Can. 173/J1
Olomouc, Czh. 83/J4
Olomoucký (pol. reg.), Czh. 83/J4
Olongapo, Phil. 121/D5
Olonne-sur-Mer, Fr. 84/C3
Olorgasailie Nat'l Mon., Kenya 146/C3
Oloron-Sainte-Marie, Fr. 84/C5
Olot, Sp. 87/G1
Oloy (range), Rus. 107/S3
Olpe (riv.), Ger. 93/F6
Olpe, Ger. 95/G1
Olsberg, Ger. 93/F6
Olst, Neth. 92/D4
Olsztyn, Pol. 81/J5
Olsztynek, Pol. 83/L2
Olt (prov.), Rom. 91/G3
Olt (riv.), Rom. 91/G3
Olte, Sierra de (hills), Arg. 200/C4
Olten, Swi. 98/D3
Olteniţa, Rom. 91/H3
Olteţ (riv.), Rom. 91/F3
Oltre il Colle, It. 99/F6
Oltu, Turk. 132/E1
Oltu (riv.), Turk. 132/E1
Olur, Turk. 132/E1
Olvera, Sp. 86/C4
Olympia (cap.), Wa, US 168/C4
Olympic (mts.), Wa, US 168/C4
Olympic Dam, Austl. 155/H4
Olympic Game Farm, Wa, US 177/A1
Olympic National Forest, Wa, US 177/A2
Olympic NP, Wa, US 168/B4
Olympic Park, SKor. 115/G6
Olympos (Mount Olympus) (peak), Gre. 89/H2
Olympus (mt.), Wa, US 168/C4
Olympus (peak), Cyp. 133/C2
Olyutorskiy (bay), Rus. 107/S3
Ōma, Japan 118/B3
Oma (riv.), Rus. 103/K2
Ōma-zaki (pt.), Japan 118/B3
Ōmachi, Japan 117/E2
Omae-zaki (pt.), Japan 117/F3
Ōmagari, Japan 118/B4
Omagh (dist.), NI, UK 76/A2
Omagh, NI, UK 76/A2
Omak, Wa, US 168/D3
Oman (ctry.) 131/G4
Oman (gulf), Asia 131/H4
Omar Torrijos Herrera (int'l arpt.), Pan. 187/G4
Omaruru, Namb. 147/C5
Omas, Peru 198/B4
Omatako (riv.), Namb. 147/C4
Omate, Peru 198/D5
Ombai (str.), Indo. 123/F5
Ombrone (riv.), It. 85/J5
Ombúes de Lavalle, Uru. 201/K10
Ōme, Japan 119/C2
Omeath, Ire. 76/B3
Omegna, It. 85/H4
Omeo, Austl. 157/C3
Ömerli, Turk. 132/E2
Ometepe (isl.), Nic. 186/E4
Ometepec, Mex. 186/B2
Ōmi, Japan 119/K5
Ōmihachiman, Japan 119/K5
Omiš, Cro. 88/E1
Omitlán (riv.), Mex. 186/B2
Ōmiya, Japan 117/G2
Ōmiya, Japan 119/H4
Ōmiya, Japan 119/K7
Ommaney (cape), Ak, US 176/M4
Ommen, Neth. 92/D3
Ömnögovi (prov.), Mong. 112/H3
Omo NP, Eth. 139/N6
Omo Wenz (riv.), Eth. 139/N6
Omodeo (lake), It. 88/A2
Omolon (riv.), Rus. 109/Q3
Omono (riv.), Japan 118/B4
Omsk, Rus. 129/F1
Omsk (int'l arpt.), Rus. 129/F2
Omskaya Oblast, Rus. 129/F1
Ōmu, Japan 118/C1
Omul (peak), Rom. 91/G3
Ōmura, Japan 116/A4
Omurtag, Bul. 91/H4
Ōmuta, Japan 116/B4
Omutninsk, Rus. 103/M4
Onagawa, Japan 118/B4
Onalaska, Tx, US 174/E4
Onaping (lake), On, Can. 172/D2
Oñate, Sp. 86/D1
Onaway, Mi, US 172/C2
Onchan, IM, UK 76/D3
Onda, Sp. 87/E3
Ondava (riv.), Slvk. 83/L4
Ondjiva, Ang. 147/C4
Ondo, Nga. 145/G5
Ondo (state), Nga. 145/G5
Öndörhaan, Mong. 113/K2
Onè, It. 101/E1
Onega, Rus. 102/H3
Onega (bay), Rus. 102/G2
Onega (lake), Rus. 202/D
Onega (pen.), Rus. 102/H2
Onega (riv.), Rus. 106/D3
Oneida, NY, US 172/F3
Oneida, Pa, US 180/B2
Oneonta, NY, US 172/F3
Onex, Swi. 98/C5
Ongjin, NKor. 115/C4
Ongole, India 124/D4
Ongtüstik Qazaqstan, Kaz. 106/G5
Onhaye, Belg. 95/D3
Onida, SD, US 169/H4
Onil, Sp. 87/E3
Onilahy (riv.), Ang. 149/G8
Onishi, Japan 119/C1
Onitsha, Nga. 145/G5
Onjuku, Japan 119/E3
Onkaparinga (riv.), Austl. 155/M8
Onnaing, Fr. 94/C3
Onny (riv.), Eng, UK 74/D2
Ōno, Japan 116/E3
Ono, Japan 116/D3
Ōno, Japan 119/L5
Onoda, Japan 116/B4
Onomichi, Japan 116/C3
Onon, Mong. 113/K2
Onon (riv.), Rus. 113/K1
Onoto, Ven. 195/E2
Onotoa (isl.), Kiri. 158/G5
Onrusrivier, SAfr. 148/L11
Onslow, Austl. 154/B2
Ontake-san (peak), Japan 117/E3
Ontario, Or, US 168/D4
Ontario, Ca, US 178/C2
Ontario (prov.), Can. 164/H3
Ontario (lake), Can.,US 172/E3
Ontelaunee (lake), Pa, US 180/C3
Onteniente, Sp. 87/E3
Ontonagon, Mi, US 169/L4
Ontong Java (isl.), Sol. 158/E5
Onyang, SKor. 115/D4
Onzaga, Col. 194/C3
Oologah (lake), Ok, US 174/D2
Oona River, BC, Can. 176/M5
Oost-Vlaanderen (prov.), Belg. 94/C2
Oost-Vlieland, Neth. 92/C2
Oostburg, Neth. 94/C1
Oostelijk Flevoland (polder), Neth. 92/C3
Oostende (Ostend), Belg. 94/B1
Oosterhout, Neth. 92/B5
Oosterscheidedam (dam),Neth. 92/A5
Oosterschelde (riv.), Neth. 82/B3
Oosterwolde, Neth. 92/D3
Oosterzele, Belg. 94/C2
Oostkamp, Belg. 94/C1
Oostvaarderplassen (lake),Neth. 92/C4
Oostzaan, Neth. 92/B4
Ootmarsum, Neth. 92/D4
Opaka, Bul. 91/H4
Opalenica, Pol. 83/J2
Opasatika (riv.), On, Can. 172/D1
Opatija, Cro. 90/B3
Opatów, Pol. 83/L3
Opava, Czh. 83/J4
Opelika, Al, US 175/G3
Opelousas, La, US 171/J5
Opera, It. 100/C2
Öpfingen, Ger. 99/F1
Opglabbeek, Belg. 95/E1
Ophir, Ak, US 176/G3
Ophir, Ut, US 179/J13
Ophthalmia (range), Austl. 154/C2
Oploo, Neth. 92/C5
Opmeer, Neth. 92/B3
Opoczno, Pol. 83/L3
Opole, Pol. 83/J3
Opole Lubelskie, Pol. 83/L3
Opolskie (prov.), Pol. 83/J3
Opovo, Serb. 90/E3
Opp, Al, US 175/G4
Oppdal, Nor. 79/D3
Oppeano, It. 101/E2
Oppenau, Ger. 98/E1
Oppenheim, Ger. 96/B3
Oppland (co.), Nor. 79/D3
Opportunity, Wa, US 168/D4
Opwijk, Belg. 95/D2
Oquirrh (mts.), Ut, US 179/J12
Or 'Aqiva, Isr. 133/F6
Or, Mont d' (peak), Fr. 98/C4
Or Yehuda, Isr. 133/F7
Ora (riv.), Mex. 184/D3
Ōra, Japan 119/C1
Oradell, NJ, US 181/J8
Oradell (res.), NJ, US 181/J8
Orahovac, Serb. 90/E4
Orahovica, Cro. 90/C3
Orai, India 126/B3
Orain (riv.), Fr. 98/B4
Oral, Kaz. 105/J2
Oran, Alg. 142/E5
Orang (riv.), NKor. 115/E2
Orange, Austl. 157/D2
Orange (cape), Braz. 193/H3
Orange, Fr. 84/F4
Orange (riv.), Nam.,SAfr. 147/C6
Orange, Ca, US 178/G8
Orange, Ct, US 181/E1
Orange, NJ, US 181/J8
Orange (co.), NY, US 180/D1
Orange, Tx, US 171/J5
Orange, Va, US 172/E4
Orange Park, Fl, US 175/H4
Orange Walk, Belz. 186/D2
Orangeburg, NY, US 181/K7
Orangeburg, SC, US 175/H3
Orangeville, On, Can. 172/D3
Orangeville, Pa, US 180/B1
Orango (isl.), GBis. 144/A4
Oranienburg, Ger. 82/Q6
Oranje (mts.), Sur. 195/H4
Oranjekanaal (riv.), Neth. 92/D3
Oranjemund, Namb. 148/B3
Oranjestad, Aruba. 194/D1
Oranmore, Ire. 73/P10
Orapa, Bots. 147/E5
Oras, Phil. 121/E5
Orăştie, Rom. 91/F3
Oraviţa, Rom. 90/E3
Orb (riv.), Fr. 84/E5
Orba (riv.), It. 100/B3
Orbe, Swi. 98/C4
Orbe (riv.), Swi. 98/C4
Orbey, Fr. 98/D1
Órbigo (riv.), Sp. 86/C1
Orbost, Austl. 157/D3
Örbyhus, Swe. 80/G1
Orcemont, Fr. 72/H6
Orcera, Sp. 86/D3
Orchamps, Fr. 98/B3
Orchamps-Vennes, Fr. 98/C3
Orchard (lake), Mi, US 177/F6
Orchard City, Co, US 170/F3
Orchard Farm, Mo, US 179/G8
Orchard Homes, Mt, US 168/E4
Orchard Lake Village, Mi, US 177/F6
Orchid (isl.), Tai. 121/D3
Orchies, Fr. 94/C3
Orchy (riv.), Sc, UK 78/B4
Orciano di Pesaro, It. 101/F5
Orco (riv.), It. 85/G4
Orcopampa, Peru 198/C4
Orcotuna, Peru 198/C3
Ord, Ne, US 169/J5
Ordaz (int'l arpt.), Mex. 184/D4
Ordes, Sp. 86/A1
Ordesa y Monte Perdido, PN de, Sp. 87/F1
Ordos (des.), China 112/J4
Ordos (Mu Us Shamo) (des.), China 112/J4
Ordu, Turk. 132/D1
Ordu (prov.), Turk. 132/D1
Ore, Nga. 145/G5
Orealla, Guy. 195/G3
Örebro, Swe. 80/F2
Örebro (prov.), Swe. 79/E4
Orebro (int'l arpt.), Swe. 80/F2
Oregon (state), US 168/C5
Oregon Caves Nat'l Mon., Or, US 168/C5
Oregon City, Or, US 168/C4
Öregrund, Swe. 80/H1
Orekhovo-Zuyevo, Rus. 102/H5
Orël, Rus. 104/F1
Orellana, Peru 198/C2
Orellana la Vieja, Sp. 86/C3
Orem, Ut, US 179/K13
Orenberg (int'l arpt.), Rus. 105/K2
Orenburg, Rus. 105/K2
Orenburgskaya Oblast, Rus. 129/B2
Orense, Sp. 86/B1
Orestiás, Gre. 89/K2
Øresund (sound), Swe. 80/E4
Oreti (riv.), NZ 159/R12
Orford, Austl. 157/C4
Orford (pt.), Eng, UK 75/H2
Organ Pipe Cactus Nat'l Mon., Az, US 170/D4
Órgãos, Serra dos (mts.), Braz. 197/K7
Orgaz, Sp. 86/D3
Orgelet, Fr. 98/B4
Orgeurs, Fr. 72/H5
Orgeval, Fr. 72/H5
Orgosolo, It. 88/A2
Orhaneli, Turk. 104/D5
Orhangazi, Turk. 91/J5
Orhei, Mol. 91/J2
Orhon (riv.), Mong. 112/J2
Oria, Sp. 86/D4
Orient (pt.), NY, US 181/F1
Oriental, Mex. 185/M7
Oriental, Cordillera (mts.), SAm. 192/C5
Orientale (prov.), D.R. Congo 146/A2
Oriente, Arg. 200/E3
Origny-Sainte-Benoîte, Fr. 94/C4
Orihuela, Sp. 87/E3
Orillia, On, Can. 172/E2
Orimattila, Fin. 81/L1
Orinda, Ca, US 177/K11
Orinoco (delta), Ven. 195/F2
Orinoco (riv.), Col.,Ven. 195/F2
Orio al Serio (int'l arpt.), It. 100/C1
Oriolo, It. 88/E2
Orion (lake), Mi, US 177/F6
Orissa (state), India 124/D3
Orissa Coast (canal), India 127/F5
Oristano, It. 88/A3
Oristano, Golfo di (gulf), It. 88/A3
Orivesi, Fin. 81/L1
Oriximiná, Braz. 193/G4
Orizaba, Mex. 185/M8
Orizona, Braz. 196/A5
Orjen (peak), Mont. 90/D4
Órjiva, Sp. 86/D4
Orke (riv.), Ger. 93/F6
Örkelljunga, Swe. 80/E3
Orkhomenós, Gre. 89/H3
Orkney, SAfr. 148/D2
Orkney (isls.), UK 202/G
Orla, Tx, US 174/C4
Orland Park, Il, US 177/Q16
Orlândia, Braz. 197/C2

262

Orlan – Palpa

Orlando (int'l arpt.), Fl, US 175/H4
Orlando, Fl, US 175/H4
Orlando, Capo d' (cape), It. 88/D3
Orléanais (reg.), Fr. 84/D2
Orleans, Ca, US 168/C5
Orleans (parish), La, US 179/P16
Orléans, Fr. 84/D3
Örlenbach, Ger. 96/D2
Orlik (res.), Czh. 97/H3
Orlová, Czh. 83/K4
Orlovskaya Oblast, Rus. 104/F1
Orly (int'l arpt.), Fr. 72/K5
Orly, Fr. 72/K5
Ormanlı, Turk. 91/K5
Ormea, It. 100/A4
Ormília, Gre. 89/H2
Ormiston, Sc, UK 78/D5
Ormoc, Phil. 121/D5
Ormond Beach, Fl, US 175/H4
Ormskirk, Eng, UK 77/F4
Ornain (riv.), Fr. 84/F2
Ornans, Fr. 98/C3
Ornavasso, It. 99/E6
Orne (riv.), Fr. 82/C4
Ørnes, Nor. 79/E2
Orneta, Pol. 81/J4
Örnsköldsvik, Swe. 79/F3
Oro (riv.), Mex. 196/C2
Oro Grande, Ca, US 178/C1
Oro, Monte d' (peak), Fr. 88/A1
Oro Valley, Az, US 170/E4
Orocó, Braz. 196/C3
Orocué, Col. 194/D3
Orodara, Burk. 144/D4
Orofino, Id, US 168/D4
Orolo (riv.), It. 101/E1
Oroluk (isl.), Micr. 158/E4
Oromocto, NB, Can. 173/H2
Oron-la-Ville, Swi. 98/C4
Orona (Hull) (isl.), Kiri. 159/H5
Orono, Me, US 173/G2
Orontes (riv.), Syria 132/D3
Oropesa, Sp. 86/C3
Oroqen Zizhiqi, China 113/M1
Orós, Braz. 196/C2
Orosei, It. 88/A2
Orosei, Golfo di (gulf), It. 88/A2
Orosháza, Hun. 90/E2
Oroszlány, Hun. 90/D2
Orovada, Nv, US 168/D5
Oroville, Wa, US 168/D3
Oroville, Ca, US 170/B3
Orphin, Fr. 72/H6
Orpund, Swi. 98/D3
Orrefors, Swe. 80/F3
Orrell, Eng, UK 77/F4
Orrick, Mo, US 179/E5
Orrin (riv.), Sc, UK 78/B2
Orrin (res.), Sc, UK 78/B2
Orroli, It. 88/A3
Orroroo, Austl. 155/H5
Orrtanna, Pa, US 180/A4
Orry-la-Ville, Fr. 72/K4
Orsa, Swe. 80/F1
Orsago, It. 101/F1
Orsay, Fr. 72/J5
Orsett, Eng, UK 72/E2
Orsha, Bela. 81/P4
Orsk, Rus. 105/L2
Orsonnens, Swi. 98/C4
Orşova, Rom. 90/F3
Ørsta, Nor. 79/C3
Örsundsbro, Swe. 80/G2
Orta (lake), It. 85/H4
Orta, Turk. 104/E4
Orta Nova, It. 88/D2
Ortaca, Turk. 132/B2
Ortaköy, Turk. 132/C1
Ortaköy, Turk. 132/C2
Ortega, Col. 194/C4
Ortegal (cape), Sp. 86/B1
Ortenberg, Ger. 96/C2
Orth an der Donau, Aus. 91/P7
Orthez, Fr. 84/C5
Ortigara (peak), It. 99/H5
Ortigueira, Sp. 86/B1
Orting, Wa, US 177/C3
Ortiz, Mex. 184/C2
Ortles (mts.), It. 85/J3
Ortles (peak), It. 99/G4
Ortón (riv.), Bol. 192/E6
Ortona, It. 88/D1
Ortonville, Mn, US 169/J4
Ortonville, Mi, US 177/F6
Örtze (riv.), Ger. 93/H3
Orūmīyeh, Iran 132/F2
Orurillo, Peru 198/D4
Oruro, Bol. 192/E7
Orust (isl.), Swe. 80/D2
Orvieto, It. 85/K5
Orvilliers, Fr. 72/G5
Orwell (riv.), Eng, UK 75/H2
Orwigsburg, Pa, US 180/B2
Oryakhovo, Bul. 91/F4
Orzinuovi, It. 100/C2
Orzysz, Pol. 81/J5
Os, Nor. 80/A1
Osa, Rus. 103/M4
Osa, Peninsula de (pen.), CR 192/B2
Osage (riv.), Mo, US 171/J3
Osage Beach, Mo, US 171/J3
Ōsaka (pref.), Japan 116/D3
Ōsaka (int'l arpt.), Japan 119/H6
Ōsaka, Japan 119/J6
Ōsaka Castle, Japan 119/H6
Osan, SKor. 115/D4
Osasco, Braz. 197/G8
Ōsato, Japan 119/C1
Osborn (mt.), Ak, US 176/E3
Osburg, Ger. 95/F4
Osby, Swe. 80/E3
Osceola, Ar, US 172/B5
Oschersleben, Ger. 82/F2
Oschiri, It. 88/A2
Oscura (mts.), NM, US 174/B3
Osdorf, Ger. 93/G1
Osh (obl.), Kyr. 129/F5
Osh, Kyr. 129/F4
Oshamambe, Japan 118/B2
Oshawa, On, Can. 173/S8
Oshika (pen.), Japan 118/B4
Oshino, Japan 119/B3
Oshkosh, Ne, US 169/H5
Oshnovīyeh, Iran 132/F2
Oshogbo, Nga. 145/G5
Osijek, Cro. 90/D3
Osio Sotto, It. 100/C1
Osipaonica, Serb. 90/E3
Oskarshamn, Swe. 80/G3
Oskarström, Swe. 80/E3
Oskol (riv.), Rus.,Ukr. 104/F2
Oslo (cap.), Nor. 80/D2
Osmānābād, India 131/L5
Osmancık, Turk. 132/C1
Osmaneli, Turk. 91/K5
Osmaniye, Turk. 133/E1
Osnabrück, Ger. 93/F4
Osnago, It. 100/C1
Osny, Fr. 72/J4
Oso (riv.), D.R. Congo 146/A3
Oso (mt.), Ca, US 177/M12
Osogna, Swi. 99/E5
Osório, Braz. 197/B4
Osorno, Sp. 86/C1
Osorno, Chile 200/B4
Osoyoos, BC, Can. 168/D3
Ospedaletti, It. 100/A5
Ospedaletto Euganeo, It. 101/E2
Ospitaletto, It. 100/D1
Osprey (reef), Austl. 151/D2
Oss, Neth. 92/C5
Ossa (mt.), Austl. 157/C4
Ossa, Sierra de (mts.), Port. 86/B3
Osse (riv.), Nga. 145/G5
Osséja, Fr. 84/D5
Ossett, Eng, UK 77/G4
Ossi, It. 88/A2
Ossining, NY, US 181/K7
Ostashkov, Rus. 102/G4
Ostbevern, Ger. 93/E4
Ostellato, It. 101/E3
Osten, Ger. 93/G1
Osterburg, Ger. 82/F2
Osterburken, Ger. 96/C4
Österbybruk, Swe. 80/G1
Österbymo, Swe. 80/F3
Ostercappeln, Ger. 93/F4
Osterdalälven (riv.), Swe. 80/F1
Osterems (chan.), Ger. 92/D1
Östergötland (co.), Swe. 79/E4
Osterhofen, Ger. 97/G5
Osterholz-Scharmbeck, Ger. 93/F2
Osteria Grande, It. 101/E4
Ostermiething, Aus. 97/F6
Osterode am Harz, Ger. 93/H5
Östersund, Swe. 79/E3
Östervåla, Swe. 80/G1
Ostfildern, Ger. 96/C5
Østfold (co.), Nor. 79/D4
Ostfriesland (reg.), Ger. 93/E2
Östhammar, Swe. 80/H1
Ostheim vor der Rhön, Ger. 96/D2
Osthofen, Ger. 96/B3
Ostia Antica (ruin), It. 88/C2
Ostiano, It. 100/D2
Ostiglia, It. 101/E2
Ostional NWR, CR 186/E4
Ostra, It. 101/G5
Östra Silen (lake), Swe. 80/E2
Ostra Vetere, It. 101/G5
Ostrach (riv.), Ger. 96/C6
Ostrava, Czh. 83/K4
Ostravský (pol. reg.), Czh. 83/J4
Ostrhauderfehn, Ger. 93/E2
Oštri Rt (cape), Mont. 90/D4
Ostricourt, Fr. 94/C3
Ostróda, Pol. 81/H5
Ostrogozhsk, Rus. 104/F2
Ostrołęka, Pol. 83/L2
Ostrov, Czh. 97/F2
Ostrov, Rus. 81/N3
Ostrów Mazowiecka, Pol. 83/L2
Ostrów Wielkopolski, Pol. 83/J3
Ostrowiec Świętokrzyski, Pol. 83/L3
Ostrzeszów, Pol. 83/J3
Ostseebad Binz, Ger. 80/E4
Ostseebad Göhren, Ger. 80/E4
Ostseebad Prerow, Ger. 80/E4
Oststeinbek, Ger. 93/H1
Ostuni, It. 89/E2
Ostwald, Fr. 96/A5
Osŭm (riv.), Bul. 91/G4
Osum (riv.), Slvk. 90/E5
Ōsumi (isls.), Japan 116/B5
Ōsumi (pen.), Japan 116/B5
Osun (state), Nga. 145/G5
Osuna, Sp. 86/C4
Osvaldo Cruz, Braz. 197/B2
Oswaldtwistle, Eng, UK 77/F4
Oswego, NY, US 172/E3
Oswego, Il, US 177/P16
Oswestry, Eng, UK 77/E6
Oświęcim (Auschwitz), Pol. 83/K3
Ōta (riv.), Japan 116/C3
Ōta, Japan 117/F2
Ōtake, Japan 116/C3
Ōtaki, Japan 117/G3
Ōtaki, Japan 119/B2
Ōtakine-yama (peak), Japan 117/G2
Otava (riv.), Czh. 85/K2
Otavalo, Ecu. 194/B4
Otavi, Namb. 147/C4
Ōtawara, Japan 117/G2
Otay, Ca, US 178/C5
Oţelu Roşu, Rom. 90/F3
Otero de Rey, Sp. 86/B1
Oteros (riv.), Mex. 184/C3
Otgon Tenger (peak), Mong. 112/G2
Othello, Wa, US 168/D4
Othis, Fr. 72/L4
Othonoí (isl.), Gre. 89/F3
Oti (riv.), Gha. 145/F4
Otjiwarongo, Namb. 147/C5
Otley, Eng, UK 77/G4
Otočac, Cro. 90/B3
Otofuke, Japan 118/C2
Otog Qi, China 112/J4
Otok, Cro. 90/D3
Ōtone, Japan 119/D1
Otopeni (int'l arpt.), Rom. 91/H3
Otoskwin (riv.), On, Can. 169/L3
Otowa, Japan 119/M6
Otra (riv.), Nor. 80/B2
Otradnyy, Rus. 105/J1
Otranto, Strait of (str.), It. 89/F2
Otrokovice, Czh. 83/J4
Otse, Bots. 148/D2
Ōtsu, Japan 119/J5
Ōtsuchi, Japan 118/B4
Ōtsuki, Japan 119/B2
Otta, Nga. 145/F5
Ottawa (cap.), Can. 172/F2
Ottawa (int'l arpt.), On, Can. 172/F2
Ottawa (isls.), Nun., Can. 165/H3
Ottawa (riv.), On, Can. 172/E2
Ottawa, Oh, US 172/C3
Ottawa, Ks, US 171/J3
Ottensheim, Aus. 97/H6
Otter (riv.), Eng, UK 74/C5
Otterbach, Ger. 95/G5
Otterberg, Ger. 95/G4
Otterndorf, Ger. 93/F1
Ottersberg, Ger. 93/G2
Ottershaw, Eng, UK 72/B2
Otterville, Il, US 179/G7
Ottignies-Louvain-la-Neuve, Belg. 95/D2
Öttingen im Bayern, Ger. 96/D5
Ottmarsheim, Fr. 98/D2
Ottnang am Hausruck, Aus. 97/G6
Otto, Mo, US 179/F9
Ottobeuren, Ger. 99/G2
Ottobrunn, Ger. 97/E6
Ottone, It. 100/C3
Ottosdal, SAfr. 148/D2
Ottsville, Pa, US 180/C3
Ottumwa, Ia, US 169/K5
Ottweiler, Ger. 95/G5
Otumba de Gómez Farías, Mex. 185/L7
Otuzco, Peru 198/B2
Otway (cape), Austl. 157/B3
Otway (bay), Chile 201/C7
Otway NP, Austl. 157/B3
Otwock, Pol. 83/L2
Ötztal Alps (mts.), Aus. 85/J3
Ötztaler Ache (riv.), Aus. 99/G3
Ou (mts.), Japan 118/B4
Ouachita (mts.), Ok, US 171/J4
Ouachita (riv.), Ar,La, US 171/J4
Ouadda, CAfr. 139/K6
Ouaddaï (reg.), Chad 139/J5
Ouadi Haddad (riv.), Chad 139/J4
Ouadi Rimé (riv.), Chad 139/J5
Ouagadougou (int'l arpt.), Burk. 145/E3
Ouagadougou (cap.), Burk. 145/E3
Ouahigouya, Burk. 145/E3
Ouaka (riv.), CAfr. 139/K6
Oualâta, Dhar (cliff), Mrta. 144/D2
Ouallam, Niger 145/F3
Ouanda Djallé, CAfr. 139/K6
Ouanne (riv.), Fr. 84/E3
Ouarane (pol. reg.), Mrta. 138/C3
Ouarane (reg.), Mrta. 140/C5
Ouargla (prov.), Alg. 141/G3
Ouargla, Alg. 141/G3
Ouarkziz, Jebel (mts.), Mor. 140/C3
Ouarzazate (int'l arpt.), Mor. 140/D3
Ouarzazate, Mor. 140/D3
Ouasiemsca (riv.), Qu, Can. 172/F1
Oubangui (riv.), CAfr. 139/J7
Oubritenga (prov.), Burk. 145/E3
Ouche (riv.), Fr. 98/B3
Oud-Beijerland, Neth. 92/B5
Oud-Turnhout, Belg. 92/B6
Ōuda, Japan 119/J7
Oudalan (prov.), Burk. 145/E3
Ouddorp, Neth. 92/A5
Oude IJssel (riv.), Neth. 92/D5
Oude Pekela, Neth. 92/E2
Oude Westereems (chan.), Neth. 92/D1
Oudenaarde, Belg. 94/C2
Oudenbosch, Neth. 92/B5
Oudenburg, Belg. 94/C1
Oudewater, Neth. 92/B4
Oudon (riv.), Fr. 84/C3
Oudtshoorn, SAfr. 148/C4
Oued el Hadjar (well), Mali 144/E2
Oued Moulouyadeu (riv.), Mor. 138/E1
Oued Sous (riv.), Mor. 138/D1
Oued Zem, Mor. 140/D2
Ouémé (riv.), Ben. 138/F6
Ouéme (prov.), Ben. 145/F5
Ouenza, Alg. 142/L7
Ouerrha (riv.), Mor. 142/B2
Ouessé, Ben. 145/F4
Ouesso, Congo 138/J7
Ouest (prov.), Camr. 145/H5
Ouest (pt.), Haiti 187/H1
Ouest (pt.), Haiti 187/H2
Ouezzane, Mor. 142/B2
Oughterard, Ire. 73/P10
Ouham (riv.), CAfr. 138/J6
Ouidah, Ben. 145/F5
Oujda, Mor. 142/D2
Oujda (prov.), Mor. 142/C2
Oujda (Angads) (int'l arpt.), Mor. 142/D2
Oulad Teïma, Mor. 140/C3
Oulangan NP, Fin. 102/F2
Ould Birni (well), Alg. 141/E4
Oulnina (peak), Austl. 155/H5
Oulu, Fin. 102/E2
Oulu (prov.), Fin. 79/H2
Oulujärvi (lake), Fin. 79/H2
Oum El Bouaghi, Alg. 142/K7
Oum er Rbia, Oued (riv.), Mor. 140/D2
Oum er Rhia (riv.), Mor. 138/D1
Ounasjoki (riv.), Fin. 79/H2
Oupeye, Belg. 95/E2
Our (riv.), Eur. 95/E4
Ource (riv.), Fr. 84/F3
Ourcq (riv.), Fr. 82/B4
Ourcq, Canal de l' (canal), Fr. 72/K5
Øure Anarjokka NP, Nor. 79/H1
Øure Dividal NP, Nor. 79/F1
Ouricuri, Braz. 196/B2
Ourinhos, Braz. 197/B2
Ourique, Port. 86/A4
Ouro Fino, Braz. 197/G7
Ouro, Ponta do (pt.), Moz. 149/F2
Ouro Preto, Braz. 197/D2
Ouroux-sur-Saône, Fr. 98/A4
Ourthe Occidentale (riv.), Belg. 95/E3
Ourthe Orientale (riv.), Belg. 95/E3
Ouse (riv.), Eng, UK 77/H4
Oust (riv.), Fr. 84/B3
Outaouais (riv.), Qu, Can. 172/E2
Outardes (riv.), Qu, Can. 173/G1
Outardes Quatre (lake), Qu, Can. 173/G1
Outeïd Arkas (well), Mali 144/D2
Outer Hebrides (isls.), Sc, UK 73/P8
Outes, Sp. 86/A1
Outjo, Namb. 147/C5
Outlook, Sk, Can. 168/G3
Outreau, Fr. 94/A2
Outremont, Qu, Can. 173/N6
Ouvèze (riv.), Fr. 84/F4
Ouyen, Austl. 157/B2
Ouzinkie, Ak, US 176/H4
Ovacık, Turk. 132/D2
Ovacık, Turk. 132/C1
Ovada, It. 100/B3
Ovalle, Chile 199/B3
Ovana (peak), Ven. 195/E3
Ovar, Port. 86/A2
Overath, Ger. 95/G2
Overflakkee (isl.), Neth. 92/B5
Overhalla, Nor. 79/D2
Overholser (lake), Ok, US 179/M14
Overijse, Belg. 95/D2
Overijssel (prov.), Neth. 92/D3
Overijssels (riv.), Neth. 92/D4
Överkalix, Swe. 79/G2
Overland, Mo, US 179/G8
Overland Park, Ks, US 179/D6
Overlea, Md, US 180/B5
Overo (peak), Arg. 200/C5
Overpelt, Belg. 92/C6
Overton, Nv, US 170/D3
Övertorneå, Swe. 102/D2
Overum, Swe. 80/G3
Oviedo, Sp. 86/C1
Ovoca, Ire. 76/B6
Övörhangay (prov.), Mong. 112/H2
Övre Fryken (lake), Swe. 80/E1
Øvre Pasvik NP, Nor. 79/J1
Ovriá, Gre. 89/G3
Owando, Congo 138/J8
Ōwani, Japan 118/B3
Owariasahi, Japan 119/M5
Owase, Japan 116/E3
Owassa (lake), NJ, US 180/D1
Owasso, Ok, US 171/J3
Owego, NY, US 172/E3
Owen (mt.), NZ 159/S11
Owen, Austl. 155/H5
Owen, Ger. 96/C5
Owen Falls (dam), Ugan. 146/B2
Owen Roberts (int'l arpt.), UK 187/F2
Owen Sound, On, Can. 172/D2
Owenkillew (riv.), NI, UK 76/A2
Owens (riv.), Ca, US 170/C3
Owensboro, Ky, US 172/C4
Owerri, Nga. 145/G5
Owingen, Ger. 99/F2
Owings, Md, US 180/B6
Owings Mills, Md, US 180/B5
Owl Creek (mts.), Wy, US 168/F4
Owo, Nga. 145/G5
Owosso, Mi, US 172/C3
Owyhee, Nv, US 168/D5
Owyhee (lake), Or, US 170/C2
Owyhee (mts.), Id, US 170/C2
Owyhee (riv.), Id,Or, US 168/D5
Owyhee, South Fork (riv.), Nv, US 168/D5
Oxapampa, Peru 198/C3
Oxbow, Sk, Can. 169/H3
Oxbow (lake), Mi, US 177/F6
Oxelösund, Swe. 80/G2
Oxford (lake), Mb, Can. 169/K2
Oxford, Eng, UK 75/E3
Oxford (canal), Eng, UK 75/E3
Oxford, Mi, US 177/F6
Oxford, Ms, US 175/F3
Oxford, Pa, US 180/C4
Oxfordshire (co.), Eng, UK 75/E3
Oxie, Swe. 80/E4
Oxkutzcab, Mex. 186/D1
Oxnard, Ca, US 178/A2
Oxnard Beach, Ca, US 178/A2
Oxon Hill (farm), Md, US 180/A6
Oxon Hill-Glassmanor, Md, US 180/B6
Oxted, Eng, UK 72/D3
Oyabe, Japan 117/E2
Oyama, Japan 117/F2
Oyama, Japan 119/B3
Ōyamada, Japan 119/K6
Ōyamazaki, Japan 119/J6
Oyapock (riv.), Fr. 193/H3
Oye-Plage, Fr. 94/B2
Oyem, Gabon 138/H7
Oyen, Ab, Can. 168/F3
Øyer, Nor. 80/D1
Oykell (riv.), Sc, UK 73/R8
Oyo (state), Nga. 145/F4
Oyo, Nga. 145/F5
Ōyodo (riv.), Japan 116/B5
Ōyodo, Japan 119/J7
Oyón, Peru 198/B3
Oyonnax, Fr. 98/B5
Oyster Bay, NY, US 181/L8
Oyster Bay (har.), NY, US 181/L8
Oyster Bay Cove, NY, US 181/L8
Oyster Bay NWR, NY, US 181/L8
Oyten, Ger. 93/G2
Oyyl (riv.), Kaz. 129/B3
Ozamiz, Phil. 121/D6
Ozanne (riv.), Fr. 84/D2
Ozark (plat.), Mo, US 171/J3
Ozark, Ar, US 171/J4
Ozark, Al, US 175/G4
Ozark (mts.), Ar,Mo, US 167/H4
Ozarks, Lake of the (lake), Mo, US 174/E2
Ózd, Hun. 83/L4
Ozernoy (cape), Rus. 107/S4
Ozette (lake), Wa, US 168/B3
Ozhiski (lake), On, Can. 169/L3
Ozieri, It. 88/A2
Ozimek, Pol. 83/K3
Özkonak, Turk. 132/C2
Ozoir-la-Ferrière, Fr. 72/L5
Ozona, Tx, US 171/G5
Ozora, Hun. 90/D2
Ozorków, Pol. 83/K3
Ozouer-le-Voulgis, Fr. 72/L6
Ōzu, Japan 116/C4
Ozuluama de Mascareñas, Mex. 186/B1
Ozzano dell'Emilia, It. 101/E4

P

P. K. Le Rouxdam (res.), SAfr. 148/D3
Pa-an, Myan. 120/B2
Pa Sak (riv.), Thai. 125/H4
Paar (riv.), Ger. 82/F4
Paarl, SAfr. 148/L10
Paauilo, Hi, US 166/U10
Pabbi, Pak. 128/A2
Pabellón de Arteaga, Mex. 184/E4
Pabianice, Pol. 83/K3
Pābna, Bang. 127/G3
Pābna (pol. reg.), Bang. 127/G3
Pacaás Novos, PN dos, Braz. 192/F6
Pacaás Novos, Serra dos (mts.), Braz. 192/F6
Pacajá (riv.), Braz. 193/H4
Pacajus, Braz. 196/C2
Pacaltsdorp, SAfr. 148/C4
Pacaraimã (mts.), Braz. 192/F3
Pacaya Samiria, Reserva Nacional, Peru 198/C2
Paccha, Peru 198/C3
Paceco, It. 88/C4
Pachacamac (ruin), Peru 198/B4
Pachaconas, Peru 198/C4
Pachamarca (riv.), Peru 198/C4
Pachino, It. 88/D4
Pachitea (riv.), Peru 198/C3
Pachiza, Peru 198/B2
Pachmarhī, India 128/C4
Pachuca, Mex. 185/L6
Pacific (ocean) 109/N8
Pacific (range), BC, Can. 168/B3
Pacific, Wa, US 177/C3
Pacific Palisades, Hi, US 166/W13
Pacifico (mtn.), Ca, US 178/B2
Pacinan (cape), Indo. 122/D5
Pacitan, Indo. 122/D5
Paço de Arcos, Port. 87/P10
Pad Īdan, Pak. 131/J3
Padampur, India 124/D3
Padang, Indo. 122/B4
Padangpanjang, Indo. 122/B4
Padangsidempuan, Indo. 122/A3
Paddock Lake, Wi, US 177/P14
Paddock Wood, Eng, UK 72/E3
Paderborn, Il, US 179/G9
Paderborn, Ger. 93/F5
Paderno, It. 101/F1
Padiham, Eng, UK 77/F4
Padilla, Bol. 192/F7
Padina, Serb. 90/E3
Padjelanta NP, Swe. 79/F2
Padova (prov.), It. 101/E2
Padova, It. 101/E2
Padrão, Ponta do (pt.), Ang. 147/B2
Padrauna, India 126/D2
Padre (isl.), Tx, US 174/D5
Padre Island Nat'l Seashore, Tx, US 174/D5
Padrón, Sp. 86/A1
Paducah, Ky, US 172/B4
Paducah, Tx, US 171/G4
Padul, Sp. 86/D4
Padula, It. 88/D2
Paektŏk-san (peak), SKor. 115/E4
Paektu-san (peak), NKor. 115/E2
Paese, It. 101/F1
Páez, Col. 194/C3
Páez, Col. 194/C4
Pafúri, Moz. 147/F5
Pag, Cro. 90/B3
Pag (isl.), Cro. 90/B3
Pagadian, Phil. 123/F2
Pagai Selatan (isl.), Indo. 122/B4
Pagai Utara (isl.), Indo. 122/B4
Pagan, Myan. 125/F3
Pagan (isl.), NMar. 158/D3
Paganica, It. 88/C1
Page, Az, US 170/E3
Pager (riv.), Ugan. 146/B2
Pagny-sur-Moselle, Fr. 95/F6
Pagosa Springs, Co, US 170/F3
Pagwachuan (riv.), On, Can. 172/C1
Pahala, Hi, US 166/U11
Pahang (riv.), Malay. 122/B3
Páhara (lag.), Nic. 187/F3
Pahārpur, Pak. 128/A3
Pahāsu, India 126/B1
Pahlgām, India 128/C2
Pahrump, Nv, US 170/D3
Pahuatlán, Mex. 185/L6
Pahute (mesa), Nv, US 170/C3
Pai (lake), China 114/C5
Paia, Hi, US 166/T10
Paignton, Eng, UK 74/C6
Paiján, Peru 198/B2
Päijänne (lake), Fin. 79/H3
Paikü (lake), China 127/E1
Pailolo (chan.), Hi, US 166/T10
Paimio, Fin. 81/K1
Paine (peak), Chile 201/B6
Paine, Chile 200/N8
Painesville, Oh, US 172/D3
Paint (lake), Mb, Can. 169/J2
Paint Rock, Tx, US 174/D4
Painted (des.), Az, US 170/E4
Paipa, Col. 194/C3
País Vasco (aut. comm.), Sp. 86/D1
Paisley, Sc, UK 78/B5
Paita, Peru 198/A2
Paithan, India 124/C4
Pajala, Swe. 79/G2
Paján, Ecu. 194/A5
Pajęczno, Pol. 83/K3
Pakanbaru, Indo. 122/B3
Pakch'ŏn, NKor. 115/C3
Pakenham, Austl. 157/G6
Pakenham (cape), Chile 201/B6
Pákhnes (peak), Gre. 89/J5
Pakhra (riv.), Rus. 103/W9
Pakistan (ctry.) 131/H3
Paklenica NP, Cro. 90/B3
Pakokku, Myan. 125/G3
Pakowki (lake), Ab, Can. 168/F3
Pākpattan, Pak. 128/B4
Pakrac, Cro. 90/C3
Paks, Hun. 90/D2
Pakwach, Ugan. 146/A2
Pakxe, Laos 120/D3
Pala, Chad 138/H6
Pala, Ca, US 178/C4
Pala Ind. Res., Ca, US 178/C4
Palace, Mona. 100/J8
Palafrugell, Sp. 87/G2
Palagonia, It. 88/D4
Palagruža (isls.), Cro. 88/E1
Pálairos, Gre. 89/G3
Palaiseau, Fr. 72/J5
Pālakollu, India 124/D4
Palamás, Gre. 89/H3
Palamós, Sp. 87/G2
Palana, Rus. 107/R4
Palangkaraya, Indo. 122/D4
Pālanpur, India 131/K4
Palaoa (pt.), Hi, US 166/T10
Palapye, Bots. 147/E5
Palar (riv.), India 124/C5
Palas de Rey, Sp. 86/B1
Palāsbāri, India 127/H2
Palatine, Il, US 177/P15
Palatka, Fl, US 175/H4
Palau (ctry.) 158/C4
Palau We (isl.), Indo. 122/A2
Palaw, Myan. 120/B3
Palawan (isl.), Phil. 121/C6
Palawan Passage (chan.), Phil. 121/C6
Pālayankottai, India 124/C6
Palazzolo Acreide, It. 88/D4
Palazzolo dello Stella, It. 101/G1
Palazzolo sull'Oglio, It. 100/C1
Palé, EqG. 138/G8
Pale, Bosn. 90/D4
Paleleh, Indo. 123/F3
Palembang, Indo. 122/B4
Palena (riv.), Chile 200/B4
Palena, Chile 200/C4
Palencia, Sp. 86/C1
Palenque, Mex. 186/D2
Palenque, PN, Mex. 186/C2
Palermo, It. 88/C3
Palermo, NJ, US 180/D5
Palese (int'l arpt.), It. 88/E2
Palestine (lake), Tx, US 174/E3
Palestro, It. 100/B2
Pālghar, India 131/K5
P'algong-san (peak), SKor. 115/D5
P'algong-san (peak), SKor. 115/E4
Palgrave (mt.), Austl. 154/B2
Palhano, Braz. 196/C2
Palhoça, Braz. 197/B3
Pāli, India 131/K3
Pali-Aike, PN, Chile 201/C7
Paliā Kalān, India 126/C1
Palić, Serb. 90/D2
Palikea (peak), Hi, US 166/V13
Palikir (cap.), Micr. 158/E4
Palioúrion (cape), Gre. 89/H3
Palisades (cliff), NJ,NY, US 181/K8
Palisades, NY, US 181/K8
Palisades Interstate Park, NJ, US 180/D1
Palisades Park, NJ, US 181/K8
Paliseul, Belg. 95/E4
Pālitāna, India 131/K4
Palizada, Mex. 182/C4
Paljenik (peak), Bosn. 90/C3
Palk (str.), India 124/C6
Pallamallawa, Austl. 157/D1
Pallarenda, Austl. 156/B2
Pallas-Ounastunturin NP, Fin. 79/H1
Pallasca, Peru 198/B3
Pallastunturi (peak), Fin. 79/H1
Palliser (cape), NZ 159/T11
Palm Bay, Fl, US 175/H4
Palm Beach (int'l arpt.), Fl, US 175/H5
Palm City, Ca, US 178/C5
Palm Harbor, Fl, US 175/H4
Palm Island Aboriginal Settlement, Austl. 156/B2
Palm Springs, Ca, US 170/C4
Palma, Moz. 146/D5
Palma (riv.), Braz. 193/J6
Palma, Sp. 87/G3
Palma del Río, Sp. 86/C4
Palma di Montechiaro, It. 88/C4
Palma Mallorca (int'l arpt.), Sp. 87/G3
Palma Soriano, Cuba 187/H1
Palmácia, Braz. 196/C2
Palmanova, It. 101/G1
Palmar (riv.), Ven. 187/H4
Palmares, Braz. 196/D3
Palmarito, Ven. 194/D3
Palmas, Braz. 197/A3
Palmas (cape), Libr. 144/D5
Palmdale, Ca, US 178/B1
Palmeira, Braz. 197/B3
Palmeira, CpV. 135/K10
Palmeira dos Índios, Braz. 196/C3
Palmeirais, Braz. 196/B2
Palmeiras (riv.), Braz. 196/A4
Palmeiras, Braz. 196/B4
Palmeirinhas, Ponta das (pt.), Ang. 147/B2
Palmela, Port. 87/Q10
Palmer, Ak, US 176/J3
Palmer, US, Ant. 202/V
Palmer, Wa, US 177/D3
Palmer Land (phys. reg.), Ant. 202/V
Palmerston, NZ 159/S12
Palmerston (cape), Austl. 156/C3
Palmerston Atoll (atoll), Cookls. 159/J6
Palmerston North, NZ 159/T11
Palmerston NP, Austl. 156/B2
Palmerton, Pa, US 180/C2
Palmetto, Fl, US 175/H5
Palmi, It. 88/D3
Palmilla, Chile 200/C2
Palmillas (pt.), Cuba 187/F1
Palmira, Col. 194/B4
Palmital, Braz. 197/B2
Palmitas, Uru. 201/K10
Palmyra, Ut, US 179/K13
Palmyra (isl.), PacUS 159/J4
Palmyra, Pa, US 180/B3
Palmyra (Tadmur) (ruin), Syria 132/D3
Palmyras (pt.), India 124/E3
Palni, India 124/C5
Palo, Phil. 121/D5
Palo Alto, Ca, US 170/B3
Palo Alto, Pa, US 180/B2
Palo Pinto, Tx, US 171/H4
Palo Verde, PN, CR 182/D5
Palomeu (riv.), Sur. 195/H4
Palon (peak), It. 101/E1
Palos (cape), Sp. 87/E4
Palos de la Frontera, Sp. 86/B4
Palos Hills, Il, US 177/Q16
Palos Verdes (hills), Ca, US 178/F8
Palos Verdes (pt.), Ca, US 178/F8
Palos Verdes Estates, Ca, US 178/F8
Palosco, It. 100/C1
Palpalá, Arg. 199/C1

Palpe – Penri
263

Palpetu (cape), Indo. 123/G4
Paltamo, Fin. 102/E2
Palu, Indo. 123/E4
Palu, Turk. 132/D2
Paluan, Phil. 121/D5
Palwal, India 126/A1
Pamangkat, Indo. 122/C3
Pambula, Austl. 157/D3
Pamiers, Fr. 84/D5
Pamir (riv.), Afg.,Taj. 106/H6
Pamir (reg.), China,Taj. 106/H6
Pamlico (riv.), NC, US 175/J3
Pamlico (sound), NC, US 175/J3
Pampa, Tx, US 171/G4
Pampachiri, Peru 198/C4
Pampacolca, Peru 198/C4
Pampas (plain), Arg. 200/E3
Pampas, Peru 198/C4
Pampas, Peru 198/B3
Pampas (riv.), Peru 198/C4
Pampilhosa da Serra, Port. 86/B2
Pamplona, Sp. 86/E1
Pamplona, Col. 194/C3
Pampulha (int'l arpt.), Braz. 197/D1
Pāmpur, India 128/C2
Pamukova, Turk. 91/K5
Pan de Azúcar, PN, Chile 199/B2
Panaba, Mex. 186/D1
Panabo, Phil. 121/E6
Panāgar, India 126/B4
Panagyurishte, Bul. 91/G4
Panaitan (isl.), Indo. 122/B5
Panaji, India 131/K5
Panama (ctry.) 187/F4
Panamá (bay), Pan. 187/G4
Panamá (cap.), Pan. 187/G4
Panama (canal), Pan. 187/F4
Panama (gulf), Pan. 187/G4
Panama City, Fl, US 175/G4
Panama, Isthmus of (isth.), Pan. 187/F4
Panamá Viejo (ruin), Pan. 194/B2
Panamint (range), Ca, US 170/C3
Panao, Peru 198/B3
Panaro (riv.), It. 85/J4
Panay (isl.), Phil. 121/D5
Pancake (range), Nv, US 170/C3
Pančevo, Serb. 90/E3
Pančicev vrh (peak), Serb. 90/E4
Pancilet (res.), India 127/F4
Panciu, Rom. 91/H3
Pandamatenga, Bots. 147/E4
Pandharpur, India 131/L5
Pandino, It. 100/C2
Pando, Uru. 201/L11
Pāndoh, India 128/D4
Pandrup, Den. 80/C3
Pandua, India 127/G4
Panevėžys, Lith. 81/L4
Panfilov, Kaz. 112/D3
Pangai, Tonga 159/H6
Pangaion (peak), Gre. 89/J2
Pangani, Tanz. 146/C4
Pangani (riv.), Tanz. 146/C3
Pangkalanberandan, Indo. 122/A3
Pangkalaseang (cape), Indo. 123/F4
Pangkalpinang, Indo. 122/C4
Pangnirtung, Nun., Can. 165/K2
Panguipulli, Chile 200/B3
Panguitch, Ut, US 170/D3
Pangutaran, Phil. 123/F2
Pangutaran (isl.), Phil. 121/C6
Paniai (lake), Indo. 123/J4
Paniau (peak), Hi, US 166/R10
Pānihāti, India 127/G4
Pānīpat, India 128/D5
Paniqui, Phil. 121/D4
Panj (riv.), Afg. 131/K1
Panjwīn, Iraq 130/E1
Panke (riv.), Ger. 82/Q6
P'anmunjŏm, NKor. 115/D4
Panna, India 126/C3
Pannawonica, Austl. 154/C2
Pannikin (isl.), Austl. 156/F7
Pano Lefkara, Cyp. 133/C2
Panorama, Braz. 197/B2
Pantanal (lowland), Braz. 193/G7
Pantanal Matogrossense, PN, Braz. 193/G7
Pantelleria, It. 88/B4
Pantelleria (isl.), It. 88/C4
Pantigliate, It. 100/C2
Pantin, Fr. 72/K5
Pantoja, Peru 194/C5
Pantón, Sp. 86/B1
Pantukan, Phil. 121/E6
Pánuco (riv.), Mex. 182/B3
Pánuco, Mex. 186/B1
Panzhihua, China 125/H2
Panzós, Guat. 186/D3
Pão de Açúcar, Braz. 196/C3
Paola, It. 88/E3
Paola, Malta 88/M7
Paoli, Pa, US 180/C3
Paonia, Co, US 170/F3
Paonta Sahib, India 128/D4
Paoua, CAfr. 138/J6
Pápa, Hun. 90/C2
Papa Westray (isl.), Sc, UK 73/V14
Papagayo (gulf), CR 182/D5
Papaikou, Hi, US 166/U11
Papanduva, Braz. 197/B3
Papantla, Mex. 185/M6
Papaplaya, Peru 198/C2
Papenburg, Ger. 93/E2
Papendrecht, Neth. 92/B5
Paphos, Cyp. 133/C2
Paphos (dist.), Cyp. 133/C2
Papingut (peak), Alb. 89/G2
Papisoi (cape), Indo. 123/H4
Pappenheim, Ger. 96/D5
Papua (gulf), PNG 158/D5
Papua New Guinea (ctry.) 158/D5
Papudo, Chile 200/C2
Papunya, Austl. 155/F2
Pará (riv.), Braz. 193/H4
Pará (state), Braz. 196/A1
Pará (dist.), Sur. 195/H3
Pará (falls), Ven. 195/E3
Pará de Minas, Braz. 197/C1
Para, South (riv.), Austl. 155/M8
Para Wirra NP, Austl. 155/M8
Paraburdoo, Austl. 154/C2
Paracambi, Braz. 197/K7
Paracas (pen.), Peru 198/B4
Paracas, Reserva Nacional, Peru 198/B4
Paracatu, Braz. 196/A5
Paracatu (riv.), Braz. 196/A5
Paracel (isls.), China 125/K4
Paracho de Verduzco, Mex. 184/E5
Paraćin, Serb. 90/E4
Paracuru, Braz. 196/C1
Paradhísion (int'l arpt.), Gre. 132/B2
Paradip, India 124/E3
Paradis, La, US 179/P17
Paradise (valley), Az, US 179/R18
Paradise, Mo, US 179/D5
Paradise, Pa, US 180/B4
Paradise Valley, Az, US 179/S18
Paragominas, Braz. 196/A1
Paraguá (riv.), Bol. 192/F6
Paragua (riv.), Ven. 192/F2
Paraguaçu, Braz. 197/H6
Paraguaçu (riv.), Braz. 189/E4
Paraguaçu Paulista, Braz. 197/B2
Paraguai (riv.), SAm. 189/D5
Paraguaipoa, Ven. 194/D2
Paraguaná, Peninsula de (pen.), Ven. 192/D1
Paraguarí, Par. 199/E2
Paraguay (ctry.) 189/C5
Paraguay (riv.), Par. 199/E1
Paraíba (state), Braz. 196/C2
Paraíba do Sul, Braz. 197/K7
Paraíba do Sul (riv.), Braz. 197/H8
Paraibano, Braz. 196/B2
Paraibuna (riv.), Braz. 197/H8
Paraim (riv.), Braz. 196/A3
Parainen (Pargas), Fin. 81/K1
Paraíso, Mex. 186/C2
Paraíso, CR 187/F4
Paraíso do Norte de Goiás, Braz. 193/J6
Paraisópolis, Braz. 197/H7
Parakou, Ben. 145/F4
Paramaribo (cap.), Sur. 193/G2
Paramaribo (dist.), Sur. 195/H3
Parambu, Braz. 196/B2
Paramillo (peak), Col. 194/C3
Paramillo, PN, Col. 192/C2
Paramirim (riv.), Braz. 193/K6
Paramirim, Braz. 196/B4
Paramithiá, Gre. 89/G3
Paramount, Ca, US 178/F8
Paramus, NJ, US 181/J8
Paramushir (isl.), Rus. 109/Q5
Paraná, Arg. 199/D3
Paranã (riv.), Braz. 193/J6
Paraná (state), Braz. 197/B3
Paraná (riv.), SAm. 199/E3
Paraná Ibicuy (riv.), Arg. 201/J10
Paraná Urariá (riv.), Braz. 195/G5
Paranaguá, Braz. 197/B3
Paranaguá, Baía de (bay), Braz. 197/B3
Paranaíba (riv.), Braz. 193/J7
Paranaíba, Braz. 197/B1
Paranapanema (riv.), Braz. 199/F1
Paranapiacaba, Serra do (mts.), Braz. 199/G2
Paranatinga (riv.), Braz. 189/D4
Paranavaí, Braz. 199/F1
Parang, Phil. 123/F2
Paraopeba, Braz. 197/C1
Parapetí (riv.), Bol. 192/F7
Parati, Braz. 197/J8
Paratico, It. 100/C1
Paratinga, Braz. 196/B4
Paratinga (riv.), Braz. 197/H8
Paray-Vieille-Poste, Fr. 72/K5
Paràzinho, Braz. 196/D2
Pārbati (riv.), India 131/L4
Parbhani, India 131/L5
Parchim, Ger. 82/F2
Parczew, Pol. 83/M3
Pardes Hanna-Karkur, Isr. 133/F7
Pārdi, India 131/K4
Pardo (riv.), Braz. 193/J8
Pardone (cape), SAfr. 148/D4
Pardubice, Czh. 83/H3
Pardubický (pol. reg.), Czh. 83/J4
Pare, Indo. 122/D5
Pare (mts.), Tanz. 146/C3
Parece Vela (Okino-Tori-Shima) (isl.), Japan 109/N7
Parecis (mts.), Braz. 189/C4
Parede, Port. 87/P10
Paredes de Nava, Sp. 86/C1
Paredón, Mex. 186/C2
Paredones, Chile 200/C2
Parelhas, Braz. 196/C2
Parempuyre, Fr. 84/C4
Parenda, India 124/C4
Parent (lake), Qu, Can. 172/E1
Parentis-en-Born, Fr. 84/C4
Parepare, Indo. 123/E4
Parera, Arg. 200/D2
Parets del Valles, Sp. 87/L6
Pargny-sur-Saulx, Fr. 95/D6
Paria (riv.), Ut, US 170/E3
Paria (gulf), Trin.,Ven. 195/F2
Paria, Peninsula de (pen.), Ven. 192/F1
Pariacoto, Peru 198/B3
Pariaguán, Ven. 195/E2
Pariaman, Indo. 122/B4
Parikkala, Fin. 79/J3
Parima (riv.), Braz. 195/F4
Parima, Serra (mts.), Braz. 192/F3
Parinacota (peak), Bol. 198/D5
Parinari, Peru 198/C2
Pariñas (pt.), Peru 198/A2
Paringa, Austl. 157/B2
Parîngu Mare (peak), Rom. 91/F3
Parintins, Braz. 193/G4
Paris (cap.), Fr. 72/K5
Paris (dept.), Fr. 94/B6
Paris, Ar, US 171/J4
Paris, Tx, US 171/J4
Parita (bay), Pan. 187/F4
Park (range), Co, US 170/F2
Park (pt.), Eng, UK 74/A5
Park City, Ut, US 179/L12
Park City, Il, US 177/Q15
Park Falls, Wi, US 169/L4
Park Rapids, Mn, US 169/K4
Park Ridge, Il, US 177/Q16
Park Ridge, NJ, US 181/J7
Park River, ND, US 169/J3
Parkano, Fin. 79/G3
Parker, Tx, US 171/H4
Parker, Az, US 170/D4
Parker, Co, US 179/C3
Parkersburg, WV, US 172/D4
Parkes, Austl. 157/D2
Parkesburg, Pa, US 180/C4
Parkgate, NI, UK 76/B2
Parksdale, Mo, US 179/F9
Parkside, Pa, US 180/C4
Parkstetten, Ger. 97/F5
Parkton, Md, US 180/B4
Parkville, Mo, US 179/D5
Parkville, Md, US 180/B5
Parkville, Pa, US 180/B4
Parkway-Sacramento, Ca, US 177/L9
Parla, Sp. 87/N9
Parlakhemundi, India 124/D4
Parli, India 131/L5
Parma, Oh, US 172/D3
Parma (prov.), It. 100/C3
Parma (riv.), It. 100/D3
Parma, It. 100/D3
Parmain, Fr. 72/J4
Parnaguá, Braz. 196/A3
Parnaíba, Braz. 196/B1
Parnaíba (riv.), Braz. 189/E3
Parnamirim, Braz. 196/C3
Parnamirim, Braz. 193/L5
Parnarama, Braz. 196/B2
Parnassós (peak), Gre. 89/H3
Parnassós NP, Gre. 89/H3
Párnis (peak), Gre. 89/N8
Párnis Óros NP, Gre. 89/N8
Párnon (mts.), Gre. 89/H4
Pärnu (bay), Est. 81/L2
Pärnu, Est. 81/L2
P'aro-ho (lake), SKor. 115/D3
Paron, Fr. 84/E2
Parona di Valpolicella, It. 101/D2
Paroo (riv.), Austl. 157/C1
Páros (isl.), Gre. 89/J4
Páros, Gre. 89/J4
Parow, SAfr. 148/L10
Parowan, Ut, US 170/D3
Parpan, Swi. 99/F4
Parral, Chile 200/C3
Parras de la Fuente, Mex. 184/E3
Parrett (riv.), Eng, UK 74/D4
Parrita, CR 187/E4
Parry (isls.), NW,Nun., Can. 165/R7
Parry (bay), Nun., Can. 165/H2
Parry (chan.), Nun., Can. 164/F1
Parry Sound, On, Can. 172/D2
Parsberg, Ger. 97/E4
Parseierspitze (peak), Aus. 99/G3
Parshall, ND, US 169/H4
Parsippany-Troy Hills, NJ, US 181/H8
Parsnip (riv.), BC, Can. 168/C2
Pårtefjället (peak), Swe. 79/F2
Partenstein, Ger. 96/C2
Parthenay, Fr. 84/C3
Partille, Swe. 80/E3
Partinico, It. 88/C3
Partizansk, Rus. 113/P3
Partizánske, Slvk. 83/K4
Partridge (riv.), On, Can. 172/D1
Partūr, India 131/L5
Paru (riv.), Braz. 193/H4
Paru de Oeste (riv.), Braz. 189/D2
Paruro, Peru 198/D4
Pārvathīpuram, India 124/D4
Parys, SAfr. 148/D2
Pas-de-Calais (dept.), Fr. 94/A3
Pas de Morgins (pass), Fr. 98/C5
Pasadena, Tx, US 171/J5
Pasadena, Nf, Can. 173/K1
Pasadena, Md, US 180/B5
Pasadena, Ca, US 178/F7
Pasado (cape), Ecu. 194/A5
Pasaje, Ecu. 198/B1
Pasaman (peak), Indo. 122/B3
Pasān, India 126/D4
Pascagoula, Ms, US 175/F4
Paşcani, Rom. 91/H2
Pasching, Aus. 97/H6
Pasco, Wa, US 168/D4
Pasco (dept.), Peru 198/C3
Pascua (riv.), Chile 201/B6
Pascua, Isla de (Easter) (isl.), Chile 159/Q7
Pascuales, Ecu. 198/B1
Pasewalk, Ger. 80/E5
Pasian di Prato, It. 101/G1
Pasiano, It. 101/F1
Pasig, Phil. 121/D5
Pasinler, Turk. 132/E2
Pasión, Río de la (riv.), Guat. 186/D2
Pasłęk, Pol. 81/H4
Pasłęka (riv.), Pol. 83/L2
Pasley (cape), Austl. 154/D5
Pašman (isl.), Cro. 90/B4
Pasni, Pak. 131/H3
Paso de Indios, Arg. 200/C4
Paso de los Libres, Arg. 199/E2
Paso de los Toros, Uru. 201/K10
Paso de Ovejas, Mex. 185/N7
Paso del Macho, Mex. 185/N8
Paso del Planchón (peak), Chile 200/C2
Paso Robles (El Paso de Robles), Ca, US 170/B4
Pasrūr, Pak. 128/C3
Pass (peak), Yk, Can. 176/M3
Passa Quatro, Braz. 197/J7
Passagem Franca, Braz. 196/B2
Passaic (riv.), NJ, US 180/D2
Passaic, NJ, US 181/J8
Passau, Ger. 97/G5
Passero (pt.), It. 88/D4
Passo Fundo, Braz. 197/A4
Passo Fundo, Barragem do (res.), Braz. 197/A3
Passons, It. 101/G1
Passoré (prov.), Burk. 145/E3
Passos, Braz. 197/C2
Passwang (peak), Swi. 98/D3
Passy, Fr. 98/C6
Pastavy, Bela. 81/M4
Pastaza (riv.), Ecu.,Peru 198/B2
Pastaza (dept.), Ecu. 194/B5
Pastek (riv.), Pol. 81/J5
Pasto, Col. 194/B4
Pastol (bay), Ak, US 176/F3
Pastoriza, Sp. 86/B1
Pastos Bons, Braz. 196/A2
Pasuruan, Indo. 122/D5
Pásztó, Hun. 83/K5
Pata, Bol. 198/D4
Patagonia (phys. reg.), Arg. 200/D4
Patah (peak), Indo. 122/B4
Pātan, India 126/B4
Pātan, India 131/K4
Pataná (peak), Braz. 197/B3
Patapsco (riv.), Md, US 180/A5
Patapsco, Md, US 180/B4
Pataudi, India 128/D5
Pataz, Peru 198/B2
Patchogue, NY, US 181/E2
Paterna, Sp. 87/E3
Paternò, It. 88/D4
Paterson, NJ, US 181/J8
Pathalgaon, India 126/D4
Pathānkot, India 128/C3
Pathein (Bassein), Myan. 125/F4
Pathfinder (res.), Wy, US 168/G5
Pati, Indo. 122/D5
Patía (riv.), Col. 192/C3
Patía, Col. 194/B4
Patiāla, India 128/D4
Patikul, Phil. 123/F2
Patna, India 127/E3
Patna, Sc, UK 78/B6
Patnongon, Phil. 123/F1
Patnos, Turk. 132/E2
Pato Branco, Braz. 197/A3
Patoka (riv.), In, US 175/G2
Patos, Braz. 196/C2
Patos, Alb. 89/F2
Patos de Minas, Braz. 197/C1
Patos, Lagoa dos (lake), Braz. 199/F3
Patrai (gulf), Gre. 89/G3
Pátrai, Gre. 89/G3
Pātrasāer, India 127/F4
Patrātu, India 127/E4
Patricia (mt.), Austl. 155/F2
Patricio Lynch (isl.), Chile 201/A6
Patrocínio, Braz. 197/C1
Patscherkofel (peak), Aus. 99/H3
Pattani, Thai. 120/C5
Pattensen, Ger. 93/G4
Patti, India 128/C4
Patti, It. 88/D3
Pattoki, Pak. 128/B4
Pattukkottai, India 124/C5
Pattullo (mt.), BC, Can. 176/N4
Patuākhāli (pol. reg.), Bang. 127/G4
Patuākhāli, Bang. 127/H4
Patuca (riv.), Hon. 182/D5
Patuca (mts.), Hon. 186/E3
Patuca (pt.), Hon. 187/E3
Patuxent (riv.), Md, US 180/B5
Patuxent NWR, Md, US 180/B5
Patuxent River State Park, Md, US 180/B5
Pátý, Hun. 91/Q9
Pátzcuaro, Mex. 185/E5
Pau, Fr. 84/C5
Pau Brasil, Braz. 196/C4
Pau dos Ferros, Braz. 196/C2
Paucarbamba, Peru 198/C4
Paucartambo, Peru 198/C3
Paucartambo, Peru 198/D4
Pauillac, Fr. 84/C4
Pauini (riv.), Braz. 192/E5
Paulaya (riv.), Hon. 187/E3
Paulínia, Braz. 197/F7
Paulins Kill (riv.), NJ, US 180/D2
Paulistana, Braz. 196/B3
Paullo, It. 100/C2
Paulo Afonso, Braz. 196/C3
Paulo Afonso, PN de, Braz. 196/C3
Paulo Ramos, Braz. 196/A2
Paulpietersburg, SAfr. 149/E2
Pauls Valley, Ok, US 171/H4
Paulsboro, NJ, US 180/C4
Pauma Valley, Ca, US 178/D4
Paungde, Myan. 125/G4
Pavão, Braz. 196/B5
Pavel Banya, Bul. 89/J1
Pavia (prov.), It. 100/C2
Pavia, It. 100/C2
Pavie, Fr. 84/D5
Pavlikeni, Bul. 91/G4
Pavlodar (obl.), Kaz. 129/G2
Pavlodar, Kaz. 129/G2
Pavlof (vol.), Ak, US 176/F4
Pavlohrad, Ukr. 104/E2
Pavlovo, Rus. 102/J5
Pavone Canavese, It. 100/A2
Pavone del Mella, It. 100/D2
Pavullo nel Frignano, It. 101/D4
Paw Paw, Mi, US 172/C3
Pawan (riv.), Indo. 122/D4
Pawāyan, India 126/C1
Pawhuska, Ok, US 171/H3
Pawnee (riv.), Ks, US 171/G3
Pawtucket, RI, US 173/G3
Paxoí (isl.), Gre. 89/F3
Paxson, Ak, US 176/J3
Paxton, Austl. 157/D2
Pay-Khoy (mts.), Rus. 106/G3
Payakumbuh, Indo. 122/B4
Payerne, Swi. 98/C4
Payette (riv.), Id, US 168/D5
Payne (lake), Qu, Can. 165/J3
Paynesville, Austl. 157/C3
Pays de Caux (reg.), Fr. 84/D2
Pays de France (reg.), Fr. 72/K4
Pays de la Loire (reg.), Fr. 84/C3
Paysandú, Uru. 201/J10
Payson, Az, US 170/E4
Payson, Ut, US 170/E2
Payún (peak), Arg. 200/C3
Paz (riv.), Guat. 186/D3
Paz de Ariporo, Col. 194/D3
Paz de Río, Col. 194/C3
Pazar, Turk. 132/D1
Pazar, Turk. 105/G4
Pazarcık, Turk. 132/D2
Pazardzhik, Bul. 91/G4
Pazaryeri, Turk. 104/D5
Pazin, Cro. 90/A3
Peabiru, Braz. 197/A2
Peace (riv.), BC, Can. 164/D3
Peace Memorial Park, Japan 116/C3
Peaceful Valley, Co, US 179/B2
Peachland, BC, Can. 168/D3
Peachtree City, Ga, US 175/G3
Peak Charles NP, Austl. 154/D5
Peak District NP, Eng, UK 77/G5
Peak Hill, Austl. 154/C3
Peal de Becerro, Sp. 86/D4
Peapack-Gladstone, NJ, US 180/D2
Pearblossom, Ca, US 178/C1
Pearl (har.), Hi, US 166/W13
Pearl (riv.), La,Ms, US 175/F4
Pearl, Ms, US 175/F3
Pearl and Hermes (reef), Hi, US 159/H2
Pearl Beach, Mi, US 177/G6
Pearl City, Hi, US 166/W13
Pearl River (estu.), China 121/B3
Pearl River, La, US 179/Q16
Pearl River, NY, US 181/J7
Pearland, Ca, US 178/B1
Pearsall, Tx, US 171/H5
Pearson (int'l arpt.), On, Can. 173/Q8
Pearston, SAfr. 148/D4
Peary (chan.), Nun., Can. 165/R7
Pease (riv.), Tx, US 171/G4
Pebane, Moz. 147/G4
Pebas, Peru 198/D1
Pebble (isl.), Mald. 201/E6
Peccia, Swi. 99/E5
Peccioli, It. 101/D5
Pécel, Hun. 91/R10
Pech de Guillaument (peak), Fr. 84/E5
Pechanga Ind. Res., Ca, US 178/C4
Pechora, Rus. 103/N2
Pechora (bay), Rus. 103/M1
Pechora (riv.), Rus. 109/C3
Peckham, Co, US 179/C2
Peconic (riv.), NY, US 181/F2
Pecos, Tx, US 174/C4
Pecos (riv.), Tx, US 174/C4
Pecq, Belg. 94/C2
Pecquencourt, Fr. 94/C3
Pécs, Hun. 90/D2
Peculiar, Mo, US 179/E6
Pecy, Fr. 72/M6
Pedasí, Pan. 187/F5
Pedder (lake), Austl. 157/C4
Pedemonte, It. 101/D2
Pedernales (riv.), Tx, US 185/F2
Pederneiras, Braz. 197/B2
Pedley, Ca, US 178/C3
Pedra Azul, Braz. 196/B5
Pedra Lume, CpV. 135/K10
Pedralva, Braz. 197/H7
Pedregal, Ven. 194/D2
Pedreguer, Sp. 87/F3
Pedreiras, Braz. 197/G7
Pedreiras, Braz. 196/A2
Pedricktown, NJ, US 180/C4
Pedro (pt.), SrL. 124/D6
Pedro Avelino, Braz. 196/C2
Pedro Bay, Ak, US 176/H4
Pedro Betancourt, Cuba 187/F1
Pedro Carbo, Ecu. 194/A5
Pedro Cays (isl.), Jam. 183/F4
Pedro II, Braz. 196/B2
Pedro IV (isl.), Braz. 195/E4
Pedro Juan Caballero, Par. 199/E1
Pedro Leopoldo, Braz. 197/C1
Pedro Luro, Arg. 200/E3
Pedro Osório, Braz. 197/A4
Peebles, Sc, UK 78/C5
Peedamulla Abor. Land, Austl. 154/B2
Peekskill, NY, US 180/E1
Peel (inlet), Austl. 154/B5
Peel (isl.), Austl. 156/F6
Peel (sound), Nun., Can. 164/G1
Peel (co.), On, Can. 173/Q8
Peel (riv.), Yk, Can. 164/C2
Peel, IM, UK 76/D3
Peel Fell (peak), Eng, UK 78/D6
Peene (riv.), Ger. 80/E5
Peer, Belg. 95/E1
Pegasus (bay), NZ 159/S11
Pegnitz, Ger. 97/E3
Pegnitz (riv.), Ger. 82/F4
Pego, Sp. 87/E3
Pego do Altar, Barragem de (res.), Port. 86/A3
Pegognaga, It. 101/D3
Pegwell (bay), Eng, UK 75/H4
Pehlivanköy, Turk. 91/H5
Pehowa, India 128/D5
Pehuajó, Arg. 200/E2
Pehuenche (pass), Chile 200/C2
Pei Xian, China 114/D4
Peine, Ger. 93/H4
Peipus (lake), Est.,Rus. 81/M2
Peiting, Ger. 99/G2
Peixe (riv.), Braz. 197/B2
Peixoto, Represa de (res.), Braz. 197/C2
Pekalongan, Indo. 122/C5
Pekan, Malay. 122/B3
Pekan Nanas, Malay. 122/B3
Pekhora (riv.), Rus. 103/W9
Pekin, Il, US 169/L5
Pelada, Pampa (plain), Arg. 200/C5
Pelado (vol.), Mex. 185/Q10
Pelagie (isls.), It. 88/C5
Peleaga (peak), Rom. 90/F3
Pelee (isl.), On, Can. 172/D3
Pelee (pt.), On, Can. 165/H4
Pelée (peak), Mart., Fr. 183/N9
Pelham, On, Can. 173/R9
Pelham, Al, US 175/G3
Pelham, NY, US 181/K8
Pelham Bay Park, NY, US 181/K8
Pelham Manor, NY, US 181/K8
Pelhřimov, Czh. 83/H4
Pelican (mts.), Ab, Can. 168/E2
Pelican (lake), Sk, Can. 169/H2
Pelican, Ak, US 176/L4
Pelican Narrows, Sk, Can. 169/H2
Pelindā, Ponta de (pt.), GBis. 144/A4
Pelister (peak), FYROM 89/G2
Pelister NP, FYROM 89/G2
Peljekaise NP, Swe. 79/F2
Pelješac (pen.), Cro. 89/E1
Pelješec (pen.), Cro. 90/C4
Pell Lake, Wi, US 177/P14
Pélla (ruin), Gre. 89/H2
Pélla, Gre. 89/H2
Pellegrini, Arg. 200/E3
Pellestrina, It. 101/F2
Pello, Fin. 102/E2
Pelly (riv.), Yk, Can. 164/C2
Pelly (bay), Nun., Can. 164/H2
Pelly Bay, Nun., Can. 164/H2
Peloponnesus (reg.), Gre. 89/G3
Peloritani, Monti (mts.), It. 88/D4
Pelotas (riv.), Braz. 199/F2
Pelotas, Braz. 197/A4
Pelplin, Pol. 81/H5
Pemali (cape), Indo. 123/F5
Pemali (cape), Indo. 123/F4
Pematangsiantar, Indo. 122/A3
Pemba, Moz. 147/H3
Pemba (isl.), Tanz. 147/G2
Pemba North (prov.), Tanz. 146/C4
Pemba South (prov.), Tanz. 146/C4
Pemberton, Austl. 154/C5
Pemberton, BC, Can. 168/C3
Pemberton, NJ, US 180/D4
Pembina (riv.), ND, US 168/E2
Pembina, ND, US 169/J3
Pembroke, On, Can. 172/E2
Pembroke, Wal, UK 74/B3
Pembrokeshire (co.), Wal, UK 74/A3
Pembrokeshire Coast NP, Wal, UK 74/A3
Pembury, Eng, UK 75/G4
Pemuco, Chile 200/B3
Pen Argyl, Pa, US 180/C2
Pen, The (lake), La, US 179/P17
Pen-y-Ghent (peak), Eng, UK 77/F3
Pen-y-Gogarth (pt.), Wal, UK 76/E5
Pen y Gurnos (peak), Wal, UK 74/C2
Peña Blanca (mtn.), Pan. 187/F4
Peña de Cerredo (mtn.), Sp. 86/C1
Peñafiel, Sp. 86/C2
Penafiel, Port. 86/A2
Peñaflor, Chile 200/N8
Penalva, Braz. 196/A1
Penamacor, Port. 86/B2
Penápolis, Braz. 197/B2
Peñaranda de Bracamonte, Sp. 86/C2
Peñarroya (peak), Sp. 87/E2
Peñarroya-Pueblonuevo, Sp. 86/C3
Penarth, Wal, UK 74/C4
Peñas (cape), Sp. 86/C1
Peñas (cape), Arg. 201/D7
Penas, Golfo de (gulf), Chile 199/A6
Peñasco (riv.), NM, US 171/F4
Pench (riv.), India 126/B5
Penchard, Fr. 72/L5
Penco, Chile 200/B3
Pend Oreille (lake), Id, US 168/D4
Pendelikón (peak), Gre. 89/N8
Pendembu, SLeo. 144/C4
Pendências, Braz. 196/C2
Pendjar (riv.), Burk. 145/F4
Pendjari, PN de la, Ben. 138/F5
Pendle (hill), Eng, UK 77/F4
Pendleton, Or, US 168/D4
Peneda-Gerês NP, Port. 86/A2
Penedo, Braz. 196/C3
Penetanguishene, On, Can. 172/E2
Penghu (Pescadores) (isls.), Tai. 121/C3
Penglai, China 114/E3
Penguin, Austl. 157/C4
Penha, Braz. 197/B3
Penhold, Ab, Can. 168/E2
Penibético, Sistema (range), Sp. 86/C4
Penice (peak), It. 100/C3
Peniche, Port. 86/A3
Penicuik, Sc, UK 78/C5
Península de Paria, PN, Ven. 195/F2
Peñíscola, Sp. 87/F2
Penitente, Serra do (mts.), Braz. 193/J5
Penmaenmawr, Wal, UK 76/E5
Penmarch, Fr. 84/A3
Penmarc'h, Pointe de (pt.), Fr. 84/A3
Penn Forest (res.), Pa, US 180/C2
Penn Hills, Pa, US 172/E3
Penn Yan, NY, US 172/E3
Penna, Punta della (cape), It. 88/D1
Penne (pt.), It. 89/E2
Penne, It. 88/C1
Penner (riv.), India 124/C5
Pennine Alps (mts.), Swi. 85/G4
Pennine Chain (mts.), Eng, UK 77/F2
Pennington, NJ, US 180/D3
Pennino (peak), It. 85/K5
Penns Creek (mtn.), Pa, US 180/A2
Penns Grove, NJ, US 180/C4
Penns Park, Pa, US 180/D3
Pennsauken, NJ, US 180/C4
Pennsburg, Pa, US 180/C3
Pennsville, NJ, US 180/C4
Pennsylvania (state), US 172/E3
Penny (str.), Nun., Can. 165/S7
Penobscot (riv.), Me, US 173/G2
Penola, Austl. 157/B3
Peñón Blanco, Mex. 184/D3
Penon de Al Hoceima (isl.), Sp. 142/C2
Penonomé, Pan. 187/F4
Penrhyn Mawr (pt.), Wal, UK 76/D6
Penrhyn Mawr (pt.), IM, UK 76/D5
Penrith, Eng, UK 77/F2

264

Pensa – Place

Pensacola, Fl, US 175/G4
Pensacola (mts.), Ant. 202/X
Pense, Sk, Can. 169/G3
Penshurst, Austl. 157/B3
Pentagon Fed. Govt. Res., Va, US 180/A6
Pentecost (isl.), Van. 158/F6
Pentecoste, Braz. 196/C1
Penteleu (peak), Rom. 91/H3
Penthalaz, Swi. 98/C4
Penticton, BC, Can. 168/D3
Pentire (pt.), Eng, UK 74/B5
Pentland, Austl. 156/B3
Pentland (hills), Sc, UK 78/C5
Pentland Firth (inlet), Sc, UK 73/V14
Peñuelas, PN, Chile 200/N8
Penwith (pen.), Eng, UK 74/A6
Penza, Rus. 105/H1
Penzance, Eng, UK 74/A6
Penzberg, Ger. 99/H2
Penzenskaya Oblast, Rus. 105/G1
Penzhina (riv.), Rus. 107/S3
Penzhina (bay), Rus. 107/S3
Penzing, Ger. 99/G1
Penzlin, Ger. 82/G2
Peoria, Az, US 179/R18
Pepe (cape), Cuba 187/F1
Pepeekeo, Hi, US 166/U11
Pepeekeo (pt.), Hi, US 166/U11
Pepel, SLeo. 144/B4
Pepinster, Belg. 95/E2
Pequannock, NJ, US 181/H8
Pequeña Isla del Maíz (isl.), Nic. 187/F3
Pequest (riv.), NJ, US 180/D2
Perabumulih, Indo. 122/B4
Perales (riv.), Sp. 87/M9
Peralta, Sp. 86/E1
Pérama, Gre. 89/J5
Pérama, Gre. 89/N9
Percé, Qu, Can. 173/H1
Percée (peak), Fr. 98/C6
Perche, Collines du (hills), Fr. 84/D2
Perchtoldsdorf, Aus. 91/N7
Percival (lakes), Austl. 154/E2
Percy (isls.), Austl. 156/C3
Percy Isles (chan.), Austl. 156/C3
Perdekop, SAfr. 149/E2
Pérdhika, Gre. 89/G3
Perdida (riv.), Braz. 196/A3
Perdido (mtn.), Sp. 87/F1
Peregian Beach, Austl. 156/D4
Pereira, Col. 192/C3
Pereira Barreto, Braz. 197/B2
Pereiro, Braz. 196/C2
Perelló, Sp. 87/F2
Perenjori, Austl. 154/C4
Peretola (int'l arpt.), It. 101/E5
Perg, Aus. 97/H6
Pergamino, Arg. 200/E2
Pergamum (ruin), Turk. 132/A2
Pergine Valsugana, It. 99/H5
Pergola, It. 85/K5
Péribonca (riv.), Qu, Can. 173/G1
Perico, Cuba 187/F1
Pericos, Mex. 184/D3
Pericos, Mex. 184/D4
Périgueux, Fr. 84/D4
Perijá, Sierra de (mts.), Col. 192/D2
Peristéra (isl.), Gre. 89/H3
Peristéri, Gre. 89/N8
Perito Moreno, Arg. 200/C5
Perito Moreno, PN, Arg. 199/B6
Perkasie, Pa, US 180/C3
Perl, Ger. 95/F5
Perlas (lag.), Nic. 182/E5
Perlas (pt.), Nic. 187/F3
Perleberg, Ger. 82/F2
Perlez, Serb. 90/E3
Perlis (state), Malay. 120/B5
Perm', Rus. 103/N4
Permskaya Oblast, Rus. 103/N4
Përmet, Alb. 89/G2
Pernambuco (state), Braz. 196/C3
Pernate, It. 100/B2
Pernes-les-Fontaines, Fr. 84/F4
Pernik, Bul. 90/F4
Perniö, Fin. 81/K1
Peron (pen.), Austl. 154/B3
Péronne, Fr. 94/B4
Perote, Mex. 185/M7
Pérouges, Fr. 98/B6
Perpignan, Fr. 84/E5
Perray (riv.), Fr. 72/H6
Perrigny, Fr. 98/B4
Perris (res.), Ca, US 178/C3
Perris, Ca, US 178/C3
Perris State Rec. Area, Ca, US 178/C3
Perros-Guirec, Fr. 84/B2
Perrot, Île (isl.), Qu, Can. 173/N7
Perry (riv.), Nun., Can. 164/F2
Perry, Fl, US 175/H4
Perry, Ga, US 175/H3
Perry, Ok, US 171/H3
Perry (co.), Pa, US 180/A3
Perry, Ut, US 179/J11
Perry Hall, Md, US 180/B5
Perryman, Md, US 180/B5
Perryton, Tx, US 171/G3
Perryville, Ak, US 176/G4
Perryville, Md, US 180/B4
Persan, Fr. 72/J4
Persian (gulf), Asia 130/E3
Perstorp, Swe. 80/E3
Perth, Austl. 154/K6
Perth, Austl. 157/C4
Perth (int'l arpt.), Austl. 154/K6
Perth, On, Can. 172/E2
Perth, Sc, UK 78/C4
Perth Amboy, NJ, US 181/H9
Perth nd Kinross (pol. reg.), Sc, UK 78/C4
Perth Zoo, Austl. 154/K6
Pertuis, Fr. 84/F5
Pertuis Breton (inlet), Fr. 84/C3
Pertusato (cape), Fr. 88/A2
Peru (ctry.) 198/C3
Peru, Il, US 169/L5
Peru, In, US 172/C3
Perućačko (lake), Bosn. 90/D4
Perugia, It. 85/K5
Peruíbe, Braz. 197/G9
Peruque, Mo, US 179/F8
Perushtitsa, Bul. 91/G4
Péruwelz, Belg. 94/C2
Pervari, Turk. 132/E2
Pervomays'k, Ukr. 91/K1
Pervomaysk, Rus. 103/J5
Pervoural'sk, Rus. 103/N4
Perwez, Belg. 95/D2
Péry, Swi. 98/D3
Pesa (riv.), It. 101/E5
Pesagi (peak), Indo. 122/B4
Pesaro, It. 101/F5
Pesaro e Urbino (prov.), It. 101/F5
Pescadores (Penghu) (isls.), China 121/C3
Pescantina, It. 101/D2
Pescara, It. 88/D1
Peschanyy (cape), Kaz. 105/J4
Pescia, It. 101/D5
Peseux, Swi. 98/C4
Pesha (riv.), Rus. 103/L2
Peshāwar, Pak. 128/A2
Peshawar (int'l arpt.), Pak. 128/A2
Peshtera, Bul. 91/G4
Peshtigo, Wi, US 169/M4
Peshtigo (riv.), Wi, US 172/B2
Pesmes, Fr. 98/B3
Peso da Régua, Port. 86/B2
Pesqueira, Braz. 196/C3
Pessac, Fr. 84/C4
Pest (prov.), Hun. 90/D2
Pestovkoye (lake), Rus. 103/W9
Pestovo, Rus. 102/G4
Petaḥ Tiqwa, Isr. 133/F7
Petal, Ms, US 175/F4
Petalión (gulf), Gre. 89/J4
Petaluma (riv.), Ca, US 177/J10
Pétange, Lux. 95/E4
Petare, Ven. 192/E1
Pétas, Gre. 89/G3
Petatlán (riv.), Mex. 184/D3
Petatlán, Mex. 185/E5
Petauke, Zam. 147/F3
Petawawa (riv.), On, Can. 172/E2
Petawawa, On, Can. 172/E2
Peten Itzá (lake), Guat. 186/D2
Petenwell (lake), Wi, US 169/L4
Peter (isl.), Nor. 202/U
Peterborough, Austl. 155/H5
Peterborough, On, Can. 172/E2
Peterborough, Eng, UK 75/F1
Peterborough (co.), Eng, UK 75/F1
Peterhead, Sc, UK 78/E1
Peterlee, Eng, UK 77/G2
Petermann Abor. Land, Austl. 155/F3
Peteroa (vol.), Chile 200/C2
Petersaurach, Ger. 96/D4
Petersberg, Ger. 96/C1
Petersburg, Ak, US 176/M4
Petersfield, Eng, UK 75/F4
Petershagen, Ger. 93/F4
Petershagen, Ger. 82/Q6
Petershausen, Ger. 97/E6
Peterson, Ut, US 179/K11
Pétervására, Hun. 83/L4
Petilia Policastro, It. 88/E3
Pétionville, Haiti 187/H2
Petit Goâve, Haiti 187/H2
Petit Lac Manicouagan (lake), Qu, Can. 173/H1
Petit Loango, PN du, Gabon 147/A1
Petit-Noir, Fr. 98/B4
Petit Rosne (riv.), Fr. 72/J4
Petitcodiac, NB, Can. 173/H2
Petite Miquelon (isl.), StP., Fr. 173/K2
Petite Rivière de l'Artibonite, Haiti 187/H2
Petite Rivière Noire (peak), Mrts. 149/T15
Petite-Rosselle, Fr. 95/F5
Petitt Morin (riv.), Fr. 84/E2
Petkeljärven NP, Fin. 102/F3
Petlād, India 131/K4
Petlalcingo, Mex. 186/B2
Peto, Mex. 186/D1
Petorca, Chile 200/C2
Petoskey, Mi, US 172/C2
Petra (Baţrā') (ruin), Jor. 133/D4
Petra (isls.), Rus. 107/M2
Petrel, Sp. 87/E3
Petrella (peak), It. 88/C2
Petrich, Bul. 91/F4
Petrified Forest NP, Az, US 170/E4
Petrila, Rom. 91/F3
Petrodvorets, Rus. 103/S7
Petrokhanski Prokhod (pass), Bul. 89/H1
Petrokrepost' (bay), Rus. 103/U7
Petrolândia, Braz. 196/C3
Petrolina, Braz. 196/B3
Petropavl, Kaz. 129/E2
Petropavlovsk-Kamchatskiy, Rus. 107/R4
Petrópolis, Braz. 197/K7
Petrovaradin, Serb. 90/D3
Petrovsk, Rus. 105/H1
Petrovsk-Zabaykal'skiy, Rus. 112/J1
Petrozavodsk, Rus. 102/G3
Petrus Steyn, SAfr. 148/E2
Petrusburg, SAfr. 148/D3
Petrusville, SAfr. 148/D3
Pettenbach, Aus. 97/H7
Petteril (riv.), Eng, UK 77/F2
Petzeck (peak), Aus. 85/K3
Peuerbach, Aus. 97/G6
Peulik (mt.), Ak, US 176/G4
Peumo, Chile 200/N9
Pevely, Mo, US 179/G9
Pewaukee (lake), Wi, US 177/X13
Pewaukee, Wi, US 177/P13
Peyrehorade, Fr. 84/C5
Peza (riv.), Rus. 103/K2
Pézenas, Fr. 84/E5
Pfaffenhausen, Ger. 99/G1
Pfaffenhofen an der Ilm, Ger. 96/D6
Pfaffenhofen an der Ilm, Ger. 97/E5
Pfaffenhoffen, Fr. 95/G6
Pfäffikon, Swi. 99/E3
Pfaffing, Ger. 97/F6
Pfaffnau, Swi. 98/D3
Pfahl (ridge), Ger. 97/F4
Pfälzer Wald (mts.), Ger. 95/G5
Pfälzerwald (mts.), Ger. 96/A4
Pfalzgrafenweiler, Ger. 96/B5
Pfarrhof Esternberg, Aus. 97/G5
Pfarrkirchen, Ger. 97/F6
Pfatter, Ger. 97/F5
Pfeffenhausen, Ger. 97/E5
Pfettrach (riv.), Ger. 97/E5
Pfieffe (riv.), Ger. 93/G6
Pfinztal, Ger. 96/B5
Pforzheim, Ger. 96/B5
Pfreimd, Ger. 97/F3
Pfreimd (riv.), Ger. 97/F3
Pfronstetten, Ger. 99/F1
Pfronten, Ger. 99/G2
Pfroslkopf (peak), Aus. 99/G4
Pfullendorf, Ger. 99/F2
Pfunds, Aus. 99/G4
Pfungstadt, Ger. 96/B3
Phagwāra, India 128/C4
Phalauda, India 128/D5
Phalempin, Fr. 94/C2
Phālia, Pak. 128/B3
Phalodi, India 131/K3
Phalsbourg, Fr. 95/G6
Phan Rang, Viet. 120/E4
Phan Thiet, Viet. 120/E4
Phanat Nikhom, Thai. 120/C3
Phang Hoei (range), Thai. 120/C3
Phangnga, Thai. 120/B4
Phanom Dongrak (mts.), Thai. 125/H5
Pharr, Tx, US 174/D5
Phatthalung, Thai. 120/C5
Phaya Fo (peak), Thai. 120/C2
Phayao, Thai. 120/B2
Phelan, Ca, US 178/C2
Phenix City, Al, US 175/G3
Phet Buri, Thai. 120/B3
Phetchabun, Thai. 120/C2
Phichit, Thai. 120/C2
Philadelphia, Ms, US 175/F3
Philadelphia, Pa, US 180/C4
Philadelphia (int'l arpt.), Pa, US 180/C4
Philip, SD, US 169/H4
Philip S.W. Goldson (int'l arpt.), Belz. 186/D2
Philippeville, Belg. 95/D3
Philippi, WV, US 172/D4
Philippine (sea), Asia 121/D4
Philippines (ctry.) 121/D5
Philippsburg, Ger. 96/B4
Philipsburg, Mt, US 168/E4
Philipsdam (dam), Neth. 92/B5
Philipstown, SAfr. 148/D3
Phillaur, India 128/C4
Phillipsburg, NJ, US 180/C2
Phimai (ruin), Thai. 120/C3
Phitsanulok, Thai. 120/C2
Phnom Penh (Phnum Pénh) (cap.), Camb. 120/D4
Phnum Penh (int'l arpt.), Camb. 120/D4
Pho (pt.), Thai. 120/C5
Phoenix (cap.), Az, US 179/R19
Phoenix, La, US 179/Q17
Phoenix (isls.), Kiri. 159/H5
Phoenix Park, Ire. 76/B5
Phoenix Sky Harbor (int'l arpt.), Az, US 179/S19
Phoenixville, Pa, US 180/C3
Phongsali, Laos 125/H3
Phou Bia (peak), Laos 120/C2
Phou Huatt (peak), Viet. 125/H4
Phou Loi (peak), Laos 125/H3
Phou Xai Lai Leng (peak), Laos 120/D2
Phra Nakhon Si Ayutthaya, Thai. 120/C3
Phra Thong (isl.), Thai. 120/B4
Phrae, Thai. 120/C2
Phu Hin Rong Kla NP, Thai. 120/C2
Phu Kradung NP, Thai. 120/C2
Phu Luong (peak), Viet. 125/H3
Phu Phan NP, Thai. 120/D2
Phu Quoc (isl.), Viet. 125/H5
Phu Rua NP, Thai. 120/C2
Phu Tho, Viet. 125/J3
Phuket (isl.), Thai. 125/G6
Phuket, Thai. 120/B5
Phularwan, Pak. 128/B3
Phūlpur, India 126/D3
Piaçabuçu, Braz. 196/C3
Piacenza (prov.), It. 100/C2
Piacenza, It. 100/C2
Piadena, It. 100/D2
Pian di Serra (peak), It. 101/F6
Pian-Upe Game Rsv., Ugan. 146/B2
Piancastagnaio, It. 88/B1
Piancó, Braz. 196/C2
Pianello val Tidone, It. 100/C3
Pianezza, It. 100/A2
Piangipane, It. 101/F4
Pianoro, It. 101/E4
Pianosa (isl.), It. 88/A1
Piarco (int'l arpt.), Trin. 195/F2
Piaseczno, Pol. 83/L2
Piatra Neamţ, Rom. 91/H2
Piauí (riv.), Braz. 196/B3
Piauí (state), Braz. 196/B2
Piave (riv.), It. 85/K3
Piazza, It. 100/D1
Piazza, It. 100/D1
Piazza al Serchio, It. 100/D4
Piazza Armerina, It. 88/D4
Piazza Brembana, It. 99/F6
Piazzola sul Brenta, It. 101/E1
Pic (riv.), On, Can. 172/C1
Pic de Nore (peak), Fr. 84/E5
Pic d'Orhy (peak), Fr. 84/C5
Pic du Canigou (peak), Fr. 84/E5
Pica, Chile 192/E8
Picacho del Centinela (peak), Mex. 184/E2
Picachos, Cerro Dos (peak), Mex. 184/B2
Picardie (pol. reg.), Fr. 84/E2
Picardy (reg.), Fr. 94/B4
Picatinny Arsenal, NJ, US 180/D2
Picayune, Ms, US 175/F4
Piccolo (lag.), It. 89/E2
Pichanaci, Peru 198/D5
Pichanal, Arg. 199/D1
Pichidegua, Chile 200/N9
Pichilemu, Chile 200/B2
Pichincha (dept.), Ecu. 194/B4
Pichincha, Ecu. 194/B5
Pichl bei Wels, Aus. 97/G6
Pichor, India 126/B3
Pichucalco, Mex. 186/C2
Pickens, Ms, US 171/K4
Pickering, On, Can. 173/R8
Pickering, Vale of (valley), Eng, UK 77/H3
Pickle Lake, On, Can. 169/L3
Picnic Bay, Austl. 156/B2
Pico (isl.), Azor., Port. 87/S12
Pico da Neblina, PN do, Braz. 192/F3
Pico de Orizaba, PN, Mex. 185/M7
Pico Rivera, Ca, US 178/F8
Pico Truncado, Arg. 200/D5
Picos, Braz. 196/B2
Picota, Peru 198/B2
Picsi, Peru 198/B2
Picton, On, Can. 172/E3
Pictou, NS, Can. 173/J2
Picture Rocks, Pa, US 180/B1
Pictured Rocks Nat'l Lakeshore, Mi, US 169/M4
Pictured Rocks Nat'l Lakeshore, Mi, US 172/C2
Picuí, Braz. 196/C2
Piddle (riv.), Eng, UK 74/D5
Pidurutagala (peak), SrL. 124/D6
Piedade, Port. 87/P10
Piedade do Rio Grande, Braz. 197/J6
Piedecuesta, Col. 194/C3
Piedimulera, It. 99/E5
Piedmont (upland), US 175/H3
Piedmont, Ok, US 179/M14
Piedmont, Ca, US 177/K11
Piedra Grande, Ven. 194/D2
Piedrabuena, Sp. 86/C3
Piedrahita, Sp. 86/C2
Piedras (pt.), Arg. 201/K11
Piedras Coloradas, Uru. 201/K10
Piedras Negras, Mex. 185/E2
Piedras Negras, Mex. 185/N8
Piedras, Río de las (riv.), Peru 192/D6
Piedritas, Arg. 200/E2
Piekary Śląskie, Pol. 83/K3
Piekenierskloof (pass), SAfr. 148/L10
Pieksämäki, Fin. 102/E3
Pielinen (lake), Fin. 79/J3
Piemonte (prov.), It. 85/G4
Pieniński NP, Pol. 83/L4
Piennes, Fr. 95/E5
Pieńsk, Pol. 83/H3
Piera, Sp. 87/K6
Pierce, Ne, US 169/J5
Pierce, Co, US 179/C1
Pierceland, Sk, Can. 168/F2
Pieris, It. 101/G1
Piermont, NY, US 181/K7
Pierowall, Sc, UK 73/V14
Pierre (cap.), SD, US 169/H4
Pierre-de-Bresse, Fr. 98/B4
Pierre-Levée, Fr. 72/M5
Pierrefitte-sur-Seine, Fr. 72/K5
Pierrefonds, Qu, Can. 173/N7
Pierrefontaine-les-Varans, Fr. 98/C3
Pierrelatte, Fr. 84/F4
Pierrelaye, Fr. 72/J4
Pierrevert, Fr. 84/F5
Pierry, Fr. 94/C5
Piešťany, Slvk. 83/J4
Piesting (riv.), Aus. 91/P7
Piet Retief, SAfr. 149/E2
Pieterlen, Swi. 98/D3
Pietermaritzburg, SAfr. 149/E3
Pietersburg, SAfr. 147/E5
Pietra Ligure, It. 100/B4
Pietralunga, It. 101/F6
Pietramelara, It. 88/D2
Pietravecchia (peak), It. 100/A5
Pietrosul (peak), Rom. 91/G2
Pietrosul (peak), Rom. 91/G2
Pieve del Cairo, It. 100/B2
Pieve di Cento, It. 101/E3
Pieve di Soligo, It. 101/F1
Pieve di Teco, It. 100/A4
Pieve Emanuele, It. 100/C2
Pieve Ligure, It. 100/C4
Pieve Porto Morone, It. 100/C2
Pieve Santo Stefano, It. 101/F5
Pieve Vergonte, It. 99/E6
Pievepelago, It. 100/D4
Pigeon (lake), Ab, Can. 168/E2
Pigeon (riv.), On, Can. 164/G4
Piggott, Ar, US 171/K3
Pigs (bay), Cuba 182/E3
Pigüé, Arg. 200/E3
Pigüm (isl.), SKor. 115/C5
Pihāni, India 126/C2
Pijijiapan, Mex. 186/C3
Pijnacker, Neth. 92/B4
Pijol (peak), Hon. 186/E3
Pike (co.), Pa, US 180/C1
Pikelot (isl.), Micr. 158/D4
Pikes Creek (res.), Pa, US 180/B1
Pikesville, Md, US 180/B5
Piketberg, SAfr. 148/L10
Pikeville, Ky, US 172/D4
Pikit, Phil. 121/D6
Pila, Arg. 201/J12
Piła, Pol. 83/J2
Pilanesberg (range), SAfr. 148/P12
Pilani, India 128/C5
Pilão Arcado, Braz. 196/B3
Pilar, Arg. 200/E1
Pilar, Braz. 196/D3
Pilar, Par. 199/E2
Pilar, Phil. 121/D5
Pilatus (peak), Swi. 99/E4
Pilaya (riv.), Bol. 192/F8
Pilchuck (riv.), Wa, US 177/D1
Pilcomayo (riv.), SAm. 197/D1
Pili, Phil. 121/D5
Pīlībhīt, India 126/B1
Pilica (riv.), Pol. 83/L3
Pilion (peak), Gre. 89/H3
Pilis, Hun. 90/D2
Pilis (peak), Hun. 91/Q9
Pilis (mts.), Hun. 91/R9
Piliscsaba, Hun. 91/Q9
Pilisvörösvár, Hun. 91/Q9
Pilkhua, India 128/D5
Pillar (cape), Austl. 157/C4
Pillar (peak), Eng, UK 77/E3
Pillar (pt.), Ca, US 177/J12
Pilliga, Austl. 157/D1
Pillon, Col du (pass), Swi. 98/D5
Pillow, Pa, US 180/B2
Pilões, Serra dos (mtn.), Braz. 196/A5
Pilos, Gre. 89/G4
Pilot (mtn.), Tn, US 172/C4
Pilot Point, Ak, US 176/G4
Pilot Station, Ak, US 176/F3
Pilsting, Ger. 97/F5
Pima, Az, US 170/E4
Pimpri-Chinchwad, India 131/K5
Piña (pt.), Pan. 187/G5
Pináculo (peak), Arg. 201/B6
Pinal, Az, US 179/R19
Pinamar, Arg. 201/F3
Pinang (cape), Malay. 122/A2
Pinang (isl.), Malay. 122/A2
Pinar del Río, Cuba 187/F1
Pınarbaşı, Turk. 132/D2
Pınarhisar, Turk. 91/H5
Piñas, Ecu. 198/B1
Pinatubo (mt.), Phil. 121/D4
Pinawa, Mb, Can. 169/K3
Pincher Creek, Ab, Can. 168/E3
Pinconning, Mi, US 172/D3
Pîncota, Rom. 90/E2
Pincourt, Qu, Can. 173/N7
Pińczów, Pol. 83/L3
Pind Dādan Khān, Pak. 128/B3
Pindamonhangaba, Braz. 197/H7
Pindaré (riv.), Braz. 193/J4
Pindaré-Mirim, Braz. 196/A1
Píndhos NP, Gre. 89/G3
Pindi Bhattiān, Pak. 128/B4
Pindi Gheb, Pak. 128/B3
Pindobaçu, Braz. 196/B3
Píndus (mts.), Gre. 89/G2
Pindwāra, India 131/K4
Pine Barrens (phys. reg.), NJ, US 180/D4
Pine Bluff, Ar, US 171/J4
Pine Bluffs, Wy, US 169/G5
Pine Creek (pt.), Ct, US 181/E1
Pine Falls, Mb, Can. 169/J3
Pine Grove, Pa, US 180/B2
Pine Hill, NJ, US 180/D4
Pine Island, Mn, US 172/A2
Pine Island Bay (flat), Ant. 202/S
Pine Lawn, Mo, US 179/G8
Pine Point, NW, Can. 164/E2
Pine Ridge, SD, US 169/H5
Pine, South Branch (riv.), Mi, US 177/G6
Pine, The (hills), Mt, US 169/G4
Pinecliff (lake), NJ, US 181/H7
Pinecliffe, Co, US 179/B3
Pinedale, Wy, US 168/F5
Pinega (riv.), Rus. 106/E3
Pineimuta (riv.), On, Can. 169/L2
Pinelands, SAfr. 148/L10
Piñera, Uru. 201/K10
Pinerolo, It. 85/G4
Pinetown, SAfr. 149/E3
Pineuilh, Fr. 84/D4
Pineview (res.), Ut, US 179/K11
Pineville, La, US 171/J5
Pinewood Springs, Co, US 179/B2
Ping (riv.), Thai. 125/G4
Ping Chau (isl.), China 113/V9
Pingbian Miaozu Zizhixian, China 125/H3
Pingding, China 114/C3
Pingdingshan, China 114/C4
Pingdu, China 114/D3
Pingelap (isl.), Micr. 158/F4
Pingelly, Austl. 154/C5
Pingguo, China 114/H6
Pingguo, China 125/J3
Pinghe, China 121/C3
Pinghu, China 114/L9
Pingjiang, China 121/B2
Pingjing (pass), China 114/C5
Pingle, China 125/K3
Pinglu, China 114/B4
Pinglu, China 114/C3
Pingnan, China 121/B3
Pingquan, China 114/D2
Pingshan, China 114/C3
Pingshun, China 114/C3
Pingtan, China 121/C2
Pingtang, China 125/J2
P'ingtung, Tai. 121/D3
Pingxiang, China 125/K2
Pingxiang, China 125/J3
Pingxing Guan (pass), China 114/C3
Pingyao, China 114/C3
Pingyi, China 114/D4
Pingyin, China 114/D3
Pingyu, China 114/C4
Pingyuan, China 114/D3
Pinhal, Braz. 197/G7
Pinhal Novo, Port. 87/Q10
Pinhão, Braz. 197/B3
Pinheiro, Braz. 196/A1
Pinheiros, Braz. 196/B5
Pinhel, Port. 86/B2
Piniós (riv.), Gre. 89/G4
Pinjar (lake), Austl. 154/K6
Pinjarra, Austl. 154/B5
Pink, Ok, US 179/N15
Pinkafeld, Aus. 90/C2
Pinkawillinie Conservation Park, Austl. 155/G5
Pinkegat (chan.), Neth. 92/C2
Pinnacles Nat'l Mon., Ca, US 170/B3
Pinnaroo, Austl. 155/J5
Pinnau (riv.), Ger. 93/G1
Pinneberg, Ger. 93/G1
Pino Hachado (pass), Arg. 200/C3
Pino Torinese, It. 100/A2
Pinole, Ca, US 177/K10
Pinon Hills, Ca, US 178/C2
Pinos (mt.), Ca, US 170/C4
Pinos, Mex. 185/E4
Pinos, Isla de (Isla de la Juventud) (isl.), Cuba 182/E3
Pinos-Puente, Sp. 86/D4
Pinoso, Sp. 87/E3
Pins, Île des (isl.), NCal., Fr. 158/F7
Pinsdorf, Aus. 97/G7
Pinsk, Bela. 104/C1
Pinta, Isla (isl.), Ecu. 198/E6
Pinto, Sp. 87/N9
Pinto, Chile 200/C3
Pinzolo, It. 99/G5
Pio Ix, Braz. 196/B2
Pio Xii, Braz. 196/A1
Piobbico, It. 101/F5
Pioche, Nv, US 170/D3
Piombino, It. 85/J5
Piombino Dese, It. 101/F1
Pioneer World, Austl. 154/L7
Pioner (isl.), Rus. 106/J2
Pionki, Pol. 83/L3
Piorini (riv.), Braz. 192/F4
Piorini (lake), Braz. 195/F5
Piota (riv.), It. 100/B3
Piotrków Trybunalski, Pol. 83/K3
Piove di Sacco, It. 101/F2
Piovene-Rocchette, It. 101/E1
Pipariā, India 126/B4
Pipe Spring Nat'l Mon., Az, US 170/D3
Piper, Ks, US 179/D5
Pipersville, Pa, US 180/C3
Pipestone (riv.), On, Can. 164/G3
Piplān, Pak. 128/A3
Pipmuacan (res.), Qu, Can. 165/J4
Pippingarra Abor. Land, Austl. 154/C2
Pipra, India 126/D3
Pipraich, India 126/D2
Piqua, Oh, US 172/C3
Piquet Carneiro, Braz. 196/C2
Piquete, Braz. 197/H7
Piquiri (riv.), Braz. 193/H7
Pīr Mahal, Pak. 128/B4
Pir Panjal (range), India 128/C3
Piracanjuba, Braz. 197/B1
Piracicaba, Braz. 197/C2
Piracuruca, Braz. 196/B1
Pirae-bong (peak), NKor. 115/C2
Piraí, Braz. 197/K7
Piraí do Sul, Braz. 197/B3
Piraiévs, Gre. 89/N9
Piraju, Braz. 197/B2
Pirajuí, Braz. 197/B2
Pirámide (peak), Chile 201/B6
Piran, Slov. 101/G1
Pirané, Arg. 199/E2
Piranga (riv.), Braz. 197/D1
Piranhas (riv.), Braz. 193/L5
Piranji (riv.), Braz. 196/C2
Pirapemas, Braz. 196/A1
Pirapora, Braz. 196/A5
Pirapòzinho, Braz. 197/B2
Pirarajá, Uru. 201/G2
Pirássununga, Braz. 197/C2
Pires do Rio, Braz. 197/B1
Pírgos, Gre. 89/G4
Pírgos, Gre. 89/J5
Piriápolis, Uru. 201/G2
Pirin (mts.), Bul. 91/F5
Pirin (peak), Bul. 91/F5
Pirin NP, Bul. 91/F5
Piripiri, Braz. 196/B2
Piritiba, Braz. 196/B3
Píritu, Ven. 194/D2
Pirkkala, Fin. 81/K1
Pirmasens, Ger. 95/G5
Pirna, Ger. 83/G3
Piro, India 127/E3
Pirot, Serb. 90/F4
Pirre (mtn.), Pan. 187/G5
Pirthīpur, India 126/B3
Piru (lake), Ca, US 178/B1
Piru, Ca, US 178/B2
Piryíon, Gre. 89/J3
Pisa, It. 100/D5
Pisa (prov.), It. 101/D6
Pisac, Peru 198/D4
Pisanino (peak), It. 100/D4
Pisau (cape), Malay. 123/E2
Pisba, PN, Col. 194/C3
Piscataway, Md, US 180/B6
Piscataway, NJ, US 180/D2
Pisco (riv.), Peru 192/C6
Pisco, Peru 198/B4
Piscobamba, Peru 198/B3
Písek (peak), Czh. 97/H3
Písek, Czh. 97/H4
Pishan, China 112/C4
Pishīn, Pak. 131/J2
Pīshīn, Iran 131/H3
Piskavica, Bosn. 90/C3
Pisoc (peak), Swi. 99/G4
Pisogne, It. 100/D1
Pissis (peak), Arg. 199/C2
Pistakee (lake), Il, US 177/P15
Pisticci, It. 88/E2
Pistoia (prov.), It. 101/D5
Pistoia, It. 101/D5
Pisuerga (riv.), Sp. 86/C1
Pisz, Pol. 83/L2
Pit (riv.), Ca, US 170/B2
Pitalito, Col. 194/B4
Pitanga, Braz. 197/B3
Pitcairn (isl.), Pitc. 159/N7
Pitcairn Islands (dpcy.), UK 159/N7
Piteå, Swe. 79/G2
Piteälven (riv.), Swe. 79/F2
Piteşti, Rom. 91/G3
Píthion, Gre. 89/K2
Pithiviers, Fr. 84/E2
Pithoragarh, India 126/C1
Pitigliano, It. 88/B1
Pitiquito, Mex. 184/B2
Pitjantjatjara Abor. Lands, Austl. 155/F3
Pitkas Point, Ak, US 176/F3
Pitlochry, Sc, UK 78/C3
Pitman, NJ, US 180/C4
Pitmedden, Sc, UK 78/D2
Pitomača, Cro. 90/C3
Piton de la Fournaise (peak), Reun., Fr. 149/S15
Piton des Neiges (peak), Reun., Fr. 149/S15
Pitrufquén, Chile 200/B3
Pitt Water (bay), Austl. 156/H8
Pittenweem, Sc, UK 78/D4
Pittsburg, Ks, US 171/J3
Pittsburgh, Pa, US 172/E3
Pittsfield, Me, US 173/G2
Pittsfield, Ma, US 172/F3
Pittston, Pa, US 172/F3
Pittstown, NJ, US 180/D2
Pittsworth, Austl. 156/C4
Pitzbach (riv.), Aus. 99/G4
Piuí, Braz. 197/C2
Piumazzo, It. 101/E3
Piura, Peru 198/A2
Piura (dept.), Peru 198/A2
Pivdenny Buh (riv.), Ukr. 104/D2
Pivijay, Col. 194/C2
Pixoyal, Mex. 182/C4
Piz d'Err (peak), Swi. 99/F4
Pizacoma, Peru 198/D5
Pizarra, Sp. 86/C4
Pizhma (riv.), Rus. 103/K4
Pizol (peak), Swi. 99/F4
Pizzighettone, It. 100/C2
Pizzo, It. 88/E3
Pizzo dei Tre Signori (peak), It. 99/F6
Pizzo della Presolana (peak), It. 99/G6
Pizzo di Coca (peak), It. 99/G5
Pizzo di Vogorno (peak), Swi. 99/E5
Pizzuto (peak), It. 88/C1
Placentia, Nf, Can. 173/L2
Placentia (bay), Nf, Can. 173/L2
Placentia, Ca, US 178/G8
Placer, Phil. 121/E6
Placer (co.), Ca, US 177/M9

265
Place – Prade

Placetas, Cuba 187/G1
Plachkovtsi, Bul. 91/G4
Plaffeien, Swi. 98/D4
Plai Mat (riv.), Thai. 120/C3
Plaidt, Ger. 95/G3
Plailly, Fr. 72/K4
Plain City, Ut, US 179/J11
Plain Dealing, La, US 171/J4
Plaine (riv.), Fr. 98/C1
Plainfield, NJ, US 181/H9
Plainfield, Il, US 177/P16
Plains, Tx, US 171/G4
Plains, Pa, US 180/C1
Plainsboro, NJ, US 180/D3
Plainview, Tx, US 171/G4
Plainview, Mn, US 172/A2
Plainview, NY, US 181/M8
Plaisir, Fr. 72/H5
Plan-les-Ouates, Swi. 98/C5
Planá, Czh. 97/F3
Plana Cays (isls.), Bahm. 187/H1
Planaltina, Braz. 196/A4
Plancher-Bas, Fr. 98/C2
Plancher-les-Mines, Fr. 98/C2
Plandište, Serb. 90/E3
Planeta Rica, Col. 194/C2
Planken, Lcht. 99/F3
Plant City, Fl, US 175/H4
Plantation, Fl, US 175/H5
Plaquemines (parish), La, US 179/Q17
Plasencia, Sp. 86/B2
Plasy, Czh. 97/G3
Plata (estu.), Arg.,Uru. 201/K11
Platani (riv.), It. 88/C4
Plate Taile, Barrage de la (dam), Belg. 95/D3
Plateau (state), Nga. 145/H4
Plati, Gre. 89/H2
Platinum, Ak, US 176/F4
Plato, Col. 194/C2
Platón Sánchez, Mex. 186/B1
Platte (riv.), Ne, US 171/H2
Platte City, Mo, US 179/D5
Platte, North (riv.), Ne,Wy, US 171/G2
Platte, South (riv.), Co, US 171/G2
Platteville, Co, US 179/C2
Plattling, Ger. 97/F5
Plattsburgh, NY, US 172/F2
Plauen, Ger. 97/F1
Plav, Serb. 90/D4
Plavna Dadaint (peak), Swi. 99/G4
Playa de los Muertos (ruin), Hon. 186/E3
Playa del Carmen, Mex. 186/E1
Playa Noriega (lake), Mex. 184/C2
Playa Vicente, Mex. 186/C2
Playas (lake), NM, US 170/E5
Playas, Ecu. 194/A5
Playgreen (lake), Mb, Can. 169/J2
Pleasant (lake), Az, US 179/R18
Pleasant Grove, Ut, US 179/K13
Pleasant Hill, Ca, US 177/K11
Pleasant Hill, Mo, US 179/E6
Pleasant Hills, Md, US 180/B5
Pleasant Valley, Mo, US 179/E5
Pleasant View, Co, US 179/B3
Pleasant View, Ut, US 179/K11
Pleasanton, Ca, US 177/L11
Pleasanton, Tx, US 171/H5
Pleasantville, NJ, US 180/D5
Pleasantville, NY, US 181/K7
Pleaux, Fr. 84/E4
Pleiku, Viet. 120/D3
Pleinfeld, Ger. 96/D4
Pleisse (riv.), Ger. 82/G3
Plenty (riv.), Austl. 157/G5
Plenty (bay), NZ 159/T10
Plentywood, Mt, US 169/G3
Plérin, Fr. 84/B2
Plesná (riv.), Czh. 97/F2
Pleso (int'l arpt.), Cro. 90/C3
Pleszew, Pol. 83/J3
Plétipi (lake), Qu, Can. 173/G1
Plettenberg, Ger. 93/E6
Pleurtuit (int'l arpt.), Fr. 84/B2
Pleven, Bul. 91/G4
Pliska, Bul. 91/H4
Plitvice Lakes NP, Cro. 90/B3
Pljevlja, Mont. 90/D4
Plobsheim, Fr. 98/D1
Plöcckenstein (peak), Ger. 97/G5
Ploče, Cro. 89/E1
Plochingen, Ger. 96/C5
Płock, Pol. 83/K2
Pločno (peak), Bosn. 90/C4
Ploemeur, Fr. 84/B3
Ploiești, Rom. 91/H3
Plomárion, Gre. 89/K3
Plombières, Belg. 95/E2
Plombières-lès-Dijon, Fr. 98/A3
Plön, Ger. 80/D4
Płońsk, Pol. 83/L2
Plouay, Fr. 84/B3
Ploučnice (riv.), Czh. 83/H3
Ploufragan, Fr. 84/B2
Plougastel-Daoulas, Fr. 84/A2
Plouguernével, Fr. 84/B2
Plouzané, Fr. 84/A2
Plovdiv, Bul. 91/G4
Plovdiv (pol. reg.), Bul. 91/G4
Plover Cove (res.), China 113/U10
Pluguffan (int'l arpt.), Fr. 84/A3
Plum (isl.), NY, US 181/F1
Plumridge Lakes Nature Rsv., Austl. 154/E4
Plumsteadville, Pa, US 180/C3
Plungė, Lith. 81/J4
Plymouth, Eng, UK 74/B6
Plymouth (co.), Eng, UK 74/B6
Plymouth (sound), Eng, UK 74/B6
Plymouth (cap.), Monts., UK 183/N8
Plymouth, In, US 172/C3
Plymouth, NC, US 175/J3
Plymouth, NH, US 173/G3
Plymouth, Pa, US 180/C1
Plymouth, Wi, US 172/C3
Plynlimon (peak), Wal, UK 74/C2
Plzeň, Czh. 97/G3
Plzeňský (pol. reg.), Czh. 97/G4
PNC Bank Arts Center, NJ, US 181/J10
Pniel, SAfr. 148/L10
Pniewy, Pol. 83/J2
Pô, Burk. 145/E4
Po (riv.), It. 85/J4
Po di Venezia (riv.), It. 101/F2
Po di Volano (riv.), It. 101/E3
Po Klong Garai Cham Towers, Viet. 120/E4
Po, Mouths of the (delta), It. 85/K4
Pô, PN de, Burk. 145/E4
Po Toi Group (isls.), China 113/V11
Po, Valle del (valley), It. 85/J4
Poá, Braz. 197/G8
Poa (riv.), Ven. 195/E2
Poag, Il, US 179/G8
Pobé, Ben. 145/F5
Pobedy (peak), Kyr. 112/D3
Pobiedziska, Pol. 83/J2
Pobla de Segur, Sp. 87/F1
Pocahontas, Ar, US 171/K3
Poção de Pedra, Braz. 196/A2
Pochep, Rus. 104/E1
P'och'ŏn, SKor. 115/G6
Pocinhos, Braz. 196/C2
Pöcking, Ger. 99/H2
Pöcking, Ger. 97/G6
Pocklington (reef), PNG 158/E6
Poço Fundo, Braz. 197/H6
Poções, Braz. 196/B4
Pocola, Ok, US 171/J4
Poconé, Braz. 193/G7
Pocono (mts.), Pa, US 180/C1
Pocono (lake), Pa, US 180/C1
Pocono Lake, Pa, US 180/C1
Pocono Pines, Pa, US 180/C1
Poços de Caldas, Braz. 197/G6
Pocri, Pan. 187/F4
Podbořany, Czh. 97/G2
Poddębice, Pol. 83/K3
Podenzano, It. 100/C3
Podgorica (cap.), Mont. 90/D4
Podkarpackie (prov.), Pol. 83/L4
Podlasie (reg.), Bela.,Pol. 83/M3
Podlaskie (prov.), Pol. 83/M2
Podol'sk, Rus. 103/W9
Podor, Sen. 144/B2
Podporozh'ye, Rus. 102/G3
Podravska Slatina, Cro. 90/C3
Podujevo, Serb. 90/E4
Pofadder, SAfr. 148/B3
Poggibonsi, It. 101/E6
Poggio Renatico, It. 101/E3
Poggio Rusco, It. 101/E3
Poggiola, It. 101/E6
Pogromni (vol.), Ak, US 176/F5
P'ohang, SKor. 115/E4
Pohénégamook, Qu, Can. 173/G2
Pohja (Pojo), Fin. 81/K1
Pohjanmaa (reg.), Fin. 79/G3
Pohjois-Karjala (prov.), Fin. 102/F3
Pohnpei (isl.), Micr. 158/E4
Pohoiki, Hi, US 166/U11
Pohopoco Mtn. (mtn.), Pa, US 180/C2
Poigny-la-Forêt, Fr. 72/H5
Poing, Ger. 97/E6
Poinsett (cape), Ant. 202/H
Point (lake), NW, Can. 164/E2
Point au Fer (isl.), La, US 171/K5
Point Baker, Ak, US 176/M4
Point Fortin, Trin. 195/F2
Point Hope, Ak, US 176/E2
Point Lay, Ak, US 176/F2
Point Lookout (peak), Austl. 157/E1
Point Mugu Naval Air Sta., Ca, US 178/A2
Point Mugu State Park, Ca, US 178/A2
Point of Aire (pt.), Wal, UK 77/E5
Point of Ayre (pt.), IM, UK 76/D3
Point Pelee NP, On, Can. 172/D3
Point Pleasant, NJ, US 180/D3
Point Pleasant, Pa, US 180/C3
Point Pleasant, WV, US 172/D4
Point Pleasant Beach, NJ, US 180/D3
Point Salines (int'l arpt.), Gren. 195/F1
Point Salvation Abor. Rsv., Austl. 154/D4
Pointe-à-Pitre, Guad., Fr. 183/N8
Pointe à Raquette, Haiti 187/H2
Pointe-aux-Trembles, Qu, Can. 173/P6
Pointe-Calumet, Qu, Can. 173/N6
Pointe-Claire, Qu, Can. 173/N7
Pointe de Chassiron (pt.), Fr. 84/C3
Pointe de l'Arcouest (pt.), Fr. 84/B2
Pointe des Verres (peak), Fr. 98/C6
Pointe-du-Lac, Qu, Can. 173/F2
Pointe du Sablon (pt.), Fr. 84/F5
Pointe-Noire, Congo 147/B1
Poirino, It. 100/A3
Poissonier (pt.), Austl. 154/C1
Poissy, Fr. 72/J5
Poitiers, Fr. 84/D3
Poitou (reg.), Fr. 84/C3
Poitou-Charentes (reg.), Fr. 84/C3
Poix-de-Picardie, Fr. 94/A4
Poix-Terron, Fr. 95/D4
Pojuca, Braz. 196/C4
Pok Liu Chau (isl.), China 113/U11
Pokaran, India 131/K3
Pokharā, Nepal 126/D1
Pokhvistnevo, Rus. 105/K1
Pol-e Khomrī, Afg. 131/J1
Pola de Laviana, Sp. 86/C1
Pola de Lena, Sp. 86/C1
Pola de Siero, Sp. 86/C1
Polabská Nížina (phys. reg.), Czh. 85/L1
Pol'ana (peak), Slvk. 104/A2
Poland (ctry.) 83/K2
Połaniec, Pol. 83/L3
Polatlı, Turk. 132/C2
Polatsk, Bela. 81/N4
Polch, Ger. 95/G3
Połczyn-Zdrój, Pol. 80/G5
Pole of Inaccessibility, Ant. 202/E
Polesella, It. 101/E3
Polesine (reg.), It. 101/E3
Poleski NP, Pol. 83/M3
Polgár, Hun. 90/E2
Pŏlgyo, SKor. 115/D5
Políaigos (isl.), Gre. 89/J4
Policastro, Golfo di (gulf), It. 88/D3
Police, Pol. 80/F5
Policoro, It. 88/E2
Poligny, Fr. 98/B4
Políkastron, Gre. 89/H2
Políkhni, Gre. 89/H2
Polikhnítos, Gre. 89/K3
Polillo (isl.), Phil. 121/D4
Polis, Cyp. 133/C2
Polistena, It. 88/E3
Políyiros, Gre. 89/H2
Polje, Slov. 85/L3
Polkowice, Pol. 83/J3
Polla, It. 88/D2
Pollença, Sp. 87/G3
Polochic (riv.), Guat. 186/D3
Polomolok, Phil. 121/E6
Polonia (cape), Uru. 201/G2
Polonnaruwa, SrL. 124/D6
Polonne, Ukr. 104/C2
Polski Trŭmbesh, Bul. 91/G4
Polson, Mt, US 168/E4
Poltava, Ukr. 104/E2
Poltavs'ka Oblasti, Ukr. 104/E2
Poluostrov Barsakel'mes (isl.), Kaz. 129/C3
Poluška (peak), Czh. 97/H5
Polvijärvi, Fin. 102/F3
Polyarnyy, Rus. 102/G1
Polynesia (reg.) 158/G6
Pomabamba, Peru 198/B3
Pomarance, It. 85/J5
Pomarico, It. 88/E2
Pomáz, Hun. 91/R9
Pomba (riv.), Som. 197/D2
Pombal, Braz. 196/C2
Pombal, Port. 86/A3
Pombas, CpV. 135/J9
Pomerania (reg.), Pol. 80/F4
Pomeranian (bay), Ger.,Pol. 80/F4
Pomerode, Braz. 197/B3
Pomeroon-Supenaam (pol. reg.), Guy. 195/G3
Pomeroy, Wa, US 168/D4
Pomeroy, NI, UK 76/B2
Pommersfelden, Ger. 96/D3
Pomona, Ca, US 178/C2
Pomona, NJ, US 180/D5
Pomona, Md, US 180/B5
Pomorie, Bul. 91/H4
Pomorskie (prov.), Pol. 83/J1
Pomos (pt.), Cyp. 133/C2
Pompano Beach, Fl, US 175/H5
Pompei (ruin), It. 88/D2
Pompeu, Braz. 197/C1
Pompey, Fr. 95/F6
Pompeys Pillar Nat'l Mon., Mt, US 168/G4
Pompiano, It. 100/C2
Pompton (riv.), NJ, US 181/H8
Pompton Lakes, NJ, US 181/H8
Poncarale, It. 100/D2
Ponce, PR 183/M8
Ponchatoula, La, US 179/P16
Poncheville (lake), Qu, Can. 172/E1
Pond, Mo, US 179/F8
Pond (inlet), Nun., Can. 165/J1
Pond (pt.), Ct, US 181/E1
Pond Inlet, Nun., Can. 165/J1
Pondicherry, India 124/C5
Pondicherry (terr.), India 124/C5
Ponente, Riviera di (coast), Fr. 100/B5
Ponferrada, Sp. 86/B1
Pongdong, SKor. 115/D5
Ponghwa, SKor. 115/E4
Pongolo (riv.), SAfr. 149/E2
Poni (prov.), Burk. 144/E4
Poniatowa, Pol. 83/M3
Ponnaiyar (riv.), India 124/C5
Ponoka, Ab, Can. 168/E2
Ponoy (riv.), Rus. 106/D3
Pons, Fr. 84/C4
Ponsacco, It. 100/D5
Pont-à-Celles, Belg. 95/D3
Pont-à-Marcq, Fr. 94/C2
Pont-D'Ain, Fr. 98/B5
Pont-de-Chéruy, Fr. 98/B6
Pont-de-Roide, Fr. 98/C3
Pont-de-Vaux, Fr. 98/A5
Pont-de-Veyle, Fr. 98/A5
Pont-du-Château, Fr. 84/E4
Pont-Remy, Fr. 94/A3
Pont-Saint-Esprit, Fr. 84/F4
Pont-Saint-Martin, It. 100/A1
Pont-Sainte-Maxence, Fr. 94/B5
Ponta Delgada, Azor., Port. 87/T13
Ponta do Pico (peak), Azor., Port. 87/S12
Ponta Grossa, Braz. 197/B3
Ponta Porã, Braz. 199/E1
Pontalina, Braz. 197/B1
Pontarlier, Fr. 98/C4
Pontarmé, Fr. 72/K4
Pontassieve, It. 101/E5
Pontault-Combault, Fr. 72/K5
Pontax (riv.), Qu, Can. 172/E1
Pontcarré, Fr. 72/L5
Pontchartrain (lake), La, US 175/F4
Pontchâteau, Fr. 84/B3
Ponte Alta do Bom Jesus, Braz. 196/A4
Ponte Alta do Tocantins, Braz. 196/A3
Ponte Buggianese, It. 101/D5
Ponte de Sor, Port. 86/A3
Ponte dell'Olio, It. 100/C3
Ponte di Legno, It. 99/G5
Ponte di Piave, It. 101/F1
Ponte do Lima, Port. 86/A2
Ponte Lambro, It. 100/C1
Ponte Nova, Braz. 197/D2
Ponte San Nicolò, It. 101/E2
Pontecagnano, It. 88/D2
Pontecorvo, It. 88/C2
Pontecurone, It. 100/B3
Pontedera, It. 100/D5
Pontefract, Eng, UK 77/G4
Ponteland, Eng, UK 77/G1
Pontelongo, It. 101/F2
Pontenure, It. 100/C3
Pontes e Lacerda, Braz. 192/G7
Pontestura, It. 100/B2
Pontevedra, Sp. 86/A1
Pontevico, It. 100/D2
Ponthévrard, Fr. 72/H6
Ponthieu (reg.), Fr. 94/A3
Pontiac, Il, US 169/L5
Pontiac, Mi, US 172/D3
Pontiac (lake), Mi, US 177/E6
Pontianak, Indo. 122/C4
Pontivy, Fr. 84/B2
Pontoise, Fr. 72/J4
Pontoon Beach, Il, US 179/G8
Pontotoc, Ms, US 175/F3
Pontpoint, Fr. 94/B5
Pontremoli, It. 100/C4
Pontresina, Swi. 99/F5
Pontypool, Wal, UK 74/C3
Ponza, It. 88/C2
Ponziane, Isole (isls.), It. 88/C2
Poole, Eng, UK 74/E5
Poole (bay), Eng, UK 75/E5
Poole (co.), Eng, UK 74/D5
Poolewe, Sc, UK 73/R8
Poona (Pune), India 131/K5
Poondarrie (peak), Austl. 154/C3
Poondinna (mt.), Austl. 155/F3
Poopó (lake), Bol. 192/E7
Poortugaal, Neth. 92/B5
Pöösapää (pt.), Est. 81/K2
Poosepatuck Ind. Res., NY, US 181/F2
Popayán, Col. 194/B4
Poperinge, Belg. 94/B2
Popigochic (riv.), Mex. 184/C2
Popilta (lake), Austl. 155/J5
Popio (lake), Austl. 157/B2
Poplar (riv.), Mb,On, Can. 164/G3
Poplar (isl.), Md, US 180/B6
Poplar, Mt, US 169/G3
Poplar Bluff, Mo, US 171/K3
Poplarville, Ms, US 175/F4
Popocatépetl (vol.), Mex. 185/L7
Popoli, It. 88/C1
Popovo, Bul. 91/H4
Poppberg (peak), Ger. 97/E4
Poppenhausen, Ger. 96/D2
Poppenhausen, Ger. 96/C2
Poppi, It. 101/E5
Poprad, Slvk. 83/L4
Poprad (riv.), Slvk. 83/L4
Poranga, Braz. 196/B2
Porangatu, Braz. 193/J6
Porbandar, India 131/J4
Porcari, It. 100/D5
Porce (riv.), Col. 194/C3
Porcheville, Fr. 72/H5
Porcia, It. 101/F1
Porcuna, Sp. 86/C4
Porcupine (riv.), Can.,US 176/K2
Porcupine Gorge NP, Austl. 156/B3
Porcupine Plain, Sk, Can. 169/H2
Pordenone (prov.), It. 101/F2
Pordenone, It. 101/F1
Pordim, Bul. 91/G4
Pore, Col. 194/D3
Poreč, Cro. 101/G2
Poretta (int'l arpt.), Fr. 88/A1
Pori (int'l arpt.), Fin. 81/J1
Pori, Fin. 81/J1
Porirua, NZ 159/S11
Porlezza, It. 99/F5
Pornic, Fr. 84/B3
Porongurup NP, Austl. 154/C5
Póros, Gre. 89/H4
Porpoise (bay), Ant. 202/J
Porrentruy, Swi. 98/D3
Porretta Terme, It. 101/D4
Porriño, Sp. 86/A1
Porsangen (inlet), Nor. 79/H1
Porsgrunn, Nor. 80/C2
Porsuk (riv.), Turk. 132/B2
Port (isl.), Japan 119/H6
Port Alberni, BC, Can. 168/B3
Port Albert, Austl. 157/C3
Port Alexander, Ak, US 176/M4
Port Alfred, SAfr. 148/D4
Port Alice, BC, Can. 168/B3
Port Angeles, Wa, US 168/C3
Port Antonio, Jam. 187/G2
Port Appin, Sc, UK 78/A3
Port Arthur, Tx, US 171/J5
Port au Choix, Nf, Can. 173/K1
Port-au-Prince (cap.), Haiti 187/H2
Port Augusta, Austl. 155/H5
Port Bannatyne, Sc, UK 78/A5
Port Blair, India 125/F5
Port Blakely, Wa, US 177/C2
Port Bolivar, Tx, US 174/E4
Port-Bouët, C.d'Iv. 144/E5
Port Bouet (Abidgan) (int'l arpt.), C.d'Iv. 144/E5
Port Broughton, Austl. 155/H5
Port Canning, India 127/G4
Port Carbon, Pa, US 180/B2
Port Charlotte, Fl, US 175/H5
Port Chester, NY, US 181/L8
Port Clements, BC, Can. 176/M5
Port Clinton, Oh, US 172/D3
Port Clinton, Pa, US 180/B2
Port Colborne, On, Can. 173/R10
Port Columbus (int'l arpt.), Oh, US 172/D4
Port Davey (har.), Austl. 157/C4
Port-de-Paix, Haiti 187/H2
Port Deposit, Md, US 180/B4
Port Dickson, Malay. 122/B3
Port Discovery (bay), Wa, US 177/B1
Port Douglas, Austl. 156/B2
Port Edward, BC, Can. 176/M4
Port Elgin, On, Can. 172/D2
Port Elizabeth, SAfr. 148/D4
Port Elizabeth, NJ, US 180/D5
Port Ellen, Sc, UK 73/Q9
Port Elliot, Austl. 155/H5
Port Erin, IM, UK 76/D3
Port-Eynon (pt.), Wal, UK 74/B3
Port Fairy, Austl. 157/B3
Port Gamble, Wa, US 177/B2
Port Gamble Ind. Res., Wa, US 177/B2
Port-Gentil, Gabon 138/G8
Port Gibson, Ms, US 171/K5
Port Glasgow, Sc, UK 78/B5
Port Graham, Ak, US 176/H4
Port Harcourt, Nga. 145/G5
Port Harcourt (int'l arpt.), Nga. 145/G5
Port Hardy, BC, Can. 168/B3
Port Hawkesbury, NS, Can. 173/J2
Port Hedland, Austl. 154/C2
Port Hedland (int'l arpt.), Austl. 154/C2
Port Heiden, Ak, US 176/G4
Port Hueneme, Ca, US 178/A2
Port Huron, Mi, US 172/D3
Port Isaac (bay), Eng, UK 74/B5
Port Jefferson, NY, US 181/E2
Port-la-Nouvelle, Fr. 84/E5
Port Lambton, On, Can. 177/H6
Port Lavaca, Tx, US 171/H5
Port Lincoln, Austl. 155/G5
Port Lions, Ak, US 176/H4
Port Loko, SLeo. 144/B4
Port-Louis, Guad., Fr. 183/N8
Port Louis (cap.), Mrts. 149/T15
Port Macdonnell, Austl. 157/B3
Port Macquarie, Austl. 157/E1
Port Madison Ind. Res., Wa, US 177/B2
Port Maria, Jam. 187/G2
Port McNeill, BC, Can. 168/B3
Port-Menier, Qu, Can. 173/H1
Port Monmouth, NJ, US 181/J10
Port Moresby (cap.), PNG 158/D5
Port Nolloth, SAfr. 148/B3
Port Norris, NJ, US 180/C5
Port of Ness, Sc, UK 73/Q7
Port-of-Spain (cap.), Trin. 195/F2
Port Orange, Fl, US 175/H4
Port Penn, De, US 180/C4
Port Phillip (bay), Austl. 157/C3
Port Pirie, Austl. 155/H5
Port Reading, NJ, US 181/J9
Port Republic, NJ, US 180/D4
Port Royal, Pa, US 180/A2
Port Saint Joe, Fl, US 175/G4
Port-Saint-Louis-du-Rhône, Fr. 84/F5
Port Saint Lucie, Fl, US 175/H5
Port Saint Mary, IM, UK 76/D3
Port Shepstone, SAfr. 149/E3
Port Stephens (bay), Austl. 157/E2
Port-sur-Saône, Fr. 98/C2
Port Townsend, Wa, US 168/C3
Port-Vendres, Fr. 84/E5
Port Victoria, Austl. 155/H5
Port-Vila (cap.), Van. 158/F6
Port Wakefield, Austl. 155/H5
Port Washington, NY, US 181/L8
Port Weld, Malay. 122/B3
Porta Westfalica (pass), Ger. 93/F4
Porta Westfalica, Ger. 93/F4
Portachuelo, Bol. 192/F7
Portadown, NI, UK 76/B3
Portaferry, NI, UK 76/C3
Portage, Mi, US 172/C3
Portage Des Sioux, Mo, US 179/G8
Portage la Prairie, Mb, Can. 169/J3
Portalegre (dist.), Port. 86/B3
Portalegre, Port. 86/B3
Portales, NM, US 171/G4
Portarlington, Ire. 73/Q10
Portbou, Sp. 87/G1
Porteirinha, Braz. 196/B4
Portel, Braz. 193/H4
Porters (lake), Pa, US 180/C1
Porterville, SAfr. 148/L10
Porterville, Ca, US 170/C3
Porterville, Ut, US 179/K12
Portes-lès-Valence, Fr. 84/F4
Portet-sur-Garonne, Fr. 84/D5
Portete (bay), Col. 187/J3
Portglenone, NI, UK 76/B2
Portimão, Port. 86/A4
Portishead, Eng, UK 74/D4
Portknockie, Sc, UK 78/D1
Portland, Austl. 157/D2
Portland, Austl. 157/B3
Portland (cape), Austl. 157/C4
Portland (pt.), Jam. 187/G2
Portland, In, US 172/C3
Portland, Me, US 173/G3
Portland, Or, US 168/C4
Portland (int'l arpt.), Or, US 168/C4
Portland, Tn, US 172/C4
Portland Canal (inlet), BC, Can. 176/M4
Portland Jetport (int'l arpt.), Me, US 173/G3
Portlaoise, Ire. 73/Q10
Portlaw, Ire. 73/Q10
Portlethen, Sc, UK 78/D2
Portmarnock, Ire. 76/B5
Portmore, Jam. 187/G2
Portneuf (riv.), Qu, Can. 173/G1
Porto (gulf), Fr. 88/A1
Porto, Port. 86/A2
Porto (dist.), Port. 86/A2
Porto (int'l arpt.), Port. 86/A2
Porto Azzurro, It. 85/J5
Porto Belo, Braz. 197/B3
Porto Calvo, Braz. 196/D3
Porto Ceresio, It. 99/E6
Pôrto da Fôlha, Braz. 196/C3
Porto de Mós, Port. 86/A3
Porto Empedocle, It. 88/C4
Porto Ercole, It. 88/B1
Porto Ferreira, Braz. 197/C2
Porto Franco, Braz. 196/A2
Porto Garibaldi, It. 101/F3
Porto Inglês, CpV. 135/K10
Porto Nacional, Braz. 193/J6
Porto-Novo (cap.), Ben. 145/F5
Porto Potenza Picena, It. 101/G6
Porto Recanati, It. 101/G6
Porto Sant'Elpidio, It. 85/K5
Porto Santo (isl.), Port. 140/A2
Porto Santo Stefano, It. 88/B1
Porto Seguro, Braz. 196/C5
Porto Tolle, It. 101/F3
Porto Torres, It. 88/A2
Porto União, Braz. 197/B3
Porto Valtravaglia, It. 99/E6
Porto-Vecchio, Fr. 88/A2
Porto Velho, Braz. 192/F5
Portobelo, PN, Pan. 187/G4
Portocannone, It. 88/D2
Portocivitanova, It. 85/K5
Portoferraio, It. 85/J5
Portofino, It. 100/C4
Portogruaro, It. 101/F1
Portomaggiore, It. 101/E3
Portovenere, It. 100/C4
Portoviejo, Ecu. 194/A5
Portpatrick, Sc, UK 76/C2
Portree, Sc, UK 73/Q8
Portrush, NI, UK 76/B1
Portsea (isl.), Eng, UK 75/E5
Portslade-by-Sea, Eng, UK 75/F5
Portsmouth, Dom. 183/N9
Portsmouth, Eng, UK 75/E5
Portsmouth (co.), Eng, UK 75/E5
Portsmouth, NH, US 173/G3
Portsoy, Sc, UK 78/D1
Portstewart, NI, UK 76/B1
Portugal (ctry.) 86/A3
Portugalete, Sp. 86/D1
Portuguesa (riv.), Ven. 194/D2
Portuguesa (state), Ven. 194/D2
Portumna, Ire. 73/P10
Porvenir, Chile 201/C7
Porvenir, Uru. 201/K10
Porzuna, Sp. 86/C3
Posada, It. 88/A2
Posadas, Arg. 199/E2
Posadas, Sp. 86/C4
Posavina (valley), Bosn. 90/C3
Poschiavo, Swi. 99/G5
Posio, Fin. 102/F2
Poso (lake), Indo. 123/F4
Posof, Turk. 132/E1
Posŏng, SKor. 115/D5
Posŏng (riv.), SKor. 115/D5
Posorja, Ecu. 194/A5
Posse, Braz. 196/A4
Possession (pt.), Wa, US 177/C2
Possession (sound), Wa, US 177/C2
Post, Tx, US 171/G4
Post Falls, Id, US 168/D4
Poste Maurice Cortier (ruin), Alg. 141/F5
Postmasburg, SAfr. 148/C3
Postojna, Slov. 85/L4
Postoloprty, Czh. 97/G2
Potam, Mex. 184/C3
Potamós, Gre. 89/H5
Potaro-Siparuni (pol. reg.), Guy. 195/G3
Potchefstroom, SAfr. 148/D2
Poteau, Ok, US 171/J4
Potenza (riv.), It. 88/C1
Potenza, It. 88/D2
Potenza Picena, It. 101/G6
Potes, Sp. 86/C1
Potholes (res.), Wa, US 168/D4
Poti (riv.), Braz. 193/K5
P'ot'i, Geo. 105/G4
Potiraguá, Braz. 196/C4
Potomac (riv.), US 172/E4
Potomac, Md, US 180/A5
Potosí, Bol. 192/E7
Potosi, Mo, US 171/K3
Potrerillos, Chile 199/C2
Potsdam, NY, US 172/F2
Potsdam, Ger. 82/G7
Pottawatomie (co.), Ok, US 179/N15
Pottendorf, Aus. 85/M3
Pottenstein, Ger. 97/E3
Potters Bar, Eng, UK 72/C1
Pöttmes, Ger. 96/E5
Pottstown, Pa, US 180/C3
Pottsville, Pa, US 180/B2
Pottuvil, SrL. 124/D6
Poudre d'Or, Mrts. 149/T15
Poughkeepsie, NY, US 172/F3
Pouilley-les-Vignes, Fr. 98/B3
Poulaphouca (res.), Ire. 76/B5
Poulter (riv.), Eng, UK 77/G5
Poulton-le-Fylde, Eng, UK 77/F4
Poŭn, SKor. 115/D4
Pourri (peak), Fr. 85/G4
Pouru-Saint-Remy, Fr. 95/E4
Pouso Alegre, Braz. 197/H7
Pouthisat (riv.), Camb. 125/H5
Pouzauges, Fr. 84/C3
Považská Bystrica, Slvk. 83/K4
Povegliano Veronese, It. 101/D2
Poverty Point Nat'l Mon., La, US 171/K4
Poviglio, It. 100/D3
Póvoa de Varzim, Port. 86/A2
Povoação, Azor., Port. 87/T13
Povorino, Rus. 105/G2
Povungnituk (riv.), Qu, Can. 165/J2
Povungnituk, Qu, Can. 165/J2
Poway, Ca, US 178/C5
Powder (riv.), Mt,Wy, US 169/G4
Powell (lake), Az,Ut, US 170/E3
Powell, Wy, US 168/F4
Powell River, BC, Can. 168/B3
Power (res.), NY, US 173/R9
Powers (lake), Wi, US 177/P14
Powys (co.), Wal, UK 77/E6
Powys, Vale of (valley), Wal, UK 74/C1
Poxoreo, Braz. 193/H7
Poyang (lake), China 121/C2
Poynton, Eng, UK 77/F5
Poyo, Sp. 86/A1
Poysdorf, Aus. 83/J4
Poza Rica, Mex. 185/M6
Požarevac, Serb. 90/E3
Požega, Serb. 90/E4
Poznań, Pol. 83/J2
Pozo Alcón, Sp. 86/D4
Pozoblanco, Sp. 86/C3
Pozohondo, Sp. 86/E3
Pozuelo de Alarcón, Sp. 87/N9
Pozuelos, Ven. 195/E2
Pozuzo, Peru 198/C3
Pozza, It. 101/D3
Pozzallo, It. 88/D4
Pozzolo Formigaro, It. 100/B3
Pozzonovo, It. 101/E2
Ppa. de Salamanca (plain), Arg. 200/F1
Prabuty, Pol. 81/H5
Pracham Hiang (pt.), Thai. 120/B4
Prachatice, Czh. 97/H4
Prachin Buri (riv.), Thai. 120/C3
Prachin Buri, Thai. 120/C3
Prachuap Khiri Khan, Thai. 120/B4
Praděd (peak), Czh. 83/J3
Pradera, Col. 194/B4

Prade – Queen

Prades, Fr. 84/E5
Prado, Braz. 196/C5
Prado del Rey, Sp. 86/C4
Prado Flood Control (basin), Ca, US 178/C3
Pragelpass (pass), Swi. 99/E4
Prague (Praha) (cap.), Czh. 97/H2
Praha (peak), Czh. 97/G3
Praha (pol. reg.), Czh. 97/H2
Prahova (prov.), Rom. 91/G3
Praia (cap.), CpV. 135/K11
Praia (int'l arpt.), CpV. 135/K11
Praia da Vitória, Azor., Port. 87/S12
Praia Grande, Braz. 197/G9
Prairie Dog Town Fk. (riv.), Tx, US 171/G4
Prairie du Chien, Wi, US 169/L5
Prairie Grove, Il, US 177/P15
Prairie View, Tx, US 171/J5
Prairie Village, Ks, US 179/D6
Prairies (riv.), Qu, Can. 173/N6
Prairietown, Il, US 179/H8
Pralboino, It. 100/D2
Pralungo, It. 100/B1
Pram (riv.), Aus. 97/G6
Prambachkirchen, Aus. 97/G6
Pran Buri (res.), Thai. 125/G5
Prangins, Swi. 98/C5
Prānhita (riv.), India 124/C4
Prapat, Indo. 122/A3
Præstø, Den. 80/E4
Praszka, Pol. 83/K3
Prat, Chile, Ant. 202/W
Prata, Braz. 197/B1
Prata (riv.), Braz. 196/A5
Prata di Pordenone, It. 101/F1
Prathersville, Mo, US 179/E5
Prätigau (valley), Swi. 99/F4
Prato, It. 101/E5
Prato (prov.), It. 101/E5
Prato allo Stelvio (Prad am Stilfserjoch), It. 99/G4
Prato (Leventina), Swi. 99/E5
Pratola Peligna, It. 88/C1
Pratomagno (mts.), It. 101/E5
Pratovecchio, It. 101/E5
Pratt (isl.), Chile 201/B6
Pratt, Ks, US 171/H3
Pratteln, Swi. 98/D2
Prattville, Al, US 175/G3
Prauthoy, Fr. 98/B2
Pravets, Bul. 89/H1
Pravia, Sp. 86/B1
Prawle (pt.), Eng, UK 74/C6
Praxedis G. Guerrero, Mex. 184/D2
Praya, Indo. 123/E5
Pré-Saint-Didier, It. 98/C6
Preah Vihear (ruin), Camb. 120/D3
Précy-sur-Oise, Fr. 94/B5
Predappio, It. 101/E4
Predazzo, It. 85/J3
Predeal, Rom. 91/G3
Predosa, It. 100/B3
Preeceville, Sk, Can. 169/H3
Preetz, Ger. 80/D4
Preganziol, It. 101/F1
Pregarten, Aus. 97/H6
Pregolya (riv.), Pol. 81/J4
Pregolya (riv.), Rus. 83/L1
Pregonero, Ven. 194/D2
Preissac (lake), Qu, Can. 172/E1
Premana, It. 99/F5
Prémery, Fr. 84/E3
Premià de Mar, Sp. 87/L7
Prenzlau, Ger. 83/G2
Přerov, Czh. 83/J4
Presanella (peak), It. 99/G5
Prescot, Eng, UK 77/F5
Prescott, Az, US 170/D4
Prescott, On, Can. 172/F2
Preševo, Serb. 90/E4
Presidencia Roque Sáenz Peña, Arg. 199/D2
Presidente Dutra, Braz. 196/A2
Presidente Epitácio, Braz. 197/A2
Presidente Olegário, Braz. 197/C1
Presidente Venceslau, Braz. 197/B2
Presidential Lake Estates, NJ, US 180/D4
Presidio, Tx, US 171/F5
Presidio (riv.), Mex. 184/D4
Preslav, Bul. 91/H4
Presles, Fr. 72/J4
Presles-en-Brie, Fr. 72/L5
Prešov, Slvk. 83/L4
Prešovský (pol. reg.), Slvk. 83/L4
Prespa (lake), Eur. 89/G2
Presque Isle, Me, US 173/G2
Pressath, Ger. 97/E3
Pressbaum, Aus. 91/N7
Prestatyn, Wal, UK 77/E5
Prestea, Gha. 145/E5
Prestfoss, Nor. 80/C1
Přeštice, Czh. 97/G3
Preston (cape), Austl. 154/C2
Preston, Md, US 180/C6
Preston, Wa, US 177/D2
Preston, Eng, UK 77/F4
Prestonpans, Sc, UK 78/D5
Prestonsburg, Ky, US 172/D4
Prestwich, Eng, UK 77/F4
Prestwick (int'l arpt.), Sc, UK 78/B5
Prestwick, Sc, UK 78/B6
Prêto (riv.), Braz. 193/J6
Pretoria (cap.), SAfr. 148/E2
Pretty Boy (res.), Md, US 180/B4
Preussisch Olendorf, Ger. 93/F4
Prevalje, Slov. 85/L3
Préveza, Gre. 89/G3
Prévost, Qu, Can. 173/M6
Prey Veng, Camb. 120/D4
Pribilof (isls.), Ak, US 176/D4
Priboj, Serb. 90/D4
Příbram, Czh. 97/H3
Price (riv.), Ut, US 170/E3
Price, Ut, US 170/E3
Price, Md, US 180/C5
Prichard, Al, US 175/F4
Prichsenstadt, Ger. 96/D3
Priego, Sp. 86/D2
Priego de Córdoba, Sp. 86/C4
Prien am Chiemsee, Ger. 97/F7
Prieska, SAfr. 148/C3
Priest (lake), Id, US 168/D3
Priest River, Id, US 168/D3
Prieta (mtn.), Sp. 86/C1
Prievidza, Slvk. 83/K4
Prignitz (reg.), Ger. 82/F2
Prijedor, Bosn. 90/C3
Prijepolje, Serb. 90/D4
Prikaspian (plain), Kaz.,Rus. 106/E5
Prikumsk, Rus. 105/H3
Prilep, FYROM 89/G2
Prilly, Swi. 98/C4
Prima Porta, It. 88/C1
Prima Tapia, Mex. 184/A1
Prime Hook NWR, De, US 180/C6
Primeira Cruz, Braz. 196/B1
Primero (cape), Chile 201/B6
Primorskiy Kray, Rus. 107/P5
Primorsko, Bul. 91/H4
Primorsko-Akhtarsk, Rus. 104/F3
Prims (riv.), Ger. 95/F4
Prince Albert, Sk, Can. 169/G2
Prince Albert (pen.), NW, Can. 164/E1
Prince Albert (sound), NW, Can. 164/E1
Prince Albert NP, Sk, Can. 164/F3
Prince Albert, SAfr. 148/C4
Prince Alfred (cape), NW, Can. 164/D1
Prince Charles (isl.), Nun., Can. 165/J2
Prince Edward (isl.), Can. 161/L5
Prince Edward Island (prov.), Can. 173/J2
Prince Edward Island NP, PE, Can. 173/J2
Prince Edward (isls.), SAfr. 65/L7
Prince George, BC, Can. 168/C2
Prince Georges (co.), Md, US 180/B6
Prince Gustav Adolf (sea), Nun., Can. 165/R7
Prince Leopold (isl.), Nun., Can. 164/G1
Prince of Wales (str.), NW, Can. 164/E1
Prince of Wales (isl.), Ak, US 164/C3
Prince Olav (coast), Ant. 202/D
Prince Patrick (isl.), NW, Can. 165/R7
Prince Regent (inlet), Nun., Can. 164/G1
Prince Rupert, BC, Can. 176/M4
Prince William (sound), Ak, US 164/B2
Princenhof (lake), Neth. 92/C2
Princes Risborough, Eng, UK 75/F3
Princes Town, Trin. 183/J5
Princesa Isabel, Braz. 196/C2
Princess Charlotte (bay), Austl. 156/A1
Princess Margaret (range), Nun., Can. 165/S6
Princess Royal (isl.), BC, Can. 164/C3
Princeton, Mn, US 169/K4
Princeton, BC, Can. 168/C3
Princeton, In, US 172/C4
Princeton, Ky, US 172/C4
Princeton, NJ, US 180/D3
Princeton Junction, NJ, US 180/D3
Princeville, Hi, US 166/S9
Príncipe (isl.), SaoT. 138/G7
Prindle (vol.), Ak, US 176/K3
Prineville, Or, US 168/C4
Pringsewu, Indo. 122/B5
Pringy, Fr. 98/C6
Prinsenbeek, Neth. 92/B5
Prinses Margriet (canal), Neth. 92/C3
Prinzapolka, Nic. 187/F3
Prinzapolka (riv.), Nic. 187/E3
Priolo di Gargallo, It. 88/D4
Prior (cape), Sp. 86/A1
Priore (peak), It. 85/K5
Priozersk, Rus. 81/P1
Pripet Marshes (swamp), Bela.,Ukr. 104/C1
Pripyat' (riv.), Ukr. 104/C2
Prisdorf, Ger. 93/G1
Priština, Serb. 90/E4
Prittriching, Ger. 99/G1
Pritzwalk, Ger. 82/G2
Privas, Fr. 84/F4
Privolzhskiy, Rus. 105/H2
Priyutovo, Rus. 105/K1
Prizren, Serb. 90/E4
Prnjavor, Serb. 90/D3
Prnjavor, Bosn. 90/C3
Probištip, FYROM 89/H1
Probolinggo, Indo. 122/D5
Probstzella, Ger. 97/E1
Proctor (lake), Tx, US 174/D3
Proctor (pt.), La, US 179/Q17
Proddatūr, India 124/C5
Proença-a-Nova, Port. 86/B3
Profondeville, Belg. 95/D3
Progreso, Mex. 185/K6
Progreso, Mex. 186/D1
Progreso, Pan. 187/F4
Progreso, Uru. 201/K11
Progress, Rus. 113/N2
Progresso, It. 101/E3
Prokhladnyy, Rus. 105/G4
Prokuplje, Serb. 90/E4
Promised Land (lake), Pa, US 180/C1
Promissão, Braz. 197/B2
Promissão, Represa (res.), Braz. 197/B2
Propriá, Braz. 196/C3
Propriano, Fr. 88/A2
Proserpine, Austl. 156/C3
Prosna (riv.), Pol. 83/J2
Prospect Park, NJ, US 181/J8
Prospector (mtn.), Yk, Can. 176/L3
Prosperidad, Phil. 121/E6
Prosperous, Ire. 73/Q10
Prostějov, Czh. 83/J4
Proston, Austl. 156/C4
Proszowice, Pol. 83/L3
Protivín, Czh. 97/H4
Provadiya, Bul. 91/H4
Provence (reg.), Fr. 84/F5
Provence (int'l arpt.), Fr. 84/F5
Provence-Alpes-Côte-d'Azur, Fr. 85/G4
Providence (cap.), RI, US 173/G3
Providencia, Isla de (isl.), Col. 182/E5
Providência, Serra de (mts.), Braz. 192/F6
Providenciales (isl.), Bahm. 187/H1
Provins, Fr. 84/E2
Provo, Ut, US 179/K13
Provo (riv.), Ut, US 179/K13
Provo (peak), Ut, US 179/K13
Provost, Ab, Can. 168/F2
Prozor, Bosn. 90/C4
Prudentópolis, Braz. 197/B3
Prudhoe (bay), Ak, US 176/J1
Prudhoe, Eng, UK 77/G2
Prudhoe Bay, Ak, US 176/J1
Prudnik, Pol. 83/J3
Prüm (riv.), Ger. 82/D4
Prüm, Ger. 95/F3
Prunay-en-Yvelines, Fr. 72/H6
Prunelli-di-Fiumorbo, Fr. 88/A1
Pruszcz Gdański, Pol. 80/H4
Pruszków, Pol. 83/L2
Prut (riv.), Eur. 91/J2
Prutz, Aus. 99/G3
Pryluky, Ukr. 104/E2
Pryor, Ok, US 171/J3
Prypyats' (riv.), Bela. 104/D2
Przasnysz, Pol. 83/L2
Przemków, Pol. 83/H3
Przemyśl, Pol. 83/M4
Przeworsk, Pol. 83/M3
Przylądek Rozewie (cape),Pol. 80/H4
Przysucha, Pol. 83/L3
Psakhná, Gre. 89/H3
Psará (isl.), Gre. 89/J3
Psárion, Gre. 89/G4
Psël (riv.), Rus.,Ukr. 104/E2
Pskov (lake), Rus. 102/F5
Pskov, Rus. 81/N3
Pskovskaya Oblast, Rus. 102/F4
Pšovka (riv.), Czh. 97/H2
Pszczyna, Pol. 83/K4
Ptolemaïs, Gre. 89/G2
Ptuj, Slov. 85/L3
Pu Xian, China 114/B3
Puan, SKor. 115/D5
Pubei, China 121/A3
Pucacaca, Peru 198/B2
Pucallpa, Peru 198/C3
Pucará, Ecu. 198/B1
Pucará, Peru 198/B2
Pucará, Peru 198/D4
Pucarani, Bol. 198/D5
Pucaurco, Peru 194/D5
Puchenau, Aus. 97/H6
Pucheng, China 121/C2
Pucheng, China 114/B4
Puchheim, Ger. 97/E6
Puch'on, SKor. 115/F7
Puchuncaví, Chile 200/N8
Pucioasa, Rom. 91/G3
Puck, Pol. 80/H4
Pucking, Aus. 97/H6
Pucón, Chile 200/C3
Pucusana, Peru 198/B4
Pudasjärvi, Fin. 102/E2
Puderbach, Ger. 95/G2
Pudsey, Eng, UK 77/G4
Pudu (riv.), China 125/H2
Puebla (state), Mex. 182/B4
Puebla, Mex. 185/L7
Puebla de Alcocer, Sp. 86/C3
Puebla de Don Fadrique, Sp. 86/D4
Puebla de la Calzada, Sp. 86/B3
Puebla de Sanabria, Sp. 86/B1
Puebla de Trives, Sp. 86/B1
Puebla del Caramiñal, Sp. 86/A1
Pueblillo, Mex. 185/M6
Pueblito, Col. 194/C2
Pueblo, Co, US 171/F3
Pueblo Nuevo, Nic. 186/E3
Pueblo Nuevo, Ven. 194/D2
Pueblo Yaqui, Mex. 184/C3
Puente (hills), Ca, US 178/G8
Puente Alto, Chile 200/N8
Puente Caldelas, Sp. 86/A1
Puente-Ceso, Sp. 86/A1
Puente de Ixtla, Mex. 185/K8
Puente del Inca, Arg. 200/C2
Puente-Genil, Sp. 86/C4
Puente Nacional, Col. 194/C3
Puente Piedra, Peru 198/B3
Puenteareas, Sp. 86/A1
Puentedeume, Sp. 86/A1
Puentes de García Rodríguez, Sp. 86/B1
Pueo (pt.), Hi, US 166/R10
Puerco (riv.), NM, US 170/E4
Puerto Acosta, Bol. 198/D4
Puerto Aisén, Chile 200/B5
Puerto América, Peru 198/B2
Puerto Ángel, Mex. 186/B3
Puerto Armuelles, Pan. 187/F4
Puerto Asís, Col. 194/B4
Puerto Ayacucho, Ven. 195/E3
Puerto Ayora, Ecu. 198/E7
Puerto Baquerizo Moreno, Ecu. 198/F7
Puerto Barrios, Guat. 186/D3
Puerto Bermúdez, Peru 198/C3
Puerto Berrío, Col. 194/C3
Puerto Cabello, Ven. 194/D2
Puerto Cabezas, Nic. 187/F3
Puerto Carreño, Col. 195/E3
Puerto Cisnes, Chile 200/B5
Puerto Cortés, Mex. 184/C3
Puerto Cortés, Hon. 186/E3
Puerto Cumarebo, Ven. 194/D2
Puerto de la Cruz, Sp. 140/A3
Puerto de la Libertad, Mex. 184/B2
Puerto de Navacerrada (pass), Sp. 87/M8
Puerto del Rosario, Sp. 140/B3
Puerto del Son, Sp. 86/A1
Puerto Deseado, Arg. 201/D5
Puerto El Carmen, Ecu. 194/C4
Puerto Escondido, Col. 194/B2
Puerto Escondido, Mex. 186/B3
Puerto Heath, Bol. 198/D4
Puerto Iguazú, Arg. 199/F2
Puerto Inca, Peru 198/C3
Puerto Ingeniero Ibáñez, Chile 200/C5
Puerto Inírida, Col. 194/E4
Puerto La Cruz, Ven. 195/E2
Puerto Leguízamo, Col. 194/C5
Puerto Lempira, Hon. 187/F3
Puerto López, Col. 194/C3
Puerto Lumbreras, Sp. 86/E4
Puerto Madero, Mex. 186/C3
Puerto Madryn, Arg. 200/D4
Puerto Magdalena, Mex. 184/B3
Puerto Maldonado, Peru 198/D4
Puerto Montt, Chile 200/B4
Puerto Morazán, Nic. 186/E3
Puerto Morelos, Mex. 182/D3
Puerto Napo, Ecu. 194/B5
Puerto Natales, Chile 201/B6
Puerto Obaldía, Pan. 187/G4
Puerto Ocopa, Peru 198/C3
Puerto Padre, Cuba 187/G1
Puerto Páez, Ven. 195/E3
Puerto Peñasco, Mex. 184/B2
Puerto Píritu, Ven. 195/E2
Puerto Portillo, Peru 198/C3
Puerto Prado, Peru 198/C3
Puerto Princesa, Phil. 123/E2
Puerto Quellón, Chile 200/B4
Puerto Real, Sp. 86/B4
Puerto Rico, Col. 194/C4
Puerto Rico, Col. 194/C4
Puerto Rico (dpcy.), US 183/M8
Puerto Rondón, Col. 194/D3
Puerto San Carlos, Mex. 184/B3
Puerto San Julián, Arg. 201/D6
Puerto Santa Cruz, Arg. 201/C6
Puerto Serrano, Sp. 86/C4
Puerto Suárez, Bol. 192/G7
Puerto Supe, Peru 198/B3
Puerto Tejada, Col. 194/B4
Puerto Vallarta, Mex. 184/D4
Puerto Varas, Chile 200/B4
Puerto Viejo, CR 187/E4
Puerto Villamil, Ecu. 198/E7
Puerto Wilches, Col. 194/C3
Puerto Williams, Chile 201/D7
Puertollano, Sp. 86/C3
Pueyrredón (lake), Arg. 200/C5
Puffin (isl.), Wal, UK 76/D5
Pugachev, Rus. 105/J1
Puget (sound), Wa, US 177/C2
Puglia (prov.), It. 88/E2
Puigcerdà, Sp. 87/F1
Puiseux-en-France, Fr. 72/K4
Pujehun, SLeo. 144/C5
Pujiang, China 121/C2
Pujilí, Ecu. 194/B5
Pujŏn (lake), NKor. 115/D2
Pujut (cape), Indo. 122/C5
Pukalani, Hi, US 166/T10
Puk'an-san (peak), SKor. 115/F6
Puk'an-san NP, SKor. 115/D4
Pukapuka (isl.), Cookls. 159/J6
Pukarua (isl.), FrPol. 159/M6
Pukaskwa NP, On, Can. 172/C1
Pukch'ŏng, NKor. 115/E2
Pukdae (riv.), NKor. 115/E2
Pukhan (riv.), NKor.,SKor. 115/D3
Pukhrāyān, India 126/B2
Pukovac, Serb. 90/E4
Pukp'ot'ae-san (peak), NKor. 115/E2
Pula, Cro. 90/A3
Pulacayo, Bol. 192/E8
Pulandian (bay), China 115/A3
Pulanduta (pt.), Phil. 123/F1
Pulap (isl.), Micr. 158/D4
Pulaski, Va, US 172/D4
Pulaski, Tn, US 175/G3
Pulau (riv.), Indo. 123/J5
Puławy, Pol. 83/L3
Pulguk-sa, SKor. 115/E5
Pulheim, Ger. 95/F2
Pulisan (cape), Indo. 123/G3
Pulkovo (int'l arpt.), Rus. 103/T7
Pullach im Isartal, Ger. 99/H1
Pullman, Wa, US 168/D4
Pully, Swi. 98/C5
Pulsnitz (riv.), Ger. 83/G3
Pułtusk, Pol. 83/L2
Pülümür, Turk. 132/D2
Puluwat (isl.), Micr. 158/D4
Pulversheim, Fr. 98/D2
Pum (riv.), China 127/F1
Puma (lake), China 127/H1
Pumu (pass), China 127/H2
Puna de Atacama (plat.), Arg. 199/C2
Puná, Isla (isl.), Ecu. 192/B4
Punākha, Bhu. 127/G2
Punata, Bol. 192/E7
Pūnch, India 128/C3
Pūnch (riv.), India 128/C3
Pūndri, India 128/D5
Pune (Poona), India 131/K5
Punggai (cape), Malay. 122/B3
P'unggi, SKor. 115/E4
P'ungsan, NKor. 115/E2
Pungwe (falls), Zim. 147/F4
Punjab (plain), Pak. 131/K2
Punjab (state), Pak. 124/B2
Puno, Peru 198/D4
Puno (dept.), Peru 198/D4
Pūnpūn (riv.), India 127/E3
Punta, Ca, US 178/A2
Punta Alta, Arg. 200/E3
Punta Arena (pt.), Mex. 184/C4
Punta Arenas, Chile 201/C7
Punta Banda (cape), Mex. 184/A2
Punta Cardón, Ven. 194/D2
Punta Celarain (pt.), Mex. 186/E1
Punta Colnett (pt.), Mex. 184/A2
Punta Colonet, Mex. 184/A2
Punta de Bombón, Peru 198/D5
Punta de Mata, Ven. 195/F2
Punta del Este, Uru. 201/G2
Punta del Este (Capitán Curbelo) (int'l arpt.), Uru. 201/G2
Punta Gorda, Fl, US 175/H5
Punta Gorda (bay), Nic. 182/E5
Punta Gorda, Belz. 186/D2
Punta Marina, It. 101/F4
Punta Raisi (int'l arpt.), It. 88/C3
Punta Umbría, Sp. 86/B4
Puntarenas, CR 187/E4
Puolo (pt.), Hi, US 166/S10
Pupiales, Col. 194/B4
Pupuya (peak), Bol. 198/D4
Puquio, Peru 198/C4
Pur (riv.), Rus. 106/H3
Puracé (vol.), Col. 194/B4
Puracé, PN, Col. 192/C3
Pūranpur, India 126/C1
Purbeck (isl.), Eng, UK 74/D5
Purcell (mts.), BC, Can. 168/D3
Purcell, Ok, US 171/H4
Puré (riv.), Col. 194/D5
Purén, Chile 200/B3
Purgatoire (riv.), Co, US 171/G3
Pürgen, Ger. 99/G1
Purgstall an der Erlauf, Aus. 85/L2
Purī, India 124/D3
Purificación, Col. 194/C4
Purikari (pt.), Est. 81/L2
Purkersdorf, Aus. 91/N7
Purmerend, Neth. 92/B3
Pūrna, India 124/C4
Purnia, India 127/F3
Purranque, Chile 199/B5
Puruê (riv.), Braz. 194/D5
Purūlia, India 127/F4
Puruni (riv.), Guy. 195/G3
Purús (riv.), Braz. 189/C3
Purushottampur, India 124/D4
Pürvomay, Bul. 91/G4
Purwa, India 126/C2
Purwokerto, Indo. 122/C5
Pusad, India 124/C4
Pusan, SKor. 115/E5
Pusan-Gwangyŏksi (prov.), SKor. 115/E5
Pusat Gayo (mts.), Indo. 122/A3
Puschendorf, Ger. 96/D3
Pushkin, Rus. 103/T7
Püspökladány, Hun. 90/E2
Pusur (riv.), Bang. 127/G4
Putaendo, Chile 200/C2
Putian, China 121/C2
Putina, Peru 198/D4
Puting (cape), Indo. 122/D4
Putla de Guerrero, Mex. 186/B2
Putomayo (dept.), Col. 194/C4
Putorana (mts.), Rus. 106/K3
Putrachoique (peak), Arg. 200/C4
Putre, Chile 198/D5
Puttalam, SrL. 124/C6
Putte, Belg. 95/D1
Puttelange-aux-Lacs, Fr. 95/F5
Putten, Neth. 92/C4
Putten (isl.), Neth. 92/B5
Püttlach (riv.), Ger. 97/E3
Püttlingen, Ger. 95/F5
Putu (range), Libr. 144/C5
Putumayo (riv.), SAm. 194/C5
Putussibau, Indo. 122/D3
Puu Kukui (peak), Hi, US 166/T10
Puu Moaulanui (peak), Hi, US 166/T10
Puu o Mahuka Heiau State Mon., Hi, US 166/V12
Puuanahulu, Hi, US 166/U11
Puuiki, Hi, US 166/T10
Puula (lake), Fin. 81/M1
Puurs, Belg. 95/D1
Puuwai, Hi, US 166/R10
Puy de Sancy (peak), Fr. 84/E4
Puyallup, Wa, US 168/C4
Puyallup (riv.), Wa, US 177/C3
Puyallup Ind. Res., Wa, US 177/C3
Puyang, China 114/C4
Puyehué (lake), Chile 200/B4
Puyehue (vol.), Chile 200/B4
Puylaurens, Fr. 84/E5
Puymorens, Col de (pass), Fr. 84/D5
Puyŏ, SKor. 115/D4
Puyo, Ecu. 194/B5
Puzal, Sp. 87/E3
Pwani (pol. reg.), Tanz. 146/C4
Pwllheli, Wal, UK 76/D6
Pyandzh (riv.), Taj. 129/F5
Pyaozero (lake), Rus. 79/J2
Pyapon, Myan. 125/G4
Pyasina (riv.), Rus. 106/J2
Pyatigorsk, Rus. 105/G3
Pyfara (peak), Fr. 84/F4
Pyhä-Häkin NP, Fin. 102/E3
Pyhäjärvi, Fin. 102/E3
Pyhäjärvi (lake), Fin. 81/K1
Pyhäntä, Fin. 102/E2
Pyhätunturi (peak), Fin. 102/E2
Pyinmana, Myan. 125/G4
P'yŏngan-bukto (prov.), NKor. 115/C2
P'yŏngan-namdo (prov.), NKor. 115/C3
P'yŏngch'ang, SKor. 115/E4
P'yŏnggang, NKor. 115/D3
P'yŏnghae, SKor. 115/E4
P'yŏngsan, NKor. 115/D3
P'yŏngsong, NKor. 115/C3
Pyŏngt'aek, SKor. 115/D4
P'yŏngyang (int'l arpt.), NKor. 115/C3
P'yŏngyang (cap.), NKor. 115/C3
P'yŏngyang-si (prov.), NKor. 115/C3
Pyŏnsanbando NP, SKor. 115/D5
Pyramid (lake), Nv, US 170/B3
Pyramid (mtn.), BC, Can. 176/M4
Pyramids of Jīzah, Egypt 133/B5
Pyrenees (mts.), Fr.,Sp. 69/D4
Pyrénées Occidental, PN des, Fr. 84/C5
Pyryatyn, Ukr. 104/E2
Pyrzyce, Pol. 83/H2
Pyshma (riv.), Rus. 103/Q4
Pyu, Myan. 125/G4
Pyuthān, Nepal 126/D1

Q

Qā 'al Jafr (salt pan), Jor. 133/E4
Qabalān, WBnk. 133/G7
Qabātiyah, WBnk. 133/G7
Qādima, Isr. 133/F7
Qādirpur Rān, Pak. 128/A4
Qā'en, Iran 131/G2
Qafa e Malit (pass), Alb. 89/G1
Qaffīn, WBnk. 133/G7
Qahar Youyi Qianqi, China 114/C2
Qahar Youyi Zhongqi, China 114/C2
Qaidam (basin), China 112/F4
Qalansuwa, Isr. 133/F7
Qal'at Dīzah, Iraq 132/F2
Qal'eh-ye Now, Afg. 129/D6
Qalqīlyah, WBnk. 133/F7
Qalyūb, Egypt 133/B4
Qamdo, China 112/G5
Qamīnis, Libya 138/K1
Qapshagay Bögeni (res.), Kaz. 129/G4
Qapshaghay, Kaz. 129/G4
Qaraghandy, Kaz. 129/F3
Qaraghandy (obl.), Kaz. 129/F3
Qarataū, Kaz. 129/F4
Qarataū Zhotasy (mts.), Kaz. 129/E4
Qareh Chāy (riv.), Iran 130/E2
Qareh Sū (riv.), Iran 105/H5
Qarqan (riv.), China 112/E4
Qarrit (pass), Alb. 89/G2
Qarshi, Uzb. 129/E5
Qārūn (lake), Egypt 143/B2
Qashqadaryo (pol. reg.), Uzb. 129/D5
Qaşr-e Qand, Iran 131/H3
Qaşr-e-Shīrīn, Iran 130/E2
Qa'ţabah, Yem. 130/D6
Qatar (ctry.) 130/F3
Qattara (depr.), Egypt 132/A4
Qaţţīnah, Buḩayrat (lake), Syria 133/E2
Qaydaq Sory (swamp), Kaz. 105/K3
Qayyārah, Iraq 132/E3
Qazaqtyng Usaqshoqylyghy (uplands), Kaz. 106/H5
Qāzi Ahmad, Pak. 124/A2
Qazvīn, Iran 130/F1
Qedma, Isr. 133/F8
Qendrevica (peak), Alb. 89/F2
Qezel Owzan (riv.), Iran 130/E1
Qi Xian, China 114/C4
Qian (mts.), China 115/B2
Qian (riv.), China 114/D5
Qian'an, China 113/M3
Qianxi, China 114/J6
Qianyang, China 121/B2
Qiaojia, China 125/H2
Qibyā, Isr. 133/G8
Qidong, China 125/K2
Qidong, China 114/L8
Qiemo, China 112/E4
Qihe, China 114/D3
Qijiang, China 121/A2
Qikiqtarjuaq, Nun., Can. 165/K2
Qila Dīdār Singh, Pak. 128/C3
Qila Sobha Singh, Pak. 128/C3
Qilian (mts.), China 112/G4
Qilian (peak), China 112/G4
Qimantag (mts.), China 112/F4
Qimen, China 121/C2
Qin (mts.), China 114/B4
Qinā (gov.), Egypt 143/C3
Qing (riv.), China 121/B1
Qing'an, China 113/N2
Qingdao, China 114/E3
Qingfeng, China 114/C4
Qinghai (mts.), China 112/G4
Qinghai (prov.), China 112/G4
Qinghe, China 114/C3
Qinglong, China 114/D2
Qingpu, China 114/L8
Qingshui (riv.), China 121/A2
Qingshuihe, China 114/B3
Qingyuan, China 125/K3
Qingyun, China 114/D3
Qingzhou, China 114/D3
Qinhuangdao, China 114/D3
Qinshui, China 114/C4
Qinyang, China 114/C4
Qinyuan, China 114/C3
Qinzhou, China 125/J3
Qionghai, China 125/K4
Qionglai (mts.), China 112/H5
Qiongshan, China 125/K4
Qiongzhong, China 120/E2
Qiqihar, China 113/M2
Qira, China 112/D4
Qiryat Ata, Isr. 133/G6
Qiryat Bialik, Isr. 133/G6
Qiryat Gat, Isr. 133/D4
Qiryat Mal'akhi, Isr. 133/F8
Qiryat Motzkin, Isr. 133/G6
Qiryat Shemona, Isr. 133/G6
Qiryat Tiv'on, Isr. 133/G6
Qiryat Yam, Isr. 133/G6
Qitai, China 112/E3
Qitaihe, China 113/P2
Qixia, China 114/E3
Qixing (riv.), China 107/P5
Qizilqum (des.), Kaz. 106/G5
Qogir (peak), China 131/L1
Qom (riv.), Iran 130/F2
Qom, Iran 130/F2
Qomsheh, Iran 130/F2
Qondūz (riv.), Afg. 131/J1
Qonggyai, China 127/H1
Qoraqalpoghiston Aut. Rep., Uzb. 105/L3
Qormi, Malta 88/L7
Qorveh, Iran 130/E1
Qostanay (obl.), Kaz. 129/D2
Qostanay (int'l arpt.), Kaz. 103/P5
Qostanay, Kaz. 103/P5
Qoţūr, Iran 132/F2
Qu (riv.), China 113/L6
Quabbin (res.), Ma, US 173/F3
Quairading, Austl. 154/C5
Quakenbrück, Ger. 93/E3
Quakertown, Pa, US 180/C3
Quambatook, Austl. 157/B2
Quanah, Tx, US 171/H4
Quanbao (mtn.), China 114/B4
Quang Ngai, Viet. 120/E3
Quang Tri, Viet. 120/D2
Quanjiao, China 114/D4
Quannan, China 121/B3
Quantocks, The (hills), Eng, UK 74/C4
Quanzhou, China 121/C3
Qu'appelle (dam), Sk, Can. 169/G3
Qu'appelle (riv.), Sk, Can. 169/G3
Qu'appelle, Sk, Can. 169/H3
Quaqtaq, Qu, Can. 165/K2
Quaregnon, Belg. 94/C3
Quarles (mts.), Indo. 123/E4
Quarona, It. 100/B1
Quarrata, It. 101/D5
Quarryville, Pa, US 180/B4
Quarto d'Altino, It. 101/F1
Quartu Sant'Elena, It. 88/A3
Quartz Hill, Ca, US 178/B1
Quatre Bornes, Mrts. 149/T15
Quattervals (peak), Swi. 99/G4
Quba, Azer. 105/J4
Qūchān, Iran 131/G1
Queanbeyan, Austl. 157/D2
Québec (int'l arpt.), Qu, Can. 173/G2
Québec (cap.), Qu, Can. 173/G2
Québec (prov.), Can. 165/J3
Quebra-Cangalha, Serra (mts.), Braz. 197/H8
Quecholac, Mex. 185/M8
Quechutenango, Mex. 185/F5
Quedal (pt.), Chile 200/B4
Queen Alia (int'l arpt.), Jor. 133/E4
Queen Anne, Md, US 180/C6
Queen Annes (co.), Md, US 180/C5
Queen Charlotte, BC, Can. 176/M5

268

Répce – Røros

Répcelak, Hun. 85/M3
Repelón, Col. 187/H4
Repentigny, Qu, Can. 173/P6
Replonges, Fr. 98/A5
Republic, Wa, US 168/D3
Republican (riv.), Ks,Ne, US 171/H2
Repulse (bay), Austl. 156/C3
Repulse Bay (isl.), Austl. 156/C3
Repulse Bay, Nun., Can. 165/H2
Requena, Peru 198/C2
Requena, Sp. 87/E3
Requinoa, Chile 200/N9
Reriutaba, Braz. 196/B2
Reşadiye, Turk. 132/D1
Reschensee (Resia) (lake), It. 99/G4
Rescue (pt.), Chile 200/B5
Resegone (peak), It. 100/C1
Resen, FYROM 89/G2
Resende, Braz. 197/J7
Resende, Port. 86/B2
Reserve, NM, US 170/E4
Resia, Passo di (pass), It. 99/G4
Resia (Reschensee) (lake), It. 99/G4
Resistencia, Arg. 199/E2
Reşiţa, Rom. 90/E3
Res Jebel, Tun. 142/M6
Resolution (isl.), Nun., Can. 165/K2
Respenda de la Peña, Sp. 86/C1
Resplendor, Braz. 197/D1
Restigouche (riv.), NB, Can. 173/H2
Reston, Mb, Can. 169/H3
Reston, Va, US 180/A6
Reszel, Pol. 81/J4
Retalhuleu, Guat. 186/D3
Rethel, Fr. 95/D4
Rethem, Ger. 93/G3
Réthimnon, Gre. 89/J5
Retie, Belg. 92/C6
Retrezap NP, Rom. 90/F3
Rétság, Hun. 90/D2
Rettenberg, Ger. 99/G2
Retz, Aus. 83/H4
Réunion (dpcy.), Fr. 149/S15
Reus, Sp. 87/F2
Reusel, Neth. 92/C6
Reuss (riv.), Swi. 99/E3
Reuterstadt Stavenhagen, Ger. 80/E5
Reutlingen, Ger. 96/C6
Reutov, Rus. 103/W9
Reutte, Aus. 99/G3
Revadim, Isr. 133/F8
Réveillon (riv.), Fr. 72/K5
Revel, Fr. 84/D5
Revelstoke, BC, Can. 168/D3
Revere, It. 101/E2
Revfülöp, Hun. 90/C2
Revigny-sur-Ornain, Fr. 95/D6
Revillagigedo (isls.), Mex. 184/B5
Revin, Fr. 95/D4
Revolyutsii (peak), Taj. 129/F5
Revsbotn (inlet), Nor. 79/G1
Rewa, India 126/C3
Rewa (riv.), Guy. 195/G4
Rex (mtn.), Ak, US 176/J3
Rey, Isla del (isl.), Pan. 187/G4
Reyes, Bol. 192/E6
Reyes (pt.), Ca, US 170/B3
Reyhanlı, Turk. 133/E1
Reykjanestá (cape), Ice. 79/M7
Reykjavík (int'l arpt.), Ice. 79/N7
Reykjavík (cap.), Ice. 79/N7
Reynosa, Mex. 185/F3
Reyssouze (riv.), Fr. 98/B5
Rezé, Fr. 84/C3
Rēzekne, Lat. 81/M3
Rezzato, It. 100/D1
Rhaetian Alps (mts.), Swi., Aus 85/H3
Rhallamane (reg.), Mrta. 140/C5
Rhallamane (lake), Mrta. 140/C4
Rhart (peak), Mor. 140/D3
Rhat (peak), Mor. 140/D3
Rhätikon (mts.), Aus.,Swi. 99/F3
Rheda-Wiedenbrück, Ger. 93/F5
Rhede, Ger. 92/D5
Rhede, Ger. 93/E2
Rheden, Neth. 92/D4
Rheidol (riv.), Wal, UK 74/C2
Rheinau, Swi. 99/E2
Rheinbach, Ger. 95/F2
Rheinberg, Ger. 92/D5
Rheinbreitbach, Ger. 95/G2
Rheinbrohl, Ger. 95/G3
Rheine, Ger. 93/E4
Rheinfall, Swi. 99/E2
Rheinfelden, Ger. 98/D2
Rheinland-Pfalz (state), Ger. 96/A3
Rheinwaldhorn (peak), Swi. 99/F5
Rheinzabern, Ger. 96/B4
Rhemiles (well), Alg. 140/D3
Rhenen, Neth. 92/C5
Rheris, Oued (riv.), Mor. 140/D3
Rhinau, Fr. 98/D1
Rhine (riv.), Eur. 69/E4
Rhine-Herne (canal), Ger. 93/E5
Rhinns (pt.), Sc, UK 73/Q9
Rhinns, The (pt.), Sc, UK 76/C2
Rhino Camp, Ugan. 146/A2
Rhiou (riv.), Alg. 142/F5
Rhiou (riv.), Alg. 142/F5
Rhir (cape), Mor. 140/C3
Rhisnes, Belg. 95/D3
Rhiw (riv.), Wal, UK 74/C1
Rho, It. 100/C1
Rhode Island (state), US 173/G3
Rhodes (isl.), Gre. 132/A3
Rhön (mts.), Ger. 96/D1
Rhondda, Wal, UK 74/C3
Rhondda Cynon Taff (co.), Wal, UK 74/C3
Rhône (dept.), Fr. 98/A6
Rhône (riv.), Fr. 84/F4
Rhone (glacier), Swi. 99/E4
Rhône-Alpes (pol. reg.), Fr. 98/B5
Rhône au Rhin (canal), Fr. 98/B3
Rhonelle (riv.), Fr. 94/C3
Rhosllanerchrugog, Wal, UK 77/E6
Rhum (isl.), Sc, UK 73/Q8
Rhume (riv.), Ger. 93/H5
Rhumel, Oued el (riv.), Alg. 142/J4
Rhyddhywel (peak), Wal, UK 74/C2
Rhyl, Wal, UK 76/E5
Riachão, Braz. 196/A2
Riachão das Neves, Braz. 196/A3
Riachão do Jacuípe, Braz. 196/C3
Riacho de Santana, Braz. 196/B4
Riachuelo, Braz. 196/D2
Rialto, Ca, US 178/C2
Rianjo, Sp. 86/A1
Riaño, Sp. 86/C1
Riāsi, India 128/C3
Riau (isls.), Indo. 122/B3
Riaza, Sp. 86/D2
Ribadeo, Sp. 86/B1
Ribadesella, Sp. 86/C1
Riban'i Manamby (mts.), Madg. 149/H9
Ribble (riv.), Eng, UK 77/F4
Ribblesdale (valley), Eng, UK 77/F3
Ribe, Den. 80/C4
Ribe (co.), Den. 80/C4
Ribeauvillé, Fr. 98/D1
Ribécourt-Dreslincourt, Fr. 94/B4
Ribeira (riv.), Braz. 197/B3
Ribeira Brava, CpV. 135/J10
Ribeira de Pena, Port. 86/B2
Ribeira do Pombal, Braz. 196/C3
Ribeira Grande, Azor., Port. 87/T13
Ribeira Grande, CpV. 135/J9
Ribeirão, Braz. 196/D3
Ribeirão do Pinha, Braz. 197/B2
Ribeiro Gonçalves, Braz. 196/A2
Ribera, It. 88/C4
Riberalta, Bol. 192/E6
Rîbniţa, Mol. 91/J2
Ribnitz-Damgarten, Ger. 80/E4
Říčany u Prahy, Czh. 97/H3
Ricaurte, Col. 194/B4
Riccia, It. 88/D2
Riccione, It. 101/F5
Ricco'del Golfo, It. 100/C4
Rice (lake), On, Can. 172/E2
Richard Toll, Sen. 144/B2
Richards (isl.), NW, Can. 164/C2
Richard's Bay, SAfr. 149/F3
Richardson (lakes), Me, US 173/G2
Richboro, Pa, US 180/C3
Riche (cape), Austl. 154/C5
Richebourg, Fr. 72/G5
Richel (isl.), Neth. 92/C2
Richelieu, Qu, Can. 173/P7
Richfield, Ut, US 170/D3
Richfield, Pa, US 180/A2
Richhill, NI, UK 76/B3
Richland, NJ, US 180/D5
Richland, Ok, US 179/M14
Richland, Pa, US 180/B3
Richland, Wa, US 168/D4
Richland Balsam (peak), NC, US 175/H3
Richland Center, Wi, US 169/L5
Richland Creek (res.), Tx, US 171/H5
Richlandtown, Pa, US 180/C3
Richmond, Austl. 156/A3
Richmond, BC, Can. 168/C3
Richmond, Qu, Can. 173/F2
Richmond, SAfr. 149/E3
Richmond, SAfr. 148/C3
Richmond, Il, US 177/P15
Richmond, Ky, US 172/C4
Richmond (co.), NY, US 180/D2
Richmond Beach-Innis Arden, Wa, US 177/B2
Richmond Heights, Mo, US 179/G8
Richmond Hill, On, Can. 173/R8
Richmond Park (bor.), Eng, UK 72/C2
Richmond Upon Thames (bor.), Eng, UK 72/B2
Richmond-Windsor, Austl. 156/G8
Richtersveld NP, SAfr. 148/B3
Richterswil, Swi. 99/E3
Richwiller, Fr. 98/D2
Rickenbach, Ger. 98/D2
Ricketts Glen State Park, Pa, US 180/B1
Rickmansworth, Eng, UK 72/B2
Ricla, Sp. 86/E2
Ricse, Hun. 83/L4
Ridā', Yem. 130/D6
Ridderkerk, Neth. 92/B5
Rideau (lake), On, Can. 172/E2
Ridgecrest, Ca, US 170/C4
Ridgefield, Ct, US 181/E1
Ridgefield, NJ, US 181/K8
Ridgefield Park, NJ, US 181/J8
Ridgeland, Ms, US 171/K4
Ridgely, Mo, US 179/D5
Ridgely, Md, US 180/C6
Ridgewood, NJ, US 181/J8
Ridgewood State Park, NJ, US 180/D2
Riding Mountain NP, Mb, Can. 169/H3
Ridlees Cairn (hill), Eng, UK 78/D6
Riecito (riv.), Col. 194/D3
Ried im Innkreis, Aus. 97/G6
Ried im Traunkreis, Aus. 97/H6
Riede, Ger. 93/F3
Riedenburg, Ger. 97/E5
Riedisheim, Fr. 98/D2
Riedlingen, Ger. 99/F1
Riegelsberg, Ger. 95/F5
Riegelsville, Pa, US 180/C2
Riegsee (lake), Ger. 99/H2
Riehen, Swi. 98/D2
Riemst, Belg. 95/E2
Rieneck, Ger. 96/C2
Riesa, Ger. 83/G3
Rieschweiler-Mühlbach, Ger. 95/G5
Riesco (isl.), Chile 199/B7
Riese Pio X, It. 101/E1
Riet (riv.), SAfr. 148/D3
Rietberg, Ger. 93/F5
Rietbron, SAfr. 148/C4
Rieti, It. 88/C1
Riffe (lake), Wa, US 168/C4
Rifle, Co, US 170/F3
Rifsnes (pt.), Ice. 79/N6
Rift Valley (prov.), Kenya 146/B2
Riga (gulf), Eur. 81/K2
Rīga (Riga) (cap.), Lat. 81/L3
Rigby, Id, US 168/F5
Rīgestan (pol. reg.), Afg. 131/H2
Riggins, Id, US 168/D4
Rigi (peak), Swi. 99/E3
Rignano sull'Arno, It. 101/E5
Rigolet, Nf, Can. 165/L3
Rihand (dam), India 126/D3
Rihand (riv.), India 126/D3
Rihand Sāgar (res.), India 124/D3
Riihimäki, Fin. 81/L1
Riiser-Larsen (pen.), Ant. 202/C
Riiser-Larsen Ice Shelf, Ant. 202/Y
Riisitunturin NP, Fin. 102/F2
Rijeka, Cro. 90/B3
Rijksmuseum Kröller Müller, Neth. 92/C4
Rijnsburg, Neth. 92/B4
Rijsbergen, Neth. 92/B5
Rijssen, Neth. 92/D4
Rijswijk, Neth. 92/B4
Rikers (isl.), NY, US 181/K8
Rikitea, FrPol. 159/M7
Rikuchū-Kaigan NP, Japan 118/C4
Rikuzentakata, Japan 118/B4
Rila, Bul. 91/F4
Rila (mts.), Bul. 91/F4
Rillieux-la-Pape, Fr. 98/A6
Rilski Manastir, Bul. 89/H1
Rimatara (isl.), FrPol. 159/K7
Rimavská Sobota, Slvk. 83/L4
Rimbach, Ger. 96/B3
Rimbey, Ab, Can. 168/E2
Rimforsa, Swe. 80/F2
Rimini, It. 101/F4
Rîmnicu Sărat, Rom. 91/H3
Rîmnicu Vîlcea, Rom. 91/G3
Rimogne, Fr. 95/D4
Rimouski, Qu, Can. 173/G1
Rimpar, Ger. 96/C3
Rimpfischhorn (peak), Swi. 98/D5
Rinas (int'l arpt.), Alb. 89/F2
Rinbung, China 127/G1
Rinchnach, Ger. 97/G5
Rincón de la Vieja, PN, CR 182/D5
Rincón de Romos, Mex. 184/E4
Ringarooma, Austl. 157/C4
Ringboy (pt.), NI, UK 76/C3
Ringebu, Nor. 80/D1
Ringelspitz (peak), Swi. 99/F4
Ringgold, La, US 171/J4
Ringkøbing (fjord), Den. 80/B3
Ringkøbing, Den. 80/C3
Ringkøbing (co.), Den. 80/B3
Ringoes, NJ, US 180/D3
Ringsend, NI, UK 76/B1
Ringsted, Den. 80/D4
Ringtown, Pa, US 180/B2
Ringvaart (riv.), Neth. 92/B4
Ringvassøy (isl.),Nor. 79/F1
Ringwood, Eng, UK 75/E5
Ringwood, NJ, US 181/H7
Ringwood State Park, NJ, US 180/D1
Rinia (isl.), Gre. 89/J4
Rinteln, Ger. 93/G4
Rinxent, Fr. 94/A2
Río Abiseo, PN, Peru 192/C5
Rio Azul, Braz. 197/B3
Río Blanco, Mex. 185/M8
Rio Bonito, Braz. 197/L7
Rio Branco, Braz. 192/E5
Rio Branco do Sul, Braz. 197/B3
Río Bravo, Mex. 185/F5
Río Bueno, Chile 200/B4
Rio Casca, Braz. 197/D2
Río Cauto, Cuba 187/G1
Río Clarillo, PN, Chile 200/N8
Rio Claro, Braz. 197/J7
Rio Claro, Trin. 195/F2
Río Colorado, Arg. 200/D3
Río Cuarto, Arg. 200/D2
Rio de Janeiro, Braz. 197/K7
Rio de Janeiro (state), Braz. 197/D2
Rio de Janeiro (int'l arpt.), Braz. 197/K7
Rio Dell, Ca, US 168/B5
Río Gallegos, Arg. 201/C6
Río Grande, Arg. 201/D7
Rio Grande, Braz. 197/A5
Rio Grande (riv.), Mex.,US 171/F5
Rio Grande, NJ, US 180/D5
Rio Grande (plain), Tx, US 182/B2
Rio Grande City, Tx, US 174/D5
Rio Grande da Serra, Braz. 197/G8
Rio Grande Do Norte , (state) Braz. 196/C2
Rio Grande do Piauí, Braz. 196/B2
Rio Grande Valley (int'l arpt.), Tx, US 174/D5
Rio Jaú, PN do, Braz. 192/F4
Río Lagartos, Mex. 186/D1
Rio Largo, Braz. 196/D3
Rio Maior, Port. 86/A3
Río Mayo, Arg. 200/C5
Rio Negrinho, Braz. 197/B3
Río Negro (prov.), Arg. 200/E3
Rio Negro, Braz. 197/B3
Río Negro, Chile 200/B4
Río Negro, Embalse de (res.), Uru. 199/E3
Rio Paranaíba, Braz. 197/C1
Rio Pardo, Braz. 197/A4
Río Pilcomayo, PN, Arg. 199/E2
Rio Prêto (range), Braz. 196/A5
Rio Rancho, NM, US 170/F4
Rio Real, Braz. 196/C3
Rio Saliceto, It. 101/D3
Río Simpson, PN, Chile 200/B5
Río Tala, Arg. 201/J10
Rio Tercero, Arg. 199/D3
Rio Tigre, Ecu. 194/B5
Rio Tinto, Braz. 196/D2
Rio Verde, Braz. 197/B1
Río Verde, Chile 201/C7
Río Verde, Mex. 185/F4
Rio Verde de Mato Grosso, Braz. 193/H7
Rio Vista, Ca, US 177/L10
Riobamba, Ecu. 194/B5
Riohacha, Col. 194/C2
Rioja, Peru 198/B2
Riolândia, Braz. 197/B1
Riolo Terme, It. 101/E4
Riom, Fr. 84/E4
Riom-ès-Montagne, Fr. 84/E4
Riomaggiore, It. 100/C4
Rion-des-Landes, Fr. 84/C5
Riondel, BC, Can. 168/D3
Rionegro, Col. 194/C3
Rionero in Vulture, It. 88/D2
Riorges, Fr. 84/F3
Ríos, Sp. 86/B2
Ríos (lake), Chile 200/B5
Ríosucio, Col. 194/B3
Rioz, Fr. 98/C3
Ripalti, Punta dei (pt.), It. 88/B1
Ripanj, Serb. 90/E3
Riparbella, It. 100/D6
Ripley, Ms, US 175/F3
Ripley, Eng, UK 77/G5
Ripoll, Sp. 87/G1
Ripoll (riv.), Sp. 87/L6
Ripollet, Sp. 87/L6
Ripon, Wi, US 169/L5
Ripon, Eng, UK 77/G3
Riposto, It. 88/D4
Ripponden, Eng, UK 77/G4
Rippowam (riv.), Ct, US 181/L7
Ris-Orangis, Fr. 72/K6
Risaralda (dept.), Col. 194/A4
Rishiri, Japan 118/B1
Rishiri-Rebun-Sarobetsu NP, Japan 118/B1
Rishon Leẕiyyon, Isr. 133/F8
Rising Sun, Md, US 180/B4
Rising Sun-Lebanon, De, US 180/C5
Risle (riv.), Fr. 84/D2
Risnjak (peak), Cro. 90/B3
Risnjak NP, Cro. 90/B3
Rîşnov, Rom. 91/G3
Rison, Ar, US 171/J4
Risør, Nor. 80/C2
Riss (riv.), Ger. 99/F1
Risse (riv.), Fr. 98/C5
Ristiina, Fin. 81/M1
Ritacuba (peak), Col. 194/C3
Ritaiō (isl.), Japan 158/D2
Ritoio (peak), It. 101/E5
Ritterhude, Ger. 93/F2
Rittō, Japan 119/J5
Ritzville, Wa, US 168/D4
Riva, It. 99/G6
Riva Ligure, It. 100/A5
Riva Presso Chieri, It. 100/A3
Riva San Vitale, Swi. 99/E6
Rivadavia, Arg. 199/C3
Rivadavia, Arg. 200/E2
Rivalta, It. 100/D2
Rivalta di Torino, It. 100/A2
Rivanazzano, It. 100/C3
Rivarolo Canavese, It. 100/A2
Rivarolo Mantovano, It. 100/D2
Rivas, Nic. 186/E4
Rive-de-Gier, Fr. 84/F4
River Cess, Libr. 144/C5
River Edge, NJ, US 181/J8
River Kwai Bridge, Thai. 120/B3
River Rouge, Mi, US 177/F7
River Vale, NJ, US 181/J8
Rivera, Uru. 199/E3
Rivera, Swi. 99/E5
Rivera (isl.), Chile 200/B5
Rivera, Arg. 200/E3
Riverdale, NJ, US 181/H8
Riverdale, Ut, US 179/K11
Rivergaro, It. 100/C3
Riverhead, NY, US 181/F2
Rivers (inlet), BC, Can. 168/B3
Rivers, Mb, Can. 169/H3
Rivers (state), Nga. 145/G5
Riversdale, SAfr. 148/C4
Riverside (co.), Ca, US 178/C3
Riverside, Ca, US 178/C3
Riverside, Mo, US 179/D5
Riverside, NJ, US 180/D3
Riverside, Pa, US 180/B2
Riverton, Mb, Can. 169/J3
Riverton, NZ 159/R12
Riverton, Ut, US 179/K12
Riverton, Austl. 155/H5
Riverview, NB, Can. 173/H2
Riverwoods, Il, US 177/Q15
Riviera Beach, Fl, US 175/H5
Riviera Beach, Md, US 180/B5
Rivière-du-Loup, Qu, Can. 173/G2
Riviersonderendreeks (mts.), SAfr. 148/L11
Rivignano, It. 101/G1
Rivne, Ukr. 104/C2
Rivnens'ka Oblasti, Ukr. 104/C2
Rivoli, It. 85/G4
Rivolta d'Adda, It. 100/C2
Rixensart, Belg. 95/D2
Rixheim, Fr. 98/D2
Riyāq, Leb. 133/D3
Rize, Turk. 132/E1
Rize (prov.), Turk. 132/E1
Rizhao, China 114/D4
Rizokarpasso, Cyp. 133/D2
Rizzuto (cape), It. 89/E3
Rjukan, Nor. 80/C2
Rkîz (lake), Mrta. 144/B2
Roa, Sp. 86/D2
Roa, Nor. 80/D1
Road Town (cap.), BVI 183/M8
Roan (plat.), Co, US 170/E3
Roan Fell (hill), Sc, UK 77/F1
Roanne, Fr. 84/F3
Roanoke, Al, US 175/G3
Roanoke (riv.), Va, US 172/E4
Roanoke (pt.), NY, US 181/F2
Roatán (isl.), Hon. 182/D4
Roatán, Hon. 186/E2
Robāţ Karīm, Iran 130/F1
Robbiate, It. 100/C1
Robbins (isl.), Austl. 157/C4
Robbio, It. 100/B2
Robe, Austl. 157/A3
Robe (mt.), Austl. 157/B1
Robe (riv.), Ire. 73/P10
Robecchetto con Induno, It. 100/B1
Röbel, Ger. 80/E4
Robert (peak), Fr. 98/B5
Robert Lee, Tx, US 171/G5
Roberts (mtn.), Ak, US 176/E4
Roberts (Monrovia) (int'l arpt.), Libr. 144/C5
Robertsfors, Swe. 79/G2
Robertsganj, India 126/D3
Robertson, SAfr. 148/L10
Robertsport, Libr. 144/C5
Robertstown, Ire. 73/Q10
Roberval, Qu, Can. 173/F1
Robesonia, Pa, US 180/B3
Robinson (ranges), Austl. 154/C3
Robinson Crusoe (isl.), Chile 189/B6
Robinson Gorge NP, Austl. 156/C4
Robinvale, Austl. 157/B2
Roblin, Mb, Can. 169/H3
Roboré, Bol. 192/G7
Robson (mt.), BC, Can. 168/D2
Robstown, Tx, US 174/D5
Roby, Tx, US 171/G4
Roc du Haut du Faite (peak), Fr. 98/D1
Roca, Cabo da (cape), Port. 87/P10
Roca Partida (isl.), Mex. 184/B5
Roca Partida, Punta (pt.), Mex. 186/C2
Rocafuerte, Ecu. 194/A5
Rocas (isl.), Braz. 193/M4
Rocca San Casciano, It. 101/E4
Roccabianca, It. 100/D2
Roccastrada, It. 85/J5
Rocciamelone (peak), It. 85/G4
Rocha, Uru. 201/G2
Rocha (dept.), Uru. 201/G2
Rochdale, Eng, UK 77/F4
Rochdale (co.), Eng, UK 77/F4
Roche, Swi. 98/C5
Roche du Sapin Sec (peak), Fr. 98/C1
Roche-lez-Beaupré, Fr. 98/C3
Rochefort, Fr. 84/C4
Rochefort, Belg. 95/E3
Rochelle Park, NJ, US 181/J8
Rochers du Bourbet (peak), Fr. 98/C3
Rochester, Austl. 157/C3
Rochester, Mn, US 169/K4
Rochester, NY, US 172/E3
Rochester, In, US 172/C3
Rochester, NH, US 173/G3
Rochester, Eng, UK 75/G4
Rochester, Mi, US 177/F6
Rochester, Wi, US 177/P14
Rochford, Eng, UK 72/F2
Rock (riv.), Il, US 172/B3
Rock (riv.), Ia,Mo, US 171/H2
Rock Creek, Yk, Can. 176/L3
Rock Forest, Qu, Can. 173/G2
Rock Glen, Pa, US 180/B2
Rock Hall, Md, US 180/B5
Rock Hill, SC, US 175/H3
Rock Island, Il, US 169/L5
Rock Springs, Wy, US 168/F5
Rockall (isl.), UK 69/C3
Rockaway, NJ, US 180/D2
Rockaway (riv.), NJ, US 181/H8
Rockaway (inlet), NY, US 181/K9
Rockaway (pt.), NY, US 181/K9
Rockdale, Il, US 177/P17
Rockefeller (plat.), Ant. 202/R
Rockenhausen, Ger. 95/G4
Rockford, Il, US 169/L5
Rockglen, Sk, Can. 169/G3
Rockhampton, Austl. 156/C3
Rockingham, NC, US 175/J3
Rockingham, Austl. 154/K7
Rockland, On, Can. 172/F2
Rockland, Me, US 173/G2
Rockland (co.), NY, US 180/D1
Rockland Lake, NY, US 181/K7
Rocklands (res.), Austl. 157/B3
Rockledge, Fl, US 175/H4
Rockledge, Pa, US 180/C3
Rockport, Tx, US 174/D4
Rocks, Md, US 180/B4
Rocksprings, Tx, US 171/G5
Rockstone, Guy. 195/G3
Rockville, Md, US 172/E4
Rockville Centre, NY, US 181/L9
Rockwall, Tx, US 171/H4
Rockwood, Tn, US 175/G3
Rocky (mtn.), Ky, US 172/D4
Rocky (mts.), Can.,US 161/E4
Rocky (pt.), NY, US 181/F1
Rocky Cape NP, Austl. 157/C4
Rocky Harbour, Nf, Can. 173/K1
Rocky Island (lake), On, Can. 172/D2
Rocky Mount, NC, US 175/J3
Rocky Mountain House, Ab, Can. 168/E2
Rocky Mountain NP, Co, US 170/F2
Rocroi, Fr. 95/D4
Rodach (riv.), Ger. 97/E2
Rodach bei Coburg, Ger. 96/D2
Rodalben, Ger. 95/G5
Rødberg, Nor. 80/C1
Rødbyhavn, Den. 80/D4
Roddickton, Nf, Can. 173/K1
Rødding, Den. 80/C4
Roden (riv.), Eng, UK 77/F6
Rodenbach, Ger. 96/C2
Rodeo, Mex. 184/D3
Rodeo, Ca, US 177/K10
Rödermark, Ger. 96/B3
Rodewisch, Ger. 97/F1
Rodez, Fr. 84/E4
Rodholívos, Gre. 89/H2
Ródhos (ruin), Gre. 132/B2
Ródhos (Rhodes), Gre. 132/B2
Rodigo, It. 100/D2
Roding (riv.), Eng, UK 72/D2
Roding, Ger. 97/F4
Rodinga (mt.), Austl. 155/G3
Rödinghausen, Ger. 93/F4
Rodoč, Bosn. 89/E1
Rodolfo Sánchez Toboada, Mex. 184/A2
Rodríguez, Uru. 201/K11
Roe (riv.), NI, UK 76/B2
Roebourne, Austl. 154/C2
Roebuck (bay), Austl. 151/B2
Roeland Park, Ks, US 179/D5
Roen (peak), It. 99/H5
Roer (riv.), Neth. 92/D6
Roermond, Neth. 92/C6
Roes Welcome Sound (str.), Nun., Can. 165/H2
Roeselare, Belg. 94/C2
Roesiger (lake), Wa, US 177/D2
Rogachev, Bela. 104/D1
Rogaland (co.), Nor. 79/C4
Rogaška Slatina, Slov. 85/L3
Rogatica, Bosn. 90/D4
Rogers (mt.), Va, US 172/D4
Rogers, Ar, US 171/J3
Rogers City, Mi, US 172/D2
Rogersville, Tn, US 172/D4
Roggwil, Swi. 98/D3
Rogliano, Fr. 85/H5
Roglio (riv.), It. 101/D5
Rognon (riv.), Fr. 84/F2
Rogoźno, Pol. 83/J2
Rogue (riv.), Or, US 170/B2
Rohl (riv.), Sudan 139/L6
Rohr, Ger. 97/E5
Rohrbach bei Mattersburg, Aus. 85/M3
Rohrbach in Oberösterreich, Aus. 97/G5
Rohrbach-lès-Bitche, Fr. 95/G5
Rohri, Pak. 131/J3
Röhrmoos, Ger. 97/E6
Rohtak, India 128/D5
Roi Et, Thai. 120/C2
Roine (lake), Fin. 81/L1
Roissy, Fr. 72/K5
Roissy-en-France, Fr. 72/K4
Rojas, Arg. 200/E2
Rojo (cape), PR 183/M8
Rojo, Cabo (cape), Mex. 186/B1
Rokan (riv.), Indo. 122/B3
Rokeby Croll Creek NP, Austl. 156/A1
Rokel (riv.), SLeo. 144/C4
Rokkasho, Japan 118/B3
Rokkō-san (peak), Japan 119/H6
Rokugō, Japan 119/A3
Rokycany, Czh. 97/G3
Rokytka (riv.), Czh. 97/H2
Rolampont, Fr. 98/B2
Rolândia, Braz. 197/B2
Rolava (riv.), Czh. 97/F2
Rolde, Neth. 92/D3
Rolla, ND, US 169/J3
Rolla, BC, Can. 168/C2
Rolla, Mo, US 171/K3
Rolle, Swi. 98/C5
Rolling Fork, Ms, US 171/K4
Rolling Hills Estates, Ca, US 178/F8
Rolling Meadows, Il, US 177/P15
Rollingbay, Wa, US 177/B2
Rollinsville, Co, US 179/A3
Rolo, It. 101/D3
Rom (peak), Ugan. 146/B2
Roma, Austl. 156/C4
Roma, Swe. 80/H3
Roma (Rome) (cap.), It. 88/C2
Romagnano Sesia, It. 100/B1
Romagnat, Fr. 84/E4
Romain (cape), SC, US 175/J3
Romaine (riv.), Qu, Can. 165/K3
Roman, Bul. 91/F4
Roman, Rom. 91/H2
Romang (str.), Indo. 123/G5
Romang (isl.), Indo. 123/G5
Romania (ctry.) 91/F3
Romano Canavese, It. 100/A2
Romano, Cayo (isl.), Cuba 187/G1
Romano d'Ezzelino, It. 101/E1
Romano di Lombardia, It. 100/C1
Romans d'Isonzo, It. 101/G1
Romans-sur-Isère, Fr. 84/F4
Romanshorn, Swi. 99/F2
Romanzof (cape), Ak, US 176/E3
Rombas, Fr. 95/F5
Romblon, Phil. 121/D5
Rome (cap.), It. 88/C2
Rome, Ga, US 175/G3
Rome, NY, US 172/F3
Rome, Wi, US 177/N14
Romenay, Fr. 98/B4
Romeoville, Il, US 177/P16
Römhild, Ger. 96/D2
Romilly-sur-Seine, Fr. 84/E2
Rommani, Mor. 140/D2
Rommerskirchen, Ger. 95/F1
Romney Marsh (phys. reg.), Eng, UK 75/G4
Romny, Ukr. 104/E2
Rømø (isl.), Den. 80/C4
Romoland, Ca, US 178/C3
Romont, Swi. 98/C4
Romorantin-Lanthenay, Fr. 84/D3
Romsey, Eng, UK 75/E5
Rømskog, Nor. 80/D2
Ronald Reagan Washington National (int'l arpt.), DC, US 180/A6
Ronan, Mt, US 168/E4
Roncade, It. 101/F1
Roncador Cay (isl.), Col. 187/G3
Roncador, Serra do (mts.), Braz. 193/H6
Ronchamp, Fr. 98/C2
Ronchi dei Legionari (int'l arpt.), It. 101/G1
Ronchi dei Legionari, It. 101/G1
Ronciglione, It. 88/C1
Ronco (riv.), It. 101/F5
Ronco All'Adige, It. 101/E2
Ronco Scrivia, It. 100/B3
Roncoferraro, It. 101/D2
Roncq, Fr. 94/C2
Ronda, Sp. 86/C4
Rondane NP, Nor. 79/D3
Ronde, Tête (peak), Swi. 98/D5
Rondonópolis, Braz. 193/H7
Rong (riv.), China 125/J2
Rong Xian, China 125/K3
Rongcheng, China 115/E3
Rongcheng, China 114/G7
Ronge (lake), Sk, Can. 164/F3
Rongelap (isl.), Mrsh. 158/F3
Rongerik (isl.), Mrsh. 158/F3
Ronkonkoma, NY, US 181/E2
Rønne, Den. 80/F4
Ronne Ice Shelf, Ant. 202/W
Ronneby, Swe. 80/F3
Ronnenberg, Ger. 93/G4
Ronquerolles, Fr. 72/J4
Ronsard (cape), Austl. 154/B3
Ronsberg, Ger. 99/G2
Ronse, Belg. 94/C2
Ronuro (riv.), Braz. 193/H6
Roodepoort, SAfr. 148/P13
Rooiberg (peak), Namb. 148/B2
Roorkee, India 124/C2
Roosendaal, Neth. 92/B5
Roosevelt, Ut, US 170/E2
Roosevelt (canal), Az, US 179/S19
Roosevelt (riv.), Braz. 189/C4
Roosevelt (mt.), BC, Can. 164/D3
Roosevelt, NJ, US 180/D3
Roosevelt (isl.), Ant. 202/N
Roosevelt, NY, US 181/L9
Root (mt.), Ak, US 176/L4
Root (riv.), Wi, US 177/P14
Root, West Branch (riv.), Wi, US 177/P14
Roque Pérez, Arg. 201/J11
Roquetas de Mar, Sp. 86/D4
Roraima (peak), Braz. 192/F2
Roraima (peak), Ven. 195/F3
Roraima (state), Braz. 195/F4
Rorke's Drift, SAfr. 149/E3
Rorke's Drift Battlesite, SAfr. 149/E3
Rorketon, Mb, Can. 169/J3
Røros, Nor. 79/D3

Samor – Sankt
271

Samora (riv.), Port. 87/Q10
Samora Correia, Port. 87/Q10
Sámos (isl.), Gre. 132/A2
Sámos, Gre. 132/A2
Samothráki, Gre. 89/J2
Sampacho, Arg. 200/D2
Samper de Calanda, Sp. 87/E2
Sampit (riv.), Indo. 122/D4
Sampit, Indo. 122/D4
Samsø (isl.), Den. 80/D4
Samsø Bælt (chan.), Den. 80/D4
Samson (mt.), Austl. 156/E6
Samsonvale (lake), Austl. 156/E6
Samsun, Turk. 132/D1
Samsun (prov.), Turk. 132/C1
Samthar, India 126/B3
Samugheo, It. 88/A3
Samui (isl.), Thai. 125/H6
Samukawa, Japan 119/C3
Samundri, Pak. 128/B4
Samur (riv.), Azer.,Rus. 106/E5
Samut Prakan, Thai. 120/C3
Samut Sakhon, Thai. 120/C3
Samut Songkhram, Thai. 120/B3
Samye Monastery, China 127/H1
San (riv.), Camb. 120/D3
San, Mali 144/D3
San (riv.), Pol. 83/M3
San Adrián, Cabo de (cape), Sp. 86/A1
San Agustin (cape), Phil. 121/E6
San Agustín, Col. 194/B4
San Agustín de Guadalix, Sp. 87/N8
San Agustín, Parque Arqeológico, Col. 194/B4
San Ambrosio (isl.), Chile 189/B5
San Andreas (lake), Ca, US 177/J11
San Andres (mts.), NM, US 170/F4
San Andrés (lake), Mex. 186/B1
San Andrés, Col. 194/C3
San Andrés, Col. 187/F3
San Andrés Cuexcontitlán, Mex. 185/Q10
San Andrés de Giles, Arg. 201/J11
San Andrés de Machaca, Bol. 198/D5
San Andrés del Rabanedo, Sp. 86/C1
San Andrés, Isla de (isl.), Col. 182/E5
San Andrés Tuxtla, Mex. 186/C2
San Angelo, Tx, US 174/C4
San Anselmo, Ca, US 177/J11
San Antonio (cape), Arg. 201/F3
San Antonio, Chile 200/N8
San Antonio, Ecu. 194/B4
San Antonio, Mex. 184/C4
San Antonio, Peru 198/B4
San Antonio, Uru. 201/K11
San Antonio, Ven. 195/F2
San Antonio (mt.), Ca, US 178/C2
San Antonio, Tx, US 171/H5
San Antonio (int'l arpt.), Tx, US 171/H5
San Antonio (riv.), Tx, US 174/D4
San Antonio Abad, Sp. 87/F3
San Antonio de Areco, Arg. 201/J11
San Antonio de Caparo, Ven. 194/D3
San Antonio del Golfo, Ven. 195/F2
San Antonio del Táchira, Ven. 194/C3
San Antonio Oeste, Arg. 200/D4
San Antonio, Punta (pt.), Mex. 184/B2
San Augustine, Tx, US 174/E4
San Bartolo, Peru 198/B4
San Bartolomé de Tirajana, Canl. 87/X17
San Bartolome Tlaltelulco, Mex. 185/Q10
San Bartolomeo in Bosco, It. 101/E3
San Bartolomeo in Galdo, It. 88/D2
San Bautista, Uru. 201/L11
San Benedetto (range), It. 101/E5
San Benedetto del Tronto, It. 85/K5
San Benedetto in Alpe, It. 101/E5
San Benedetto Po, It. 101/D2
San Benedicto (isl.), Mex. 184/C5
San Bernardo, Chile 200/N8
San Bernardo (pt.), Col. 194/C2
San Bernardino, Ca, US 178/C2
San Bernardino (co.), Ca, US 178/C2
San Bernardino (mts.), Ca, US 178/C2
San Bernardino Nat'l Forest, Ca, US 178/C2
San Blas, Mex. 184/D4
San Blas, Mex. 184/C3
San Blas (cape), Fl, US 175/G4
San Bonifacio, It. 101/E2
San Borja, Bol. 192/E6
San Bruno, Mex. 184/B3
San Bruno, Ca, US 177/K11
San Buenaventura, Mex. 185/E3
San Buenaventura (Ventura), Ca, US 178/A2
San Candido (Innichen), It. 85/K3
San Carlos, Chile 200/C3
San Carlos, Mex. 185/E2
San Carlos, Mex. 185/F3
San Carlos, Nic. 187/E4
San Carlos, Pan. 194/B2
San Carlos, Phil. 121/D4
San Carlos, Uru. 201/G2
San Carlos, Ven. 194/D2
San Carlos (lake), Az, US 170/E4
San Carlos, Ca, US 177/K11
San Carlos de Bariloche, Arg. 200/C4
San Carlos de Bariloche (int'l arpt.), Arg. 200/C4
San Carlos de Río Negro, Ven. 195/E4
San Carlos del Zulia, Ven. 194/D2
San Casciano in Val di Pesa, It. 101/E5
San Cataldo, It. 89/F2
San Cayetano, Arg. 200/F3
San Cesario sul Panaro, It. 101/E3
San Ciro de Acosta, Mex. 185/F4
San Clemente (isl.), Ca, US 170/C4
San Clemente, Ca, US 178/C4
San Clemente, Sp. 86/D3
San Clemente, Chile 200/C2
San Clemente del Tuyú, Arg. 201/F3
San Colombano al Lambro, It. 100/C2
San Cristóbal, Arg. 199/D3
San Cristobal (isl.), Sol. 158/F6
San Cristóbal (vol.), Nic. 186/E3
San Cristóbal, Cuba 187/F1
San Cristóbal (isl.), Ecu. 198/F7
San Cristóbal, Ven. 194/C3
San Cristóbal de las Casas, Mex. 186/C2
San Cristobal Wash (riv.), Az, US 184/B1
San Damiano d'Asti, It. 100/B3
San Diego (cape), Arg. 201/D7
San Diego, Ca, US 178/C5
San Diego (aqueduct), Ca, US 178/C4
San Diego (bay), Ca, US 178/C5
San Diego (co.), Ca, US 178/C4
San Diego, Tx, US 174/D5
San Diego International-Lindbergh Field (int'l arpt.), Ca, US 178/C5
San Diego Naval Station, Ca, US 178/C5
San Diego Wild Animal Park, Ca, US 178/C4
San Diego Zoo, Ca, US 178/C5
San Diequito (riv.), Ca, US 178/C5
San Dimas, Ca, US 178/C2
San Donà di Piave, It. 101/F1
San Donnino, It. 101/E5
San Dorligo della Valle, It. 101/G1
San Esteban de Gormaz, Sp. 86/D2
San Felice Circeo, It. 88/C2
San Felice del Benaco, It. 100/D1
San Felice sul Panaro, It. 101/E3
San Felipe, Mex. 184/B2
San Felipe, Ven. 194/D2
San Felipe, Chile 200/N8
San Felipe de Puerto Plata, DRep. 183/G4
San Felipe de Vichayal, Peru 198/A2
San Felipe Jalapa de Díaz, Mex. 185/F5
San Felipe Torres Mochas, Mex. 185/E4
San Felix (isl.), Chile 189/A5
San Fernando, Arg. 201/J11
San Fernando, Chile 200/C2
San Fernando (riv.), Mex. 174/D5
San Fernando, Phil. 121/D4
San Fernando, Phil. 121/D4
San Fernando, Sp. 86/B4
San Fernando, Trin. 195/F2
San Fernando, Ca, US 178/F7
San Fernando (valley), Ca, US 178/B2
San Fernando de Apure, Ven. 195/E3
San Fernando de Atabapo, Ven. 194/E3
San Fernando de Henares, Sp. 87/N9
San Fernando de Presas, Mex. 185/F3
San Fior di Sopra, It. 101/F1
San Francesco al Campo, It. 100/A2
San Francisco, Arg. 199/D3
San Francisco, Col. 194/B4
San Francisco, ESal. 186/D3
San Francisco, Phil. 121/E6
San Francisco, Ven. 194/D2
San Francisco (riv.), Az,NM, US 170/E4
San Francisco, Ca, US 170/B3
San Francisco (co.), Ca, US 177/K11
San Francisco (int'l arpt.), Ca, US 170/B3
San Francisco Acuautla, Mex. 185/R10
San Francisco Bay NWR, Ca, US 177/K11
San Francisco, Cabo de (cape), Ecu. 194/A4
San Francisco Chimalpa, Mex. 185/Q10
San Francisco de la Paz, Hon. 186/E3
San Francisco de Macorís, DRep. 183/G4
San Francisco de Mostazal, Chile 200/N8
San Francisco del Mezquital, Mex. 184/D4
San Francisco del Monte de Oro, Arg. 200/D2
San Francisco del Oro, Mex. 184/D3
San Francisco del Rincón, Mex. 185/E4
San Francisco Telixtlahuaca, Mex. 182/B4
San Fratello, It. 88/D3
San Gabriel (riv.), Ca, US 178/C2
San Gabriel (pt.), Mex. 184/B2
San Gabriel (res.), Ca, US 178/C2
San Gabriel, Ecu. 194/B4
San Gabriel, Ca, US 178/F7
San Gavino Monreale, It. 88/A3
San Germán, Cuba 187/G1
San Germano Vercellese, It. 100/B2
San Gil, Col. 194/C3
San Gimignano, It. 101/E6
San Giorgio delle Pertiche, It. 101/E1
San Giorgio di Piano, It. 101/E3
San Giorgio Ionico, It. 89/E2
San Giorgio Piacentino, It. 100/C3
San Giovanni al Natisone, It. 101/G1
San Giovanni Bianco, It. 100/C1
San Giovanni Gemini, It. 88/C4
San Giovanni in Croce, It. 100/D2
San Giovanni in Fiore, It. 88/E3
San Giovanni in Marignano, It. 101/F5
San Giovanni in Persiceto, It. 101/E3
San Giovanni Lupatoto, It. 101/E2
San Giovanni Valdarno, It. 101/E5
San Giuliano, It. 100/B3
San Giuliano Terme, It. 100/D5
San Giustino, It. 101/F5
San Giusto Canavese, It. 100/A2
San Gorgonio (mtn.), Ca, US 170/C4
San Gottardo, Passo del (pass), Swi. 99/E4
San Gregorio, Arg. 200/E2
San Gregorio, Uru. 201/L10
San Gregorio, Ca, US 177/K12
San Guiliano Milanese, It. 100/C2
San Hipólito Punta (pt.), Mex. 184/B3
San Ignacio, Belz. 186/D2
San Ignacio, Bol. 192/E6
San Ignacio, Bol. 192/F7
San Ignacio, Chile 200/B3
San Ignacio, Mex. 184/B3
San Ignacio, Mex. 184/D4
San Ignacio, Peru 198/B2
San Ildefonso, Sp. 86/D2
San Isidro, Nic. 186/E3
San Isidro, CR 187/F4
San Jacinto, Col. 194/C2
San Jacinto, Uru. 201/L11
San Javier, Chile 200/C2
San Javier, Sp. 87/E4
San Javier, Uru. 201/J10
San Jerónimo, Mex. 184/E3
San Joaquín, Bol. 192/F6
San Joaquin (riv.), Ca, US 170/C3
San Joaquín, Col. 194/C3
San Joaquin (hills), Ca, US 178/G8
San Joaquin (co.), Ca, US 177/L11
San Joaquín (peak), Ecu. 198/F7
San Jorge (cape), Arg. 200/D5
San Jorge (gulf), Arg. 200/D5
San Jorge (riv.), Col. 194/C3
San Jorge (bay), Mex. 184/B2
San Jorge, Golfo di (gulf), Sp. 87/F2
San José (gulf), Arg. 200/D4
San José, Col. 194/B4
San José (cap.), CR 187/E4
San José (isl.), Mex. 184/C3
San José, Peru 198/D4
San José, Peru 198/B2
San Jose, Phil. 121/D4
San Jose, Phil. 121/D5
San José, Sp. 87/F3
San Jose (riv.), Uru. 201/K10
San José (dept.), Uru. 201/K11
San Jose, Ca, US 170/B3
San Jose (hills), Ca, US 178/G7
San Jose (int'l arpt.), Ca, US 170/B3
San Jose de Buenavista, Phil. 121/D5
San José de Chiquitos, Bol. 192/F7
San José de Guanipa, Ven. 195/E2
San José de Guaribe, Ven. 195/E2
San José de Jáchal, Arg. 199/C3
San José de la Esquina, Arg. 200/E2
San Jose de Los Molinos, Peru 198/C4
San José de los Remates, Nic. 186/E3
San José de Maipo, Chile 200/N8
San José de Mayo, Uru. 201/K11
San José de Raíces, Mex. 185/E3
San José de Seque, Ven. 194/D2
San José del Cabo, Mex. 184/C4
San José del Guaviare, Col. 194/C4
San José Iturbide, Mex. 185/E4
San José Viejo, Mex. 184/C4
San Juan, Arg. 199/C3
San Juan (riv.), Arg. 199/C3
San Juan, Peru 198/C4
San Juan (basin), NM, US 174/A2
San Juan (riv.), NM, US 174/B2
San Juan, Phil. 121/D5
San Juan, PR 183/M8
San Juan (riv.), Nic. 182/E5
San Juan (pt.), ESal. 186/D3
San Juan (mts.), Co, US 170/F3
San Juan (cape), Arg. 201/E7
San Juan Abajo, Mex. 184/D4
San Juan Bautista, Par. 199/E2
San Juan Bautista Coixtlahuaca, Mex. 186/B2
San Juan Bautista Tuxtepec, Mex. 186/B2
San Juan Bautista Valle Nacional, Mex. 186/B2
San Juan Capistrano, Ca, US 178/C3
San Juan de Alicante, Sp. 87/E3
San Juan de Aznalfarache, Sp. 86/B4
San Juan de la Costa, Mex. 184/C3
San Juan de Lima (pt.), Mex. 184/E5
San Juan de los Cayos, Ven. 194/D2
San Juan de los Lagos, Mex. 184/E4
San Juan de los Morros, Ven. 192/E2
San Juan del Norte, Nic. 187/F4
San Juan del Río, Mex. 185/F4
San Juan Guichicovi, Mex. 182/B4
San Juan Hot Springs, Ca, US 178/C3
San Juan Ixcaquixtla, Mex. 185/M8
San Juan Juquila Mixes, Mex. 186/C2
San Juan Nepomuceno, Col. 194/C2
San Juanico, Mex. 184/B3
San Juanico Punta (pt.), Mex. 184/B3
San Juanito, Mex. 184/D2
San Justo, Arg. 199/D3
San Lázaro (cape), Mex. 184/B3
San Lazzaro, It. 101/E4
San Leandro, Ca, US 177/K11
San Leandro (res.), Ca, US 177/K11
San Lorenzo (cape), Ecu. 192/B4
San Lorenzo, Bol. 192/E6
San Lorenzo (peak), Chile 201/B5
San Lorenzo, Ecu. 194/B4
San Lorenzo, Hon. 186/E3
San Lorenzo (cape), It. 88/A3
San Lorenzo (riv.), Mex. 184/D3
San Lorenzo, Nic. 186/E3
San Lorenzo, Peru 198/D3
San Lorenzo, Ca, US 177/K11
San Lorenzo al Mare, It. 100/A5
San Lorenzo de El Escorial, Sp. 87/M8
San Lorenzo in Campo, It. 101/F5
San Lucas, Nic. 186/E3
San Lucas, Cabo (cape), Mex. 184/C4
San Luis, Arg. 200/D2
San Luis, Cuba 187/H1
San Luis, Guat. 186/D2
San Luis, Peru 198/B4
San Luis, Ven. 194/D2
San Luis (valley), Co, US 174/B2
San Luis Acatlán, Mex. 186/B2
San Luis al Medio, Uru. 201/G2
San Luis de la Paz, Mex. 185/E4
San Luis Obispo, Ca, US 170/B4
San Luis Potosí (state), Mex. 182/A3
San Luis Potosí, Mex. 185/E4
San Luis Rey (riv.), Ca, US 178/C4
San Luis Rey, Ca, US 178/C4
San Luis Río Colorado, Mex. 184/B1
San Luis, Sierra de (mts.), Arg. 200/D2
San Manuel, Az, US 170/E4
San Marcello Pistoiese, It. 101/D4
San Marcos, Peru 198/B3
San Marcos, Peru 198/B2
San Marcos, Tx, US 171/H5
San Marcos, Ca, US 178/C4
San Marcos, Mex. 182/B4
San Marcos, Guat. 186/D3
San Marcos, CR 187/E4
San Marcos, Col. 194/C2
San Maria di Porto Novo, It. 101/G5
San Mariano, Phil. 121/D4
San Marino (ctry.) 101/F5
San Marino (cap.), SMar. 101/F5
San Marino, Ca, US 178/F7
San Martín (riv.), Bol. 192/F6
San Martín (dept.), Peru 198/B2
San Martín, Mex. 185/R9
San Martín, Col. 194/C4
San Martín (lake), Arg. 201/B6
San Martín, Arg. 200/C2
San Martin Cuautlalpan, Mex. 185/R10
San Martín de los Andes, Arg. 200/C4
San Martín de Valdeiglesias, Sp. 86/C2
San Martino Buon Albergo, It. 101/E2
San Martino-di-Lota, Fr. 88/A1
San Martino di Lupari, It. 101/E1
San Martino di Venezze, It. 101/E2
San Martino in Passiria (Sankt Martin in Passieir), It. 99/H4
San Martino in Rio, It. 101/D3
San Martino in Strada, It. 100/C2
San Martino Siccomario, It. 100/C2
San Mateo, Peru 198/B3
San Mateo, Sp. 87/F2
San Mateo, Ven. 195/E2
San Mateo, Ca, US 170/B3
San Mateo (co.), Ca, US 177/K12
San Mateo (mts.), NM, US 174/B3
San Mateo Atarasquillo, Mex. 185/Q10
San Mateo Xoloc, Mex. 185/Q9
San Matías, Bol. 192/G7
San Matías, Golfo (gulf), Arg. 200/D4
San Maurizio d'Opaglio, It. 100/B1
San Mauro Pascoli, It. 101/F4
San Mauro Torinese, It. 100/A2
San Michele al Tagliamento, It. 101/F1
San Miguel (riv.), Bol. 192/F6
San Miguel, Peru 198/B2
San Miguel, Peru 198/C4
San Miguel, Mex. 184/E2
San Miguel, ESal. 186/D3
San Miguel (gulf), Pan. 187/G4
San Miguel (riv.), Col. 194/B4
San Miguel Coatlincham, Mex. 185/R10
San Miguel de Allende, Mex. 185/E4
San Miguel de los Bancos, Ecu. 194/B4
San Miguel de Tucumán, Arg. 199/C2
San Miguel del Monte, Arg. 201/J11
San Miguel Tlaixpan, Mex. 185/R9
San Miguel Totolapan, Mex. 182/A4
San Miniato, It. 101/D5
San Nicolás (isl.), Ca, US 170/B4
San Nicolás de los Arroyos, Arg. 200/E2
San Nicolò, It. 100/C2
San Onofre (mtn.), Ca, US 178/C4
San Onofre, Ca, US 178/C4
San Onofre, Col. 194/C2
San Pablo, Chile 200/B4
San Pablo, Col. 194/B4
San Pablo, Peru 198/B2
San Pablo, Phil. 121/D5
San Pablo (int'l arpt.), Sp. 86/C4
San Pablo, Ven. 195/E2
San Pablo, Ca, US 177/K11
San Pablo (res.), Ca, US 177/K11
San Pablo Bay NWR, Ca, US 177/K10
San Pablo de las Salinas, Mex. 185/Q9
San Pablo Huixtepec, Mex. 186/B2
San Paolo, It. 100/D2
San Pawl il-Baħar, Malta 88/L7
San Pedro, Arg. 201/J10
San Pedro, Arg. 199/D1
San Pedro, Belz. 186/E2
San Pedro, Chile 200/N8
San Pedro (vol.), Chile 199/C1
San Pédro, C.d'Iv. 144/D5
San Pedro (riv.), Guat. 186/D2
San Pedro, Mex. 184/E3
San Pedro (riv.), Mex. 184/D3
San Pedro, Par. 199/E1
San Pedro Arriba, Mex. 185/Q10
San Pedro Carchá, Guat. 186/D3
San Pedro de Cajas, Peru 198/C3
San Pedro de la Cueva, Mex. 184/C2
San Pedro de Lloc, Peru 198/B2
San Pedro de Lóvago, Nic. 187/E3
San Pedro de Macorís, DRep. 183/H4
San Pedro del Pinatar, Sp. 87/E4
San Pedro Huamelula, Mex. 186/C2
San Pedro Pochutla, Mex. 186/B3
San Pedro, Sierra de (mts.), Sp. 86/B3
San Pedro Sula, Hon. 186/D3
San Pedro Tapanatepec, Mex. 186/C2
San Pedro Totoltepec, Mex. 185/Q10
San Pellegrino Terme, It. 100/C1
San Piero a Sieve, It. 101/E5
San Piero in Bagno, It. 101/E5
San Pietro (isl.), It. 88/A3
San Pietro in Casale, It. 101/E3
San Pietro in Gù, It. 101/E1
San Pietro in Vincoli, It. 101/F4
San Pietro in Volta, It. 101/F2
San Polo d'Enza, It. 100/D3
San Polo di Piave, It. 101/F1
San Possidonio, It. 101/D3
San Quentin, Ca, US 177/K11
San Quintín (cape), Mex. 184/B2
San Quintín, Mex. 184/B2
San Rafael (riv.), Ut, US 170/E3
San Rafael, Arg. 200/C2
San Rafael, Mex. 185/N6
San Rafael, Peru 198/B3
San Rafael, Peru 198/B2
San Rafael (hills), Ca, US 178/F7
San Rafael del Moján, Ven. 194/D2
San Ramón, CR 187/E4
San Ramón, Peru 198/C3
San Ramón, Uru. 201/L11
San Ramon, Ca, US 177/L11
San Ramón de la Nueva Orán, Arg. 199/D1
San Remo, It. 100/A5
San Rocco al Porto, It. 100/C2
San Romano, It. 101/D5
San Roque, Sp. 86/C4
San Rosendo, Chile 200/B3
San Saba (riv.), Tx, US 171/H5
San Salvador (cap.), ESal. 186/D3
San Salvador (riv.), Uru. 201/J10
San Salvador de Jujuy, Arg. 199/C1
San Salvador el Seco, Mex. 185/M7
San Salvador, Isla (isl.), Bahm. 183/G3
San Salvador (Watling) (isl.), Bahm. 183/G3
San Salvatore Monferrato, It. 100/B3
San Salvo, It. 88/D1
San Sebastián, Sp. 86/E1
San Sebastián de los Reyes, Sp. 87/N8
San Sebastián de Yalí, Nic. 186/E3
San Sebastiano, It. 100/D1
San Secondo Parmense, It. 100/D3
San Severo, It. 88/D2
San Telmo (pt.), Mex. 184/E5
San Timoteo, Ven. 194/D2
San Valentín (peak), Chile 200/B5
San Valentino, It. 101/G1
San Vicente (res.), Ca, US 178/D5
San Vicente, Mex. 184/A2
San Vicente, ESal. 186/D3
San Vicente, Chile 200/C2
San Vicente de Alcántara, Sp. 86/B3
San Vicente de Cañete, Peru 198/B4
San Vicente del Caguán, Col. 194/C4
San Vicente del Raspeig, Sp. 87/E3
San Vicino (peak), It. 85/K5
San Vincenzo, It. 85/J5
San Vito (cape), It. 88/C3
San Vito, CR 187/F4
San Vito al Tagliamento, It. 101/F1
San Ysidro, Ca, US 178/C5
Saña, Peru 198/B2
Sana (riv.), Bosn. 90/C3
Sanaa (Şan'ā) (cap.), Yem. 130/D5
Sanae IV, SAfr., Ant. 202/Z
Sanaga (riv.), Camr. 135/C4
Sanak (isl.), Ak, US 176/F5
Sanana (isl.), Indo. 123/G4
Sanandaj, Iran 130/E1
Sananduva, Braz. 197/B3
Sanaur, India 128/D4
Sānāwad, India 131/L4
Sanborn, NY, US 173/S9
Sanch'ŏng, SKor. 115/D5
Sancti Spíritu, Arg. 200/E2
Sancti Spíritus, Cuba 187/G1
Sand (riv.), Ab, Can. 168/F2
Sand (riv.), SAfr. 148/D3
Sand (pt.), Eng, UK 74/D4
Sand (hills), Ne, US 171/G2
Sand, Nor. 80/B2
Sand am Main, Ger. 96/D3
Sand Point, Ak, US 176/F4
Sanda, Japan 119/H6
Sanda (isl.), Sc, UK 76/C1
Sandakan, Malay. 123/E2
Sandane, Nor. 79/C3
Sandanski, Bul. 91/F5
Sandarne, Swe. 80/G1
Sanday (isl.), Sc, UK 73/V14
Sandbach, Eng, UK 77/F5
Sandberg, Ger. 96/C2
Sande, Ger. 93/F1
Sandefjord, Nor. 80/D2
Sandersville, Ga, US 175/H3
Sandhurst, Eng, UK 75/F4
Sandia, Peru 198/D4
Sandıklı, Turk. 132/B2
Sandīla, India 126/C2
Sandino, Cuba 182/E3
Sandnes, Nor. 80/A2
Sandomierz, Pol. 83/L3
Sandoná, Col. 194/B4
Sándorfalva, Hun. 90/E2
Sandougou (riv.), Sen. 144/B3
Sandover (riv.), Austl. 155/G2
Sandoway, Myan. 125/F4
Sandpoint, Id, US 168/D3
Sandrakatsy, Madg. 149/J7
Sandrigo, It. 101/E1
Sands (pt.), NY, US 181/L8
Sands Point, NY, US 181/L8
Sandspit, BC, Can. 176/M5
Sandstedt, Ger. 93/F2
Sandstone, Austl. 154/C3
Sandu Shuizu Zizhixian, China 125/J2
Sandusky, Mi, US 172/D3
Sandusky, Oh, US 172/D3
Sandvika, Nor. 80/D2
Sandviken, Swe. 80/G1
Sandweiler, Lux. 95/F4
Sandwell (co.), Eng, UK 74/D2
Sandwich (cape), Austl. 156/B2
Sandwich, Eng, UK 75/H4
Sandwīp (isl.), Bang. 127/H4
Sandy, Ut, US 179/K12
Sandy (cape), Austl. 156/D4
Sandy (lake), On, Can. 164/G3
Sandy (pt.), RI, US 181/G1
Sandy Bay, Sk, Can. 169/H2
Sandy Hook (bay), NJ, US 180/D3
Sandy Hook (bar), NJ, US 181/J10
Sandy Hook Lighthouse, NJ, US 181/J10
Sandy Springs, Ga, US 175/G3
Sanem, Lux. 95/E4
Sånfjällets NP, Swe. 79/E3
Sanford (mt.), Ak, US 176/K3
Sanford, Me, US 173/G3
Sanford, NC, US 175/J3
Sanford, Fl, US 175/H4
Sangamner, India 131/K5
Sangamon (riv.), Il, US 171/K3
Sangān (mtn.), Afg. 131/H2
Sangaria, India 128/C5
Sangatte, Fr. 94/A2
Sangay (vol.), Ecu. 194/B5
Sangay, PN, Ecu. 192/C4
Sangenjo, Sp. 86/A1
Sanggan (riv.), China 114/C2
Sanggau, Indo. 122/D3
Sanggou (bay), China 115/B4
Sangha (riv.), Congo 138/J7
Sangihe (isl.), Indo. 123/G3
Sangihe (isl.), Phil. 109/M9
Sangju, SKor. 115/E4
Sangkulirang, Indo. 123/E3
Sāngla, Pak. 128/B4
Sāngli, India 131/K5
Sangmélima, Camr. 138/H7
Sangō, Japan 119/J6
Sangre de Cristo (mts.), US 171/F3
Sangre Grande, Trin. 195/F2
Sangri, China 127/J1
Sangro (riv.), It. 88/D2
Sangrūr, India 128/C4
Sangster (int'l arpt.), Jam. 187/G2
Sangue, Rio do (riv.), Braz. 192/G6
Sangüesa, Sp. 86/E1
Sanguie (prov.), Burk. 145/E4
Sanguinetto, It. 101/E2
Sangzhi, China 121/B2
Sanhe, China 114/H7
Sani (pass), Les. 148/E3
Sāni Bheri (riv.), Nepal 126/D1
San'in Kaigin NP, Japan 116/D3
Saniquellie, Libr. 144/C5
Sanjō, Japan 117/F2
Sankanbiriwa (peak), SLeo. 144/C4
Sankh (riv.), India 127/E4
Sankoroni (riv.), Gui. 144/C4
Sankosh (riv.), India 127/G2
Sankt Aegyd am Neuwalde, Aus. 85/L3
Sankt Agatha, Aus. 97/G6
Sankt Andrä, Aus. 85/L3
Sankt Andrä-Wördern, Aus. 91/N7
Sankt Andreasberg, Ger. 93/H5
Sankt Anton am Arlberg, Aus. 99/G3
Sankt Augustin, Ger. 95/G2
Sankt Blasien, Ger. 98/E2
Sankt Florian am Inn, Aus. 97/G6
Sankt Gallen, Swi. 99/F3
Sankt Gallenkirch, Aus. 99/F3
Sankt Georgen bei Salzburg, Aus. 97/F7
Sankt Georgen im Attergau, Aus. 97/G7
Sankt Georgen im Schwarzwald, Ger. 99/E1
Sankt Goar, Ger. 95/G3
Sankt Goarshausen, Ger. 95/G3
Sankt Ingbert, Ger. 95/G5
Sankt Johann im Pongau, Aus. 85/K3
Sankt Johann in Tirol, Aus. 85/K3
Sankt Leonhard im Pitztal, Aus. 99/G3
Sankt Leonhard in Passeier (San Leonardo in Passiria), It. 99/H4
Sankt Marien, Aus. 97/H6

272

Sankt – Sassa

Sankt Martin im Mühlkreis, Aus. 97/H6
Sankt Michael in Obersteiermark, Aus. 85/L3
Sankt Moritz, Swi. 99/F5
Sankt Oswald bei Freistadt, Aus. 97/H5
Sankt Pantaleon, Aus. 97/F6
Sankt Peter am Hart, Aus. 97/G6
Sankt Peter in der Au, Aus. 97/H6
Sankt Peter-Ording, Ger. 80/C4
Sankt Pölten, Aus. 83/H4
Sankt Stephan, Swi. 98/D4
Sankt Ulrich bei Steyr, Aus. 97/H6
Sankt Valentin, Aus. 97/H6
Sankt Veit, Aus. 90/B1
Sankt Veit an der Glan, Aus. 85/L3
Sankt Wendel, Ger. 95/G5
Sankt Wolfgang, Ger. 97/F6
Sanlúcar de Barrameda, Sp. 86/B4
Sanmatenga (prov.), Burk. 145/E3
Sanmen, China 121/D2
Sanmenxia, China 114/B4
Sanming, China 121/C2
Sannan, Japan 119/H5
Sannazzaro de'Burgondi, It. 100/B2
Sannicandro Garganico, It. 88/D2
Sannikova (str.), Rus. 107/P2
San'nohe, Japan 118/B3
Sannois, Fr. 72/J5
Sano, Japan 117/F2
Sanok, Pol. 83/M4
Sanquhar, Sc, UK 78/C6
Sanquianga, PN, Col. 192/C3
Sans Bois (mts.), Ok, US 174/E3
Sansepolcro, It. 101/F5
Sanshui, China 121/B3
Sant Adrià de Besòs, Sp. 87/L7
Sant Boi de Llobregat, Sp. 87/L7
Sant Carles de la Ràpita, Sp. 87/F2
Sant Celoni, Sp. 87/L6
Sant Cugat del Vallès, Sp. 87/L7
Sant Feliu de Guíxols, Sp. 87/G2
Sant Feliu de Llobregat, Sp. 87/L7
Sant Julia, And. 84/D5
Sant Pere de Ribes, Sp. 87/K7
Sant Sadurní d'Anoia, Sp. 87/K7
Sant Vicenç de Castellet, Sp. 87/K6
Sant Vicenç dels Horts, Sp. 87/L7
Santa (riv.), Peru 198/B3
Santa, Peru 198/B3
Santa Ana, Bol. 192/E6
Santa Ana, Ecu. 194/A5
Santa Ana, ESal. 186/D3
Santa Ana, Hon. 186/E3
Santa Ana (vol.), ESal. 186/D3
Santa Ana, Mex. 184/C2
Santa Ana, Ca, US 178/G8
Santa Ana (riv.), Ca, US 178/C3
Santa Ana (mts.), Ca, US 178/C3
Santa Ana, Ven. 194/C3
Santa Ana, Ven. 194/D2
Santa Ana del Alto Beni, Bol. 192/E7
Santa Anna, Tx, US 171/H5
Santa Bárbara, Braz. 197/D1
Santa Bárbara, Chile 200/B3
Santa Bárbara, Hon. 186/D3
Santa Bárbara, Mex. 184/D3
Santa Barbara, Ca, US 178/A2
Santa Barbara (co.), Ca, US 178/A1
Santa Bárbara, Ven. 194/D3
Santa Bárbara, Ven. 194/D2
Santa Bárbara d'Oeste, Braz. 197/C2
Santa Barbara Mountains Nat'l Rec. Area, Ca, US 178/E7
Santa Catalina, Phil. 121/D6
Santa Catalina, Ven. 194/D3
Santa Catalina, Pan. 187/F4
Santa Catalina (isl.), CA, US 170/C4
Santa Catalina, Gulf of (gulf), Ca, US 170/C4
Santa Catarina (state), Braz. 197/B3
Santa Catarina, Mex. 185/E3
Santa Catarina, Ilha de (isl.), Braz. 199/G2
Santa Cecília, Braz. 197/B3
Santa Clara, Cuba 187/G1
Santa Clara, Mex. 184/E3
Santa Clara, Ven. 195/E2
Santa Clara, Ca, US 177/L12
Santa Clara (co.), Ca, US 177/L12
Santa Clara, Barragem de (res.), Port. 86/A4
Santa Clara de Olimar, Uru. 201/G2
Santa Clarita, Ca, US 178/B2
Santa Clotilde, Peru 194/C5
Santa Coloma de Farners, Sp. 87/G2
Santa Coloma de Gramanet, Sp. 87/L7
Santa Comba, Sp. 86/A1
Santa Croce di Magliano, It. 88/D2
Santa Croce sull'Arno, It. 101/D5
Santa Cruz (riv.), Az, US 171/E5
Santa Cruz, Braz. 196/C2
Santa Cruz, Peru 198/C2
Santa Cruz, Mex. 184/C2
Santa Cruz, Phil. 121/E6
Santa Cruz, Phil. 121/D5
Santa Cruz, Ca, US 170/B3
Santa Cruz, Phil. 121/D5
Santa Cruz (isls.), Sol. 158/F6
Santa Cruz (riv.), Arg. 201/C6
Santa Cruz (mts.), Guat. 186/D3
Santa Cruz, CR 186/E4
Santa Cruz, Chile 200/C2
Santa Cruz (prov.), Arg. 200/C5
Santa Cruz (isl.), Ecu. 198/E7
Santa Cruz da Graciosa, Azor., Port. 87/S12
Santa Cruz da Vitória, Braz. 196/C4
Santa Cruz das Flores, Azor., Port. 87/R12
Santa Cruz de Bucaral, Ven. 194/D2
Santa Cruz de El Seibo, DRep. 183/H4
Santa Cruz de la Palma, Sp. 140/A3
Santa Cruz de la Sierra, Bol. 192/F7
Santa Cruz de la Zarza, Sp. 86/D3
Santa Cruz de Mudela, Sp. 86/D3
Santa Cruz de Orinoco, Ven. 195/E2
Santa Cruz de Tenerife, Sp. 140/A3
Santa Cruz del Quiché, Guat. 186/D3
Santa Cruz del Sur, Cuba 187/G1
Santa Cruz do Capibaribe, Braz. 196/C2
Santa Cruz do Piauí, Braz. 196/B2
Santa Cruz do Rio Pardo, Braz. 197/B2
Santa Cruz do Sul, Braz. 197/A4
Santa Cruz Island (isl.), Ca, US 170/C4
Santa Elena, Peru 198/C2
Santa Elena (bay), CR 186/E4
Santa Elena, Hon. 186/E2
Santa Elena (cape), CR 186/E4
Santa Elena, Ecu. 194/A5
Santa Elena (peak), Arg. 200/D5
Santa Elena de Uairén, Ven. 195/F3
Santa Eugenia de Ribeira, Sp. 86/A1
Santa Eulalia del Río, Sp. 87/F3
Santa Fe, Arg. 199/D3
Santa Fe (cap.), NM, US 171/F4
Santa Fe (riv.), Fl, US 175/H4
Santa Fé, Sp. 86/D4
Santa Fe, Cuba 187/F1
Santa Fé do Sul, Braz. 197/B2
Santa Fe Springs, Ca, US 178/F8
Santa Felicia (dam), Ca, US 178/B2
Santa Filomena, Braz. 196/A3
Santa Giustina (lake), It. 99/H5
Santa Helena, Braz. 196/A1
Santa Helena de Goiás, Braz. 197/B1
Santa Inés (isl.), Chile 199/B7
Santa Inês, Braz. 196/C4
Santa Inês, Braz. 196/A1
Santa Isabel, Braz. 197/G8
Santa Isabel, Ecu. 198/B1
Santa Isabel (isl.), Sol. 158/E5
Santa Isabel (riv.), Guat. 186/D2
Santa Isabel, Arg. 200/D3
Santa Isabel, Arg. 200/E2
Santa Isabel de Sihuas, Peru 198/C5
Santa Isabel, Pico de (peak), EqG. 138/G7
Santa Juliana, Braz. 197/C1
Santa Lucía, Canl. 87/X17
Santa Lucía, Ecu. 194/B5
Santa Lucía, Peru 198/D4
Santa Lucía, Uru. 201/K11
Santa Lucía, Ven. 194/D2
Santa Lucia di Piave, It. 101/F1
Santa Luz, Braz. 196/C3
Santa Luzia, Braz. 196/A1
Santa Luzia, Braz. 197/D1
Santa Luzia, Braz. 196/C2
Santa Luzia (isl.), CpV. 135/J10
Santa Magdalena (isl.), Mex. 184/B3
Santa Magdalena, Arg. 200/E2
Santa Margarita (isl.), Mex. 184/B3
Santa Margarita (riv.), Ca, US 178/C4
Santa Margherita Ligure, It. 100/C4
Santa Maria, Braz. 199/F2
Santa Maria, Ca, US 170/B4
Santa Maria (riv.), Mex. 174/B4
Santa María (riv.), Mex. 184/D2
Santa María (bay), Mex. 184/C3
Santa Maria (cape), Port. 86/B4
Santa Maria (isl.), Azor., Port. 87/T13
Santa Maria (isl.), Chile 200/B3
Santa Maria, CpV. 135/K10
Santa María, Chile 200/N8
Santa María, Ecu. 198/F2
Santa María (isl.), Ecu. 198/E7
Santa Maria a Monte, It. 101/D5
Santa Maria, Cabo de (cape), Moz. 149/F2
Santa Maria Capua Vetere, It. 88/D2
Santa Maria, Chapadão de (hills), Braz. 196/A4
Santa Maria da Boa Vista, Braz. 196/C3
Santa Maria da Vitória, Braz. 196/A4
Santa María de Cayón, Sp. 86/D1
Santa María de Ipire, Ven. 195/E2
Santa María de Nanay, Peru 198/C1
Santa María del Oro, Mex. 184/D3
Santa Maria della Versa, It. 100/C3
Santa Maria di Leuca, Capo (cape), It. 89/F3
Santa Maria do Suaçui, Braz. 196/B5
Santa Maria Maddalena, It. 101/E3
Santa Maria Maggiore, It. 99/E5
Santa Maria Nuova, It. 101/G6
Santa María Xadani, Mex. 182/B4
Santa Marta, Col. 194/C2
Santa Marta Grande (cape), Braz. 197/B4
Santa Marta, Sierra Nevada de (mts.), Col. 194/C2
Santa Monica (bay), Ca, US 178/B3
Santa Monica (mts.), Ca, US 178/B2
Santa Monica, Ca, US 178/F7
Santa Monica Mountains Nat'l Rec. Area, Ca, US 178/B2
Santa Olalla del Cala, Sp. 86/B4
Santa Paula (peak), Ca, US 178/A2
Santa Paula, Ca, US 178/A2
Santa Pola, Sp. 87/E3
Santa Pola, Cabo de (cape), Sp. 87/E3
Santa Quitéria, Braz. 196/B2
Santa Quitéria do Maranhão, Braz. 196/B1
Santa Rita, Braz. 196/A1
Santa Rita, Braz. 196/D2
Santa Rita, Ven. 194/D2
Santa Rita de Cássia, Braz. 196/A3
Santa Rita do Sapucaí, Braz. 197/H7
Santa Rosa, Arg. 192/F8
Santa Rosa, Arg. 200/D3
Santa Rosa, Arg. 199/C3
Santa Rosa, Braz. 199/F2
Santa Rosa, PN, CR 186/E4
Santa Rosa, Ecu. 198/B1
Santa Rosa, Peru 198/D4
Santa Rosa, Uru. 201/K11
Santa Rosa, Ven. 194/D2
Santa Rosa, Ca, US 170/B3
Santa Rosa, NM, US 171/F4
Santa Rosa (range), Nv, US 170/C2
Santa Rosa and San Jacinto Mountains Nat'l Mon., Ca, US 170/C4
Santa Rosa, Bajo de (plain), Arg. 200/D4
Santa Rosa de Aguán, Hon. 186/E3
Santa Rosa de Copán, Hon. 186/D3
Santa Rosa de Osos, Col. 194/C3
Santa Rosa de Viterbo, Braz. 197/C2
Santa Rosa Island (isl.), Ca, US 170/B4
Santa Rosalía (pt.), Mex. 184/B2
Santa Rosalía, Mex. 184/B3
Santa Rosalía, Ven. 194/D2
Santa Rosalía, Ven. 195/E3
Santa Sofia, It. 101/E5
Santa Susana (mts.), Ca, US 178/B2
Santa Teresa (riv.), Braz. 193/J6
Santa Teresa, Austl. 155/G3
Santa Teresa Abor. Land, Austl. 155/G2
Santa Teresa, PN, Uru. 201/G2
Santa Teresinha, Braz. 193/H6
Santa Teresita, Arg. 201/F3
Santa Vitória, Braz. 197/B1
Santa Vitória do Palmar, Braz. 201/G2
Santa Ynez (mts.), Ca, US 178/A2
SantAantioco (isl.), It. 88/A3
Santaella, Sp. 86/C4
Sant'Agata Bolognese, It. 101/E3
Sant'Agata di Militello, It. 88/D3
Sant'Agata Feltria, It. 101/F5
Sant'Agostino, It. 101/E3
Sant'Alberto, It. 101/F3
Santan (canal), Az, US 179/S19
Santana, Braz. 196/A4
Santana (isl.), Braz. 196/B1
Santana do Acaraú, Braz. 196/B1
Santana do Ipanema, Braz. 196/C3
Santana do Livramento, Braz. 199/E3
Santander, Sp. 86/D1
Santander (dept.), Col. 194/C3
Santander de Quilichao, Col. 194/B4
Santander Jiménez, Mex. 185/F3
Sant'Angelo in Vado, It. 101/F5
Sant'Angelo Lodigiano, It. 100/C2
Sant'Antioco, It. 88/A3
Sant'Antonio, It. 101/D2
Santañy, Sp. 87/G3
Sant'Apollinare in Classe, It. 101/F4
Santarcángelo, It. 101/F4
Santarém, Braz. 193/H4
Santarém (dist.), Port. 86/A3
Santarém, Port. 86/A3
Sant'arsenio, It. 88/D2
Santee (riv.), SC, US 175/J3
Santee, Ca, US 178/D5
Sant'Eufemia (gulf), It. 88/D3
Santena, It. 100/A3
Santerno (riv.), It. 85/J4
Santeuil, Fr. 72/H4
Santhia, It. 100/B2
Santiago, Braz. 199/F2
Santiago, Peru 198/C4
Santiago, Phil. 121/D4
Santiago (res.), Ca, US 178/C3
Santiago (peak), Ca, US 178/C3
Santiago (int'l arpt.), Sp. 86/A1
Santiago, Pan. 187/F4
Santiago (mtn.), Pan. 187/F4
Santiago (riv.), Peru 194/B5
Santiago (mts.), Tx, US 174/C4
Santiago (cap.), Chile 200/N8
Santiago (cape), Chile 201/B6
Santiago Cuautlalpan, Mex. 185/R10
Santiago Cuautlalpan, Mex. 185/Q9
Santiago de Cao, Peru 198/B2
Santiago de Chocorvos, Peru 198/C4
Santiago de Chuco, Peru 198/B3
Santiago de Compostela, Sp. 86/A1
Santiago de Cuba, Cuba 187/H1
Santiago de los Caballeros, DRep. 183/G4
Santiago de Machaca, Bol. 198/D5
Santiago del Estero, Arg. 199/D2
Santiago do Cacém, Port. 86/A3
Santiago Ixcuintla, Mex. 184/D4
Santiago Jamiltepec, Mex. 186/B2
Santiago Juxtlahuaca, Mex. 186/B2
Santiago Miahuatlán, Mex. 185/M8
Santiago Papasquiaro, Mex. 184/D3
Santiago Pinotepa Nacional, Mex. 186/B2
Santiago Tilapa, Mex. 185/Q10
Santiago Tolman, Mex. 185/R9
Santiago Vázquez, Uru. 201/K11
Santiago Zacatepec, Mex. 186/C2
Sant'Ilario d'Enza, It. 100/D3
Sāntipur, India 127/G4
Säntis (peak), Swi. 99/F3
Santisteban del Puerto, Sp. 86/D3
Santō, Japan 119/G5
Santō, Japan 119/K5
Santo Amaro, Braz. 196/C4
Santo Amaro, Ilha de (isl.), Braz. 197/G8
Santo Anastácio, Braz. 197/B2
Santo André, Braz. 197/G8
Santo Ângelo, Braz. 199/F2
Santo Antão (isl.), CpV. 135/J9
Santo António, SaoT. 138/G7
Santo Antônio de Jesus, Braz. 196/C4
Santo Antônio de Pádua, Braz. 197/D2
Santo Antônio do Içá, Braz. 194/E5
Santo Antônio do Jacinto, Braz. 196/B5
Santo Antônio dos Lopes, Braz. 196/A2
Santo Domingo (cap.), DRep. 183/H4
Santo Domingo, Mex. 185/E4
Santo Domingo (pt.), Mex. 184/B3
Santo Domingo, Cuba 187/F1
Santo Domingo, Chile 200/N8
Santo Domingo de la Calzada, Sp. 86/D1
Santo Domingo de los Colorados, Ecu. 194/B5
Santo Domingo Petapa, Mex. 186/C2
Santo Domingo Tehuantepec, Mex. 186/C2
Santo Domingo Zanatepec, Mex. 186/C2
Santo Estêvão, Braz. 196/C4
Santo Onofre (riv.), Braz. 196/B4
Santo Stefano Belbo, It. 100/B3
Santo Stefano d'Aveto, It. 100/C3
Santo Stefano di Magra, It. 100/C4
Santo Stino di Livenza, It. 101/F1
Santo Tomás, Peru 198/C4
Santo Tomás, Peru 198/B2
Santo Tomás, Mex. 184/A2
Santo Tomás (pt.), Mex. 184/A2
Santo Tomás (vol.), Ecu. 198/E7
Santo Tomé, Arg. 199/E2
Santo Tomé, Arg. 199/D3
Santoña, Sp. 86/D1
Santorso, It. 101/E1
Santos, Braz. 197/G8
Santos Dumont (int'l arpt.), Braz. 197/K7
Santos Dumont, Braz. 197/K6
Santos Reyes Nopala, Mex. 186/B2
Santuario di Crea, It. 100/B2
Santuario di Oropa, It. 100/A1
Şanūr, WBnk. 133/G7
Sanwa, Japan 119/D1
São Benedito, Braz. 196/B2
São Benedito do Rio Prêto, Braz. 196/B1
São Bento, Braz. 196/C2
São Bento, Braz. 196/A1
São Bento do Sapucaí, Braz. 197/H7
São Bento do Sul, Braz. 197/B3
São Bento do Una, Braz. 196/C3
São Bernardo do Campo, Braz. 197/G8
São Borja, Braz. 199/E2
São Carlos, Braz. 197/C2
São Cristóvão, Braz. 196/C3
São Desidério, Braz. 196/A4
São Domingos (riv.), Braz. 196/A4
São Domingos, Braz. 196/A4
São Domingos do Maranhão, Braz. 196/A2
São Félix do Xingu, Braz. 193/H5
São Fidélis, Braz. 197/D2
São Filipe, CpV. 135/J11
São Francisco, Braz. 196/A4
São Francisco (riv.), Braz. 189/F3
São Francisco do Sul, Braz. 197/B3
São Francisco, Ilha de (isl.), Braz. 199/G2
São Fransisco de Paula, Braz. 197/B4
São Gabriel, Braz. 199/F3
São Gabriel da Palha, Braz. 197/D1
São Gonçalo, Braz. 197/K7
São Gonçalo do Abaeté, Braz. 196/A5
São Gonçalo do Sapucaí, Braz. 197/H6
São Gotardo, Braz. 197/C1
São Joachim da Barra, Braz. 197/C2
São João Batista, Braz. 196/A1
São João Batista, Braz. 197/B3
São João da Aliança, Braz. 196/A4
São João da Barra, Braz. 197/D2
São João da Boa Vista, Braz. 197/G6
São João da Madeira, Port. 86/A2
São João da Pesqueira, Port. 86/B2
São João da Ponte, Braz. 196/A4
São João das Lampas, Port. 87/P10
São João de Meriti, Braz. 197/K7
São João del Rei, Braz. 197/C2
São João do Paraíso, Braz. 196/B4
São João do Piauí, Braz. 196/B3
São João dos Patos, Braz. 196/B2
São João Evangelista, Braz. 197/D1
São João, Ilhas de (isl.), Braz. 193/K4
São João Nepomuceno, Braz. 197/K6
São João, Serra de (mts.), Braz. 192/F5
São Joaquim, Braz. 197/B4
São Joaquim, PN de, Braz. 197/B4
São Jorge (isl.), Azor., Port. 87/S12
São José, Braz. 197/B3
São José da Laje, Braz. 196/C3
São José de Mipibu, Braz. 196/D2
São José de Piranhas, Braz. 196/C2
São José de Ribamar, Braz. 196/A1
São José do Belmonte, Braz. 196/C2
São José do Egito, Braz. 196/C2
São José do Norte, Braz. 197/A5
São José do Peixe, Braz. 196/B2
São José do Rio Pardo, Braz. 197/G6
São José do Rio Prêto, Braz. 197/B2
São José dos Campos, Braz. 197/H8
São José dos Pinhais, Braz. 197/B3
São Julião, Braz. 196/B2
São Leopoldo, Braz. 197/B4
São Lourenço (riv.), Braz. 193/G7
São Lourenço, Braz. 197/H7
São Lourenço, Port. 87/P11
São Lourenço do Sul, Braz. 197/B4
São Luís, Braz. 196/A1
São Luís do Curu, Braz. 196/C1
São Luís do Quitunde, Braz. 196/D3
São Manoel, Braz. 197/B2
São Marcos (riv.), Braz. 196/A5
São Marcos (bay), Braz. 189/E3
São Martinho do Porto, Port. 86/A3
São Mateus, Braz. 197/E1
São Mateus (riv.), Braz. 197/D1
São Mateus do Maranhão, Braz. 196/A2
São Mateus do Sul, Braz. 197/B3
São Miguel, Braz. 196/C2
São Miguel (isl.), Azor., Port. 87/T13
São Miguel Arcanjo, Braz. 197/C2
São Miguel do Tapuio, Braz. 196/B2
São Miguel dos Campos, Braz. 196/C3
São Nicolau (isl.), CpV. 135/J10
São Paulo (state), Braz. 197/B2
São Paulo, Braz. 197/G8
São Paulo de Olivença, Braz. 192/E4
São Paulo do Potengi, Braz. 196/D2
São Pedro da Aldeia, Braz. 197/D2
São Pedro do Piauí, Braz. 196/B2
São Pedro do Sul, Port. 86/A2
São Raimundo das Mangabeiras, Braz. 196/A2
São Raimundo Nonato, Braz. 196/B3
São Romão, Braz. 196/A5
São Roque, Cabo de (cape), Braz. 196/D2
São Roque do Pico, Azor., Port. 87/S12
São Sebastião (pt.), Moz. 147/G5
São Sebastião, Braz. 197/H8
São Sebastião do Paraíso, Braz. 197/C2
São Sebastião, Ilha de (isl.), Braz. 197/C2
São Simão, Barragem de (res.), Braz. 197/B1
São Teotónio, Port. 86/A4
São Tiago, Braz. 197/C2
São Tiago (isl.), CpV. 135/K10
São Tomé (cap.), SaoT. 138/G7
São Tomé (isl.), SaoT. 138/G7
São Tomé and Príncipe (ctry.) 138/F7
São Tomé, Cabo de (cape), Braz. 197/D2
São Vicente, Braz. 197/G8
São Vicente (cape), Port. 86/A4
São Vicente (isl.), CpV. 135/J10
Saône (riv.), Fr. 84/F3
Saône-et-Loire (dept.), Fr. 98/B4
Saori, Japan 119/L5
Saouru (riv.), Alg. 138/E1
Sápai, Gre. 89/J2
Sapallanga, Peru 198/C4
Sapanca, Turk. 91/K5
Sapatgrām, India 127/H2
Sapé, Braz. 196/D2
Sapele, Nga. 145/G5
Sapelo (isl.), Ga, US 175/H4
Şaphane, Turk. 104/D5
Sapiéndza (isl.), Gre. 89/G4
Sapkyo, SKor. 115/D4
Sapo (mts.), Pan. 187/G5
Sapo NP, Libr. 144/C5
Saposoa, Peru 198/B2
Sappemeer, Neth. 92/D2
Sapphire, Austl. 156/B3
Sappington, Mo, US 179/G8
Sapporo, Japan 118/B2
Sapri, It. 88/D2
Sapsi (isl.), SKor. 115/D3
Sapt Kosi (riv.), Nepal 127/F2
Sapucaí (riv.), Braz. 197/H7
Sapucaia, Braz. 197/L6
Saqqez, Iran 130/E1
Saquena, Peru 198/C2
Saquisilí, Ecu. 194/B5
Šar (mts.), Serb 89/G1
Sar Dasht, Iran 132/F2
Sar-e Pol, Afg. 129/E5
Sara Buri, Thai. 120/C3
Sarāb, Iran 130/E1
Saraguro, Ecu. 198/B1
Sarāi Alamgir, Pak. 128/B3
Sarāi Sidhu, Pak. 128/A4
Sarajevo (cap.), Bosn. 90/D4
Saraland, Al, US 175/F4
Saramacca (dist.), Sur. 195/H3
Saran (peak), Indo. 122/D4
Saran', Kaz. 129/F3
Saranac Lake, NY, US 172/F2
Sarandapótamos (riv.), Gre. 89/N8
Sarandë, Alb. 89/G3
Sarandí de Navarro, Uru. 201/K10
Sarandí del Yi, Uru. 201/G2
Sarandí Grande, Uru. 201/K10
Sarangani (isls.), Phil. 123/G2
Sārangpur, India 131/L4
Saransk, Rus. 105/H1
Sarapul, Rus. 103/M4
Sarare (riv.), Ven. 194/D3
Sarasota, Fl, US 175/H5
Saratoga, Wy, US 168/G5
Saratoga, Ca, US 177/K12
Saratoga Springs, NY, US 172/F3
Saratov (res.), Rus. 105/J1
Saratov, Rus. 105/H2
Saratovskaya Oblast, Rus. 129/A2
Saravan, Laos 120/D3
Sarawak (reg.), Malay. 122/D3
Saray, Turk. 91/H5
Sarayacu, Ecu. 194/B5
Sarāyan (riv.), India 126/C2
Sarayköy, Turk. 132/B2
Sarayönü, Turk. 132/C2
Sárbogárd, Hun. 90/D2
Sarcelles, Fr. 72/K5
Sārda (riv.), India 126/C1
Sārda (canal), India 126/C2
Sarda (riv.), India 124/D2
Sardara, It. 88/A3
Sardārshahar, India 128/C5
Sardegna (prov.), It. 88/A2
Sardhana, India 128/D5
Sardinata, Col. 194/C2
Sardinaux, Cap des (cape), Fr. 85/G5
Sardinia (isl.), It. 88/A2
Sardis (lake), Ms, US 171/K4
Sardis (lake), Ok, US 171/J4
Sareks NP, Swe. 79/F2
Sarektjåkko (peak), Swe. 79/F2
Sarempaka (peak), Indo. 123/E4
Sarentino, It. 99/H4
Sarezzo, It. 100/D1
Sargans, Swi. 99/F3
Sargodha, Pak. 128/B3
Sarh, Chad 139/J6
Sārī, Iran 130/F1
Sari-Solenzara, Fr. 88/A2
Sariaya, Phil. 121/D5
Saribi (cape), Indo. 123/J4
Sarigan (isl.), NMar. 158/D3
Sarıgöl, Turk. 132/B2
Sarıkamış, Turk. 132/E1
Sarıkaya, Turk. 104/E5
Sarikaya (prov.), Turk. 132/C2
Sarikei, Malay. 122/D3
Sarina, Austl. 156/C3
Sarine (riv.), Swi. 85/G3
Sariñena, Sp. 87/E2
Sarīr Kalanshiyū (des.), Libya 138/K2
Sarīr Tibastī (des.), Libya 138/J3
Sarita, Tx, US 174/D5
Sariwŏn, NKor. 115/C3
Sarju (riv.), India 126/C1
Sark (isl.), Chl, UK 84/B2
Sarkad, Hun. 90/E2
Sarkant, Kaz. 112/C2
Şarkîkaraağaç, Turk. 132/B2
Şarkışla, Turk. 132/D2
Şarköy, Turk. 91/H5
Sarlat-la-Canéda, Fr. 84/D4
Sarleinsbach, Aus. 97/G5
Sarmato, It. 100/C2
Sarmeola, It. 101/E2
Sarmiento, Arg. 200/C5
Sarmiento (peak), Chile 201/C7
Särna, Swe. 80/E1
Sarnano, It. 85/K5
Sarnen, Swi. 99/E4
Sarnia, On, Can. 172/D3
Sarnico, It. 100/C1
Sarny, Ukr. 104/C2
Saroma (lake), Japan 118/C1
Saronic (gulf), Gre. 89/H4
Saronno, It. 100/C1
Saros (gulf), Turk. 91/H5
Sárospatak, Hun. 83/L4
Sarpsborg, Nor. 80/D2
Sarralbe, Fr. 95/G6
Sarre (riv.), Fr. 94/F6
Sarre-Union, Fr. 95/G6
Sarrebourg, Fr. 95/G6
Sarria, Sp. 86/B1
Sarroch, It. 88/A3
Sarry, Fr. 95/D6
Sarsāwa, India 128/D4
Sarsina, It. 101/F5
Sarstedt, Ger. 93/G4
Sarstún (riv.), Guat. 186/D3
Sartang (riv.), Rus. 107/P3
Sarteano, It. 88/B1
Sartène, Fr. 88/A2
Sarthe (riv.), Fr. 84/C3
Sartrouville, Fr. 72/J5
Sarufutsu, Japan 118/C1
Saruhanlı, Turk. 132/A2
Sārvār, Hun. 85/M3
Sárvár, Hun. 90/D2
Saryesik Atgraü Qumy (des.), Kaz. 112/C2
Saryshaghan, Kaz. 129/F3
Sarysu (riv.), Kaz. 106/G5
Sarzana, It. 100/C4
Sas Van Gent, Neth. 94/C1
Sasaginnigack (lake), Mb, Can. 169/K3
Sasarām, India 127/E3
Sasayama, Japan 119/H5
Sasayama (riv.), Japan 119/H5
Sásd, Hun. 90/D2
Sasebo, Japan 116/A4
Sashima, Japan 119/D1
Saskatchewan (prov.), Can. 164/F3
Saskatchewan (riv.), Can. 164/E3
Saskatoon, Sk, Can. 168/G2
Saslaya (mtn.), Nic. 187/E3
Saslaya, PN, Nic. 187/E3
Sāsni, India 126/B2
Sasolburg, SAfr. 148/D2
Sasovo, Rus. 105/G1
Saspamco, Tx, US 179/U21
Sassafras, Md, US 180/C5

Sassa – Serra
273

Sassafras (riv.), Md, US 180/B5
Sassandra (riv.), C.d'Iv. 138/D6
Sassandra, C.d'Iv. 144/D5
Sassari, It. 88/A2
Sassello, It. 100/B4
Sassenberg, Ger. 93/F4
Sassenheim, Neth. 92/B4
Sassnitz, Ger. 80/E4
Sasso Marconi, It. 101/E4
Sassocorvaro, It. 101/F5
Sassoferrato, It. 101/F6
Sassuolo, It. 101/D3
Sástago, Sp. 87/E2
Sasyk (lake), Ukr. 91/J3
Sata-misaki (cape), Japan 116/B5
Sātāra, India 131/K5
Satawan (isl.), Micr. 158/E4
Säter, Swe. 80/F1
Saticoy, Ca, US 178/A2
Satilla (riv.), Ga, US 175/H4
Satipo, Peru 198/C3
Sātkhira, Bang. 127/G4
Sátoraljaújhely, Hun. 83/L4
Satpayev, Kaz. 129/E3
Satpura (range), India 131/K4
Satte, Japan 119/D1
Satteins, Aus. 99/F3
Satteldorf, Ger. 96/D4
Sattler, Tx, US 179/U20
Satu Mare, Rom. 83/M5
Satu Mare (co.), Rom. 83/M5
Satun, Thai. 120/C5
Sauce, Peru 198/B2
Sauce Grande (riv.), Arg. 200/E3
Saucillo, Mex. 184/D2
Sauda, Nor. 80/B2
Saúde, Braz. 196/B3
Saudhárkrókur, Ice. 79/N6
Saudi Arabia (ctry.) 130/D4
Sauer (riv.), Ger. 93/F5
Sauerlach, Ger. 99/H2
Sauerland (reg.), Ger. 82/D3
Sauêruiná (riv.), Braz. 192/G6
Saugatuck (riv.), Ct, US 181/E1
Saujon, Fr. 84/C4
Sauk (riv.), Mn, US 169/K4
Sauk Centre, Mn, US 169/K4
Sauk Rapids, Mn, US 169/K4
Saül, FrG. 193/H3
Sauland, Nor. 80/C2
Sauldre (riv.), Fr. 84/D3
Saulgau, Ger. 99/F1
Saulheim, Ger. 96/B3
Saulieu, Fr. 84/F3
Sault-lès-Rethel, Fr. 95/D5
Sault Sainte Marie, On, Can. 172/C2
Sault Ste. Marie, Mi, US 172/C2
Saulx, Fr. 98/C2
Saulx (riv.), Fr. 82/C4
Saulxures-sur-Moselotte, Fr. 98/C2
Saumur, Fr. 84/C3
Saunders (peak), Austl. 154/E3
Saura (riv.), India 127/F3
Saurimo, Ang. 147/D2
Sausalito, Ca, US 177/J11
Sausseron (riv.), Fr. 72/J4
Sauteurs, Gren. 195/F1
Sava, It. 89/E2
Sava (riv.), Slov. 85/L3
Savá, Hon. 186/E3
Savage (dam), Ca, US 178/D5
Savage River, Austl. 157/C4
Savai'i (isl.), Sam. 159/H6
Savalou, Ben. 145/F5
Savane (riv.), Qu, Can. 173/G1
Savanna-la-Mar, Jam. 187/G2
Savannah, Ga, US 175/H3
Savannah, Tn, US 175/F3
Savannah (riv.), US 175/H3
Savannakhet, Laos 120/D2
Savant (lake), On, Can. 169/L3
Sāvantvādi, India 124/B4
Sävar, Swe. 79/G3
Savaştepe, Turk. 132/A2
Save (riv.), Moz. 147/F5
Sāveh, Iran 130/F1
Savena (riv.), It. 101/E4
Săveni, Rom. 91/H2
Saverdun, Fr. 84/D5
Saverne, Fr. 95/G6
Savièse, Swi. 98/D5
Savigliano, It. 85/G4
Savignano sul Panaro, It. 101/E4
Savignano sul Rubicone, It. 101/F4
Savigny-le-Temple, Fr. 72/K6
Savigny-sur-Orge, Fr. 72/K5
Savio (riv.), It. 85/K5
Sävja, Swe. 80/G2
Savognin, Swi. 99/F4
Savoie (dept.), Fr. 98/C6
Savona, BC, Can. 168/C3
Savona (prov.), It. 100/B4
Savona, It. 100/B4
Savoonga, Ak, US 176/D3
Savoy (reg.), Fr. 84/F4
Savoy Alps (mts.), Fr. 98/C6
Şavşat, Turk. 132/E1
Sävsjö, Swe. 80/F3
Savu (sea), Indo. 123/F5
Sawahlunto, Indo. 122/B4
Sawankhalok, Thai. 120/B2
Sawara, Japan 117/G3
Sawasaki-bana (pt.), Japan 117/F2
Sawatch (range), Co, US 170/F3
Sawdā', Jabal (peak), SAr. 130/D5
Saweba (cape), Indo. 123/H4
Sawel (mtn.), NI, UK 76/A2
Sawtell, Austl. 157/E1
Sawtooth (range), Id, US 168/E4
Sawtooth Nat'l Rec. Area, Id, US 168/E5
Sawu (isls.), Indo. 123/F6
Sax, Sp. 87/E3
Saxman, Ak, US 176/M4
Saxon, Swi. 98/D5
Say, Niger 145/F3
Saya, Japan 119/L5
Sayama, Japan 117/F3
Sayama, Japan 119/J6
Sayán, Peru 198/B3
Şaydā, Leb. 133/D3
Sayil (ruin), Mex. 186/D1
Saynbach (riv.), Ger. 95/G3
Sayreville, NJ, US 181/H10
Sayula, Mex. 184/E5
Sayville, NY, US 181/E2
Saywūn, Yem. 130/E5
Sazan (isl.), Alb. 89/F2
Sázava (riv.), Czh. 85/L2
Sbaa, Alg. 141/E3
Scafell Pikes (peak), Eng, UK 77/E3
Scalasaig, Sc, UK 73/Q8
Scald Law (peak), Sc, UK 78/C5
Scalea, It. 88/D3
Scalino (peak), It. 99/F5
Scalloway, Sc, UK 73/W13
Scammon Bay, Ak, US 176/E3
Scandia, Wa, US 177/B2
Scandiano, It. 101/D3
Scandicci, It. 101/E5
Scapa Flow (chan.), Sc, UK 73/V14
Scar Water (riv.), Sc, UK 76/E1
Scarborough, Can. 173/R8
Scarborough, Eng, UK 77/H3
Scarborough Shoal (isl.), Phil. 121/C4
Scardovari, It. 101/F3
Scarpe (riv.), Fr. 82/B3
Scarperia, It. 101/E5
Scarriff, Ire. 73/P10
Scarsdale, La, US 179/Q17
Scarsdale, NY, US 181/K7
Sceaux, Fr. 72/J5
Scenic Oaks, Tx, US 179/T20
Scey-sur-Saône-et-St-Albin, Fr. 98/B2
Schaefferstown, Pa, US 180/B3
Schaerbeek, Belg. 95/D2
Schaffhausen (canton), Swi. 99/E2
Schaffhausen, Swi. 99/E2
Schäftlarn, Ger. 99/H2
Schagen, Neth. 92/B3
Schaijk, Neth. 92/C5
Schalchen, Aus. 97/G6
Schalkau, Ger. 96/E2
Schalksmühle, Ger. 93/E6
Schanck (cape), Austl. 157/C3
Schangnau, Swi. 98/D4
Scharans, Swi. 99/F4
Schardenberg, Aus. 97/G5
Schärding, Aus. 97/G6
Scharfreiter (peak), Aus. 99/H3
Scharhorn (isl.), Ger. 93/F1
Scharnebeck, Ger. 93/H2
Scharnitz (pass), Ger. 99/H3
Scharnstein, Aus. 97/G7
Schashagen, Ger. 82/F1
Schattdorf, Swi. 99/E4
Schauenstein, Ger. 97/E2
Schaumburg, Il, US 177/P15
Scheemda, Neth. 92/D2
Scheer, Ger. 99/F1
Scheessel, Ger. 93/G2
Schefferville, Qu, Can. 123/K3
Scheibbs, Aus. 83/H4
Scheidegg, Ger. 99/F2
Scheinfeld, Ger. 96/D3
Schelde (riv.), Belg. 84/E1
Schelklingen, Ger. 96/C6
Schell Creek (range), Nv, US 170/D3
Schellerten, Ger. 93/H4
Schellville, Ca, US 177/K10
Schenectady, NY, US 172/F3
Schenefeld, Ger. 93/G1
Schermbeck, Ger. 92/D5
Scherpenzeel, Neth. 92/C3
Schertz, Tx, US 179/U20
Schesaplana (peak), Aus. 99/F3
Schesslitz, Ger. 96/E3
Scheyern, Ger. 97/E5
Schiedam, Neth. 92/B5
Schieder-Schwalenberg, Ger. 93/G5
Schiehallion (peak), Sc, UK 78/B3
Schier Monnikoog (isl.), Neth. 82/D2
Schierling, Ger. 97/F5
Schiermonnikoog (isl.), Neth. 92/D1
Schiermonnikoog, Neth. 92/D2
Schiers, Swi. 99/F4
Schifferstadt, Ger. 96/B4
Schiffweiler, Ger. 95/G5
Schijndel, Neth. 92/C5
Schilde, Belg. 92/B6
Schildmeer (lake), Neth. 92/D2
Schillighörn (cape), Ger. 93/F1
Schillingfürst, Ger. 96/D4
Schiltach, Ger. 99/E1
Schiltigheim, Fr. 98/D1
Schinnen, Neth. 95/E2
Schinznach-Dorf, Swi. 98/E3
Schio, It. 101/E1
Schipbeek (riv.), Neth. 92/D4
Schirmeck, Fr. 98/D1
Schkumbin (riv.), Alb. 89/G2
Schladen, Ger. 93/H4
Schladming, Aus. 85/K3
Schlanders (Silandro), It. 85/J3
Schlangen, Ger. 93/F5
Schlangenbad, Ger. 96/B2
Schleiden, Ger. 95/F2
Schleitheim, Swi. 99/E2
Schleiz, Ger. 97/E1
Schlema, Ger. 97/F1
Schleswig, Ger. 80/C4
Schleswig-Holstein (state), Ger. 80/B4
Schleswig-Holsteinisches Wattenmeer NP, Ger. 80/C4
Schleuse (riv.), Ger. 96/D2
Schleusingen, Ger. 96/D1
Schliengen, Ger. 98/D2
Schlierbach, Aus. 97/H7
Schlieren, Swi. 99/E3
Schloss Herrenchiemsee, Ger. 97/F7
Schloss Holte-Stukenbrock, Ger. 93/F5
Schloss Sansoucci, Ger. 82/Q7
Schloss Wilhelmstein, Ger. 93/G4
Schlotheim, Ger. 93/H6
Schluchsee, Ger. 98/E2
Schlüchtern, Ger. 96/C2
Schlüsselfeld, Ger. 96/D3
Schlüsslberg, Aus. 97/G6
Schmalkalden, Ger. 85/J1
Schmallenberg, Ger. 93/F6
Schmeich (riv.), Ger. 96/C6
Schmelz, Ger. 95/F5
Schmiech (riv.), Ger. 99/F1
Schmitten, Swi. 98/D4
Schmitten, Ger. 96/B2
Schmutter (riv.), Ger. 96/D5
Schnaitsee, Ger. 97/F6
Schnaittach, Ger. 97/E3
Schnaittenbach, Ger. 97/F3
Schnarrtanne, Ger. 97/F1
Schnecksville, Pa, US 180/C2
Schneeberg (peak), Ger. 97/E2
Schneeberg, Ger. 97/F1
Schneeberg, Ger. 96/C3
Schneifel (upland), Ger. 82/D3
Schneverdingen, Ger. 93/G2
Schofield Barracks, Hi, US 166/V12
Schollene, Ger. 82/G2
Schöllkrippen, Ger. 96/C2
Schömberg, Ger. 99/E1
Schömberg, Ger. 96/B5
Schönaich, Ger. 96/C5
Schönau im Schwarzwald, Ger. 98/D2
Schönberg, Ger. 80/D4
Schönberg, Ger. 97/G5
Schondorf am Ammersee, Ger. 99/H1
Schondra (riv.), Ger. 96/C2
Schönebeck, Ger. 82/F2
Schöneck, Ger. 96/B2
Schönecken, Ger. 95/F3
Schönefeld (int'l arpt.), Ger. 82/Q7
Schongau, Ger. 99/G2
Schöningen, Ger. 82/F2
Schönsee, Ger. 97/F3
Schönwald, Ger. 97/E2
Schoonebeek, Neth. 92/D3
Schoonhoven, Neth. 92/B5
Schoorl, Neth. 92/B3
Schopfheim, Ger. 95/G4
Schopfloch, Ger. 96/D4
Schöppenstedt, Ger. 93/H4
Schörfling, Aus. 97/G7
Schorndorf, Ger. 96/C5
Schortens, Ger. 93/E1
Schoten, Belg. 92/B6
Schotten, Ger. 96/C1
Schouten (isl.), Austl. 157/D4
Schouten (isls.), Indo. 158/C5
Schouwen (isl.), Neth. 92/A5
Schramberg, Ger. 99/E1
Schrankogel (peak), Aus. 99/H3
Schreckhorn (peak), Swi. 98/E4
Schriesheim, Ger. 96/B4
Schrobenhausen, Ger. 96/E5
Schroffenstein (peak), Namb. 148/B2
Schrozberg, Ger. 96/C4
Schruns, Aus. 99/F3
Schübelbach, Swi. 99/E3
Schuby, Ger. 80/C4
Schulenburg, Tx, US 171/H5
Schulzendorf, Ger. 82/Q7
Schunter (riv.), Ger. 93/H4
Schüpfheim, Swi. 98/E4
Schussen (riv.), Ger. 99/F2
Schussenried, Ger. 99/F1
Schutter (riv.), Ger. 96/A6
Schutterwald, Ger. 98/D1
Schüttorf, Ger. 93/E4
Schuylkill (riv.), Pa, US 180/C3
Schuylkill Haven, Pa, US 180/B2
Schwabach, Ger. 96/D4
Schwabhausen bei Dachau, Ger. 97/E6
Schwäbisch Gmünd, Ger. 96/C5
Schwäbisch Hall, Ger. 96/C4
Schwäbische Alb (range), Ger. 82/E4
Schwabmünchen, Ger. 99/G1
Schwaig bei Nürnberg, Ger. 96/E4
Schwaigern, Ger. 96/C4
Schwalbach, Ger. 95/F5
Schwalbach am Taunus, Ger. 96/B2
Schwalm (riv.), Ger. 82/E3
Schwalmtal, Ger. 92/D6
Schwanden, Swi. 99/F4
Schwandorf im Bayern, Ger. 97/F4
Schwanebeck, Ger. 82/Q6
Schwanenstadt, Aus. 97/G6
Schwaner (mts.), Indo. 122/D4
Schwanewede, Ger. 93/F2
Schwanfeld, Ger. 96/D3
Schwangau, Ger. 99/G2
Schwarmstedt, Ger. 93/G3
Schwartz Elster (riv.), Ger. 83/G3
Schwartzerberg (peak), Namb. 148/B2
Schwarza (riv.), Ger. 96/E1
Schwarzach, Ger. 97/F5
Schwarzach (riv.), Ger. 97/E4
Schwarzach im Pongau, Aus. 85/K3
Schwarze Laber (riv.), Ger. 97/E4
Schwarzenbach am Wald, Ger. 97/E2
Schwarzenbek, Ger. 93/H1
Schwarzenberg, Ger. 97/F1
Schwarzenbruck, Ger. 96/E4
Schwarzenburg, Swi. 98/D4
Schwarzenfeld, Ger. 97/F4
Schwarzer Mann (peak), Ger. 95/F3
Schwarzhorn (peak), Aus. 99/H3
Schwarzwald (Black Forest) (for.), Ger. 96/B6
Schwaz, Aus. 85/J3
Schwebheim, Ger. 96/D3
Schwechat, Aus. 91/N7
Schwechat (int'l arpt.), Aus. 91/P7
Schwedt, Ger. 83/H2
Schwegenheim, Ger. 96/B4
Schweich, Ger. 95/F4
Schweighouse-sur-Moder, Fr. 95/G6
Schweinfurt, Ger. 96/D2
Schweitenkirchen, Ger. 97/E5
Schweizer-Reneke, SAfr. 148/D2
Schwelm, Ger. 93/E6
Schwendi, Ger. 99/F1
Schwenksville, Pa, US 180/C3
Schwerin, Ger. 80/D5
Schweriner (lake), Ger. 82/F2
Schwertberg, Aus. 97/H6
Schwerte, Ger. 93/E6
Schwetzingen, Ger. 96/B4
Schwinge (riv.), Ger. 93/G1
Schwörstadt, Ger. 98/D2
Schwülme (riv.), Ger. 93/G5
Schwülper, Ger. 93/H4
Schwyz (canton), Swi. 99/E3
Schwyz, Swi. 99/E3
Sciacca, It. 88/C4
Scicli, It. 88/D4
Scilly (isls.), Eng, UK 73/Q11
Ścinawa, Pol. 83/J3
Scionzier, Fr. 98/C5
Sciota, Pa, US 180/C2
Scioto (riv.), Oh, US 172/D4
Scobey, Mt, US 169/G3
Scolt (pt.), Eng, UK 75/G1
Scone, Austl. 157/D2
Scopello, It. 100/B2
Scordia, It. 88/D4
Scorzè, It. 101/F2
Scotch Corner, Eng, UK 77/G3
Scotch Plains, NJ, US 181/H9
Scotia (sea) 202/W
Scotland, UK 76/D1
Scott (cape), BC, Can. 164/D3
Scott (cape), NW, Can. 123/R7
Scott (lake), NW,Sk, Can. 164/F2
Scott, NZ, Ant. 202/M
Scott City, Ks, US 171/G3
Scott NP, Austl. 154/B5
Scott (reef), Austl. 151/B2
Scottburgh, SAfr. 149/E3
Scotts (cr.), Austl. 155/M9
Scottish Borders (pol. reg.), Sc, UK 78/C5
Scotts Bluff Nat'l Mon., Ne, US 171/F2
Scottsbluff, Ne, US 171/G2
Scottsboro, Al, US 175/G3
Scottsburg, In, US 172/C4
Scottsdale, Austl. 157/C4
Scottsdale, Az, US 170/E4
Scottsville, Ky, US 175/G2
Scottville, Mi, US 172/C2
Scourie, Sc, UK 73/R7
Scranton, Pa, US 172/F3
Scrivia (riv.), It. 100/B3
Scunthorpe, Eng, UK 77/H4
Scuol, Swi. 99/G4
Scuppernong (riv.), Wi, US 177/N14
Scurdie Ness (pt.), Sc, UK 78/D3
Scutari (lake), Alb., Mont. 90/D4
Sea Cliff, Ca, US 178/A2
Sea Cliff, NY, US 181/L8
Sea Girt, NJ, US 180/D3
Sea Isle City, NJ, US 180/D5
Sea Lake, Austl. 157/B2
Sea-Tac, Wa, US 177/C3
Seabeck, Wa, US 177/B2
Seabold, Wa, US 177/B2
Seabra, Braz. 196/B4
Seabrook, NJ, US 180/C5
Seaford, Eng, UK 75/G5
Seaford, NY, US 181/M9
Seaforde, NI, UK 76/C3
Seaforth, Austl. 156/C3
Seagraves, Tx, US 171/G4
Seaham, Eng, UK 77/G2
Seahorse (pt.), Nun, Can. 123/J2
Seahurst, Wa, US 177/C3
Seal, Eng, UK 72/D3
Seal (riv.), MB, Can. 164/G3
Seal (pt.), Chile 200/B5
Seal (cape), SAfr. 148/C4
Seal Beach, Ca, US 178/F8
Seale, Eng, UK 72/A3
Seamer, Eng, UK 77/H3
Seano, It. 101/E6
Searcy, Ar, US 171/K4
Seascale, Eng, UK 76/E3
Seaside, Or, US 168/B4
Seaside Heights, NJ, US 180/D4
Seaside Park, NJ, US 180/D4
Seaton, Eng, UK 74/C5
Seaton (riv.), Eng, UK 74/B6
Seaton Carew, Eng, UK 77/G2
Seattle, Wa, US 168/C4
Sébaco, Nic. 186/E3
Sebaou (riv.), Alg. 142/H4
Sebastian, Fl, US 175/H5
Sebastián Vizcaíno (bay), Mex. 184/B2
Sebayan (peak), Indo. 122/D4
Sebdou, Alg. 142/D2
Sébékoro, Mali 144/C3
Seben, Turk. 91/K5
Sebeş, Rom. 91/F3
Sebezh, Rus. 81/N3
Şebinkarahisar, Turk. 132/D1
Sebiş, Rom. 90/F2
Sebkhet al Kalīyah (drylake), Alg. 142/M7
Sebnitz, Ger. 83/H3
Seboruco, Ven. 194/C2
Sebou (riv.), Mor. 142/B2
Sebou, Oued (riv.), Mor. 140/D2
Sebring, Fl, US 175/H5
Sebuku (isl.), Indo. 123/E4
Secaucus, NJ, US 181/J8
Secchia (riv.), It. 85/J4
Sechura, Peru 198/A2
Sechura (bay), Peru 198/A2
Sechura, Desierto de (des.), Peru 198/A2
Seclin, Fr. 94/C2
Seco (riv.), Arg. 201/D6
Seco (riv.), Mex.,US 184/C2
Second Mountain (mtn.), Pa, US 180/B3
Second Watchung (mtn.), NJ, US 181/H9
Secunda, SAfr. 148/E2
Secure (riv.), Bol. 192/E7
Seda, Lith. 81/K3
Sedalia, Mo, US 171/J3
Sedan, Fr. 95/D4
Sedano, Sp. 86/D1
Sedaung (mtn.), Myan. 120/B3
Sedbergh, Eng, UK 77/F3
Seddülbahir, Turk. 89/K2
Sedeh, Iran 131/G2
Sederot, Isr. 133/D4
Sedgefield, Eng, UK 77/G2
Sedhiou, Sen. 144/B3
Sedlčany, Czh. 97/H3
Sedlo (peak), Czh. 97/H1
Sedona, Az, US 170/E4
Sedrata, Alg. 142/K6
Šeduva, Lith. 81/K4
Sędziszów, Pol. 83/L3
Sée (riv.), Fr. 84/C2
Seeb (int'l arpt.), Oman 131/G4
Seeboden, Aus. 85/K3
Seefeld in Tirol, Aus. 99/H3
Seeg, Ger. 99/G2
Seehausen, Ger. 82/F2
Seeheim, Namb. 148/B2
Seeheim-Jugenheim, Ger. 96/B3
Seekirchen Markt, Aus. 97/G7
Seekoei (riv.), SAfr. 148/D3
Seelow, Ger. 83/H2
Seeon-Seebruck, Ger. 97/F7
Seer Green, Eng, UK 72/B2
Sées, Fr. 84/D2
Seesen, Ger. 93/H5
Seeshaupt, Ger. 99/H2
Seeve (riv.), Ger. 93/G2
Seewalchen, Aus. 97/G7
Seewis im Prättigau, Swi. 99/F4
Şefaatlı, Turk. 132/C2
Sefrou, Mor. 142/B3
Sefton (co.), Eng, UK 77/E4
Segamat, Malay. 122/B3
Segarcea, Rom. 91/F3
Ségbana, Ben. 145/F4
Ségélo-Koro, C.d'Iv. 144/D4
Segelstad Bru, Nor. 80/D1
Seget, Indo. 123/H4
Segezha, Rus. 102/G3
Segorbe, Sp. 87/E3
Ségou, Mali 144/D3
Ségou (pol. reg.), Mali 144/D3
Segovia, Col. 194/C3
Segovia, Sp. 86/C2
Segozero (lake), Rus. 102/G3
Segrate, It. 100/C3
Segré, Fr. 84/C3
Segre (riv.), Sp. 87/F2
Seguam (isl.), Ak, US 176/D5
Séguédine, Niger 138/H3
Séguéla, C.d'Iv. 144/D5
Séguénéga, Burk. 145/E3
Seguin, Tx, US 174/D4
Segura (riv.), Sp. 86/D3
Segusino, It. 101/E2
Sehithwa, Bots. 147/D5
Sehnde, Ger. 93/G4
Sehonghong, Les. 148/E3
Sehore, India 124/C3
Sehwān, Pak. 131/J3
Seibersbach, Ger. 95/G4
Seiersberg, Aus. 90/B2
Seika, Japan 119/J6
Seiling, Ok, US 171/H3
Seille (riv.), Fr. 82/C5
Seinäjoki, Fin. 102/D3
Seine (riv.), On, Can. 169/L3
Seine (bay), Fr. 84/C2
Seine (riv.), Fr. 84/D2
Seine-et-Marne (dept.), Fr. 94/B5
Seine-Maritime (dept.), Fr. 94/A4
Seine-st-Denis (dept.), Fr. 94/B6
Seitenstetten, Aus. 97/H6
Seiwa, Japan 119/K7
Seix, Fr. 84/D5
Seixal, Port. 87/P10
Sejaka, Indo. 123/E4
Sejerø (isl.), Den. 80/D4
Sejny, Pol. 81/K4
Sekayu, Indo. 122/B4
Seke, Tanz. 146/A2
Sekenke, Tanz. 146/A3
Seki (riv.), Turk. 133/A1
Seki, Japan 119/L5
Seki, Japan 119/K6
Sekigahara, Japan 119/K5
Sekijo, Japan 119/D1
Sekiyado, Japan 119/D1
Sekondi, Gha. 145/E5
Sel, Nor. 79/D3
Selah, Wa, US 168/C4
Selaphum, Thai. 120/C2
Selargius, It. 88/A3
Selaru (isl.), Indo. 123/H5
Selatan (cape), Indo. 122/D4
Selawik (lake), Ak, US 176/F2
Selayar (isl.), Indo. 123/F5
Selb, Ger. 97/F2
Selbitz, Ger. 97/E2
Selbitz (riv.), Ger. 97/E2
Selbu, Nor. 79/D3
Selby, SD, US 169/H4
Selby, Eng, UK 77/G4
Selby-on-the-Bay, Md, US 180/B6
Selci, It. 101/F6
Selçuk, Turk. 132/A2
Selden, NY, US 181/E2
Sele (riv.), It. 88/D2
Selebi-Phikwe, Bots. 147/E5
Seleli (hill), Tanz. 146/B5
Selemdzha (riv.), Rus. 107/N4
Selenča, Serb. 90/D3
Selenge (prov.), Mong. 112/J2
Selenge (riv.), Mong. 112/J2
Selenginsk, Rus. 107/L4
Selenicë, Alb. 89/F2
Sélestat, Fr. 98/D1
Selety (riv.), Kaz. 129/F2
Seleznëvo, Rus. 81/N1
Selfoss, Ice. 79/N7
Sélibabi, Mrta. 144/B3
Seligenstadt, Ger. 96/B2
Seliger (lake), Rus. 102/G4
Selimbau, Indo. 122/D3
Selimiye, Turk. 132/A2
Selinsgrove, Pa, US 180/B2
Seljord, Nor. 80/C2
Selkan (tun.), Japan 118/B3
Selkirk, Sc, UK 78/D5
Selkirk, Mb, Can. 164/G3
Selkirk (mts.), BC, Can. 168/D3
Selleck, Wa, US 177/D3
Sellersville, Pa, US 180/C3
Sellières, Fr. 98/B4
Sells, Az, US 170/E5
Selly Oak, Eng, UK 74/E2
Sellye, Hun. 90/C3
Selm, Ger. 93/E5
Selma, Al, US 175/G3
Selmer, Tn, US 175/F3
Selongey, Fr. 98/B2
Selouma, Gui. 144/C4
Selous Game Reserve, Tanz. 146/B4
Selsey, Eng, UK 75/F5
Selsey Bill (pt.), Eng, UK 75/F5
Selsingen, Ger. 93/G2
Sel'tso, Rus. 104/E1
Seltz, Fr. 96/B5
Sélune (riv.), Fr. 84/C2
Selvas (for.), Braz. 189/C3
Selvik, Nor. 79/R9
Selwyn, Austl. 156/A3
Selwyn (range), Austl. 156/A3
Selz (riv.), Ger. 85/H2
Semara, WSah. 138/C2
Semarang, Indo. 122/D5
Semarsot, India 126/D4
Sembehun, SLeo. 144/B5
Sembera (riv.), Czh. 97/H2
Semberong (riv.), Malay. 122/B3
Şemdinli, Turk. 132/F2
Séméac, Fr. 84/D5
Semenivka, Ukr. 104/E1
Semenivka, Ukr. 104/E2
Semenov, Rus. 103/K4
Semeru (peak), Indo. 122/D5
Semey, Kaz. 129/H2
Semikarakorsk, Rus. 105/G3
Semilovo, Rus. 105/G1
Semiluki, Rus. 104/F2
Seminole (lake), Ga, US 175/G4
Seminole, Tx, US 174/C3
Seminoe (res.), Wy, US 170/F2
Semitau, Indo. 122/D4
Semliki (riv.), D.R. Congo 146/A2
Semnān, Iran 130/F1
Semnon (riv.), Fr. 84/C3
Semois (riv.), Belg. 84/F2
Semporna, Malay. 123/E3
Semsales, Swi. 98/C4
Semskefjellet (peak), Nor. 79/E2
Sen (riv.), Camb. 125/H5
Sen-san (peak), Japan 119/G7
Sena, Thai. 125/H5
Senador Pompeu, Braz. 196/C2
Senaja, Malay. 123/E2
Senaki, Geo. 105/G4
Senanga, Zam. 147/D4
Sénas, Fr. 132/B5
Senatobia, Ms, US 175/F3
Sence (riv.), Eng, UK 75/E1
Send, Eng, UK 72/B3
Sendai (riv.), Japan 116/D3
Sendai, Japan 117/G1
Sendai, Japan 116/B5
Sendai (int'l arpt.), Japan 117/G1
Sendai (bay), Japan 118/B4
Sendai (riv.), Japan 116/B5
Senden, Ger. 96/D6
Senden, Ger. 93/E5
Sendenhorst, Ger. 93/E5
Senec, Slvk. 83/J4
Seneca Creek State Park, Md, US 180/A5
Seneffe, Belg. 95/D2
Senegal (ctry.) 144/B3
Sénégal (riv.), Afr. 144/B2
Senekal, SAfr. 148/D3
Seney NWR, Mi, US 172/C2
Senezhskoye (lake), Rus. 103/W8
Senfi, Gha. 145/E5
Senftenberg, Ger. 83/H3
Sengenthal, Ger. 97/E4
Sengilev, Rus. 105/J1
Sengor, Bhu. 127/H2
Senguer (riv.), Arg. 200/D3
Senhor do Bonfim, Braz. 196/B3
Senica, Slvk. 83/J4
Senirkent, Turk. 132/B2
Senise, It. 88/E2
Senj, Cro. 85/L4
Senja (isl.), Nor. 79/F1
Senkaku-Shotō (isl.), Japan 117/G8
Şenkaya, Turk. 132/E1
Şenköy, Turk. 133/E1
Senlis, Fr. 94/B5
Senmonoron, Camb. 123/D3
Sennan, Japan 119/H7
Sennar (dam), Sudan 139/M5
Senne (riv.), Belg. 95/D2
Sennecy-le-Grand, Fr. 98/A4
Sennfeld, Ger. 96/D2
Senno, Bela. 81/N4
Sennoy, Rus. 105/G2
Sennoy, Rus. 105/H1
Sennwald, Swi. 99/F3
Sennybridge, Wal, UK 74/C3
Séno (prov.), Burk. 145/F3
Senones, Fr. 98/C1
Senorbì, It. 88/A3
Senou (Bamako) (int'l arpt.), Mali 144/D3
Senovo, Bul. 91/H4
Sens, Fr. 84/E2
Sensuntepeque, ESal. 186/D3
Senta, Serb. 90/E3
Sentani, Indo. 123/K4
Sentery, D.R. Congo 147/E2
Senya Beraku, Gha. 145/E5
Senyavin (isls.), Micr. 158/E4
Senzig, Ger. 82/Q7
Seohāra, India 126/B1
Seon, Swi. 98/E3
Seondha, India 126/B2
Seoni, India 126/B4
Seonī Mālwā, India 126/A4
Seoul (Sŏul) (cap.), SKor. 115/D4
Seoul Grand Park, SKor. 115/G7
Seoul Jikhalsi (prov.), SKor. 115/D4
Sepetiba (bay), Braz. 197/J8
Sepik (riv.), PNG 158/D5
Sep'o, NKor. 115/D3
Sepo, Indo. 123/G3
Sępólno Krajeńskie, Pol. 83/J2
Sept-Îles, Qu, Can. 173/H2
Septemvri, Bul. 49/G4
Septeuil, Fr. 72/H5
Sepulveda (dam), Ca, US 178/F7
Sequeros, Sp. 86/B2
Sequoia NP, Ca, US 170/C3
Serafimovich, Rus. 105/G2
Seraincourt, Fr. 72/H4
Seraing, Belg. 95/E2
Serampore, India 127/G4
Seran (riv.), Fr. 98/D3
Serasan (str.), Indo.,Malay. 122/C3
Serasan, Indo. 122/C3
Seravezza, It. 100/D6
Serbia (ctry.) 90/D3
Serbia (reg.), Serb. 90/E4
Serchio (riv.), It. 100/D4
Serdobsk, Rus. 105/H1
Serebryansk, Kaz. 106/J5
Serednikovo, Rus. 102/H5
Seregno, It. 100/C2
Serein (riv.), Fr. 82/D4
Serémange-Erzange, Fr. 95/F5
Seremban, Malay. 122/B3
Serengeti NP, Tanz. 139/M8
Serenje, Zam. 147/F3
Serere, Ugan. 146/A1
Sergach, Rus. 103/K5
Sergeantsville, NJ, US 180/D3
Sergen, Turk. 91/H5
Sergeya Kirova (isls.), Rus. 106/J2
Sergeyevka, Kaz. 103/Q5
Sergipe (state), Braz. 196/C3
Sergiyev Posad, Rus. 102/H4
Sergnano, It. 100/C3
Seria, Bru. 122/D3
Seriate, It. 100/C2
Sérifontaine, Fr. 94/A5
Sérifos, Gre. 89/J4
Sérifos (isl.), Gre. 89/J4
Sérignan, Fr. 84/E5
Serik, Turk. 132/B2
Seringa, Serra da (mts.), Braz. 193/H5
Serio (riv.), It. 100/C2
Serkout (peak), Alg. 141/G5
Sermaize-les-Bains, Fr. 95/D6
Sermide, It. 101/E4
Sernovodsk, Rus. 105/J1
Sernur, Rus. 103/L4
Serón, Sp. 86/D4
Serós, Sp. 87/F2
Serottini (peak), It. 99/G5
Serov, Rus. 106/G4
Serowe, Bots. 147/E5
Serpa, Port. 86/B4
Serpeddì (peak), It. 88/A3
Serpent's Mouth (str.), Trin.,Ven. 195/F2
Serpentine (dam), Austl. 157/C4
Serpentine Lakes, Austl. 155/F4
Serpukhov, Rus. 102/H5
Serra (peak), It. 100/D6
Serra, Braz. 197/D2
Serra Branca, Braz. 196/C2
Serra da Bocaína, PN da, Braz. 197/C2
Serra da Canastra, PN da, Braz. 197/C2
Serra da Capivara, PN da, Braz. 196/B3
Serra da Estrela (peak), Port. 86/B2
Serra da Estrela (mts.), Port. 86/A3
Serra do Cipó, PN da, Braz. 197/D1
Serra dos Órgãos, PN da, Braz. 197/K7
Serra San Bruno, It. 88/E3
Serra San Quirico, It. 101/G7
Serra Talhada, Braz. 196/C2
Serrai, Gre. 89/H2
Serralta di San Vito (peak), It. 88/E3

274
Serra – Sincé

Serramanna, It. 88/A3
Serramazzoni, It. 101/D5
Serrana Bank (isl.), Col. 187/G3
Serranía de la Cerbatana (mts.), Ven. 195/E3
Serranía de la Neblina, PN, Ven. 195/E4
Serranías del Burro (mts.), Mex. 184/E2
Serranilla Bank (isl.), Col. 187/G3
Serrano, Arg. 200/E2
Serranópolis, Braz. 197/B1
Serrat (cape), Tun. 142/L6
Serravalle, It. 101/F4
Serravalle, SMar. 101/F6
Serravalle Scrivia, It. 100/B4
Serravalle Sesia, It. 100/B2
Serre (riv.), Fr. 82/B4
Serrenti, It. 88/A3
Serrinha, Braz. 196/C3
Serris, Fr. 72/L5
Sersale, It. 88/E3
Sertã, Port. 86/A3
Sertânia, Braz. 196/C3
Sertãozinho, Braz. 197/H2
Sertavul (pass), Turk. 132/C2
Serteng (mts.), China 112/F4
Serui, Indo. 123/J4
Seruyan (riv.), Indo. 122/D4
Servance, Fr. 98/C2
Servi, Turk. 132/E2
Sérvia, Gre. 89/G2
Serviceton, Austl. 157/B3
Sese (isls.), Ugan. 146/A3
Sesebi (ruin), Sudan 143/B4
Sesepe, Indo. 123/G4
Sesheke, Zam. 147/D4
Sesia (riv.), It. 85/H4
Sesimbra, Port. 86/A3
Sesimbra, Port. 87/P11
Seskar (isl.), Rus. 81/N1
Sespe, Ca, US 178/B2
Sespe (cr.), Ca, US 178/A1
Sespe Condor Sanctuary, Ca, US 178/C3
Sesslach, Ger. 96/D2
Sesto Calende, It. 100/B2
Sesto Fiorentino, It. 101/E6
Sesto San Giovanni, It. 100/C2
Sesto Ulteriano, It. 100/C3
Sestola, It. 101/D5
Sestra (riv.), Rus. 102/W9
Sestri Levante, It. 100/C5
Sestroretsk, Rus. 103/S6
Sestroretskiy (lake), Rus. 103/T6
Sestu, It. 88/A3
Sesvenna (peak), It. 99/G4
Sesvete, Cro. 90/C3
Šeta, Lith. 81/L4
Setana, Japan 118/A2
Sète, Fr. 84/E5
Sete Lagoas, Braz. 197/C1
Sethārja, Pak. 131/J3
Seti (riv.), Nepal 126/C1
Seti (zone), Nepal 126/C1
Sétif, Alg. 142/H4
Sétif (wilaya), Alg. 142/H4
Seto, Japan 119/M5
Seto-Naikai NP, Japan 116/C4
Setouchi, Japan 117/K6
Settat, Mor. 140/D2
Settepani (peak), It. 100/B5
Settimo Torinese, It. 100/A2
Settimo Vittone, It. 100/A1
Settle, Eng, UK 77/F3
Settsu, Japan 119/J6
Setúbal (dist.), Port. 86/A3
Setúbal (bay), Port. 86/A3
Setúbal, Port. 87/Q10
Seubersdorf, Ger. 97/E4
Seudre (riv.), Fr. 84/C4
Seugne (riv.), Fr. 84/C4
Seuil-d'Argonne, Fr. 95/E6
Seul (lake), On, Can. 164/G3
Seulimeum, Indo. 122/A2
Seurre, Fr. 98/B4
Seuzach, Swi. 99/E2
Sevan, Arm. 105/H4
Sevana (lake), Arm. 105/H4
Sevastopol', Ukr. 104/E3
Sevelen, Swi. 99/F3
Seven (riv.), Eng, UK 77/H3
Seven Heads (pt.), Ire. 73/P11
Seven Valleys, Pa, US 180/B4
Sevenoaks, Eng, UK 72/D3
Sevenoaks Weald, Eng, UK 72/D3
Severn (riv.), Wal, UK 77/F6
Severn (riv.), On, Can. 164/G3
Severn (riv.), Md, US 180/B5
Severn, Md, US 180/B5
Severna Park, Md, US 180/B5
Severnaya Osetiya-Alaniya, Resp., Rus. 105/G4
Severnaya Sos'va (riv.), Rus. 103/N3
Severnaya Zemlya (isls.), Rus. 106/J2
Severnyy, Rus. 103/P2
Severo-Kuril'sk, Rus. 107/R4
Severo-Yeniseyskiy, Rus. 106/K3
Severobaykal'sk, Rus. 107/L4
Severodvinsk, Rus. 102/H2
Severomorsk, Rus. 102/G1
Severomuysk, Rus. 107/M4
Severoural'sk, Rus. 103/N3
Severskaya, Rus. 104/F3
Severukha, Rus. 103/P4
Seveso, It. 100/C2
Sevier (des.), Ut, US 170/D3
Sevierville, Tn, US 175/H3
Sevilla, Col. 194/C3
Seville, Sp. 86/C4
Seville, Austl. 157/G5
Sevlievo, Bul. 91/G4
Sevnica, Slov. 90/B2
Sevojno, Serb. 90/D4
Sevran, Fr. 72/K5
Sevsk, Rus. 104/E1
Sewa (riv.), SLeo. 144/C5
Seward (pen.), Ak, US 176/E2
Seward, Ak, US 176/J3
Seward, Ne, US 171/H2
Sewaren, NJ, US 181/J9
Sewell, Chile 200/N9
Seyah Cheshmeh, Iran 105/H5
Seybaplaya, Mex. 186/D2
Seybouse, Oued (riv.), Alg. 142/K6
Seychelles (ctry.) 65/M6
Seydhisfjördhur, Ice. 79/O6
Seydişehir, Turk. 132/B2
Seyhan (dam), Turk. 132/C2
Seyhan (riv.), Turk. 133/D1
Seyitgazi, Turk. 132/B2
Seym (riv.), Rus. 104/E2
Seymour, Austl. 157/C3
Seymour, Tx, US 171/H4
Seynod, Fr. 98/C6
Seyssel, Fr. 98/B6
Sežana, Slov. 85/K4
Sézanne, Fr. 94/C6
Sezimovo Ústí, Czh. 97/H4
Sezze, It. 88/C2
Sfax, Tun. 141/H2
Sfax (gov.), Tun. 141/H2
Sfîntu Gheorghe, Rom. 91/J3
Sfîntu Gheorghe, Rom. 91/G3
Sfîntu Gheorghe Branch (riv.), Rom. 91/J3
Sfizef, Alg. 142/E5
Sgurr na Lapaich (peak), Sc, UK 78/A2
Sha (riv.), China 114/C4
Sha Tin, China 113/U10
Shaanxi (prov.), China 112/J5
Shaba Nat'l Rsv., Kenya 146/C2
Shābāzpur (riv.), Bang. 127/H4
Shabeelle (riv.), Som. 139/P7
Shabla, Bul. 91/J4
Shabqadar, Pak. 128/A2
Shabunda, D.R. Congo 139/L8
Shache, China 129/G5
Shade (mtn.), Pa, US 180/A2
Shadrinsk, Rus. 103/P4
Shafter, Tx, US 174/B4
Shagamu, Nga. 145/F5
Shagany (lake), Ukr. 91/J3
Shageluk, Ak, US 176/G3
Shah Alam, Malay. 122/B3
Shāh Kot, Pak. 128/B4
Shāhābād, India 126/B2
Shāhābād, India 126/B1
Shāhābād, India 128/D4
Shāhdād, Iran 131/G2
Shahdādkot, Pak. 131/J3
Shahdol, India 126/C4
Shāhganj, India 126/D2
Shaḥḥāt, Libya 139/K1
Shāhjahānpur, India 126/B2
Shāhpur, Pak. 128/B3
Shāhpur Chākar, Pak. 124/A2
Shāhpura, India 126/C4
Shahr-e Kord, Iran 130/F2
Shahr Sultān, Pak. 128/A5
Shāhrūd (Emāmshahr), Iran 131/F1
Shā'ib al Banāt (peak), Egypt 143/C3
Shaikhpura, India 127/E3
Shājāpur, India 131/L4
Shakargarh, Pak. 128/C3
Shakaskraal, SAfr. 149/E3
Shakawe, Bots. 147/D4
Shakhrisabz, Uzb. 129/E5
Shakhtinsk, Kaz. 129/F3
Shakhty, Rus. 104/G3
Shakhun'ya, Rus. 103/K4
Shaki, Nga. 145/F4
Shakotan (pen.), Japan 118/B2
Shaktoolik, Ak, US 176/F3
Shalbuzdag (peak), Rus. 105/H4
Shallow Reach (inlet), Austl. 155/M8
Shalqar, Kaz. 105/L3
Shaluli (mts.), China 112/G5
Shām, Jabal ash (peak), Oman 131/G4
Shama (riv.), Tanz. 147/F2
Shamattawa (riv.), On, Can. 123/H3
Shāmgarh, India 131/L4
Shamīl, Iran 131/G3
Shāmli, India 128/D5
Shammar, Jabal (mts.), SAr. 130/D3
Shamokin, Pa, US 180/B2
Shamokin Dam, Pa, US 180/B2
Shamrock (mtn.), Yk, Can. 176/L3
Shamrock, Tx, US 171/G4
Shamsābād, India 128/C4
Shamva, Zim. 147/F4
Shan (plat.), Myan. 112/G7
Shan (state), Myan. 125/G3
Sha'nabī, Jabal ash (peak), Tun. 142/L7
Shandong (prov.), China 113/L4
Shandong (isl.), China 114/E3
Shangcai, China 114/C4
Shangcheng, China 114/C5
Shangdu, China 113/K3
Shanghai (prov.), China 113/M5
Shanghai, China 114/L8
Shanghang, China 121/C2
Shanghe, China 114/D3
Shangqiu, China 114/C4
Shangshui, China 114/C4
Shangyi, China 114/C2
Shangyou, China 121/B2
Shannon (riv.), Ire. 73/P10
Shanshan, China 112/F3
Shantar (isls.), Rus. 107/P4
Shantar (isl.), Rus. 109/N4
Shantou, China 121/C3
Shanxi (prov.), China 113/K4
Shanyin, China 114/C3
Shaoguan, China 125/K3
Shaowu, China 121/C2
Shaoxing, China 121/D2
Shaoyang, China 121/B2
Shaoyang, China 125/K2
Shapkina (riv.), Rus. 103/M2
Shaqlāwah, Iraq 132/F2
Sharafkhāneh, Iran 132/F2
Sharbatāt, Ra's ash (pt.), Oman 131/G5
Sharga, Mong. 112/G2
Shari, Japan 118/D2
Sharīngol, Mong. 112/J2
Shark (bay), Austl. 154/B3
Shark River (inlet), NJ, US 180/D3
Sharon, Pa, US 172/D3
Sharp (mtn.), Ut, US 179/K11
Sharpe (lake), SD, US 169/J4
Sharqpur, Pak. 128/C4
Shar'ya, Rus. 103/K4
Shashi, China 121/B1
Shasta (lake), Ca, US 168/C5
Shasta (mt.), Ca, US 168/C5
Shatskiy NP, Ukr. 83/M3
Shatt al Arab (riv.), Iraq 130/E2
Shaṭṭ al Jarīd (dry lake), Gabon 138/G1
Shattuck, Ok, US 171/H3
Shaunavon, Sk, Can. 168/F3
Shavano Park, Tx, US 179/T20
Shaw, Eng, UK 75/E4
Shawano, Wi, US 169/L4
Shawinigan, Qu, Can. 173/F2
Shawnee, Ok, US 171/H4
Shawnee (res.), Ok, US 179/N15
Shawnee, Ks, US 179/D5
Shay Gap, Austl. 154/D2
Shaykhān, Iraq 132/E2
Shchara (riv.), Bela. 104/C1
Shchekino, Rus. 104/F1
Shchelkovo, Rus. 103/W9
Shchigry, Rus. 104/F2
Shchūchīnsk, Kaz. 129/F2
She Xian, China 121/C2
Shea Stadium, NY, US 181/K9
Shebelē Wenz (riv.), Eth. 139/P6
Sheberghān, Afg. 131/J1
Sheboygan, Wi, US 169/M5
Shediac, NB, Can. 173/H2
Shee (riv.), Sc, UK 78/C3
Sheelin (lake), Ire. 76/A4
Sheep (mtn.), Ak, US 176/F2
Shefar'am, Isr. 133/G6
Shefayim, Isr. 133/F7
Sheffield, Austl. 157/C4
Sheffield, Eng, UK 77/G5
Sheffield (co.), Eng, UK 77/G5
Sheffield, Al, US 175/G3
Sheffield (isl.), Ct, US 181/M7
Shehuén (riv.), Arg. 199/B6
Shek Uk (peak), China 113/V10
Shekak (riv.), On, Can. 172/C1
Shekhūpura, Pak. 128/B4
Shelagskiy (cape), Rus. 107/S2
Shelburne, NS, Can. 173/H3
Shelby, Mt, US 168/F3
Shelby, Ms, US 171/K4
Shelby, Mi, US 172/C3
Shelby, NC, US 175/H3
Shelbyville (lake), Il, US 175/F2
Shelbyville, Tn, US 175/G3
Shelbyville, In, US 172/C4
Sheldon Point, Ak, US 176/F3
Shelekhov (gulf), Rus. 109/Q3
Shelikof (str.), Ak, US 176/H4
Shell (pt.), Eng, UK 75/G4
Shell Lake, Wi, US 169/L4
Shell Rock (riv.), Ia, US 169/K5
Shellbrook, Sk, Can. 169/G2
Shelley (isl.), Pa, US 180/B3
Shelter (isl.), NY, US 181/F1
Shelter Island (sound), NY, US 181/F1
Shelton, Wa, US 168/C4
Shelton, Ct, US 181/E1
Shen Xian, China 114/C3
Shenandoah, Pa, US 180/B2
Shenandoah NP, Va, US 172/E4
Shenchi, China 114/C3
Sheng Xian, China 121/D2
Shenge (pt.), SLeo. 144/B5
Shengena (peak), Tanz. 146/C4
Shennongjia, China 114/B5
Shenqiu, China 114/C4
Shenyang, China 115/B2
Shenzhen, China 125/K3
Shepetivka, Ukr. 104/C2
Shepherd (isls.), Van. 158/F6
Sheppey, Isle of (isl.), Eng, UK 75/G4
Shepshed, Eng, UK 75/E1
Sheqi, China 114/C4
Sherbro (isl.), SLeo. 144/B5
Sherbrooke, Qu, Can. 173/G2
Shere (hill), Nga. 145/H4
Sheremetyevo (int'l arpt.), Rus. 103/W9
Sherghāti, India 127/E3
Sheridan, Wy, US 168/G4
Sheridan, Co, US 179/B3
Sherman, Tx, US 171/H4
Sherpur, Bang. 127/H3
Sherwood (pt.), Ct, US 181/E1
Shetland (isls.), UK 202/G
Sheung Shui-Fanling, China 113/U10
Shevchenko (int'l arpt.), Kaz. 105/J4
Sheyang (riv.), China 114/D4
Sheyang, China 114/E4
Sheyenne (riv.), ND, US 169/J4
Shi (riv.), China 114/C4
Shi San Ling, China 114/H6
Shibakawa, Japan 119/B3
Shibata, Japan 117/F2
Shibayama, Japan 119/E2
Shibecha, Japan 118/D2
Shibetsu, Japan 118/C1
Shibetsu, Japan 118/D2
Shibīn al Kawm, Egypt 133/B4
Shibīn al Qanāṭir, Egypt 133/B4
Shibogama (lake), On, Can. 169/L2
Shibotsu (isl.), Rus. 118/E2
Shibushi (bay), Japan 116/B5
Shicheng, China 121/C2
Shicheng (isl.), China 115/B3
Shickshinny, Pa, US 180/B1
Shiderty (riv.), Kaz. 129/F2
Shido, Japan 116/D3
Shiga, Japan 119/J5
Shigaraki, Japan 119/K6
Shihezi, China 112/E3
Shijak, Alb. 89/F2
Shijiazhuang, China 114/C3
Shijōnawate, Japan 119/J6
Shikabe, Japan 118/B2
Shikārpur, India 126/B1
Shikārpur, Pak. 131/J3
Shikata, Japan 119/G6
Shikatsu, Japan 119/L5
Shikishima, Japan 119/B2
Shikohābād, India 126/B2
Shikoku (isl.), Japan 116/C4
Shikoku (mts.), Japan 116/C4
Shikotsu (lake), Japan 118/B2
Shikotsu-Tōya NP, Japan 118/B2
Shildon, Eng, UK 77/G2
Shilka (riv.), Rus. 109/L4
Shilla (peak), India 131/L2
Shillington, Pa, US 180/C3
Shillong, India 125/F3
Shiloh, Il, US 179/H8
Shiloh, NJ, US 180/C5
Shilou, China 114/B3
Shimabara, Japan 116/B4
Shimagahara, Japan 119/K6
Shimamoto, Japan 119/J6
Shimane (pref.), Japan 116/C3
Shimasahi, Japan 119/K5
Shimba Hills Nat'l Rsv., Kenya 146/C4
Shimbara (bay), Japan 116/B4
Shimber Berris (peak), Som. 139/Q5
Shimizu, Japan 118/C2
Shimizu, Japan 119/B3
Shimo-Koshiki (isl.), Japan 116/A5
Shimobe, Japan 119/A3
Shimoda, Japan 117/F3
Shimodate, Japan 117/F2
Shimofusa, Japan 119/E2
Shimoichi, Japan 119/J7
Shimokita (pen.), Japan 118/B3
Shimonita, Japan 119/B1
Shimonoseki, Japan 116/B4
Shimotsuma, Japan 119/D1
Shimoyama, Japan 119/M5
Shimukappu, Japan 118/C2
Shin, Japan 119/C1
Shin (lake), Sc, UK 73/R7
Shingū, Japan 116/D4
Shinhyōn, SKor. 116/A3
Shinji (lake), Japan 116/C3
Shinjō, Japan 118/B4
Shinjō, Japan 119/J7
Shinkawa, Japan 119/L5
Shinminato, Japan 117/E2
Shinnecock (bay), NY, US 181/F2
Shinnecock Ind. Res., NY, US 181/F2
Shinsei, Japan 119/L5
Shintoku, Japan 118/C2
Shintone, Japan 119/E2
Shinyanga, Tanz. 146/B3
Shinyanga (pol. reg.), Tanz. 146/B3
Shio-no-misaki (cape), Japan 116/D4
Shiogama, Japan 117/G1
Shioya-saki (pt.), Japan 117/G2
Ship Bottom, NJ, US 180/D4
Shipley, Eng, UK 77/G4
Shippan (pt.), Ct, US 181/L7
Shippegan, NB, Can. 173/H2
Shippo, Japan 119/L5
Shiprock, NM, US 170/E3
Shīr (mtn.), Iran 130/F2
Shirakami-misaki (cape), Japan 118/B3
Shirakawa, Japan 117/G2
Shirakawa, Japan 119/M4
Shirakawa-tōge (pass), Japan 116/E3
Shirako, Japan 119/E3
Shirane, Japan 119/A2
Shirane-san (peak), Japan 117/F3
Shirane-san (peak), Japan 117/F2
Shiranuka, Japan 118/D2
Shiraoi, Japan 118/B2
Shiraoka, Japan 119/D1
Shīrāz, Iran 130/F3
Shirbīn, Egypt 133/B4
Shiretoko-misaki (cape), Japan 118/D1
Shiretoko NP, Japan 118/D1
Shiriya-zaki (pt.), Japan 118/B3
Shirjiu (lake), China 114/D5
Shirley, NY, US 181/F2
Shiroi, Japan 119/E2
Shiroishi, Japan 117/G1
Shirone, Japan 117/F2
Shiroyama, Japan 119/C2
Shīrvān, Iran 131/G1
Shishaldin (vol.), Ak, US 176/F5
Shīshgarh, India 126/B1
Shishi, China 121/C3
Shishmaref, Ak, US 176/E2
Shishou, China 121/B2
Shisui, Japan 119/E2
Shithātha, Iraq 132/E3
Shivpurī, India 126/A3
Shivpuri NP, India 126/A3
Shixing, China 125/K3
Shiyan, China 114/B4
Shizhu, China 121/A2
Shizugawa, Japan 118/B4
Shizuishan, China 112/J4
Shizukuishi, Japan 118/B4
Shizunai, Japan 118/C2
Shizuoka (pref.), Japan 117/E3
Shkumbin (riv.), Alb. 90/E5
Shmidta (cape), Rus. 176/C2
Shoal (pt.), Austl. 154/B4
Shoal Lake, Mb, Can. 169/H3
Shoalhaven (riv.), Austl. 157/D2
Shōbara, Japan 116/C3
Shōbu, Japan 119/D1
Shōdo (isl.), Japan 116/D3
Shoemakersville, Pa, US 180/C3
Shokanbetsu-dake (peak), Japan 118/B2
Sholāpur, India 131/L5
Sholl (peak), Arg. 201/D6
Shomron (ruin), WBnk. 133/G7
Shōnan, Japan 119/E2
Shorāpur, India 124/C4
Shoreham-by-Sea, Eng, UK 75/F5
Shorewood, Wi, US 177/Q13
Shorewood, Il, US 177/P16
Shorkot, Pak. 128/B4
Short (mtn.), Tn, US 175/G3
Shortland (isls.), Sol. 158/E5
Shoshone (riv.), Wy, US 168/F4
Shoshone (mts.), Nv, US 170/C3
Shoshoni, Wy, US 168/F5
Shostka, Ukr. 104/E2
Shotts, Sc, UK 78/C5
Shou Xian, China 114/D4
Shouguang, China 114/D3
Shouyang, China 114/C3
Show Low, Az, US 170/E4
Shōwa, Japan 119/B2
Shōwa, Japan 119/D2
Shpanberga (chan.), Rus. 118/E2
Shpola, Ukr. 104/D2
Shreveport, La, US 171/J4
Shrewsbury, Mo, US 179/G8
Shrewsbury, Eng, UK 74/D1
Shrewsbury, Pa, US 180/B4
Shriner (mtn.), Pa, US 180/A2
Shropshire (co.), Eng, UK 77/E6
Shropshire Union (canal), Eng, UK 77/F6
Shū (riv.), Kaz. 107/H5
Shu (riv.), China 114/D5
Shuangbai, China 125/H3
Shuangcheng, China 113/N2
Shuangliao, China 114/E2
Shuangpai, China 125/K2
Shuangyashan, China 113/P2
Shu'ayb, Jabal an (peak), Yem. 130/D5
Shubrā al Khaymah, Egypt 133/B4
Shubrā Khīt, Egypt 133/B4
Shucheng, China 114/D5
Shu'fāṭ, Isr. 133/G8
Shufu, China 129/G5
Shuiyang (riv.), China 114/D5
Shujāābād, Pak. 128/A5
Shulan, China 113/N3
Shule, China 129/G5
Shule (riv.), China 106/K6
Shumagin (isls.), Ak, US 176/G4
Shumen, Bul. 91/H4
Shumerlya, Rus. 103/K5
Shuna (isl.), Sc, UK 78/A3
Shunak (peak), Kaz. 129/F3
Shungnak, Ak, US 176/G2
Shunyi, China 114/H6
Shuo Xian, China 114/C3
Shupīyan, India 128/C3
Shūr (riv.), Iran 131/G2
Shurugwi, Zim. 147/E4
Shūshtar, Iran 130/E2
Shuswap (lake), BC, Can. 168/D3
Shuwaykah, WBnk. 133/G7
Shuya, Rus. 102/J4
Shuyang, China 114/D4
Shwebo, Myan. 125/G3
Shwegyin, Myan. 125/G4
Shyghys Qazaqstan (obl.), Kaz. 106/J5
Shymkent, Kaz. 129/E4
Shyok (riv.), India 131/L2
Si Satchanalai (ruin), Thai. 120/B2
Si Xian, China 114/D4
Siāh Kūh (mts.), Afg. 131/H2
Siak (riv.), Indo. 122/B3
Siālkot, Pak. 128/C3
Sianów, Pol. 80/G4
Siapa (riv.), Ven. 195/E4
Siargao (isl.), Phil. 121/E6
Siasi, Phil. 123/F2
Siaton (pt.), Phil. 123/F2
Siaton, Phil. 121/D6
Siau (isl.), Indo. 123/G3
Šiauliai, Lith. 81/K4
Sibalom, Phil. 121/D5
Sibay, Rus. 105/L1
Sibbo (Sipoo), Fin. 81/L1
Šibenik, Cro. 90/B4
Siberia (reg.), Rus. 109/H3
Siberut (isl.), Indo. 122/A4
Sibi, Pak. 131/J3
Sibiloi NP, Kenya 139/N7
Sibiti, Congo 147/B1
Sibiu, Rom. 91/G3
Sibiu (prov.), Rom. 91/G2
Sibley, Mo, US 179/E5
Sibolga, Indo. 122/A3
Sibu, Malay. 122/D3
Sibuco, Phil. 123/F2
Sibut, CAfr. 139/J6
Sibuyan (isl.), Phil. 123/F1
Sibuyan (sea), Phil. 123/F1
Sicamous, BC, Can. 168/D3
Sichuan (prov.), China 112/H5
Sicilia (pol. reg.), It. 88/C4
Sicily (isl.), It. 88/C3
Sicily, Strait of (str.), It. 88/B3
Sico (riv.), Hon. 182/D4
Sicuani, Peru 198/D4
Šid, Serb. 90/D3
Siddipet, India 124/C4
Siderno Marina, It. 88/E3
Siderópolis, Braz. 197/B4
Sidewinder (mtn.), Ca, US 178/C1
Sidhaulī, India 126/C2
Sidhi, India 126/C3
Sidhirókastron, Gre. 89/H2
Sidhpur, India 131/K4
Sidi Aïssa, Alg. 142/G5
Sīdī Barrānī, Egypt 143/A2
Sidi Bel-Abbes, Alg. 142/E5
Sidi Bennour, Mor. 140/C2
Sidi Bouzid, Tun. 142/L7
Sidi Bou Zid (gov.), Tun. 142/L7
Sidi Ifni, Mor. 140/C3
Sidi Kacem, Mor. 142/B2
Sidi Kacem (prov.), Mor. 142/B2
Sīdī Sālim, Egypt 133/B4
Sidi Slimane, Mor. 142/B2
Sidi Yahya du Rharb, Mor. 142/A2
Sidlaw (hills), Sc, UK 78/C3
Sidmouth, Eng, UK 74/C5
Sidney, BC, Can. 168/C3
Sidney, Mt, US 169/G4
Sidney, Oh, US 172/C3
Sidney Lanier (lake), Ga, US 175/H3
Sidra (gulf), Libya 138/J1
Sieci, It. 101/E5
Siedlce, Pol. 83/M2
Sieg (riv.), Ger. 85/G1
Siegburg, Ger. 95/G2
Siegen, Ger. 95/H2
Siegenburg, Ger. 97/E5
Siegendorf im Burgenland, Aus. 85/M3
Siemianówka (lake), Pol. 83/M2
Siemiatycze, Pol. 83/M2
Siemreab, Camb. 120/C3
Siena (prov.), It. 101/E6
Siena, It. 85/J5
Sienne (riv.), Fr. 84/C2
Sieradz, Pol. 83/K3
Sieraków, Pol. 83/J2
Sierning, Aus. 97/H6
Sierpc, Pol. 83/K2
Sierra (peak), Ca, US 178/C3
Sierra Blanca, Tx, US 171/F5
Sierra de la Macarena, PN, Col. 192/D3
Sierra de San Pedro Mártir, Mex. 184/B2
Sierra Estrella (mts.), Az, US 179/R19
Sierra Grande, Arg. 200/D4
Sierra Leone (ctry.) 144/B4
Sierra Leone (cape), SLeo. 144/B4
Sierra Madre, Ca, US 178/F7
Sierra Mojada, Mex. 184/E3
Sierra Nevada (mts.), US 170/B3
Sierra Nevada de Santa Marta, PN, Col. 194/C2
Sierra Nevada, PN, Ven. 194/D2
Sierra Vieja (mts.), Mex.,US 174/B4
Sierra Vista, Az, US 170/E5
Sierras Bayas, Arg. 200/E3
Sierre, Swi. 98/D5
Siete Picos (peak), Sp. 87/M8
Siete Tazas, PN, Chile 200/C2
Sieve (riv.), It. 101/E5
Sif Fatima, Alg. 141/H3
Sífnos (isl.), Gre. 89/J4
Sig, Alg. 142/E5
Siga Hills (hills), Tanz. 146/B3
Sigean, Fr. 84/E5
Siġġiewi, Malta 88/L7
Sighetu Marmaţiei, Rom. 91/F2
Sighişoara, Rom. 91/G2
Sighty Crag (hill), Eng, UK 77/F1
Sigillo, It. 101/F6
Sigli, Indo. 122/A2
Sigli (cape), Alg. 142/H4
Siglufjördhur, Ice. 79/N6
Sigmaringen, Ger. 99/F1
Sigmarszell, Ger. 99/F2
Signa, It. 101/E5
Signal de la Mère Boitier (peak), Fr. 84/F3
Signal de Toussaines (peak), Fr. 84/B2
Signal d'Écouves (peak), Fr. 84/D2
Signal Hill, Ca, US 178/F8
Signau, Swi. 98/D4
Signy-L'Abbaye, Fr. 95/D4
Signy-le-Petit, Fr. 95/D4
Signy-Signets, Fr. 72/M5
Sigriswil, Swi. 98/D4
Sigtuna, Swe. 80/G2
Siguatepeque, Hon. 186/E3
Sigüenza, Sp. 86/D2
Sihl (riv.), Swi. 99/E3
Sihlsee (lake), Swi. 99/E3
Sihochac, Mex. 186/D2
Sihong, China 114/D4
Sihorā, India 126/C4
Sihuas, Peru 198/B3
Siilinjärvi, Fin. 102/E3
Siirt (prov.), Turk. 132/E2
Siirt, Turk. 132/E2
Sikandarābād, India 126/A1
Sikandarpur, India 127/E2
Sikandra Rao, India 126/B2
Sikanni Chief (riv.), BC, Can. 164/D3
Sīkar, India 131/L3
Sikasso, Mali 144/D4
Sikasso (pol. reg.), Mali 144/D4
Sikeston, Mo, US 171/K3
Sikhote-Alin' (mts.), Rus. 107/P5
Sikinos, Gre. 89/J4
Síkinos (isl.), Gre. 89/J4
Sikkim (state), India 127/G2
Siklós, Hun. 90/D3
Sikoúrion, Gre. 89/H3
Sil (riv.), Sp. 86/B1
Silai (riv.), India 127/F4
Silandro (Schlanders), It. 99/G4
Silao, India 127/E3
Silao, Mex. 185/E4
Silat Aẓ Ẓahr, WBnk. 133/G7
Silay, Phil. 121/D5
Silchar, India 125/F3
Şile, Turk. 91/J5
Silea, It. 101/F1
Silenen, Swi. 99/E4
Silesia (reg.), Pol. 83/H3
Siletitengiz (lake), Kaz. 129/F2
Silgadhī, Nepal 126/C1
Siliana, Tun. 142/L6
Siliana (gov.), Tun. 142/L6
Silifke, Turk. 133/C1
Silīguri, India 127/G2
Silistra, Bul. 91/H3
Silivri, Turk. 91/J5
Siljan (lake), Swe. 80/F1
Siljansnäs, Swe. 80/F1
Silkeborg, Den. 80/C3
Sill (riv.), Aus. 99/H3
Silla, Sp. 87/E3
Silla Tombs, SKor. 115/E5
Sillamäe, Est. 81/M2
Sillānwāli, Pak. 128/B4
Sillaro (riv.), It. 101/E4
Silleda, Sp. 86/A1
Sillian, Aus. 85/K3
Sillustani (ruin), Peru 198/D4
Silly-le-Long, Fr. 72/L4
Siloam Springs, Ar, US 171/J3
Silopi, Turk. 132/E2
Silsbee, Tx, US 171/J5
Silsden, Eng, UK 77/G4
Silsersee (lake), Swi. 99/F5
Siltou (well), Chad 138/J4
Šilutė, Lith. 81/J4
Silvan (dam), Turk. 132/E2
Silvaplana, Swi. 99/F5
Silvassa, India 124/B3
Silver (lake), Or, US 170/B2
Silver (riv.), Or, US 170/C2
Silver (mtn.), Ca, US 178/C1
Silver Bay, Mn, US 169/L4
Silver City, NM, US 170/E4
Silver Lake, Wi, US 177/P14
Silver Lake-Fircrest, Wa, US 177/C2
Silver Meadow (lake), NJ, US 180/C5
Silver Run, Md, US 180/A4
Silver Spring, Md, US 180/A6
Silverado, Ca, US 178/C3
Silverton, Or, US 168/C4
Silverton, Co, US 170/F3
Silverton, NJ, US 180/D3
Silverwood (lake), Ca, US 178/C2
Silves, Port. 86/A4
Silvi, It. 88/D1
Silvia, Col. 194/B4
Silvies (riv.), Or, US 170/C2
Silvretta (mts.), Aus. 99/G4
Silz, Aus. 99/G3
Sim (cape), Mor. 140/C3
Simão Dias, Braz. 196/C3
Simard (lake), Qu, Can. 172/E2
Simav, Turk. 132/B2
Simbach am Inn, Ger. 97/G6
Simcoe, On, Can. 172/D3
Simcoe (lake), Qu, Can. 123/J4
Simdega, India 127/E4
Simēn (mts.), Eth. 139/N5
Simeria, Rom. 90/F3
Simeulue (isl.), Indo. 122/A3
Simferopol', Ukr. 104/E3
Simi (hills), Ca, US 178/B2
Simi Valley, Ca, US 178/B2
Similaun (peak), It. 85/J3
Similaun (peak), Aus.,It. 99/G4
Simití, Col. 194/C3
Simitli, Bul. 91/F5
Simiyu (riv.), Tanz. 146/B3
Simla, India 128/D4
Simleu Silvaniei, Rom. 91/F2
Simme (riv.), Swi. 85/G3
Simmelsdorf, Ger. 97/E3
Simmerath, Ger. 95/F2
Simmerbach (riv.), Ger. 95/G4
Simmern, Ger. 95/G4
Simmertal, Ger. 95/G4
Simmszand (isl.), Neth. 92/D2
Simni (isl.), NKor. 115/C3
Simo, Fin. 102/E2
Simões, Braz. 196/B2
Simões Filho, Braz. 196/C4
Simojovel de Allende, Mex. 186/C2
Simón Bolívar (int'l arpt.), Ecu. 194/B5
Simoncello (peak), It. 101/F5
Simonstown, SAfr. 148/L11
Simpang-Kiri (riv.), Indo. 122/A3
Simpelveld, Neth. 95/E2
Simplício Mendes, Braz. 196/B2
Simplon, Swi. 98/E5
Simplonpass (pass), Swi. 98/E5
Simpson (des.), Austl. 155/H3
Simpson (pen.), Nun., Can. 164/G2
Simpson (riv.), Nun., Can. 164/G2
Simpson Desert Conservation Park, Austl. 155/H3
Simpson Desert NP, Austl. 155/H3
Simpsons Gap NP, Austl. 155/G2
Simrishamn, Swe. 80/F4
Simunul, Phil. 123/E3
Sin-le-Noble, Fr. 94/C3
Sinai (pen.), Egypt 139/M1
Sinaia, Rom. 91/G3
Sinaloa (state), Mex. 184/D3
Sinaloa de Leyva, Mex. 184/C3
Sinalunga, It. 85/J5
Sinan, China 121/A2
Sīnāwin, Libya 141/H3
Sincé, Col. 194/C2

275
Since – Sot

Sincelejo, Col. 194/C2
Sinceny, Fr. 94/C4
Sinch'ŏn, NKor. 115/C3
Sinclair, Wy, US 168/G5
Sinclair (lake), Ga, US 175/H3
Sinclair (pt.), Austl. 155/G5
Sincorá, Serra do (range), Braz. 196/B4
Sind (riv.), India 124/C2
Sindal, Den. 80/D3
Sindañgan, Phil. 121/D6
Sindangbarang, Indo. 122/C5
Sindelfingen, Ger. 96/C5
Sındh (prov.), Pak. 124/A2
Sindhulimādi, Nepal 127/E2
Sındırgı, Turk. 132/B2
Sinekçi, Turk. 91/H5
Sinendé, Ben. 145/F4
Sines, Port. 86/A4
Sines (cape), Port. 86/A4
Sinfra, C.d'Iv. 144/D5
Sing Buri, Thai. 120/C3
Singapore (ctry.) 122/B3
Singapore (cap.), Sing. 122/B3
Singen, Ger. 99/E2
Sîngeorz-Băi, Rom. 91/G2
Singida (pol. reg.), Tanz. 146/B4
Singida, Tanz. 146/B4
Singitic (gulf), Gre. 89/H2
Singkawang, Indo. 122/C3
Singkep (isl.), Indo. 122/B4
Singleton, Austl. 157/D2
Singleton (mt.), Austl. 154/C4
Singleton (mt.), Austl. 155/F2
Singou, Réserve Totale de Faune du, Burk. 145/F4
Sinincay, Ecu. 194/B5
Siniscola, It. 88/A2
Sinjār, Iraq 132/E2
Sinjil, WBnk. 133/G7
Sinn (riv.), Ger. 82/E3
Sinnam-dok-san (peak), NKor. 115/D2
Sinnamary, FrG. 193/H2
Sinnard, Co, US 179/C1
Sînnicolau Mare, Rom. 90/E2
Sinnūris, Egypt 133/B5
Sinnyŏng, SKor. 115/E4
Sino (co.), Libr. 144/C5
Sinoe (lake), Rom. 91/J3
Sinop, Braz. 193/G6
Sinop, Turk. 132/C1
Sinop (prov.), Turk. 132/C1
Sinop (pt.), Turk. 132/C1
Sinp'o, NKor. 115/E2
Sint-Genesius-Rode, Belg. 95/D2
Sint-Gillis-Waas, Belg. 92/B6
Sint-Katelijne-Waver, Belg. 95/D1
Sint-Laureins, Belg. 94/C1
Sint-Martens-Voeren, Belg. 95/E2
Sint-Michielsgestel, Neth. 92/C5
Sint-Niklaas, Belg. 92/B6
Sint-Oedenrode, Neth. 92/C5
Sint-Pieters-Leeuw, Belg. 95/D2
Sint-Truiden, Belg. 95/E2
Sint'aein, SKor. 115/D5
Sintang, Indo. 122/D3
Sinton, Tx, US 174/D4
Sintra, Port. 87/P10
Sintra (range), Port. 87/P10
Sinú (riv.), Col. 192/C2
Sinŭiju, NKor. 115/C2
Sinzheim, Ger. 96/B5
Sinzig, Ger. 95/G2
Sió (riv.), Hun. 90/D2
Siocon, Phil. 123/F2
Siófok, Hun. 90/D2
Sioma Ngwezi NP, Zam. 147/D4
Sion, Swi. 98/D5
Sion Mills, NI, UK 73/Q9
Sioule (riv.), Fr. 84/E4
Sioux City, Ia, US 169/J5
Sioux Lookout, On, Can. 169/L3
Sipalay, Phil. 121/D6
Sipaliwini (dist.), Sur. 195/H4
Sipaliwini (riv.), Sur. 195/G4
Sipanok (chan.), Mb,Sk, Can. 169/H2
Siparia, Trin. 195/F2
Sipí, Col. 194/B3
Siping, China 114/F2
Sipiwesk (lake), Mb, Can. 164/G3
Siple (isl.), Ant. 202/R
Siponto (ruin), It. 88/D2
Sipsey (riv.), Al, US 175/G3
Sipura (isl.), Indo. 122/A4
Siqueira Campos, Braz. 197/B2
Siquia (riv.), Nic. 182/E5
Siquisique, Ven. 194/D2
Sir Alexander (mt.), BC, Can. 168/C2
Sir Edward Pellew Group (isls.), Austl. 151/C2
Sir James Macbrien (mt.), NW, Can. 164/D2
Sir James Mitchell NP, Austl. 154/C5
Sir John (cape), Austl. 157/D4
Sir Seewoosagur Ramgoolam (int'l arpt.), Mrts. 149/T15
Sir Thomas (mt.), Austl. 155/F3
Sira (riv.), Nor. 79/C4
Siracusa (Syracuse), It. 88/D4
Sirājganj, Bang. 127/G3
Şiran, Turk. 132/D1
Sirdaryo (pol. reg.), Uzb. 129/E4
Siret, Rom. 91/H2
Siret (riv.), Rom. 91/H2
Sirha, Nepal 127/F2
Sirhind, India 128/D4
Sirik (cape), Malay. 122/D3
Sīrīk, Iran 131/G3
Sirikit (res.), Thai. 125/H4
Sirinhaém, Braz. 196/D3
Sīrīs, WBnk. 133/G7
Sirius (pt.), Ak, US 176/B5
Sirmilik Nat'l Park, Nun., Can. 123/J1
Sirmione, It. 100/D2
Sirnach, Swi. 99/F3
Şırnak, Turk. 132/E2
Sirolo, It. 101/G5
Sironj, India 126/A3
Síros (isl.), Gre. 89/J4
Siroua (peak), Mor. 140/D3
Sirsa, India 128/C5
Sirsāganj, India 126/B2
Sirsi, India 126/B1
Sirsi, India 131/K6
Sisak, Cro. 90/C3
Sisaket, Thai. 120/D3
Sishui, China 114/D4
Sisikon, Swi. 99/E4
Sisipuk (lake), Mb,Sk, Can. 169/H2
Sissach, Swi. 98/D3
Sisseton, SD, US 169/J4
Sissili (prov.), Burk. 145/E4
Sissonne, Fr. 94/C4
Sissonville, WV, US 172/D4
Sisterdale, Tx, US 179/T20
Sisteron, Fr. 84/F4
Siswā Bāzār, India 126/D2
Sitacocha, Peru 198/B2
Sītākund, Bang. 127/H4
Sītāmarhi, India 127/E2
Sītāpur, India 126/C2
Sitārganj, India 126/B1
Siteki, Swaz. 149/E2
Site of World Trade Center, NY, US 181/J9
Sitges, Sp. 87/K7
Sithoniá (pen.), Gre. 89/J2
Sitía, Gre. 89/K5
Sitidgi (lake), NW, Can. 176/M2
Sítio Novo do Grajaú, Braz. 196/A2
Sitka, Ak, US 176/L4
Sitno (peak), Slvk. 90/D1
Sittard, Neth. 95/E2
Sittensen, Ger. 93/G2
Sitter (riv.), Swi. 99/F3
Sittingbourne, Eng, UK 75/G4
Sitton (peak), Ca, US 178/C3
Sittwe (Akyab), Myan. 125/F3
Sivac, Serb. 90/D3
Sivakāsi, India 124/C6
Sīvand, Iran 130/F2
Sivas, Turk. 132/D2
Sivas (prov.), Turk. 132/D2
Siverek, Turk. 132/D2
Siviriez, Swi. 98/C4
Sivrihisar, Turk. 132/B2
Sivry-Courtry, Fr. 72/L6
Siwa Oasis (oasis), Egypt 143/A2
Sīwah, Egypt 139/L2
Siwalik (range), Nepal 124/B1
Siwān, India 127/E2
Siwāni, India 128/C5
Six Flags Great Adventure, NJ, US 180/D3
Six Flags Great America, Il, US 177/Q15
Six Flags Magic Mountain, Ca, US 178/B2
Sixmilecross, NI, UK 76/A2
Sixth (falls), Sudan 139/M4
Siyabuswa, SAfr. 147/E6
Siyāna, India 126/B1
Siyang, China 114/D4
Siziano, It. 100/C2
Siziwang, China 113/K3
Sjælland (isl.), Den. 79/D5
Sjenica, Serb. 90/E4
Sjöbo, Swe. 80/E4
Sjónfridh (peak), Ice. 79/M6
Sjuntorp, Swe. 80/E2
Skaftafell NP, Ice. 79/P7
Skagen, Den. 80/D3
Skagens (The Skaw) (cape), Den. 80/D3
Skagern (lake), Swe. 80/F2
Skagerrak (str.), Den.,Nor. 80/C3
Skaget (peak), Nor. 80/C1
Skagway, Ak, US 176/L3
Skála, Gre. 89/H4
Skälderviken (bay), Swe. 80/E3
Skálfandafljót (riv.), Ice. 79/P7
Skalica, Slvk. 83/J4
Skalice (riv.), Czh. 85/K2
Skalka (res.), Czh. 97/F2
Skælskør, Den. 80/D4
Skanderborg, Den. 80/C3
Skåne (reg.), Swe. 80/E4
Skanes (int'l arpt.), Tun. 142/M7
Skånland, Nor. 79/F1
Skänninge, Swe. 80/F2
Skanör, Swe. 80/E4
Skantzoura (isl.), Gre. 89/J3
Skara, Swe. 80/E2
Skaraborg (co.), Swe. 79/E4
Skärblacka, Swe. 80/F2
Skåre, Swe. 80/E2
Skarszewy, Pol. 80/H4
Skarżysko-Kamienna, Pol. 83/L3
Skateraw, Sc, UK 78/D5
Skattkärr, Swe. 80/E2
Skawina, Pol. 83/K4
Skeena (riv.), BC, Can. 164/D3
Skeena (mts.), BC, Can. 164/D3
Skegness, Eng, UK 77/J5
Skellefteå, Swe. 79/G2
Skellefteälven (riv.), Swe. 79/F2
Skelleftehamn, Swe. 79/G2
Skelmersdale, Eng, UK 77/F4
Skelmorlie, Sc, UK 78/B5
Skerne (riv.), Eng, UK 77/G2
Skerries, Ire. 76/B4
Skhimatárion, Gre. 89/H3
Skhirat, Mor. 142/A3
Skhirat Temara (prov.), Mor. 142/A3
Skhiza (isl.), Gre. 89/G4
Skhodnya (riv.), Rus. 103/W9
Ski, Nor. 80/D2
Skiathos, Gre. 89/H3
Skiatook, Ok, US 171/H3
Skibbereen, Ire. 73/P11
Skidegate, BC, Can. 176/M5
Skidhra, Gre. 89/H2
Skien, Nor. 80/C2
Skierniewice, Pol. 83/L3
Skikda, Alg. 142/K6
Skinári (cape), Gre. 89/G4
Skinnskatteberg, Swe. 80/F2
Skipton, Eng, UK 77/F4
Skirfare (riv.), Eng, UK 77/F3
Skíros, Gre. 89/J3
Skive, Den. 80/C3
Skjærhollen, Nor. 80/D2
Skjeberg, Nor. 80/D2
Skjelåtinden (peak), Nor. 79/E2
Skjern, Den. 80/C4
Skjern (riv.), Den. 80/C4
Škofja Loka, Slov. 85/L3
Skoghall, Swe. 80/E2
Skogstorp, Swe. 80/G2
Skokholm (isl.), Wal, UK 74/A3
Skokie (riv.), Il, US 177/Q15
Skokloster, Swe. 80/G2
Sköllersta, Swe. 80/F2
Skolniki Park, Rus. 103/W9
Skomer (isl.), Wal, UK 74/A3
Skópelos (isl.), Gre. 89/H3
Skópelos, Gre. 89/H3
Skopin, Rus. 104/F1
Skopje (cap.), FYROM 89/G1
Skopje (int'l arpt.), FYROM 90/E5
Skotterud, Nor. 80/E2
Skoútari, Gre. 89/H2
Skövde, Swe. 80/E2
Skowhegan, Me, US 173/G2
Skukum (mt.), Yk, Can. 176/L3
Skull, Ire. 73/P11
Skultorp, Swe. 80/E2
Skultuna, Swe. 80/G2
Skunk (riv.), Ia, US 172/A3
Skurup, Swe. 83/G1
Skutskär, Swe. 80/G1
Skwentna, Ak, US 176/H3
Skwierzyna, Pol. 83/H2
Skye (isl.), Sc, UK 73/G8
Skyring (sound), Chile 201/B7
Skytop, Pa, US 180/C1
Slagelse, Den. 80/D4
Slakovský Les (for.), Czh. 97/F2
Slamannan, Sc, UK 78/C5
Slana, Ak, US 176/K3
Slaná (riv.), Slvk. 83/L4
Slane, Ire. 76/B4
Slaney (riv.), Ire. 73/Q10
Slănic, Rom. 91/G3
Slănic-Moldova, Rom. 91/H2
Slantsy, Rus. 81/N2
Slaný, Czh. 97/H2
Slapy (res.), Czh. 97/H3
Śląskie (prov.), Pol. 83/K3
Slatedale, Pa, US 180/C2
Slatina, Rom. 91/G3
Slatington, Pa, US 180/C2
Slaton, Tx, US 171/G4
Slattum, Nor. 80/D1
Slaughter Beach, De, US 180/C6
Slaughterville, Ok, US 179/N15
Slave (coast), Afr. 145/F5
Slave (riv.), NW, Can. 164/E2
Slave Lake, Ab, Can. 168/E2
Slavgorod, Rus. 129/G2
Slavkov u Brna, Czh. 85/M2
Slavonia (reg.), Cro. 90/C3
Slavonska Požega, Cro. 90/C3
Slavonski Brod, Cro. 90/D3
Slavuta, Ukr. 104/C2
Slavyanovo, Bul. 91/G4
Slavyansk-na-Kubani, Rus. 104/F3
Sławno, Pol. 80/G4
Sleen, Neth. 92/D3
Sleeper (isls.), On, Can. 123/H3
Sleeping Bear Dunes Nat'l Lakeshore, US 172/C2
Sleepy Hollow, NY, US 181/K7
Sleepy Hollow, Il, US 177/P15
Sleetmute, Ak, US 176/G3
Slidell, La, US 179/Q16
Sliedrecht, Neth. 92/B5
Sliema, Malta 88/M7
Slieve Binnian (peak), NI, UK 76/C3
Slieve Croob (peak), NI, UK 76/C3
Slieve Donard (peak), NI, UK 76/C3
Slieve Gullion (peak), NI, UK 76/B3
Slieve Snaght (peak), Ire. 76/A1
Slioch (peak), Sc, UK 78/A1
Slite, Swe. 81/H3
Sliven, Bul. 91/H4
Slivnitsa, Bul. 90/F4
Sloan, NY, US 173/S10
Sloatsburg, NY, US 181/J7
Slobodskoy, Rus. 103/L4
Slobozia, Rom. 91/H3
Slochteren, Neth. 92/D2
Slonim, Bela. 104/C1
Sloten, Neth. 92/C3
Slotermeer (lake), Neth. 92/C3
Slough, Eng, UK 72/B2
Slough (co.), Eng, UK 72/B2
Slovakia (ctry.) 83/K4
Slovenia (ctry.) 90/B3
Slovenj Gradec, Slov. 85/L3
Slovenska Bistrica, Slov. 85/L3
Slovenska L'upča, Slvk. 83/K4
Slovenske Konjice, Slov. 85/L3
Slovenské Rudohorie (mts.), Slvk. 83/L4
Slov'yans'k, Ukr. 104/F2
Słowiński PN, Pol. 80/G4
Słubice, Pol. 83/H2
Sluch' (riv.), Ukr. 104/C2
Sluderno (Schluderns), It. 99/G4
Sluis, Neth. 94/C1
Słupca, Pol. 83/J2
Słupia (riv.), Pol. 80/G4
Słupsk, Pol. 80/G4
Slutsk, Bela. 104/C1
Slyne Head (pt.), Ire. 72/F10
Smålandsstenar, Swe. 80/E3
Smallwood (res.), Nf, Can. 123/K3
Smeaton, Sk, Can. 169/G2
Smederevo, Serb. 90/E3
Smederevska Palanka, Serb. 90/E3
Smedjebacken, Swe. 80/F1
Smendou (riv.), Alg. 142/J4
Śmigiel, Pol. 83/J2
Smila, Ukr. 104/D2
Smilde, Neth. 92/D3
Smith (riv.), Mt, US 168/F4
Smith (inlet), BC, Can. 168/B3
Smith (isl.), Qu, Can. 123/J2
Smith Mountain (lake), Va, US 172/E4
Smith Village, Ok, US 179/N15
Smithburg, NJ, US 180/D3
Smithers, BC, Can. 168/B2
Smithfield, Ut, US 168/F5
Smithfield, NC, US 175/J3
Smiths Creek, Mi, US 177/G6
Smiths Falls, On, Can. 172/E2
Smithton, Austl. 157/C4
Smithton, Il, US 179/H9
Smithtown (bay), NY, US 181/E2
Smithtown, NY, US 181/E2
Smithville, Ok, US 174/E3
Smithville (lake), Mo, US 179/D5
Smithville, Mo, US 179/D5
Smoky (cape), Austl. 157/E1
Smoky (hills), Ks, US 171/H3
Smoky (riv.), Ab, Can. 164/E3
Smoky Hill (riv.), Ks, US 171/G3
Smoky Lake, Ab, Can. 168/E2
Smøla (isl.), Nor. 79/C3
Smolensk, Rus. 102/G5
Smolenskaya Oblast, Rus. 102/F5
Smólikas (peak), Gre. 89/G2
Smolyan, Bul. 91/G5
Smooth Rock Falls, On, Can. 172/D1
Smrčina (peak), Czh. 97/G5
Smutná (riv.), Czh. 97/H4
Smyadovo, Bul. 91/H4
Smyrna, Ga, US 175/G3
Smyrna (riv.), De, US 180/C5
Smyrna, De, US 180/C5
Snaefell (peak), IM, UK 76/D3
Snake (riv.), US 168/D4
Snake River (plain), Id, US 168/E5
Snares (isls.), NZ 159/R12
Snåsa, Nor. 79/E2
Snedsted, Den. 80/C3
Sneek, Neth. 92/C2
Sneekermeer (lake), Neth. 92/C2
Sneeuberg (peak), SAfr. 148/B4
Sneeuberg (mts.), SAfr. 148/D3
Sneeuwkop (peak), SAfr. 148/L11
Snejbjerg, Den. 80/C3
Sněžka (peak), Czh. 83/H3
Snežnik (peak), Slov. 85/L4
Sni Mills, Mo, US 179/E6
Śniardwy (lake), Pol. 83/L2
Snodland, Eng, UK 75/G4
Snøhetta (peak), Nor. 79/D3
Snohomish, Wa, US 177/C2
Snohomish (co.), Wa, US 177/C2
Snohomish (riv.), Wa, US 177/C2
Snoqualmie (riv.), Wa, US 177/D2
Snoqualmie (falls), Wa, US 177/D2
Snoqualmie, Wa, US 177/D2
Snoqualmie Falls, Wa, US 177/D2
Snoqualmie, Middle Fk. (riv.), Wa, US 177/D2
Snoqualmie, North Fork (riv.), Wa, US 177/D2
Snoqualmie, South Fork (riv.), Wa, US 177/D3
Snøtind (peak), Nor. 79/E2
Snowdon (peak), IM, UK 76/D5
Snowdonia NP, Wal, UK 76/D6
Snowflake, Az, US 170/E4
Snowtown, Austl. 155/H5
Snowy (peak), Ak, US 176/K2
Snowy (riv.), Austl. 157/D3
Snowy River NP, Austl. 157/D3
Snyder (co.), Pa, US 180/A2
Snydertown, Pa, US 180/B2
Snyderville, Ut, US 179/K12
Soalala, Madg. 149/H7
Soanierana-Ivongo, Madg. 149/J7
Soanindrariny, Madg. 149/H7
Soar (riv.), Eng, UK 77/G6
Soavina, Madg. 149/H8
Soavina, Madg. 149/J8
Soavinandriana, Madg. 149/H7
Sobaek (mts.), SKor. 115/D5
Soběslav, Czh. 97/H4
Sobger (riv.), Indo. 123/K4
Sobhādero, Pak. 131/J3
Sobradinho, Represa (res.), Braz. 189/E3
Sobral, Braz. 196/B1
Sobretta (peak), It. 99/G5
Sobue, Japan 119/L5
Soc Trang, Viet. 120/D4
Soča (riv.), Slov. 85/K3
Socabaya, Peru 198/D5
Sochaczew, Pol. 83/L2
Sochi, Rus. 104/F4
Sŏch'ŏn, SKor. 115/D4
Söchtenau, Ger. 97/F7
Soci, It. 101/E5
Society (isls.), FrPol. 159/K6
Socorro, Braz. 197/G7
Socorro, Col. 194/C3
Socorro, NM, US 170/F4
Socorro (isl.), NM, Mex. 184/C5
Socorro, Tx, US 171/F5
Socota, Peru 198/B2
Socotá, Col. 194/C3
Socotra (isl.), Yem. 109/E8
Socuéllamos, Sp. 86/D3
Soda Springs, Id, US 168/F5
Sodankylä, Fin. 102/E2
Sodegaura, Japan 119/D3
Söderbärke, Swe. 80/F1
Söderfors, Swe. 80/G1
Söderhamn, Swe. 80/G1
Söderköping, Swe. 80/G2
Södermanland (co.), Swe. 79/E4
Södertälje, Swe. 80/G2
Sodo, Eth. 139/N6
Södu (riv.), NKor. 115/E2
Sodwana Bay NP, SAfr. 149/F2
Soest, Ger. 93/F5
Soest, Neth. 92/C4
Soeste (riv.), Ger. 82/D2
Sofádhes, Gre. 89/H3
Sofia (Sofiya) (cap.), Bul. 49/F4
Sofia (int'l arpt.), Bul. 91/F4
Sofiya (prov.), Bul. 49/F4
Sogamoso (riv.), Col. 194/C3
Sogamoso, Col. 194/C3
Sögel, Ger. 93/E3
Sogn Og Fjordane (co.), Nor. 79/C3
Sognafjorden (inlet), Nor. 79/C3
Sogndal, Nor. 80/B1
Søgne, Nor. 80/B2
Sogollé (well), Chad 138/J4
Soğuksu NP, Turk. 132/C1
Söğüt, Turk. 132/B1
Söğütlü, Turk. 91/K5
Sogwass (peak), Ugan. 146/B2
Sohāgpur, India 126/B4
Sohren, Ger. 95/G4
Sŏhŭng, NKor. 115/D3
Soignies, Belg. 95/D2
Soignolles-en-Brie, Fr. 72/L6
Soissons, Fr. 94/C5
Sōja, Japan 116/C3
Sojat, India 131/K3
Sŏjosŏn (bay), NKor. 115/C3
Sok (riv.), Rus. 105/J1
Sok (pt.), Thai. 120/C3
Sōka, Japan 119/D2
Sokch'o, SKor. 115/E3
Söke, Turk. 132/A2
Sokhós, Gre. 89/H2
Sokhumi, Geo. 105/G4
Sokna, Nor. 80/C1
Soko (isls.), China 113/T11
Soko Banja, Serb. 90/E4
Sokodé, Togo 145/F4
Sokol, Rus. 102/J4
Sokol (peak), Czh. 97/G4
Sokółka, Pol. 83/M2
Sokolov, Czh. 97/F2
Sokołów Podlaski, Pol. 83/M2
Sokoto (plain), Nga. 138/F5
Sokoto (riv.), Nga. 138/F5
Sokoto, Nga. 145/G3
Sokoto (state), Nga. 145/G3
Sol, Costa del (coast), Sp. 86/C4
Sol'-Iletsk, Rus. 105/K2
Sola, Nor. 80/A2
Sola (int'l arpt.), Nor. 80/A2
Solana, Phil. 121/D4
Solana Beach, Ca, US 178/C5
Solânea, Braz. 196/D2
Solano (pt.), Col. 194/B3
Solano, Phil. 121/D4
Solano (co.), Ca, US 177/L10
Solarolo, It. 101/E4
Solca, Rom. 91/G2
Sölden, Aus. 99/H4
Soldier (riv.), Ia, US 171/J2
Soldotna, Ak, US 176/H3
Soledad, Col. 194/C2
Soledad, Ven. 195/F2
Soledad Canyon (canyon), Ca, US 178/B2
Soledad de Doblado, Mex. 185/N7
Soledad de Graciano, Mex. 185/E4
Soledade, Braz. 197/A4
Solent, The (chan.), Eng, UK 75/E5
Solesino, It. 101/E2
Solesmes, Fr. 94/C3
Soleuvre (peak), Lux. 95/E4
Solferino, It. 100/D2
Solhan, Turk. 132/E2
Soliera, It. 101/D3
Soligo, It. 101/F1
Solihull, Eng, UK 75/E2
Solihull (co.), Eng, UK 75/E2
Solimões (riv.), Braz. 195/E5
Solingen, Ger. 92/E6
Sollefteå, Swe. 79/F3
Sollentuna, Swe. 80/G2
Sóller, Sp. 87/G3
Sollerön, Swe. 80/F1
Solling (mts.), Ger. 82/E3
Solmsbach (riv.), Ger. 96/B2
Soln (peak), Nor. 79/D3
Solnan (riv.), Fr. 84/F3
Solntsevo, Rus. 103/W9
Solo (riv.), Indo. 122/D5
Solok, Indo. 122/B4
Sololá, Guat. 186/D3
Solomon, Ak, US 176/F3
Solomon (riv.), Ks, US 171/H3
Solomon (sea), PNG,Sol. 158/D5
Solomon Islands (ctry.) 158/E6
Solomon, North Fork (riv.), US 171/G3
Solonchak Goklenkui (swamp), Trkm. 129/C4
Solonópole, Braz. 196/C2
Solothurn, Swi. 98/D3
Solothurn (canton), Swi. 98/D3
Solovetskiy (isls.), Rus. 102/G2
Solre-le-Château, Fr. 95/D3
Solsona, Sp. 87/F2
Solt, Hun. 90/D2
Šolta (isl.), Cro. 88/E1
Soltau, Ger. 93/G3
Soltustik Qazaqstan (obl.), Kaz. 106/G4
Soltvadkert, Hun. 90/D2
Solunska (peak), FYROM 89/G2
Solva (riv.), Wal, UK 74/A3
Solvang, Ca, US 170/B4
Sölvesborg, Swe. 80/F3
Solway Firth (inlet), Eng.,Sc, UK 76/E2
Solwezi, Zam. 147/E3
Solymár, Hun. 91/Q9
Sōma, Japan 117/G2
Soma, Turk. 132/A2
Somain, Fr. 94/C3
Somalia (ctry.) 139/Q6
Sombor, Serb. 90/D3
Sombra, On, Can. 177/H6
Sombreffe, Belg. 95/D2
Sombrerete, Mex. 184/E4
Sombrio, Braz. 197/B4
Someren, Neth. 92/C6
Somero, Fin. 81/K1
Somers, Mt, US 168/E3
Somers, Wi, US 177/Q14
Somers Point, NJ, US 180/D5
Somerset (isl.), Nun., Can. 164/G1
Somerset (co.), Eng, UK 74/D4
Somerset, Ky, US 172/C4
Somerset, NY, US 173/S9
Somerset, NJ, US 180/D3
Somerset, Tx, US 179/T21
Somerset East, SAfr. 148/D4
Somerset West, SAfr. 148/L11
Somersworth, NH, US 173/G3
Somerton, Az, US 170/D4
Somerville (lake), Tx, US 171/H5
Somerville, NJ, US 180/D2
Someş (riv.), Rom. 91/F2
Someşul Mare (riv.), Serb. 91/G2
Someswar (range), India 127/E2
Somis, Ca, US 178/B2
Sōmjin (riv.), SKor. 115/D5
Somma Lombardo, It. 100/B1
Sommacampagna, It. 101/D2
Sommam (riv.), Alg. 142/H4
Sommariva del Bosco, It. 100/A3
Somme (bay), Fr. 84/D1
Somme (dept.), Fr. 94/B4
Somme (riv.), Fr. 82/B3
Somme, Canal de la (canal), Fr. 94/B4
Somme-Leuze, Belg. 95/E3
Somme-Soude (riv.), Fr. 95/D6
Sommedieue, Fr. 95/E5
Sommen (lake), Swe. 80/F2
Sommet de Finiels (peak), Fr. 84/E4
Sommevoire, Fr. 98/A1
Somogy (prov.), Hun. 90/C2
Somoto, Nic. 186/E3
Son (riv.), India 124/D3
Son Servera, Sp. 87/G3
Sona, It. 101/D2
Sonāmukhi, India 127/F4
Sonāmura, India 127/H4
Sonār (riv.), India 126/B4
Sonchamp, Fr. 72/H6
Sŏnch'ŏn, NKor. 115/C3
Soncino, It. 100/C2
Sondalo, It. 99/G5
Sønder Nissum, Den. 80/C3
Sonderborg (int'l arpt.), Den. 80/C4
Sønderborg, Den. 80/C4
Sonderend (riv.), SAfr. 148/L11
Sønderjylland (co.), Den. 80/C4
Sondica (int'l arpt.), Sp. 86/D1
Sondrio, It. 99/F5
Sondrio (dept.), It. 99/F5
Sonepur, India 124/D3
Song (peak), China 114/C4
Song Xian, China 114/C4
Songea, Tanz. 146/B5
Songeons, Fr. 94/A4
Songhua (riv.), China 113/P2
Sŏnghwan, SKor. 115/D4
Songi (isl), SKor. 115/C5
Songino, Mong. 112/G2
Songjiang, China 114/L8
Sŏngju, SKor. 115/E5
Songkhla, Thai. 120/C5
Songkhram (riv.), Thai. 125/H4
Songling, China 113/M2
Songming, China 125/H2
Sŏngnam, SKor. 115/G7
Songnim, NKor. 115/C3
Songololo, D.R. Congo 147/B2
Songt'an, SKor. 115/D4
Songtao Miaozu Zizhixian, China 121/A2
Songxi, China 121/C2
Songzi, China 121/B1
Songzi (pass), China 114/C5
Soni, Japan 119/K6
Sonid Youqi, China 113/K3
Sonid Zuoqi, China 113/K3
Sonīpat, India 128/D5
Sonneberg, Ger. 96/E2
Sonnefeld, Ger. 96/E2
Sonnjoch (peak), Aus. 99/H3
Sonntagshorn (peak), Ger. 85/K3
Sonobe, Japan 119/H5
Sonoma (co.), Ca, US 177/J10
Sonoma (mts.), Ca, US 177/J10
Sonora (state), Mex. 184/C2
Sonora, Ca, US 170/B3
Sonora, Tx, US 171/G5
Sonoran Desert Nat'l Mon., Az, US 170/D4
Sonoyta, Mex. 184/B2
Sonoyta (riv.), Mex. 184/B2
Sonpur, India 127/E3
Sonqor, Iran 130/E2
Sŏnsan, SKor. 115/E4
Sonsbeck, Ger. 92/D5
Sonseca, Sp. 86/D3
Sonsonate, ESal. 186/D3
Sonsorol (isls.), Palau 158/C4
Sonta, Serb. 90/D3
Sontheim, Ger. 99/G2
Sontheim an der Brenz, Ger. 96/D5
Sonthofen, Ger. 99/G2
Sontra, Ger. 93/G6
Sonvico, Swi. 99/E5
Sopetrán, Col. 194/C3
Sopi (cape), Indo. 123/G3
Sopor, India 128/C2
Sopot, Bul. 91/G4
Sopot, Pol. 80/H4
Sopron, Hun. 85/M3
Sôr (riv.), Wal, UK 74/D3
Sor Karatuley (salt pan), Kaz. 129/C4
S'ør-Trøndelag (co.), Nor. 79/D3
Sør-Varanger, Nor. 79/J1
Sora, It. 88/C2
Soragna, It. 100/D3
Sŏrak-san (peak), SKor. 115/E3
Sŏraksan NP, SKor. 115/E3
Sorata, Bol. 192/E7
Sorbas, Sp. 86/D4
Sorbolo, It. 100/D3
Sorcy-Saint-Martin, Fr. 95/E6
Sorel, Qu, Can. 172/F2
Sorell-Midway Point, Austl. 157/C4
Soresina, It. 100/C2
Sörforsa, Swe. 80/G1
Sorgues, Fr. 84/F5
Sorgun, Turk. 132/C2
Sori, It. 100/C4
Soria, Sp. 86/D2
Soriano (cept.), Uru. 200/G3
Soriano, Uru. 201/J10
Sorikmerapi (peak), Indo. 122/A3
Soritor, Peru 198/B2
Sormonne (riv.), Fr. 95/D4
Sorø, Den. 80/D4
Soro, Rio do (riv.), Braz. 193/J5
Soroca, Mol. 91/J1
Sorocaba, Braz. 197/C2
Sorochinsk, Rus. 105/K1
Sorol (isls.), Micr. 158/D4
Soron, India 126/B2
Sorong, Indo. 123/H4
Soroti, Ugan. 146/B2
Sørøya (isl.), Nor. 79/G1
Sørøysundet (chan.), Nor. 79/G1
Sorpestausee (lake), Ger. 93/E6
Sorraia (riv.), Port. 86/A3
Sorrento, It. 88/D2
Sorsele, Swe. 79/F2
Sorso, It. 88/A2
Sorsogon, Phil. 121/D5
Sort, Sp. 87/F1
Sörve (pt.), Est. 81/K3
Sos del Rey Católico, Sp. 86/E1
Sōsan, SKor. 115/D4
Sŏsan Haean NP, SKor. 115/C4
Sösdala, Swe. 80/E3
Söse (riv.), Ger. 93/H5
Soshanguve, SAfr. 147/E6
Sosna (riv.), Rus. 104/F1
Sosneado (peak), Arg. 200/C2
Sosnogorsk, Rus. 103/M3
Sosnovka, Rus. 103/L4
Sosnowiec, Pol. 83/K3
Sospiro, It. 100/D2
Sosúa, DRep. 183/G4
Sos'va (riv.), Rus. 106/G3
Sot (riv.), India 126/B1

276
Soto – Strat

Soto del Real, Sp. 87/N8
Soto la Marina, Mex. 185/F4
Sotouboua, Togo 145/F4
Sottrum, Ger. 93/G2
Sotuta, Mex. 186/D1
Soude (riv.), Fr. 95/D6
Souderton, Pa, US 180/C3
Soúdha, Gre. 89/J5
Souffelweyersheim, Fr. 95/G6
Soufflenheim, Fr. 95/G6
Souflíon, Gre. 89/K2
Soufrière (peak), StV. 183/N9
Soufrière (peak), Guad., Fr. 183/N8
Souillac, Fr. 84/D4
Souillac, Mrts. 149/T15
Souk Ahras, Alg. 142/K6
Souk Ahras (prov.), Alg. 142/K6
Souk el Arba du Rharb, Mor. 142/A2
Sŏul (Seoul) (cap.), SKor. 113/N4
Soultz-Haut-Rhin, Fr. 98/D2
Soultz-sous-Forêts, Fr. 96/A5
Soum (prov.), Burk. 145/E3
Soumagne, Belg. 95/E2
Sound, The (chan.), Den. 79/E5
Souppes-sur-Loing, Fr. 84/E2
Sour El Ghozlane, Alg. 142/G4
Sources, Mont aux (peak), Les. 148/E3
Soure, Braz. 193/J4
Soure, Port. 86/A2
Souris, Mb, Can. 169/H3
Souris, PE, Can. 173/J2
Souris (riv.), Can.,US 169/H3
Sourou (prov.), Burk. 144/E3
Sous le Vent, Îles (isls.), FrPol. 159/K6
Sousa, Braz. 196/C2
Sousse, Tun. 142/M7
Sousse (gov.), Tun. 142/M7
Sout (riv.), SAfr. 148/C3
South (mts.), NS, Can. 173/H2
South (bay), Nun., Can. 165/H2
South (cape), NZ 159/R12
South (isl.), NZ 159/S11
South (mtn.), Pa, US 180/A3
South Africa (ctry.) 147/D6
South Amboy, NJ, US 181/H10
South America (cont.) 147
South Andaman (isl.), India 125/F5
South Anna (riv.), Va, US 175/J2
South Augusta, Ga, US 175/H3
South Aulatsivik (isl.), Nf, Can. 165/K3
South Australia (state), Austl. 151/C3
South Ayrshire (pol. reg.), Sc, UK 78/B6
South Bend, In, US 172/C3
South Bend, Wa, US 168/C4
South Benfleet, Eng, UK 75/G3
South Buganda (prov.), Ugan. 146/A3
South Burlington, Vt, US 172/F2
South Caicos (isl.), UK 187/J1
South Carolina (state), US 175/H3
South China (sea), Asia 109/L8
South Colby, Wa, US 177/B2
South Dakota (state), US 169/H4
South Dorset Downs (uplands), Eng, UK 74/D5
South Downs (hills), Eng, UK 75/F5
South Dum Dum, India 127/G4
South East (pt.), Austl. 157/C3
South East (cape), Austl. 157/C4
South Elgin, Il, US 177/P16
South Esk (riv.), Austl. 157/C4
South Esk (riv.), Sc, UK 78/C3
South Farmingdale, NY, US 181/M9
South Fork, Co, US 174/B2
South Fulton, Tn, US 172/B4
South Gate, Md, US 180/B5
South Gate, Ca, US 178/F8
South Georgia (isl.), UK 64/H8
South Gloucestershire (co.), Eng, UK 74/D3
South Hams (plain), Eng, UK 74/C6
South Holland, Il, US 177/Q16
South Island NP, Kenya 146/C2
South Jordan, Ut, US 179/K12
South Koel (riv.), India 127/E4
South Korea (ctry.) 115/D4
South Lake Tahoe, Ca, US 170/C3
South Lanarkshire (pol. reg.), Sc, UK 78/E5
South Loup (riv.), Ne, US 169/J5
South Luangwa NP, Zam. 147/F3
South Lyon, Mi, US 177/E7
South Magnetic Pole, Ant. 202/K
South Moose (lake), Mb, Can. 169/J2
South Moresby NP and Prsv., BC, Can. 176/M5
South Naknek, Ak, US 176/G4
South Normanton, Eng, UK 77/G5
South Nyack, NY, US 181/K7
South Ockenden, Eng, UK 72/D2
South Ogden, Ut, US 179/K11
South Orange, NJ, US 181/H9
South Orkney (isls.), UK 202/X
South Ossetia (reg.), Geo. 105/G4
South Oxhey, Eng, UK 72/B2
South Oyster (bay), NY, US 181/M9
South Pacific (ocean) 64/B7
South Para (res.), Austl. 155/M8
South Pasadena, Ca, US 178/F7
South Pine (riv.), Austl. 156/E6
South Plainfield, NJ, US 181/H9
South Platte (riv.), Co, US 179/C2
South Polar (plat.), Ant. 202/Y
South Pole, Ant. 202/A
South Prairie, Wa, US 177/C3
South River, NJ, US 181/H10
South Rockwood, Mi, US 177/F7
South Ronaldsay (isl.), Sc, UK 73/V14
South Roxana, Il, US 179/G8
South Salt Lake, Ut, US 179/K12
South San Francisco, Ca, US 177/K11
South Sandwich (isls.), UK 64/H8
South Saskatchewan (riv.), Sk, Can. 164/E3
South Seaville, NJ, US 180/D5
South Shetland (isls.), UK 202/W
South Shields, Eng, UK 77/G2
South Sioux City, Ne, US 169/J5
South Skunk (riv.), Ia, US 171/J2
South Taranaki Bight (bay), NZ 159/S10
South Turkana Nat'l Rsv., Kenya 146/B2
South Tyne (riv.), Eng, UK 77/F2
South Tyneside (co.), Eng, UK 77/G2
South Ubian, Phil. 123/F2
South Uist (isl.), Sc, UK 73/Q8
South Umpqua (riv.), Or, US 170/B2
South Valley Stream, NY, US 181/L9
South Weber, Ut, US 179/K11
South West (cape), Austl. 157/C4
South West NP, Austl. 157/C4
South West Rocks, Austl. 157/E1
South Whittier, Ca, US 178/F8
South Williamsport, Pa, US 180/B1
South Woodham Ferrers, Eng, UK 72/E2
South Yorkshire (co.), Eng, UK 77/G5
Southampton (cape), Nun., Can. 165/H2
Southampton (isl.), Nun., Can. 165/H2
Southampton, On, Can. 172/D2
Southampton, Eng, UK 75/E5
Southampton (co.), Eng, UK 75/E5
Southampton, NY, US 181/F2
Southampton Water (inlet), Eng, UK 75/E5
Southaven, Ms, US 171/K4
Southeast (cape), Ak, US 176/E3
Southeast (pt.), Bahm. 187/H1
Southeast (pt.), Jam. 187/G2
Southend (int'l arpt.), Eng, UK 75/G3
Southend-on-Sea, Eng, UK 75/G3
Southend-on-Sea (co.), Eng, UK 75/G3
Southern (ocean) 64/C9
Southern (riv.), Austl. 154/K7
Southern (dist.), Isr. 133/D4
Southern (prov.), Ugan. 146/A3
Southern Alps (mts.), NZ 159/R11
Southern Cook (isls.), CookIs. 159/J6
Southern Cross, Austl. 154/C4
Southern Indian (lake), Mb, Can. 164/G3
Southern NP, Sudan 139/L6
Southern Pines, NC, US 175/J3
Southern Uplands (hills), Sc, UK 77/D1
Southern Ural (mts.), Rus. 103/N5
Southesk Tablelands (plat.), Austl. 151/B2
Southold, NY, US 181/F1
Southport, NC, US 175/J3
Southport, Eng, UK 77/E4
Southton, Tx, US 179/U21
Southwark (bor.), Eng, UK 72/A1
Southwood NP, Austl. 156/C4
Southworth, Wa, US 177/C3
Sovata, Rom. 91/G2
Soverato Marina, It. 88/E3
Sovere, It. 100/D1
Sovetsk, Rus. 81/J4
Sōwa, Japan 119/D1
Sowerby Bridge, Eng, UK 77/G4
Soweto, SAfr. 148/D2
Sōya-misaki (cape), Japan 118/B1
Soyana (riv.), Rus. 102/J2
Soyang (lake), SKor. 115/D4
Soyaux, Fr. 84/D4
Soyen, Ger. 97/F6
Soyhières, Swi. 98/D3
Sozh (riv.), Bela. 104/D1
Sozopol, Bul. 91/H4
Spa, Belg. 95/E3
Spada (lake), Wa, US 177/D2
Spain (ctry.) 86/C2
Spalding, Austl. 155/H5
Spalding, Eng, UK 77/H6
Spalt, Ger. 96/D4
Spanish Lake, Mo, US 179/G8
Spanish Town, Jam. 187/G2
Spannort (peak), Swi. 99/E4
Sparanise, It. 88/D2
Sparks, Nv, US 170/C3
Sparlingville, Mi, US 177/G6
Sparreholm, Swe. 80/G2
Sparta, NC, US 172/D4
Sparta, NJ, US 180/D1
Sparta, Tn, US 172/C5
Sparta, Wi, US 169/L5
Spartanburg, SC, US 175/H3
Spartel (cape), Mor. 142/B2
Spárti (Sparta), Gre. 89/H4
Spartivento (cape), It. 88/E4
Sparwood, BC, Can. 168/E3
Spassk-Dal'niy, Rus. 113/P3
Spáta, Gre. 89/N9
Spátha (cape), Gre. 89/H5
Spean (riv.), Sc, UK 78/B3
Speer (peak), Swi. 99/F3
Speer Canal (canal), Co, US 179/C2
Speicher, Swi. 99/F3
Speicher, Ger. 95/F4
Speichersdorf, Ger. 97/E3
Speke (gulf), Tanz. 146/B3
Speke (int'l arpt.), Eng, UK 77/F5
Spelle, Ger. 93/E4
Spencer (cape), Austl. 155/H5
Spencer (gulf), Austl. 155/H5
Spencer (pt.), Ak, US 176/E2
Spencer, Ia, US 169/K5
Spencer, Ok, US 179/N14
Spenge, Ger. 93/F4
Spennymoor, Eng, UK 77/G2
Spentrup, Den. 80/D3
Sperkhiás, Gre. 89/H3
Sperkhiós (riv.), Gre. 89/H3
Sperrin (mts.), NI, UK 76/A2
Spessart (range), Ger. 96/C3
Spétsai, Gre. 89/H4
Spey (riv.), Sc, UK 78/B2
Spey (bay), Sc, UK 78/C1
Speyer, Ger. 96/B4
Speyerbsch (riv.), Ger. 96/B4
Spezzano Albanese, It. 88/E3
Špičák (peak), Czh. 97/F2
Spicer (isls.), Nun., Can. 165/H2
Spiekeroog (isl.), Ger. 93/E1
Spiez, Swi. 98/D4
Spigno Monferrato, It. 100/B3
Spijkenisse, Neth. 92/B5
Spike (mtn.), Ak, US 176/K2
Spilamberto, It. 101/E3
Spilion, Gre. 89/J5
Spilve (int'l arpt.), Lat. 81/L3
Spina (peak), It. 88/A2
Spinetta Marengo, It. 100/B3
Spino d'Adda, It. 100/C2
Spirano, It. 100/C1
Spirit River, Ab, Can. 168/D2
Spiritwood, Sk, Can. 168/G2
Spišská Nová Ves, Slvk. 83/L4
Spiti (riv.), India 128/D3
Spitsbergen (isl.), Sval. 202/E
Split, Cro. 90/C4
Split (int'l arpt.), Cro. 90/C4
Split (lake), Mb, Can. 164/G3
Splitrock (res.), NJ, US 181/H8
Spluga, Passo dello (pass), Swi. 99/F5
Splügen, Swi. 99/F4
Spokane, Wa, US 168/D4
Spokane (riv.), Wa, US 168/D4
Spöl (riv.), It. 99/G5
Spoleto, It. 85/K5
Spoon (riv.), Il, US 172/B3
Spooner, Wi, US 169/L4
Spotorno, It. 100/B4
Spotswood, NJ, US 181/H10
Sprague, Mb, Can. 169/K3
Sprang, Neth. 92/C5
Spratly (isls.) 122/D2
Spree (riv.), Ger. 83/H2
Sprendlingen, Ger. 95/G4
Spresiano, It. 101/F1
Sprimont, Belg. 95/E3
Spring, Tx, US 171/J5
Spring City, Pa, US 180/C3
Spring Grove, Pa, US 180/B4
Spring Grove, Il, US 177/P15
Spring Hill, Ks, US 179/D6
Spring Lake, NJ, US 180/D3
Spring Valley, Ca, US 178/D5
Spring Valley, NY, US 181/J7
Springbok, SAfr. 148/B3
Springdale, Nf, Can. 173/K1
Springdale, Ar, US 171/J3
Springe, Ger. 93/G4
Springer, NM, US 171/F3
Springerville, Az, US 170/E4
Springfield, Ma, US 173/F3
Springfield, Mo, US 171/J3
Springfield, NJ, US 181/H9
Springfield, Or, US 168/C4
Springfield, Tn, US 172/C4
Springfield, Vt, US 173/F3
Springfield, Va, US 180/A6
Springfontein, SAfr. 148/D3
Springhill, La, US 171/J4
Springhill, NS, Can. 173/H2
Springs, SAfr. 148/E2
Springs, NY, US 181/F1
Springside, Sk, Can. 169/H3
Springsure, Austl. 156/C4
Springville, Ut, US 179/K13
Sprockhövel, Ger. 93/E6
Spruce (peak), WV, US 172/E4
Spruce Run (res.), NJ, US 180/C2
Spui (riv.), Neth. 92/B5
Spurn (pt.), Eng, UK 77/J4
Squamish, BC, Can. 168/C3
Squaw Harbor, Ak, US 176/F4
Squaxin Island Ind. Res., Wa, US 177/A3
Squillace, Golfo di (gulf), It. 88/E3
Squinzano, It. 89/F2
Squires (mt.), Austl. 155/E3
Srbobran, Serb. 90/D3
Srebrenica, Bosn. 90/D3
Sredna (mts.), Bul. 91/G4
Srednogorie, Bul. 91/G4
Śrem, Pol. 83/J2
Sremčica, Serb. 90/E3
Sremska Mitrovica, Serb. 90/D3
Sreng (riv.), Camb. 120/C3
Srepok (riv.), Camb. 120/D3
Sri Dungargarh, India 131/K3
Sri Gangānagar, India 128/B5
Sri Jayewardenepura Kotte, (cap.), SrL. 124/C6
Sri Lanka (ctry.) 124/D6
Srīkākulam, India 124/D4
Srīnagar, India 128/C2
Srīvardhan, India 131/K5
Środa Śląska, Pol. 83/J3
Środa Wielkopolska, Pol. 83/J2
St. Albans, Vale of (valley), Eng, UK 72/B1
St. John's (cap.), Nf, Can. 173/L2
Stabbursdalen NP, Nor. 79/H1
Staberhuk (pt.), Ger. 80/D4
Stabroek, Belg. 92/B6
Stade, Ger. 93/G1
Staden, Belg. 94/C2
Stadl-Paura, Aus. 97/G6
Stadskanaal, Neth. 92/D3
Stadtbergen, Ger. 96/D6
Stadthagen, Ger. 93/G4
Stadtlauringen, Ger. 96/D2
Stadtlohn, Ger. 92/D5
Stadtoldendorf, Ger. 93/G5
Stadtsteinach, Ger. 97/E2
Stäfa, Swi. 99/E3
Staffanstorp, Swe. 80/E4
Staffelberg (peak), Ger. 96/E2
Staffelegg (pass), Swi. 98/E3
Staffelsee (lake), Ger. 99/H2
Staffhorst, Ger. 93/F3
Staffora (riv.), It. 100/C3
Stafford, Eng, UK 77/F6
Stagno, It. 100/D5
Stagnone Isole Della (isl.), It. 88/B4
Stahnsdorf, Ger. 82/Q7
Staines, Eng, UK 72/B2
Stains, Fr. 72/K5
Stakes (mt.), Ca, US 177/M12
Stakhanov, Ukr. 104/F2
Stalden, Swi. 98/D5
Stalingrad (Volgograd), Rus. 105/H2
Stallings, Il, US 179/G8
Stallworthy (cape), Nun., Can. 165/S6
Stalowa Wola, Pol. 83/M3
Stalybridge, Eng, UK 77/F5
Stamboliyski, Bul. 91/G4
Stamford, Eng, UK 75/F1
Stamford, Ct, US 181/L7
Stamford, Tx, US 171/H4
Stampa, Swi. 99/F5
Stampriet, Namb. 147/C5
Stamullen, Ire. 76/B4
Standerton, SAfr. 148/E2
Standish-with-Langtree, Eng, UK 77/F4
Standley (lake), Co, US 179/B3
Stanford-le-Hope, Eng, UK 75/G3
Stange, Nor. 80/D1
Stanger, SAfr. 149/E3
Stanghella, It. 101/E2
Stanhope, NJ, US 180/D2
Stanišić, Serb. 90/D3
Stanislaus (co.), Ca, US 177/M12
Stanislaus (riv.), Ca, US 170/B3
Stanley, Austl. 157/C4
Stanley (mt.), Austl. 157/C4
Stanley (mt.), Austl. 155/F2
Stanley, NB, Can. 173/H2
Stanley (falls), D.R. Congo 139/L8
Stanley (cap.), Falk. 201/F6
Stanley, Eng, UK 77/G2
Stanley, Sc, UK 78/C4
Stanley, ND, US 169/H3
Stanley, Ks, US 179/D6
Stanley (res.), India 124/C5
Stanley Draper (lake), Ok, US 179/N15
Stanovo, Serb. 90/E4
Stanovoy (range), Rus. 109/M4
Stans, Swi. 99/E4
Stansted (int'l arpt.), Eng, UK 75/G3
Stanthorpe, Austl. 156/C5
Stanton, Ky, US 172/D4
Stanton, Tx, US 171/G4
Stanton, De, US 180/C4
Stanton, NJ, US 180/D2
Stanton, Ca, US 178/G8
Staphorst, Neth. 92/D3
Staplehurst, Eng, UK 75/G4
Staples, On, Can. 177/G7
Stąporków, Pol. 83/L3
Stara Pazova, Serb. 90/E3
Stara Planina (mts.), Serb. 90/F3
Stara Zagora, Bul. 91/G4
Starachowice, Pol. 83/L3
Staranzano, It. 101/G1
Staraya Russa, Rus. 81/P2
Starbuck (isl.), Kiri. 159/K5
Starcke NP, Austl. 156/B1
Stargard Szczeciński, Pol. 80/F5
Starke, Fl, US 175/H4
Starkville, Ms, US 175/F3
Starnbergersee (lake), Ger. 99/H2
Starodub, Rus. 104/E1
Starogard Gdański, Pol. 80/H5
Start (bay), Eng, UK 74/C6
Start (pt.), Eng, UK 74/C6
Start (pt.), Sc, UK 73/V14
Startup, Wa, US 177/D2
Staryy Oskol', Rus. 104/F2
Staszów, Pol. 83/L3
State College, Pa, US 172/E3
State Fairgrounds, De, US 180/C6
State Park Place, Il, US 179/G8
Staten (isl.), NY, US 180/D2
States (int'l arpt.), Chl, UK 84/B2
Statesboro, Ga, US 175/H3
Statesville, NC, US 175/H3
Statue of Liberty Nat'l Mon., NY, US 181/J9
Staufen im Breisgau, Ger. 98/D2
Staufenberg, Ger. 82/E3
Stavanger, Nor. 80/A2
Staveley, Eng, UK 77/G5
Stavelot, Belg. 95/E3
Staveren, Neth. 92/C3
Stavern, Nor. 80/D2
Stavropol', Rus. 105/G3
Stavropol'skiy Kray, Rus. 106/E5
Stavrós, Gre. 89/H2
Stawell, Austl. 157/B3
Stayton, Or, US 168/C4
Ste-Marguerite (riv.), Qu, Can. 173/H1
Steamboat Slough (riv.), Ca, US 177/L10
Steamboat Springs, Co, US 170/F2
Stebbins, Ak, US 176/F3
Steckborn, Swi. 99/E2
Stederau (riv.), Ger. 93/H3
Steeg, Aus. 99/G3
Steele, ND, US 169/J4
Steele's Knowe (hill), Sc, UK 78/C4
Steelpoortrivier (riv.), SAfr. 149/E2
Steelton, Pa, US 180/B3
Steenbergen, Neth. 92/B5
Steens (mtn.), Or, US 170/C2
Steensby (inlet), Nun., Can. 165/J1
Steenvoorde, Fr. 94/B2
Steenwijk, Neth. 92/D3
Steep (pt.), Austl. 154/B3
Steep Holm (isl.), Eng, UK 74/C4
Steephill (lake), Sk, Can. 169/G1
Steeping (riv.), Eng, UK 77/J5
Steese Nat'l Conservation Area, Ak, US 176/J2
Stefansson (isl.), Nun., Can. 164/F1
Steffen (peak), Chile 200/C5
Steffisburg, Swi. 98/D4
Steg, Swi. 98/D5
Stege, Den. 80/E4
Steiermark (prov.), Aus. 83/H5
Steigerwald (for.), Ger. 85/J2
Steilacoom, Wa, US 177/B3
Steimbke, Ger. 93/G3
Stein, Neth. 95/E2
Stein am Rhein, Swi. 99/E2
Stein bei Nünnberg, Ger. 96/E4
Steina (riv.), Ger. 99/E2
Steinach, Ger. 97/F5
Steinach (riv.), Ger. 96/E2
Steinach am Brenner, Aus. 99/H3
Steinbach, Mb, Can. 169/J3
Steinbach an der Steyr, Aus. 97/H7
Steinbourg, Fr. 95/G6
Steinen, Ger. 98/D2
Steinerkirchen an der Traun, Aus. 97/G6
Steinfeld, Ger. 93/F3
Steinfeld, Ger. 96/B4
Steinfeld, Ger. 96/C3
Steinfort, Lux. 95/E4
Steingaden, Ger. 99/G2
Steinhagen, Ger. 93/F4
Steinhausen, Swi. 99/E3
Steinhausen an der Rottum, Ger. 99/F1
Steinheim, Ger. 93/G5
Steinheim am Albuch, Ger. 96/D5
Steinheim an der Murr, Ger. 96/C5
Steinhorst, Ger. 93/H3
Steinhuder (lake), Ger. 93/G4
Steinkjer, Nor. 79/D2
Steinsland, Nor. 80/A1
Steinweiler, Ger. 96/B4
Stekene, Belg. 92/B6
Stella, SAfr. 148/D2
Stella (peak), It. 99/F5
Stellarton, NS, Can. 173/J2
Stelle, Ger. 93/H2
Stellenbosch, SAfr. 148/L10
Stello (peak), Fr. 85/H5
Stelvio, Passo di (pass), It. 99/G4
Stelvio, PN Dello, It. 85/J3
Stenay, Fr. 95/E5
Stendal, Ger. 82/F2
Steneto NP, Bul. 91/G4
Stenhousemuir, Sc, UK 78/C4
Stenungsund, Swe. 80/D2
Stephansposching, Ger. 97/F5
Stephenville, Nf, Can. 173/K1
Stephenville, Tx, US 171/H4
Sterkstroom, SAfr. 148/D3
Sterling, Ak, US 176/H3
Sterling, Co, US 171/G2
Sterlitamak, Rus. 105/K1
Sternstein (peak), Aus. 97/H5
Sterzing (Vipiteno), It. 99/H4
Stęszew, Pol. 83/J2
Štěti, Czh. 97/H2
Stettler, Ab, Can. 168/E2
Steubenville, Oh, US 172/D3
Stevenage, Eng, UK 75/F3
Stevens Village, Ak, US 176/J2
Stevenson (lake), Mb, Can. 169/J2
Stevenson Entrance (str.), Ak, US 176/H4
Stevenston, Sc, UK 78/B5
Stevensville, Mt, US 168/E4
Stevensville, Md, US 180/B6
Stevinsluizen (dam), Neth. 92/C3
Stevzing (Vipiteno), It. 85/J3
Stewart, BC, Can. 176/N4
Stewart (riv.), Yk, Can. 164/C2
Stewart (isl.), NZ 159/R12
Stewart Crossing, Yk, Can. 176/L3
Stewarton, Sc, UK 78/B5
Stewartstown, Pa, US 180/B4
Stewartstown, NI, UK 76/B2
Stewartville, Mn, US 169/K5
Steynrus, SAfr. 148/D2
Steynsburg, SAfr. 148/D3
Steyr, Aus. 97/H6
Steyr (riv.), Aus. 83/H5
Steyregg, Aus. 97/H6
Steytlerville, SAfr. 148/D4
Stia, It. 101/E5
Stiava, It. 100/D5
Stickney (mt.), Wa, US 177/D2
Stiens, Neth. 92/C2
Stigler, Ok, US 171/J4
Stigtomta, Swe. 80/G2
Stikine (riv.), Can.,US 176/M4
Stilbaai, SAfr. 148/C4
Stilfontein, SAfr. 148/D2
Stilís, Gre. 89/H3
Still Creek (res.), Pa, US 180/C2
Still Pond, Md, US 180/B5
Stilling, Den. 80/D3
Stillings, Mo, US 179/D5
Stillwater (range), Nv, US 170/C3
Stillwater, Ok, US 171/H3
Stillwater, Pa, US 180/B1
Stillwater (lake), Pa, US 180/C1
Stilo (cape), It. 88/E3
Stilwell, Ok, US 171/J4
Stilwell, Ks, US 179/D6
Štimlje, Serb. 90/E4
Stimpfach, Ger. 96/D4
Stinchar (riv.), Sc, UK 76/D1
Stinnett, Tx, US 171/G4
Štip, FYROM 89/H2
Stiring-Wendel, Fr. 95/F5
Stírka (peak), Czh. 97/G4
Stirling (mt.), Austl. 154/C4
Stirling, Sc, UK 78/C4
Stirling (pol. reg.), Sc, UK 78/B4
Stirling Range NP, Austl. 154/C5
Stirone (riv.), It. 100/C3
Stjørdal, Nor. 79/D3
Stob a' Choin (peak), Sc, UK 78/B4
Stob Choire Claurigh (peak), Sc, UK 78/B3
Stochov, Czh. 97/G2
Stock, Eng, UK 72/E2
Stock (lake), Fr. 95/F6
Stockach, Ger. 99/F2
Stockerau, Aus. 91/N7
Stockertown, Pa, US 180/C2
Stockholm (cap.), Swe. 79/F4
Stockholm (co.), Swe. 80/G2
Stockhorn (peak), Swi. 98/D4
Stockport, Eng, UK 77/F5
Stockport (co.), Eng, UK 77/F5
Stocks (res.), Eng, UK 77/F4
Stocksbridge, Eng, UK 77/G5
Stockstadt am Rhein, Ger. 96/B3
Stockton, Ca, US 170/B3
Stockton (lake), Mo, US 171/J3
Stockton, NJ, US 180/D3
Stockton (plat.), Tx, US 174/C4
Stockton, Ut, US 179/J13
Stockton-on-Tees, Eng, UK 77/G2
Stockton-on-Tees (co.), Eng, UK 77/G2
Stod, Czh. 97/G3
Stoddard, Ut, US 179/K11
Stoke (pt.), Eng, UK 74/B6
Stoke-on-Trent, Eng, UK 77/F5
Stoke-on-Trent (co.), Eng, UK 77/F5
Stoke Poges, Eng, UK 72/B2
Stokenchurch, Eng, UK 72/A2
Stokes (pt.), Austl. 157/B4
Stokes NP, Austl. 154/D5
Stolac, Bosn. 89/E1
Stolberg, Ger. 95/F2
Stolbovoy (isl.), Rus. 107/P2
Stöllet, Swe. 80/E1
Stolzenau, Ger. 93/G3
Stompneuspunt (pt.), SAfr. 148/K10
Ston, Cro. 89/E1
Stone, Eng, UK 77/F6
Stone Harbor, NJ, US 180/D5
Stonehaven, Sc, UK 78/D3
Stonehenge (ruin), Eng, UK 75/E4
Stonehouse, Sc, UK 78/C5
Stonewall, Mb, Can. 169/J3
Stoney Creek, On, Can. 173/Q9
Stoney Point, On, Can. 177/G7
Stoneyburn, Sc, UK 78/C5
Stonington, Ct, US 181/G1
Stony (pt.), Mb, Can. 169/J2
Stony Brook, NY, US 181/E2
Stony Creek (lake), Mi, US 177/E7
Stony Mountain, Mb, Can. 169/J3
Stony Point, NY, US 180/E1
Stony River, Ak, US 176/G3
Stony Tunguska (riv.), Rus. 109/J3
Stonybrook-Wilshire, Pa, US 180/B4
Stooping (riv.), Co, US 172/D1
Stor (isl.), Nun., Can. 165/S7
Stör (riv.), Ger. 93/G1
Stor-Elvdal, Nor. 80/D1
Storå, Swe. 80/F2
Stora Le (lake), Swe. 80/D2
Stora Sjöfallets NP, Swe. 79/F2
Storavan (lake), Swe. 79/F2
Stord (isl.), Nor. 80/A2
Store Bælt (chan.), Den. 80/D4
Storebø, Nor. 80/A1
Støren, Nor. 79/D3
Storfors, Swe. 80/F2
Storm (bay), Austl. 159/C4
Stormberg (mtn.), SAfr. 148/D3
Stormont, NI, UK 76/C2
Stornoway, Sc, UK 73/Q7
Storo, It. 100/D1
Storr, The (peak), Sc, UK 73/Q8
Storsjön (lake), Swe. 79/E3
Storsteinsfjellet (peak), Nor. 79/F1
Storstrøm (co.), Den. 80/D4
Storvik, Swe. 80/G1
Storvreta, Swe. 80/G2
Story, Wy, US 168/G4
Stosch (isl.), Chile 201/A6
Stötten am Auerberg, Ger. 99/G2
Stoughton, Sk, Can. 169/H3
Stoumont, Belg. 95/E3
Stour (riv.), Eng, UK 74/D5
Stourbridge, Eng, UK 74/D2
Stourport-on-Severn, Eng, UK 74/D2
Stovring, Den. 80/C3
Stowe, Pa, US 180/C3
Stowmarket, Eng, UK 75/G2
Stra, It. 101/F2
Strabane (dist.), NI 76/A2
Strabane, NI, UK 73/Q9
Stradella, It. 100/C2
Straelen, Ger. 92/D6
Strahan, Austl. 157/C4
Strakonice, Czh. 97/G4
Straldzha, Bul. 91/H4
Stralsund, Ger. 80/E4
Strambino, It. 100/A2
Strand, SAfr. 148/L11
Strangford, NI, UK 76/C3
Strangford (lake), NI, UK 76/C3
Strängnäs, Swe. 80/G2
Strangways (mt.), Austl. 155/G2
Stranocum, NI, UK 76/B1
Stranraer, Sc, UK 76/C2
Strasbourg, Fr. 98/D1
Strasbourg (Entzheim) (int'l arpt.), Fr. 98/D1
Strasburg, Mo, US 179/E6
Strasburg, Pa, US 180/B4
Strassen, Lux. 95/F4
Strasshof an der Nordbahn, Aus. 91/P7
Strasswalchen, Aus. 97/G7
Stratford, Tx, US 171/G3
Stratford, On, Can. 172/D3
Stratford, NZ 159/S10
Stratford, Ct, US 181/E1
Stratford, NJ, US 180/C4
Stratford (pt.), Ct, US 181/E1
Stratford (har.), Ct, US 181/L8
Stratford and Worcester (canal), Eng, UK 74/D2
Stratford-upon-Avon, Eng, UK 75/E2

278
T'aina – Tenmi

T'ainan, Tai. 121/D3
Taínaron (cape), Gre. 89/H4
Taingainony, Madg. 149/H8
Taino, It. 100/B1
Taiobeiras, Braz. 196/B4
T'aipei (cap.), Tai. 121/D2
Taiping, Malay. 122/B3
Taiping, China 121/C1
Taisha, Japan 116/C3
Taishan, China 121/B3
Taishi, Japan 119/J6
Taishun, China 121/C2
Taiskirchen im Innkreis, Aus. 97/G6
Taissy, Fr. 95/D5
Taitao (pen.), Chile 200/B5
Taiti (peak), Kenya 146/B2
T'aitung, Tai. 121/D3
Taiwan (ctry.) 121/D3
Taiwan (str.), China,Tai. 121/C3
Taixing, China 114/E4
Taíyetos (mts.), Gre. 89/H4
Taiyuan, China 114/C3
Taizhou, China 114/D4
Taizi (riv.), China 114/F2
Ta'izz, Yem. 130/D6
Tāj Mahal, India 126/B2
Tajikistan (ctry.) 129/E5
Tajima, Japan 117/F2
Tajimi, Japan 119/M5
Tajiri, Japan 119/H7
Tājpur, India 126/B1
Tajrīsh, Iran 130/F1
Tajumulco (vol.), Guat. 186/D3
Tajuña (riv.), Sp. 86/D2
Tak, Thai. 120/B2
Takahagi, Japan 117/G2
Takahama, Japan 119/J5
Takahama, Japan 119/L6
Takahashi (riv.), Japan 116/C3
Takahashi, Japan 116/C3
Takahata, Japan 117/G1
Takaishi, Japan 119/H6
Takamatsu, Japan 116/D3
Takami-yama (peak), Japan 119/K7
Takanabe, Japan 116/B4
Takane, Japan 119/A2
Takanosu, Japan 118/B3
Takanosu-yama (peak), Japan 119/C2
Takaoka, Japan 117/E2
Takapuna, NZ 159/S10
Takarazuka, Japan 119/H6
Takaroa (isl.), FrPol. 159/L6
Takasaki, Japan 117/F2
Takashima, Japan 119/K5
Takatomi, Japan 119/L5
Takatori, Japan 119/J7
Takatsuki, Japan 119/K5
Takatsuki, Japan 119/J6
Takayama, Japan 117/E2
Takefu, Japan 116/E3
Takehara, Japan 116/C3
Tākestān, Iran 130/E1
Taketa, Japan 116/B4
Taketoyo, Japan 119/L6
Takhatgarh, India 124/B2
Takhatpur, India 126/C4
Takht-e Jamshīd (ruin), Iran 130/F3
Takht-i-Bhāi, Pak. 128/A2
Taki, Japan 119/L7
Takijuq (lake), Nun., Can. 164/E2
Takikawa, Japan 118/B2
Takino, Japan 119/G6
Takla (lake), BC, Can. 168/B2
Takla Makan (des.), China 112/D4
Tako, Japan 119/E2
Takoradi, Gha. 145/E5
Takouch (cape), Alg. 142/K6
Taksony, Hun. 91/R10
Tala, Mex. 184/E4
Talā, Egypt 133/B4
Tala, Uru. 201/L11
Talagang, Pak. 128/B3
Talagante, Chile 200/N8
Talāja, India 131/K4
Talak (phys. reg.), Niger 138/G4
Talamanca (mts.), CR 187/F4
Talamba, Pak. 128/B4
Talamona, It. 99/F5
Talang (peak), Indo. 122/B4
Talanga, Hon. 186/E3
Talange, Fr. 95/F5
Talant, Fr. 98/A3
Talara, Peru 198/A2
Talas (obl.), Kyr. 129/F4
Talas, Turk. 132/C2
Talas, Kyr. 129/F4
Talas (riv.), Kaz. 129/F4
Talaud (isl.), Phil. 123/G3
Talavera de la Reina, Sp. 86/C3
Talawakele, SrL. 124/D6
Talayuela, Sp. 86/C3
Talbingo, Austl. 157/D2
Talbot (mt.), Austl. 154/E3
Talbot (co.), Md, US 180/B6
Talca, Chile 200/C2
Talcahuano, Chile 200/B3
Tālcher, India 124/E3
Taldyqorghan (obl.), Kaz. 129/G3
Taldyqorghan, Kaz. 129/G3
Talence, Fr. 84/C4
Talent (riv.), Swi. 98/C4
Talfer (Talvera) (riv.), It. 99/H4
Talgar, Kaz. 129/G4
Taliabu (isl.), Indo. 123/F4
Taliouine, Mor. 140/D3
Talkeetna, Ak, US 176/H3
Ţalkhā, Egypt 133/B4
Tall 'Afar, Iraq 132/E2
Tall al Muqayyar (ruin), Iraq 130/E2
Tall 'Āsūr (peak), Isr. 133/G8
Tall Kayf, Iraq 132/E2
Talladega, Al, US 175/G3
Tallahassee (cap.), Fl, US 175/G4
Tallahatchie (riv.), Ms, US 171/K4
Tallangatta, Austl. 157/C3
Tallanstown, Ire. 76/B4
Tallering (peak), Austl. 154/B4
Talleyville, De, US 180/C4
Tallinn (cap.), Est. 81/L2
Tallman Mountain State Park, NY, US 181/K7
Talloires, Fr. 98/C6
Tallow, Ire. 73/Q10
Tallulah, La, US 171/K4
Tallulah (falls), Ga, US 175/H3
Talmassons, It. 101/G1
Talo (peak), Eth. 139/N5
Taloda, India 131/K4
Tāloqān, Afg. 131/J1
Taloyoak, Nun., Can. 164/G2
Talpa de Allende, Mex. 184/D4
Talsperre Pöhl (res.), Ger. 97/F1
Taltal, Chile 199/B2
Taltson (riv.), NW, Can. 164/E2
Talumphuk (pt.), Thai. 120/C4
Talvera (Talfer) (riv.), It. 99/H4
Talwāra, India 128/C4
Tam Ky, Viet. 120/E3
Tama, Japan 119/C2
Tama (riv.), Japan 119/D2
Tamagawa, Japan 119/C2
Tamaho, Japan 119/B2
Tamaki, Japan 119/L7
Tamalameque, Col. 194/C2
Tamale, Gha. 145/E4
Tamamura, Japan 119/C1
Taman, Indo. 122/D5
Taman-Rasset, Oued (riv.), Alg. 141/F5
Tamaná (peak), Col. 194/B3
Tamana (isl.), Kiri. 158/G5
Tamanar, Mor. 140/C3
Tamanghasset (prov.), Alg. 145/F1
Tamanghasset, Oued (riv.), Alg. 141/F5
Tamanrasset, Alg. 141/G5
Tamanrasset (prov.), Alg. 141/F4
Tamaqua, Pa, US 180/C2
Tamar (riv.), Eng, UK 74/B5
Tamara (isl.), Japan 117/H8
Tamari, Japan 119/E1
Tamarindo NWR, CR 186/E4
Tamarite de Litera, Sp. 87/F2
Tamaro (peak), Swi. 99/E5
Tamási, Hun. 90/D2
Tamatsukuri, Japan 119/E1
Tamaulipas (state), Mex. 182/B3
Tamazula de Gordiano, Mex. 184/E5
Tamazunchale, Mex. 186/B1
Tamba, Japan 119/H5
Tamba (uplands), Japan 119/H5
Tambacounda (pol. reg.), Sen. 144/B3
Tambacounda, Sen. 144/B3
Tambaoura, Falaise de (cliff), Mali 144/C3
Tambelan (isls.), Indo. 122/C3
Tambellup, Austl. 154/C5
Tambo (riv.), Peru 198/C3
Tambo (peak), Swi. 99/F5
Tambo, Austl. 156/B4
Tambo Colorado (ruin), Peru 198/C4
Tambo de Mora, Peru 198/B4
Tambo Grande, Peru 198/A2
Tambobamba, Peru 198/C4
Tambohorano, Madg. 149/G7
Tambopata (riv.), Peru 198/D4
Tambora (peak), Indo. 123/E5
Tamboril, Braz. 196/B2
Tamboritha (mt.), Austl. 157/C3
Tambov, Rus. 105/G1
Tambovskaya Oblast, Rus. 105/G1
Tambre (riv.), Sp. 86/A1
Tame (riv.), Eng, UK 75/E1
Tame, Col. 194/D3
Tâmega (riv.), Port. 86/B2
Tamentit, Alg. 141/E4
Tameside (co.), Eng, UK 77/F5
Tamgak (peak), Niger 145/H2
Tamgue (mass.), Gui. 144/B3
Tamiahua, Mex. 186/B1
Tamiahua (lag.), Mex. 186/B1
Tamil Nādu (state), India 124/C5
Taminango, Col. 194/B4
Ţāmiyah, Egypt 133/B5
Tamlūk, India 127/F4
Tammany (mt.), NJ, US 180/C2
Tammela, Fin. 81/K1
Ţammūn, WBnk. 133/D3
Tampa, Fl, US 175/H5
Tampa (int'l arpt.), Fl, US 175/H5
Tampere, Fin. 81/K1
Tampere-Pirkkala (int'l arpt.), Fin. 81/K1
Tampico, Mex. 186/B1
Tampoc (riv.), FrG. 195/H4
Tampon Ambohitra (peak), Madg. 149/J6
Tampulonanjing (peak), Indo. 122/A3
Tamra, Isr. 133/G6
Tamshiyacu, Peru 198/C2
Tamuín (riv.), Mex. 186/B1
Tamuín, Mex. 186/B1
Tamur (riv.), Nepal 127/F2
Tamworth, Austl. 157/D1
Tamworth, Eng, UK 75/E1
Tamyang, SKor. 115/D5
Tan (riv.), China 125/K3
Tan An, Viet. 120/D4
Tan-Tan, Mor. 140/C3
Tana (lake), Eth. 139/N5
Tana (riv.), Kenya 146/D3
Tana River Primate Nat'l Rsv., Kenya 146/D3
Tanabe, Japan 116/D4
Tanabe, Japan 119/J6
Tanabi, Braz. 197/B2
Tanacross, Ak, US 176/K3
Tanafjorden (estu.), Nor. 79/J1
Tanaga (vol.), Ak, US 176/C6
Tanaga (isl.), Ak, US 176/C6
Tanagura, Japan 117/G2
Tanah Merah, Malay. 125/H6
Tanahbala (isl.), Indo. 122/A4
Tanakpur, India 126/C1
Tanambe, Madg. 149/J7
Tanami (des.), Austl. 151/C2
Tanana, Ak, US 176/H2
Tanana (riv.), Ak, US 176/J3
Tanandava, Madg. 149/G8
Tanaro (riv.), It. 85/G4
Tancheng, China 114/D4
Tanch'ŏn, NKor. 115/E2
Tancítaro, Pico de (peak), Mex. 184/E5
Tancitaro, PN de, Mex. 182/A4
Tanda (lake), Mali 144/D3
Tānda, India 126/D2
Tānda, India 126/B1
Ţăndărei, Rom. 91/H3
Tandil, Arg. 200/F3
Tāndliānwāla, Pak. 128/B4
Tando Ādam, Pak. 131/J3
Tando Allāhyār, Pak. 131/J3
Tando Muhammad Khān, Pak. 131/J3
Tandou (lake), Austl. 157/B2
Tandragee, NI, UK 76/B3
Tanem Taunggyi (range), Thai. 125/G4
Tanezrouft (des.), Alg. 141/E5
Tanezrouft-n-Ahenet (des), Alg. 141/F5
Tang (riv.), China 114/C4
Tanga, Tanz. 146/C4
Tanga (pol. reg.), Tanz. 146/C4
Tangail, Bang. 127/G3
Tangail (pol. reg.), Bang. 127/G3
Tanganyika (lake), D.R. Congo,Tanz. 146/A4
Tangará da Serra, Braz. 192/G6
Tangent (pt.), Ak, US 176/G1
Tanger, Mor. 142/B2
Tanger (prov.), Mor. 142/A2
Tangerhütte, Ger. 82/F2
Tangermünde, Ger. 82/F2
Tanggula (mts.), China 112/E5
Tanghe, China 114/C4
Tangi, Pak. 128/A2
Tangipahoa (riv.), La, US 179/P16
Tangipahoa (parish), La, US 179/P16
Tangjin, SKor. 115/D4
Tanglewilde-Thompson Place, Wa, US 177/B3
Tangshan, China 114/J7
Tangub, Phil. 121/D6
Tangyin, China 114/C4
Tangyuan, China 113/N2
Tanhaçu, Braz. 196/B4
Tanigumi, Japan 119/L4
Tanimbar (isl.), Indo. 123/H5
Taninges, Fr. 98/C5
Tanintharyi (div.), Myan. 125/G5
Tanjay, Phil. 121/D6
Tanjungbalai, Indo. 122/A3
Tanjungkarang-Telukbetung, Indo. 122/C5
Tanjungpandan, Indo. 122/C4
Tanjungpinang, Indo. 122/B3
Tanjungpura, Indo. 122/A3
Tānk, Pak. 128/A3
Tankwa Karoo NP, SAfr. 148/B4
Tann, Ger. 97/F6
Tanna (isl.), Van. 158/F6
Tannan, Japan 119/H5
Tannersville, Pa, US 180/C1
Tannheim, Aus. 99/G3
Tannu-Ola (mts.), Mong.,Rus. 112/F1
Tano (riv.), Gha. 138/E6
Tânout, Niger 145/H3
Tanquián de Escobedo, Mex. 186/B1
Tansen, Nepal 126/D2
Ţanţā, Egypt 133/B4
Tantallon, Md, US 180/A6
Tantō, Japan 119/G5
Tantoyuca, Mex. 186/B1
Tanuku, India 124/D4
Tanumshede, Swe. 80/D2
Tanunda, Austl. 157/A2
Tanyang, SKor. 115/E4
Tanzania (ctry.) 146/B4
Tanzawa-yama (peak), Japan 119/C3
Tao (isl.), Myan. 120/B4
Taolañaro, Madg. 149/H9
Taormina, It. 88/D4
Tāoru, India 128/D5
Taos, NM, US 171/F3
Taounate (town), Mor. 142/B2
Taounate, Mor. 142/B2
Taourirt, Alg. 141/F4
Taourirt, Mor. 142/C2
T'aoyüan, Tai. 121/D2
Taoyuan, China 125/K2
Tap Mun Chau (isl.), China 113/V10
Tap O'Noth (hill), Sc, UK 78/D2
Tapa, Est. 81/L2
Tapachula, Mex. 186/C3
Tapajós (riv.), Braz. 189/D3
Tapanahoni (riv.), Sur. 193/G3
Tapanti Nat'l Wild. Ref., CR 187/F4
Tapauá (riv.), Braz. 192/E5
Tapauá, Braz. 192/F5
Tapaz, Phil. 121/D5
Tapejara, Braz. 197/A4
Tapes, Braz. 197/B4
Tapeta, Libr. 144/C5
Tapia de Casariego, Sp. 86/B1
Tapiche (riv.), Peru 198/C2
Tapilula, Mex. 186/C2
Tapis (peak), Malay. 122/B3
Tapo, Peru 198/C3
Tapoa (prov.), Burk. 145/F3
Tapolca, Hun. 90/C2
Tappahannock, Va, US 172/E4
Tappan, NY, US 181/K7
Tappan Zee (lake), NY, US 181/E1
Tappan Zee (riv.), NY, US 181/K7
Tappi-zaki (pt.), Japan 118/B3
Tapps (lake), Wa, US 177/C3
Tāpti (riv.), India 131/J4
Ţāq Kisrá (Ctesiphon) (ruin), Iraq 132/F3
Taquara, Braz. 197/B4
Taquari (riv.), Braz. 193/G7
Taquari, Braz. 197/B4
Taquaritinga, Braz. 197/B2
Taquarituba, Braz. 197/B2
Taquil, Ecu. 198/B1
Tar (riv.), Kyr. 129/F4
Tara, Rus. 129/F1
Tara (riv.), Bosn.,Mont. 90/D4
Tara, Austl. 156/C4
Taraba (state), Nga. 145/H5
Taraba (riv.), Nga. 145/H4
Ţarābulus, Leb. 133/D2
Ţarābulus (Tripoli) (cap.), Libya 138/H1
Tarakan, Indo. 123/E3
Taraklı, Turk. 91/K5
Taraku (isl.), Rus. 118/E2
Taralga, Austl. 157/D2
Taranagar, India 128/C5
Tarancón, Sp. 86/D2
Tarangire NP, Tanz. 147/G1
Taranto, It. 89/E2
Taranto, Golfo di (gulf), It. 88/E2
Tarapoto, Peru 198/B2
Tarare, Fr. 84/F4
Tarariras, Uru. 201/K11
Tarascon, Fr. 84/F5
Tarascon-sur-Ariège, Fr. 84/D5
Tarata, Peru 198/D5
Tarauacá, Braz. 198/D3
Tarauacá (riv.), Braz. 198/D2
Taravai (isl.), FrPol. 159/M7
Tarawa (cap.), Kiri. 158/G4
Tarawa (isl.), Kiri. 158/G4
Tarazona, Sp. 86/E3
Tarazona, Sp. 86/E2
Tarbagatay (mts.), Kaz. 112/D2
Tarbat Ness (pt.), Sc, UK 78/C1
Tarbela (dam), Pak. 128/B2
Tarbela (res.), Pak. 128/B2
Tarbes, Fr. 84/D5
Tarbolton, Sc, UK 78/B5
Tarboro, NC, US 175/J3
Tarcento, It. 85/K3
Tarcutta, Austl. 157/C2
Tardes (riv.), Fr. 84/E3
Tardienta, Sp. 87/E2
Tardoire (riv.), Fr. 84/D4
Taree, Austl. 157/E1
Tarf Water (riv.), Sc, UK 76/D2
Tarfâwi (well), Egypt 143/B4
Tarfaya, Mor. 140/B4
Target Rock NWR, NY, US 181/M8
Targuist, Mor. 142/B2
Tarhūnah, Libya 138/H1
Tarifa, Ecu. 198/B1
Tarifa, Sp. 86/C4
Tarija, Bol. 192/F8
Tariku (riv.), Indo. 123/J4
Tariku-Taritatu (plain), Indo. 123/J4
Tarim (basin), China 112/D4
Tarim (riv.), China 112/D3
Tarin (riv.), Afg. 131/J2
Tarin (Torino), It. 85/G4
Taritatu (riv.), Indo. 123/J4
Tarkastad, SAfr. 148/D4
Tarkhankut (cape), Ukr. 91/L3
Tarkwa, Gha. 145/E5
Tarlac, Phil. 121/D4
Tarma, Peru 198/C3
Tarmstedt, Ger. 93/G2
Tarn (riv.), Fr. 84/D5
Tarn Tāran, India 128/C4
Tarnak (riv.), Afg. 131/J2
Tarnobrzeg, Pol. 83/L3
Tarnów, Pol. 83/L3
Tärnsjö, Swe. 80/G1
Taro (riv.), It. 85/J4
Tarō, Japan 118/B4
Ţārom, Iran 131/G3
Taroom, Austl. 156/C4
Tarouca, Port. 86/B2
Taroudannt, Mor. 140/C3
Tarp, Ger. 80/C4
Tarpa, Hun. 90/F1
Tarpon Springs, Fl, US 175/H4
Tarquinia, It. 88/B1
Tarqūmiyah, WBnk. 133/D4
Tarrafal, CpV. 135/K10
Tarragona, Sp. 87/F2
Tarraleah, Austl. 157/C4
Tàrrega, Sp. 87/F2
Tarrenz, Aus. 99/G3
Tarrytown, NY, US 181/K7
Tarsney Lakes, Mo, US 179/E6
Tarsus, Turk. 133/D1
Tarsus (riv.), Turk. 133/D1
Tartagal, Arg. 199/D1
Tartaro (riv.), It. 101/E2
Tartas, Fr. 84/C5
Tartu, Est. 81/M2
Ţarţūs (prov.), Syria 132/C3
Ţarţūs, Syria 133/D2
Tarui, Japan 119/L5
Tarumizu, Japan 116/B5
Tarutao NP, Thai. 120/B5
Tarvagatay (mts.), Mong. 112/G2
Taşağıl, Turk. 133/B1
Täsch, Swi. 98/D5
Taşçı, Turk. 132/C2
Tashkent (cap.), Uzb. 129/E4
Tashkent (int'l arpt.), Uzb. 129/E4
Tasikmalaya, Indo. 122/C5
Taşkent, Turk. 133/C1
Taşköprü, Turk. 104/E4
Taşlıçay, Turk. 132/E2
Tasman (pen.), Austl. 157/C4
Tasman (sea), Austl.,NZ 158/E8
Tasman (bay), NZ 159/S11
Tasman Head (cape), Austl. 157/C4
Tasmania, Austl. 157/C3
Tasmania (state), Austl. 157/C4
Tăşnad, Rom. 90/F2
Taşova, Turk. 132/D1
Tasquillo, Mex. 185/K6
Tassili-n-Ajjer (mts.), Alg. 141/G4
Tassili Oua-n Ahaggar (mts.), Alg. 141/G5
Tasu, BC, Can. 176/M5
Taşucu, Turk. 133/C1
Tata, Mor. 140/D3
Tata, Hun. 90/D2
Tatabánya, Hun. 90/D2
Tatachikapika (riv.), On, Can. 172/D2
Tatakoto (isl.), FrPol. 159/L6
Tatamy, Pa, US 180/C2
Tataouine, Tun. 141/H2
Tataouine (gov.), Tun. 141/H2
Tatar (str.), Rus. 109/P5
Tatarlar, Turk. 89/K2
Tatarsk, Rus. 129/G1
Tatarstan, Resp., Rus. 106/Q6
Tate-yama (peak), Japan 117/E2
Tatebayashi, Japan 119/D1
Tateshina, Japan 119/A1
Tateyama, Japan 117/F3
Tathlina (lake), NW, Can. 164/E2
Tathra, Austl. 157/D3
Tatilt (well), Mrta. 144/B2
Tatitlek, Ak, US 176/J3
Tatnam (cape), Mb, Can. 164/G3
Tatomi, Japan 119/B2
Tatranský NP, Slvk. 83/K4
Tatsuno, Japan 117/E3
Tatsuta, Japan 119/L5
Tatura, Austl. 157/C3
Tatvan, Turk. 132/E2
Tauá, Braz. 196/B2
Taubaté, Braz. 197/H8
Tauber (riv.), Ger. 82/E4
Tauberbischofsheim, Ger. 96/C3
Tauca, Peru 198/B3
Taufkirchen, Ger. 97/F6
Taufkirchen an der Pram, Aus. 97/G6
Taufstein (peak), Ger. 96/C1
Taulihawa, Nepal 126/D2
Taung, SAfr. 148/D2
Taungdwingyi, Myan. 125/G3
Taunggyi, Myan. 125/G3
Taungup, Myan. 125/F4
Taunsa, Pak. 128/A4
Taunton, Ma, US 173/G3
Taunton, Eng, UK 74/C4
Taunus (range), Ger. 96/A2
Taunusstein, Ger. 96/B2
Taupo, NZ 159/T10
Taupo (lake), NZ 159/T10
Tauragė, Lith. 81/K4
Tauranga, NZ 159/T10
Taurion (riv.), Fr. 84/D3
Taurisano, It. 89/F3
Taurus (mts.), Turk. 132/C2
Tauste, Sp. 86/E2
Taute (riv.), Fr. 84/C2
Tauu (isls.), PNG 158/E5
Tavanbulag, Mong. 112/H2
Tavannes, Swi. 98/D3
Tavaputs (plat.), Ut, US 170/E3
Tavarnelle, It. 101/E5
Tavarnuzze, It. 101/E5
Tavas, Turk. 132/B2
Tavaux, Fr. 98/B3
Tavazzano, It. 100/C2
Tavda (riv.), Rus. 106/G4
Tavernerio, It. 100/C1
Taverny, Fr. 72/J4
Taviano, It. 89/F3
Tavira, Port. 86/B4
Tavoy (pt.), Myan. 120/B3
Tavoy (Dawei), Myan. 120/B3
Tavşanlı, Turk. 132/D2
Tavy (riv.), Eng, UK 74/B6
Taw (riv.), Eng, UK 74/C5
Tawaramoto, Japan 119/J6
Tawas City, Mi, US 172/D2
Tawau, Malay. 123/E3
Tawe (riv.), Wal, UK 74/C3
Tawern, Ger. 95/F4
Tāwi (riv.), India 128/C3
Tawi-Tawi (isl.), Phil. 121/C6
Ţāwūq, Iraq 132/F3
Taxco, Mex. 185/K8
Taxila (ruin), Pak. 128/B3
Taxila, Pak. 128/B3
Taxkorgan Tajik Zizhixian, China 131/L1
Tay (lake), Sc, UK 78/B3
Tay (riv.), Sc, UK 78/C3
Tay, Firth of (inlet), Sc, UK 78/C4
Tay Ninh, Viet. 120/D4
Tayabamba, Peru 198/B3
Taylor, Mi, US 177/F7
Taylorsville-Bennion, Ut, US 179/K12
Taymyr (riv.), Rus. 106/K2
Taymyr (isl.), Rus. 107/L2
Taymyr (pen.), Rus. 106/K2
Taymyrskiy Aut. Okrug, Rus. 106/J2
Tayoltita, Mex. 184/D3
Tayport, Sc, UK 78/D4
Tayrona, PN, Col. 194/C2
Tayshet, Rus. 107/K4
Taytay, Phil. 123/E1
Taz (riv.), Rus. 109/H3
Taza (prov.), Mor. 142/C2
Taza, Mor. 142/B2
Tazawako, Japan 118/B4
Tazekka (peak), Mor. 142/B2
Tazenakht, Mor. 140/D3
Tazewell, Tn, US 172/D4
Tāzirbū (oasis), Libya 139/K2
Tazumal (ruin), ESal. 186/D3
T'bilisi (cap.), Geo. 105/H4
T'boli, Phil. 121/D6
Tchamba, Togo 145/F4
Tchaourou, Ben. 145/F4
Tchefuncta (riv.), La, US 179/P16
Tchibanga, Gabon 138/H8
Tcholliré, Camr. 138/H6
Tczew, Pol. 81/H4
Te Anau, NZ 159/R12
Te Araroa, NZ 159/T10
Te Aroha, NZ 159/T10
Te Awamutu, NZ 159/T10
Te Kao, NZ 159/S9
Te Kuiti, NZ 159/T10
Tea (riv.), Braz. 192/E4
Teacapán, Mex. 184/D4
Teague, Tx, US 171/H5
Teaneck, NJ, US 181/J8
Teano, It. 88/D2
Teapa, Mex. 186/C2
Tearce, FYROM 89/G1
Tebak (peak), Indo. 122/B4
Tébessa (prov.), Alg. 141/G2
Tébessa (mts.), Alg. 142/L7
Tébessa, Alg. 142/L7
Tebesselamane (well), Mali 145/F2
Tebicuary (riv.), Par. 199/E2
Tebingtinggi, Indo. 122/A3
Tebourba, Tun. 88/A4
Tebulos-mta (peak), Rus. 105/H4
Tecalitlán, Mex. 184/E5
Tecamac, Mex. 185/R9
Tecamachalco, Mex. 185/M8
Tecate, Mex. 184/A1
Tech (riv.), Fr. 84/E5
Techirghiol, Rom. 91/J3
Tecirli, Turk. 132/D2
Tecka, Arg. 200/C4
Tecka (riv.), Arg. 200/C4
Tecklenberg, Ger. 93/E4
Tecolutla, Mex. 185/M6
Tecomán, Mex. 184/E5
Tecozautla, Mex. 185/K6
Tecpan de Galeana, Mex. 185/E5
Tecuala, Mex. 184/D4
Tecuci, Rom. 91/H3
Tecumseh, Mi, US 172/D3
Tecumseh, Ne, US 171/H2
Tecumseh, On, Can. 177/G7
Tedjert (well), Alg. 141/H1
Tedzhen (riv.), Trkm. 106/G6
Tees (bay), Eng, UK 77/G2
Tees (riv.), Eng, UK 77/G3
Teesside (int'l arpt.), Eng, UK 77/G3
Tefé (riv.), Braz. 192/E4
Tefé, Braz. 192/F4
Teferič, Serb. 90/E4
Tega (lake), Japan 119/E2
Tegal, Indo. 122/C5
Tegel (int'l arpt.), Ger. 82/Q6
Tegelen, Neth. 92/D6
Tegeler (lake), Ger. 82/Q6
Tegheri (well), Libya 141/H4
Teghra, India 127/E3
Tegid, Llyn (lake), Wal, UK 76/E6
Teglio, It. 99/G5
Tégouma (riv.), Niger 145/H3
Tegsh, Mong. 112/G2
Tegucigalpa (cap.), Hon. 186/E3
Tehek (lake), Nun., Can. 164/G2
Tehrān (cap.), Iran 130/F1
Tehuacán, Mex. 185/M8
Tehuantepec (isth.), Mex. 185/G5
Tehuantepec (riv.), Mex. 186/C2
Tehuantepec (gulf), Mex. 186/C3
Teide, Pico de (peak), Sp. 140/A3
Teifi (riv.), Wal, UK 74/B2
Teifiside (valley), Wal, UK 74/B2
Teiga (plat.), Sudan 139/L4
Teign (riv.), Eng, UK 74/C5
Teignmouth, Eng, UK 74/C5
Teisendorf, Ger. 97/F7
Teith (riv.), Sc, UK 78/B4
Tejen, Trkm. 131/H1
Tejn, Den. 80/F4
Tejupilco de Hidalgo, Mex. 185/E5
Tekamah, Ne, US 169/J5
Tekāri, India 127/E3
Tekax de Álvaro Obregón, Mex. 186/D1
Teke, Turk. 91/J5
Tekeli, Kaz. 129/G4
Tekes (riv.), China 106/J5
Tekezē Wenz (riv.), Eth. 139/N5
Tekiliktag (peak), China 112/D4
Tekirdağ, Turk. 91/H5
Tekirdağ (prov.), Turk. 91/H5
Tekit, Mex. 186/D1
Tekkali, India 124/D4
Tekke, Turk. 132/D1
Tekkeköy, Turk. 132/D1
Tekman, Turk. 132/E2
Tel Aviv (dist.), Isr. 133/D3
Tel Aviv-Yafo, Isr. 133/F7
Tel Megiddo (ruin), Isr. 133/G6
Tela, Hon. 186/E3
Télagh, Alg. 142/D2
T'elavi, Geo. 105/H4
Telde, Sp. 140/B3
Télé (lake), Mali 144/D2
Telêmaco Borba, Braz. 197/B3
Telemark (co.), Nor. 79/D4
Telen (riv.), Indo. 123/E3
Teleorman (prov.), Rom. 91/G4
Telertheba (peak), Alg. 141/G4
Teles Pires (riv.), Braz. 189/D3
Telford, Pa, US 180/C3
Telford Dawley, Eng, UK 74/D1
Telfs, Aus. 99/H3
Telgate, It. 100/C1
Telgte, Ger. 93/E5
Telica, Nic. 186/E3
Télig (well), Mali 140/E5
Télimélé, Gui. 144/B4
Telkwa, BC, Can. 168/B2
Tell City, In, US 172/C4
Teller, Ak, US 176/E2
Telli (lake), Mrta. 140/C4
Tellicherry, India 124/C5
Tellin, Belg. 95/E3
Telluride, Co, US 170/F3
Telok Anson, Malay. 122/B3
Teloloapan, Mex. 185/F5
Telšiai, Lith. 81/K4
Teltow, Ger. 82/Q7
Teltow (reg.), Ger. 83/G2
Tema, Gha. 145/E5
Temagami (lake), On, Can. 172/D2
Temax, Mex. 186/D1
Tembilahan, Indo. 122/B4
Tembisa, SAfr. 148/E2
Temblador, Ven. 195/F2
Teme (riv.), Eng, UK 74/C2
Temecula, Ca, US 178/C4
Temelkovo, Bul. 90/F4
Temerin, Serb. 90/D3
Temerloh, Malay. 122/B3
Temirtaū, Kaz. 129/F2
Témiscamie (riv.), Qu, Can. 173/F1
Témiscaming, Qu, Can. 172/E2
Temoaya, Mex. 185/Q10
Temoe (isl.), FrPol. 159/M7
Temora, Austl. 157/C2
Tempe, Az, US 179/S19
Tempio Pausania, It. 88/A2
Temple, Pa, US 180/C3
Temple City, Ca, US 178/F7
Temple of Lady Chua Xu, Viet. 120/D4
Templemore, Ire. 73/Q10
Templepatrick, NI, UK 76/B2
Templeuve, Fr. 94/C2
Templeville, Md, US 180/C5
Templin, Ger. 83/G2
Templiner (lake), Ger. 82/Q7
Tempoal de Sánchez, Mex. 186/B1
Temryuk, Rus. 104/F3
Temse, Belg. 95/D1
Temuco, Chile 200/B3
Temuka, NZ 159/S11
Ten Boer, Neth. 92/D2
Tena, Ecu. 194/B5
Tena Kourou (peak), Mali 138/D5
Tenabo, Mex. 186/D1
Tenafly, NJ, US 181/K8
Tenakee Springs, Ak, US 176/L4
Tenancingo, Mex. 185/K8
Tenango, Mex. 185/R10
Tenango de Arista, Mex. 185/Q10
Tenasserim (range), Myan. 120/B3
Tenasserim, Myan. 120/B3
Tenay, Fr. 98/B6
Tenby, Wal, UK 74/B3
Tende, Fr. 85/G4
Tende, Col de (pass), Fr. 100/A4
Tenderovsk (bay), Ukr. 91/K2
Tenderovsk Spit (isl.), Ukr. 91/K2
Tendō, Japan 118/B4
Tendre (peak), Swi. 98/C4
Ténenkou, Mali 144/D3
Ténéré (des.), Niger 138/G4
Ténéré du Tafassasset (des.), Niger 138/G3
Tenerife, Col. 194/C2
Tenerife (isl.), Sp. 140/A3
Ténès, Alg. 142/F4
Tenes (riv.), Sp. 87/L6
Teng (riv.), Myan. 125/G3
Teng Xian, China 114/D4
Tenggarong, Indo. 123/E4
Tengger (des.), China 112/H4
Tengiz Köli (lake), Kaz. 106/G4
Tenguel, Ecu. 194/B5
Tenibres (peak), It. 85/G4
Teniente Enciso, PN, Par. 199/D1
Teningen, Ger. 98/D1
Tenja, Cro. 90/D3
Tenkodogo, Burk. 145/E4
Tenmile (riv.), Az, US 170/D4

Tenne – Tŏkch
279

Tennessee (state), US 175/G3
Tennessee (riv.), US 175/F3
Tenneville, Belg. 95/E3
Tennuaca (well), Mor. 140/B5
Teno, Chile 200/C2
Tenojoki (riv.), Fin. 79/H1
Tenosique de Pino Suárez, Mex. 186/D2
Tenri, Japan 119/J6
Tenryū, Japan 117/E3
Tenryū (riv.), Japan 117/E3
Tensift (pol. reg.), Mor. 140/C3
Tensift, Oued (riv.), Mor. 140/C3
Tenterfield, Austl. 157/E1
Tentolomatinan (peak), Indo. 123/F3
Tenus (peak), Kenya 146/B2
Teo, Sp. 86/A1
Teocaltiche, Mex. 182/A3
Teocelo, Mex. 185/N7
Teodelina, Arg. 200/E2
Teodoro Sampaio, Braz. 197/A2
Teófilo Otoni, Braz. 196/B5
Teopisca, Mex. 186/C2
Teotihuacán (ruin), Mex. 185/R9
Teotihuacán, Mex. 185/R9
Teotitlán del Camino, Mex. 186/B2
Tepache, Mex. 184/C2
Tepalcatepec, Mex. 184/E5
Tepalcingo, Mex. 185/L8
Tepatitlán de Morelos, Mex. 182/A3
Tepatlaxco, Mex. 185/M7
Tepeapulco, Mex. 185/L7
Tepebaşı, Turk. 133/C1
Tepehuaje, Mex. 185/F4
Tepehuanes, Mex. 184/D3
Tepeji del Río de Ocampo, Mex. 185/K7
Tepelenë, Alb. 89/G2
Tepelská Plošina (mts.), Czh. 97/F2
Tepetlaoxtoc, Mex. 185/R9
Tepexi, Mex. 185/M8
Tepexpan, Mex. 185/R9
Tepic, Mex. 184/D4
Teplá (riv.), Czh. 82/G3
Teplá Vltava (riv.), Czh. 97/G5
Teplice, Czh. 83/G3
Tepoca (cape), Mex. 184/B2
Tepoca, Cabo (cape), Mex. 184/B2
Tepoto (isl.), FrPol. 159/L6
Tepotzotlán, Mex. 185/Q9
Tepoztlán, Mex. 185/K8
Tequila, Mex. 184/E4
Tequisquiapan, Mex. 185/F4
Tequixquiac, Mex. 185/K7
Ter (riv.), Sp. 87/G1
Ter Aar, Neth. 92/B4
Téra, Niger 145/F3
Tera (riv.), Sp. 86/B1
Teraina (Washington) (isl.), Kiri. 159/J4
Teramo, It. 85/K5
Terang, Austl. 157/B3
Tercan, Turk. 132/E2
Terceira (isl.), Azor., Port. 87/S12
Terek (riv.), Rus. 105/H4
Terepaima, PN, Ven. 194/D2
Teresina, Braz. 196/B2
Teresópolis, Braz. 197/L7
Terespol, Pol. 83/M2
Tergnier, Fr. 94/C4
Tergun Daba (mts.), China 112/F4
Terheijden, Neth. 92/B5
Teriberskiy (pt.), Rus. 102/G1
Terkaplesterpoelen (lake), Neth. 92/C2
Terlan (Terlano), It. 99/H4
Termas de Río Hondo, Arg. 199/D2
Termini Imerese, It. 88/C4
Términos (lag.), Mex. 186/D2
Termiz, Uzb. 131/J1
Termo, Ca, US 168/C5
Termoli, It. 88/D1
Termonfeckin, Ire. 76/B4
Termunten, Neth. 92/E2
Ternate, Indo. 123/G3
Ternberg, Aus. 97/H7
Terneuzen, Neth. 92/A6
Terni, It. 88/C1
Ternin (riv.), Fr. 84/F3
Ternoise (riv.), Fr. 94/B3
Ternopil', Ukr. 104/C2
Ternopil's'ka Oblasti, Ukr. 104/C2
Terpeniya (bay), Rus. 107/Q5
Terpní, Gre. 89/H2
Terra Nova, Braz. 196/B4
Terra Nova, Braz. 196/C3
Terra Nova NP, Nf, Can. 173/L1
Terrace, BC, Can. 168/A2
Terrace Bay, On, Can. 169/M3
Terracina, It. 88/C2
Terråk, Nor. 79/E2
Terralba, It. 88/A3
Terranuova Bracciolini, It. 101/E5
Terrassa, Sp. 87/L6
Terrasson-la-Villedieu, Fr. 84/D4
Terre Hill, Pa, US 180/B3
Terrebonne, Qu, Can. 173/N6
Terrell Hills, Tx, US 179/U21
Terri (peak), Swi. 99/F4
Terry, Mt, US 169/G4
Terry (lake), Co, US 179/B2
Terrytown, La, US 179/P17
Terschelling (isl.), Neth. 92/C2
Tertenia, It. 88/A3
Teruel, Sp. 87/E2
Terutao (isl.), Thai. 125/G6
Tervel, Bul. 91/H4
Terza Grande (peak), It. 85/K3
Terzo d'Aquileia, It. 101/G1
Tešanj, Bosn. 90/C3
Tescou (riv.), Fr. 84/D5
Tesero, It. 99/H5
Teshekpuk (lake), Ak, US 176/G1
Teshikaga, Japan 118/D2
Teshio (riv.), Japan 118/C1
Teshio, Japan 118/B1
Teshio-dake (peak), Japan 118/C2
Teslić, Bosn. 90/C3
Teslin (riv.), Yk, Can. 164/C2
Teslin (lake), BC, Can. 164/C3
Tessaoua, Niger 145/G3
Tessenderlo, Belg. 95/E1
Tessenie (Teseney), Erit. 130/C5
Test (riv.), Eng, UK 75/E4
Testa del Gargano (pt.), It. 88/E2
Tét, Hun. 90/C2
Tete, Moz. 147/F4
Tête de l'Estrop (peak), Fr. 85/G4
Tetela, Mex. 185/M7
Teterow, Ger. 80/E5
Teteven, Bul. 91/G4
Tetiaroa (isl.), FrPol. 159/L6
Tetlin, Ak, US 176/K3
Teton (riv.), Mt, US 168/F4
Tétouan (prov.), Mor. 142/B2
Tétouan, Mor. 142/B2
Tetovo, FYROM 89/G1
Tettnang, Ger. 99/F2
Tetulia (riv.), Bang. 127/H4
Teublitz, Ger. 97/F4
Teuco (riv.), Arg. 199/D1
Teufen, Swi. 99/F3
Teúl de González Ortega, Mex. 184/E4
Teulada (cape), It. 88/A3
Teulon, Mb, Can. 169/J3
Teupasenti, Hon. 186/E3
Teuri (isl.), Japan 118/B1
Teuschnitz, Ger. 97/E2
Teutoburger Wald (for.), Ger. 93/F4
Tevere (Tiber) (riv.), It. 85/K5
Teverya, Isr. 133/D3
Teviot (riv.), Sc, UK 78/D6
Teviotdale (valley), Sc, UK 78/D6
Tewantin-Noosa, Austl. 156/D4
Tewkesbury, Eng, UK 74/D3
Texarkana, Tx, US 171/J4
Texas, Austl. 157/D1
Texas (state), US 174/C4
Texas City, Tx, US 171/J5
Texcoco, Mex. 185/R9
Texel (isl.), Neth. 82/C2
Texhoma, Ok, US 174/C2
Texmelucan, Mex. 185/L7
Texoma (lake), Ok,Tx, US 171/H4
Teyateyaneng, Les. 148/D3
Teykovo, Rus. 102/J4
Tezio (peak), It. 85/K5
Teziutlán, Mex. 185/M7
Tezonapa, Mex. 185/N8
Tezontepec, Mex. 185/L7
Tezontepec de Aldama, Mex. 185/K6
Tezoyuca, Mex. 185/R9
Tezpur, India 112/F6
Tezu, India 125/G2
Tezze, It. 101/E1
Tha-Anne (riv.), Nun., Can. 164/G2
Tha Chin (riv.), Thai. 120/B3
Thabana-Ntlenyana (peak), Les. 148/E3
Thabankulu (peak), SAfr. 149/E2
Thaen (pt.), Thai. 120/B4
Thai Binh, Viet. 125/J3
Thai Nguyen, Viet. 125/J3
Thailand (gulf), Asia 120/C4
Thailand (ctry.) 120/C3
Thākurdwāra, India 126/B1
Thal, Pak. 128/A3
Thal (des.), Pak. 128/A4
Thaleban NP, Thai. 120/C5
Thaleischweiler-Fröschen, Ger. 95/G5
Thalerhof (int'l arpt.), Aus. 85/L3
Thalgau, Aus. 97/G7
Thalheim bei Wels, Aus. 97/H6
Thalmässing, Ger. 96/E4
Thalwil, Swi. 99/E3
Thamar, Jabal (peak), Yem. 130/E6
Thame (riv.), Eng, UK 75/F3
Thames (riv.), On, Can. 172/D3
Thames, NZ 159/T10
Thames (riv), Eng., UK 75/G4
Thames Barrier, Eng, UK 72/D2
Thāna, India 131/K5
Thāna Bhawan, India 128/D5
Thānesar, India 128/D5
Thangool, Austl. 156/C4
Thanh Hoa, Viet. 125/J4
Thanjavur, India 124/C5
Thann, Fr. 98/D2
Thannhausen, Ger. 99/G1
Thaon-les-Vosges, Fr. 98/C1
Thar (des.), Pak. 128/A5
Tharād, India 131/K4
Thargomindah, Austl. 156/A5
Tharrawaddy, Myan. 125/G4
Thásos, Gre. 89/J2
Thásos (isl.), Gre. 89/J2
Thatcham, Eng, UK 75/E4
Thatcher, Az, US 170/E4
Thaton, Myan. 120/B2
Thaur, Aus. 99/H3
Thaya (riv.), Aus. 83/H4
Thayetmyo, Myan. 125/G4
Thayngen, Swi. 99/E2
Thazi, Myan. 125/G3
The Alamo, Tx, US 179/U21
The Dalles, Or, US 168/C4
The Hague ('s-Gravenhage) (cap.), Neth. 92/B4
The Oaks, Ca, US 178/B1
The Pas, Mb, Can. 169/H2
The Rock, Austl. 157/C2
The Valley (cap.), Angu. 183/N8
The Village, Ok, US 179/M14
The Woodlands, Tx, US 171/J5
The Wrekin (co.), Eng, UK 77/F6
Thebes (ruin), Egypt 143/C3
Theilheim, Ger. 96/D3
Thelma, Tx, US 179/T21
Thelon (riv.), NW,Nun., Can. 164/F2
Thémericourt, Fr. 72/H4
Theo (mt.), Austl. 155/F2
Theodore, Sk, Can. 169/H3
Theodore, Austl. 156/C4
Theodore Roosevelt (lake), Az, US 170/E4
Theodore Roosevelt NP, ND, US 169/G4
Thérain (riv.), Fr. 84/D2
Thermaic (gulf), Gre. 89/H2
Thérmi, Gre. 89/H2
Thermopilai (Thermopylae) (pass), Gre. 89/H3
Thermopolis, Wy, US 168/F5
Thérouanne (riv.), Fr. 72/L4
Thesprotikón, Gre. 89/G3
Thessalon, On, Can. 172/D2
Thessaloníki, Gre. 89/H2
Thessaly (reg.), Gre. 89/H3
Thet (riv.), Eng, UK 75/G2
Thetford, Eng, UK 75/G2
Thetford Mines, Qu, Can. 173/G2
Theunissen, SAfr. 148/D3
Theux, Belg. 95/E2
Thève (riv.), Fr. 72/K4
Theydon Bois, Eng, UK 72/D2
Thiais, Fr. 72/K5
Thíamis (riv.), Gre. 89/G3
Thiant, Fr. 94/C3
Thiaucourt-Regniéville, Fr. 95/E6
Thief River Falls, Mn, US 169/J3
Thielle (riv.), Swi. 98/C4
Thielsen (mt.), Or, US 168/C5
Thiene, It. 101/E1
Thiérache (reg.), Fr. 94/C4
Thierhaupten, Ger. 96/D5
Thiers, Fr. 84/E4
Thiers-sur-Thève, Fr. 72/K4
Thierville-sur-Meuse, Fr. 95/E5
Thiès (pol. reg.), Sen. 144/A3
Thiès, Sen. 144/A3
Thika, Kenya 146/C3
Thimphu (cap.), Bhu. 127/G2
Thingvellir NP, Ice. 79/N7
Thionville, Fr. 95/F5
Thíra, Gre. 89/J4
Thíra (isl.), Gre. 89/J4
Third Cataract (falls), Sudan 143/B5
Third Lake, Il, US 177/Q15
Thirlmere (lake), Eng, UK 77/E2
Thirsty (mt.), Austl. 154/D5
Thirtymile (pt.), NY, US 173/V9
Thise, Fr. 98/C3
Thisted, Den. 80/C3
Thistilfjördhur (estu.), Ice. 79/P6
Thistle (isl.), Austl. 155/H5
Thistle (mtn.), Yk, Can. 176/L3
Thitu (isl.) 121/B5
Thívai, Gre. 89/H3
Thiverval-Grignon, Fr. 72/H5
Thjósa (riv.), Ice. 79/N7
Thlewiaza (riv.), Nun., Can. 164/G2
Thoiry, Fr. 72/H5
Tholen (isl.), Neth. 92/B5
Tholen, Neth. 92/B5
Tholey, Ger. 95/G5
Thomaston, Ga, US 175/G3
Thomastown, Ire. 73/Q10
Thomasville, Al, US 175/G4
Thomasville, Ga, US 175/H4
Thomasville, NC, US 175/H3
Thomasville, Pa, US 180/B4
Thompson, Mb, Can. 169/J2
Thompson (riv.), BC, Can. 168/C3
Thompson (lake), Austl. 154/K7
Thompson Falls, Mt, US 168/E4
Thomsen (riv.), NW, Can. 164/E1
Thomson (riv.), Austl. 156/A4
Thomson, Ga, US 175/H3
Thongwa, Myan. 120/B2
Thonnance-lès-Joinville, Fr. 98/B1
Thonon-les-Bains, Fr. 98/C5
Thoreau, NM, US 170/E4
Thorens-Glières, Fr. 98/C6
Thorhild, Ab, Can. 168/E2
Thorigny-sur-Marne, Fr. 72/L5
Thorlákshöfn, Ice. 79/N7
Thornaby-on-Tees, Eng, UK 77/G2
Thornbury, Eng, UK 74/D3
Thorndale, Pa, US 180/C4
Thorne, Eng, UK 77/H4
Thorne Bay, Ak, US 176/M4
Thornhill, Sc, UK 78/B4
Thornhill, Sc, UK 76/E1
Thornhurst, Pa, US 180/C1
Thornton, Co, US 179/C3
Thornton, Ca, US 177/M10
Thornton Cleveleys, Eng, UK 77/E4
Thorold, On, Can. 173/R9
Thórshöfn, Ice. 79/P6
Thouars, Fr. 84/C3
Thouet (riv.), Fr. 84/C3
Thourotte, Fr. 94/B5
Thousand Oaks, Ca, US 178/B2
Thowa (riv.), Kenya 146/C3
Thrace (reg.), Gre.,Turk. 89/J2
Thracian (sea), Gre. 89/J2
Thredbo Village, Austl. 157/D3
Three Bridges, NJ, US 180/D2
Three Forks, Mt, US 168/F4
Three Guardsmen (mtn.), BC, Can. 176/L4
Three Hills, Ab, Can. 168/E3
Three Hummock (isl.), Austl. 157/C4
Three Kings (isls.), NZ 159/S9
Three Mile (isl.), Pa, US 180/B3
Three Pagodas (pass), Myan. 120/B3
Three Points (cape), Gha. 145/E5
Three Rivers, Mi, US 172/C3
Three Rivers, Austl. 154/C3
Three Springs, Austl. 154/B4
Thriuvananthapuram, India 124/C6
Throssell (lake), Austl. 156/E3
Thrushel (riv.), Eng, UK 74/B5
Thu Dau Mot, Viet. 120/D4
Thuin, Belg. 95/D3
Thuir, Fr. 84/E5
Thulba (riv.), Ger. 96/C2
Thule Air Base, Den. 165/T7
Thun, Swi. 98/D4
Thunderbird (lake), Ok, US 179/N15
Thuner See (lake), Swi. 85/G3
Thung Salaeng Luang NP, Thai. 120/C2
Thüngersheim, Ger. 96/C3
Thur (riv.), Swi. 85/H3
Thurgau (canton), Swi. 99/E2
Thüringen (state), Ger. 85/J1
Thüringen, Aus. 99/F3
Thüringer Schiefergebirge (mts.), Ger. 96/E2
Thüringer Wald (for.), Ger. 85/J1
Thurles, Ire. 73/Q10
Thurnau, Ger. 97/E2
Thurø By, Den. 80/D4
Thurrock (co.), Eng, UK 75/G3
Thurso, Sc, UK 73/V14
Thurston (isl.), Ant. 202/T
Thurston (co.), Wa, US 177/A3
Thury-en-Valois, Fr. 72/M4
Thusis, Swi. 99/F4
Thyez, Fr. 98/C5
Thyolo, Malw. 147/G4
Ti-m-Merhsoï (riv.), Niger 145/G2
Ti-n-Jedane, Oued (riv.), Alg. 141/G4
Ti-n-Zaouâten, Alg. 138/F4
Ti-Tree Abor. Land, Austl. 155/G2
Tiahuanco (ruin), Bol. 198/D5
Tian (pt.), BC, Can. 176/M5
Tian Shan (mts.), China 112/C3
Tianchang, China 114/D4
Tianguá, Braz. 196/B1
Tianguistenco, Mex. 185/Q10
Tianjin (mun.), China 113/L4
Tianjin, China 114/H7
Tianlin, China 125/J3
Tianmen, China 121/B1
Tianmu (mts.), China 114/K9
Tianshui, China 112/J5
Tianyang, China 121/A3
Tianzhen, China 114/C2
Tianzhu, China 125/J2
Tiaret, Alg. 142/F5
Tibagi, Braz. 197/B3
Tibaji (riv.), Braz. 197/B3
Tibaná, Col. 194/C3
Tibati, Camr. 138/H6
Tibba, Pak. 128/A5
Tibé, Pic de (peak), Gui. 144/C4
Tiber (Tevere) (riv.), It. 85/J5
Tiberias (lake), Isr. 133/D3
Tibesti (mts.), Chad 138/J3
Tibet (reg.), China 109/H6
Tibet (Xizang) (aut. reg.), China 112/D5
Tibro, Swe. 80/F2
Tiburon (cape), Haiti 183/G4
Tiburon, Ca, US 177/K11
Tiburón, Isla (isl.), Mex. 184/B2
Ticaco, Peru 198/D5
Tichigan (lake), Wi, US 177/P14
Tîchît, Dhar (cliff), Mrta. 144/C2
Ticino (canton), Swi. 99/E5
Ţicleni, Rom. 91/F3
Ticllos, Peru 198/B3
Ticonderoga, NY, US 172/F3
Ticul, Mex. 186/D1
Tidaholm, Swe. 80/E2
Tidikelt (plain), Alg. 138/F2
Tidjikdja, Mrta. 144/C2
Tidone (riv.), It. 100/C3
Tidore (isl.), Indo. 123/G3
Tidra, Île (isl.), Mrta. 144/A2
Tidsit (lake), WSah. 140/B5
Tiede, PN del, Sp. 140/A3
Tiefencastel, Swi. 99/F4
Tiel, Neth. 92/C5
Tieling, China 114/E2
Tielt, Belg. 94/C2
Tielt-Winge, Belg. 95/D2
Tiemba (riv.), C.d'Iv. 144/D4
Tienen, Belg. 95/D2
Tieri, Austl. 156/C3
Tieroko (peak), Chad 139/J3
Tierp, Swe. 80/G1
Tierra Amarilla, NM, US 170/F3
Tierra Blanca, Mex. 185/N8
Tierra Colorada, Mex. 185/F5
Tierra del Fuego (isl.), Arg. 201/D7
Tierra del Fuego, Antártida e Islas del Atlántico Sur, Arg. 201/C7
Tierra del Fuego, PN, Arg. 201/C7
Tierradentro, Col. 194/B4
Tierranueva, Mex. 185/E4
Tiétar (riv.), Sp. 86/C2
Tietê (riv.), Braz. 189/D5
Tiffin, Oh, US 172/D3
Tiflet, Mor. 142/A3
Tifton, Ga, US 175/H4
Tigeaux, Fr. 72/L5
Tighina (Bendery), Mol. 91/J2
Tighvein (hill), Sc, UK 78/A6
Tignère, Camr. 138/H6
Tignieu-Jameyzieu, Fr. 98/B6
Tigre (riv.), Ven. 192/C4
Tigre (riv.), Ven. 195/F2
Tigre, Arg. 201/J11
Tigris (riv.), Iraq 130/E2
Tigui (well), Chad 139/J4
Tiguidit, Falaise de (cliff), Niger 145/G2
Tigzirt, Alg. 142/H4
Tihosuco, Mex. 186/D1
Tihuatlán, Mex. 186/B1
Tiilikkajärven NP, Fin. 102/F3
Tijāra, India 126/A2
Tijuana, Mex. 178/C5
Tijuca, PN da, Braz. 197/K7
Tijucas, Braz. 197/B3
Tijuco (riv.), Braz. 197/B1
Tikal (ruin), Guat. 186/D2
Tikamgarh, India 126/B3
Tikchik (lakes), Ak, US 176/G3
Tikehau (isl.), FrPol. 159/L6
Tikhoretsk, Rus. 104/G3
Tikhvin, Rus. 102/G4
Tikrīt, Iraq 132/E3
Tikveš (lake), FYROM 89/H2
Tila, Mex. 186/C2
Tilburg, Neth. 92/C5
Tilbury, Eng, UK 72/E2
Tilden, Tx, US 174/D4
Tilghman, Md, US 180/B6
Tilghman (isl.), Md, US 180/B6
Tilhar, India 126/B2
Tilin, Myan. 125/F3
Tilisarao, Arg. 200/D2
Till (riv.), Eng, UK 78/D5
Tillabéri (dept.), Niger 145/F3
Tillabéri, Niger 145/F3
Tillamook, Or, US 168/C4
Tille (riv.), Fr. 82/C5
Tillicoultry, Sc, UK 78/C4
Tilst, Den. 80/D3
Tilt (riv.), Sc, UK 78/C3
Tiltil, Chile 200/N8
Tim, Den. 80/C3
Timan (ridge), Rus. 106/F3
Timaná, Col. 194/C4
Timanfaya, PN de, Sp. 140/B3
Timaru, NZ 159/S11
Timashevsk, Rus. 104/F3
Timbákion, Gre. 89/J5
Timbaúba, Braz. 196/D2
Timbédra, Mrta. 144/C2
Timber Lake, SD, US 169/H4
Timberlane, La, US 179/Q17
Timberwood Park, Tx, US 179/U20
Timbiquí, Col. 194/B4
Timbiras, Braz. 196/B2
Timbó, Braz. 197/B3
Timboon, Austl. 157/B3
Timehri (int'l arpt.), Guy. 195/G3
Timelkam, Aus. 97/G6
Timfristós (peak), Gre. 89/G3
Timimoun, Alg. 141/F3
Timiris (cape), Mrta. 144/A2
Timiş (prov.), Rom. 90/E3
Timiş (riv.), Rom. 90/E3
Timişoara (int'l arpt.), Rom. 90/E3
Timişoara, Rom. 90/E3
Timmins, On, Can. 172/D1
Timms (hill), Wi, US 169/L4
Timnath, Co, US 179/C1
Timon, Braz. 196/B2
Timonium, Md, US 180/B5
Timor (isl.), ETim.,Indo. 123/F5
Timor (sea), Asia,Austl. 123/G5
Timóteo, Braz. 197/D1
Timpanogos Cave Nat'l Mon., Ut, US 170/E2
Timpanogos Nat'l Mon., Ut, US 179/K13
Timpson, Tx, US 171/J5
Timpton (riv.), Rus. 107/N4
Tims Ford (lake), Tn, US 175/G3
Timurnī, India 126/A4
Tin Can Bay, Austl. 156/D4
Tin Shui Wai, China 113/T10
Tina (riv.), SAfr. 148/B1
Tinaca (pt.), Phil. 121/E6
Tinaco, Ven. 194/D2
Tindivanam, India 124/C5
Tindouf, Alg. 140/C4
Tindouf (prov.), Alg. 140/D3
Tineo, Sp. 86/B1
Tingalpa (res.), Austl. 156/F7
Tingaringy NP, Austl. 157/D3
Tingha, Austl. 157/D1
Tingi (mts.), SLeo. 144/C4
Tingmerkpuk (mtn.), Ak, US 176/F2
Tingo María, Peru 198/C3
Tingsryd, Swe. 80/F3
Tinguiririca (vol.), Chile 200/C2
Tinharé, Ilha de (isl.), Braz. 193/L6
Tinian (isl.), NMar. 158/D3
Tinicum Nat'l Consv. Area, Pa, US 180/C4
Tinkisso (riv.), Gui. 144/C4
Tinley Park, Il, US 177/Q16
Tinogasta, Arg. 199/C2
Tinos, Gre. 89/J4
Tínos (isl.), Gre. 89/J4
Tinqueux, Fr. 94/C5
Tinrhir, Mor. 140/D3
Tinta, Peru 198/D4
Tintagel (pt.), Eng, UK 74/B5
Tintern Abbey, Eng, UK 74/D3
Tintigny, Belg. 95/E4
Tintinara, Austl. 157/B2
Tinto (riv.), Sp. 86/B4
Tinto (peak), Sc, UK 78/C5
Tinton Falls (New Shrewsbury), NJ, US 180/D3
Tinyahuarco, Peru 198/B3
Tioga, ND, US 169/H3
Tioman (isl.), Malay. 122/B3
Tione di Trento, It. 99/G5
Tipasa (prov.), Alg. 142/F4
Tipasa, Alg. 142/G4
Tipperary, Ire. 73/P10
Tiptūr, India 124/C5
Tir Rhiwiog (peak), Wal, UK 74/C1
Tiracambu, Serra do (mts.), Braz. 193/J4
Tiran (str.), Egypt, SA 143/C3
Tiran (isl.), Egypt,SAr 143/C3
Tirān (isl.), Egypt 139/M2
Tiranë (cap.), Alb. 89/F2
Tirano, It. 99/G5
Tirari (des.), Austl. 155/H4
Tiraspol, Mol. 91/J2
Tirat Karmel, Isr. 133/F6
Tire, Turk. 132/A2
Tirebolu, Turk. 104/F4
Tiree (isl.), Sc, UK 73/Q8
Tirest (well), Mali 145/F1
Tîrgovişte, Rom. 91/G3
Tîrgu Bujor, Rom. 91/H3
Tîrgu Cărbuneşti, Rom. 91/F3
Tîrgu Frumos, Rom. 91/H2
Tîrgu Jiu, Rom. 91/F3
Tîrgu Lăpuş, Rom. 91/F2
Tîrgu Mureş, Rom. 91/G2
Tîrgu Neamţ, Rom. 91/H2
Tîrgu Ocna, Rom. 91/H2
Tîrgu Secuiesc, Rom. 91/H2
Tirich Mīr (peak), Pak. 131/K1
Tiris (reg.), WSah. 140/B5
Tiris Zemmour (pol. reg.), Mrta. 140/C4
Tîrnava Mare (riv.), Rom. 91/G2
Tîrnava Mică (riv.), Rom. 91/F2
Tîrnăveni, Rom. 91/G2
Tírnavos, Gre. 89/H3
Tiros, Braz. 197/C1
Tirschenreuth, Ger. 97/F3
Tirstrup (int'l arpt.), Den. 80/D3
Tiruchchirāppalli, India 124/C5
Tiruchendūr, India 124/C6
Tiruchengodu, India 124/C5
Tirunelveli, India 124/C6
Tiruntán, Peru 198/C2
Tirupati, India 124/C5
Tiruppattūr, India 124/C5
Tiruppūr, India 124/C5
Tiruvannāmalai, India 124/C5
Tisa (riv.), Ukr. 91/G1
Tisdale, Sk, Can. 169/G2
Tishomingo, Ok, US 171/H4
Tissa, Mor. 142/B2
Tissemsilt (prov.), Alg. 142/F5
Tissemsilt, Alg. 142/F5
Tista (riv.), Bang. 127/G2
Tisza (riv.), Hun. 104/B3
Tiszaföldvár, Hun. 90/E2
Tiszafüred, Hun. 90/E2
Tiszakécske, Hun. 90/E2
Tiszalök, Hun. 90/E1
Tiszavasvári, Hun. 83/L5
Titano (peak), SMar. 101/F5
Titel, Serb. 90/E3
Titicaca (lake), Bol.,Peru 198/D4
Titisee-Neustadt, Ger. 98/E2
Titlagarh, India 124/D3
Titlis (peak), Swi. 99/E4
Tito, It. 88/D2
Titov Veles, FYROM 89/G2
Titov vrh (peak), FYROM 89/G2
Titting, Ger. 96/E5
Tittmoning, Ger. 97/F6
Titu, Rom. 91/G3
Titusville, Fl, US 175/H4
Titusville, NJ, US 180/D3
Tiva (riv.), Kenya 146/C3
Tivaouane, Sen. 144/A3
Tivat, Mont. 90/D4
Tiverton, Eng, UK 74/C5
Tiwanacu, Bol. 198/D5
Tixán, Ecu. 198/B1
Tixtla de Guerrero, Mex. 185/F5
Tizayuca, Mex. 185/L7
Tizi Ouzou (prov.), Alg. 142/H4
Tizi Ouzou, Alg. 142/H4
Tizimín, Mex. 186/D1
Tiznap (riv.), China 131/L1
Tiznit, Mor. 140/C3
Tjæreborg, Den. 80/C4
Tjeldstø, Nor. 80/A1
Tjeukemeer (lake), Neth. 92/C3
Tjøme, Nor. 80/D2
Tjorn (isl.), Swe. 80/D3
Tlachichuca, Mex. 185/M7
Tlacolula de Matamoros, Mex. 186/B2
Tlacotalpan, Mex. 185/P8
Tlacotepec, Mex. 185/F5
Tlahualilo de Zaragoza, Mex. 184/E3
Tlalixcoyan, Mex. 185/N8
Tlalmanalco, Mex. 185/Q10
Tlalnepantla, Mex. 185/Q9
Tláloc (vol.), Mex. 185/Q10
Tlaltenango de Sánchez Román, Mex. 184/E4
Tlaltizapan, Mex. 185/K8
Tlapa de Comonfort, Mex. 186/B2
Tlapacoya (ruin), Mex. 185/Q10
Tlapacoyan, Mex. 185/M7
Tlapehuala, Mex. 185/E5
Tlaquepaque, Mex. 184/E4
Tlaquiltenango, Mex. 185/K8
Tlatlauquitepec, Mex. 185/M7
Tlaxcala (state), Mex. 182/A5
Tlaxcala, Mex. 185/L7
Tlaxco, Mex. 185/L7
Tlaxcoapan, Mex. 185/K6
Tlell, BC, Can. 176/M5
Tlemcen, Alg. 142/D2
Toabré, Pan. 187/F4
Toaca (peak), Rom. 91/G2
Toachi (riv.), Ecu. 194/B4
Toamasina, Madg. 149/J7
Toamasina (prov.), Madg. 149/J7
Toandos (pen.), Wa, US 177/B2
Toau (isl.), FrPol. 159/L6
Toay, Arg. 200/D3
Toba (lake), Indo. 122/A3
Toba (inlet), BC, Can. 168/B3
Toba, China 112/G5
Toba, Japan 119/L7
Toba Kākar (range), Pak. 131/J2
Toba Tek Singh, Pak. 128/B4
Tobago (isl.), Trin. 192/F1
Tobarra, Sp. 86/E3
Tobbio (peak), It. 100/B3
Tobermore, NI, UK 76/B2
Tōbetsu, Japan 118/B2
Tobias Barreto, Braz. 196/C3
Tobin (lake), Austl. 154/E2
Tobique (riv.), NB, Can. 173/H2
Tobishima, Japan 119/L5
Tobol (riv.), Rus. 103/Q5
Tobu, Japan 119/A1
Tobyhanna (lake), Pa, US 180/C1
Tobyhanna (riv.), Pa, US 180/C1
Tobyhanna, Pa, US 180/C1
Tobyhanna St. Park, Pa, US 180/C1
Tobyl (riv.), Kaz. 105/M1
Tobysh (riv.), Rus. 103/L2
Tocache, Peru 198/B3
Tocantinópolis, Braz. 196/A2
Tocantins (riv.), Braz. 189/E4
Tocantins (state), Braz. 196/A3
Toccoa, Ga, US 175/H3
Toce (riv.), It. 85/H3
Tochigi (pref.), Japan 117/F2
Tochigi, Japan 117/F2
Tochimilco, Mex. 185/L8
Tochio, Japan 117/F2
Tocina, Sp. 86/C4
Töcksfors, Swe. 80/D2
Toco, Trin. 195/F2
Tocopilla, Chile 199/B1
Tocumen, Pan. 187/G4
Tocumwal, Austl. 157/C2
Tocuyito, Ven. 194/D2
Tocuyo (riv.), Ven. 192/E1
Toda, Japan 119/D2
Toda Bhīm, India 124/C2
Todi, It. 88/C1
Tödi (peak), Swi. 99/E4
Todmorden, Eng, UK 77/F4
Todos os Santos, Baiaa de (bay), Braz. 196/C4
Todos Santos, Mex. 184/C4
Todtmoos, Ger. 98/E2
Todtnau, Ger. 98/D2
Toffal (hill), Mrta. 140/C5
Toffo, Ben. 145/F5
Tofield, Ab, Can. 168/E2
Tofua (isl.), Tonga 159/H6
Tōgane, Japan 119/E2
Togba (well), Mrta. 144/C2
Toggenburg (valley), Swi. 99/F3
Togher, Ire. 76/B5
Togiak, Ak, US 176/F4
Togo (ctry.) 145/F4
Tōgō, Japan 119/M5
Tögrög, Mong. 112/F2
Togtoh, China 114/B2
Tōgyu-san NP, SKor. 115/D5
Tohāna, India 128/C5
Tohatchi, NM, US 174/A3
Tōhoku (prov.), Japan 117/F1
Toi, Japan 117/F3
Tōin, Japan 119/L5
Toiyabe (range), Nv, US 170/C3
Tojō, Japan 116/C3
Tōjō, Japan 119/H6
Tok, Ak, US 176/K3
Tokachi (riv.), Japan 118/C2
Tōkai, Japan 119/L5
Tokaj, Hun. 83/L4
Tōkamachi, Japan 117/F2
Tokar Nat'l Rsv., Sudan 143/B4
Tokara (isls.), Japan 117/K6
Tokat, Turk. 132/D1
Tokat (prov.), Turk. 132/D1
Tŏkchŏk (isl.), NKor. 115/C4

280
Tŏkch – Tsuen

Tŏkchŏk (arch.), NKor. 115/C4
Tokeen, Ak, US 176/M4
Tokelau (terr.), NZ 159/H5
Toki, Japan 119/M5
Toki (riv.), Japan 119/M5
Tokigawa, Japan 119/C2
Tokoname, Japan 119/L6
Tokoro (riv.), Japan 118/C2
Tokoro, Japan 118/D1
Tokoroa, NZ 159/T10
Tokorozawa, Japan 117/F3
Toksook Bay, Ak, US 176/E3
Toksun, China 112/E3
Tokuno (isl.), Japan 117/K7
Tokunoshima, Japan 117/K7
Tokushima (pref.), Japan 116/C4
Tokushima, Japan 116/D3
Tokuyama, Japan 116/B3
Tōkyō (cap.), Japan 117/F3
Tōkyō (pref.), Japan 117/F3
Tōkyō (bay), Japan 119/D2
Tōkyō Disneyland, Japan 119/D2
Tola, Nic. 186/E4
Tolbo, Mong. 112/F2
Toledo, Braz. 199/F1
Toledo, Phil. 121/D5
Toledo, Oh, US 172/D3
Toledo, Sp. 86/C3
Toledo, Col. 194/C3
Toledo, Uru. 201/K11
Toledo Bend (dam), La,Tx, US 171/J5
Toledo Bend (res.), La,Tx, US 171/J5
Toledo, Montes de (mts.), Sp. 86/C3
Tolentino, It. 85/K5
Tolfa, It. 88/B1
Tolhuaca, PN, Chile 200/C3
Toli, China 112/D2
Toliara (prov.), Madg. 149/H8
Toliara, Madg. 149/G8
Tolima (dept.), Col. 194/C3
Tolitoli, Indo. 123/F3
Tolka (riv.), Ire. 76/B5
Tolleson, Az, US 179/R19
Tolmezzo, It. 85/K3
Tolna (prov.), Hun. 90/D2
Tolna, Hun. 90/D2
Tolo (chan.), China 113/U10
Tolo, Gulf of (gulf), Indo. 123/F4
Tolosa, Sp. 86/D1
Tolsan (isl.), SKor. 115/D5
Tolt (riv.), Wa, US 177/D2
Tolt (res.), Wa, US 177/D2
Tolt, North Fork (riv.), Wa, US 177/D2
Tolt, South Fork (riv.), Wa, US 177/D2
Toltén, Chile 200/B3
Toltén (riv.), Chile 200/B3
Tolú, Col. 194/C2
Toluca, Mex. 185/Q10
Tolúviejo, Col. 194/C2
Tol'yatti, Rus. 105/J1
Tom' (riv.), Rus. 106/J4
Tom Price, Austl. 154/C2
Tom White (mt.), Ak, US 176/K3
Tomakomai, Japan 118/B2
Tomamae, Japan 118/B1
Tomar, Port. 86/A3
Tómaros (peak), Gre. 89/G3
Tomarza, Turk. 132/C2
Tomás, Peru 198/C4
Tomás de Berlanga, Ecu. 198/E7
Tomaszów Lubelski, Pol. 83/M3
Tomaszów Mazowiecki, Pol. 83/L3
Tomatlán, Mex. 184/D5
Tomb of Qinshihuang, China 114/B4
Tombador, Serra do (mts.), Braz. 192/G6
Tombigbee (riv.), Al,Ms, US 175/F3
Tombolo, It. 101/E1
Tombouctou, Mali 144/E2
Tombouctou (pol. reg.), Mali 140/D5
Tombstone, Az, US 170/E5
Tombua, Ang. 147/B4
Tomé, Chile 200/B3
Tomé, Île (isl.), Fr. 84/B2
Tomelilla, Swe. 80/E4
Tomelloso, Sp. 86/D3
Tomika, Japan 119/L5
Tomini (gulf), Indo. 123/F4
Tomiño, Sp. 86/A2
Tomioka, Japan 119/B1
Tomisato, Japan 119/E2
Tomiura, Japan 119/D3
Tomiyama, Japan 117/F3
Tomizawa, Japan 119/A3
Tommot, Rus. 107/N4
Tomo (riv.), Col. 192/E2
Tompa, Hun. 90/D2
Tompkinsville, Ky, US 172/C4
Toms (riv.), NJ, US 180/D3
Toms River, NJ, US 180/D4
Tomsk, Rus. 106/J4
Tomskskaya Oblast, Rus. 106/H4
Tömük, Turk. 133/D1
Tonalá, Mex. 186/C2
Tonale, Passo del (pass), It. 99/G5
Tonasket, Wa, US 168/D3
Tonawanda, NY, US 173/S9
Tonawanda Ind. Res., NY, US 173/S9
Tonbridge, Eng, UK 72/D3
Toncontín (int'l arpt.), Hon. 186/E3
Tondabayashi, Japan 119/J7
Tondano, Indo. 123/F3
Tondou, Massif du (plat.), CAfr.,Sudan 139/K6
Tondu (peak), Fr. 98/C6
Tone (riv.), Japan 117/G3
Tone, Japan 119/E2
Tonekābon, Iran 130/F1
Tonelagee (peak), Ire. 76/B5
Tonga (ctry.) 159/H7
Tongaat, SAfr. 149/E3
Tongareva (Penrhyn) (isl.), CookIs. 159/J5
Tongariro NP, NZ 159/T10
Tongatapu (isl.), Tonga 159/H7
Tongbai, China 114/C4
Tongbu, SKor. 115/G6
Tongcheng, China 121/B2
Tongcheng, China 114/D5
T'ongch'ŏn, NKor. 115/D3
Tongchuan, China 114/B4
Tongdao Dongzu Zizhixian, China 125/J2
Tongduch'on, SKor. 115/G6
Tongeren, Belg. 95/E2
Tonggu (peak), China 113/L7
Tonggu, China 125/K2
Tonghae, SKor. 115/E4
Tonghua, China 115/C2
Tonghua, China 115/C2
Tongliao, China 114/E2
Tongling, China 113/L5
Tongno (riv.), NKor. 115/D2
Tongo (peak), Indo. 123/E5
Tongobory, Madg. 149/H8
Tongren, China 125/J2
Tongsa (riv.), Bhu. 127/H2
Tongsa Dzong, Bhu. 127/H2
Tongshan, China 121/B2
Tongue (riv.), Mt, US 168/G4
Tongue, Sc, UK 73/R7
Tongxu, China 114/C4
Tongyu, China 113/M3
Tongzi, China 121/A2
Tonino-Anivskiy (pen.), Rus. 118/C1
Tönisvorst, Ger. 92/D6
Tonk, India 131/L3
Tonkawa, Ok, US 171/H3
Tonkin (gulf), China,Viet. 120/D1
Tonkoui (peak), C.d'Iv. 144/D5
Tonle Sap (lake), Camb. 125/H5
Tonneins, Fr. 84/D4
Tonnerre, Fr. 84/E3
Tönning, Ger. 80/C4
Tōno, Japan 118/B4
Tonopah, Nv, US 170/C3
Tonoshō, Japan 116/D3
Tonosí, Pan. 187/F5
Tonota, Bots. 147/E5
Tons (riv.), India 126/C3
Tønsberg, Nor. 80/D2
Tonsina, Ak, US 176/J3
Tonstad, Nor. 80/B2
Tonto Nat'l For., Az, US 179/S18
Tonto Nat'l Mon., Az, US 170/E4
Tonya, Turk. 132/D1
Ton-y-Pandy, Wal, UK 74/C3
Toodyay, Austl. 154/C4
Tooele, Ut, US 179/J12
Tooele (co.), Ut, US 179/J13
Tooradin, Austl. 157/C3
Toowoomba, Austl. 156/C4
Top (mt.), Austl. 155/G2
Topanaga State Park, Ca, US 178/B2
Topanga, Ca, US 178/B2
Topanga Beach, Ca, US 178/E7
Tope de Coroa (mtn.), CpV. 135/J10
Topia, Mex. 184/D3
Topley, BC, Can. 168/B2
Toplița, Rom. 91/G2
Topol'čany, Slvk. 83/K4
Topolobampo, Mex. 184/C3
Topoloveni, Rom. 91/G3
Topolovgrad, Bul. 91/H4
Topozero (lake), Rus. 79/J2
Toppenish, Wa, US 168/C4
Toprakkale, Turk. 133/E1
Topton, Pa, US 180/C3
Tor (bay), Eng, UK 74/C6
Torahime, Japan 119/K5
Torata, Peru 198/D5
Torawitan (cape), Indo. 123/G3
Torbalı, Turk. 132/A2
Torbat-e Ḩeydarīyeh, Iran 131/G1
Torbat-e Jām, Iran 129/D5
Torbay, Nf, Can. 173/L2
Torbay (co.), Eng, UK 74/C6
Torbeck, Haiti 187/H2
Torbert (mt.), Ak, US 176/H3
Torcy, Fr. 72/K5
Tordera (riv.), Sp. 87/L6
Tordesillas, Sp. 86/C2
Töreboda, Swe. 80/F2
Torelló, Sp. 87/G1
Torfaen (co.), Wal, UK 74/C3
Torgelow, Ger. 80/E5
Torghay, Kaz. 129/D3
Torghay (riv.), Kaz. 129/D3
Torghay Üstirti (plat.), Kaz. 129/D2
Torhamnsudde (pt.), Swe. 80/F3
Torhout, Belg. 94/C1
Tori-shima (isl.), Japan 158/D1
Toride, Japan 119/E2
Torigni-sur-Vire, Fr. 84/C2
Torii-tōge (pass), Japan 117/E3
Toriñana (cape), Sp. 86/A1
Torino (prov.), It. 100/A2
Torino (Turin), It. 85/G4
Torkestān (mts.), Afg. 131/H1
Tormes (riv.), Sp. 86/C2
Torndirrup NP, Austl. 154/C5
Torne (riv.), Eng, UK 77/H4
Torneälven (riv.), Swe. 102/D2
Tornesch, Ger. 93/G1
Tornik (peak), Serb. 90/D4
Tornio, Fin. 79/H2
Tornionjoki (riv.), Fin. 79/G2
Toro, Sp. 86/C2
Toro, Cerro del (peak), Arg.,Chile 199/C2
Toro Nat'l Rsv., Ugan. 146/A2
Toro, PN, Ven. 194/D2
Törökbálint, Hun. 91/Q10
Törökszentmiklό, Hun. 90/E2
Toronaic (gulf), Gre. 89/H2
Torondoy, Ven. 194/D2
Toronto (cap.), On, Can. 173/R8
Toronto (isl.), On, Can. 173/R8
Toropets, Rus. 81/P3
Tororo, Ugan. 146/B2
Torote (riv.), Sp. 87/N8
Torp (int'l arpt.), Nor. 80/D2
Torpa, Swe. 80/E3
Torquay, Austl. 157/C3
Torquay, Eng, UK 74/C6
Torquemada, Sp. 86/C1
Torr (pt.), NI, UK 76/B1
Torrance, Ca, US 178/F8
Torraz, Tête du (peak), Fr. 98/C6
Torrazza Piemonte, It. 100/A2
Torre de Moncorvo, Port. 86/B2
Torre dè Passeri, It. 88/C1
Torre del Campo, Sp. 86/D4
Torre del Greco, It. 88/D2
Torre del Lago Puccini, It. 100/D5
Torre-Pacheco, Sp. 87/E4
Torrebelvicino, It. 101/E1
Torreblanca, Sp. 87/F2
Torredonjimeno, Sp. 86/D4
Torreglia, It. 101/E2
Torrejón de Ardoz, Sp. 87/N9
Torrejoncillo, Sp. 86/B3
Torrelaguna, Sp. 86/D2
Torrelavega, Sp. 86/C1
Torrelodones, Sp. 87/N8
Torremaggiore, It. 88/D2
Torremolinos, Sp. 86/C4
Torrens (isl.), Austl. 155/M8
Torrens (lake), Austl. 155/H4
Torrens (riv.), Austl. 155/M8
Torrente, Sp. 87/E3
Torreón, Mex. 184/E3
Torreperogil, Sp. 86/D3
Tôrres, Braz. 197/B4
Torres (str.), Austl.,PNG 158/D6
Torres (isls.), Van. 158/F6
Torres del Paine, PN, Chile 201/B6
Torres Novas, Port. 86/A3
Torres Vedras, Port. 86/A3
Torrevieja, Sp. 87/E4
Torri di Quartesolo, It. 101/E1
Torridge (riv.), Eng, UK 74/B5
Torrijos, Sp. 86/C3
Torrington, Wy, US 169/G5
Torrita di Siena, It. 85/J5
Torroella de Montgrí, Sp. 87/G1
Torrone Alto (peak), Swi. 99/F5
Torrox, Sp. 86/D4
Torsa (riv.), Bhu. 127/G2
Torsås, Swe. 80/F3
Torsby, Swe. 80/E1
Tórshavn, Den. 202/G
Tortola (isl.), UK 183/J4
Tortolì, It. 88/A3
Tortona, It. 100/B3
Tortosa (cape), Sp. 87/F2
Tortosa, Sp. 87/F2
Tortuga (isl.), Haiti 183/H5
Tortuguero, PN, CR 187/F4
Tortum, Turk. 105/G4
Torūd, Iran 131/F1
Torugart (pass), Kyr. 129/G4
Torul, Turk. 132/D1
Toruń, Pol. 83/K2
Torup, Swe. 80/E3
Tory (isl.), Ire. 73/P9
Torysa (riv.), Slvk. 83/L4
Torzhok, Rus. 102/G4
Tosa, Japan 116/C4
Tosagua, Ecu. 194/A5
Tosashimizu, Japan 116/C4
Toscana (reg.), It. 100/C4
Toscana (prov.), It. 85/J5
Toscanella, It. 101/E4
Toscolano-Maderno, It. 100/D1
Toshi (isl.), Japan 119/L6
Toshibetsu (riv.), Japan 118/A2
Toshkent (pol. reg.), Uzb. 129/E4
Tosna (riv.), Rus. 103/T7
Tosno, Rus. 81/P2
Tosontsengel, Mong. 112/G2
Töss (riv.), Swi. 85/H3
Tosson (hill), Eng, UK 78/E6
Tostado, Arg. 199/D2
Tostedt, Ger. 93/G2
Tosu, Japan 116/B4
Tosya, Turk. 132/C1
Totana, Sp. 86/E4
Totness, Sur. 195/G3
Totowa, NJ, US 181/J8
Totten (inlet), Wa, US 177/A3
Tottenham, Austl. 157/C2
Tottington, Eng, UK 77/F4
Tottori, Japan 116/D3
Tottori (pref.), Japan 116/C3
Totutla, Mex. 185/N7
Touat (reg.), Alg. 141/E4
Touba, C.d'Iv. 144/D4
Toubkal (peak), Mor. 140/D3
Toubkal, PN du, Mor. 140/D3
Touchwood (hills), Sk, Can. 169/G3
Toucy, Fr. 84/E3
Toudao (riv.), China 115/D1
Tougan, Burk. 144/E3
Touggourt, Alg. 141/G2
Toughkenamon, Pa, US 180/C4
Touiel (riv.), Alg. 142/G5
Toul, Fr. 95/E6
Toulnustouc (riv.), Qu, Can. 173/H1
Toulon, Fr. 84/F5
Toulouse, Fr. 84/D5
Toumo (well), Niger 138/H3
Toumodi, C.d'Iv. 144/D5
Toungoo, Myan. 125/G4
Touquin, Fr. 72/M5
Toura, Monts du (mts.), C.d'Iv. 144/D5
Tourcoing, Fr. 94/C2
Tourfourine (well), Mali 140/D4
Tourlaville, Fr. 84/C2
Tournai, Belg. 94/C2
Tournan-en-Brie, Fr. 72/L5
Tournus, Fr. 98/A4
Touros, Braz. 196/D2
Tours, Fr. 84/D3
Tous, Embalse de (res.), Sp. 87/E3
Toussidé (peak), Chad 138/J3
Toussoro (peak), CAfr. 139/K6
Touws (riv.), SAfr. 148/C4
Touwsrivier, SAfr. 148/M10
Toužim, Czh. 97/G2
Töv (prov.), Mong. 112/J2
Tovar, Ven. 194/D2
Tove (riv.), Eng, UK 75/E2
Towaco, NJ, US 181/H8
Towada, Japan 117/G2
Towada (lake), Japan 118/B3
Towada-Hachimantai NP, Japan 118/B3
Tower City, Pa, US 180/B2
Tower Hamlets (bor.), Eng, UK 72/A1
Tower of London, Eng, UK 72/C2
Towner, ND, US 169/H3
Townsend, Mt, US 168/F4
Townsend, De, US 180/C5
Townsend (mt.), Wa, US 177/A2
Townsends (inlet), NJ, US 180/D5
Townshend (cape), Austl. 156/C3
Townsville, Austl. 156/B2
Towson, Md, US 180/B5
Towuti (lake), Indo. 123/F4
Toya (lake), Japan 118/B2
Toyah, Tx, US 174/C4
Toyahvale, Tx, US 174/C4
Toyama, Japan 117/E2
Toyama (pref.), Japan 117/E2
Toyang, SKor. 115/D5
Toyoake, Japan 119/M5
Toyohashi, Japan 117/E3
Toyokawa, Japan 117/E3
Toyonaka, Japan 119/H6
Toyono, Japan 119/H6
Toyo'oka, Japan 116/D3
Toyosato, Japan 119/E1
Toyosato, Japan 119/K5
Toyoshina, Japan 117/E2
Toyota, Japan 119/M5
Toyotomi, Japan 119/B2
Toyoyama, Japan 119/L5
Tozeur, Tun. 141/H2
Tozeur (gov.), Tun. 141/G2
Tozi (mt.), Ak, US 176/H2
Tra Vinh, Viet. 120/D4
Traben-Trarbach, Ger. 95/G4
Trabuco Canyon, Ca, US 178/C3
Trabzon, Turk. 132/D1
Trabzon (prov.), Turk. 132/D1
Tracadie, NB, Can. 173/H2
Trachselwald, Swi. 98/D3
Tracy, Qu, Can. 172/F2
Tracy, Mo, US 179/D5
Tracyton, Wa, US 177/B2
Tradate, It. 100/B1
Trafalgar (cape), Sp. 86/B4
Trafford (co.), Eng, UK 77/F5
Tragwein, Aus. 97/H6
Traiguén, Chile 200/B3
Trail, BC, Can. 168/D3
Traipu, Braz. 196/C3
Trairi, Braz. 196/C1
Traisen (riv.), Aus. 83/H5
Traiskirchen, Aus. 91/N7
Traismauer, Aus. 83/H4
Trakai NP, Lith. 81/L4
Traki, Lith. 81/L4
Tralee, Ire. 73/P10
Tramandaí, Braz. 197/B4
Tramelan, Swi. 98/D3
Tramin (Termeno), It. 99/H5
Tranås, Swe. 80/F2
Tranbjerg, Den. 80/D3
Trancoso, Port. 86/B2
Tranebjerg, Den. 80/D4
Tranemo, Swe. 80/E3
Tranent, Sc, UK 78/D5
Tranet (peak), Fr. 95/D4
Trang, Thai. 120/B5
Trangan (isl.), Indo. 123/H5
Trangie, Austl. 157/C2
Trängsletsjön (lake), Swe. 80/E1
Trani, It. 88/E2
Tranoroa, Madg. 149/H9
Transantarctic (mts.), Ant. 202/W
Transylvania (reg.), Rom. 90/F2
Transylvanian Alps (mts.), Rom. 90/F3
Trapani, It. 88/C3
Trapper (peak), Mt, US 168/E4
Trappes, Fr. 72/J5
Traralgon, Austl. 157/C3
Trarza (pol. reg.), Mrta. 138/B4
Trasacco, It. 88/C2
Trasimeno (lake), It. 85/K5
Träslövsläge, Swe. 80/E3
Trat, Thai. 120/C3
Traun (riv.), Aus. 82/H4
Traun, Aus. 97/H6
Traunreut, Ger. 97/F6
Traunsee (lake), Aus. 85/K3
Traunstein, Ger. 97/F7
Trautmannsdorf an der Leitha, Aus. 91/P7
Travagliato, It. 100/D1
Trave (riv.), Ger. 82/F2
Travedona Monate, It. 100/B1
Travellers (lake), Austl. 157/B2
Travemunde, Ger. 82/F2
Traverse (peak), Ak, US 176/G2
Traverse (lake), Mn, SD, US 169/J4
Traverse City, Mi, US 172/C2
Traversetolo, It. 100/D3
Travis (lake), Tx, US 174/D4
Travis AFB, Ca, US 177/L10
Travnik, Bosn. 90/C3
Trawsalt (peak), Wal, UK 74/C2
Trawsfynydd, Llyn (lake), Wal, UK 76/D6
Trbovlje, Slov. 85/L3
Tré-la-Tête (peak), Fr. 98/C6
Treachery (mt.), Austl. 155/G2
Trebaseleghe, It. 101/F1
Trebbia (riv.), It. 85/H4
Trebel (riv.), Ger. 82/G1
Třebíč, Czh. 83/H4
Trebinje, Bosn. 89/F1
Trebisacce, It. 88/E3
Třeboň, Czh. 97/H4
Trebonne, Austl. 156/B2
Trebujena, Sp. 86/B4
Trebur, Ger. 96/B3
Trecate, It. 100/B2
Tregnago, It. 101/E1
Treia, Ger. 80/C4
Treig (lake), Sc, UK 78/B3
Treinta de Agosto, Arg. 200/E3
Treinta y Tres (dept.), Uru. 201/G2
Treinta y Tres, Uru. 201/G2
Trélazé, Fr. 84/C3
Trelew, Arg. 200/D4
Trélissac, Fr. 84/D4
Trelleborg, Swe. 80/E4
Tremadoc (bay), Wal, UK 76/D6
Tremblestown (riv.), Ire. 76/B4
Trembleur (lake), BC, Can. 168/B2
Tremelo, Belg. 95/D2
Tremiti (isl.), It. 88/D1
Tremont, Pa, US 180/B2
Třemošná (riv.), Czh. 97/G3
Tremp, Sp. 87/F1
Třemšín (peak), Czh. 97/G3
Trenche (riv.), Qu, Can. 172/F1
Trenčiansky (pol. reg.), Slvk. 83/J4
Trenčín, Slvk. 83/K4
Trenel, Arg. 200/D2
Trenque Lauquen, Arg. 200/E2
Trent (riv.), Eng, UK 77/F6
Trent and Mersey (canal), Eng, UK 77/F6
Trentino-Alto Adige (pol. reg.), It. 85/J3
Trento, It. 99/H5
Trento (prov.), It. 99/G5
Trenton, On, Can. 172/E2
Trenton, Ga, US 175/G3
Trenton, Fl, US 175/H4
Trenton, Tn, US 172/B5
Trenton, Mo, US 171/J2
Trenton (cap.), NJ, US 180/D3
Trenzano, It. 100/D2
Trepuzzi, It. 89/F2
Tres Algarrobos, Arg. 200/E2
Tres Arroyos, Arg. 200/E3
Três Corações, Braz. 197/H6
Três Irmãos, Represa (res.), Braz. 197/B2
Tres Isletas, Arg. 199/D2
Três Lagoas, Braz. 197/B2
Tres Lomas, Arg. 200/E3
Tres Marias, Braz. 196/A5
Tres Marías (isls.), Mex. 184/D4
Tres Marías, Mex. 185/Q10
Três Marias, Represa (res.), Braz. 193/J7
Tres Montes (cape), Chile 201/B5
Tres Morros, Alto de (peak), Col. 194/B3
Tres Picos, Mex. 186/C3
Tres Picos (peak), Arg. 200/C4
Tres Picos (peak), Arg. 200/E3
Três Pontas, Braz. 197/H6
Tres Puntas (cape), Arg. 200/D5
Três Rios, Braz. 197/K7
Tres Valles, Mex. 186/B2
Tresa (riv.), Swi. 99/E5
Tresckow, Pa, US 180/C2
Trescore Balneario, It. 100/C1
Trescore Cremasco, It. 100/C2
Tresigallo, It. 101/E3
Tresinaro (riv.), It. 100/D4
Trestina, It. 101/F6
Trets, Fr. 84/F5
Treuchtlingen, Ger. 96/D5
Treuen, Ger. 97/F1
Treuenbrietzen, Ger. 82/G2
Treungen, Nor. 80/C2
Trevelín, Arg. 200/C4
Treviglio, It. 100/C1
Trevignano, It. 101/F1
Treviso (int'l arpt.), It. 101/F1
Treviso (prov.), It. 101/F2
Treviso, It. 101/F1
Trevorton, Pa, US 180/B2
Trevose (pt.), Eng, UK 74/A5
Trezzano sul Naviglio, It. 100/C2
Trezzo sull'Adda, It. 100/C1
Trhové Sviny, Czh. 97/H5
Triabunna, Austl. 157/C4
Triadelphia (res.), Md, US 180/A5
Triángulos (reef), Mex. 186/C1
Tribbey, Ok, US 179/N15
Triberg, Ger. 99/E1
Tribhuvan (int'l arpt.), Nepal 127/E2
Tribugá (bay), Col. 194/B3
Tribulation (cape), Austl. 156/B2
Tribulaun (peak), Aus. 99/H4
Tricase, It. 89/F3
Trichūr, India 124/C5
Tricora (peak), Indo. 123/J4
Tricot, Fr. 94/B4
Trie-Château, Fr. 94/A5
Trier, Ger. 95/F4
Trierweiler, Ger. 95/F4
Triesen, Lcht. 99/F3
Trieste, It. 101/G1
Trieste (prov.), It. 101/G1
Trieste, It. 85/K4
Trieux, Fr. 95/E5
Triftern, Ger. 97/G6
Triggiano, It. 90/C5
Trigla NP, Slov. 85/K3
Triglav (peak), Slov. 85/K3
Trigolo, It. 100/C2
Tríkala, Gre. 89/G3
Trikhonís (lake), Gre. 89/G3
Trilport, Fr. 94/B6
Trimbach, Swi. 98/D3
Trimble, Mo, US 179/D5
Trimmis, Swi. 99/F4
Trin, Swi. 99/F4
Trincomalee, SrL. 124/D6
Trindade, Braz. 193/J7
Trindade, Ilha da (isl.), Braz. 193/N8
Třinec, Czh. 83/K4
Tring, Eng, UK 75/F3
Trinidad (isl.), Arg. 199/D4
Trinidad, Bol. 192/F6
Trinidad (chan.), Chile 201/B6
Trinidad (gulf), Chile 201/A6
Trinidad, Col. 194/D3
Trinidad (isl.), Trin. 192/F2
Trinidad, Uru. 201/K10
Trinidad, Co, US 171/F3
Trinidad and Tobago (ctry.) 183/N10
Trinity (bay), Nf, Can. 173/L2
Trinity (isls.), Ak, US 176/H4
Trinity (riv.), Ca, US 168/C5
Trinity (range), Nv, US 170/C2
Trinity (riv.), Tx, US 174/E4
Trinity, West Fork (riv.), Tx, US 171/H4
Trino, It. 100/B2
Triolet, Mrts. 149/T15
Tripolis, Gre. 89/H4
Tripolitania (reg.), Libya 138/H1
Trippstadt, Ger. 95/G5
Tripunittura, India 124/C6
Tripura (state), India 125/F3
Trisanna (riv.), Aus. 99/G4
Trissino, It. 101/E1
Tristan da Cunha (isl.), StH. 64/J7
Triste (peak), Arg. 200/D4
Trisuli (riv.), Nepal 127/E2
Trittau, Ger. 93/H1
Trivero, It. 100/B1
Trnava, Slvk. 83/J4
Trnavský (pol. reg.), Slvk. 83/J4
Trobriand (isls.), PNG 158/E5
Trochtelfingen, Ger. 99/F1
Troesne (riv.), Fr. 94/A5
Trofaiach, Aus. 85/L3
Trofarello, It. 100/A3
Trøgstad, Nor. 80/D2
Troia, It. 88/D2
Trois Fourches, Cap des (cape), Mor. 142/C2
Trois-Pistoles, Qu, Can. 173/G1
Trois-Ponts, Belg. 95/E3
Trois-Rivières, Qu, Can. 173/F2
Troisdorf, Ger. 95/G2
Troistorrents, Swi. 98/C5
Troisvierges, Lux. 95/F3
Troitsk, Rus. 103/P5
Trollhättan, Swe. 80/E2
Trombetas (riv.), Braz. 193/G3
Tromello, It. 100/B2
Tromie (riv.), Sc, UK 78/B3
Troms (co.), Nor. 79/F1
Tromsø, Nor. 79/F1
Tronador (peak), Arg. 200/C4
Trondheim, Nor. 79/D3
Trondheims-Fjorden (estu.), Nor. 79/D3
Tronville-en-Barrios, Fr. 95/E6
Tronzano Vercellese, It. 100/B2
Troodos (mts.), Cyp. 133/C2
Trool (lake), Sc, UK 76/D1
Troon, Sc, UK 78/B5
Trooper, Pa, US 180/C3
Tropea, It. 88/D3
Trosa, Swe. 80/G2
Trosly-Breuil, Fr. 94/B5
Trossingen, Ger. 99/E1
Trostan (peak), NI, UK 76/B1
Trostberg an der Alz, Ger. 97/F6
Trou du Nord, Haiti 187/H2
Troup (pt.), Sc, UK 78/D1
Trout (lake), NW, Can. 164/D2
Trout Lake, Ab, Can. 168/E1
Trowbridge, Eng, UK 74/D4
Troxelville, Pa, US 180/A2
Troy, Al, US 175/G4
Troy, Mi, US 172/D3
Troy, NY, US 172/F3
Troy, Oh, US 175/G1
Troy, Il, US 179/H8
Troy Center, Wi, US 177/N14
Troyan, Bul. 91/G4
Troyanski Prokhod (pass), Bul. 91/G4
Troyes, Fr. 84/F2
Trstenik, Serb. 90/E4
Trub, Swi. 98/D4
Truitt (peak), Yk, Can. 176/M3
Trujillo, Peru 198/B3
Trujillo, Sp. 86/C3
Trujillo, Ven. 194/D2
Trujillo (state), Ven. 194/D2
Trujillo, Hon. 186/E3
Truk (isls.), Micr. 158/E4
Trulben, Ger. 95/G5
Truman Library and Museum, Mo, US 179/E5
Trumau, Aus. 91/N8
Trumbauersville, Pa, US 180/C3
Trumbull, Ct, US 181/E1
Trümmelbachfälle (falls), Swi. 98/D4
Trūn, Bul. 90/F4
Trundle, Austl. 157/C2
Truro, NS, Can. 173/J2
Truro, Eng, UK 74/A6
Truskmore (peak), Ire. 73/P9
Trŭstenik, Bul. 91/G4
Truth or Consequences, NM, US 170/F4
Trutnov, Czh. 83/H3
Truyère (riv.), Fr. 84/E4
Trwyn Cilan (pt.), Wal, UK 76/D6
Tryavna, Bul. 91/G4
Trysil, Nor. 80/E1
Trysilelva (riv.), Nor. 80/D1
Trzcianka, Pol. 83/J2
Trzebiatów, Pol. 80/F4
Trzebnica, Pol. 83/J3
Trzemeszno, Pol. 83/J2
Tsabong, Bots. 148/C2
Tsagaan Bogd (peak), Mong. 112/G3
Tsakane, SAfr. 148/Q13
Tsalgar, Mong. 112/F2
Tsant, Mong. 112/J2
Tsao, Bots. 147/D5
Tsarahonenana, Madg. 149/J6
Tsaramandroso, Madg. 149/H7
Tsaratanana, Madg. 149/H7
Tsaratanana (mass.), Madg. 149/J6
Tsast (peak), Mong. 112/F2
Tsatsana (peak), Les. 148/E3
Tsavo East NP, Kenya 147/G1
Tsavo West NP, Kenya 147/G1
Tschagguns, Aus. 99/F3
Tschierv, Swi. 99/G4
Tschlin, Swi. 99/G4
Tselfat (peak), Mor. 142/B2
Tsetserleg, Mong. 112/F2
Tsetserleg, Mong. 112/H2
Tseung Kwan O, China 113/U10
Tsévié, Togo 145/F5
Tshane, Bots. 147/D5
Tshela, D.R. Congo 147/B1
Tshikapa, D.R. Congo 147/D2
Tshuapa (riv.), D.R. Congo 139/K8
Tsiafajavona (peak), Madg. 149/H7
Tsil'ma (riv.), Rus. 103/L2
Tsimlyansk (res.), Rus. 106/E5
Tsing Yi (isl.), China 113/U10
Tsiombe, Madg. 149/H9
Tsiribihina (riv.), Madg. 149/H7
Tsiroanomandidy, Madg. 149/H7
Tsitsikamma Forest and Coastal NP, SAfr. 148/C4
Tsivory, Madg. 149/H9
Ts'khinvali, Geo. 105/G4
Tsna (riv.), Rus. 102/G4
Tsomo (riv.), SAfr. 148/D3
Tsomog, Mong. 113/J2
Tsu, Japan 119/L6
Tsu (isl.), Japan 116/A3
Tsubame, Japan 117/F2
Tsubata, Japan 117/E2
Tsuchiura, Japan 117/G2
Tsuchiyama, Japan 119/K6
Tsuen Wan, China 113/U10

281
Tsuga – Uslar

Tsugaru (pen.), Japan 118/B3
Tsuge, Japan 119/J6
Tsukidate, Japan 118/B4
Tsukigase, Japan 119/K6
Tsukuba, Japan 119/E1
Tsukude, Japan 119/M6
Tsukui, Japan 119/C2
Tsukumi, Japan 116/B4
Tsumeb, Namb. 147/C4
Tsuna, Japan 119/G7
Tsuru, Japan 117/F3
Tsuruga, Japan 116/E3
Tsurugashima, Japan 119/C2
Tsurugi, Japan 116/E2
Tsurugi-san (peak), Japan 116/D4
Tsuruoka, Japan 118/A4
Tsushima, Japan 119/L5
Tsuyama, Japan 116/D3
Tua (cape), Indo. 122/C5
Tua (riv.), Port.,Sp. 86/B2
Tuam, Ire. 73/P10
Tuamapu (chan.), Chile 200/B4
Tuamotu (arch.), FrPol. 159/L6
Tuan (pt.), Indo. 122/A3
Tuan (riv.), China 114/B4
Tuangku (isl.), Indo. 122/A3
Tuao, Phil. 121/D4
Tuapse, Rus. 104/F3
Tuba City, Az, US 170/E3
Tuban, Indo. 122/D5
Tuban (riv.), Yem. 130/D6
Tubarão, Braz. 197/B4
Tubbergen, Neth. 92/D4
Tübingen, Ger. 96/C5
Tubize, Belg. 95/D2
Tubmanburg, Libr. 144/C5
Ţubruq (Tobruk), Libya 139/K1
Tubuaï (isl.), FrPol. 159/K7
Tubualá, Pan. 187/G4
Tucacas, Ven. 194/D2
Tucano, Braz. 196/C3
Tuchola, Pol. 83/J2
Tuchów, Pol. 83/L4
Tuckahoe, NJ, US 180/D5
Tuckahoe (riv.), NJ, US 180/D5
Tuckahoe, NY, US 181/K8
Tuckerton, NJ, US 180/D4
Tucquegnieux, Fr. 95/E5
Tucson, Az, US 170/E4
Tucumcari, NM, US 171/G4
Tucupido, Ven. 195/E2
Tucupita, Ven. 195/F2
Tucuruí, Braz. 193/J4
Tucuruí (res.), Braz. 193/J4
Tudela, Sp. 86/E1
Tudela de Duero, Sp. 86/C2
Tuen Mun, China 113/T10
Tuenno, It. 99/H5
Tufanbeyli, Turk. 132/D2
Tug Fork (riv.), Ky,WV, US 175/H2
Tugela, SAfr. 149/E3
Tugela (falls), SAfr. 148/E3
Tugela (riv.), SAfr. 149/E3
Tughlakabad (ruin), India 128/D5
Tuguegarao, Phil. 121/D4
Tukangbesi (isls.), Indo. 123/F5
Ţūkh, Egypt 133/B4
Tuktoyaktuk, NW, Can. 176/M2
Tukums, Lat. 81/K3
Tukung (peak), Indo. 122/D4
Tukuyu, Tanz. 146/B5
Tukwila, Wa, US 177/C3
Tula (riv.), Kenya 146/C3
Tula, Mex. 185/F4
Tula, Rus. 104/F1
Tula (riv.), Mex. 185/K6
Tula, Mex. 185/K6
Tula, PN, Mex. 185/K6
Tulancingo, Mex. 185/L6
Tulare, Ca, US 170/C3
Tularosa (valley), NM, US 171/F4
Tularosa, NM, US 171/F4
Tulcán, Ecu. 194/B4
Tulcea, Rom. 91/J3
Tulcea (prov.), Rom. 91/J3
Tule (canal), Ca, US 177/L9
Tüledi (isls.), Rus. 129/B3
Tulia, Tx, US 171/G4
Tulik (vol.), Ak, US 176/E5
Tulin (isls.), PNG 158/E5
Tulita, NW, Can. 164/D2
Ţūlkarm, WBnk. 133/G7
Tulla (lake), Sc, UK 78/B3
Tullahoma, Tn, US 175/G3
Tullamarine (int'l arpt.), Austl. 157/F5
Tullamore, Austl. 157/C2
Tullamore, Ire. 73/Q10
Tulle, Fr. 84/D4
Tullibody, Sc, UK 78/C4
Tullnerbach, Aus. 91/N7
Tullow, Ire. 73/Q10
Tully, Austl. 156/B2
Tullytown, Pa, US 180/D3
Tuloma (riv.), Rus. 106/D3
Tulsa, Ok, US 171/J3
Tulsipur, Nepal 126/D1
Tulsīpur, India 126/D2
Tul'skaya Oblast, Rus. 104/F1
Tultitlán, Mex. 185/Q9
Tuluá, Col. 194/B3
Tuluksak, Ak, US 176/F3
Tulum, Mex. 186/E1
Tulum (ruin), Mex. 186/E1
Tulun, Rus. 107/L4
Tumacacori Nat'l Hist. Park, Az, US 170/E5
Tumaco, Col. 194/B4
Tumatumari, Guy. 195/G3
Tumauini, Phil. 121/D4
Tumba (lake), D.R. Congo 139/J8
Tumba, Swe. 80/G2
Tumbarumba, Austl. 157/D2
Tumbes (dept.), Peru 198/A1
Tumbes, Peru 198/A1
Tumbot (peak), Camb. 120/C3
Tumby Bay, Austl. 155/H5
Tumd Youqi, China 114/B2
Tumd Zuoqi, China 114/B2
Tumen, China 113/N3
Tumen (riv.), China 115/E1
Tumeremo, Ven. 195/F3
Tumereng, Guy. 195/F3
Tumkūr, India 124/C5
Tummel (riv.), Sc, UK 78/C3
Tumpat, Malay. 125/H6
Tumpu (peak), Indo. 123/F4
Tumu, Gha. 145/E4
Tumuc-Humac (mts.), Braz. 193/G3
Tumut, Austl. 157/D2
Tunadal, Swe. 102/C3
Tunceli (prov.), Turk. 132/D2
Tunceli, Turk. 132/D2
Tunchang, China 125/K4
Tundla, India 126/B2
Tundyk (riv.), Kaz. 129/G2
Tundzha (riv.), Bul. 91/H4
Tung Chung, China 113/T10
Tung Lung (riv.), China 113/V11
Tungabhadra (res.), India 124/C4
Tungabhadra (riv.), India 124/C4
Tungamah, Austl. 157/C3
Tŭngsan-got (pt.), NKor. 115/C4
Tungsten, NW, Can. 164/D2
Tungurahua (prov.), Ecu. 194/B5
Tünhel, Mong. 112/J2
Tūnis (cap.), Tun. 142/M6
Tūnis (gov.), Tun. 142/M6
Tunis, Gulf of (gulf), Tun. 142/M6
Tunisia (ctry.) 141/H2
Tunjá, Col. 194/C3
Tunliu, China 114/C3
Tunnels of Vinh Moc, Viet. 120/D2
Tuntum, Braz. 196/A2
Tuntutuliak, Ak, US 176/F3
Tunungayualuk (isl.), Nf, Can. 165/K3
Tunuyán (riv.), Arg. 200/C2
Tunuyán, Arg. 200/C2
Tuolumne (riv.), Ca, US 170/B3
Tuoniang (riv.), China 125/J3
Tupã, Braz. 197/B2
Tupaciguara, Braz. 197/B1
Tupai (isl.), FrPol. 159/K6
Tupambaé, Uru. 201/G2
Tuparro (riv.), Col. 194/D3
Tupelo, Ms, US 175/F3
Tupi Paulista, Braz. 197/B2
Tupiza, Bol. 192/E8
Tupper Lake, NY, US 172/F2
Tupungato, Arg. 200/C2
Tupungato (peak), Arg. 200/P8
Tura, India 127/H3
Tura (riv.), Rus. 106/G4
Tura, Rus. 107/L3
Turaiçu (riv.), Braz. 196/A1
Turan Lowland (plain), Uzb. 106/G5
Turangi, NZ 159/T10
Turbaco, Col. 194/C2
Turbat, Pak. 131/H3
Turbenthal, Swi. 99/E3
Turbo, Col. 194/B2
Turbotville, Pa, US 180/B1
Turčiansky Svätý Martin, Slvk. 104/A2
Turckheim, Fr. 98/D1
Turda, Rom. 91/F2
Tureia (isl.), FrPol. 159/M7
Turek, Pol. 83/K2
Turgeon (riv.), Qu, Can. 172/E1
Türgovishte, Bul. 91/H4
Turgutlu, Turk. 132/A2
Turhal, Turk. 132/D1
Turia (riv.), Sp. 87/E3
Turiaçu, Braz. 193/J4
Turkana (Rudolf) (lake), Kenya 146/C2
Türkeli, Turk. 104/E4
Túrkeve, Hun. 90/E2
Turkey (ctry.) 132/C2
Turkey (riv.), Ia, US 171/K2
Türkheim, Ger. 99/G1
Türkistan, Kaz. 129/E4
Türkmenbashi (Krasnowodsk), Trkm. 105/K5
Turkmenistan (ctry.) 129/C5
Türkoğlu, Turk. 132/D2
Turks (isls.), Haiti 183/G3
Turks and Caicos (isls.), UK 183/G3
Turks Island Passage (chan.), UK 187/J1
Turku (Åbo), Fin. 81/K1
Turku (int'l arpt.), Fin. 81/K1
Turku Ja Pori (prov.), Fin. 79/G3
Turkwel (riv.), Kenya 146/B2
Turlock, Ca, US 170/B3
Turmalina, Braz. 196/B5
Turneffe (isls.), Belz. 182/D4
Turner (mt.), Austl. 154/C2
Turnersville, NJ, US 180/C4
Turnhouse (int'l arpt.), Sc, UK 78/C5
Turnhout, Belg. 92/B6
Turnor Lake, Sk, Can. 168/F1
Turnov, Czh. 83/H3
Turnu Măgurele, Rom. 91/G4
Tuross Head, Austl. 157/D3
Tuross Head, Austl. 157/D3
Turpan, China 112/E3
Turpan (depr.), China 112/E3
Turquino (peak), Cuba 187/G2
Turriaco, It. 101/G1
Turriff, Sc, UK 78/D1
Turt, Mong. 112/H1
Turtle (isls.), SLeo. 144/B5
Turtleford, Sk, Can. 168/F2
Turugart (pass), China 129/G4
Turukhansk, Rus. 106/J3
Tuscaloosa, Al, US 175/G3
Tuscano (arch.), It. 88/B1
Tuscarora, Nv, US 168/D5
Tuscarora (mtn.), Pa, US 180/A3
Tuscarora Ind. Res., US 173/S9
Tuskegee, Al, US 175/G3
Tustin, Ca, US 178/G8
Tuszyn, Pol. 83/K3
Tutak, Turk. 132/E2
Tutayev, Rus. 102/H4
Tuticorin, India 124/C6
Tutin, Serb. 90/E4
Tutóia, Braz. 196/B1
Tutong, Bru. 122/D3
Tutrakan, Bul. 91/H3
Tuttle Creek (lake), Ks, US 171/H3
Tuttlingen, Ger. 99/E2
Tutuila (isl.), ASam. 159/H6
Tutupaca (vol.), Peru 198/D5
Tututalak (mtn.), Ak, US 176/F2
Tutzing, Ger. 99/H2
Tuusula, Fin. 81/L1
Tuvalu (ctry.) 158/G5
Ţuwayq, Jabal (mts.), SAr. 130/E3
Tuxpan, Mex. 184/E5
Tuxpan, Mex. 184/D4
Tuxpan de Rodríguez Cano, Mex. 186/B1
Tuxtla Gutiérrez, Mex. 186/C2
Túy, Sp. 86/A1
Tuy Hoa, Viet. 120/E3
Tuyen Quang, Viet. 120/D1
Tuymazy, Rus. 103/M5
Tūysarkān, Iran 130/E2
Tuz (lake), It. 132/C2
Ţūz Khurmātū, Iraq 132/F3
Tuzigoot Nat'l Mon., Az, US 170/D4
Tuzla, Bosn. 90/D3
Tuzla, Turk. 133/D1
Tuzluca, Turk. 132/E1
Tuzlukçu, Turk. 132/B2
Tvååker, Swe. 80/E3
Tvedestrand, Nor. 80/C2
Tver', Rus. 102/G4
Tverskaya Oblast, Rus. 81/P3
Tvertsa (riv.), Rus. 102/G4
Tvŭrditsa, Bul. 91/G4
Twardogóra, Pol. 83/J3
Tweed (riv.), Sc, UK 78/C5
Tweed Heads, Austl. 156/D5
Twello, Neth. 92/D4
Twente (canal), Neth. 92/D4
Twente (pol. reg.), Neth. 92/D4
Twin Buttes (res.), Tx, US 171/G5
Twin Hills, Ak, US 176/F4
Twin Lakes, Wi, US 177/P14
Twin Rivers, NJ, US 180/D3
Twiste (riv.), Ger. 93/G6
Twistringen, Ger. 93/F3
Twizel, NZ 159/S11
Two Hills, Ab, Can. 168/F2
Two Rivers, Wi, US 169/M4
Twofold (bay), Austl. 157/D3
Twyford, Eng, UK 75/F4
Twymyn (riv.), Wal, UK 74/C1
Tyatya (vol.), Rus. 118/E1
Tychy, Pol. 83/K3
Tyendinaga, On, Can. 172/E2
Tyger (riv.), SC, US 175/H3
Tyldesley, Eng, UK 77/F4
Tylersville, Pa, US 180/A2
Týn, Czh. 83/H4
Tyne (riv.), Sc, UK 78/D5
Tyne and Wear (co.), Eng, UK 77/G2
Tynemouth, Eng, UK 77/G1
Tynset, Nor. 79/D3
Tyonek, Ak, US 176/H3
Tyrifjorden (lake), Nor. 80/C1
Tyringe, Swe. 80/E3
Tyrnyauz, Rus. 105/G4
Tyrrell (lake), Austl. 157/B2
Tyrrhenian (sea), It. 88/B2
Tysnes, Nor. 80/A1
Tysnesøy (isl.), Nor. 80/A2
Tysons Corner, Va, US 180/A6
Tysse, Nor. 80/A1
Tystberga, Swe. 80/G2
Tyub-Karagan (pt.), Kaz. 105/J3
Tyuleniy (isl.), Rus. 105/H3
Tyumen (int'l arpt.), Rus. 103/Q4
Tyumen', Rus. 103/Q4
Tyumenskaya Oblast, Rus. 129/E1
Tyva, Resp., Rus. 106/K4
Tywi (riv.), Wal, UK 74/B3
Tzaneen, SAfr. 147/F5
Tzucacab, Mex. 186/D1

U

U.C.-Irvine, Ca, US 178/G8
U.K. Sovereign Base Area (gov.), Cyp. 133/C2
U.S. Naval Weapons Station, Ca, US 178/F8
U.S.S. Arizona Nat'l Mem., Hi, US 166/W13
Uad Assag (riv.), WSah. 140/B4
Uad Atui (riv.), WSah. 140/B5
Uad el Jat (riv.), WSah. 140/B4
Uad Tenuaiur (riv.), WSah. 140/A5
Uamh Bheag (peak), Sc, UK 78/B4
Uatumã (riv.), Braz. 192/G4
Uauá, Braz. 196/C3
Uaupés (riv.), Braz. 192/E3
Uaxactún (ruin), Guat. 186/D2
Ub, Serb. 90/E3
Ubá, Braz. 197/D2
Übach-Palenberg, Ger. 95/F2
Ubagan (riv.), Kaz. 103/Q5
Ubaíra, Braz. 196/C4
Ubaitaba, Braz. 196/C4
Ubajara, Braz. 196/B1
Ubajara, PN de, Braz. 196/B1
Ubangi (riv.), D.R. Congo 135/D4
Ubatã, Braz. 196/C4
Ubatuba, Braz. 197/H8
Ubay, Phil. 121/D5
Ubaye (riv.), Fr. 85/G4
Ubbergen, Neth. 92/C5
Ube, Japan 116/B4
Úbeda, Sp. 86/D3
Uberaba (lake), Braz. 192/G7
Uberaba, Braz. 197/C1
Überherrn, Ger. 95/F5
Uberlândia, Braz. 197/B1
Überlingen, Ger. 99/F2
Überlingersee (lake), Ger. 99/E2
Ubia (peak), Indo. 123/J4
Ubinas, Peru 198/D5
Ubombo, SAfr. 149/F2
Ubon Ratchathani, Thai. 120/D3
Ubrique, Sp. 86/C4
Ubundu, D.R. Congo 139/L8
Ucayali (dept.), Peru 198/C3
Ucayali (riv.), Peru 198/C3
Uccle, Belg. 95/D2
Ucha (riv.), Rus. 103/W9
Uchaly, Rus. 103/N5
Uchāna, India 128/D5
Uchinskoye (res.), Rus. 103/W9
Uchiza, Peru 198/B3
Uchte, Ger. 93/F3
Uchte (riv.), Ger. 82/F2
Uchumarca, Peru 198/B2
Uchumayo, Peru 198/D5
Uchur (riv.), Rus. 107/P4
Ücker (riv.), Ger. 80/E5
Uckermark (reg.), Ger. 83/G2
Uckfield, Eng, UK 75/G5
Ucluelet, BC, Can. 168/B3
Uda (riv.), Rus. 107/M4
Udagamandalam, India 124/C5
Udaipur, India 131/K4
Udaipura, India 126/B4
Uddevalla, Swe. 80/D2
Uddingston, Sc, UK 78/B5
Uddjaure (lake), Swe. 79/F2
Üdem, Ger. 92/D5
Uden, Neth. 92/C5
Udenhout, Neth. 92/C5
Udgīr, India 124/C4
Udhampur, India 128/C3
Udine (prov.), It. 101/G1
Udine, It. 85/K3
Udipi, India 124/B5
Udmurtia, Resp., Rus. 106/Q6
Udon Thani, Thai. 120/C2
Ueckermünde, Ger. 80/F5
Ueda, Japan 117/F2
Uele (riv.), D.R. Congo 139/K7
Uelsen, Ger. 92/D3
Uelzen, Ger. 93/H3
Ueno, Japan 119/B1
Ueno, Japan 119/K6
Uenohara, Japan 117/F3
Uetendorf, Swi. 98/D4
Uetersen, Ger. 93/G1
Uetze, Ger. 93/H4
Ufa (riv.), Rus. 129/C1
Ufa, Rus. 103/M5
Uffenheim, Ger. 96/D3
Uffing, Ger. 99/H2
Ugalla (riv.), Tanz. 146/A4
Ugalla River Game Rsv., Tanz. 146/A4
Uganda (ctry.) 146/B2
Ugento, It. 89/F3
Ugie (riv.), Sc, UK 78/E1
Ugine, Fr. 98/C6
Uglich, Rus. 102/H4
Ugod, Hun. 90/C2
Ugra (riv.), Rus. 102/G5
Ugŭrchin, Bul. 91/G4
Uherské Hradiště, Czh. 83/J4
Uhingen, Ger. 96/C5
Úhlava (riv.), Czh. 83/G4
Úhlavka (riv.), Czh. 97/F3
Uibaí, Braz. 196/B3
Uíge, Ang. 147/C2
Ŭihŭng, SKor. 115/E4
Ŭijŏngbu, SKor. 115/G6
Ŭiju, NKor. 115/C2
Uilkraal (riv.), SAfr. 148/L11
Uilpata (peak), Rus. 105/G4
Uinta (mts.), Ut, US 170/E2
Uintah, Ut, US 179/K11
Uiraúna, Braz. 196/C2
Ŭiryŏng, SKor. 115/E5
Ŭisŏng, SKor. 115/E4
Uitenhage, SAfr. 148/D4
Uitgeest, Neth. 92/B3
Uithoorn, Neth. 92/B4
Uithuizen, Neth. 92/D2
Ujae (isl.), Mrsh. 158/F4
Ujelang (isl.), Mrsh. 158/F4
Újfehértó, Hun. 83/L5
Ujhāni, India 126/B1
Uji, Japan 119/J6
Uji (riv.), Japan 116/D3
Ujitawara, Japan 119/J6
Ujjain, India 131/L4
Ujung Pandang, Indo. 123/E5
Ukara (isl.), Tanz. 146/B3
Ukerewe (isl.), Tanz. 146/B3
Ukhta, Rus. 103/M3
Ukiah, Ca, US 170/B3
Uklāna, India 128/C5
Ukmergė, Lith. 81/L4
Ukraine (ctry.) 104/D2
Ulaanbaatar (cap.), Mong. 112/J2
Ulaangom, Mong. 112/F2
Ulaanjirem, Mong. 112/J2
Ulanhot, China 113/M2
Ulchin, SKor. 115/E4
Ulcumayo, Peru 198/C3
Ulefoss, Nor. 80/C2
Ulemiste (int'l arpt.), Est. 81/L2
Ulhāsnagar, India 131/K5
Uliastay, Mong. 112/G2
Ulindi (riv.), D.R. Congo 139/L8
Ulithi (isl.), Micr. 158/C3
Uljma, Serb. 90/E3
Ülken Borsyq Qumy (des.), Kaz. 129/C3
Ülken-Qobda (riv.), Kaz. 105/K2
Ulla (riv.), Sp. 86/A1
Ulla Ulla, Bol. 198/D4
Ulla Ulla, Reserva Nacional, Bol. 198/D4
Ulladulla, Austl. 157/D2
Ullapool, Sc, UK 73/R8
Ullared, Swe. 80/E3
Ulldecona, Sp. 87/F2
Ullensvang, Nor. 80/B1
Üllő, Hun. 91/R10
Ullsfjorden (estu.), Nor. 79/F1
Ullswater (lake), Eng, UK 77/F2
Ulm, Ger. 96/C6
Ulmarra, Austl. 157/E1
Ulmen, Ger. 95/F3
Ulricehamn, Swe. 80/E3
Ulrichen, Swi. 99/E5
Ulrichsberg, Aus. 97/G5
Ulrichstein, Ger. 96/C1
Ulrum, Neth. 92/D2
Ulsan, SKor. 115/E5
Ulstein, Nor. 79/C3
Ulster (reg.), Ire. 76/A3
Ulster (riv.), Ger. 96/C1
Ulster American Folk Park, NI, UK 76/A2
Ulúa (riv.), Hon. 186/E3
Uluçınar, Turk. 133/D1
Uludağ (peak), Turk. 132/B1
Uludoruk (peak), Turk. 130/D1
Uluguru (mts.), Tanz. 146/C4
Ulukışla, Turk. 132/C2
Ulundi, SAfr. 149/E3
Uluru NP, Austl. 155/F3
Ulverston, Eng, UK 77/E3
Ulverstone, Austl. 157/C4
Ulvik, Nor. 80/B1
Ulvila, Fin. 81/J1
Ul'yanovka, Rus. 81/P2
Ul'yanovsk, Rus. 103/L5
Ul'yanovskaya Oblast, Rus. 105/H1
Ulytaū (mts.),Kaz. 129/E3
Ulytau (peak), Kaz. 129/E3
Umag, Cro. 90/A3
Uman', Ukr. 104/D2
Umán, Mex. 186/D1
Umarizal, Braz. 196/C2
Umarkot, India 124/D4
Umāsi La (pass), India 128/D3
Umbertide, It. 85/K5
Umbogintwini, SAfr. 149/E3
Umboi (isl.), PNG 158/D5
Umbrail (peak), Swi. 99/G4
Umbrailpass (pass), Swi. 99/G4
Umbria (prov.), It. 85/K5
Umeå, Swe. 79/G3
Umeälven (riv.), Swe. 79/F2
Umfolozi (riv.), SAfr. 149/E3
Umgeni (riv.), SAfr. 149/E3
Umhausen, Aus. 99/G3
Umiat, Ak, US 176/H2
Umkirch, Ger. 98/D1
Umkomaas, SAfr. 149/E3
Umm Durmān, Sudan 139/M4
Umm el Faḥm, Isr. 133/G6
Umm Hibal (well), Egypt 143/C4
Ummendorf, Ger. 99/F1
Umnak (isl.), Ak, US 176/E5
Umnak Pass (chan.), Ak, US 176/E5
Umpqua (riv.), Or, US 168/C5
Umraniye, Turk. 132/B2
Ŭmsŏng, SKor. 115/D4
Umtata, SAfr. 148/E3
Umuahia, Nga. 145/G5
Umuarama, Braz. 199/F1
Umurbey, Turk. 89/K2
Umzimvubu (riv.), SAfr. 148/E3
Umzinto, SAfr. 149/E3
Una, Braz. 196/C4
Una, India 128/D4
Una (mt.), NZ 159/S11
Una (riv.), Bosn.,Cro. 85/L4
Unai, Braz. 196/A5
Unalakleet, Ak, US 176/F3
Unalaska, Ak, US 176/E5
Unalaska (isl.), Ak, US 176/E5
Uncastillo, Sp. 87/E1
Unchahra, India 126/C3
Uncompahgre (plat.), Co, US 170/E3
Unden (lake), Swe. 80/F2
Undenheim, Ger. 96/B3
Underberg, SAfr. 148/E3
Underbool, Austl. 157/B2
Underwood, ND, US 169/H4
Unecha, Rus. 104/E1
Unga (isl.), Ak, US 176/F4
Ungama (bay), Kenya 147/H1
Ungarie, Austl. 157/C2
Ungava (pen.), Qu, Can. 165/J2
Ungava (bay), Qu, Can. 165/K3
Ungheni, Mol. 91/H2
Unhošť, Czh. 97/H2
União, Braz. 196/B2
União da Vitória, Braz. 197/B3
União dos Palmares, Braz. 196/C3
Unimak (isl.), Ak, US 176/E4
Unimak Pass (str.), Ak, US 176/E5
Unini (riv.), Braz. 192/F4
Union, Or, US 168/D4
Union, Mo, US 171/K3
Union, SC, US 175/H3
Union (lake), NJ, US 180/C5
Unión, Arg. 200/D2
Union, NJ, US 181/H9
Union (canal), Sc, UK 78/C5
Union Beach, NJ, US 181/J10
Union Bridge, Md, US 180/A4
Union City, Tn, US 172/B4
Union City, Ca, US 177/K11
Union City, NJ, US 181/J8
Unión de Reyes, Cuba 187/F1
Unión de Tula, Mex. 184/D5
Unión Hidalgo, Mex. 186/C2
Union Mills, Md, US 180/A4
Union Springs, Al, US 175/G3
Uniondale, SAfr. 148/C4
Uniondale, NY, US 181/L9
Uniontown, Pa, US 172/E4
Uniontown, Md, US 180/A4
Unionville, Mo, US 169/K5
United Arab Emirates (ctry.) 130/F4
United Kingdom (ctry.) 73/R9
United Nations, NY, US 181/K9
United Nations Mem. Cemetery, SKor. 115/E5
United States (range), Nun., Can. 165/T6
United States (ctry.) 124
United States Coast Guard Receiving Center, NJ, US 180/D6
United States Department of Energy, Md, US 180/A5
United States Naval Academy, Md, US 180/B6
United States Naval Reservation Mil. Res., PR 183/M8
Unity, Sk, Can. 168/F2
University City, Mo, US 179/G8
University Place, Wa, US 177/B3
Unjha, India 131/K4
Unkel, Ger. 95/G2
Unna, Ger. 93/E5
Unnão, India 126/C2
Ŭnsan-ŭp, NKor. 115/D3
Unst (isl.), Sc, UK 73/W13
Unter Pleichfeld, Ger. 96/D3
Unterägeri, Swi. 99/E3
Unterargen (riv.), Ger. 99/F2
Untergriesbach, Ger. 97/G5
Unterhaching, Ger. 97/E6
Unteriberg, Swi. 99/E3
Unterkulm, Swi. 98/E3
Unterlüss, Ger. 93/H3
Unterschleissheim, Ger. 97/E6
Untersee (lake), Swi. 99/E2
Unterseen, Swi. 98/D4
Untersiggenthal, Swi. 99/E3
Unterthingau, Ger. 99/G2
Untervaz, Swi. 99/F4
Unterweissenbach, Aus. 97/H6
Ünye, Turk. 132/D1
Unzen-Amakusa NP, Japan 116/A4
Unzen-dake (peak), Japan 116/B4
Unzha (riv.), Rus. 106/E4
Uozu, Japan 117/E2
Upala, CR 187/E4
Upanema, Braz. 196/C2
Upata, Ven. 195/F2
Upemba, Lac (lake), D.R. Congo 147/E2
Upemba, PN de l', D.R. Congo 147/E2
Uphall, Sc, UK 78/C5
Upington, SAfr. 148/C3
Upland, Pa, US 180/C4
Upleta, India 131/K4
Upolu (pt.), Hi, US 166/U10
Upolu (isl.), Sam. 159/H6
Upper (lake), Ca, US 170/B2
Upper (pen.), Mi, US 172/C2
Upper (bay), NY, US 180/D2
Upper Arrow (lake), BC, Can. 168/D3
Upper Darby, Pa, US 180/C4
Upper Demerara-Berbice (pol. reg.), Guy. 195/G3
Upper East (pol. reg.), Gha. 145/E4
Upper Engadine (valley), Swi. 99/F5
Upper Falls, Md, US 180/B5
Upper Ganges (canal), India 126/A1
Upper Hutt, NZ 159/T11
Upper Iowa (riv.), Ia, US 171/J2
Upper Klamath (lake), Or, US 168/C5
Upper Lough Erne (lake), NI, UK 73/Q9
Upper Missouri River Breaks Nat'l Mon., Mt, US 168/F4
Upper Peoria (lake), Il, US 169/L5
Upper Red (lake), Mn, US 169/K3
Upper Rouge (riv.), Mi, US 177/F7
Upper Saddle River, NJ, US 181/J7
Upper Takutu-Upper Essequibo (pol. reg.), Guy. 195/G4
Upper Thames (valley), Eng, UK 75/E3
Upper Trajan's Wall, Mol. 104/D3
Upper West (pol. reg.), Gha. 145/E4
Upperlands, NI, UK 76/B2
Upplands-Väsby, Swe. 80/G2
Uppsala, Swe. 80/G2
Uppsala (co.), Swe. 79/F3
Upright (cape), Ak, US 176/D3
Upstart (cape), Austl. 156/B2
Upton, Wy, US 169/G4
Urabá (gulf), Col. 194/B2
Uracoa, Ven. 195/F2
Urad Qianqi, China 114/B2
Uraga (chan.), Japan 119/D3
Urahoro, Japan 118/C2
Uraim (riv.), Braz. 196/A1
Urakawa, Japan 118/C2
Ural (mts.), Rus. 69/L2
Uralla, Austl. 157/D1
Urana, Austl. 157/C2
Urandi, Braz. 196/B4
Uraricoera (riv.), Braz. 192/F3
Urasoe, Japan 117/J7
Urawa, Japan 117/F3
Uray, Rus. 106/G3
Urayasu, Japan 119/D2
Urbach, Ger. 96/C5
Urbana, Md, US 180/A5
Urbania, It. 101/F5
Urbano Santos, Braz. 196/B1
Urbenville, Austl. 156/D5
Urbino, It. 101/F5
Urcos, Peru 198/D4
Urda, Sp. 86/D3
Urdinarrain, Arg. 201/J10
Urdorf, Swi. 99/E3
Ure (riv.), Eng, UK 77/G3
Ures, Mex. 184/C2
Ureshino, Japan 119/K6
Urewera NP, NZ 159/T10
Urfa (prov.), Turk. 132/D2
Urfa, Turk. 132/D2
Urft (riv.), Ger. 93/G6
Urft (lake), Ger. 95/F2
Urganch, Uzb. 129/D4
Urgnano, It. 100/C1
Urho Kekkosen NP, Fin. 79/H1
Uri, India 128/C2
Uri-Rotstock (peak), Swi. 99/E4
Uriangato, Mex. 185/E4
Uribante (riv.), Ven. 194/D3
Uribia, Col. 194/C2
Urie (riv.), Sc, UK 78/D2
Uriménil, Fr. 98/C1
Urique (riv.), Mex. 184/D3
Urjala, Fin. 81/K1
Urk, Neth. 92/C3
Urla, Turk. 132/A2
Urlaţi, Rom. 91/H3
Urmar, India 128/C4
Urmia (lake), Iran 132/F2
Urmitz, Ger. 95/G3
Urmston, Eng, UK 77/F5
Urnäsch, Swi. 99/F3
Urnersee (lake), Swi. 99/E4
Uroševac, Serb. 90/E4
Urr Water (riv.), Sc, UK 76/E1
Ursensollen, Ger. 97/E4
Ursulo Galván, Mex. 185/N7
Uruaçu, Braz. 193/J6
Uruapan, Mex. 184/E5
Urubamba (riv.), Peru 192/D6
Urubamba, Peru 198/C4
Urubu (riv.), Braz. 192/G4
Uruburetama, Braz. 196/C1
Uruçuca, Braz. 196/C4
Uruçuí, Braz. 196/A2
Uruçuí Preto (riv.), Braz. 196/A3
Uruçuí, Serra do (mts.), Braz. 193/K5
Urucuia (riv.), Braz. 193/J7
Uruguaiana, Braz. 199/E2
Uruguay (ctry.) 199/E3
Uruguay (riv.), SAm. 199/E2
Urumaco, Ven. 194/D2
Ürümqi, China 112/E3
Urunga, Austl. 157/E1
Uruoca, Braz. 196/B1
Urup (isl.), Rus. 109/Q5
Ururi, It. 88/D2
Urussanga, Braz. 197/B4
Uryupinsk, Rus. 105/G2
Urziceni, Rom. 91/H3
Us, Fr. 72/H4
Usa, Japan 116/B4
Usa (riv.), Rus. 106/F3
Uşak, Turk. 132/B2
Uşak (prov.), Turk. 132/B2
Usakos, Namb. 147/C5
Usborne (mt.), UK 201/F6
Uscio, It. 100/C4
Usedom (isl.), Ger. 80/E4
Useldange, Lux. 95/E4
Useless Loop, Austl. 154/B3
Ushibori, Japan 119/F2
Ushibuka, Japan 116/B4
Ushiku, Japan 119/E2
Ushtobe, Kaz. 129/G3
Ushuaia, Arg. 201/C7
Usibelli, Ak, US 176/J3
Usicayos, Peru 198/D4
Usilampatti, India 124/C6
Usingen, Ger. 96/B2
Üsküp, Turk. 91/H5
Uslar, Ger. 93/G5

282
Usman' – Vicha

Usman', Rus. 104/F1
Uspallata, Arg. 200/C2
Uspallata, Paso de (pass), Chile 200/N8
Usquil, Peru 198/B2
Ussel, Fr. 84/E4
Ussel (riv.), Ger. 96/D5
Usses (riv.), Fr. 98/C5
Ussuri (riv.), China,Rus. 107/P5
Ussuriysk, Rus. 113/P3
Ussy-sur-Marne, Fr. 72/M5
Ust'-Ilimsk, Rus. 107/L4
Ust'-Kamchatsk, Rus. 107/S4
Ust'-Kut, Rus. 107/L4
Ust'-Ordynskiy Buryatskiy Aut. Okrug, Rus. 107/Q7
Úštěk, Czh. 97/H1
Uster, Swi. 99/E3
Ústí nad Labem, Czh. 85/L1
Ustica (isl.), It. 88/C3
Ustica, It. 88/C3
Ustka, Pol. 80/G4
Ustrzyki Dolne, Pol. 83/M4
Ust'ya (riv.), Rus. 103/K3
Ustyurt (plat.), Kaz. 109/D5
Usu, China 112/D3
Usuda, Japan 119/A1
Usuki, Japan 116/B4
Usulután, ESal. 186/D3
Usumacinta (riv.), Mex. 182/C4
Utah (state), US 170/E3
Utah (co.), Ut, US 179/K13
Utah (lake), Ut, US 170/D2
Utangan (riv.), India 126/A2
Utano, Japan 119/J7
Utashinai, Japan 118/C2
Utena, Lith. 81/L4
Uterský (riv.), Czh. 97/G3
Uthai Thani, Thai. 120/C3
Utica, NY, US 172/F3
Utica, Mi, US 177/F6
Utiel, Sp. 86/E3
Utik (lake), Mb, Can. 169/J2
Utila (isl.), Hon. 186/E2
Utinga, Braz. 196/B4
Utirik (isl.), Mrsh. 158/G3
Utiroa, Kiri. 158/G5
Utmānzai, Pak. 128/A2
Utopia Abor. Land, Austl. 155/G2
Utraulā, India 126/D2
Utrecht, SAfr. 149/E2
Utrecht, Neth. 92/C4
Utrecht (prov.), Neth. 92/C4
Utrera, Sp. 86/C4
Utsunomiya, Japan 117/F2
Uttar Pradesh (state), India 124/C2
Uttaradit, Thai. 120/C2
Uttarranchal (state), India 126/B1
Uttenweiler, Ger. 99/F1
Uttoxeter, Eng, UK 77/G6
Utuado, PR 183/M8
Utupua (isl.), Sol. 158/F6
Uturoa, FrPol. 159/K6
Utzenstorf, Swi. 98/D3
Uusikaupunki, Fin. 81/J1
Uusimaa (prov.), Fin. 79/H3
Uva (riv.), Col. 192/E3
Uvalde, Tx, US 171/H5
Uvarovo, Rus. 105/G2
Uverito, Ven. 195/E2
Uvira, D.R. Congo 146/A3
Uvongo, SAfr. 149/E3
Uvs (prov.), Mong. 112/F2
Uwajima, Japan 116/C4
Uwimmerah (riv.), Indo. 123/K5
Uxin Qi, China 114/B3
Uxmal (ruin), Mex. 186/D1
Üydzin, Mong. 112/J3
Uyo, Nga. 145/G5
Üyönch, Mong. 112/F2
Uyuni, Bol. 192/E8
Uzbekistan (ctry.) 129/D4
Uzbekistan Nat'l Park, Uzb. 129/E5
Uzein (int'l arpt.), Fr. 84/C5
Uzerche, Fr. 84/D4
Uzès, Fr. 84/F4
Uzhhorod, Ukr. 83/M4
Uzhok (pass), Ukr. 83/M4
Užice, Serb. 90/D4
Uzlovaya, Rus. 104/F1
Uznach, Swi. 99/E3
Üzümlü, Turk. 132/D2
Uzunköprü, Turk. 89/K2
Uzwil, Swi. 99/F3

V

V.P. Rosales, PN, Chile 200/B4
Vaal (riv.), SAfr. 148/D2
Vaala, Fin. 79/H2
Vaalbos NP, SAfr. 148/D3
Vaaldam (res.), SAfr. 148/D2
Vaals, Neth. 95/F2
Vaalserberg (hill), Neth. 95/F2
Vaasa (prov.), Fin. 79/G3
Vaasa (int'l arpt.), Fin. 79/G3
Vaasa (Vasa), Fin. 79/G3
Vaassen, Neth. 92/C4
Vác, Hun. 90/D2
Vaca (mt.), Ca, US 177/K10
Vaca (mts.), Ca, US 177/K10
Vacaria, Braz. 197/B4
Vacaville, Ca, US 170/B3
Vachon (riv.), Qu, Can. 165/J2
Vada, It. 100/D6
Vado Ligure, It. 100/B4
Vadret (peak), Swi. 99/F4
Vadsø, Nor. 79/J1
Vadstena, Swe. 80/F2
Vaduz (cap.), Lcht. 99/F3
Vaernes (int'l arpt.), Nor. 79/D3
Vaga (riv.), Rus. 102/J3
Vågå, Nor. 79/D3
Vågan, Nor. 79/E1
Vaganski vrh (peak), Cro. 90/B3
Vagay (riv.), Rus. 103/R4
Vaggeryd, Swe. 80/F3
Vagney, Fr. 98/C1
Vagos, Port. 86/A2
Vågsøy, Nor. 79/C3
Vah (riv.), Slvk. 83/J4
Vahitahi (isl.), FrPol. 159/M6
Vaiano, It. 101/E5
Vaiano Cremasco, It. 100/C2
Vaich (lake), Sc, UK 78/B1
Vaihingen an der Enz, Ger. 96/B5
Vaijāpur, India 131/K5
Vail, Co, US 171/F3
Vailate, It. 100/C2
Vair (riv.), Fr. 98/B1
Vaisali (ruin), India 126/E2
Vaitupu (isl.), Tuv. 158/G5
Vaivre-et-Montoille, Fr. 98/C2
Vakfıkebir, Turk. 104/F4
Vakh (riv.), Rus. 106/J3
Vākhān (mts.), Afg. 131/K1
Vakhsh (riv.), Taj. 131/J1
Vál, Hun. 90/D2
Val-de-Marne (dept.), Fr. 94/B6
Val-d'Or, Qu, Can. 172/E1
Val Lagarina (valley), It. 101/D1
Val Marie, Sk, Can. 168/G3
Val Venosta (valley), It. 99/G4
Val Verda, Ut, US 179/K12
Val Verde, Ca, US 178/B2
Valais (canton), Swi. 98/D5
Valbo, Swe. 80/G1
Valburg, Neth. 92/C5
Valcheta, Arg. 200/D4
Valdagno, It. 101/E1
Valdahon, Fr. 98/C3
Valdai (hills), Rus. 102/G4
Valdarno (valley), It. 101/E5
Valdecañas, Embalse de (res.), Sp. 86/C3
Valdemarsvik, Swe. 80/G2
Valdemorillo, Sp. 87/M8
Valdense, Uru. 201/K11
Valdepeñas, Sp. 86/D3
Valderas, Sp. 86/C1
Valderrobres, Sp. 87/F2
Valdés (pen.), Arg. 200/E4
Valdeverdeja, Sp. 86/C3
Valdez, Ak, US 176/J3
Valdez, Ecu. 194/B4
Valdivia, Col. 194/C3
Valdivia, Chile 200/B3
Valdobbiadene, It. 101/F1
Valdoie, Fr. 98/C2
Valdosta, Ga, US 175/H4
Valdoviño, Sp. 86/A1
Vale, Or, US 168/D5
Vale of Glamorgan (co.), Wal, UK 74/C4
Valeggio sul Mincio, It. 101/D2
Valemount, BC, Can. 168/D2
Valença, Braz. 196/C4
Valença, Braz. 197/K7
Valença, Port. 86/A1
Valença do Piauí, Braz. 196/B2
Valence, Fr. 84/D4
Valence, Fr. 84/F4
Valence-sur-Baïse, Fr. 84/D5
Valencia, Ven. 192/E1
Valencia (int'l arpt.), Sp. 87/E3
Valencia, Sp. 87/E3
Valencia (aut. comm.), Sp. 86/E2
Valencia, Ecu. 194/B5
Valencia (isl.), Ire. 72/P11
Valencia de Alcántara, Sp. 86/B3
Valencia de Don Juan, Sp. 86/C1
Valencia, Golfo de (gulf), Sp. 87/F3
Valenciennes, Fr. 94/C3
Valendas, Swi. 99/F4
Vălenii de Munte, Rom. 91/H3
Valente, Braz. 196/C3
Valentigney, Fr. 98/C3
Valentim (range), Braz. 196/B2
Valentine, Tx, US 174/B4
Valentines, Uru. 201/G2
Valenton, Fr. 72/K5
Valenza, It. 100/B2
Våler, Nor. 80/D1
Våler, Nor. 80/D2
Valera, Ven. 194/D2
Valff, Fr. 98/D1
Valga, Est. 81/M3
Valhalla, NY, US 181/K7
Valinco, Golfe de (gulf), Fr. 88/A2
Valinhos, Braz. 197/F7
Valjevo, Serb. 90/D3
Valkeakoski, Fin. 81/K1
Valkeala, Fin. 81/M1
Valkenburg, Neth. 95/E2
Valkenswaard, Neth. 92/C6
Vall de Uxó, Sp. 87/E3
Valladolid, Sp. 86/C2
Valladolid (int'l arpt.), Sp. 86/C2
Valladolid, Mex. 186/D1
Vallangoujard, Fr. 72/J4
Valle, Ecu. 194/B5
Valle, Nor. 80/B2
Valle d'Aosta (pol. reg.), It. 85/G4
Valle de Bravo, Mex. 185/E5
Valle de Cauca (dept.), Col. 194/B4
Valle de Guanape, Ven. 195/E2
Valle de La Pascua, Ven. 192/E2
Valle de Santiago, Mex. 185/E4
Valle de Zaragoza, Mex. 174/B5
Valle Hermoso, Mex. 185/F3
Valle Lomellina, It. 100/B2
Valle Mosso, It. 100/B1
Vallecitos de Zaragoza, Mex. 185/E5
Vallecrosia, It. 85/G5
Valledupar, Col. 194/C2
Valleé de l'Azaouak (riv.), Mali 145/G2
Vallée du Ferlo (riv.), Sen. 144/B3
Valleé du Mboune (riv.), Sen. 144/B3
Valleé du Saloum (riv.), Sen. 144/B3
Valleé du Serpent (riv.), Mali 144/C3
Vallegrande, Bol. 192/F7
Vallehermoso, Sp. 140/A3
Vallejo, Ca, US 170/B3
Vallenar, Chile 199/B2
Vallendar, Ger. 95/G3
Valleroy, Fr. 95/E5
Valletta (cap.), Malta 88/M7
Valley Brook, Ok, US 179/N15
Valley Center, Ca, US 178/C4
Valley City, ND, US 169/J4
Valley Cottage, NY, US 181/K7
Valley East, On, Can. 172/D2
Valley Forge Nat'l Hist. Park, Pa, US 180/C3
Valley of Desolation, SAfr. 148/D4
Valley of the Kings, Egypt 143/C3
Valley Park, Mo, US 179/G8
Valley Spring, Tx, US 171/H5
Valley Stream, NY, US 181/L9
Vallière (riv.), Fr. 98/B4
Vallorbe, Swi. 98/C4
Valls, Sp. 87/F2
Valluga (peak), Aus. 99/G3
Valmayor (res.), Sp. 87/M8
Valme (riv.), Ger. 93/F6
Valmeyer, Il, US 179/G9
Valmiera, Lat. 81/L3
Valmondois, Fr. 72/J4
Valognes, Fr. 84/C2
Valois (reg.), Fr. 94/B5
Valona, Bay of (bay), Alb. 89/F2
Valpaços, Port. 86/B2
Vālpārai, India 124/C5
Valparaiso, Fl, US 175/G4
Valparaiso, In, US 172/C3
Valparaíso, Mex. 184/E4
Valparaíso (pol. reg.), Chile 200/C2
Valparaíso, Chile 200/N8
Valpovo, Cro. 90/D3
Valréas, Fr. 84/F4
Vals (riv.), SAfr. 148/D2
Vals, Swi. 99/F4
Vals-les-Bains, Fr. 84/F4
Valsād, India 131/K4
Valsaquillo (res.), Mex. 185/L8
Valsbaai (bay), SAfr. 147/C7
Valserine (riv.), Fr. 98/B5
Valserrhein (riv.), Swi. 99/F4
Valsura (riv.), It. 99/G4
Valtellina (valley), It. 99/F5
Valtice, Czh. 85/M2
Valuyki, Rus. 104/F2
Valverde, Sp. 140/A4
Valverde del Camino, Sp. 86/B4
Valyermo, Ca, US 178/C2
Våmhus, Swe. 80/F1
Vammala, Fin. 81/K1
Vámos, Gre. 89/J5
Vámosmikola, Hun. 90/D2
Vámospércs, Hun. 90/E2
Van, Turk. 132/E2
Van (lake), Turk. 132/E2
Van Buren, Me, US 173/H2
Van Buren, Ar, US 171/J4
Van Cortlandt Park, NY, US 181/K8
Van Diemen (cape), Austl. 151/C2
Van Diemen (gulf), Austl. 151/C2
Van Harinxmakanaal (riv.), Neth. 92/C2
Van Horn, Tx, US 171/F5
Van Norman Lakes, Ca, US 178/B2
Van Rees (mts.), Indo. 123/J4
Van Wert, Oh, US 172/C3
Vana-Javesi (lake), Fin. 81/K1
Vanadzor, Arm. 105/H4
Vanavaro (isl.), FrPol. 159/L7
Vancouver (mt.), Yk, Can. 176/L3
Vancouver, Wa, US 168/C4
Vancouver, BC, Can. 168/C3
Vancouver (int'l arpt.), BC, Can. 168/C3
Vancouver (cape), Austl. 154/C5
Vancouver (isl.), BC, Can. 164/D4
Vandalia, Mo, US 171/K3
Vandans, Aus. 99/F3
Vanderbijlpark, SAfr. 148/D2
Vanderbilt Museum, NY, US 181/E2
Vanderhoof, BC, Can. 168/B2
Vandœuvre-lès-Nancy, Fr. 95/F6
Vanegas, Mex. 185/E4
Vänern (lake), Swe. 80/E2
Vänersborg, Swe. 80/E2
Vangaindrano, Madg. 149/H8
Vanier (isl.), Nun., Can. 165/R7
Vanikolo (isl.), Sol. 158/F6
Vanil Noir (peak), Swi. 98/D4
Vanimo, PNG 158/D5
Vännäs, Swe. 79/F3
Vanne (riv.), Fr. 84/E2
Vannes, Fr. 84/B3
Vanoise, PN de la, Fr. 85/G4
Vanreenenpas (pass), SAfr. 148/E3
Vanrhynsdorp, SAfr. 148/B3
Vansbro, Swe. 80/F1
Vanse, Nor. 80/B2
Vansittart (isl.), Nun., Can. 165/H2
Vantaa, Fin. 81/L1
Vanua Levu (isl.), Fiji 158/G6
Vanuatu (ctry.) 158/F6
Vanwyksvlei, SAfr. 148/C3
Var (riv.), Fr. 85/G5
Vara (riv.), It. 100/C4
Vara, Swe. 80/E2
Varadero, Cuba 187/F1
Varaita (riv.), It. 100/A3
Varallo, It. 100/B1
Varāmīn, Iran 130/F1
Vārānasi, India 126/D3
Varanger-Halvøya (pen.), Nor. 79/J1
Varangerfjorden (estu.), Nor. 79/J1
Varangéville, Fr. 95/F6
Varano (lake), It. 88/D2
Varano Borghi, It. 100/B1
Varaždin, Cro. 85/M3
Varazze, It. 100/B4
Varberg, Swe. 80/E3
Vardar (riv.), FYROM 89/G2
Varde, Den. 80/C4
Várdha, Gre. 89/G3
Vardø, Nor. 79/J1
Varel, Ger. 93/F2
Varenne (riv.), Fr. 84/C2
Varennes, Qu, Can. 173/P6
Varennes-Jarcy, Fr. 72/K5
Varennes-Vauzelles, Fr. 84/E3
Vareš, Bosn. 90/D3
Varese, It. 100/B1
Varese (prov.), It. 99/E6
Varese Ligure, It. 100/C4
Vårgårda, Swe. 80/E2
Vargem Grande, Braz. 196/B1
Vargem do Sul, Braz. 197/G6
Varginha, Braz. 197/H6
Vári, Gre. 89/N9
Varilhes, Fr. 84/D5
Värmeln (lake), Swe. 80/E2
Värmland (co.), Swe. 79/E3
Varna, Bul. 91/H4
Varna (pol. reg.), Bul. 91/H4
Värnamo, Swe. 80/F3
Varois-et-Chaignot, Fr. 98/B3
Varoška Rijeka, Bosn. 90/C3
Várpalota, Hun. 90/D2
Varraddes, Fr. 72/L5
Varsi, It. 100/C3
Vårsta, Swe. 80/G2
Vartholomión, Gre. 89/G4
Varto, Turk. 132/E2
Vartry (res.), Ire. 76/B5
Vartry (riv.), Ire. 76/B5
Várzea Alegre, Braz. 196/C2
Várzea da Palma, Braz. 196/A5
Várzea Grande, Braz. 196/B2
Várzea Grande, Braz. 193/G7
Varzelândia, Braz. 196/A4
Varzi, It. 100/C3
Varzo, It. 99/E5
Varzuga (riv.), Rus. 102/H2
Vas (prov.), Hun. 90/C2
Vasa Barris (riv.), Braz. 193/L5
Vásárosnamény, Hun. 83/M4
Vaşcău, Rom. 90/F2
Vashka (riv.), Rus. 103/K2
Vashon, Wa, US 177/C3
Vashon (isl.), Wa, US 177/C3
Vasiliká, Gre. 89/H2
Vasil'yevskiy (isl.), Rus. 103/S7
Vaslui (prov.), Rom. 91/H2
Vaslui, Rom. 91/H2
Vassar, Mi, US 172/D3
Vassdalsegga (peak), Nor. 80/B2
Vassouras, Braz. 197/K7
Västerås, Swe. 80/G2
Västerbotten (co.), Swe. 79/F2
Västerdalälven (riv.), Swe. 80/E1
Västernorrland (co.), Swe. 79/F3
Västervik, Swe. 80/G3
Västmanland (co.), Swe. 79/E3
Vasto, It. 88/D1
Västra Silen (lake), Swe. 80/E2
Vasvár, Hun. 90/C2
Vasyl'kiv, Ukr. 104/D2
Vaterstetten, Ger. 97/E6
Vatican City (ctry.) 88/C2
Vatnajökull (glacier), Ice. 79/P7
Vatomandry, Madg. 149/J7
Vatra Dornei, Rom. 91/G2
Vättern (lake), Swe. 79/E4
Vaucouleurs (riv.), Fr. 72/H5
Vaud (canton), Swi. 98/C4
Vaudoy-en-Brie, Fr. 72/M5
Vaudreuil-Dorion, Qu, Can. 173/M7
Vaughan, On, Can. 173/Q8
Vaughn, NM, US 171/F4
Vaughn, Wa, US 177/B3
Vaulruz, Swi. 98/C4
Vaulx-en-Velin, Fr. 98/A6
Vaupés (dept.), Col. 194/D4
Vaupés (riv.), Col. 194/D4
Vauréal, Fr. 72/J4
Vauvert, Fr. 84/F5
Vauvillers, Fr. 98/C2
Vaux (riv.), Fr. 82/C4
Vaux-sur-Seine, Fr. 72/H4
Vaux-sur-Sûre, Belg. 95/E4
Vauxhall, Ab, Can. 168/E3
Vavatenina, Madg. 149/J7
Vava'u Group (isls.), Tonga 159/H6
Vavuniya, SrL. 124/D6
Vawkavysk, Bela. 83/N2
Vaxjo (int'l arpt.), Swe. 80/F3
Växjö, Swe. 80/F3
Vaygach (isl.), Rus. 202/B
Vazante, Braz. 196/A5
Vázea Paulista, Braz. 197/G8
Vazuza (res.), Rus. 102/G5
Vazzola, It. 101/F1
Vecchiano, It. 100/D5
Vechigen, Swi. 98/D4
Vecht (riv.), Neth. 92/D3
Vechta, Ger. 93/F3
Vechte (riv.), Ger. 92/D3
Vecsés, Hun. 90/D2
Vedano Olona, It. 100/B1
Veddige, Swe. 80/E3
Vedea (riv.), Rom. 91/G3
Vedelago, It. 101/F1
Vedia, Arg. 200/E2
Vedra, Sp. 86/A1
Veendam, Neth. 92/D2
Veenendaal, Neth. 92/C4
Veere, Neth. 92/A5
Veerse Meer (res.), Neth. 92/A5
Vefsn, Nor. 79/E2
Vega, Tx, US 171/G4
Vega (pt.), Ak, US 176/B6
Vega (isl.), Nor. 79/D2
Vega de Alatorre, Mex. 185/N6
Vegafjorden (estu.), Nor. 79/D2
Veghel, Neth. 92/C5
Vègreville, Ab, Can. 168/E2
Végueta, Peru 198/B3
Vehkalahti, Fin. 81/M1
Vehne (riv.), Ger. 93/F2
Veigné, Fr. 84/D3
Veinticinco de Mayo, Arg. 200/E2
Veinticinco de Mayo, Arg. 200/D3
Veinticinco de Mayo, Uru. 201/K11
Veintiocho de Mayo, Ecu. 198/B1
Veintiocho de Noviembre, Arg. 201/B6
Veitsch, Aus. 90/B2
Veitshöchheim, Ger. 96/C3
Vejen, Den. 80/C4
Vejer de la Frontera, Sp. 86/C4
Vejle, Den. 80/C4
Vejle (co.), Den. 80/C4
Vejprty, Czh. 97/G2
Vela, Cabo de la (pt.), Col. 194/C1
Vela Luka, Cro. 88/E1
Velaines, Fr. 95/E6
Vélan (peak), Swi. 98/D6
Velardeña, Mex. 184/E3
Velas, Azor., Port. 87/S12
Velasco Ibarra, Ecu. 194/B5
Velázquez, Uru. 201/G2
Velbert, Ger. 92/E6
Velburg, Ger. 97/E4
Velddrif, SAfr. 148/L10
Velden, Ger. 97/F6
Velden am Wörthersee, Aus. 85/L3
Veldhoven, Neth. 92/C6
Velen, Ger. 92/D5
Velešta, FYROM 89/G2
Velestínon, Gre. 89/H3
Vélez, Col. 194/C3
Vélez-Blanco, Sp. 86/D4
Vélez-Málaga, Sp. 86/C4
Vélez-Rubio, Sp. 86/D4
Velhas, Rio das (riv.), Braz. 193/K7
Velika Gorica, Cro. 90/C3
Velika Kladuša, Bosn. 85/L4
Velika Plana, Serb. 90/E3
Velikaya (riv.), Rus. 102/F4
Velikiy Ustyug, Rus. 103/K3
Velikiye Luki, Rus. 81/P3
Veliko Tŭrnovo, Bul. 91/G4
Velille, Peru 198/D4
Vélingara, Sen. 144/B3
Vélizy-Villacoublay, Fr. 72/J5
Vel'ké Kapušany, Slvk. 90/F1
Veľký Krtíš, Slvk. 83/K4
Velký Zvon (peak), Czh. 97/F3
Vellberg, Ger. 96/C4
Velletri, It. 88/C2
Vellinge, Swe. 80/E4
Vellmar, Ger. 93/G6
Vellón (res.), Sp. 87/N8
Vellore, India 124/C5
Vélon, Gre. 89/H4
Vel'sk, Rus. 102/J3
Veluwe (phys. reg.), Neth. 92/C4
Veluwemeer (lake), Neth. 92/C4
Veluwezoom, NP, Neth. 92/C4
Velva, ND, US 169/H3
Velvary, Czh. 97/H2
Velvendós, Gre. 89/H2
Vémars, Fr. 72/K4
Vemb, Den. 80/C3
Vémend, Hun. 90/D2
Venachar (lake), Sc, UK 78/B4
Venado Tuerto, Arg. 200/E2
Venafro, It. 88/D2
Venamo (peak), Ven. 195/F3
Venâncio Aires, Braz. 197/A4
Venaria, It. 85/G4
Vence, Fr. 85/G5
Venceslau Brás, Braz. 197/B2
Vendas Novas, Port. 86/A3
Vendôme, Fr. 84/D3
Vendrell, Sp. 87/F2
Vendrest, Fr. 72/M4
Veneta, Laguna (lake), It. 101/F2
Venetie, Ak, US 176/J2
Veneto (pol. reg.), It. 85/J4
Venezia (prov.), It. 101/F1
Venezia, Golfo di (gulf), Eur. 101/F2
Venezia (Venice), It. 101/F2
Venezuela (gulf), Col.,Ven. 195/D2
Venezuela (ctry.) 195/E3
Vengurla, India 131/K5
Veniaminof (vol.), Ak, US 176/G4
Venice, Fl, US 175/H5
Venice, Il, US 179/G8
Venice (Venezia), It. 85/K4
Vénissieux, Fr. 84/F4
Venjan, Swe. 80/E1
Venjansjön (lake), Swe. 80/E1
Venkatagiri, India 124/C5
Venlo, Neth. 92/D6
Vennesla, Nor. 80/B2
Veno (bay), Den. 80/C3
Venoge (riv.), Swi. 98/C4
Venosa, It. 88/D2
Venray, Neth. 92/C5
Vent, Îles du (isls.), FrPol. 159/L6
Venta (riv.), Lat. 81/J3
Venta de Baños, Sp. 86/C2
Ventauri (riv.), Ven. 192/E3
Ventersburg, SAfr. 148/D3
Ventersdorp, SAfr. 148/D2
Venterstad, SAfr. 148/D3
Ventiseri, Fr. 88/A2
Ventnor, Eng, UK 75/E5
Ventnor City, NJ, US 180/D5
Ventspils, Lat. 81/J3
Ventuari (riv.), Ven. 195/E3
Ventura, Ca, US 178/A2
Ventura (co.), Ca, US 178/A2
Ventura (riv.), Ca, US 178/A2
Venturina, It. 85/J5
Venturosa, Braz. 196/C3
Venustiano Carranza, Mex. 182/C4
Venustiano Carranza (res.), Mex. 185/E3
Vép, Hun. 85/M3
Ver-sur-Launette, Fr. 72/L4
Vera, Arg. 199/D2
Vera, Sp. 86/E4
Vera Cruz, Pan. 194/B2
Veracruz, Mex. 185/N7
Veracruz-Llave (state), Mex. 182/B3
Veranópolis, Braz. 197/B4
Verāval, India 131/K4
Verbania, It. 99/E6
Verberie, Fr. 94/B5
Verbicaro, It. 88/D3
Vercelli, It. 100/B2
Vercelli (prov.), It. 98/E6
Verdal, Nor. 79/D3
Verde (riv.), Par. 199/D1
Verde (cape), Sen. 138/B5
Verde (riv.), Braz. 193/G6
Verde (riv.), Mex. 185/F4
Verde (coast), Sp. 86/B1
Verde (cape), It. 100/A5
Verde (bay), Arg. 200/E3
Verde Grande (riv.), Braz. 193/K7
Verden, Ger. 93/G3
Verdhikoússa, Gre. 89/G3
Verdigris (riv.), Ks, US 171/J3
Verdinho (riv.), Braz. 197/B1
Verdon (riv.), Fr. 84/F5
Verdugo (mts.), Ca, US 178/F7
Verdun, Qu, Can. 173/N7
Vereeniging, SAfr. 148/D2
Verena (peak), It. 99/H6
Vereshchagino, Rus. 103/M4
Veretskiy (pass), Ukr. 83/M4
Verga (cape), Gui. 144/B4
Vergara, Uru. 201/G2
Vergato, It. 101/E4
Vergennes, Vt, US 172/F2
Vergiate, It. 100/B1
Vergina (ruin), Gre. 89/H2
Verigenstadt, Ger. 99/F1
Verín, Sp. 86/B2
Veríssimo, Braz. 197/B1
Verkhnetulomskiy (res.), Rus. 102/F1
Verkhoyansk (range), Rus. 109/M2
Verkhoyansk, Rus. 107/P3
Verl, Ger. 93/F5
Vermenagna (riv.), It. 100/A4
Vermilion, Ab, Can. 168/F2
Vermilion (riv.), Ab, Can. 168/F2
Vermilion (range), Mn, US 169/K4
Vermilion Cliffs Nat'l Mon., Az, US 168/E3
Vermillion, SD, US 169/J5
Vermont (state), US 173/F2
Vernal, Ut, US 170/E2
Vernayaz, Swi. 98/D5
Vernazza, It. 100/C4
Verneuil-sur-Avre, Fr. 84/D2
Verneuil-sur-Seine, Fr. 72/H5
Verneukpan (salt pan), SAfr. 148/C3
Vernier, Swi. 98/C5
Vernon, BC, Can. 168/D3
Vernon, Fr. 72/H4
Vernon Hills, Il, US 177/Q15
Vernon Valley, NJ, US 180/D1
Vernouillet, Fr. 72/H5
Vero Beach, Fl, US 175/H5
Véroia, Gre. 89/H2
Verolanuova, It. 100/D2
Verolavecchia, It. 100/D2
Verolengo, It. 100/A2
Verona (prov.), It. 101/D1
Verona (int'l arpt.), It. 101/D2
Verona, It. 101/D2
Verona, NJ, US 181/J8
Verónica, Arg. 201/K11
Verrès, It. 100/A1
Verret, La, US 179/Q17
Verrières-le-Buisson, Fr. 72/J5
Versa (riv.), It. 100/B3
Versailles, Ky, US 172/C4
Versailles, Fr. 72/J5
Versigny, Fr. 72/L4
Verskla (riv.), Rus.,Ukr. 106/D4
Versmold, Ger. 93/F4
Versoix, Swi. 98/C5
Vert-le-Grand, Fr. 72/K6
Vert-le-Petit, Fr. 72/K6
Vert-Saint-Denis, Fr. 72/K6
Vertana (peak), It. 99/G4
Verte (peak), Fr. 98/C6
Vertemate, It. 100/C1
Vertientes, Cuba 187/G1
Vertou, Fr. 84/C3
Vertova, It. 100/C1
Vertus, Fr. 94/D6
Verviers, Belg. 95/E2
Vervins, Fr. 94/C4
Verwoerdburg, SAfr. 148/Q12
Veryan (bay), Eng, UK 74/B6
Verzasca (riv.), Swi. 99/E5
Verzasca (Gerra), Swi. 99/E5
Verzenay, Fr. 95/D5
Verzuolo, It. 85/G4
Verzy, Fr. 95/D5
Vescovato, Fr. 88/A1
Vescovato, It. 100/D2
Vesdre (riv.), Belg. 84/F1
Veselí nad Lužnicí, Czh. 97/H4
Veselyy (res.), Rus. 105/G3
Vesgre (riv.), Fr. 94/A6
Vesijärvi (lake), Fin. 81/L1
Vesle (riv.), Fr. 82/C4
Vesoul, Fr. 98/C2
Vespolate, It. 100/B2
Vest-Agder (co.), Nor. 79/C4
Vest-Sjælland (prov.), Den. 80/D4
Vest-Vlaanderen (prov.), Belg. 94/B2
Vestbjerg, Den. 80/C3
Vestby, Nor. 80/D2
Vesterålen (isls.), Nor. 79/E1
Vestfjorden (inlet), Nor. 79/E2
Vestfold (co.), Nor. 79/D4
Vestmannaeyjar, Ice. 79/N7
Vestone, It. 100/D1
Vestvågøy, Nor. 79/E1
Vestvågøya (isl.), Nor. 79/E1
Vesuvio (Vesuvius) (vol.), It. 88/D2
Veszprém (prov.), Hun. 90/C2
Veszprém, Hun. 90/C2
Vészto, Hun. 90/E2
Vet (riv.), SAfr. 148/D3
Vétheuil, Fr. 72/H4
Vetlanda, Swe. 80/F3
Vetluga (riv.), Rus. 106/E4
Vetralla, It. 88/C1
Vétraz, Fr. 98/C5
Větřní, Czh. 97/H5
Vettore (peak), It. 85/K5
Veude (riv.), Fr. 84/D3
Veurne, Belg. 94/B1
Vevey, Swi. 98/C5
Vex, Swi. 98/D5
Veybach (riv.), Ger. 95/F2
Veyle (riv.), Fr. 98/B5
Veyrier-du-Lac, Fr. 98/C6
Vézelise, Fr. 98/C1
Vézère (riv.), Fr. 84/D4
Vezirköprü, Turk. 132/C2
Vezza d'Oglio, It. 99/G5
Vezzano Ligure, It. 100/C4
Viacha, Bol. 192/E7
Viadana, It. 100/D3
Viana, Braz. 196/A1
Viana del Bollo, Sp. 86/B1
Viana do Alentejo, Port. 86/A3
Viana do Castelo, Port. 86/A2
Viana do Castelo (dist.), Port. 86/A2
Vianden, Lux. 95/F4
Vianen, Neth. 92/C4
Viangchan (Vientiane) (cap.), Laos 120/C2
Viar (riv.), Sp. 86/C4
Viareggio, It. 100/D5
Viarmes, Fr. 72/K4
Viaur (riv.), Fr. 84/E4
Vibbard, Mo, US 179/E5
Vibo Valentia, It. 88/E3
Viborg, Den. 80/C3
Viborg (co.), Den. 80/C3
Vic, Sp. 87/G2
Vic-en-Bigorre, Fr. 84/D5
Vic-Fezensac, Fr. 84/D5
Vicam, Mex. 184/C3
Vicar, Sp. 86/D4
Vicarello, It. 100/D5
Vicchio, It. 101/E6
Vice, Peru 198/A2
Vicente (pt.), Ca, US 178/F8
Vicente Guerrero, Mex. 184/E4
Vicente Guerrero, Mex. 184/A2
Vicente López, Arg. 201/J11
Vicenza, It. 101/E1
Vicenza (prov.), It. 99/H6
Vichada (riv.), Col. 192/E3
Vichada (dept.), Col. 194/D3
Vichaya, Bol. 198/D5

283
Vichu – Wagen

Vichuga, Rus. 102/J4
Vichy, Fr. 84/E3
Vickham (cape), Austl. 157/B3
Vicksburg, Ms, US 171/K4
Vicksburg Nat'l Mil. Park, Ms, US 171/K4
Vico, Fr. 88/A1
Vico (lake), It. 88/C1
Vico del Gargano, It. 90/B5
Vicopisano, It. 100/D5
Viçosa, Braz. 196/C3
Viçosa, Braz. 197/D2
Viçosa do Ceará, Braz. 196/B1
Vicosoprano, Swi. 99/F5
Vicou Gorge NP, Gre. 89/G3
Vicq, Fr. 72/H5
Victor Harbor, Austl. 155/H5
Víctor Rosales, Mex. 184/E4
Victoria, Malay. 122/E2
Victoria (peak), Phil. 123/E2
Victoria, Austl. 157/B2
Victoria (falls), Zim. 147/E4
Victoria, Arg. 199/D3
Victoria (cap.), BC, Can. 168/C3
Victoria (riv.), Austl. 151/C2
Victoria (state), Austl. 157/C3
Victoria, China 125/K3
Victoria (mt.), Myan. 125/F3
Victoria, Rom. 91/G3
Victoria, Hon. 186/E3
Victoria, Chile 200/B3
Victoria (peak), Belz. 186/D2
Victoria, Gren. 195/F1
Victoria (isl.), NW,Nun., Can. 164/E1
Victoria (str.), Nun., Can. 164/F2
Victoria (lake), Afr. 146/B3
Victoria de las Tunas, Cuba 187/G1
Victoria Land (pol. reg.), Ant. 202/M
Victoria Nile (riv.), Ugan. 139/M7
Victoria West, SAfr. 148/C3
Victorias, Phil. 121/D5
Victoriaville, Qu, Can. 173/G2
Victorica, Arg. 200/D3
Victorville, Ca, US 178/C1
Victory Junction, Ks, US 179/D5
Vicuña Mackenna, Arg. 200/D2
Vidal (cape), SAfr. 149/F3
Vidalia, La, US 171/K5
Vidalia, Ga, US 175/H3
Videira, Braz. 197/B3
Videle, Rom. 91/G3
Vidhošť (peak), Czh. 97/G4
Vidigueira, Port. 86/B3
Vidigulfo, It. 100/C2
Vidin, Bul. 91/F4
Vidisha, India 126/A4
Vidnoye, Rus. 103/W9
Vidor, Tx, US 171/J5
Vidor, It. 101/F1
Vidöstern (lake), Swe. 80/F3
Vidourle (riv.), Fr. 84/E5
Vie (riv.), Fr. 84/D2
Viechtach, Ger. 97/F4
Viedma, Arg. 200/E4
Viedma (lake), Arg. 201/B6
Viehberg (peak), Aus. 97/H5
Vieille-Eglise-en-Yvelines, Fr. 72/H6
Viejo (peak), Peru 198/B2
Viella, Sp. 87/F1
Vielsalm, Belg. 95/E3
Vienenburg, Ger. 93/H5
Vienna (Wien) (cap.), Aus. 91/N7
Vienna, Va, US 180/A6
Vienna, WV, US 172/D4
Vienne, Fr. 84/F4
Vienne (riv.), Fr. 84/D3
Vientiane (int'l arpt.), Laos 120/C2
Vientiane (Viangchan) (cap.), Laos 120/C2
Vieques (isl.), PR 183/M8
Vière (riv.), Fr. 95/D6
Vierlingsbeek, Neth. 92/D5
Viernheim, Ger. 96/B3
Vierre (riv.), Belg. 95/E4
Viersen, Ger. 92/D6
Vierzon, Fr. 84/E3
Viesca, Mex. 184/E3
Vieste, It. 88/E2
Viet Tri, Viet. 125/J3
Vietnam (ctry.) 120/D2
Vieux-Boucau-les-Bains, Fr. 84/C5
Vieux Carré, La, US 179/P17
Vieux-Charmont, Fr. 98/C2
Vieux-Condé, Fr. 94/C3
Vieux Fort, StL. 183/N9
Vieux-Thann, Fr. 98/D2
Vieze (riv.), Swi. 98/C5
Viga, Phil. 121/D5
Vigan, Phil. 121/D4
Vigarano Mainarda, It. 101/E3
Vigasio, It. 101/D2
Vigevano, It. 100/B2
Viggiù, It. 99/E6
Vigia, Braz. 193/J4
Vigliano Biellese, It. 100/B1
Viglio (peak), It. 88/C2
Vignacourt, Fr. 94/B3
Vignanello, It. 88/C1
Vignemale (peak), Fr. 84/C5
Vigneulles-lès-Hattonchâtel, Fr. 95/E6
Vigneux-sur-Seine, Fr. 72/K5
Vignola, It. 101/D4
Vignot, Fr. 95/E6
Vigo, Sp. 86/A1
Vigodarzere, It. 101/E2
Vigonovo, It. 101/E2
Vigonza, It. 101/E2
Vigrestad, Nor. 80/A2
Viguzzolo, It. 100/B3
Vihanti, Fin. 102/E2
Vihāri, Pak. 128/B4
Vihti, Fin. 81/L1
Viitasaari, Fin. 102/E3
Vijayawada, India 124/D4
Vík, Ice. 79/N7
Vik, Nor. 80/B1
Vikersund, Nor. 80/C2
Vikesā, Nor. 80/B2
Vikhren (peak), Bul. 91/F5
Viking, Ab, Can. 168/F2
Vikmanshyttan, Swe. 80/F1
Vila Bittencourt, Braz. 194/D5
Vila de Sena, Moz. 147/G4
Vila do Bispo, Port. 86/A4
Vila do Conde, Port. 86/A2
Vila do Porto, Azor., Port. 87/T13
Vila Franca de Xira, Port. 87/P10
Vila Franca do Campo, Azor., Port. 87/T13
Vila Nova de Fozcoa, Port. 86/B2
Vila Nova de Gaia, Port. 86/A2
Vila Nova de Milfontes, Port. 86/A4
Vila Pouca de Aguiar, Port. 86/B2
Vila Real, Port. 86/B2
Vila Real (dist.), Port. 86/B2
Vila Velha Argolas, Braz. 197/D2
Vila Velha de Ródão, Port. 86/B3
Vila Verde, Port. 86/A2
Vila Viçosa, Port. 86/B3
Viladecans, Sp. 87/K7
Vilafranca del Penedès, Sp. 87/K7
Vilaine (riv.), Fr. 84/B3
Vilanandro (cape), Madg. 149/H7
Vilanculos, Moz. 147/G5
Vilanova i la Geltrù, Sp. 87/K7
Vilar Formoso, Port. 86/B2
Vilcabamba, Peru 198/B3
Vilcea (prov.), Rom. 91/F3
Vilches, Sp. 86/D3
Vilhelmina, Swe. 79/F2
Vilhena, Braz. 192/F6
Viliya (riv.), Bela. 102/E5
Viljandi, Est. 81/L2
Viljoenskroon, SAfr. 148/D2
Vil'kitsogo (str.), Rus. 107/K2
Villa Alemana, Chile 200/N8
Villa Alhué, Chile 200/N9
Villa Ángela, Arg. 199/D2
Villa Atuel, Arg. 200/D2
Villa Bartolomea, It. 101/E2
Villa Bruzual, Ven. 194/D2
Villa Cañás, Arg. 200/E2
Villa Carcina, It. 100/D1
Villa Carlos Paz, Arg. 199/D3
Villa Chañar Ladeado, Arg. 200/E2
Villa Constitución, Arg. 200/E2
Villa Corzo, Mex. 186/C2
Villa Cuauhtemoc, Mex. 185/Q10
Villa d'Almè, It. 100/C1
Villa de Arista, Mex. 185/E4
Villa de Cos, Mex. 184/E4
Villa de Costa Rica, Mex. 184/D3
Villa de La Paz, Mex. 185/E4
Villa de Reyes, Mex. 185/E4
Villa del Carbón, Mex. 185/Q9
Villa del Carmen, Uru. 201/K10
Villa del Río, Sp. 86/C4
Villa di Serio, It. 100/C1
Villa Dolores, Arg. 199/C3
Villa Dolores, Arg. 200/D1
Villa Flores, Mex. 186/C2
Villa Gesell, Arg. 201/F3
Villa Guardia, It. 100/C1
Villa Hidalgo, Mex. 184/D4
Villa Hidalgo, Mex. 184/C2
Villa Huidobro, Arg. 200/D2
Villa Iris, Arg. 200/E3
Villa Isabela, DRep. 187/J2
Villa Jaragua, DRep. 187/J2
Villa Juárez, Mex. 184/C3
Villa Juárez, Mex. 184/D3
Villa La Angostura, Arg. 200/C4
Villa Lázaro Cárdenas, Mex. 185/M6
Villa López, Mex. 184/D3
Villa Mantero, Arg. 201/J10
Villa María, Arg. 199/D3
Villa Minozzo, It. 100/D4
Villa Montes, Bol. 192/F8
Villa Nueva, Arg. 200/C2
Villa Nueva, Guat. 186/D3
Villa Nueva, Nic. 186/E3
Villa Opicina, It. 101/G1
Villa Park, Il, US 177/Q16
Villa Park, Ca, US 178/G8
Villa Regina, Arg. 200/D3
Villa Rica, Peru 198/C3
Villa Rosario, Col. 194/C3
Villa Sandino, Nic. 187/E3
Villa Sarmiento, Arg. 200/D2
Villa Serrano, Bol. 192/F7
Villa Unión, Arg. 199/C2
Villa Unión, Mex. 184/D4
Villa Valeria, Arg. 200/D2
Villa Verucchio, It. 101/F5
Villaba, Sp. 86/E1
Villablino, Sp. 86/B1
Villacañas, Sp. 86/D3
Villacarrillo, Sp. 86/D3
Villada, Sp. 86/C1
Villadiego, Sp. 86/C1
Villadose, It. 101/E2
Villadossola, It. 99/E5
Villafamés, Sp. 87/E2
Villafranca, Sp. 86/E1
Villafranca d'Asti, It. 100/B3
Villafranca de los Barros, Sp. 86/B3
Villafranca del Bierzo, Sp. 86/B1
Villafranca del Cid, Sp. 87/E2
Villafranca di Verona, It. 101/D2
Villafranca in Lunigiana, It. 100/C4
Villagarcía, Sp. 86/A1
Villagrán, Mex. 185/F3
Villaguay, Arg. 199/E3
Villahermosa, Sp. 86/D3
Villahermosa, Mex. 186/C2
Villajoyosa, Sp. 87/E3
Villalba, Sp. 86/B1
Villalcampo, Embalse de (res.), Sp. 86/B2
Villaldama, Mex. 174/C5
Villalón de Campos, Sp. 86/C1
Villalonga, Arg. 200/E3
Villalpando, Sp. 86/C2
Villamartín, Sp. 86/C4
Villandro (peak), It. 99/H4
Villanova, It. 101/E4
Villanova, It. 101/E4
Villanova d'Asti, It. 100/A3
Villanova Mondovì, It. 100/A4
Villanterio, It. 100/C2
Villanueva, Mex. 184/E4
Villanueva, Col. 194/C2
Villanueva, Hon. 186/E3
Villanueva de Arosa, Sp. 86/A1
Villanueva de Córdoba, Sp. 86/C3
Villanueva de la Serena, Sp. 86/C3
Villanueva de los Infantes, Sp. 86/D3
Villanueva de Oscos, Sp. 86/B1
Villanueva del Arzobispo, Sp. 86/D3
Villanuova sul Clisi, It. 100/D1
Villány, Hun. 90/D3
Villar del Arzobispo, Sp. 87/E3
Villarcayo, Sp. 86/D1
Villardevós, Sp. 86/B2
Villarreal de los Infantes, Sp. 87/E3
Villarrica, Par. 199/E2
Villarrica, Chile 200/B3
Villarrica (vol.), Chile 200/C3
Villarrica (lake), Chile 200/B3
Villarrica, PN, Chile 200/C3
Villarrobledo, Sp. 86/D3
Villarrubia de los Ojos, Sp. 86/D3
Villars-les-Dombes, Fr. 98/B6
Villars-sur-Glâne, Swi. 98/D4
Villas, NJ, US 180/D5
Villasana de Mena, Sp. 86/D1
Villasanta, It. 100/C1
Villastellone, It. 100/A3
Villaverde del Río, Sp. 86/C4
Villaverla, It. 101/E1
Villavicencio, Col. 194/C3
Villaviciosa, Sp. 86/C1
Villaviciosa de Odón, Sp. 87/N9
Villazón, Bol. 199/C1
Villecresnes, Fr. 72/K5
Villefranche-de-Rouergue, Fr. 84/E4
Villefranche-sur-Saône, Fr. 84/F4
Villejuif, Fr. 72/K5
Villemur-sur-Tarn, Fr. 84/D5
Villena, Sp. 87/E3
Villeneuve, Swi. 98/C5
Villeneuve-d'Ascq, Fr. 94/C2
Villeneuve-le-Comte, Fr. 72/L5
Villeneuve-le-Roi, Fr. 72/K5
Villeneuve-lès-Avignon, Fr. 84/F5
Villeneuve-Saint-Denis, Fr. 72/L5
Villeneuve-Saint-Georges, Fr. 72/K5
Villeneuve-Saint-Germain, Fr. 94/C5
Villeneuve-sur-Lot, Fr. 84/D4
Villeneuve-sur-Yonne, Fr. 84/E2
Villeneuve-Tolosane, Fr. 84/D5
Villennes-sur-Seine, Fr. 72/H5
Villeparisis, Fr. 72/K5
Villepinte, Fr. 72/K5
Villepreux, Fr. 72/J5
Villeroy, Fr. 72/L4
Villers-Bretonneux, Fr. 94/B4
Villers-Cotterêts, Fr. 94/C5
Villers-en-Arthies, Fr. 72/H4
Villers-le-Bouillet, Belg. 95/E2
Villers-le-Lac, Fr. 98/C3
Villers-lès-Nancy, Fr. 95/F6
Villers-Saint-Genest, Fr. 72/L4
Villers-Saint-Paul, Fr. 94/B5
Villers-Semeuse, Fr. 95/D4
Villersexel, Fr. 98/C2
Villerupt, Fr. 95/E5
Villette, Fr. 72/H5
Villeurbanne, Fr. 98/A6
Villevaudé, Fr. 72/K5
Villiers, SAfr. 148/E2
Villiers-en-Lieu, Fr. 95/D6
Villiers-le-Bel, Fr. 72/K4
Villiers-Saint-Georges, Fr. 94/C6
Villiers-sur-Marne, Fr. 72/K5
Villiers-sur-Morin, Fr. 72/L5
Villiersdorp, SAfr. 148/L10
Villieu-Loyes-Mollon, Fr. 98/B6
Villingen-Schwenningen, Ger. 99/E1
Villmar, Ger. 96/B2
Villongo, It. 100/C1
Villorba, It. 101/F1
Vilnius (int'l arpt.), Lith. 81/L4
Vilnius (cap.), Lith. 81/L4
Vils, Aus. 99/G2
Vils (riv.), Ger. 82/F4
Vilsbiburg, Ger. 97/F6
Vilseck, Ger. 97/E3
Vilshofen, Ger. 97/G5
Vilters, Swi. 99/F3
Vilvoorde, Belg. 95/D2
Vilyuy (riv.), Rus. 109/L3
Vilyuy (range), Rus. 107/M3
Vimercate, It. 100/C1
Vimeu (reg.), Fr. 94/A3
Vimmerby, Swe. 80/F3
Vimodrone, It. 100/C2
Vimperk, Czh. 97/G4
Vina (riv.), Camr. 138/H6
Viña del Mar, Chile 200/N8
Vinanivao, Madg. 149/J6
Vinaroz, Sp. 87/F2
Vincennes, In, US 172/C4
Vincennes (lake), Fr. 72/L5
Vincennes (bay), Ant. 202/H
Vincennes, Fr. 72/K5
Vincent, Ca, US 178/B1
Vincentown, NJ, US 180/D4
Vinces, Ecu. 194/B5
Vincey, Fr. 98/C1
Vinchos, Peru 198/C4
Vinci, It. 101/D5
Vindeby, Den. 80/D4
Vindeln, Swe. 79/F2
Vindhya (range), India 126/A4
Vineland, NJ, US 180/D5
Vineland Station, On, Can. 173/R9
Vineuil, Fr. 84/D3
Vingåker, Swe. 80/F2
Vinh, Viet. 120/D2
Vinh An, Viet. 121/A4
Vinh Long, Viet. 120/D4
Vinh Yen, Viet. 120/D1
Vinhais, Port. 86/B2
Vinhedo, Braz. 197/G8
Vinica, FYROM 89/H2
Vinita, Ok, US 171/J3
Vinju Mare, Rom. 90/F3
Vinkovci, Cro. 90/D3
Vinningen, Ger. 95/G5
Vinnyts'ka Oblasti, Ukr. 104/D2
Vinnytsya, Ukr. 104/D2
Vinon-sur-Verdon, Fr. 84/F5
Vinson Massif (peak), Ant. 202/U
Viola, De, US 180/C5
Viola, NY, US 181/J7
Violet, La, US 179/Q17
Violet Town, Austl. 157/C3
Viosne (riv.), Fr. 94/A5
Virac, Phil. 121/D5
Viracopos (int'l arpt.), Braz. 197/F7
Viranşehir, Turk. 132/D2
Virār, India 131/K5
Virden, Mb, Can. 169/H3
Vire, Fr. 84/C2
Vire (riv.), Fr. 84/C2
Viren (lake), Swe. 80/F2
Vireux-Wallerand, Fr. 95/D3
Virgem da Lapa, Braz. 196/B5
Virgin (riv.), US 170/D3
Virgin (isls.), UK,US 183/M8
Virgin Gorda (isl.), UK 183/M8
Virgin Islands NP, USVI 183/M8
Virginia, SAfr. 148/D3
Virginia (state), US 172/E4
Virginia City, Nv, US 170/C3
Virginia Water, Eng, UK 72/B2
Viriat, Fr. 98/B5
Virieu-le-Grand, Fr. 98/B6
Viroflay, Fr. 72/J5
Viroin (riv.), Belg. 95/D3
Viroqua, Wi, US 171/K2
Virovitica, Cro. 90/C3
Virserum, Swe. 80/F3
Virton, Belg. 95/E4
Virú, Peru 198/B3
Virudunagar, India 124/C6
Virunga, D.R. Congo 146/A3
Virunga NP, D.R. Congo 146/A3
Viry-Châtillon, Fr. 72/K6
Vis (isl.), Cro. 90/C4
Visaginas, Lith. 81/M4
Visalia, Ca, US 170/C3
Visandre (riv.), Fr. 72/M5
Visayan (sea), Phil. 121/D5
Visbek, Ger. 93/F3
Visby, Swe. 80/H3
Visconde do Rio Branco, Braz. 197/D2
Viscount Melville (sound), NW,Nun., Can. 165/R7
Visé, Belg. 95/E2
Višegrad, Bosn. 90/D4
Viseu, Port. 86/B2
Viseu (dist.), Port. 86/B2
Vişeu de Sus, Rom. 91/G2
Vishākhapatnam, India 124/D4
Vishera (riv.), Rus. 103/L3
Vishoek, SAfr. 148/L11
Viskafors, Swe. 80/E3
Vislanda, Swe. 80/F3
Visnagar, India 131/K4
Višnjevac, Cro. 90/D3
Visoko, Bosn. 90/D4
Visp, Swi. 98/D5
Visperterminen, Swi. 98/D5
Visselhövede, Ger. 93/G3
Vissenbjerg, Den. 80/D4
Vissoie, Swi. 98/D5
Vista, Ca, US 178/C4
Vistonís (lake), Gre. 89/J2
Vistula (riv.), Pol. 83/K2
Vit (riv.), Bul. 91/G4
Vita, Mb, Can. 169/J3
Viterbo, It. 88/C1
Vitez, Bosn. 90/C3
Viti Levu (isl.), Fiji 158/G6
Vitigudino, Sp. 86/B2
Vitim (plat.), Rus. 107/M4
Vitim (riv.), Rus. 109/L4
Vitkuv Kamen (peak), Czh. 97/H5
Vitomirica, Serb. 90/E4
Vitor, Peru 198/D5
Vitória, Braz. 197/D2
Vitoria, Sp. 86/D1
Vitória da Conquista, Braz. 196/B4
Vitória de Santo Antão, Braz. 196/D3
Vitória do Mearim, Braz. 196/A1
Vitorino Freire, Braz. 196/A2
Vitosha NP, Bul. 91/F4
Vitré, Fr. 84/C2
Vitrey-sur-Mance, Fr. 98/B2
Vitrolles, Fr. 84/F5
Vitry-en-Artois, Fr. 94/B3
Vitry-le-François, Fr. 95/D6
Vitry-sur-Seine, Fr. 72/K5
Vitsyebsk, Bela. 81/P4
Vitsyebskaya Voblasts, Bela. 102/E5
Vittangi, Swe. 79/G2
Vittel, Fr. 98/B1
Vittoria, It. 88/D4
Vittorio Veneto, It. 85/K4
Vivarais, Monts du (mts.), Fr. 84/F4
Viveiro, Sp. 86/B1
Viverone (lake), It. 100/B2
Viverone, It. 100/B2
Vivian, La, US 171/J4
Vivonne, Fr. 84/D3
Vizcaíno, Sierra (mts.), Mex. 184/B3
Vize, Turk. 91/H5
Vizhas (riv.), Rus. 103/K2
Vizianagaram, India 124/D4
Vlaardingen, Neth. 92/B5
Vlădeasa (peak), Rom. 91/F2
Vladikavkaz, Rus. 105/H4
Vladimir, Rus. 102/J4
Vladimirskaya Oblast, Rus. 102/J5
Vladivostok, Rus. 113/P3
Vlagtwedde, Neth. 93/E2
Vlăhiţa, Rom. 91/G2
Vlajna (peak), Serb. 90/E4
Vlasenica, Bosn. 90/D3
Vlašim, Czh. 85/L2
Vlasotince, Serb. 90/F4
Vlieland (isl.), Neth. 82/C2
Vliestroom (chan.), Neth. 92/C2
Vlijmen, Neth. 92/C5
Vlissingen, Neth. 92/A6
Vlotho, Ger. 93/F4
Vltava (riv.), Czh. 83/H4
Vnukovo (int'l arpt.), Rus. 103/W9
Vobarno, It. 100/D1
Vöcklabruck, Aus. 97/G6
Vöcklamarkt, Aus. 97/G6
Vodice, Cro. 90/B3
Vodlozero (lake), Rus. 102/H3
Vodňany, Czh. 97/H4
Vodskov, Den. 80/D3
Voerde, Ger. 92/D5
Vogan, Togo 145/F5
Vogelsberg (mts.), Ger. 85/H1
Voghera, It. 100/C3
Vogogna, It. 99/E6
Vogorno (lake), Swi. 99/E5
Vogtareuth, Ger. 97/F7
Vogtland (reg.), Ger. 82/F3
Vohenstrauss, Ger. 97/F3
Vohilava, Madg. 149/H8
Vohimena (cape), Madg. 149/H9
Vohipeno, Madg. 149/H8
Vohiposa, Madg. 149/H8
Voi, Kenya 146/C3
Void-Vacon, Fr. 95/E6
Voil (lake), Sc, UK 78/B4
Voinjama, Libr. 144/C4
Voinsles, Fr. 72/M5
Voiron, Fr. 84/F4
Voise (riv.), Fr. 84/D2
Voisey (bay), Nf, Can. 165/K3
Voiteur, Fr. 98/B4
Vojosë (riv.), Alb. 90/D5
Vojvodina (prov.), Serb. 90/D3
Völklingen, Ger. 95/F5
Volano, It. 99/H6
Volary, Czh. 97/G5
Volcán Barú, PN, Pan. 187/F4
Volcán Poás, PN, CR 187/E4
Volcano, Hi, US 166/U11
Volcano (isls.), Japan 158/C2
Volcans NP, Rwa. 146/A3
Volchiy Nos (cape), Rus. 81/Q1
Volda, Nor. 79/C3
Volendam, Neth. 92/C3
Volga (riv.), Rus. 69/J3
Volga-Baltic Waterway (canal), Rus. 102/H3
Volgelsheim, Fr. 98/D1
Volgodonsk, Rus. 105/G3
Volgograd (int'l arpt.), Rus. 105/H2
Volgograd (res.), Rus. 105/H2
Volgogradskaya Oblast, Rus. 105/G2
Volkach (riv.), Ger. 96/D3
Volkach, Ger. 96/D3
Volkeradam (dam), Neth. 92/B5
Völkermarkt, Aus. 85/L3
Volketswil, Swi. 99/E3
Volkhov, Rus. 81/Q2
Volkhov (riv.), Rus. 102/G4
Volkmarsen, Ger. 93/G6
Volksrust, SAfr. 149/E2
Volodymyr-Volyns'kyy, Ukr. 104/C2
Vologda, Rus. 102/H4
Vologdskaya Oblast, Rus. 102/J3
Vologne (riv.), Fr. 82/D4
Volos (gulf), Gre. 89/H3
Vólos, Gre. 89/H3
Volpago del Montello, It. 101/F1
Volpiano, It. 100/A2
Völs, Aus. 99/H3
Vol'sk, Rus. 105/H1
Volta (riv.), Gha. 138/F6
Volta (pol. reg.), Gha. 145/F5
Volta (lake), Gha. 145/E4
Volta Mantovana, It. 100/D2
Volta Redonda, Braz. 197/J7
Voltana, It. 101/E3
Volterra, It. 101/D6
Voltlage, Ger. 93/E4
Volturino (peak), It. 88/D2
Volturno (riv.), It. 88/D2
Volubilis (ruin), Mor. 142/B2
Vólvi (lake), Gre. 89/H2
Volyně, Czh. 97/G4
Volyňka (riv.), Czh. 97/G4
Volyns'ka Oblasti, Ukr. 104/C2
Volzhsk, Rus. 103/L5
Volzhskiy, Rus. 105/H2
Von Frank (mtn.), Ak, US 176/H3
Von Ormy, Tx, US 179/T21
Vondrozo, Madg. 149/H8
Vónitsa, Gre. 89/G3
Vonne (riv.), Fr. 84/D3
Voorburg, Neth. 92/B4
Voorne (isl.), Neth. 92/B5
Voorschoten, Neth. 92/B4
Voorst, Neth. 92/D4
Vopnafjördhur, Ice. 79/P6
Vorab (peak), Swi. 99/F4
Vorarlberg (prov.), Aus. 82/E5
Vorbach (riv.), Ger. 96/C4
Vorchdorf, Aus. 97/G6
Vorden, Neth. 92/D4
Vorderrhein (riv.), Swi. 85/H3
Vorderweissenbach, Aus. 97/H5
Vordingborg, Den. 80/D4
Voreppe, Fr. 84/F4
Vorkuta, Rus. 103/P2
Vorkuta (int'l arpt.), Rus. 103/Q2
Vormsi (isl.), Est. 81/K2
Vóroi, Gre. 89/J5
Vorona (riv.), Rus. 105/G1
Voronezh (int'l arpt.), Rus. 104/F2
Voronezh (riv.), Rus. 104/F1
Voronezh, Rus. 104/F2
Voronezhskaya Oblast, Rus. 105/G2
Voron'ya (riv.), Rus. 102/G1
Vorskla (riv.), Ukr. 104/E2
Vorst, Belg. 95/E1
Võrts (lake), Est. 81/L2
Võru, Est. 81/M3
Vorya (riv.), Rus. 103/X8
Vosburg, SAfr. 148/C3
Vösendorf, Aus. 91/N7
Vosges (dept.), Fr. 98/C1
Vosges (mts.), Fr. 82/D5
Voskresensk, Rus. 102/H5
Voss, Nor. 80/B1
Vostok (isl.), Kiri. 159/K6
Vostok (cape), Ant. 202/V
Vostok, Rus., Ant. 202/H
Votice, Czh. 97/H3
Votkinsk, Rus. 103/M4
Votkinsk (res.), Rus. 103/M4
Votorantim, Braz. 197/C2
Votuporanga, Braz. 197/B2
Vouga (riv.), Port. 86/A2
Vouglans (lake), Fr. 98/B5
Vouglans, Barrage de (dam), Fr. 98/B5
Voujeaucourt, Fr. 98/C3
Voúla, Gre. 89/N9
Voulangis, Fr. 72/L5
Vouvry, Swi. 98/C5
Voúxa (cape), Gre. 89/H5
Vouziers, Fr. 95/D5
Voy-Vozh, Rus. 103/M3
Voyageurs NP, Mn, US 172/A1
Voyeykov Ice Shelf, Ant. 202/J
Voytolovka (riv.), Rus. 103/T7
Vozhe (lake), Rus. 102/H3
Voznesens'k, Ukr. 91/K2
Vozrozhdeniya (isl.), Uzb. 129/C4
Vrå, Den. 80/C3
Vraine (riv.), Fr. 98/B1
Vrancea (prov.), Rom. 91/H3
Vrangelya (isl.), Rus. 107/T2
Vranjska Banja, Serb. 90/E4
Vranov nad Teplou, Slvk. 83/L4
Vrapčište, FYROM 89/G2
Vratsa, Bul. 91/F4
Vrbas, Serb. 90/D3
Vrbas (riv.), Bosn. 90/C3
Vrchy (peak), Czh. 97/H4
Vrede, SAfr. 148/E2
Vredefort, SAfr. 148/D2
Vreden, Ger. 92/D4
Vredenburg-Saldanha, SAfr. 148/K10
Vredendal, SAfr. 148/B3
Vresse-sur-Semois, Belg. 95/D4
Vrhnika, Slov. 85/L4
Vries, Neth. 92/D2
Vriezenveen, Neth. 92/D4
Vrigstad, Swe. 80/F3
Vrin (riv.), Fr. 82/B5
Vrindāban, India 126/A2
Vrnjačka Banja, Serb. 90/E4
Vrondádhos, Gre. 89/K3
Vršac, Serb. 90/E3
Vryburg, SAfr. 148/D2
Vryheid, SAfr. 149/E2
Vsetín, Czh. 83/K4
Vsevidof (mt.), Ak, US 176/E5
Vsevolozhsk, Rus. 103/T6
Vtáčnik (peak), Slvk. 83/K4
Vught, Neth. 92/C5
Vukovar, Cro. 90/D3
Vulcan, Ab, Can. 168/E3
Vulcan, Rom. 91/F3
Vulcano (isl.), It. 88/D3
Vülchedrüm, Bul. 91/F4
Vülchi Dol, Bul. 91/H4
Vulci (ruin), It. 88/B1
Vung Tau, Viet. 120/D4
Vuohijärvi (lake), Fin. 81/M1
Vuollerim, Swe. 79/G2
Vuoska (lake), Rus. 81/N1
Vuotso, Fin. 102/E1
Vürbitsa, Bul. 91/H4
Vuria (peak), Kenya 146/C3
Vürshets, Bul. 91/F4
Vyāra, India 131/K4
Vyatka (riv.), Rus. 106/E4
Vyatskiye Polyany, Rus. 103/L4
Vyazemskiy, Rus. 113/P2
Vyaz'ma, Rus. 102/G5
Vyborg, Rus. 81/N1
Vyborg (bay), Rus. 81/N1
Vychegda (riv.), Rus. 106/F3
Vygozero (lake), Rus. 102/G3
Vyhorlat (peak), Slvk. 83/M4
Vyksa, Rus. 102/J5
Vym' (riv.), Rus. 103/L3
Vynohradiv, Ukr. 83/M4
Vyrnwy (riv.), Wal, UK 74/C1
Vyshniy Volochek, Rus. 102/G4
Vyškov, Czh. 83/J4

W

W du Benin, PN du, Ben. 145/F4
W du Burkino Faso, PN du, Burk. 145/F4
W du Niger, PN du, Ben. 138/F5
W du Niger, PN du, Niger 145/F3
W. J. van Blommestein (lake), Sur. 193/G2
Wa, Gha. 145/E4
Waal, Ger. 99/G2
Waal (riv.), Neth. 92/C5
Waalre, Neth. 92/C6
Waalwijk, Neth. 92/C5
Waarschoot, Belg. 94/C1
Wabasca, Ab, Can. 168/E2
Wabasca (riv.), Ab, Can. 164/E3
Wabash, In, US 172/C3
Wabash (riv.), Il,In, US 172/C4
Wabē Shebelē Wenz (riv.), Eth. 139/P6
Wabern, Ger. 93/G6
Wabigoon (lake), On, Can. 169/K3
Wabowden, Mb, Can. 169/J2
Wąbrzeźno, Pol. 83/K2
Wabu (lake), China 114/D4
Wabu, SKor. 115/G6
Wachenheim an der Weinstrasse, Ger. 96/B4
Wachi, Japan 119/H5
Wachtebeke, Belg. 94/C1
Wachtendonk, Ger. 92/D6
Wächtersbach, Ger. 96/C2
Wackernheim, Ger. 96/B3
Wackersdorf, Ger. 97/F4
Waco, Tx, US 171/H5
Waconda (lake), Ks, US 171/H3
Waconia, Mn, US 169/K4
Wad Medanī, Sudan 139/M5
Wada, Japan 119/E3
Wadayama, Japan 119/G5
Wadbilliga NP, Austl. 157/D3
Waddān, Libya 138/J2
Waddell, Az, US 179/R18
Waddell (dam), Az, US 179/R18
Waddenzee (sound), Neth. 82/C2
Waddington (mt.), BC, Can. 168/B3
Waddinxveen, Neth. 92/B4
Waddy (pt.), Austl. 156/D4
Wadena, Sk, Can. 169/H3
Wadena, Mn, US 169/K4
Wädenswil, Swi. 99/E3
Wadern, Ger. 95/F4
Wadersloh, Ger. 93/F5
Wadgassen, Ger. 95/F5
Wādī al Layl, Tun. 142/M6
Wādī As Sīr, Jor. 133/D4
Wādī Majardah (riv.), Tun. 142/L6
Wādī Mūsá, Jor. 133/D4
Wading (riv.), NJ, US 180/D4
Wading River, NY, US 181/F2
Wadowice, Pol. 83/K4
Wadsworth, Il, US 177/Q15
Waegwan, SKor. 115/E5
Wafangdian, China 115/A3
Wagenfeld-Hasslingen, Ger. 93/F3
Wageningen, Neth. 92/C5

285
West L – Wooli

West Lincoln, Ne, US 171/H2
West Lothian (pol. reg.), Sc, UK 171/H2
West Lunga NP, Zam. 147/D3
West Memphis, Ar, US 171/K4
West Midlands (co.), Eng, UK 75/E1
West Milford, NJ, US 181/H7
West Milton, Pa, US 180/B1
West Monroe, La, US 171/J4
West New York, NJ, US 181/J8
West Nyack, NY, US 181/K7
West Orange, NJ, US 181/J8
West Palm Beach, Fl, US 175/H5
West Paterson, NJ, US 181/J8
West Pensacola, Fl, US 175/G4
West Plains, Mo, US 171/K3
West Point, Ne, US 169/J5
West Point (lake), Al,Ga, US 175/G3
West Point, Ms, US 175/F3
West Point (mil. res.), NY, US 181/D1
West Point, Ut, US 179/J11
West Reading, Pa, US 180/C3
West Redding, Ct, US 181/E1
West Road (riv.), BC, Can. 168/B2
West Sacramento, Ca, US 177/L9
West Sayville, NY, US 181/E2
West Seneca, NY, US 173/S10
West Siberian (plain), Rus. 106/H3
West Sussex (co.), Eng, UK 75/E5
West-Terschelling, Neth. 92/C2
West Valley City, Ut, US 179/K12
West Vancouver, BC, Can. 168/C3
West Virginia (state), US 172/D4
West Warren, Ut, US 179/J11
West Water (riv.), Sc, UK 78/D3
West Weber, Ut, US 179/J11
West Wyalong, Austl. 157/C2
West York, Pa, US 180/B4
Westall (pt.), Austl. 155/G5
Westbrook, Ct, US 181/F1
Westbury, NY, US 181/L9
Westchester (co.), NY, US 181/E1
Westcott, Eng, UK 72/B3
Westerbork, Neth. 92/D3
Westerburg, Ger. 95/G2
Westerham, Eng, UK 72/D3
Westerheim, Ger. 99/G1
Westerholt, Ger. 93/E1
Westerkappeln, Ger. 93/E4
Westerland, Ger. 80/C4
Westerlo, Belg. 95/D1
Western (prov.), Kenya 146/B2
Western (des.), Egypt 139/L2
Western (prov.), Ugan. 146/A2
Western (pol. reg.), Gha. 145/E5
Western (chan.), SKor. 115/E5
Western Area (prov.), SLeo. 144/B4
Western Australia (state), Austl. 151/B3
Western Cape (prov.), SAfr. 148/C4
Western Ghats (mts.), India 131/K5
Western Run (riv.), Md, US 180/B4
Western Sahara (reg.) 138/B3
Western Sayans (mts.), Rus. 106/J4
Westerschelde (chan.), Belg. 92/A6
Westerstede, Ger. 93/E2
Westerville, Oh, US 172/D3
Westervoort, Neth. 92/C5
Westerwald (mts.), Ger. 82/D3
Westfield, NJ, US 181/H9
Westgat (chan.), Neth. 92/D2
Westhampton, NY, US 181/F2
Westhampton Beach, NY, US 181/F2
Westhausen, Ger. 96/D5
Westheim, Ger. 96/B4
Westhill, Sc, UK 78/D2
Westhofen, Ger. 96/B3
Westhoughton, Eng, UK 77/F4
Westkapelle, Neth. 92/A5
Westlake Village, Ca, US 178/B2
Westland, Mi, US 177/F7
Westland NP, NZ 159/R11
Westminster, Co, US 179/B3
Westminster, Md, US 180/B4
Westminster, Ca, US 178/F8
Westminster, City of (bor.), Eng, UK 72/A1
Westmont, Il, US 177/P16
Westmont (Haddon), NJ, US 180/C4
Westmorland (reg.), Eng, UK 77/F3
Westmount, Qu, Can. 173/N7
Weston, Mo, US 179/D5
Weston, Ct, US 181/E1
Weston-super-Mare, Eng, UK 74/D4
Westonaria, SAfr. 148/P13
Westport, Ire. 73/P10
Westport, NZ 159/S11
Westport, Ct, US 181/E1
Westray (isl.), Sc, UK 73/V14
Westview, Il, US 179/G8
Westwego, La, US 179/P17
Westwood, Ks, US 179/D5
Westwood, NJ, US 181/J8
Wet (mts.), Co, US 174/B2
Wetar (isl.), Indo. 123/G5
Wetar (str.), Indo. 123/G5
Wetaskiwin, Ab, Can. 168/E2
Wete, Tanz. 146/C4
Wétetnagami (riv.), Qu, Can. 172/E1
Wetherell (lake), Austl. 157/B2
Wetter, Ger. 93/E6
Wetter (riv.), Ger. 96/B2
Wetterau (reg.), Ger. 96/C2
Wetteren, Belg. 94/C2
Wetterhorn (peak), Swi. 98/E4
Wettingen, Swi. 99/E3
Wettringen, Ger. 93/E4
Wetzikon, Swi. 99/E3
Wetzlar, Ger. 96/B1
Wetzstein (peak), Ger. 97/E2
Wevelgem, Belg. 94/C2
Wewak, PNG 158/D5
Wewoka, Ok, US 171/H4
Wexford, Ire. 73/Q10
Wey (riv.), Eng, UK 72/A3
Weybridge, Eng, UK 72/B2
Weyburn, Sk, Can. 169/H3
Weygand (ruin), Alg. 141/F4
Weyhausen, Ger. 93/H4
Weyland (pt.), Austl. 155/G5
Weymouth, Eng, UK 74/D5
Weymouth (bay), Eng, UK 74/D5
Wha Ti, NW, Can. 164/E2
Whakatane, NZ 159/T10
Whale Cove, Nun., Can. 164/G2
Whalsey (isl.), Sc, UK 73/W13
Whangarei, NZ 159/S10
Wharfe (riv.), Eng, UK 77/G3
Wheat Ridge, Co, US 179/B3
Wheatland, Wy, US 169/G5
Wheaton, Il, US 172/B3
Wheaton-Glenmont, Md, US 180/A5
Wheaton Village, NJ, US 180/C5
Wheeler (peak), Nv, US 170/D3
Wheeler (peak), NM, US 171/F3
Wheeler (lake), Al, US 175/G3
Wheeler Springs, Ca, US 178/A1
Wheeling, WV, US 172/D3
Wheeling, Il, US 177/Q15
Wheelwright, Arg. 200/E2
Whernside (peak), Eng, UK 77/F3
Whickham, Eng, UK 77/G2
Whidbey (pt.), Austl. 155/G5
Whinham (mt.), Austl. 155/F3
Whitburn, Sc, UK 78/C5
Whitby, On, Can. 173/S8
Whitby, Eng, UK 77/H3
White (lake), La, US 171/J5
White (riv.), Ar, US 171/J4
White (riv.), SD, US 169/H5
White (riv.), Tx, US 171/G4
White (lake), Austl. 155/F2
White (lake), On, Can. 172/C1
White (riv.), In, US 172/C4
White (pass), Ak, US 176/L3
White (sea), Rus. 102/H2
White (bay), Nf, Can. 165/L3
White Bear (riv.), Nf, Can. 173/K1
White City, Sk, Can. 169/G3
White Cliffs, Austl. 157/B1
White Coomb (peak), Sc, UK 78/C6
White Esk (riv.), Sc, UK 78/C6
White Fox, Sk, Can. 169/G2
White Hall, Md, US 180/B4
White Haven, Pa, US 180/C1
White Marsh, Md, US 180/B5
White Mountain, Ak, US 176/F3
White Mountains Nat'l Rec. Area, Ak, US 176/J2
White Nile (riv.), Sudan 139/M7
White Oak, Md, US 180/B5
White Otter (lake), On, Can. 169/K3
White Plains, NY, US 181/K7
White River, On, Can. 172/C1
White Rock, NM, US 174/B3
White Sands, NM, US 170/F4
White Sands Nat'l Mon., NM, US 170/F4
White Sulphur Springs, Mt, US 168/F4
White Volta (riv.), Gha. 145/E4
White, West Fork (riv.), In, US 172/C4
Whiteadder Water (riv.), Sc, UK 78/D5
Whitecourt, Ab, Can. 168/E2
Whiteface (riv.), Mn, US 169/K4
Whitefield, Eng, UK 77/F4
Whitefish, Mt, US 168/E3
Whitefish (bay), US,Can. 172/C2
Whiteford (pt.), Wal, UK 74/B3
Whiteford, Md, US 180/B4
Whitehall, Mt, US 168/E4
Whitehall, Mi, US 172/C3
Whitehaven, Eng, UK 76/E2
Whitehead, NI, UK 76/C2
Whitehills, Sc, UK 78/D1
Whitehorse (cap.), Yk, Can. 176/L3
Whitehorse (hill), Eng, UK 75/E3
Whitehouse, Tx, US 171/J4
Whitemouth (riv.), Mb, Can. 169/K3
Whiteriver, Az, US 170/E4
Whiteside (chan.), Chile 201/C7
Whitesville, NJ, US 180/D3
Whiteville, NC, US 175/J3
Whitewater (lake), On, Can. 169/L3
Whitewood, Sk, Can. 169/H3
Whithorn, Sc, UK 76/D2
Whiting, In, US 177/R16
Whitley Bay, Eng, UK 77/G1
Whitmore Village, Hi, US 166/V12
Whitney (lake), Tx, US 171/H4
Whitney, Tx, US 171/H5
Whitsand (bay), Eng, UK 74/B6
Whitstable, Eng, UK 75/H4
Whitsunday (isl.), Austl. 151/D3
Whittaker, Mi, US 177/E7
Whittier, Ak, US 176/J3
Whittier, Ca, US 178/F8
Whittlesea, Austl. 157/G5
Whitton, Austl. 157/C2
Whitworth, Eng, UK 77/F4
Wholdaia (lake), NW, Can. 164/F2
Whyalla, Austl. 155/H5
Wi (isl.), SKor. 115/D5
Wiang Kosai NP, Thai. 120/B2
Wiarton, On, Can. 172/D2
Wiawso, Gha. 145/E5
Wichabai, Guy. 195/G4
Wichelen, Belg. 94/C2
Wichita (riv.), Tx, US 171/H4
Wichita (mts.), Ok, US 171/H4
Wichita Falls, Tx, US 171/H4
Wick, Sc, UK 73/S7
Wickenburg, Az, US 170/D4
Wickepin, Austl. 154/C5
Wickford, Eng, UK 72/E2
Wickham, Austl. 154/C2
Wicklow (mts.), Ire. 73/Q10
Wicklow (pass), Ire. 76/B5
Wicklow, Ire. 76/B6
Wicklow (pt.), Ire. 76/B6
Wickriede (riv.), Ger. 93/F4
Wid (riv.), Eng, UK 72/E2
Widnau, Swi. 99/F3
Widnes, Eng, UK 77/F5
Więcbork, Pol. 83/J2
Wied (riv.), Ger. 85/G1
Wiedau (riv.), Ger. 93/G2
Wiefelstede, Ger. 93/F2
Wiehengebirge (ridge), Ger. 93/F4
Wiehl, Ger. 95/G2
Wielenbach, Ger. 99/H2
Wieliczka, Pol. 83/L4
Wielkopolski NP, Pol. 83/J2
Wielkopolskie (prov.), Pol. 83/J2
Wielsbeke, Belg. 94/C2
Wieluń, Pol. 83/K3
Wien (riv.), Aus. 91/N7
Wien (prov.), Aus. 83/J4
Wien (Vienna) (cap.), Aus. 91/N7
Wiener Neudorf, Aus. 91/N7
Wiener Neustadt, Aus. 85/M3
Wienerwald (reg.), Aus. 91/N7
Wienwald (reg.), Aus. 85/L2
Wieprz (riv.), Pol. 83/M3
Wierden, Neth. 92/D4
Wieringermeerpolder (polder), Neth. 92/B3
Wieringerwerf, Neth. 92/C3
Wieruszów, Pol. 83/K3
Wiesbaden, Ger. 96/B2
Wiese (riv.), Ger. 85/G3
Wiese (isl.), Rus. 202/A
Wieseck (riv.), Ger. 96/B1
Wiesendangen, Swi. 99/E2
Wiesensteig, Ger. 96/C5
Wiesent (riv.), Ger. 96/E4
Wiesentheid, Ger. 96/D3
Wiesloch, Ger. 96/B4
Wiesmoor, Ger. 93/E2
Wietmarschen, Ger. 93/D4
Wietze, Ger. 93/G3
Wietze (riv.), Ger. 93/G3
Wietzendorf, Ger. 93/G3
Wieżyca (peak), Pol. 80/H4
Wigan, Eng, UK 77/F4
Wigan (co.), Eng, UK 77/F4
Wiggins, Ms, US 175/F4
Wight (isl.), UK 75/E5
Wigierski NP, Pol. 83/M1
Wignehies, Fr. 94/D3
Wigry (lake), Pol. 81/K5
Wigston, Eng, UK 75/E1
Wigtown, Sc, UK 76/D2
Wigtown (bay), Sc, UK 76/D2
Wijchen, Neth. 92/C5
Wijhe, Neth. 92/D4
Wijk bij Duurstede, Neth. 92/C5
Wil, Swi. 99/F3
Wilber, Ne, US 171/H2
Wilberforce, Austl. 156/G8
Wilbur, Wa, US 168/D4
Wilburton, Ok, US 171/J4
Wilcannia, Austl. 157/B1
Wilchingen, Swi. 99/E2
Wilczek (isl.), Rus. 106/G1
Wild (coast), SAfr. 148/E4
Wild Creek (res.), Pa, US 180/C2
Wild Rice (riv.), Mn, US 169/J4
Wild World, Md, US 180/B6
Wildau, Ger. 82/Q7
Wildbad im Schwarzwald, Ger. 96/B5
Wildberg, Ger. 96/B5
Wilder, Ks, US 179/D5
Wilderswil, Swi. 98/D4
Wildeshausen, Ger. 93/F3
Wildflecken, Ger. 96/C2
Wildgrat (peak), Aus. 99/G3
Wildhaus, Swi. 99/F3
Wildhorn (peak), Swi. 98/D5
Wildomar, Ca, US 178/C3
Wildspitze (peak), Aus. 99/G4
Wildstrubel (peak), Swi. 98/D5
Wildwood, NJ, US 180/D6
Wildwood Crest, NJ, US 180/D6
Wilge (riv.), SAfr. 148/E2
Wilhelm II (coast), Ant. 202/F
Wilhelmina (mts.), Sur. 192/G3
Wilhelminakanaal (canal), Neth. 92/C5
Wilhelmshaven, Ger. 93/F1
Wilhering, Aus. 97/H6
Wilkes-Barre, Pa, US 180/C1
Wilkes Land (phys. reg.), Ant. 202/J
Wilkesboro, NC, US 172/D4
Wilkeson, Wa, US 177/C3
Wilkie, Sk, Can. 168/F2
Wilkins (sound), Ant. 202/U
Will (mt.), BC, Can. 176/N4
Will (co.), Il, US 177/P16
Willamette (riv.), Or, US 168/C4
Willandra NP, Austl. 157/C2
Willapa (bay), Wa, US 168/B4
Willard (bay), Ut, US 179/J11
Willard (res.), Ut, US 179/J11
Willard, Ut, US 179/J11
Willaura, Austl. 157/B3
Willcox, Az, US 170/E4
Willebadessen, Ger. 93/G5
Willebroek, Belg. 95/D1
Willemstad, Neth. 92/B5
Willemstad (cap.), NAnt. 194/D1
William (mt.), Austl. 157/B3
William B. Hartsfield Atlanta (int'l arpt.), Ga, US 175/G3
William Bay NP, Austl. 154/C5
Williams, Az, US 170/D4
Williams, Austl. 154/C5
Williams Lake, BC, Can. 168/C2
Williamsburg, Ky, US 172/C4
Williamsport, Pa, US 180/A1
Williamston, NC, US 175/J3
Williamstown, Pa, US 180/B2
Williamstown, NJ, US 180/D4
Williamsville, NY, US 173/S10
Willich, Ger. 92/D6
Willingboro, NJ, US 180/D3
Willingen, Ger. 93/F6
Willis, Tx, US 171/J5
Willis Islets (isls.), Austl. 151/E2
Willisau, Swi. 98/D3
Williston, ND, US 169/H3
Williston, Fl, US 175/H4
Williston, SAfr. 148/C3
Williston (lake), BC, Can. 164/D3
Williston Park, NY, US 181/L9
Willits, Ca, US 170/B3
Willmar, Mn, US 169/K4
Willow, Ak, US 176/H3
Willow (riv.), BC, Can. 168/C2
Willow Bunch, Sk, Can. 169/G3
Willow Grove, Pa, US 180/C3
Willow Grove, De, US 180/C5
Willow Grove Naval Air Sta., Pa, US 180/C3
Willow River, BC, Can. 168/C2
Willow Street, Pa, US 180/B4
Willow Tree, Austl. 157/D1
Willowbrook, Ca, US 178/F8
Willowbrook, Il, US 177/P16
Willowmore, SAfr. 148/C4
Willows, Ca, US 170/B3
Wills (lake), Austl. 151/B3
Wills Point, La, US 179/Q17
Willstätt, Ger. 98/D1
Willunga, Austl. 155/H5
Wilmette, Il, US 177/Q15
Wilmington, NC, US 175/J3
Wilmington, Austl. 155/H5
Wilmington, De, US 180/C4
Wilmington Island, Ga, US 175/H4
Wilmslow, Eng, UK 77/F5
Wilnsdorf, Ger. 95/H2
Wilrijk, Belg. 92/B6
Wilseder (peak), Ger. 93/G2
Wilson, NC, US 175/J3
Wilson (co.), Tx, US 179/U21
Wilson, NY, US 173/S9
Wilson (mt.), Ca, US 178/B2
Wilson, Pa, US 180/C2
Wilson (cape), Nun., Can. 165/H2
Wilsons Promontory (pen.), Austl. 151/D4
Wilsons Promontory NP, Austl. 157/C3
Wilsonville, Il, US 179/H7
Wilstedt, Ger. 93/G2
Wilster, Ger. 93/G1
Wilsum, Ger. 92/D3
Wilton, Eng, UK 75/E4
Wilton, Ct, US 181/E1
Wiltshire (co.), Eng, UK 75/E4
Wiltz, Lux. 95/E4
Wiltz (riv.), Lux. 95/E4
Wiluna, Austl. 154/D3
Wimborne Minster, Eng, UK 74/E5
Wimereux, Fr. 94/A2
Wimmis, Swi. 98/D4
Winam (gulf), Kenya 146/B3
Winburg, SAfr. 148/D3
Winchester, Ky, US 172/C4
Winchester, Tn, US 175/G3
Winchester, Ca, US 178/C3
Winchester, Eng, UK 75/E4
Winchester Mystery House, Ca, US 177/L12
Wind (riv.), Wy, US 168/F5
Wind (lake), Wi, US 177/P14
Wind Cave NP, SD, US 171/G2
Wind Gap, Pa, US 180/C2
Wind Lake, Wi, US 177/P14
Wind Point, Wi, US 177/Q14
Wind River (range), Wy, US 170/E2
Windach (riv.), Ger. 99/G2
Windach, Ger. 96/E6
Winder, Ga, US 175/H3
Windermere (lake), Eng, UK 77/F3
Windermere, Eng, UK 77/F3
Windesheim, Ger. 95/G4
Windhoek (cap.), Namb. 147/C5
Windlesham, Eng, UK 72/B2
Window Rock, Az, US 170/E4
Windrush (riv.), Eng, UK 75/E3
Windsbach, Ger. 96/D4
Windsor, Nf, Can. 173/L1
Windsor, NS, Can. 173/H2
Windsor, Qu, Can. 173/G2
Windsor, On, Can. 172/D3
Windsor, Eng, UK 75/F4
Windsor, Co, US 179/C2
Windsor (res.), Co, US 179/C1
Windsor, Pa, US 180/B4
Windsor and Maidenhead (co.), Eng, UK 75/F3
Windward (isls.), StV. 183/J5
Windward Passage (passg.), Cuba,Haiti 187/H2
Winfield, BC, Can. 168/D3
Winfield, Ks, US 171/H3
Winfield, Pa, US 180/B2
Winfield, Md, US 180/A5
Wingene, Belg. 94/C1
Winger, On, Can. 173/R10
Wingham, Austl. 157/E1
Winifred (lake), Austl. 154/D2
Winifreda, Arg. 200/D3
Winisk (riv.), On, Can. 165/H3
Winkler, Mb, Can. 169/J3
Winneba, Gha. 145/E5
Winnebago (lake), Wi, US 169/L5
Winnenden, Ger. 96/C5
Winner, SD, US 169/J5
Winnetka, Il, US 177/Q15
Winnett, Mt, US 168/F4
Winnfield, La, US 171/J5
Winningen, Ger. 95/G3
Winnipeg (cap.), Mb, Can. 169/J3
Winnipeg (int'l arpt.), Mb, Can. 169/J3
Winnipeg (riv.), Mb,On, Can. 169/K3
Winnipeg (lake), Mb, Can. 169/J3
Winnipeg Beach, Mb, Can. 169/J3
Winnipegosis, Mb, Can. 169/J3
Winnipegosis (lake), Mb, Can. 169/H2
Winnsboro, La, US 171/K4
Winnsboro, SC, US 175/H3
Winnweiler, Ger. 95/G4
Winschoten, Neth. 92/E2
Winsford, Eng, UK 77/F5
Winslow, Az, US 170/E4
Winslow, NJ, US 180/D4
Winslow, Wa, US 177/B2
Winston-Salem, NC, US 175/H2
Winsum, Neth. 92/D2
Winter Haven, Fl, US 175/H4
Winter Park, Fl, US 175/H4
Winterberg, Ger. 93/F6
Winterberge (mts.), SAfr. 148/D4
Winterlingen, Ger. 99/F1
Winters, Tx, US 171/H5
Winters, Ca, US 177/K9
Winters Run (riv.), Md, US 180/B4
Winterstaude (peak), Aus. 99/F3
Winterswijk, Neth. 92/D5
Winterthur, Swi. 99/E3
Winterthur Museum and Gardens, De, US 180/C4
Winthrop, Me, US 173/G2
Winton, Austl. 156/A3
Wintzenheim, Fr. 98/D1
Wipper (riv.), Ger. 82/F3
Wipperau (riv.), Ger. 93/H2
Wipperfürth, Ger. 95/G1
Wirges, Ger. 95/G3
Wirrabara, Austl. 155/H5
Wirral (co.), Eng, UK 77/E5
Wirral (pen.), Eng, UK 77/E5
Wisbech, Eng, UK 75/G1
Wisch, Neth. 92/D5
Wischhafen, Ger. 93/G1
Wisconsin (riv.), Wi, US 169/L5
Wisconsin (state), US 169/L4
Wiseman, Ak, US 176/H2
Wisenta (riv.), Ger. 97/E1
Wishaw, Sc, UK 78/C5
Wishek, ND, US 169/J4
Wisła, Pol. 83/K4
Wiślany (lag.), Pol. 81/H4
Wisłoka (riv.), Pol. 83/L4
Wismar, Ger. 80/D5
Wisner, La, US 171/K5
Wissant, Fr. 94/A2
Wissembourg, Fr. 95/G5
Wissen, Ger. 95/G2
Wissey (riv.), Eng, UK 75/G1
Wit Kei (riv.), SAfr. 148/D3
Witbank, SAfr. 148/E2
Witham, Eng, UK 75/G3
Witham (riv.), Eng, UK 77/H5
Witherspoon (mt.), Ak, US 176/J3
Withlacoochee (riv.), Fl,Ga, US 175/H4
Withnell, Eng, UK 77/F4
Witjira NP, Austl. 155/G3
Witkowo, Pol. 83/J2
Witney, Eng, UK 75/E3
Witnica, Pol. 83/H2
Witry-lès-Reims, Fr. 95/D5
Wittelsheim, Fr. 98/D2
Wittem, Neth. 95/E2
Witten, Ger. 93/E6
Wittenbach, Swi. 99/F3
Wittenberg, Ger. 82/G3
Wittenberge, Ger. 82/F2
Wittenburg, Ger. 80/D5
Wittenheim, Fr. 98/D2
Wittenoom, Austl. 154/C2
Wittingen, Ger. 93/H3
Wittislingen, Ger. 96/D5
Wittlich, Ger. 95/F4
Wittman, Md, US 180/B6
Wittmund, Ger. 93/E1
Wittmunder (riv.), Ger. 93/E1
Witton (pen.), Ger. 83/G1
Wittstock, Ger. 82/G2
Witu, Kenya 146/D3
Witwatersrand (reg.), SAfr. 148/P12
Witzenhausen, Ger. 93/G6
Wivenhoe (lake), Austl. 151/E3
Wixom, Mi, US 177/E6
Wkra (riv.), Pol. 83/L2
Władysławowo, Pol. 80/H4
Włocławek, Pol. 83/K2
Włocławskie (lake), Pol. 83/K2
Włodawa, Pol. 83/M3
Włoszczowa, Pol. 83/K3
Wobulenzi, Ugan. 146/B2
Wodonga, Austl. 157/C3
Wodzisław Śląski, Pol. 83/K4
Woensdrecht, Neth. 92/B6
Woerden, Neth. 92/B4
Wognum, Neth. 92/C3
Wohlen, Swi. 99/E3
Wohlen bei Bern, Swi. 98/D4
Wohlford (lake), Ca, US 178/C4
Woippy, Fr. 95/F5
Wokam (isl.), Indo. 123/H5
Woking, Eng, UK 72/B3
Wokingham, Eng, UK 75/F4
Wokingham (co.), Eng, UK 75/F4
Wŏlch'ul-san NP, SKor. 115/D5
Wolcott, Ks, US 179/D5
Wolcottsville, NY, US 173/S9
Wołczyn, Pol. 83/K3
Woleai (isl.), Micr. 158/D4
Wolf (mtn.), Ak, US 176/H2
Wolf (riv.), Wi, US 172/B2
Wolf (vol.), Ecu. 198/E7
Wolf (isl.), Ecu. 198/E6
Wolf (lake), In, US 177/Q16
Wolf Creek (mtn.), Ak, US 176/F3
Wolf Creek, Mt, US 168/E4
Wolf Point, Mt, US 169/G3
Wolfach, Ger. 99/E1
Wolfach (riv.), Ger. 96/B6
Wolfegg, Ger. 99/F2
Wolfen, Ger. 82/G3
Wolfenbüttel, Ger. 93/H4
Wolfern, Aus. 97/H6
Wölfersheim, Ger. 96/B2
Wolfhagen, Ger. 93/G6
Wolframs-Eschenbach, Ger. 96/D4
Wolfsburg, Ger. 93/H4
Wolfsegg am Hausruck, Aus. 97/G6
Wolfurt, Aus. 99/F3
Wolgast, Ger. 80/E4
Wolhusen, Swi. 98/E3
Wolin, Pol. 80/F5
Woliński PN, Pol. 83/H2
Wolkersdorf, Aus. 91/P7
Wollaston (isl.), Chile 199/C8
Wollaston (lake), Sk, Can. 164/F3
Wollaston (pen.), NW,Nun., Can. 164/E2
Wollemi NP, Austl. 157/D2
Wollerau, Swi. 99/E3
Wollongong, Austl. 157/D2
Wöllstadt, Ger. 96/B2
Wöllstein, Ger. 95/G4
Wolmaransstad, SAfr. 148/D2
Wolnzach, Ger. 97/E5
Wologizi (range), Libr. 138/C6
Wołomin, Pol. 83/L2
Wołów, Pol. 83/J3
Wolseley, SAfr. 148/L10
Wolsztyn, Pol. 83/J2
Woluwé-Saint-Lambert, Belg. 95/D2
Wolvega, Neth. 92/D3
Wolverhampton, Eng, UK 74/D1
Wolverhampton (co.), Eng, UK 74/D1
Wolverine Lake, Mi, US 177/F6
Wolziger (lake), Ger. 82/Q7
Woman (riv.), On, Can. 172/D2
Wombourne, Eng, UK 74/D1
Wombwell, Eng, UK 77/G4
Womelsdorf, Pa, US 180/B3
Wondai, Austl. 156/C4
Wonder (lake), Il, US 177/P16
Wondervu, Co, US 179/B3
Wondreb (riv.), Ger. 97/F3
Wong Chu (riv.), Bhu. 127/G2
Wongan Hills, Austl. 154/C4
Wŏnju, SKor. 115/D4
Wonnangatta-Moroka NP, Austl. 157/C3
Wŏnsan, NKor. 115/D3
Wonthaggi, Austl. 157/C3
Wonyulgunna (peak), Austl. 154/C3
Wood (mt.), Yk, Can. 176/K3
Wood (riv.), Sk, Can. 169/H2
Wood (mtn.), Sk, Can. 168/G3
Wood (riv.), Il, US 179/G8
Wood Buffalo NP, NW,Ab, Can. 164/E2
Wood Dale, Il, US 177/P16
Wood-Ridge, NJ, US 181/J8
Wood River, Il, US 179/G8
Woodbine, NJ, US 180/D5
Woodbine, Md, US 180/A5
Woodbridge, Ct, US 181/E1
Woodbridge, Ca, US 177/M10
Woodbridge, NJ, US 181/H9
Woodburn, Austl. 157/E1
Woodburn, Or, US 168/C4
Woodburn, Il, US 179/G7
Woodburn, On, Can. 173/Q9
Woodbury, NJ, US 180/C4
Woodcliff Lake, NJ, US 181/J7
Woodenbong, Austl. 157/E1
Woodenbridge, Ire. 76/B6
Woodend, Austl. 157/C3
Woodgate, Austl. 156/D4
Woodgate NP, Austl. 156/D4
Woodinville, Wa, US 177/C2
Woodland, Ca, US 170/B3
Woodlark (isl.), Sol. 158/E5
Woodlawn, Md, US 180/B5
Woodlawn Park, Ok, US 179/M14
Woodmere, NY, US 181/L9
Woodmont, Ct, US 181/F1
Woodridge, Il, US 177/P16
Woodroffe (mt.), Austl. 155/F3
Woods, Ok, US 179/N15
Woods (lake), On, Can. 164/G4
Woods Cross, Ut, US 179/K12
Woods Heights, Mo, US 179/E5
Woodsboro, Md, US 180/A4
Woodside, De, US 180/C5
Woodside, Austl. 155/M8
Woodside, Ca, US 177/K12
Woodside-Drifton, Pa, US 180/C2
Woodstock, Austl. 157/D2
Woodstock, NB, Can. 173/H2
Woodstock, Il, US 171/K2
Woodstock, Eng, UK 75/E3
Woodstock, Md, US 180/B5
Woodstown, NJ, US 180/C4
Woodville, Ms, US 171/K5
Woodway, Wa, US 177/C2
Woolgoolga, Austl. 157/E1
Wooli, Austl. 157/E1

Woolrich, Pa, US 180/A1
Woomera, Austl. 155/H4
Woomera Prohibited Area, Austl. 155/G4
Woonsocket, SD, US 171/H1
Woorabinda Aboriginal Community, Austl. 156/C4
Wooramel (riv.), Austl. 154/B3
Wooster, Oh, US 172/D3
Worb, Swi. 98/D4
Worcester, Ma, US 173/G3
Worcester, Eng, UK 74/D2
Worcester, SAfr. 148/L10
Worcestershire (co.), Eng, UK 74/D2
Worcester and Birmingham (canal), Eng, UK 74/D2
Worden, Il, US 179/H8
Wörgl, Aus. 85/K3
Workington, Eng, UK 76/E2
Worksop, Eng, UK 77/G5
Workum, Neth. 92/C3
Worland, Wy, US 168/G4
World 22
Wormer, Neth. 92/B3
Wormhoudt, Fr. 94/B2
Worms (pt.), Wal, UK 74/B3
Worms, Ger. 96/B3
Wörnitz (riv.), Ger. 85/J2
Worpswede, Ger. 93/F2
Wörrstadt, Ger. 96/B3
Wörsbach (riv.), Ger. 96/B2
Worsbrough, Eng, UK 77/G4
Worth, Il, US 177/Q16
Wörth am Rhein, Ger. 96/B4
Wörth an der Donau, Ger. 97/F4
Wörth an der Isar, Ger. 97/F5
Wortham, Tx, US 171/H5
Worthing, Eng, UK 75/F5
Wörthsee (lake), Ger. 96/E6
Worton, Md, US 180/B5
Wotho (isl.), Mrsh. 158/F3
Wotje (isl.), Mrsh. 158/G4
Woudenberg, Neth. 92/C4
Woudrichem, Neth. 92/B5
Wounta (lake), Nic. 187/F3
Wouw, Neth. 92/B5
Wowoni (isl.), Indo. 123/F4
Wrangel (isl.), Rus. 202/U
Wrangell, Ak, US 176/M4
Wrangell (mts.), Ak, US 164/B2
Wrangell-St. Elias NP and Prsv., Ak, US 176/K3
Wrath (cape), Sc, UK 73/R7
Wray, Co, US 171/G2
Wraysbury, Eng, UK 72/B2
Wraysbury (res.), Eng, UK 72/B2
Wreck (reef), Austl. 151/E3
Wreck (pt.), SAfr. 148/B3
Wrekin, The (hill), Eng, UK 74/D1
Wremen, Ger. 93/E2
Wrexham, Wal, UK 77/F5
Wrexham (co.), Wal, UK 77/E5
Wright, Wy, US 169/G5
Wrightstown, NJ, US 180/D3
Wrightwood, Ca, US 178/C2
Wrigley, NW, Can. 164/D2
Writtle, Eng, UK 75/G3
Wrocław, Pol. 83/J3
Września, Pol. 83/J2
Wschowa, Pol. 83/J3
Wu (riv.), China 121/A2
Wu'an, China 114/C3
Wuchang, China 113/N3
Wuchang (lake), China 114/D5
Wucheng, China 114/D3
Wuchuan, China 121/A2
Wuchuan, China 121/B3
Wuchuan, China 114/B2
Wudang (mtn.), China 114/B4
Wudi, China 114/D3
Wuding (riv.), China 114/B3
Wudinna, Austl. 155/G5
Wufeng, China 121/B1
Wugang, China 121/B2
Wuhai, China 112/J4
Wuhan, China 121/B1
Wuhe, China 114/D4
Wuhle (riv.), Ger. 82/Q6
Wuhu, China 114/D5
Wuhu, China 114/D5
Wuhua, China 121/C3
Wujal Wujal Aboriginal Community, Austl. 156/B1
Wujiang, China 114/L8
Wular (lake), India 128/C2
Wülfrath, Ger. 92/E6
Wulften, Ger. 93/H5
Wulian, China 114/D4
Wuling (mts.), China 121/B2
Wulong, China 125/J2
Wum, Camr. 145/H5
Wumang (isl.), China 115/B3
Wümme (riv.), Ger. 93/F2
Wūn, India 124/C3
Wungong (res.), Austl. 154/L7
Wuning, China 121/C2
Wünnenberg, Ger. 93/F5
Wünnewil, Swi. 98/D4
Wunsiedel, Ger. 97/F2
Wunstorf, Ger. 93/G4
Wupatki Nat'l Mon., Az, US 170/E4
Wuppertal, Ger. 93/E6
Wuqi, China 114/B3
Wuqia, China 129/G5
Wuqiang, China 114/C3
Wuqiao, China 114/D3
Würm (riv.), Ger. 95/H6
Würm K. (canal), Ger. 99/H1
Würselen, Ger. 95/F2
Würzburg, Ger. 96/C3
Wusheng (pass), China 114/C5
Wushi, China 112/C3
Wüstegarten (peak), Ger. 93/G6
Wüstenrot, Ger. 96/C4
Wusuli (riv.), China 113/P2
Wutach (riv.), Ger. 99/E2
Wutai (peak), China 114/C3
Wutai, China 114/C3
Wuteve (mt.), Libr. 144/C4
Wutha-Farnroda, Ger. 96/D1
Wutöschingen, Ger. 99/E2
Wuustwezel, Belg. 92/B6
Wuwei, China 112/H4
Wuwei, China 114/D5
Wuxi, China 114/L8
Wuxiang, China 114/C3
Wuyang, China 114/C4
Wuyi (mts.), China 121/C2
Wuyi, China 114/C3
Wuyuan, China 112/J3
Wuyuan, China 121/C2
Wuzhai, China 114/B3
Wuzhi (peak), China 125/J4
Wuzhi, China 114/C4
Wuzhi (peak), China 114/J6
Wuzhou, China 125/K3
Wyalkatchem, Austl. 154/C4
Wyandanch, NY, US 181/M8
Wyandotte (co.), Ks, US 179/D5
Wyandotte County (lake), Ks, US 179/D5
Wyandotte NWR, Mi, US 177/F7
Wyangala (dam), Austl. 157/D2
Wycheproof, Austl. 157/B3
Wyckoff, NJ, US 181/J8
Wye (riv.), Eng, UK 74/C2
Wye Mills, Md, US 180/B6
Wyee, Austl. 157/D2
Wyk, Ger. 80/C4
Wynigen, Swi. 98/D3
Wynne, Ar, US 171/K4
Wynyard, Austl. 157/C4
Wynyard, Sk, Can. 169/G3
Wyoming (state), US 168/F5
Wyoming, De, US 180/C5
Wyoming, Mi, US 172/C3
Wyoming, Pa, US 180/C1
Wyoming (range), Wy, US 170/E2
Wyomissing, Pa, US 180/C3
Wyperfeld NP, Austl. 157/B2
Wyralinu (peak), Austl. 154/D5
Wyre (riv.), Eng, UK 77/F4
Wyrzysk, Pol. 83/J2
Wysokie Mazowieckie, Pol. 83/M2
Wyszków, Pol. 83/L2

X

X-Can, Mex. 186/E1
Xa Binh Long, Viet. 120/D4
Xaçmaz, Azer. 105/J4
Xagħra, Malta 88/L6
Xai-Xai, Moz. 147/F6
Xainza, China 112/E5
Xaitongmoin, China 127/G1
Xaltianguis, Mex. 185/F5
Xan (riv.), Viet. 120/D3
Xankändi, Azer. 105/H5
Xanten, Ger. 92/D5
Xánthi, Gre. 89/J2
Xanxerê, Braz. 197/A3
Xar Moron (riv.), China 113/L3
Xarba (pass), China 127/E1
Xavantes, Represa de (res.), Braz. 197/B2
Xavantes, Serra dos (mts.), Braz. 193/J6
Xayar, China 112/D3
Xenia, Oh, US 172/D4
Xerta, Sp. 87/F2
Xertigny, Fr. 98/C1
Xi (lake), China 114/E2
Xi (riv.), China 113/K7
Xiaguan, China 125/H2
Xiajin, China 114/C3
Xiamen, China 121/C3
Xiamen (int'l arpt.), China 121/C3
Xi'an, China 114/B4
Xiang (riv.), China 113/K6
Xiangcheng, China 125/G2
Xiangcheng, China 114/C4
Xiangcheng, China 114/C4
Xiangfan, China 114/C4
Xiangfen, China 114/B4
Xianghe, China 114/H7
Xiangkhoang, Laos 120/C2
Xiangkhoang (plat.), Laos 120/C2
Xiangning, China 114/B4
Xiangshan, China 121/D2
Xiangshui, China 114/D4
Xiangtan, China 125/K2
Xiangxiang, China 121/B2
Xiangyuan, China 114/C3
Xiangyun, China 125/H2
Xianju, China 121/D2
Xianning, China 121/B2
Xiantao, China 121/B1
Xianyang, China 112/J5
Xiao Hinggan (mts.), China 113/N2
Xiao Xian, China 114/D4
Xiaogan, China 113/K5
Xiaoqing (riv.), China 114/D3
Xiaoshan, China 114/L9
Xiaowutai (peak), China 114/C3
Xiaoyi, China 114/B3
Xiapu, China 121/C2
Xiayi, China 114/D4
Xichang, China 125/H2
Xichou, China 125/H3
Xico, Mex. 185/N7
Xicohténcatl, Mex. 185/F4
Xicotepec, Mex. 185/M6
Xifei (riv.), China 114/C4
Xifeng, China 112/J4
Xifeng, China 125/J2
Xifeng, China 114/F2
Xigazê, China 127/G1
Xihua, China 114/C4
Xilin, China 125/J3
Xilitla, Mex. 186/B1
Xilókastron, Gre. 89/H3
Ximeng Vazu Zizhixian, China 125/G3
Xin (riv.), China 121/C2
Xin Barag Zuoqi, China 113/L2
Xin'an, China 114/C4
Xin'an (riv.), China 114/D5
Xin'anjiang (res.), China 121/C2
Xin'anjiang (res.), China 114/D5
Xinbin, China 115/C2
Xincai, China 114/C4
Xinchang, China 121/D2
Xincheng, China 121/A3
Xincheng, China 114/G7
Xinfeng, China 121/B2
Xinfeng, China 125/K3
Xinfengjiang (res.), China 121/B3
Xing'an, China 121/B2
Xingcheng, China 114/E2
Xinghua, China 114/D4
Xinglong, China 114/H6
Xingshan, China 114/B5
Xingtai, China 114/C3
Xingu (riv.), Braz. 193/H4
Xingu, PN do, Braz. 193/H6
Xingyang, China 114/C4
Xingzi, China 121/C2
Xinhe, China 112/D3
Xinhe, China 114/C3
Xinhua, China 121/B2
Xinhuang Dongzu Zizhixian, China 121/A2
Xining, China 112/H4
Xinji, China 114/C3
Xinjiang, China 114/B4
Xinjiang Uygur (reg.), China 109/H5
Xinjin, China 115/A3
Xinle, China 114/C3
Xinmin, China 115/B1
Xintai, China 114/D4
Xinxiang, China 114/C4
Xinyang, China 113/K5
Xinyang, China 114/C4
Xinye, China 114/C4
Xinyi, China 125/K3
Xinyi, China 114/D4
Xinyu, China 121/B2
Xinyuan, China 112/D3
Xinzheng, China 114/C4
Xinzo de Limia, Sp. 86/B1
Xiong Xian, China 114/H7
Xiping, China 114/C4
Xiqing (mts.), China 112/H5
Xique-Xique, Braz. 196/B3
Xitang, China 114/L9
Xitiao (riv.), China 114/K9
Xiu (riv.), China 121/B2
Xiuning, China 121/C2
Xiuwen, China 125/J2
Xiuwu, China 114/C4
Xiuyan, China 115/B2
Xixabangma (peak), China 127/E1
Xixia, China 114/B4
Xiyang (riv.), China 125/J3
Xizang (Tibet) (aut. reg.), China 112/D5
Xochicalco (ruin), Mex. 185/K8
Xonacatlán, Mex. 185/Q10
Xpujil, Mex. 186/D2
Xu (riv.), China 121/C2
Xuan'en, China 121/A2
Xuanhua, China 114/G6
Xuchang, China 114/C4
Xun (riv.), China 121/B3
Xun Xian, China 114/C4
Xunke, China 113/N2
Xunwu, China 121/C3
Xunyang, China 114/B4
Xupu, China 121/B2
Xuwen, China 125/K3
Xuyi, China 114/D4
Xuzhou, China 114/D4

Y

Y Llethr (peak), Wal, UK 76/E6
Ya'an, China 112/H6
Ya'bad, Isr. 133/G7
Yabassi, Camr. 138/G7
Yablanitsa, Bul. 91/G4
Yablonovyy (range), Rus. 109/L4
Yabrūd, Isr. 133/G8
Yabucoa, PR 183/M8
Yabuki, Japan 117/G2
Yabuzukahon, Japan 119/C1
Yachi (riv.), China 112/J6
Yachiho, Japan 119/A1
Yachimata, Japan 119/E2
Yachiyo, Japan 119/D1
Yachiyo, Japan 119/G5
Yachiyo, Japan 119/E2
Yacimiento Río Turbio, Arg. 201/B6
Yacuiba, Bol. 192/F8
Yacuma (riv.), Bol. 192/E6
Yacumbu, PN, Ven. 194/D2
Yādgīr, India 124/C4
Yadkin (riv.), NC, US 175/H2
Yaeyama (isls.), Japan 117/G8
Yāfā, Isr. 133/G6
Yağcılar, Turk. 132/B2
Yagi, Japan 119/J5
Yagorlytsk (gulf), Ukr. 91/K2
Yagoua, Camr. 138/J5
Yagradagzê (peak), China 112/G4
Yaguale (riv.), Hon. 186/E3
Yaguarón (riv.), Uru. 201/G2
Yaguas (riv.), Peru 194/D5
Yague del Sur (riv.), DRep. 187/J2
Yagur, Isr. 133/G6
Yahagi (riv.), Japan 119/M6
Yahualica de Gonzalez Gallo, Mex. 184/E4
Yahyalı, Turk. 132/C2
Yáios (Paxoí), Gre. 89/G3
Yaita, Japan 117/F2
Yaizu, Japan 117/F3
Yajalón, Mex. 186/C2
Yakacık, Turk. 133/E1
Yakapınar, Turk. 133/D1
Yakima (riv.), Wa, US 168/C4
Yakima, Wa, US 168/C4
Yakishiri (isl.), Japan 118/B1
Yako, Burk. 145/E3
Yakoruda, Bul. 91/F4
Yakumo, Japan 118/B2
Yakuno, Japan 119/G5
Yakutat (bay), Ak, US 164/B3
Yakutsk, Rus. 107/N3
Yala, Thai. 120/C5
Yalahua (lag.), Mex. 186/E1
Yalangoz, Turk. 133/E1
Yalata Abor. Land, Austl. 155/F4
Yalbac (hills), Belz. 186/D2
Yalgoo, Austl. 154/C4
Yalgorup NP, Austl. 154/B5
Yalnızçam, Turk. 132/E1
Yaloké, CAfr. 139/J6
Yalong (riv.), China 112/H5
Yalova, Turk. 91/J5
Yalova, Turk. 91/H5
Yalpuh (lake), Ukr. 91/J3
Yalta, Ukr. 104/E3
Yalu (riv.), China,NKor. 115/C2
Yalutorovsk, Rus. 129/E1
Yalvaç, Turk. 132/B2
Yamada, Japan 118/B4
Yamaga, Japan 116/B4
Yamagata, Japan 113/Q4
Yamagata, Japan 117/G1
Yamagata (pref.), Japan 118/A4
Yamaguchi (pref.), Japan 116/B3
Yamaguchi, Japan 116/B3
Yamakita, Japan 119/C3
Yamal (pen.), Rus. 106/G2
Yamalo-Nenetskiy Aut. Okrug, Rus. 106/H3
Yamanaka (lake), Japan 119/B3
Yamanashi, Japan 119/B2
Yamanie (falls), Austl. 156/B2
Yamanie Falls NP, Austl. 156/B2
Yamantau (peak), Rus. 103/N5
Yamaoka, Japan 119/M5
Yamarna Abor. Rsv., Austl. 154/D4
Yamashiro, Japan 119/J6
Yamato, Japan 119/B2
Yamato, Japan 119/E1
Yamato, Japan 119/C3
Yamato (riv.), Japan 119/J6
Yamato-Kōriyama, Japan 119/J6
Yamatotakada, Japan 119/J6
Yamazoe, Japan 119/K6
Yamba, Austl. 157/E1
Yambio, Sudan 139/L7
Yambol, Bul. 91/H4
Yambrasbamba, Peru 198/B2
Yamdena (isl.), Indo. 123/H5
Yamethin, Myan. 125/G3
Yamin (peak), Indo. 123/K4
Yamma Yamma (lake), Austl. 156/A4
Yamoto, Japan 118/B4
Yamoussoukro (cap.), C.d'Iv. 144/D5
Yampa (riv.), Co, US 170/F2
Yamuna (riv.), India 124/D2
Yamunānagar, India 128/D4
Yamzho Yumco (lake), China 124/F2
Yan (riv.), SrL. 124/D6
Yan Yean (res.), Austl. 157/G5
Yana (riv.), Rus. 109/N3
Yanagawa, Japan 116/B4
Yanahuanca, Peru 198/B3
Yanai, Japan 116/C4
Yanaizu, Japan 119/L5
Yan'an, China 114/B3
Yanaoca, Peru 198/D4
Yanaul, Rus. 103/M4
Yanbian, China 125/H2
Yancheng, China 114/C4
Yancheng, China 114/E4
Yanchep NP, Austl. 154/B4
Yanco, Austl. 157/C2
Yandeearra Abor. Rsv., Austl. 154/C2
Yandoon, Myan. 125/G4
Yanfolila, Mali 144/C4
Yangambi, D.R. Congo 139/K7
Yangbi (riv.), China 125/G2
Yangcheng, China 114/C4
Yangcheng (lake), China 114/L8
Yangchun, China 121/B3
Yangdang (mts.), China 121/C2
Yangdŏk, NKor. 115/D3
Yanggang-do (prov.), NKor. 115/D2
Yanggao, China 114/C2
Yanggu, SKor. 115/D3
Yanggu, China 114/C3
Yangiyul', Uzb. 129/E4
Yangjiang, China 125/K3
Yangma (isl.), China 115/A4
Yangon (div.), Myan. 125/G4
Yangp'yŏng, SKor. 115/D4
Yangqu, China 114/C3
Yangquan, China 114/C3
Yangsan, SKor. 115/E5
Yangshan, China 125/K3
Yangtze (Chang) (riv.), China 121/C1
Yangudi Rassa NP, Eth. 139/P5
Yangxin, China 121/C2
Yangxin, China 114/D3
Yangyang, SKor. 115/E3
Yangyuan, China 114/C2
Yangzhong, China 114/E4
Yangzhou, China 114/D4
Yanhe, China 121/A2
Yanji, China 113/N3
Yanjin, China 125/H2
Yanjin, China 114/C4
Yankari Game Reserve, Nga. 139/H6
Yankee Stadium, NY, US 181/K8
Yanling, China 114/C4
Yanmen (pass), China 114/C3
Yanshan, China 121/C2
Yanshan, China 125/H3
Yanshan, China 114/D3
Yanshi, China 114/C4
Yanshou, China 113/N2
Yantai, China 114/E3
Yanyuan, China 125/H2
Yanzhou, China 114/D4
Yao, Japan 119/J6
Yao'an, China 125/H2
Yaotsu, Japan 119/M5
Yaoundé (cap.), Camr. 138/H7
Yap (isls.), Micr. 158/C4
Yapacana, PN, Ven. 192/E3
Yapei, Gha. 145/E4
Yapen (isl.), Indo. 123/J4
Yapen (str.), Indo. 123/J4
Yapraklı, Turk. 132/C1
Yaqui (riv.), Mex. 184/C2
Yara, Cuba 187/G1
Yaracuy (state), Ven. 194/D2
Yaralıgöz (peak), Turk. 132/C1
Yaransk, Rus. 103/K4
Yardımcı (pt.), Turk. 133/B1
Yardley, Pa, US 180/D3
Yardville-Groveville, NJ, US 180/D3
Yare (riv.), Eng, UK 75/H1
Yarí (riv.), Col. 192/D3
Yari-ga-take (peak), Japan 117/E2
Yarımca, Turk. 91/J5
Yaritagua, Ven. 194/D2
Yarkant (riv.), China 112/C4
Yarloop, Austl. 154/B5
Yarlung Zangbo (Brahmaputra) (riv.), China 127/G1
Yarmouth, NS, Can. 173/H3
Yaroslavl', Rus. 102/H4
Yaroslavskaya Oblast, Rus. 102/H4
Yarpuz, Turk. 133/E1
Yarra (riv.), Austl. 157/G5
Yarra Glen, Austl. 157/G5
Yarram, Austl. 157/C3
Yarraman, Austl. 156/D4
Yarrawonga, Austl. 157/C3
Yarrow Point, Wa, US 177/C2
Yartsevo, Rus. 106/K3
Yarumal, Col. 194/C3
Yasato, Japan 119/E1
Yasawa Group (isls.), Fiji 158/G6
Yasel'da (riv.), Bela. 104/C1
Yashima, Japan 118/B4
Yashio, Japan 119/D2
Yashiro, Japan 119/G6
Yasnyy, Rus. 105/L2
Yasothon, Thai. 120/D3
Yass, Austl. 157/D2
Yasu (riv.), Japan 119/K6
Yasu, Japan 119/K5
Yasugi, Japan 116/C3
Yāsūj, Iran 130/F2
Yasun Burnu (pt.), Turk. 132/D1
Yasuni, PN, Ecu. 192/C4
Yatabe, Japan 117/G2
Yatağan, Turk. 132/B2
Yateley, Eng, UK 75/F4
Yatenga (prov.), Burk. 145/E3
Yathkyed (lake), Nun., Can. 164/G2
Yatomi, Japan 119/L5
Yatsu-ga-take (peak), Japan 119/A2
Yatsuo, Japan 117/E2
Yatsushiro, Japan 116/B4
Yatsushiro, Japan 119/B2
Yaṭṭah, WBnk. 133/D4
Yauca (riv.), Peru 198/C4
Yauca, Peru 198/C4
Yauco, PR 183/M8
Yauli, Peru 198/B3
Yaupi, Ecu. 194/B5
Yaután, Peru 198/B3
Yauyos, Peru 198/C4
Yauza (riv.), Rus. 103/W9
Yavari (riv.), Braz.,Peru 198/C2
Yavari Mirim (riv.), Peru 198/C2
Yavaros, Mex. 184/C3
Yavay (pen.), Rus. 106/H2
Yaviza, Pan. 187/G4
Yavne, Isr. 133/F8
Yavuzeli, Turk. 132/D2
Yawahara, Japan 119/E2
Yawata, Japan 119/J6
Yawatahama, Japan 116/C4
Yaxchilán (ruin), Guat. 186/D2
Yaygın, Turk. 132/E2
Yayladağı, Turk. 133/E2
Yayladere, Turk. 132/E2
Yazd, Iran 131/F2
Yazmān, Pak. 128/A5
Yazoo (riv.), Ms, US 171/K4
Yazoo City, Ms, US 171/K4
Ybbs (riv.), Aus. 83/H4
Ybbsitz, Aus. 85/L3
Yding Skovhøj (peak), Den. 80/C3
Ye, Myan. 120/B3
Ye Xian, China 114/D3
Yeay Sen (cape), Camb. 120/C4
Yecheng, China 129/G5
Yech'ŏn, SKor. 115/E4
Yecla, Sp. 87/E3
Yécora, Mex. 184/C2
Yecuatla, Mex. 185/N7
Yedigöller Nat'l Park, Turk. 91/K5
Yeditepe, Turk. 133/E2
Yéfira, Gre. 89/H2
Yefremov, Rus. 104/F1
Yegizkara (peak), Kaz. 129/D3
Yegorlyk (riv.), Rus. 105/G3
Yehualtepec, Mex. 185/M8
Yehud, Isr. 133/F7
Yejmiadzin, Arm. 105/H4
Yekaterinburg (Sverdlovsk), Rus. 103/P4
Yekateriny (chan.), Rus. 118/E1
Yelabuga, Rus. 103/M5
Yelan', Rus. 105/G2
Yelarbon, Austl. 156/C5
Yelets, Rus. 104/F1
Yélimané, Mali 144/C3
Yelizovo, Rus. 107/R4
Yell (isl.), Sc, UK 73/W13
Yellel, Alg. 142/F5
Yellow (riv.), Fl, US 175/G4
Yellow (sea), Asia 113/M5
Yellow Grass, Sk, Can. 169/G3
Yellowknife (riv.), NW, Can. 164/E2
Yellowknife (cap.), NW, Can. 164/E2
Yellowstone (lake), Wy, US 168/F4
Yellowstone (riv.), Mt, US 169/G4
Yellowstone NP, US 170/E1
Yellville, Ar, US 171/J3
Yemen (ctry.) 130/E5
Yenakiyeve, Ukr. 104/F2
Yenangyaung, Myan. 125/F3
Yenda, Austl. 157/C2
Yendi, Gha. 145/E4
Yengisar, China 129/G5
Yeniçağa, Turk. 91/L5
Yenice, Turk. 133/D1
Yenice, Turk. 91/L5
Yenice, Turk. 91/H6
Yenice (riv.), Turk. 104/E4
Yeniceoba, Turk. 132/C2
Yeniköy, Turk. 91/H5
Yenişehir, Turk. 91/J5
Yenisey (riv.), Rus. 109/H3
Yeniseysk, Rus. 106/K4
Yeo (lake), Austl. 154/E3
Yeo Lake Nature Rsv., Austl. 154/E3
Yeoval, Austl. 157/D2
Yeovil, Eng, UK 74/D5
Yeppoon, Austl. 156/C3
Yeraifia (well), WSah. 140/B4
Yerakovoúni (peak), Gre. 89/H3
Yères (riv.), Fr. 94/A4
Yerevan (cap.), Arm. 105/H4
Yerevan (int'l arpt.), Arm. 105/H4
Yerington, Nv, US 170/C3
Yerköy, Turk. 132/C2
Yerlisu, Turk. 89/K2
Yermak, Kaz. 129/G2
Yeroḥam, Isr. 133/D4
Yerolímin, Gre. 89/H4
Yerre (riv.), Fr. 84/D2
Yerres, Fr. 72/K5
Yerupaja (peak), Peru 198/B3
Yesagyo, Myan. 125/G3
Yesan, SKor. 115/D4
Yeşilhisar, Turk. 132/C2
Yeşilırmak (riv.), Turk. 104/F4
Yeşilkent, Turk. 133/E1
Yeşilova, Turk. 132/B2
Yesodot, Isr. 133/F8
Yesŏng (riv.), NKor. 115/D3
Yessentuki, Rus. 105/G3
Yeste, Sp. 86/D3
Yetti (reg.), Mrta. 140/D4
Yeu, Île d' (isl.), Fr. 84/B3
Yevla, India 124/B3
Yevlax, Azer. 105/H4
Yevpatoriya, Ukr. 104/E3
Yèvre (riv.), Fr. 95/D5
Yeya (riv.), Rus. 104/G3
Yeysk, Rus. 104/F3
Ygos-Saint-Saturnin, Fr. 84/C5
Yi (riv.), Uru. 201/F2
Yialousa, Cyp. 133/D2
Yiannitsá, Gre. 89/H2
Yiánnouli, Gre. 89/H3
Yíaros (isl.), Gre. 89/J4
Yibin, China 112/H6
Yicheng, China 113/K5
Yicheng, China 114/C5
Yicheng, China 114/B4
Yichuan, China 114/C4
Yichun, China 113/N2
Yichun, China 125/K2
Yifeng, China 125/K2
Yığılca, Turk. 91/K5
Yihuang, China 121/C2
Yıldız (peak), Turk. 132/D1
Yıldızeli, Turk. 132/D2
Yilehuli (mts.), China 113/M1
Yiliang, China 125/H2
Yima, China 114/B4
Yimen, China 125/H3
Yin (mts.), China 112/J3
Yinan, China 114/D4
Yinchuan, China 112/J4
Yindarlgooda (lake), Austl. 154/D4
Yingcheng, China 113/K5
Yingde, China 121/B3
Yingkou, China 115/B2
Yingshan, China 114/C5
Yingshang, China 114/D4
Yingtan, China 121/C2
Yining, China 112/D3
Yishan, China 121/A3
Yishui, China 114/D4
Yíthion, Gre. 89/H4
Yitong (riv.), SKor. 114/C5
Yiwu, China 112/F3
Yixing, China 114/K8
Yiyang, China 125/K2
Yiyang, China 114/C4
Yiyuan, China 114/D3
Yizhang, China 125/K2
Yizheng, China 114/D4
Ylöjärvi, Fin. 81/K1
Ÿnder (lake), Kaz. 105/K2
Yngaren (lake), Swe. 80/G2
Yobe (state), Nga. 145/H3
Yŏch'ŏn, SKor. 115/D5
Yodo (riv.), Japan 119/J6
Yoduma (riv.), Rus. 107/P4
Yoff (Dakar) (int'l arpt.), Sen. 144/A3
Yogo, Japan 119/K4
Yogoum (well), Chad 139/J4
Yoğuntaş, Turk. 91/H5
Yogyakarta, Indo. 122/D5
Yoho NP, BC, Can. 168/D3
Yoichi, Japan 118/B2
Yojoa (lake), Hon. 186/D3
Yŏju, SKor. 115/D4
Yokadouma, Camr. 138/J7
Yōkaichi, Japan 119/K5
Yokawa, Japan 119/H6
Yokkaichi, Japan 119/L6
Yokohama, Japan 117/F3
Yokoshiba, Japan 119/E2
Yokosuka, Japan 117/F3
Yokote, Japan 118/B4
Yokoze, Japan 119/C2
Yola, Nga. 138/H6
Yolaina (mts.), Nic. 187/E4
Yolboyu, Turk. 132/D2
Yolo, Ca, US 177/L9
Yolo (co.), Ca, US 177/L9
Yom (riv.), Thai. 125/H4
Yon (riv.), China 121/A3
Yon (riv.), Fr. 84/C3
Yonago, Japan 116/C3
Yonaguni (isl.), Japan 117/G8
Yonaha-dake (peak), Japan 117/K7
Yoneshiro (riv.), Japan 118/B3
Yonezawa, Japan 117/G2
Yŏng-yang, SKor. 115/E4
Yŏngam, SKor. 115/D5
Yongamp'o, NKor. 115/C3
Yong'an, China 121/C2
Yongchang, China 112/H4
Yongcheng, China 114/D4
Yŏngch'ŏn, SKor. 115/E5
Yongchun, China 121/C2
Yongde, China 125/G3
Yongding, China 121/C3
Yongding (riv.), China 114/G6
Yŏngdŏk, SKor. 115/E4
Yŏngdong, SKor. 115/D4
Yŏnggwang, SKor. 115/D5
Yŏnghae, SKor. 115/E4
Yonghe, China 114/B3
Yŏnghŭng (riv.), NKor. 115/D3
Yŏnghŭng, NKor. 115/D3
Yongji, China 114/B4
Yŏngjong (isl.), SKor. 115/F6
Yŏngju, SKor. 115/E4
Yongkang, China 121/D2
Yongmun-san (peak), SKor. 115/D4
Yongnian, China 114/C3
Yongqing, China 114/H7
Yongren, China 125/H2
Yŏngsan (riv.), SKor. 115/D5
Yongsheng, China 125/H2
Yongshun, China 125/J2
Yongtai, China 121/C2
Yŏngwŏl, SKor. 115/E4
Yongxing, China 121/B2
Yongxiu, China 121/C2
Yonkers, NY, US 181/K8
Yonne (riv.), Fr. 82/B5
Yono, Japan 119/D2
Yopal, Col. 194/C3
Yopurga, China 129/G5
Yoqne'am 'Illit, Isr. 133/G6
Yorba Linda, Ca, US 178/G8
Yorii, Japan 119/C1
York, Austl. 154/C4
York (cape), Austl. 151/D2
York (sound), Austl. 151/B2
York (riv.), Qu, Can. 173/H1
York, Eng, UK 77/G4
York (co.), Eng, UK 77/G4
York, Al, US 175/F3
York, Ne, US 169/J5
York, Pa, US 180/B4
York (co.), Pa, US 180/B4
York, SC, US 175/H3
York (riv.), Va, US 172/E4
York Haven, Pa, US 180/B3
York Landing, Mb, Can. 169/J1
York Minster, Eng, UK 77/G4
York Springs, Pa, US 180/A4
York, Vale of (valley), Eng, UK 77/G3
Yorke (pen.), Austl. 155/H5
Yorketown, Austl. 155/H5
Yorkshire Dales NP, Eng, UK 77/F3
Yorkshire Wolds (hills), Eng, UK 77/H3
Yorkton, Sk, Can. 169/H3
Yorktown, Tx, US 171/H5
Yorktown Heights, NY, US 181/E1
Yoro, Hon. 186/E3
Yōrō (riv.), Japan 119/E3
Yorō, Japan 119/L5
Yoroi-zaki (pt.), Japan 119/L7
Yoron (isl.), Japan 117/K7
Yorosso, Mali 144/D3
Yorubaland (plat.), Nga. 138/F6
Yos Sudarso (isl.), Indo. 123/J5

287
Yosem – Żywie

Yosemite NP, Ca, US 170/C3
Yoshida, Japan 116/C4
Yoshida, Japan 119/C1
Yoshii (riv.), Japan 116/D3
Yoshii, Japan 119/B1
Yoshikawa, Japan 119/D2
Yoshima (riv.), Japan 116/D3
Yoshimi, Japan 119/C1
Yoshino (riv.), Japan 116/C4
Yoshino, Japan 119/J7
Yoshino-Kumano NP, Japan 119/J7
Yoshkar-Ola, Rus. 103/L4
Yŏsu, SKor. 115/D5
Yōtei-san (peak), Japan 118/B2
Yotsukaidō, Japan 119/E2
You (riv.), China 121/A3
Young, Austl. 157/D2
Young, Uru. 201/K10
Youngs (lake), Wa, US 177/C3
Youngstown, Oh, US 172/D3
Youngstown, NY, US 173/R9
Youngtown, Az, US 179/R18
Yountville, Ca, US 177/K10
Youssoufia, Mor. 140/C2
Youyang, China 125/J2
Yoví (peak), Ven. 195/E3
Yozgat, Turk. 132/C2
Ypsilanti, Mi, US 177/E7
Yr Eifl (peak), Wal, UK 76/D6
Yreka, Ca, US 170/B2
Yser (riv.), Fr. 82/B3
Ysieux (riv.), Fr. 72/K4
Ystad, Swe. 80/E4
Ysyk-Köl (lake), Kyr. 112/C3
Ysyk-Köl (obl.), Kyr. 129/G4
Ythan (riv.), Sc, UK 78/D2
Ytrac, Fr. 84/E4
Ytre Sula (isl.), Nor. 80/A1
Ytterby, Swe. 80/D3
Ytterbyn, Swe. 79/G2
Yü (peak), Tai. 121/D3
Yu (riv.), China 125/J3
Yu Xian, China 114/C3
Yu Xian, China 114/C4
Yuan (riv.), China 113/K6
Yuan (lake), China 114/C5
Yuan'an, China 114/B5
Yüanlin, Tai. 121/D3
Yuanping, China 114/C3
Yuanqu, China 114/B4
Yuanshi, China 114/C3
Yuanyang, China 114/C4
Yuba City, Ca, US 170/B3
Yūbari, Japan 118/B2
Yūbetsu, Japan 118/C1
Yūbetsu (riv.), Japan 118/C2
Yucaipa, Ca, US 178/C2
Yucatán (state), Mex. 186/D1
Yucatan (pen.), Mex. 186/D2
Yucatan (chan.), NAm. 186/E1
Yucca House Nat'l Mon., Co, US 170/E3
Yucheng, China 114/D3
Yucheng, China 114/C4
Yuci, China 114/C3
Yuen Long, China 113/U10
Yuendumu, Austl. 155/F2
Yuendumu Abor. Land, Austl. 155/F2
Yueqing, China 121/D2
Yueyang, China 121/B2
Yug (riv.), Rus. 106/E4
Yugan, China 121/C2
Yugawara, Japan 119/C3
Yugorskiy (pen.), Rus. 103/P1
Yuhang, China 114/L9
Yuhuan, China 121/D2
Yui, Japan 119/B3
Yujiang, China 121/C2
Yūki, Japan 117/F2
Yukon, Ok, US 179/M14
Yukon (riv.), Can.,US 176/L3
Yukon-Charley Rivers Nat'l Prsv., Ak, US 176/K2
Yukon Territory (terr.), Can. 176/L2
Yüksekova, Turk. 132/F2
Yukuhashi, Japan 116/B4
Yulara, Austl. 155/F3
Yuleba, Austl. 156/C4
Yulin, China 125/K3
Yulin, China 125/J4
Yulin, China 114/B3
Yuma, Az, US 170/D4
Yuma, Co, US 171/G2
Yumbarra Consv. Park, Austl. 155/G4
Yumbel, Chile 200/B3
Yumbo, Col. 194/B4
Yumen, China 112/G4
Yumin, China 112/D2
Yumurtalık, Turk. 133/D1
Yun (riv.), China 114/C5
Yun Xian, China 125/H3
Yun Xian, China 114/B4
Yunak, Turk. 132/B2
Yuncheng, China 114/C4
Yuncheng, China 114/B4
Yundum (Banjul) (int'l arpt.), Gam. 144/A3
Yungang Caves, China 114/C2
Yungas (phys. reg.), Bol. 192/E7
Yungay, Chile 200/B3
Yungk'ang, Tai. 121/D3
Yunguyo, Peru 198/D5
Yunkanjini Abor. Land, Austl. 155/F2
Yunlong, China 125/G2
Yunnan (prov.), China 112/H7
Yuntai (peak), China 114/D4
Yunxi, China 114/B4
Yunxiao, China 121/C3
Yunyan (riv.), China 114/D4
Yunzhong (mtn.), China 114/C3
Yuping, China 125/J2
Yupukarri, Guy. 195/G4
Yuqiao (res.), China 114/H7
Yuracyacu, Peru 198/B2
Yurga, Rus. 106/J4
Yuri (isl.), Rus. 118/E2
Yurimaguas, Peru 198/B2
Yuruari (riv.), Ven. 195/F3
Yürük, Turk. 91/H5
Yur'yevets, Rus. 102/J4
Yuryuzan' (riv.), Rus. 103/N5
Yuscarán, Hon. 186/E3
Yushan, China 121/C2
Yushe, China 114/C3
Yushu, China 113/N3
Yusŏng, SKor. 115/D4
Yusufeli, Turk. 132/E1
Yutai, China 114/D4
Yutian, China 112/D4
Yutian, China 114/H7
Yutz, Fr. 95/F5
Yuza, Japan 118/A4
Yuzawa, Japan 118/B4
Yuzhno-Sakhalinsk, Rus. 113/R2
Yverdon, Swi. 98/C4
Yvette (riv.), Fr. 94/B6
Yvoir, Belg. 95/D3
Yvonand, Swi. 98/C4
Yvron (riv.), Fr. 72/L6
Yzeure, Fr. 84/E3

Z

Za (riv.), Mor. 142/C2
Zaachila, Mex. 186/B2
Zaandam, Neth. 82/C2
Zaanstad, Neth. 92/B4
Żabbar, Malta 88/M7
Zaber (riv.), Ger. 96/C4
Ząbki, Pol. 83/L2
Ząbkowice Śląskie, Pol. 83/J3
Žabljak, Mont. 90/D4
Zábřeh, Czh. 83/J4
Zabrze, Pol. 83/K3
Zacapa, Guat. 186/D3
Zacapoaxtla, Mex. 185/M7
Zacapu, Mex. 185/E5
Zacatecas (state), Mex. 182/A3
Zacatecas, Mex. 184/E4
Zacatecoluca, ESal. 186/D3
Zacatelco, Mex. 185/L7
Zacatepec, Mex. 185/K8
Zacatlán, Mex. 185/M7
Zachary, La, US 175/F4
Zachodniopomorskie (prov.), Pol. 83/H2
Zacoalco de Torres, Mex. 184/E4
Zacualtipán, Mex. 186/B1
Zadar, Cro. 85/L4
Zadetkyi (isl.), Myan. 122/A2
Zafarwāl, Pak. 128/C3
Zafra, Sp. 86/B3
Żagań, Pol. 83/H3
Zaghouan, Tun. 142/M6
Zaghouan (gov.), Tun. 142/M6
Zagora, Mor. 140/D3
Zagorá, Gre. 89/H3
Zagorje ob Savi, Slov. 85/L3
Zagreb (cap.), Cro. 90/B3
Zagros (mts.), Iran 130/E1
Zāhedān, Iran 131/H3
Zahirābād, India 124/C4
Zaḩlah, Leb. 133/D3
Záhony, Hun. 83/M4
Zahrez Chergui (dry lake), Alg. 142/G5
Zaidín, Sp. 87/F2
Zaidpur, India 126/C2
Zaïo, Mor. 142/C2
Zaire (see Congo, Democratic Republic of the)
Zakamensk, Rus. 112/H1
Zakarpats'ka Oblasti, Ukr. 104/B2
Zakháro, Gre. 89/G4
Zakhodnyaya Dzvina (riv.), Bela. 102/E5
Zākhū, Iraq 132/E2
Zákinthos (isl.), Gre. 89/G4
Zákinthos, Gre. 89/G4
Zakopane, Pol. 83/K4
Zakouma, PN de, Chad 139/J5
Zala (riv.), Hun. 90/C2
Zala (prov.), Hun. 90/C2
Zalaapáti, Hun. 90/C2
Zalaegerszeg, Hun. 90/C2
Zalamea de la Serena, Sp. 86/C3
Zalamea la Real, Sp. 86/B4
Zalaszentgrót, Hun. 90/C2
Zalău, Rom. 91/F2
Žalec, Slov. 85/L3
Zalţan (well), Libya 139/J2
Zaltbommel, Neth. 92/C5
Zalun, Myan. 125/G4
Zama, Japan 119/C3
Zamānia, India 126/D3
Zambezi, Zam. 147/D3
Zambezi (riv.), Afr. 147/F4
Zambia (ctry.) 147/E3
Zamboanga, Phil. 123/F2
Zambrów, Pol. 83/M2
Zamfora (riv.), Nga. 145/G3
Zami (riv.), Myan. 120/B3
Zamora (riv.), Ecu. 192/C4
Zamora, Ecu. 198/B2
Zamora, Sp. 86/C2
Zamora-Chinchipe (prov.), Ecu. 198/B2
Zamora de Hidalgo, Mex. 184/E5
Zamość, Pol. 83/M3
Zams, Aus. 99/G3
Záncara (riv.), Sp. 86/D3
Zanda, China 112/C5
Zandkreekdam (dam), Neth. 92/A5
Zandvoort, Neth. 92/B4
Zanè, It. 101/E1
Zanhuang, China 114/C3
Zanjān, Iran 130/E1
Zanjón (riv.), Mex. 170/E5
Zánka, Hun. 90/C2
Zanzibar, Tanz. 146/C4
Zanzibar (isl.), Tanz. 146/C4
Zanzibar (Kisauni) (int'l arpt.), Tanz. 146/C4
Zanzibar Central/South (pol. reg.),Tanz. 146/C4
Zanzibar North (prov.), Tanz. 146/C4
Zanzibar Urban/West (pol. reg.), Tanz. 146/C4
Zanzuzi (hill), Tanz. 146/B3
Zaō-san (peak), Japan 117/G1
Zaoqiang, China 114/C3
Zaouiet Kounta, Alg. 141/E4
Zaoyang, China 114/C4
Zaozhuang, China 114/D4
Zapala, Arg. 200/C3
Zapaleri (peak), SA 199/C1
Zapallar, Chile 200/C2
Zapata, Tx, US 174/D5
Zapata (pen.), Cuba 187/F1
Zapatoca, Col. 194/C3
Zapatosa (lake), Col. 194/C2
Záplatský Rybník (lake), Czh. 97/H4
Zapolyarnyy, Rus. 102/F1
Zapopan, Mex. 184/E4
Zaporizhzhya, Ukr. 104/E3
Zaporizhzhya (int'l arpt.), Ukr. 104/E3
Zaporiz'ka Oblasti, Ukr. 104/E3
Zapotal, Ecu. 194/B5
Zapotillo, Ecu. 198/A2
Zapponeta, It. 88/D2
Zaprešić, Cro. 90/B3
Zara, Turk. 132/D2
Zaragoza, Mex. 185/E2
Zaragoza (int'l arpt.), Sp. 87/E2
Zaragoza, Mex. 185/M7
Zaragoza, Col. 194/C3
Zaragoza (Saragossa), Sp. 87/E2
Zarah, Ks, US 179/D6
Zarand, Iran 131/G2
Zaranda (hill), Nga. 145/H4
Zárate, Arg. 201/J11
Zarauz, Sp. 86/D1
Zaraza, Ven. 195/E2
Zard (mtn.), Iran 130/F2
Zareh Sharan, Afg. 131/J2
Zargān, Iran 130/F3
Zaria, Nga. 145/G4
Zarmast (pass), Afg. 131/H2
Zărneşti, Rom. 91/G3
Žarnovica, Slvk. 90/D1
Zarós, Gre. 89/J5
Záruby (peak), Slvk. 90/C1
Zaruma, Ecu. 198/B1
Zarumilla, Peru 198/A1
Żary, Pol. 83/H3
Zarza la Mayor, Sp. 86/B3
Zarzal, Col. 194/B3
Zarzis, Tun. 139/H2
Zāskār (range), India 128/D3
Zāskār (riv.), India 128/D3
Zastron, SAfr. 148/D3
Žatec, Czh. 97/G2
Zauche (reg.), Ger. 82/P7
Zavalla, Arg. 200/E2
Zavdi'el, Isr. 133/F8
Zaventem, Belg. 95/D2
Zavet, Bul. 91/H4
Zavidovići, Bosn. 90/D3
Zavitinsk, Rus. 113/N1
Zawadzkie, Pol. 83/K3
Zawiercie, Pol. 83/K3
Zaysan, Kaz. 112/D2
Zaysan (lake), Kaz. 112/D2
Zayü (riv.), China 125/G2
Zaza (riv.), Cuba 187/G1
Zazárida, Ven. 194/D2
Zbąszyń, Pol. 83/H2
Žďár nad Sázavou, Czh. 83/H4
Zdice, Czh. 97/G3
Zduńska Wola, Pol. 83/K3
Zeballos (peak), Arg. 201/C5
Żebbuġ, Malta 88/L7
Zeddine (riv.), Alg. 142/F5
Zedelgem, Belg. 94/C1
Zeehan, Austl. 157/C4
Zeeland, Mi, US 172/C3
Zeeland (prov.), Neth. 92/A5
Zeeland, Neth. 92/C5
Zeerust, SAfr. 147/E6
Zeewolde, Neth. 92/C4
Zefat, Isr. 133/D3
Zegrzyńskie (res.), Pol. 83/L2
Zehdenick, Ger. 83/G2
Zeil (mt.), Austl. 155/G2
Zeil, Ger. 96/D2
Zeiselmauer, Aus. 91/N7
Zeist, Neth. 92/C4
Zeitz, Ger. 82/G3
Żejtun, Malta 88/M7
Zekharya, Isr. 133/F8
Zele, Belg. 94/D1
Zelenodol'sk, Rus. 103/L5
Zelenogorsk, Rus. 103/S6
Zelenokumsk, Rus. 105/G3
Zelhem, Neth. 92/D4
Zell, Swi. 99/E3
Zell, Swi. 98/D3
Zell, Ger. 95/G3
Zell am Harmersbach, Ger. 98/E1
Zell am Main, Ger. 96/C3
Zell am Moos, Aus. 97/G7
Zell am See, Aus. 85/K3
Zell an der Pram, Aus. 97/G6
Zell in Wiesental, Ger. 98/D2
Zellersee (lake), Aus. 96/G7
Zellingen, Ger. 96/C3
Zelów, Pol. 83/K3
Zeltingen-Rachtig, Ger. 95/G4
Zeltweg, Aus. 85/L3
Zelzate, Belg. 94/C1
Zemaitija NP, Lith. 81/J3
Zembra (isls.), Tun. 142/M6
Zemen, Bul. 90/F4
Zemio, CAfr. 139/L6
Zemmer, Ger. 95/F4
Zemmora, Alg. 142/F5
Zempoala, Mex. 185/N7
Zempoala (peak), Mex. 185/Q10
Zempoaltepec, Cerro (peak), Mex. 186/C2
Zemst, Belg. 95/D2
Zenica, Bosn. 90/C3
Zenith, Wa, US 177/C3
Zenn (riv.), Ger. 85/J2
Zenne (riv.), Belg. 95/D1
Zenon Park, Sk, Can. 169/H2
Zentsūji, Japan 116/C3
Žepče, Bosn. 90/D3
Zepu, China 129/G5
Zeralda, Alg. 142/G4
Zeravshan (riv.), Taj.,Uzb. 129/E5
Zermatt, Swi. 98/D5
Zernez, Swi. 99/G4
Zernien, Ger. 93/H2
Zernograd, Rus. 104/G3
Zero Branco, It. 101/F1
Zeta (lake), Nun., Can. 164/F1
Zetel, Ger. 93/E2
Zeuthen, Ger. 82/Q7
Zeven, Ger. 93/G2
Zevenaar, Neth. 92/D5
Zevenbergen, Neth. 92/B5
Zevgolatión, Gre. 89/H4
Zevio, It. 101/E2
Zeya (res.), Rus. 109/M4
Zeya (riv.), Rus. 107/N4
Zeya-Bureya (plain), Rus. 107/N4
Zeytindağ, Turk. 132/A2
Zêzere (riv.), Port. 86/A3
Zghartā, Leb. 133/D2
Zgierz, Pol. 83/K3
Zgorzelec, Pol. 83/H3
Zhambyl (obl.), Kaz. 129/F4
Zhambyl, Kaz. 129/F4
Zhangaözen, Kaz. 105/K4
Zhangaqazaly, Kaz. 129/D3
Zhangatas, Kaz. 129/E4
Zhanghei, China 114/C2
Zhangjiakou, China 114/C2
Zhangping, China 121/C2
Zhangpu, China 121/C3
Zhangqiu, China 114/D3
Zhangshu, China 121/C2
Zhangwei (riv.), China 114/D3
Zhangye, China 112/H4
Zhangzhou, China 121/C3
Zhangzi (isl.), China 115/B3
Zhangzi, China 114/C3
Zhanhua, China 114/D3
Zhanjiang, China 125/K3
Zhao Xian, China 114/C3
Zhao'an, China 121/C3
Zhaojue, China 125/H2
Zhaoqing, China 125/K3
Zhaotong, China 125/H2
Zhaoyuan, China 114/E3
Zhaozhou, China 113/N2
Zhāyya (Ural) (riv.), Kaz.,Rus. 106/F5
Zhayyq (riv.), Kaz. 106/F5
Zhecheng, China 114/C4
Zhejiang (prov.), China 113/L6
Zhelaniya (cape), Rus. 106/G2
Zheleznodorozhnyy, Rus. 103/L3
Zheleznogorsk, Rus. 104/E1
Zheleznogorsk-Ilimskiy, Rus. 107/L4
Zhenfeng Bouyeizu Miaozu Zizhixian, China 125/J2
Zhengding, China 114/C3
Zhenglan, China 113/L3
Zhengning, China 114/B4
Zhengyang, China 114/C4
Zhengzhou, China 114/C4
Zhenhai, China 121/D2
Zhenjiang, China 114/D4
Zhenkang, China 125/G3
Zhenning Bouyeizu Miaozu Zizhixian, China 125/J2
Zhenping, China 114/C4
Zhentou (riv.), China 114/C4
Zhenwu (mtn.), China 114/B3
Zhenxiong, China 125/H2
Zhenyuan, China 121/A2
Zhenyuan, China 125/H3
Zhetiqara, Kaz. 105/M1
Zhezqazghan, Kaz. 129/E3
Zhezqazghan (obl.), Kaz. 129/E3
Zhicheng, China 121/B1
Zhigulevsk, Rus. 105/J1
Zhijiang, China 121/B1
Zhijin, China 125/J2
Zhiloy (isl.), Azer. 105/J4
Zhlobin, Bela. 104/D1
Zhmerynka, Ukr. 104/D2
Zhob, Pak. 131/J2
Zhob (riv.), Pak. 131/J2
Zhodino, Bela. 81/N4
Zhokhov (isl.), Rus. 107/R2
Zhongba, China 121/C3
Zhongshan, China 125/K3
Zhongxiang, China 114/C5
Zhongyang, China 114/B3
Zhoukou, China 114/C4
Zhoushan (isls.), China 121/D2
Zhouzhou, China 114/G7
Zhovtneve, Ukr. 91/L2
Zhuanghe, China 115/B3
Zhucheng, China 114/D4
Zhuhai, China 125/K3
Zhuji, China 121/D2
Zhujiang Kou (bay), China 113/T10
Zhukovka, Rus. 104/E1
Zhukovskiy, Rus. 103/X9
Zhumadian, China 114/C4
Zhuolu, China 114/G6
Zhuozi, China 114/C2
Zhushan, China 114/B4
Zhuxi, China 114/B4
Zhuzhou, China 125/K2
Zhuzhou, China 125/K2
Zhytomyr, Ukr. 104/D2
Zhytomyrs'ka Oblasti, Ukr. 104/C2
Zi (riv.), China 121/B2
Zia (int'l arpt.), Bang. 127/H4
Zibo, China 114/D3
Ziębice, Pol. 83/J3
Zielona Góra, Pol. 83/H3
Zierenberg, Ger. 93/G6
Zierikzee, Neth. 92/A5
Ziftá, Egypt 133/B4
Zigong, China 125/H2
Zigui, China 114/B5
Ziguinchor (int'l arpt.), Sen. 144/A3
Ziguinchor, Sen. 144/A3
Ziguinchor (pol. reg.), Sen. 144/A3
Zihuatanejo, Mex. 185/E5
Zijing (mtn.), China 114/B3
Zikhron Ya'aqov, Isr. 133/F6
Zile, Turk. 132/C1
Žilina, Slvk. 83/K4
Žilinský (pol. reg.), Slvk. 83/K4
Zillah, Libya 138/J2
Ziller (riv.), Aus. 85/J3
Zillisheim, Fr. 98/D2
Zimapán, Mex. 185/F4
Zimatlán de Álvarez, Mex. 186/B2
Zimba, Zam. 147/E4
Zimbabwe (ctry.) 147/E4
Zimla (well), Alg. 140/E4
Zimnicea, Rom. 91/G4
Zinapécuaro de Figueroa, Mex. 185/E5
Zinave, PN de, Moz. 147/F5
Zinder, Niger 145/H3
Zinder (dept.), Niger 145/H3
Ziniaré, Burk. 145/E3
Zinjin, China 121/C3
Zion, Md, US 180/C4
Zion NP, Ut, US 170/D3
Zippori, Isr. 133/G6
Zirc, Hun. 90/C2
Žirje (isl.), Cro. 90/B4
Zirl, Aus. 99/H3
Ziro, India 125/F2
Zitácuaro, Mex. 185/E5
Žitava (riv.), Slvk. 83/K5
Zittau, Ger. 83/H3
Živinice, Bosn. 90/D3
Ziwa Magharibi (pol. reg.), Tanz. 146/A3
Zixi, China 121/C2
Zixing, China 125/K2
Ziya (riv.), China 114/D3
Ziyyon, Isr. 133/G8
Ziz, Oued (riv.), Mor. 140/D2
Zlatna, Rom. 91/F2
Zlatograd, Bul. 91/G5
Zlatorsko (lake), Serb. 90/D4
Zlatoust, Rus. 103/N5
Zlín, Czh. 83/J4
Zlínský (pol. reg.), Czh. 83/J4
Zliv, Czh. 97/H4
Złocieniec, Pol. 83/J2
Zlot, Serb. 90/E3
Złotoryja, Pol. 83/H3
Złotów, Pol. 83/J2
Žlutice, Czh. 97/G2
Żmigród, Pol. 83/J3
Znam'yanka, Ukr. 104/E2
Żnin, Pol. 83/J2
Znojmo, Czh. 83/J4
Zocca, It. 101/D4
Zoersel, Belg. 92/B6
Zoetermeer, Neth. 92/B4
Zoeterwoude, Neth. 92/B4
Zofingen, Swi. 98/D3
Zogang, China 125/G2
Zogno, It. 100/C1
Zográfos, Gre. 89/N9
Zohreh (riv.), Iran 130/F2
Zola, It. 101/E4
Zollikon, Swi. 99/E3
Zolotonosha, Ukr. 104/E2
Zomba, Malw. 147/G4
Zone (pt.), Eng, UK 74/A6
Zongolica, Mex. 185/N8
Zonguldak, Turk. 91/K5
Zonguldak (prov.), Turk. 91/K5
Zonhoven, Belg. 95/E2
Zonnebeke, Belg. 94/B2
Zonza, Fr. 88/A2
Zorge (riv.), Ger. 93/H5
Zorgo, Burk. 145/E3
Zorn (riv.), Fr. 82/D4
Zorneding, Ger. 97/E6
Zornheim, Ger. 96/B3
Zorritos, Peru 198/A1
Zossen, Ger. 82/Q7
Zottegem, Belg. 94/C2
Zou (prov.), Ben. 145/F5
Zou Xian, China 114/D4
Zouérat, Mrta. 140/B5
Zound-Wéogo (prov.), Burk. 145/E4
Zouping, China 114/D3
Zousfana, Oued (riv.), Alg. 141/E3
Zrenjanin, Serb. 90/E3
Zschopau (riv.), Ger. 97/F1
Zuata, Ven. 195/E2
Zubia, Sp. 86/D4
Zubūbā, Isr. 133/G6
Zucchero (peak), Swi. 99/E5
Zuckerhütl (peak), Aus. 99/H4
Zuehl, Tx, US 179/U21
Zug, Swi. 99/E3
Zugdidi, Geo. 105/G4
Zugersee (lake), Swi. 85/H3
Zughrār (well), Libya 141/H3
Zugspitze (peak), Ger. 99/G3
Zuid Holland (prov.), Neth. 92/A5
Zuid-Willemsvaart (canal), Belg.,Neth. 92/C6
Zuidbeveland (isl.), Neth. 92/A6
Zuidelijk Flevoland (polder), Neth. 92/C4
Zuidhorn, Neth. 92/D2
Zuidlaardermeer (lake), Neth. 92/D2
Zuidlaren, Neth. 92/D2
Zuidwolde, Neth. 92/D3
Zuienkerke, Belg. 94/C1
Zújar (riv.), Sp. 86/C3
Zújar, Sp. 86/D4
Zújar, Embalse (res.), Sp. 86/C3
Zulia (riv.), Ven. 192/D2
Zulia (state), Ven. 194/C2
Zülpich, Ger. 95/F2
Zulte, Belg. 94/C2
Zululand (reg.), SAfr. 149/E2
Zumárraga, Sp. 86/D1
Zumba, Ecu. 198/B2
Zumbo, Moz. 147/F4
Zumpango de Ocampo, Mex. 185/K7
Zumpango del Río, Mex. 185/F5
Zundert, Neth. 92/B6
Zunhua, China 114/H6
Zuni (riv.), Az,NM, US 170/E4
Zuni, NM, US 170/E4
Zuni (mts.), NM, US 174/A3
Zunyi, China 125/J2
Zuo (riv.), China 121/A3
Zuo Jiang (riv.), China 120/D1
Zuoquan, China 114/C3
Zuoyun, China 114/C3
Zuoz, Swi. 99/F4
Županja, Cro. 90/D3
Žur, Serb. 90/E4
Zurbāţīyah, Iraq 130/E2
Zürich (canton), Swi. 99/E2
Zürich (int'l arpt.), Swi. 99/E3
Zürich, Swi. 99/E3
Zurichsee (lake), Swi. 85/H3
Żuromin, Pol. 83/K2
Żurrieq, Malta 88/L7
Zurzach, Swi. 99/E2
Zusam (riv.), Ger. 85/J2
Zushi, Japan 119/D3
Zusmarshausen, Ger. 96/D6
Zutiua (riv.), Braz. 196/A2
Zutphen, Neth. 92/D4
Zuurberg NP, SAfr. 148/D4
Zuwārah, Libya 138/H1
Zuyevka, Rus. 103/L4
Zvijesda NP, Bosn. 90/D4
Zvishavane, Zim. 147/F5
Zvolen, Slvk. 104/A2
Zvorničko (lake), Bosn. 90/D3
Zvornik, Bosn. 90/D3
Zwarte Meer (lake), Neth. 92/C3
Zwartsluis, Neth. 92/D3
Zwedru, Libr. 144/C5
Zweibrücken, Ger. 95/G5
Zweisimmen, Swi. 98/D4
Zwesten, Ger. 93/G6
Zwevegem, Belg. 94/C2
Zwickau, Ger. 85/K1
Zwickauer Mulde (riv.), Ger. 82/G3
Zwijndrecht, Belg. 95/D1
Zwischenahner Meer (lake), Ger. 93/F2
Zwischenwasser, Aus. 99/F3
Zwoleń, Pol. 83/L3
Żychlin, Pol. 83/K2
Żyrardów, Pol. 83/L2
Żywiec, Pol. 83/K4

Acknowledgements

Maps and Photo Credits

Maps in the Map Section: © Hammond World Atlas Corporation 2008, Springfield, New Jersey

Satellite Images: © GEOSPACE, Austria, 2000, Original Data: Eurimage – © GEOSPACE / World Sat International Corp. 2000 – © Deutsches Zentrum für Luft- und Raumfahrt, Oberpfaffenhofen

Theme Section and other pages in the atlas: action press, Hamburg – aisa, Archivo iconografico, Barcelona – Archiv für Kunst und Geschichte, Berlin – theeartarchive, London – Art Publishers, Durban – Astrofoto Bildagentur, Sörth – Prof. Dr. J. Bähr, Altwittenbek – Prof. Dr. W. Barthlott, Bonn – J. Bautze, Berlin – BAVARIA Bildagentur, Gauting – Berliner Missionswerk – Hans Bertram Luftbildverlag, Munich – Bibliographisches Institut & F. A. Brockhaus, Mannheim – Bibliothèque Nationale de France, Paris – Bildarchiv Preußischer Kulturbesitz, Berlin – Bilderberg, Archiv der Fotografen, Hamburg – Prof. Dr. G. Bosinski, Neuwied – Prof. Dr. G. Bräuer, Hartenholm – British Library, London – Luftbildarchiv Albrecht Brugger im Hause Fotofachlabor Schnepf, Stuttgart – R. Brugger, Königswinter – Bundesanstalt für Geowissenschaften und Rohstoffe, Hanover – J.-L. Charmet, Paris – Prof. M. Deuchler, London – Deutscher Wetterdienst, Offenbach am Main – Deutsches Museum, Munich – Digimago, Eppelheim – dpa Bildarchiv, Frankfurt am Main und Stuttgart – Dr. H. Eichler, Heidelberg – Prof. Dr. Ch. Feest, Frankfurt am Main – Photo- und Presseagentur FOCUS, Hamburg – Photo- und Presseagentur Focus, Hamburg / B. Barbey / Magnum – Photo- und Presseagentur Focus, Hamburg / J. Blair – Photo- und Presseagentur Focus, Hamburg / B. Edmaier – M. Fries, Wiesbaden – Dr. K. Gallas, München – Studio X, Gamma, Limours – Dr. G. Gerster, Zumikon, Schweiz – Dr. S. von der Heide, Cologne – Prof. Dr. K. Heine, Regensburg – D. Heunemann, Starnberg – Prof. Dr. P. Höllermann, Bonn – IFA-Bilderteam, Taufkirchen – Prof. Dr. A. Jockenhövel, Münster – W. Keimer, Dossenheim – KNA Kath. Nachrichten Agentur, Frankfurt am Main – Dr. H.-J. Kress, Fulda – Helga Lade Fotoagentur, Frankfurt am Main – laenderpress, Mainz – J. Lauré, Woodfin Camp & Associates, New York – Löppert, Optik-Foto-Dia, Munich – Dr. L. Marfaing, Hamburg – Bildagentur Mauritius, Mittenwald – P. Meyer, Frankfurt. – MEV Verlag, Augsburg – Prof. Dr. F.-D. Miotke, Garbsen – W. Müller, Ettlingen – Museum für Völkerkunde, Vienna – NASA / Earth from Space Images, Washington D.C. – NASA / JPL / RPIF / DLR – Neanderthal Museum, Mettmann – Prof. Dr. G. Niemz, Neu-Isenburg – Oberösterreichisches Landesmuseum, Linz – G. Dagli Orti, Paris – Österreichische Nationalbibliothek, Vienna – Physikalisch-Technische Bundesanstalt, Braunschweig und Berlin – Picture Press, Hamburg / Meyer-Andersen – J. Poupard – J. M. Prieto, Asunción – Dr. D. Rafiqpoor, Bonn – Prof. Dr. S. Rahmstorf, Potsdam – Agentur RAPHO, Paris – Rosgartenmuseum, Konstanz – Prof. Dr. H.-J. Sander, Bonn – K. Schlosser, Kiel – G. Schrüfer, Bayreuth – Forschungsinstitut und Natur-Museum Senckenberg, Frankfurt am Main – Silvestris Verlag, Bildarchiv, Kastl – Sipa Press, Paris – E. SLAWIK, Waldenburg – K. Stevens, USA – H. Stierlin, Genf – Dr. K.-H. Striedter, Frankfurt am Main – L. A. Thomas / Doug Peebles Photography, Hawaii – Tony Stone Bilderwelten, Munich – Uitgeverij Het Spectrum, Utrecht – Ullstein Bilderdienst, Berlin – Ulmer Museum, Ulm – Prof. Dr. W. H. Valentin, Berlin – Prof. Dr. M. Yaldiz, Berlin – ZEFA-Zentrale Farbbild Agentur, Düsseldorf – Carl Zeiss, Oberkochen

Locator maps based on MHM © 1993 Digital Wisdom, Inc.

Other graphic illustrations, maps, and drawings: Bibliographisches Institut & F. A. Brockhaus, Mannheim

Publisher	Hammond World Atlas Corporation
Chairman	Andreas Langenscheidt
President	Marc Jennings
VP of Cartography	Vera Lorenz
Director Database Resources	Theophrastos E. Giouvanos
Cartography	Walter H. Jones Jr.
	Sharon Lightner
	Harry E. Morin
	James Padykula
	Thomas R. Rubino
	Thomas J. Scheffer
Layout and Composition	John A. DiGiorgio
	Maribel López Castillo
Cover Design	Marian Purcell
Map Text Blocks	Helmut Vieser;
	Klartext Journalistenbüro, Stuttgart

Thematic Section
Conception and Editorial Supervision

Writers	Dr. Eva Maria Brugger
	Dr. Joachim Born, Technische Universität Dresden
	Dr. Eva Maria Brugger, Heidelberg
	Prof. Dr. Eckart Ehlers, Universität Bonn
	Dr. Horst Eichler, Universität Heidelberg
	Dr. Gernot Gruber, Wiesbaden
	Prof. Uwe Jäschke, Hochschule für Technik und Wirtschaft Dresden
	Wolfhard Keimer, Dossenheim
	Prof. Dr. Wilhelm Lauer & Daud Rafiqpoor, Universität Bonn
	Prof. Dr. Franz-Dieter Miotke, Garbsen
	Prof. Dr. Stefan Rahmsdorf, Institut für Klimafolgenforschung Potsdam
	Prof. Dr. Theo Sundermeier, Universität Heidelberg
Layout and Composition	Matthias Hugo; Hugo Grafische Formgebung, Köln
Informational Graphics	Matthias Hugo; Hugo Grafische Formgebung, Köln
	Joachim Knappe, Hamburg
Cartography	Dipl.-Ing. (FH) Jörg Radtke
	Dipl.-Ing. (FH) Manuela Lipp
	Erika Korbien

Satellite Section
Conception and Design Supervision

	Dipl.-Geogr. Ellen Astor
Consultation and Photo Procurement	Dr. Lothar Beckel; GEOSPACE, Salzburg
Layout and Composition	Sigrid Hecker / doppelpack, Mannheim

Translation

German to English	John S. Southard
Editorial Assistance	Michael Venhoff
	Ellen Astor
Technology	Sigrid Hecker
	Jörg Radtke
Author of Thematic and Satellite Sections	Bibliographisches Institut & F. A. Brockhaus AG

ARCTIC REGION **202**

Greenland
(Kalaallit Nunaat)

79

79 Iceland

EUROPE **69**

Norw

Lo*ndon* **72**

Paris **72**

Monaco **100**

Alaska **176**

176

Canada **164**

NORTH AMERICA **161**

United States of America **166**

Metropolitan
New York **181**

178
Metropolitan Los Angeles

Azores
87

NORTHERN
AFRICA **138**

Madeira
87 Morocco

87

Canary

Algeria

184

182

Bahamas

Mexico

Mexico
Veracruz **205**

Mexic **185**

Cuba
Hon. Haiti

Dom.
Rep.

183

Cape Verde **135**

Mauritania

Mali

Nige

Oahu **166** Hawaii **166**
166

Jamaica

Sen.

B.F.

Benin

Guat.
Nicar. **186**

Costa Rica
Panama

Venezuela

Guy.
Sur.

194

NORTHERN
SOUTH AMERICA **192**

Guinea
Libr.

Côte
d'Iv.
Togo
Ghana Niger

144

AFRICA **135**

CENTRAL
PACIFIC OCEAN **158**

Columbia

Ecu. **198**

Galápagos Is.

Peru **198**

Bolivia

Brazil **196**

Rio de Janeiro-
São Paulo **197**

SOUTHER
AFRICA **147**

SOUTH AMERICA **189**

Par.

Chile

Argentina

Ur. **201**
Rio de la Plata

197

Santiago-
Valparaíso **200**

200

SOUTHERN
SOUTH AMERICA **199**

201

168 BC

Canada

AB SK MB

QU

NF

a WA

172 ON

NB
ME

NS

MT ND MN

WI

170 OR ID

WY SD

NE IA

MI

NY
PA

n

New York **180**
181

United States
of America

IL

IN OH

NV UT b

174 CO KS MO

WV VA

KY

CA
Los
Angeles **178** **178**

AZ NM

OK

AR

TN

NC

SC

d

MS AL GA

TX

LA

g

FL

Mexico